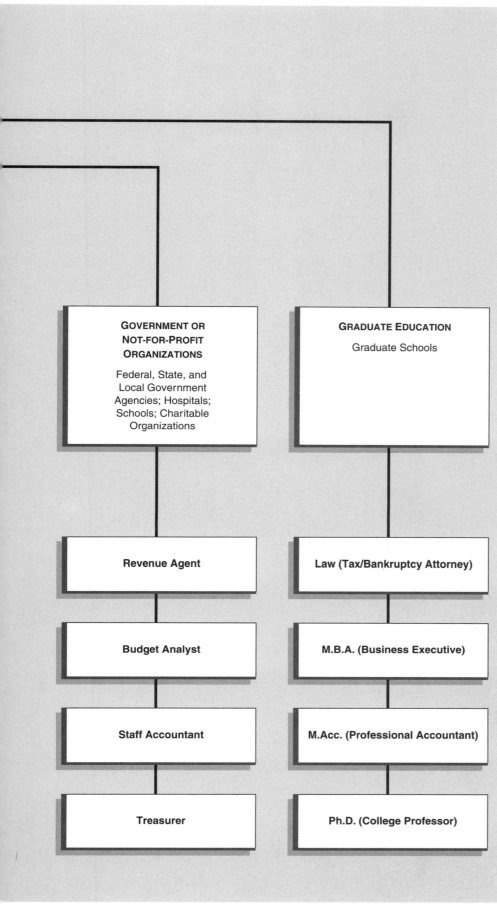

GOVERNMENT OR NOT-FOR-PROFIT ORGANIZATIONS

Federal, State, and Local Government Agencies; Hospitals; Schools; Charitable Organizations

GRADUATE EDUCATION

Graduate Schools

Revenue Agent

Law (Tax/Bankruptcy Attorney)

Budget Analyst

M.B.A. (Business Executive)

Staff Accountant

M.Acc. (Professional Accountant)

Treasurer

Ph.D. (College Professor)

FINANCIAL ACCOUNTING

FIFTH EDITION

Financial

Accounting

Belverd E. Needles, Jr.

Ph.D., C.P.A., C.M.A.

Arthur Andersen & Co. Alumni

Distinguished Professor of Accounting

DePaul University

Houghton Mifflin Company

Boston   Toronto   Geneva, Illinois   Palo Alto

Princeton, New Jersey

To my wife, Marian,
To my mother, Mrs. Belverd E. Needles, Sr., and
In memory of my father, Mr. Belverd E. Needles, Sr.,
 and my grandparents, Mr. and Mrs. Benjamin E. Needles

SPONSORING EDITOR: Karen Natale

ASSOCIATE SPONSORING EDITOR: Margaret E. Monahan

SENIOR PROJECT EDITOR: Margaret M. Kearney

SENIOR PRODUCTION/DESIGN COORDINATOR: Sarah Ambrose

SENIOR MANUFACTURING COORDINATOR: Priscilla Bailey

COVER DESIGN: Edda V. Sigurdardottir.

COVER IMAGE: Timothy Hursley, The Arkansas Office, Inc.

PHOTO CREDITS: Page 3, Photo courtesy of Gerber Products Company; page 13, Tony Hutchings/Tony Stone Images; page 51, Courtesy the Boeing Company; page 99, Tony Freeman/PhotoEdit; page 114, G. & M. David DeLossy/The Image Bank; page 143, Courtesy Ecolab; page 189, Copyright Steve Neidorf, 1994; page 205, Andy Sacks/Tony Stone Images; page 241, Lawrence Migdale; page 293, Zigy Kaluzny/Tony Stone Images; page 304, Rich LaSalle/Tony Stone Images; page 345, Gabriel M. Covian/The Image Bank; page 360, Bob Thomason/Tony Stone Images; page 387, Bruce Herman/Tony Stone Images; page 408, Ulf Sjostedt/FPG International; page 439, David Joel/Tony Stone Images; page 461, Explorer/Photo Researchers; page 485, Amy Reichman/Envision; page 505, Vanessa Vick/Photo Researchers; page 533, Andy Sacks/Tony Stone Images; page 541, R. Sidney/The Image Works; page 573, Stephen Studd/Tony Stone Images; page 589, Courtesy Pennzoil Company; page 619, Photo courtesy of Marriott International, Inc.; page 627, Brett Froomer/The Image Bank; page 679, Dave Schaefer/Uniphoto; page 683, Karen Leeds/The Stock Market; page 732, Hideo Kurihara/Tony Stone Images; page 741, Gary Gay/The Image Bank.

Exhibits 15-3 through 15-12: Copyright © 1991, 1992 and 1993 by Apple Computers, Inc. Used with permission.

Toys "R" Us Annual Report (excerpts and complete) year ended January 29, 1994 reprinted by permission.

This book is written to provide accurate and authoritative information concerning the covered topics. It is not meant to take the place of professional advice.

Printed in the U.S.A.

Library of Congress Catalog Card Number: 94-76533

Student Book ISBN: 0-395-69802-2

Instructor's Edition ISBN: 0-395-71682-9

3456789-VH-98 97 96 95

CONTENTS IN BRIEF

CONTENTS

CHAPTER 6   Financial Reporting and Analysis   240

DECISION POINT   *The Gap, Inc.*   *241*

PREFACE

This textbook is intended for use in the first course in financial accounting, at the undergraduate or graduate level. It is designed for both business and accounting majors, and requires no previous training in either area. *Financial Accounting*, Fifth Edition, is part of a well integrated learning package that includes numerous print and computerized supplements. It has proven successful in a one-quarter or one-semester course and has been used equally well in a two-quarter course.

FOCUS ON DECISION MAKING AND THE USES OF ACCOUNTING INFORMATION

Through the first four editions, I approached the writing of this book with the recognition that the majority of students who take the financial accounting course are business and management majors who will read, analyze, and interpret financial statements throughout their careers, and that the fundamental purpose of accounting is to provide information for decision making. While not neglecting topics important for accounting majors, my goal was for all students to become intelligent *users* of financial statements. I have striven to make the content authoritative, practical, and contemporary and to apply rigorously a system of integrated learning objectives that enhances the role of the overall package, and particularly that of the textbook, by fostering complete and thorough coordination between the instructor and the student. The success of the first four editions has justified my confidence in this fundamental approach. In fact, this approach is being adopted at more and more colleges and universities.

DESIGNED TO DEVELOP A BROAD SKILL SET IN STUDENTS

The Fifth Edition of *Financial Accounting* represents a major expansion of the fundamental ideas upon which the book is built. The pedagogical system underlying the Fifth Edition of *Financial Accounting* is the Learning

Improvement Model, which encompasses an enlarged set of instructional strategies designed to achieve a broad skill set in students. This model, which includes the Teaching/Learning Cycle™, cognitive levels of learning, output skills, instructional strategies, and evaluation and feedback, is described in the special "Partners in Change" insert in the Instructors' Edition of this text. Among the goals of the Fifth Edition that result from the application of this model are (1) to develop a much stronger user orientation and reduce the procedural detail, (2) to increase the real-world emphasis, (3) to reorganize and expand the assignment material to develop a broad set of skills, including critical thinking, communication, and financial statement analysis, and (4) to make the book more visually interesting. How these goals are achieved is described in the following sections.

A MUCH STRONGER USER ORIENTATION

Financial Accounting has always emphasized the use of accounting information by external users. The Fifth Edition places additional emphasis on the uses of accounting information by management and on decisions that management makes regarding accounting information.

New Management Sections   New sections on management's use of accounting information appear at or near the beginning of the following chapters:

Chapter 1   Uses of Accounting Information
Chapter 5   Accounting for Merchandising Operations
Chapter 7   Short-Term Liquid Assets
Chapter 8   Inventories
Chapter 9   Long-Term Assets
Chapter 10   Current Liabilities
Chapter 11   Long-Term Liabilities

Financial Ratios   Beginning with Chapter 6, financial analysis ratios are introduced and are integrated in subsequent chapters at appropriate points. These ratios are usually discussed in the "management issues" section at the beginning of the chapters.

Reduced Procedural Detail   The first seven chapters have been substantially revised to reduce procedural detail. Unnecessary topics are deleted, and procedures that are not essential to conceptual understanding are treated as supplemental objectives at chapter's end. The extent of change resulting from increased emphasis on management's use of accounting information and decreased emphasis on procedural detail throughout the text can be seen in the following detailed descriptions of the revisions in three sample chapters:

- *CHAPTER 1   Uses of Accounting Information and the Basic Financial Statements* Rewritten and reorganized to reflect its new title, this chapter contains new material that emphasizes business and management uses of accounting information. All-new illustrations highlight the business goals of profitability and liquidity and the activities of financing, investing, and operating. A new section discusses the use of accounting information in all management functions. The section on the basic financial statements has been rewritten and is accompanied by a new illustration to underscore the interrelationship of the statements. The section on GAAP and organizations that influence GAAP has been moved toward the end of the chapter to smooth the flow of information earlier in the chapter. The section on professional ethics and the accounting profession has been rewritten and, through more concise writing, shortened.

- **CHAPTER 5   *Accounting for Merchandising Operations***   Rewritten to focus on the merchandising income statement, to provide increased coverage of the perpetual inventory system, and to remove much of the procedural detail usually associated with the topic of merchandising, Chapter 5 now contains a new opening section that focuses on management issues related to merchandising businesses, including the concept of the operating cycle and its relationship to cash flows. The structure of the merchandising income statement is presented early in the chapter, and a new illustration of the components of cost of goods sold is included. The chapter now offers equal and parallel coverage of the periodic and perpetual inventory systems. Since sales discounts and purchases discounts are usually immaterial and add procedural complexity to the problems, these topics have been transferred from the discussion of merchandising transactions to the end of the chapter and treated as a supplemental objective. The merchandising work sheet and closing entries have been moved from the chapter to an appendix at the end of the book.

- **CHAPTER 7   *Short-Term Liquid Assets***   A new section on the management issues related to short-term liquid assets has been added at the beginning of Chapter 7. It focuses on managing cash needs, setting credit policies, and financing receivables, and introduces two key ratios—receivable turnover and average days' sales uncollected. The discussion of cash and cash equivalents has been updated to incorporate the new topic of banking and electronic funds transfer, and the discussion of short-term investments has been rewritten to incorporate the requirements of SFAS No. 115. The topic of bank reconciliations has been moved to the discussion of cash and cash equivalents. The learning objective that previously covered miscellaneous topics related to accounts receivable has been eliminated, and the topics have been either integrated into the discussion of accounts receivable or omitted in order to reduce procedural detail. One new illustration shows the relationship of the subsidiary ledger to the controlling account, and another illustration contrasts two approaches to estimating uncollectible accounts. The entries for discounting notes receivable and petty cash procedures have been deleted to reduce the procedural detail, and the topic of credit card sales has been made a supplemental objective.

Eliminated Procedural Topics   Other examples of eliminated procedural topics are:

Chapter 9	Sum-of-the-years'-digits method
Chapter 9	Methods of computing goodwill
Chapter 9	Accounting for assets of low unit cost
Chapter 10	Employee payroll records

New or Revised Conceptual and Analytical Topics   Examples of new or substantially revised conceptual or analytical topics are:

Chapter 2	The use of the chart of accounts as a data base for accounting information
Chapter 3	The relationships of cash flows to accrual accounting
Chapter 6	Management's responsibility for ethical reporting
Chapter 6	Components of an annual report (using Toys "R" Us)
Chapter 8	Parallel presentation of inventory pricing methods for both the periodic and the perpetual inventory systems
Chapter 9	Integration of the concepts of capital and revenue expenditures into the section on acquisition cost
Chapter 14	Analysis of cash flows
Chapter 15	Nature of nonoperating items under quality of earnings
Chapter 15	Comprehensive illustration of ratio analysis using the financial statements of Apple Computer, Inc.
Chapter 15	Ratios related to cash flow adequacy

Sections about accounting for marketable securities in Chapters 7, 14, 15, and the appendix on bond investments have been updated for the effects of SFAS No. 115.

Supplemental Objectives Some topics are treated under supplemental objectives so they can be covered at the instructor's discretion. Exercises and problems that cover supplemental topics are identified and placed at the end of their respective assignment sets. Examples of topics that have been made supplemental objectives include:

Chapter 3	Relationships of cash flows to accrual accounting
Chapter 4	The work sheet
Chapter 4	Reversing entries
Chapter 5	Sales discounts and purchases discounts
Chapter 5	Merchandising work sheet and closing entries
Chapter 7	Credit card sales
Chapter 8	Valuing inventories by estimation
Chapter 9	Special problems of depreciating plant assets
Chapter 14	Workbook approach to statement of cash flows

INCREASE IN REAL-WORLD EMPHASIS

Many steps have been taken to increase the real-world emphasis of the text, including the following:

Decision Points Every chapter contains at least two Decision Points based on real companies. Decision Points present a situation requiring a decision by management or other users of accounting information and then show how the decision can be made using accounting information.

Business Bulletins Also new in this edition are features called Business Bulletins—short items related to chapter topics that show the relevance of accounting in four areas: Business Practice, International Practice, Technology in Practice, and Ethics in Practice.

Other Real-World Topics Information from actual annual reports and articles from such periodicals as *Business Week*, *Forbes*, and the *Wall Street Journal* enhances students' appreciation for the usefulness and relevance of accounting information. In total, more than one hundred publicly held companies have been used as examples. In addition, Chapter 15 demonstrates financial statement analysis using the financial statements of Apple Computer, Inc. Among the real-world topics introduced for the first time in this edition are:

Chapter 1	Business strategies, goals, and activities
Chapter 5	Complete and parallel coverage of the perpetual and periodic inventory systems
Chapter 7	Banking and electronic funds transfer
Chapter 10	Relationship of interest rates to length of maturities and risk for U.S. Treasury debt and corporate debt
Chapter 11	Financial leverage
Chapter 12	Initial public offerings and "tombstone" advertisements
Chapter 15	The segment information of PepsiCo, Inc.

Real Companies in Assignments The use of real companies in the assignment materials has been greatly increased, as discussed below.

International Accounting In recognition of the global economy in which all businesses operate today, international accounting examples are introduced in Chapter 1 and integrated throughout the text. Among the foreign companies mentioned in the text and assignments are Takashimaya Co. (Japanese), Wellcome (British), Mitsubishi (Japanese), and Groupe Michelin (French).

Real-World Graphic Illustrations   Graphs or tables illustrating how actual business practices relate to chapter topics are presented in most chapters. Many of these illustrations are based on data from studies of 600 annual reports published in *Accounting Trends and Techniques*. Beginning in Chapter 6, most chapters have a new graphic that shows selected ratios for selected industries based on Dun and Bradstreet data. Service industry examples include accounting and bookkeeping and interstate trucking companies. Merchandising industry examples include auto and home supply and grocery store companies. Manufacturing industry examples include pharmaceutical and appliance companies. Most Interpretation Cases from Business are based on the published financial reports of real companies.

Governmental and Not-for-Profit Organizations   In recognition of the importance of governmental and not-for-profit organizations in our society, discussions and examples regarding such organizations are included at appropriate points. Among the organizations cited are the city of Chicago and the Lyric Opera of Chicago. An appendix at the end of the book provides an introduction to accounting for governmental and not-for-profit organizations.

REORGANIZED AND EXPANDED ASSIGNMENT MATERIAL TO EMPHASIZE CRITICAL THINKING, COMMUNICATION, AND FINANCIAL STATEMENT ANALYSIS

To accommodate students' need for an expanded skill set and instructors' need for greater pedagogical flexibility, the end-of-chapter assignments and accompanying materials have been reorganized and greatly expanded. My objective has been to provide the most comprehensive and flexible set of assignments available and to include more cases that involve real companies. Because students need to be better prepared in writing and communication skills, I have provided ample assignments to enhance student communication skills. In the new organization, each type of assignment has a specific title and purpose, and has been placed in one of four categories. The end-of-chapter assignments and principal accompanying materials are as follows:

KNOWLEDGE AND UNDERSTANDING

Questions (Q)   Fifteen to twenty-four review questions that cover the essential topics of the chapter.

Short Exercises (SE)   Ten brief exercises suitable for classroom use that cover the key points of the chapter.

APPLICATION

Exercises (E)   Fifteen single-topic exercises that stress the application of all topics in the chapter.

Problem Set A (A)   Five more extensive applications of chapter topics, often covering more than one learning objective. Selected problems in each chapter contain writing components.

Problem Set B (B)   An alternative set of problems.

CRITICAL THINKING AND COMMUNICATION

Conceptual Mini-Cases (CMC)   Designed so a written solution is appropriate, but usable in other communication modes, these short cases address conceptual accounting issues and are based on real companies and situations.

Ethics Mini-Cases (EMC)   In recognition that accounting and business students need to be exposed in all their courses to ethical considerations, every chapter has a short case, often based on a real company, in which students must address an ethical dilemma directly related to the chapter content.

Decision-Making Case (DMC)   In the role of decision maker, the student is asked to extract relevant data from a longer case, make computations as necessary, and arrive at a determination. The decision maker may be a manager, an investor, an analyst, or a creditor.

Basic Research Activity (RA)   These exercises are designed to acquaint students with the use of business periodicals, annual reports and business references, and the library. Through field activities at actual businesses, students can improve interviewing and observation skills.

FINANCIAL REPORTING AND ANALYSIS

Interpretation Cases from Business (ICB)   Short cases abstracted from business articles and annual reports of well-known corporations and organizations such as K-Mart, Sears, IBM, Toys "R" Us, Chrysler, and UAL (United Airlines) require students to extract relevant data, make computations, and interpret the results.

International Company Case (ICC)   Short cases similar to the ICBs, but involving companies from other countries.

Toys "R" Us Case (TC)   Cases that emphasize the reading and analysis of the actual annual report of Toys "R" Us contained in an appendix at the end of the book.

COMPREHENSIVE PROBLEM

A comprehensive problem covering Chapters 11 and 12 has been added after Chapter 12. Comprehensive stockholders' equity transactions for Sundial Corporation are recorded and a statement of stockholders' equity is prepared.

COMPUTER ASSIGNMENTS

Exercises, cases, and problems that can be solved with Lotus® or General Ledger Software are identified by icons in the text.

MOODY'S COMPANY DATA™ ASSIGNMENT BOOKLET

A series of cases that make use of the Moody's Company Data Base software containing the complete financial records of approximately one-hundred publicly held U.S. companies, keyed to topics in the text.

BUSINESS READINGS

Accompanying the text is a booklet of approximately thirty readings from business and accounting periodicals, such as *Business Week*, *Forbes*, the *Wall Street Journal*, the *Journal of Accountancy*, and *Management Accounting*. These readings, which are coordinated to chapter topics, highlight the relevance of accounting to business issues for real companies. In addition, they address ethical issues, international accounting, not-for-profit applications, and historical perspectives.

FINANCIAL ANALYSIS CASES

Also accompanying the text are a series of comprehensive financial analysis cases that may be integrated throughout the course after Chapter 6 or used as a capstone for the entire course. The first, *General Mills: Decision Case in Financial Analysis*, uses the actual annual report of General Mills, Inc. The other cases, *Heartland Airways, Inc.* and *Richland Home Centers, Inc.*, present complete annual reports for an airline company and a home improvement retailing chain and guide students through a complete financial analysis. These cases may be assigned individually, and provide excellent group assignments, as well. *Soft-Tec, Inc.*, a practice case based on a small merchandising business operating as a corporation, is also available for use after Chapter 5 in the text.

A MORE VISUALLY INTERESTING BOOK

New four-color photographs have been added to every chapter to illustrate the relevance of accounting to business. Bright, lively colors and more contemporary graphics are used throughout. Most illustrations of concepts and relationships have been redrawn for greater clarity, and many new illustrations have been added to enhance comprehension and visual appeal. Examples of the new visual approach in the first five chapters include all illustrations in Chapter 1, the figure depicting the analysis and processing of accounting transactions in Chapter 2, the five figures showing account relationships for adjusting entries in Chapter 3, the figures of the accounting cycle and the closing process in Chapter 4, and the figure illustrating the components of cost of goods sold in Chapter 5.

SUPPLEMENTARY LEARNING AIDS

Study Guide

Business Readings in Financial Accounting

Working Papers for Exercises and A Problems

Blank Working Papers

Check List of Key Figures

Accounting Transaction Tutor

General Ledger Software

Lotus® Templates to Accompany Financial Accounting, with Student Manual

Moody's Company Data™ **Software and Assignment Booklet**
Moody's Handbook of Dividend Achievers™—**1994 Houghton Mifflin**
Educational Edition
Student Resource Videos for Chapters 1–4
Business Bulletin Videos

INSTRUCTOR'S SUPPORT MATERIALS

Instructor's Solutions Manual
Instructor's Handbook
Test Bank
Computerized Test Bank
A.S.S.E.T.: Accounting Software System for Electronic Transparencies
Solutions Transparencies Boxes 1 & 2
Teaching Transparencies
Videodisc
Master Teacher Video

SPECIAL ACKNOWLEDGMENT

I express my thanks and admiration to my two colleagues, Henry R. Anderson of the University of Central Florida and James C. Caldwell of Andersen Consulting, Dallas, Texas, for their support and contribution to this textbook. The learning by objectives system in this text is based on the one developed by the three of us and used in all our texts.

ACKNOWLEDGMENTS

Preparing a financial accounting text is a long and demanding project that cannot really succeed without the help of one's colleagues. I am grateful to a large number of professors, other professional colleagues, and students for their many constructive comments on the text. Unfortunately, any attempt to list all who have helped risks slighting some by omission. Nonetheless, some try must be made to mention those who have been so helpful.

I wish to express my deep appreciation to my colleagues at DePaul University, who have been extremely supportive and encouraging.

The thoughtful and meticulous work of Edward Julius (California Lutheran University) is reflected not only in the Study Guide and Test Bank, but also in many other ways. I also would like to thank Marguerite Savage (Elgin Community College) for her work on the Instructor's Handbook, as well as Marion Taube (University of Pittsburgh) for her contribution to the Working Papers.

I want to thank Marian Powers for her constant assistance, inspiration, and support for this book. Also very important to the quality of this book is the supportive collaboration of my sponsoring editor, Karen Natale. I further benefited from the ideas and guidance of my associate sponsoring editor, Peggy Monahan, and my developmental editor, Cynthia Fostle. Thanks also go to Fred Shafer and Laurie Grano for their help with the preparation of the manuscript.

Others, who have been supportive and have had an impact on this book throughout their reviews, suggestions, and class testing are:

Martin E. Batross	*Franklin University*
Reba Love Cunningham	*Austin College*
Mark Dawson	
David Fetyko	*Kent State University*
Thomas M. Finnicum	*Oklahoma State University*
Rita Grant	*Grand Valley State University*
Dennis Gutting	*Orange County Community College*
Thomas Hilgeman	*St. Louis Community College at Meramec*
Paul E. Holt	*Texas A & I*
Cathy Xanthaky Larson	*Middlesex Community College*
Alvin Lieberman	*The University of Akron*
Rene P. Manes	*Florida State University*
Mary D. Maury	*St. John's University*
Michael F. Monahan	
Jenine Moscove	
Rebecca L. Phillips	*University of Louisville*
Harold Ripley	*Orange County Community College*
Sharon L. Robinson	*Frostburg State University*
Margo Rock	*Hillsborough Community College*
Larry Roman	*Cuyahoga Community College*
Marguerite Savage	*Elgin Community College*
Donald Shannon	*DePaul University*
Philip H. Siegel	*University of Houston—Downtown*
S. Murray Simons	*Northeastern University*
Elaine Simpson	*St. Louis CC at Florissant Valley*
Dr. Ralph S. Spanswick	*California State University at Los Angeles*
Marion Taube	*University of Pittsburgh*
Teresa D. Thamer	*Embry Riddle University*
John M. Trussel	*Hood College*
T. Sterling Wetzel	*Oklahoma State University*
Glenn Young	
Marilyn Young	*Tulsa Junior College*
William G. Zorr	*University of Wisconsin—Oshkosh*

How to Study Accounting Successfully

Whether you are majoring in accounting or in another business discipline, your financial accounting course is one of the most important classes you will take, because it is fundamental to the business curriculum and to your success in the business world beyond college. The course has multiple purposes because its students have diverse interests, backgrounds, and purposes for taking it. What are your goals in studying financial accounting? Being clear about your goals can contribute to your success in this course.

Success in this class also depends on your desire to learn and your willingness to work hard. And it depends on your understanding of how the text complements the way your instructor teaches and the way you learn. A familiarity with how this text is structured will help you to study more efficiently, make better use of classroom time, and improve your performance on examinations and other assignments.

To be successful in the business world after you graduate, you will need a broad set of skills, which may be summarized as follows:

Technical/Analytical Skills A major objective of your financial accounting course is to give you a firm grasp of the essential business and accounting terminology and techniques that you will need to succeed in a business environment. With this foundation, you then can begin to develop the higher-level perception skills that will help you to acquire further knowledge on your own.

An even more crucial objective of this course is to help you develop analytical skills that will allow you to evaluate data. Well-developed analytical and decision-making skills are among the professional skills most highly valued by employers, and will serve you well throughout your academic and professional careers.

Communication Skills Another skill highly prized by employers is the ability to express oneself in a manner that is understood correctly by others. This can include writing skills, speaking skills, and presentation skills. Communication skills are developed through particular tasks and assignments and are improved through constructive criticism. Reading skills and listening skills support the direct communication skills.

Interpersonal Skills Effective interaction between two people requires a solid foundation of interpersonal skills. The success of such interaction depends on empathy, or the ability to identify with and understand the problems, concerns, and motives of others. Leadership, supervision, and interviewing skills also facilitate a professional's interaction with others.

Personal/Self Skills   Personal/self skills form the foundation for growth in the use of all other skills. To succeed, a professional must take initiative, possess self-confidence, show independence, and be ethical in all areas of life. Personal/self skills can be enhanced significantly by the formal learning process and by peers and mentors who provide models upon which you can build. Financial Accounting is just one course in your entire curriculum, but it can play an important role in your development of the above skills. Your instructor is interested in helping you gain both a knowledge of accounting and the more general skills you will need to succeed in the business world. The following sections describe how you can get the most out of this course.

THE TEACHING/LEARNING CYCLE™

Both teaching and learning have natural, parallel, and mutually compatible cycles. This teaching/learning cycle, as shown in Figure 1 on page xxxii, interacts with the basic structure of learning objectives in this text.

The Teaching Cycle   The inner (blue) circle in Figure 1 shows the steps an instructor takes in teaching a chapter. Your teacher *assigns* material, *presents* the subject in lecture, *explains* by going over assignments and answering questions, *reviews* the subject prior to an exam, and *tests* your knowledge and understanding using examinations and other means of evaluation.

The Learning Cycle   Moving outward, the next circle (pink) in Figure 1 shows the steps you should take in studying a chapter. You should *preview* the material, *read* the chapter, *apply* your understanding by working the assignments, *review* the chapter, and *recall* and *demonstrate* your knowledge and understanding of the material on examinations and other assessments.

Integrated Learning Objectives   Your textbook supports the teaching/learning cycle through the use of integrated learning objectives. Learning objectives are simply statements of what you should be able to do after you have completed a chapter. In Figure 1, the outside (green) circle shows how learning objectives are integrated into your text and other study aids and how they interact with the teaching/learning cycle.

1. Learning objectives appear at the beginning of the chapter, as an aid to your teacher in making assignments and as a preview of the chapter for you.
2. Each learning objective is repeated in the text at the point where that subject is covered to assist your teacher in presenting the material and to help you organize your thoughts as you read the material.
3. Every exercise, problem, and case in the chapter assignments shows the applicable learning objective(s) so you can refer to the text if you need help.
4. A summary of the key points for each learning objective, a list of new concepts and terms referenced by learning objectives, and a review problem covering key learning objectives assist you in reviewing each chapter. Your Study Guide, also organized by learning objectives, provides for additional review.

Why Students Succeed   Students succeed in their accounting course when they coordinate their personal learning cycle with their instructor's cycle. Students who do a good job of previewing their assignments, reading the chapters before the instructor is ready to present them, preparing homework assignments before they are discussed in class, and reviewing carefully will ultimately achieve their potential on exams. Those who get out of phase with

Figure 1. The Teaching/Learning Cycle™ with Integrated Learning Objectives

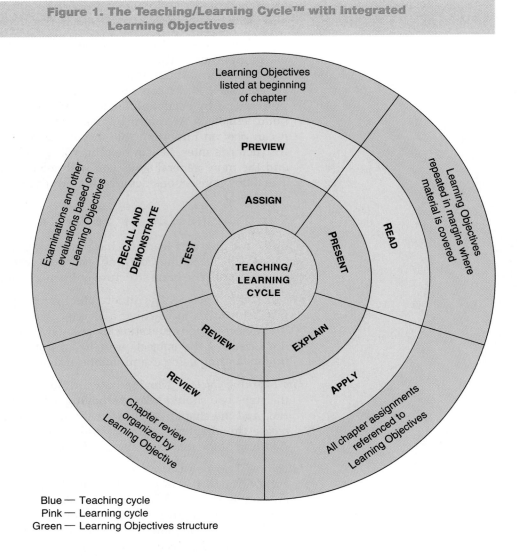

Blue — Teaching cycle
Pink — Learning cycle
Green — Learning Objectives structure

their instructor, for whatever reason, will do poorly or fail. To ensure that your learning cycle is synchronized with your instructor's teaching cycle, check your study habits against these suggestions.

PREVIEWING THE CHAPTER

1. Read the learning objectives at the beginning of the chapter. These learning objectives specifically describe what you should be able to do after completing the chapter.
2. Study your syllabus. Know where you are in the course and where you are going. Know the rules of the course.
3. Realize that in an accounting course, each assignment builds on previous ones. If you do poorly in Chapter 1, you may have difficulty in Chapter 2 and be lost in Chapter 3.

READING THE CHAPTER

1. As you read each chapter, be aware of the learning objectives in the margins. They will tell you why the material is relevant.

2. Allow yourself plenty of time to read the text. Accounting is a technical subject. Accounting books are so full of information that almost every sentence is important.

3. Strive to understand why as well as how each procedure is done. Accounting is logical and requires reasoning. If you understand why something is done in accounting, there is little need to memorize.

4. Relate each new topic to its learning objective and be able to explain it in your own words.

5. Be aware of colors as you read. They are designed to help you understand the text. (See the chart on the back of your textbook.)

   Yellow: All source documents and inputs are in yellow.

   Aqua: All accounting forms, working papers, and accounting processes are shown in aqua.

   Purple: All financial statements, the output or final product of the accounting process, are shown in purple.

   Gray: In selected tables and illustrations, gray is used to heighten contrasts and aid understanding.

6. If there is something you do not understand, prepare specific questions for your instructor. Pinpoint the topic or concept that confuses you. Some students keep a notebook of points with which they have difficulty.

APPLYING THE CHAPTER

1. In addition to understanding why each procedure is done, you must be able to do it yourself by working exercises, problems, and cases. Accounting is a "do-it-yourself" course.

2. Read assignments and instructions carefully. Each assignment has a specific purpose. The wording is precise, and a clear understanding of it will save time and improve your performance. Acquaint yourself with the end-of-chapter assignment materials in this text by reading the description of them in the Preface.

3. Try to work exercises, problems, and cases without referring to their discussions in the chapter. If you cannot work an assignment without looking in the chapter, you will not be able to work a similar problem on an exam. After you have tried on your own, refer to the chapter (based on the learning objective reference) and check your answer. Try to understand any mistakes you may have made.

4. Be neat and orderly. Sloppy calculations, messy papers, and general carelessness cause most errors on accounting assignments.

5. Allow plenty of time to work the chapter assignments. You will find that assignments seem harder and that you make more errors when you are feeling pressed for time.

6. Keep up with your class. Check your work against the solutions presented in class. Find your mistakes. Be sure you understand the correct solutions.

7. Note the part of each exercise, problem, or case that causes you difficulty so you can ask for help.

8. Attend class. Most instructors design classes to help you and to answer your questions. Absence from even one class can hurt your performance.

REVIEWING THE CHAPTER

1. Read the summary of learning objectives in the chapter review. Be sure you know all the words in the review of concepts and terminology.

2. Review all assigned exercises, problems, and cases. Know them cold. Be sure you can work the assignments without the aid of the book.

3. Determine the learning objectives for which most of the problems were assigned. They refer to topics that your instructor is most likely to emphasize

on an exam. Scan the text for such learning objectives and pay particular attention to the examples and illustrations.

4. Look for and scan other similar assignments that cover the same learning objectives. They may be helpful on an exam.
5. Review quizzes. Similar material will often appear on longer exams.
6. Attend any labs or visit any tutors your school provides, or see your instructor during office hours to get assistance. Be sure to have specific questions ready.

TAKING EXAMINATIONS

1. Arrive at class early so you can get the feel of the room and make a last-minute review of your notes.
2. Have plenty of sharp pencils and your calculator (if allowed) ready.
3. Review the exam quickly when it is handed out to get an overview of your task. Start with a part you know. It will give you confidence and save time.
4. Allocate your time to the various parts of the exam, and stick to your schedule. Every exam has time constraints. You need to move ahead and make sure you attempt all parts of the exam.
5. Read the questions carefully. Some may not be exactly like your homework assignments. They may approach the material from a slightly different angle to test your understanding and ability to reason, rather than your ability to memorize.
6. To avoid unnecessary errors, be neat, use good form, and show calculations.
7. Relax. If you have followed the above guidelines, your effort will be rewarded.

PREPARING OTHER ASSIGNMENTS

1. Understand the assignment. Written assignments, term papers, computer projects, oral presentations, case studies, group activities, individual field trips, video critiques, and other activities are designed to enhance skills beyond your technical knowledge. It is essential to know exactly what your instructor expects. Know the purpose, audience, scope, and expected end product.
2. Allow plenty of time. "Murphy's Law" applies to such assignments: If anything can go wrong, it will.
3. Prepare an outline of each report, paper, or presentation. A well-done project always has a logical structure.
4. Write a rough draft of each paper and report, and practice each presentation. Professionals always try out their ideas in advance and thoroughly rehearse their presentations. Good results are not accomplished by accident.
5. Make sure that each paper, report, or presentation is of professional quality. Instructors appreciate attention to detail and polish. A good rule of thumb is to ask yourself: Would I give this work to my boss?

Accounting as an Information System

Accounting is an information system for measuring, processing, and communicating information that is useful in making economic decisions. **Part One** focuses on the users and uses of accounting information and presents the fundamental concepts and techniques of the basic accounting system, including the presentation and analysis of financial statements.

CHAPTER 1
Uses of Accounting Information and the Basic Financial Statements

explores the nature and environment of accounting, with special emphasis on the users and uses of accounting information. It introduces the four basic financial statements, the concept of accounting measurement, and the effects of business transactions on financial position. This chapter concludes with a discussion of ethical considerations in accounting.

CHAPTER 2
Measuring Business Transactions

continues the exploration of accounting measurement by focusing on the problems of recognition, valuation, and classification and how they are solved in the measuring and recording of business transactions.

CHAPTER 3
Measuring Business Income

defines the accounting concept of business income, discusses the role of adjusting entries in the measurement of income, and demonstrates the preparation of financial statements.

CHAPTER 4
Completing the Accounting Cycle

focuses on the preparation of closing entries and the completion of the accounting cycle. The work sheet is presented as a supplemental learning objective.

CHAPTER 5
Accounting for Merchandising Operations

introduces the merchandising business and the merchandising income statement. The periodic and perpetual inventory systems receive equal treatment. Internal control for merchandising businesses is the final topic of the chapter.

CHAPTER 6
Financial Reporting and Analysis

introduces the objectives and qualitative aspects of financial information. It demonstrates how much more useful classified financial statements are than simple financial statements in presenting information to statement users. This chapter also includes an introduction to financial statement analysis.

CHAPTER 1

Uses of Accounting Information and the Basic Financial Statements

LEARNING OBJECTIVES

1. Define *accounting*, identify business goals and activities, and describe the role of accounting in making informed decisions.

2. Identify the many users of accounting information in society.

3. Explain the importance of business transactions, money measure, and separate entity to accounting measurement.

4. Describe the corporate form of business organization.

5. Define *financial position*, state the accounting equation, and show how they are affected by simple transactions.

6. Identify the four basic financial statements.

7. State the relationship of generally accepted accounting principles (GAAP) to financial statements and the independent CPA's report, and identify the organizations that influence GAAP.

8. Define *ethics* and describe the ethical responsibilities of accountants.

DECISION POINT

Gerber Products Co.

Top management of Gerber Products Co., a leader in baby and toddler food products, children's clothes, and other markets, states the following financial goals in its annual report to stockholders:

1. Seek real earnings growth of 6 to 8 percent annually.
2. Sustain a return on equity of at least 24 percent.
3. Maintain cash flow from operations (earnings before interest, taxes, and depreciation) at a minimum of 15 percent of revenues.
4. Increase dividends commensurate with earnings growth.

Management views these goals as essential to building the long-term wealth of the company's owners. What financial knowledge do the company's managers need in order to achieve these goals?

Each goal is stated in terms of financial results. Gerber's managers must have a thorough knowledge of accounting to understand how the operations for which they are responsible contribute to the firm's overall financial health as reflected by these goals. This requires a mastery of the terminology and concepts that underlie accounting, of the way in which financial information is generated, and of the way in which that information is interpreted and analyzed. The purpose of this textbook is to assist you in acquiring that mastery. : : : : :

ACCOUNTING AS AN INFORMATION SYSTEM

OBJECTIVE

1 *Define accounting, identify business goals and activities, and describe the role of accounting in making informed decisions*

Today's accountant focuses on the ultimate needs of decision makers who use accounting information, whether those decision makers are inside or outside the business. Accounting "is not an end in itself,"[1] but is *an information system that measures, processes, and communicates financial information about an identifiable economic entity.* An economic entity is a unit that exists independently—for example, a business, a hospital, or a governmental body. The central focus of this book is on business entities and business activities, although other economic units, such as hospitals and governmental units, will be mentioned at appropriate points in the text and assignment material.

Accounting provides a vital service by supplying the information decision makers need to make "reasoned choices among alternative uses of scarce

1. *Statement of Financial Accounting Concepts No. 1,* "Objectives of Financial Reporting by Business Enterprises" (Stamford, Conn.: Financial Accounting Standards Board, 1978), par. 9.

resources in the conduct of business and economic activities."[2] As shown in Figure 1-1, accounting is a link between business activities and decision makers. First, accounting measures business activities by recording data about them for future use. Second, the data are stored until needed and then processed to become useful information. Third, the information is communicated, through reports, to decision makers. We might say that data about business activities are the input to the accounting system and that useful information for decision makers is the output.

BUSINESS BULLETIN: BUSINESS PRACTICE

Accounting is a very old discipline. Forms of it have been essential to commerce for more than five thousand years. Accounting, in a version close to what we know today, gained widespread use in the 1400s, especially in Italy, where it was instrumental to the development of shipping, trade, construction, and other forms of commerce. This system of double-entry bookkeeping was documented by the famous Italian mathematician, scholar, and philosopher Fra Luca Pacioli. In 1494, Pacioli published his most important work, *Summa de Arithmetica, Geometrica, Proportioni et Proportionalita*, which contained a detailed description of accounting as practiced in that age. This book became the most widely read book on mathematics in Italy and firmly established Pacioli as the "Father of Accounting." ══════

BUSINESS GOALS AND ACTIVITIES

A business is an economic unit that aims to sell goods and services to customers at prices that will provide an adequate return to its owners. For example, listed below are some companies and the principal goods or services they sell:

Gerber Products Co.	Baby food and baby-care products
Reebok International Ltd.	Athletic footwear and clothing
Sony Corp.	Consumer electronics
Wendy's International Inc.	Food service
Hilton Hotels Corp.	Hotels and resorts service
USAir, Inc.	Passenger airline service

Despite their differences, all these businesses have similar goals and engage in similar activities, as shown in Figure 1-2. Each must take in enough money from customers to pay all the costs of doing business, with enough left over as profit for the owners to want to stay in the business. This need to earn enough income to attract and hold investment capital is the goal of profitability. In addition, businesses must meet the goal of liquidity. Liquidity means having enough funds on hand to pay debts when they are due. For example, Toyota may meet the goal of profitability by selling many cars at a price that earns a profit, but if its customers do not pay for their cars quickly

2. Ibid.

Figure 1-1. Accounting as an Information System

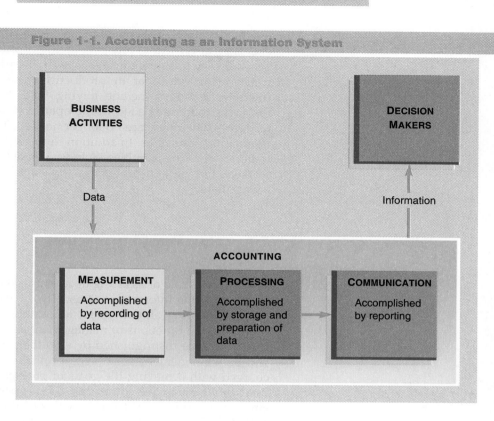

enough to enable Toyota to pay its suppliers and employees, the company may fail to meet the goal of liquidity. Both goals must be met if a company is to survive and be successful.

All businesses pursue their goals by engaging in similar activities. First, each business must engage in financing activities to obtain adequate funds, or capital, to begin and to continue operating. Financing activities include

Figure 1-2. Business Goals and Activities

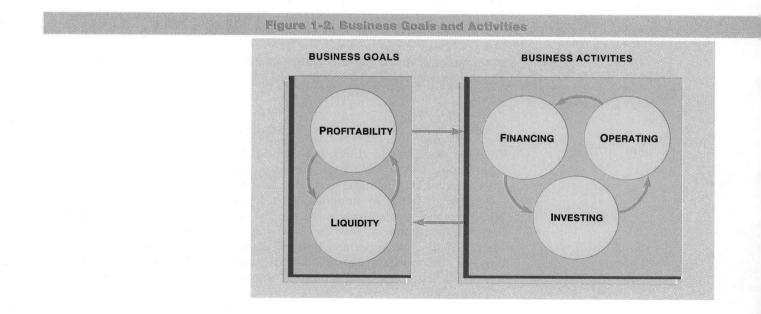

obtaining capital from owners and from creditors, such as banks and suppliers. They also include repaying creditors and paying a return to the owners. Second, each business must engage in investing activities to spend the capital it receives in ways that are productive and will help to achieve its objectives. Investing activities include buying land, buildings, equipment, and other resources that are needed in the operation of the business, and selling these resources when they are no longer needed. Third, each business must engage in operating activities. In addition to the selling of goods and services to customers, operating activities include such actions as employing managers and workers, buying and producing goods and services, and paying taxes to the government.

FINANCIAL AND MANAGEMENT ACCOUNTING

Accounting's role of assisting decision makers by measuring, processing, and communicating information is usually divided into the categories of management accounting and financial accounting. Although there is considerable overlap in the functions of management accounting and financial accounting, the two can be distinguished by who the principal users of their information will be. Management accounting provides internal decision makers who are charged with achieving the goals of profitability and liquidity with information about financing, investing, and operating activities. Managers and employees who conduct the activities of the business need information that tells them how they have done in the past and what they can expect in the future. For example, The Gap needs an operating report on each mall outlet that tells how much was sold at that outlet, and what costs were incurred, and it needs a budget for each outlet that projects the sales and costs for the next year. Financial accounting generates reports and communicates them to external decision makers so that they can evaluate how well the business has achieved its goals. These reports to external users are called financial statements. The Gap, for instance, will send its financial statements to its owners (called *stockholders*), its banks and other creditors, and government regulators. Financial statements report directly on the goals of profitability and liquidity and are used extensively both inside and outside a business to evaluate the business's success. It is important for every person involved with a business to understand financial statements. They are a central feature of accounting and are the primary focus of this book.

PROCESSING ACCOUNTING INFORMATION

To avoid misunderstandings, it is important to distinguish accounting itself from the ways in which accounting information is processed by bookkeeping, the computer, and management information systems.

People often fail to understand the difference between accounting and bookkeeping. Bookkeeping is the process of recording financial transactions and keeping financial records. Mechanical and repetitive, bookkeeping is only a small—but important—part of accounting. Accounting, on the other hand, includes the design of an information system that meets the user's needs. The major goals of accounting are the analysis, interpretation, and use of information.

The computer is an electronic tool that is used to collect, organize, and communicate vast amounts of information with great speed. Accountants were among the earliest and most enthusiastic users of computers, and today they use microcomputers in all aspects of their work. It may appear that the computer is doing the accountant's job; in fact, it is only a tool that is instructed to do routine bookkeeping and to perform complex calculations.

With the widespread use of the computer today, a business's many information needs are organized into what is called a management information system (MIS). A management information system consists of the interconnected subsystems that provide the information needed to run a business. The accounting information system is the most important subsystem because it plays the key role of managing the flow of economic data to all parts of a business and to interested parties outside the business.

DECISION MAKERS: THE USERS OF ACCOUNTING INFORMATION

OBJECTIVE

2 *Identify the many users of accounting information in society*

The people who use accounting information to make decisions fall into three categories: (1) those who manage a business; (2) those outside a business enterprise who have a direct financial interest in the business; and (3) those people, organizations, and agencies that have an indirect financial interest in the business, as shown in Figure 1-3.

MANAGEMENT

Management, collectively, is the people who have overall responsibility for operating a business and for meeting its profitability and liquidity goals. In a small business, management may include the owners. In a large business, management more often consists of people who have been hired. Managers

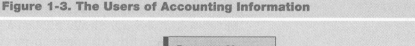

Figure 1-3. The Users of Accounting Information

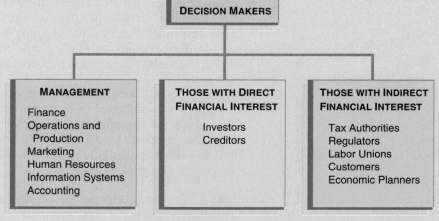

must decide what to do, how to do it, and whether the results match their original plans. Successful managers consistently make the right decisions based on timely and valid information. To make good decisions, managers need answers to such questions as: What was the company's net income during the past quarter? Is the rate of return to the owners adequate? Does the company have enough cash? Which products are most profitable? What is the cost of manufacturing each product? Because so many key decisions are based on accounting data, management is one of the most important users of accounting information.

In carrying out its decision-making process, management performs a set of functions essential to the operation of the business. Although larger businesses will have more elaborate operations, the same basic functions must be accomplished in all cases, and each requires accounting information for decision making. The basic management functions are:

> *Financing the business.* Financial management obtains financial resources so that the company can begin, and continue, operating.
>
> *Investing the resources of the business.* Asset management invests the financial resources of the business in productive assets that support the company's goals.
>
> *Producing goods and services.* Operations and production management develops and produces products and services.
>
> *Marketing goods and services.* Marketing management sells, advertises, and distributes goods and services.
>
> *Managing employees.* Human resource management encompasses the hiring, evaluation, and compensation of employees.
>
> *Providing information to decision makers.* Information management captures data about all aspects of the company's operations, organizes the data into usable information, and provides reports to internal managers and appropriate outside parties. Accounting plays a key role in this function.

USERS WITH A DIRECT FINANCIAL INTEREST

Another group of decision makers who need accounting information are those with a direct financial interest in a business. They depend on accounting to measure and report information about how a business has performed. Most businesses periodically publish a set of general-purpose financial statements that report their success in meeting the goals of profitability and liquidity. These statements show what has happened in the past and are important indicators of what is going to happen in the future. Many people outside the company carefully study these financial reports. The two most important outside groups are investors and creditors.

Investors   Those who invest or may invest in a business and acquire a part ownership are interested in its past success and its potential earnings. A thorough study of a company's financial statements helps potential investors judge the prospects for a profitable investment. After investing in a company, investors must continually review their commitment, again by examining the company's financial statements.

Creditors   Most companies borrow money for both long- and short-term operating needs. Creditors, those who lend money or deliver goods and services before being paid, are interested mainly in whether a company will have the cash to pay interest charges and repay debt at the appropriate time. They study a company's liquidity and cash flow as well as its profitability. Banks, finance companies, mortgage companies, securities firms, insurance firms, suppliers, and other lenders must analyze a company's financial position before they make a loan.

USERS WITH AN INDIRECT FINANCIAL INTEREST

In recent years, society as a whole, through government and public groups, has become one of the biggest and most important users of accounting information. Users who need accounting information to make decisions on public issues include (1) tax authorities, (2) regulatory agencies, and (3) other groups.

Tax Authorities Government at every level is financed through the collection of taxes. Under federal, state, and local laws, companies and individuals pay many kinds of taxes, including federal, state, and city income taxes, social security and other payroll taxes, excise taxes, and sales taxes. Each tax requires special tax returns and often a complex set of records as well. Proper reporting is generally a matter of law and can be very complicated. The Internal Revenue Code, for instance, contains thousands of rules governing the preparation of the accounting information used in computing federal income taxes.

Regulatory Agencies Most companies must report to one or more regulatory agencies at the federal, state, and local levels. For example, all public corporations must report periodically to the Securities and Exchange Commission (SEC). This body, which was set up by Congress to protect the public, regulates the issuing, buying, and selling of stocks in the United States. Companies that are listed on a stock exchange also must meet the special reporting requirements of their exchange.

Other Groups Labor unions study the financial statements of corporations as part of preparing for contract negotiations. A company's income and costs often play an important role in these negotiations. Those who advise investors and creditors—financial analysts and advisers, brokers, underwriters, lawyers, economists, and the financial press—also have an indirect interest in the financial performance and prospects of a business. Consumers' groups, customers, and the general public have become more concerned about the financing and earnings of corporations as well as the effects that corporations have on inflation, the environment, social problems, and the quality of life. And economic planners, among them members of the President's Council of Economic Advisers and the Federal Reserve Board, use aggregated accounting information to set economic policies and evaluate economic programs.

GOVERNMENT AND NOT-FOR-PROFIT ORGANIZATIONS

More than 30 percent of the U.S. economy is generated by government and not-for-profit organizations (hospitals, universities, professional organizations, and charities). Like the heads of private firms, the managers of these diverse entities need accounting information. They need to raise funds and deploy scarce resources. They need to plan to pay for operations and repay creditors on a timely basis. Moreover, they have an obligation to report their financial performance to legislators, boards, and contributors. Although most of the examples in this text focus on business enterprises, the same basic principles apply to government and not-for-profit organizations. We discuss accounting for these types of organizations in an appendix to the textbook.

ACCOUNTING MEASUREMENT

Accounting is an information system that measures, processes, and communicates financial information. In this section, you begin the study of the measurement aspects of accounting. Here you learn what accounting actually measures and study the effects of certain transactions on a company's financial position.

To make an accounting measurement, the accountant must answer four basic questions:

1. What is measured?
2. When should the measurement be made?
3. What value should be placed on what is measured?
4. How should what is measured be classified?

All these questions deal with basic assumptions and generally accepted accounting principles, and their answers establish what accounting is and what it is not. Accountants in industry, professional associations, public accounting, government, and academic circles debate the answers to these questions constantly, and the answers change as new knowledge and practice require. But the basis of today's accounting practice rests on a number of widely accepted concepts and conventions, which are described in this book. Questions **2**, **3**, and **4** are examined in the chapter on measuring and recording business transactions. Here we focus on question **1**: What is measured?

WHAT IS MEASURED?

The world contains an unlimited number of things to measure and ways to measure them. For example, consider a machine that makes bottle caps. How many measurements of this machine could you make? You might start with size and then go on to location, weight, cost, or one of many other units of measurement. Some of these measurements are relevant to accounting; some are not. Every system must define what it measures, and accounting is no exception. Basically, financial accounting uses money measures to gauge the impact of business transactions on separate business entities. The concepts of business transactions, money measure, and separate entity are discussed in the next sections.

BUSINESS TRANSACTIONS AS THE OBJECT OF MEASUREMENT

Business transactions are economic events that affect the financial position of a business entity. Business entities can have hundreds or even thousands of transactions every day. These business transactions are the raw material of accounting reports.

A transaction can be an exchange of value (a purchase, sale, payment, collection, or loan) between two or more independent parties. A transaction also can be an economic event that has the same effect as an exchange transaction but does not involve an exchange. Some examples of "nonexchange" transactions are losses from fire, flood, explosion, and theft; physical wear and tear on machinery and equipment; and the day-by-day accumulation of interest.

To be recorded, a transaction must relate directly to a business entity. For example, suppose a customer buys a shovel from Ace Hardware but has to buy a hoe from a competing store because Ace is out of hoes. The transaction in which the shovel was sold is entered in Ace's records. However, the purchase of the hoe from the competitor is not entered in Ace's records because even though it indirectly affects Ace economically, it does not involve a direct exchange of value between Ace and the customer.

MONEY MEASURE

All business transactions are recorded in terms of money. This concept is termed money measure. Of course, information of a nonfinancial nature may be recorded, but it is through the recording of monetary amounts that the diverse transactions and activities of a business are measured. Money is the only factor that is common to all business transactions, and thus it is the only practical unit of measure that can produce financial data that are alike and can be compared.

The monetary unit a business uses depends on the country in which the business resides. For example, in the United States, the basic unit of money is the dollar. In Japan, it is the yen; in France, the franc; in Germany, the mark; and in the United Kingdom, the pound. If there are transactions between countries, exchange rates must be used to translate from one currency to another. An exchange rate is the value of one currency in terms of another. For example, an English person purchasing goods from a U.S. company and paying in U.S. dollars must exchange British pounds for U.S. dollars before making payment. In effect, the currencies are goods that can be bought and sold. Table 1-1 illustrates the exchange rates for several currencies in terms of dollars. It shows the exchange rate for British pounds as $1.50 per pound on a particular date. Like the price of any good or service, these prices change daily according to supply and demand for the currencies. For example, a few

Table 1-1. Partial Listing of Foreign Exchange Rates

Country	Price in $ U.S.	Country	Price in $ U.S.
Britain (pound)	1.50	Italy (lira)	0.0006
Canada (dollar)	0.574	Japan (yen)	0.0095
France (franc)	0.18	Mexico (peso)	0.31
Germany (mark)	0.59	Philippines (peso)	0.034
Hong Kong (dollar)	0.13	Taiwan (dollar)	0.038

Source: The *Wall Street Journal*, Mar. 11, 1994. Reprinted by permission of *Wall Street Journal*. © 1993 Dow Jones & Company, Inc. All Rights Reserved.

years earlier the exchange rate for British pounds was $1.20. Although our discussion in this book focuses on dollars, selected examples and assignments will be in foreign currencies.

THE CONCEPT OF SEPARATE ENTITY

For accounting purposes, a business is a separate entity, distinct not only from its creditors and customers but also from its owner or owners. It should have a completely separate set of records, and its financial records and reports should refer only to its own financial affairs.

For example, the Jones Florist Company should have a bank account that is separate from the account of Kay Jones, the owner. Kay Jones may own a home, a car, and other property, and she may have personal debts, but these are not the Jones Florist Company's resources or debts. Kay Jones also may own another business, say a stationery shop. If she does, she should have a completely separate set of records for each business.

THE CORPORATION AS A SEPARATE ENTITY

OBJECTIVE

4 *Describe the corporate form of business organization*

There are three basic forms of business enterprise. Besides the corporate form, there are the sole proprietorship form and the partnership form. Whichever form is used, the business should be viewed for accounting purposes as a separate entity, and all its records and reports should be developed separate and apart from those of its owners.

CORPORATIONS DIFFERENTIATED FROM SOLE PROPRIETORSHIPS AND PARTNERSHIPS

A sole proprietorship is a business owned by one person. The individual receives all profits or losses and is liable for all obligations of the business. Proprietorships represent the largest number of businesses in the United States, but typically they are the smallest in size. A partnership is like a proprietorship in most ways except that it has two or more co-owners. The partners share the profits and losses of the partnership according to an agreed-upon formula. Generally, any partner can bind the partnership to another party, and, if necessary, the personal resources of each partner can be called on to pay obligations of the partnership. A partnership must be dissolved if the ownership changes, as when a partner leaves or dies. If the business is to continue as a partnership after this occurs, a new partnership must be formed. Both the sole proprietorship and the partnership are convenient ways of separating the business owners' commercial activities from their personal activities. But legally there is no economic separation between the owners and the businesses.[3]

A corporation, on the other hand, is a business unit that is legally separate from its owners (the stockholders). The stockholders, whose ownership is represented by shares of stock, do not directly control the corporation's operations. Instead they elect a board of directors to run the corporation for their

---

3. Accounting for sole proprietorships and partnerships is discussed in an appendix to this book.

benefit. In exchange for their limited involvement in the corporation's actual operations, stockholders enjoy limited liability. That is, their risk of loss is limited to the amount they paid for their shares. If they wish, stockholders can sell their shares without affecting corporate operations. Because of this limited liability, stockholders are often willing to invest in riskier, but potentially more profitable, activities. Also, because ownership can be transferred without dissolving the corporation, the life of a corporation is unlimited and not subject to the whims or health of a proprietor or a partner.

The characteristics of corporations make them very efficient in amassing capital, which enables them to grow extremely large. Even though corporations are fewer in number than sole proprietorships and partnerships, they contribute much more to the U.S. economy in monetary terms (see Figure 1-4). For example, in 1993, General Motors generated more revenues than all but fourteen of the world's countries. Because of the economic significance of corporations, this book will emphasize accounting for the corporate form of business.

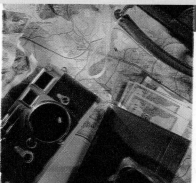

Santini Tours Company

DECISION POINT

Carlos Santos, the owner of a successful travel agency that operates in Chicago as a sole proprietorship, has just merged his company with Tiniger Tours Agency of Detroit, which is operated by three brothers as a partnership. Santos and the Tiniger brothers hope to make the new Santini Tours Company the Midwest's largest provider of specialized tours. To achieve this objective, they will need to raise money from investors and creditors. They are talking about organizing the new company as a corporation. Considering the differences between a sole proprietorship, a partnership, and a corporation, should they organize as a corporation?

Because Santini Tours Company has multiple owners and expects future growth, organizing as a corporation has advantages for the company. The corporate structure allows the transfer of ownership among multiple owners with a minimum of difficulty. In addition, it is often easier for a corporation to raise investment funds and secure loans from outside parties than it is for a sole proprietorship or a partnership. ⁚⁚⁚⁚⁚

FORMATION OF A CORPORATION

To form a corporation, most states require individuals, called incorporators, to sign an application and file it with the proper state official. This application contains the articles of incorporation. If approved by the state, these articles become, in effect, a contract, called the company charter, between the state and the incorporators. The company is then authorized to do business.

ORGANIZATION OF A CORPORATION

The authority to manage the corporation is delegated by the stockholders to the board of directors and by the board of directors to the corporate officers

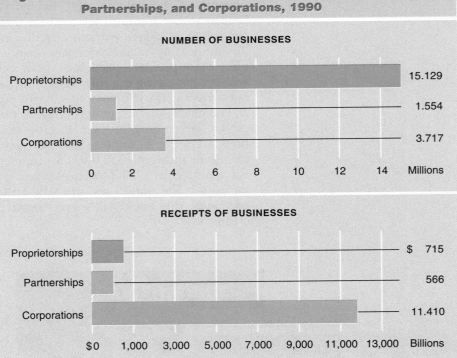

Figure 1-4. Number and Receipts of U.S. Proprietorships, Partnerships, and Corporations, 1990

Source: U.S. Treasury Department, Internal Revenue Service, *Statistics of Income Bulletin,* Winter 1992–1993, pp. 197–199.

(see Figure 1-5). That is, the stockholders elect the board of directors, which sets company policies and chooses the corporate officers, who in turn carry out the corporate policies by managing the business.

Stockholders   A unit of ownership in a corporation is called a share of stock. The articles of incorporation state the maximum number of shares of stock that the corporation will be allowed, or authorized, to issue. The number of shares held by stockholders is the outstanding capital stock; this may be less than the number authorized in the articles of incorporation. To invest in a corporation, a stockholder transfers cash or other resources to the corporation. In return, the stockholder receives shares of stock representing a proportionate share of ownership in the corporation. Afterward, the stockholder may transfer the shares at will. Corporations may have more than one kind of capital stock, but the first part of this book will refer only to common stock.

Board of Directors   As noted, the stockholders elect the board of directors, which in turn decides on the major business policies of the corporation. Among the specific duties of the board are authorizing contracts, setting executive salaries, and arranging major loans with banks. The declaration of dividends is also an important function of the board of directors. Only the board has the authority to declare dividends. Dividends are distributions of resources, generally in the form of cash, to the stockholders. Paying dividends is one way of rewarding stockholders for their investment when the corpora-

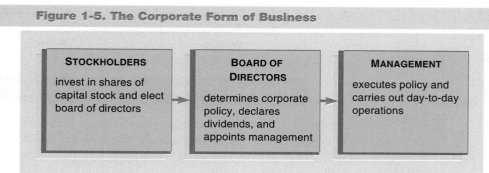

Figure 1-5. The Corporate Form of Business

STOCKHOLDERS	BOARD OF DIRECTORS	MANAGEMENT
invest in shares of capital stock and elect board of directors	determines corporate policy, declares dividends, and appoints management	executes policy and carries out day-to-day operations

tion has been successful in earning a profit. (The other way is through a rise in the market value of the stock.) Although there is usually a delay of two or three weeks between the time the board declares a dividend and the date of the actual payment, we shall assume in the early chapters of this book that declaration and payment are made on the same day.

The board of directors will vary in composition from company to company, but in most cases it will contain several officers of the corporation and several outsiders. Today, the formation of an audit committee with several outside directors is encouraged to make sure that the board will be objective in evaluating management's performance. One function of the audit committee is to engage the company's independent auditors and review their work. Another is to make sure that proper systems exist to safeguard the company's resources and ensure that reliable accounting records are kept.

Management   The board of directors appoints managers to carry out the corporation's policies and run day-to-day operations. The management consists of the operating officers, who are generally the president, vice presidents, controller, treasurer, and secretary. Besides being responsible for running the business, management has the duty of reporting the financial results of its administration to the board of directors and the stockholders. Though management must, at a minimum, make a comprehensive annual report, it may and generally does report more often. The annual reports of large public corporations are available to the public. Excerpts from many of them will be used throughout this book.

BUSINESS BULLETIN: BUSINESS PRACTICE

Most people think of corporations as large national or global companies whose shares of stock are held by thousands of people and institutions. Indeed, corporations can be huge and have many stockholders. However, of the approximately 3.7 million corporations in the United States, only about 15,000 have stock that is publicly bought and sold. The vast majority of corporations are small businesses that are privately held by a few stockholders. In Illinois alone there are more than 250,000 corporations. For this reason, the study of corporations is just as relevant to small businesses as it is to large ones. =====

OBJECTIVE

5 *Define* financial position, *state the accounting equation, and show how they are affected by simple transactions*

FINANCIAL POSITION AND THE ACCOUNTING EQUATION

Financial position refers to the economic resources that belong to a company and the claims against those resources at a point in time. Another term for claims is *equities.* Therefore, a company can be viewed as economic resources and equities:

$$\text{Economic resources} = \text{equities}$$

Every company has two types of equities, creditors' equities and owners' equity. Thus,

$$\text{Economic resources} = \text{creditors' equities} + \text{owners' equity}$$

In accounting terminology, economic resources are called *assets* and creditors' equities are called *liabilities.* So the equation can be written like this:

$$\text{Assets} = \text{liabilities} + \text{owners' equity}$$

This equation is known as the **accounting equation.** The two sides of the equation always must be equal, or "in balance."

ASSETS

Assets are economic resources owned by a business that are expected to benefit future operations. Certain kinds of assets—for example, cash and money owed to the company from customers (called *accounts receivable*)—are monetary items. Other assets—inventories (goods held for sale), land, buildings, and equipment—are nonmonetary physical things. Still other assets—the rights granted by patent, trademark, or copyright—are nonphysical.

LIABILITIES

Liabilities are present obligations of a business to pay cash, transfer assets, or provide services to other entities in the future. Among these obligations are debts of the business, amounts owed to suppliers for goods or services bought on credit (called *accounts payable*), borrowed money (for example, money owed on loans payable to banks), salaries and wages owed to employees, taxes owed to the government, and services to be performed.

As debts, liabilities are claims recognized by law. That is, the law gives creditors the right to force the sale of a company's assets if the company fails to pay its debts. Creditors have rights over owners and must be paid in full before the owners receive anything, even if payment of a debt uses up all the assets of a business.

OWNERS' EQUITY

Owners' equity represents the claims by the owners of a business to the assets of the business. It equals the residual interest, or residual equity, in the assets of an entity that remains after deducting the entity's liabilities. Theoretically, it is what would be left over if all the liabilities were paid and sometimes is said to equal net assets. By rearranging the accounting equation, we can define owners' equity this way:

$$\text{Owners' equity} = \text{assets} - \text{liabilities}$$

The owners' equity of a corporation is called stockholders' equity, so the accounting equation becomes

$$\text{Assets} = \text{liabilities} + \text{stockholders' equity}$$

Stockholders' equity has two parts, contributed capital and retained earnings:

$$\text{Stockholders' equity} = \text{contributed capital} + \text{retained earnings}$$

Contributed capital is the amount invested in the business by the stockholders. Their ownership in the business is represented by shares of capital stock. An example of a Federal Express stock certificate, which represents such ownership, is shown in Figure 1-6.

Typically, contributed capital is divided between par value and additional paid-in capital. Par value is an amount per share that is entered in the corporation's capital stock account and is the minimum amount that can be reported as contributed capital. Additional paid-in capital results when the stock is issued at an amount greater than par value. In the initial chapters of this book, contributed capital will be shown as common stock that has been issued at par value.

Figure 1-6. A Federal Express Stock Certificate

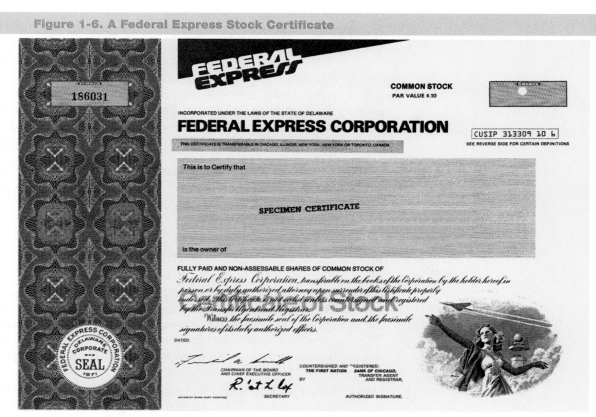

Source: Courtesy of Federal Express Corporation.

Retained earnings represent the equity of the stockholders generated from the income-producing activities of the business and kept for use in the business. As you can see in Figure 1-7, retained earnings are affected by three kinds of transactions: revenues, expenses, and dividends.

Simply stated, revenues and expenses are the increases and decreases in stockholders' equity that result from operating a business. For example, the cash a customer pays (or agrees to pay in the future) to a company in return for a service provided by the company is a revenue to the company. The assets (cash or accounts receivable) of the company increase, and the stockholders' equity in those assets also increases. On the other hand, the cash a company pays out (or agrees to pay in the future) in the process of providing a service is an expense. In this case, the assets (cash) decrease or the liabilities (accounts payable) increase, and the stockholders' equity decreases. Generally speaking, a company is successful if its revenues exceed its expenses. When revenues exceed expenses, the difference is called net income; when expenses exceed revenues, the difference is called net loss. Dividends are distributions to stockholders of assets (usually cash) generated by past earnings. It is important not to confuse expenses and dividends, both of which reduce retained earnings.

SOME ILLUSTRATIVE TRANSACTIONS

Let us now examine the effect of some of the most common business transactions on the accounting equation. Suppose that James and John Shannon open a real estate agency called Shannon Realty, Inc. on December 1. During December, their business engages in the transactions described in the following paragraphs.

Owners' Investments   James and John Shannon file articles of incorporation with the state and receive their charter. To begin their new business, they invest $50,000 in Shannon Realty, Inc. in exchange for 5,000 shares of $10 par value stock. The first balance sheet of the new company would show the asset Cash and the contributed capital (Common Stock) of the owners:

Assets	=	Stockholders' Equity (SE)	
Cash	Common Stock	Type of SE Transaction
1. $50,000	$50,000	Stockholders' Investments

At this point, the company has no liabilities, and assets equal stockholders' equity. The labels Cash and Common Stock are called accounts and are used by accountants to accumulate amounts that result from similar transactions. Transactions that affect stockholders' equity are identified by type so that similar types may later be grouped together on accounting reports.

Purchase of Assets with Cash   After a good location is found, the company pays cash to purchase a lot for $10,000 and a small building on the lot for $25,000. This transaction does not change the total assets, liabilities, or stock-

Figure 1-7. Three Types of Transactions That Affect Retained Earnings

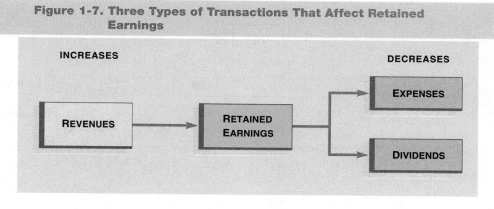

holders' equity of Shannon Realty, Inc., but it does change the composition of the assets—it decreases Cash and increases Land and Building:

	Assets			=	Stockholders' Equity	
	Cash	Land	Building		Common Stock	Type of SE Transaction
bal.	$50,000				$50,000	
2.	−35,000	+$10,000	+$25,000			
bal.	$15,000	$10,000	$25,000		$50,000	
		$50,000				

Purchase of Assets by Incurring a Liability   Assets do not always have to be purchased with cash. They may also be purchased on credit, that is, on the basis of an agreement to pay for them later. Suppose the company buys some office supplies for $500 on credit. This transaction increases the assets (Supplies) and increases the liabilities of Shannon Realty, Inc. This liability is designated by an account called Accounts Payable:

	Assets				=	Liabilities	+	Stockholders' Equity	
	Cash	Supplies	Land	Building		Accounts Payable		Common Stock	Type of SE Transaction
bal.	$15,000		$10,000	$25,000				$50,000	
3.		+$500				+$500			
bal.	$15,000	$500	$10,000	$25,000		$500		$50,000	
		$50,500					$50,500		

Notice that this transaction increases both sides of the accounting equation to $50,500.

Payment of a Liability   If the company later pays $200 of the $500 owed for the supplies, both assets (Cash) and liabilities (Accounts Payable) decrease, but Supplies is unaffected:

	Assets				= Liabilities +	Stockholders' Equity	
	Cash	Supplies	Land	Building	Accounts Payable	Common Stock	Type of SE Transaction
bal.	$15,000	$500	$10,000	$25,000	$500	$50,000	
4.	−200				−200		
bal.	$14,800	$500	$10,000	$25,000	$300	$50,000	
		$50,300				$50,300	

Notice that both sides of the accounting equation are still equal, although now at a total of $50,300.

Revenues   Shannon Realty, Inc. earns revenues in the form of commissions by selling houses for clients. Sometimes these commissions are paid to Shannon Realty, Inc. immediately in the form of cash, and sometimes the client agrees to pay the commission later. In either case, the commission is recorded when it is earned and Shannon Realty, Inc. has a right to a current or future receipt of cash. First, assume that Shannon Realty, Inc. sells a house and receives a commission of $1,500 in cash. This transaction increases both assets (Cash) and stockholders' equity (Retained Earnings):

	Assets				= Liabilities +	Stockholders' Equity		
	Cash	Supplies	Land	Building	Accounts Payable	Common Stock	Retained Earnings	Type of SE Transaction
bal.	$14,800	$500	$10,000	$25,000	$300	$50,000		
5.	+1,500						+$1,500	Commissions Earned
bal.	$16,300	$500	$10,000	$25,000	$300	$50,000	+$1,500	
		$51,800				$51,800		

Now assume that Shannon Realty, Inc. sells a house, in the process earning a commission of $2,000, and agrees to wait for payment of the commission. Because the commission has been earned now, a bill or invoice is sent to the client, and the transaction is recorded now. This revenue transaction increases both assets and stockholders' equity as before, but a new asset account, Accounts Receivable, shows that Shannon Realty, Inc. is awaiting receipt of the commission:

	Assets				= Liabilities +	Stockholders' Equity		
Cash	Accounts Receiv- able	Supplies	Land	Building	Accounts Payable	Common Stock	Retained Earnings	Type of SE Transaction
bal. $16,300		$500	$10,000	$25,000	$300	$50,000	$1,500	
6.	+$2,000						+2,000	Commissions Earned
bal. $16,300	$2,000	$500	$10,000	$25,000	$300	$50,000	$3,500	

$53,800 $53,800

The use of separate accounts for revenues, like Commissions Earned, will be introduced in the chapter on measuring business transactions.

Collection of Accounts Receivable   Let us assume that a few days later Shannon Realty, Inc. receives $1,000 from the client in transaction **6.** At that time, the asset Cash increases and the asset Accounts Receivable decreases:

	Assets				= Liabilities +	Stockholders' Equity		
Cash	Accounts Receiv- able	Supplies	Land	Building	Accounts Payable	Common Stock	Retained Earnings	Type of SE Transaction
bal. $16,300	$2,000	$500	$10,000	$25,000	$300	$50,000	$3,500	
7. +1,000	−1,000							
bal. $17,300	$1,000	$500	$10,000	$25,000	$300	$50,000	$3,500	

$53,800 $53,800

Notice that this transaction does not affect stockholders' equity because the commission revenue was already recorded in transaction **6.** Also, notice that the balance of Accounts Receivable is $1,000, indicating that $1,000 is still to be collected.

Expenses   Just as revenues are recorded when they are earned, expenses are recorded when they are incurred. Expenses can be paid in cash when they occur, or they can be paid later. If payment is going to be made later, a liability—for example, Accounts Payable or Wages Payable—increases. In both cases, stockholders' equity decreases. Assume that Shannon Realty, Inc. pays $1,000 to rent some equipment for the office and $400 in wages to a part-time helper. These transactions reduce assets (Cash) and stockholders' equity (Retained Earnings):

	Assets					= Liabilities +	Stockholders' Equity		
	Cash	Accounts Receiv- able	Supplies	Land	Building	Accounts Payable	Common Stock	Retained Earnings	Type of SE Transaction
bal.	$17,300	$1,000	$500	$10,000	$25,000	$300	$50,000	$3,500	
8.	−1,000							−1,000	Equipment Rental Expense
9.	−400							−400	Wages Expense
bal.	$15,900	$1,000	$500	$10,000	$25,000	$300	$50,000	$2,100	

$52,400 $52,400

Now assume that Shannon Realty, Inc. has not paid the $300 bill for utility expenses incurred for December. In this case, the effect on stockholders' equity is the same as when the expense is paid in cash, but instead of a reduction in assets, there is an increase in liabilities (Accounts Payable):

	Assets					= Liabilities +	Stockholders' Equity		
	Cash	Accounts Receiv- able	Supplies	Land	Building	Accounts Payable	Common Stock	Retained Earnings	Type of SE Transaction
bal.	$15,900	$1,000	$500	$10,000	$25,000	$300	$50,000	$2,100	
10.						+300		−300	Utility Expense
bal.	$15,900	$1,000	$500	$10,000	$25,000	$600	$50,000	$1,800	

$52,400 $52,400

The use of separate accounts for expenses will be introduced in the chapter on measuring business transactions.

Dividends   A dividend of $600 is declared, and it is paid by taking $600 out of the company's bank account and paying it to the stockholders for deposit in their personal bank accounts. The payment of dividends reduces assets (Cash) and stockholders' equity (Retained Earnings). Note that although these dividends reduce retained earnings in the same way as the expenses in transactions **8**, **9**, and **10**, they perform a different function. They are distributions of assets (Cash) to the stockholders, whereas the function of the expenses is to pay for services that helped produce the revenues in transactions **5** and **6**.

		Assets			= Liabilities +		Stockholders' Equity	
Cash	Accounts Receivable	Supplies	Land	Building	Accounts Payable	Common Stock	Retained Earnings	Type of SE Transaction
bal. $15,900	$1,000	$500	$10,000	$25,000	$600	$50,000	$1,800	
11. −600							−600	Dividends
bal. $15,300	$1,000	$500	$10,000	$25,000	$600	$50,000	$1,200	

$51,800 $51,800

Summary   A summary of these eleven illustrative transactions is presented in Exhibit 1-1 (on page 24).

COMMUNICATION THROUGH FINANCIAL STATEMENTS

OBJECTIVE

6 *Identify the four basic financial statements*

Financial statements are the primary means of communicating important accounting information to users. It is helpful to think of these statements as models of the business enterprise because they show the business in financial terms. As is true of all models, however, financial statements are not perfect pictures of the real thing, but rather the accountant's best effort to represent what is real. Four major financial statements are used to communicate accounting information about a business: the income statement, the statement of retained earnings, the balance sheet, and the statement of cash flows.

Exhibit 1-2 illustrates the relationship among the four financial statements by showing how they would appear for Shannon Realty, Inc. after the eleven sample transactions shown in Exhibit 1-1. It is assumed that the time period covered is the month of December, 19xx. Notice that each statement is headed in a similar way. Each heading identifies the company and the kind of statement. The income statement, the statement of retained earnings, and the statement of cash flows give the time period to which they apply; the balance sheet gives the specific date to which it applies. Much of this book deals with developing, using, and interpreting more complete versions of these basic statements.

THE INCOME STATEMENT

The income statement summarizes the revenues earned and expenses incurred by a business over a period of time. Many people consider it the most important financial report because it shows whether or not a business achieved its profitability goal of earning an acceptable income. In Exhibit 1-2, Shannon Realty, Inc. had revenues in the form of commissions earned of $3,500 ($2,000 of revenue earned on credit and $1,500 of cash). From this amount, total expenses of $1,700 were deducted (equipment rental expense of $1,000, wages expense of $400, and utility expense of $300), to arrive at a net income of $1,800. To show that it applies to a period of time, the statement is dated "For the Month Ended December 31, 19xx."

Exhibit 1-1. Summary of Effects of Illustrative Transactions on Financial Position

	Assets					= Liabilities +	Stockholders' Equity		
	Cash	Accounts Receiv-able	Supplies	Land	Building	Accounts Payable	Common Stock	Retained Earnings	Type of Stockholders' Equity Transaction
1.	$50,000						$50,000		Stockholders' Investments
2.	−35,000			+$10,000	+$25,000				
bal.	$15,000			$10,000	$25,000		$50,000		
3.			+$500			+$500			
bal.	$15,000		$500	$10,000	$25,000	$500	$50,000		
4.	−200					−200			
bal.	$14,800		$500	$10,000	$25,000	$300	$50,000		
5.	+1,500							+$1,500	Commissions Earned
bal.	$16,300		$500	$10,000	$25,000	$300	$50,000	$1,500	
6.		+$2,000						+2,000	Commissions Earned
bal.	$16,300	$2,000	$500	$10,000	$25,000	$300	$50,000	$3,500	
7.	+1,000	−1,000							
bal.	$17,300	$1,000	$500	$10,000	$25,000	$300	$50,000	$3,500	
8.	−1,000							−1,000	Equipment Rental Expense
9.	−400							−400	Wages Expense
bal.	$15,900	$1,000	$500	$10,000	$25,000	$300	$50,000	$2,100	
10.						+300		−300	Utility Expense
bal.	$15,900	$1,000	$500	$10,000	$25,000	$600	$50,000	$1,800	
11.	−600							−600	Dividends
	$15,300	$1,000	$500	$10,000	$25,000	$600	$50,000	$1,200	

$51,800

$51,800

Exhibit 1-2. Income Statement, Statement of Retained Earnings, Balance Sheet, and Statement of Cash Flows for Shannon Realty, Inc.

Shannon Realty, Inc.
Income Statement
For the Month Ended December 31, 19xx

Revenues		
Commissions Earned		$3,500
Expenses		
Equipment Rental Expense	$1,000	
Wages Expense	400	
Utility Expense	300	
Total Expenses		1,700
Net Income		**$1,800**

Shannon Realty, Inc.
Statement of Retained Earnings
For the Month Ended December 31, 19xx

Retained Earnings, December 1, 19xx	$ 0
Net Income for the Month	**1,800**
Subtotal	$1,800
Less Dividends	600
Retained Earnings, December 31, 19xx	**$1,200**

Shannon Realty, Inc.
Statement of Cash Flows
For the Month Ended December 31, 19xx

Cash Flows from Operating Activities		
Net Income		$ 1,800
Noncash Expenses and Revenues		
Included in Income		
Increase in Accounts Receivable	$ (1,000)*	
Increase in Supplies	(500)	
Increase in Accounts Payable	600	(900)
Net Cash Flows from Operating		
Activities		$ 900
Cash Flows from Investing Activities		
Purchase of Land	$(10,000)	
Purchase of Building	(25,000)	
Net Cash Flows from		
Investing Activities		(35,000)
Cash Flows from Financing Activities		
Investments by Stockholders	$ 50,000	
Dividends	(600)	
Net Cash Flows from		
Financing Activities		49,400
Net Increase (Decrease) in Cash		**$15,300**
Cash at Beginning of Month		0
Cash at End of Month		$15,300

Shannon Realty, Inc.
Balance Sheet
December 31, 19xx

Assets		Liabilities	
Cash	$15,300	Accounts Payable	$ 600
Accounts			
Receivable	1,000		
Supplies	500	**Stockholders' Equity**	
Land	10,000	Common Stock $50,000	
Building	25,000	**Retained**	
		Earnings 1,200	
		Total Stockholders'	
		Equity	51,200
		Total Liabilities and	
Total Assets	$51,800	Stockholders' Equity	$51,800

*Parentheses indicate a negative amount.

THE STATEMENT OF RETAINED EARNINGS

The statement of retained earnings shows the changes in retained earnings over a period of time. In Exhibit 1-2, the beginning retained earnings is zero because the company was started in this accounting period. During the month, the company earned an income (as shown in the income statement) of $1,800. Deducted from this amount are the dividends for the month of $600, leaving an ending balance of $1,200 of earnings retained in the business.

THE BALANCE SHEET

The purpose of a balance sheet is to show the financial position of a business on a certain date usually the end of the month or year. For this reason, it often is called the *statement of financial position* and is dated as of a certain date. The balance sheet presents a view of the business as the holder of resources, or assets, that are equal to the claims against or sources of those assets. The claims or sources consist of the company's liabilities and the stockholders' equity in the company. In Exhibit 1-2, Shannon Realty, Inc. has several categories of assets, which total $51,800. These assets equal the total liabilities of $600 (Accounts Payable) plus the ending balance of stockholders' equity of $51,200. Notice that the Retained Earnings account on the balance sheet comes from the ending balance on the statement of retained earnings.

THE STATEMENT OF CASH FLOWS

Whereas the income statement focuses on a company's profitability goal, the statement of cash flows is directed toward the company's liquidity goal. It shows the cash produced by operating a business as well as important investing and financing transactions that take place during an accounting period. Exhibit 1-2 shows the statement of cash flows for Shannon Realty, Inc. Notice that the statement explains how the Cash account changed during the period. Cash increased by $15,300. Operating activities produced net cash flows of $900, and financing activities produced net cash flows of $49,400. Investment activities used cash flows of $35,000.

This statement is related directly to the other three statements. Notice that net income comes from the income statement and that dividends come from the statement of retained earnings. The other items in the statement represent changes in the balance sheet accounts: Accounts Receivable, Supplies, Accounts Payable, Land, Building, and Common Stock. Here we focus on the importance and overall structure of the statement. Its construction and use are discussed in detail in the chapter on the statement of cash flows.

GENERALLY ACCEPTED ACCOUNTING PRINCIPLES

OBJECTIVE

7 *State the relationship of generally accepted accounting principles (GAAP) to financial statements and the independent CPA's report, and identify the organizations that influence GAAP*

To ensure that financial statements will be understandable to their users, a set of practices, called generally accepted accounting principles, has been developed to provide guidelines for financial accounting. Although the term has several meanings in the literature of accounting, perhaps this is the best definition: "Generally accepted accounting principles encompass the conventions, rules, and procedures necessary to define accepted accounting practice at a particular time."[4] In other words, GAAP arise from wide agreement on the theory and practice of accounting at a particular time. These "principles"

4. *Statement of the Accounting Principles Board No. 4,* par. 138.

are not like the unchangeable laws of nature found in chemistry or physics. They are developed by accountants and businesses to serve the needs of decision makers, and they can be altered as better methods evolve or as circumstances change.

In this book, we present accounting practice, or GAAP, as it is today. We also try to explain the reasons or theory on which the practice is based. Both theory and practice are part and parcel of the study of accounting. However, you should realize that accounting is a discipline that is always growing, changing, and improving. Just as years of research are necessary before a new surgical method or lifesaving drug can be introduced, it may take years for research and new discoveries in accounting to become common practice. As a result, you may come across practices that seem contradictory. In some cases, we point out new directions in accounting. Your instructor also may mention certain weaknesses in current theory or practice.

FINANCIAL STATEMENTS, GAAP, AND THE INDEPENDENT CPA'S REPORT

Because financial statements are prepared by the management of a company and could be falsified for personal gain, all companies that sell ownership to the public and many companies that apply for sizable loans have their financial statements audited by an independent certified public accountant. Certified public accountants (CPAs) are licensed by all states for the same reason that lawyers and doctors are—to protect the public by ensuring the quality of professional service. One important attribute of CPAs is independence: They have no financial or other compromising ties with the companies they audit. This gives the public confidence in their work. The firms listed in Table 1-2 employ about 25 percent of all CPAs.

An independent CPA makes an audit, which is an examination of a company's financial statements and the accounting systems, controls, and records that produced them. The purpose of the audit is to ascertain that the financial statements have been prepared in accordance with generally accepted accounting principles. If the independent accountant is satisfied

Table 1-2. Large International Certified Public Accounting Firms

Firm	Home Office	Some Major Clients
Arthur Andersen & Co.	Chicago	ITT, Texaco, United Airlines
Coopers & Lybrand	New York	AT&T, Ford
Deloitte & Touche	New York	General Motors, Procter & Gamble, Sears
Ernst & Young	New York	Coca-Cola, McDonald's, Mobil
KPMG Peat Marwick	New York	General Electric, Xerox
Price Waterhouse	New York	Du Pont, Exxon, IBM
Grant Thornton	Chicago	Fretter, Grainger, Home Shopping Network

that this standard has been met, his or her report contains the following language:

> In our opinion, the financial statements . . . present fairly, in all material respects . . . in conformity with generally accepted accounting principles.

This wording emphasizes the fact that accounting and auditing are not exact sciences. Because the framework of GAAP provides room for interpretation and the application of GAAP necessitates the making of estimates, the auditor can render an opinion or judgment only that the financial statements *present fairly* or conform *in all material respects* to GAAP. The accountant's report does not preclude minor or immaterial errors in the financial statements. However, it does imply that on the whole, investors and creditors can rely on those statements. Historically, auditors have enjoyed a strong reputation for competence and independence. As a result, banks, investors, and creditors are willing to rely on an auditor's opinion when deciding to invest in a company or to make loans to a firm that has been audited. The independent audit is an important factor in the worldwide growth of financial markets.

ORGANIZATIONS THAT INFLUENCE CURRENT PRACTICE

Many organizations directly or indirectly influence GAAP and so influence much of what is in this book. The Financial Accounting Standards Board (FASB) is the most important body for developing and issuing rules on accounting practice. This independent body issues Statements of Financial Accounting Standards. The American Institute of Certified Public Accountants (AICPA) is the professional association of certified accountants and influences accounting practice through the activities of its senior technical committees. The Securities and Exchange Commission (SEC) is an agency of the federal government that has the legal power to set and enforce accounting practices for companies whose securities are offered for sale to the general public. As such, it has enormous influence on accounting practice. The Governmental Accounting Standards Board (GASB), which was established in 1984 under the same governing body as the Financial Accounting Standards Board, is responsible for issuing accounting standards for state and local governments.

With the growth of financial markets throughout the world, worldwide cooperation in the development of accounting principles has become a priority. The International Accounting Standards Committee (IASC) has approved more than thirty international standards, which have been translated into six languages.

U.S. tax laws that govern the assessment and collection of revenue for operating the federal government also influence accounting practice. Because a major source of the government's revenue is the income tax, these laws specify the rules for determining taxable income. These rules are interpreted and enforced by the Internal Revenue Service (IRS). In some cases, these rules conflict with good accounting practice, but they still are an important influence on that practice. Businesses use certain accounting practices simply because they are required by the tax laws. Sometimes companies follow an accounting practice specified in the tax laws to take advantage of rules that can help them financially. Cases where the tax laws affect accounting practice are noted throughout this book.

PROFESSIONAL ETHICS AND THE ACCOUNTING PROFESSION

OBJECTIVE

8 *Define* ethics *and describe the ethical responsibilities of accountants*

Ethics is a code of conduct that applies to everyday life. It addresses the question of whether actions are right or wrong. Ethical actions are the product of individual decisions. You are faced with many ethical situations every day. Some may be potentially illegal—the temptation to take office supplies from your employer to use when you do homework, for example. Others are not illegal but are equally unethical—for example, deciding not to tell a fellow student who missed class that a test has been announced for the next class meeting. When an organization is said to act ethically or unethically, it means that individuals within the organization have made a decision to act ethically or unethically. When a company uses false advertising, cheats customers, pollutes the environment, treats employees poorly, or misleads investors by presenting false financial statements, members of management and other employees have made a conscious decision to act unethically. In the same way, ethical behavior within a company is a direct result of the actions and decisions of the company's employees.

Professional ethics is a code of conduct that applies to the practice of a profession. Like the ethical conduct of a company, the ethical actions of a profession are a collection of individual actions. As members of a profession, accountants have a responsibility, not only to their employers and clients but to society as a whole, to uphold the highest ethical standards. A survey of over one thousand prominent people in business, education, and government ranked the accounting profession second only to the clergy as having the highest ethical standards.[5] It is the responsibility of every person who becomes an accountant to uphold the high standards of the profession, regardless of the field of accounting the individual enters.

To ensure that its members understand the responsibilities of being professional accountants, the AICPA and each state have adopted codes of professional conduct that must be followed by certified public accountants. Fundamental to these codes is responsibility to the public, including clients, creditors, investors, and anyone else who relies on the work of the public accountant. In resolving conflicts among these groups, the accountant must act with integrity, even to the sacrifice of personal benefit. **Integrity** means that the accountant is honest and candid, and subordinates personal gain to service and the public trust. The accountant must also be objective. **Objectivity** means that he or she is impartial and intellectually honest. Furthermore, the accountant must be independent. **Independence** means avoiding all relationships that impair or even appear to impair the accountant's objectivity. One way in which the auditor of a company maintains independence is by having no direct financial interest in the company and not being an employee of the company. The accountant must exercise **due care** in all activities, carrying out professional responsibilities with competence and diligence. For example, an accountant must not accept a job for which he or she is not qualified, even at the risk of losing a client to another firm, and careless work is not acceptable. These broad principles are supported by more specific rules that public accountants must follow. (For instance, with certain

5. Touche Ross & Co., "Ethics in American Business" (New York: Touche Ross & Co., 1988), p. 7.

exceptions, client information must be kept confidential.) Accountants who violate the rules can be disciplined or suspended from practice.

The Institute of Management Accountants has adopted the Code of Professional Conduct for Management Accountants. This ethical code emphasizes that management accountants have a responsibility to be competent in their jobs, to keep information confidential except when authorized or legally required to disclose it, to maintain integrity and avoid conflicts of interest, and to communicate information objectively and without bias.[6]

BUSINESS BULLETIN: ETHICS IN PRACTICE

 A recent survey has shown that 45 percent of the 1,000 largest U.S. companies have ethics programs or workshops. NYNEX, for example, has appointed an ethics officer, written a new code of conduct, put more that 1,500 managers through a formal training program, and provided its 94,000 employees with a whistle blowers' hotline. Companies with such comprehensive programs tend to receive significantly lower fines from federal judges if their employees are caught in illegal acts because the judges want to reward companies that are trying to be good corporate citizens.[7]

CHAPTER REVIEW

REVIEW OF LEARNING OBJECTIVES

1. **Define *accounting*, identify business goals and activities, and describe the role of accounting in making informed decisions.** Accounting is an information system that measures, processes, and communicates information, primarily financial in nature, about an identifiable entity for the purpose of making economic decisions. Management accounting focuses on the preparation of information primarily for internal use by management. Financial accounting is concerned with the development and use of accounting reports that are communicated to those external to the business organization as well as to management. Accounting is not an end in itself but a tool that provides the information that is necessary to make reasoned choices among alternative uses of scarce resources in the conduct of business and economic activities.

2. **Identify the many users of accounting information in society.** Accounting plays a significant role in society by providing information to managers of all institutions and to individuals with a direct financial interest in those institutions, including present or potential investors or creditors. Accounting information is also important to those with an indirect financial interest in the business—for example, tax authorities, regulatory agencies, and economic planners.

3. **Explain the importance of business transactions, money measure, and separate entity to accounting measurement.** To make an accounting measurement, the

6. *Statement Number IC*, "Standards of Ethical Conduct for Management Accountants" (Montvale, N.J.: Institute of Management Accountants, June 1, 1983).
7. *Business Week*, Sept. 23, 1991, p. 65.

accountant must determine what is measured, when the measurement should be made, what value should be placed on what is measured, and how what is measured should be classified. Generally accepted accounting principles define the objects of accounting measurement as business transactions, money measure, and separate entities. Relating these three concepts, financial accounting uses money measure to gauge the impact of business transactions on a separate business entity.

4. **Describe the corporate form of business organization.** Corporations, whose ownership is represented by shares of stock, are separate entities for both legal and accounting purposes. The stockholders own the corporation and elect the board of directors, whose duty it is to determine corporate policy. The corporate officers or management of the corporation are appointed by the board of directors and are responsible for the operation of the business in accordance with the board's policies.

5. **Define *financial position*, state the accounting equation, and show how they are affected by simple transactions.** Financial position is the economic resources that belong to a company and the claims against those resources at a point in time. The accounting equation shows financial position in the equation form Assets = liabilities + owners' equity. For a corporation, the accounting equation is Assets = liabilities + stockholders' equity. Business transactions affect financial position by decreasing or increasing assets, liabilities, or stockholders' equity in such a way that the accounting equation is always in balance.

6. **Identify the four basic financial statements.** Financial statements are the means by which accountants communicate the financial condition and activities of a business to those who have an interest in the business. The four basic financial statements are the income statement, the statement of retained earnings, the balance sheet, and the statement of cash flows.

7. **State the relationship of generally accepted accounting principles (GAAP) to financial statements and the independent CPA's report, and identify the organizations that influence GAAP.** Acceptable accounting practice consists of those conventions, rules, and procedures that make up generally accepted accounting principles at a particular time. GAAP are essential to the preparation and interpretation of financial statements and the independent CPA's report. Among the organizations that influence the formulation of GAAP are the Financial Accounting Standards Board, the American Institute of Certified Public Accountants, the Securities and Exchange Commission, and the Internal Revenue Service.

8. **Define *ethics* and describe the ethical responsibilities of accountants.** All accountants are required to follow a code of professional ethics, the foundation of which is responsibility to the public. Accountants must act with integrity, objectivity, and independence, and they must exercise due care in all their activities.

REVIEW OF CONCEPTS AND TERMINOLOGY

The following concepts and terms were introduced in this chapter.

L O 1 **Accounting:** An information system that measures, processes, and communicates financial information about an identifiable economic entity.

L O 5 **Accounting equation:** Assets = liabilities + owners' equity or, for corporations, Assets = liabilities + stockholders' equity.

L O 5 **Accounts:** The labels used by accountants to accumulate the amounts produced from similar transactions.

L O 7 **American Institute of Certified Public Accountants (AICPA):** The professional association of certified public accountants.

L O 4 **Articles of incorporation:** An official document filed with and approved by a state that authorizes the incorporators to do business as a corporation.

L O 5 **Assets:** Economic resources owned by a business that are expected to benefit future operations.

L O 7   **Audit:** An examination of a company's financial statements in order to render an independent professional opinion that they have been presented fairly and prepared in conformity with generally accepted accounting principles.

L O 4   **Audit committee:** A subgroup of the board of directors of a corporation that is charged with ensuring that the board will be objective in reviewing management's performance; it engages the company's independent auditors and reviews their work.

L O 6   **Balance sheet:** The financial statement that shows the assets, liabilities, and stockholders' equity of a business at a point in time. Also called a *statement of financial position.*

L O 1   **Bookkeeping:** The process of recording financial transactions and keeping financial records.

L O 1   **Business:** An economic unit that aims to sell goods and services to customers at prices that will provide an adequate return to its owners.

L O 3   **Business transactions:** Economic events that affect the financial position of a business entity.

L O 7   **Certified public accountant (CPA):** A public accountant who has met the stringent licensing requirements set by the individual states.

L O 1   **Computer:** An electronic tool for the rapid collection, organization, and communication of large amounts of information.

L O 5   **Contributed capital:** The part of stockholders' equity that represents the amount invested in the business by the owners (stockholders).

L O 4   **Corporation:** A business unit granted a state charter recognizing it as a separate legal entity having its own rights, privileges, and liabilities distinct from those of its owners.

L O 5   **Dividends:** Distributions to stockholders of assets (usually cash) generated by past earnings.

L O 8   **Due care:** The act of carrying out professional responsibilities competently and diligently.

L O 8   **Ethics:** A code of conduct that addresses whether everyday actions are right or wrong.

L O 3   **Exchange rate:** The value of one currency in terms of another.

L O 5   **Expenses:** Decreases in stockholders' equity that result from operating a business.

L O 1   **Financial accounting:** The process of generating and communicating accounting information in the form of financial statements to those outside the organization.

L O 7   **Financial Accounting Standards Board (FASB):** The most important body for developing and issuing rules on accounting practice, called *Statements of Financial Accounting Standards.*

L O 5   **Financial position:** The economic resources that belong to a company and the claims against those resources at a point in time.

L O 1   **Financial statements:** The primary means of communicating important accounting information to users. They include the income statement, statement of retained earnings, balance sheet, and statement of cash flows.

L O 1   **Financing activities:** Activities undertaken by management to obtain adequate funds to begin, and continue, operating a business.

L O 7   **Generally accepted accounting principles (GAAP):** The conventions, rules, and procedures that define accepted accounting practice at a particular time.

L O 7   **Governmental Accounting Standards Board (GASB):** The board responsible for issuing accounting standards for state and local governments.

L O 6   **Income statement:** The financial statement that summarizes the revenues earned and expenses incurred by a business over a period of time.

L O 8   **Independence:** The avoidance of all relationships that impair or appear to impair an accountant's objectivity.

L O 8   **Institute of Management Accountants:** A professional organization made up primarily of management accountants.

L O 8   **Integrity:** Honesty, candidness, and the subordination of personal gain to service and the public trust.

L O 7   **Internal Revenue Service (IRS):** The federal agency that interprets and enforces the tax laws governing the assessment and collection of revenue for operating the national government.

L O 7   **International Accounting Standards Committee (IASC):** The organization that encourages worldwide cooperation in the development of accounting principles; it has approved more than thirty international standards of accounting.

L O 1   **Investing activities:** Activities undertaken by management to spend the capital received in such a way that the money will be productive and helpful in achieving the business's objectives.

L O 5   **Liabilities:** Present obligations of a business to pay cash, transfer assets, or provide services to other entities in the future.

L O 1   **Liquidity:** Having enough funds on hand to pay debts when they are due.

L O 2   **Management:** Collectively, the people who have overall responsibility for operating a business and meeting its goals.

L O 1   **Management accounting:** The process of producing accounting information for the internal use of a company's management.

L O 1   **Management information system (MIS):** The interconnected subsystems that provide the information needed to run a business.

L O 3   **Money measure:** The recording of all business transactions in terms of money.

L O 5   **Net assets:** Stockholders' equity, or assets minus liabilities.

L O 5   **Net income:** The difference between revenues and expenses when revenues exceed expenses.

L O 5   **Net loss:** The difference between expenses and revenues when expenses exceed revenues.

L O 8   **Objectivity:** Impartiality and intellectual honesty.

L O 1   **Operating activities:** Activities undertaken by management in the course of running the business.

L O 5   **Owners' equity:** The residual interest in the assets of a business entity that remains after deducting the entity's liabilities. Also called *residual equity* or, for corporations, *stockholders' equity.*

L O 4   **Partnership:** A business owned by two or more people.

L O 8   **Professional ethics:** A code of conduct that applies to the practice of a profession.

L O 1   **Profitability:** The ability to earn enough income to attract and hold investment capital.

L O 5   **Retained earnings:** The equity of the stockholders generated from the income-producing activities of the business and kept for use in the business.

L O 5   **Revenues:** Increases in stockholders' equity that result from operating a business.

L O 2   **Securities and Exchange Commission (SEC):** An agency of the federal government set up by the U.S. Congress to protect the public by regulating the issuing, buying, and selling of stocks. It has the legal power to set and enforce accounting practices for firms whose securities are sold to the general public.

L O 3   **Separate entity:** A business that is treated as distinct from its creditors, customers, and owners.

L O 4   **Share of stock:** A unit of ownership in a corporation.

L O 4   **Sole proprietorship:** A business owned by one person.

L O 6   **Statement of cash flows:** The financial statement that shows the inflows and outflows of cash from operating activities, investing activities, and financing activities over a period of time.

L O 6   **Statement of retained earnings:** The financial statement that shows the changes in retained earnings over a period of time.

L O 5 **Stockholders' equity:** The owners' equity of a corporation, consisting of contributed capital and retained earnings.

REVIEW PROBLEM
THE EFFECT OF TRANSACTIONS ON THE ACCOUNTING EQUATION

L O 5 Charlene Rudek finished law school in June and immediately set up her own law practice. During the first month of operation, she completed the following transactions:

a. Began the law practice by exchanging $2,000 for 1,000 shares of $2 par value common stock of the corporation.
b. Purchased a law library for $900 cash.
c. Purchased office supplies for $400 on credit.
d. Accepted $500 in cash for completing a contract.
e. Billed clients $1,950 for services rendered during the month.
f. Paid $200 of the amount owed for office supplies.
g. Received $1,250 in cash from one client who had been billed previously for services rendered.
h. Paid rent expense for the month in the amount of $1,200.
i. Declared and paid a dividend of $400.

REQUIRED Show the effect of each of these transactions on the balance sheet equation by completing a table similar to Exhibit 1-1. Identify each stockholders' equity transaction.

ANSWER TO REVIEW PROBLEM

	Cash	Accounts Receiv- able	Office Supplies	Law Library	Accounts Payable	Common Stock	Retained Earnings	Type of SE Transaction
			Assets		**= Liabilities +**		**Stockholders' Equity (SE)**	
a.	$2,000					$2,000		Stockholders' Investment
b.	−900			+$900				
bal.	$1,100			$900		$2,000		
c.			+$400		+$400			
bal.	$1,100		$400	$900	$400	$2,000		
d.	+500						+$ 500	Service Revenue
bal.	$1,600		$400	$900	$400	$2,000	$ 500	
e.		+$1,950					+1,950	Service Revenue
bal.	$1,600	$1,950	$400	$900	$400	$2,000	$2,450	
f.	−200				−200			
bal.	$1,400	$1,950	$400	$900	$200	$2,000	$2,450	
g.	+1,250	−1,250						
bal.	$2,650	$ 700	$400	$900	$200	$2,000	$2,450	
h.	−1,200						−1,200	Rent Expense
bal.	$1,450	$ 700	$400	$900	$200	$2,000	$1,250	
i.	−400						−400	Dividends
bal.	$1,050	$ 700	$400	$900	$200	$2,000	$ 850	

$3,050 = $3,050

CHAPTER ASSIGNMENTS

KNOWLEDGE AND UNDERSTANDING

Questions

1. Why is accounting considered an information system?
2. What is the role of accounting in the decision-making process, and what broad business goals and activities does it help management to achieve and manage?
3. Distinguish between management accounting and financial accounting.
4. Distinguish among these terms: *accounting, bookkeeping,* and *management information systems.*
5. Which decision makers use accounting information?
6. A business is an economic unit whose goal is to sell goods and services to customers at prices that will provide an adequate return to the business owners. What functions must management perform to achieve that goal?
7. Why are investors and creditors interested in reviewing the financial statements of a company?
8. Among those who use accounting information are people and organizations with an indirect interest in the business entity. Briefly describe these people and organizations.
9. Why has society as a whole become one of the largest users of accounting information?
10. Use the terms *business transaction, money measure,* and *separate entity* in a single sentence that demonstrates their relevance to financial accounting.
11. How do sole proprietorships, partnerships, and corporations differ?
12. In a corporation, what are the functions of stockholders, the board of directors, and management?
13. Define *assets, liabilities,* and *stockholders' equity.*
14. Arnold Smith's corporation has assets of $22,000 and liabilities of $10,000. What is the amount of the stockholders' equity?
15. What three elements affect retained earnings? How?
16. Give examples of the types of transactions that (a) increase assets and (b) increase liabilities.
17. Why is the balance sheet sometimes called the statement of financial position?
18. Contrast the purpose of the balance sheet with that of the income statement.
19. A statement for an accounting period that ends in June can be headed "June 30, 19xx" or "For the Year Ended June 30, 19xx." Which heading is appropriate for (a) a balance sheet and (b) an income statement?
20. What is the function of the statement of retained earnings?
21. How does the income statement differ from the statement of cash flows?
22. What are GAAP? Why are they important to the readers of financial statements?
23. What do auditors mean by the phrase "in all material respects" when they state that financial statements "present fairly, in all material respects . . . in conformity with generally accepted accounting principles"?
24. What organization has the most influence on GAAP?
25. Discuss the importance of professional ethics in the accounting profession.

Short Exercises

SE 1-1.

L O 3, 4   *Accounting Concepts*

Tell whether each of the following words or phrases relates most closely to (a) a business transaction, (b) a separate entity, or (c) a money measure.

1. Partnership 2. U.S. dollar 3. Payment for expense 4. Corporation 5. Sale of an asset

SE 1-2.
L O 5 *The Accounting Equation*

Determine the amount missing from each accounting equation below.

	Assets	=	Liabilities	+	Stockholders' Equity
1.	?		$25,000		$35,000
2.	$ 78,000		$42,000		?
3.	$146,000		?		$96,000

SE 1-3.
L O 5 *The Accounting Equation*

Use the accounting equation to answer each question below.

1. The assets of Cruse Company are $480,000, and the liabilities are $360,000. What is the amount of the stockholders' equity?
2. The liabilities of Nabors Company equal one-fifth of the total assets. The stockholders' equity is $80,000. What is the amount of the liabilities?

SE 1-4.
L O 5 *The Accounting Equation*

Use the accounting equation to answer each question below.

1. At the beginning of the year, Gilbert Company's assets were $180,000, and its stockholders' equity was $100,000. During the year, assets increased $60,000 and liabilities increased $10,000. What was the stockholders' equity at the end of the year?
2. At the beginning of the year, Sailor Company had liabilities of $50,000 and stockholders' equity of $48,000. If assets increased by $20,000 and liabilities decreased by $15,000, what was stockholders' equity at the end of the year?

SE 1-5.
L O 5 *The Accounting Equation and Net Income*

Use the following information and the accounting equation to determine the net income for the year for each alternative below.

	Assets	Liabilities
Beginning of the year	$ 70,000	$30,000
End of the year	100,000	50,000

1. No investments were made in the business and no dividends were paid during the year.
2. Investments of $10,000 were made in the business, but no dividends were paid during the year.
3. No investments were made in the business, but dividends of $2,000 were paid during the year.

SE 1-6.
L O 5 *The Accounting Equation and Net Income*

Murillo Company had assets of $140,000 and liabilities of $60,000 at the beginning of the year, and assets of $200,000 and liabilities of $70,000 at the end of the year. During the year, there was an investment of $20,000 in the business, and dividends of $24,000 were paid. What amount of net income was earned during the year?

SE 1-7.
L O 5 *Effect of Transactions on the Accounting Equation*

On a sheet of paper, list the numbers 1 through 6, with columns labeled Assets, Liabilities, and Stockholders' Equity. In the columns, indicate whether each transaction below caused an increase (+), a decrease (−), or no change (NC) in assets, liabilities, and stockholders' equity.

1. Purchased equipment on credit.
2. Purchased equipment for cash.
3. Billed customers for services performed.
4. Received and immediately paid a utility bill.
5. Received payment from a previously billed customer.
6. Received an additional investment from a stockholder.

SE 1-8.
L O 5 *Effect of Transactions on the Accounting Equation*

On a sheet of paper, list the numbers 1 through 6, with columns labeled Assets, Liabilities, and Stockholders' Equity. In the columns, indicate whether each transaction below caused an increase (+), a decrease (−), or no change (NC) in assets, liabilities, and stockholders' equity.

1. Purchased supplies on credit.
2. Paid for previously purchased supplies.
3. Paid employee's weekly wages.
4. Paid a dividend to stockholders.
5. Purchased a truck with cash.
6. Received a telephone bill to be paid next month.

SE 1-9.
L O 6   *Preparation of a*
Balance Sheet

Use the following accounts and balances to prepare a balance sheet for Jay Company at December 31, 19x1, using Exhibit 1-2 as a model.

Accounts Payable	$2,500
Common Stock	3,000
Cash	1,200
Retained Earnings	600
Equipment	3,300
Accounts Receivable	1,600

SE 1-10.
L O 6   *Preparation and*
Completion of a
Balance Sheet

Use the following accounts and balances to prepare a balance sheet for DeLay Company at June 30, 19x1, using Exhibit 1-2 as a model.

Accounts Receivable	$ 800
Wages Payable	250
Retained Earnings	1,750
Common Stock	12,000
Building	10,000
Cash	?

APPLICATION

Exercises

E 1-1.
L O 1, 2, 7   *The Nature of*
Accounting

Match the terms on the left with the descriptions on the right.

_____ 1. Bookkeeping	a. Function of accounting
_____ 2. Creditors	b. Often confused with accounting
_____ 3. Measurement	c. User(s) of accounting information
_____ 4. Financial Accounting	d. Organization that influences
Standards Board (FASB)	current practice
_____ 5. Tax authorities	e. Tool that facilitates the practice of
_____ 6. Computer	accounting
_____ 7. Communication	
_____ 8. Securities and Exchange	
Commission (SEC)	
_____ 9. Investors	
_____ 10. Processing	
_____ 11. Management	
_____ 12. Management information	
system	

E 1-2.
L O 3   *Business Transactions*

Theresa owns and operates a minimart. State which of the actions below are business transactions. Explain why any other actions are not regarded as transactions.

1. Theresa reduces the price of a gallon of milk to match the price offered by a competitor.
2. Theresa pays a high school student cash for cleaning up the driveway behind the market.
3. Theresa fills her son's car with gasoline in payment for restocking the vending machines and the snack food shelves.
4. Theresa pays interest to herself on a loan she made three years ago to the business.

E 1-3.
L O 3, 4 *Accounting Concepts*

Financial accounting uses money measures to gauge the impact of business transactions on a separate business entity. Tell whether each of the following words or phrases relates most closely to (a) a business transaction, (b) a separate entity, or (c) a money measure.

1. Corporation
2. French franc
3. Sale of products
4. Receipt of cash
5. Sole proprietorship

6. U.S. dollar
7. Partnership
8. Stockholders' investments
9. Japanese yen
10. Purchase of supplies

E 1-4.
L O 3 *Money Measure*

You have been asked to compare the sales and assets of four companies that make computer chips in order to determine which company is the largest in each category. You have gathered the following data, but they cannot be used for direct comparison because each company's sales and assets are in its own currency:

Company (Currency)	Sales	Assets
Inchip (U.S. dollar)	20,000,000	13,000,000
Wong (Taiwan dollar)	50,000,000	24,000,000
Mitzu (Japanese yen)	3,500,000,000	2,500,000,000
Works (German mark)	35,000,000	39,000,000

Assuming that the exchange rates in Table 1-1 are current and appropriate, convert all the figures to U.S. dollars and determine which company is the largest in sales and which is the largest in assets.

E 1-5.
L O 5 *The Accounting Equation*

Use the accounting equation to answer each question below. Show any calculations you make.

1. The assets of Newport Corporation are $650,000, and the stockholders' equity is $360,000. What is the amount of the liabilities?
2. The liabilities and stockholders' equity of Fitzgerald Corporation are $95,000 and $32,000, respectively. What is the amount of the assets?
3. The liabilities of Emerald Corp. equal one-third of the total assets, and stockholders' equity is $120,000. What is the amount of the liabilities?
4. At the beginning of the year, Pickett Corporation's assets were $220,000 and its stockholders' equity was $100,000. During the year, assets increased $60,000 and liabilities decreased $10,000. What is the stockholders' equity at the end of the year?

E 1-6.
L O 5 *Stockholders' Equity Transactions*

Identify the following transactions by marking each as a stockholders' investment (I), dividend (D), revenue (R), expense (E), or not stockholders' equity transaction (NSE).

a. Received cash for providing a service.
b. Took assets out of the business as a dividend.
c. Received cash from a customer previously billed for a service.
d. Transferred assets to the business from a personal account.
e. Paid a service station for gasoline for a business vehicle.
f. Performed a service and received a promise of payment.
g. Paid cash to purchase equipment.
h. Paid cash to an employee for services performed.

E 1-7.
L O 5 *Effect of Transactions on the Accounting Equation*

During the month of April, Andres Corporation had the following transactions:

a. Paid salaries for April, $5,400.
b. Purchased equipment on credit, $9,000.
c. Purchased supplies with cash, $300.
d. Additional investment by stockholders, $12,000.
e. Received payment for services performed, $1,800.
f. Made partial payment on equipment purchased in transaction **b**, $3,000.
g. Billed customers for services performed, $4,800.
h. Received payment from customers billed in transaction **g**, $900.
i. Received utility bill, $210.
j. Declared and paid dividends of $4,500.

On a sheet of paper, list the letters **a** through **j**, with columns labeled Assets, Liabilities, and Stockholders' Equity. In the columns, indicate whether each transaction caused an increase (+), a decrease (−), or no change (NC) in assets, liabilities, and stockholders' equity.

E 1-8.
L O 5 *Examples of Transactions*

For each of the following categories, describe a transaction that would have the required effect on the elements of the accounting equation.

1. Increase one asset and decrease another asset.
2. Decrease an asset and decrease a liability.
3. Increase an asset and increase a liability.
4. Increase an asset and increase stockholders' equity.
5. Decrease an asset and decrease stockholders' equity.

E 1-9.
L O 5 *Effect of Transactions on the Accounting Equation*

The total assets and liabilities at the beginning and end of the year for Pizarro Company are listed below.

	Assets	Liabilities
Beginning of the year	$110,000	$ 45,000
End of the year	200,000	120,000

Determine Pizarro Company's net income for the year under each of the following alternatives:

1. The stockholders made no investments in the business, and no dividends were paid during the year.
2. The stockholders made no investments in the business, but dividends of $22,000 were paid during the year.
3. The stockholders made investments of $13,000, but no dividends were paid during the year.
4. The stockholders made investments of $10,000 in the business, and dividends of $22,000 were paid during the year.

E 1-10.
L O 5, 6 *Identification of Accounts*

1. Indicate whether each of the following accounts is an asset (A), a liability (L), or a part of stockholders' equity (SE).

   a. Cash
   b. Salaries Payable
   c. Accounts Receivable
   d. Common Stock
   e. Land
   f. Accounts Payable
   g. Supplies

2. Indicate whether each account would be shown on the income statement (IS), the statement of retained earnings (RE), or the balance sheet (BS).

   a. Repair Revenue
   b. Automobile
   c. Fuel Expense
   d. Cash
   e. Rent Expense
   f. Accounts Payable
   g. Dividends

E 1-11.
L O 6 *Preparation of a Balance Sheet*

Listed in random order below are the balance sheet figures for the Glick Company as of June 30, 19xx.

Accounts Payable	$20,000
Building	45,000
Common Stock	50,000
Supplies	5,000
Accounts Receivable	25,000
Cash	10,000
Equipment	20,000
Retained Earnings	35,000

Sort the balances and prepare a balance sheet similar to the one in Exhibit 1-2.

E 1-12.
L O 6 *Completion of Financial Statements*

Determine the amounts that correspond to the letters by completing the following independent sets of financial statements. (Assume no new investments by the stockholders.)

Income Statement	Set A	Set B	Set C
Revenues	$1,100	$ g	$240
Expenses	a	5,200	m
Net Income	$ b	$ h	$ 80

Statement of Retained Earnings			
Beginning Balance	$ 900	$ 5,400	$100
Net Income	c	1,600	n
Dividends	(200)	i	o
Ending Balance	$1,000	$ j	$ p

Balance Sheet			
Total Assets	$ d	$21,000	$ q
Liabilities	$1,600	$ 5,000	$ r
Stockholders' Equity			
Common Stock	2,000	10,000	100
Retained Earnings	e	k	180
Total Liabilities and Stockholders' Equity	$ f	$ l	$480

E 1-13.
L O 6 *Preparation of Financial Statements*

Strickland Corporation engaged in the following activities during the year: Service Revenue, $52,800; Rent Expense, $4,800; Wages Expense, $33,080; Advertising Expense, $5,400; Utility Expense, $3,600; and Dividends, $2,800. In addition, the year-end balances of selected accounts were as follows: Cash, $6,200; Accounts Receivable, $3,000; Supplies, $400; Land, $4,000; Accounts Payable, $1,800; and Common Stock, $4,000.

Using good form, prepare the income statement, statement of retained earnings, and balance sheet for Strickland Corporation (assume the year ends on June 30, 19x2). (**Hint:** You must solve for the year-end balances of retained earnings for 19x1 and 19x2.)

E 1-14.
L O 6 *Revenues, Expenses, and Cash Flows*

Lorraine, an attorney, bills her clients at a rate of $100 per hour. During July, she worked 150 hours for clients and billed them appropriately. By the end of July, 80 of these hours remained unpaid. At the beginning of the month, clients owed Lorraine $8,000, of which $5,600 was paid during July.

Lorraine has one employee, a secretary who is paid $20 per hour. During July, the secretary worked 170 hours, of which 16 hours were to be paid in August. The rest were paid in July. Also, during July, Lorraine paid the secretary for 8 hours worked in June.

Determine for the month of July: (1) the amount of revenue from clients, (2) wages expense for the secretary, (3) cash received from clients, and (4) cash paid to the secretary.

E 1-15.
L O 6 *Statement of Cash Flows*

Diamond Corporation began the year 19x2 with cash of $86,000. In addition to earning a net income of $50,000 and paying a cash dividend of $30,000, Diamond borrowed $120,000 from the bank and purchased equipment for $180,000 with cash. Also, Accounts Receivable increased by $12,000 and Accounts Payable increased by $18,000.

Determine the amount of cash on hand at December 31, 19x2, by preparing a statement of cash flows similar to the one in Exhibit 1-2.

E 1-16.
L O 7 *Accounting Abbreviations*

Identify the accounting meaning of each of the following abbreviations: AICPA, SEC, GAAP, FASB, IRS, GASB, IASC, IMA, and CPA.

Problem Set A

1A-1.

LO5 *Effect of Transactions on the Accounting Equation*

The Creative Frames Shop, Inc. was started by Rosa Partridge in a small shopping center. In the first weeks of operation, she completed the following transactions:

a. Deposited $21,000 in cash in the name of the company, in exchange for 2,100 shares of $10 par value stock of the corporation.
b. Paid the current month's rent, $1,500.
c. Purchased store equipment on credit, $10,800.
d. Purchased framing supplies for cash, $5,100.
e. Received framing revenues, $2,400.
f. Billed customers for services, $2,100.
g. Paid utility expense, $750.
h. Received payment from customers in transaction **f**, $600.
i. Made payment on store equipment purchased in transaction **c**, $5,400.
j. Declared and paid dividends of $1,200.

REQUIRED

1. Arrange the following asset, liability, and stockholders' equity accounts in an equation similar to Exhibit 1-1: Cash, Accounts Receivable, Framing Supplies, Store Equipment, Accounts Payable, Common Stock, and Retained Earnings.
2. Show by addition and subtraction, as in Exhibit 1-1, the effects of the transactions on the accounting equation. Show new balances after each transaction, and identify each stockholders' equity transaction by type.

1A-2.

LO5 *Effect of Transactions on the Accounting Equation*

The Quality Courier Corporation was founded by Johnny Hui on March 1 and engaged in the following transactions:

a. Deposited $12,000 in cash in the name of Quality Courier Corporation, in exchange for 12,000 shares of $1 par value stock of the corporation.
b. Purchased a motorbike on credit, $3,200.
c. Purchased delivery supplies for cash, $400.
d. Billed a customer for a delivery, $200.
e. Received delivery fees in cash, $600.
f. Made a payment on the motorbike, $1,400.
g. Paid repair expense, $240.
h. Received payment from customer billed in transaction **d**, $100.
i. Declared and paid dividends of $300.

REQUIRED

1. Arrange the following asset, liability, and stockholders' equity accounts in an equation similar to Exhibit 1-1: Cash, Accounts Receivable, Delivery Supplies, Motorbike, Accounts Payable, Common Stock, and Retained Earnings.
2. Show by addition and subtraction, as in Exhibit 1-1, the effects of the transactions on the accounting equation. Show new balances after each transaction, and identify each stockholders' equity transaction by type.

1A-3.

LO5 *Effect of Transactions on the Accounting Equation*

After completing his Ph.D. in management, Tony Rosello set up a consulting practice. At the end of his first month of operation, Dr. Rosello had the following account balances: Cash, $5,860; Accounts Receivable, $2,800; Office Supplies, $540; Office Equipment, $8,400; Accounts Payable, $3,800; Common Stock, $12,000; and Retained Earnings, $1,800. Soon thereafter, the following transactions were completed:

a. Paid current month's rent, $800.
b. Made payment toward accounts payable, $900.
c. Billed clients for services performed, $1,600.
d. Received payment from clients billed last month, $2,000.
e. Purchased office supplies for cash, $160.
f. Paid secretary's salary, $1,700.
g. Paid utility expense, $180.
h. Paid telephone expense, $100.
i. Purchased additional office equipment for cash, $800.
j. Received cash from clients for services performed, $2,400.
k. Declared and paid dividends of $1,000.

REQUIRED

1. Arrange the following asset, liability, and stockholders' equity accounts in an equation similar to Exhibit 1-1: Cash, Accounts Receivable, Office Supplies, Office Equipment, Accounts Payable, Common Stock, and Retained Earnings.
2. Enter the beginning balances of the assets, liabilities, and stockholders' equity.
3. Show by addition and subtraction, as in Exhibit 1-1, the effects of the transactions on the accounting equation. Show new balances after each transaction, and identify each stockholders' equity transaction by type.

1A-4.

L O 6 *Preparation of Financial Statements*

At the end of its first month of operation, March 19xx, Ellis Plumbing Corporation had the following account balances:

Cash	$58,600
Accounts Receivable	10,800
Delivery Truck	38,000
Tools	7,600
Accounts Payable	8,600

In addition, during the month of March, the following transactions affected stockholders' equity:

Initial investment by J. Ellis	$40,000
Further investment by J. Ellis	60,000
Contract revenue	23,200
Repair revenue	5,600
Salaries expense	16,600
Rent expense	1,400
Fuel expense	400
Dividends	4,000

REQUIRED

Using Exhibit 1-2 as a model, prepare an income statement, a statement of retained earnings, and a balance sheet for Ellis Plumbing Corporation. (**Hint:** The final balance of Stockholders' Equity is $106,400.)

1A-5.

L O 5, 6 *Effect of Transactions on the Accounting Equation and Preparation of Financial Statements*

Arrow Copying Service, Inc. began operations and engaged in the following transactions during August 19xx:

a. Myra Lomax deposited $10,000 in cash in the name of the corporation, in exchange for 1,000 shares of $10 par value stock of the corporation.
b. Paid current month's rent, $900.
c. Purchased copier for cash, $5,000.
d. Copying job payments received in cash, $1,780.
e. Copying job billed to major customer, $1,360.
f. Paid cash for paper and other copier supplies, $380.
g. Paid wages to part-time employees, $560.
h. Purchased additional copier supplies on credit, $280.
i. Received partial payment from customer in transaction **e**, $600.
j. Paid current month's utility bill, $180.
k. Made partial payment on supplies purchased in transaction **h**, $140.
l. Declared and paid dividends of $1,400.

REQUIRED

1. Arrange the asset, liability, and stockholders' equity accounts in an equation similar to Exhibit 1-1, using these account titles: Cash, Accounts Receivable, Supplies, Copier, Accounts Payable, Common Stock, and Retained Earnings.
2. Show by addition and subtraction, as in Exhibit 1-1, the effects of the transactions on the accounting equation. Show new balances after each transaction, and identify each stockholders' equity transaction by type.
3. Using Exhibit 1-2 as a guide, prepare an income statement, a statement of retained earnings, and a balance sheet for Arrow Copying Service, Inc.

Problem Set B

1B-1.

L O 5 *Effect of Transactions on the Accounting Equation*

John Unger, after receiving his degree in computer science, started his own business, Regency Business Services Corporation. He completed the following transactions soon after starting the business:

a. Invested $18,000 in cash and a systems library that is valued at $1,840 in exchange for 1,984 shares of $10 par value stock in the corporation.
b. Paid current month's rent on an office, $720.
c. Purchased a minicomputer for cash, $14,000.
d. Purchased computer supplies on credit, $1,200.
e. Received from a client for programming done, $1,600.
f. Billed a client on completion of a short programming project, $1,420.
g. Paid wages, $800.
h. Received a partial payment from the client billed in transaction **f**, $160.
i. Made a partial payment on the computer supplies purchased in transaction **d**, $400.
j. Declared and paid dividends of $500.

REQUIRED

1. Arrange the asset, liability, and stockholders' equity accounts in an equation similar to Exhibit 1-1, using the following account titles: Cash, Accounts Receivable, Supplies, Equipment, Systems Library, Accounts Payable, Common Stock, and Retained Earnings.
2. Show by addition and subtraction, as in Exhibit 1-1, the effects of the transactions on the accounting equation. Show new balances after each transaction, and identify each stockholders' equity transaction by type.

1B-2.

L O 5 *Effect of Transactions on the Accounting Equation*

On October 1, Oscar Melendez started a new business, the Melendez Transport Corporation. During the month of October, the firm completed the following transactions:

a. Deposited $132,000 in cash in the name of Melendez Transport Corporation, in exchange for 13,200 shares of $10 par value stock of the corporation.
b. Purchased two trucks for cash, $86,000.
c. Purchased equipment on credit, $18,000.
d. Billed a customer for hauling goods, $2,400.
e. Received cash for hauling goods, $4,600.
f. Received cash payment from the customer billed in transaction **d**, $1,200.
g. Made a payment on the equipment purchased in transaction **c**, $10,000.
h. Paid wages expense in cash, $3,400.
i. Declared and paid dividends of $2,400.

REQUIRED

1. Arrange the asset, liability, and stockholders' equity accounts in an equation similar to Exhibit 1-1, using the following account titles: Cash, Accounts Receivable, Trucks, Equipment, Accounts Payable, Common Stock, and Retained Earnings.
2. Show by addition and subtraction, as in Exhibit 1-1, the effects of the transactions on the accounting equation. Show new balances after each transaction, and identify each stockholders' equity transaction by type.

1B-3.

L O 5 *Effect of Transactions on the Accounting Equation*

Dr. Barbara Getz, a psychologist, moved from her hometown to set up an office in Saint Louis. After one month, the business had the following assets: Cash, $5,600; Accounts Receivable, $1,360; Office Supplies, $600; and Office Equipment, $15,000. Stockholders' equity consisted of Common Stock, $16,000, and Retained Earnings, $1,360. The Accounts Payable balance was $5,200 for purchases of office equipment on credit. During a short period of time, the following transactions were completed:

a. Paid one month's rent, $700.
b. Billed patient for services rendered, $120.
c. Made payment on accounts owed, $600.
d. Paid for office supplies, $200.
e. Paid the secretary's salary, $600.
f. Received payment for services rendered from patients not previously billed, $1,600.

g. Made payment on accounts owed, $720.
h. Paid telephone bill for current month, $140.
i. Received payment from patients previously billed, $580.
j. Purchased additional office equipment on credit, $600.
k. Declared and paid dividends of $1,000.

REQUIRED

1. Arrange the asset, liability, and stockholders' equity accounts in an equation similar to Exhibit 1-1, using the following account titles: Cash, Accounts Receivable, Office Supplies, Office Equipment, Accounts Payable, Common Stock, and Retained Earnings.
2. Enter the beginning balances for assets, liabilities, and stockholders' equity in your equation.
3. Show by addition and subtraction, as in Exhibit 1-1, the effects of the transactions on the accounting equation. Show new balances after each transaction, and identify each stockholders' equity transaction by type.

1B-4.
L O 6 *Preparation of Financial Statements*

At the end of August 19xx, the Common Stock account of the Moon Valley Riding Club, Inc. had a balance of $60,000, and Retained Earnings were $14,600. After operating during September, the club had the following account balances:

Cash	$17,400
Accounts Receivable	2,400
Supplies	2,000
Land	42,000
Building	60,000
Horses	20,000
Accounts Payable	35,600

In addition, the following transactions affected stockholders' equity during September:

Stockholders' investment in common stock	$32,000
Riding lesson revenue	12,400
Locker rental revenue	3,400
Salaries expense	4,600
Feed expense	2,000
Utility expense	1,200
Dividends	6,400

REQUIRED

Using Exhibit 1-2 as a model, prepare an income statement, a statement of retained earnings, and a balance sheet for Moon Valley Riding Club, Inc. (**Hint:** The final balance of stockholders' equity is $108,200.)

1B-5.
L O 5, 6 *Effect of Transactions on the Accounting Equation and Preparation of Financial Statements*

On April 1, 19xx, Dependable Taxi Service, Inc. began operation and engaged in the following transactions during April:

a. Madeline Curry deposited $42,000 in a bank account in the name of the corporation, in exchange for 4,200 shares of $10 par value stock in the corporation.
b. Purchase of taxi for cash, $19,000.
c. Purchase of uniforms on credit, $400.
d. Taxi fares received in cash, $3,200.
e. Paid wages to part-time drivers, $500.
f. Purchased gasoline during month for cash, $800.
g. Purchased car washes during month on credit, $120.
h. Further investment by owner, $5,000.
i. Paid part of the amount owed for the uniforms purchased in transaction **c**, $200.
j. Billed major client for fares, $900.
k. Paid for automobile repairs, $250.
l. Declared and paid dividends of $1,000.

REQUIRED

1. Arrange the asset, liability, and stockholders' equity accounts in an equation similar to Exhibit 1-1, using the following account titles: Cash, Accounts Receivable, Uniforms, Taxi, Accounts Payable, Common Stock, and Retained Earnings.

2. Show by addition and subtraction, as in Exhibit 1-1, the effects of the transactions on the accounting equation. Show new balances after each transaction, and identify each stockholders' equity transaction by type.
3. Using Exhibit 1-2 as a guide, prepare an income statement, a statement of retained earnings, and a balance sheet for Dependable Taxi Service, Inc.

CRITICAL THINKING AND COMMUNICATION

Conceptual Mini-Cases

CMC 1-1.

L O 1, 2 *Business Activities and Management Functions*

Aetna Life and Casualty Co. is a leading insurance company. According to its letter to shareholders, 1992 financial results were completely unsatisfactory, and the company is working hard to revitalize itself.

> Our strategy centers on four key elements: sharp focus on core businesses, disciplined financial programs to improve earnings and reduce expenses, reengineering to radically improve our business processes, and targeted programs to give Aetna's people the tools, training, and support they need to succeed. Our strategy is to allocate key resources—capital, people, time, technology—to those businesses that offer the best profit potential.[8]

To achieve its strategy, Aetna must organize its management into functions that relate to the principal activities of a business. Discuss the three basic activities Aetna will engage in to achieve its goals, and suggest some examples of each. What is the role of Aetna's management, and what functions must its management perform to accomplish these activities?

CMC 1-2.

L O 2 *Users of Accounting Information*

Public companies report annually on their success or failure in making a net income. Suppose that the following item appeared in the newspaper:

> *New York. Commonwealth Power Company,* a major electric utility, reported yesterday that its net income for the year just ended represented a 50 percent increase over last year. . . .

Discuss why each of the following individuals or groups might be interested in seeing the accounting reports that support this statement.

1. The management of Commonwealth Power
2. The stockholders of Commonwealth Power
3. The creditors of Commonwealth Power
4. Potential stockholders of Commonwealth Power
5. The Internal Revenue Service
6. The Securities and Exchange Commission
7. The electrical workers' union
8. A consumers' group called Public Cause
9. An economic adviser to the President of the United States

CMC 1-3.

L O 5 *Concept of an Asset*

Foote, Cone & Belding is one of the largest and most successful advertising agencies in the world. Its annual report carries the following statement: "Our principal asset is our people. Our success depends in large part on our ability to attract and retain personnel who are competent in the various aspects of our business."[9] Are personnel considered assets in financial statements? Discuss in what sense Foote, Cone & Belding considers its employees its principal asset.

8. Aetna Life and Casualty Co., *Annual Report*, 1992.
9. Foote, Cone & Belding, *Annual Report*, 1989.

Ethics Mini-Case

EMC 1-1.

L O 8   *Professional Ethics*

Discuss the ethical choices in the situations below. In each instance, determine the alternative courses of action, describe the ethical dilemma, and tell what you would do.

1. You are the payroll accountant for a small business. A friend asks you how much another employee is paid per hour.
2. As an accountant for the branch office of a wholesale supplier, you discover that several of the receipts the branch manager has submitted for reimbursement as selling expense actually stem from nights out with his spouse.
3. You are an accountant in the purchasing department of a construction company. When you arrive home from work on December 22, you find a large ham in a box marked "Happy Holidays—It's a pleasure to work with you." The gift is from a supplier who has bid on a contract your employer plans to award next week.
4. As an auditor with one year's experience at a local CPA firm, you are expected to complete a certain part of an audit in twenty hours. Because of your lack of experience, you know you cannot finish the job within that time. Rather than admit this, you are thinking about working late to finish the job and not telling anyone.
5. You are a tax accountant at a local CPA firm. You help your neighbor fill out her tax return, and she pays you $200 in cash. Because there is no record of this transaction, you are considering not reporting it on your tax return.
6. The accounting firm for which you work as a CPA has just won a new client, a firm in which you own 200 shares of stock that you received as an inheritance from your grandmother. Because it is only a small number of shares and you think the company will be very successful, you are considering not disclosing the investment.

Decision-Making Case

DMC 1-1.

L O 6   *Effect of Transactions on the Balance Sheet*

Instead of hunting for a summer job after finishing her junior year in college, Lucy Henderson started a lawn service business in her neighborhood. On June 1, she deposited $1,350 in a new bank account in the name of her corporation. The $1,350 consisted of a $500 loan from her father and $850 of her own money. In return for her investment, Lucy issued 850 shares of $1 par value common stock to herself.

Using the money in this checking account, Lucy rented lawn equipment, purchased supplies, and hired neighborhood high school students to mow and trim the lawns of neighbors who had agreed to pay her for the service. At the end of each month, she mailed bills to her customers.

On August 31, Lucy was ready to dissolve her business and go back to school for the fall term. Because she had been so busy, she had not kept any records other than her checkbook and a list of amounts owed by customers.

Her checkbook had a balance of $1,760, and her customers owed her $435. She expected these customers to pay her during September. She planned to return unused supplies to Suburban Landscaping Company for a full credit of $25. When she brought back the rented lawn equipment, Suburban Landscaping also would return a deposit of $100 she had made in June. She owed Suburban Landscaping $260 for equipment rentals and supplies. In addition, she owed the students who had worked for her $50, and she still owed her father $350. Although Lucy feels she did quite well, she is not sure just how successful she was.

REQUIRED

1. Prepare one balance sheet dated June 1 and another dated August 31 for Henderson Lawn Care, Inc.
2. Compare the two balance sheets and comment on the performance of Henderson Lawn Care, Inc. Did the company have a profit or a loss? (Assume that Lucy used none of the company's assets for personal purposes.)
3. If Lucy wants to continue her business next summer, what kind of information from her recordkeeping system would make it easier for her to tell whether or not she is earning a profit?

Basic Research Activity

RA 1-1.
L O 1, 2 *Need for Knowledge of Accounting*

From the business section of your local paper or a nearby metropolitan daily, clip an article about a company. List all the financial and accounting terms used in the article. Bring the article to class and be prepared to discuss how a knowledge of accounting would help a reader understand the content of the article.

FINANCIAL REPORTING AND ANALYSIS

Interpretation Cases from Business

ICB 1-1.
L O 1, 2 *Uses of Accounting Information*

The *Wall Street Journal* is the leading daily financial newspaper in the United States. The following excerpts from an article entitled "Public Service E & G Asks $464.5 Million Annual Rates Rise" appeared in the *Wall Street Journal* on January 10, 1983:

> Newark, N.J. Public Service Electric & Gas Co. said it asked the New Jersey Board of Public Utilities to authorize increases in gas and electric rates that would add $464.5 million to annual revenue, an 11.5% jump.
>
> The utility said that more than half of the added revenue would go to paying federal income taxes, and the state gross receipts and franchise tax.
>
> The request asks for a 15.6% increase in electric rates, amounting to added revenue of $398 million a year, and a 4.5% increase in gas rates, which would bring added annual revenue of $67 million. . . .
>
> Explaining its need for expanded revenue, the utility said it has suffered a decline in electricity demand as a result of the recession. Kilowatt-hour sales fell 2.7% in 1982, and gas sales dropped 2%, the utility said. . . .[10]

REQUIRED

1. Assume that you are a member of the New Jersey Board of Public Utilities and are faced with the above request for a rate increase. Be prepared to discuss what five factors you would consider most important or relevant to making an informed decision. Be as specific as possible.
2. What do you suppose would be the best source or sources of information about each of the factors you listed in **1**?

ICB 1-2.
L O 6 *Nature of Cash, Assets, and Net Income*

Merrill Lynch & Co., Inc. is a U.S.-based global financial services firm. Information for 1992 and 1991 from the company's 1992 annual report is presented on page 48.[11] (All numbers are in thousands.)

Three students who were looking at Merrill Lynch's annual report were overheard to make the following comments:

Student A: What a great year Merrill Lynch had in 1992! The company earned net income of $20,764,830 because its total assets increased from $86,259,343 to $107,024,173.

Student B: But the change in total assets isn't the same as net income! The company had a net income of only $177,648 because cash increased from $1,073,924 to $1,251,572.

Student C: I see from the annual report that Merrill Lynch paid cash dividends of $126,237 in 1992. Don't you have to take that into consideration when analyzing the company's performance?

REQUIRED

1. Comment on the interpretations of Students A and B, and then answer Student C's question.
2. Calculate Merrill Lynch's net income for 1992. (**Hint:** Reconstruct the statement of retained earnings.)

---

10. The *Wall Street Journal*, January 10, 1983. Reprinted by permission of *Wall Street Journal*, © 1983 Dow Jones and Company, Inc. All Rights Reserved Worldwide.
11. Merrill Lynch & Co., Inc, *Annual Report*, 1992.

Merrill Lynch & Co., Inc.
Condensed Balance Sheets
December 31, 1992 and 1991
(in thousands)

	1992	1991
Assets		
Cash	$ 1,251,572	$ 1,073,924
Other Assets	105,772,601	85,185,419
Total Assets	$107,024,173	$86,259,343
Liabilities		
Total Liabilities	$102,455,069	$82,441,255
Stockholders' Equity		
Common Stock	$ 998,124	$ 1,014,696
Retained Earnings	3,570,980	2,803,392
Total Liabilities and Stockholders' Equity	$107,024,173	$86,259,343

ICB 1-3.

L O 6 *Financial Statements: Missing Data*

Ponderosa Inc. is the well-known operator of Ponderosa Steakhouses, located throughout the United States. Selected amounts from the company's condensed financial statements for 1985 and 1986 are presented below, with several amounts missing (all figures are in thousands). The 1984 end-of-year balance of retained earnings is $82,883.[12]

Income Statement	1986	1985
Revenues	$490,304	$ a
Costs and Expenses	h	(501,295)
Income Taxes	(853)	(3,603)
Net Income	$ i	$ b
Statement of Retained Earnings		
Beginning-of-Year Balance	$ j	$ c
Net Income	3,747	d
Dividends	k	(3,845)
End-of-Year Balance	$ l	$ e
Balance Sheet		
Total Assets	$ m	$246,481
Total Liabilities	110,192	102,239
Common Stock	57,968	56,800
Retained Earnings	n	f
Total Liabilities and Stockholders' Equity	$255,473	$ g

12. Ponderosa Inc., *Annual Report*, 1985 and 1986.

REQUIRED

1. Determine the missing amounts indicated by the letters.
2. Given the data presented, did the company's profitability improve from 1985 to 1986? Would you characterize the company as a "growth" company? Why or why not? Be prepared to discuss your opinion.

International Company Case

ICC 1-1.
L O 1 *The Goal of Profitability*

The Swedish company *Volvo AB*, the largest company in Scandinavia, had a difficult year in 1992. In the company's annual report, the president said in part, "The results in 1992 for Volvo's core businesses are profoundly unsatisfactory. The operating loss in Volvo Cars was considerable and Volvo Trucks also reported a loss. . . . The measures to return Volvo to favorable profitability have the highest priority."[13] Discuss the meaning of *profitability*. What other goal must a business achieve? Why is the goal of profitability important to Volvo's president? What is the accounting measure of profitability, and on which statement is it determined?

Toys "R" Us Case

TC 1-1.
L O 6 *The Four Basic Financial Statements*

Refer to the financial statements in the appendix on Toys "R" Us to answer the questions below. Keep in mind that every company, while following basic principles, adapts financial statements and terminology to its own special needs. Therefore, the complexity of the financial statements and the terminology in the Toys "R" Us statements will sometimes differ from those in the text.

1. What names does Toys "R" Us give its four basic financial statements? (Note that the use of the word "Consolidated" in the names of the financial statements simply means that these statements combine those of several companies owned by Toys "R" Us.)
2. Prove that the accounting equation works for Toys "R" Us in 1994 by finding the amounts for the following equation: Assets = liabilities + stockholders' equity.
3. What were the total revenues of Toys "R" Us for 1994?
4. Was Toys "R" Us profitable in 1994? How much was net income in that year, and did it increase or decrease from 1993?
5. Did the company's cash and equivalents increase from 1993 to 1994? By how much? In what two places in the statements can this number be found or computed?

---

13. Volvo AB, *Annual Report*, 1992.

CHAPTER 2 *Measuring Business Transactions*

LEARNING OBJECTIVES

1. Explain, in simple terms, the generally accepted ways of solving the measurement issues of recognition, valuation, and classification.

2. Describe the chart of accounts and recognize commonly used accounts.

3. Define *double-entry system* and state the rules for double entry.

4. Apply the steps for transaction analysis and processing to simple transactions.

5. Record transactions in the general journal.

6. Post transactions from the general journal to the ledger.

7. Prepare a trial balance and describe its value and limitations.

DECISION POINT

UAL Corporation and The Boeing Co.

In October 1990, UAL Corporation, United Airlines' parent company, announced that it had ordered up to 128 Boeing wide-body jets: 68 of the long-awaited 777 models and 60 of the 747-400 models. This order, which was estimated to come to more than $22 billion, was the largest order ever placed for commercial aircraft. The agreement included firm orders for half the aircraft and options to buy the other half. Boeing was manufacturing the aircraft for UAL, and the new planes were to be delivered beginning in 1995. How should this important order have been recorded, if at all, in the records of UAL and of Boeing? When should the forthcoming purchase and sale have been recorded in the companies' records?

The order obviously was an important event, one that carried long-term consequences for both companies. But, as you will see in this chapter, it was not recorded in the accounting records of either company. At the time the order was placed, the aircraft were yet to be manufactured and would not begin to be delivered for five years. For half the aircraft, UAL was given an option that could be accepted or refused. Even for the "firm" orders, Boeing cautioned in its 1989 annual report that "an economic downturn could result in airline equipment requirements less than currently anticipated resulting in requests to negotiate the rescheduling or possible cancellation of firm orders." The aircraft were not assets of UAL, and the company had not incurred a liability. No aircraft had been delivered or even built, so UAL was not obligated to pay at that point. And Boeing could not record any revenue until the aircraft were manufactured and delivered to UAL, until title to (ownership of) the aircraft shifted from Boeing to UAL. As it turned out, some orders and options were canceled or extended in 1993 because of the adverse effects of the economy on UAL Corporation.[1]

To understand and use financial statements, it is important to know how to analyze events to determine the extent of their impact on those statements. ⦂ ⦂ ⦂ ⦂ ⦂

1. The *Wall Street Journal,* October 16, 1990, p. A3, and The Boeing Co., *Annual Report,* 1989.

OBJECTIVE

1 *Explain, in simple terms, the generally accepted ways of solving the measurement issues of recognition, valuation, and classification*

In the chapter on uses of accounting information and the basic financial statements, we defined business transactions as economic events that affect the financial position of a business entity. To measure a business transaction, the accountant must decide when the transaction occurred (the recognition issue), what value to place on the transaction (the valuation issue), and how the components of the transaction should be categorized (the classification issue).

These three issues—recognition, valuation, and classification—underlie almost every major decision in financial accounting today. They lie at the heart of accounting for pension plans, of mergers of giant companies, and of international transactions; and they allow the accountant to project and plan for the effects of inflation. In discussing the three basic issues, we follow generally accepted accounting principles and use an approach that promotes an understanding of the basic ideas of accounting. Keep in mind, however, that controversy does exist, and that some solutions to problems are not as cut-and-dried as they appear.

THE RECOGNITION ISSUE

The recognition issue refers to the difficulty of deciding when a business transaction should be recorded. Often the facts of a situation are known, but there is disagreement about *when* the event should be recorded. Suppose, for instance, that a company orders, receives, and pays for an office desk. Which of the following actions constitutes a recordable event?

1. An employee sends a purchase requisition to the purchasing department.
2. The purchasing department sends a purchase order to the supplier.
3. The supplier ships the desk.
4. The company receives the desk.
5. The company receives the bill from the supplier.
6. The company pays the bill.

The answer to this question is important because amounts in the financial statements are affected by the date on which a purchase is recorded. According to accounting tradition, the transaction is recorded when title to the desk passes from the supplier to the purchaser, creating an obligation to pay. Thus, depending on the details of the shipping agreement, the transaction is recognized (recorded) at the time of either action **3** or action **4.** This is the guideline that we generally use in this book. However, in many small businesses that have simple accounting systems, the transaction is not recorded until the bill is received (action **5**) or paid (action **6**) because these are the implied points of title transfer. The predetermined time at which a transaction should be recorded is the recognition point.

The recognition issue is not always solved easily. Consider the case of an advertising agency that is asked by a client to prepare a major advertising campaign. People may work on the campaign several hours a day for a number of weeks. Value is added to the plan as the employees develop it. Should this added value be recognized as the campaign is being produced or at the time it is completed? Normally, the increase in value is recorded at the time the plan is finished and the client is billed for it. However, if a plan is going to take a long period to develop, the agency and the client may agree that the client will be billed at key points during its development.

THE VALUATION ISSUE

Valuation is perhaps the most controversial issue in accounting. The **valuation issue** focuses on assigning a monetary value to a business transaction. Generally accepted accounting principles state that the appropriate value to assign to all business transactions—and therefore to all assets, liabilities, and components of stockholders' equity, including revenues and expenses, acquired by a business—is the original cost (often called *historical cost*). **Cost** is defined here as the exchange price associated with a business transaction at the point of recognition. According to this guideline, the purpose of accounting is not to account for value in terms of worth, which can change after a transaction occurs, but to account for value in terms of cost at the time of the transaction. For example, the cost of an asset is recorded when the asset is acquired, and the value is held at that level until the asset is sold, expires, or is consumed. In this context, *value* means the cost at the time of the transaction. The practice of recording transactions at cost is referred to as the **cost principle**.

Suppose that a person offers a building for sale at $120,000. It may be valued for real estate taxes at $75,000, and it may be insured for $90,000. One prospective buyer may offer $100,000 for the building, and another may offer $105,000. At this point, several different, unverifiable opinions of value have been expressed. Finally, suppose the seller and a buyer settle on a price and complete the sale for $110,000. All of these figures are values of one kind or another, but only the last is sufficiently reliable to be used in the records. The market value of the building may vary over the years, but it will remain on the new buyer's records at $110,000 until it is sold again. At that point, the accountant will record the new transaction at the new exchange price, and a profit or loss will be recognized.

The cost principle is used because the cost is verifiable. It results from the actions of independent buyers and sellers who come to an agreement on price. An exchange price is an objective price that can be verified by evidence created at the time of the transaction. It is this final price, verified by agreement of the two parties, at which the transaction is recorded.

THE CLASSIFICATION ISSUE

The **classification** issue has to do with assigning all the transactions in which a business engages to appropriate categories, or accounts. For example, a company's ability to borrow money can be affected by the way in which its debts are categorized. Or a company's income can be affected by whether purchases of small items such as tools are considered repair expenses (a component of stockholders' equity) or equipment (assets). Proper classification depends not only on correctly analyzing the effect of each transaction on the business, but also on maintaining a system of accounts that reflects that effect. The rest of this chapter explains the classification of accounts and the analysis and recording of transactions.

ACCOUNTS AND THE CHART OF ACCOUNTS

OBJECTIVE

2 *Describe the chart of accounts and recognize commonly used accounts*

In the measurement of business transactions, large amounts of data are gathered. These data require a method of storage. Business people should be able to retrieve transaction data quickly and in usable form. In other words, there should be a filing system to sort out or classify all the transactions that occur in a business. This filing system consists of accounts. Recall that accounts are the basic storage units for accounting data and are used to accumulate amounts from similar transactions. An accounting system has a separate account for each asset, each liability, and each component of stockholders' equity, including revenues and expenses. Whether a company keeps records by hand or by computer, management must be able to refer to accounts so that it can study the company's financial history and plan for the future. A very small company may need only a few dozen accounts; a multinational corporation may need thousands.

In a manual accounting system, each account is kept on a separate page or card. These pages or cards are placed together in a book or file called the general ledger. In the computerized systems that most companies have today, accounts are maintained on magnetic tapes or disks. However, as a matter of convenience, accountants still refer to the group of company accounts as the general ledger, or simply the *ledger*.

To help identify accounts in the ledger and to make them easy to find, the accountant often numbers them. A list of these numbers with the corresponding account names is called a chart of accounts. A very simple chart of accounts appears in Exhibit 2-1. Notice that the first digit refers to the major financial statement classifications. An account number that begins with the digit 1 is an asset, an account number that begins with a 2 is a liability, and so forth. The second and third digits refer to individual accounts. Notice the gaps in the sequence of numbers. These gaps allow the accountant to expand the number of accounts. The accounts in Exhibit 2-1 will be used in this chapter and in the next two chapters, through the sample case of the Joan Miller Advertising Agency, Inc.

BUSINESS BULLETIN: BUSINESS PRACTICE

 Today, most businesses, even the smallest, use computerized accounting systems. In small businesses, these systems are called *general ledger packages* and run on personal computers. The starting point for these systems is a chart of accounts that reflects the activities in which the business engages. Every company develops a chart of accounts for its own needs. Seldom do two companies have exactly the same chart of accounts. A small business may get by with a simple chart of accounts like that in Exhibit 2-1. A large, complicated business like Commonwealth Edison, the electric utility in Chicago, will have twelve or more digits in its account numbers and thousands of accounts in its chart of accounts. ====

STOCKHOLDERS' EQUITY ACCOUNTS

In the chart of accounts in Exhibit 2-1, the revenue and expense accounts are separated from the stockholders' equity accounts. The relationships of these accounts to each other and to the basic financial statements are shown in Figure 2-1 on page 58. The distinctions among them are important for legal and financial reporting purposes.

Exhibit 2-1. Chart of Accounts for a Small Business

Account Number	Account Name	Description
	Assets	
111	Cash	Money and any medium of exchange, including coins, currency, checks, postal and express money orders, and money on deposit in a bank
112	Notes Receivable	Amounts due from others in the form of promissory notes (written promises to pay definite sums of money at fixed future dates)
113	Accounts Receivable	Amounts due from others from credit sales (sales on account)
114	Fees Receivable	Amounts arising from services performed but not yet billed to customers
115	Art Supplies	Prepaid expense; art supplies purchased and not used
116	Office Supplies	Prepaid expense; office supplies purchased and not used
117	Prepaid Rent	Prepaid expense; rent paid in advance and not used
118	Prepaid Insurance	Prepaid expense; insurance purchased and not expired; unexpired insurance
141	Land	Property owned for use in the business
142	Buildings	Structures owned for use in the business
143	Accumulated Depreciation, Buildings	Sum of the periodic allocation of the cost of buildings to expense
144	Art Equipment	Art equipment owned for use in the business
145	Accumulated Depreciation, Art Equipment	Sum of the periodic allocation of the cost of art equipment to expense
146	Office Equipment	Office equipment owned for use in the business
147	Accumulated Depreciation, Office Equipment	Sum of the periodic allocation of the cost of office equipment to expense

(continued)

Exhibit 2-1. Chart of Accounts for a Small Business (continued)

Account Number	Account Name	Description
	Liabilities	
211	Notes Payable	Amounts due to others in the form of promissory notes
212	Accounts Payable	Amounts due to others for purchases on credit
213	Unearned Art Fees	Unearned revenue; advance deposits for artwork to be provided in the future
214	Wages Payable	Amounts due to employees for wages earned and not paid
215	Income Taxes Payable	Amounts due to government for income taxes owed and not paid
221	Mortgage Payable	Amounts due on loans that are backed by the company's property and buildings
	Stockholders' Equity	
311	Common Stock	Stockholders' investments in a corporation for which they receive shares of capital stock
312	Retained Earnings	Stockholders' claims against company assets derived from profitable operations
313	Dividends	Distributions of assets (usually cash) that reduce retained earnings
314	Income Summary	Temporary account used at the end of the accounting period to summarize the revenues and expenses for the period
	Revenues	
411	Advertising Fees Earned	Revenues derived from performing advertising services
412	Art Fees Earned	Revenues derived from performing art services
	Expenses	
511	Wages Expense	Amounts earned by employees
512	Utility Expense	Amounts of utilities, such as water, electricity, and gas used
513	Telephone Expense	Amounts of telephone services used

(continued)

Exhibit 2-1. Chart of Accounts for a Small Business *(continued)*

Account Number	Account Name	Description
	Expenses (continued)	
514	Rent Expense	Amounts of rent on property and buildings used
515	Insurance Expense	Amounts for insurance used
516	Art Supplies Expense	Amounts for art supplies used
517	Office Supplies Expense	Amounts for office supplies used
518	Depreciation Expense, Buildings	Amount of buildings' cost allocated to expense
519	Depreciation Expense, Art Equipment	Amount of art equipment costs allocated to expense
520	Depreciation Expense, Office Equipment	Amount of office equipment costs allocated to expense
521	Interest Expense	Amount of interest on debts

First, the stockholders' equity accounts represent legal claims by the stockholders against the assets of the company. Common Stock is a capital stock account (corporations may have more than one type of capital stock) that represents stockholders' claims arising from their investments in the company, and Retained Earnings represents stockholders' claims arising from profitable operations. Both are claims against the general assets of the company, not against specific assets. They do not represent pools of funds that have been set aside. Dividends are included among the stockholders' equity accounts because they are distributions of assets that reduce ownership claims on retained earnings and are shown on the statement of retained earnings.

Second, the law requires that capital investments and dividends be separated from revenues and expenses for income tax reporting, financial reporting, and other purposes.

Third, management needs a detailed breakdown of revenues and expenses for budgeting and operating purposes. From these accounts, which are included on the income statement, management can identify the sources of all revenues and the nature of all expenses.

ACCOUNT TITLES

The names of accounts often confuse beginning accounting students because some of the words are new or have technical meanings. Also, the same asset, liability, or stockholders' equity account can have different names in different companies. (Actually, this is not so strange. People, too, often are called different names by their friends, families, and associates.) For example, Fixed Assets, Plant and Equipment, Capital Assets, and Long-Lived Assets are all names for long-term asset accounts. Even the most acceptable names change over time, and, out of habit, some companies use names that are out of date.

Figure 2-1. Relationships of Stockholders' Equity Accounts

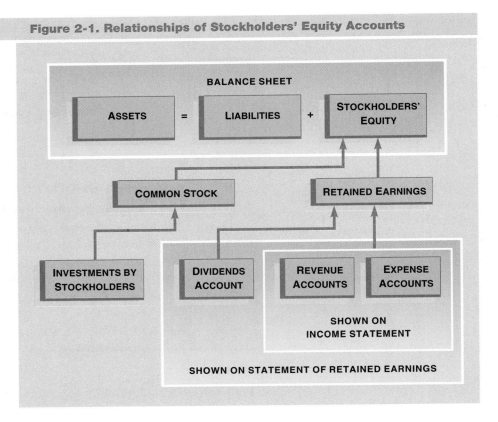

In general, an account title should describe what is recorded in the account. When you come across an account title that you do not recognize, you should examine the context of the name—whether it is classified as an asset, liability, or stockholders' equity component, including revenue or expense, on the financial statements—and look for the kind of transaction that gave rise to the account.

THE DOUBLE-ENTRY SYSTEM: THE BASIC METHOD OF ACCOUNTING

OBJECTIVE

3 *Define double-entry system and state the rules for double entry*

The double-entry system, the backbone of accounting, evolved during the Renaissance. As noted previously, the first systematic description of double-entry bookkeeping appeared in 1494, two years after Columbus discovered America, in a mathematics book written by Fra Luca Pacioli. Goethe, the famous German poet and dramatist, referred to double-entry bookkeeping as "one of the finest discoveries of the human intellect." And Werner Sombart, an eminent economist-sociologist, believed that "double-entry bookkeeping is born of the same spirit as the system of Galileo and Newton."

What is the significance of the double-entry system? The system is based on the *principle of duality*, which means that every economic event has two aspects—effort and reward, sacrifice and benefit, source and use—that offset or balance each other. In the double-entry system, each transaction must be recorded with at least one debit and one credit, so that the total dollar amount of debits and the total dollar amount of credits equal each other. Because of the way it is designed, the whole system is always in balance. All accounting systems, no matter how sophisticated, are based on the principle of duality.

THE T ACCOUNT

The T account is a good place to begin the study of the double-entry system. In its simplest form, an account has three parts: (1) a title, which describes the asset, the liability, or the stockholders' equity account; (2) a left side, which is called the debit side; and (3) a right side, which is called the credit side. This form of an account, called a T account because it resembles the letter *T*, is used to analyze transactions. It looks like this:

Title of Account

Debit (left) side	Credit (right) side

Any entry made on the left side of the account is a debit, or debit entry; and any entry made on the right side of the account is a credit, or credit entry. The terms *debit* (abbreviated Dr., from the Latin *debere*) and *credit* (abbreviated Cr., from the Latin *credere*) are simply the accountant's words for "left" and "right" (not for "increase" or "decrease"). We present a more formal version of the T account later in this chapter, where we examine the ledger account form.

THE T ACCOUNT ILLUSTRATED

In the chapter on uses of accounting information and the basic financial statements, Shannon Realty, Inc. had several transactions that involved the receipt or payment of cash. (See the exhibit "Summary of Effects of Illustrative Transactions on Financial Position" in the chapter on uses of accounting information and the basic financial statements for a summary of the numbered transactions listed below.) These transactions can be summarized in the Cash account by recording receipts on the left (debit) side of the account and payments on the right (credit) side of the account:

Cash

(1)	50,000	(2)	35,000
(5)	1,500	(4)	200
(7)	1,000	(8)	1,000
		(9)	400
		(11)	600
	52,500		37,200
Bal.	15,300		

The cash receipts on the left total $52,500. (The total is written in small figures so that it cannot be confused with an actual debit entry.) The cash payments on the right side total $37,200. These totals are simply working totals, or footings. Footings, which are calculated at the end of each month, are an easy way to determine cash on hand. The difference in dollars between the total debit footing and the total credit footing is called the balance, or *account balance*. If the balance is a debit, it is written on the left side. If it is a credit, it is written on the right side. Notice that Shannon Realty, Inc.'s Cash account has a debit balance of $15,300 ($52,500 − $37,200). This is the amount of cash the business has on hand at the end of the month.

ANALYZING AND PROCESSING TRANSACTIONS

The two rules of double-entry bookkeeping are that every transaction affects at least two accounts and that total debits must equal total credits. In other words, for every transaction, one or more accounts must be debited and one or more accounts must be credited, and the total dollar amount of the debits must equal the total dollar amount of the credits.

Look again at the accounting equation:

$$\text{Assets} = \text{liabilities} + \text{stockholders' equity}$$

You can see that if a debit increases assets, then a credit must be used to increase liabilities or stockholders' equity because they are on opposite sides of the equal sign. Likewise, if a credit decreases assets, then a debit must be used to decrease liabilities or stockholders' equity. These rules can be shown as follows:

Assets		=	Liabilities		+	Stockholders' Equity	
Debit for increases (+)	Credit for decreases (−)		Debit for decreases (−)	Credit for increases (+)		Debit for decreases (−)	Credit for increases (+)

1. Increases in assets are debited to asset accounts. Decreases in assets are credited to asset accounts.
2. Increases in liabilities and stockholders' equity are credited to liability and stockholders' equity accounts. Decreases in liabilities and stockholders' equity are debited to liability and stockholders' equity accounts.

One of the more difficult points to understand is the application of double-entry rules to the stockholders' equity components. The key is to remember that dividends and expenses are deductions from stockholders' equity. Thus, transactions that *increase* dividends or expenses *decrease* stockholders' equity. Consider this expanded version of the accounting equation:

Stockholders' Equity

$$\text{Assets} = \text{liabilities} + \text{common stock} + \text{retained earnings} - \text{dividends} + \text{revenues} - \text{expenses}$$

This equation may be rearranged by shifting dividends and expenses to the left side, as follows:

Assets		+	Dividends		+	Expenses		=	Liabilities		+	Common Stock		+	Retained Earnings		+	Revenues	
+ (debits)	− (credits)		+ (debits)	− (credits)		+ (debits)	− (credits)		− (debits)	+ (credits)		− (debits)	+ (credits)		− (debits)	+ (credits)		− (debits)	+ (credits)

Note that the rules for double entry for all the accounts on the left of the equal sign are just the opposite of the rules for all the accounts on the right of the equal sign. Assets, dividends, and expenses are increased by debits and decreased by credits. Liabilities, common stock, retained earnings, and revenues are increased by credits and decreased by debits.

With this basic information about double entry, it is possible to analyze and process transactions by following the five steps illustrated in Figure 2-2. To show how the steps are applied, assume that on June 1, Shell Oil Company borrows $100,000 from its bank on a promissory note. The transaction is analyzed and processed as follows:

1. *Analyze the transaction to determine its effect on assets, liabilities, and stockholders' equity.* In this case, both an asset (Cash) and a liability (Notes Payable) increase. A transaction is usually supported by some kind of source document—an invoice, a receipt, a check, or a contract. Here, a copy of the signed note would be the source document.

2. *Apply the rules of double entry.* Increases in assets are recorded by debits. Increases in liabilities are recorded by credits.

3. *Record the entry.* Transactions are recorded in chronological order in a journal. One form of journal, which is explained in more detail later in this chapter, records the date, the debit account, and the debit amount on one line and the credit account and credit amount indented on the next line, as follows:

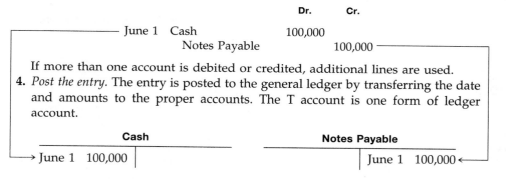

	Dr.	**Cr.**
June 1 Cash	100,000	
Notes Payable		100,000

If more than one account is debited or credited, additional lines are used.

4. *Post the entry.* The entry is posted to the general ledger by transferring the date and amounts to the proper accounts. The T account is one form of ledger account.

Cash	**Notes Payable**
June 1 100,000	June 1 100,000

For purposes of analysis, accountants often bypass step **3** and record entries directly in T accounts because doing so clearly and quickly shows the effects of transactions on the accounts. Some of the assignments in this chapter use the same approach to emphasize the analytical aspects of double entry. In formal records, step **3** is not omitted.

5. *Prepare the trial balance to confirm the balance of the accounts.* Periodically, accountants prepare a trial balance to confirm that the accounts are still in balance after the recording and posting of transactions. Preparation of the trial balance is explained at the end of this chapter.

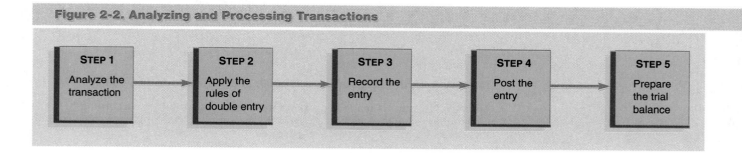

Figure 2-2. Analyzing and Processing Transactions

STEP 1	**STEP 2**	**STEP 3**	**STEP 4**	**STEP 5**
Analyze the transaction	Apply the rules of double entry	Record the entry	Post the entry	Prepare the trial balance

OBJECTIVE

4 *Apply the steps for transaction analysis and processing to simple transactions*

TRANSACTION ANALYSIS ILLUSTRATED

In the next few pages, we examine the transactions for Joan Miller Advertising Agency, Inc. during the month of January. In the discussion, we illustrate the principle of duality and show how transactions are recorded in the accounts.

January 1: Joan Miller obtains a charter from the state and invests $10,000 in her own advertising agency in exchange for 10,000 shares of $1 par value stock.

	Dr.	Cr.
Jan. 1 Cash	10,000	
Common Stock		10,000

Cash

Jan. 1	10,000	

Common Stock

		Jan. 1	10,000

Transaction: Investment in business.
Analysis: Assets increase. Stockholders' equity increases.
Rules: Increases in assets are recorded by debits. Increases in stockholders' equity are recorded by credits.
Entry: The increase in assets is recorded by a debit to Cash. The increase in stockholders' equity is recorded by a credit to Common Stock.

Analysis: If Joan Miller had invested assets other than cash in the business, the appropriate asset accounts would be debited.

January 2: Rents an office, paying two months' rent, $800, in advance.

	Dr.	Cr.
Jan. 2 Prepaid Rent	800	
Cash		800

Cash

Jan. 1	10,000	Jan. 2	800

Prepaid Rent

Jan. 2	800	

Transaction: Rent paid in advance.
Analysis: Assets increase. Assets decrease.
Rules: Increases in assets are recorded by debits. Decreases in assets are recorded by credits.
Entry: The increase in assets is recorded by a debit to Prepaid Rent. The decrease in assets is recorded by a credit to Cash.

January 3: Orders art supplies, $1,800, and office supplies, $800.

Analysis: No entry is made because no transaction has occurred. According to the recognition issue, there is no liability until the supplies are shipped or received and there is an obligation to pay for them.

January 4: Purchases art equipment, $4,200, with cash.

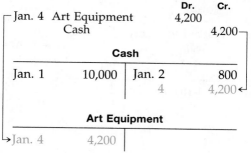

		Dr.	Cr.
Jan. 4	Art Equipment	4,200	
	Cash		4,200

Cash

Jan. 1	10,000	Jan. 2	800
		4	4,200

Art Equipment

Jan. 4	4,200	

Transaction: Purchase of equipment.
Analysis: Assets increase. Assets decrease.
Rules: Increases in assets are recorded by debits. Decreases in assets are recorded by credits.
Entry: The increase in assets is recorded by a debit to Art Equipment. The decrease in assets is recorded by a credit to Cash.

January 5: Purchases office equipment, $3,000, from Morgan Equipment; pays $1,500 in cash and agrees to pay the rest next month.

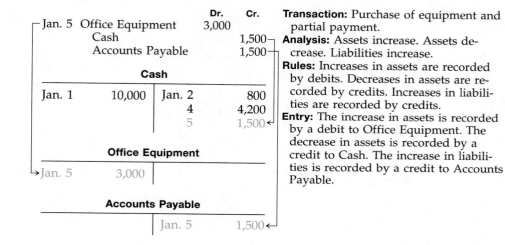

		Dr.	Cr.
Jan. 5	Office Equipment	3,000	
	Cash		1,500
	Accounts Payable		1,500

Cash

Jan. 1	10,000	Jan. 2	800
		4	4,200
		5	1,500

Office Equipment

Jan. 5	3,000	

Accounts Payable

		Jan. 5	1,500

Transaction: Purchase of equipment and partial payment.
Analysis: Assets increase. Assets decrease. Liabilities increase.
Rules: Increases in assets are recorded by debits. Decreases in assets are recorded by credits. Increases in liabilities are recorded by credits.
Entry: The increase in assets is recorded by a debit to Office Equipment. The decrease in assets is recorded by a credit to Cash. The increase in liabilities is recorded by a credit to Accounts Payable.

January 6: Purchases art supplies, $1,800, and office supplies, $800, from Taylor Supply Company, on credit.

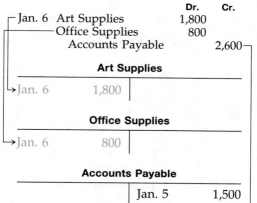

		Dr.	Cr.
Jan. 6	Art Supplies	1,800	
	Office Supplies	800	
	Accounts Payable		2,600

Art Supplies

Jan. 6	1,800	

Office Supplies

Jan. 6	800	

Accounts Payable

		Jan. 5	1,500
		6	2,600

Transaction: Purchase of supplies on credit.
Analysis: Assets increase. Liabilities increase.
Rules: Increases in assets are recorded by debits. Increases in liabilities are recorded by credits.
Entry: The increase in assets is recorded by debits to Art Supplies and Office Supplies. The increase in liabilities is recorded by a credit to Accounts Payable.

January 8: Pays for a one-year life insurance policy, $480, with coverage effective January 1.

	Dr.	Cr.
Jan. 8 Prepaid Insurance	480	
Cash		480

Cash

Jan. 1	10,000	Jan. 2	800
		4	4,200
		5	1,500
		8	480

Prepaid Insurance

Jan. 8	480	

Transaction: Insurance purchased in advance.
Analysis: Assets increase. Assets decrease.
Rules: Increases in assets are recorded by debits. Decreases in assets are recorded by credits.
Entry: The increase in assets is recorded by a debit to Prepaid Insurance. The decrease in assets is recorded by a credit to Cash.

January 9: Pays Taylor Supply Company $1,000 of the amount owed.

	Dr.	Cr.
Jan. 9 Accounts Payable	1,000	
Cash		1,000

Cash

Jan. 1	10,000	Jan. 2	800
		4	4,200
		5	1,500
		8	480
		9	1,000

Accounts Payable

Jan. 9	1,000	Jan. 5	1,500
		6	2,600

Transaction: Partial payment on a liability.
Analysis: Assets decrease. Liabilities decrease.
Rules: Decreases in assets are recorded by credits. Decreases in liabilities are recorded by debits.
Entry: The decrease in liabilities is recorded by a debit to Accounts Payable. The decrease in assets is recorded by a credit to Cash.

January 10: Performs a service for an automobile dealer by placing advertisements in the newspaper and collects a fee, $1,400.

	Dr.	Cr.
Jan. 10 Cash	1,400	
Advertising Fees Earned		1,400

Cash

Jan. 1	10,000	Jan. 2	800
10	1,400	4	4,200
		5	1,500
		8	480
		9	1,000

Advertising Fees Earned

		Jan. 10	1,400

Transaction: Revenue earned and cash collected.
Analysis: Assets increase. Stockholders' equity increases.
Rules: Increases in assets are recorded by debits. Increases in stockholders' equity are recorded by credits.
Entry: The increase in assets is recorded by a debit to Cash. The increase in stockholders' equity is recorded by a credit to Advertising Fees Earned.

January 12: Pays the secretary two weeks' wages, $600.

		Dr.	Cr.
Jan. 12	Office Wages		
	Expense	600	
	Cash		600

Cash

Jan. 1	10,000	Jan. 2	800
10	1,400	4	4,200
		5	1,500
		8	480
		9	1,000
		12	600

Office Wages Expense

Jan. 12	600	

Transaction: Payment of wages expense.
Analysis: Assets decrease. Stockholders' equity decreases.
Rules: Decreases in assets are recorded by credits. Decreases in stockholders' equity are recorded by debits.
Entry: The decrease in stockholders' equity is recorded by a debit to Office Wages Expense. The decrease in assets is recorded by a credit to Cash.

January 15: Accepts an advance fee, $1,000, for artwork to be done for another agency.

		Dr.	Cr.
Jan. 15	Cash	1,000	
	Unearned Art		
	Fees		1,000

Cash

Jan. 1	10,000	Jan. 2	800
10	1,400	4	4,200
15	1,000	5	1,500
		8	480
		9	1,000
		12	600

Unearned Art Fees

		Jan. 15	1,000

Transaction: Payment received for future services.
Analysis: Assets increase. Liabilities increase.
Rules: Increases in assets are recorded by debits. Increases in liabilities are recorded by credits.
Entry: The increase in assets is recorded by a debit to Cash. The increase in liabilities is recorded by a credit to Unearned Art Fees.

January 19: Performs a service by placing several major advertisements for Ward Department Stores. The fee, $2,800, is billed now but will be collected next month.

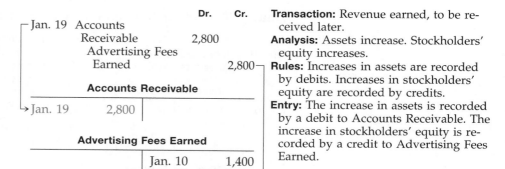

		Dr.	Cr.
Jan. 19	Accounts		
	Receivable	2,800	
	Advertising Fees		
	Earned		2,800

Accounts Receivable

Jan. 19	2,800	

Advertising Fees Earned

		Jan. 10	1,400
		19	2,800

Transaction: Revenue earned, to be received later.
Analysis: Assets increase. Stockholders' equity increases.
Rules: Increases in assets are recorded by debits. Increases in stockholders' equity are recorded by credits.
Entry: The increase in assets is recorded by a debit to Accounts Receivable. The increase in stockholders' equity is recorded by a credit to Advertising Fees Earned.

January 26: Pays the secretary two more weeks' wages, $600.

		Dr.	Cr.
Jan. 26	Office Wages Expense	600	
	Cash		600

Cash

Jan.	1	10,000	Jan.	2	800
	10	1,400		4	4,200
	15	1,000		5	1,500
				8	480
				9	1,000
				12	600
				26	600

Office Wages Expense

Jan. 12	600	
26	600	

Transaction: Payment of wages expense.
Analysis: Assets decrease. Stockholders' equity decreases.
Rules: Decreases in assets are recorded by credits. Decreases in stockholders' equity are recorded by debits.
Entry: The decrease in stockholders' equity is recorded by a debit to Office Wages Expense. The decrease in assets is recorded by a credit to Cash.

January 29: Receives and pays the utility bill, $100.

		Dr.	Cr.
Jan. 29	Utility Expense	100	
	Cash		100

Cash

Jan.	1	10,000	Jan.	2	800
	10	1,400		4	4,200
	15	1,000		5	1,500
				8	480
				9	1,000
				12	600
				26	600
				29	100

Utility Expense

Jan. 29	100	

Transaction: Payment of utility expense.
Analysis: Assets decrease. Stockholders' equity decreases.
Rules: Decreases in assets are recorded by credits. Decreases in stockholders' equity are recorded by debits.
Entry: The decrease in stockholders' equity is recorded by a debit to Utility Expense. The decrease in assets is recorded by a credit to Cash.

January 30: Receives (but does not pay) the telephone bill, $70.

		Dr.	Cr.
Jan. 30	Telephone Expense	70	
	Accounts Payable		70

Accounts Payable

Jan. 9	1,000	Jan.	5	1,500
			6	2,600
			30	70

Telephone Expense

Jan. 30	70	

Transaction: Expense incurred, to be paid later.
Analysis: Liabilities increase. Stockholders' equity decreases.
Rules: Increases in liabilities are recorded by credits. Decreases in stockholders' equity are recorded by debits.
Entry: The decrease in stockholders' equity is recorded by a debit to Telephone Expense. The increase in liabilities is recorded by a credit to Accounts Payable.

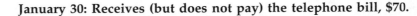

January 31: Declared and paid a dividend of $1,400.

		Dr.	Cr.
Jan. 31	Dividends	1,400	
	Cash		1,400

Transaction: Declaration and payment of dividends.

Analysis: Assets decrease. Stockholders' equity decreases.

Rules: Decreases in assets are recorded by credits. Decreases in stockholders' equity are recorded by debits.

Entry: The decrease in stockholders' equity is recorded by a debit to Dividends. The decrease in assets is recorded by a credit to Cash.

Cash

Jan.	1	10,000	Jan.	2	800
	10	1,400		4	4,200
	15	1,000		5	1,500
				8	480
				9	1,000
				12	600
				26	600
				29	100
				31	1,400

Dividends

Jan. 31	1,400	

SUMMARY OF TRANSACTIONS

The transactions for January are shown in Exhibit 2-2 in their accounts and in relation to the accounting equation.

American Collegiate Sales Corporation (ACS) used student representatives to market grooming aids, casual clothes, and other such products on college campuses. These representatives organized parties at which they displayed the products. Students who bought products paid the representative, who in turn ordered the products and paid ACS for them. When the products arrived, the student representative delivered them to the buyers. The representative paid ACS less than he or she charged the buyer. The difference represented the earnings of the representatives, who were not employees of ACS. Wall Street investors admired ACS because the company had enjoyed several years of rapid growth in sales and earnings.

Early last year ACS predicted further increases of 30 percent. By December, however, it was apparent that the forecasted sales goals would not be met. So, during the last two weeks of December, ACS shipped $20 million of merchandise to the sales representatives to be held for future sales parties. The company billed the student representatives and recorded the shipments as sales. In this way, ACS was able to meet its sales goal for the year and maintain the high value of its stock.

The shipments, however, were improperly recorded as sales. The goods had not been ordered by or sold to actual customers, and the student repre-

Exhibit 2-2. Summary of Sample Accounts and Transactions for Joan Miller Advertising Agency, Inc.

Assets	=	Liabilities	+	Stockholders' Equity

Cash

Jan.	1	10,000	Jan.	2	800
	10	1,400		4	4,200
	15	1,000		5	1,500
				8	480
				9	1,000
				12	600
				26	600
				29	100
				31	1,400

	12,400		10,680
Bal.	1,720		

Accounts Receivable

Jan. 19	2,800

Art Supplies

Jan. 6	1,800

Office Supplies

Jan. 6	800

Prepaid Rent

Jan. 2	800

Prepaid Insurance

Jan. 8	480

Art Equipment

Jan. 4	4,200

Office Equipment

Jan. 5	3,000

Accounts Payable

Jan. 9	1,000	Jan.	5	1,500
			6	2,600
			30	70

	1,000		4,170
		Bal.	3,170

Unearned Art Fees

		Jan. 15	1,000

Common Stock

	Jan. 1	10,000

Dividends

Jan. 31	1,400

Advertising Fees Earned

	Jan. 10	1,400
	19	2,800

	Bal.	4,200

Office Wages Expense

Jan. 12	600
26	600

Bal.	1,200

Utility Expense

Jan. 29	100

Telephone Expense

Jan. 30	70

sentatives had the right to return all the products unconditionally. In technical terms, this type of arrangement is called a *consignment*. To report consignment shipments as legitimate sales is certainly unethical and can be, as in this case, illegal when the intent is to deceive. As it turned out, most of the $20 million of products were returned during January and February, and ACS went into bankruptcy. Officials of the company were later convicted of fraud.

RECORDING AND POSTING TRANSACTIONS

OBJECTIVE

5 *Record transactions in the general journal*

The formal processing of transactions in the general journal, the general ledger, and the trial balance is now illustrated.

THE GENERAL JOURNAL

As you have seen, transactions can be entered directly into the accounts. But this method makes identifying individual transactions or finding errors very difficult because the debit is recorded in one account and the credit in another. The solution is to record all transactions chronologically in a journal. The journal is sometimes called the *book of original entry* because it is where transactions first enter the accounting records. Later, the debit and credit portions of each transaction can be transferred to the appropriate accounts in the ledger.

A separate journal entry is used to record each transaction, and the process of recording transactions is called journalizing.

Most businesses have more than one kind of journal. Several types of journals are discussed in the appendix on special-purpose journals. The simplest and most flexible type is the general journal, the one we focus on in this chapter. Entries in the general journal include the following information about each transaction:

1. The date
2. The names of the accounts debited and the dollar amounts on the same lines in the debit column
3. The names of the accounts credited and the dollar amounts on the same lines in the credit column
4. An explanation of the transaction
5. The account identification numbers, if appropriate

We have recorded two transactions for Joan Miller Advertising Agency, Inc. in Exhibit 2-3. As shown in that exhibit, the procedure for recording transactions in the general journal is as follows:

1. Record the date by writing the year in small figures on the first line at the top of the first column, the month on the next line of the first column, and the day in the second column opposite the month. For subsequent entries on the same page for the same month and year, the month and year can be omitted.
2. Write the exact names of the accounts debited and credited under the heading "Description." Write the name of the account debited next to the left margin of the second line, and indent the name of the account credited. The explanation is placed on the next line and further indented. It should be brief but sufficient to explain and identify the transaction. A transaction can have more than one debit or credit entry; this is called a compound entry. In a compound entry, all debit accounts are listed before any credit accounts. (The January 6 transaction of Joan Miller Advertising Agency, Inc. is an example of a compound entry; see Exhibit 2-3.)
3. Write the debit amounts in the appropriate column opposite the accounts to be debited, and write the credit amounts in the appropriate column opposite the accounts to be credited.
4. At the time the transactions are recorded in the general journal, nothing is placed in the Post. Ref. (posting reference) column. (This column is sometimes

Exhibit 2-3. The General Journal

Date		Description	Post. Ref.	Debit	Credit
19xx Jan.	6	Art Supplies		1,800	
		Office Supplies		800	
		Accounts Payable			2,600
		Purchase of art and office supplies on credit			
	8	Prepaid Insurance		480	
		Cash			480
		Paid one-year life insurance premium			

General Journal — Page 1

called *LP* or *Folio*.) Later, if the company uses account numbers to identify accounts in the ledger, fill in the account numbers to provide a convenient cross-reference from the general journal to the ledger and to indicate that the entry has been posted to the ledger. If the accounts are not numbered, use a checkmark (✔).

5. It is customary to skip a line after each journal entry.

THE GENERAL LEDGER

The general journal is used to record the details of each transaction. The general ledger is used to update each account.

The Ledger Account Form   The T account is a simple, direct means of recording transactions. In practice, a somewhat more complicated form of the account is needed in order to record more information. The ledger account form, which contains four columns for dollar amounts, is illustrated in Exhibit 2-4.

Exhibit 2-4. Accounts Payable in the General Ledger

General Ledger

Accounts Payable — Account No. 212

Date		Item	Post. Ref.	Debit	Credit	Balance Debit	Balance Credit
19xx Jan.	5		J1		1,500		1,500
	6		J1		2,600		4,100
	9		J1	1,000			3,100
	30		J2		70		3,170

The account title and number appear at the top of the account form. The date of the transaction appears in the first two columns as it does in the journal. The Item column is used only rarely to identify transactions, because explanations already appear in the journal. The Post. Ref. column is used to note the journal page where the original entry for the transaction can be found. The dollar amount of the entry is entered in the appropriate Debit or Credit column, and a new account balance is computed in the final two columns after each entry. The advantage of this form of account over the T account is that the current balance of the account is readily available.

Posting to the Ledger   After the transactions have been entered in the journal, they must be transferred to the general ledger. The process of transferring journal entry information from the journal to the ledger is called posting. Posting is usually done after several entries have been made—for example, at the end of each day or less frequently, depending on the number of transactions.

Through posting, each amount in the Debit column of the journal is transferred into the Debit column of the appropriate account in the ledger, and each amount in the Credit column of the journal is transferred into the Credit column of the appropriate account in the ledger (Exhibit 2-5). These are the steps in the posting process:

1. In the ledger, locate the debit account named in the journal entry.
2. Enter the date of the transaction and, in the Post. Ref. column of the ledger, the journal page number from which the entry comes.
3. Enter in the Debit column of the ledger account the amount of the debit as it appears in the journal.
4. Calculate the account balance and enter it in the appropriate balance column.
5. Enter in the Post. Ref. column of the journal the account number to which the amount has been posted.
6. Repeat the same five steps for the credit side of the journal entry.

Notice that step **5** is the last step in the posting process for each debit and credit. In addition to serving as an easy reference between the journal entry and the ledger account, this entry in the Post. Ref. column of the journal indicates that all steps for the item have been completed. This allows accountants who have been called away from their work to easily find where they were before the interruption.

THE TRIAL BALANCE

For every amount debited in the ledger, an equal amount must be credited. This means that the total of debits and credits in the ledger must be equal. To test this, the accountant periodically prepares a trial balance. Exhibit 2-6 shows a trial balance for Joan Miller Advertising Agency, Inc. It was prepared from the accounts in Exhibit 2-2, on page 68.

The trial balance may be prepared at any time but is usually prepared on the last day of the month. Here are the steps in preparing a trial balance:

1. List each ledger account that has a balance, with debit balances in the left column and credit balances in the right column. Accounts are listed in the order in which they appear in the ledger.
2. Add each column.
3. Compare the totals of the columns.

Exhibit 2-5. Posting from the General Journal to the Ledger

General Journal
② Page 2

Date		Description	Post. Ref.	Debit	Credit
19xx ②		①	⑤	③	
Jan.	30	Telephone Expense	513	70	
		Accounts Payable	212		70
		Received bill for			
		telephone expense			

General Ledger

Accounts Payable Account No. 212

Date		Item	Post. Ref.	Debit	Credit	Balance Debit	Balance Credit
19xx							
Jan.	5		J1		1,500		1,500
	6		J1		2,600		4,100
	9		J1	1,000			3,100
	30		J2		70		3,170

General Ledger

Telephone Expense Account No. 513

Date		Item	Post. Ref.	Debit	Credit	Balance Debit	Balance Credit
19xx						④	
Jan.	30		J2	70		70	

In carrying out steps **1** and **2**, remember that the account form in the ledger has two balance columns, one for debit balances and one for credit balances. In accounts in which increases are recorded by debits, the normal balance (the usual balance) is a debit balance; where increases are recorded by credits, the normal balance is a credit balance. Table 2-1 summarizes the normal account balances of the major account categories. According to the table, the ledger account Accounts Payable (a liability) typically has a credit balance and is copied into the trial balance as a credit balance.

Once in a while, a transaction leaves an account with a balance that is not "normal." For example, when a company overdraws its account at the bank, its Cash account (an asset) will show a credit balance instead of a debit balance. The "abnormal" balance should be copied into the trial balance columns as it stands, as a debit or a credit.

The trial balance proves whether or not the ledger is in balance. *In balance* means that equal debits and credits have been recorded for all transactions, so that total debits equal total credits. But the trial balance does not prove that the transactions were analyzed correctly or recorded in the proper accounts.

Exhibit 2-6. Trial Balance

Joan Miller Advertising Agency, Inc.
Trial Balance
January 31, 19xx

Cash	$ 1,720	
Accounts Receivable	2,800	
Art Supplies	1,800	
Office Supplies	800	
Prepaid Rent	800	
Prepaid Insurance	480	
Art Equipment	4,200	
Office Equipment	3,000	
Accounts Payable		$ 3,170
Unearned Art Fees		1,000
Common Stock		10,000
Dividends	1,400	
Advertising Fees Earned		4,200
Office Wages Expense	1,200	
Utility Expense	100	
Telephone Expense	70	
	$18,370	$18,370

For example, there is no way of determining from the trial balance that a debit should have been made in the Art Equipment account rather than the Office Equipment account. And the trial balance does not detect whether transactions have been omitted, because equal debits and credits will have been omitted. Also, if an error of the same amount is made in both a debit and a credit, it will not be discovered by the trial balance. The trial balance proves only that the debits and credits in the accounts are in balance.

If the debit and credit columns of the trial balance are not equal, look for one or more of the following errors: (1) a debit was entered in an account as a

Table 2-1. Normal Account Balances of Major Account Categories

Account Category	Increases Recorded by		Normal Balance	
	Debit	Credit	Debit	Credit
Asset	x		x	
Liability		x		x
Stockholders' Equity:				
Common Stock		x		x
Dividends	x		x	
Revenues		x		x
Expenses	x		x	

credit, or vice versa; (2) the balance of an account was computed incorrectly; (3) an error was made in carrying the account balance to the trial balance; or (4) the trial balance was summed incorrectly.

Other than simply adding the columns wrong, the two most common mistakes in preparing a trial balance are (1) recording an account with a debit balance as a credit, or vice versa, and (2) transposing two numbers when transferring an amount to the trial balance (for example, entering \$23,459 as \$23,549). The first of these mistakes causes the trial balance to be out of balance by an amount divisible by 2. The second causes the trial balance to be out of balance by a number divisible by 9. Thus, if a trial balance is out of balance and the addition has been verified, determine the amount by which the trial balance is out of balance and divide it first by 2 and then by 9. If the amount is divisible by 2, look in the trial balance for an amount equal to the quotient. If you find the amount, it is probably in the wrong column. If the amount is divisible by 9, trace each amount to the ledger account balance, checking carefully for a transposition error. If neither of these techniques identifies the error, first recompute the balance of each account in the ledger, then, if the error still has not been found, retrace each posting from the journal to the ledger.

BUSINESS BULLETIN: TECHNOLOGY IN PRACTICE

In computerized accounting systems, posting is done automatically and the trial balance can be easily prepared as often as needed. Any accounts with abnormal balances are highlighted for investigation. Some general ledger software packages for small businesses list the trial balance amounts in a single column, with credit balances shown as minuses. In such cases, the trial balance is in balance if the total is zero.

SOME NOTES ON PRESENTATION

Ruled lines appear in financial reports before each subtotal or total to indicate that the amounts above are added or subtracted. It is common practice to use a double line under a final total to show that it has been checked, or verified.

Dollars signs (\$) are required in all financial statements, including the balance sheet and income statement, and in the trial balance and other schedules. On these statements, a dollar sign should be placed before the first amount in each column and before the first amount in a column following a ruled line. Dollar signs in the same column are aligned. Dollar signs are not used in journals and ledgers.

On unruled paper, commas and decimal points are used in dollar amounts. On paper with ruled columns—like the paper in journals and ledgers—commas and decimal points are not needed. In this book, because most problems and illustrations are in whole dollar amounts, the cents column usually is omitted. When accountants deal with whole dollars, they often use a dash in the cents column to indicate whole dollars rather than take the time to write zeros.

CHAPTER REVIEW

REVIEW OF LEARNING OBJECTIVES

1. **Explain, in simple terms, the generally accepted ways of solving the measurement issues of recognition, valuation, and classification.** To measure a business transaction, the accountant must determine when the transaction occurred (the recognition issue), what value should be placed on the transaction (the valuation issue), and how the components of the transaction should be categorized (the classification issue). In general, recognition occurs when title passes, and a transaction is valued at the exchange price, the cost at the time the transaction is recognized. Classification refers to the categorizing of transactions according to a system of accounts.

2. **Describe the chart of accounts and recognize commonly used accounts.** An account is a device for storing data from transactions. There is one account for each asset, liability, and component of stockholders' equity, including revenues and expenses. The general ledger is a book or file consisting of all of a company's accounts arranged according to a chart of accounts. Commonly used asset accounts are Cash, Notes Receivable, Accounts Receivable, Prepaid Expenses, Land, Buildings, and Equipment. Common liability accounts are Notes Payable, Accounts Payable, Wages Payable, and Mortgages Payable. Common stockholders' equity accounts are Common Stock, Retained Earnings, Dividends, and revenue and expense accounts.

3. **Define *double-entry system* and state the rules for double entry.** In the double-entry system, each transaction must be recorded with at least one debit and one credit so that the total dollar amount of the debits equals the total dollar amount of the credits. The rules for double entry are (1) increases in assets are debited to asset accounts; decreases in assets are credited to asset accounts; and (2) increases in liabilities and stockholders' equity are credited to those accounts; decreases in liabilities and stockholders' equity are debited to those accounts.

4. **Apply the steps for transaction analysis and processing to simple transactions.** The procedure for analyzing transactions is (1) analyze the effect of the transaction on assets, liabilities, and stockholders' equity; (2) apply the appropriate double-entry rule; (3) record the entry; (4) post the entry; and (5) prepare a trial balance.

5. **Record transactions in the general journal.** The general journal is a chronological record of all transactions. That record contains the date of each transaction, the names of the accounts and the dollar amounts debited and credited, an explanation of each entry, and the account numbers to which postings have been made.

6. **Post transactions from the general journal to the ledger.** After transactions have been entered in the general journal, they are posted to the general ledger. Posting is done by transferring each amount in the Debit column of the general journal to the Debit column of the appropriate account in the general ledger, and transferring each amount in the Credit column of the general journal to the Credit column of the appropriate account in the general ledger. After each entry is posted, a new balance is entered in the appropriate Balance column.

7. **Prepare a trial balance and describe its value and limitations.** A trial balance is used to check that the debit and credit balances in the ledger are equal. It is prepared by listing each account with its balance in the Debit or Credit column. Then, the two columns are added and compared to test their balances. The major limitation of the trial balance is that even if debit and credit balances are equal, this does not necessarily mean that the transactions were analyzed correctly or recorded in the proper accounts.

REVIEW OF CONCEPTS AND TERMINOLOGY

The following concepts and terms were introduced in this chapter:

L O 3   **Balance:** The difference in dollars between the total debit footing and the total credit footing of an account. Also called *account balance*.

L O 2 **Chart of accounts:** A scheme that assigns a unique number to each account to facilitate finding the account in the ledger; also, the list of account numbers and titles.

L O 1 **Classification:** The process of assigning transactions to the appropriate accounts.

L O 5 **Compound entry:** A journal entry that has more than one debit or credit entry.

L O 1 **Cost:** The exchange price associated with a business transaction at the point of recognition.

L O 1 **Cost principle:** The practice of recording a transaction at cost and maintaining this cost in the records until the asset, liability, or component of stockholders' equity is sold, expires, is consumed, is satisfied, or is otherwise disposed of.

L O 3 **Credit:** The right side of an account.

L O 3 **Debit:** The left side of an account.

L O 3 **Double-entry system:** The accounting system in which each transaction is recorded with at least one debit and one credit so that the total dollar amount of debits and the total dollar amount of credits equal each other.

L O 3 **Footings:** Working totals of columns of numbers. To *foot* means to total a column of numbers.

L O 5 **General journal:** The simplest and most flexible type of journal.

L O 2 **General ledger:** The book or file that contains all or groups of the company's accounts, arranged in the order of the chart of accounts. Also called *ledger.*

L O 5 **Journal:** A chronological record of all transactions; the place where transactions first enter the accounting records. Also called *book of original entry.*

L O 5 **Journal entry:** The notations in the journal that are used to record a single transaction.

L O 5 **Journalizing:** The process of recording transactions in a journal.

L O 6 **Ledger account form:** The form of account that has four columns: one column for debit entries, one column for credit entries, and two columns (debit and credit) for showing the balance of the account.

L O 7 **Normal balance:** The usual balance of an account; also the side (debit or credit) that increases the account.

L O 6 **Posting:** The process of transferring journal entry information from the journal to the ledger.

L O 1 **Recognition:** The determination of when a business transaction should be recorded.

L O 1 **Recognition point:** The predetermined time at which a transaction should be recorded; usually, the point at which title passes to the buyer.

L O 3 **Source document:** An invoice, check, receipt, or other document that supports a transaction.

L O 3 **T account:** The simplest form of an account, used to analyze transactions.

L O 7 **Trial balance:** A comparison of the total of debit and credit balances in the ledger to check that they are equal.

L O 1 **Valuation:** The process of assigning a monetary value to a business transaction.

REVIEW PROBLEM

TRANSACTION ANALYSIS, GENERAL JOURNAL, LEDGER ACCOUNTS, AND TRIAL BALANCE

L O 4, 5, 6, 7 After graduation from veterinary school, Laura Cox entered private practice. The transactions of the business through May 27 are as follows:

19xx

May 1   Laura Cox invested $2,000 in 2,000 shares of $1 par value common stock of her newly chartered company, Pet Clinic, Inc.

3   Paid $300 for two months' rent in advance for an office.

9   Purchased medical supplies for $200 in cash.

May 12 Purchased $400 of equipment on credit, making a 25 percent down payment.
    15 Delivered a calf for a fee of $35.
    18 Made a partial payment of $50 on the equipment purchased May 12.
    27 Paid a utility bill of $40.

REQUIRED

1. Record these entries in the general journal.
2. Post the entries from the journal to the following accounts in the ledger: Cash (111); Medical Supplies (115); Prepaid Rent (117); Equipment (144); Accounts Payable (212); Common Stock (311); Veterinary Fees Earned (411); and Utility Expense (512).
3. Prepare a trial balance as of May 31.

ANSWER TO REVIEW PROBLEM

1. Record the journal entries.

		General Journal			Page 1
\multicolumn{2}{c}{Date}	Description	Post. Ref.	Debit	Credit
19xx May	1	Cash	111	2,000	
		Common Stock	311		2,000
		Invested $2,000 in 2,000 shares of $1 par value stock			
	3	Prepaid Rent	117	300	
		Cash	111		300
		Paid two months' rent in advance for an office			
	9	Medical Supplies	115	200	
		Cash	111		200
		Purchased medical supplies for cash			
	12	Equipment	144	400	
		Accounts Payable	212		300
		Cash	111		100
		Purchased equipment on credit, paying 25 percent down			
	15	Cash	111	35	
		Veterinary Fees Earned	411		35
		Collected fee for delivery of a calf			
	18	Accounts Payable	212	50	
		Cash	111		50
		Partial payment for equipment purchased May 12			
	27	Utility Expense	512	40	
		Cash	111		40
		Paid utility bill			

2. Post the transactions to the ledger accounts.

General Ledger

Cash   **Account No. 111**

Date		Item	Post. Ref.	Debit	Credit	Balance Debit	Balance Credit
19xx May	1		J1	2,000		2,000	
	3		J1		300	1,700	
	9		J1		200	1,500	
	12		J1		100	1,400	
	15		J1	35		1,435	
	18		J1		50	1,385	
	27		J1		40	1,345	

Medical Supplies   **Account No. 115**

Date		Item	Post. Ref.	Debit	Credit	Balance Debit	Balance Credit
19xx May	9		J1	200		200	

Prepaid Rent   **Account No. 117**

Date		Item	Post. Ref.	Debit	Credit	Balance Debit	Balance Credit
19xx May	3		J1	300		300	

Equipment   **Account No. 144**

Date		Item	Post. Ref.	Debit	Credit	Balance Debit	Balance Credit
19xx May	12		J1	400		400	

Accounts Payable   **Account No. 212**

Date		Item	Post. Ref.	Debit	Credit	Balance Debit	Balance Credit
19xx May	12		J1		300		300
	18		J1	50			250

(continued)

Common Stock   Account No. 311

Date		Item	Post. Ref.	Debit	Credit	Balance Debit	Balance Credit
19xx May	1		J1		2,000		2,000

Veterinary Fees Earned   Account No. 411

Date		Item	Post. Ref.	Debit	Credit	Balance Debit	Balance Credit
19xx May	15		J1		35		35

Utility Expense   Account No. 512

Date		Item	Post. Ref.	Debit	Credit	Balance Debit	Balance Credit
19xx May	27		J1	40		40	

3. Complete the trial balance.

Pet Clinic, Inc.
Trial Balance
May 31, 19xx

	Debit	Credit
Cash	$1,345	
Medical Supplies	200	
Prepaid Rent	300	
Equipment	400	
Accounts Payable		$ 250
Common Stock		2,000
Veterinary Fees Earned		35
Utility Expense	40	
	$2,285	$2,285

CHAPTER ASSIGNMENTS

KNOWLEDGE AND UNDERSTANDING

Questions

1. What three issues underlie most accounting measurement decisions?
2. Why is recognition an issue for accountants?

3.   A customer asks the owner of a store to save an item for him and says that he will pick it up and pay for it next week. The owner agrees to hold it. Should this transaction be recorded as a sale? Explain your answer.

4.   Why is it practical for accountants to rely on original cost for valuation purposes?

5.   Under the cost principle, changes in value after a transaction is recorded are not usually recognized in the accounts. Comment on this possible limitation of using original cost in accounting measurements.

6.   What is an account, and how is it related to the ledger?

7.   Tell whether each of the following accounts is an asset account, a liability account, or a stockholders' equity account:
   a. Notes Receivable   d. Bonds Payable   f. Insurance Expense
   b. Land   e. Prepaid Rent   g. Service Revenue
   c. Dividends

8.   In the stockholders' equity accounts, why do accountants maintain separate accounts for revenues and expenses rather than using the Retained Earnings account?

9.   Why is the system of recording entries called the double-entry system? What is significant about this system?

10. "Double-entry accounting refers to entering a transaction in both the journal and the ledger." Comment on this statement.

11. "Debits are bad; credits are good." Comment on this statement.

12. What are the rules of double entry for (a) assets, (b) liabilities, and (c) stockholders' equity?

13. Why are the rules of double entry the same for liabilities and stockholders' equity?

14. What is the meaning of the statement, "The Cash account has a debit balance of $500"?

15. Explain why debits, which decrease stockholders' equity, also increase expenses, which are a component of stockholders' equity.

16. What are the five steps in analyzing and processing a transaction?

17. Is it a good idea to forgo the journal and enter a transaction directly into the ledger? Explain your answer.

18. In recording entries in a journal, which is written first, the debit or the credit? How is indentation used in the general journal?

19. What is the relationship between the journal and the ledger?

20. Describe each of the following:
   a. Account   d. Book of original entry   g. Posting
   b. Journal   e. Post. Ref. column   h. Footings
   c. Ledger   f. Journalizing   i. Compound entry

21. What does a trial balance prove?

22. What is the normal balance of Accounts Payable? Under what conditions could Accounts Payable have a debit balance?

23. Can errors be present even though a trial balance balances? Explain your answer.

24. List the following six items in sequence to illustrate the flow of events through the accounting system:
   a. Analysis of the transaction
   b. Debits and credits posted from the journal to the ledger
   c. Occurrence of the business transaction
   d. Preparation of the financial statements
   e. Entry made in the journal
   f. Preparation of the trial balance

Short Exercises

SE 2-1.
L O 1   *Recognition*

Which of the following events would be recognized and entered in the accounting records of Hawthorne Company? Why?

Jan. 10   Hawthorne Company places an order for office supplies.
Feb. 15   Hawthorne Company receives the office supplies and a bill for them.
Mar. 1   Hawthorne pays for the office supplies.

SE 2-2.
L O 2   *Classification of Accounts*

Tell whether each of the following accounts is an asset, a liability, a revenue, an expense, or none of these.

a. Accounts Payable
b. Supplies
c. Dividends
d. Fees Earned
e. Supplies Expense
f. Accounts Receivable
g. Unearned Revenue
h. Equipment

SE 2-3.
L O 7   *Normal Balances*

Tell whether the normal balance of each account in SE 2-2 above is a debit or a credit.

SE 2-4.
L O 4   *Transaction Analysis*

For each transaction below, tell which account is debited and which account is credited.

May 2   Joe Hurley started a computer programming business, Hurley's Programming Service, Inc., by investing $5,000 in exchange for common stock.
5   Purchased a computer for $2,500 in cash.
7   Purchased supplies on credit for $300.
19   Received cash for programming services performed, $500.
22   Received cash for programming services to be performed, $600.
25   Paid the rent for May, $650.
31   Billed a customer for programming services performed, $250.

SE 2-5.
L O 4   *Recording Transactions in T Accounts*

Set up T accounts and record each transaction in SE 2-4 above. Determine the balance of each account.

SE 2-6.
L O 7   *Preparing a Trial Balance*

From the T accounts created in SE 2-5, prepare a trial balance dated May 31, 19x1.

SE 2-7.
L O 5   *Recording Transactions in the General Journal*

Prepare a general journal form like the one in Exhibit 2-3 and label it Page 4. Record the following transactions in the journal.

Sept. 6   Billed a customer for services performed, $1,900.
16   Received partial payment from the customer billed on Sept. 6, $900.

SE 2-8.
L O 6   *Posting to the Ledger Accounts*

Prepare ledger account forms like the one in Exhibit 2-4 for the following accounts: Cash (111), Accounts Receivable (113), and Service Revenue (411). Post the transactions recorded in SE 2-7 to the ledger accounts, at the same time making proper posting references.

SE 2-9.
L O 7   *Preparing a Trial Balance*

Using the account balances presented below, all of which are normal, prepare a trial balance for El-Tech Company at June 30, 19x1. List the accounts in proper order. Compute the balance of the Cash account.

Accounts Payable	$ 70
Accounts Receivable	140
Cash	?
Common Stock	100
Equipment	200
Office Expense	90
Retained Earnings	120
Service Revenue	150

SE 2-10.

LO 7 *Correcting Errors in
a Trial Balance*

The trial balance below is out of balance. Assuming all balances are normal, place the
accounts in proper order and correct the trial balance so that debits equal credits.

Sanders Boating Service, Inc.
Trial Balance
January 31, 19x1

Cash	$2,000	
Accounts Payable	400	
Fuel Expense	800	
Unearned Service Revenue	250	
Accounts Receivable		$1,300
Prepaid Rent		150
Common Stock		1,500
Service Revenue	1,750	
Wages Expense		300
Retained Earnings	650	
	$5,850	$3,250

APPLICATION

Exercises

E 2-1.

LO 1 *Recognition*

Which of the following events would be recognized and recorded in the accounting
records of the Sabatini Corporation on the date indicated?

Feb. 17   Sabatini Corporation offers to purchase a tract of land for $280,000. There is
a high likelihood that the offer will be accepted.

Mar. 7   Sabatini Corporation receives notice that its rent will be increased from
$1,000 per month to $1,200 per month effective April 1.

Apr. 28   Sabatini Corporation receives its utility bill for the month of April. The bill
is not due until May 10.

May 2   Ray Sabatini, a major stockholder in Sabatini Corporation, dies. Ray's son,
Andrew, inherits all of Ray's stock in the company.

May 14   Andrew, who inherited Ray's stock in Sabatini Corporation, sells 2,000
shares of stock to Bob Rader for $120,000.

May 19   Sabatini Corporation places a firm order for new office equipment costing
$42,000.

June 27   The office equipment ordered on May 19 arrives. Payment is not due until
September 1.

E 2-2.

LO 1 *Application of
Recognition Point*

Infelice's Body Shop, Inc. uses a large amount of supplies in its business. The following table summarizes selected transaction data for orders of supplies purchased:

Order	Date Shipped	Date Received	Amount
a	April 28	May 7	$300
b	May 8	13	750
c	10	16	400
d	15	21	600
e	25	June 1	750
f	June 3	9	500

Determine the total purchases of supplies for May alone under each of the following
assumptions:

1. Infelice's Body Shop, Inc. recognizes purchases when orders are shipped.
2. Infelice's Body Shop, Inc. recognizes purchases when orders are received.

E 2-3.

L O 2, 7 *Classification of Accounts*

Listed below are the ledger accounts of the Kedzie Service Corporation:

a. Cash
b. Wages Expense
c. Accounts Receivable
d. Common Stock
e. Service Revenue
f. Prepaid Rent
g. Accounts Payable
h. Investments in Stock and Bonds
i. Bonds Payable
j. Income Taxes Expense
k. Land
l. Supplies Expense
m. Prepaid Insurance

n. Utility Expense
o. Fees Earned
p. Dividends
q. Wages Payable
r. Unearned Revenue
s. Office Equipment
t. Rent Payable
u. Notes Receivable
v. Interest Expense
w. Notes Payable
x. Supplies
y. Interest Receivable

Complete the following table, using Xs to indicate each account's classification and normal balance (whether a debit or credit increases the account):

Type of Account

				Stockholders' Equity			Normal Balance (increases balance)	
					Retained Earnings			
Item	Asset	Liability	Common Stock	Dividends	Revenue	Expense	Debit	Credit
a.	x							x

E 2-4.

L O 4 *Transaction Analysis*

Analyze each of the following transactions, using the form shown in the example below the list.

a. Benny James established Benny's Barber Shop, Inc. by investing $2,400 in exchange for 2,400 shares of $1 par value common stock.
b. Paid two months' rent in advance, $840.
c. Purchased supplies on credit, $120.
d. Received cash for barbering services, $300.
e. Paid for supplies purchased in **c.**
f. Paid utility bill, $72.
g. Declared and paid a dividend of $100.

Example

a. The asset Cash was increased. Increases in assets are recorded by debits. Debit Cash $2,400. A component of stockholders' equity, Common Stock, was increased. Increases in stockholders' equity are recorded by credits. Credit Common Stock $2,400.

E 2-5.

L O 4 *Recording Transactions in T Accounts*

Open the following T accounts: Cash; Repair Supplies; Repair Equipment; Accounts Payable; Common Stock; Dividends; Repair Fees Earned; Salary Expense; and Rent Expense. Record the following transactions for the month of June directly in the T accounts; use the letters to identify the transactions in your T accounts. Determine the balance in each account.

a. Michelle Donato opened Eastmoor Repair Service, Inc. by investing $4,300 in cash and $1,600 in repair equipment in return for 5,900 shares of the company's $1 par value common stock.
b. Paid $400 for current month's rent.
c. Purchased repair supplies on credit, $500.
d. Purchased additional repair equipment for cash, $300.
e. Paid salary to a helper, $450.
f. Paid $200 of amount purchased on credit in **c.**
g. Accepted cash for repairs completed, $960.
h. Declared and paid a dividend of $100.

E 2-6.
L O 7 *Trial Balance*

After recording the transactions in E 2-5, prepare a trial balance in proper sequence for Eastmoor Repair Service, Inc. at June 30, 19xx.

E 2-7.
L O 4 *Analysis of Transactions*

Explain each transaction (**a** through **h**) entered below.

	Cash				Accounts Receivable			Equipment	
a.	60,000	b.	15,000	c.	6,000	g. 1,500	b.	15,000	h. 900
g.	1,500	e.	3,000				d.	9,000	
h.	900	f.	4,500						

	Accounts Payable			Service Revenue			Wages Expense	
f.	4,500	d.	9,000		c. 6,000	e.	3,000	

Common Stock	
	a. 60,000

E 2-8.
L O 4 *Analysis of Transactions*

Dover Cleanup Corporation provided monthly waste-removal services for Permamove Corporation, which resulted in the following transactions in Dover's records:

Cash			Accounts Receivable			
Sept. 27	1,000		Aug. 31	1,500	Sept. 27	1,000

Waste Removal Service Revenue	
	Aug. 31 1,500

Using T accounts, prepare the corresponding entries in Permamove's records.

E 2-9.
L O 4, 5 *Analysis of Unfamiliar Transactions*

Managers and accountants often encounter transactions with which they are unfamiliar. Use your analytical skills to analyze and record in general journal form the transactions below, which have not yet been discussed in the text.

May 1 Purchased merchandise inventory on account, $1,600.
2 Purchased marketable securities for cash, $4,800.
3 Returned part of merchandise inventory purchased in **a** for full credit, $500.
4 Sold merchandise inventory on account, $1,600 (record sale only).
5 Purchased land and a building for $600,000. Payment is $120,000 cash and a thirty-year mortgage for the remainder. The purchase price is allocated $200,000 to the land and $400,000 to the building.
6 Received an order for $24,000 in services to be provided. With the order was a deposit of $8,000.

E 2-10.
L O 5, 6 *Recording Transactions in the General Journal and Posting to the Ledger Accounts*

Open a general journal form like the one in Exhibit 2-3, and label it Page 10. After opening the form, record the following transactions in the journal.

Dec. 14 Purchased an item of equipment for $6,000, paying $2,000 as a cash down payment.
28 Paid $3,000 of the amount owed on the equipment.

Prepare three ledger account forms like the one shown in Exhibit 2-4. Use the following account numbers: Cash, 111; Equipment, 143; and Accounts Payable, 212. Then post the two transactions from the general journal to the ledger accounts, at the same time making proper posting references.

Assume that the Cash account has a debit balance of $8,000 on the day prior to these transactions.

E 2-11.
LO 6 *Preparation of a Ledger Account*

Below is a T account showing cash transactions for the month of July.

Cash

July	1	18,800	July	3	1,800
	9	2,400		7	400
	16	8,000		13	3,400
	23	400		15	10,000
	29	12,800		27	1,200

Prepare the account in ledger form for Cash (Account 111). (See Exhibit 2-4 for an example.)

E 2-12.
LO 7 *Preparing a Trial Balance*

The accounts of the Barnes Service Corporation as of October 31, 19xx are listed below in alphabetical order. The amount of Accounts Payable is omitted.

Accounts Payable	?	Equipment	$24,000
Accounts Receivable	$ 6,000	Land	10,400
Building	68,000	Notes Payable	40,000
Cash	18,000	Prepaid Insurance	2,200
Common Stock	40,000	Retained Earnings	22,900

Prepare a trial balance with the proper heading (see Exhibit 2-6) and with the accounts listed in the chart of accounts sequence (see Exhibit 2-1). Compute the balance of Accounts Payable.

E 2-13.
LO 7 *Effect of Errors on a Trial Balance*

Which of the following errors would cause a trial balance to have unequal totals? Explain your answers.

a. A payment to a creditor was recorded as a debit to Accounts Payable for $172 and a credit to Cash for $127.

b. A payment of $200 to a creditor for an account payable was debited to Accounts Receivable and credited to Cash.

c. A purchase of office supplies of $560 was recorded as a debit to Office Supplies for $56 and a credit to Cash for $56.

d. A purchase of equipment for $600 was recorded as a debit to Supplies for $600 and a credit to Cash for $600.

E 2-14.
LO 7 *Correcting Errors in a Trial Balance*

This was the trial balance for Gilliam Services, Inc. at the end of September:

Gilliam Services, Inc.
Trial Balance
September 30, 19xx

Cash	$ 3,840	
Accounts Receivable	5,660	
Supplies	120	
Prepaid Insurance	180	
Equipment	8,400	
Accounts Payable		$ 4,540
Common Stock		4,000
Retained Earnings		7,560
Dividends		700
Revenues		5,920
Salaries Expense	2,600	
Rent Expense	600	
Advertising Expense	340	
Utility Expense	26	
	$21,766	$22,720

The trial balance does not balance because of a number of errors. Gilliam's accountant compared the amounts in the trial balance with the ledger, recomputed the account balances, and compared the postings. He found the following errors:

a. The balance of Cash was understated by $400.
b. A cash payment of $420 was credited to Cash for $240.
c. A debit of $120 to Accounts Receivable was not posted.
d. Supplies purchased for $60 were posted as a credit to Supplies.
e. A debit of $180 to Prepaid Insurance was not posted.
f. The Accounts Payable account had debits of $5,320 and credits of $9,180.
g. The Notes Payable account, with a credit balance of $2,400, was not included in the trial balance.
h. The debit balance of Dividends was listed in the trial balance as a credit.
i. A $200 debit to Dividends was posted as a credit.
j. The actual balance of Utility Expense, $260, was listed as $26 in the trial balance.

Prepare a corrected trial balance.

E 2-15.
L O 7 *Preparing a Trial Balance*

The Ferraro Construction Corporation builds foundations for buildings and parking lots. The following alphabetical list shows the account balances as of November 30, 19xx.

Accounts Payable	$11,700	Office Trailer	$ 6,600
Accounts Receivable	30,360	Prepaid Insurance	13,800
Cash	?	Retained Earnings	30,000
Common Stock	90,000	Revenue Earned	52,200
Construction Supplies	5,700	Supplies Expense	21,600
Dividends	23,400	Utility Expense	1,260
Equipment	73,500	Wages Expense	26,400
Notes Payable	60,000		

Prepare a trial balance for the company with the proper heading and with the accounts in balance sheet sequence. Determine the correct balance for the Cash account on November 30, 19xx.

Problem Set A

2A-1.
L O 4, 7 *Transaction Analysis, T Accounts, and Trial Balance*

Elena Garcia established a small business, Garcia Training Center, Inc., to teach individuals how to use spreadsheet analysis, word processing, and other techniques on microcomputers.

a. Garcia began by transferring the following assets to the business in exchange for 39,200 shares of $1 par value common stock:

Cash $18,400
Furniture   6,200
Microcomputer   14,600

b. Paid the first month's rent on a small storefront, $560.
c. Purchased computer software on credit, $1,500.
d. Paid for an advertisement in the local newspaper, $200.
e. Received enrollment applications from five students for a five-day course to start next week. Each student will pay $400 if he or she actually begins the course.
f. Paid wages to a part-time helper, $300.
g. Received cash payments from three of the students enrolled in **e**, $1,200.
h. Billed the two other students in **e**, who attended but did not pay in cash, $800.
i. Paid the utility bill for the current month, $220.
j. Made a payment on the software purchased in **c**, $500.
k. Received payment from one student billed in **h**, $400.
l. Purchased a second microcomputer for cash, $9,400.
m. Declared and paid a dividend of $600.

REQUIRED

1. Set up the following T accounts: Cash; Accounts Receivable; Software; Furniture; Microcomputers; Accounts Payable; Common Stock; Dividends; Tuition Revenue; Wages Expense; Utility Expense; Rent Expense; and Advertising Expense.
2. Record the transactions listed above by entering debits and credits directly in the T accounts, using the transaction letter to identify each debit and credit.
3. Prepare a trial balance using the current date.

2A-2.

L O 1, 4, 5   *Transaction Analysis and Concepts*

Cindy Liang opened a photography and portrait studio on July 1. The studio completed the following transactions during the month:

July	1	Opened the business by depositing $51,000 in a bank account in the name of the business in exchange for 5,100 shares of $10 par value stock.
	3	Paid two months' rent in advance for a studio, $2,700.
	5	Transferred to the business personal photography equipment valued at $12,900 in exchange for 1,290 shares of $10 par value common stock.
	7	Ordered additional photography equipment, $7,500.
	8	Purchased office equipment for cash, $5,400.
	10	Received and paid for the photography equipment ordered on July 7, $7,500.
	12	Purchased photography supplies on credit, $2,100.
	13	Received cash for previously unbilled portraits, $1,140.
	17	Billed customers for portraits, $2,250.
	19	Paid for half the supplies purchased on July 12, $1,050.
	25	Paid the utility bill for July, $360.
	26	Paid the telephone bill for July, $210.
	28	Received payments from the customers billed on July 17, $750.
	29	Paid wages to assistant, $1,200.
	30	Received an advance deposit from a customer for work to be done, $150.
	31	Declared and paid a dividend of $3,600.

REQUIRED

1. Record these transactions in the general journal.
2. Discuss how recognition applies to the transactions of July 7 and 8 and how classification applies to the transactions of July 13 and 30.

2A-3.

L O 1, 4,
5, 7   *Transaction Analysis, T Accounts, General Journal, and Trial Balance*

Bob Reeves won a concession to rent bicycles in the local park during the summer. In the month of May, Reeves completed the following transactions for his bicycle rental business:

May	3	Began business by placing $14,400 in a business checking account in the name of the corporation in exchange for 14,400 shares of $1 par value stock.
	6	Purchased supplies on account for $300.
	7	Purchased ten bicycles for a total of $5,000, paying $2,400 down and agreeing to pay the rest in thirty days.
	8	Received $940 in cash for rentals during the first week of operation.
	9	Hired a part-time assistant to help out on weekends at $8 per hour.
	10	Purchased a small shed to hold the bicycles and to use for other operations for $5,800 in cash.
	11	Paid $800 in cash for shipping and installation costs (considered an addition to the cost of the shed) to place the shed at the park entrance.
	14	Received $1,000 in cash for rentals during the second week of operation.
	15	Paid a maintenance person $150 to clean the grounds.
	16	Paid the assistant $160 for a weekend's work.
	19	Paid $300 for the supplies purchased on May 6.
	20	Paid $110 on a previously unrecorded repair bill on bicycles.
	21	Received $1,100 in cash for rentals during the third week of operation.
	23	Paid the assistant $160 for a weekend's work.
	24	Billed a company $220 for bicycle rentals for an employees' outing.
	26	Paid the $200 fee for May to the Park District for the right to the bicycle concession.
	28	Received $820 in cash for rentals during the week.
	30	Paid the assistant $160 for a weekend's work.
	31	Declared and paid a dividend of $1,000.

REQUIRED

1. Record these transactions in the general journal. Use the accounts listed below.
2. Set up the following T accounts and post all the journal entries: Cash; Accounts Receivable; Supplies; Shed; Bicycles; Accounts Payable; Common Stock; Dividends; Rental Revenue; Wages Expense; Maintenance Expense; Repair Expense; and Concession Fee Expense.
3. Prepare a trial balance for Reeves Rentals, Inc. as of May 31, 19xx.
4. Discuss how recognition applies to the transactions of May 24 and 28 and how classification applies to the transactions of May 11 and 15.

2A-4.
L O 4, 5, 6, 7

Transaction Analysis, General Journal, Ledger Accounts, and Trial Balance

Fulton Security Service, Inc. provides ushers and security personnel for athletic events and other functions. Here is Fulton's trial balance at the end of October:

Fulton Security Service, Inc.
Trial Balance
October 31, 19xx

Cash (111)	$ 26,600	
Accounts Receivable (113)	18,800	
Supplies (115)	1,120	
Prepaid Insurance (116)	1,200	
Equipment (141)	15,600	
Accounts Payable (211)		$ 10,600
Common Stock (311)		20,000
Retained Earnings (312)		22,320
Dividends (313)	4,000	
Security Services Revenue (411)		56,000
Wages Expense (512)	32,000	
Rent Expense (513)	6,400	
Utility Expense (514)	3,200	
	$108,920	$108,920

During November, Fulton, Inc. engaged in the following transactions:

Nov. 1   Received cash from customers billed last month, $8,400.
    3   Made a payment on accounts payable, $6,200.
    5   Purchased a new one-year insurance policy in advance, $7,200.
    7   Purchased supplies on credit, $860.
    8   Billed a client for security services, $4,400.
   10   Made a rent payment for November, $1,600.
   11   Received cash from customers for security services, $3,200.
   12   Paid wages to the security staff, $2,800.
   14   Ordered equipment, $1,600.
   15   Paid the current month's utility bill, $800.
   17   Received and paid for the equipment ordered on November 14, $1,600.
   19   Returned for full credit some of the supplies purchased on November 7 because they were defective, $240.
   21   Paid for the supplies purchased on November 7, less the return on November 19, $620.
   23   Billed a customer for security services performed, $3,600.
   30   Paid wages to the security staff, $2,100.
   30   Declared and paid a dividend of $2,000.

REQUIRED

1. Record these transactions in the general journal (Pages 26 and 27).
2. Open ledger accounts for the accounts shown in the trial balance. Enter the October 31 trial balance amounts in the ledger.
3. Post the journal entries to the ledger.
4. Prepare a trial balance as of November 30, 19xx.

2A-5.

L O 4, 5, 6, 7

Relationship of General Journal, Ledger Accounts, and Trial Balance

Boulevard Communications Corporation is a public relations firm. On April 30, 19xx, the company's trial balance looked like this:

Boulevard Communications Corporation
Trial Balance
April 30, 19xx

Cash (111)	$20,400	
Accounts Receivable (113)	11,000	
Supplies (115)	1,220	
Office Equipment (141)	8,400	
Accounts Payable (211)		$ 5,200
Common Stock (311)		24,000
Retained Earnings (312)		11,820
	$41,020	$41,020

During the month of May, the company completed the following transactions:

May	3	Paid rent for May, $1,300.
	5	Received cash from customers on account, $4,600.
	6	Ordered supplies, $760.
	8	Billed customers for services provided, $5,600.
	10	Made a payment on accounts payable, $2,200.
	13	Received the supplies ordered on May 6 and agreed to pay for them in thirty days, $760.
	15	Paid salaries for the first half of May, $3,800.
	16	Discovered some of the supplies were not as ordered and returned them for full credit, $160.
	18	Received cash from a customer for previously unbilled services, $9,600.
	22	Paid the utility bill for May, $320.
	23	Paid the telephone bill for May, $240.
	27	Received a bill, to be paid in June, for advertisements placed in the local newspaper during the month of May, $1,400.
	28	Billed a customer for services provided, $5,400.
	30	Paid salaries for the last half of May, $3,800.
	31	Declared and paid a dividend of $2,400.

REQUIRED

1. Enter these transactions in the general journal (Pages 22 and 23).
2. Open accounts in the ledger for the accounts in the trial balance and the following accounts: Dividends (313); Public Relations Fees (411); Salaries Expense (511); Rent Expense (512); Utility Expense (513); Telephone Expense (514); and Advertising Expense (515).
3. Enter the April 30 account balances from the trial balance in the appropriate ledger accounts.
4. Post the entries to the ledger accounts. Be sure to make the appropriate posting references in the journal and ledger as you post.
5. Prepare a trial balance as of May 31, 19xx.

Problem Set B

2B-1.

L O 4, 7 *Transaction Analysis, T Accounts, and Trial Balance*

Donna Polonsky opened a secretarial school called Village Business School, Inc.

a. She contributed the following assets to the business, in exchange for 27,200 shares of $1 par value stock.

Cash	$11,400
Word processors	8,600
Office equipment	7,200

b. Found a location for the business and paid the first month's rent, $520.
c. Paid for an advertisement announcing the opening of the school, $380.
d. Received applications from three students for a four-week secretarial program and from two students for a ten-day keyboarding course. The students will be billed a total of $2,600.
e. Purchased supplies on credit, $660.
f. Billed the enrolled students, $2,600.
g. Paid an assistant one week's salary, $440.
h. Purchased a word processor, $960, and office equipment, $760, on credit.
i. Paid for the supplies purchased on credit in **e**, $660.
j. Paid cash to repair a broken word processor, $80.
k. Billed new students who enrolled late in the course, $880.
l. Received partial payment from students previously billed, $2,160.
m. Paid the utility bill for the current month, $180.
n. Paid an assistant one week's salary, $440.
o. Received cash revenue from another new student, $500.
p. Declared and paid a dividend of $600.

REQUIRED

1. Set up the following T accounts: Cash; Accounts Receivable; Supplies; Word Processors; Office Equipment; Accounts Payable; Common Stock; Dividends; Tuition Revenue; Salaries Expense; Utility Expense; Rent Expense; Repair Expense; and Advertising Expense.
2. Record the transactions by entering debits and credits directly in the T accounts, using the transaction letter to identify each debit and credit.
3. Prepare a trial balance using today's date.

2B-2.

L O 1, 4, 5 *Transaction Analysis and Concepts*

Kwan Lee began a rug-cleaning business on October 1 and engaged in the following transactions during the month:

Oct. 1   Began business by depositing $6,000 in a bank account in the name of the corporation in exchange for 600 shares of $10 par value common stock.
2   Ordered cleaning supplies, $500.
3   Purchased cleaning equipment for cash, $1,400.
4   Leased a van by making two months' lease payment in advance, $600.
7   Received the cleaning supplies ordered on October 2 and agreed to pay half the amount in ten days and the rest in thirty days.
9   Paid for repairs on the van with cash, $40.
12   Received cash for cleaning carpets, $480.
17   Paid half of the amount owed on supplies purchased on October 7, $250.
21   Billed customers for cleaning carpets, $670.
24   Paid for additional repairs on the van in cash, $40.
27   Received $300 from the customers billed on October 21.
30   Received an advance deposit from a customer for carpets to be cleaned, $280.
31   Declared and paid a dividend of $350.

REQUIRED

1. Record these transactions in the general journal.
2. Discuss how recognition applies to the transactions of October 2 and 3 and how classification applies to the transactions of October 12 and 30.

2B-3.

L O 1, 4,
5, 7

Transaction Analysis, T Accounts, General Journal, and Trial Balance

Jerry Green, a house painter, obtained a charter from the state and opened a business called Green Painting Service, Inc. During the month of June, he completed the following transactions:

June 3 Began his business by contributing equipment valued at $2,460 and placing $14,200 in a business checking account in the name of the corporation in exchange for 1,666 shares of $10 par value common stock.

5 Purchased a used truck costing $3,800. Paid $1,000 in cash and signed a note for the balance.

7 Purchased supplies on account for $640.

8 Completed a painting job and billed the customer $960.

10 Received $300 in cash for painting two rooms.

11 Hired an assistant to work with him at $12 per hour.

12 Purchased supplies for $320 in cash.

13 Received a $960 check from the customer billed on June 8.

14 Paid $800 for an insurance policy for eighteen months' coverage.

16 Billed a customer $1,240 for a painting job.

18 Paid the assistant $300 for twenty-five hours' work.

19 Paid $80 for a tune-up for the truck.

20 Paid for the supplies purchased on June 7.

21 Purchased a new ladder (equipment) for $120 and supplies for $580, on account.

23 Received a telephone bill for $120, due next month.

24 Received $660 in cash from the customer billed on June 16.

26 Received $720 in cash for painting a five-room apartment.

28 Paid $400 on the note signed for the truck.

29 Paid the assistant $360 for thirty hours' work.

30 Declared and paid a dividend of $600.

REQUIRED

1. Record these transactions in the general journal. Use the accounts listed below.
2. Set up the following T accounts and post all the journal entries: Cash; Accounts Receivable; Supplies; Prepaid Insurance; Equipment; Truck; Notes Payable; Accounts Payable; Common Stock; Dividends; Painting Fees Earned; Wages Expense; Telephone Expense; and Truck Expense.
3. Prepare a trial balance for Green Painting Service, Inc. as of June 30, 19xx.
4. Discuss how recognition applies to the transactions of June 8 and 10 and how classification applies to the transactions of June 14 and 18.

2B-4.

L O 4, 5,
6, 7

Transaction Analysis, General Journal, Ledger Accounts, and Trial Balance

The account balances for Ramirez Lawn Service, Inc. at the end of February are presented in the trial balance on page 92.

During March, Ramirez Lawn Service, Inc. completed the following transactions:

Mar. 3 Paid for supplies purchased on credit last month, $280.

5 Billed customers for services, $820.

6 Paid for one month's lease on a pickup truck, $580.

7 Purchased supplies on credit, $300.

8 Received cash from customers not previously billed, $580.

9 Purchased new equipment from Carson Manufacturing Company on account, $2,600.

11 Received a bill for an oil change on the truck, $80.

13 Returned a portion of the equipment that was purchased on March 9 for a credit, $640.

14 Received payments from customers previously billed, $380.

16 Paid the bill received on March 11.

20 Paid for the supplies purchased on March 7.

21 Billed customers for services, $540.

Mar. 22 Purchased equipment on account, $560.
  24 Received payments from customers previously billed, $780.
  28 Purchased gasoline for the truck with cash, $60.
  30 Made a payment to reduce the principal of the note payable, $1,200.
  31 Declared and paid a dividend of $220.

Ramirez Lawn Service, Inc.
Trial Balance
February 28, 19xx

Cash (111)	$ 6,200	
Accounts Receivable (113)	440	
Supplies (115)	920	
Prepaid Insurance (116)	800	
Equipment (141)	8,800	
Notes Payable (211)		$ 6,000
Accounts Payable (212)		1,400
Common Stock (311)		6,000
Retained Earnings (312)		2,400
Dividends (313)	840	
Service Revenue (411)		2,980
Lease Expense (412)	580	
Pickup Truck Expense (413)	200	
	$18,780	$18,780

REQUIRED

1. Record the March transactions in the general journal (Pages 11, 12, and 13).
2. Open ledger accounts for the accounts shown in the trial balance. Enter the February 28 trial balance amounts in the ledger accounts.
3. Post the entries to the ledger accounts.
4. Prepare a trial balance as of March 31, 19xx.

2B-5.

L O 4, 5, 6, 7 *Relationship of General Journal, Ledger Accounts, and Trial Balance*

The Progressive Child Care Corporation provides babysitting and child-care programs. On August 31, 19xx, this was the company's trial balance:

Progressive Child Care Corporation
Trial Balance
August 31, 19xx

Cash (111)	$ 3,740	
Accounts Receivable (113)	3,400	
Equipment (141)	2,080	
Buses (143)	34,800	
Notes Payable (211)		$30,000
Accounts Payable (212)		3,280
Common Stock (311)		8,000
Retained Earnings (312)		2,740
	$44,020	$44,020

During the month of September, the company completed the following transactions:

Sept. 3   Paid this month's rent, $540.

5   Received fees for this month's services, $1,300.

7   Purchased supplies on account, $170.

8   Reimbursed the bus driver for gas expenses, $80.

9   Ordered playground equipment, $2,000.

10   Paid part-time assistants for two weeks' services, $460.

12   Made a payment on account, $340.

13   Received payments from customers on account, $2,400.

15   Billed customers who had not yet paid for this month's services, $1,400.

16   Paid for the supplies purchased on September 7.

18   Purchased playground equipment for cash, $2,000.

20   Purchased equipment on account, $580.

21   Paid this month's utility bill, $290.

24   Paid part-time assistants for two weeks' services, $460.

25   Received payment for one month's services from customers previously billed, $1,000.

26   Purchased gas and oil for the bus on account, $70.

29   Paid for a one-year insurance policy, $580.

30   Declared and paid a dividend of $220.

REQUIRED

1. Enter these transactions in the general journal (Pages 17, 18, and 19).
2. Open accounts in the ledger for the accounts in the trial balance and the following accounts: Supplies (115); Prepaid Insurance (116); Dividends (313); Service Revenue (411); Rent Expense (511); Bus Expense (512); Wages Expense (513); and Utility Expense (514).
3. Enter the August 31, 19xx, account balances from the trial balance.
4. Post the entries to the ledger accounts. Be sure to make the appropriate posting references in the journal and ledger as you post.
5. Prepare a trial balance as of September 30, 19xx.

CRITICAL THINKING AND COMMUNICATION

Conceptual Mini-Cases

CMC 2-1.

L O 1   *Valuation Issue*

The Foxboro Company manufactures and markets a comprehensive family of products for automating the industrial process. In one of the company's annual reports, under Summary of Significant Accounting Policies, the following statement was made: "Property, plant and equipment was stated at cost."[2] Given that the property, plant, and equipment undoubtedly were purchased over several years and that the current value of those assets was likely to be very different from their original cost, tell what authoritative basis there is for carrying the assets at cost. Does accounting generally recognize changes in value subsequent to the purchase of property, plant, and equipment?

CMC 2-2.

L O 1   *Recognition, Valuation, Classification Issues*

Stauffer Chemical Company relies on agricultural chemicals, such as fertilizer and pesticides, for more than half its profits. One year, Stauffer was hammered by bad weather, depressed farm prices, and decreased farm output caused by a federal price-support program. In an article in the *Wall Street Journal*, it was reported that Stauffer had overstated its 1982 earnings by $31.1 million by improperly accounting for certain

2. The Foxboro Company, *Annual Report*, 1989.

sales. In settling a suit brought by the Securities and Exchange Commission (SEC), the company agreed, without admitting or denying the charges, to restate the 1982 financial results, lowering the 1982 profit by 25 percent. The *Wall Street Journal* summarized the situation as follows:

> In the summer of 1982, "aware that agricultural chemical sales for its 1982–83 season would probably fall off sharply," Stauffer undertook a plan to accelerate sales of certain products to dealers during fiscal 1982, according to the SEC. . . .
>
> Stauffer, the SEC charged, offered its dealers incentives to take products during the fourth quarter of 1982. As a result, the company reported $72 million of revenue that ordinarily wouldn't have been booked until early 1983. By March 1983, according to the commission, Stauffer realized that it would have to "offer its distributors relief" from the oversupply of unsaleable products. Stauffer offered dealers refunds for as much as 100% of unsold products taken in 1982, compared with 32% the previous year.
>
> Stauffer ended up refunding nearly 40% of its 1982 agricultural chemical sales, but failed to disclose the "substantial uncertainties" surrounding the sales in the annual report it filed with the SEC in April 1983. The omission was "materially false and misleading," according to the SEC.
>
> "Their business was down and they wanted to accelerate sales," said a government official familiar with the year-long SEC investigation.[3]

REQUIRED

1. Prepare the journal entry that Stauffer made in 1982 that the SEC feels should not have been made until 1983.
2. Three issues that must be addressed when recording a transaction are recognition, valuation, and classification. Which of these issues were of most concern to the SEC in the Stauffer case? Explain how each applies to the transaction in part **1**.

CMC 2-3.
L O 4, 5

Analysis of an Unfamiliar Transaction

The quotations below are from the annual report of Shelley Corporation, a manufacturer of entertainment products.

Long-Term Obligations:
"Total long-term debt increased to $160 million at December 31, 1993, from $110 million at year-end 1992. In 1993, $50 million of long-term debt, due 2008, was sold to the public."

Capital Expenditures
"Shelley plans to use the $50 million in proceeds from the sale of the long-term debt, described previously, largely for investments in buildings and equipment related to product assembly and manufacturing. Pending such use, at year-end 1993, the debt proceeds were invested in marketable securities."

REQUIRED

1. Discuss what effect the transaction described under "Long-Term Obligations" had on Shelley's balance sheet. Prepare the entry in general journal form to record the transaction.
2. From reading the information under "Capital Expenditures," you know what Shelley did with the proceeds of the sale of long-term debt in 1993 and what the company plans to do with the proceeds in 1994. Before it can carry out these plans, what transactions must occur? Prepare three entries in general journal form to record the one transaction completed in 1993 and the two transactions planned for 1994. Use the Marketable Securities account to record entries related to the investments.

---

3. Wynter, Leon E., "Stauffer Profit Overstated in '82, SEC Says in Suit," the *Wall Street Journal*, Aug. 14, 1984. Reprinted by permission of the *Wall Street Journal*, © 1984 Dow Jones and Company, Inc. All Rights Reserved Worldwide.

Ethics Mini-Case

EMC 2-1.

L O 1   *Recognition Point and Ethical Considerations*

One of **Penn Office Supplies Corporation**'s sales representatives, Jerry Hasbrow, is compensated on a commission basis and receives a substantial bonus for meeting his annual sales goal. The company's recognition point for sales is the day of shipment. On December 31, Jerry realizes that he needs sales of $2,000 to reach his sales goal and receive the bonus. He calls a purchaser for a local insurance company, whom he knows well, and asks him to buy $2,000 worth of copier paper today. The purchaser says, "But Jerry, that's more than a year's supply for us." Jerry says, "Buy it today. If you decide it's too much, you can return however much you want for full credit next month." The purchaser says, "Okay, ship it." The paper is shipped on December 31 and recorded as a sale. On January 15, the purchaser returns $1,750 worth of paper for full credit (okayed by Jerry) against the bill. Should the shipment on December 31 be recorded as a sale? Discuss the ethics of Jerry's action.

Decision-Making Case

DMC 2-1.

L O 4, 5, 6, 7   *Transaction Analysis and Evaluation of a Trial Balance*

Benjamin Obi hired an attorney to help him start Obi Repairs Corporation. On June 1, Mr. Obi deposited $23,000 in a bank account in the name of the corporation in exchange for 2,300 shares of $10 par value stock. When he paid the attorney's bill of $1,400, the attorney advised him to hire an accountant to keep his records. However, Mr. Obi was so busy that it was June 30 before he asked you to straighten out his records. Your first task is to develop a trial balance based on the June transactions.

After the investment and payment to the attorney, Mr. Obi borrowed $10,000 from the bank. He later paid $520, which included interest of $120, on this loan. He also purchased a pickup truck in the company's name, paying $5,000 down and financing $14,800. The first payment on the truck is due July 15. Mr. Obi then rented an office and paid three months' rent, $1,800, in advance. Credit purchases of office equipment for $1,400 and repair tools for $1,000 must be paid by July 13.

In June, Obi Repairs Corporation completed repairs of $2,600, of which $800 were cash transactions. Of the credit transactions, $600 was collected during June, and $1,200 remained to be collected at the end of June. Wages of $800 were paid to employees. On June 30, the company received a $150 bill for June utility expense and a $100 check from a customer for work to be completed in July.

REQUIRED

1. Record the June transactions in the general journal (no dates are required).
2. Set up and determine the balance of each T account by posting the general journal entries to T accounts and determining the balance of each account.
3. Prepare a June 30 trial balance for Obi Repairs Corporation.
4. Benjamin Obi is unsure how to evaluate the trial balance. His Cash account balance is $24,980, which exceeds his original investment of $23,000 by $1,980. Did he make a profit of $1,980? Explain why the Cash account is not an indicator of business earnings. Cite specific examples to show why it is difficult to determine net income by looking solely at figures in the trial balance.

Basic Research Activity

RA 2-1.

L O 4, 5   *Transactions in a Business Article*

Obtain a recent issue of one of the following business journals: *Barron's, Business Week, Forbes, Fortune,* or the *Wall Street Journal*. Find an article on a company you recognize or on a company in a business that interests you. Read the article carefully, noting any references to transactions that the company engages in. These may be normal transactions (sales, purchases) or unusual transactions (a merger, the purchase of another company). Bring a copy of the article to class and be prepared to describe how you would analyze and record the transactions you have noted.

FINANCIAL REPORTING AND ANALYSIS

Interpretation Cases from Business

ICB 2-1.
L O 2, 4, 5   *Interpreting a Bank's Financial Statements*

First Chicago Corp. is the largest bank holding company in Illinois. Selected accounts from the company's 1992 annual report are as follows (in millions):[4]

Cash and Due from Banks	$ 9,338
Loans to Customers	21,901
Investment Securities	2,400
Deposits by Customers	29,740

REQUIRED

1. Indicate whether each of the accounts listed above is an asset, a liability, or a component of stockholders' equity on First Chicago's balance sheet.
2. Assume that you are in a position to do business with First Chicago. Prepare the general journal entry (in First Chicago's records) to record each of the following transactions:

   a. You sell securities in the amount of $2,000 to the bank.
   b. You deposit the $2,000 received in step **a** in the bank.
   c. You borrow $5,000 from the bank.

ICB 2-2.
L O 4, 5   *Analyzing a Freight Company's Transactions*

Yellow Freight System, Inc. of Delaware operates one of the largest freight transportation and related services companies in the United States. Selected data from the company's 1992 statement of cash flows appear below (in thousands):[5]

Investing Activities:	
Acquisition of operating property	($ 86,248)
Proceeds from disposal of operating property	7,597
Purchases of short-term investments	(16,740)
Proceeds from sale of short-term investments	11,341

Financing Activities:	
Repayment of long-term debt	($ 3,241)
Cash dividends paid to shareholders	(26,380)

REQUIRED

1. Record each of the above entries in the general journal (assuming that each is done in a single transaction and that there are no gains or losses on the transactions).
2. From 1991 to 1992, Yellow Freight's cash balance increased by $14,181,000. How is this possible given that both investing and financing activities resulted in net cash outflows?
3. The following statement is made by Yellow Freight's management in its 1992 annual report:

   > Projected facility expenditures will target expansion of a few specific hub and terminal locations. Equipment expenditures are expected to consist primarily of replacement units. It is anticipated that 1993 capital expenditures will be financed through internally generated funds.

   Be prepared to discuss what you think is meant by "internally generated funds." How would it differ from external financing? How will the balance sheet differ at the end of the year if the capital expenditures are paid with internally generated funds as opposed to being paid with external financing?

International Company Case

ICC 2-1.
L O 5   *Transaction Analysis*

United Biscuits, a United Kingdom company with operations in twenty-eight countries, is a leading producer of snack foods. Under the Keebler brand, it is the second - largest manufacturer of cookies and crackers in the United States. The following

---

4. First Chicago Corp., *Annual Report*, 1992.
5. Yellow Freight System, *Annual Report*, 1992.

selected aggregate cash transactions were reported in the investing and financing sections of its statement of cash flows in its 1992 annual report (amounts in millions):[6]

Dividends paid, £71.1
Purchase of investments, £1.7
Proceeds from new borrowings (Loans Payable), £87.1
Repayments of borrowings (Loans Payable), £9.5
Proceeds from issue of shares of stock, £83.4

Prepare journal entries to record the above transactions.

Toys "R" Us Case

TC 2-1.

L O 4, 5   *Transaction Analysis*

Refer to the Balance Sheet in the appendix on Toys "R" Us and answer the following questions. Prepare T accounts for the accounts Cash and Cash Equivalents, Accounts and Other Receivables, Prepaid Expenses and Other, Accounts Payable, and Income Taxes Payable. Properly place the balance of the account at January 29, 1994 in the T accounts. Below are some typical transactions in which Toys "R" Us would engage. Analyze each transaction, enter in the T accounts, and determine the balance of each account. Assume all entries are in thousands.

a. Paid cash in advance for certain expenses, $20,000.
b. Received cash from customers billed previously, $35,000.
c. Paid cash for income taxes previously owed, $24,000.
d. Paid cash to suppliers for amounts owed, $120,000.

---

6. United Biscuits, *Annual Report*, 1992.

LEARNING OBJECTIVES

1. Define *net income* and its two major components, *revenues* and *expenses*.
2. Explain the difficulties of income measurement caused by (a) the accounting period issue, (b) the continuity issue, and (c) the matching issue.
3. Define *accrual accounting* and explain two broad ways of accomplishing it.
4. State four principal situations that require adjusting entries.
5. Prepare typical adjusting entries.
6. Prepare financial statements from an adjusted trial balance.

SUPPLEMENTAL OBJECTIVE

7. Analyze cash flows from accrual-based information.

Gannett Co., Inc.

DECISION POINT

Gannett Co., Inc. is the United States' largest newspaper publisher, with eighty-two dailies, including *USA Today*. The company also operates broadcasting stations and outdoor advertising businesses, and provides other services. Gannett has 36,700 employees, and payroll is its largest expense.[1] During most of the year, payroll is recorded as an expense when it is paid. However, at the end of the year employees may have earned compensation (wages or salaries) that will not be paid until after the end of the year. If these wages and salaries are not accounted for correctly, they will appear in the wrong year—the year in which they are paid instead of the year in which the company benefited from them. How does accounting solve this problem?

According to the concepts of accrual accounting and the matching rule, which you will learn in this chapter, the accountant must determine the amount of wages and salaries earned but not paid and record an adjusting entry for this amount as an expense of the current year and a liability to be paid the next year. In this way, expenses are correctly stated on the income statement and liabilities are correctly stated on the balance sheet. In the case of Gannett, the effect is significant. At the end of 1992, Gannett had a liability for compensation of $46,746,000. If an adjusting entry had not been made to record this liability and its related expense in 1992, income (before taxes) would have been overstated by $46,746,000. Given that income after deducting this expense in 1992 was $527,534,000, without the adjusting entry, readers of the financial statements would have been misled into thinking that Gannett's income was 8.9 percent greater than it actually was. :::::

THE MEASUREMENT OF BUSINESS INCOME

For a business to succeed, or even to survive, it must earn a profit. The word profit, though, has many meanings. One is the increase in stockholders' equity that results from business operations. However, even this definition can be interpreted differently by economists, lawyers, business people, and

---

1. Gannett Co., Inc., *Annual Report*, 1992.

the public. Because the word *profit* has more than one meaning, accountants prefer to use the term *net income,* which can be precisely defined from an accounting point of view. Net income is reported on the income statement and is used by management, stockholders, and others to monitor business performance. Readers of income statements need to understand how the accountant defines net income and be aware of its strengths and weaknesses as a measure of company performance.

OBJECTIVE

1 *Define* net income *and its two major components,* revenues *and* expenses

NET INCOME

Net income is the net increase in stockholders' equity that results from the operations of a company and is accumulated in the Retained Earnings account. Net income, in its simplest form, is measured by the difference between revenues and expenses when revenues exceed expenses:

$$\text{Net income} = \text{revenues} - \text{expenses}$$

When expenses exceed revenues, a net loss occurs.

Revenues   Revenues are increases in stockholders' equity resulting from selling goods, rendering services, or performing other business activities. In the simplest case, revenues equal the price of goods sold and services rendered over a specific period of time. When a business delivers a product or provides a service to a customer, it usually receives either cash or a promise to pay cash in the near future. The promise to pay is recorded in either Accounts Receivable or Notes Receivable. The revenue for a given period equals the total of cash and receivables from goods and services provided to customers during that period.

Liabilities generally are not affected by revenues, and some transactions that increase cash and other assets are not revenues. For example, a bank loan increases liabilities and cash but does not produce revenue. The collection of accounts receivable, which increases cash and decreases accounts receivable, does not produce revenue either. Remember that when a sale on credit takes place, the asset account Accounts Receivable increases; at the same time, a stockholders' equity revenue account increases. So counting the collection of the receivable as revenue later would be counting the same sale twice.

Not all increases in stockholders' equity arise from revenues. Stockholders' investments increase stockholders' equity but are not revenue.

Expenses   Expenses are decreases in stockholders' equity resulting from the costs of selling goods, rendering services, or performing other business activities. In other words, expenses are the costs of the goods and services used up in the course of earning revenues. Often called the *cost of doing business,* expenses include the costs of goods sold, the costs of activities necessary to carry on a business, and the costs of attracting and serving customers. Examples are salaries, rent, advertising, telephone service, and depreciation (allocation of cost) of a building or office equipment.

Just as not all cash receipts are revenues, not all cash payments are expenses. A cash payment to reduce a liability does not result in an expense. The liability, however, may have come from incurring a previous expense, such as advertising, that is to be paid later. There may also be two steps before an expenditure of cash becomes an expense. For example, prepaid expenses or plant assets (such as machinery and equipment) are recorded as assets when they are acquired. Later, as their usefulness expires in the operation of the business, their cost is allocated to expenses. In fact, expenses sometimes are called *expired costs.*

Not all decreases in stockholders' equity arise from expenses. Dividends decrease stockholders' equity, but they are not expenses.

Temporary and Permanent Accounts   Revenues and expenses can be recorded directly in stockholders' equity as increases and decreases to retained earnings. In practice, however, management and others want to know the details of the increases and decreases in stockholders' equity produced by revenues and expenses. For this reason, a separate account for each revenue and expense is needed to accumulate the amounts. Because the balances of these income statement accounts apply only to the current accounting period, they are called temporary accounts. Temporary accounts, or *nominal accounts,* show the accumulation of revenues and expenses over the accounting period. At the end of the accounting period, their balances are transferred to stockholders' equity. Thus, nominal accounts start each accounting period with zero balances and then accumulate the specific revenues and expenses of that period. On the other hand, the balance sheet accounts—assets, liabilities, and stockholders' equity—are called permanent accounts, or *real accounts,* because their balances extend beyond the end of an accounting period. The process of transferring totals from the temporary revenue and expense accounts to the permanent stockholders' equity accounts is described in the chapter on completion of the accounting cycle.

OBJECTIVE

2a   *Explain the difficulties of income measurement caused by the accounting period issue*

THE ACCOUNTING PERIOD ISSUE

The accounting period issue addresses the difficulty of assigning revenues and expenses to a short period of time, such as a month or a year. Not all transactions can be easily assigned to specific time periods. Purchases of buildings and equipment, for example, have effects that extend over many years. Accountants solve this problem by estimating the number of years the buildings or equipment will be in use and the cost that should be assigned to each year. In the process, they make an assumption about periodicity: that the net income for any period of time less than the life of the business, although tentative, is still a useful estimate of the net income for the period.

Generally, to make comparisons easier, the time periods are of equal length. And the time period should be noted in the financial statements. Financial statements may be prepared for any time period. Accounting periods of less than one year—for example, a month or a quarter—are called *interim periods.* The twelve-month accounting period used by a company is called its fiscal year. Many companies use the calendar year, January 1 to December 31, for their fiscal year. Others find it convenient to choose a fiscal year that ends during a slack season rather than a peak season. In this case, the fiscal year corresponds to the company's yearly cycle of business activity.

OBJECTIVE

2b   *Explain the difficulties of income measurement caused by the continuity issue*

THE CONTINUITY ISSUE

The process of measuring business income requires that certain expense and revenue transactions be allocated over several accounting periods. The number of accounting periods raises the continuity issue: How long will the business entity last? Many businesses last less than five years; in any given year, thousands go bankrupt. To prepare financial statements for an accounting period, the accountant must make an assumption about the ability of the business to survive. Specifically, unless there is evidence to the contrary, the accountant assumes that the business will continue to operate indefinitely, that the business is a going concern. Justification for all the techniques of income measurement rests on the assumption of continuity. For example, this assumption allows the cost of certain assets to be held on the balance sheet to a future year when it will become an expense on the income statement.

Another example has to do with the value of assets on the balance sheet. In the chapter on measuring business transactions, we pointed out that the accountant records assets at cost and does not record subsequent changes in their value. But the value of assets to a going concern is much higher than the value of assets to a firm facing bankruptcy. In the latter case, the accountant may be asked to set aside the assumption of continuity and to prepare financial statements based on the assumption that the firm will go out of business and sell all of its assets at liquidation value—that is, for what they will bring in cash.

BUSINESS BULLETIN: BUSINESS PRACTICE

The list below shows the diverse fiscal years used by some well-known companies.

Company	Last Month of Fiscal Year
American Greetings Corp.	February
Caesars World, Inc.	July
The Walt Disney Company	September
Eastman Kodak Company	December
Fleetwood Enterprises, Inc.	April
Lorimar	March
Mattel Inc.	December
MGM/UA Communications Co.	August
Polaroid Corp.	December

Many governmental and educational units use fiscal years that end June 30 or September 30.

THE MATCHING ISSUE

Revenues and expenses can be accounted for on a cash received and cash paid basis. This practice is known as the cash basis of accounting. In certain cases, an individual or business may use the cash basis of accounting for income tax purposes. Under this method, revenues are reported in the period in which cash is received, and expenses are reported in the period in which cash is paid. Taxable income, therefore, is calculated as the difference between cash receipts from revenues and cash payments for expenses.

Although the cash basis of accounting works well for some small businesses and many individuals, it does not meet the needs of most businesses. As explained above, revenues can be earned in a period other than the one in which cash is received, and expenses can be incurred in a period other than the one in which cash is paid. To measure net income adequately, revenues and expenses must be assigned to the appropriate accounting period. The accountant solves this problem by applying the matching rule:

> Revenues must be assigned to the accounting period in which the goods are sold or the services performed, and expenses must be assigned to the accounting period in which they are used to produce revenue.

Direct cause-and-effect relationships seldom can be demonstrated for certain, but many costs appear to be related to particular revenues. The accountant recognizes these expenses and the related revenues in the same accounting period. Examples are the costs of goods sold and sales commissions. When there is no direct means of connecting expenses and revenues, the accountant tries to allocate costs in a systematic way among the accounting periods that benefit from the costs. For example, a building is converted from an asset to an expense by allocating its cost over the years that benefit from its use.

ACCRUAL ACCOUNTING

OBJECTIVE

3 *Define* accrual accounting *and explain two broad ways of accomplishing it*

To apply the matching rule, accountants have developed accrual accounting. Accrual accounting "attempts to record the financial effects on an enterprise of transactions and other events and circumstances . . . in the periods in which those transactions, events, and circumstances occur rather than only in the periods in which cash is received or paid by the enterprise."[2] That is, accrual accounting consists of all the techniques developed by accountants to apply the matching rule. It is done in two general ways: (1) by recording revenues when earned and expenses when incurred and (2) by adjusting the accounts.

RECOGNIZING REVENUES WHEN EARNED AND EXPENSES WHEN INCURRED

We illustrated the first method of accrual accounting several times in the chapter on measuring business transactions. For example, when Joan Miller Advertising Agency, Inc. made a sale on credit by placing advertisements for a client (in the January 19 transaction), revenue was recorded at the time of the sale by debiting Accounts Receivable and crediting Advertising Fees Earned. This is how the accountant recognizes the revenue from a credit sale before the cash is collected. Accounts Receivable serves as a holding account until payment is received. The process of determining when a sale takes place is called revenue recognition.

When Joan Miller Advertising Agency, Inc. received the telephone bill on January 30, the expense was recognized both as having been incurred and as helping to produce revenue in January. The transaction was recorded by debiting Telephone Expense and crediting Accounts Payable. Until the bill is paid, Accounts Payable serves as a holding account. Notice that recognition of the expense does not depend on the payment of cash.

---

2. *Statement of Financial Accounting Concepts No. 1,* "Objectives of Financial Reporting by Business Enterprises" (Stamford, Conn.: Financial Accounting Standards Board, 1978), par. 44.

Exhibit 3-1. Trial Balance for Joan Miller Advertising Agency, Inc.

Joan Miller Advertising Agency, Inc.
Trial Balance
January 31, 19xx

Cash	$ 1,720	
Accounts Receivable	2,800	
Art Supplies	1,800	
Office Supplies	800	
Prepaid Rent	800	
Prepaid Insurance	480	
Art Equipment	4,200	
Office Equipment	3,000	
Accounts Payable		$ 3,170
Unearned Art Fees		1,000
Common Stock		10,000
Dividends	1,400	
Advertising Fees Earned		4,200
Office Wages Expense	1,200	
Utility Expense	100	
Telephone Expense	70	
	$18,370	$18,370

ADJUSTING THE ACCOUNTS

An accounting period, by definition, ends on a particular day. The balance sheet must list all assets and liabilities as of the end of that day, and the income statement must contain all revenues and expenses applicable to the period ending on that day. Although operating a business is a continuous process, there must be a cutoff point for the periodic reports. Some transactions invariably span the cutoff point; thus, some accounts need adjustment.

For example, some of the accounts in the end-of-the-period trial balance for Joan Miller Advertising Agency, Inc. (Exhibit 3-1) do not show the correct balances for preparing the financial statements. The January 31 trial balance lists prepaid rent of $800. At $400 per month, this represents rent for the months of January and February. So on January 31, one-half of the $800, or $400, represents rent expense for January; the remaining $400 represents an asset that will be used in February. An adjustment is needed to reflect the $400 balance in the Prepaid Rent account on the balance sheet and the $400 rent expense on the income statement. As you will see on the following pages, several other accounts in the Joan Miller Advertising Agency, Inc. trial balance do not reflect their correct balances. Like the Prepaid Rent account, they need to be adjusted.

THE ADJUSTMENT PROCESS

Accountants use adjusting entries to apply accrual accounting to transactions that span more than one accounting period. Adjusting entries have at least

OBJECTIVE

 State four principal situations that require adjusting entries

one balance sheet (or permanent) account entry and at least one income statement (or temporary) account entry. Adjusting entries never involve the Cash account. They are needed when deferrals or accruals exist. A deferral is the postponement of the recognition of an expense already paid or incurred, or of a revenue already received. Deferrals are used in two instances:

1. Costs have been recorded that must be apportioned between two or more accounting periods. Examples are prepaid rent, prepaid insurance, supplies, and costs of a building. The adjusting entry in this case involves an asset account and an expense account.
2. Revenues have been recorded that must be apportioned between two or more accounting periods. An example is payments collected for services yet to be rendered. The adjusting entry involves a liability account and a revenue account.

An accrual is the recognition of a revenue or expense that has arisen but has not yet been recorded. Accruals are required in these two cases:

1. There are unrecorded revenues. An example is fees earned but not yet collected or billed to customers. The adjusting entry involves an asset account and a revenue account.
2. There are unrecorded expenses. Examples are the wages earned by employees in the current accounting period but after the last pay period. The adjusting entry involves an expense account and a liability account.

Once again, we use Joan Miller Advertising Agency, Inc. to illustrate the kinds of adjusting entries that most businesses must make.

APPORTIONING RECORDED EXPENSES BETWEEN TWO OR MORE ACCOUNTING PERIODS (DEFERRED EXPENSES)

OBJECTIVE

 Prepare typical adjusting entries

Companies often make expenditures that benefit more than one period. These expenditures are usually debited to an asset account. At the end of the accounting period, the amount that has been used is transferred from the asset account to an expense account. Two of the more important kinds of adjustments are for prepaid expenses and the depreciation of plant and equipment.

Prepaid Expenses   Some expenses customarily are paid in advance. These expenditures are called prepaid expenses. Among them are rent, insurance, and supplies. At the end of an accounting period, a portion (or all) of these goods or services will have been used up or will have expired. An adjusting entry reducing the asset and increasing the expense, as shown in Figure 3-1, is always required. The amount of the adjustment equals the cost of the goods or services used up or expired. If adjusting entries for prepaid expenses are not made at the end of the period, both the balance sheet and the income statement will present information that is incorrect: The assets of the company will be overstated, and the expenses of the company will be understated. This means that stockholders' equity on the balance sheet and net income on the income statement will be overstated.

At the beginning of the month, Joan Miller Advertising Agency, Inc. paid two months' rent in advance. This expenditure resulted in an asset consisting of the right to occupy the office for two months. As each day in the month passed, part of the asset's cost expired and became an expense. By January

Figure 3-1. Adjustment for Prepaid (Deferred) Expense

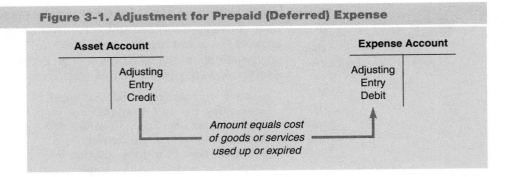

31, one-half had expired and should be treated as an expense. Here is the analysis of this economic event:

Prepaid Rent (Adjustment a)

	Dr.	Cr.
Jan. 31 Rent Expense	400	
Prepaid Rent		400

Prepaid Rent

Jan. 2	800	Jan. 31	400

Rent Expense

Jan. 31	400	

Transaction: Expiration of one month's rent.
Analysis: Assets decrease. Stockholders' equity decreases.
Rules: Decreases in assets are recorded by credits. Decreases in stockholders' equity are recorded by debits.
Entries: The decrease in stockholders' equity is recorded by a debit to Rent Expense. The decrease in assets is recorded by a credit to Prepaid Rent.

The Prepaid Rent account now has a balance of $400, which represents one month's rent paid in advance. The Rent Expense account reflects the $400 expense for the month of January.

Besides rent, Joan Miller Advertising Agency, Inc. prepaid expenses for insurance, art supplies, and office supplies, all of which call for adjusting entries.

On January 8, the agency purchased a one-year life insurance policy, paying for it in advance. Like prepaid rent, prepaid insurance offers benefits (in this case, protection) that expire day by day. By the end of the month, one-twelfth of the protection had expired. The adjustment is analyzed and recorded like this:

Prepaid Insurance (Adjustment b)

	Dr.	Cr.
Jan. 31 Insurance Expense	40	
Prepaid Insurance		40

Prepaid Insurance

Jan. 8	480	Jan. 31	40

Insurance Expense

Jan. 31	40	

Transaction: Expiration of one month's life insurance.
Analysis: Assets decrease. Stockholders' equity decreases.
Rules: Decreases in assets are recorded by credits. Decreases in stockholders' equity are recorded by debits.
Entries: The decrease in stockholders' equity is recorded by a debit to Insurance Expense. The decrease in assets is recorded by a credit to Prepaid Insurance.

The Prepaid Insurance account now shows the correct balance, $440, and Insurance Expense reflects the expired cost, $40 for the month.

Early in the month, Joan Miller Advertising Agency, Inc. purchased art supplies and office supplies. As Joan Miller did artwork for various clients during the month, art supplies were consumed. And her secretary used office supplies. There is no need to account for these supplies every day because the financial statements are not prepared until the end of the month and the recordkeeping would involve too much work. Instead, Joan Miller makes a careful inventory of the art and office supplies at the end of the month. This inventory records the number and cost of those supplies that are still assets of the company—that are yet to be consumed.

Suppose the inventory shows that art supplies costing $1,300 and office supplies costing $600 are still on hand. This means that of the $1,800 of art supplies originally purchased, $500 worth were used up (became an expense) in January. Of the original $800 of office supplies, $200 worth were consumed. These transactions are analyzed and recorded as follows:

Art Supplies and Office Supplies (Adjustments c and d)

		Dr.	Cr.	**Transaction:** Consumption of supplies.
Jan. 31	Art Supplies			**Analysis:** Assets decrease. Stockholders' equity decreases.
	Expense	500		
	Art Supplies		500	**Rules:** Decreases in assets are recorded by credits. Decreases in stockholders' equity are recorded by debits.
Jan. 31	Office Supplies			
	Expense	200		**Entries:** The decreases in stockholders' equity are recorded by debits to Art Supplies Expense and Office Supplies Expense. The decreases in assets are recorded by credits to Art Supplies and Office Supplies.
	Office Supplies		200	

Art Supplies

Jan. 6	1,800	Jan. 31	500

Art Supplies Expense

Jan. 31	500	

Office Supplies

Jan. 6	800	Jan. 31	200

Office Supplies Expense

Jan. 31	200	

The asset accounts Art Supplies and Office Supplies now reflect the correct balances, $1,300 and $600, respectively, of supplies that are yet to be consumed. In addition, the amount of art supplies used up during the accounting period is shown as $500 and the amount of office supplies used up is shown as $200.

Depreciation of Plant and Equipment   When a company buys a long-term asset—a building, equipment, trucks, automobiles, a computer, store fixtures, or office furniture—it is, in effect, prepaying for the usefulness of that asset for as long as it benefits the company. Because a long-term asset is a deferral of an expense, the accountant must allocate the cost of the asset over its estimated useful life. The amount allocated to any one accounting period is called depreciation, or *depreciation expense.* Depreciation, like other expenses, is incurred during an accounting period to produce revenue.

It is often impossible to tell how long an asset will last or how much of the asset is used in any one period. For this reason, depreciation must be estimated. Accountants have developed a number of methods for estimating depreciation and for dealing with the related complex problems. Here we look at the simplest case.

Suppose, for example, that Joan Miller Advertising Agency, Inc. estimates that its art equipment and office equipment will last five years (60 months) and will be worthless at the end of that time. The monthly depreciation of art equipment and office equipment is $70 ($4,200 ÷ 60 months) and $50 ($3,000 ÷ 60 months), respectively. These amounts represent the costs allocated to the month, and they are the amounts by which the asset accounts must be reduced and the expense accounts increased (reducing stockholders' equity).

Art Equipment and Office Equipment (Adjustments e and f)

	Dr.	Cr.
Jan. 31 Depreciation Expense, Art Equipment	70	
Accumulated Depreciation, Art Equipment		70
Jan. 31 Depreciation Expense, Office Equipment	50	
Accumulated Depreciation, Office Equipment		50

Transaction: Recording depreciation expense.
Analysis: Assets decrease. Stockholders' equity decreases.
Rules: Decreases in assets are recorded by credits. Decreases in stockholders' equity are recorded by debits.
Entries: The stockholders' equity is decreased by debits to Depreciation Expense, Art Equipment and Depreciation Expense, Office Equipment. The assets are decreased by credits to Accumulated Depreciation, Art Equipment and Accumulated Depreciation, Office Equipment.

Art Equipment

Jan. 4 4,200	

Accumulated Depreciation, Art Equipment

	Jan. 31 70

Office Equipment

Jan. 5 3,000	

Accumulated Depreciation, Office Equipment

	Jan. 31 50

Depreciation Expense, Art Equipment

Jan. 31 70	

Depreciation Expense, Office Equipment

Jan. 31 50	

The privatization of businesses in Eastern Europe and the republics of the former Soviet Union has created a great need for Western accounting knowledge. Many managers from these countries are anxious to study accounting. Under the old system, the concept of net income as Westerners know it did not exist because the State owned everything and there was no such thing as income. The new businesses, because they are private, require accounting systems that recognize the importance of net income. In these new systems, it is necessary to make adjusting entries to record such things as depreciation and accrued expenses. Many of these entities have been suffering losses for years without knowing it and are now in bad condition, because they have ignored these expenses. =====

Accumulated Depreciation—A Contra Account

Notice that in the analysis above, the asset accounts are not credited directly. Instead, as shown in Figure 3-2, new accounts—Accumulated Depreciation, Art Equipment and Accumulated Depreciation, Office Equipment—are credited. These accumulated depreciation accounts are contra-asset accounts used to total the past depreciation expense on a specific long-term asset. A contra account is a separate account that is paired with a related account—in this case an asset account. The balance of the contra account is shown on the financial statement as a deduction from the related account. There are several types of contra accounts. In this case, the balance of Accumulated Depreciation, Art Equipment is shown on the balance sheet as a deduction from the associated account Art Equipment. Likewise, Accumulated Depreciation, Office Equipment is a deduction from Office Equipment. Exhibit 3-2 shows the plant and equipment section of the balance sheet for Joan Miller Advertising Agency, Inc. after these adjusting entries have been made.

A contra account is used for two very good reasons. First, it recognizes that depreciation is an estimate. Second, a contra account preserves the original cost of an asset: In combination with the asset account, it shows both how much of the asset has been allocated as an expense and the balance left to be

Figure 3-2. Adjustment for Depreciation

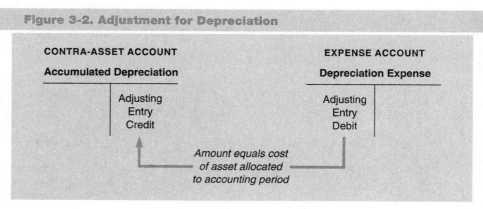

Exhibit 3-2. Plant and Equipment Section of the Balance Sheet

Joan Miller Advertising Agency, Inc.
Partial Balance Sheet
January 31, 19xx

Plant and Equipment		
Art Equipment	$4,200	
Less Accumulated Depreciation	70	$4,130
Office Equipment	$3,000	
Less Accumulated Depreciation	50	2,950
Total Plant and Equipment		$7,080

depreciated. As the months pass, the amount of the accumulated depreciation grows, and the net amount shown as an asset declines. In six months, Accumulated Depreciation, Art Equipment will show a balance of $420; when this amount is subtracted from Art Equipment, a net amount of $3,780 will remain. This net amount is called the carrying value, or *book value*, of the asset.

Other names are also used for accumulated depreciation, among them *allowance for depreciation*. But *accumulated depreciation* is the newer, better term.

APPORTIONING RECORDED REVENUES BETWEEN TWO OR MORE ACCOUNTING PERIODS (DEFERRED REVENUES)

Just as expenses can be paid before they are used, revenues can be received before they are earned. When revenues are received in advance, the company has an obligation to deliver goods or perform services. Therefore, unearned revenues are shown in a liability account. For example, publishing companies usually receive payment in advance for magazine subscriptions. These receipts are recorded in a liability account. If the company fails to deliver the magazines, subscribers are entitled to their money back. As the company delivers each issue of the magazine, it earns a part of the advance payments. This earned portion must be transferred from the Unearned Subscriptions account to the Subscription Revenue account, as shown in Figure 3-3.

During the month of January, Joan Miller Advertising Agency, Inc. received $1,000 as an advance payment for artwork to be done for another

Figure 3-3. Adjustment for Unearned (Deferred) Revenue

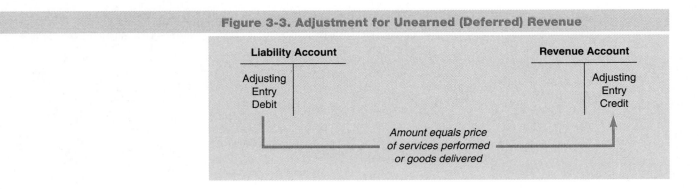

agency. Assume that by the end of the month, $400 of the artwork was done and accepted by the other agency. Here is the transaction analysis:

Unearned Art Fees (Adjustment g)

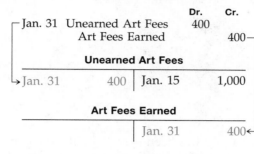

		Dr.	Cr.
Jan. 31	Unearned Art Fees	400	
	Art Fees Earned		400

Unearned Art Fees

Jan. 31	400	Jan. 15	1,000

Art Fees Earned

		Jan. 31	400

Transaction: Performance of services paid for in advance.
Analysis: Liabilities decrease. Stockholders' equity increases.
Rules: Decreases in liabilities are recorded by debits. Increases in stockholders' equity are recorded by credits.
Entries: The decrease in liabilities is recorded by a debit to Unearned Art Fees. The increase in stockholders' equity is recorded by a credit to Art Fees Earned.

The liability account Unearned Art Fees now reflects the amount of work still to be performed, $600. The revenue account Art Fees Earned reflects the services performed and the revenue earned for those services during the month, $400.

RECOGNIZING UNRECORDED REVENUES (ACCRUED REVENUES)

Accrued revenues are revenues for which a service has been performed or goods delivered but for which no entry has been recorded. Any revenues that have been earned but not recorded during the accounting period call for an adjusting entry that debits an asset account and credits a revenue account, as shown in Figure 3-4. For example, the interest on a note receivable is earned day by day but may not be received until another accounting period. Interest Receivable should be debited and Interest Income should be credited for the interest accrued at the end of the current period.

Suppose that Joan Miller Advertising Agency, Inc. has agreed to place a series of advertisements for Marsh Tire Company and that the first appears on January 31, the last day of the month. The fee of $200 for this advertisement, which has been earned but not recorded, should be recorded this way:

Accrued Advertising Fees (Adjustment h)

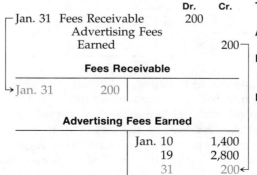

		Dr.	Cr.
Jan. 31	Fees Receivable	200	
	Advertising Fees Earned		200

Fees Receivable

Jan. 31	200	

Advertising Fees Earned

		Jan. 10	1,400
		19	2,800
		31	200

Transaction: Accrual of unrecorded revenue.
Analysis: Assets increase. Stockholders' equity increases.
Rules: Increases in assets are recorded by debits. Increases in stockholders' equity are recorded by credits.
Entries: The increase in assets is recorded by a debit to Fees Receivable. The increase in stockholders' equity is recorded by a credit to Advertising Fees Earned.

Now both the asset and the revenue accounts show the correct balance: The $200 in Fees Receivable is owed to the company, and the $4,400 in Advertising

Figure 3-4. Adjustment for Unrecorded (Accrued) Revenues

Asset Receivable Account		Revenue Account
Adjusting Entry Debit		Adjusting Entry Credit

Amount equals price of services performed

Fees Earned has been earned by the company during the month. Marsh will be billed for the series of advertisements when they are completed. At that time, Accounts Receivable will be debited and Fees Receivable will be credited.

RECOGNIZING UNRECORDED EXPENSES (ACCRUED EXPENSES)

At the end of an accounting period, there are usually expenses that have been incurred but not recorded in the accounts. These expenses require adjusting entries. One such case is interest on borrowed money. Each day, interest accumulates on the debt. As shown in Figure 3-5, at the end of the accounting period, an adjusting entry is made to record this accumulated interest, which is an expense of the period, and the corresponding liability to pay the interest. Other unrecorded expenses are taxes, wages, and salaries. As the expense and the corresponding liability accumulate, they are said to *accrue*—hence the term accrued expenses.

Accrued Wages   Suppose the calendar for January looks like this:

January

Su	M	T	W	Th	F	Sa
	1	2	3	4	5	6
7	8	9	10	11	12	13
14	15	16	17	18	19	20
21	22	23	24	25	26	27
28	29	30	31			

By the end of business on January 31, the secretary at Joan Miller Advertising Agency, Inc. will have worked three days (Monday, Tuesday, and Wednesday) beyond the last biweekly pay period, which ended on January 26. The employee has earned the wages for these days, but she will not be paid until the regular payday in February. The wages for these three days are rightfully an expense for January, and the liabilities should reflect the fact that the company owes the secretary for those days. Because the secretary's wage rate is $600 every two weeks, or $60 per day ($600 ÷ 10 working days), the expense is $180 ($60 × 3 days).

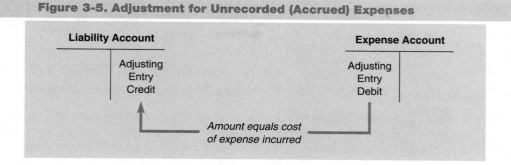

Figure 3-5. Adjustment for Unrecorded (Accrued) Expenses

Accrued Wages (Adjustment i)

		Dr.	Cr.
Jan. 31	Office Wages Expense	180	
	Wages Payable		180

Wages Payable

		Jan. 31	180

Office Wages Expense

Jan. 12	600	
26	600	
31	180	

Transaction: Accrual of unrecorded expense.
Analysis: Liabilities increase. Stockholders' equity decreases.
Rules: Increases in liabilities are recorded by credits. Decreases in stockholders' equity are recorded by debits.
Entries: The decrease in stockholders' equity is recorded by a debit to Office Wages Expense. The increase in liabilities is recorded by a credit to Wages Payable.

The liability of $180 is now reflected correctly in the Wages Payable account. The actual expense incurred for office wages during the month, $1,380, is also correct.

Estimated Income Taxes As a corporation, Joan Miller Advertising Agency, Inc. is subject to federal income taxes. Although the actual amount owed cannot be determined until after net income is computed at the end of the fiscal year, each month should bear its part of the total year's expense, in accordance with the matching concept. Therefore, the amount of income taxes expense for the current month must be estimated. Assume that after analyzing the first month's operations and conferring with her CPA, Joan Miller estimates January's share of the federal income taxes for the year to be $400. This estimated expense can be analyzed and recorded as follows:

Estimated Income Taxes (Adjustment j)

		Dr.	Cr.
Jan. 31	Income Taxes Expense	400	
	Income Taxes Payable		400

Income Taxes Payable

		Jan. 31	400

Income Taxes Expense

Jan. 31	400	

Transaction: Accrual of estimated income taxes.
Analysis: Liabilities increase. Stockholders' equity decreases.
Rules: Increases in liabilities are recorded by credits. Decreases in stockholders' equity are recorded by debits.
Entries: The decrease in stockholders' equity is recorded by a debit to Income Taxes Expense. The increase in liabilities is recorded by a credit to Income Taxes Payable.

Expenses for January will now reflect the estimated income taxes attributable to that month, and the liability for these estimated income taxes will appear on the balance sheet.

USING THE ADJUSTED TRIAL BALANCE TO PREPARE FINANCIAL STATEMENTS

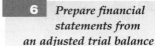
OBJECTIVE

6 *Prepare financial statements from an adjusted trial balance*

In the chapter on measuring business transactions, a trial balance was prepared before any adjusting entries were recorded. Here, we prepare an adjusted trial balance, a list of the accounts and balances after the adjusting entries have been recorded and posted. The adjusted trial balance for Joan Miller Advertising Agency, Inc. is shown on the left side of Exhibit 3-3. Notice that some accounts, such as Cash and Accounts Receivable, have the same balances they have in the trial balance (see Exhibit 3-1 on page 104) because no adjusting entries affected them. Other accounts, such as Art Supplies, Office Supplies, Prepaid Rent, and Prepaid Insurance, have different balances from those in the trial balance because adjusting entries did affect them. If the adjusting entries have been posted to the accounts correctly, the adjusted trial balance should have equal debit and credit totals.

From the adjusted trial balance, the financial statements can be easily prepared. The income statement is prepared from the revenue and expense accounts, as shown in Exhibit 3-3. Then, as shown in Exhibit 3-4, the statement of retained earnings and the balance sheet are prepared. Notice that the net income from the income statement is combined with dividends on the statement of retained earnings to give the net change in Joan Miller Advertising Agency's Retained Earnings account. The resulting balance of Retained Earnings at January 31 is used on the balance sheet, as are the asset and liability accounts. In more complex situations, accountants use a work sheet to prepare financial statements. The preparation of a work sheet is covered in the chapter on completion of the accounting cycle.

DECISION POINT

Joan Miller Advertising Agency, Inc.

In one example used in this chapter, on January 31, an accrual of $180 is made for wages payable. Joan Miller might ask, "Why go to the trouble of making this adjustment? Why worry about it? Doesn't everything come out in the end, when the secretary is paid in February? Because wages expense in total is the same for the two months, isn't the net income in total unchanged?" Give three reasons why adjusting entries can help Joan Miller assess the performance of her business.

Adjusting entries are important because they help accountants compile information that is useful to management and stockholders. First, adjusting entries are necessary to measure income and financial position in a relevant and useful way. Joan Miller should know how much the agency has earned each month and what its liabilities and assets are on the last day of the month. For instance, if the three days' accrued wages for the secretary are not recorded, the agency's income will be overstated by $180, or 11.3 percent ($180 ÷ $1,590). Second, adjusting entries allow

Exhibit 3-3. Relationship of Adjusted Trial Balance to Income Statement

Joan Miller Advertising Agency, Inc.
Adjusted Trial Balance
January 31, 19xx

Cash	$ 1,720	
Accounts Receivable	2,800	
Fees Receivable	200	
Art Supplies	1,300	
Office Supplies	600	
Prepaid Rent	400	
Prepaid Insurance	440	
Art Equipment	4,200	
Accumulated Depreciation, Art Equipment		$ 70
Office Equipment	3,000	
Accumulated Depreciation, Office Equipment		50
Accounts Payable		3,170
Wages Payable		180
Income Taxes Payable		400
Unearned Art Fees		600
Common Stock		10,000
Dividends	1,400	
Advertising Fees Earned		4,400
Art Fees Earned		400
Office Wages Expense	1,380	
Utility Expense	100	
Telephone Expense	70	
Rent Expense	400	
Insurance Expense	40	
Art Supplies Expense	500	
Office Supplies Expense	200	
Depreciation Expense, Art Equipment	70	
Depreciation Expense, Office Equipment	50	
Income Taxes Expense	400	
	$19,270	$19,270

Joan Miller Advertising Agency, Inc.
Income Statement
For the Month Ended January 31, 19xx

Revenues		
Advertising Fees Earned	$4,400	
Art Fees Earned	400	
Total Revenues		$4,800
Expenses		
Office Wages Expense	$1,380	
Utility Expense	100	
Telephone Expense	70	
Rent Expense	400	
Insurance Expense	40	
Art Supplies Expense	500	
Office Supplies Expense	200	
Depreciation Expense, Art Equipment	70	
Depreciation Expense, Office Equipment	50	
Income Taxes Expense	400	
Total Expenses		3,210
Net Income		$1,590

financial statements to be compared from one accounting period to the next. Joan Miller can see whether the company is making progress toward earning a profit or if the company has improved its financial position. To return to our example, if the adjustment for accrued wages is not recorded, not only will the net income for January be overstated by $180, but the net income for February (the month when payment will be made) will be understated by $180. This error will make February's earnings, whatever they may be, appear lower than they actually are. Third, even

Exhibit 3-4. Relationship of Adjusted Trial Balance to Balance Sheet and Statement of Retained Earnings

Joan Miller Advertising Agency, Inc.
Adjusted Trial Balance
January 31, 19xx

Cash	$ 1,720	
Accounts Receivable	2,800	
Fees Receivable	200	
Art Supplies	1,300	
Office Supplies	600	
Prepaid Rent	400	
Prepaid Insurance	440	
Art Equipment	4,200	
Accumulated Depreciation, Art Equipment		$ 70
Office Equipment	3,000	
Accumulated Depreciation, Office Equipment		50
Accounts Payable		3,170
Wages Payable		180
Income Taxes Payable		400
Unearned Art Fees		600
Common Stock		10,000
Dividends	1,400	
Advertising Fees Earned		4,400
Art Fees Earned		400
Office Wages Expense	1,380	
Utility Expense	100	
Telephone Expense	70	
Rent Expense	400	
Insurance Expense	40	
Art Supplies Expense	500	
Office Supplies Expense	200	
Depreciation Expense, Art Equipment	70	
Depreciation Expense, Office Equipment	50	
Income Taxes Expense	400	
	$19,270	$19,270

From Income Statement in Exhibit 3–3.

Joan Miller Advertising Agency, Inc.
Balance Sheet
January 31, 19xx

Assets

Cash		$ 1,720
Accounts Receivable		2,800
Fees Receivable		200
Art Supplies		1,300
Office Supplies		600
Prepaid Rent		400
Prepaid Insurance		440
Art Equipment	$4,200	
Less Accumulated Depreciation	70	4,130
Office Equipment	$3,000	
Less Accumulated Depreciation	50	2,950
Total Assets		$14,540

Liabilities

Accounts Payable	$3,170	
Unearned Art Fees	600	
Wages Payable	180	
Income Taxes Payable	400	
Total Liabilities		$ 4,350

Stockholders' Equity

Common Stock	$10,000	
Retained Earnings	190	
Total Stockholders' Equity		10,190
Total Liabilities and Stockholders' Equity		$14,540

Joan Miller Advertising Agency, Inc.
Statement of Retained Earnings
For the Month Ended January 31, 19xx

Retained Earnings, January 1, 19xx	—
Net Income	$1,590
Subtotal	$1,590
Less Dividends	1,400
Retained Earnings, January 31, 19xx	$ 190

though one adjusting entry may seem insignificant, the cumulative effect of all adjusting entries can be great. Look back over all the adjustments made by Joan Miller Advertising Agency, Inc. for prepaid rent and insurance, art and office supplies, depreciation of art and office equipment, unearned art fees, accrued advertising fees, accrued wages, and estimated income taxes. These are normal adjustments. Their effect on net income in January is to increase expenses by $1,840 and revenues by $600, for a net effect of minus $1,240, or 78 percent ($1,240 ÷ $1,590) of net income. If adjusting entries had not been made, Joan Miller would have had a false impression of her company's performance. :::::

CASH FLOWS, ACCRUAL ACCOUNTING, AND MANAGEMENT OBJECTIVES

Supplemental OBJECTIVE

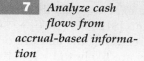

7 *Analyze cash flows from accrual-based information*

The purpose of accrual accounting is to measure the earnings of a business during an accounting period. This measurement of net income is directly related to management's profitability goal. A company must earn a sufficient net income to survive over the long term. Management also has the short-range goal of achieving sufficient liquidity to meet its needs for cash, to pay its ongoing obligations, and to plan for borrowing money from the bank. An important measure of liquidity is cash flow. Cash flow is the amount of cash paid out or received during an accounting period and the resulting availability of cash. It is important for managers to be able to use accrual-based financial information to analyze cash flows in order to plan payments to creditors and assess the need for short-term borrowing.

Every revenue or expense account on the income statement has one or more related accounts on the balance sheet. For instance, Supplies Expense is related to Supplies, Wages Expense to Wages Payable, and Service Revenues to Unearned Revenues. As shown in this chapter, these accounts are related through adjusting entries whose purpose is to apply the matching rule in the measurement of net income. The cash flows generated or paid by company operations may also be determined by analyzing these relationships. For example, suppose that after receiving the financial statements in Exhibits 3-3 and 3-4, Joan Miller wants to know how much cash was expended for art supplies. On the income statement, Art Supplies Expense is $500, and on the balance sheet, Art Supplies is $1,300. Because January was the first month of operation for the company, there was no prior balance of supplies, so the amount of cash expended for supplies during the month was $1,800. The cash flow used to purchase art supplies ($1,800) was much greater than the amount expensed in determining income ($500). In planning for February, Joan Miller can anticipate that the cash needed may be less than the amount expensed because, given the large inventory of art supplies, it will probably not be necessary to buy art supplies for more than a month. Understanding these cash flow effects enables Joan to better predict her business's need for cash during February.

The general rule for determining the cash flow received from any revenue or paid for any expense (except depreciation, which is a special case not covered here) is to determine the potential cash payments or cash receipts and deduct the amount not paid or received. The application of the general rule varies with the type of asset or liability account, as shown on the next page:

Type of Account	Potential Payment or Receipt	Not Paid or Received	Result
Prepaid Expense	Ending Balance + Expense for the Period	− Beginning Balance	= Cash Payments for Expenses
Unearned Revenue	Ending Balance + Revenue for the Period	− Beginning Balance	= Cash Receipts from Revenues
Accrued Liability	Beginning Balance + Expense for the Period	− Ending Balance	= Cash Payments for Expenses
Accrued Receivable	Beginning Balance + Revenue for the Period	− Ending Balance	= Cash Receipts from Revenues

For instance, assume that on May 31 a company had a balance of $480 in Prepaid Insurance and that on June 30 the balance was $670. If the insurance expense during June was $120, the amount of cash expended on insurance during June can be computed as follows:

Prepaid Insurance at June 30	$670
Insurance Expense during June	120
Potential cash payments for insurance	$790
Less Prepaid Insurance at May 31	480
Cash payments for insurance during June	$310

The beginning balance is deducted because it was paid in a prior accounting period. Note that the cash payments equal the expense plus the increase in the balance of the Prepaid Insurance account [$120 + ($670 − $480) = $310]. In this case, the cash paid was almost three times the amount of insurance expense. In future months, cash payments are likely to be less than the expense.

BUSINESS BULLETIN: TECHNOLOGY IN PRACTICE

In a computerized accounting system, adjusting entries may be entered just like any other transactions. However, since some adjusting entries, such as those for insurance expense and depreciation expense, may be similar for each accounting period, and others, such as those for accrued wages and income taxes, may always involve the same accounts, the computer may be programmed to display the adjusting entries automatically so that all the accountant has to do is verify the amounts or enter the correct amounts. Then the adjusting entries are entered and posted and the adjusted trial balance is prepared with the touch of a button.

A NOTE ABOUT JOURNAL ENTRIES

Throughout this chapter and the chapter on measuring business transactions, we have presented a full analysis of each journal entry. The analyses showed you the thought process behind each entry. By now, you should be fully aware of the effects of transactions on the accounting equation and the rules of debit and credit. For this reason, in the rest of the book, journal entries are presented without full analysis.

CHAPTER REVIEW

REVIEW OF LEARNING OBJECTIVES

1. **Define *net income* and its two major components, *revenues* and *expenses.*** Net income is the net increase in stockholders' equity that results from the operations of a company. Net income equals revenues minus expenses, unless expenses exceed revenues, in which case a net loss results. Revenues equal the price of goods sold and services rendered during a specific period. Expenses are the costs of goods and services used up in the process of producing revenues.

2. **Explain the difficulties of income measurement caused by (a) the accounting period issue, (b) the continuity issue, and (c) the matching issue.** The accounting period issue recognizes that net income measurements for short periods of time are necessarily tentative. The continuity issue recognizes that even though businesses face an uncertain future, without evidence to the contrary, accountants must assume that a business will continue indefinitely. The matching issue has to do with the difficulty of assigning revenues and expenses to a period of time. It is solved by applying the matching rule: Revenues must be assigned to the accounting period in which the goods are sold or the services performed, and expenses must be assigned to the accounting period in which they are used to produce revenue.

3. **Define *accrual accounting* and explain two broad ways of accomplishing it.** Accrual accounting consists of all the techniques developed by accountants to apply the matching rule. The two general ways of accomplishing accrual accounting are (1) by recognizing revenues when earned and expenses when incurred and (2) by adjusting the accounts.

4. **State four principal situations that require adjusting entries.** Adjusting entries are required (1) when recorded expenses have to be apportioned between two or more accounting periods, (2) when recorded revenues must be apportioned between two or more accounting periods, (3) when unrecorded revenues exist, and (4) when unrecorded expenses exist.

5. **Prepare typical adjusting entries.** The preparation of adjusting entries is summarized in the following table:

Type of Adjusting Entry	Type of Account		Examples
	Debited	**Credited**	
Deferrals			
1. Apportioning recorded expenses (expired, not recorded)	Expense	Asset (or contra asset)	Prepaid Rent Prepaid Insurance Supplies Buildings Equipment
2. Apportioning recorded revenues (earned, not recorded)	Liability	Revenue	Commissions Received in Advance
Accruals			
1. Accrued revenues (earned, not received)	Asset	Revenue	Commissions Receivable Interest Receivable
2. Accrued expenses (incurred, not paid)	Expense	Liability	Wages Payable Interest Payable

6. **Prepare financial statements from an adjusted trial balance.** An adjusted trial balance is prepared after adjusting entries have been posted to the ledger accounts. Its purpose is to test the balance of the ledger after the adjusting entries are made and before the financial statements are prepared. The income statement is prepared from the revenue and expense accounts. The balance sheet is prepared from the asset and liability accounts in the adjusted trial balance and from the statement of retained earnings.

SUPPLEMENTAL OBJECTIVE

7. **Analyze cash flows from accrual-based information.** Cash flow information bears on management's liquidity goal. The general rule for determining the cash flow effect of any revenue or expense (except depreciation, which is a special case not covered here) is to determine the potential cash payments or cash receipts and deduct the amount not paid or received.

REVIEW OF CONCEPTS AND TERMINOLOGY

The following concepts and terms were introduced in this chapter:

L O 2 **Accounting period issue:** The difficulty of assigning revenues and expenses to a short period of time.

L O 4 **Accrual:** The recognition of an expense or revenue that has arisen but has not yet been recorded.

L O 3 **Accrual accounting:** The attempt to record the financial effects of transactions and other events in the periods in which those transactions or events occur, rather than only in the periods in which cash is received or paid by the business. All the techniques developed by accountants to apply the matching rule.

L O 5 **Accrued expenses:** Expenses that have been incurred but are not recognized in the accounts; unrecorded expenses.

L O 5 **Accrued revenues:** Revenues for which a service has been performed or goods delivered but for which no entry has been made; unrecorded revenues.

L O 5 **Accumulated depreciation account:** A contra-asset account used to accumulate the depreciation expense of a specific long-lived asset.

L O 6 **Adjusted trial balance:** A trial balance prepared after all adjusting entries have been posted to the accounts.

L O 4 **Adjusting entries:** Entries made to apply accrual accounting to transactions that span more than one accounting period.

L O 5 **Carrying value:** The unexpired portion of the cost of an asset. Also called *book value.*

L O 2 **Cash basis of accounting:** Accounting for revenues and expenses on a cash received and cash paid basis.

L O 2 **Continuity issue:** The difficulty associated with not knowing how long a business entity will survive.

L O 5 **Contra account:** An account whose balance is subtracted from an associated account in the financial statements.

L O 4 **Deferral:** The postponement of the recognition of an expense that already has been paid or incurred, or of a revenue that already has been received.

L O 5 **Depreciation:** The portion of the cost of a tangible long-term asset allocated to any one accounting period. Also called *depreciation expense.*

L O 1 **Expenses:** The cost of goods and services used up in the course of earning revenues.

L O 2 **Fiscal year:** Any twelve-month accounting period used by an economic entity.

L O 2 **Going concern:** The assumption, unless there is evidence to the contrary, that a business entity will continue to operate indefinitely.

L O 2 **Matching rule:** Revenues must be assigned to the accounting period in which the goods are sold or the services performed, and expenses must be assigned to the accounting period in which they are used to produce revenue.

L O 1   **Net income:** The net increase in stockholders' equity that results from business operations and is accumulated in the Retained Earnings account; revenues less expenses when revenues exceed expenses.

L O 1   **Net loss:** The net decrease in stockholders' equity that results from business operations when expenses exceed revenues. It is accumulated in the Retained Earnings account.

L O 2   **Periodicity:** The recognition that net income for any period less than the life of the business, although tentative, is still a useful estimate of net income for that period.

L O 1   **Permanent accounts:** Balance sheet accounts; accounts whose balances can extend past the end of an accounting period. Also called *real accounts*.

L O 5   **Prepaid expenses:** Expenses paid in advance that have not yet expired; an asset account.

L O 1   **Profit:** The increase in stockholders' equity that results from business operations.

L O 3   **Revenue recognition:** In accrual accounting, the process of determining when a sale takes place.

L O 1   **Revenues:** The increases in stockholders' equity from selling goods, rendering services, or performing other business activities.

L O 1   **Temporary accounts:** Accounts that show the accumulation of revenues and expenses over one accounting period; at the end of the accounting period, these account balances are transferred to stockholders' equity. Also called *nominal accounts*.

L O 5   **Unearned revenues:** Revenues received in advance for which the goods have not yet been delivered or the services performed; a liability account.

REVIEW PROBLEM
DETERMINING ADJUSTING ENTRIES, POSTING TO T ACCOUNTS, PREPARING ADJUSTED TRIAL BALANCE, AND PREPARING FINANCIAL STATEMENTS

L O 5, 6   This was the unadjusted trial balance for Certified Answering Service, Inc. on December 31, 19x2.

Certified Answering Service, Inc.
Trial Balance
December 31, 19x2

Cash	$2,160	
Accounts Receivable	1,250	
Office Supplies	180	
Prepaid Insurance	240	
Office Equipment	3,400	
Accumulated Depreciation, Office Equipment		$ 600
Accounts Payable		700
Unearned Revenue		460
Common Stock		2,000
Retained Earnings		2,870
Dividends	400	
Answering Service Revenue		2,900
Wages Expense	1,500	
Rent Expense	400	
	$9,530	$9,530

The information on the next page is also available:

a. Insurance that expired during December amounted to $40.
b. Office supplies on hand at the end of December totaled $75.
c. Depreciation for the month of December totaled $100.
d. Accrued wages at the end of December totaled $120.
e. Services performed in December but not yet billed on December 31 totaled $300.
f. Revenues earned for services performed that were paid in advance totaled $160.
g. Income taxes are estimated to be $250.

REQUIRED

1. Prepare T accounts for the accounts in the trial balance and enter the balances.
2. Determine the required adjusting entries and record them directly to the T accounts. Open new T accounts as needed.
3. Prepare an adjusted trial balance.
4. Prepare an income statement, a statement of retained earnings, and a balance sheet for the month ended December 31, 19x2.

ANSWER TO REVIEW PROBLEM

1. T accounts set up and amounts from trial balance entered
2. Adjusting entries recorded

Cash			
Bal.	2,160		

Accounts Receivable			
Bal.	1,250		

Service Revenue Receivable			
(e)	300		

Office Supplies			
Bal.	180	(b)	105
Bal.	**75**		

Prepaid Insurance			
Bal.	240	(a)	40
Bal.	**200**		

Office Equipment			
Bal.	3,400		

Accumulated Depreciation, Office Equipment			
		Bal.	600
		(c)	100
		Bal.	**700**

Accounts Payable			
		Bal.	700

Unearned Revenue			
(f)	160	Bal.	460
		Bal.	**300**

Wages Payable			
		(d)	120

Income Taxes Payable			
		(g)	250

Common Stock			
		Bal.	2,000

Retained Earnings			
		Bal.	2,870

Dividends			
Bal.	400		

Answering Service Revenue			
		Bal.	2,900
		(e)	300
		(f)	160
		Bal.	**3,360**

Wages Expense			
Bal.	1,500		
(d)	120		
Bal.	**1,620**		

Rent Expense			
Bal.	400		

Insurance Expense			
(a)	40		

Office Supplies Expense			
(b)	105		

Depreciation Expense, Office Equipment			
(c)	100		

Income Taxes Expense			
(g)	250		

3. Adjusted trial balance prepared

Certified Answering Service, Inc.
Adjusted Trial Balance
December 31, 19x2

Cash	$ 2,160	
Accounts Receivable	1,250	
Service Revenue Receivable	300	
Office Supplies	75	
Prepaid Insurance	200	
Office Equipment	3,400	
Accumulated Depreciation, Office Equipment		$ 700
Accounts Payable		700
Unearned Revenue		300
Wages Payable		120
Income Taxes Payable		250
Common Stock		2,000
Retained Earnings		2,870
Dividends	400	
Answering Service Revenue		3,360
Wages Expense	1,620	
Rent Expense	400	
Insurance Expense	40	
Office Supplies Expense	105	
Depreciation Expense, Office Equipment	100	
Income Taxes Expense	250	
	$10,300	$10,300

4. Financial statements prepared

Certified Answering Service, Inc.
Income Statement
For the Month Ended December 31, 19x2

Revenues

Answering Service Revenue		$3,360

Expenses

Wages Expense	$1,620	
Rent Expense	400	
Insurance Expense	40	
Office Supplies Expense	105	
Depreciation Expense, Office Equipment	100	
Income Taxes Expense	250	
Total Expenses		2,515
Net Income		$ 845

Certified Answering Service, Inc.
Statement of Retained Earnings
For the Month Ended December 31, 19x2

Retained Earnings, November 30, 19x2	$2,870
Net Income	845
Subtotal	$3,715
Less Dividends	400
Retained Earnings, December 31, 19x2	$3,315

Certified Answering Service, Inc.
Balance Sheet
December 31, 19x2

Assets

Cash		$2,160
Accounts Receivable		1,250
Service Revenue Receivable		300
Office Supplies		75
Prepaid Insurance		200
Office Equipment	$3,400	
Less Accumulated Depreciation	700	2,700
Total Assets		$6,685

Liabilities

Accounts Payable	$ 700
Unearned Revenue	300
Wages Payable	120
Income Taxes Payable	250
Total Liabilities	$1,370

Stockholders' Equity

Common Stock	$2,000	
Retained Earnings	3,315	
Total Stockholders' Equity		5,315
Total Liabilities and Stockholders' Equity		$6,685

CHAPTER ASSIGNMENTS

KNOWLEDGE AND UNDERSTANDING

Questions

1. Why does the accountant use the term *net income* instead of *profit*?
2. Define the terms *revenues* and *expenses*.

3. Why are income statement accounts called *temporary accounts*?

4. Why does the need for an accounting period cause problems?

5. What is the significance of the continuity assumption?

6. "The matching rule is the most significant concept in accounting." Do you agree with this statement? Explain your answer.

7. What is the difference between the cash basis and the accrual basis of accounting?

8. In what two ways is accrual accounting accomplished?

9. Why do adjusting entries have to be made?

10. What are the four situations that require adjusting entries? Give an example of each.

11. "Some assets are expenses that have not expired." Explain this statement.

12. What do plant and equipment, office supplies, and prepaid insurance have in common?

13. What is the difference between accumulated depreciation and depreciation expense?

14. What is a contra account? Give an example.

15. Why are contra accounts used to record depreciation?

16. How does unearned revenue arise? Give an example.

17. Where does unearned revenue appear on the balance sheet?

18. What accounting problem does a magazine publisher who sells three-year subscriptions have?

19. Under what circumstances does a company have accrued revenues? Give an example. What asset arises when the adjustment is made?

20. What is an accrued expense? Give three examples.

21. "Why worry about adjustments? Doesn't it all come out in the wash?" Discuss these questions.

22. Why is the income statement usually the first statement prepared from the adjusted trial balance?

23. To what management goals do the measurements of net income and cash flow relate?

Short Exercises

SE 3-1.
L O 2, 3 *Accrual Accounting Concepts*

Match the concepts of accrual accounting on the right with the assumptions or actions on the left.

1. Assumes expenses can be assigned to the accounting period in which they are used to produce revenues
2. Assumes a business will last indefinitely
3. Assumes revenues are earned at a point in time
4. Assumes net income measured for a short period of time, such as one quarter, is a useful measure

a. periodicity
b. going concern
c. matching rule
d. revenue recognition

SE 3-2.
L O 5 *Adjustment for Prepaid Insurance*

The Prepaid Insurance account began the year with a balance of $230. During the year, insurance in the amount of $570 was purchased. At the end of the year (December 31), the amount of insurance still unexpired was $350. Make the year-end journal entry to record the adjustment for insurance expense for the year.

SE 3-3.
L O 5 *Adjustment for Supplies*

The Supplies account began the year with a balance of $190. During the year, supplies in the amount of $490 were purchased. At the end of the year (December 31), the inventory of supplies on hand was $220. Make the year-end journal entry to record the adjustment for supplies expense for the year.

SE 3-4.
L O 5 *Adjustment for Depreciation*

The depreciation expense on office equipment for the month of March is $50. This is the third month that the office equipment, which cost $950, has been owned. Prepare the adjusting journal entry to record depreciation for March and show the balance sheet presentation for office equipment and related accounts after the adjustment.

SE 3-5.
L O 5 *Adjustment for Accrued Wages*

Wages are paid each week on a Saturday for a six-day work week. Wages are currently running $690 per week. Make the adjusting entry required on June 30, assuming July 1 falls on a 5Tuesday.

SE 3-6.
L O 5 *Adjustment for Unearned Revenue*

During the month of August, advance deposits in the amount of $550 were received for services to be performed. By the end of the month, services in the amount of $380 had been performed. Prepare the necessary adjustment for Service Revenues at the end of the month.

SE 3-7.
L O 6 *Preparation of Income Statement from Adjusted Trial Balance*

The adjusted trial balance for Cirtis Company at December 31, 19x1 contains the following accounts and balances: Retained Earnings, $4,300; Dividends, $350; Service Revenue, $2,300; Rent Expense, $400; Wages Expense, $900; Utility Expense, $200; and Telephone Expense, $100. Prepare an income statement in proper form for the month of December.

SE 3-8.
L O 6 *Preparation of Statement of Retained Earnings*

Using the data in SE 3-7, prepare a statement of retained earnings for Cirtis Company.

SE 3-9.
S O 7 *Determination of Cash Flows*

Wages Payable were $590 at the end of May and $920 at the end of June. Wages Expense for June was $2,300. How much in cash payments were made for wages during June?

SE 3-10.
S O 7 *Determination of Cash Flows*

Unearned Revenue was $1,300 at the end of November and $900 at the end of December. Service Revenue was $5,100 for the month of December. How much cash was received for service provided during December?

APPLICATION

Exercises

E 3-1.
L O 2, 3, 4 *Applications of Accounting Concepts Related to Accrual Accounting*

The accountant for Marina Company makes the following assumptions or performs the following activities:

1. In estimating the life of a building, assumes that the business will last indefinitely.
2. Records a sale when the customer is billed.
3. Postpones the recognition of a one-year insurance policy as an expense by initially recording the expenditure as an asset.
4. Recognizes the usefulness of financial statements prepared on a monthly basis even though they are based on estimates.
5. Recognizes, by making an adjusting entry, wages expense that has been incurred but not yet recorded.
6. Prepares an income statement that shows the revenues earned and the expenses incurred during the accounting period.

Tell which of the following concepts of accrual accounting most directly relates to each of the assumptions and actions above: (a) periodicity, (b) going concern, (c) matching rule, (d) revenue recognition, (e) deferral, and (f) accrual.

E 3-2.
L O 5 *Revenue Recognition*

Lifestyle Corporation of Toledo, Ohio publishes a monthly magazine featuring local restaurant reviews and upcoming social, cultural, and sporting events. Subscribers pay for subscriptions either one year or two years in advance. Cash received from subscribers is credited to an account called Magazine Subscriptions Received in Advance. On December 31, 19x3, the end of the company's fiscal year, the balance of this account was $1,000,000. Expiration of subscriptions was as follows:

During 19x3	$200,000
During 19x4	500,000
During 19x5	300,000

Prepare the adjusting journal entry for December 31, 19x3.

E 3-3.
L O 5 *Adjusting Entries for Prepaid Insurance*

An examination of the Prepaid Insurance account shows a balance of $4,112 at the end of an accounting period, before adjustment. Prepare journal entries to record the insurance expense for the period under each of the following independent assumptions:

1. An examination of the insurance policies shows unexpired insurance that cost $1,974 at the end of the period.
2. An examination of the insurance policies shows that insurance that cost $694 has expired during the period.

E 3-4.
L O 5 *Supplies Account: Missing Data*

Each column below represents a supplies account:

	a	b	c	d
Supplies on hand October 1	$396	$651	$294	$?
Supplies purchased during the month	78	?	261	2,892
Supplies consumed during the month	291	1,458	?	2,448
Supplies on hand October 31	?	654	84	1,782

1. Determine the amounts indicated by the question marks in the columns.
2. Make the adjusting entry for Column **a**, assuming supplies purchased are debited to an asset account.

E 3-5.
L O 5 *Adjusting Entry for Accrued Salaries*

Tru Vent has a five-day workweek and pays salaries of $70,000 each Friday.

1. Make the adjusting entry required on July 31, assuming that August 1 falls on a Wednesday.
2. Make the entry to pay the salaries on August 3.

E 3-6.
L O 5 *Revenue and Expense Recognition*

Orlando Company produces computer software that is sold by Bond Systems, Inc. Orlando receives a royalty of 15 percent of sales. Royalties are paid by Bond Systems, Inc. and received by Orlando semiannually on May 1 for sales made July through December of the previous year and on November 1 for sales made January through June of the current year. Royalty expense for Bond Systems, Inc. and royalty income for Orlando in the amount of $12,000 were accrued on December 31, 19x2. Cash in the amounts of $12,000 and $20,000 was paid and received on May 1 and November 1, 19x3, respectively. Software sales during the July to December, 19x3 period totaled $300,000.

1. Calculate the amount of royalty expense for Bond Systems, Inc. and royalty income for Orlando during 19x3.
2. Record the appropriate adjusting entries made by each of the companies on December 31, 19x3.

E 3-7.
L O 5 *Adjusting Entries*

Prepare year-end adjusting entries for each of the following:

1. Office Supplies had a balance of $168 on January 1. Purchases debited to Office Supplies during the year amount to $830. A year-end inventory reveals supplies of $570 on hand.
2. Depreciation of office equipment is estimated to be $4,260 for the year.
3. Property taxes for six months, estimated at $1,750, have accrued but have not been recorded.
4. Unrecorded interest receivable on U.S. government bonds is $1,700.
5. Unearned Revenue has a balance of $1,800. Services for $600 received in advance have now been performed.
6. Services totaling $400 have been performed; the customer has not yet been billed.

E 3-8.
L O 5, 6 *Accounting for Revenue Received in Advance*

Antonia Soria, a lawyer, was paid $72,000 on April 1 to represent a client in real estate negotiations over the next twelve months.

1. Record the entries required in Soria's records on April 1 and at the end of the fiscal year, June 30.
2. How would this transaction be reflected in the income statement and balance sheet on June 30?

E 3-9.

L O 5 *Identification of Accruals*

Northwest Refrigeration Company has the following liabilities at year end:

Notes Payable	$30,000
Accounts Payable	20,000
Contract Revenue Received in Advance	18,000
Wages Payable	4,900
Interest Payable	1,400
Income Taxes Payable	2,500

1. Which of these accounts probably was created at the end of the fiscal year as a result of an accrual? Which probably was adjusted at year end?
2. Which adjustments probably reduced net income? Which probably increased net income?

E 3-10.

L O 6 *Preparation of Financial Statements*

Prepare the monthly income statement, statement of retained earnings, and balance sheet for Rogers Custodial Services, Inc. from the data provided in this adjusted trial balance:

Rogers Custodial Services, Inc.
Adjusted Trial Balance
August 31, 19xx

Cash	$ 4,590	
Accounts Receivable	2,592	
Prepaid Insurance	380	
Prepaid Rent	200	
Cleaning Supplies	152	
Cleaning Equipment	3,200	
Accumulated Depreciation, Cleaning Equipment		$ 320
Truck	7,200	
Accumulated Depreciation, Truck		720
Accounts Payable		420
Wages Payable		80
Unearned Janitorial Revenue		920
Income Taxes Payable		800
Common Stock		4,000
Retained Earnings		11,034
Dividends	2,000	
Janitorial Revenue		14,620
Wages Expense	5,680	
Rent Expense	1,200	
Gas, Oil, and Other Truck Expense	580	
Insurance Expense	380	
Supplies Expense	2,920	
Depreciation Expense, Cleaning Equipment	320	
Depreciation Expense, Truck	720	
Income Taxes Expense	800	
	$32,914	$32,914

E 3-11.

S O 7 *Relationship of Cash to Expenses Paid or Revenues Received*

After adjusting entries had been made, the balance sheets of Hampton Company showed the following asset and liability amounts at the end of 19x3 and 19x4:

	19x3	19x4
Prepaid Insurance	$1,450	$1,200
Wages Payable	1,100	600
Unearned Fees	950	2,100

From the 19x4 income statement, the following amounts were taken:

Insurance Expense	$2,150
Wages Expense	9,250
Fees Earned	3,300

Calculate the amount of cash paid for insurance and wages and received for fees during 19x4.

E 3-12.
S O 7 *Cash Flow Analysis of Deferrals and Accruals*

The following amounts are taken from the balance sheets of Green Bay Corporation:

	December 31	
	19x1	**19x2**
Prepaid Expenses	$ 45,000	$56,000
Accrued Liabilities	103,000	88,000

During 19x2, expenses related to Prepaid Expenses were $103,000, and expenses related to Accrued Liabilities were $197,000. Determine the amount of cash payments related to Prepaid Expenses and to Accrued Liabilities for 19x2.

E 3-13.
S O 7 *Determining Cash Flows*

Horowitz Newspaper Agency, Inc. delivers morning, evening, and Sunday city newspapers to subscribers who live in the suburbs. Customers can pay a yearly subscription fee in advance (at a savings) or pay monthly after delivery of their newspapers. The following data are available for the Subscriptions Receivable and Unearned Subscriptions accounts at the beginning and end of October 19xx:

	October 1	October 31
Subscriptions Receivable	$ 7,600	$ 9,200
Unearned Subscriptions	22,800	19,600

The income statement shows subscription revenue for October of $44,800. Determine the amount of cash received from customers for subscriptions during October. Why is it important for management to make a calculation like this?

E 3-14.
S O 7 *Relationship of Expenses to Cash Paid*

The income statement for Jarvis Company included the following expenses for 19xx:

Rent Expense	$ 5,200
Interest Expense	7,800
Salaries Expense	83,000

Listed below are the related balance sheet account balances at year end for last year and this year:

	Last Year	This Year
Prepaid Rent	—	$ 900
Interest Payable	$1,200	—
Salaries Payable	5,000	9,600

1. Compute the cash paid for rent during the year.
2. Compute the cash paid for interest during the year.
3. Compute the cash paid for salaries during the year.

Problem Set A

3A-1.
L O 5 *Preparation of Adjusting Entries*

On May 31, the end of the current fiscal year, the following information was available to help Costa Corporation's accountants make adjusting entries:

a. The Supplies account showed a beginning balance of $4,348. Purchases during the year were $9,052. The end-of-year inventory revealed supplies on hand that cost $2,794.
b. The Prepaid Insurance account showed the following on May 31:

Beginning Balance	$ 7,160
February 1	8,400
April 1	14,544

The beginning balance represents the portion of a one-year policy that remained unexpired at the beginning of the current fiscal year. The February 1 entry represents a new one-year policy, and the April 1 entry represents additional coverage in the form of a three-year policy.

c. The table below contains the cost and annual depreciation for buildings and equipment, all of which were purchased before the current year.

Account	Cost	Annual Depreciation
Buildings	$572,000	$29,000
Equipment	748,000	70,800

d. On March 1, the company completed negotiations with a client and accepted payment of $33,600, which represented one year's services paid in advance. The $33,600 was credited to Unearned Service Revenue.

e. The company calculated that as of May 31, it had earned $8,000 on a $22,000 contract that would be completed and billed in September.

f. Among the liabilities of the company is a note payable in the amount of $600,000. On May 31, the accrued interest on this note amounted to $30,000.

g. On Saturday, June 2, the company, which is on a six-day workweek, will pay its regular salaried employees $24,600.

h. On May 29, the company completed negotiations and signed a contract to provide services to a new client at an annual rate of $35,000.

i. Management estimates income taxes for the year to be $50,000.

REQUIRED

Prepare adjusting entries for each item listed above.

3A-2.

L O 5 *Determining Adjusting Entries, Posting to T Accounts, and Preparing Adjusted Trial Balance*

Here is the trial balance for Crown Advisory Services, Inc. on July 31:

Crown Advisory Services, Inc.
Trial Balance
July 31, 19xx

Cash	$ 8,250	
Accounts Receivable	4,125	
Office Supplies	1,331	
Prepaid Rent	660	
Office Equipment	4,620	
Accumulated Depreciation, Office Equipment		$ 770
Accounts Payable		2,970
Notes Payable		5,500
Unearned Fees		1,485
Common Stock		5,000
Retained Earnings		7,001
Dividends	11,000	
Fees Revenue		36,300
Salaries Expense	24,700	
Rent Expense	2,200	
Utility Expense	2,140	
	$59,026	$59,026

The following information is also available:

a. Ending inventory of office supplies, $132.
b. Prepaid rent expired, $220.
c. Depreciation of office equipment for the period, $330.
d. Accrued interest expense at the end of the period, $275.
e. Accrued salaries at the end of the month, $165.

f. Fees still unearned at the end of the period, $583.

g. Fees earned but unrecorded, $1,100.

h. Estimated federal income taxes, $2,000.

REQUIRED

1. Open T accounts for the accounts in the trial balance plus the following: Fees Receivable; Interest Payable; Salaries Payable; Income Taxes Payable; Office Supplies Expense; Depreciation Expense, Office Equipment; Interest Expense; and Income Taxes Expense. Enter the balances.

2. Determine the adjusting entries and post them directly to the T accounts.

3. Prepare an adjusted trial balance.

3A-3.

L O 5, 6 *Determining Adjusting Entries and Tracing Their Effects to Financial Statements*

The Foremost Janitorial Service, Inc. is owned by Ron Hudson. After six months of operations, the September 30, 19xx trial balance for the company was prepared.

Foremost Janitorial Service, Inc.
Trial Balance
September 30, 19xx

Cash	$ 4,524	
Accounts Receivable	3,828	
Prepaid Insurance	760	
Prepaid Rent	1,400	
Cleaning Supplies	2,792	
Cleaning Equipment	3,480	
Truck	7,200	
Accounts Payable		$ 340
Unearned Janitorial Fees		960
Common Stock		14,190
Dividends	1,000	
Janitorial Fees		14,974
Wages Expense	4,800	
Gas, Oil, and Other Truck Expenses	680	
	$30,464	$30,464

The balance of the Common Stock account reflects investments made by Ron Hudson. The following information is also available:

a. Cleaning supplies of $234 are on hand.

b. Prepaid Insurance represents the cost of a one-year policy purchased on April 1.

c. Prepaid Rent represents a $200 payment made on April 1 toward the last month's rent of a three-year lease plus $200 rent per month for each of the past six months.

d. The cleaning equipment and trucks are depreciated at the rate of 20 percent per year (10 percent for each six-month period).

e. The unearned revenue represents a six-month payment in advance made by a customer on August 1.

f. During the last week of September, Ron completed the first stage of work on a project that will not be billed until the contract is completed. The price of this stage is $800.

g. On Saturday, October 3, Ron will owe his employees $1,080 for one week's work (six-day workweek).

h. Federal income taxes for the six months are estimated to be $1,500.

REQUIRED

1. Open T accounts for the accounts in the trial balance plus the following: Fees Receivable; Accumulated Depreciation, Cleaning Equipment; Accumulated Depreciation, Truck; Wages Payable; Income Taxes Payable; Rent Expense; Insurance Expense; Cleaning Supplies Expense; Depreciation Expense, Cleaning Equipment; Depreciation Expense, Truck; and Income Taxes Expense.

2. Determine the adjusting entries and post them directly to the T accounts.
3. Prepare an adjusted trial balance, an income statement, a statement of retained earnings, and a balance sheet.

3A-4.

L O 5, 6 *Determining Adjusting Entries and Tracing Their Effects to Financial Statements*

At the end of the first three months of operations, this was the trial balance of the A-1 Answering Service, Inc.:

A-1 Answering Service, Inc.
Trial Balance
October 31, 19x4

Cash (111)	$ 5,524	
Accounts Receivable (112)	8,472	
Office Supplies (115)	1,806	
Prepaid Rent (116)	1,600	
Prepaid Insurance (117)	1,440	
Office Equipment (141)	4,600	
Communications Equipment (143)	4,800	
Accounts Payable (211)		$ 5,346
Unearned Answering Service Revenue (213)		1,776
Common Stock (311)		11,866
Dividends (313)	4,260	
Answering Service Revenue (411)		18,004
Wages Expense (511)	3,800	
Office Cleaning Expense (513)	690	
	$36,992	$36,992

Terry Mei, the owner of A-1, hired an accountant to prepare financial statements in order to determine how well the company was doing after three months. On examining the records, the accountant found the following items of interest:

a. An inventory of office supplies reveals supplies on hand of $266.
b. The Prepaid Rent account includes the rent for the first three months plus the amount for the last month's rent.
c. Prepaid Insurance reflects a one-year policy purchased on August 4.
d. Depreciation is estimated at $204 on the office equipment and $212 on the communications equipment for the first three months.
e. The balance of the Unearned Answering Service Revenue account represents a twelve-month service contract paid in advance on September 1.
f. On October 31, accrued wages totaled $160.
g. Federal income taxes for the period are estimated to be $3,000.

The balance of the Common Stock account represents investments by Terry Mei.

REQUIRED

1. Record the adjusting entries in the general journal (Pages 12 and 13).
2. Open ledger accounts for the accounts in the trial balance plus the following: Accumulated Depreciation, Office Equipment (142); Accumulated Depreciation, Communications Equipment (144); Wages Payable (212); Income Taxes Payable (214); Rent Expense (512); Insurance Expense (514); Office Supplies Expense (515); Depreciation Expense, Office Equipment (516); Depreciation Expense, Communications Equipment (517); and Income Taxes Expense (520). Record the balances shown in the trial balance.
3. Post the adjusting entries from the general journal to the ledger accounts, showing the correct references.
4. Prepare an adjusted trial balance.
5. Prepare an income statement, a statement of retained earnings, and a balance sheet.
6. Give examples to show how the techniques of accrual accounting affect A-1 Inc.'s income statement.

3A-5.

L O 5, 6 *Determining Adjusting Entries and Tracing Their Effects to Financial Statements*

Here is the trial balance for Century Dance School, Inc. at the end of its current fiscal year:

Century Dance School, Inc.
Trial Balance
July 31, 19x4

Cash (111)	$ 5,084	
Accounts Receivable (112)	3,551	
Supplies (115)	510	
Prepaid Rent (116)	1,200	
Prepaid Insurance (117)	1,080	
Equipment (141)	18,300	
Accumulated Depreciation, Equipment (142)		$ 1,200
Accounts Payable (211)		1,140
Unearned Dance Fees (213)		2,700
Common Stock (311)		4,500
Retained Earnings (312)		3,000
Dividends (313)	26,000	
Dance Fees (411)		62,985
Wages Expense (511)	9,600	
Rent Expense (512)	6,600	
Utility Expense (515)	3,600	
	$75,525	$75,525

Loretta Harper, the owner, made no investments in the business during the year. The following information is available to help in the preparation of adjusting entries:

a. An inventory of supplies reveals $276 still on hand.
b. Prepaid Rent reflects the rent for July plus the rent for the last month of the lease.
c. Prepaid Insurance consists of a two-year policy purchased on February 1, 19x4.
d. Depreciation on equipment is estimated at $2,400.
e. Accrued wages are $195 on July 31.
f. Two-thirds of the unearned dance fees had been earned by July 31.
g. Management estimates federal income taxes for the year to be $9,000.

REQUIRED

1. Record the adjusting entries in the general journal (Pages 53 and 54).
2. Open ledger accounts for the accounts in the trial balance plus the following: Wages Payable (212); Income Taxes Payable (214); Supplies Expense (513); Insurance Expense (514); Depreciation Expense, Equipment (516); and Income Taxes Expense (520). Record the balances shown in the trial balance.
3. Post the adjusting entries from the general journal to the ledger accounts, showing the correct references.
4. Prepare an adjusted trial balance, an income statement, a statement of retained earnings, and a balance sheet.

Problem Set B

3B-1.

L O 5 *Preparation of Adjusting Entries*

On June 30, the end of the current fiscal year, the following information was available to aid the Sterling Corporation accountants in making adjusting entries:

a. Among the liabilities of the company is a mortgage payable in the amount of $240,000. On June 30, the accrued interest on this mortgage amounted to $12,000.
b. On Friday, July 2, the company, which is on a five-day workweek and pays employees weekly, will pay its regular salaried employees $19,200.
c. On June 29, the company completed negotiations and signed a contract to provide services to a new client at an annual rate of $3,600.

d. The Supplies account showed a beginning balance of $1,615 and purchases during the year of $3,766. The end-of-year inventory revealed supplies on hand that cost $1,186.

e. The Prepaid Insurance account showed the following entries on June 30:

Beginning Balance	$1,530
January 1	2,900
May 1	3,366

The beginning balance represents the portion of a one-year policy that remained unexpired at the beginning of the current fiscal year. The January 1 entry represents a new one-year policy, and the May 1 entry represents additional coverage in the form of a three-year policy.

f. The table below contains the cost and annual depreciation for buildings and equipment, all of which were purchased before the current year:

Account	Cost	Annual Depreciation
Buildings	$185,000	$ 7,300
Equipment	218,000	21,800

g. On June 1, the company completed negotiations with another client and accepted a payment of $21,000, representing one year's services paid in advance. The $21,000 was credited to Service Fees Collected in Advance.

h. The company calculated that as of June 30 it had earned $3,500 on a $7,500 contract that would be completed and billed in August.

i. Federal income taxes for the year are estimated to be $5,000.

REQUIRED

Prepare adjusting entries for each item listed above.

3B-2.

L O 5 *Determining Adjusting Entries, Posting to T Accounts, and Preparing Adjusted Trial Balance*

This is the trial balance for the Executive Advisory Corporation on March 31, 19x3:

Executive Advisory Corporation
Trial Balance
March 31, 19x3

Cash	$ 25,572	
Accounts Receivable	49,680	
Office Supplies	1,982	
Prepaid Rent	2,800	
Office Equipment	13,400	
Accumulated Depreciation, Office Equipment		$ 3,200
Accounts Payable		3,640
Notes Payable		20,000
Unearned Fees		5,720
Common Stock		20,000
Retained Earnings		38,774
Dividends	30,000	
Fees Revenue		117,000
Salaries Expense	66,000	
Utility Expense	3,500	
Rent Expense	15,400	
	$208,334	$208,334

The following information is also available:

a. Ending inventory of office supplies, $172.
b. Prepaid rent expired, $1,400.
c. Depreciation of office equipment for the period, $1,200.
d. Interest accrued on the note payable, $1,200.

e. Salaries accrued at the end of the period, $400.
f. Fees still unearned at the end of the period, $2,820.
g. Fees earned but not billed, $1,200.
h. Estimated federal income taxes for the year, $6,000.

REQUIRED

1. Open T accounts for the accounts in the trial balance plus the following: Fees Receivable; Interest Payable; Salaries Payable; Income Taxes Payable; Office Supplies Expense; Depreciation Expense, Office Equipment; Interest Expense; and Income Taxes Expense. Enter the balances.
2. Determine the adjusting entries and post them directly to the T accounts.
3. Prepare an adjusted trial balance.

3B-3.

L O 5, 6 *Determining Adjusting Entries and Tracing Their Effects to Financial Statements*

Having graduated from college with a degree in accounting, Joyce Ozaki opened a small tax preparation service. At the end of its second year of operations, the Ozaki Tax Service, Inc. has the following trial balance:

Ozaki Tax Service, Inc.
Trial Balance
December 31, 19xx

Cash	$ 2,268	
Accounts Receivable	1,031	
Prepaid Insurance	240	
Office Supplies	782	
Office Equipment	4,100	
Accumulated Depreciation, Office Equipment		$ 410
Copier	3,000	
Accumulated Depreciation, Copier		360
Accounts Payable		635
Unearned Tax Fees		219
Common Stock		2,000
Retained Earnings		3,439
Dividends	6,000	
Fees Revenue		21,926
Office Salaries Expense	8,300	
Advertising Expense	650	
Rent Expense	2,400	
Telephone Expense	218	
	$28,989	$28,989

Joyce Ozaki made no investments in her business during the year. The following information was also available:

a. Supplies on hand, December 31, 19xx, were $227.
b. Insurance still unexpired amounted to $120.
c. Estimated depreciation of office equipment was $410.
d. Estimated depreciation of the copier was $360.
e. The telephone expense for December was $19. This bill has been received but not recorded.
f. The services for all unearned tax fees had been performed by the end of the year.
g. Federal income taxes for the year were estimated to be $1,800.

REQUIRED

1. Open T accounts for the accounts in the trial balance plus the following: Income Taxes Payable; Insurance Expense; Office Supplies Expense; Depreciation Expense, Office Equipment; Depreciation Expense, Copier; and Income Taxes Expense. Record the balances as shown in the trial balance.
2. Determine the adjusting entries and post them directly to the T accounts.

3. Prepare an adjusted trial balance, an income statement, a statement of retained earnings, and a balance sheet.

3B-4.

L O 5, 6 *Determining Adjusting Entries and Tracing Their Effects to Financial Statements*

At the end of its fiscal year, the trial balance for North Star Dry Cleaners, Inc. appears as shown below.

North Star Dry Cleaners, Inc.
Trial Balance
June 30, 19x3

Cash (111)	$ 27,682	
Accounts Receivable (112)	39,741	
Prepaid Insurance (115)	5,100	
Cleaning Supplies (116)	11,061	
Land (141)	27,000	
Building (142)	243,000	
Accumulated Depreciation, Building (143)		$ 60,600
Delivery Trucks (144)	34,500	
Accumulated Depreciation, Delivery Trucks (145)		7,800
Accounts Payable (212)		30,600
Unearned Dry Cleaning Revenue (216)		2,400
Mortgage Payable (221)		180,000
Common Stock (311)		60,000
Retained Earnings (312)		24,840
Dividends (313)	20,000	
Dry Cleaning Revenue (411)		180,501
Laundry Revenue (412)		55,950
Plant Wages Expense (511)	97,680	
Sales and Delivery Wages Expense (512)	54,315	
Cleaning Equipment Rent Expense (513)	9,000	
Delivery Trucks Expense (514)	6,561	
Interest Expense (519)	16,500	
Other Expenses (520)	10,551	
	$602,691	$602,691

Jason Graves, the owner, made no investments during the year. The following information is also available:

a. A study of insurance policies shows that $1,020 is unexpired at the end of the year.
b. An inventory of cleaning supplies shows $1,866 on hand.
c. Estimated depreciation for the year is $12,900 on the building and $6,300 on the delivery trucks.
d. Accrued interest on the mortgage payable amounts to $1,500.
e. On May 1, the company signed a contract effective immediately with Kane County Park District to dry-clean, for a fixed monthly charge of $600, the uniforms used by park district officers. The park district paid for four months' service in advance.
f. Unrecorded plant wages total $2,946.
g. Sales and delivery wages are paid on Saturday. The weekly payroll is $1,440. June 30 falls on a Thursday, and the company has a six-day workweek.
h. Federal income taxes for the period are estimated to be $1,000.

REQUIRED

1. Determine adjusting entries and enter them in the general journal (Pages 42 and 43).
2. Open ledger accounts for the accounts in the trial balance plus the following: Wages Payable (213); Interest Payable (214); Income Taxes Payable (215); Insurance Expense (515); Cleaning Supplies Expense (516); Depreciation Expense, Building

(517); Depreciation Expense, Delivery Trucks (518); and Income Taxes Expense (521). Record the balances shown in the trial balance.

3. Post the adjusting entries to the ledger accounts, showing the correct references.
4. Prepare an adjusted trial balance.
5. Prepare an income statement, a statement of retained earnings, and a balance sheet for the year ended June 30, 19x3.
6. Give examples of how the techniques of accrual accounting affect the income statement.

3B-5.

L O 5, 6 *Determining Adjusting Entries and Tracing Their Effects to Financial Statements*

Westland Limo Service, Inc. was organized on January 1, 19x2 to provide limousine service between the airport and various suburban locations. It has just completed its second year of business. Its trial balance appears below.

Westland Limo Service, Inc.
Trial Balance
December 31, 19x3

Cash (111)	$ 19,624	
Accounts Receivable (112)	28,454	
Prepaid Rent (117)	24,000	
Prepaid Insurance (118)	9,800	
Prepaid Maintenance (119)	24,000	
Spare Parts (141)	22,620	
Limousines (142)	400,000	
Accumulated Depreciation, Limousines (143)		$ 50,000
Notes Payable (211)		90,000
Unearned Passenger Service Revenue (212)		60,000
Common Stock (311)		60,000
Retained Earnings (312)		96,422
Dividends (313)	40,000	
Passenger Service Revenue (411)		856,996
Gas and Oil Expense (511)	178,600	
Salaries Expense (512)	412,720	
Advertising Expense (513)	53,600	
	$1,213,418	$1,213,418

John Cummings, the owner, made no investments during the year. The following information is also available:

a. To obtain space at the airport, Westland paid two years' rent in advance when it began business.
b. An examination of the firm's insurance policies reveals that $5,600 expired during the year.
c. To provide regular maintenance for the vehicles, a deposit of $24,000 was made with a local garage. An examination of maintenance invoices reveals that there are $21,888 in charges against the deposit.
d. An inventory of spare parts shows $3,804 on hand.
e. All of Westland's limousines are depreciated at the rate of 12.5 percent a year. No limousines were purchased during the year.
f. A payment of $21,000 for one year's interest on notes payable is now due.
g. Unearned Passenger Service Revenue on December 31 includes $35,630 in tickets that employers purchased for their executives but that have not been redeemed.
h. Federal income taxes for the period are estimated to be $24,000.

REQUIRED

1. Record the adjusting entries in the general journal (Pages 14 and 15).
2. Open ledger accounts for the accounts in the trial balance plus the following: Interest Payable (213); Income Taxes Payable (214); Rent Expense (514); Insurance

Expense (515); Spare Parts Expense (516); Depreciation Expense, Limousines (517); Maintenance Expense (518); Interest Expense (519); and Income Taxes Expense (520). Record the balances shown in the trial balance.

3. Post the adjusting entries from the general journal to the ledger accounts, showing the correct references.

4. Prepare an adjusted trial balance, an income statement, a statement of retained earnings, and a balance sheet.

CRITICAL THINKING AND COMMUNICATION

Conceptual Mini-Cases

CMC 3-1.
L O 2, 3, 4   *Importance of Adjustments*

Never Flake Company, which operated in the northeastern part of the United States, provided a rust prevention coating for the underside of new automobiles. The company advertised widely and offered its services through new car dealers. When a dealer sold a new car, the dealer attempted to sell the rust prevention coating as an option. The protective coating was supposed to make cars last longer in the severe northeastern winters. A key selling point was Never Flake's warranty, which stated that it would repair any damage due to rust at no charge as long as the buyer owned the car.

During the 1970s and most of the 1980s, Never Flake was very successful in generating enough cash to continue operations. But in 1988 the company suddenly declared bankruptcy. Company officials said that the firm had only $5.5 million in assets against liabilities of $32.9 million. Most of the liabilities represented potential claims under the company's lifetime warranty. It seemed that owners were keeping their cars longer in the 1980s than they had in the 1970s. Therefore, more damage was being attributed to rust. Discuss what accounting decisions could have helped Never Flake to survive under these circumstances.

CMC 3-2.
L O 3, 4   *Application of Accrual Accounting*

The Lyric Opera of Chicago is one of the largest and best managed opera companies in the United States. Managing opera productions requires advance planning, including the development of scenery, costumes, and stage properties; the sale of tickets; and the collection of contributions. To measure how well the company is operating in any given year, accrual accounting must be applied to these and other transactions. At year end, April 30, 1992, Lyric Opera of Chicago's balance sheet showed Deferred Production and Other Costs of $1,147,783, Deferred Revenue from Sales of Tickets of $13,261,773, and Deferred Revenue from Contributions of $4,969,866. Be prepared to discuss what accounting policies and adjusting entries are applicable to these accounts. Why are they important to Lyric Opera's management?

CMC 3-3.
L O 2, 3   *Cash Versus Accrual Accounting*

In 1979, Jane Byrne won the mayoral election in the *City of Chicago* partly on the basis of her charge that Michael Bilandic, the former mayor, was responsible for the budget deficit. Taking office in 1980, she hired a major international accounting firm, Peat, Marwick, Mitchell & Co. (now known as KPMG Peat Marwick), to straighten things out. This excerpt appeared in an article from a leading Chicago business publication:

> [A riddle]
> Q: When is a budget deficit not a deficit?
> A: When it is a surplus, of course.

Chicago Mayor Jane Byrne was once again caught with egg on her face last week as she and her financial advisers tried to defend that riddle. On one hand, Comptroller Daniel J. Grim [a Byrne appointee], explaining $75 million in assets the mayor [Byrne] hopes to hold in reserve in the 1981 Chicago city budget, testified in hearings that the city had actually ended 1979 with a $6 million surplus, not the much-reported deficit. He said further that the modest surplus grew to $54 million as a result of tax-enrichment supplements to the 1979 balance sheet.

On the other hand, the mayor stuck by the same guns she used last year on her predecessor. The city had ended 1979, under the Michael Bilandic Administration, not merely without a surplus, but with a deficit. The apparent discrepancy can be explained.[3]

Like most U.S. cities, Chicago operates under a modified accrual accounting basis. This is a combination of the straight cash basis and the accrual basis. The modified accrual basis differs from the accrual method in that an account receivable is recorded only when it is collected in the next accounting period. The collection of Chicago's parking tax, which is assessed on all city parking lots and garages, is an example:

> The tax is assessed and collected on a quarterly basis but the city doesn't collect the amount due for the last quarter of 1980 until the first quarter of 1981. Under ideal accrual methods, the parking revenues should be recorded in the 1980 financial statement. Under a cash approach, the revenues would be recorded in the 1981 budget. What the city did before was to record the money whenever it was advantageous politically. That, combined with the infamous revolving funds, allowed the city to hide the fact it was running large deficits under [former] Mayor Bilandic. That also means that no one really knew where the city stood.[4]

The auditors are now reallocating the parking revenues to the 1981 budget but are accruing other revenues by shifting the period of collection from a year in the past. Overall, more revenues were moved into earlier fiscal years than into later years, inflating those budgets. Thus, the 1979 deficit is a surplus. The article concluded:

> The upshot is that both Mayor Byrne and Mr. Grim [the comptroller] were correct. There was a deficit in the 1979 corporate or checkbook fund, but because of corrections taking place now, a surplus exists.[5]

REQUIRED

1. Do you agree with the way the auditors handled parking revenues? Support your answer by explaining which method of accounting you think a city should use.
2. "Systematically applied accounting principles will allow all to know exactly where the city stands." Comment on this statement, made in another part of the article quoted above.

Ethics Mini-Case

EMC 3-1.
L O 2, 3, 4
Importance of Adjustments

Central Appliance Service Co., Inc. has achieved fast growth in the St. Louis area by selling service contracts on large appliances, such as washers, dryers, and refrigerators. For a fee, Central Appliance agrees to provide all parts and labor on an appliance after the regular warranty runs out. For example, by paying a fee of $200, a person who buys a dishwasher can add two years (years 2 and 3) to the regular one-year (year 1) warranty on the appliance. In 1991, the company sold service contracts in the amount of $1.8 million, all of which applied to future years. Management wanted all the sales recorded as revenues in 1991, contending that the amount of the contracts could be determined and the cash had been received. Discuss whether or not you agree with this logic. How would you record these cash receipts? What assumptions do you think should be made? Would you consider it unethical to follow management's recommendation? Who might be hurt or helped by this action?

Decision-Making Case

DMC 3-1.
L O 1, 5
Adjusting Entries and Dividend Policy

Karen Jamison, the owner of a newsletter for managers of hotels and restaurants, has prepared condensed amounts from the financial statements for 19x3, as shown at the top of the next page:

---

3. Reprinted with permission from the December 8, 1980 issue of *Crain's Chicago Business.* Copyright © 1980 by Crain Communications, Inc.
4. Ibid.
5. Ibid.

Revenues	$346,000
Expenses	282,000
Net Income	$ 64,000
Total Assets	$172,000
Liabilities	$ 48,000
Stockholders' Equity	124,000
Total Liabilities and Stockholders' Equity	$172,000

Given these figures, Jamison is planning a cash dividend of $50,000. However, Jamison's accountant has found that the following items were overlooked:

a. Although the balance of the Printing Supplies account is $32,000, only $14,000 in supplies is on hand at the end of the year.
b. Depreciation of $20,000 on equipment has not been recorded.
c. Wages in the amount of $9,400 have been earned by employees but not recognized in the accounts.
d. No provision has been made for estimated income taxes payable of $10,800.
e. A liability account called Unearned Subscriptions has a balance of $16,200, although it is determined that one-third of these subscriptions have been mailed to subscribers.

REQUIRED

1. Prepare the necessary adjusting entries.
2. Recast the condensed financial statement figures after making the necessary adjustments.
3. Discuss the performance of Jamison's business after the adjustments have been made. **Hint:** Compare net income to revenues and total assets before and after the adjustments. Do you think that paying the dividend is advisable?

Basic Research Activity

RA 3-1.
L O 4 *Service Businesses and Adjusting Entries*

Consult the Yellow Pages of your local telephone directory. Find the names of five different kinds of service businesses. List the types of adjusting entries you think each business regularly makes. Be prepared to discuss any adjustments you think may be unique to each business.

FINANCIAL REPORTING AND ANALYSIS

Interpretation Cases from Business

ICB 3-1.
L O 2, 5 *Analysis of an Asset Account*

Orion Pictures Corporation is engaged in the financing, production, and distribution of theatrical motion pictures and television programming. In Orion's 1993 annual report, the balance sheet contains an asset called Film Inventories. Film Inventories, which consist of the cost associated with producing films less the amount expensed, were $498,890,000 in 1993. The statement of cash flows reveals that the amount of film inventories expensed (amortized) during 1993 was $161,173,000 and the amount spent for new film productions was only $7,348,000 because of the company's financial problems.[6]

REQUIRED

1. What is the nature of the asset Film Inventories?
2. Prepare an entry to record the amount spent on new film production during 1993 (assume all expenditures are paid for in cash).
3. Prepare the adjusting entry that would be made to record the expense for film productions in 1993.
4. Can you suggest a method by which Orion Pictures Corporation might have determined the expense in **3** in accordance with the matching rule?

6. Orion Pictures Corporation, *Annual Report*, 1993.

ICB 3-2.
L O 1, 2, 5
*Analysis of
Unearned Revenue*

Sperry & Hutchinson Co., Inc. is known as "The Green Stamp Company" because its principal business is selling S & H Green Stamps to merchants, who give them to customers, who, in turn, may redeem them for merchandise. When S & H sells green stamps, it incurs a liability to redeem the stamps. It makes a profit to the extent that people do not redeem the stamps. In the past, S & H has assumed that 95 percent of all stamps will be redeemed. Thus, a sale of $1,000 worth of stamps would be recorded as follows:

Cash	1,000	
Liability to Redeem Stamps		950
Stamp Revenue		50

Since it may be years before some stamps are redeemed, the company keeps the liability on its balance sheet indefinitely. An article in *Forbes*, a leading business biweekly magazine, commented on S & H's situation as follows:

> The company [S & H] is sitting on a mountain of money held in reserve to redeem stamps already issued but not yet cashed in. How many of these stamps will ultimately be redeemed? Nobody knows for sure. But Sperry [S & H] has made some assumptions in drawing up its financial statements, and at last count it had stashed away no less than $308 million to match unredeemed stamps. That's more than last year's stamp sales. It's one-third more than the company's total [stockholders'] equity of $231 million. What's more, to the extent that the company has over-estimated the need for that liability—setting aside cash for Green Stamps that have been thrown into the garbage—some of the cash is clearly equity in all but name.[7]

The Liability to Redeem Stamps account eventually became so large that S & H began setting aside only 90 percent (instead of 95 percent) of stamp sales for redemption. The immediate effect of this change was to boost profits. The reason for this effect is, as stated in *Forbes*, "the extra 5 percent of stamps now assumed to be lost forever goes straight through as pure profit."

REQUIRED

1. Assume that S & H has an asset account called Merchandise that represents the goods that can be purchased. What entry would be made if $700 worth of stamps were redeemed for merchandise?
2. What does *Forbes* mean when it says that "some of the cash is clearly equity in all but name"? Is the word "cash" used properly? Show that you know what *Forbes* means by presenting the adjusting entry that would be made if S & H decided to reduce the liability for redemption of stamps.
3. Explain *Forbes*'s comment that the extra 5 percent "goes straight through as pure profit."

International Company Case

ICC 3-1.
L O 2, 3, 4
*Account
Identification and
Accrual Accounting*

Takashimaya Company, Limited is Japan's largest department store chain. On Takashimaya's balance sheet is an account called Gift Certificates, which contains ¥26,156 million ($176 million). Is this account an asset or a liability? What transaction gives rise to the account? How is this account an example of the application of accrual accounting? Explain the conceptual issues that must be resolved for an adjusting entry to be valid.

Toys "R" Us Case

TC 3-1.
L O 4
*Analysis of Balance
Sheet and Adjusting
Entries*

Refer to the balance sheet in the appendix on Toys "R" Us. Examine the accounts listed in the current assets, property and equipment, and current liabilities sections. Which accounts are most likely to have had year-end adjusting entries? Tell the nature of the adjusting entries. For more information about the property and equipment section, refer to the notes to the consolidated financial statements.

---

7. *Forbes*, October 12, 1981, page 73. Reprinted by permission of *Forbes* magazine. © Forbes Inc., 1981.

Completing the Accounting Cycle

1. State all the steps in the accounting cycle.

2. Explain the purposes of closing entries.

3. Prepare the required closing entries.

4. Prepare the post-closing trial balance.

5. Prepare reversing entries as appropriate.

6. Prepare a work sheet.

7. Use a work sheet for three different purposes.

Ecolab, Inc.

DECISION POINT

Ecolab, Inc. provides restaurants and hotels, food service and health care facilities, dairy plants and farms, food and beverage processors, and businesses around the world with premium products and services for cleaning, sanitizing, and maintenance. As a company whose shares are traded on the New York Stock Exchange, Ecolab is required to prepare both annual and quarterly financial statements for its stockholders. Whether required by law or not, the preparation of *interim* financial statements every quarter, or even every month, is a good idea for all businesses because they provide an ongoing view of financial performance. What costs and time are involved in preparing interim financial statements?

The preparation of interim financial statements throughout the year requires more effort than the preparation of a single set of financial statements for the entire year. Each time the financial statements are prepared, adjusting entries must be determined, prepared, and recorded. In addition, the ledger accounts must be prepared to begin the next accounting period. These procedures are time-consuming and costly. The advantages of preparing interim financial statements, even when they are not required, usually outweigh the costs, however, because these statements give management timely information that can help it make decisions that will improve operations. This chapter explains the procedures that are carried out to prepare financial statements at the end of an accounting period, whether that period is a month, a quarter, or a year.

OVERVIEW OF THE ACCOUNTING CYCLE

OBJECTIVE

1 *State all the steps in the accounting cycle*

The main focus of previous chapters was on accounting measurement. This chapter emphasizes the process of accounting, or the accounting cycle. The purpose of the accounting cycle is to measure business activities in the form of transactions and to transform these transactions into financial statements that will communicate useful information to decision makers. The steps in the accounting cycle, as illustrated in Figure 4-1, are:

1. *Analyze* business transactions from source documents.
2. *Record* the entries in the journal.
3. *Post* the entries to the ledger and prepare a trial balance.
4. *Adjust* the accounts and prepare an adjusted trial balance.

Figure 4-1. Overview of the Accounting Cycle

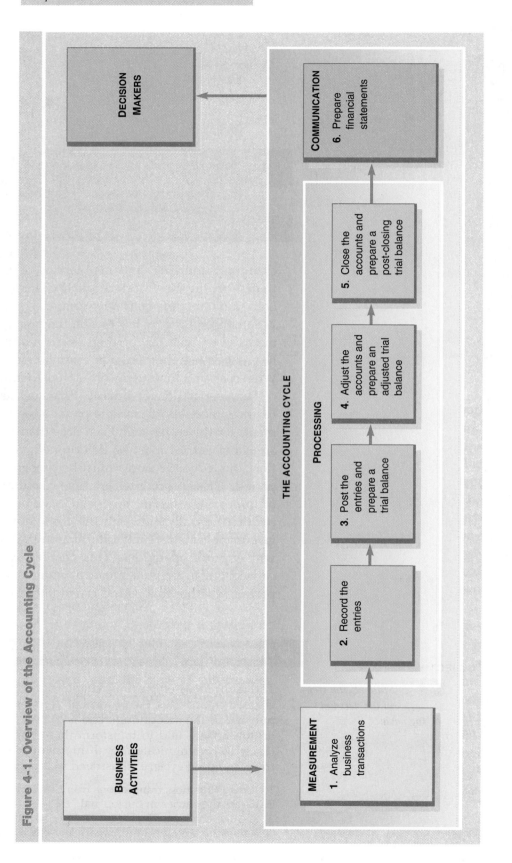

5. *Close* the accounts and prepare a post-closing trial balance.
6. *Prepare* financial statements.

At key points during the accounting cycle, trial balances are prepared to ensure that the ledger remains in balance. You are already familiar with the first four steps, including the initial trial balance and the adjusted trial balance, which were introduced in the chapters on measuring business transactions and measuring business income. Step **6** was also covered in the chapter on measuring business income, when financial statements were prepared from the adjusted trial balance. This chapter concentrates on step **5**. It also covers reversing entries, an optional first step of the next accounting period, and the work sheet, a tool accountants use to facilitate the adjusting, closing, and preparation steps in the accounting cycle.

BUSINESS BULLETIN: BUSINESS PRACTICE

Performing routine accounting functions for other companies has become big business. This practice of managing a customer's data processing operations for a fixed fee is called *outsourcing.* By leaving the data processing to an outside company, management can devote its attention to income-earning activities. Electronic Data Systems, Inc., founded by H. Ross Perot in 1962 and the source of his fortune, is the largest company in this business (it is now owned by General Motors). EDS had revenues exceeding $8 billion in 1993 and is very profitable. ═══

CLOSING ENTRIES

OBJECTIVE

2 *Explain the purposes of closing entries*

Closing entries are journal entries made at the end of an accounting period. They accomplish two purposes. First, closing entries set the stage for the next accounting period by clearing revenue, expense, and dividend accounts of their balances. Remember that the income statement reports net income (or loss) for a single accounting period and shows revenues and expenses for that period only. For the income statement to present the activity of a single accounting period, each new period must begin with zero balances in the revenue and expense accounts. These zero balances are obtained by using closing entries to clear the balances in the revenue and expense accounts at the end of each accounting period. The Dividends account is closed in a similar manner.

Second, closing entries summarize a period's revenues and expenses. This is done by transferring the balances of revenues and expenses to the Income Summary account. This temporary account, which appears in the chart of accounts between the Dividends account and the first revenue account, provides a place to summarize all revenues and expenses. It is used only in the closing process and never appears in the financial statements.

The balance of Income Summary equals the net income or loss reported on the income statement. The net income or loss is then transferred to the Retained Earnings account. This is done because even though revenues and

Chapter 4

expenses are recorded in revenue and expense accounts, they actually represent increases and decreases in stockholders' equity. Closing entries transfer the net effect of increases (revenues) and decreases (expenses) to stockholders' equity. An overview of the closing process is illustrated in Figure 4-2.

As explained in the chapter on measuring business income, revenue and expense accounts are temporary, or nominal, accounts because they begin each period with a zero balance, accumulate a balance during the period, and are then cleared by means of closing entries. On the other hand, balance sheet accounts are considered to be permanent accounts because they carry their end-of-period balances into the next accounting period.

OBJECTIVE

3 *Prepare the required closing entries*

REQUIRED CLOSING ENTRIES

There are four important steps in closing the accounts:

1. Closing the credit balances from income statement accounts to the Income Summary account
2. Closing the debit balances from income statement accounts to the Income Summary account
3. Closing the Income Summary account balance to the Retained Earnings account
4. Closing the Dividends account balance to the Retained Earnings account

Each step is accomplished by a closing entry. The data for recording the closing entries are found in the adjusted trial balance. Exhibit 4-1 shows the relationships of the four kinds of entries to the adjusted trial balance.

Step 1: Closing the Credit Balances from Income Statement Accounts to the Income Summary Account   On the credit side of the adjusted trial balance in Exhibit 4-1, two revenue accounts show balances: Advertising Fees Earned and Art Fees Earned. To close these two accounts, a

Figure 4-2. Overview of the Closing Process

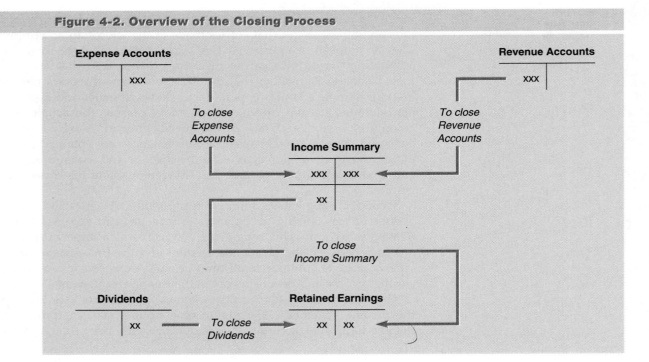

Exhibit 4-1. Preparing Closing Entries from the Adjusted Trial Balance

Joan Miller Advertising Agency, Inc.
Adjusted Trial Balance
January 31, 19xx

Cash	$ 1,720	
Accounts Receivable	2,800	
Fees Receivable	200	
Art Supplies	1,300	
Office Supplies	600	
Prepaid Rent	400	
Prepaid Insurance	440	
Art Equipment	4,200	
Accumulated Depreciation, Art Equipment		$ 70
Office Equipment	3,000	
Accumulated Depreciation, Office Equipment		50
Accounts Payable		3,170
Unearned Art Fees		600
Wages Payable		180
Income Taxes Payable		400
Common Stock		10,000
Dividends	1,400	
Advertising Fees Earned		4,400
Art Fees Earned		400
Office Wages Expense	1,380	
Utility Expense	100	
Telephone Expense	70	
Rent Expense	400	
Insurance Expense	40	
Art Supplies Expense	500	
Office Supplies Expense	200	
Depreciation Expense, Art Equipment	70	
Depreciation Expense, Office Equipment	50	
Income Taxes Expense	400	
	$19,270	$19,270

Entry 1:
Jan.	31	Advertising Fees Earned	411	4,400	
		Art Fees Earned	412	400	
		Income Summary	314		4,800
		To close the revenue accounts			

Entry 2:
Jan.	31	Income Summary	314	3,210	
		Office Wages Expense	511		1,380
		Utility Expense	512		100
		Telephone Expense	513		70
		Rent Expense	514		400
		Insurance Expense	515		40
		Art Supplies Expense	516		500
		Office Supplies Expense	517		200
		Depreciation Expense, Art Equipment	519		70
		Depreciation Expense, Office Equipment	520		50
		Income Taxes Expense	521		400
		To close the expense accounts			

Income Summary

Jan. 31	3,210	Jan. 31	4,800
Jan. 31	1,590	**Bal.**	—

Entry 3:
Jan.	31	Income Summary	314	1,590	
		Retained Earnings	312		1,590
		To close the Income Summary account			

Entry 4:
Jan.	31	Retained Earnings	312	1,400	
		Dividends	313		1,400
		To close the Dividends account			

journal entry must be made debiting each in the amount of its balance and crediting the total to the Income Summary account. The effect of posting the entry is shown in Exhibit 4-2. Notice that the entry (1) sets the balances of the revenue accounts to zero and (2) transfers the total revenues to the credit side of the Income Summary account.

Step 2: Closing the Debit Balances from Income Statement Accounts to the Income Summary Account Several expense accounts show balances on the debit side of the adjusted trial balance in Exhibit 4-1. A compound entry is needed to credit each of these expense accounts for its

Exhibit 4-2. Posting the Closing Entry of the Credit Balances from the Income Statement Accounts to the Income Summary Account

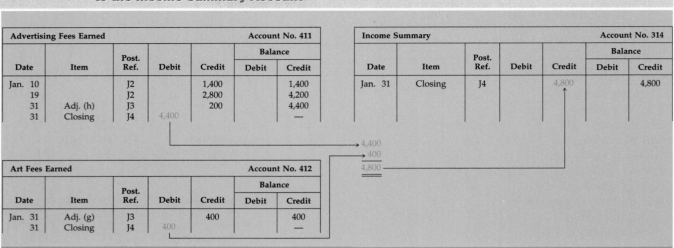

balance and to debit the Income Summary account for the total. The effect of posting the closing entry is shown in Exhibit 4-3. Notice how the closing entry (1) reduces the expense account balances to zero and (2) transfers the total of the account balances to the debit side of the Income Summary account.

Step 3: Closing the Income Summary Account to the Retained Earnings Account

After the entries closing the revenue and expense accounts have been posted, the balance of the Income Summary account equals the net income or loss for the period. Since revenues are represented by the credit to Income Summary and the expenses are represented by the debit to Income Summary, a net income is indicated by a credit balance (where revenues exceed expenses); a net loss, by a debit balance (where expenses exceed revenues). At this point, the Income Summary balance, whatever its nature, must be closed to the Retained Earnings account, as shown in Exhibit 4-1. The effect of posting the closing entry, when the company has a net income, is shown in Exhibit 4-4. Notice the dual effect of (1) closing the Income Summary account and (2) transferring the balance, net income in this case, to Retained Earnings.

Step 4: Closing the Dividends Account to the Retained Earnings Account

The Dividends account shows the amount by which retained earnings is reduced during the period by cash dividends. The debit balance of the Dividends account is closed to the Retained Earnings account, as shown in Exhibit 4-1. The effect of this closing entry, as shown in Exhibit 4-5, is to (1) close the Dividends account and (2) transfer the balance to the Retained Earnings account.

THE ACCOUNTS AFTER CLOSING

After all the steps in the closing process have been completed and all closing entries have been posted to the accounts, the stage is set for the next accounting period. The ledger accounts of Joan Miller Advertising Agency, Inc., as

Exhibit 4-3. Posting the Closing Entry of the Debit Balances from the Income Statement Accounts to the Income Summary Account

Office Wages Expense — Account No. 511

Date	Item	Post. Ref.	Debit	Credit	Balance Debit	Balance Credit
Jan. 12		J2	600		600	
26		J2	600		1,200	
31	Adj. (i)	J3	180		1,380	
31	Closing	J4		1,380	—	

Income Summary — Account No. 314

Date	Item	Post. Ref.	Debit	Credit	Balance Debit	Balance Credit
Jan. 31	Closing	J4		4,800		4,800
31	Closing	J4	3,210			1,590

Utility Expense — Account No. 512

Date	Item	Post. Ref.	Debit	Credit	Balance Debit	Balance Credit
Jan. 29		J2	100		100	
31	Closing	J4		100	—	

Telephone Expense — Account No. 513

Date	Item	Post. Ref.	Debit	Credit	Balance Debit	Balance Credit
Jan. 30		J2	70		70	
31	Closing	J4		70	—	

Rent Expense — Account No. 514

Date	Item	Post. Ref.	Debit	Credit	Balance Debit	Balance Credit
Jan. 31	Adj. (a)	J3	400		400	
31	Closing	J4		400	—	

Insurance Expense — Account No. 515

Date	Item	Post. Ref.	Debit	Credit	Balance Debit	Balance Credit
Jan. 31	Adj. (b)	J3	40		40	
31	Closing	J4		40	—	

Art Supplies Expense — Account No. 516

Date	Item	Post. Ref.	Debit	Credit	Balance Debit	Balance Credit
Jan. 31	Adj. (c)	J3	500		500	
31	Closing	J4		500	—	

Office Supplies Expense — Account No. 517

Date	Item	Post. Ref.	Debit	Credit	Balance Debit	Balance Credit
Jan. 31	Adj. (d)	J3	200		200	
31	Closing	J4		200	—	

Depreciation Expense, Art Equipment — Account No. 519

Date	Item	Post. Ref.	Debit	Credit	Balance Debit	Balance Credit
Jan. 31	Adj. (e)	J3	70		70	
31	Closing	J4		70	—	

Depreciation Expense, Office Equipment — Account No. 520

Date	Item	Post. Ref.	Debit	Credit	Balance Debit	Balance Credit
Jan. 31	Adj. (f)	J3	50		50	
31	Closing	J4		50	—	

Income Taxes Expense — Account No. 521

Date	Item	Post. Ref.	Debit	Credit	Balance Debit	Balance Credit
Jan. 31	Adj. (j)	J3	400		400	
31	Closing	J4		400	—	

1,380
100
70
400
40
500
400
50
70
200
3,210

Exhibit 4-4. Posting the Closing Entry of the Income Summary Account to the Retained Earnings Account

Income Summary						Account No. 314
		Post.			Bal	ance
Date	Item	Ref.	Debit	Credit	Debit	Credit
Jan. 31	Closing	J4		4,800		4,800
31	Closing	J4	3,210			1,590
31	Closing	J4	1,590			—

Retained Earnings						Account No. 312
		Post.			Bal	ance
Date	Item	Ref.	Debit	Credit	Debit	Credit
Jan. 31	Closing	J4		1,590		1,590

they appear at this point, are shown in Exhibit 4-6. The revenue, expense, and Dividends accounts (temporary accounts) have zero balances. Retained Earnings has been increased to reflect the agency's net income and decreased for dividends. The balance sheet accounts (permanent accounts) show the correct balances, which are carried forward to the next period.

THE POST-CLOSING TRIAL BALANCE

OBJECTIVE

4 *Prepare the post-closing trial balance*

Because it is possible to make errors in posting the closing entries to the ledger accounts, it is necessary to determine that all temporary accounts have zero balances and to double check that total debits equal total credits by preparing a new trial balance. This final trial balance, called the post-closing trial balance, is shown in Exhibit 4-7 on page 153. Notice that only the balance sheet accounts show balances because the income statement accounts and the Dividends account have all been closed.

BUSINESS BULLETIN: INTERNATIONAL PRACTICE

For companies with far-flung international operations like Caterpillar, Inc., Dow Chemical, Phillips Petroleum, Gillette Co., and Bristol Myers Squibb, closing the records and preparing financial statements on a timely basis used to be a problem. It was common practice for foreign divisions of companies like these to end their fiscal year one month before the end of the fiscal year of their counterparts in the United States. This gave them the extra time they needed to perform closing procedures and mail

Exhibit 4-5. Posting the Closing Entry of the Dividends Account to the Retained Earnings Account

Dividends						Account No. 313
		Post.			Bal	ance
Date	Item	Ref.	Debit	Credit	Debit	Credit
Jan. 25		J2	1,400		1,400	
31	Closing	J4		1,400	—	

Retained Earnings						Account No. 312
		Post.			Bal	ance
Date	Item	Ref.	Debit	Credit	Debit	Credit
Jan. 31	Closing	J4		1,590		1,590
31	Closing	J4	1,400			190

Exhibit 4-6. The Accounts After Closing Entries Are Posted

Cash — Account No. 111

Date	Item	Post. Ref.	Debit	Credit	Balance Debit	Balance Credit
Jan. 1		J1	10,000		10,000	
2		J1		800	9,200	
4		J1		4,200	5,000	
5		J1		1,500	3,500	
8		J1		480	3,020	
9		J1		1,000	2,020	
10		J2	1,400		3,420	
12		J2		600	2,820	
15		J2	1,000		3,820	
26		J2		600	3,220	
29		J2		100	3,120	
31		J2		1,400	1,720	

Accounts Receivable — Account No. 113

Date	Item	Post. Ref.	Debit	Credit	Balance Debit	Balance Credit
Jan. 19		J2	2,800		2,800	

Fees Receivable — Account No. 114

Date	Item	Post. Ref.	Debit	Credit	Balance Debit	Balance Credit
Jan. 31	Adj. (h)	J3	200		200	

Art Supplies — Account No. 115

Date	Item	Post. Ref.	Debit	Credit	Balance Debit	Balance Credit
Jan. 6		J1	1,800		1,800	
31	Adj. (c)	J3		500	1,300	

Office Supplies — Account No. 116

Date	Item	Post. Ref.	Debit	Credit	Balance Debit	Balance Credit
Jan. 6		J1	800		800	
31	Adj. (d)	J3		200	600	

Prepaid Rent — Account No. 117

Date	Item	Post. Ref.	Debit	Credit	Balance Debit	Balance Credit
Jan. 2		J1	800		800	
31	Adj. (a)	J3		400	400	

Prepaid Insurance — Account No. 118

Date	Item	Post. Ref.	Debit	Credit	Balance Debit	Balance Credit
Jan. 8		J1	480		480	
31	Adj. (b)	J3		40	440	

Art Equipment — Account No. 144

Date	Item	Post. Ref.	Debit	Credit	Balance Debit	Balance Credit
Jan. 4		J1	4,200		4,200	

Accumulated Depreciation, Art Equipment — Account No. 145

Date	Item	Post. Ref.	Debit	Credit	Balance Debit	Balance Credit
Jan. 31	Adj. (e)	J3		70		70

Office Equipment — Account No. 146

Date	Item	Post. Ref.	Debit	Credit	Balance Debit	Balance Credit
Jan. 5		J1	3,000		3,000	

Accumulated Depreciation, Office Equipment — Account No. 147

Date	Item	Post. Ref.	Debit	Credit	Balance Debit	Balance Credit
Jan. 31	Adj. (f)	J3		50		50

Accounts Payable — Account No. 212

Date	Item	Post. Ref.	Debit	Credit	Balance Debit	Balance Credit
Jan. 5		J1		1,500		1,500
6		J1		2,600		4,100
9		J1	1,000			3,100
30		J2		70		3,170

Unearned Art Fees — Account No. 213

Date	Item	Post. Ref.	Debit	Credit	Balance Debit	Balance Credit
Jan. 15		J2		1,000		1,000
31	Adj. (g)	J3	400			600

Wages Payable — Account No. 214

Date	Item	Post. Ref.	Debit	Credit	Balance Debit	Balance Credit
Jan. 31	Adj. (i)	J3		180		180

Income Taxes Payable — Account No. 215

Date	Item	Post. Ref.	Debit	Credit	Balance Debit	Balance Credit
Jan. 31	Adj. (j)	J3		400		400

(continued)

Exhibit 4-6. The Accounts After Closing Entries Are Posted *(continued)*

Common Stock — Account No. 311

Date	Item	Post. Ref.	Debit	Credit	Balance Debit	Balance Credit
Jan. 1		J1		10,000		10,000

Retained Earnings — Account No. 312

Date	Item	Post. Ref.	Debit	Credit	Balance Debit	Balance Credit
Jan. 31	Closing	J4		1,590		1,590
31	Closing	J4	1,400			190

Dividends — Account No. 313

Date	Item	Post. Ref.	Debit	Credit	Balance Debit	Balance Credit
Jan. 31		J2	1,400		1,400	
31	Closing	J4		1,400	—	

Income Summary — Account No. 314

Date	Item	Post. Ref.	Debit	Credit	Balance Debit	Balance Credit
Jan. 31	Closing	J4		4,800		4,800
31	Closing	J4	3,210			1,590
31	Closing	J4	1,590			

Advertising Fees Earned — Account No. 411

Date	Item	Post. Ref.	Debit	Credit	Balance Debit	Balance Credit
Jan. 10		J2		1,400		1,400
19		J2		2,800		4,200
31	Adj. (h)	J3		200		4,400
31	Closing	J4	4,400			—

Art Fees Earned — Account No. 412

Date	Item	Post. Ref.	Debit	Credit	Balance Debit	Balance Credit
Jan. 31	Adj. (g)	J3		400		400
31	Closing	J4	400			—

Office Wages Expense — Account No. 511

Date	Item	Post. Ref.	Debit	Credit	Balance Debit	Balance Credit
Jan. 12		J2	600		600	
26		J2	600		1,200	
31	Adj. (i)	J3	180		1,380	
31	Closing	J4		1,380	—	

Utility Expense — Account No. 512

Date	Item	Post. Ref.	Debit	Credit	Balance Debit	Balance Credit
Jan. 29		J2	100		100	
31	Closing	J4		100		

Telephone Expense — Account No. 513

Date	Item	Post. Ref.	Debit	Credit	Balance Debit	Balance Credit
Jan. 30		J2	70		70	
31	Closing	J4		70		

Rent Expense — Account No. 514

Date	Item	Post. Ref.	Debit	Credit	Balance Debit	Balance Credit
Jan. 31	Adj. (a)	J3	400		400	
31	Closing	J4		400	—	

Insurance Expense — Account No. 515

Date	Item	Post. Ref.	Debit	Credit	Balance Debit	Balance Credit
Jan. 31	Adj. (b)	J3	40		40	
31	Closing	J4		40		

Art Supplies Expense — Account No. 516

Date	Item	Post. Ref.	Debit	Credit	Balance Debit	Balance Credit
Jan. 31	Adj. (c)	J3	500		500	
31	Closing	J4		500	—	

Office Supplies Expense — Account No. 517

Date	Item	Post. Ref.	Debit	Credit	Balance Debit	Balance Credit
Jan. 31	Adj. (d)	J3	200		200	
31	Closing	J4		200	—	

Depreciation Expense, Art Equipment — Account No. 519

Date	Item	Post. Ref.	Debit	Credit	Balance Debit	Balance Credit
Jan. 31	Adj. (e)	J3	70		70	
31	Closing	J4		70	—	

(continued)

Exhibit 4-6. The Accounts After Closing Entries Are Posted *(continued)*

Depreciation Expense, Office Equipment					Account No. 520	
		Post.			**Balance**	
Date	Item	Ref.	Debit	Credit	Debit	Credit
Jan. 31	Adj. (f)	J3	50		50	
31	Closing	J4		50	—	

Income Taxes Expense					Account No. 521	
		Post.			**Balance**	
Date	Item	Ref.	Debit	Credit	Debit	Credit
Jan. 31	Adj. (j)	J3	400		400	
31	Closing	J4		400	—	

Exhibit 4-7. Post-Closing Trial Balance

Joan Miller Advertising Agency, Inc.
Post-Closing Trial Balance
January 31, 19xx

Cash	$ 1,720	
Accounts Receivable	2,800	
Fees Receivable	200	
Art Supplies	1,300	
Office Supplies	600	
Prepaid Rent	400	
Prepaid Insurance	440	
Art Equipment	4,200	
Accumulated Depreciation, Art Equipment		$ 70
Office Equipment	3,000	
Accumulated Depreciation, Office Equipment		50
Accounts Payable		3,170
Unearned Art Fees		600
Wages Payable		180
Income Taxes Payable		400
Common Stock		10,000
Retained Earnings		190
	$14,660	$14,660

the results back to U.S. headquarters to be used in preparation of the company's overall financial statements. This setup is usually unnecessary today because high-speed computers and electronic communications enable companies to close records and prepare financial statements for both foreign and domestic operations in less than a week. ══

REVERSING ENTRIES: THE OPTIONAL FIRST STEP IN THE NEXT ACCOUNTING PERIOD

At the end of each accounting period, adjusting entries are made to bring revenues and expenses into conformity with the matching rule. A reversing

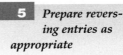
entry is a general journal entry made on the first day of a new accounting period that is the exact reverse of an adjusting entry made at the end of the previous period. Reversing entries are optional. They simplify the bookkeeping process for transactions involving certain types of adjustments. Not all adjusting entries can be reversed. For the recording system used in this book, only adjustments for accruals (accrued revenues and accrued expenses) can be reversed. Deferrals cannot be reversed because such reversals would not simplify the bookkeeping process in future accounting periods.

To see how reversing entries can be helpful, consider the adjusting entry made in the records of Joan Miller Advertising Agency, Inc. to accrue office wages expense:

Jan. 31	Office Wages Expense	180	
	Wages Payable		180
	To accrue unrecorded wages		

When the secretary is paid on the next regular payday, the accountant would make this entry:

Feb. 9	Wages Payable	180	
	Office Wages Expense	420	
	Cash		600
	Payment of two weeks' wages to secretary, $180 of which accrued in the previous period		

Notice that when the payment is made, if there is no reversing entry, the accountant must look in the records to find out how much of the $600 applies to the current accounting period and how much is applicable to the previous period. This may seem easy in our example, but think of how difficult and time-consuming it would be if a company had hundreds of employees, especially if some were paid on different schedules. A reversing entry helps solve the problem of applying revenues and expenses to the correct accounting period. It is exactly what its name implies: a reversal made by debiting the credits and crediting the debits of a previously made adjusting entry.

For example, notice the following sequence of entries and their effects on the ledger account Office Wages Expense:

1. Adjusting Entry

Jan. 31	Office Wages Expense	180	
	Wages Payable		180

2. Closing Entry

Jan. 31	Income Summary	1,380	
	Office Wages Expense		1,380

3. Reversing Entry

Feb. 1	Wages Payable	180	
	Office Wages Expense		180

4. Payment Entry

Feb. 9	Office Wages Expense	600	
	Cash		600

Office Wages Expense   **Account No. 511**

Date		Post. Ref.	Debit	Credit	Balance Debit	Balance Credit
Jan.	12	J2	600		600	
	26	J2	600		1,200	
	31	J3	180		1,380	
	31	J4		1,380	—	
Feb.	1	J5		180		180
	9	J6	600		420	

Entry 1 adjusted Office Wages Expense to accrue $180 in the January accounting period.

Entry 2 closed the $1,380 in Office Wages Expense for January to Income Summary, leaving a zero balance.

Entry 3, the reversing entry, set up a credit balance of $180 on February 1 in Office Wages Expense equal to the expense recognized through the adjusting entry in January (and also reduced the liability account Wages Payable to a zero balance). Notice that the reversing entry always sets up an abnormal balance in the income statement account and produces a zero balance in the balance sheet account.

Entry 4 recorded the $600 payment of two weeks' wages as a debit to Office Wages Expense, automatically leaving a balance of $420, which represents the correct wages expense to date in February.

The reversing entry simplified the process of making the payment entry on February 9.

Reversing entries apply to any accrued expenses or revenues. In the case of Joan Miller Advertising Agency, Inc., Income Taxes Expense is also an accrued expense that needs to be reversed. In addition, the asset Fees Receivable was created as a result of the adjusting entry made to accrue fees earned but not yet billed. The adjusting entry for this accrued revenue would require a reversing entry as well. The two additional reversing entries are as follows:

Feb. 1	Income Taxes Payable	400	
	Income Taxes Expense		400
	To reverse adjusting entry for estimated income taxes		
1	Advertising Fees Earned	200	
	Fees Receivable		200
	To reverse adjusting entry for accrued accrued fees receivable		

When the series of advertisements is finished, the company can credit all the proceeds to Advertising Fees Earned without regard to the amount accrued in the previous period. The credit will automatically be reduced to the amount earned during February by the $200 debit in the account.

As noted earlier, under the system of recording used in this book, reversing entries apply only to accruals. Reversing entries do not apply to deferrals, such as those that involve supplies, prepaid rent, prepaid insurance, depreciation, and unearned art fees.

Supplemental OBJECTIVE

6 *Prepare a work sheet*

THE WORK SHEET: AN ACCOUNTANT'S TOOL

As seen earlier, the flow of information that affects a business does not stop arbitrarily at the end of an accounting period. In preparing financial reports, accountants must collect relevant data to determine what should be included. For example, they need to examine insurance policies to see how much prepaid insurance has expired, examine plant and equipment records to determine depreciation, take an inventory of supplies on hand, and calculate the amount of accrued wages. These calculations, together with other computations, analyses, and preliminary drafts of statements, make up the accountants' working papers. Working papers are important for two reasons. First, they help accountants organize their work and thus avoid omitting important data or steps that affect the financial statements. Second, they provide evidence of past work so that accountants or auditors can retrace their steps and support the information in the financial statements.

A special kind of working paper is the work sheet. The work sheet is often used as a preliminary step in the preparation of financial statements. Using a work sheet lessens the possibility of leaving out an adjustment, helps the accountant check the arithmetical accuracy of the accounts, and facilitates the preparation of financial statements. The work sheet is never published and is rarely seen by management. It is a tool for the accountant.

Because preparing a work sheet is a very mechanical process, many accountants use a microcomputer. In some cases, accountants use a spreadsheet program to prepare the work sheet. In other cases, general ledger software is used to prepare financial statements from the adjusted trial balance.

PREPARING THE WORK SHEET

So far, adjusting entries have been entered directly in the journal and posted to the ledger, and the financial statements have been prepared from the adjusted trial balance. The process has been relatively simple because Joan Miller Advertising Agency, Inc. is a small company. For larger companies, which may require many adjusting entries, a work sheet is essential. To illustrate the preparation of the work sheet, we continue with the Joan Miller Advertising Agency, Inc. example.

A common form of work sheet has one column for account names and/or numbers and ten more columns with the headings shown in Exhibit 4-8. Notice that the work sheet is identified by a heading that consists of (1) the name of the company, (2) the title "Work Sheet," and (3) the period of time covered (as on the income statement).

There are five steps in the preparation of a work sheet:

1. Enter and total the account balances in the Trial Balance columns.
2. Enter and total the adjustments in the Adjustments columns.
3. Enter and total the adjusted account balances in the Adjusted Trial Balance columns.
4. Extend the account balances from the Adjusted Trial Balance columns to the Income Statement columns or the Balance Sheet columns.
5. Total the Income Statement columns and the Balance Sheet columns. Enter the net income or net loss in both pairs of columns as a balancing figure, and recompute the column totals.

1. **Enter and total the account balances in the Trial Balance columns.** The titles and balances of the accounts as of January 31 are copied directly from the ledger into the Trial Balance columns, as shown in Exhibit 4-8. This trial balance is the same as that illustrated in the chapter on measuring business income. When a work sheet is used, the accountant does not have to prepare a separate trial balance.

2. **Enter and total the adjustments in the Adjustments columns.** The required adjustments for Joan Miller Advertising Agency, Inc. were explained in the chapter on measuring business income. The same adjustments are entered in the Adjustments columns of the work sheet as shown in Exhibit 4-9. As each adjustment is entered, a letter is used to identify its debit and credit parts. The first adjustment, identified by the letter **a,** is to recognize rent expense, which results in a debit to Rent Expense and a credit to Prepaid Rent. In practice, this letter may be used to reference supporting computations or documentation

Exhibit 4-8. Entering the Account Balances in the Trial Balance Columns

Joan Miller Advertising Agency, Inc.
Work Sheet
For the Month Ended January 31, 19xx

Account Name	Trial Balance		Adjustments		Adjusted Trial Balance		Income Statement		Balance Sheet	
	Debit	Credit	Debit	Credit	Debit	Credit	Debit	Credit	Debit	Credit
Cash	1,720									
Accounts Receivable	2,800									
Art Supplies	1,800									
Office Supplies	800									
Prepaid Rent	800									
Prepaid Insurance	480									
Art Equipment	4,200									
Accumulated Depreciation, Art Equipment										
Office Equipment	3,000									
Accumulated Depreciation, Office Equipment										
Accounts Payable		3,170								
Unearned Art Fees		1,000								
Common Stock		10,000								
Dividends	1,400									
Advertising Fees Earned		4,200								
Office Wages Expense	1,200									
Utility Expense	100									
Telephone Expense	70									
	18,370	18,370								

underlying the adjusting entry and may simplify the recording of adjusting entries in the general journal.

If an adjustment calls for an account that has not been used in the trial balance, the new account is added below the accounts listed in the trial balance. The trial balance includes only those accounts that have balances. For example, Rent Expense has been added in Exhibit 4-9. The only exception to this rule is the Accumulated Depreciation accounts, which have a zero balance only in the initial period of operation. Accumulated Depreciation accounts are listed immediately after their associated asset accounts.

When all the adjustments have been made, the two Adjustments columns must be totaled. This step proves that the debits and credits of the adjustments are equal and generally reduces errors in the preparation of the work sheet.

3. **Enter and total the adjusted account balances in the Adjusted Trial Balance columns.** Exhibit 4-10 (page 159) shows the adjusted trial balance. It is prepared by combining the amount of each account in the original Trial Balance columns with the corresponding amount in the Adjustments columns and entering each result in the Adjusted Trial Balance columns.

Some examples from Exhibit 4-10 illustrate crossfooting, or adding and subtracting a group of numbers horizontally. The first line shows Cash with a

Exhibit 4-9. Entries in the Adjustments Columns

Joan Miller Advertising Agency, Inc.
Work Sheet
For the Month Ended January 31, 19xx

Account Name	Trial Balance Debit	Credit	Adjustments Debit	Credit	Adjusted Trial Balance Debit	Credit	Income Statement Debit	Credit	Balance Sheet Debit	Credit
Cash	1,720									
Accounts Receivable	2,800									
Art Supplies	1,800			(c) 500						
Office Supplies	800			(d) 200						
Prepaid Rent	800			(a) 400						
Prepaid Insurance	480			(b) 40						
Art Equipment	4,200									
Accumulated Depreciation, Art Equipment				(e) 70						
Office Equipment	3,000									
Accumulated Depreciation, Office Equipment				(f) 50						
Accounts Payable		3,170								
Unearned Art Fees		1,000	(g) 400							
Common Stock		10,000								
Dividends	1,400									
Advertising Fees Earned		4,200		(h) 200						
Office Wages Expense	1,200		(i) 180							
Utility Expense	100									
Telephone Expense	70									
	18,370	18,370								
Rent Expense			(a) 400							
Insurance Expense			(b) 40							
Art Supplies Expense			(c) 500							
Office Supplies Expense			(d) 200							
Depreciation Expense, Art Equipment			(e) 70							
Depreciation Expense, Office Equipment			(f) 50							
Art Fees Earned				(g) 400						
Fees Receivable			(h) 200							
Wages Payable				(i) 180						
Income Taxes Expense			(j) 400							
Income Taxes Payable				(j) 400						
			2,440	2,440						

debit balance of $1,720. Because there are no adjustments to the Cash account, $1,720 is entered in the debit column of the Adjusted Trial Balance columns. The second line is Accounts Receivable, which shows a debit of $2,800 in the Trial Balance columns. Because there are no adjustments to Accounts Receivable, the $2,800 balance is carried over to the debit column of the Adjusted Trial Balance columns. The next line is Art Supplies, which shows a debit of $1,800 in the Trial Balance columns and a credit of $500 from adjust-

Exhibit 4-10. Entries in the Adjusted Trial Balance Columns

Joan Miller Advertising Agency, Inc.
Work Sheet
For the Month Ended January 31, 19xx

Account Name	Trial Balance Debit	Trial Balance Credit	Adjustments Debit	Adjustments Credit	Adjusted Trial Balance Debit	Adjusted Trial Balance Credit	Income Statement Debit	Income Statement Credit	Balance Sheet Debit	Balance Sheet Credit
Cash	1,720				1,720					
Accounts Receivable	2,800				2,800					
Art Supplies	1,800			(c) 500	1,300					
Office Supplies	800			(d) 200	600					
Prepaid Rent	800			(a) 400	400					
Prepaid Insurance	480			(b) 40	440					
Art Equipment	4,200				4,200					
Accumulated Depreciation, Art Equipment				(e) 70		70				
Office Equipment	3,000				3,000					
Accumulated Depreciation, Office Equipment				(f) 50		50				
Accounts Payable		3,170				3,170				
Unearned Art Fees		1,000	(g) 400			600				
Common Stock		10,000				10,000				
Dividends	1,400				1,400					
Advertising Fees Earned		4,200		(h) 200		4,400				
Office Wages Expense	1,200		(i) 180		1,380					
Utility Expense	100				100					
Telephone Expense	70				70					
	18,370	18,370								
Rent Expense			(a) 400		400					
Insurance Expense			(b) 40		40					
Art Supplies Expense			(c) 500		500					
Office Supplies Expense			(d) 200		200					
Depreciation Expense, Art Equipment			(e) 70		70					
Depreciation Expense, Office Equipment			(f) 50		50					
Art Fees Earned				(g) 400		400				
Fees Receivable			(h) 200		200					
Wages Payable				(i) 180		180				
Income Taxes Expense			(j) 400		400					
Income Taxes Payable				(j) 400		400				
			2,440	2,440	19,270	19,270				

ment **c** in the Adjustments columns. Subtracting $500 from $1,800 results in a $1,300 debit balance in the Adjusted Trial Balance columns. This process is followed for all the accounts, including those added below the trial balance. The Adjusted Trial Balance columns are then footed (totaled) to check the accuracy of the crossfooting.

4. **Extend the account balances from the Adjusted Trial Balance columns to the Income Statement columns or the Balance Sheet columns.** Every account in the

Exhibit 4-11. Entries in the Income Statement and Balance Sheet Columns

Joan Miller Advertising Agency, Inc.
Work Sheet
For the Month Ended January 31, 19xx

Account Name	Trial Balance Debit	Trial Balance Credit	Adjustments Debit	Adjustments Credit	Adjusted Trial Balance Debit	Adjusted Trial Balance Credit	Income Statement Debit	Income Statement Credit	Balance Sheet Debit	Balance Sheet Credit
Cash	1,720				1,720				1,720	
Accounts Receivable	2,800				2,800				2,800	
Art Supplies	1,800			(c) 500	1,300				1,300	
Office Supplies	800			(d) 200	600				600	
Prepaid Rent	800			(a) 400	400				400	
Prepaid Insurance	480			(b) 40	440				440	
Art Equipment	4,200				4,200				4,200	
Accumulated Depreciation, Art Equipment				(e) 70		70				70
Office Equipment	3,000				3,000				3,000	
Accumulated Depreciation, Office Equipment				(f) 50		50				50
Accounts Payable		3,170				3,170				3,170
Unearned Art Fees		1,000	(g) 400			600				600
Common Stock		10,000				10,000				10,000
Dividends	1,400				1,400				1,400	
Advertising Fees Earned		4,200		(h) 200		4,400		4,400		
Office Wages Expense	1,200		(i) 180		1,380		1,380			
Utility Expense	100				100		100			
Telephone Expense	70				70		70			
	18,370	18,370								
Rent Expense			(a) 400		400		400			
Insurance Expense			(b) 40		40		40			
Art Supplies Expense			(c) 500		500		500			
Office Supplies Expense			(d) 200		200		200			
Depreciation Expense, Art Equipment			(e) 70		70		70			
Depreciation Expense, Office Equipment			(f) 50		50		50			
Art Fees Earned				(g) 400		400		400		
Fees Receivable			(h) 200		200				200	
Wages Payable				(i) 180		180				180
Income Taxes Expense			(j) 400		400		400			
Income Taxes Payable				(j) 400		400				400
			2,440	2,440	19,270	19,270				

adjusted trial balance is either a balance sheet account or an income statement account. Each account is extended to its proper place as a debit or credit in either the Income Statement columns or the Balance Sheet columns. The result of extending the accounts is shown in Exhibit 4-11. Revenue and expense accounts are copied to the Income Statement columns. Assets, liabilities, and the Common Stock and Dividends accounts are extended to the Balance Sheet columns. To avoid overlooking an account, extend the accounts line by line, beginning with the first line (which is Cash) and not omitting any subsequent lines. For instance, the Cash debit balance of $1,720 is extended to the debit column of the Balance Sheet columns; the Accounts Receivable debit balance of $2,800 is extended to the same debit column, and so forth. Each amount is carried across to only one column.

5. **Total the Income Statement columns and the Balance Sheet columns. Enter the net income or net loss in both pairs of columns as a balancing figure, and recompute the column totals.** This last step, as shown in Exhibit 4-12 (page 162), is necessary to compute net income or net loss and to prove the arithmetical accuracy of the work sheet.

Net income (or net loss) is equal to the difference between the total debits and credits of the Income Statement columns. It also equals the difference between the total debits and credits of the Balance Sheet columns.

Revenue (Income Statement credit column total)	$4,800
Expenses (Income Statement debit column total)	(3,210)
Net Income	$1,590

In this case, revenues (credit column) exceed expenses (debit column). Consequently, the company has a net income of $1,590. The same difference is shown between the total debits and credits of the Balance Sheet columns.

The $1,590 is entered in the debit side of the Income Statement columns to balance the columns, and it is entered in the credit side of the Balance Sheet columns. Remember that the excess of revenue over expenses (net income) increases stockholders' equity and that increases in stockholders' equity are recorded by credits.

When a net loss occurs, the opposite rule applies. The excess of expenses over revenue—net loss—is placed in the credit side of the Income Statement columns as a balancing figure. It is then placed in the debit side of the Balance Sheet columns because a net loss decreases stockholders' equity, and decreases in stockholders' equity are recorded by debits.

As a final check, the four columns are totaled again. If the Income Statement columns and the Balance Sheet columns do not balance, an account may have been extended or sorted to the wrong column, or an error may have been made in adding the columns. Of course, equal totals in the two pairs of columns are not absolute proof of accuracy. If an asset has been carried to the debit Income Statement column and a similar error with revenues or liabilities has been made, the work sheet still balances, but the net income figure is wrong.

BUSINESS BULLETIN: TECHNOLOGY IN PRACTICE

The work sheet is a good application for electronic spreadsheet software programs like Lotus 1-2-3 and Microsoft Excel. Constructing a work sheet on spreadsheet software takes time, but once it is done, the work sheet can be used over and over. The principal advantage of electronic preparation over manual preparation is that each time a number is entered or revised, the entire electronic work sheet is updated automatically without the possibility of addition or extension mistakes. For example, if

Exhibit 4-12. Totals of the Income Statement and Balance Sheet Columns and Net Income

Joan Miller Advertising Agency, Inc.
Work Sheet
For the Month Ended January 31, 19xx

Account Name	Trial Balance Debit	Trial Balance Credit	Adjustments Debit	Adjustments Credit	Adjusted Trial Balance Debit	Adjusted Trial Balance Credit	Income Statement Debit	Income Statement Credit	Balance Sheet Debit	Balance Sheet Credit
Cash	1,720				1,720				1,720	
Accounts Receivable	2,800				2,800				2,800	
Art Supplies	1,800			(c) 500	1,300				1,300	
Office Supplies	800			(d) 200	600				600	
Prepaid Rent	800			(a) 400	400				400	
Prepaid Insurance	480			(b) 40	440				440	
Art Equipment	4,200				4,200				4,200	
Accumulated Depreciation, Art Equipment				(e) 70		70				70
Office Equipment	3,000				3,000				3,000	
Accumulated Depreciation, Office Equipment				(f) 50		50				50
Accounts Payable		3,170				3,170				3,170
Unearned Art Fees		1,000	(g) 400			600				600
Common Stock		10,000				10,000				10,000
Dividends	1,400				1,400				1,400	
Advertising Fees Earned		4,200		(h) 200		4,400		4,400		
Office Wages Expense	1,200		(i) 180		1,380		1,380			
Utility Expense	100				100		100			
Telephone Expense	70				70		70			
	18,370	18,370								
Rent Expense			(a) 400		400		400			
Insurance Expense			(b) 40		40		40			
Art Supplies Expense			(c) 500		500		500			
Office Supplies Expense			(d) 200		200		200			
Depreciation Expense, Art Equipment			(e) 70		70		70			
Depreciation Expense, Office Equipment			(f) 50		50		50			
Art Fees Earned				(g) 400		400		400		
Fees Receivable			(h) 200		200				200	
Wages Payable				(h) 180		180				180
Income Taxes Expense			(j) 400		400		400			
Income Taxes Payable				(j) 400		400				400
			2,440	2,440	19,270	19,270	3,210	4,800	16,060	14,470
Net Income							1,590			1,590
							4,800	4,800	16,060	16,060

an error in an adjusting entry is corrected, the proper extensions to the other columns are made, all columns are re-added, and net income is recomputed. Of course, the software is purely mechanical. People are still responsible for inputting the correct numbers in the first place. ═══

Supplemental
OBJECTIVE

7 *Use a work sheet
for three different
purposes*

USING THE WORK SHEET

The completed work sheet assists the accountant in three principal tasks: (1) preparing the financial statements, (2) recording the adjusting entries, and (3) recording the closing entries in the general journal to prepare the records for the beginning of the next period.

Preparing the Financial Statements   Once the work sheet has been completed, preparing the financial statements is simple because the account balances have been sorted into Income Statement and Balance Sheet columns. The income statement shown in Exhibit 4-13 was prepared from the accounts in the Income Statement columns of Exhibit 4-12. The statement of retained earnings and the balance sheet of Joan Miller Advertising Agency, Inc. are presented in Exhibits 4-14 and 4-15. The account balances for these statements are drawn from the Balance Sheet columns of the work sheet shown in Exhibit 4-12. Notice that the total assets and the total liabilities and stockholders' equity in the balance sheet are not the same as the totals of the Balance Sheet columns in the work sheet. The reason for this is that the Accumulated Depreciation and Dividends accounts appear in different columns from their associated accounts on the balance sheet. In addition, the Retained Earnings account on the balance sheet is the amount determined on the statement of retained earnings. At this point, the financial statements have been prepared from the work sheet, not from the ledger accounts. For the ledger accounts to show the correct balances, the adjusting entries must be journalized and posted to the ledger.

Exhibit 4-13. Income Statement for Joan Miller Advertising Agency, Inc.

Joan Miller Advertising Agency, Inc.
Income Statement
For the Month Ended January 31, 19xx

Revenues		
Advertising Fees Earned	$4,400	
Art Fees Earned	400	
Total Revenues		$4,800
Expenses		
Office Wages Expense	$1,380	
Utility Expense	100	
Telephone Expense	70	
Rent Expense	400	
Insurance Expense	40	
Art Supplies Expense	500	
Office Supplies Expense	200	
Depreciation Expense, Art Equipment	70	
Depreciation Expense, Office Equipment	50	
Income Taxes Expense	400	
Total Expenses		3,210
Net Income		**$1,590**

Exhibit 4-14. Statement of Retained Earnings for Joan Miller Advertising Agency, Inc.

Joan Miller Advertising Agency, Inc.
Statement of Retained Earnings
For the Month Ended January 31, 19xx

Retained Earnings, January 1, 19xx	$ 0
Net Income	1,590
Subtotal	$1,590
Less Dividends	1,400
Retained Earnings, January 31, 19xx	$ 190

Exhibit 4-15. Balance Sheet for Joan Miller Advertising Agency, Inc.

Joan Miller Advertising Agency, Inc.
Balance Sheet
January 31, 19xx

Assets

Cash		$ 1,720
Accounts Receivable		2,800
Fees Receivable		200
Art Supplies		1,300
Office Supplies		600
Prepaid Rent		400
Prepaid Insurance		440
Art Equipment	$4,200	
Less Accumulated Depreciation	70	4,130
Office Equipment	$ 3,000	
Less Accumulated Depreciation	50	2,950
Total Assets		$14,540

Liabilities

Accounts Payable	$ 3,170	
Unearned Art Fees	600	
Wages Payable	180	
Income Taxes Payable	400	
Total Liabilities		$ 4,350

Stockholders' Equity

Common Stock	$10,000	
Retained Earnings	190	
Total Stockholders' Equity		10,190
Total Liabilities and Stockholders' Equity		$14,540

Completing the Accounting Cycle

Recording the Adjusting Entries   For Joan Miller Advertising Agency, Inc., the adjustments were determined while completing the work sheet because they are essential to the preparation of the financial statements. The adjusting entries could have been recorded in the general journal at that point. However, it is usually convenient to delay recording them until after the work sheet and the financial statements have been prepared because this task can be done at the same time the closing entries are recorded, a process described earlier in this chapter. Recording the adjusting entries with appropriate explanations in the general journal, as shown in Exhibit 4-16, is an easy step. The information can simply be copied from the work sheet. Adjusting entries are then posted to the general ledger.

Recording the Closing Entries   The four closing entries for Joan Miller Advertising Agency, Inc. are entered in the journal and posted to the ledger as shown in Exhibits 4-2 through 4-5. All accounts that need closing, except for Dividends, may be found in the Income Statement columns of the work sheet.

Exhibit 4-16. Adjustments from Work Sheet Entered in the General Journal

General Journal					Page 3
Date		Description	Post. Ref.	Debit	Credit
19xx Jan.	31	Rent Expense	514	400	
		Prepaid Rent	117		400
		To recognize expiration of one month's rent			
	31	Insurance Expense	515	40	
		Prepaid Insurance	118		40
		To recognize expiration of one month's insurance			
	31	Art Supplies Expense	516	500	
		Art Supplies	115		500
		To recognize art supplies used during the month			
	31	Office Supplies Expense	517	200	
		Office Supplies	116		200
		To recognize office supplies used during the month			
	31	Depreciation Expense, Art Equipment	519	70	
		Accumulated Depreciation, Art Equipment	145		70
		To record depreciation of art equipment for a month			

(continued)

Exhibit 4-16. Adjustments from the Work Sheet Entered in the General Journal *(continued)*

	General Journal				Page 3
Date		Description	Post. Ref.	Debit	Credit
19xx Jan.	31	Depreciation Expense, Office Equipment	520	50	
		Accumulated Depreciation, Office Equipment	147		50
		To record depreciation of office equipment for a month			
	31	Unearned Art Fees	213	400	
		Art Fees Earned	412		400
		To recognize performance of services paid for in advance			
	31	Fees Receivable	114	200	
		Advertising Fees Earned	411		200
		To accrue advertising fees earned but unrecorded			
	31	Office Wages Expense	511	180	
		Wages Payable	214		180
		To accrue unrecorded wages			
	31	Income Taxes Expense	521	400	
		Income Taxes Payable	215		400
		To accrue estimated income taxes			

CHAPTER REVIEW

REVIEW OF LEARNING OBJECTIVES

1. **State all the steps in the accounting cycle.** The steps in the accounting cycle are (1) analyze business transactions from source documents, (2) record the entries in the journal, (3) post the entries to the ledger and prepare a trial balance, (4) adjust the accounts and prepare an adjusted trial balance, (5) close the accounts and prepare a post-closing trial balance, and (6) prepare the financial statements.

2. **Explain the purposes of closing entries.** Closing entries have two purposes. First, they clear the balances of all temporary accounts (revenue and expense accounts and Dividends) so that they have zero balances at the beginning of the next accounting period. Second, they summarize a period's revenues and expenses in the Income Summary account so that the net income or loss for the period can be transferred as a total to Retained Earnings.

3. **Prepare the required closing entries.** Closing entries are prepared by first transferring the revenue and expense account balances to the Income Summary account. Then the balance of the Income Summary account is transferred to the Retained Earnings account. And, finally, the balance of the Dividends account is transferred to the Retained Earnings account.

4. **Prepare the post-closing trial balance.** As a final check on the balance of the ledger and to ensure that all temporary (nominal) accounts have been closed, a post-closing trial balance is prepared after the closing entries are posted to the ledger accounts.

SUPPLEMENTAL OBJECTIVES

5. **Prepare reversing entries as appropriate.** Reversing entries are optional entries made on the first day of a new accounting period to simplify routine bookkeeping procedures. They reverse certain adjusting entries made in the previous period. Under the system used in this text, they apply only to accruals.

6. **Prepare a work sheet.** There are five steps in the preparation of a work sheet: (1) Enter and total the account balances in the Trial Balance columns; (2) enter and total the adjustments in the Adjustments columns; (3) enter and total the adjusted account balances in the Adjusted Trial Balance columns; (4) extend the account balances from the Adjusted Trial Balance columns to the Income Statement or Balance Sheet columns; and (5) total the Income Statement and Balance Sheet columns, enter the net income or net loss in both pairs of columns as a balancing figure, and recompute the column totals.

7. **Use a work sheet for three different purposes.** A work sheet is useful in (1) preparing the financial statements, (2) recording the adjusting entries, and (3) recording the closing entries. The balance sheet and income statement can be prepared directly from the Balance Sheet and Income Statement columns of the completed work sheet. The statement of retained earnings is prepared using Dividends, net income, additional investments, and the beginning balance of Retained Earnings. Notice that the ending balance of Retained Earnings does not appear on the work sheet. Adjusting entries can be recorded in the general journal directly from the Adjustments columns of the work sheet. Closing entries may be prepared from the Income Statement columns, except for Dividends, which is found in the Balance Sheet columns.

REVIEW OF CONCEPTS AND TERMINOLOGY

The following concepts and terms were introduced in this chapter.

L O 1 **Accounting cycle:** The sequence of steps followed in the accounting process to measure business transactions and transform them into financial statements.

L O 2 **Closing entries:** Journal entries made at the end of an accounting period that set the stage for the next accounting period by clearing the temporary accounts of their balances, and that summarize a period's revenues and expenses.

S O 6 **Crossfooting:** Adding and subtracting numbers across a row.

L O 2 **Income Summary:** A temporary account used during the closing process that holds a summary of all revenues and expenses before the net income or loss is transferred to the Retained Earnings account.

L O 4 **Post-closing trial balance:** A trial balance prepared at the end of the accounting period after all adjusting and closing entries have been posted; a final check on the balance of the ledger.

S O 5 **Reversing entries:** Journal entries made on the first day of a new accounting period that reverse certain adjusting entries and simplify the bookkeeping process for the next accounting period.

S O 6   **Working papers:** Documents used by accountants to organize their work and to support the information in the financial statements.

S O 6   **Work sheet:** A type of working paper used as a preliminary step in the preparation of financial statements.

REVIEW PROBLEM
PREPARATION OF CLOSING ENTRIES

L O 3   At the end of the current fiscal year, the adjusted trial balance for Westwood Movers, Inc. appeared as follows:

Westwood Movers, Inc.
Adjusted Trial Balance
June 30, 19xx

Cash	$ 14,200	
Accounts Receivable	18,600	
Packing Supplies	10,400	
Prepaid Insurance	7,900	
Land	4,000	
Building	80,000	
Accumulated Depreciation, Building		$ 7,500
Trucks	106,000	
Accumulated Depreciation, Trucks		27,500
Accounts Payable		7,650
Unearned Storage Fees		5,400
Income Taxes Payable		9,000
Mortgage Payable		70,000
Common Stock		80,000
Retained Earnings		24,740
Dividends	18,000	
Moving Services Earned		159,000
Storage Fees Earned		26,400
Driver Wages Expense	94,000	
Fuel Expense	19,000	
Office Wages Expense	14,400	
Office Equipment Rental Expense	3,000	
Utility Expense	4,450	
Insurance Expense	4,200	
Depreciation Expense, Building	4,000	
Depreciation Expense, Trucks	6,040	
Income Taxes Expense	9,000	
	$417,190	$417,190

REQUIRED   Prepare the necessary closing entries.

ANSWER TO REVIEW PROBLEM

June	30	Moving Services Earned	159,000	
		Storage Fees Earned	26,400	
		Income Summary		185,400
		To close revenue accounts		

June 30   Income Summary   158,090
    Driver Wages Expense   94,000
    Fuel Expense   19,000
    Office Wages Expense   14,400
    Office Equipment Rental Expense   3,000
    Utility Expense   4,450
    Insurance Expense   4,200
    Depreciation Expense, Building   4,000
    Depreciation Expense, Trucks   6,040
    Income Taxes Expense   9,000
     To close expense accounts

June 30   Income Summary   27,310
    Retained Earnings   27,310
     To close Income Summary and
     transfer balance to Retained Earnings

June 30   Retained Earnings   18,000
    Dividends   18,000
     To close the Dividends account

CHAPTER ASSIGNMENTS

KNOWLEDGE AND UNDERSTANDING

Questions

1. Resequence the following activities 1 through 6 to indicate the correct order of the accounting cycle.
   a. The transactions are entered in the journal.
   b. The financial statements are prepared.
   c. The transactions are analyzed from the source documents.
   d. The adjusting entries are prepared.
   e. The closing entries are prepared.
   f. The transactions are posted to the ledger.

2. What are the two purposes of closing entries?

3. What is the difference between adjusting entries and closing entries?

4. What is the purpose of the Income Summary account?

5. Which of the following accounts do not show a balance after the closing entries are prepared and posted?
   a. Insurance Expense   e. Dividends
   b. Accounts Receivable   f. Supplies
   c. Commission Revenue   g. Supplies Expense
   d. Prepaid Insurance   h. Retained Earnings

6. What is the significance of the post-closing trial balance?

7. Which of the following accounts would you expect to find on the post-closing trial balance?
   a. Insurance Expense   e. Dividends
   b. Accounts Receivable   f. Supplies
   c. Commission Revenue   g. Supplies Expense
   d. Prepaid Insurance   h. Retained Earnings

8. How do reversing entries simplify the bookkeeping process?

9. To what types of adjustments do reversing entries apply? To what types do they not apply?

10. Why are working papers important to accountants?

11. Why are work sheets never published and rarely seen by management?

12. Can the work sheet be used as a substitute for the financial statements? Explain your answer.

13. What is the normal balance (debit or credit) of the following accounts?
    a. Cash
    b. Accounts Payable
    c. Prepaid Rent
    d. Common Stock
    e. Commission Revenue
    f. Dividends
    g. Rent Expense
    h. Accumulated Depreciation, Office Equipment
    i. Office Equipment

14. What is the probable cause of a credit balance in the Cash account?

15. Should the Adjusted Trial Balance columns of the work sheet be totaled before or after the adjusted amounts are carried to the Income Statement and Balance Sheet columns? Discuss your answer.

16. What sequence should be followed in extending the Adjusted Trial Balance columns to the Income Statement and Balance Sheet columns? Discuss your answer.

17. Do the Income Statement columns and the Balance Sheet columns of the work sheet balance after the amounts from the Adjusted Trial Balance columns are extended?

18. Do the totals of the Balance Sheet columns of the work sheet agree with the totals on the balance sheet? Explain your answer.

19. Should adjusting entries be posted to the ledger accounts before or after the closing entries? Explain your answer.

20. At the end of the accounting period, does the posting of adjusting entries to the ledger precede or follow the preparation of the work sheet?

Short Exercises

SE 4-1.
L O 1 *Accounting Cycle*

Resequence the following activities to indicate the correct order of the accounting cycle.

a. Close the accounts.
b. Analyze the transactions.
c. Post the entries.
d. Prepare the financial statements.
e. Adjust the accounts.
f. Record the transactions.
g. Prepare the post-closing trial balance.
h. Prepare the initial trial balance.
i. Prepare the adjusted trial balance.

SE 4-2.
L O 3 *Closing Revenue Accounts*

Assuming credit balances at the end of the accounting period of $3,400 in Patient Services and $1,800 in Laboratory Fees, prepare the required closing entry. The accounting period ends December 31.

SE 4-3.
L O 3 *Closing Expense Accounts*

Assuming debit balances at the end of the accounting period of $1,400 in Rent Expense, $1,100 in Wages Expense, and $500 in Other Expenses, prepare the required closing entry. The accounting period ends December 31.

SE 4-4.
L O 3 *Closing the Income Summary Account*

Assuming total revenues were $5,200 and total expenses were $3,000, prepare the journal entry to close the Income Summary account. The accounting period ends December 31.

SE 4-5.

L O 3 *Closing the Dividends Account*

Assuming dividends during the accounting period were $800, prepare the journal entry to close the Dividends account. The accounting period ends December 31.

SE 4-6.

L O 3 *Posting Closing Entries*

Show the effects of the transactions in SE 4-2 to SE 4-5 by entering beginning balances in appropriate T accounts and recording the transactions. Assume that Retained Earnings has a beginning balance of $1,300.

SE 4-7.

S O 5 *Preparation of Reversing Entries*

Below, indicated by letters, are the adjusting entries at the end of March. Prepare the required reversing entries.

Account Name	Debit		Credit	
Prepaid Insurance			(a)	180
Accumulated Depreciation, Office Equipment			(b)	1,050
Salaries Expense	(c)	360		
Insurance Expense	(a)	180		
Depreciation Expense, Office Equipment	(b)	1,050		
Salaries Payable			(c)	360
Income Taxes Expense	(d)	470		
Income Taxes Payable			(d)	470
		2,060		2,060

SE 4-8.

S O 5 *Effects of Reversing Entries*

Assume that prior to the adjustments in SE4-7, Salaries Expense had a debit balance of $1,800 and Salaries Payable had a zero balance. Prepare a T account for each of these accounts. Enter the beginning balance; post the adjustment for accrued salaries, the appropriate closing entry, and the reversal; and enter the transaction in the T accounts for a payment of $480 for salaries on April 3.

SE 4-9.

S O 7 *Preparing Closing Entries from a Work Sheet*

Prepare the required closing entries for the year ended December 31, using the following items from the Income Statement columns of a work sheet and assuming that dividends were $6,000.

Account Name	Income Statement	
	Debit	Credit
Repair Revenue		36,860
Wages Expense	12,260	
Rent Expense	1,800	
Supplies Expense	6,390	
Insurance Expense	1,370	
Depreciation Expense, Repair Equipment	2,020	
Income Taxes Expense	4,000	
	27,840	36,860
Net Income	9,020	
	36,860	36,860

APPLICATION

Exercises

E 4-1.
L O 3 *Preparation of Closing Entries*

Below is the adjusted trial balance for the Nafzger Realty Company at the end of its fiscal year. Prepare the required closing entries.

Nafzger Realty Company
Adjusted Trial Balance
December 31, 19xx

Cash	$ 4,275	
Accounts Receivable	2,325	
Prepaid Insurance	585	
Office Supplies	440	
Office Equipment	6,300	
Accumulated Depreciation, Office Equipment		$ 765
Automobile	6,750	
Accumulated Depreciation, Automobile		750
Accounts Payable		1,700
Unearned Management Fees		1,500
Common Stock		10,000
Retained Earnings		4,535
Dividends	7,000	
Sales Commissions Earned		31,700
Office Salaries Expense	13,500	
Advertising Expense	2,525	
Rent Expense	2,650	
Telephone Expense	1,600	
Income Taxes Expense	3,000	
	$50,950	$50,950

E 4-2.
S O 5 *Reversing Entries*

Selected June T accounts for Holmes Corporation are presented below.

Supplies

6/1 Bal.	860	6/30 Adjust.	1,280
June purchases	940		
Bal.	**520**		

Supplies Expense

6/30 Adjust.	1,280	6/30 Closing	1,280
Bal.	—		

Wages Payable

		6/30 Adjust.	640
		Bal.	**640**

Wages Expense

June wages	3,940	6/30 Closing	4,580
6/30 Adjust.	640		
Bal.	—		

1. In which of these accounts would a reversing entry be helpful? Why?
2. Prepare the appropriate reversing entry.
3. Prepare the entry to record payments on July 3 for wages totaling $3,140. How much of this amount represents wages expense for July?

E 4-3.

S O 6   *Preparation of a*
         Trial Balance

The following alphabetical list presents the accounts and balances for Natraj Realty, Inc. on June 30, 19x3. All the accounts have normal balances.

Accounts Payable	$15,420
Accounts Receivable	7,650
Accumulated Depreciation, Office Equipment	1,350
Advertising Expense	1,800
Cash	7,635
Common Stock	20,000
Dividends	27,000
Office Equipment	15,510
Prepaid Insurance	1,680
Rent Expense	7,200
Retained Earnings	10,630
Revenue from Commissions	57,900
Supplies	825
Wages Expense	36,000

Prepare the trial balance by listing the accounts in the correct order for work sheet preparation, with the balances in the appropriate debit or credit column.

E 4-4.

S O 6   *Completion of a*
         Work Sheet

The following is a highly simplified alphabetical list of trial balance accounts and their normal balances for the month ended October 31, 19xx.

Trial Balance Accounts and Balances

Accounts Payable	$ 4
Accounts Receivable	7
Accumulated Depreciation, Office Equipment	1
Cash	4
Common Stock	5
Dividends	6
Office Equipment	8
Prepaid Insurance	2
Retained Earnings	7
Service Revenue	23
Supplies	4
Unearned Revenue	3
Utility Expense	2
Wages Expense	10

1. Prepare a work sheet, entering the trial balance accounts in the order in which they would normally appear, and arranging the balances in the correct debit or credit column.
2. Complete the work sheet using the following information:
   a. Expired insurance, $1.
   b. Of the unearned revenue balance, $2 has been earned by the end of the month.
   c. Estimated depreciation on office equipment, $1.
   d. Accrued wages, $1.
   e. Unused supplies on hand, $1.
   f. Estimated income taxes, $1.

E 4-5.

L O 3   *Preparation of a*
S O 7   *Statement of*
         Retained Earnings

The Retained Earnings, Dividends, and Income Summary accounts for Wendell's Barber Shop, Inc. are shown in T account form below. The closing entries have been recorded for the year ended December 31, 19xx.

Retained Earnings

12/31	4,500	1/1	13,000
		12/31	9,500
		Bal.	**18,000**

Dividends

4/1	1,500	12/31	4,500
7/1	1,500		
10/1	1,500		
Bal.	—		

Income Summary

12/31	21,500	12/31	31,000
12/31	9,500		
Bal.	—		

Prepare a statement of retained earnings for Wendell's Barber Shop, Inc.

E 4-6.

S O 7 *Derivation of Adjusting Entries from Trial Balance and Income Statement Columns*

Below is a partial work sheet in which the Trial Balance and Income Statement columns have been completed. All amounts shown are in dollars.

Account Name	Trial Balance		Income Statement	
	Debit	Credit	Debit	Credit
Cash	16			
Accounts Receivable	24			
Supplies	22			
Prepaid Insurance	16			
Building	50			
Accumulated Depreciation, Building		16		
Accounts Payable		8		
Unearned Revenue		4		
Common Stock		40		
Retained Earnings		24		
Revenue		90		94
Wages Expense	54		60	
	182	182		
Insurance Expense			8	
Supplies Expense			16	
Depreciation Expense, Building			4	
Income Taxes Expense			2	
			90	94
Net Income			4	
			94	94

1. Determine what adjustments have been made. (Assume that no adjustments have been made to Accounts Receivable or Accounts Payable.)
2. Prepare a balance sheet.

E 4-7.

S O 5, 7 *Preparation of Adjusting and Reversing Entries from Work Sheet Columns*

These items are from the Adjustments columns of a work sheet dated June 30, 19xx.

	Adjustments			
Account Name	**Debit**		**Credit**	
Prepaid Insurance			(a)	240
Office Supplies			(b)	630
Accumulated Depreciation, Office Equipment			(c)	1,400
Accumulated Depreciation, Store Equipment			(d)	2,200
Office Salaries Expense	(e)	240		
Store Salaries Expense	(e)	480		
Insurance Expense	(a)	240		
Office Supplies Expense	(b)	630		
Depreciation Expense, Office Equipment	(c)	1,400		
Depreciation Expense, Store Equipment	(d)	2,200		
Salaries Payable			(e)	720
Income Taxes Expense	(f)	800		
Incomes Taxes Payable			(f)	800
		5,990		5,990

1. Prepare the adjusting entries.
2. Where required, prepare appropriate reversing entries.

E 4-8.

L O 3
S O 7 *Preparation of Closing Entries from the Work Sheet*

The items below are from the Income Statement columns of the work sheet for DiPietro Repair Shop, Inc. for the year ended December 31, 19xx.

	Income Statement	
Account Name	**Debit**	**Credit**
Repair Revenue		25,620
Wages Expense	8,110	
Rent Expense	1,200	
Supplies Expense	4,260	
Insurance Expense	915	
Depreciation Expense, Repair Equipment	1,345	
Income Taxes Expense	1,000	
	16,830	25,620
Net Income	8,790	
	25,620	25,620

Prepare entries to close the revenue, expense, Income Summary, and Dividends accounts. Dividends of $5,000 were paid during the year.

Problem Set A

4A-1.

L O 3
S O 5

*Preparation of
Financial Statements
and End-of-Period
Entries*

Benzinger Trailer Rental, Inc. owns thirty small trailers that are rented by the day for local moving jobs. The adjusted trial balance for Benzinger Trailer Rental, Inc. on December 31, 19x4, which is the end of the current fiscal year, is shown below.

Benzinger Trailer Rental, Inc.
Adjusted Trial Balance
December 31, 19x4

Cash	$ 1,384	
Accounts Receivable	1,944	
Supplies	238	
Prepaid Insurance	720	
Trailers	24,000	
Accumulated Depreciation, Trailers		$ 14,400
Accounts Payable		542
Wages Payable		400
Common Stock		2,000
Retained Earnings		6,388
Dividends	11,400	
Trailer Rentals		91,092
Wages Expense	46,800	
Insurance Expense	1,440	
Supplies Expense	532	
Depreciation Expense, Trailers	4,800	
Other Expenses	21,564	
Income Taxes Expense	4,000	
Income Taxes Payable		4,000
	$118,822	$118,822

REQUIRED

1. Prepare an income statement, a statement of retained earnings, and a balance sheet.
2. From the information given, record the closing entries.
3. Assuming Wages Payable and Income Taxes Payable represent wages and taxes accrued at the end of the period, record the required reversing entries on January 1.

4A-2.

L O 3

*Preparation of
Financial Statements
and Closing Entries*

The adjusted trial balance on page 177 pertains to Holiday Bowling Lanes, Inc. at the end of the company's fiscal year.

REQUIRED

1. Prepare an income statement, a statement of retained earnings, and a balance sheet.
2. From the information given, record the closing entries.

Holiday Bowling Lanes, Inc.
Adjusted Trial Balance
June 30, 19x4

Cash	$ 32,428	
Accounts Receivable	14,776	
Supplies	312	
Prepaid Insurance	600	
Land	10,000	
Building	200,000	
Accumulated Depreciation, Building		$ 54,400
Equipment	250,000	
Accumulated Depreciation, Equipment		66,000
Accounts Payable		30,088
Notes Payable		140,000
Unearned Revenues		600
Wages Payable		7,924
Property Taxes Payable		20,000
Income Taxes Payable		30,000
Common Stock		40,000
Retained Earnings		81,626
Dividends	48,000	
Revenues		1,236,526
Wages Expense	762,152	
Advertising Expense	30,400	
Utility Expense	84,400	
Maintenance Expense	168,200	
Supplies Expense	2,296	
Insurance Expense	3,000	
Depreciation Expense, Building	9,600	
Depreciation Expense, Equipment	22,000	
Property Taxes Expense	20,000	
Miscellaneous Expense	19,000	
Income Taxes Expense	30,000	
	$1,707,164	$1,707,164

4A-3.

L O 3

S O 5, 6, 7

Preparation of a Work Sheet; Financial Statements; and Adjusting, Closing, and Reversing Entries

Donald Leung began his consulting practice immediately after earning his M.B.A. To help him get started, several clients paid him retainers (payments in advance) for future services. Other clients paid when service was provided. The firm's trial balance after one year appears on page 178.

REQUIRED

1. Enter the trial balance amounts in the Trial Balance columns of a work sheet. Remember that accumulated depreciation is listed with its asset account. Complete the work sheet using the following information:
   a. Inventory of unused office supplies, $174.
   b. Estimated depreciation on office equipment, $1,800.
   c. Services rendered during the month but not yet billed, $2,175.
   d. Services rendered that should be applied against unearned retainers, $9,450.
   e. Wages earned by employees but not yet paid, $360.
   f. Estimated income taxes for the year, $3,000.

2. Prepare an income statement, a statement of retained earnings, and a balance sheet.
3. Prepare adjusting, closing, and, if required, reversing entries.
4. How would you evaluate Mr. Leung's first year in practice?

Donald Leung, Consultant, Inc.
Trial Balance
June 30, 19x5

Cash	$ 9,750	
Accounts Receivable	8,127	
Office Supplies	1,146	
Office Equipment	11,265	
Accounts Payable		$ 3,888
Unearned Retainers		15,000
Common Stock		12,000
Dividends	18,000	
Consulting Fees		54,525
Rent Expense	5,400	
Utility Expense	2,151	
Wages Expense	29,574	
	$85,413	$85,413

4A-4.

L O 3
S O 5, 6, 7

Preparation of a Work Sheet; Financial Statements; and Adjusting, Closing, and Reversing Entries

At the end of the current fiscal year, this was the trial balance of the Drexel Theater Corporation:

Drexel Theater Corporation
Trial Balance
June 30, 19x5

Cash	$ 31,800	
Accounts Receivable	18,544	
Prepaid Insurance	19,600	
Office Supplies	780	
Cleaning Supplies	3,590	
Land	20,000	
Building	400,000	
Accumulated Depreciation, Building		$ 39,400
Theater Furnishings	370,000	
Accumulated Depreciation, Theater Furnishings		65,000
Office Equipment	31,600	
Accumulated Depreciation, Office Equipment		15,560
Accounts Payable		45,506
Gift Books Liability		41,900
Mortgage Payable		300,000
Common Stock		200,000
Retained Earnings		112,648
Dividends	60,000	
Ticket Sales Revenue		411,400
Theater Rental Revenue		45,200
Usher Wages Expense	157,000	
Office Wages Expense	24,000	
Utility Expense	112,700	
Interest Expense	27,000	
	$1,276,614	$1,276,614

REQUIRED

1. Enter the trial balance amounts in the Trial Balance columns of a work sheet, and complete the work sheet using the following information:
   a. Expired insurance, $17,400.
   b. Inventory of unused office supplies, $244.
   c. Inventory of unused cleaning supplies, $468.
   d. Estimated depreciation on the building, $14,000.
   e. Estimated depreciation on the theater furnishings, $36,000.
   f. Estimated depreciation on the office equipment, $3,160.
   g. The company credits all gift books sold during the year to the Gift Books Liability account. A gift book is a booklet of ticket coupons that is purchased in advance as a gift. The recipient redeems the coupons at some point in the future. On June 30 it was estimated that $37,800 worth of the gift books had been redeemed.
   h. Accrued but unpaid usher wages at the end of the accounting period, $860.
   i. Estimated federal income taxes, $20,000.
2. Prepare an income statement, a statement of retained earnings, and a balance sheet.
3. Prepare adjusting, closing, and, if required, reversing entries.

4A-5.
L O 3
S O 5, 6, 7
The Complete Accounting Cycle: Two Months

During its first two months of operation, the Rawls Repair Corporation, which specializes in bicycle repairs, completed the following transactions:

Oct. 1 Began business by making a deposit in a company bank account of $12,000, in exchange for 1,200 shares of $10 par value common stock.
1 Paid the premium on a one-year insurance policy, $1,200.
1 Paid the current month's rent, $1,040.
3 Purchased repair equipment from Conklin Company, $4,400. The terms were $600 down and $200 per month for nineteen months. The first payment is due November 1.
8 Purchased repair supplies from McKenna Company on credit, $390.
12 Paid utility bill for October, $154.
16 Cash bicycle repair revenue for the first half of October, $1,362.
19 Made payment to McKenna Company, $200.
31 Cash bicycle repair revenue for the last half of October, $1,310.
31 Declared and paid cash dividend of $800.

Nov. 1 Paid the monthly rent, $1,040.
1 Made the monthly payment to Conklin Company, $200.
7 Purchased repair supplies on credit from McKenna Company, $894.
15 Cash bicycle repair revenue for the first half of November, $1,050.
16 Paid the utility bill for November, $166.
17 Paid McKenna Company on account, $400.
30 Cash bicycle repair revenue for the last half of November, $1,874.
30 Declared and paid cash dividend of $800.

REQUIRED

1. Prepare journal entries to record the October transactions.
2. Open the following accounts: Cash (111); Prepaid Insurance (117); Repair Supplies (119); Repair Equipment (144); Accumulated Depreciation, Repair Equipment (145); Accounts Payable (212); Income Taxes Payable (213); Common Stock (311); Retained Earnings (312); Dividends (313); Income Summary (314); Bicycle Repair Revenue (411); Store Rent Expense (511); Utility Expense (512); Insurance Expense (513); Repair Supplies Expense (514); Depreciation Expense, Repair Equipment (515); and Income Taxes Expense (516). Post the October journal entries to the ledger accounts.
3. Prepare a trial balance in the Trial Balance columns of a work sheet, and complete the work sheet using the following information:
   a. One month's insurance has expired.
   b. The remaining inventory of repair supplies is $194.
   c. The estimated depreciation on repair equipment is $70.
   d. The estimated income taxes are $40.
4. From the work sheet, prepare an income statement, a statement of retained earnings, and a balance sheet for October.
5. From the work sheet, prepare and post adjusting and closing entries for October.

6. Prepare a post-closing trial balance.
7. Prepare and post the journal entries to record the November transactions.
8. Prepare a trial balance for November in the Trial Balance columns of a work sheet, and complete the work sheet based on the following information:
   a. One month's insurance has expired.
   b. The inventory of repair supplies is $418.
   c. The estimated depreciation on repair equipment is $70.
   d. The estimated income taxes are $40.
9. From the work sheet, prepare an income statement, a statement of retained earnings, and a balance sheet for November.
10. From the work sheet, prepare and post adjusting and closing entries for November.
11. Prepare a post-closing trial balance.

Problem Set B

4B-1.

L O 3
S O 5

Preparation of Financial Statements and End-of-Period Entries

Lancaster Recreational Park, Inc. rents campsites in a wooded park. The adjusted trial balance for Lancaster Recreational Park, Inc. on June 30, 19x3, the end of the current fiscal year, is shown below.

Lancaster Recreational Park, Inc.
Adjusted Trial Balance
June 30, 19x3

Cash	$ 4,080	
Accounts Receivable	7,320	
Supplies	228	
Prepaid Insurance	1,188	
Land	30,000	
Building	91,800	
Accumulated Depreciation, Building		$ 21,000
Accounts Payable		3,450
Wages Payable		1,650
Common Stock		40,000
Retained Earnings		53,070
Dividends	36,000	
Campsite Rentals		88,200
Wages Expense	23,850	
Insurance Expense	3,784	
Utility Expense	1,800	
Supplies Expense	1,320	
Depreciation Expense, Building	6,000	
Income Taxes Expense	10,000	
Income Taxes Payable		10,000
	$217,370	$217,370

REQUIRED

1. From the information given, prepare an income statement, a statement of retained earnings, and a balance sheet.
2. Record the closing entries in the general journal.
3. Assuming that Wages Payable and Income Taxes Payable represent wages and income taxes accrued at the end of the accounting period, record the reversing entries required on July 1.

4B-2.

L O 3 *Preparation of Financial Statements and Closing Entries*

The following adjusted trial balance pertains to County Line Tennis Club, Inc. at the end of the company's fiscal year.

County Line Tennis Club, Inc.
Adjusted Trial Balance
June 30, 19x5

Cash	$ 26,200	
Prepaid Advertising	9,600	
Supplies	1,200	
Land	745,200	
Buildings	300,000	
Accumulated Depreciation, Buildings		$ 45,000
Equipment	156,000	
Accumulated Depreciation, Equipment		50,400
Accounts Payable		303,000
Unearned Revenue, Locker Fees		3,000
Wages Payable		9,000
Property Taxes Payable		22,500
Income Taxes Payable		40,000
Common Stock		464,000
Retained Earnings		271,150
Dividends	54,000	
Revenues from Court Fees		678,100
Revenues from Locker Fees		9,600
Wages Expense	351,000	
Maintenance Expense	51,600	
Advertising Expense	39,750	
Water and Utility Expense	64,800	
Supplies Expense	6,000	
Depreciation Expense, Buildings	9,000	
Depreciation Expense, Equipment	12,000	
Property Taxes Expense	22,500	
Miscellaneous Expense	6,900	
Income Taxes Expense	40,000	
	$1,895,750	$1,895,750

REQUIRED

1. Prepare an income statement, a statement of retained earnings, and a balance sheet.
2. From the information provided, prepare closing entries.

4B-3.

L O 3
S O 5, 6, 7 *Preparation of a Work Sheet; Financial Statements; and Adjusting, Closing, and Reversing Entries*

José Vargas opened his executive search service on July 1, 19x1. Some customers paid for his services after they were rendered, and others paid in advance for one year of service. After six months of operation, Mr. Vargas wanted to know how his business stood. The trial balance on December 31 appears on page 182.

REQUIRED

1. Enter the trial balance amounts in the Trial Balance columns of the work sheet. Remember that accumulated depreciation is listed with its asset account. Complete the work sheet using the following information:
   a. One year's rent had been paid in advance when the business began.
   b. Inventory of unused office supplies, $75.

c. One-half year's depreciation on office equipment, $300.

d. Service rendered that had been paid for in advance, $863.

e. Executive search services rendered during the month of December but not yet billed, $270.

f. Wages earned by employees but not yet paid, $188.

g. Estimated income taxes for the half-year, $1,000.

2. From the work sheet, prepare an income statement, a statement of retained earnings, and a balance sheet.

3. From the work sheet, prepare adjusting and closing entries and, if required, reversing entries.

4. What is your evaluation of Mr. Vargas's first six months in business?

Vargas Executive Search Service, Inc.
Trial Balance
December 31, 19x1

Cash	$ 3,713	
Prepaid Rent	1,800	
Office Supplies	413	
Office Equipment	10,750	
Accounts Payable		$ 3,173
Unearned Revenue		1,823
Common Stock		10,000
Dividends	3,200	
Search Revenue		15,140
Telephone and Utility Expense	1,260	
Wages Expense	9,000	
	$30,136	$30,136

4B-4.

L O 3

S O 5, 6, 7

Preparation of a Work Sheet; Financial Statements; and Adjusting, Closing, and Reversing Entries

The trial balance on page 183 was taken from the ledger of Robinson Delivery Service Corporation on December 31, 19x4, the end of the company's fiscal year.

REQUIRED

1. Enter the trial balance amounts in the Trial Balance columns of a work sheet, and complete the work sheet using the following information:

a. Expired insurance, $3,060.

b. Inventory of unused delivery supplies, $1,430.

c. Inventory of unused office supplies, $186.

d. Estimated depreciation, building, $14,400.

e. Estimated depreciation, trucks, $15,450.

f. Estimated depreciation, office equipment, $2,700.

g. The company credits the lockbox fees of customers who pay in advance to the Unearned Lockbox Fees account. Of the amount credited to this account during the year, $5,630 had been earned by December 31.

h. Lockbox fees earned but unrecorded and uncollected at the end of the accounting period, $816.

i. Accrued but unpaid truck drivers' wages at the end of the year, $1,920.

j. Management estimates federal income taxes to be $12,000.

2. Prepare an income statement, a statement of retained earnings, and a balance sheet.

3. Prepare adjusting, closing, and, if required, reversing entries from the work sheet.

Robinson Delivery Service Corporation
Trial Balance
December 31, 19x4

Cash	$ 10,072	
Accounts Receivable	29,314	
Prepaid Insurance	5,340	
Delivery Supplies	14,700	
Office Supplies	2,460	
Land	15,000	
Building	196,000	
Accumulated Depreciation, Building		$ 53,400
Trucks	103,800	
Accumulated Depreciation, Trucks		30,900
Office Equipment	15,900	
Accumulated Depreciation, Office Equipment		10,800
Accounts Payable		9,396
Unearned Lockbox Fees		8,340
Mortgage Payable		72,000
Common Stock		40,000
Retained Earnings		88,730
Dividends	30,000	
Delivery Services Revenue		283,470
Lockbox Fees Earned		28,800
Truck Drivers' Wages Expense	120,600	
Office Salaries Expense	44,400	
Gas, Oil, and Truck Repairs Expense	31,050	
Interest Expense	7,200	
	$625,836	$625,836

4B-5.

L O 3
S O 5, 6, 7
The Complete Accounting Cycle: Two Months

On August 1, 19xx, Carl Luzinski opened Luzinski Appliance Service, Inc. During August and September, he completed the following transactions for the company:

Aug. 1 Deposited $10,000 of his savings in a bank account for the company in exchange for 1,000 shares of $10 par value stock.
1 Paid the rent for a store for one month, $850.
1 Paid the premium on a one-year insurance policy, $960.
5 Purchased repair equipment from Jensen Company for $8,400 on the basis of a $1,200 down payment and $600 per month for one year. The first payment is due September 1.
9 Purchased repair supplies from Marco Company on credit, $936.
12 Paid cash for an advertisement in a local newspaper, $120.
16 Received cash repair revenue for the first half of the month, $800.
25 Made a payment to Marco Company, $450.
31 Received cash repair revenue for the second half of August, $1,950.
31 Declared and paid a cash dividend, $500.
Sept. 1 Paid the monthly rent, $850.
1 Made monthly payment to Jensen Company, $600.
7 Purchased additional repair supplies on credit from Marco Company, $1,726.
15 Received cash repair revenue for the first half of the month, $1,828.
18 Paid cash for an additional advertisement in the local newspaper, $120.
20 Paid Marco Company on account, $1,200.
30 Received cash repair revenue for the last half of the month, $1,634.
30 Declared and paid a cash dividend, $500.

REQUIRED

1. Prepare journal entries to record the August transactions.
2. Open the following accounts: Cash (111); Prepaid Insurance (117); Repair Supplies (119); Repair Equipment (144); Accumulated Depreciation, Repair Equipment (145); Accounts Payable (212); Income Taxes Payable (213); Common Stock (311); Retained Earnings (312); Dividends (313); Income Summary (314); Repair Revenue (411); Store Rent Expense (511); Advertising Expense (512); Insurance Expense (513); Repair Supplies Expense (514); Depreciation Expense, Repair Equipment (515); and Income Taxes Expense (516). Post the August journal entries to the ledger accounts.
3. Prepare a trial balance in the Trial Balance columns of a work sheet, and complete the work sheet using the following information:
   a. One month's insurance has expired.
   b. The remaining inventory of repair supplies is $338.
   c. The estimated depreciation on repair equipment is $140.
   d. The estimated income taxes are $100.
4. From the work sheet, prepare an income statement, a statement of retained earnings, and a balance sheet for August.
5. From the work sheet, prepare and post the adjusting and closing entries.
6. Prepare a post-closing trial balance.
7. Prepare and post journal entries to record the September transactions.
8. Prepare a trial balance in the Trial Balance columns of a work sheet, and complete the work sheet based on the following information:
   a. One month's insurance has expired.
   b. The inventory of unused repair supplies is $826.
   c. The estimated depreciation on repair equipment is $140.
   d. The estimated income taxes are $100.
9. From the work sheet, prepare the September income statement, a statement of retained earnings, and a balance sheet.
10. From the work sheet, prepare and post the adjusting and closing entries.
11. Prepare a post-closing trial balance.

CRITICAL THINKING AND COMMUNICATION

Conceptual Mini-Cases

CMC 4-1.

L O 1

Interim Financial Statements

Ocean Oil Services Corporation provides services for offshore drilling operations off the coast of Louisiana. The company has a significant amount of debt to River National Bank in Baton Rouge. The bank requires the company to provide it with financial statements every quarter. Explain what is involved in preparing financial statements every quarter.

CMC 4-2.

S O 5

Accounting Efficiency

Way Heaters, Inc., located just outside Milwaukee, Wisconsin, is a small, successful manufacturer of industrial heaters. The company's heaters are used, for instance, to heat chocolate for candy manufacturers. The company sells its heaters to some of its customers on credit with generous terms. The terms usually specify payment six months after purchase and an interest rate based on current bank rates. Because the interest on these loans accrues a little bit every day but is not paid until the due date of the note, it is necessary to make an adjusting entry at the end of each accounting period to debit Interest Receivable and credit Interest Income for the amount of the interest accrued but not paid to date. The company prepares financial statements every month. Keeping track of what has been accrued in the past is time-consuming because the notes carry different dates and interest rates. Be prepared to discuss what the accountant can do to simplify the process of making the adjusting entry for accrued interest each month.

Ethics Mini-Case

EMC 4-1.

L O 2 *Ethics and Time Pressure*

Jay Wheeler, the assistant accountant for WB, Inc., has made adjusting entries and is preparing the adjusted trial balance for the first six months of the year. Financial statements must be delivered to the bank by 5 o'clock to support a critical loan agreement. By noon, Jay cannot balance the adjusted trial balance. The figures are off by $1,320, so he increases the balance of the Retained Earnings account by $1,320. He prepares the statements and sends them to the bank on time. Jay hopes that no one will notice the problem and believes he can find the error and correct it by the end of next month. Are Jay's actions ethical? Why or why not? Did Jay have other alternatives?

Decision-Making Case

DMC 4-1.

S O 7 *Conversion from Accrual to Cash Statement*

Adele's Secretarial Service, Inc. is a very simple business. Adele provides typing services for students at the local university. Her accountant prepared the income statement that appears below for the year ended June 30, 19x4.

Adele's Secretarial Service, Inc.
Income Statement
For the Year Ended June 30, 19x4

Revenues		
Typing Services		$20,980
Expenses		
Rent Expense	$2,400	
Depreciation Expense, Office Equipment	2,200	
Supplies Expense	960	
Other Expenses	1,240	
Total Expenses		6,800
Net Income		$14,180

In reviewing this statement, Adele is puzzled. She knows the company paid cash dividends of $15,600 to her, the sole stockholder, yet the cash balance in the company's bank account increased from $460 to $3,100 from last June 30 to this June 30. She wants to know how her net income could be less than the cash dividends she took out of the business if there is an increase in the cash balance.

Her accountant shows her the balance sheet for June 30, 19x4 and compares it to the one for June 30, 19x3. She explains that besides the change in the cash balance, accounts receivable from customers decreased by $1,480 and accounts payable increased by $380 (supplies are the only items Adele buys on credit). The only other asset or liability account that changed during the year was Accumulated Depreciation, Office Equipment, which increased by $2,200.

REQUIRED

1. Explain to Adele why the accountant is answering her question by pointing out year-to-year changes in the balance sheet.
2. Verify the cash balance increase by preparing a statement that lists the receipts of cash and the expenditures of cash during the year.
3. How did you treat depreciation expense? Why?

Basic Research Activity

RA 4-1.

L O 2, 3, 4 *Interview of a Local*
S O 5 *Business Person*

Arrange to spend about an hour interviewing the owner, manager, or accountant of a local service or retail business. Your goal is to learn as much as you can about the accounting cycle of the person's business. Ask the interviewee to show you his or her accounting records and to tell you how such transactions as sales, purchases, payments, and payroll are handled. Examine the documents used to support these transactions. Look at any journals, ledgers, or work sheets. Does the business use a computer? Does it use its own accounting system, or does it use an outside or centralized service? Does it use the cash or the accrual basis of accounting? When does it prepare adjusting entries? When does it prepare closing entries? How often does it prepare financial statements? Does it prepare reversing entries? How do its procedures differ from those described in the text? When the interview is finished, organize and write up your findings and be prepared to present them to your class.

FINANCIAL REPORTING AND ANALYSIS

Interpretation Cases from Business

ICB 4-1.
L O 2, 3 *Closing Entries*

H&R Block, Inc. is the world's largest tax preparation service firm. In its 1993 annual report, the statement of earnings (in thousands, without earnings per share information) for the year ended April 30, 1993 looked like this:[1]

Revenues

Service Revenues	$1,382,306
Royalties	112,560
Investment Income	15,038
Other Revenues	15,426
Total Revenues	$1,525,330

Expenses

Employee Compensation and Benefits	$ 754,002
Occupancy and Equipment Expense	220,815
Marketing and Advertising	52,260
Supplies, Freight, and Postage	59,209
Other Operating Expenses	143,774
Total Expenses	1,230,060
Earnings Before Income Taxes	295,270
Income Taxes	114,565
Net Earnings	$ 180,705

In its statement of retained earnings, the company reported cash dividends for 1993 of $103,462,000.

REQUIRED

1. Prepare, in general journal form, the closing entries that would have been made by H&R Block on April 30, 1993.
2. Based on the way you handled expenses and dividends in **1** and their ultimate effect on retained earnings, what theoretical reason can you give for not including expenses and dividends in the same closing entry?

ICB 4-2.
L O 2 *Identification of Adjusting Entries*

Halliburton Company is one of the world's larger and more diversified oil field services and engineering/construction organizations. The following items appeared on the December 31, 1992, balance sheet of Halliburton Company (in millions).[2] The contracts referred to are agreements to perform services for engineering/construction clients.

Among the assets:
   Unbilled Work on Uncompleted Contracts $198.9

Among the liabilities:
   Advance Billings on Uncompleted Contracts $379.6

---

1. H&R Block, Inc., *Annual Report,* 1993.
2. Halliburton Company, *Annual Report,* 1992.

Contained in Note 2:
> Unbilled work on uncompleted contracts generally represents currently billable work, and such work is usually billed during normal billing processes in the next month.

REQUIRED

1. Which of the two accounts above arises from an adjusting entry? What would be the debit and credit accounts of the entry?
2. Which of the two accounts above would normally require an adjusting entry at the end of the accounting period? What are the debit and credit accounts of the entry?
3. How does the accounting policy described in Note 2 differ from the general rule covered in this text? Why does it differ?
4. Of the four accounts you mentioned in the adjusting entries in **1** and **2** above, which require closing at the end of the year?

International Company Case

ICC 4-1.
L O 1, 3 *Accounting Cycle and Closing Entries*

Nestlé S.A., maker of such well-known products as Nescafé, Lean Cuisine, Perrier, and many others, is one of the largest and most internationally diverse companies in the world. Only 2 percent of its $54.5 billion in revenues comes from its home country of Switzerland, with the rest coming from sales in almost every other country of the world. Nestlé has 482 factories in 69 countries[3] and is highly decentralized; that is, many of its divisions operate as separate companies in their countries. Managing the accounting operations of such a vast empire is a tremendous challenge. In what ways do you think the accounting cycle, including the closing process, would be the same for Nestlé as it is for Joan Miller Advertising Agency, Inc., and in what ways would it be different?

Toys "R" Us Case

TC 4-1.
L O 1, 3 *Fiscal Year, Closing Process, and Interim Reports*

Refer to the Notes to Consolidated Financial Statements in the appendix on Toys "R" Us. When does Toys "R" Us end its fiscal year? What reasons can you give for the company's having chosen this date? From the standpoint of completing the accounting cycle, what advantages does this date have? Does Toys "R" Us prepare interim financial statements? What are the implications of interim financial statements for the accounting cycle?

---

3. Nestlé S.A., *Annual Report,* 1992.

Accounting for Merchandising Operations

LEARNING OBJECTIVES

1. Identify the management issues related to merchandising businesses.
2. Compare the income statements for service and merchandising concerns and define the components of the merchandising income statement.
3. Distinguish between the perpetual and the periodic inventory systems and explain the importance of taking a physical inventory.
4. Contrast and record transactions related to sales and purchases under the periodic and the perpetual inventory systems.
5. Define *internal control* and identify the three elements of the internal control structure, including seven examples of control procedures.
6. Describe the inherent limitations of internal control.
7. Apply control procedures to certain merchandising transactions.

SUPPLEMENTAL OBJECTIVE

8. Apply sales and purchases discounts to merchandising transactions.

Target Stores

The management of merchandising companies has two key decisions to make: the price at which merchandise is sold and the level of service the company provides. For instance, a department store can set the price of its merchandise at a relatively high level and provide a great deal of service. A discount store, on the other hand, may price its merchandise at a relatively low level and provide limited service. Target Stores, a division of Dayton-Hudson Corp., is a successful discount merchandiser of brand-name apparel and other products. What decisions did Target Stores make about pricing and service to achieve this success?

By emphasizing brand-name merchandise at low prices, the company chose to differentiate itself from department and specialty stores that sell at full price and from other discount chains that sell low-priced but less well-known merchandise. Target Stores decided to operate very large stores that could be controlled by a minimum number of employees. The company planned to earn income by selling a large volume of merchandise. In 1992, it operated over five hundred stores and earned income (before interest and income taxes) of $574 million on sales of $10.4 billion.[1]

MANAGEMENT ISSUES IN MERCHANDISING BUSINESSES

OBJECTIVE

1 *Identify the management issues related to merchandising businesses*

Up to this point you have studied business and accounting issues related to the simplest type of business—the service business. Service businesses, such as advertising agencies and law firms, perform services for fees or commissions. Merchandising businesses, on the other hand, earn income by buying and selling products or merchandise. These companies, whether wholesale or retail, use the same basic accounting methods as do service companies, but the buying and selling of merchandise adds to the complexity of the process. As a foundation for discussing the accounting issues of merchandising businesses, we must first identify the management issues involved in running a merchandising business.

1. Dayton-Hudson Corp., *Annual Report*, 1992.

CASH FLOW MANAGEMENT

Merchandising businesses differ from service businesses in that they have goods on hand for sale to customers, or merchandise inventory, and engage in a series of transactions called the operating cycle, as shown in Figure 5-1. The transactions in the operating cycle consist of (1) purchases of merchandise inventory, (2) sales of merchandise inventory for cash or on credit, and (3) collection of the cash from the sales. In the case of sales of merchandise for cash, or cash sales, this cash is collected immediately. In the case of sales of merchandise on credit, or credit sales, the company must wait a period of time before receiving the cash. Some very small retail stores may have mostly cash sales and very few credit sales, whereas large wholesale concerns may have almost all credit sales. Most merchandising concerns, however, have a combination of cash and credit sales.

Regardless of the proportions of cash and credit sales, the operators of a merchandising business must carefully manage cash flow, or liquidity. Such cash flow management involves planning the company's receipts and payments of cash. If the company is not able to pay its bills when they are due, it may be forced out of business. Often merchandise that is purchased must be paid for before it is sold and the cash from its sale is collected. For example, if a retail business must pay for its purchases in thirty days, it must have cash available or arrange for borrowing if it cannot sell and collect for the merchandise in thirty days.

The operating cycle for a merchandising firm can be 120 days, or even longer. For example, Dillard Department Stores, Inc., a successful chain of department stores in the South and Southwest, has an operating cycle of about 220 days. Its inventory is on hand on average 79 days, and it takes on average 141 days to collect its receivables. Since the company pays for its merchandise in an average of 65 days, a much shorter time, management must carefully plan its cash flow, including borrowing.

Figure 5-1. The Operating Cycle of Merchandising Concerns

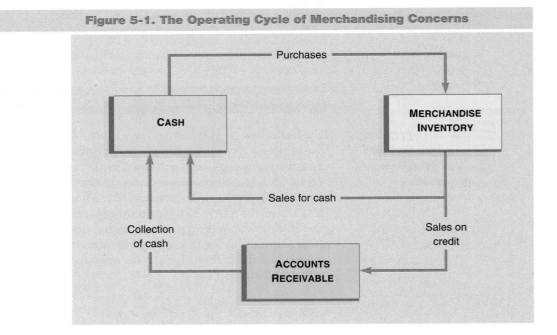

PROFITABILITY MANAGEMENT

In addition to managing its cash flow, management must endeavor to sell its merchandise at a price that exceeds its cost by a sufficient margin to pay operating expenses, such as wages, utilities, advertising, and taxes, and have enough left over to provide sufficient income, or profitability. Profitability management is a complex activity that includes setting appropriate prices on merchandise, purchasing merchandise at favorable prices and terms, and maintaining acceptable levels of expenses. For example, Land's End, Inc., a direct merchant of casual clothing, increased its net income dramatically from 1991 to 1993 by increasing its prices and reducing its selling and general and administrative expenses.

CHOICE OF INVENTORY SYSTEM

A third issue management of merchandising businesses must address is the choice of inventory system. There are two basic systems of accounting for the many items in the merchandise inventory. Under the periodic inventory system, the inventory on hand is counted periodically, usually at the end of the accounting period. No detailed records of the actual inventory on hand are maintained during the accounting period. Under the perpetual inventory system, continuous records are kept of the quantity and, usually, the cost of individual items as they are bought and sold. The periodic inventory system is less costly to maintain than the perpetual inventory system, but it gives management less information about the current status of merchandise inventory. Given the number and diversity of items contained in the merchandise inventory of most businesses, the perpetual inventory system is usually more effective for keeping track of quantities and ensuring optimal customer service. Management must choose the system or combination of systems that is best for achieving the company's goals.

CONTROL OF MERCHANDISING OPERATIONS

The principal transactions of merchandising businesses, which involve buying and selling, are covered by asset accounts—Cash, Accounts Receivable, and Merchandise Inventory—that are vulnerable to theft and embezzlement. One reason for this vulnerability is that cash and inventory are fairly easy to steal. Another is that these asset accounts usually are involved in a large number of transactions, such as cash receipts, receipts on account, payments for purchases, and receipts and shipments of inventory, which can become difficult to monitor. If a merchandising company does not take steps to protect its assets, it can have high losses of cash and inventory. Management's responsibility is to establish an environment, accounting systems, and control procedures that will protect these assets. These systems and procedures are called the internal control structure.

INCOME STATEMENT FOR A MERCHANDISING CONCERN

Service companies, as illustrated thus far in this book, require only a simple income statement. For those companies, as shown in Figure 5-2, net income

Figure 5-2. The Components of Income Statements for Service and Merchandising Companies

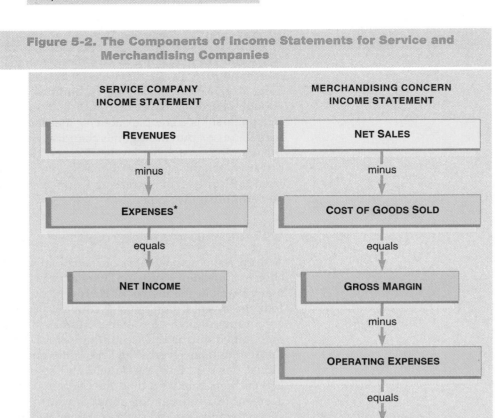

*Includes income taxes.

OBJECTIVE

2 *Compare the income statements for service and merchandising concerns and define the components of the merchandising income statement*

represents the difference between revenues and expenses. But merchandising companies, because they buy and sell merchandise inventory, require a more complex income statement. As shown in Figure 5-2, the income statement for a merchandiser has four major parts: (1) net sales, (2) cost of goods sold, (3) operating expenses, and (4) income taxes. There are also subtotals for (1) gross margin, (2) income before income taxes, and (3) net income. The main difference between a merchandiser's income statement and that of a service business is that the merchandiser must compute gross margin before operating expenses and income taxes are deducted. In the following discussion, the income statement for Fenwick Fashions Corporation, presented in Exhibit 5-1, will serve as an example of a merchandising income statement.

Exhibit 5-1. Merchandising Income Statement

Fenwick Fashions Corporation
Income Statement
For the Year Ended December 31, 19x2

Net Sales

Gross Sales			$246,350
Less Sales Returns and Allowances			7,025
Net Sales			$239,325

Cost of Goods Sold

Merchandise Inventory, December 31, 19x1		$ 52,800	
Purchases	$126,400		
Less Purchases Returns and Allowances	7,776		
Net Purchases	$118,624		
Freight In	8,236		
Net Cost of Purchases		126,860	
Goods Available for Sale		$179,660	
Less Merchandise Inventory, December 31, 19x2		48,300	
Cost of Goods Sold			131,360

Gross Margin			$107,965

Operating Expenses

Selling Expenses			
Sales Salaries Expense	$ 22,500		
Freight Out Expense	5,740		
Advertising Expense	10,000		
Insurance Expense, Selling	1,600		
Store Supplies Expense	1,540		
Total Selling Expenses		$ 41,380	
General and Administrative Expenses			
Office Salaries Expense	$ 26,900		
Insurance Expense, General	4,200		
Office Supplies Expense	1,204		
Depreciation Expense, Building	2,600		
Depreciation Expense, Office Equipment	2,200		
Total General and Administrative Expenses		37,104	
Total Operating Expenses			78,484

Income Before Income Taxes			$ 29,481
Income Taxes			5,000
Net Income			$ 24,481

NET SALES

The first major part of the merchandising income statement is net sales, or often simply *sales*. Net sales consist of the gross proceeds from sales of merchandise, or gross sales, less sales returns and allowances and any discounts allowed. Gross sales consist of total cash sales and total credit sales during a given accounting period. Even though the cash may not be collected until the following accounting period, revenue is recognized, under the revenue recognition rule, as being earned when title for merchandise passes from seller to buyer at the time of sale. Sales returns and allowances are cash refunds, credits on account, and allowances off selling prices made to customers who have received defective or otherwise unsatisfactory products. If other discounts or allowances are given to customers (see supplemental objective 8, for instance), they also should be deducted from gross sales.

Management, investors, and others often use the amount of sales and trends suggested by sales as indicators of a firm's progress. Increasing sales suggest growth; decreasing sales indicate the possibility of decreased future earnings and other financial problems. To detect trends, comparisons are frequently made between the net sales of different accounting periods.

COST OF GOODS SOLD

Cost of goods sold, or often simply *cost of sales,* which is the amount a merchant paid for the merchandise that was sold during an accounting period, is the second part of the merchandising income statement. The method of computing cost of goods sold is sometimes confusing because it must take into account both merchandise inventory on hand at the beginning of the accounting period, or beginning inventory, and merchandise inventory on hand at the end of the accounting period, or ending inventory. The ending inventory appears on the balance sheet at the end of the accounting period and becomes the beginning inventory for the next accounting period.

The computation of cost of goods sold for Fenwick Fashions based on the income statement in Exhibit 5-1 is illustrated in Figure 5-3. The goods available for sale during the year is the sum of two factors, beginning inven-

Figure 5-3. Components of Cost of Goods Sold

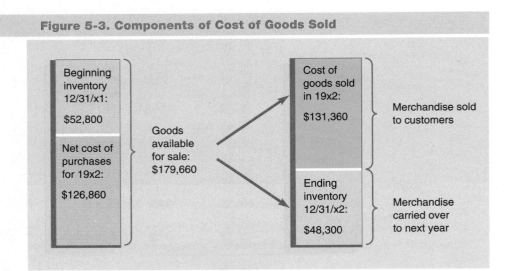

tory and the net cost of purchases during the year. In this case, the goods available for sale is $179,660 ($52,800 + $126,860).

If a company sold all the goods available for sale during a given accounting period, the cost of goods sold would equal the cost of goods available for sale. In most businesses, however, some merchandise will remain unsold and on hand at the end of the year. This merchandise, or ending inventory, must be deducted from the cost of goods available for sale to determine cost of goods sold. In the case of Fenwick Fashions, the ending inventory on December 31, 19x2, is $48,300. Thus, cost of goods sold is $131,360 ($179,660 − $48,300).

An important component of the cost of goods sold section is net cost of purchases, which consists of net purchases plus any freight charges on the purchases. Net purchases equals total purchases less any deductions, such as purchases returns and allowances or any discounts allowed by suppliers for early payment (see supplemental objective 8). Because freight charges, or freight in (or transportation in), are a necessary cost to receive merchandise for sale, they are added to net purchases to arrive at the net cost of purchases.

GROSS MARGIN

The third major area of the merchandising income statement is gross margin, or *gross profit,* which is the difference between net sales and cost of goods sold. To be successful, merchants must sell goods for an amount greater than cost—that is, gross margin must be great enough to pay operating expenses and provide an adequate income after income taxes have been paid. Management is interested in both the amount and the percentage of gross margin. The percentage of gross margin is computed by dividing the amount of gross margin by net sales. In the case of Fenwick Fashions, the amount of gross margin is $107,965 and the percentage of gross margin is 45.1 percent ($107,965 ÷ $239,325). This information is helpful in planning business operations. For instance, management may try to increase total sales dollars by reducing the selling price. This strategy reduces the percentage of gross margin, but it will work only if the total items sold increase enough to raise the absolute amount of gross margin. This is the strategy followed by a discount warehouse store like Sam's Warehouse Club. On the other hand, management may decide to keep a high gross margin from sales and attempt to increase sales and the amount of gross margin by increasing operating expenses such as advertising. This is the strategy followed by upscale specialty stores like Neiman Marcus. Other strategies to increase gross margin from sales, such as reducing cost of goods sold by better purchasing methods, can also be explored.

OPERATING EXPENSES

The fourth major area of the merchandising income statement consists of operating expenses, which are the expenses other than cost of goods sold that are incurred in running a business. They are similar to the expenses of a service company. It is customary to group operating expenses into categories, such as selling expenses and general and administrative expenses. Selling expenses include the costs of storing and preparing goods for sale; displaying, advertising, and otherwise promoting sales; making sales; and delivering goods to the buyer, if the seller pays the cost of delivery. The latter cost is often called freight out expense, or delivery expense. Among general and administrative expenses are general office expense, which includes expenses for accounting, personnel, and credit and collections, and any other expenses that apply to overall operation. Although general occupancy expenses, such as rent expense, insurance expense, and utility expenses, are often classified as general and administrative expenses, they may also be allocated between both the selling and the general and administrative categories. Careful planning and control of operating expenses can improve a company's profitability.

INCOME BEFORE INCOME TAXES

Income before income taxes—the difference between gross margin and operating expenses—is an important measure of profitability because it tells how much income a business has earned from operations. Income before income taxes is also referred to as *operating income* or *income from operations* because it represents the income from a company's normal, or main, business. Because companies may be subject to different tax rates, income before income taxes is often used to compare the profitability of two or more companies or divisions within a company.

INCOME TAXES

Income taxes are stated separately on the income statement because they are determined by law and are therefore less subject to management control than other items. Current federal income tax rates for corporations can vary from 15 percent to 38 percent depending on the amount of income before income taxes and other factors.

NET INCOME

Net income, the final figure, or "bottom line," of the income statement is what remains after operating expenses and income taxes are deducted from the gross margin. It is an important performance measure because it represents the amount of business earnings that accrue to stockholders. It is the amount that is transferred to retained earnings from all the income-generating activities during the year. Both management and investors often use net income to measure whether a business has been operating successfully during the past accounting period.

INVENTORY SYSTEMS

OBJECTIVE

3 *Distinguish between the perpetual and the periodic inventory systems and explain the importance of taking a physical inventory*

As we have seen, merchandise inventory is a key factor in determining the cost of goods sold. Consequently, every merchandiser needs a useful and reliable system for determining both the quantity and the cost of the goods on hand. The two basic systems of accounting for the number of items in the merchandise inventory are the periodic inventory system and the perpetual inventory system.

PERIODIC INVENTORY SYSTEM

As discussed earlier, under the periodic inventory system, the inventory on hand is counted periodically, usually at the end of the accounting period. No detailed records of the actual inventory on hand are maintained during the period. Cost of goods sold under the periodic inventory system is determined according to the format followed by Fenwick Fashions in Exhibit 5-1 and Figure 5-3. In the simplest case, the cost of inventory purchased is accumulated in a Purchases account. At the end of the accounting period, the cost of the physical inventory, based on an actual count, is deducted from the cost of goods available for sale to arrive at cost of goods sold. Entries are made at the end of the accounting period to remove the beginning inventory (the last period's ending inventory) and to enter the ending inventory of the current period. As explained in the appendix on the merchandising work sheet and closing entries, these are the only entries that will be made to the merchandise inventory account during the period. Consequently, the figure for inventory on hand is accurate only on the balance sheet date. As soon as any purchases or sales are made, the figure becomes a historical amount and remains so until the new ending inventory is entered at the end of the next accounting period.

Many retail and wholesale businesses use periodic inventory systems because they do not require much clerical work. If a business is fairly small, management can maintain control over inventory simply by observation or by use of an off-line system of cards or computer records. On the other hand, for larger businesses, the lack of detailed records may cause inefficiencies that lead either to lost sales or to high operating costs.

PERPETUAL INVENTORY SYSTEM

Under the perpetual inventory system, records are kept of the quantity and, usually, the cost of individual items as they are bought or sold. The detailed data available under the perpetual inventory system enable management to respond to customers' inquiries about product availability, to order inventory more effectively and thus avoid running out of stock, and to control financial costs associated with investments in the inventory. Under this system, the cost of each item is recorded in the Merchandise Inventory account when it is purchased. As merchandise is sold, its cost is transferred from the Merchandise Inventory account to the Cost of Goods Sold account. Thus, at all times the balance of the Merchandise Inventory account equals the cost of goods on hand, and the balance in Cost of Goods Sold equals the cost of merchandise sold to customers. The Purchases account is not used in a perpetual inventory system.

Traditionally, the periodic inventory system has been used by companies that sell items of low value in high volume because of the difficulty and expense of accounting for the purchase and sale of each item. Examples of such companies are drugstores, automobile parts stores, department stores, discount stores, and grain companies. In contrast, companies that sell items of high unit value, such as appliances or automobiles, tended to use the perpetual inventory system. This distinction between high and low unit value for inventory systems has blurred considerably in recent years because of the widespread use of the computer. Although the periodic inventory system is still widely used, the use of the perpetual inventory system has increased greatly.

TAKING PHYSICAL INVENTORY

Actually counting all merchandise on hand is called taking a physical inventory. This can be a difficult task because it is easy to leave items out or to count them twice. A physical inventory must be taken under both the periodic and the perpetual inventory systems.

Merchandise inventory includes all salable goods owned by the concern, regardless of where they are located—on shelves, in storerooms, in warehouses, in trucks en route between warehouses and stores. It includes goods in transit from suppliers if title to the goods has passed to the merchant. Ending inventory includes neither merchandise sold but not yet delivered to customers nor goods that cannot be sold because they are damaged or obsolete. If the damaged or obsolete goods can be sold at a reduced price, however, they should be included in ending inventory at their reduced value.

The actual count usually is taken after the close of business on the last day of the fiscal year. To facilitate taking the physical inventory, many companies end their fiscal year in a slow season, when inventories are at relatively low levels. Retail department stores often end their fiscal year in January or February, for example. After hours, at night or on the weekend, employees count and record all items on numbered inventory tickets or sheets, following procedures to make sure that no items are missed. Sometimes a store closes for all or part of a day for inventory taking. The use of bar coding to take inventory electronically has greatly facilitated the taking of a physical inventory in many companies.

BUSINESS BULLETIN: TECHNOLOGY IN PRACTICE

Many grocery stores, which traditionally used the periodic inventory system, now employ bar coding. Electronic markings on each product, called bar codes or universal product codes (UPC), are used to update the physical inventory as items are sold by running them through cash registers linked to a computer. Bar coding has become common in all types of retail companies, as well as in manufacturing firms and hospitals. It has become common for some retail businesses to use the perpetual system for keeping track of the physical flow of inventory and the periodic system for preparing the financial statements.

MERCHANDISING TRANSACTIONS

OBJECTIVE

4 *Contrast and record transactions related to sales and purchases under the periodic and the perpetual inventory systems*

Merchandising transactions can be divided into the two broad categories of sales transactions and purchases transactions. The ways in which these transactions are recorded differ somewhat under the periodic and the perpetual inventory systems. Before we discuss these transactions, some terms related to sales of merchandise need to be introduced.

SALES TERMS

When goods are sold on credit, both parties should understand the amount and timing of payment as well as other terms of the purchase, such as who pays delivery or freight charges and what warranties or rights of return apply. Sellers quote prices in different ways. Many merchants quote the price at which they expect to sell their goods. Others, particularly manufacturers and wholesalers, provide a price list or catalogue and quote prices as a percentage (usually 30 percent or more) off the list or catalogue prices. These discounts are called trade discounts. For example, if an article was listed at $1,000 with a trade discount of 40 percent, or $400, the seller would record the sale at $600 and the buyer would record the purchase at $600. If the seller wishes to change the selling price, the trade discount can be raised or lowered. At times the trade discount may vary depending on the quantity purchased. The list price and related trade discounts are used only to arrive at the agreed-on price; they do not appear in the accounting records.

The terms of sale are usually printed on the sales invoice and thus constitute part of the sales agreement. Customary terms differ from industry to industry. In some industries payment is expected in a short period of time, such as ten or thirty days. In these cases, the invoice is marked "n/10" or "n/30" (read as "net ten" or "net thirty"), meaning that the amount of the invoice is due either ten days or thirty days after the invoice date. If the invoice is due ten days after the end of the month, it is marked "n/10 eom."

In some industries it is customary to give discounts for early payments. These discounts, called sales discounts, are intended to increase the seller's liquidity by reducing the amount of money tied up in accounts receivable. An invoice that offered a sales discount might be labeled "2/10, n/30," which means that the buyer either can pay the invoice within ten days of the invoice date and take a 2 percent discount off of merchandise, which does not include freight charges, or can wait thirty days and then pay the full amount of the invoice. It is almost always advantageous for a buyer to take the discount because the saving of 2 percent over a period of 20 days (from the eleventh day to the thirtieth day) represents an effective annual rate of 36 percent (360 days ÷ 20 days × 2% = 36%). Most companies would be better off borrowing money to take the discount. The practice of giving sales discounts has been declining because it is costly to the seller and because, from the buyers' viewpoint, the amount of the discount is usually very small in relation to the price of the purchase. Accounting for sales discounts is covered as a supplemental objective at the end of this chapter.

In some industries, it is customary for the seller to pay transportation costs and to charge a price that includes those costs. In other industries, it is customary for the purchaser to pay transportation charges on merchandise. Special terms designate whether the supplier or the purchaser pays the freight charges. FOB shipping point means that the supplier places the merchandise "free on board" at the point of origin, and the buyer pays the shipping costs. The title to the merchandise passes to the buyer at that point as well. For example, when the sales agreement for the purchase of a car says "FOB factory," the buyer must pay the freight from where the car was made to wherever he or she is located, and the buyer owns the car from the time it leaves the factory. On the other hand, FOB destination means that the supplier pays the transportation costs to the place where the merchandise is delivered. The supplier retains title until the merchandise reaches its destination and usually prepays the shipping costs, in which case the buyer makes no accounting entry for freight. The effects of these special shipping terms are summarized below:

Shipping Term	Where Title Passes	Who Pays the Cost of Transportation
FOB shipping point	At origin	Buyer
FOB destination	At destination	Seller

TRANSACTIONS RELATED TO PURCHASES OF MERCHANDISE

The primary difference in accounting between the perpetual and the periodic inventory systems is that under the perpetual inventory system, the Merchandise Inventory account is continuously adjusted because purchases, sales, and other inventory transactions are entered in this account as they occur. Purchases increase Merchandise Inventory, and purchases returns decrease it. As sales of goods occur, the cost of these goods is transferred from Merchandise Inventory to the Cost of Goods Sold account. Under the periodic inventory system, the Merchandise Inventory account stays at the beginning level until the physical inventory is recorded at the end of the period. A Purchases account is used to accumulate the purchases of merchandise during the accounting period, and a Purchases Returns and Allowances account is used to accumulate returns and allowances of purchases. To illustrate these differences, purchase transactions made by Fenwick Fashions are shown below. Differences in the two systems are shown in bold print.

PURCHASES OF MERCHANDISE ON CREDIT

Oct. 3   Purchased merchandise on credit from Neebok Company, invoice dated October 1, terms n/10, FOB shipping point, $4,890.

Periodic Inventory System			Perpetual Inventory System		
Oct. 3 **Purchases**	4,890		**Merchandise Inventory**	4,890	
Accounts Payable		4,890	Accounts Payable		4,890
Purchase of merchandise from Neebok Company, terms n/10, FOB shipping point, invoice dated Oct. 1			Purchase of merchandise from Neebok Company, terms n/10, FOB shipping point, invoice dated Oct. 1		

Under the periodic inventory system, Purchases is a temporary account. Its sole purpose is to accumulate the total cost of merchandise purchased for resale during an accounting period. (Purchases of other assets, such as equipment, should be recorded in the appropriate asset account, not in the Purchases account.) The Purchases account does not indicate whether merchandise has been sold or is still on hand. Under the perpetual inventory system, the Purchases account is not necessary, because purchases are recorded directly in the Merchandise Inventory account.

TRANSPORTATION COSTS ON PURCHASES

Oct. 4   Received bill from Transfer Freight Company for transportation costs on October 3 shipment, invoice dated October 1, terms n/10, $160.

Periodic Inventory System			Perpetual Inventory System		
Oct. 4 Freight In	160		Freight In	160	
Accounts Payable		160	Accounts Payable		160
Transportation charges on Oct. 3 purchase, Transfer Freight Co., terms n/10, invoice dated Oct. 1			Transportation charges on Oct. 3 purchase, Transfer Freight Co., terms n/10, invoice dated Oct. 1		

In this example, transportation costs, even though they are billed separately by the freight company, are part of the costs to acquire the goods and should be included in the Purchases or the Merchandise Inventory accounts. However, since most shipments contain many different items of merchandise, it is usually not practical to identify the specific cost of shipping each item. As a result, transportation costs on purchases are usually accumulated, under both the periodic and the perpetual inventory systems, in a Freight In account.

In some cases, the seller pays the freight charges and bills them to the buyer as a separate item on the invoice. When this occurs, the entries are the same as in the October 3 example above, except that an additional debit is made to Freight In for the amount of the freight charges and Accounts Payable is increased by a like amount.

PURCHASES RETURNS AND ALLOWANCES

Oct. 6 Returned merchandise received from Neebok Company on October 3 for credit, $480.

Periodic Inventory System			**Perpetual Inventory System**		
Oct. 6 Accounts Payable	480		Accounts Payable	480	
Purchases Returns and Allowances		480	**Merchandise Inventory**		480
Merchandise returned to Neebok Company for full credit on purchase of Oct. 3			Merchandise returned to Neebok Company for full credit on purchase of Oct. 3		

If a seller sends the wrong product or one that is otherwise unsatisfactory, the buyer may be allowed to return the item for a cash refund or credit on account, or the buyer may be given an allowance off the sales price. Under the periodic inventory system, the amount of the return or allowance is recorded in the Purchases Returns and Allowances account. This account is a contra-purchases account with a normal credit balance and is deducted from purchases on the income statement. Under the perpetual inventory system, the returned merchandise is removed from the Merchandise Inventory account.

PAYMENTS ON ACCOUNT

Oct. 10 Paid in full the amount due to Neebok Company for the purchase of October 3, part of which was returned on October 6.

Periodic Inventory System			**Perpetual Inventory System**		
Oct. 10 Accounts Payable	4,410		Accounts Payable	4,410	
Cash		4,410	Cash		4,410
Made payment on account to Neebok Company $4,890 − $480 = $4,410			Made payment on account to Neebok Company $4,890 − $480 = $4,410		

Payments for merchandise purchased are the same under both systems.

TRANSACTIONS RELATED TO SALES OF MERCHANDISE

The primary difference in accounting for transactions related to sales under the perpetual and the periodic inventory systems pertains to the Cost of

Goods Sold account. Under the perpetual inventory system, at the time of the sale, the cost of the merchandise is transferred from the Merchandise Inventory account to the Cost of Goods Sold account. In the case of a return, it is transferred back from Cost of Goods Sold to Merchandise Inventory. Under the periodic inventory system, the Cost of Goods Sold account is not used because the Merchandise Inventory account is not updated until the end of the accounting period. To illustrate these differences, transactions related to sales made by Fenwick Fashions are shown below. Differences in the two systems are indicated in bold print.

SALES OF MERCHANDISE ON CREDIT

Oct. 7   Sold merchandise on credit to Gonzales Distributors, terms n/30, FOB destination, $1,200; the cost of the merchandise was $720.

Periodic Inventory System			**Perpetual Inventory System**		
Oct. 7 Accounts Receivable	1,200		Accounts Receivable	1,200	
Sales		1,200	Sales		1,200
Sale of merchandise to Gonzales Distributors, terms n/30, FOB destination			Sale of merchandise to Gonzales Distributors, terms n/30, FOB destination		
			Cost of Goods Sold	**720**	
			Merchandise Inventory		**720**
			To transfer cost of merchandise inventory sold to Cost of Goods Sold account		

Sales of merchandise are handled in the same way under both inventory systems, except that under the perpetual inventory system, Cost of Goods Sold is updated by a transfer from Merchandise Inventory. In the case of cash sales, Cash rather than Accounts Receivable is debited for the amount of the sale.

PAYMENT OF DELIVERY COSTS

Oct. 8   Payment of transportation costs for sales on October 7, $78.

Periodic Inventory System			**Perpetual Inventory System**		
Oct. 8 Freight Out Expense	78		Freight Out Expense	78	
Cash		78	Cash		78
Delivery costs on Oct. 7 sale			Delivery costs on Oct. 7 sale		

A seller will often absorb delivery or freight out costs in the belief that doing so will facilitate the sale of its products. These costs are accumulated in an account called Delivery Expense or Freight Out Expense, which is shown as a selling expense on the income statement.

RETURNS OF MERCHANDISE SOLD

Oct. 9   Merchandise sold on October 7 accepted back from Gonzales Distributors for full credit and returned to merchandise inventory, $300; the cost of the merchandise was $180.

Periodic Inventory System				**Perpetual Inventory System**		
Oct. 9	Sales Returns and Allowances	300		Sales Returns and Allowances	300	
	Accounts Receivable		300	Accounts Receivable		300
	Return of merchandise from			Return of merchandise from		
	Gonzales Distributors			Gonzales Distributors		
				Mechandise Inventory	**180**	
				Cost of Goods Sold		**180**
				To transfer cost of		
				merchandise returned to		
				Merchandise Inventory		
				account		

Because returns and allowances to customers for wrong or unsatisfactory merchandise are often an indicator of customer dissatisfaction, such amounts are accumulated, under both methods, in a Sales Returns and Allowances account. This account is a contra-sales account with a normal debit balance and is deducted from sales on the income statement. In addition, under the perpetual inventory system, the cost of the merchandise must be transferred from the Cost of Goods Sold account into the Merchandise Inventory account. If an allowance is made instead of accepting a return, or if merchandise cannot be returned to inventory and resold, this transfer is not made.

RECEIPTS ON ACCOUNT

Nov. 5   Received payment in full from Gonzales Distributors for sale of merchandise on Oct. 7, less the return on Oct. 9.

Periodic Inventory System				**Perpetual Inventory System**		
Nov. 5	Cash	900		Cash	900	
	Accounts Receivable		900	Accounts Receivable		900
	Receipt on account from			Receipt on account from		
	Gonzales Distributors			Gonzales Distributors		
	$1,200 − $300 = $900			$1,200 − $300 = $900		

Receipts on account are recorded in the same way under both systems.

BUSINESS BULLETIN: BUSINESS PRACTICE

In some industries a high percentage of sales returns is an accepted business practice. A book publisher like Simon & Schuster will produce and ship more copies of a best seller than it expects to sell because, to gain the attention of potential buyers, copies must be distributed to a wide variety of outlets, such as bookstores, department stores, and discount stores. As a result, returns of unsold books may run as high as 30 to 50 percent of books shipped. The same sales principles apply to magazines sold on newsstands, like *People,* and to popular recordings produced by companies like Motown Records. In all these businesses, management scrutinizes the Sales Returns account for ways to reduce returns and increase profitability. ═══

PERPETUAL INVENTORY SYSTEM'S EFFECT ON THE INCOME STATEMENT

The merchandising income statement illustrated in Exhibit 5-1 uses the periodic inventory method. This may be determined by the presence of the computation of net cost of purchases and the figures for beginning and ending inventory. Under the perpetual inventory system, the Cost of Goods Sold account replaces these items. The gross margin for Fenwick Fashions would be presented as shown in Exhibit 5-2. In this example, Freight In is included in Cost of Goods Sold. Theoretically, freight in should be allocated between ending inventory and cost of goods sold, but most companies do not disclose it on the income statement because it is a relatively small amount.

INVENTORY LOSSES

Most companies experience losses in merchandise inventory from spoilage, shoplifting, and employee pilferage. When such losses occur, the periodic inventory system provides no means of tracking them because the costs are automatically included in the cost of goods sold. For example, assume that a company has lost $1,250 in stolen merchandise during an accounting period. When the physical inventory is taken, the missing items are not in stock, so they cannot be counted. Because the ending inventory does not contain these items, the amount subtracted from cost of goods available for sale is less than it would be if the goods were in stock. The cost of goods sold, then, is overstated by $1,250. In a sense, the cost of goods sold is inflated by the amount of merchandise that has been lost.

The perpetual inventory system makes it easier to identify such losses. Because the Merchandise Inventory account is continuously updated for sales, purchases, and returns, the loss will show up as the difference between the inventory records and the physical inventory taken at the end of the

Exhibit 5-2. Partial Income Statement Under the Perpetual Inventory System

Fenwick Fashions Corporation Partial Income Statement For the Year Ended Decemer 31, 19xx	
Net Sales	
Gross Sales	$246,350
Less Sales Returns and Allowances	7,025
Net Sales	$239,325
Cost of Goods Sold*	131,360
Gross Margin	$107,965

* Freight In has been included in Cost of Goods Sold.

accounting period. Once the amount of the loss has been identified, the ending inventory needs to be updated by crediting the Merchandise Inventory account. The offsetting debit is usually listed as an increase in Cost of Goods Sold because the loss is considered a cost that reduces the company's gross margin.

Audio Trak

DECISION POINT

Audio Trak, a specialty retailer of customized audio systems for automobiles, installed a perpetual inventory system in the second quarter of 1992. The new system allowed the firm to adjust its merchandise inventories to sales patterns more effectively and to prepare monthly financial statements. Although the system led to an improvement in sales and income, the gross margin on the monthly income statements was falling below both management's expectations and the industry average. At the end of 1993, a physical inventory revealed that actual merchandise inventory was considerably lower than the perpetual inventory records indicated. The merchandise inventories of some stores were off more than others, but all had deficiencies. Management wondered what had caused these losses and what steps could be taken to prevent them in the future.

The merchandise inventory losses probably were due to shoplifting and embezzlement. Management must carefully review its controls at the individual stores and install a system that will protect its merchandise inventory from these forms of theft. As you will see in the next section, this goal can be accomplished through an internal control structure that creates an environment that encourages compliance with a company's policies, a good accounting system, and specific procedures designed to safeguard the merchandise inventory. • • • • •

INTERNAL CONTROL STRUCTURE: BASIC ELEMENTS AND PROCEDURES

A merchandising company can have high losses of cash and inventory if it does not take steps to protect its assets. The best way to do this is to set up and maintain a good internal control structure.

OBJECTIVE

5 *Define* **internal control** *and identify the three elements of the internal control structure, including seven examples of control procedures*

INTERNAL CONTROL DEFINED

Internal control has traditionally been defined as all the policies and procedures management uses to protect a firm's assets and to ensure the accuracy and reliability of the accounting records. It also includes controls that deal with operating efficiency and adherence to management's policies. In other words, management wants not only to safeguard assets and have reliable records, but also to maintain an efficient operation that follows its policies. To this end, it establishes an internal control structure that consists of three elements: the control environment, the accounting system, and control procedures.[2]

The control environment is created by the overall attitude, awareness, and actions of management. It includes management's philosophy and operating style, organizational structure, methods of assigning authority and responsibility, and personnel policies and practices. Personnel should be qualified to handle responsibilities, which means that employees must be trained and informed. For example, the manager of a retail store should train employees to follow prescribed procedures for handling cash sales, credit card sales, and returns and refunds. It is clear that an accounting system, no matter how well designed, is only as good as the people who run it. The control environment also includes regular reviews for compliance with procedures. For example, large companies often have a staff of internal auditors who review the company's system of internal control to see that it is working properly and that procedures are being followed. In smaller businesses, owners and managers should conduct these reviews.

The accounting system consists of the methods and records established by management to identify, assemble, analyze, classify, record, and report a company's transactions, and to make sure that the goals of internal control are being met.

Finally, management uses control procedures to safeguard the company's assets and to ensure the reliability of the accounting records. These include:

1. **Authorization**   All transactions and activities should be properly authorized by management. In a retail store, for example, some transactions, such as normal cash sales, are authorized routinely; others, such as issuing a refund, may require the manager's approval.
2. **Recording transactions**   To facilitate preparation of financial statements and to establish accountability for assets, all transactions should be recorded. In a retail store, for example, the cash register records sales, refunds, and other transactions internally on a paper tape or computer disk so that the cashier can be held responsible for the cash that has been received and the merchandise that has been removed during his or her shift.
3. **Documents and records**   The design and use of adequate documents help ensure the proper recording of transactions. For example, to ensure that all transactions are recorded, invoices and other documents should be prenumbered and all numbers should be accounted for.
4. **Limited access**   Access to assets should be permitted only with management's authorization. For example, retail stores should use cash registers, and only the cashier responsible for the cash in the register should have access to it. Other employees should not be able to open the cash drawer if the cashier is not present. Likewise, warehouses and storerooms should be accessible only to authorized personnel. Access to accounting records, including company computers, should also be controlled.
5. **Periodic independent verification**   The records should be checked against the assets by someone other than the persons responsible for the records and the assets. For example, at the end of each shift or day, the owner or store manager should count the cash in the cash drawer and compare the amount to the amounts recorded on the tape or computer disk in the cash register. Other examples of independent verification are the monthly bank reconciliation and periodic counts of physical inventory.

---

2. *Professional Standards* (New York: American Institute of Certified Public Accountants, June 1, 1989), Vol. 1, Sec. AU 319.06–.11.

6. **Separation of duties** The organizational plan should separate functional responsibilities. Within a department, no one person should be in charge of authorizing transactions, operating the department, handling assets, and keeping records of assets. For example, in a stereo store, each employee should oversee only a single part of a transaction. A sales employee takes the order and writes out an invoice. A cashier receives the customer's cash or credit card payment and issues a receipt. Once the customer has a paid receipt, and only then, another employee obtains the item from the warehouse and gives it to the customer. A person in the accounting department subsequently records the sales from the tape in the cash register, comparing them with the sales invoices and updating the inventory in the records. The separation of duties means that a mistake, careless or not, cannot be made without being seen by at least one other person.

7. **Sound personnel procedures** Sound practices should be followed in managing the people who carry out the functions of each department. Among these practices are supervision, rotation of key people among different jobs, insistence that employees take vacations, and bonding of personnel who handle cash or inventories. Bonding is the process of carefully checking an employee's background and insuring the company against any theft by that person. Bonding does not guarantee the prevention of theft, but it does prevent or reduce economic loss if theft occurs. Prudent personnel procedures help ensure that employees know their jobs, are honest, and will find it difficult to carry out and conceal embezzlement over time.

OBJECTIVE

6 *Describe the inherent limitations of internal control*

LIMITATIONS OF INTERNAL CONTROL

No system of internal control is without weaknesses. As long as control procedures are performed by people, the internal control system is vulnerable to human error. Errors may arise from misunderstandings, mistakes in judgment, carelessness, distraction, or fatigue. Separation of duties can be defeated through collusion by employees who secretly agree to deceive the company. Also, established procedures may be ineffective against employees' errors or dishonesty. Or, controls that may have been effective at first may later become ineffective because conditions have changed.[3] In some cases, the costs of establishing and maintaining elaborate systems may exceed the benefits. In a small business, for example, active involvement by the owner can be a practical substitute for separation of some duties.

BUSINESS BULLETIN: ETHICS IN PRACTICE

 A recent survey of the country's largest companies by the accounting firm KPMG Peat Marwick revealed that 76 percent of the respondents thought that fraud was a major problem for business today and that the problem was increasing. The five most frequent means of fraud were misappropriation of funds, check forgery, misuse of credit cards, false invoices, and theft. The median loss from a fraud was $200,000. Poor internal controls, collusion between employees and third parties, and management override of internal controls were the most cited causes of fraud. ▬▬▬

3. Ibid., Sec. AU 320.35.

INTERNAL CONTROL OVER MERCHANDISING TRANSACTIONS

OBJECTIVE

7 *Apply control procedures to certain merchandising transactions*

Sound internal control procedures are needed in all aspects of a business, but particularly when assets are involved. Assets are especially vulnerable when they enter or leave the business. When sales are made, for example, cash or other assets enter the business, and goods or services leave the business. Procedures must be set up to prevent theft during these transactions. Likewise, purchases of assets and payments of liabilities must be controlled. The majority of these transactions can be safeguarded by adequate purchasing and payroll systems. In addition, assets on hand, such as cash, investments, inventory, plant, and equipment, must be protected.

In this section, we apply internal control procedures to such merchandising transactions as cash sales, receipts, purchases, and cash payments. Internal control for other kinds of transactions is covered later in the book. As mentioned previously, similar procedures are applicable to service and manufacturing businesses.

When a system of internal control is applied effectively to merchandising transactions, it can achieve important goals for accounting as well as for general management. For example, here are two goals for accounting:

1. To prevent losses of cash or inventory from theft or fraud
2. To provide accurate records of merchandising transactions and account balances

And here are three broader goals for management:

1. To keep enough inventory on hand to sell to customers without overstocking
2. To keep enough cash on hand to pay for purchases in time to receive discounts
3. To keep credit losses as low as possible by making credit sales only to customers who are likely to pay on time

One control used in meeting broad management goals is the cash budget, which projects future cash receipts and disbursements. By maintaining adequate cash balances, the company is able to take advantage of discounts on purchases, prepare to borrow money when necessary, and avoid the damaging effects of being unable to pay bills when they are due. On the other hand, if the company has excess cash, it can be invested, earning interest until it is needed.

A more specific accounting control is the separation of duties involving the handling of cash. This separation means that theft without detection is extremely unlikely except through the collusion of two or more employees. The separation of duties is easier in large businesses than in small ones, where one person may have to carry out several duties. The effectiveness of internal control over cash varies, depending on the size and nature of the company. Most firms, however, should use the following procedures:

1. Separate the functions of authorization, recordkeeping, and custodianship of cash.
2. Limit the number of people who have access to cash.
3. Specifically designate the people who are responsible for handling cash.
4. Use banking facilities as much as possible, and keep the amount of cash on hand to a minimum.
5. Bond all employees who have access to cash.
6. Physically protect cash on hand by using cash registers, cashiers' cages, and safes.

7. Have a person who does not handle or record cash make surprise audits of the cash on hand.
8. Record all cash receipts promptly.
9. Deposit all cash receipts promptly.
10. Make payments by check rather than by currency.
11. Have a person who does not authorize, handle, or record cash transactions reconcile the Cash account.

Notice that each of these procedures helps safeguard cash by making it more difficult for any one person who has access to cash to steal or misuse it undetected.

CONTROL OF CASH SALES RECEIPTS

Cash receipts for sales of goods and services can be received by mail or over the counter in the form of checks or currency. Whatever the source, cash should be recorded immediately upon receipt. This usually is done by making an entry in a cash receipts journal. This step establishes a written record of cash receipts that should prevent errors and make theft more difficult. The cash receipts journal is discussed in the appendix on special-purpose journals.

Control of Cash Received Through the Mail   Cash receipts that arrive by mail are vulnerable to theft by the employees who handle them. This way of doing business is increasing, however, because of the expansion of mail order sales. To control these receipts, customers should be urged to pay by check instead of currency.

Cash that comes in through the mail should be handled by two or more employees. The employee who opens the mail should make a list in triplicate of the money received. The list should contain each payer's name, the purpose for which the money was sent, and the amount. One copy goes with the cash to the cashier, who deposits the money. The second copy goes to the accounting department for recording. The third copy is kept by the person who opens the mail. Errors can be caught easily because the amount deposited by the cashier must agree with the amount received and the amount recorded in the cash receipts journal.

Control of Cash Received over the Counter   Two common means of controlling cash sales receipts are the use of cash registers and prenumbered sales tickets. The amount of a cash sale should be rung up on a cash register at the time of the sale. The cash register should be placed so that the customer can see the amount recorded. Each cash register should have a locked-in tape on which it prints the day's transactions. At the end of the day, the cashier counts the cash in the cash register and turns it in to the cashier's office. Another employee takes the tape out of the cash register and records the cash receipts for the day in the cash receipts journal. The amount of cash turned in and the amount recorded on the tape should agree; if not, any differences must be accounted for. Large retail chains commonly perform this function by having each cash register tied directly into a computer. In this way, each transaction is recorded as it occurs. This method separates the responsibility for cash receipts, cash deposits, and recordkeeping, ensuring good internal control.

In some stores, internal control is strengthened further by the use of prenumbered sales tickets and a central cash register or cashier's office, where all sales are rung up and collected by a person who does not participate in the sale. Under this procedure, the salesperson completes a prenumbered sales ticket at the time of sale, giving one copy to the customer and keeping a copy. At the end of the day, all sales tickets must be accounted for, and the sales total computed from the sales tickets should equal the total sales recorded on the cash register.

CONTROL OF PURCHASES AND CASH DISBURSEMENTS

Cash disbursements are particularly vulnerable to fraud and embezzlement. In one recent case, the treasurer of one of the nation's largest jewelry retailers was charged with having stolen over $500,000 by systematically overpaying federal income taxes and pocketing the refund checks as they came back to the company.

To avoid this kind of theft, cash should be paid only on the basis of specific authorization supported by documents that establish the validity and amount of the claim. In addition, maximum possible use should be made of the principle of separation of duties in the purchase of goods and services and the payment for them. The degree of separation of duties varies, depending on the size of the business. Figure 5-4 shows how this kind of control can be maximized in large companies. In this example, five internal units (the requesting department, the purchasing department, the accounting department, the receiving department, and the treasurer) and two external contacts (the supplier and the banking system) all play a role in the internal control plan. Notice that business documents are also crucial components of the plan.

Figure 5-4. Internal Control for Purchasing and Paying for Goods and Services

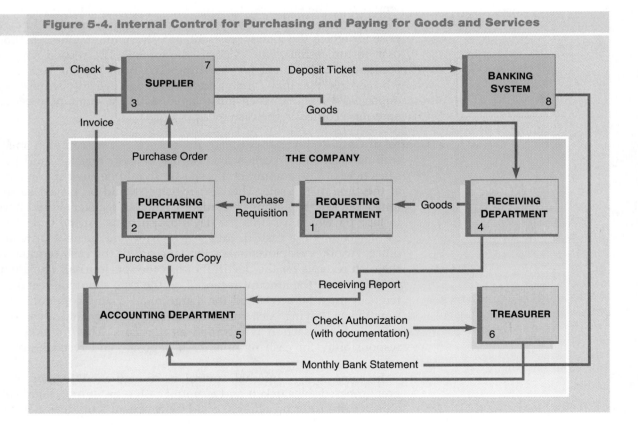

Under this plan, as summarized in Table 5-1, every action is documented and subject to verification by at least one other person. For instance, the requesting department cannot work out a kickback scheme with the supplier because the receiving department independently records receipts and the accounting department verifies prices. The receiving department cannot steal goods because the receiving report must equal the invoices. For the same reason, the supplier cannot bill for more goods than it ships. The work of the accounting

Table 5-1. Internal Control Plan for Purchases and Cash Disbursements

Business Document	Prepared by	Sent to	Verification and Related Procedures
1. Purchase requisition	Requesting department	Purchasing department	Purchasing verifies authorization.
2. Purchase order	Purchasing department	Supplier	Supplier sends goods or services in accordance with purchase order.
3. Invoice	Supplier	Accounting department	Accounting receives invoice from supplier.
4. Receiving report	Receiving department	Accounting department	Accounting compares invoice, purchase order, and receiving report. Accounting verifies prices.
5. Check authorization (or voucher)	Accounting department	Treasurer	Accounting attaches check authorization to invoice, purchase order, and receiving report.
6. Check	Treasurer	Supplier	Treasurer verifies all documents before preparing check.
7. Deposit ticket	Supplier	Supplier's bank	Supplier compares check with invoice. Bank deducts check from buyer's account.
8. Bank statement	Buyer's bank	Accounting department	Accounting compares amount and payee's name on returned check with check authorization.

department is verified by the treasurer, and the treasurer ultimately is checked by the accounting department.

Figures 5-5 through 5-9, which show typical documents used in this internal control plan, follow the purchase of twenty boxes of FAX paper rolls. To begin, the credit office (requesting department) of Martin Maintenance Company fills out a formal request for a purchase, or purchase requisition, for twenty boxes of FAX paper rolls (Figure 5-5). The department head approves it and forwards it to the purchasing department. The people in the purchasing department prepare a purchase order, as shown in Figure 5-6. The purchase order is addressed to the vendor (seller) and contains a description of the items ordered; the expected price, terms, and shipping date; and other shipping instructions. Martin Maintenance Company does not pay any bill that is not accompanied by a purchase order number.

After receiving the purchase order, the vendor, Henderson Supply Company, ships the goods (in this case, delivers them) and sends an invoice, or bill (Figure 5-7, page 213), to Martin Maintenance Company. The invoice gives the quantity and description of the goods delivered and the terms of payment. If goods cannot all be shipped immediately, the estimated date for shipment of the remainder is indicated.

When the goods reach the receiving department of Martin Maintenance Company, an employee writes the description, quantity, and condition of the goods on a form called a receiving report. The receiving department does not receive a copy of the purchase order or invoice, so its employees do not know what should be received. Thus, they are not tempted to steal any excess that may be delivered.

The receiving report is sent to the accounting department, where it is compared with the purchase order and the invoice. If all is correct, the accounting

Figure 5-5. Purchase Requisition

PURCHASE REQUISITION	No. 7077

Martin Maintenance Company

From: Credit Office   Date: September 6, 19xx

To: Purchasing Department   Suggested Vendor: Henderson Supply Company

Please purchase the following items:

Quantity	Number	Description
20 boxes	X 144	FAX paper rolls

Reason for Request	To be filled in by Purchasing Department
Six months' supply for office Approved *B.M.*	 Date ordered 9/8/xx P.O. No. J 102

Figure 5-6. Purchase Order

PURCHASE ORDER   No. __J 102__

Martin Maintenance Company
8428 Rocky Island Avenue
Chicago, Illinois 60643

To: Henderson Supply Company   Date ___September 8, 19xx___
     2525 25th Street
     Mesa, Illinois 61611   FOB ___Destination___

Ship to: Martin Maintenance Company   Ship by ___September 12, 19xx___
          Above Address   Terms ___2/10, n/30___

Please ship the following:

Quantity	✓	Number	Description	Price	Per	Amount
20 boxes		X 144	FAX paper rolls	12.00	box	$240.00

Purchase order number must appear
on all shipments and invoices.

Ordered by
Marsha Owen

Figure 5-7. Invoice

INVOICE   No. __0468__

Henderson Supply Company   Date ___September 12, 19xx___
2525 25th Street
Mesa, Illinois 61611   Your Order No. __J 102__

Sold to: Ship to:

Martin Maintenance Company   Same
8428 Rocky Island Avenue
Chicago, Illinois 60643

                             Sales Representative: Joe Jacobs

Quantity		Description	Price	Per	Amount
Ordered	Shipped				
20	20	X 144 FAX paper rolls	12.00	box	$240.00

FOB Destination	Terms: 2/10, n/30	Date Shipped: 9/12/xx Via: Self

Figure 5-8. Check Authorization

CHECK AUTHORIZATION

	NO.	CHECK
Requisition	7077	✓
Purchase Order	J 102	✓
Receiving Report	JR 065	✓
INVOICE	0468	
Price		✓
Calculations		✓
Terms		✓

Approved for Payment _____ *J. Joseph*

department completes a **check authorization** and attaches it to the three supporting documents. The check authorization form shown in Figure 5-8 has a space for each item to be checked off as it is examined. Notice that the accounting department has all the documentary evidence for the transaction but does not have access to the assets purchased. Nor does it write the checks for payment. This means that the people performing the accounting function cannot gain by falsifying documents in an effort to conceal fraud.

Finally, the treasurer examines all the documents and issues an order to the bank for payment, called a **check** (Figure 5-9), for the amount of the invoice less any appropriate discount. In some systems, the accounting department fills out the check so that all the treasurer has to do is inspect and

Figure 5-9. Check with Attached Remittance Advice

NO. _1787_

_9/21_ 19 _xx_

PAY TO
THE ORDER OF ___Henderson Supply Company___ $ _235.20_

Two hundred thirty-five and 20/100 — — — — — — — — — Dollars

THE LAKE PARK NATIONAL BANK
Chicago, Illinois

Martin Maintenance Company

.⑆03 130 1532⑆ ⑈8030 647 4⑈

by ___Arthur Martin___

- -

Remittance Advice

Date	P.O. No.	DESCRIPTION	AMOUNT
9/21/xx	J 102	20 X 144 FAX paper rolls	
		Supplied Inv. No. 0468	$240.00
		Less 2% discount	4.80
		Net	$235.20
		Martin Maintenance Company	

sign it. The check is then sent to the supplier, with a remittance advice that shows what the check is for. A supplier who is not paid the proper amount will complain, of course, thus providing a form of outside control over the payment. The supplier deposits the check in the bank, which returns the canceled check with Martin Maintenance Company's next bank statement. If the treasurer has made the check out for the wrong amount (or altered a prefilled-in check), the problem shows up in the bank reconciliation.

There are many variations of the system just described. This example is offered as a simple system that provides adequate internal control.

Supplemental OBJECTIVE

8 *Apply sales and purchases discounts to merchandising transactions*

ACCOUNTING FOR DISCOUNTS

SALES DISCOUNTS

As mentioned earlier, some industries give sales discounts for early payment. Because it usually is not possible to know at the time of the sale whether the customer will pay in time to take advantage of them, sales discounts are recorded only at the time the customer pays. For example, assume that Fenwick Fashions Corporation sells merchandise to a customer on September 20 for $300, on terms of 2/10, n/60. This is the entry at the time of the sale:

Sept. 20	Accounts Receivable	300	
	Sales		300
	Sale of merchandise on credit, terms 2/10, n/60		

The customer can take advantage of the sales discount any time on or before September 30, ten days after the date of the invoice. For example, if the customer pays on September 29, the entry in Fenwick's records would look like this:

Sept. 29	Cash	294	
	Sales Discounts	6	
	Accounts Receivable		300
	Payment for Sept. 20 sale; discount taken		

If the customer does not take advantage of the sales discount but waits until November 19 to pay for the merchandise, the entry would be as follows:

Nov. 19	Cash	300	
	Accounts Receivable		300
	Payment for Sept. 20 sale; no discount taken		

At the end of the accounting period, the Sales Discounts account has accumulated all the sales discounts taken during the period. Because sales discounts reduce revenues from sales, Sales Discounts is a contra-revenue account with a normal debit balance that is deducted from gross sales on the income statement.

PURCHASES DISCOUNTS

Merchandise purchases are usually made on credit and sometimes involve **purchases discounts** for early payment. Purchases discounts are discounts taken for early payment for merchandise purchased for resale. They are to the buyer what sales discounts are to the seller. The amount of discounts taken forms a separate account. Assume a credit purchase of merchandise was made on November 12 for $1,500, terms 2/10, n/30, and a return of $200 in merchandise was granted on November 14. When payment is made, the journal entry looks like this:

Nov. 22	Accounts Payable	1,300	
	Purchases Discounts		26
	Cash		1,274
	Paid the invoice of Nov. 12		

Purchase Nov. 12	$1,500
Less return Nov. 14	200
Net purchase	$1,300
Discount: 2%	26
Cash paid	$1,274

If the purchase is not paid for within the discount period, the entry is as follows:

Dec. 12	Accounts Payable	1,300	
	Cash		1,300
	Paid the invoice of Nov. 12		
	on due date; no discount taken		

Like Purchases Returns and Allowances, Purchases Discounts is a contra-purchases account with a normal credit balance that is deducted from Purchases on the income statement. If a company makes only a partial payment on an invoice, most creditors allow the company to take the discount applicable to the partial payment. The discount usually does not apply to freight, postage, taxes, or other charges that might appear on the invoice.

CHAPTER REVIEW

REVIEW OF LEARNING OBJECTIVES

1. **Identify the management issues related to merchandising businesses.** Merchandising companies differ from service companies in that they earn income by buying and selling products or merchandise. The buying and selling of merchandise adds to the complexity of the business and raises four issues that management must address. First, the series of transactions that merchandising companies engage in (the operating cycle) requires careful cash flow management. Second, profitability management requires pricing goods and controlling costs and expenses so as to ensure that the company earns an adequate income after operating expenses and income taxes have been paid. Third, the company must choose between using the periodic or the perpetual inventory system. Fourth, an internal control structure must be established that protects the assets of cash, merchandise inventory, and accounts receivable.

2. **Compare the income statements for service and merchandising concerns and define the components of the merchandising income statement.** In the simplest case, the income statement for a service company consists only of revenues and expenses. The income statement for a merchandising company has four major parts: (1) net sales, (2) cost of goods sold, (3) operating expenses, and (4) income taxes. Gross margin is the difference between revenues from net sales and the cost

of goods sold. Income before income taxes is the difference between gross margin and operating expenses. Net income is the "bottom line" after income taxes. Some important relationships associated with the computation of cost of goods sold are as follows:

$$\begin{array}{c}\text{Gross} \\ \text{purchases}\end{array} - \begin{array}{c}\text{purchases returns} \\ \text{and allowances}\end{array} + \begin{array}{c}\text{freight} \\ \text{in}\end{array} = \begin{array}{c}\text{net cost of} \\ \text{purchases}\end{array}$$

$$\begin{array}{c}\text{Beginning} \\ \text{merchandise inventory}\end{array} + \begin{array}{c}\text{net cost of} \\ \text{purchases}\end{array} = \begin{array}{c}\text{goods} \\ \text{available for sale}\end{array}$$

$$\begin{array}{c}\text{Goods} \\ \text{available for sale}\end{array} - \begin{array}{c}\text{ending} \\ \text{merchandise inventory}\end{array} = \text{cost of goods sold}$$

3. **Distinguish between the perpetual and the periodic inventory systems and explain the importance of taking a physical inventory.** Merchandise inventory includes all salable goods owned, regardless of where they are located. Merchandise inventory can be determined by one of two systems. Under the *periodic inventory system,* the company usually waits until the end of an accounting period to take a physical inventory; it does not maintain detailed records of physical inventory on hand during the period. Under the *perpetual inventory system,* records are kept of the quantity and, usually, the cost of individual items of inventory throughout the year. The cost of goods sold is recorded as goods are transferred to customers, and the inventory balance is kept current throughout the year as items are bought and sold. Under both systems, a physical inventory, or physical count, is taken at the end of the accounting period—to determine cost of goods sold under the periodic inventory system and to detect inventory losses under the perpetual inventory system.

4. **Contrast and record transactions related to sales and purchases under the periodic and the perpetual inventory systems.** Sales terms define the amount and timing of payment, who pays delivery or freight charges, and what warranties or rights of return apply. Under the perpetual inventory system, the Merchandise Inventory account is continuously adjusted by entering purchases, sales, and other inventory transactions as they occur. Purchases increase the Merchandise Inventory account, and purchases returns decrease it. As sales of goods occur, their cost is transferred from the Merchandise Inventory account to the Cost of Goods Sold account. Under the periodic inventory system, in contrast, the Merchandise Inventory account stays at the beginning level until the physical inventory is recorded at the end of the period. A Purchases account is used to accumulate the purchases of merchandise during the accounting period, and a Purchases Returns and Allowances account is used to accumulate returns and allowances of purchases. Under both systems, transportation costs on purchases are accumulated in the Freight In account and transportation costs on sales are recorded as delivery expense or freight out expense.

5. **Define *internal control* and identify the three elements of the internal control structure, including seven examples of control procedures.** Internal control is all the policies and procedures management uses to protect the organization's assets and to ensure the accuracy and reliability of accounting records. It also works to maintain efficient operations and compliance with management's policies. The internal control structure consists of three elements: the control environment, the accounting system, and control procedures. Examples of control procedures are proper authorization of transactions; recording transactions to facilitate preparation of financial statements and to establish accountability for assets; use of well-designed documents and records; limited access to assets; periodic independent comparison of records and assets; separation of duties into the functions of authorization, operations, custody of assets, and recordkeeping; and use of sound personnel policies.

6. **Describe the inherent limitations of internal control.** A system of internal control relies on the people who implement it. Thus, the effectiveness of internal control is

limited by the people involved. Human error, collusion, the interference of management, and failure to recognize changed conditions all can contribute to a system's failure.

7. **Apply control procedures to certain merchandising transactions.** Certain procedures strengthen internal control over sales, cash receipts, purchases, and cash disbursements. First, the functions of authorization, recordkeeping, and custody should be kept separate. Second, the accounting system should provide for physical protection of assets (especially cash and merchandise inventory), use of banking services, prompt recording and deposit of cash receipts, and payment by check. Third, the people who have access to cash and merchandise inventory should be specifically designated and their number limited. Fourth, employees who have access to cash or merchandise inventory should be bonded. Fifth, the Cash account should be reconciled each month, and surprise audits of cash on hand should be made by an individual who does not authorize, handle, or record cash transactions.

SUPPLEMENTAL OBJECTIVE

8. **Apply sales and purchases discounts to merchandising transactions.** Sales discounts are discounts for early payment. Terms of 2/10, n/30 mean that the buyer can take a 2 percent discount if the invoice is paid within ten days of the invoice date. Otherwise, the buyer is obligated to pay the full amount in thirty days. Discounts on sales are recorded in the Sales Discounts account, and discounts on purchases are recorded in the Purchases Discounts account.

REVIEW OF CONCEPTS AND TERMINOLOGY

The following concepts and terms were introduced in this chapter:

L O 5   **Accounting system:** The methods and records established to identify, assemble, analyze, classify, record, and report a company's transactions, and to ensure that the goals of internal control are being met.

L O 2   **Beginning inventory:** Merchandise on hand at the beginning of an accounting period.

L O 5   **Bonding:** The process of carefully checking an employee's background and insuring the company against theft by that person.

L O 1   **Cash flow management:** The planning of a company's receipts and payments of cash.

L O 7   **Check:** A written order to a bank to pay the amount specified from funds on deposit.

L O 7   **Check authorization:** A form prepared by the accounting department after it has compared the receiving report for goods received with the purchase order and the invoice.

L O 5   **Control environment:** The overall attitude, awareness, and actions of the management of a business, as reflected in philosophy and operating style, organizational structure, methods of assigning authority and responsibility, and personnel policies and practices.

L O 5   **Control procedures:** Procedures and policies established by management to safeguard the company's assets and ensure the reliability of the accounting records.

L O 2   **Cost of goods sold:** The amount paid for the merchandise sold during an accounting period. Also called *cost of sales.*

L O 2   **Ending inventory:** Merchandise on hand at the end of an accounting period.

L O 4   **FOB destination:** A shipping term that means that the seller pays transportation costs to the destination.

L O 4   **FOB shipping point:** A shipping term that means that the buyer pays transportation costs from the point of origin.

L O 2   **Freight in:** Transportation charges on merchandise purchased for resale. Also called *transportation in.*

L O 2   **Freight out expense:** Transportation charges on merchandise sold; an operating expense. Also called *delivery expense.*

L O 2   **Goods available for sale:** The sum of beginning inventory and the net cost of purchases during the year; the total goods available for sale to customers during an accounting period.

L O 2   **Gross margin:** The difference between net sales and cost of goods sold. Also called *gross profit.*

L O 2   **Gross sales:** Total sales for cash and on credit during an accounting period.

L O 2   **Income before income taxes:** Gross margin less operating expenses. Also called *operating income* or *income from operations.*

L O 5   **Internal control:** All the policies and procedures management uses to protect a firm's assets, ensure the accuracy and reliability of its accounting data, promote operational efficiency, and encourage adherence to its policies.

L O 1   **Internal control structure:** A structure established to safeguard the assets of a business and provide reliable accounting records; consists of the control environment, the accounting system, and the control procedures.

L O 7   **Invoice:** A form sent to the purchaser by the vendor that describes the quantity and price of the goods or services delivered and the terms of payment.

L O 1   **Merchandise inventory:** The goods on hand at any one time that are available for sale to customers.

L O 1   **Merchandising business:** A business that earns income by buying and selling products or merchandise.

L O 2   **Net cost of purchases:** Net purchases plus any freight charges on the purchases.

L O 2   **Net income:** For merchandising companies, what is left after deducting operating expenses and income taxes from the gross margin.

L O 2   **Net purchases:** Total purchases less any deductions, such as purchases returns and allowances and purchases discounts.

L O 2   **Net sales:** The gross proceeds from sales of merchandise less sales returns and allowances and any discounts. Also called *sales* on income statements.

L O 1   **Operating cycle:** A series of transactions that includes purchases of merchandise inventory, sales of merchandise inventory for cash or on credit, and collection of the cash from the sales.

L O 2   **Operating expenses:** The expenses other than the cost of goods sold that are incurred in running a business.

L O 1   **Periodic inventory system:** A system for determining ending inventory by a physical count at the end of an accounting period.

L O 1   **Perpetual inventory system:** A system for determining inventory by keeping continuous records of the physical inventory as goods are bought and sold.

L O 3   **Physical inventory:** An actual count of all merchandise on hand at the end of an accounting period.

L O 1   **Profitability management:** The process of setting the appropriate prices on merchandise, purchasing merchandise at favorable prices and terms, and maintaining acceptable levels of expenses.

L O 7   **Purchase order:** A form prepared by a company's purchasing department and sent to a vendor that describes the items ordered; their expected price, terms, and shipping date; and other shipping instructions.

L O 7   **Purchase requisition:** A formal written request for a purchase, prepared by a department in a company and sent to its purchasing department.

L O 4   **Purchases:** A temporary account used to accumulate the total cost of all merchandise purchased for resale during an accounting period.

S O 8   **Purchases discount:** A discount taken for prompt payment for merchandise purchased for resale; the Purchases Discounts account is a contra-purchases account.

L O 4 **Purchases Returns and Allowances:** A contra-purchases account used to accumulate cash refunds, credits on account, or other allowances made by suppliers on merchandise originally purchased for resale.

L O 7 **Receiving report:** A form prepared by the receiving department of a company that describes the quantity and condition of goods received.

L O 4 **Sales discount:** A discount given to a buyer for early payment for a sale made on credit; the Sales Discounts account is a contra-revenue account.

L O 2 **Sales Returns and Allowances:** A contra-revenue account used to accumulate cash refunds, credits on account, and other allowances made to customers who have received defective or otherwise unsatisfactory products.

L O 1 **Service business:** A business that earns income by performing a service for fees or commissions.

L O 4 **Trade discount:** A deduction (usually 30 percent or more) off a list or catalogue price.

REVIEW PROBLEM
MERCHANDISING TRANSACTIONS: PERIODIC AND PERPETUAL INVENTORY SYSTEMS

L O 4   Dawkins Company engaged in the following transactions:

Oct. 1   Sold merchandise to Ernie Devlin on credit, terms n/30, FOB shipping point, $1,050 (cost, $630).

2   Purchased merchandise on credit from Ruland Company, terms n/30, FOB shipping point, $1,900.

2   Paid Custom Freight $145 for freight charges on merchandise received.

6   Purchased store supplies on credit from Arizin Supply House, terms n/30, $318.

9   Purchased merchandise on credit from LNP Company, terms n/30, FOB shipping point, $1,800, including $100 freight costs paid by LNP Company.

11   Accepted from Ernie Devlin a return of merchandise, which was returned to inventory, $150 (cost, $90).

14   Returned for credit $300 of merchandise received on October 2.

15   Returned for credit $100 of store supplies purchased on October 6.

16   Sold merchandise for cash, $500 (cost, $300).

22   Paid Ruland Company for purchase of October 2 less return of October 14.

23   Received full payment from Ernie Devlin for his October 1 purchase, less return on October 11.

REQUIRED

1. Prepare general journal entries to record the transactions, assuming the periodic inventory system is used.
2. Prepare general journal entries to record the transactions, assuming the perpetual inventory system is used.

ANSWER TO REVIEW PROBLEM

1. Periodic Inventory System

2. Perpetual Inventory System

19xx

Oct. 1	Accounts Receivable	1,050	
	Sales		1,050
	Sale on account to Ernie Devlin, terms n/30, FOB shipping point		

Accounts Receivable	1,050	
Sales		1,050
Sale on account to Ernie Devlin, terms n/30, FOB shipping point		

1. Periodic Inventory System *(continued)*

Oct. 1

2 Purchases	1,900	
Accounts Payable		1,900
Purchase on account from Ruland Company, terms n/30		

2 Freight In	145	
Cash		145
Freight on previous purchase		

6 Store Supplies	318	
Accounts Payable		318
Purchased store supplies from Arizin Supply House, terms n/30		

9 Purchases	1,700	
Freight In	100	
Accounts Payable		1,800
Purchase on account from LNP Company, terms n/30, FOB shipping point, freight paid by supplier		

11 Sales Returns and Allowances	150	
Accounts Receivable		150
Accepted return of merchandise from Ernie Devlin		

14 Accounts Payable	300	
Purchases Returns and Allowances		300
Returned portion of merchandise purchased from Ruland Company		

15 Accounts Payable	100	
Store Supplies		100
Returned store supplies (not merchandise) purchased on October 6 for credit		

16 Cash	500	
Sales		500
Sold merchandise for cash		

2. Perpetual Inventory System *(continued)*

Cost of Goods Sold	630	
Merchandise Inventory		630
To transfer cost of merchandise sold to Cost of Goods Sold account		

Merchandise Inventory	1,900	
Accounts Payable		1,900
Purchase on account from Ruland Company, terms n/30		

Freight In	145	
Cash		145
Freight on previous purchase		

Store Supplies	318	
Accounts Payable		318
Purchased store supplies from Arizin Supply House, terms n/30		

Merchandise Inventory	1,700	
Freight In	100	
Accounts Payable		1,800
Purchase on account from LNP Company, terms n/30, FOB shipping point, freight paid by supplier		

Sales Returns and Allowances	150	
Accounts Receivable		150
Accepted return of merchandise from Ernie Devlin		

Merchandise Inventory	90	
Cost of Goods Sold		90
To transfer cost of merchandise returned to Merchandise Inventory		

Accounts Payable	300	
Merchandise Inventory		300
Returned portion of merchandise purchased from Ruland Company		

Accounts Payable	100	
Store Supplies		100
Returned store supplies (not merchandise) purchased on October 6 for credit		

Cash	500	
Sales		500
Sold merchandise for cash		

(continued)

1. Periodic Inventory System *(continued)*

Oct. 16

22	Accounts Payable	1,600	
	Cash		1,600
	Payment on account to Ruland Company $1,900 - $300 = $1,600		

23	Cash	900	
	Accounts Receivable		900
	Receipt on account of Ernie Devlin $1,050 - $150 = $900		

2. Perpetual Inventory System *(continued)*

Cost of Goods Sold	300	
Merchandise Inventory		300
To transfer cost of merchandise sold to Cost of Goods Sold account		

Accounts Payable	1,600	
Cash		1,600
Payment on account to Ruland Company $1,900 - $300 = $1,600		

Cash	900	
Accounts Receivable		900
Receipt on account of Ernie Devlin $1,050 - $150 = $900		

CHAPTER ASSIGNMENTS

KNOWLEDGE AND UNDERSTANDING

Questions

1. What four issues must be faced by managers of merchandising businesses?
2. What is the operating cycle of a merchandising business and why is it important?
3. What is the primary difference between the operations of a merchandising concern and those of a service concern, and how is it reflected on the income statement?
4. Is freight in an operating expense? Explain your answer.
5. Define *gross margin*. Why is it important?
6. During its first year in operation, Kumler Nursery had a cost of goods sold of $64,000 and a gross margin equal to 40 percent of sales. What was the dollar amount of the company's sales?
7. Could Kumler Nursery (in Question 6) have a net loss for the year? Explain your answer.
8. What is the difference between the periodic inventory system and the perpetual inventory system?
9. Under the periodic inventory system, how must the amount of inventory at the end of the year be determined?
10. What are the principal differences in the handling of merchandise inventory in the accounting records under the periodic inventory system and the perpetual inventory system?
11. Discuss this statement: "The perpetual inventory system is the best system because management always needs to know how much inventory it has."
12. What is the difference between a trade discount and a sales discount?
13. The following prices and terms on 50 units of product were quoted by two companies:

	Price	Terms
Supplier A	$20 per unit	FOB shipping point
Supplier B	$21 per unit	FOB destination

Which supplier is quoting the better deal? Explain your answer.

14. What is the principal difference in accounting for the purchase and sale of merchandise under the perpetual inventory system and the periodic inventory system?

15. Hornberger Hardware purchased the following items: (a) a delivery truck, (b) two dozen hammers, (c) supplies for its office workers, and (d) a broom for the janitor. Which items should be debited to the Purchases account under the periodic inventory system?

16. Under which inventory system is a Cost of Goods Sold account maintained? Why?

17. Why is it advisable to maintain a Sales Returns and Allowances account when the same result could be obtained by debiting each return or allowance to the Sales account?

18. Most people think of internal control as a means of making fraud harder to commit and easier to detect. Can you think of some other important purposes of internal control?

19. What are the three elements of the internal control structure?

20. What are some examples of control procedures?

21. Why is the separation of duties necessary to ensure sound internal control? What does this principle assume about the relationships of employees in a company and the possibility of two or more of them stealing from the company?

22. In a small business, it is sometimes impossible to separate duties completely. What are three other practices that a small business can follow to achieve the objectives of internal control over cash?

23. At Thrifty Variety Store, each sales clerk counts the cash in his or her cash drawer at the end of the day, then removes the cash register tape and prepares a daily cash form, noting any discrepancies. This information is checked by an employee in the cashier's office, who counts the cash, compares the total with the form, and then gives the cash to the cashier. What is the weakness in this system of internal control?

24. How does a movie theater control cash receipts?

25. What is the normal balance of the Sales Discounts account? Is it an asset, liability, expense, or contra-revenue account?

Short Exercises

SE 5-1.
L O 1 *Identification of Management Issues*

Identify each of the following decisions as most directly related to (a) cash flow management, (b) profitability management, (c) choice of inventory systems, or (d) control of merchandising operations.

1. Determination of how to protect cash from theft or embezzlement.
2. Determination of the selling price of goods for sale.
3. Determination of policies with regard to sales of merchandise on credit.
4. Determination of whether to use the periodic or the perpetual inventory system.

SE 5-2.
L O 2 *Merchandising Income Statement*

Using the following data, prepare an income statement for Taylor Dry Goods for the month ended February 28:

Cost of Goods Sold	$30,000
General and Administrative Expenses	8,000
Income Taxes	1,000
Net Sales	50,000
Selling Expenses	7,000

SE 5-3.
L O 2 *Cost of Goods Sold: Periodic Inventory System*

Using the following data, prepare the cost of goods sold section of a merchandising income statement (periodic inventory system) for the month of July:

Freight In	$ 3,000
Merchandise Inventory, June 30, 19xx	25,000
Merchandise Inventory, July 31, 19xx	29,000
Purchases	97,000
Purchases Returns and Allowances	5,000

SE 5-4.
L O 2   *Cost of Goods Sold: Periodic Inventory System: Missing Data*

Using the following data and assuming cost of goods sold is $230,000, prepare the cost of goods sold section of a merchandising income statement (periodic inventory system), including computation of the amount of purchases for the month of October:

Freight In	$12,000
Merchandise Inventory, Sept. 30, 19xx	33,000
Merchandise Inventory, Oct. 31, 19xx	44,000
Purchases	?
Purchases Returns and Allowances	9,000

SE 5-5.
L O 4   *Purchases of Merchandise: Periodic Inventory System*

Record each of the following transactions, assuming the periodic inventory system is used:

Aug. 2   Purchased merchandise on credit from Gear Company, invoice dated August 1, terms n/10, FOB shipping point, $2,300.

    3   Received bill from State Shipping Company for transportation costs on August 2 shipment, invoice dated August 1, terms n/30, $210.

    7   Returned damaged merchandise received from Gear Company on August 2 for credit, $360.

  10   Paid in full the amount due to Gear Company for the purchase of August 2, part of which was returned on August 7.

SE 5-6.
L O 4   *Purchases of Merchandise: Perpetual Inventory System*

Record the transactions in **SE 5-5** above, assuming the perpetual inventory system is used.

SE 5-7.
L O 4   *Sales of Merchandise: Periodic Inventory System*

Record each of the following transactions, assuming the periodic inventory system is used:

Aug. 4   Sold merchandise on credit to Kwai Corporation, terms n/30, FOB destination, $1,200.

    5   Payment of transportation costs for sale of August 4, $110.

    9   Merchandise sold on August 4 was accepted back from Kwai Corporation for full credit and returned to the merchandise inventory, $350.

Sept. 4   Received payment in full from Kwai Corporation for merchandise sold on August 4, less the return on August 9.

SE 5-8.
L O 4   *Sales of Merchandise: Perpetual Inventory System*

Record the transactions in **SE 5-7** above using the perpetual inventory system, assuming that the merchandise sold on August 4 cost $720 and the merchandise returned on August 9 cost $210.

SE 5-9.
L O 5, 7   *Internal Control Procedures*

Indicate which of the following control procedures apply to each of the check-writing policies for a small business listed below:

a. Authorization
b. Recording transactions
c. Documents and records
d. Limited access

e. Periodic independent verification
f. Separation of duties
g. Sound personnel policies

1. The person who writes the checks to pay bills is different from the persons who authorize the payments and who keep the records of the payments.
2. The checks are kept in a locked drawer. The only person who has the key is the person who writes the checks.
3. The person who writes the checks is bonded.
4. Once each month the owner compares and reconciles the amount of money shown in the accounting records with the amount in the bank account.
5. Each check is approved by the owner of the business before it is mailed.
6. A check stub recording pertinent information is completed for each check.
7. Every day, all checks are recorded in the accounting records, using the information on the check stubs.

SE 5-10.

S O 8   *Sales and Purchases Discounts*

On April 15, the Sural Company sold merchandise to Astor Corporation for $1,500 on terms of 2/10, n/30. Record the entries in both Sural's and Astor's records for (1) the sale, (2) a return of merchandise on April 20 of $300, and (3) payment in full on April 25. Assume both companies use the periodic inventory system.

APPLICATION

Exercises

E 5-1.

L O 1   *Management Issues and Decisions*

The decisions and actions below were undertaken by the management of Byrne Shoe Company. Indicate whether each action pertains primarily to (a) cash flow management, (b) profitability management, (c) choice of inventory systems, or (d) control of merchandise operations.

1. Decided to place on each item of inventory a magnetic tag that sets off an alarm if the tag is removed from the store before being deactivated.
2. Decided to reduce the credit terms offered to customers from thirty days to twenty days in order to speed up collection of accounts.
3. Decided that the benefits of keeping track of each item of inventory as it is bought and sold would exceed the costs of such a system and acted to implement the decision.
4. Decided to raise the price of each item of inventory to achieve a higher gross margin to offset an increase in rent expense.
5. Decided to purchase a new type of cash register that can be operated only by a person who knows a predetermined code.
6. Decided to switch to a new cleaning service that will provide the same service at a lower cost.

E 5-2.

L O 2   *Parts of the Income Statement: Missing Data*

Compute the dollar amount of each item indicated by a letter in the table below. Treat each horizontal row of numbers as a separate problem.

Sales	Beginning Inventory	Net Cost of Purchases	Ending Inventory	Cost of Goods Sold	Gross Margin	Operating Expenses	Income (Loss)
$250,000	$ a	$ 70,000	$ 20,000	$ b	$ 80,000	$ c	$24,000
d	24,000	e	36,000	216,000	120,000	80,000	40,000
460,000	44,000	334,000	f	g	100,000	h	(2,000)
780,000	80,000	i	120,000	j	k	240,000	80,000

E 5-3.

L O 2   *Gross Margin from Sales Computation: Missing Data*

Determine the amount of gross purchases by preparing a partial income statement under the periodic inventory system, showing the calculation of gross margin from sales from the following data: freight in, $13,000; cost of goods sold, $185,000; sales, $275,000; beginning inventory, $25,000; purchases returns and allowances, $7,500; ending inventory, $12,000.

E 5-4.

L O 2   *Preparation of Income Statement: Periodic Inventory System*

Using the selected year-end account balances at December 31, 19x2 for the Mill Pond General Store shown below, prepare a 19x2 income statement.

Account Name	Debit	Credit
Sales		$297,000
Sales Returns and Allowances	$ 15,200	
Purchases	114,800	
Purchases Returns and Allowances		4,000
Freight In	5,600	
Selling Expenses	48,500	
General and Administrative Expenses	37,200	
Income Taxes	15,000	

The company uses the periodic inventory system. Beginning merchandise inventory was $26,000; ending merchandise inventory is $22,000.

E 5-5.

L O 4 *Preparation of Income Statement: Perpetual Inventory System*

Using the selected account balances at December 31, 19xx for Nature's Adventure Store below, prepare an income statement for the year ended December 31, 19xx.

Account Name	Debit	Credit
Sales		$475,000
Sales Returns and Allowances	$ 23,500	
Cost of Goods Sold	280,000	
Freight In	13,500	
Selling Expenses	43,000	
General and Administrative Expenses	87,000	
Income Taxes	12,000	

The company uses the perpetual inventory system, and Freight In has not been included in Cost of Goods Sold.

E 5-6.

L O 2 *Merchandising Income Statement: Missing Data, Multiple Years*

Determine the missing data for each letter in the three income statements below for Lopata Office Supplies Company (in thousands):

	19x5	19x4	19x3
Gross Sales	$ p	$ h	$572
Sales Returns and Allowances	48	38	a
Net Sales	q	634	b
Merchandise Inventory, Jan. 1	r	i	76
Purchases	384	338	c
Purchases Returns and Allowances	62	j	34
Freight In	s	58	44
Net Cost of Purchases	378	k	d
Goods Available for Sale	444	424	364
Merchandise Inventory, Dec. 31	78	l	84
Cost of Goods Sold	t	358	e
Gross Margin	284	m	252
Selling Expenses	u	156	f
General and Administrative Expenses	78	n	66
Total Operating Expenses	260	256	g
Income Before Income Taxes	v	o	54
Income Taxes	6	4	10
Net Income	w	16	44

E 5-7.

L O 4 *Recording Purchases: Periodic and Perpetual Inventory Systems*

Give the entries to record each of the following transactions (1) under the periodic inventory system and (2) under the perpetual inventory system:

a. Purchased merchandise on credit, terms n/30, FOB shipping point, $7,500.
b. Paid freight on the shipment in transaction **a,** $405.
c. Purchased merchandise on credit, terms n/30, FOB destination, $4,200.
d. Purchased merchandise on credit, terms n/30, FOB shipping point, $7,800, which includes freight paid by the supplier of $600.
e. Returned part of the merchandise purchased in transaction **c,** $1,500.
f. Paid the amount owed on the purchase in transaction **a.**
g. Paid the amount owed on the purchase in transaction **d.**
h. Paid the amount owed on the purchase in transaction **c** less the return in transaction **e.**

E 5-8.

L O 4 *Recording Sales: Periodic and Perpetual Inventory Systems*

On June 15, the Jackson Company sold merchandise for $2,600 on terms of n/30 to Clement Company. On June 20, Clement Company returned some of the merchandise for a credit of $600, and on June 25, Clement paid the balance owed. Give Jackson's entries to record the sale, return, and receipt of payment (1) under the periodic inventory system and (2) under the perpetual inventory system. The cost of the merchandise sold on June 15 was $1,500 and the cost of the merchandise returned to inventory on June 20 was $350.

E 5-9.

L O 5 *Use of Accounting Records in Internal Control*

Careful scrutiny of accounting records and financial statements can lead to the discovery of fraud or embezzlement. Each situation below may indicate a breakdown in internal control. Indicate what the possible fraud or embezzlement is in each situation.

1. Wages expense for a branch office was 30 percent higher in 19x2 than in 19x1, even though the office was authorized to employ only the same four employees and raises were only 5 percent in 19x2.
2. Sales returns and allowances increased from 5 percent to 20 percent of sales in the first two months of 19x2, after record sales in 19x1 resulted in large bonuses being paid to the sales staff.
3. Gross margin decreased from 40 percent of net sales in 19x1 to 30 percent in 19x2, even though there was no change in pricing. Ending inventory was 50 percent less at the end of 19x2 than it was at the beginning of the year. There is no immediate explanation for the decrease in inventory.
4. A review of daily cash register receipts records shows that one cashier consistently accepts more discount coupons for purchases than do the other cashiers.

E 5-10.

L O 5 *Control Procedures*

Sean O'Mara, who operates a small grocery store, has established the following policies with regard to the check-out cashiers:

1. Each cashier has his or her own cash drawer, to which no one else has access.
2. Each cashier may accept checks for purchases under $50 with proper identification. Checks over $50 must be approved by O'Mara before they are accepted.
3. Every sale must be rung up on the cash register and a receipt given to the customer. Each sale is recorded on a tape inside the cash register.
4. At the end of each day O'Mara counts the cash in the drawer and compares it to the amount on the tape inside the cash register.

Identify by letter which of the following conditions for internal control applies to each of the above policies:

a. Transactions are executed in accordance with management's general or specific authorization.
b. Transactions are recorded as necessary to (1) permit preparation of financial statements and (2) maintain accountability for assets.
c. Access to assets is permitted only as allowed by management.
d. The recorded accountability for assets is compared with the existing assets at reasonable intervals.

E 5-11.

L O 5 *Internal Control Procedures*

Ruth's Video Store maintains the following policies with regard to purchases of new videotapes at each of its branch stores:

1. Employees are required to take vacations, and duties of employees are rotated periodically.
2. Once each month a person from the home office visits each branch to examine the receiving records and to compare the inventory of video tapes with the accounting records.
3. Purchases of new tapes must be authorized by purchase order in the home office and paid for by the treasurer in the home office. Receiving reports are prepared in each branch and sent to the home office.
4. All new personnel receive a one-hour orientation on receiving and cataloging new video tapes.
5. The company maintains a perpetual inventory system that keeps track of all video tapes purchased, sold, and on hand.

Indicate by letter which of the following control procedures apply to each of the above policies (some may have several answers):

a. Authorization
b. Recording transactions
c. Documents and records
d. Limited access
e. Periodic independent verification
f. Separation of duties
g. Sound personnel policies

E 5-12.
L O 5 *Internal Control Evaluation*

Developing a convenient means of providing sales representatives with cash for their incidental expenses, such as entertaining a client at lunch, is a problem many companies face. One company has a plan whereby the sales representatives receive advances in cash from the petty cash fund. Each advance is supported by an authorization from the sales manager. The representative returns the receipt for the expenditure and any unused cash, which is replaced in the petty cash fund. The cashier of the petty cash fund is responsible for seeing that the receipt and the cash returned equal the advance. At the time that the petty cash fund is reimbursed, the amount of the representative's expenditure is debited to Direct Sales Expense.

What is the weak point in this system? What fundamental principle of internal control is being ignored? What improvement in the procedure can you suggest?

E 5-13.
L O 5 *Internal Control Evaluation*

An accountant is responsible for the following procedures: (1) receiving all cash; (2) maintaining the general ledger; (3) maintaining the accounts receivable subsidiary ledger that includes the individual records of each customer; (4) maintaining the journals for recording sales, purchases, and cash receipts (some companies maintain separate journals to record frequent transactions); and (5) preparing monthly statements to be sent to customers. As a service to customers and employees, the company allows the accountant to cash checks of up to $50 with money from the cash receipts. When deposits are made, the checks are included in place of the cash receipts.

What weaknesses in internal control exist in this system?

E 5-14.
S O 8 *Purchases and Sales Involving Discounts*

The Fellini Company purchased $9,200 of merchandise, terms 2/10, n/30, from the Vance Company and paid for the merchandise within the discount period. Give the entries (1) by the Fellini Company to record the purchase and payment and (2) by the Vance Company to record the sale and receipt of payment. Both companies use the periodic inventory system.

E 5-15.
S O 8 *Sales Involving Discounts*

Give the entries to record the following transactions engaged in by Westland Corporation, which uses the periodic inventory system:

Mar. 1 Sold merchandise on credit to Grano Company, terms 2/10, n/30, FOB shipping point, $500.
    3 Accepted a return from Grano Company for full credit, $200.
    10 Received payment from Grano Company for the purchase less the return and discount.
    11 Sold merchandise on credit to Grano Company, terms 2/10, n/30, FOB destination, $800.
    31 Received payment for amount due from Grano Company for sale of March 11.

E 5-16.
S O 8 *Purchases Involving Discounts*

Give the entries to record the following transactions engaged in by Westland Corporation, which uses the periodic inventory system:

July 2 Purchased merchandise on credit from Matts Company, terms 2/10, n/30, FOB destination, invoice dated July 1, $800.
    6 Returned merchandise to Matts Company for full credit, $100.
    11 Paid Matts Company for purchase less return and discount.
    14 Purchased merchandise on credit from Matts Company, terms 2/10, n/30, FOB destination, invoice dated July 12, $900.
    31 Paid amount owed to Matts Company for purchase of July 14.

Problem Set A

5A-1.
L O 1, 2 *Merchandising Income Statement: Periodic Inventory System*

Selected accounts from the adjusted trial balance for Helen's New Styles Shop, Inc. for the end of the fiscal year, March 31, 19x4, are shown on page 229.

The merchandise inventory for Helen's New Styles Shop, Inc. was $76,400 at the beginning of the year and $58,800 at the end of the year.

Helen's New Styles Shop, Inc.
Partial Adjusted Trial Balance
March 31, 19x4

Sales		330,000
Sales Returns and Allowances	4,000	
Purchases	140,400	
Purchases Returns and Allowances		5,200
Freight In	4,600	
Store Salaries Expense	65,250	
Office Salaries Expense	25,750	
Advertising Expense	48,600	
Rent Expense	4,800	
Insurance Expense	2,400	
Utility Expense	3,120	
Store Supplies Expense	5,760	
Office Supplies Expense	2,350	
Depreciation Expense, Store Equipment	2,100	
Depreciation Expense, Office Equipment	1,600	
Income Taxes	2,000	

REQUIRED

1. Using the information given, prepare an income statement for Helen's New Styles Shop, Inc. Store Salaries Expense; Advertising Expense; Store Supplies Expense; and Depreciation Expense, Store Equipment are selling expenses. The other expenses, except Income Taxes, are general and administrative expenses.
2. Based on your knowledge at this point in the course, how would you use the income statement for Helen's New Styles Shop, Inc. to evaluate the company's profitability?

5A-2.

L O 2, 4 *Merchandising Income Statement: Perpetual Inventory System*

At the end of the fiscal year, August 31, 19x2, selected accounts from the adjusted trial balance for Polly's Fashion Shop, Inc. appeared as follows:

Polly's Fashion Shop, Inc.
Partial Adjusted Trial Balance
August 31, 19x2

Sales		162,000
Sales Returns and Allowances	2,000	
Cost of Goods Sold	61,400	
Freight In	2,300	
Store Salaries Expense	32,625	
Office Salaries Expense	12,875	
Advertising Expense	24,300	
Rent Expense	2,400	
Insurance Expense	1,200	
Utility Expense	1,560	
Store Supplies Expense	2,880	
Office Supplies Expense	1,175	
Depreciation Expense, Store Equipment	1,050	
Depreciation Expense, Office Equipment	800	
Income Taxes	4,500	

REQUIRED

Using the information given, prepare an income statement for Polly's Fashion Shop, Inc. Freight In should be combined with Cost of Goods Sold. Store Salaries Expense; Advertising Expense; Store Supplies Expense; and Depreciation Expense, Store Equipment are selling expenses. The other expenses, except Income Taxes, are general and administrative expenses.

5A-3.

L O 4 *Merchandising Transactions: Periodic and Perpetual Inventory Systems*

Heritage Company engaged in the following transactions in October:

Oct. 7 Sold merchandise on credit to Larry Hill, terms n/30, FOB shipping point, $3,000 (cost, $1,800).

8 Purchased merchandise on credit from Tower Company, terms n/30, FOB shipping point, $6,000.

9 Paid Kendall Company for shipping charges on merchandise purchased on October 8, $254.

10 Purchased merchandise on credit from Center Company, terms n/30, FOB shipping point, $9,600, which includes $600 freight costs paid by Center.

13 Purchased office supplies on credit from Phelan Company, terms n/10, $2,400.

14 Sold merchandise on credit to Mary Walton, terms n/30, FOB shipping point, $2,400 (cost, $1,440).

14 Returned damaged merchandise received from Tower Company on October 8 for credit, $600.

17 Received check from Larry Hill for his purchase of October 7.

18 Returned a portion of the office supplies received on October 13 for credit because the wrong items were sent, $400.

19 Sold merchandise for cash, $1,800 (cost, $1,080).

20 Paid Center Company for purchase of October 10.

21 Paid Tower Company the balance from transactions of October 8 and October 14.

24 Accepted from Mary Walton a return of merchandise, which was put back in inventory, $200 (cost, $120).

REQUIRED

1. Prepare general journal entries to record the transactions, assuming the periodic inventory system is used.
2. Prepare general journal entries to record the transactions, assuming the perpetual inventory system is used.

5A-4.

L O 5, 6, 7 *System for Control of Supplies*

Industrial Services Company provides maintenance services to factories located in the West Bend, Wisconsin area. The company, which buys a large amount of cleaning supplies, consistently has been over budget in its expenditures for these items. In the past, supplies were left open in the warehouse to be taken each evening as needed by the on-site supervisors. Orders of additional supplies were made periodically by a clerk in the accounting department from a long-time supplier. No records were maintained other than to record purchases. Once a year, an inventory of supplies was made for the preparation of the financial statements.

To solve the budgetary problem, management recently implemented a new system for controlling and purchasing supplies. Under this system, a secured storeroom for cleaning supplies was designated, and a supplies clerk was put in charge of the storeroom. Supplies are requisitioned by the supervisors for the jobs that they oversee. Each job receives a predetermined amount of supplies based on a study of its needs. In the storeroom, the supplies clerk notes the levels of supplies and completes a purchase requisition when supplies are needed. The purchase requisition goes to the purchasing clerk, a new position, who is solely responsible for authorizing purchases and who prepares the purchase orders for suppliers. The prices of several suppliers are monitored constantly to ensure that the lowest price is obtained. When supplies are received from a vendor, the supplies clerk checks them in and prepares a receiving report, which is sent to accounting, where each payment to a supplier is documented by the purchase requisition, the purchase order, and the receiving report. The accounting department also maintains a record of supplies inventory, supplies requisitioned by supervisors, and supplies received. Once each month, a physical inventory of cleaning supplies in the storeroom is made by the warehouse manager and compared against the supplies inventory records maintained by the accounting department.

REQUIRED

Demonstrate how the new system applies or does not apply to each of the seven control procedures described in this chapter. Is each new control procedure an improvement over the old system?

5A-5.
L O 4
S O 8

Comprehensive Merchandising Transactions, Including Discounts

Here is a list of transactions for Attention Promotions, Inc. for the month of March 19xx:

Mar. 1   Sold merchandise on credit to M. Gaberman, terms 2/10, n/60, FOB shipping point, $2,200.
      3   Purchased merchandise on credit from King Company, terms 2/10, n/30, FOB shipping point, $12,800.
      4   Received freight bill for shipment received on March 3, $900.
      6   Sold merchandise for cash, $1,100.
      7   Sold merchandise on credit to B. Gomez, terms 2/10, n/60, $2,400.
      9   Purchased merchandise from Armstrong Company, terms 1/10, n/30, FOB shipping point, $6,180, which includes freight charges of $400.
     10   Sold merchandise on credit to G. Horn, terms 2/10, n/20, $4,400.
     10   Received check from M. Gaberman for payment in full for sale of March 1.
     11   Purchased merchandise from King Company, terms 2/10, n/30, FOB shipping point, $16,400.
     12   Received freight bill for shipment of March 11, $1,460.
     13   Paid King Company for purchase of March 3.
     14   Returned merchandise from the March 9 shipment that was the wrong size and color, for credit, $580.
     16   G. Horn returned some of the merchandise sold to him on March 10 for credit, $400.
     17   Received payment from B. Gomez for half of his purchase on March 7. A discount is allowed on partial payment.
     18   Paid Armstrong Company balance due on account from transactions on March 9 and 14.
     20   In checking the purchase of March 11 from King Company, the accounting department found an overcharge of $800. King agreed to issue a credit.
     21   Paid freight company for freight charges of March 4 and 12.
     23   Purchased cleaning supplies on credit from Moon Company, terms n/5, $500.
     24   Discovered that some of the cleaning supplies purchased on March 23 had not been ordered. Returned them to Moon Company for credit, $100.
     25   Sold merchandise for cash, $1,600.
     27   Paid Moon Company for the March 23 purchase less the March 24 return.
     28   Received payment in full from G. Horn for transactions on March 10 and 16.
     29   Paid King Company for purchase of March 11 less allowance of March 20.
     31   Received payment for balance of amount owed from B. Gomez from transactions of March 7 and 17.

REQUIRED

Prepare general journal entries to record the transactions, assuming that the periodic inventory system is used.

Problem Set B

5B-1.
L O 1, 2

Merchandising Income Statement: Periodic Inventory System

The data on page 232 come from Dubinsky Lighting Shop, Inc.'s adjusted trial balance as of the fiscal year ended September 30, 19x5.

The company's beginning inventory was $162,444; ending merchandise inventory is $153,328.

Dubinsky Lighting Shop, Inc.
Partial Adjusted Trial Balance
September 30, 19x5

Sales		867,824
Sales Returns and Allowances	22,500	
Purchases	442,370	
Purchases Returns and Allowances		60,476
Freight In	20,156	
Store Salaries Expense	215,100	
Office Salaries Expense	53,000	
Advertising Expense	36,400	
Rent Expense	28,800	
Insurance Expense	5,600	
Utility Expense	37,520	
Store Supplies Expense	928	
Office Supplies Expense	1,628	
Depreciation Expense, Store Equipment	3,600	
Depreciation Expense, Office Equipment	3,700	
Income Taxes	10,000	

REQUIRED

1. Prepare an income statement for Dubinsky Lighting Shop, Inc. Store Salaries Expense; Advertising Expense; Store Supplies Expense; and Depreciation Expense, Store Equipment are selling expenses. The other expenses, except Income Taxes, are general and administrative expenses.
2. Based on your knowledge at this point in the course, how would you use Dubinsky's income statement to evaluate the company's profitability?

5B-2.

L O 2, 4

*Merchandising
Income Statement:
Perpetual Inventory
System*

At the end of the fiscal year, June 30, 19x3, selected accounts from the adjusted trial balance for Rafi's Camera Store, Inc. appeared as follows:

Rafi's Camera Store, Inc.
Partial Adjusted Trial Balance
June 30, 19x3

Sales		433,912
Sales Returns and Allowances	11,250	
Cost of Goods Sold	221,185	
Freight In	10,078	
Store Salaries Expense	107,550	
Office Salaries Expense	26,500	
Advertising Expense	18,200	
Rent Expense	14,400	
Insurance Expense	2,800	
Utility Expense	8,760	
Store Supplies Expense	2,464	
Office Supplies Expense	1,814	
Depreciation Expense, Store Equipment	1,800	
Depreciation Expense, Office Equipment	1,850	
Income Taxes	2,000	

REQUIRED

Using the information given, prepare an income statement for Rafi's Camera Store, Inc. Freight In should be combined with Cost of Goods Sold. Store Salaries Expense; Advertising Expense; Store Supplies Expense; and Depreciation Expense, Store Equipment are selling expenses. The other expenses, except Income Taxes, are general and administrative expenses.

5B-3.

L O 4 *Merchandising Transactions: Periodic and Perpetual Inventory Systems*

Nakayama Company engaged in the following transactions in July:

July 1   Sold merchandise to Bernice Wilson on credit, terms n/30, FOB shipping point, $2,100 (cost, $1,260).

    3   Purchased merchandise on credit from Simic Company, terms n/30, FOB shipping point, $3,800.

    5   Paid Banner Freight for freight charges on merchandise received, $290.

    6   Purchased store supplies on credit from Hayes Supply Company, terms n/20, $636.

    8   Purchased merchandise on credit from Salinas Company, terms n/30, FOB shipping point, $3,600, which includes $200 freight costs paid by Salinas Company.

   12   Returned some of the merchandise received on July 3 for credit, $600.

   15   Sold merchandise on credit to Marc Singer, terms n/30, FOB shipping point, $1,200 (cost, $720).

   16   Returned some of the store supplies purchased on July 6 for credit, $200.

   17   Sold merchandise for cash, $1,000 (cost, $600).

   18   Accepted for full credit a return from Bernice Wilson and returned merchandise to inventory, $200 (cost, $120).

   24   Paid Simic Company for purchase of July 3 less return of July 12.

   25   Received full payment from Bernice Wilson for her July 1 purchase less the return on July 18.

REQUIRED

1. Prepare general journal entries to record the transactions, assuming use of the periodic inventory system.
2. Prepare general journal entries to record the transactions, assuming use of the perpetual inventory system.

5B-4.

L O 5, 6, 7 *Internal Control Evaluation*

Finley's is a retail department store with several departments. Its internal control procedures for cash sales and purchases are described below.

Cash sales. Every cash sale is rung up on the department cash register by the sales clerk assigned to that department. The cash register produces a sales slip that is given to the customer with the merchandise. A carbon copy of the sales ticket is made on a continuous tape locked inside the machine. At the end of each day, a "total" key is pressed, and the machine prints the total sales for the day on the continuous tape. Then, the sales clerk unlocks the machine, takes off the total sales figure, makes the entry in the accounting records for the day's cash sales, counts the cash in the drawer, retains the basic $100 change fund, and gives the cash received to the cashier. The sales clerk then files the cash register tape and is ready for the next day's business.

Purchases. All goods are ordered by the purchasing agent at the request of the various department heads. When the goods are received, the receiving clerk prepares a receiving report in triplicate. One copy is sent to the purchasing agent, one copy is forwarded to the department head, and one copy is kept by the receiving clerk. Invoices are forwarded immediately to the accounting department to ensure payment before the discount period elapses. After payment, the invoice is forwarded to the purchasing agent for comparison with the purchase order and the receiving report and then is returned to the accounting office for filing.

REQUIRED

For each of the above situations, identify at least one major internal control weakness. What would you suggest to improve the system?

5B-5.

L O 4   *Comprehensive*

S O 8   *Merchandising Transactions, Including Discounts*

Below is a list of transactions for Reynolds Structures, Inc. for the month of December 19xx:

Dec. 1   Purchased merchandise on credit from Bickford Company, terms 2/10, n/30, FOB destination, $14,800.

   2   Sold merchandise on credit to D. Loo, terms 1/10, n/30, FOB shipping point, $2,000.

   3   Sold merchandise for cash, $1,400.

   5   Purchased and received merchandise on credit from Parillo Company, terms 2/10, n/30, FOB shipping point, $8,400.

   6   Received freight bill from Runyon Freight for shipment received on December 5, $1,140.

   8   Sold merchandise on credit to T. Mitchell, terms 1/10, n/30, FOB destination, $7,600.

   9   Purchased merchandise from Bickford Company, terms 2/10, n/30, FOB shipping point, $5,300, which includes freight costs of $300.

   10   Received freight bill from Runyon Freight for sales to T. Mitchell on December 8, $582.

   11   Paid Bickford Company for purchase of December 1.

   12   Received payment in full for D. Loo's purchase on December 2.

   15   Paid Parillo Company half the amount owed on the December 5 purchase. A discount is allowed on partial payment.

   16   Returned faulty merchandise worth $600 to Bickford Company for credit against purchase of December 9.

   17   Purchased office supplies from Zucker Company, terms n/10, $956.

   18   Received payment from T. Mitchell for half of the purchase on December 8. A discount is allowed on partial payment.

   19   Paid Bickford Company in full for the amount owed on the purchase of December 9 less the return on December 16.

   19   Sold merchandise to R. Godfrey on credit, terms 2/10, n/30, FOB shipping point, $1,560.

   20   Returned for credit several items of office supplies purchased on December 17, $256.

   23   Issued a credit to R. Godfrey for returned merchandise, $360.

   24   Paid for purchase of December 17 less return on December 20.

   27   Paid freight company for freight charges for December 6 and 10.

   28   Received payment of amount owed by R. Godfrey from purchase of December 19 less credit of December 23.

   29   Paid Parillo Company for balance of December 5 purchase.

   31   Sold merchandise for cash, $1,946.

REQUIRED

Prepare general journal entries to record the transactions, assuming that the periodic inventory system is used.

CRITICAL THINKING AND COMMUNICATION

Conceptual Mini-Cases

CMC 5-1.

L O 2   *Merchandising Income Statement*

Village TV and *TV Warehouse* sell television sets and other video equipment in the Phoenix area. Village TV gives each customer individual attention, with employees explaining the features, advantages, and disadvantages of each video component. When a customer buys a television set or video system, Village provides free delivery, installs and adjusts the equipment, and teaches the family how to use it. TV Warehouse sells the same video components through showroom display. If a customer wants to buy a video component or a system, he or she fills out a form and takes it to the cashier for payment. After paying, the customer drives to the back of the warehouse to pick up the component, which he or she then takes home and installs. Village TV charges higher prices than TV Warehouse for the same components. Discuss how you would expect the income statements of Village TV and TV Warehouse to differ. Is it possible to tell which approach is more profitable?

CMC 5-2.
L O 3

Periodic versus Perpetual Inventory Systems

The Book Nook is a well-established chain of twenty bookstores in eastern Michigan. In recent years the company has grown rapidly, adding five new stores in regional malls. Management has relied on the manager of each store to place orders keyed to the market in his or her neighborhood, selected from a master list of available titles provided by the central office. Every six months, a physical inventory is taken, and financial statements are prepared using the periodic inventory system. At that time, books that have not sold well are placed on sale or, whenever possible, returned to the publisher. As a result of the company's fast growth, management has found that the newer store managers do not have the same ability to judge the market as do managers of the older, established stores. Thus, management is considering a recommendation to implement a perpetual inventory system and carefully monitor sales from the central office. Do you think The Book Nook should switch to the perpetual inventory system or stay with the periodic inventory system? Discuss the advantages and disadvantages of each system.

CMC 5-3.
L O 5
Basic Control Procedures

The Book Nook, which is described in the previous Conceptual Mini-Case, sets up its stores so that each has one cash register and accepts cash, checks, or approved credit cards in payment. In addition to the store manager, the employees of each store include a cashier and several stock clerks. Suggest control procedures for authorization, recording transactions, documents and records, limited access, periodic independent verification, separation of duties, and sound personnel policies to control the firm's sales receipts.

Ethics Mini-Case

EMC 5-1.
S O 8
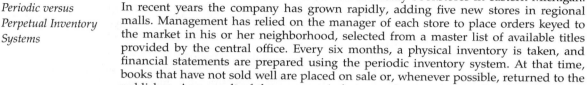
Ethics and Timely Payments

Files, Folders & Clips, with five branch stores, is the area's largest office supply chain. Francesca Gonzales, a new accountant in charge of accounts payable, is told by her supervisor that many of the company's suppliers allow a 2 percent discount if payment for a purchase is made within ten days. She is instructed to write all checks for the net amount after deducting the amount of the discount, and to date them ten days following the invoice date. The checks are not to be mailed until there is enough money in the bank to pay them. The supervisor says that, although most checks must be held a week or more after the discount date, suppliers usually allow the discount because they do not want to lose business. He tells Gonzales: "This is business as usual and just good cash management. Last year we got discounts of $30,000." Gonzales wonders if this is true and, more importantly, whether or not the practice is ethical. Is this practice ethical? Would anyone be harmed by it? What other courses of action are available to Gonzales?

Decision-Making Case

DMC 5-1.
L O 2
Analysis of Merchandising Income Statement

In 19x3 Paul Diamond opened a small retail store in a suburban mall. Called *Diamond Apparel Company,* the shop sold designer jeans. Paul worked fourteen hours a day and controlled all aspects of the operation. All sales were for cash or bank credit card. The business was such a success that in 19x4 Paul decided to open a second store in another mall. Because the new shop needed his attention, he hired a manager to work in the original store with two sales clerks. During 19x4 the new store was successful, but the operations of the original store did not match the first year's performance.

Concerned about this turn of events, Paul compared the two years' results for the original store. The figures are as follows:

	19x4	19x3
Net Sales	$650,000	$700,000
Cost of Goods Sold	450,000	450,000
Gross Margin	$200,000	$250,000
Operating Expenses	150,000	100,000
Net Income before Income Taxes	$ 50,000	$150,000

In addition, Paul's analysis revealed that the cost and selling price of jeans were about the same in both years and that the level of operating expenses was roughly the same in both years except for the new manager's $50,000 salary. Sales returns and allowances were insignificant amounts in both years.

Studying the situation further, Paul discovered the following facts about the cost of goods sold:

	19x4	19x3
Gross purchases	$400,000	$542,000
Total purchases allowances	30,000	40,000
Freight in	38,000	54,000
Physical inventory, end of year	64,000	106,000

Still not satisfied, Paul went through all the individual sales and purchase records for the year. Both sales and purchases were verified. However, the 19x4 ending inventory should have been $114,000, given the unit purchases and sales during the year. After puzzling over all this information, Paul comes to you for accounting help.

REQUIRED

1. Using Paul's new information, recompute the cost of goods sold for 19x3 and 19x4, and account for the difference in net income between 19x3 and 19x4.
2. Suggest at least two reasons for the difference. (Assume that the new manager's salary is correct.) How might Paul improve the management of the original store?

Basic Research Activities

RA 5-1.
L O 3 *Inventory Systems*

Identify three retail businesses in your local shopping area or a local shopping mall. Choose three different types of retail concerns, such as a bookstore, a clothing shop, a gift shop, a grocery, a hardware store, or a car dealership. In each business, ask to speak to someone who is knowledgeable about the store's inventory methods. Find out the answers to the following questions: How is each item of inventory identified? Does the business have a computerized or a manual inventory system? Which inventory system, periodic or perpetual, is used? How often do employees take a physical inventory? What procedures are followed in taking a physical inventory? What kinds of inventory reports are prepared or received? Prepare a table that summarizes your findings. In the table, use columns to represent the types of businesses and rows to represent the questions. Be prepared to discuss your findings in class.

RA 5-2.
L O 5, 6, 7 *Internal Control Systems*

Visit a local outlet of a national retail chain—a fast-food restaurant, a music store, or a jeans or other clothing store. Observe for one hour and record as much as you can about the company's internal control structure. It is usually best to conduct the observation at a busy time of day. How would you go about assessing the control environment? Are any aspects of the company's accounting system apparent? What control procedures, including authorization, recording transactions, documents and records, limited access, periodic independent verification, separation of duties, and sound personnel policies, can you observe? Be prepared to discuss your observations in class.

FINANCIAL REPORTING AND ANALYSIS

Interpretation Cases from Business

ICB 5-1.

L O 1, 2 *Contrast of Operating Philosophies and Income Statements*

Wal-Mart Stores, Inc. and **Kmart Corp.,** two of the largest and most successful retailers in the United States, have different approaches to retailing. You can see the difference by analyzing their respective income statements and merchandise inventories. Selected information from their annual reports for the year ended January 31, 1993 is presented below. (All amounts are in millions.)

Wal-Mart: Net Sales, $55,484; Cost of Goods Sold, $44,175; Operating Expenses, $8,321; Ending Inventory, $9,268

Kmart: Net Sales, $37,724; Cost of Goods Sold, $28,485; Operating Expenses, $7,781; Ending Inventory, $8,752

REQUIRED

1. Prepare a schedule computing the gross margin and net income (ignore income taxes) for both companies as dollar amounts and as percentages of net sales. Also, compute inventory as a percentage of the cost of goods sold.
2. From what you know about the different retailing approaches of these two companies, do the gross margins and net incomes you computed in item **1** seem compatible with these approaches? What is it about the nature of Wal-Mart's operations that produces lower gross margin from sales and lower operating expenses in percentages in comparison to Kmart? Which company's approach was more successful in 1993? Explain your answer.
3. Both companies have chosen a fiscal year that ends on January 31. Why do you suppose they made this choice? How realistic do you think the inventory figures are as indicators of inventory levels during the rest of the year?

ICB 5-2.

L O 1, 2 *Business Objectives and Income Statements*

Best Products, Inc. is one of the nation's largest discount retailers, operating 194 stores in 27 states. In a letter to stockholders in the 1986 annual report (fiscal year ended January 31, 1987), the chairman and chief executive officer of the company stated, "Our operating plan for fiscal 1987 (year ended January 30, 1988) calls for moderate sales increases, continued improvement in gross margins, and a continuation of aggressive expense reduction programs." The following data are taken from the income statements presented in the 1987 annual report (in millions):[4]

	Year Ended		
	January 30, 1988	January 31, 1987	February 1, 1986
Net Sales	$2,067	$2,142	$2,235
Cost of Goods Sold	1,500	1,593	1,685
Operating Expenses	466	486	502

REQUIRED

Did Best Products, Inc. achieve the objective stated by its chairman? **Hint:** Prepare an income statement for each year and compute gross margin and operating expenses as percentages of net sales.

ICB 5-3.

L O 5, 7 *Classic Internal Control Lapse*

J. Walter Thompson Co. (JWT) is one of the world's largest advertising agencies, with more than $1 billion in billings per year. One of its smaller units is a television syndication unit that acquires rights to distribute television programming and sells those rights to local television stations, receiving in exchange advertising time that it sells to

4. Best Products, Inc., *Annual Report*, 1987.

the agency's clients. Cash rarely changes hands between the unit and the television station, but the unit is supposed to recognize revenue when the television programs are exchanged for advertising time that later will be used by clients.

The *Wall Street Journal* reported on February 17, 1982 that the company "had discovered 'fictitious' accounting entries that inflated revenue at the television program syndication unit."[5] The article went on to say that "the syndication unit booked revenue of $29.3 million over a five-year period, but that $24.5 million of that amount was fictitious" and that "the accounting irregularities didn't involve an outlay of cash . . . and its [JWT's] advertising clients weren't improperly billed. . . . The fictitious sales were recorded in such a manner as to prevent the issuance of billings to advertising clients. The sole effect of these transactions was to overstate the degree to which the unit was achieving its revenue and profit objectives."

The chief financial officer of JWT indicated that "the discrepancies began to surface . . . when the company reorganized so that all accounting functions reported to the chief financial officer's central office. Previously, he said, 'we had been decentralized in accounting,' with the unit keeping its own books."

REQUIRED

1. Show an example entry to recognize revenue from the exchange of the right to televise a show for advertising time and an example entry to bill a client for using the advertising time. Explain how the fraud was accomplished.
2. What would motivate the head of the syndication unit to perpetrate this fraud if no cash or other assets were stolen?
3. What principles of internal control were violated that would allow this fraud to exist for five years? How did correction of the weaknesses in internal control allow the fraud to be discovered?

International Company Case

ICC 5-1.

L O 4

Terminology for Merchandising Transactions in England

Marks & Spencer is a large English retailer with department stores throughout England and in other European countries, especially France. The company also owns Brooks Brothers, the business clothing stores, in the United States. Merchandising terms in England differ from those in the United States. For instance, in England, the income statement is called the profit and loss account, sales is called turnover, merchandise inventory is called stocks, accounts receivable is called debtors, and accounts payable is called creditors. Of course, the amounts are stated in terms of pounds (£). In today's business world, it is important to understand and use terminology employed by professionals from other countries. Explain in your own words why the English may use the terms *profit and loss account, turnover, stocks, debtors,* and *creditors* in place of the American terms. Show that you can use these terms by recording in general journal form the following transactions that Marks & Spencer would engage in, using the English terminology (ignore credit terms and assume use of the perpetual inventory system):

a. Sold merchandise on credit, £230 (cost, £120).
b. Received payment for merchandise sold in transaction a.
c. Purchased merchandise on credit, £190.
d. Paid for merchandise purchased in transaction c.

Toys "R" Us Case

TC 5-1.

L O 1

Operating Cycle

Refer to the Annual Report in the appendix on Toys "R" Us. Is merchandise inventory or accounts receivable a more important component of the Toys "R" Us operating cycle? Explain your answer. In the "To Our Stockholders" section, a part titled

5. Paul Blustein, "JWT Sees Pretax Write-Off of $18 Million; Fictitious Accounting Entries at Unit Cited," *Wall Street Journal*, February 17, 1982, p. 16.

"Operational Highlights" refers to the opening of an automated state-of-the-art distribution center in Southern Germany and to the installation of satellite technology in North America that instantaneously links stores with computer databases at headquarters and with customer transaction authorization networks in a most cost-effective manner. The enhanced inventory and distribution systems increased inventory productivity and improved the company's ability to replenish inventory. What effects are these actions intended to have on the operating cycle and the profitability of Toys "R" Us?

CHAPTER 6

Financial Reporting and Analysis

The Gap, Inc.

DECISION POINT

Corporations issue annual reports in order to distribute their financial statements and communicate other relevant information to stockholders and others outside the business. Because these users have no direct access to the accounting records, they must depend on the information contained in the report. Beyond the financial statements and accompanying notes and text, management must devise its own methods to help the reader understand the data in the statements.

The management of The Gap, Inc., one of the most successful U.S. specialty retailers of casual and active wear for men, women, and children, helps readers of its annual report by presenting on the first page a series of statistics called "Financial Highlights." Most of the statistics in the series are based on figures from the financial statements for the preceding three years. Along with such important information as net sales, net earnings, and total assets, a number of ratios appear, including working capital, current ratio, debt to equity, net earnings as a percentage of net sales, and return on average stockholders' equity. Of course, these ratios are meaningless unless the reader understands financial statements and generally accepted accounting principles, on which the statements are based. Because learning how to read and interpret financial statements is so important, this chapter describes the categories and classifications used in balance sheets and income statements and explains some of the most important ratios for financial statement analysis. The chapter begins by describing the objectives, characteristics, and conventions that underlie the preparation of financial statements. It ends with an overview of the Toys "R" Us, Inc. annual report. ⁞ ⁞ ⁞ ⁞ ⁞

OBJECTIVES OF FINANCIAL INFORMATION

OBJECTIVE

1 *State the objectives of financial reporting*

The United States has a highly developed exchange economy. In this kind of economy, most goods and services are exchanged for money or claims to money instead of being used or bartered by their producers. Most business is carried on through corporations, including many extremely large firms that buy, sell, and obtain financing in U.S. and world markets.

By issuing stocks and bonds that are traded in the financial market, businesses can raise capital for production and marketing activities. Investors are interested mainly in returns from dividends and increases in the market price of their investments. Creditors want to know if the business can repay a loan plus interest according to required terms. Thus, investors and creditors both need to know if a company can generate favorable cash flows. Financial statements are important to both groups in making this judgment. They offer valuable information that helps investors and creditors judge a company's ability to pay dividends and repay debts with interest. In this way, the market puts scarce resources to work in companies that can use them most efficiently.

The needs of users and the general business environment are the basis for the Financial Accounting Standards Board's three objectives of financial reporting:[1]

1. *To furnish information useful in making investment and credit decisions* Financial reporting should offer information that can help present and potential investors and creditors make rational investment and credit decisions. The reports should be in a form that makes sense to those who have some understanding of business and are willing to study the information carefully.
2. *To provide information useful in assessing cash flow prospects* Financial reporting should supply information to help present and potential investors and creditors judge the amounts, timing, and risk of expected cash receipts from dividends or interest and the proceeds from the sale, redemption, or maturity of stocks or loans.
3. *To provide information about business resources, claims to those resources, and changes in them* Financial reporting should give information about the company's assets, liabilities, and stockholders' equity, and the effects of transactions on the company's assets, liabilities, and stockholders' equity.

Financial statements are the most important way of periodically presenting to parties outside the business the information that has been gathered and processed in the accounting system. For this reason, these statements—the balance sheet, the income statement, the statement of retained earnings, and the statement of cash flows—are the most important output of the accounting system. These financial statements are "general purpose" because of their wide audience. They are "external" because their users are outside the business. Because of a potential conflict of interest between managers, who must prepare the statements, and investors or creditors, who invest in or lend money to the business, these statements often are audited by outside accountants to increase confidence in their reliability.

QUALITATIVE CHARACTERISTICS OF ACCOUNTING INFORMATION

It is easy for students in their first accounting course to get the idea that accounting is 100 percent accurate. This idea is reinforced by the fact that all the problems in this and other introductory books can be solved. The numbers all add up; what is supposed to equal something else does. Accounting seems very much like mathematics in its precision. In this course, the basics

---

1. "Objectives of Financial Reporting by Business Enterprises," *Statement of Financial Accounting Concepts No. 1* (Stamford, Conn.: Financial Accounting Standards Board, 1978), pars. 32–54.

OBJECTIVE

2 *State the qualitative characteristics of accounting information and describe their interrelationships*

of accounting are presented in a simple form at first, to help you understand them. In practice, however, accounting information is neither simple nor precise, and it rarely satisfies all criteria. The FASB emphasizes this fact in the following statement:

> The information provided by financial reporting often results from approximate, rather than exact, measures. The measures commonly involve numerous estimates, classifications, summarizations, judgments and allocations. The outcome of economic activity in a dynamic economy is uncertain and results from combinations of many factors. Thus, despite the aura of precision that may seem to surround financial reporting in general and financial statements in particular, with few exceptions the measures are approximations, which may be based on rules and conventions, rather than exact amounts.[2]

The goal of accounting information—to provide the basic data that different users need to make informed decisions—is an ideal. The gap between the ideal and the actual provides much of the interest and controversy in accounting. To facilitate interpretation, the FASB has described the qualitative characteristics of accounting information, which are standards for judging that information. In addition, there are generally accepted conventions for recording and reporting that simplify interpretation. The relationships among these concepts are shown in Figure 6-1.

The most important qualitative characteristics are understandability and usefulness. Understandability depends on both the accountant and the decision maker. The accountant prepares the financial statements in accordance with accepted practices, generating important information that is believed to be understandable. But the decision maker must interpret the information and use it in making decisions. The decision maker must judge what information to use, how to use it, and what it means.

Figure 6-1. Qualitative Characteristics and the Conventions of Accounting Information

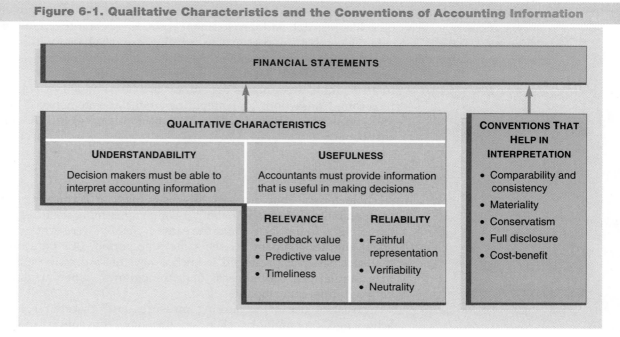

2. "Qualitative Characteristics of Accounting Information," *Statement of Financial Accounting Concepts No. 1* (Stamford, Conn.: Financial Accounting Standards Board, 1980), par. 20.

For accounting information to meet the standard of usefulness, it must have two major qualitative characteristics: relevance and reliability. Relevance means that the information can make a difference in the outcome of a decision. In other words, another decision would be made if the relevant information were not available. To be relevant, information must provide feedback, help predict future conditions, and be timely. For example, the income statement provides information about how a company did over the past year (feedback), and it helps in planning for the next year (prediction). To be useful, however, it also must be communicated soon enough after the end of the accounting period to enable the reader to make decisions (timeliness).

In addition to being relevant, accounting information must have reliability. In other words, the user must be able to depend on the information. It must represent what it is meant to represent. It must be credible and verifiable by independent parties using the same methods of measuring. It also must be neutral. Accounting should convey business activity as faithfully as possible without influencing anyone in a specific direction. For example, the balance sheet should represent the economic resources, obligations, and stockholders' equity of a business as faithfully as possible in accordance with generally accepted accounting principles, and this balance sheet should be verifiable by an auditor.

CONVENTIONS THAT HELP IN THE INTERPRETATION OF FINANCIAL INFORMATION

To a large extent, financial statements are based on estimates and arbitrary accounting rules of recognition and allocation. In this book, we point out a number of difficulties with financial statements. One is failing to recognize the changing value of the dollar due to inflation. Another is treating intangibles, like research and development costs, as assets if they are purchased outside the company and as expenses if they are developed within the company. These problems do not mean that financial statements are useless; they are essential. However, users must know how to interpret them. To help in this interpretation, accountants depend on five conventions, or rules of thumb, in recording transactions and preparing financial statements: (1) comparability and consistency, (2) materiality, (3) conservatism, (4) full disclosure, and (5) cost-benefit.

COMPARABILITY AND CONSISTENCY

A characteristic that increases the usefulness of accounting information is comparability. Information about a company is more useful if it can be compared with similar facts about the same company over several time periods or about another company for the same time period. Comparability means that the information is presented in such a way that a decision maker can recognize similarities, differences, and trends over different time periods or between different companies.

Consistent use of accounting measures and procedures is important in achieving comparability. The consistency convention requires that an accounting procedure, once adopted by a company, remain in use from one period to the next unless users are informed of the change. Thus, without a note to the contrary, users of financial statements can assume that there has been no arbitrary change in the treatment of a particular transaction, account, or item that would affect the interpretation of the statements.

If management decides that a certain procedure is no longer appropriate and should be changed, generally accepted accounting principles require that the change and its dollar effect be described in the notes to the financial statements:

> The nature of and justification for a change in accounting principle and its effect on income should be disclosed in the financial statements of the period in which the change is made. The justification for the change should explain clearly why the newly adopted accounting principle is preferable.[3]

For example, in its 1992 annual report, Rubbermaid Incorporated stated that it changed its method of accounting for inventories in 1992 because management felt the new method improved the matching of revenues and costs.

MATERIALITY

The term materiality refers to the relative importance of an item or event. If an item or event is material, it is probably relevant to the user of financial statements. In other words, an item is material if the user would have done something differently if he or she had not known about the item. The accountant is often faced with decisions about small items or events that make little difference to users no matter how they are handled. For example, a large company may decide that expenditures for durable items of less than $500 should be charged as expenses rather than recorded as long-term assets and depreciated.

In general, an item is material if there is a reasonable expectation that knowing about it would influence the decisions of users of financial statements. The materiality of an item normally is determined by relating its dollar value to an element of the financial statements, such as net income or total assets. Some accountants feel that when an item is 5 percent or more of net income, it is material. However, materiality also depends on the nature of the item, not just its value. For example, in a multimillion-dollar company, a mistake in recording an item of $5,000 may not be important, but the discovery of a $5,000 bribe or theft can be very important. Also, many small errors can combine into a material amount. Accountants judge the materiality of many things, and the users of financial statements depend on their judgments being fair and accurate.

CONSERVATISM

Accountants try to base their decisions on logic and evidence that lead to the fairest report of what happened. In judging and estimating, however, accountants often are faced with uncertainties. In these cases, they look to the convention of conservatism. This convention means that when accountants face major uncertainties about which accounting procedure to use, they generally choose the one that is least likely to overstate assets and income.

One of the most common applications of the conservatism convention is the use of the lower-of-cost-or-market method in accounting for inventories (see the chapter on inventories). Under this method, if the market value is greater than cost, the more conservative cost figure is used. If the market value falls below cost, the more conservative market value is used. The latter situation often occurs in the computer industry.

3. Accounting Principles Board, "Accounting Changes," *Opinion No. 20* (New York: American Institute of Certified Public Accountants, 1971), par. 17.

Conservatism can be a useful tool in doubtful cases, but the abuse of this convention leads to incorrect and misleading financial statements. Suppose that someone incorrectly applies the conservatism convention by expensing a long-term asset in the period of purchase. In this case, there is no uncertainty. Income and assets for the current period would be understated, and income in future periods would be overstated. For this reason, accountants depend on the conservatism convention only when there is uncertainty about which accounting procedure to use.

FULL DISCLOSURE

The convention of full disclosure requires that financial statements and their notes present all information that is relevant to the users' understanding of the statements. In other words, accounting information should offer any explanation that is needed to keep it from being misleading. Explanatory notes are considered an integral part of the financial statements. For instance, as mentioned above, a change from one accounting procedure to another should be reported. In general, the form of the financial statements can affect their usefulness in making certain decisions. Also, certain items, such as the amount of depreciation expense on the income statement and the accumulated depreciation on the balance sheet, are essential to the readers of financial statements.

Other examples of disclosures required by the Financial Accounting Standards Board and other official bodies are the accounting procedures used in preparing the statements, important terms of the company's debt, commitments and contingencies, and important events taking place after the date of the statements. However, there is a point at which the statements become so cluttered that notes impede rather than help understanding. Beyond required disclosures, the application of the full-disclosure convention is based on the judgment of management and of the accountants who prepare the financial statements.

In recent years, the principle of full disclosure also has been influenced by users of accounting information. To protect investors and creditors, independent auditors, the stock exchanges, and the SEC have made more demands for disclosure by publicly owned companies. The SEC has been pushing especially hard for the enforcement of full disclosure. So today, more and better information about corporations is available to the public than ever before.

COST-BENEFIT

The cost-benefit convention underlies all the qualitative characteristics and conventions. It holds that the benefits to be gained from providing new accounting information should be greater than the costs of providing it. Of course, minimum levels of relevance and reliability must be reached for accounting information to be useful. Beyond these minimum levels, however, it is up to the FASB and the SEC, which require the information, and the accountant, who provides the information, to judge the costs and benefits in each case. Most of the costs of providing information fall at first on the preparers; the benefits are reaped by both preparers and users. Finally, both the costs and the benefits are passed on to society in the form of prices and social benefits from more efficient allocation of resources.

The costs and benefits of a particular requirement for accounting disclosure are both direct and indirect, immediate and deferred. For example, it is hard to judge the final costs and benefits of a far-reaching and costly regulation. The FASB, for instance, allows certain large companies to make a supplemental disclosure in their financial statements of the effects of changes on current costs (we talk about this in the chapter on international accounting and intercompany investments). Most companies choose not to present this information because they believe the costs of producing and providing it exceed its benefits to the readers of their financial statements. Cost-benefit is a question faced by all regulators, including the FASB and the SEC. Even though there are no definitive ways of measuring costs and benefits, much of an accountant's work deals with these concepts.

MANAGEMENT'S RESPONSIBILITY FOR ETHICAL REPORTING

OBJECTIVE

4 *Explain management's responsibility for ethical financial reporting and define fraudulent financial reporting*

The users of financial statements depend on the good faith of those who prepare these statements. This dependence places a duty on a company's management and its accountants to act ethically in the reporting process. This duty is often expressed in the report of management that accompanies financial statements. For example, the report of the management of Quaker Oats Company, a company known for strong financial reporting and controls, states

> Management is responsible for the preparation and integrity of the Company's financial statements. The financial statements have been prepared in accordance with generally accepted accounting principles and necessarily include some amounts that are based on management's estimates and judgment.[4]

Quaker Oats' management also tells how it meets this responsibility:

> To fulfill its responsibility, management maintains a strong system of internal controls, supported by formal policies and procedures that are communicated throughout the Company. Management also maintains a staff of internal auditors who evaluate the adequacy of and investigate the adherence to these controls, policies, and procedures.[5]

The intentional preparation of misleading financial statements is called fraudulent financial reporting.[6] It can result from the distortion of records (the manipulation of inventory records), falsified transactions (fictitious sales or orders), or the misapplication of accounting principles (treating as an asset an item that should be expensed). The motivation for fraudulent reporting springs from various sources—for instance, the desire to obtain a higher price in the sale of a company, to meet the expectations of stockholders, or to obtain a loan. Other times, the incentive is personal gain, such as additional compensation, promotion, or avoidance of penalties for poor performance. The personal costs of such actions can be high—individuals who authorize or prepare fraudulent financial statements may face criminal penalties and financial loss. Others, including investors and lenders to the company, employees, and customers, suffer from fraudulent financial reporting as well.

The motivations for fraudulent financial reporting exist to some extent in every company. It is management's responsibility to insist on honest financial

4. Quaker Oats Company, *Annual Report*, 1992.
5. Ibid.
6. National Commission of Fraudulent Financial Reporting, *Report of the National Commission on Fraudulent Financial Reporting* (Washington, D.C., 1987), p. 2.

reporting, but it is also the company accountants' responsibility to maintain high ethical standards. Ethical reporting demands that accountants apply financial accounting concepts to present a fair view of the company's operations and financial position and to avoid misleading readers of the financial statements.

BUSINESS BULLETIN: ETHICS IN PRACTICE

There is a difference between management's choosing to follow accounting principles that are favorable to its actions and fraudulent financial reporting. For example, a company may choose to recognize revenue as soon as possible after a sale is made; however, when Oracle Corporation, a software company, inflated its revenues and earnings by double-billing customers and failing to record product returns, it engaged in fraudulent financial reporting. The company agreed to settle charges brought by the Securities and Exchange Commission by paying a $100,000 fine. Management said the company's explosive growth in sales exceeded the ability of its internal control systems to detect errors.

CLASSIFIED BALANCE SHEET

OBJECTIVE

5 *Identify and describe the basic components of a classified balance sheet*

The balance sheets you have seen in the chapters thus far categorize accounts as assets, liabilities, and stockholders' equity. Because even a fairly small company can have hundreds of accounts, simply listing accounts in these broad categories is not particularly helpful to a statement user. Setting up subcategories within the major categories often makes financial statements much more useful. Investors and creditors study and evaluate the relationships among the subcategories. General-purpose external financial statements that are divided into useful subcategories are called classified financial statements.

The balance sheet presents the financial position of a company at a particular time. The subdivisions of the classified balance sheet shown in Exhibit 6-1 are typical of most companies in the United States. The subdivisions under owners' or stockholders' equity, of course, depend on the form of business.

ASSETS

A company's assets are often divided into four categories: (1) current assets; (2) investments; (3) property, plant, and equipment; and (4) intangible assets. For simplicity, some companies group investments, intangible assets, and other miscellaneous assets into a category called "other assets." These categories are listed in the order of their presumed ease of conversion into cash. For example, current assets are usually more easily converted to cash than are property, plant, and equipment.

Current Assets Current assets are cash or other assets that are reasonably expected to be realized in cash, sold, or consumed over the next year or the

Exhibit 6-1. Classified Balance Sheet for Shafer Auto Parts Corporation

Shafer Auto Parts Corporation
Balance Sheet
December 31, 19x2

Assets

Current Assets

Cash	$10,360	
Short-Term Investments	2,000	
Notes Receivable	8,000	
Accounts Receivable	35,300	
Merchandise Inventory	60,400	
Prepaid Insurance	6,600	
Store Supplies	1,060	
Office Supplies	636	
Total Current Assets		$124,356

Investments

Land Held for Future Use		5,000

Property, Plant, and Equipment

Land		$ 4,500	
Building	$20,650		
Less Accumulated Depreciation	8,640	12,010	
Delivery Equipment	$18,400		
Less Accumulated Depreciation	9,450	8,950	
Office Equipment	$ 8,600		
Less Accumulated Depreciation	5,000	3,600	
Total Property, Plant, and Equipment			29,060

Intangible Assets

Trademark		500
Total Assets		$158,916

Liabilities

Current Liabilities

Notes Payable	$15,000	
Accounts Payable	25,683	
Salaries Payable	2,000	
Total Current Liabilities		$ 42,683

Long-Term Liabilities

Mortgage Payable		17,800
Total Liabilities		$ 60,483

Stockholders' Equity

Contributed Capital

Common Stock, $10 par value		
5,000 shares authorized, issued,		
and outstanding	$50,000	
Paid-in Capital in Excess of Par Value	10,000	
Total Contributed Capital	$60,000	
Retained Earnings	38,433	
Total Stockholders' Equity		98,433
Total Liabilities and Stockholders' Equity		$158,916

normal operating cycle of the business, whichever is longer. The normal operating cycle of a company is the average time needed to go from cash to cash. For example, cash is used to buy merchandise inventory, which is sold for cash or for a promise of cash if the sale is made on account. If a sale is made on account, the resulting receivable must be collected before the cycle is completed.

The normal operating cycle for most companies is less than one year, but there are exceptions. Tobacco companies, for example, must cure their tobacco for two or three years before it can be sold. The tobacco inventory is nonetheless considered a current asset because it will be sold within the normal operating cycle. Another example is a company that sells on the installment basis. The payments for a television set or stove can be extended over twenty-four or thirty-six months, but these receivables are still considered current assets.

Cash is obviously a current asset. Temporary investments, notes and accounts receivable, and inventory are also current assets because they are expected to be converted to cash within the next year or during the normal operating cycle. On the balance sheet, they are listed in the order of their ease of conversion into cash. Accounting for these short-term assets is presented in the chapter on short-term liquid assets.

Prepaid expenses, such as rent and insurance paid for in advance, and inventories of supplies bought for use rather than for sale also should be classified as current assets. These kinds of assets are current in the sense that if they had not been bought earlier, a current outlay of cash would be needed to obtain them.[7]

In deciding whether an asset is current or noncurrent, the idea of "reasonable expectation" is important. For example, Short-Term Investments is an account used for temporary investments of idle cash, or cash that is not immediately required for operating purposes. Management can reasonably expect to sell these securities as cash needs arise over the next year or operating cycle. Investments in securities that management does not expect to sell within the next year and that do not involve the temporary use of idle cash should be shown in the investments category of a classified balance sheet.

Investments   The investments category includes assets, usually long term, that are not used in the normal operation of the business and that management does not plan to convert to cash within the next year. Items in this category are securities held for long-term investment, long-term notes receivable, land held for future use, plant or equipment not used in the business, and special funds established to pay off a debt or buy a building. Also in this category are large permanent investments in another company for the purpose of controlling that company. These topics are covered in the chapter on international accounting and intercompany investments.

Property, Plant, and Equipment   The property, plant, and equipment category includes long-term assets that are used in the continuing operation of the business. They represent a place to operate (land and buildings) and equipment to produce, sell, deliver, and service the company's goods. For this reason, these assets are called *operating assets* or, sometimes, *fixed assets, tangible assets, long-lived assets,* or *plant assets.* Through depreciation, the costs of these assets (except land) are spread over the periods they benefit. Past depreciation is recorded in the Accumulated Depreciation accounts. The exact

7. *Accounting Research and Terminology Bulletin,* final ed. (New York: American Institute of Certified Public Accountants, 1961), p. 20.

order in which property, plant, and equipment are listed on the balance sheet is not the same everywhere. In practice, accounts are often combined to make the financial statements less cluttered. For example:

Property, Plant, and Equipment

Land		$ 4,500
Buildings and Equipment	$47,650	
Less Accumulated Depreciation	23,090	24,560
Total Property, Plant, and Equipment		$29,060

Many companies simply show a single line with a total for property, plant, and equipment and provide the details in a note to the financial statements.

Property, plant, and equipment also includes natural resources owned by the company, such as forest lands, oil and gas properties, and coal mines. Assets that are not used in the regular course of business are listed in the investments category, as noted above. The chapter on long-term assets is devoted largely to property, plant, and equipment.

Intangible Assets   Intangible assets are long-term assets that have no physical substance but have a value based on the rights or privileges that belong to their owner. Examples are patents, copyrights, goodwill, franchises, and trademarks. These assets are recorded at cost, which is spread over the expected life of the right or privilege. We talk about these assets in detail in the chapter on long-term assets.

Other Assets   Some companies use the category other assets to group all owned assets other than current assets and property, plant, and equipment. Other assets can include investments and intangible assets.

LIABILITIES

Liabilities are divided into two categories: current liabilities and long-term liabilities.

Current Liabilities   The category current liabilities consists of obligations due to be paid or performed within a year or within the normal operating cycle of the business, whichever is longer. These liabilities are typically paid from current assets or by incurring new short-term liabilities. Under this heading are notes payable, accounts payable, the current portion of long-term debt, salaries and wages payable, taxes payable, and customer advances (unearned revenues). Current liabilities are discussed in more detail in the chapter on current liabilities and the time value of money.

Long-Term Liabilities   The debts of a business that fall due more than one year in the future or beyond the normal operating cycle, or that are to be paid out of noncurrent assets, are long-term liabilities. Mortgages payable, long-term notes, bonds payable, employee pension obligations, and long-term lease liabilities generally fall in this category. Deferred income taxes are often disclosed as a separate category in the long-term liability section of the balance sheet of publicly held corporations. This liability arises because the rules for measuring income for tax purposes differ from those for financial reporting. The cumulative annual difference between the income taxes payable to governments and the income taxes expense reported on the income statement is included in the account Deferred Income Taxes. Long-term liabilities are described in a later chapter.

STOCKHOLDERS' EQUITY

The stockholders' equity section of a corporation would appear as shown in the balance sheet for Shafer Auto Parts Corporation. As you learned earlier, corporations are separate, legal entities that are owned by their stockholders. The stockholders' equity section of a balance sheet has two parts: contributed or paid-in capital and retained earnings. Generally, contributed capital is shown on corporate balance sheets by two amounts: (1) the par value of the issued stock and (2) the amounts paid in or contributed in excess of the par value per share.

OTHER FORMS OF BUSINESS ORGANIZATION

The accounting treatment of assets and liabilities is not usually affected by the form of business organization. However, the equity section of the balance sheet is very different for a business that is organized as a sole proprietorship or a partnership than it is for a corporation.

Sole Proprietorship   The equity section for a sole proprietorship simply shows the capital in the owner's name at an amount equal to the net assets of the company. The equity section of a sole proprietorship might appear as follows:

Owner's Equity

Hershell Serton, Capital $98,433

Since there is no legal separation between an owner and his or her sole proprietorship, there is no need for contributed capital to be separated from earnings retained for use in a business. This capital account is increased by both the owner's investments and net income. It is decreased by net losses and withdrawals of assets from the business for personal use by the owner. In this kind of business, the formality of declaring and paying dividends is not required.

In fact, the terms *owner's equity, proprietorship, capital,* and *net worth* are used interchangeably. They all stand for the owner's interest in the company. The first three terms are preferred to *net worth* because most assets are recorded at original cost rather than at current value. For this reason, the ownership section will not represent "worth." It is really a claim against the assets of the company.

Partnership   The equity section of the balance sheet for a partnership is called partners' equity and is much like that of the sole proprietorship. It might appear as follows:

Partners' Equity

A. J. Martin, Capital	$21,666	
R. C. Moore, Capital	35,724	
Total Partners' Equity		$57,390

Accounting can be an issue even in the movies. Despite worldwide receipts of $300 million and additional millions in merchandise sales, Warner Bros. Inc. says the original *Batman* has not made a profit and may never do so. However, a lawsuit by two executive producers says that the studio's accounting is fraudulent and unconscionable. At issue is the measurement of "net profits," a percentage of which the producers are to receive. The problem is that the top actors, like Jack Nicholson, the director, and others receive a share of every dollar that the movie generates and, as a result, have earned millions of dollars. Because of these shares, it is impossible for the movie ever to earn a "net profit." Thus, while others are paid handsomely, the two executive producers receive nothing. It pays to know your accounting before signing your movie contract.

FORMS OF THE INCOME STATEMENT

OBJECTIVE

6 *Prepare multistep and single-step classified income statements*

For internal management, a detailed income statement like the one you learned about in the chapter on the merchandising income statement and internal control is helpful in analyzing the company's performance.

For external reporting purposes, however, the income statement usually is presented in condensed form. Condensed financial statements present only the major categories of the detailed financial statements. There are two common forms of the condensed income statement, the multistep form and the single-step form. The multistep form, illustrated in Exhibit 6-2, derives net income in the same step-by-step fashion as a detailed income statement would, except that only the totals of significant categories are given. Usually, some breakdown is shown for operating expenses, such as the totals for selling expenses and for general and administrative expenses. In the Shafer statement, gross margin less operating expenses is called income from operations, and a new section, other revenues and expenses, has been added to include nonoperating revenues and expenses. The latter section includes revenues from investments (such as dividends and interest from stocks, bonds, and savings accounts) and interest earned on credit or notes extended to customers. It also includes interest expense and other expenses that result from borrowing money or from credit extended to the company. If the company has other revenues and expenses that are not related to normal business operations, they too are included in this part of the income statement. Thus, an analyst who wants to compare two companies independent of their financing methods—that is, before considering other revenues and expenses—would focus on income from operations.

Income taxes, also called *provision for income taxes*, represents the expense for federal and state income taxes on corporate income and is shown as a separate item on the income statement. Usually the word *expense* is not used. This account would not appear in the income statements of sole proprietorships and partnerships because they are not tax-paying units. The individuals who own these businesses are the tax-paying units, and they pay income

Exhibit 6-2. Condensed Multistep Income Statement for Shafer Auto Parts Corporation

Shafer Auto Parts Corporation
Income Statement
For the Year Ended December 31, 19x2

Net Sales		$289,656
Cost of Goods Sold		181,260
Gross Margin		$108,396
Operating Expenses		
Selling Expenses	$54,780	
General and Administrative Expenses	34,504	
Total Operating Expenses		89,284
Income from Operations		$ 19,112
Other Revenues and Expenses		
Interest Income	$ 1,400	
Less Interest Expense	2,631	
Excess of Other Expenses over Other Revenues		1,231
Income Before Income Taxes		$ 17,881
Income Taxes		3,381
Net Income		$ 14,500
Earnings per share		$ 2.90

taxes on their share of the business income. Corporations, however, must report and pay income taxes on earnings. Because federal, state, and local income taxes for corporations are substantial, they have a significant effect on business decisions. Most other taxes, such as property taxes, employment taxes, licenses, and fees, are shown among the operating expenses.

Earnings per share, often called *net income per share* of common stock, is also unique to corporate reporting. Ownership in corporations is represented by shares of stock, and the net income per share is reported immediately below net income on the income statement. In the simplest case, it is computed by dividing the net income by the average number of shares of common stock outstanding during the year. For example, Shafer's earnings per share of $2.90 was computed by dividing the net income of $14,500 by the 5,000 shares of common stock outstanding, as reported in the stockholders' equity section of the balance sheet (Exhibit 6-1). Investors find the figure useful as a quick way of assessing both a company's profit-earning success and its earnings in relation to the market price of its stock.

The single-step form of income statement, illustrated in Exhibit 6-3, derives income before income taxes in a single step by putting the major categories of revenues in the first part of the statement and the major categories of costs and expenses in the second part. Income taxes are shown as a separate item, as is done on the multistep income statement.

The multistep form and the single-step form each have advantages. The multistep form shows the components used in deriving net income; the sin-

Exhibit 6-3. Condensed Single-Step Income Statement for Shafer Auto Parts Corporation

Shafer Auto Parts Corporation
Income Statement
For the Year Ended December 31, 19x2

Revenues		
Net Sales		$289,656
Interest Income		1,400
Total Revenues		$291,056
Costs and Expenses		
Cost of Goods Sold	$181,260	
Selling Expenses	54,780	
General and Administrative Expenses	34,504	
Interest Expense	2,631	
Total Costs and Expenses		273,175
Income Before Income Taxes		$ 17,881
Income Taxes		3,381
Net Income		$ 14,500
Earnings per share		$ 2.90

gle-step form has the advantage of simplicity. About an equal number of large U.S. companies use each form in their public reports.

Net income from the income statement becomes an input to the statement of retained earnings.

USING CLASSIFIED FINANCIAL STATEMENTS

OBJECTIVE

7 *Use classified financial statements for the simple evaluation of liquidity and profitability*

Earlier in this chapter, you learned that financial reporting, according to the Financial Accounting Standards Board, seeks to provide information that is useful in making investment and credit decisions, in judging cash flow prospects, and in understanding business resources, claims to those resources, and changes in them. This is related to two of the more important goals of management—maintaining adequate liquidity and achieving satisfactory profitability—because investors and creditors base their decisions largely on their assessment of a company's potential liquidity and profitability. The following analysis focuses on these two important goals.

In this section a series of charts shows average ratios for six industries based on data obtained from *Industry Norms and Ratios,* a publication of Dun and Bradstreet. There are two examples from service industries, advertising agencies and interstate trucking; two from merchandising industries, auto and home supply and grocery stores; and two from manufacturing, pharmaceuticals and household appliances. Shafer Auto Parts Corporation, the example used in this chapter, falls into the auto and home supply industry.

EVALUATION OF LIQUIDITY

Liquidity means having enough money on hand to pay bills when they are due and to take care of unexpected needs for cash. Two measures of liquidity are working capital and the current ratio.

Working Capital   The first measure, working capital, is the amount by which total current assets exceed total current liabilities. This is an important measure of liquidity because current liabilities are debts that must be paid within one year and current assets are assets that will be realized in cash or used up within one year or one operating cycle, whichever is longer. By definition, current liabilities are paid out of current assets. So the excess of current assets over current liabilities is the net current assets on hand to continue business operations. It is the working capital that can be used to buy inventory, obtain credit, and finance expanded sales. Lack of working capital can lead to a company's failure.

For Shafer Auto Parts Corporation, working capital is computed as follows:

Current assets	$124,356
Less current liabilities	42,683
Working capital	$ 81,673

Current Ratio   The second measure of liquidity, the current ratio, is closely related to working capital and is believed by many bankers and other creditors to be a good indicator of a company's ability to pay its bills and to repay outstanding loans. The current ratio is the ratio of current assets to current liabilities. For Shafer Auto Parts Corporation, it would be computed like this:

$$\text{Current ratio} = \frac{\text{current assets}}{\text{current liabilities}} = \frac{\$124,356}{\$42,683} = 2.9$$

Thus, Shafer has $2.90 of current assets for each $1.00 of current liabilities. Is this good or bad? The answer requires the comparison of this year's ratio with those of earlier years and with similar measures for successful companies in the same industry. The average current ratio varies widely from industry to industry, as shown in Figure 6-2. For interstate trucking companies, which have no merchandise inventory, the current ratio is 1.4. In contrast, auto and home supply companies, which carry large merchandise inventories, have an average current ratio of 2.6. Shafer Auto Parts Corporation, with a ratio of 2.9, exceeds the average for its industry. A very low current ratio, of course, can be unfavorable, but so can a very high one. The latter may indicate that a company is not using its assets effectively.

EVALUATION OF PROFITABILITY

Equally as important as paying bills on time is profitability—the ability to earn a satisfactory income. As a goal, profitability competes with liquidity for managerial attention because liquid assets, although important, are not the best profit-producing resources. Cash, for example, means purchasing power, but a satisfactory profit can be made only if purchasing power is used to buy profit-producing (and less liquid) assets, such as inventory and long-term assets.

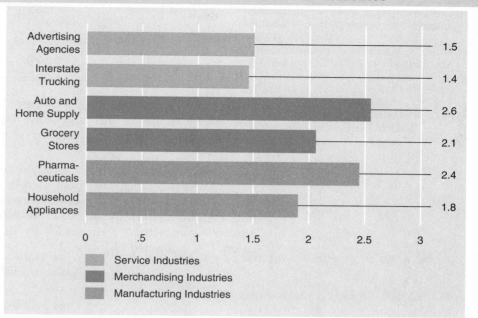

Figure 6-2. Average Current Ratio for Selected Industries

Source: Data from Dun and Bradstreet, *Industry Norms and Ratios*, 1992–93.

Among the common measures of a company's ability to earn income are (1) profit margin, (2) asset turnover, (3) return on assets, (4) debt to equity, and (5) return on equity. To evaluate a company meaningfully, one must relate its profit performance to its past performance and prospects for the future as well as to the averages for other companies competing in the same industry.

Profit Margin   The profit margin shows the percentage of each sales dollar that results in net income. It is figured by dividing net income by net sales. It should not be confused with gross margin, which is not a ratio but rather the amount by which revenues exceed the cost of goods sold.

Shafer Auto Parts Corporation has a profit margin of 5.0 percent:

$$\text{Profit margin} = \frac{\text{net income}}{\text{net sales}} = \frac{\$14,500}{\$289,656} = .05\ (5.0\%)$$

On each dollar of net sales, Shafer Auto Parts Corporation made 5.0 cents. A difference of 1 or 2 percent in a company's profit margin can mean the difference between a fair year and a very profitable one.

Asset Turnover   Asset turnover measures how efficiently assets are used to produce sales. Computed by dividing net sales by average total assets, it shows how many dollars of sales were generated by each dollar of assets. A company with a higher asset turnover uses its assets more productively than one with a lower asset turnover. Average total assets is computed by adding total assets at the beginning of the year to total assets at the end of the year and dividing by 2.

Assuming that total assets for Shafer Auto Parts Corporation were $148,620 at the beginning of the year, its asset turnover is computed as follows:

$$\text{Asset turnover } = \frac{\text{net sales}}{\text{average total assets}}$$

$$= \frac{\$289,656}{(\$148,620 \ + \ \$158,916)/2}$$

$$= \frac{\$289,656}{\$153,768} = 1.9 \text{ times}$$

Shafer Auto Parts Corporation produces $1.90 in sales for each $1.00 invested in average total assets. This ratio shows a meaningful relationship between an income statement figure and a balance sheet figure.

Return on Assets   Both the profit margin and the asset turnover ratios have some limitations. The profit margin ratio does not take into consideration the assets necessary to produce income, and the asset turnover ratio does not take into account the amount of income produced. The return on assets ratio overcomes these deficiencies by relating net income to average total assets. It is computed like this:

$$\text{Return on assets } = \frac{\text{net income}}{\text{average total assets}}$$

$$= \frac{\$14,500}{(\$148,620 \ + \ \$158,916)/2}$$

$$= \frac{\$14,500}{\$153,768} = .094 \text{ (or 9.4\%)}$$

For each dollar invested, Shafer Auto Parts Corporation's assets generated 9.4 cents of net income. This ratio indicates the income-generating strength (profit margin) of the company's resources and how efficiently the company is using all its assets (asset turnover).

Return on assets, then, combines profit margin and asset turnover:

Profit margin $\times$ asset turnover $=$ return on assets

5.0% $\times$ 1.9 times $=$ 9.5%*

*The slight difference between 9.4 and 9.5 is due to rounding.

Thus, a company's management can improve overall profitability by increasing the profit margin, the asset turnover, or both. Similarly, in evaluating a company's overall profitability, the financial statement user must consider the interaction of both ratios to produce return on assets.

Careful study of Figures 6-3, 6-4, and 6-5 shows the different ways in which the selected industries combine profit margin and asset turnover to produce return on assets. For instance, grocery stores and pharmaceutical companies have a similar return on assets, but they achieve it in very different ways. Grocery stores have a very small profit margin, 1.4 percent, which when multiplied by a high asset turnover, 5.5 times, gives a return on assets of 7.7 percent. Pharmaceutical manufacturers, on the other hand, have a high profit margin, 8.6 percent, and a low asset turnover, .8 times, producing a return on assets of 6.9 percent. Advertising agencies have the best return on assets, 11.2 percent, because their low profit margin, 2.9 percent, is combined with a good asset turnover, 3.8 times.

Shafer Auto Parts Corporation's profit margin of 5.0 percent is well above the auto and home supply industry average of 2.3 percent, but its turnover of

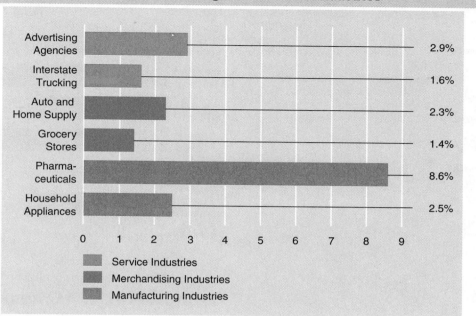

Figure 6-3. Average Profit Margin for Selected Industries

Source: Data from Dun and Bradstreet, *Industry Norms and Ratios*, 1992–93.

1.9 times lags behind the industry average of 2.4 times. Shafer is sacrificing asset turnover to achieve a high profit margin. It is clear that this strategy is working, because Shafer's return on assets of 9.4 percent exceeds the industry average of 5.5 percent.

Debt to Equity   Another useful measure is the debt to equity ratio, which shows the proportion of the company financed by creditors in comparison to that financed by stockholders. This ratio is computed by dividing total liabilities by stockholders' equity. Since the balance sheets of most public companies do not show total liabilities, a short way of determining total liabilities is to deduct the total of stockholders' equity from total assets. A debt to equity ratio of 1.0 means that total liabilities equal stockholders' equity—that half of the company's assets are financed by creditors. A ratio of .5 would mean that one-third of the assets are financed by creditors. A company with a high debt to equity ratio is more vulnerable in poor economic times because it must continue to repay creditors. Stockholders' investments, on the other hand, do not have to be repaid, and dividends can be deferred if the company is suffering because of a poor economy.

The Shafer Auto Parts debt to equity ratio is computed as follows:

$$\text{Debt to equity} = \frac{\text{total liabilities}}{\text{stockholders' equity}} = \frac{\$60,483}{\$98,433} = .614 \text{ (or 61.4\%)}$$

Because its ratio of debt to equity is 61.4 percent, about 38 percent of Shafer Auto Parts Corporation is financed by creditors and roughly 62 percent is financed by investors.

The debt to equity ratio does not fit neatly into either the liquidity or the profitability category. It is clearly very important to liquidity analysis because

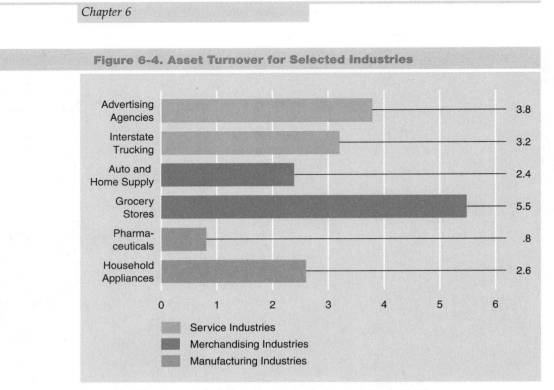

Figure 6-4. Asset Turnover for Selected Industries

Source: Data from Dun and Bradstreet, *Industry Norms and Ratios*, 1992–93.

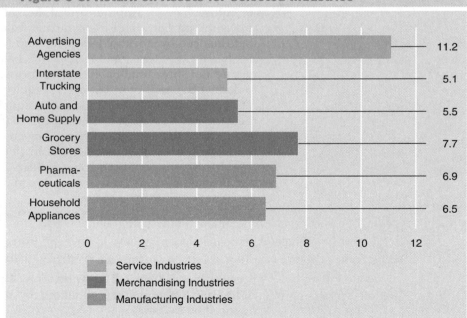

Figure 6-5. Return on Assets for Selected Industries

Source: Data from Dun and Bradstreet, *Industry Norms and Ratios*, 1992–93.

it relates to debt and its repayment. However, the debt to equity ratio is also relevant to profitability for two reasons. First, creditors are interested in the proportion of the business that is debt financed because the more debt a company has, the more profit it must earn to protect the payment of interest to its creditors. Second, stockholders are interested in the proportion of the business that is debt financed. The amount of interest that must be paid on the debt affects the amount of profit that is left to provide a return on stockholders' investments. The debt to equity ratio also shows how much expansion is possible by borrowing additional long-term funds. Figure 6-6 shows that the debt to equity ratio in our selected industries varies from a low of 63.0 percent in the pharmaceutical industry to a high of 124.6 percent in advertising agencies.

Return on Equity   Of course, stockholders are interested in how much they have earned on their investment in the business. Their **return on equity** is measured by the ratio of net income to average stockholders' equity. Taking the ending stockholders' equity from the balance sheet and assuming that beginning stockholders' equity is $100,552, Shafer's return on equity is computed as follows:

$$\text{Return on equity} = \frac{\text{net income}}{\text{average stockholders' equity}}$$

$$= \frac{\$14,500}{(\$100,552 + \$98,433)/2}$$

$$= \frac{\$14,500}{\$99,492.50} = .146 \text{ (or 14.6\%)}$$

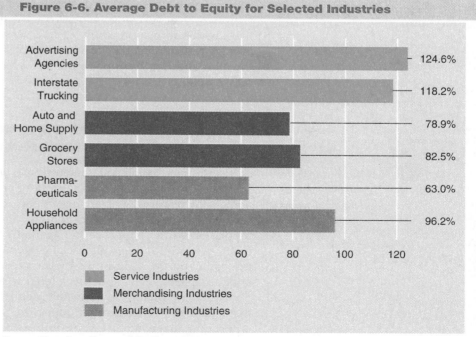

Figure 6-6. Average Debt to Equity for Selected Industries

Source: Data from Dun and Bradstreet, *Industry Norms and Ratios*, 1992–93.

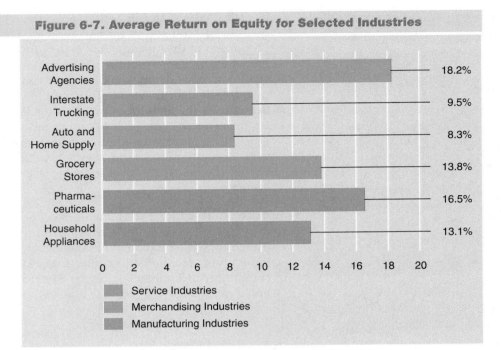

Figure 6-7. Average Return on Equity for Selected Industries

- Advertising Agencies — 18.2%
- Interstate Trucking — 9.5%
- Auto and Home Supply — 8.3%
- Grocery Stores — 13.8%
- Pharma-ceuticals — 16.5%
- Household Appliances — 13.1%

0 2 4 6 8 10 12 14 16 18 20

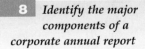

Service Industries
Merchandising Industries
Manufacturing Industries

Source: Data from Dun and Bradstreet, *Industry Norms and Ratios*, 1992–93.

In 19x2, Shafer Auto Parts Corporation earned 14.6 cents for every dollar invested by the stockholders.

Whether or not this is an acceptable return depends on several factors, such as how much the company earned in prior years and how much other companies in the same industry earned. As measured by return on equity (Figure 6-7), advertising agencies are the most profitable of our sample industries, with a return on equity of 18.2 percent. Shafer Auto Parts Corporation's average return on equity of 14.6 percent exceeds the average of 8.3 percent for the auto and home supply industry, which is the least profitable industry in our sample.

Supplemental OBJECTIVE

8 *Identify the major components of a corporate annual report*

COMPONENTS OF AN ANNUAL REPORT

So far, simple financial statements have been presented. Financial statements for major corporations can be quite complicated, however, and have many additional features. The management of a corporation has a responsibility each year to report to stockholders on the company's performance. This report, called the annual report, contains the annual financial statements, the notes related to those financial statements, and other information about the company. In addition to the financial statements and related notes, the annual report usually contains a letter to the stockholders (or shareholders), a multiyear summary of financial highlights, a description of the business, management's discussion of operating results and financial condition, a report of management's responsibility, the auditors' report, and a list of directors and officers of the company. This report and other data must also be filed annually with the Securities and Exchange Commission.

To illustrate the annual report of a major corporation, excerpts from the 1994 annual report of Toys "R" Us, Inc., presented in an appendix at the end of this book, will be used in the following sections. Toys "R" Us, Inc., one of the most successful retailers of this generation, is famous for its stores filled with huge inventories of toys and other items for children. In recent years, the company has opened a chain of stores that sell children's clothes, called Kids "R" Us.

LETTER TO THE STOCKHOLDERS

Traditionally, at the beginning of the annual report, there is a letter in which the top officers of a corporation tell stockholders about the performance of and prospects for the company. The president and the chairman of the board of Toys "R" Us wrote to the stockholders about the highlights of the past year, the outlook for the new year, corporate citizenship, human resources, and expansion plans. For example, they reported on future prospects as follows:

> With our financial strength, we intend to capitalize on our strong competitive position throughout the world, by continued expansion to achieve greater sales, earnings, and market share gains.

FINANCIAL HIGHLIGHTS

The financial highlights section of the annual report presents key financial statistics for a ten-year period and is often accompanied by graphs. The Toys "R" Us annual report, for example, gives key figures for operations, financial position, and number of stores at year end and uses a graph to illustrate consolidated net sales for the last ten years. Other key figures are also shown graphically at appropriate points in the report. Note that the financial highlights section often includes nonfinancial data, such as number of stores.

In addition to financial highlights, an annual report will contain a detailed description of the products and divisions of the company. Some analysts tend to scoff at this section of the annual report because it often contains glossy photographs and other image-building material, but it should not be overlooked because it may provide useful information about past results and future plans.

FINANCIAL STATEMENTS

All companies present four basic financial statements. Toys "R" Us presents statements of earnings, balance sheets, statements of stockholders' equity, and statements of cash flows. Refer to these statements in the Toys "R" Us appendix during the following discussion.

All of Toys "R" Us financial statements are preceded by the word *consolidated.* A corporation issues consolidated financial statements when it consists of several companies and has combined their data for reporting purposes. For example, Toys "R" Us also operates Kids "R" Us and has combined that company's financial data with those of the Toys "R" Us stores.

Toys "R" Us also provides several years of data for each financial statement: two years for the balance sheet and three years for the others. Financial statements presented in this fashion are called comparative financial statements. Such statements are in accordance with generally accepted accounting principles and help readers to assess the company's performance over several years.

You may notice that the fiscal year for Toys "R" Us, instead of ending on the same date each year, ends on the Saturday nearest to the end of January. This arrangement is convenient because it allows the company to always take the annual physical inventory on a weekend.

In a footnote at the bottom of each page of the financial statements, the company reminds the reader that the accompanying notes are an integral part of the statements and must be consulted in interpreting the data.

Consolidated Statements of Earnings   Toys "R" Us uses a single-step form of the income statement and so includes all costs and expenses as a deduction from net sales to arrive at earnings before taxes on income.

Consolidated Balance Sheets   Toys "R" Us has a typical balance sheet for a merchandising company. Several items in the stockholders' equity section need further explanation. Common stock represents the number of shares outstanding at par value. Additional paid-in capital represents amounts invested by stockholders in excess of the par value of the common stock. Foreign currency translation adjustments occur because Toys "R" Us has foreign operations (see the chapter on international accounting and intercompany investments). Treasury shares is a contra-stockholders' equity account that represents the cost of previously issued shares that have been bought back by the company.

Consolidated Statements of Stockholders' Equity   Instead of a simple statement of retained earnings, Toys "R" Us presents a **statement of stockholders' equity**. This statement explains the changes in four components of stockholders' equity.

Consolidated Statements of Cash Flows   The preparation of the consolidated statement of cash flows is presented in the chapter on the statement of cash flows. Whereas the income statement reflects a company's profitability, the statement of cash flows reflects its liquidity. The statement provides information about a company's cash receipts, cash payments, and investing and financing activities during an accounting period.

Refer to the consolidated statements of cash flows in the Toys "R" Us appendix. The first section shows cash flows from operating activities. It begins with the net earnings (income) from the consolidated statements of earnings and adjusts that figure, which is based on accrual accounting, to a figure that represents the net cash flows provided by operating activities. Among the adjustments are increases for depreciation and amortization, which are expenses that do not require the use of cash, and increases and decreases for the changes in the working capital accounts. In the year ended January 29, 1994, Toys "R" Us had net earnings of $482,953,000, and its net cash inflow from these operations was $657,115,000. Added to net income are expenses that do not require a current outlay of cash, such as depreciation and amortization ($133,370,000) and deferred income taxes ($36,534,000). An increase of $29,149,000 in accounts and other receivables had a negative effect on cash flow. Cash was also used to increase inventories ($278,898,000) and prepaid expenses and other operating assets ($39,448,000). A large increase of

$325,165,000 in accounts payable, accrued expenses and other liabilities had the most significant positive effect on cash flows.

The second major section of the consolidated statements of cash flows is cash flows from investing activities. The main item in this category is capital expenditures, net, of $555,258,000. This shows that Toys "R" Us is a growing company.

The third major section of the consolidated statements of cash flows is cash flows from financing activities. You can see here that the sources of cash from financing activities are short-term borrowings, net of $119,090,000, long-term borrowings of $40,576,000, and exercise of stock options of $29,879,000, which was helpful in paying for part of the capital expenditures in the investing activities section. The amount of $183,233,000 was spent to repurchase the company stock. In total, the company raised only $4,977,000 from financing activities during the year.

At the bottom of the consolidated statements of cash flows, the net effect of the operating, investing, and financing activities on the Cash balance may be seen. Toys "R" Us had an increase in cash (and short-term investments) during the year of $28,172,000 and ended the year with $791,893,000 of cash (and short-term investments) on hand.

The supplemental disclosures of cash flow information explain that Toys "R" Us intends the word *cash* to include not only cash but also highly liquid short-term investments called *cash equivalents*. This section also shows income tax and interest payments for the last three years.

NOTES TO CONSOLIDATED FINANCIAL STATEMENTS

To meet the requirements of full disclosure, the company must add notes to the financial statements to help users interpret some of the more complex items. The notes are considered an integral part of the financial statements. In recent years, the need for explanation and further details has become so great that the notes often take more space than the statements themselves. The notes to the financial statements can be put into three broad groups: summary of significant accounting policies, explanatory notes, and supplementary information notes.

Summary of Significant Accounting Policies   In its *Opinion No. 22,* the Accounting Principles Board requires that the financial statements include a summary of significant accounting policies. In most cases, this summary is presented in the first note to the financial statements or as a separate section just before the notes. In this summary, the company tells which generally accepted accounting principles it has followed in preparing the statements. For example, in the Toys "R" Us report the company states the principles followed for property and equipment:

> Property and equipment are recorded at cost. Depreciation and amortization are provided using the straight-line method over the estimated useful lives of the assets, or, where applicable, the terms of the respective leases, whichever is shorter.

Other important accounting policies listed by Toys "R" Us deal with fiscal year, principles of consolidation, merchandise inventories, preopening costs, capitalized interest, financial instruments, and forward foreign exchange contracts.

Explanatory Notes   Other notes explain some of the items in the financial statements. For example, Toys "R" Us showed the details of its Property and Equipment account in the first note, as follows:

	Useful Life (In years)	January 29, 1994	January 30, 1993
		(in thousands)	
Land		$ 693,737	$ 642,368
Buildings	45–50	1,446,277	1,280,850
Furniture and equipment	5–20	953,360	809,772
Leaseholds and leasehold improvements	12½–50	658,191	510,780
Construction in progress		41,855	72,895
Leased property under capital leases		24,360	20,193
		$3,817,780	$3,336,858
Less accumulated depreciation and amortization		633,313	533,308
		$3,184,467	$2,803,550

Other notes had to do with long-term debt, leases, stockholders' equity, taxes on income, the profit sharing plan, stock options, and foreign operations.

Supplementary Information Notes   In recent years, the FASB and the SEC have ruled that certain supplemental information must be presented with financial statements. Examples are the quarterly reports that most companies present to their stockholders and to the Securities and Exchange Commission. These quarterly reports, which are called interim financial statements, are in most cases reviewed but not audited by the company's independent CPA firm. In its annual report, Toys "R" Us presented unaudited quarterly financial data from its 1994 quarterly statements, which are shown in the following table (for the year ended January 29, 1994; dollars in thousands, except per share amounts):

	First Quarter	Second Quarter	Third Quarter	Fourth Quarter
Net Sales	$1,286,479	$1,317,012	$1,449,118	$3,893,458
Cost of Sales	882,876	902,414	982,151	2,727,325
Net Earnings	35,436	35,505	37,457	374,555
Earnings per share	.12	.12	.13	1.27

Interim data were presented for 1993 as well. Toys "R" Us also provides supplemental information on the market price of its common stock during the years. Other companies that engage in more than one line or type of business may present information for each business segment.

REPORT OF MANAGEMENT'S RESPONSIBILITIES

A statement of management's responsibility for the financial statements and the internal control structure may accompany the financial statements. The management report of Toys "R" Us acknowledges management's responsibility for the integrity and objectivity of the financial information and for the system of internal controls. It mentions the company's internal audit program and its distribution of policies to employees. It also states that the financial statements have been audited.

MANAGEMENT'S DISCUSSION AND ANALYSIS

Management also presents a discussion and analysis of financial condition and results of operations. In this section, management explains the difference from one year to the next. For example, the management of Toys "R" Us describes the company's sales performance in the following way:

> The Company has experienced sales growth in each of its last three years; sales were up 10.8% in 1993, 17.1% in 1992 and 11.1% in 1991. Part of the growth is attributable to the opening of 130 new U.S.A. toy stores, 137 international toy stores and 57 children's clothing stores during the three-year period, and a portion of the increase is due to comparable U.S.A. toy store sales increases of 3.3%, 6.9% and 2.4% in 1993, 1992 and 1991, respectively.

Its management of cash flows is described as follows:

> The seasonal nature of the business (approximately 49% of sales take place in the fourth quarter) typically causes cash to decline from the beginning of the year through October as inventory increases for the Christmas season and funds are used for land purchases and construction of new stores which usually open in the first ten months of the year. Therefore, the Company has commitments and backup lines from numerous financial institutions to adequately support its short-term financing needs. Management expects that seasonal cash requirements will continue to be met primarily through operations, issuance of short-term commercial paper and bank borrowings for its foreign subsidiaries.

REPORT OF CERTIFIED PUBLIC ACCOUNTANTS

The independent auditors' report deals with the credibility of the financial statements. This report by independent certified public accountants gives the accountants' opinion about how fairly these statements have been presented. Using financial statements prepared by managers without an independent audit would be like having a judge hear a case in which he or she was personally involved. Management, through its internal accounting system, is logically responsible for recordkeeping because it needs similar information for its own use in operating the business. The certified public accountants, acting independently, add the necessary credibility to management's figures for interested third parties. They report to the board of directors and the stockholders rather than to management.

In form and language, most auditors' reports are like the one shown in Figure 6-8. Usually such a report is short, but its language is very important. The report is divided into three parts.

Figure 6-8. Auditors' Report for Toys "R" Us, Inc.

REPORT OF INDEPENDENT AUDITORS

The Board of Directors and Stockholders
Toys "R" Us, Inc.

(1) We have audited the accompanying consolidated balance sheets of Toys "R" Us, Inc. and subsidiaries, as of January 29, 1994 and January 30, 1993, and the related consolidated statements of earnings, stockholders' equity and cash flows for the years then ended. These financial statements are the responsibility of the Company's management. Our responsibility is to express an opinion on these financial statements based on our audit. The consolidated statements of earnings, stockholders' equity and cash flows of Toys "R" Us, Inc. and subsidiaries for the year ended February 1, 1992 were audited by other auditors whose report dated March 11, 1992, expressed an unqualified opinion on those statements.

(2) We conducted our audits in accordance with generally accepted auditing standards. Those standards require that we plan and perform the audit to obtain reasonable assurance about whether the financial statements are free of material misstatement. An audit includes examining, on a test basis, evidence supporting the amounts and disclosures in the financial statements. An audit also includes assessing the accounting principles used and significant estimates made by management, as well as evaluating the overall financial statement presentation. We believe that our audits provide a reasonable basis for our opinion.

(3) In our opinion, the 1993 and 1992 financial statements referred to above present fairly, in all material respects, the consolidated financial position of Toys "R" Us, Inc. and subsidiaries at January 29, 1994 and January 30, 1993 and the consolidated results of their operations and their cash flows for the years then ended in conformity with generally accepted accounting principles.

Ernst + Young

New York, New York
March 9, 1994

Reprinted courtesy of Toys "R" Us, Inc. The notes to the financial statement, which are an integral part of the report, are not included.

1. The first paragraph identifies the financial statements subject to the auditors' report. This paragraph also identifies responsibilities. Company management is responsible for the financial statements, and the auditor is responsible for expressing an opinion on the financial statements based on the audit.

2. The second paragraph, or scope section, states that the examination was made in accordance with generally accepted auditing standards. These standards call for an acceptable level of quality in ten areas established by the American Institute of Certified Public Accountants. This paragraph also contains a brief description of the objectives and nature of the audit.

3. The third paragraph, or opinion section, states the results of the auditors' examination. The use of the word *opinion* is very important because the auditor does not certify or guarantee that the statements are absolutely correct. To do so would go beyond the truth, since many items, such as depreciation, are based on estimates. Instead, the auditors simply give an opinion about whether, overall, the financial statements "present fairly," in all material respects, the financial position, results of operations, and cash flows. This means that the statements are prepared in accordance with generally accepted accounting principles. If, in the auditors' opinion, the statements do not meet accepted standards, the auditors must explain why and to what extent.

CHAPTER REVIEW

REVIEW OF LEARNING OBJECTIVES

1. **State the objectives of financial reporting.** The objectives of financial reporting are (1) to furnish the information needed to make investment and credit decisions, (2) to provide information that can be used to assess cash flow prospects, and (3) to

provide information about business resources, claims to those resources, and changes in them.

2. **State the qualitative characteristics of accounting information and describe their interrelationships.** Understandability depends on the knowledge of the user and the ability of the accountant to provide useful information. Usefulness is a function of two primary characteristics, relevance and reliability. Information is relevant when it affects the outcome of a decision. Information that is relevant has feedback value and predictive value, and is timely. To be reliable, information must represent what it is supposed to represent, must be verifiable, and must be neutral.

3. **Define and describe the use of the conventions of *comparability* and *consistency, materiality, conservatism, full disclosure*, and *cost-benefit*.** Because accountants' measurements are not exact, certain conventions have come to be applied in current practice to help users interpret financial statements. One of these conventions is consistency, which requires the use of the same accounting procedures from period to period and enhances the comparability of financial statements. The second is materiality, which has to do with the relative importance of an item. The third is conservatism, which entails using the procedure that is least likely to overstate assets and income. The fourth is full disclosure, which means including all relevant information in the financial statements. The fifth is cost-benefit, which suggests that above a minimum level of information, additional information should be provided only if the benefits derived from the information exceed the costs of providing it.

4. **Explain management's responsibility for ethical financial reporting and define *fraudulent financial reporting*.** Management is responsible for the preparation of financial statements in accordance with generally accepted accounting principles and for the internal controls that provide assurance that this objective is achieved. Fraudulent financial reporting is the intentional preparation of misleading financial statements.

5. **Identify and describe the basic components of a classified balance sheet.** The classified balance sheet is subdivided as follows:

Assets	Liabilities
Current Assets	Current Liabilities
Investments	Long-Term Liabilities
Property, Plant, and Equipment	
Intangible Assets	**Stockholders' Equity**
(Other Assets)	Contributed Capital
	Retained Earnings

A current asset is an asset that can reasonably be expected to be realized in cash or consumed during the next year or the normal operating cycle, whichever is longer. Investments are long-term assets that are not usually used in the normal operation of a business. Property, plant, and equipment are long-term assets that are used in day-to-day operations. Intangible assets are long-term assets whose value stems from the rights or privileges they extend to stockholders. A current liability is a liability that can reasonably be expected to be paid or performed during the next year or the normal operating cycle, whichever is longer. Long-term liabilities are debts that fall due more than one year in the future or beyond the normal operating cycle. The equity section for a corporation differs from that of a proprietorship in that it has subdivisions of contributed capital (the value of assets invested by stockholders) and retained earnings (stockholders' claim to assets earned from operations and reinvested in operations).

6. **Prepare multistep and single-step classified income statements.** Condensed income statements for external reporting can be in multistep or single-step form. The multistep form arrives at net income through a series of steps; the single-step form arrives at income before income taxes in a single step. There is usually a separate section in the multistep form for other revenues and expenses.

7. **Use classified financial statements for the simple evaluation of liquidity and profitability.** One major use of classified financial statements is to evaluate a company's liquidity and profitability. Two simple measures of liquidity are working capital

and the current ratio. Five simple measures of profitability are profit margin, asset turnover, return on assets, debt to equity, and return on equity.

SUPPLEMENTAL OBJECTIVE

8. **Identify the major components of a corporate annual report.** In its annual report, a corporation's management reports to stockholders on the company's financial results for the year. The annual report has the following principal components: letter to the stockholders, financial highlights, the four basic financial statements, notes to the financial statements, report of management's responsibilities, management's discussion and analysis of earnings, and the report of the certified public accountants.

REVIEW OF CONCEPTS AND TERMINOLOGY

The following concepts and terms were introduced in this chapter:

S O 8 **Annual report:** The medium in which the general-purpose external financial statements of a business are communicated once a year to stockholders and other interested parties.

L O 7 **Asset turnover:** A measure of profitability that shows how efficiently assets are used to produce sales; net sales divided by average total assets.

L O 5 **Classified financial statements:** General-purpose external financial statements that are divided into subcategories.

L O 3 **Comparability:** The convention of presenting information in a way that enables decision makers to recognize similarities, differences, and trends over different time periods or between different companies.

S O 8 **Comparative financial statements:** Financial statements in which data for two or more years are presented in adjacent columns.

L O 6 **Condensed financial statements:** Financial statements for external reporting purposes that present only the major categories of information.

L O 3 **Conservatism:** The convention that mandates that, when faced with two equally acceptable alternatives, the accountant must choose the one less likely to overstate assets and income.

L O 3 **Consistency:** The convention that requires that an accounting procedure, once adopted, not be changed from one period to another unless users are informed of the change.

S O 8 **Consolidated financial statements:** The combined financial statements of a parent company and its subsidiaries.

L O 3 **Convention:** Rule of thumb or customary way of recording transactions or preparing financial statements.

L O 3 **Cost-benefit:** The convention that holds that benefits gained from providing accounting information should be greater than the costs of providing that information.

L O 5 **Current assets:** Cash or other assets that are reasonably expected to be realized in cash, sold, or consumed within one year or within a normal operating cycle, whichever is longer.

L O 5 **Current liabilities:** Obligations due to be paid or performed within one year or within the normal operating cycle, whichever is longer.

L O 7 **Current ratio:** A measure of liquidity; current assets divided by current liabilities.

L O 7 **Debt to equity:** A ratio that measures the relationship of assets provided by creditors to those provided by stockholders; total liabilities divided by stockholders' equity.

L O 6 **Earnings per share:** Net income earned on each share of common stock; net income divided by the average number of common shares outstanding. Also called *net income per share* or *net earnings per share*.

L O 4 **Fraudulent financial reporting:** The intentional preparation of misleading financial statements.

L O 3 **Full disclosure:** The convention that requires that financial statements and their notes present all information that is relevant to the users' understanding of the company's financial condition.

L O 6 **Income from operations:** Gross margin less operating expenses.

L O 6 **Income taxes:** An account that represents the expense for federal and state income taxes on corporate income; this account appears only on income statements of corporations. Also called *provision for income taxes.*

S O 8 **Independent auditors' report:** The section of an annual report in which the independent certified public accountants describe the nature of the audit (scope section) and state an opinion about how fairly the financial statements have been presented (opinion section).

L O 5 **Intangible assets:** Long-term assets that have no physical substance but have a value based on rights or privileges that belong to their owner.

S O 8 **Interim financial statements:** Financial statements prepared for an accounting period of less than one year.

L O 5 **Investments:** Assets, usually long-term, that are not used in the normal operation of a business and that management does not intend to convert to cash within the next year.

L O 7 **Liquidity:** Having enough money on hand to pay bills when they are due and to take care of unexpected needs for cash.

L O 5 **Long-term liabilities:** Debts that fall due more than one year in the future or beyond the normal operating cycle; debts to be paid out of noncurrent assets.

L O 3 **Materiality:** The convention that requires that an item or event in a financial statement be important to the users of financial statements.

L O 6 **Multistep form:** A form of income statement that arrives at net income in steps.

S O 8 **Notes to the financial statements:** Section of a corporate annual report containing information that aids users in interpreting the financial statements.

S O 8 **Opinion section:** Part of the auditors' report that states the results of the auditors' examination.

L O 5 **Other assets:** The balance sheet category that may include various types of assets other than current assets and property, plant, and equipment.

L O 6 **Other revenues and expenses:** The section of a classified income statement that includes nonoperating revenues and expenses.

L O 7 **Profitability:** The ability of a business to earn a satisfactory income.

L O 7 **Profit margin:** A measure of profitability that shows the percentage of each sales dollar that results in net income; net income divided by net sales.

L O 5 **Property, plant, and equipment:** Tangible long-term assets that are used in the continuing operation of a business. Also called *operating assets, fixed assets, tangible assets, long-lived assets,* or *plant assets.*

L O 2 **Qualitative characteristics:** Standards for judging the information that accountants give to decision makers.

L O 2 **Relevance:** The qualitative characteristic of bearing directly on the outcome of a decision.

L O 2 **Reliability:** The qualitative characteristic of being representationally faithful, verifiable, and neutral.

L O 7 **Return on assets:** A measure of profitability that shows how efficiently a company uses its assets to produce income; net income divided by average total assets.

L O 7 **Return on equity:** A measure of profitability that relates the amount earned by a business to the stockholders' investments in the business; net income divided by average stockholders' equity.

S O 8 **Scope section:** Part of the auditors' report that tells that the examination was made in accordance with generally accepted auditing standards.

L O 6 **Single-step form:** A form of income statement that arrives at income before income taxes in a single step.

S O 8 **Statement of stockholders' equity:** Financial statement that shows the same basic information as the statement of retained earnings, but also shows the changes in all stockholders' equity accounts.

S O 8 **Summary of significant accounting policies:** Section of a corporate annual report that discloses which generally accepted accounting principles the company has followed in preparing the financial statements.

L O 2 **Understandability:** The qualitative characteristic of communicating an intended meaning.

L O 2 **Usefulness:** The qualitative characteristic of being relevant and reliable.

L O 7 **Working capital:** A measure of liquidity that shows the current assets on hand to continue business operations; total current assets minus total current liabilities.

REVIEW PROBLEM
ANALYZING LIQUIDITY AND PROFITABILITY USING RATIOS

L O 7 Flavin Shirt Company has faced increased competition from overseas shirtmakers in recent years. Presented below is summary information for the last two years:

	19x2	19x1
Current Assets	$ 200,000	$ 170,000
Total Assets	880,000	710,000
Current Liabilities	90,000	50,000
Long-Term Liabilities	150,000	50,000
Stockholders' Equity	640,000	610,000
Sales	1,200,000	1,050,000
Net Income	60,000	80,000

Total assets and stockholders' equity at the beginning of 19x1 were $690,000 and $590,000, respectively.

REQUIRED Use (1) liquidity analysis and (2) profitability analysis to document the declining financial position of Flavin Shirt Company.

ANSWER TO REVIEW PROBLEM

1. Liquidity analysis

	Current Assets	Current Liabilities	Working Capital	Current Ratio
19x1	$170,000	$50,000	$120,000	3.40
19x2	200,000	90,000	110,000	2.22
Increase (decrease) in working capital			($10,000)	
Decrease in current ratio				1.18

Both working capital and the current ratio declined because, although current assets increased by $30,000 ($200,000 − $170,000), current liabilities increased by a greater amount, $40,000 ($90,000 − $50,000), from 19x1 to 19x2.

2. Profitability analysis

	Net Income	Sales	Profit Margin	Average Total Assets	Asset Turnover	Return on Assets	Average Stock-holders' Equity	Return on Equity
19x1	$80,000	$1,050,000	7.6%	$700,000[1]	1.50	11.4%	$600,000[3]	13.3%
19x2	60,000	1,200,000	5.0%	795,000[2]	1.51	7.5%	625,000[4]	9.6%
Increase (decrease)	($20,000)	$ 150,000	(2.6)%	$ 95,000	0.01	(3.9)%	$ 25,000	(3.7)%

[1]($690,000 + $710,000) ÷ 2   [3]($590,000 + $610,000) ÷ 2
[2]($710,000 + $880,000) ÷ 2   [4]($610,000 + $640,000) ÷ 2

Net income decreased by $20,000 despite an increase in sales of $150,000, and an increase in average total assets of $95,000. The results were decreases in profit margin from 7.6 percent to 5.0 percent and in return on assets from 11.4 percent to 7.5 percent. Asset turnover showed almost no change, and so did not contribute to the decline in profitability. The decrease in return on equity from 13.3 percent to 9.6 percent was not as great as the decrease in return on assets because the growth in total assets was financed by debt instead of stockholders' equity, as shown by the capital structure analysis below.

	Total Liabilities	Stockholders' Equity	Debt to Equity Ratio
19x1	$100,000	$610,000	16.4%
19x2	240,000	640,000	37.5%
Increase	$140,000	$ 30,000	21.1%

Total liabilities increased by $140,000, while stockholders' equity increased by $30,000. As a result, the amount of the business financed by debt in relation to the amount of the business financed by stockholders' equity increased from 16.4 percent to 37.5 percent.

CHAPTER ASSIGNMENTS

KNOWLEDGE AND UNDERSTANDING

Questions

1. What are the three objectives of financial reporting?
2. What are the qualitative characteristics of accounting information, and what is their significance?
3. What are the accounting conventions? How does each help in the interpretation of financial information?

4. Who is responsible for preparation of reliable financial statements, and what is a principal way of achieving this objective?
5. What is the purpose of classified financial statements?
6. What are four common categories of assets?
7. What criteria must an asset meet to be classified as current? Under what condition is an asset considered current even though it will not be realized as cash within a year? What are two examples of assets that fall into this category?
8. In what order should current assets be listed?
9. What is the difference between a short-term investment in the current assets section and a security in the investments section of the balance sheet?
10. What is an intangible asset? Give at least three examples.
11. Name the two major categories of liabilities.
12. What are the primary differences between the equity section for a sole proprietorship or partnership and the corresponding section for a corporation?
13. Explain how the multistep form of income statement differs from the single-step form. What are the relative merits of each?
14. Why are other revenues and expenses separated from operating revenues and expenses in the multistep income statement?
15. What are some of the differences between the income statement for a sole proprietorship and that for a corporation?
16. Explain earnings per share and how this figure appears on the income statement.
17. Define *liquidity* and name two measures of liquidity.
18. How is the current ratio computed and why is it important?
19. Which is the more important goal—liquidity or profitability? Explain your answer.
20. Name five measures of profitability.
21. "Return on assets is a better measure of profitability than profit margin." Evaluate this statement.
22. Explain the difference between contributed capital and retained earnings.
23. Why are notes to financial statements necessary?
24. What is the purpose of the independent auditors' report?

Short Exercises

SE 6-1.

L O 3   *Accounting Conventions*

State which of the accounting conventions—comparability and consistency, materiality, conservatism, full disclosure, or cost-benefit—is being followed in each case below:

1. Management provides detailed information about the company's long-term debt in the notes to the financial statements.
2. A company does not account separately for discounts received for prompt payment of accounts payable because few of these transactions occur and the total amount of the discounts is small.
3. Management eliminates a weekly report on property, plant, and equipment acquisitions and disposals because no one finds it useful.
4. A company follows the policy of recognizing a loss on inventory when the market value of an item falls below its cost but doing nothing if the market value rises.
5. When several accounting methods are acceptable, management chooses a single method and follows that method from year to year.

SE 6-2.

L O 5   *Classification of Accounts: Balance Sheet*

Tell whether each of the following accounts is a current asset; an investment; property, plant, and equipment; an intangible asset; a current liability; a long-term liability; stockholders' equity; or not on the balance sheet.

1. Delivery Trucks
2. Accounts Payable
3. Note Payable (due in ninety days)
4. Delivery Expense
5. Common Stock
6. Prepaid Insurance
7. Trademark
8. Investment to Be Held Six Months
9. Income Taxes Payable
10. Factory Not Used in Business

SE 6-3.
L O 5 *Classified Balance Sheet*

Using the following accounts, prepare a classified balance sheet at May 31 year-end: Accounts Payable, $400; Accounts Receivable, $550; Accumulated Depreciation, Equipment, $350; Cash, $100; Common Stock, $500; Equipment, $2,000; Franchise, $100; Investments (long-term), $250; Merchandise Inventory, $300; Notes Payable (long-term), $200; Retained Earnings, ?; Wages Payable, $50.

SE 6-4.
L O 6 *Classification of Accounts: Income Statement*

Tell whether each of the following accounts is part of net sales, cost of goods sold, operating expenses, other revenues and expenses, or not on the income statement:

1. Delivery Expense
2. Interest Expense
3. Unearned Revenue
4. Sales Returns and Allowances
5. Purchases
6. Depreciation Expense
7. Investment Income
8. Retained Earnings

SE 6-5.
L O 6 *Single-Step Income Statement*

Using the following accounts, prepare a single-step income statement at May 31 year-end: Cost of Goods Sold, $280; General Expenses, $150; Income Taxes, $35; Interest Expense, $70; Interest Income, $30; Net Sales, $800; Selling Expenses, $185. Ignore earnings per share.

SE 6-6.
L O 6 *Multistep Income Statement*

Using the accounts presented in SE 6-5, prepare a multistep income statement.

SE 6-7.
L O 7 *Liquidity Ratios*

Using the following accounts and balances taken from a year-end balance sheet, compute working capital and the current ratio:

Accounts Payable	$ 7,000
Accounts Receivable	10,000
Cash	4,000
Common Stock	20,000
Marketable Securities	2,000
Merchandise Inventory	12,000
Notes Payable in Three Years	13,000
Property, Plant, and Equipment	40,000
Retained Earnings	28,000

SE 6-8.
L O 7 *Profitability Ratios*

Using the following information from a balance sheet and an income statement, compute the (1) profit margin, (2) asset turnover, (3) return on assets, (4) debt to equity, and (5) return on equity. (The previous year's total assets were $100,000 and stockholders' equity was $70,000.)

Total Assets	$120,000
Total Liabilities	30,000
Total Stockholders' Equity	90,000
Net Sales	130,000
Cost of Goods Sold	70,000
Operating Expenses	40,000
Income Taxes	5,000

SE 6-9.
S O 8 *Components of an Annual Report*

Tell whether the following information typically included in an annual report would be found in (a) the letter to the stockholders, (b) the financial highlights, (c) the financial statements, (d) the summary of significant accounting policies, (e) the explanatory notes, (f) the supplementary information notes, (g) the report of management's responsibilities, (h) management's discussion and analysis, or (i) the report of certified public accountants.

1. Detailed information about an account on the balance sheet.
2. A statement about the company's method of revenue recognition.
3. A statement about whether or not the statements are fairly presented in accordance with generally accepted accounting principles.
4. A ten-year summary of various financial data.
5. The company president's description of future plans.
6. Data about cash flows from operations.

7. Management's analysis of cash flows from operations.
8. Quarterly financial results.
9. A statement that management is responsible for the financial statements.

APPLICATION

Exercises

E 6-1.
L O 3 *Accounting Concepts and Conventions*

Each of the statements below violates a convention in accounting. State which of the following concepts or conventions is violated: comparability and consistency, materiality, conservatism, full disclosure, or cost-benefit.

1. A series of reports that are time-consuming and expensive to prepare is presented to the board of directors each month even though the reports are never used.
2. A company changes its method of accounting for depreciation.
3. The company in **2** does not indicate in the financial statements that the method of depreciation was changed, nor does it specify the effect of the change on net income.
4. A new office building next to the factory is debited to the Factory account because it represents a fairly small dollar amount in relation to the factory.
5. The asset account for a pickup truck still used in the business is written down to what it could be sold for even though the carrying value under conventional depreciation methods is higher.

E 6-2.
L O 1, 2, 3 *Financial Accounting Concepts*

The lettered items below represent a classification scheme for the concepts of financial accounting. Match each numbered term with the letter of the category in which it belongs.

a. Decision makers (users of accounting information)
b. Business activities or entities relevant to accounting measurement
c. Objectives of accounting information
d. Accounting measurement considerations
e. Accounting processing considerations
f. Qualitative characteristics
g. Accounting conventions
h. Financial statements

1. Conservatism
2. Verifiability
3. Statement of cash flows
4. Materiality
5. Reliability
6. Recognition
7. Cost-benefit
8. Understandability
9. Business transactions
10. Consistency
11. Full disclosure
12. Furnishing information that is useful to investors and creditors
13. Specific business entities
14. Classification
15. Management
16. Neutrality
17. Internal accounting control
18. Valuation
19. Investors
20. Timeliness
21. Relevance
22. Furnishing information that is useful in assessing cash flow prospects

E 6-3.
L O 5 *Classification of Accounts: Balance Sheet*

The lettered items below represent a classification scheme for a balance sheet, and the numbered items are account titles. Match each account with the letter of the category in which it belongs.

a. Current assets
b. Investments
c. Property, plant, and equipment
d. Intangible assets
e. Current liabilities
f. Long-term liabilities
g. Stockholders' equity
h. Not on balance sheet

1. Patent
2. Building Held for Sale
3. Prepaid Rent
4. Wages Payable
5. Note Payable in Five Years
6. Building Used in Operations
7. Fund Held to Pay Off Long-Term Debt
8. Inventory
9. Prepaid Insurance
10. Depreciation Expense
11. Accounts Receivable
12. Interest Expense
13. Unearned Revenue
14. Short-Term Investments
15. Accumulated Depreciation
16. Retained Earnings

E 6-4.
L O 5 *Classified Balance Sheet Preparation*

The following data pertain to AMAX, Inc.: Accounts Payable, $51,000; Accounts Receivable, $38,000; Accumulated Depreciation, Building, $14,000; Accumulated Depreciation, Equipment, $17,000; Bonds Payable, $60,000; Building, $70,000; Cash, $31,200; Common Stock—$10 par, 10,000 shares authorized, issued, and outstanding, $100,000; Copyright, $6,200; Equipment, $152,000; Inventory, $40,000; Investment in Corporate Securities (long-term), $20,000; Investment in Six-Month Government Securities, $16,400; Land, $8,000; Paid-in Capital in Excess of Par Value, $50,000; Prepaid Rent, $1,200; Retained Earnings, $88,200; and Revenue Received in Advance, $2,800.

Prepare a classified balance sheet at December 31, 19xx.

E 6-5.
L O 6 *Classification of Accounts: Income Statement*

Using the classification scheme below for a multistep income statement, match each account with the letter of the category in which it belongs.

a. Revenues from sales
b. Cost of goods sold
c. Selling expenses
d. General and administrative expenses
e. Other revenues and expenses
f. Not on income statement

1. Purchases
2. Sales Discounts
3. Merchandise Inventory (beginning)
4. Dividend Income
5. Advertising Expense
6. Office Salaries Expense
7. Freight Out Expense
8. Prepaid Insurance
9. Utility Expense
10. Sales Salaries Expense
11. Rent Expense
12. Purchases Returns and Allowances
13. Freight In
14. Depreciation Expense, Delivery Equipment
15. Taxes Payable
16. Interest Expense

E 6-6.
L O 6 *Preparation of Income Statements*

The following data pertain to a corporation: Net Sales, $405,000; Cost of Goods Sold, $220,000; Selling Expenses, $90,000; General and Administrative Expenses, $60,000; Income Taxes, $7,500; Interest Expense, $4,000; Interest Income, $3,000; and Common Stock Outstanding, 100,000 shares.

1. Prepare a condensed single-step income statement.
2. Prepare a condensed multistep income statement.

E 6-7.

L O 6 *Condensed Multistep Income Statement*

A condensed single-step income statement appears below. Present this information in a condensed multistep income statement, and tell what insights can be obtained from the multistep form as opposed to the single-step form.

Narajan Furniture Corporation
Income Statement
For the Year Ended June 30, 19xx

Revenues		
Net Sales	$1,197,132	
Interest Income	5,720	
Total Revenues		$1,202,852
Costs and Expenses		
Cost of Goods Sold	$ 777,080	
Selling Expenses	203,740	
General and Administrative Expenses	100,688	
Interest Expense	13,560	
Total Costs and Expenses		1,095,068
Income Before Income Taxes		$ 107,784
Income Taxes		24,000
Net Income		$ 83,784
Earnings per share		$ 8.38

E 6-8.

L O 7 *Liquidity Ratios*

The following accounts and balances are taken from the general ledger of Mount Cedar Corporation:

Accounts Payable	$ 49,800
Accounts Receivable	30,600
Cash	4,500
Current Portion of Long-Term Debt	30,000
Long-Term Investments	31,200
Marketable Securities	37,800
Merchandise Inventory	76,200
Notes Payable, 90 days	45,000
Notes Payable, 2 years	60,000
Notes Receivable, 90 days	78,000
Notes Receivable, 2 years	30,000
Prepaid Insurance	1,200
Property, Plant, and Equipment	180,000
Property Taxes Payable	3,750
Retained Earnings	84,900
Salaries Payable	2,550
Supplies	1,050
Unearned Revenue	2,250

Compute the (1) working capital and (2) current ratio.

E 6-9.

L O 7 *Profitability Ratios*

The following end-of-year amounts are taken from the financial statements of Overton Corporation: Total Assets, $852,000; Total Liabilities, $344,000; Stockholders' Equity, $508,000; Net Sales, $1,564,000; Cost of Goods Sold, $972,000; Operating Expenses, $357,000; Income Taxes, $47,000; and Dividends, $80,000. During the past year, total assets increased by $150,000. Total stockholders' equity was affected only by net income and dividends.

Compute the (1) profit margin, (2) asset turnover, (3) return on assets, (4) debt to equity, and (5) return on equity.

E 6-10.
L O 7 *Computation of Ratios*

The simplified balance sheet and income statement for a corporation appear as follows:

Balance Sheet
December 31, 19xx

Assets		Liabilities	
Current Assets	$100,000	Current Liabilities	$ 40,000
Investments	20,000	Long-Term Liabilities	60,000
Property, Plant, and		Total Liabilities	$100,000
Equipment	293,000		
Intangible Assets	27,000	**Stockholders' Equity**	
Total Assets	$440,000	Common Stock	$200,000
		Retained Earnings	140,000
		Total Stockholders'	
		Equity	$340,000
		Total Liabilities and	
		Stockholders' Equity	$440,000

Income Statement
For the Year Ended December 31, 19xx

Revenue from Sales (net)	$820,000
Cost of Goods Sold	500,000
Gross Margin	$320,000
Operating Expenses	260,000
Income Before Income Taxes	$ 60,000
Income Taxes	10,000
Net Income	$ 50,000

Total assets and stockholders' equity at the beginning of 19xx were $360,000 and $280,000, respectively.

1. Compute the following liquidity measures: (a) working capital and (b) current ratio.
2. Compute the following profitability measures: (a) profit margin, (b) asset turnover, (c) return on assets, (d) debt to equity, and (e) return on equity.

E 6-11.
S O 8 *Components of an Annual Report*

Tell whether the following information that is typically included in an annual report would be found in (a) the letter to the stockholders, (b) the financial highlights, (c) the financial statements, (d) the summary of significant accounting policies, (e) the explanatory notes, (f) the supplementary information notes, (g) the report of management's responsibilities, (h) management's discussion and analysis, or (i) the report of certified public accountants.

1. A ten-year summary of financial data about operations.
2. Data about cash flows from financing activities.
3. A statement that management is responsible for the company's internal controls.
4. A statement about the company's method of accounting for depreciation.
5. Management's analysis of income from operations.
6. The company president's description of prospects for next year.
7. Sales and net income for the last four quarters.
8. Detailed information about the company's long-term liabilities.
9. A statement about whether or not the statements are fairly presented in accordance with generally accepted accounting principles.

Problem Set A

6A-1.

L O 3 *Accounting Conventions*

In each case below, accounting conventions may have been violated.

1. After careful study, Gerson Company, which has offices in forty states, has determined that in the future its method of depreciating office furniture should be changed. The new method is adopted for the current year, and the change is noted in the financial statements.
2. In the past, Jafari Corporation has recorded operating expenses in general accounts for each classification (for example, Salaries Expense, Depreciation Expense, and Utility Expense). Management has determined that in spite of the additional recordkeeping costs, the company's income statement should break down each operating expense into its selling expense and administrative expense components.
3. Corey, the auditor of Addison Corporation, discovered that an official of the company may have authorized the payment of a $3,000 bribe to a local official. Management argued that because the item was so small in relation to the size of the company ($3,000,000 in sales), the illegal payment should not be disclosed.
4. Farrell Bookstore built a small addition to its main building to house a new computer games division. Because of uncertainty about whether the computer games division would succeed, the accountant took a conservative approach, recording the addition as an expense.
5. Since its origin ten years ago, Vazquez Company has used the same generally accepted inventory method. Because there has been no change in the inventory method, the company does not declare in its financial statements what inventory method it uses.

REQUIRED

In each case, state the convention that is applicable, tell whether or not the treatment is in accord with that convention and with generally accepted accounting principles, and briefly explain why.

6A-2.

L O 6 *Forms of the Income Statement*

The July 31, 19x3 year-end income statement accounts that follow are for Kissell Hardware Corporation. Beginning merchandise inventory was $172,800 and ending merchandise inventory is $145,000. The corporation had 20,000 shares of common stock outstanding throughout the year.

Account Name	Debit	Credit
Sales		$982,200
Sales Returns and Allowances	$ 53,800	
Purchases	449,000	
Purchases Returns and Allowances		23,840
Freight In	34,800	
Sales Salaries Expense	124,320	
Sales Supplies Expense	3,280	
Rent Expense, Selling Space	14,400	
Utility Expense, Selling Space	5,920	
Advertising Expense	33,600	
Depreciation Expense, Delivery Equipment	8,800	
Office Salaries Expense	58,480	
Office Supplies Expense	19,520	
Rent Expense, Office Space	4,800	
Utility Expense, Office Space	2,000	
Postage Expense	4,640	
Insurance Expense	5,360	
Miscellaneous Expense	2,880	
General Management Salaries Expense	84,000	
Interest Expense	11,200	
Interest Income		840
Income Taxes	14,000	

REQUIRED

From the information provided, prepare the following:

1. A detailed income statement.
2. A condensed income statement in multistep form.
3. A condensed income statement in single-step form.

6A-3.
L O 5   *Classified Balance Sheet*

Accounts from the July 31, 19x3 post-closing trial balance of Kissell Hardware Corporation appear below.

Account Name	Debit	Credit
Cash	$ 31,000	
Short-Term Investments	33,000	
Notes Receivable	10,000	
Accounts Receivable	276,000	
Merchandise Inventory	145,000	
Prepaid Rent	1,600	
Prepaid Insurance	4,800	
Sales Supplies	1,280	
Office Supplies	440	
Deposit for Future Advertising	3,680	
Building, Not in Use	49,600	
Land	22,400	
Delivery Equipment	41,200	
Accumulated Depreciation, Delivery Equipment		$ 28,400
Franchise Fee	4,000	
Accounts Payable		114,600
Salaries Payable		5,200
Interest Payable		840
Long-Term Notes Payable		80,000
Common Stock, $1 par value		20,000
Paid-in Capital in Excess of Par Value		160,000
Retained Earnings		214,960

REQUIRED

From the information provided, prepare a classified balance sheet.

6A-4.
L O 7   *Ratio Analysis: Liquidity and Profitability*

Criss Products Corporation has been disappointed with its operating results for the past two years. As accountant for the company, you have the following information available to you:

	19x3	19x2
Current Assets	$ 45,000	$ 35,000
Total Assets	145,000	110,000
Current Liabilities	20,000	10,000
Long-Term Liabilities	20,000	—
Stockholders' Equity	105,000	100,000
Net Sales	262,000	200,000
Net Income	16,000	11,000

Total assets and stockholders' equity at the beginning of 19x2 were $90,000 and $80,000, respectively.

REQUIRED

1. Compute the following measures of liquidity for 19x2 and 19x3: (a) working capital and (b) the current ratio. Comment on the differences between the years.
2. Compute the following measures of profitability for 19x2 and 19x3: (a) profit margin, (b) asset turnover, (c) return on assets, (d) debt to equity, and (e) return on equity. Comment on the change in performance from 19x2 to 19x3.

6A-5.

L O 5, 6, 7 *Classified Financial Statement Preparation and Evaluation*

Wu Corporation sells outdoor sports equipment. At the December 31, 19x4 year-end, the following financial information was available from the income statement: Administrative Expenses, $161,600; Cost of Goods Sold, $700,840; Income Taxes, $14,000; Interest Expense, $45,280; Interest Income, $5,600; Net Sales, $1,428,780; and Selling Expenses, $440,400.

The following information was available from the balance sheet (after closing entries were made): Accounts Payable, $65,200; Accounts Receivable, $209,600; Accumulated Depreciation, Delivery Equipment, $34,200; Accumulated Depreciation, Store Fixtures, $84,440; Cash, $56,800; Common Stock—$1 par value, 20,000 shares authorized, issued, and outstanding, $20,000; Delivery Equipment, $177,000; Dividends, $120,000; Inventory, $273,080; Investment in Securities (long term), $112,000; Investment in U.S. Government Securities (short term), $79,200; Long-Term Notes Payable, $200,000; Paid-in Capital in Excess of Par Value, $180,000; Retained Earnings, $518,600 (ending balance); Notes Payable (short term), $100,000; Prepaid Expenses (short term), $11,520; and Store Fixtures, $283,240.

Total assets and total stockholders' equity at December 31, 19x3 were $1,048,800 and $766,340, respectively.

REQUIRED

1. From the information above, prepare (a) an income statement in single-step form, (b) a statement of retained earnings, and (c) a classified balance sheet.
2. From the statements you have prepared, compute the following measures: (a) working capital and current ratio (for liquidity); and (b) profit margin, asset turnover, return on assets, debt to equity, and return on equity (for profitability).

Problem Set B

6B-1.

L O 3 *Accounting Conventions*

In each case below, accounting conventions may have been violated.

1. Wolin Manufacturing Company uses the cost method for computing the balance sheet amount of inventory unless the market value of the inventory is less than the cost, in which case the market value is used. At the end of the current year, the market value is $221,000 and the cost is $240,000. Wolin uses the $221,000 figure to compute net income because management feels it is the more cautious approach.
2. Mesic Company has annual sales of $15,000,000. It follows a practice of charging any items that cost less than $300 to expense in the year purchased. During the current year, it purchased several chairs for the executive conference rooms at $291 each, including freight. Although the chairs were expected to last for at least ten years, they were charged as an expense in accordance with company policy.
3. Hayden Company closed its books on July 31, 19x2, before preparing its annual report. On July 30, 19x2, a fire had destroyed one of the company's two factories. Although the company had fire insurance and would not suffer a loss on the building, a significant decrease in sales in 19x3 was expected because of the fire. The fire damage was not reported in the 19x2 financial statements because the operations for that year were not affected by the fire.
4. Padron Drug Company spends a substantial portion of its profits on research and development. The company has been reporting its $7,500,000 expenditure for research and development as a lump sum, but management recently decided to begin classifying the expenditures by project even though its recordkeeping costs will increase.
5. During the current year, Schiff Company changed from one generally accepted method of accounting for inventories to another generally accepted method.

REQUIRED

In each case, state the convention that is applicable, and explain briefly whether or not (and why) the treatment is in accord with the convention and generally accepted accounting principles.

6B-2.

L O 6 *Forms of the Income Statement*

Income statement accounts from the June 30, 19x2 year-end adjusted trial balance of Tasheki Hardware Corporation appear as follows. Beginning merchandise inventory was $175,200 and ending merchandise inventory is $157,650. The company had 20,000 shares of common stock outstanding throughout the year.

Account Name	Debit	Credit
Sales		$541,230
Sales Returns and Allowances	$ 15,298	
Purchases	212,336	
Purchases Returns and Allowances		6,159
Freight In	11,221	
Sales Salaries Expense	102,030	
Sales Supplies Expense	1,642	
Rent Expense, Selling Space	18,000	
Utility Expense, Selling Space	11,256	
Advertising Expense	21,986	
Depreciation Expense, Selling Fixtures	6,778	
Office Salaries Expense	47,912	
Office Supplies Expense	782	
Rent Expense, Office Space	4,000	
Depreciation Expense, Office Equipment	3,251	
Utility Expense, Office Space	3,114	
Postage Expense	626	
Insurance Expense	2,700	
Miscellaneous Expense	481	
Interest Expense	3,600	
Interest Income		800
Income Taxes	15,000	

REQUIRED

From the information provided, prepare the following:

1. A detailed income statement.
2. A condensed income statement in multistep form.
3. A condensed income statement in single-step form.

6B-3.
L O 5 *Classified Balance Sheet*

Accounts from the June 30, 19x2 post-closing trial balance of Tasheki Hardware Corporation appear below.

Account Name	Debit	Credit
Cash	$ 24,000	
Short-Term Investments	13,150	
Notes Receivable	45,000	
Accounts Receivable	76,570	
Merchandise Inventory	156,750	
Prepaid Rent	2,000	
Prepaid Insurance	1,200	
Sales Supplies	426	
Office Supplies	97	
Land Held for Future Expansion	11,500	
Selling Fixtures	72,400	
Accumulated Depreciation, Selling Fixtures		$ 22,000
Office Equipment	24,100	
Accumulated Depreciation, Office Equipment		12,050
Trademark	4,000	
Accounts Payable		109,745
Salaries Payable		787
Interest Payable		600
Notes Payable (due in three years)		36,000
Common Stock, $1 par value		20,000
Paid-in Capital in Excess of Par Value		130,000
Retained Earnings		100,011

REQUIRED

From the information provided, prepare a classified balance sheet.

6B-4.

L O 7 *Ratio Analysis: Liquidity and Profitability*

Here is a summary of data taken from the income statements and balance sheets for D'Angelo Construction Supply, Inc. for the past two years:

	19x4	19x3
Current Assets	$ 366,000	$ 310,000
Total Assets	2,320,000	1,740,000
Current Liabilities	180,000	120,000
Long-Term Liabilities	800,000	580,000
Stockholders' Equity	1,340,000	1,040,000
Net Sales	4,600,000	3,480,000
Net Income	300,000	204,000

Total assets and stockholders' equity at the beginning of 19x3 were $1,360,000 and $840,000, respectively.

REQUIRED

1. Compute the following liquidity measures for 19x3 and 19x4: (a) working capital and (b) current ratio. Comment on the differences between the years.
2. Compute the following measures of profitability for 19x3 and 19x4: (a) profit margin, (b) asset turnover, (c) return on assets, (d) debt to equity, and (e) return on equity. Comment on the change in performance from 19x3 to 19x4.

6B-5.

L O 5, 6, 7 *Classified Financial Statement Preparation and Evaluation*

The following accounts (in alphabetical order) and amounts were taken or calculated from the June 30, 19x4 year-end adjusted trial balance of Skowron Lawn Equipment Center, Inc.: Accounts Payable, $72,600; Accounts Receivable, $169,400; Accumulated Depreciation, Building, $52,400; Accumulated Depreciation, Equipment, $34,800; Building, $220,000; Cash, $21,280; Common Stock ($10 par value), $80,000; Cost of Goods Sold, $492,000; Dividend Income, $2,560; Dividends, $47,800; Equipment, $151,200; General and Administrative Expenses, $121,200; Income Taxes, $12,000; Interest Expense, $24,400; Inventory, $112,300; Land (used in operations), $58,000; Land Held for Future Use, $40,000; Mortgage Payable, $180,000; Notes Payable (short-term), $50,000; Notes Receivable (short-term), $24,000; Paid-in Capital in Excess of Par Value, $120,000; Retained Earnings, $222,420 (as of June 30, 19x3); Sales (net), $896,000; Selling Expenses, $190,700; Short-Term Investment (100 shares of General Motors), $13,000; and Trademark, $13,500. Total assets and total stockholders' equity on June 30, 19x3 were $687,900 and $422,420, respectively.

REQUIRED

1. From the information above, prepare (a) an income statement in condensed multi-step form, (b) a statement of retained earnings, and (c) a classified balance sheet.
2. Calculate these measures of liquidity: (a) working capital and (b) current ratio.
3. Calculate these measures of profitability: (a) profit margin, (b) asset turnover, (c) return on assets, (d) debt to equity, and (e) return on equity.

CRITICAL THINKING AND COMMUNICATION

Conceptual Mini-Cases

CMC 6-1.

L O 3 *Accounting Conventions*

Mason Parking, Inc., which operates a seven-story parking building in downtown Chicago, has a calendar year end. It serves daily and hourly parkers, as well as monthly parkers who pay a fixed monthly rate in advance. The company traditionally has recorded all cash receipts as revenues when received. Most monthly parkers pay in full during the month prior to that in which they have the right to park. The company's auditors have said that beginning in 1993, the company should consider recording the cash receipts from monthly parking on an accrual basis, crediting Unearned Revenues. Total cash receipts for 1993 were $2,500,000, and the cash receipts received in 1993 and applicable to January 1994 were $125,000. Discuss the relevance of the accounting conventions of consistency, materiality, and full disclosure to the decision to record the monthly parking revenues on an accrual basis.

CMC 6-2.

L O 3 *Materiality*

Mackey Electronics, Inc. operates a chain of consumer electronics stores in the Atlanta area. This year the company achieved annual sales of $50 million, on which it earned a net income of $2 million. Until this year, the company used the periodic inventory system for financial reporting. At the beginning of the year, management implemented a new inventory system that enabled it to track all purchases and sales. At the end of the year, a physical inventory revealed that the actual inventory was $80,000 below what the new system indicated it should be. The inventory loss, which probably resulted from shoplifting, is reflected in a higher cost of goods sold. This problem concerns management but seems to be less important to the company's auditors. What is materiality? Why might the inventory loss concern management more than it does the auditors? Do you think the amount is material?

CMC 6-3.

L O 7 *Evaluation of Profitability*

Carla Cruz is the principal stockholder and president of *Cruz Tapestries, Inc.,* which wholesales fine tapestries to retail stores. Because Cruz was not satisfied with the company earnings in 19x3, she raised prices in 19x4, increasing gross margin from sales from 30 percent in 19x3 to 35 percent in 19x4. Cruz is pleased that net income did go up from 19x3 to 19x4, as shown in the following comparative income statements:

	19x4	19x3
Revenues		
Net Sales	$611,300	$693,200
Costs and Expenses		
Cost of Goods Sold	397,345	485,240
Selling and Administrative Expenses	154,199	152,504
Total Costs and Expenses	$551,544	$637,744
Income Before Income Taxes	$ 59,756	$ 55,456
Income Taxes	15,000	14,000
Net Income	$ 44,756	$ 41,456

Total assets for Cruz Tapestries, Inc. at year end for 19x2, 19x3, and 19x4 were $623,390, $693,405, and $768,455, respectively. Has Cruz Tapestries, Inc.'s profitability really improved? (**Hint:** Compute profit margin and return on assets, and comment.) What factors has Cruz overlooked in evaluating the profitability of the company? (**Hint:** Compute asset turnover and comment on the role it plays in profitability.)

Ethics Mini-Cases

EMC 6-1.

L O 4 *Ethics and Financial Reporting*

Salem Software, Inc., located outside Boston, develops computer software and licenses it to financial institutions. The firm uses an aggressive accounting method that records revenues from the software it has sold on a percentage of completion basis. This means that revenue for partially completed projects is recognized based on the proportion of the project that is completed. If a project is 50 percent completed, then 50 percent of the contracted revenue is recognized. In 19x2, preliminary estimates for a $5 million project are that the project is 75 percent complete. Because the estimate of completion is a matter of judgment, management asks for a new report showing the project to be 90 percent complete. This change will enable senior managers to meet their financial goals for the year and thus receive substantial year-end bonuses. Do you think management's action is ethical? If you were the company controller and were asked to prepare the new report, would you do it? What action would you take?

EMC 6-2.

L O 4 *Ethics and Financial Reporting*

Treon Microsystems, Inc., a Silicon Valley manufacturer of microchips for personal computers, has just completed its year-end physical inventory in advance of preparing financial statements. To celebrate, the entire accounting department goes out for a New Year's Eve party at a local establishment. As senior accountant, you join the fun. At the party, you fall into conversation with an employee of one of your main competitors. After a while, the employee reveals that the competitor plans to introduce a new product in sixty days that will make Treon's principal product obsolete.

On Monday morning, you go to the financial vice president with this information, stating that the inventory may have to be written down and net income reduced. To your surprise, the financial vice president says that you were right to come to her, but urges you to say nothing about the problem. She says, "It is probably a rumor, and even if it is true, there will be plenty of time to write down the inventory in sixty days." You wonder if this is the appropriate thing to do. You feel confident that your source knew what he was talking about. You know that the salaries of all top managers, including the financial vice president, are tied to net income. What is fraudulent financial reporting? Is this an example of fraudulent financial reporting? What action would you take?

Decision-Making Case

DMC 6-1.

L O 7 *Financial Analysis for Loan Decision*

Steve Sullivan was recently promoted to loan officer at the **First National Bank.** He has authority to issue loans up to $50,000 without approval from a higher bank official. This week two small companies, Handy Harvey, Inc. and Sheila's Fashions, Inc., have each submitted a proposal for a six-month $50,000 loan. To prepare financial analyses of the two companies, Steve has obtained the information summarized below.

Handy Harvey, Inc. is a local lumber and home improvement company. Because sales have increased so much during the past two years, Handy Harvey has had to raise additional working capital, especially as represented by receivables and inventory. The $50,000 loan is needed to assure the company of enough working capital for the next year. Handy Harvey began the year with total assets of $740,000 and stockholders' equity of $260,000, and during the past year the company had a net income of $40,000 on net sales of $760,000. The company's current unclassified balance sheet appears as follows:

Assets		**Liabilities and Stockholders' Equity**	
Cash	$ 30,000	Accounts Payable	$200,000
Accounts Receivable (net)	150,000	Note Payable (short-term)	100,000
Inventory	250,000	Mortgage Payable	200,000
Land	50,000	Common Stock	250,000
Buildings (net)	250,000	Retained Earnings	50,000
Equipment (net)	70,000	Total Liabilities and	
Total Assets	$800,000	Stockholders' Equity	$800,000

Sheila's Fashions, Inc. has for three years been a successful clothing store for young professional women. The leased store is located in the downtown financial district. Sheila's loan proposal asks for $50,000 to pay for stocking a new line of professional suits for working women during the coming season. At the beginning of the year, the company had total assets of $200,000 and total stockholders' equity of $114,000. Over the past year, the company earned a net income of $36,000 on sales of $480,000. The firm's unclassified balance sheet at the current date appears as follows:

Assets		**Liabilities and Stockholders' Equity**	
Cash	$ 10,000	Accounts Payable	$ 80,000
Accounts Receivable (net)	50,000	Accrued Liabilities	10,000
Inventory	135,000	Common Stock	50,000
Prepaid Expenses	5,000	Retained Earnings	100,000
Equipment (net)	40,000	Total Liabilities and	
Total Assets	$240,000	Stockholders' Equity	$240,000

REQUIRED

1. Prepare a financial analysis of each company's liquidity before and after receiving the proposed loan. Also, compute profitability ratios before and after, as appropriate. Write a brief summary of the effect of the proposed loan on each company's financial position.
2. To which company do you suppose Steve would be more willing to make a $50,000 loan? What are the positive and negative factors related to each company's ability to pay back the loan in the next year? What other information of a financial or nonfi-

nancial nature would be helpful for making a final decision?

Basic Research Activity

RA 6-1.
L O 7   *Annual Reports and*
S O 8   *Financial Analysis*

Most college and public libraries file annual reports of major public corporations. In some libraries, these annual reports are on microfiche. Go to the library and obtain the annual report for a company that you recognize. In the annual report, identify the four basic financial statements and the notes to the financial statements. Perform a liquidity analysis, including the calculation of working capital and the current ratio. Perform a profitability analysis, calculating profit margin, asset turnover, return on assets, debt to equity, and return on equity. Be prepared to present your findings in class.

FINANCIAL REPORTING AND ANALYSIS

Interpretation Cases from Business

ICB 6-1.
L O 6, 7   *Analysis of a*
Multistep Income
Statement

Toys "R" Us, Inc. has consistently been one of the best and fastest growing retailers in the country. Management is proud of its record of cost control, as witnessed by the following quotation from the company's 1987 annual report:

> Toys "R" Us expense levels are among the best controlled in retailing. . . . For example, in 1986 (year ended February 1, 1987) our expenses as a percentage of sales declined by almost 3% from 21.7% to 18.8%. As a result, we were able to operate with lower merchandise margins and still increase our earnings and return on sales.[8]

The company's condensed single-step income statements appear in an appendix.

REQUIRED

1. Prepare multistep income statements for Toys "R" Us for 1993 and 1994, and compute the ratios of gross margin from sales, operating expenses, income from operations, and net earnings to net sales.
2. Comment on whether the trend indicated by management in 1987 continued to be true in 1994. In 1987, gross margin was 31.2 percent, total operating expenses were 20.0 percent of net sales, and net earnings were 9.9 percent of sales.

ICB 6-2.
L O 7   *Profitability*
Analysis

Two of the largest chains of grocery/drug stores in the United States are *Albertson's, Inc.* and *American Stores Co.* (Jewel, Lucky, Acme, Osco, Sav-on, and others). In its fiscal year ending in January 1993, Albertson's had net income of $269.2 million, and in its fiscal year ending in December 1992, American had net income of $206.4 million. It is difficult to judge which company is more profitable from these figures alone because they do not take into account the relative sales, sizes, and investments of the companies. Data (in millions) are presented below to complete a financial analysis of the two companies.[9]

	Albertson's	**American Stores**
Net sales	$10,173.7	$19,051.2
Ending total assets	2,945.6	6,545.0
Beginning total assets	2,216.2	6,954.6
Ending total liabilities	1,557.2	4,853.0
Beginning total liabilities	1,016.7	3,439.0
Ending stockholders' equity	1,388.4	1,692.0
Beginning stockholders' equity	1,199.5	1,515.6

REQUIRED

1. Determine which company was more profitable by computing profit margin, asset turnover, return on assets, debt to equity, and return on equity for the two companies. Comment on the relative profitability of the two companies.

8. Toys "R" Us, Inc., *Annual Report, 1987.*
9. Albertson's, Inc., *Annual Report,* 1993, and American Stores Co., *Annual Report,* 1992.

2. What do the ratios tell you about the factors that go into achieving an adequate return on assets in the grocery industry? Refer to Figures 6-2, 6-3, and 6-4 in the text.
3. How would you characterize the use of debt financing in the grocery industry and the use of debt by the two companies?

International Company Case

ICC 6-1.
L O 5, 7 *Interpretation and Analysis of British Financial Statements*

Presented below is the classified balance sheet for the British company *Wellcome plc,* a major pharmaceutical firm with marketing and manufacturing operations in eighteen countries.[10]

Wellcome plc
Group Company Balance Sheets
as at 1 September 1992

	1992 £m	1991 £m
FIXED ASSETS		
Tangible assets	818.0	811.0
Investments	2.2	3.1
	820.2	814.1
CURRENT ASSETS		
Stocks	196.6	228.1
Debtors	366.5	367.9
Investments	569.7	362.1
Cash at Bank	23.3	33.4
	1,156.1	991.5
CREDITORS—AMOUNTS FALLING DUE WITHIN ONE YEAR:		
Loans and overdrafts	(89.7)	(80.5)
Other	(430.0)	(375.8)
NET CURRENT ASSETS	636.4	535.2
TOTAL ASSETS LESS CURRENT LIABILITIES	1,456.6	1,349.3
Creditors—amounts falling due after more than one year:		
Loans	(93.2)	(117.2)
Other	(4.3)	(3.9)
Provisions for liabilities and charges	(155.1)	(100.6)
Minority interests	(26.6)	(26.9)
TOTAL NET ASSETS	1,177.4	1,100.7
CAPITAL AND RESERVES		
Called up share capital	215.2	214.3
Share premium account	64.5	54.5
Profit and loss account	897.7	831.9
SHAREHOLDERS' FUNDS	1,177.4	1,100.7

10. Wellcome plc, *Annual Report*, 1992.

In the United Kingdom, the format used for classified financial statements is usually different from that used in the United States. In order to compare the financial statements of companies in different countries, it is important to be able to interpret a variety of formats.

REQUIRED

1. For each line on Wellcome plc's balance sheet, indicate the corresponding term that would be found on a U.S. balance sheet. (For this exercise, consider Provisions for Liabilities and Charges and Minority Interests to be long-term liabilities.) What is the focus or rationale behind the format of the U.K. balance sheet?
2. Assuming that Wellcome plc earned a net income of £250.5 million and £258.2 million in 1991 and 1992, respectively, compute the current ratio, debt to equity, return on assets, and return on equity for 1991 and 1992. (Use year-end amounts to compute ratios.)

Toys "R" Us Case

TC 6-1.
LO 5, 6, 7
SO 8
*Reading and
Analyzing an
Annual Report*

Refer to the Annual Report in the appendix on Toys "R" Us to answer the following questions. (Note that 1994 refers to the year ended January 29, 1994, and 1993 refers to the year ended January 30, 1993.)

REQUIRED

1. Consolidated balance sheets: (a) Did the amount of working capital increase or decrease from 1993 to 1994? By how much? (b) Did the current ratio improve from 1993 to 1994? (c) Does the company have long-term investments or intangible assets? (d) Did the capital structure of Toys "R" Us change from 1993 to 1994? (e) What is the contributed capital for 1994? How does it compare with retained earnings?
2. Consolidated statements of earnings: (a) Did Toys "R" Us use a multistep or a single-step form of income statement? (b) Is it a comparative statement? (c) What is the trend of net earnings? (d) How significant are income taxes for Toys "R" Us? (e) What is the trend of net earnings per share? (f) Did the profit margin increase from 1993 to 1994? (g) Did asset turnover improve from 1993 to 1994? (h) Did the return on assets increase from 1993 to 1994? (i) Did the return on equity increase from 1993 to 1994? Total assets and total stockholders' equity for 1994 may be obtained from the financial highlights or the notes.
3. Consolidated statements of cash flows: (a) Compare net income in 1994 with cash provided by operating activities in 1994. Why is there a difference? (b) What are the most important investing activities in 1994? (c) What are the most important financing activities in 1994? (d) How did these investing and financing activities compare with those in prior years? (e) Where did Toys "R" Us get cash to pay for the capital expenditures? (f) How did the change in Cash and Short-Term Investments in 1994 compare to that in other years?
4. Auditors' report: (a) What was the name of Toys "R" Us's independent auditor? (b) Who is responsible for the financial statements? (c) What is the auditor's responsibility? (d) Does the auditor examine all the company's records? (e) Did the accountants think that the financial statements presented fairly the financial situation of the company? (f) Did the company comply with generally accepted accounting principles?

Measuring and Reporting Assets, Liabilities, and Stockholders' Equity

Accounting, as you have seen, is an information system that measures, processes, and communicates information for decision-making purposes. **Part One** presented the principles and practices of the basic accounting system and financial statements. **Part Two** considers each of the major types of assets, liabilities, and stockholders' equity, with special attention to the effect of their measurement on net income, to their presentation in the financial statements, and to their importance to the management of the business enterprise.

CHAPTER 7
Short-Term Liquid Assets

focuses on the management of and accounting for four types of short-term assets: cash and cash equivalents, short-term investments, accounts receivable, and notes receivable.

CHAPTER 8
Inventories

presents a detailed discussion of the management and prices of inventories.

CHAPTER 9
Long-Term Assets

explores the management, acquisition, and disposal of property, plant, equipment, natural resources, and intangible assets, as well as the concepts and techniques of depreciation, depletion, and amortization.

CHAPTER 10
Current Liabilities and the Time Value of Money

presents the concepts and techniques associated with current liabilities and the time value of money.

CHAPTER 11
Long-Term Liabilities

introduces the long-term liabilities of corporations, paying special attention to accounting for bond liabilities. It also deals with other long-term liabilities, such as mortgages, installment notes, and postretirement benefits.

CHAPTER 12
Contributed Capital

illustrates accounting for the contributed capital section of stockholders' equity.

CHAPTER 13
Retained Earnings and Corporate Income Statements

focuses on accounting for retained earnings, a number of other transactions that affect stockholders' equity, and the component of the corporate income statement.

Short-Term Liquid Assets

LEARNING OBJECTIVES

1. Identify and explain the management issues related to short-term liquid assets.
2. Explain cash and cash equivalents and prepare a bank reconciliation.
3. Account for short-term investments.
4. Define *accounts receivable* and apply the allowance method of accounting for uncollectible accounts, using both the percentage of net sales method and the accounts receivable aging method.
5. Define and describe a *promissory note,* and make calculations and journal entries involving promissory notes.

SUPPLEMENTAL OBJECTIVE

6. Account for credit card transactions.

DECISION POINT

Bell Atlantic Corporation

A company must use its assets to maximize income earned while maintaining liquidity. Bell Atlantic Corporation, a leading provider of voice and data communications, mobile telephone services, computer maintenance services, and equipment leasing and financing products, manages almost $3 billion in short-term liquid assets. Short-term liquid assets are financial assets that arise from cash transactions, the investment of cash, and the extension of credit. What is the composition of these assets, and why are they important to Bell Atlantic's management?

As reported on the balance sheet in the company's 1992 annual report, short-term liquid assets (in millions) were[1]:

Cash and Cash Equivalents	$ 296.0
Short-Term Investments	33.7
Accounts Receivable, Net of Allowances of $123.9	2,023.8
Notes Receivable, Net	605.0
Total Short-Term Liquid Assets	$2,958.5

Although these assets make up only a little more than 10 percent of Bell Atlantic's total assets, they are crucial to the company's strategy for meeting its goals. The asset management techniques employed at Bell Atlantic ensure that these assets remain liquid and usable for operations.

A commonly used ratio for measuring the adequacy of short-term liquid assets is the quick ratio. It is the ratio of short-term liquid assets (defined as quick assets) to current liabilities. Since Bell Atlantic's current liabilities are $5,872,200,000, its quick ratio is .5, computed as follows:

$$\text{Quick ratio} = \frac{\text{quick assets}}{\text{current liabilities}} = \frac{\$2,958,500,000}{\$5,872,200,000} = .5$$

A quick ratio of about 1.0 is a common benchmark, but it is more important to look at the trends for a particular company to see if the ratio is improving or deteriorating. Bell Atlantic has maintained a quick ratio of .5 over several years. Through good cash management, the company has been able to get by with fewer funds tied up in quick assets relative to current liabilities. This chapter emphasizes management of, and accounting for, short-term liquid assets to achieve the objective of liquidity. : : : : :

1. Bell Atlantic Corporation, *Annual Report*, 1993.

MANAGEMENT ISSUES RELATED TO SHORT-TERM LIQUID ASSETS

The management of short-term liquid assets is critical to the goal of providing adequate liquidity. In dealing with short-term liquid assets, management must address three key issues: managing cash needs during seasonal cycles, setting credit policies, and financing receivables.

MANAGING CASH NEEDS DURING SEASONAL CYCLES

Most companies experience seasonal cycles of business activity during the year. These cycles involve some periods when sales are weak and other periods when sales are strong. There are also periods when expenditures are greater and periods when expenditures are smaller. In some companies, such as toy companies, college publishers, amusement parks, construction companies, and sports equipment companies, these cycles are dramatic, but all companies experience them to some degree.

Seasonal cycles require careful planning of cash inflows, outflows, borrowing, and investing. For example, Figure 7-1 might represent the seasonal cycles for a home improvement company like The Home Depot. As you can see, cash receipts from sales are highest in the late spring, summer, and fall because this is the period when most people make home improvements. Sales are relatively low in the winter months. On the other hand, cash expenditures are highest in late winter and spring as the company builds up inventory for spring and summer selling. During the late summer, fall, and winter, the company has excess cash on hand that it needs to invest in a way that will enable it to earn a return while still giving it access to the cash when it is needed. During the late spring and early summer, the company needs to plan for short-term borrowing to tide it over until cash receipts pick up later in the year. The discussion of accounting for cash, cash equivalents, and short-term investments in this chapter is directly related to managing for the seasonal cycles of a business.

SETTING CREDIT POLICIES

Companies that sell on credit do so to be competitive and to increase sales. In setting credit terms, the management of these companies must keep in mind both the terms their competitors are offering and the needs of their customers. Obviously, companies that sell on credit want customers who will pay the debts they incur. Therefore, most companies develop control procedures to increase the likelihood of selling only to customers who will pay when they are supposed to. As a result, most companies have a credit department. This department's responsibilities include the examination of each person or company that applies for credit and the approval or rejection of a credit sale to that customer. Typically, the credit department will ask for information on the customer's financial resources and debts. In addition, it may check personal references and established credit bureaus, which may provide further information about the customer. On the basis of this information, the credit department will decide whether to extend credit to the customer.

Figure 7-1. Seasonal Cycles and Cash Requirements for a Home Improvement Company

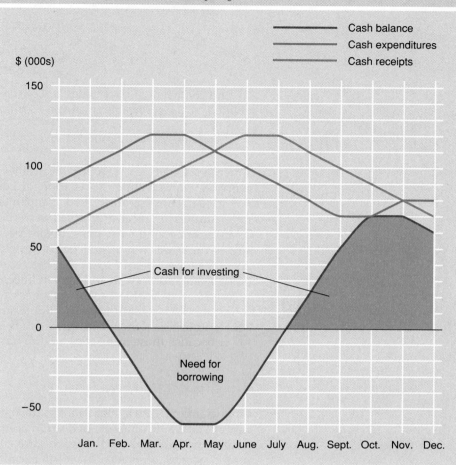

Two common measures of the effect of a company's credit policies are receivable turnover and average days' sales uncollected. The receivable turnover reflects the relative size of a company's accounts receivable and the success of its credit and collection policies. It may also be affected by external factors, such as seasonal conditions and interest rates. It shows how many times, on average, the receivables were turned into cash during the accounting period. The average days' sales uncollected is a related measure that shows, on average, how long it takes to collect accounts receivable.

Turnover ratios usually consist of one balance sheet account and one income statement account. The receivable turnover is computed by dividing net sales by average net accounts receivable. Theoretically, the numerator should be net credit sales, but the amount of net credit sales is rarely made available in public reports, so total net sales is used. American Greetings is the second largest producer of greeting cards in the United States. The company's net sales in 1993 were $1,671,692,000, and its net trade accounts receivable in 1992 and 1993 were $264,125,000 and $276,932,000, respectively.[2] Its receivable turnover is computed as follows:

2. American Greetings, *Annual Report,* 1992.

$$\text{Receivable turnover} = \frac{\text{net sales}}{\text{average net accounts receivable}}$$

$$= \frac{\$1,671,692,000}{(\$264,125,000 + \$276,932,000)/2}$$

$$= \frac{\$1,671,692,000}{\$270,528,500} = 6.2 \text{ times}$$

To find the average days' sales uncollected, the number of days in a year is divided by the receivable turnover, as follows:

$$\text{Average days' sales uncollected} = \frac{365 \text{ days}}{\text{receivable turnover}} = \frac{365 \text{ days}}{6.2} = 58.9 \text{ days}$$

American Greetings turns its receivables 6.2 times a year, or an average of every 58.9 days. While this is a longer period than for many companies, it is not unusual for greeting card companies because their credit terms allow retail outlets to receive and sell cards at various holidays, such as Easter, Thanksgiving, and Christmas, before paying for them. This example demonstrates the need to interpret ratios in light of the specific industry's practice. As may be seen from Figure 7-2, the receivable turnover ratio varies substantially from industry to industry. Grocery stores, for example, have a high turnover because this type of business has few receivables; the turnover in interstate trucking and auto and home supply is about 12 times because typical credit terms in these industries are thirty days. Manufacturers' turnover is lower because these industries tend to have longer credit terms.

FINANCING RECEIVABLES

Financial flexibility is important to most companies. Companies that have significant amounts of assets tied up in accounts receivable may be unwilling or unable to wait until the receivables are collected to receive the cash they represent. Many companies have set up finance companies to help their customers finance the purchase of their products. For example, Ford Motor Co. has Ford Motor Credit Company (FMCC), General Motors Corp. has General Motors Acceptance Corporation (GMAC), and Sears, Roebuck & Co. has Sears Roebuck Acceptance Corporation (SRAC). Some companies borrow funds by pledging their accounts receivable as collateral. If a company does not pay back its loan, the creditor can take the collateral, in this case the accounts receivable, and convert it to cash to satisfy the loan.

Companies can also raise funds by selling or transferring accounts receivable to another entity, called a factor. This sale or transfer of accounts receivable, called factoring, can be done with or without recourse. *Without recourse* means that the factor who buys the accounts receivable bears any losses from uncollectible accounts. A company's acceptance of credit cards like VISA, MasterCard, or American Express is an example of factoring without recourse because the credit card issuers accept the risk of nonpayment.

With recourse means that the seller of the receivables is liable to the purchaser if the receivable is not collected. The factor, of course, charges a fee for its service. The fee for sales with recourse is usually about 1 percent of the accounts receivable. The fee is higher for sales without recourse because the factor's risk is greater. In accounting terminology, the seller of the receivables with recourse is said to be contingently liable. A contingent liability is a potential liability that can develop into a real liability if a possible subsequent

Figure 7-2. Receivable Turnover for Selected Industries

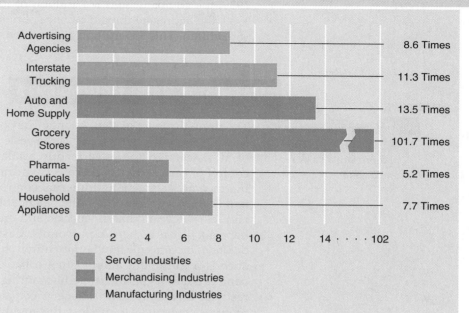

Source: Data from Dun and Bradstreet, *Industry Norms and Ratios*, 1992–93.

event occurs. In this case, the subsequent event would be nonpayment of the receivable by the customer.

Fleetwood Enterprises, Inc., the nation's leading producer of recreational vehicles and manufactured homes, provides an example of the selling of receivables. The company established Fleetwood Credit Corporation to finance sales of its RVs and by 1990 financed over 35 percent of all Fleetwood sales. Since buyers of RVs can take several years to pay, Fleetwood's management decided to sell significant amounts of the receivables held by Fleetwood Credit Corporation to obtain financial flexibility and funds for future growth. In 1993, Fleetwood sold $111.9 million of receivables to investors, and its outstanding balance of sold receivables was $393.3 million. Even though the receivables have been sold, the company has a contingent liability of up to $31.5 million for receivables sold with recourse that have not yet been paid.[3] If the receivables are paid as expected, Fleetwood will have no further liability.

Another method of financing receivables is through the discounting, or selling, of promissory notes held as notes receivable. Selling notes receivable is called discounting because the bank deducts the interest from the maturity value of the note to determine the proceeds. The holder of the note (usually the payee) endorses the note and delivers it to the bank. The bank expects to collect the maturity value of the note (principal plus interest) on the maturity date but also has recourse against the endorser or seller of the note. If the maker fails to pay, the endorser is liable to the bank for payment. The endorser has a contingent liability in the amount of the discounted notes that must be disclosed in the notes to the financial statements.

Marriott Corporation, the world's largest operator of hotels and a leader in food and services management, is an example of a company that has sold

3. Fleetwood Enterprises, *Annual Report*, 1993.

portions of the notes receivable from its various affiliates to obtain cash. In 1989, the company sold $61 million of its notes receivable. At December 29, 1989, the aggregate unpaid balance of notes receivable sold with recourse was $55 million. This $55 million represented a contingent liability.

CASH AND CASH EQUIVALENTS

2 *Explain cash and cash equivalents and prepare a bank reconciliation*

The annual report of Bell Atlantic Corporation refers to *cash and cash equivalents*. Of these two terms, *cash* is the easier to understand. It is the most liquid of all assets and the most readily available to pay debts. We discussed the control of cash receipts and cash payments in the chapter on the merchandising income statement and internal control, but we did not deal with the content of the Cash account on the balance sheet. Cash normally consists of coin and currency on hand, checks and money orders from customers, and deposits in bank checking accounts. Cash may also include a compensating balance, an amount that is not entirely free to be spent. A compensating balance is a minimum amount that a bank requires a company to keep in its bank account as part of a credit-granting arrangement. Such an arrangement restricts cash and may reduce a company's liquidity. Therefore, the SEC requires companies to disclose the amount of any compensating balances in a note to the financial statements.

The term *cash equivalents* is a little harder to understand. At times a company may find that it has more cash on hand than it needs to pay current obligations. This excess cash should not remain idle, especially during periods of high interest rates. Thus, management may periodically invest the idle funds in time deposits or certificates of deposit at banks and other financial institutions, in government securities such as U.S. Treasury notes, or in other securities. These actions are rightfully called investments. However, if these investments have a term of less than ninety days when they are purchased, they are called cash equivalents because the funds revert to cash so quickly that they are regarded as cash on the balance sheet. Bell Atlantic follows this practice. Its policy is stated as follows: "The Company considers all highly liquid investments with a maturity of 90 days or less when purchased to be cash equivalents. Cash equivalents are stated at cost, which approximates market value." A recent survey of the practices of 600 large U.S. corporations found that 96 of them, or 16 percent, used the term *cash* as the balance sheet caption and 425, or 71 percent, used the phrase *cash and cash equivalents* or *cash and equivalents*. Sixty-six companies, or 11 percent, combined cash with marketable securities.[4] The average amount of cash held can also vary by industry.

Most companies need to keep some currency and coins on hand. Currency and coins are needed for cash registers and for paying expenses that are impractical to pay by check. A company may need to advance cash to sales representatives for travel expenses, to divisions to cover their payrolls, and to individual employees to cash their paychecks. One way to control a cash fund or cash advances is through the use of an imprest system. A common form of imprest system is a petty cash fund, which is established at a fixed amount. Each cash payment from the fund is documented by a receipt. Then the fund

4. *Accounting Trends & Techniques* (New York: American Institute of Certified Public Accountants, 1992), p. 125.

is periodically reimbursed, based on the documented expenditures, for the exact amount necessary to restore its original cash balance. The person responsible for the petty cash fund must always be able to account for its contents by having cash and receipts whose total equals the originally fixed amount.

BANKING AND ELECTRONIC FUNDS TRANSFER

Banks greatly help businesses to control both cash receipts and cash disbursements. Banks serve as safe depositories for cash, negotiable instruments, and other valuable business documents, such as stocks and bonds. The checking accounts that banks provide improve control by minimizing the amount of currency a company needs to keep on hand and by supplying permanent records of all cash payments. Banks can also serve as agents in a variety of transactions, such as the collection and payment of certain kinds of debts and the exchange of foreign currencies.

Many companies commonly conduct transactions through a means of electronic communication called electronic funds transfer (EFT). Instead of writing checks to pay for purchases or to repay loans, cash is transferred electronically from one company's bank to another company's bank. Wal-Mart operates the largest electronic funds network in the retail industry and makes 75 percent of its payments to suppliers by this method. The actual cash, of course, is not transferred. For the banks, an electronic transfer is simply a bookkeeping entry.

In serving customers, banks may also offer automated teller machines (ATMs) for making deposits, withdrawing cash, transferring funds among accounts, and paying bills. Large consumer banks like Citibank, First Chicago, and Bank of America will process hundreds of thousands of ATM transactions each week. Many banks also provide customers the option of paying bills over the telephone and with *debit cards*. When a customer makes a retail purchase using a debit card, the amount of the purchase is deducted directly from the buyer's bank account. The bank usually documents debit card transactions for the retailer, but the retailer must develop new internal controls to ensure that the transactions are recorded properly and that unauthorized transfers are not permitted.

BUSINESS BULLETIN: INTERNATIONAL PRACTICE

Electronic funds transfer has been an important facilitator of international business. Caterpillar Inc., for example, sells earth-moving equipment throughout the world. To ensure payment and reduce the funds tied up in receivables, Caterpillar uses electronic funds transfer. Under prearranged terms, funds are electronically transferred from the customers' accounts to Caterpillar's account at the time orders are shipped. Worldwide, trillions of dollars in business transactions are electronically transferred every day.

PREPARING A BANK RECONCILIATION

Once a month, the bank sends each depositor a statement and returns the canceled checks that it has paid and charged to the depositor's account. The returned checks are said to be "canceled" because the bank stamps, or cancels, them to show that they have been paid. The bank statement shows the balance at the beginning of the month, the deposits, the checks paid, other debits and credits during the month, and the balance at the end of the month. A bank statement is illustrated in Figure 7-3.

Rarely will the balance of a company's Cash account exactly equal the cash balance shown on the bank statement. Certain transactions shown in the company's records may not have been recorded by the bank, and certain bank transactions may not appear in the company's records. Therefore, a necessary

Figure 7-3. Bank Statement

Statement of Account with
THE LAKE PARK NATIONAL BANK
Chicago, Illinois

Martin Maintenance Company
8428 Rocky Island Avenue
Chicago, Illinois 60643

Checking Acct No
8030-647-4
Period covered
Sept.30-Oct.31,19xx

Previous Balance	Checks/Debits—No.	Deposits/Credits—No.	S.C.	Current Balance
$2,645.78	$4,319.33 --15	$5,157.12 --7	$12.50	$3,471.07

CHECKS/DEBITS			DEPOSITS/CREDITS		DAILY BALANCES	
Posting Date	Check No.	Amount	Posting Date	Amount	Date	Amount
					09/30	2,645.78
10/01	564	100.00	10/01	586.00	10/01	2,881.78
10/01	565	250.00	10/05	1,500.00	10/04	2,825.60
10/04	567	56.18	10/06	300.00	10/05	3,900.46
10/05	566	425.14	10/16	1,845.50	10/06	4,183.34
10/06	568	17.12	10/21	600.00	10/12	2,242.34
10/12	569	1,705.80	10/24	300.00CM	10/16	3,687.84
10/12	570	235.20	10/31	25.62IN	10/17	3,589.09
10/16	571	400.00			10/21	4,189.09
10/17	572	29.75			10/24	3,745.59
10/17	573	69.00			10/25	3,586.09
10/24	574	738.50			10/28	3,457.95
10/24		5.00DM			10/31	3,471.07
10/25	575	7.50				
10/25	577	152.00				
10/28		128.14NSF				
10/31		12.50SC				

Explanation of Symbols:

CM – Credit Memo   SC – Service Charge   The last amount
DM – Debit Memo   EC – Error Correction   in this column
NSF – Non-Sufficient Funds   OD – Overdraft   is your balance.
                        IN – Interest on Average Balance

Please examine; if no errors are reported within ten (10) days, the account will be considered to be correct.

step in internal control is to prove both the balance shown on the bank statement and the balance of Cash in the accounting records. A bank reconciliation is the process of accounting for the differences between the balance appearing on the bank statement and the balance of Cash according to the company's records. This process involves making additions to and subtractions from both balances to arrive at the adjusted cash balance.

The most common examples of transactions shown in the company's records but not entered in the bank's records are the following:

1. **Outstanding checks**   These are checks that have been issued and recorded by the company, but do not yet appear on the bank statement.
2. **Deposits in transit**   These are deposits that were mailed or taken to the bank but were not received in time to be recorded on the bank statement.

Transactions that may appear on the bank statement but that have not been recorded by the company include the following:

1. **Service Charges (SC)**   Banks often charge a fee, or service charge, for the use of a checking account. Many banks base the service charge on a number of factors, such as the average balance of the account during the month or the number of checks drawn.
2. **NSF (Non-Sufficient Funds) checks**   An NSF check is a check deposited by the company that is not paid when the company's bank presents it to the maker's bank. The bank charges the company's account and returns the check so that the company can try to collect the amount due. If the bank has deducted the NSF check from the bank statement but the company has not deducted it from its book balance, an adjustment must be made in the bank reconciliation. The depositor usually reclassifies the NSF check from Cash to Accounts Receivable because the company must now collect from the person or company that wrote the check.
3. **Interest income**   It is very common for banks to pay interest on a company's average balance. These accounts are sometimes called N.O.W. or money market accounts but can take other forms. Such interest is reported on the bank statement.
4. **Miscellaneous charges and credits**   Banks also charge for other services, such as collection and payment of promissory notes, stopping payment on checks, and printing checks. The bank notifies the depositor of each deduction by including a debit memorandum with the monthly statement. A bank will sometimes serve as an agent in collecting on promissory notes for the depositor. In such a case, a credit memorandum will be included.

An error by either the bank or the depositor will, of course, require immediate correction.

Steps in Reconciling the Bank Balance   The steps to be followed in performing a bank reconciliation are as follows:

1. Compare the deposits listed on the bank statement with deposits shown in the accounting records. Any deposits in transit should be added to the bank balance. (Immediately investigate any deposits in transit from last month that are still not listed on the bank statement.)
2. Trace returned checks to the bank statement, making sure that all checks have been issued by the company, properly charged to the company's account, and properly signed.
3. Arrange the canceled checks returned with the bank statement in numerical order, and compare them with the record of checks issued. List checks issued but not on the bank statement. (Be sure to include any checks still outstanding

from prior months; investigate any checks outstanding for more than a few months.) Deduct outstanding checks from the bank balance.

4. Add to the balance per books any interest earned or credit memoranda issued by the bank, such as collection of a promissory note, that are not yet recorded on the company's books.

5. Deduct from the balance per books any debit memoranda issued by the bank, such as NSF checks and service charges, that are not yet recorded on the company's records.

6. Make sure the adjusted balance per books and per bank are in agreement.

7. Make journal entries for any items on the bank statement that have not been recorded in the company's books.

Illustration of a Bank Reconciliation

The October bank statement for Martin Maintenance Company, as shown in Figure 7-3, indicates a balance on October 31 of $3,471.07. We shall assume that in its records, Martin Maintenance Company has a cash balance on October 31 of $2,405.91. The purpose of a bank reconciliation is to identify the items that make up the difference between these amounts and to determine the correct cash balance. The bank reconciliation for Martin Maintenance Company is given in Exhibit 7-1. The numbered items in the exhibit refer to the following:

1. A deposit in the amount of $276.00 was mailed to the bank on October 31 and has not been recorded by the bank.

2. Five checks issued in October or prior months have not yet been paid by the bank, as follows:

Check No.	Date	Amount
551	Sept. 14	$150.00
576	Oct. 30	40.68
578	Oct. 31	500.00
579	Oct. 31	370.00
580	Oct. 31	130.50

3. The deposit for cash sales of October 6 was incorrectly recorded in Martin Maintenance Company's records as $330.00. The bank correctly recorded the deposit as $300.00.

4. Among the returned checks was a credit memorandum showing that the bank had collected a promissory note from A. Jacobs in the amount of $280.00, plus $20.00 in interest on the note. A debit memorandum was also enclosed for the $5.00 collection fee. No entry had been made on Martin Maintenance Company's records.

5. Also returned with the bank statement was an NSF check for $128.14. This check had been received from a customer named Arthur Clubb. The NSF check from Clubb was not reflected in the company's accounting records.

6. A debit memorandum was enclosed for the regular monthly service charge of $12.50. This charge was not yet recorded by Martin Maintenance Company.

7. Interest earned by the company on the average balance was reported as $25.62.

Note in Exhibit 7-1 that, starting from their separate balances, both the bank and book amounts are adjusted to the amount of $2,555.89. This adjusted balance is the amount of cash owned by the company on October 31 and thus is the amount that should appear on its October 31 balance sheet.

Recording Transactions After Reconciliation

The adjusted balance of cash differs from both the bank statement and Martin Maintenance Company's

Exhibit 7-1. Bank Reconciliation

Martin Maintenance Company
Bank Reconciliation
October 31, 19xx

Balance per bank, October 31		$3,471.07
① Add deposit of October 31 in transit		276.00
		$3,747.07
② Less outstanding checks:		
No. 551	$150.00	
No. 576	40.68	
No. 578	500.00	
No. 579	370.00	
No. 580	130.50	1,191.18
Adjusted bank balance, October 31		**$2,555.89**
Balance per books, October 31		$2,405.91
Add:		
④ Notes receivable collected by bank	$280.00	
Interest income on note	20.00	
⑦ Interest income	25.62	325.62
		$2,731.53
Less:		
③ Overstatement of deposit of October 6	$ 30.00	
④ Collection fee	5.00	
⑤ NSF check of Arthur Clubb	128.14	
⑥ Service charge	12.50	175.64
Adjusted book balance, October 31		**$2,555.89**

Note: The circled numbers refer to the items listed in the text on page 302.

records. The bank balance will automatically become correct when outstanding checks are presented for payment and the deposit in transit is received and recorded by the bank. Entries must be made, however, for the transactions necessary to correct the book balance. All the items reported by the bank but not yet recorded by the company must be recorded in the general journal by means of the following entries:

Oct. 31	Cash	300.00	
	Notes Receivable		280.00
	Interest Income		20.00
	Note receivable of $280.00 and interest of $20.00 collected by bank from A. Jacobs		
31	Cash	25.62	
	Interest Income		25.62
	Interest on average bank account balance		

Oct. 31	Sales	30.00	
	Cash		30.00
	Correction of error in recording a $300.00 deposit as $330.00		
31	Accounts Receivable	128.14	
	Cash		128.14
	NSF check of Arthur Clubb returned by bank		
31	Bank Service Charges Expense	17.50	
	Cash		17.50
	Bank service charge ($12.50) and collection fee ($5.00) for October		

It is acceptable to record these entries in one or two compound entries to save time and space, as follows:

Oct. 31	Cash	149.98	
	Sales	30.00	
	Accounts Receivable	128.14	
	Bank Service Charges Expense	17.50	
	Notes Receivable		280.00
	Interest Income		45.62
	To record items from bank reconciliation		

DECISION POINT

Campbell Soup Co.

During the 1980s, Campbell Soup Co. was drowning in paperwork. The company had forty locations that processed accounts payable and weekly payroll, which meant that eighty cash accounts had to be maintained and the daily transactions of each tracked manually. Each month, checks were written to settle more than 1,300 transactions among divisions of the company, and any differences in cash records and cash on hand in thirty bank accounts had to be explained. What could Campbell Soup do to become more efficient and provide better information to management?

The company developed a system that concentrates its cash management activities in two personal computer networks that perform cash management, reporting, and information management. The system is integrated, and the flow of information is automatic. Cash and general ledger transactions are automatically generated, and a system was developed so that balances among divisions could be netted and checks would not have to be written to settle accounts. Because banking fees and balances are now closely monitored, the fees paid to banks dropped from $5.0 million per year to less than $1.0 million in 1991. And because duplication of effort has been reduced, the staff has been cut in half, which has led to savings of more than $400,000 per year.[5] : : : : :

5. James D. Moss, "Campbell Soup's Cutting Edge Cash Management," *Financial Executive,* September/October 1992

SHORT-TERM INVESTMENTS

OBJECTIVE

 Account for short-term investments

When investments have a maturity of more than ninety days but are intended to be held only until cash is needed for current operations, they are called short-term investments, or marketable securities. Bell Atlantic states its policy on short-term investments as follows: "Short-term investments consist of investments that mature in 91 days to 12 months from the date of purchase." Investments that are intended to be held for more than one year are called long-term investments.

As discussed in the chapter on financial reporting and analysis, long-term investments are classified in an investments section of the balance sheet, not in the current assets section. Although these investments may be just as marketable as short-term assets, management intends to hold them for an indefinite period of time.

Securities that may be held as short-term or long-term investments fall into three categories, as specified by the Financial Accounting Standards Board: held-to-maturity securities, trading securities, and available-for-sale securities.[6] Trading securities are classified as short-term investments. Held-to-maturity securities and available-for-sale securities, depending on their length of maturity or management's intent to hold them, may be classified as either short-term or long-term investments. The three categories of securities when held as short-term investments are discussed here; long-term investments are discussed in the chapter on international accounting and intercompany investments.

HELD-TO-MATURITY SECURITIES

Held-to-maturity securities are debt securities that management intends to hold to their maturity date and whose cash value is not needed until that date. These securities are recorded at cost and valued on the balance sheet at cost adjusted for the effects of interest. For example, suppose that on December 1, 19x1 Lowes Corporation pays $97,000 for U.S. Treasury bills, which are short-term debt of the federal government. The bills will mature in 120 days at $100,000. The following entry would be made by Lowes:

19x1			
Dec. 1	Short-Term Investments	97,000	
	Cash		97,000
	Purchase of U.S. Treasury bills that mature in 120 days		

At Lowes' year end on December 31, the entry to accrue the interest income earned to date would be as follows:

19x1			
Dec. 31	Short-Term Investments	750	
	Interest Income		750
	Accrual of interest on U.S. Treasury bill $3,000 \times 30/120 = \$750$		

On December 31, the U.S. Treasury bill would be shown on the balance sheet as a short-term investment at its amortized cost of $97,750 ($97,000 + $750).

---

6. *Statement of Financial Accounting Standards No. 115,* "Accounting for Certain Investments in Debt and Equity Securities" (Stamford, Conn.: Financial Accounting Standards Board, 1993).

When Lowes receives the maturity value on March 31, 19x2, the entry is as follows:

19x2
Mar. 31 Cash   100,000
                Short-Term Investments   97,750
                Interest Income   2,250
                    Receipt of cash at maturity of
                    U. S. Treasury bill and recognition of
                    related income

TRADING SECURITIES

Trading securities are debt and equity securities that are bought and held principally for the purpose of being sold in the near term. Such securities are bought and sold frequently in order to generate profits on short-term changes in their prices. These securities are classified as current assets on the balance sheet and valued at fair value or at market value, if market value is readily available because the securities are traded on a stock exchange or in the over-the-counter market. An increase or decrease in the total trading portfolio (or group of securities held for trading purposes) is included in net income in the accounting period in which the increase or decrease occurs. For example, assume that Franklin Corporation purchases 10,000 shares of Mobil Corporation for $700,000 ($70 per share) and 5,000 shares of Texaco Inc. for $300,000 ($60 per share) on October 25, 19x1. The purchase is made for trading purposes; that is, management intends to make a gain by holding the shares for only a short period. The entry to record the investment at cost is as follows:

19x1
Oct. 25   Short-Term Investments   1,000,000
                Cash   1,000,000
                    Investment in stocks for trading
                    $700,000 + $300,000 = $1,000,000

Assume that at year end Mobil's stock price has decreased to $60 per share and Texaco's has risen to $64 per share. The trading portfolio may now be valued at $920,000, as shown below:

Security	Cost	Market Value
Mobil (10,000 shares)	$ 700,000	$600,000
Texaco (5,000 shares)	300,000	320,000
Totals	$1,000,000	$920,000

Since the current fair value of the portfolio is $80,000 less than the original cost of $1,000,000, an adjusting entry is needed, as follows:

19x1
Dec. 31   Unrealized Loss on Investments   80,000
                Allowance to Adjust Short-Term   80,000
                Investments to Market
                    Recognition of unrealized loss
                    on trading portfolio

The unrealized loss will appear on the income statement as a reduction in income. (The loss is unrealized because the securities have not been sold.)

The Allowance to Adjust Short-Term Investments to Market account appears on the balance sheet as a contra-asset, as follows:

Short-Term Investments (at cost)	$1,000,000
Less Allowance to Adjust Short-Term Investments to Market	80,000
Short-Term Investments (at market)	$ 920,000

or more simply,

Short-Term Investments (at market value, cost is $1,000,000)	$ 920,000

If Franklin sells its 5,000 shares of Texaco for $70 per share on March 2, 19x2, a realized gain on trading securities is recorded as follows:

19x2			
Mar. 2	Cash	350,000	
	Short-Term Investments		300,000
	Realized Gain on Investments		50,000
	Sale of 5,000 shares of Texaco for $70 per share; cost was $60 per share		

The realized gain will appear on the income statement. Note that the realized gain is unaffected by the adjustment for the unrealized loss at the end of 19x1. The two transactions are treated independently. If the stock had been sold for less than cost, a realized loss on investments would have been recorded. Realized losses also appear on the income statement.

Let's assume that during 19x2 Franklin buys 2,000 shares of Exxon Corporation at $64 per share and has no transactions involving Mobil. Also, assume that by December 31, 19x2, the price of Mobil's stock has risen to $75 per share, or $5 per share more than the original cost, and that Exxon's stock price has fallen to $58, or $6 less than the original cost. The trading portfolio now can be analyzed as follows:

Security	Cost	Market Value
Mobil (10,000 shares)	$700,000	$750,000
Exxon (2,000 shares)	128,000	116,000
Totals	$828,000	$866,000

The market value of the portfolio now exceeds the cost by $38,000 ($866,000 − $828,000). This amount represents the targeted ending balance for the Allowance to Adjust Short-Term Investments to Market account. Recall that at the end of 19x1, this account had a credit balance of $80,000, meaning that the market value of the trading portfolio was less than the cost. This account has no entries during 19x2 and thus retains its balance until adjusting entries are made at the end of the year. The adjustment for 19x2 must be $118,000—enough to result in a debit balance in this account of $38,000:

19x2			
Dec. 31	Allowance to Adjust Short-Term Investments to Market	118,000	
	Unrealized Gain on Investments		118,000
	Recognition of unrealized gain on trading portfolio		
	$80,000 + $38,000 = $118,000		

The 19x2 ending balance of the allowance account may be determined as follows:

Allowance to Adjust Short-Term Investments to Market

Dec. 31, 19x2 adj.	118,000	Dec. 31, 19x1 bal.	80,000
Dec. 31, 19x2 bal.	38,000		

The balance sheet presentation of short-term investments is as follows:

Short-Term Investments (at cost)	$828,000
Allowance to Adjust Short-Term Investments to Market	38,000
Short-Term Investments (at market)	$866,000

or, more simply,

Short-Term Investments (at market value, cost is $828,000)	$866,000

If the company also holds held-to-maturity securities, they are included in short-term investments at cost adjusted for the effects of interest.

AVAILABLE-FOR-SALE SECURITIES

Available-for-sale securities are debt and equity securities that do not meet the criteria for either held-to-maturity or trading securities. These securities are accounted for in exactly the same way as trading securities, except that the unrealized gain or loss is not reported on the income statement, but is reported as a special item in the stockholders' equity section of the balance sheet.

DIVIDEND AND INTEREST INCOME

Dividend and interest income for all three categories of investments are shown as income in the Other Income and Expenses section of the income statement.

ACCOUNTS RECEIVABLE

OBJECTIVE

4 *Define* accounts receivable *and apply the allowance method of accounting for uncollectible accounts, using both the percentage of net sales method and the accounts receivable aging method*

The other major types of short-term liquid assets are accounts receivable and notes receivable. Both result from credit sales to customers. Retail companies such as Sears, Roebuck and Co. have made credit available to nearly every responsible person in the United States. Every field of retail trade has expanded by allowing customers to make payments a month or more after the date of sale. What is not so apparent is that credit has expanded even more in the wholesale and manufacturing industries than at the retail level. The levels of accounts receivable in several industries are shown in Figure 7-4.

Accounts receivable are short-term liquid assets that arise from sales on credit to customers by wholesalers or retailers. This type of credit is often called trade credit. Terms on trade credit usually range from five to sixty days, depending on industry practice. For some companies that sell to consumers, installment accounts receivable constitute a significant portion of accounts receivable. Installment accounts receivable arise from the sale of goods on terms that allow the buyer to make a series of time payments. Department

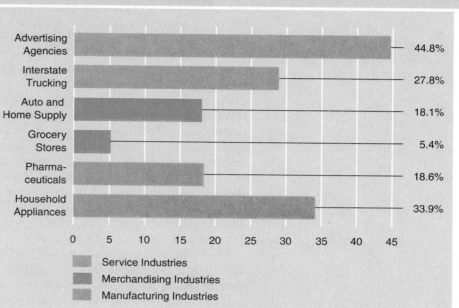

Figure 7-4. Accounts Receivable as a Percentage of Total Assets for Selected Industries

Source: Data from Dun and Bradstreet, *Industry Norms and Ratios,* 1992–93.

stores, appliance stores, furniture stores, used car companies, and other retail businesses often offer installment credit. Retailers such as J. C. Penney Company, Inc. and Sears, Roebuck and Co. have millions of dollars in installment accounts receivable. Although the payment period may be twenty-four months or more, installment accounts receivable are classified as current assets if such credit policies are customary in the industry. The special accounting rules that apply to some installment sales are usually deferred until a more advanced course.

On the balance sheet, the title Accounts Receivable is reserved for sales made to regular customers in the ordinary course of business. If loans or sales that do not fall into this category are made to employees, officers of the corporation, or owners, they should be shown separately with an asset title such as Receivables from Employees.

Normally, individual customer accounts receivable have debit balances, but sometimes customers overpay their accounts by mistake or in anticipation of future purchases. When individual customer accounts show credit balances, the total of these credits should be shown on the balance sheet as a current liability because the amounts must be refunded if future sales are not made to those customers.

THE ACCOUNTS RECEIVABLE SUBSIDIARY LEDGER

In previous chapters, a single Accounts Receivable account has been used. However, this single account does not readily tell how much each customer bought and paid for or how much each customer owes. In practice, all companies that sell to customers on credit keep an individual accounts receivable record for each customer. If the company has 6,000 credit customers, there are 6,000 accounts receivable. To include all these accounts with the other assets, liabilities, and stockholders' equity accounts would make the ledger very bulky. Consequently, most companies take the individual customers' accounts out of the general ledger, which contains the financial statement accounts, and place them in a separate ledger called a subsidiary ledger. A subsidiary ledger consists of accounts whose totals tie in with the balance of an account in the general ledger. The customers' accounts are filed alphabetically or by account number in the accounts receivable subsidiary ledger.

When a company puts its individual customers' accounts in an accounts receivable ledger, their balance is maintained in an Accounts Receivable account in the general ledger. This Accounts Receivable account in the general ledger is said to control the subsidiary ledger and is called a controlling, or control, account. It is a controlling account in the sense that its balance should equal the total of the individual account balances in the subsidiary ledger, as shown in Figure 7-5. When the amounts in the subsidiary ledger and the controlling account do not match, the accountant knows that there is an error and can find and correct it.

Most companies, as you will see, use an accounts payable subsidiary ledger as well. It is possible to use a subsidiary ledger for almost any account in the general ledger for which management wants specific information for individual items, such as Notes Receivable, Short-Term Investments, and Equipment.

UNCOLLECTIBLE ACCOUNTS AND THE DIRECT CHARGE-OFF METHOD

Regardless of how thorough and efficient its credit control system is, a company will always have some customers who cannot or will not pay. The

Figure 7-5. Relationship of Subsidiary Accounts to the Controlling Account

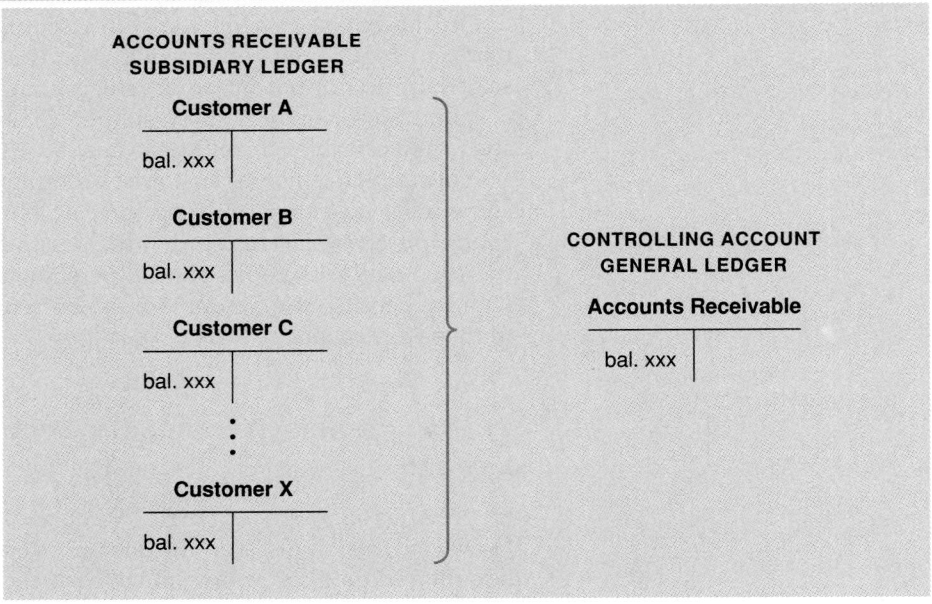

accounts owed by such customers are called uncollectible accounts, or *bad debts*, and are a loss or an expense of selling on credit. Why does a company sell on credit if it expects that some of its accounts will not be paid? The answer is that the company expects to sell much more than it would if it did not sell on credit, thereby increasing its earnings.

Some companies recognize the loss from an uncollectible account receivable at the time it is determined to be uncollectible. Assume that management determines on March 15 that it will not be able to collect $300 that is owed by an individual. Under this direct charge-off method, the loss is recognized in an entry similar to the following:

Mar. 15 Uncollectible Accounts Expense	300	
Accounts Receivable		300
To write off an account deemed to be uncollectible		

Many small companies use this method because it is required in computing taxable income under federal tax regulations. However, companies that follow generally accepted accounting principles do not use the direct charge-off method in their financial statements because it makes no attempt to match revenues and expenses. They prefer the allowance method, which is explained in the next section.

UNCOLLECTIBLE ACCOUNTS AND THE ALLOWANCE METHOD

Under the allowance method of accounting for uncollectible accounts, bad debt losses are matched against the sales they help to produce. As mentioned earlier, when management extends credit to increase sales, it knows that it will incur some losses from uncollectible accounts. These losses are expenses that occur at the time sales on credit are made and should be matched to the revenues they help to generate. Of course, at the time the sales are made, management cannot identify which customers will not pay their debts, nor can it predict the exact amount of money that will be lost. Therefore, to observe the matching rule, losses from uncollectible accounts must be estimated, and this estimate becomes an expense in the fiscal year in which the sales are made.

For example, let us assume that Cottage Sales Company made most of its sales on credit during its first year of operation. At the end of the year, accounts receivable amounted to $100,000. On this date, management reviewed the collectible status of the accounts receivable. Approximately $6,000 of the $100,000 of accounts receivable were estimated to be uncollectible. Therefore, the uncollectible accounts expense for the first year of operation was estimated to be $6,000. The following adjusting entry would be made on December 31 of that year:

Dec. 31 Uncollectible Accounts Expense	6,000	
Allowance for Uncollectible Accounts		6,000
To record the estimated uncollectible accounts expense for the year 19x1		

Uncollectible Accounts Expense appears on the income statement as an operating expense. Allowance for Uncollectible Accounts appears on the balance sheet as a contra-asset account that is deducted from Accounts Receivable.[7] It reduces the accounts receivable to the amount that is expected to be realized, or collected in cash, as follows:

Current Assets

Cash		$ 10,000
Short-Term Investments		15,000
Accounts Receivable	$100,000	
Less Allowance for Uncollectible Accounts	6,000	94,000
Inventory		56,000
Total Current Assets		$175,000

Accounts receivable may also be shown on the balance sheet as follows:

Accounts Receivable (net of allowance for uncollectible accounts of $6,000)	$94,000

Or they may be shown at "net" with the amount of the allowance for uncollectible accounts identified in a note to the financial statements. The estimated uncollectible amount cannot be credited to the account of any particular customer. Nor can it be credited to the Accounts Receivable controlling account because that would cause the controlling account to be out of balance with the total customers' accounts in the subsidiary ledger. The estimated uncollectible amount is therefore credited to a separate contra-asset account—Allowance for Uncollectible Accounts.

The allowance account will often have other titles, such as Allowance for Doubtful Accounts or Allowance for Bad Debts. Once in a while, the older phrase Reserve for Bad Debts will be seen, but in modern practice it should not be used. Bad Debts Expense is another title often used for Uncollectible Accounts Expense.

ESTIMATING UNCOLLECTIBLE ACCOUNTS EXPENSE

As noted, it is necessary to estimate the expense to cover the expected losses for the year. Of course, estimates can vary widely. If management takes an optimistic view and projects a small loss from uncollectible accounts, the resulting net accounts receivable will be larger than if management takes a pessimistic view. The net income will also be larger under the optimistic view because the estimated expense will be smaller. The company's accountant makes an estimate based on past experience and current economic conditions. For example, losses from uncollectible accounts are normally expected to be greater in a recession than during a period of economic growth. The final decision, made by management, of what the expense will be will depend on objective information, such as the accountant's analyses, and on certain qualitative factors, such as how investors, bankers, creditors, and others may view the performance of the company. Regardless of the qualitative considerations, the estimated losses from uncollectible accounts should be realistic.

---

7. The purpose of Allowance for Uncollectible Accounts is to reduce the gross accounts receivable to the amount estimated to be collectible (net realizable value). The purpose of another contra account, Accumulated Depreciation, is *not* to reduce the gross plant and equipment accounts to realizable value. Rather, its purpose is to show how much of the cost of the plant and equipment has been allocated as an expense to previous accounting periods.

The accountant may choose from two common methods for estimating uncollectible accounts expense for an accounting period: the percentage of net sales method and the accounts receivable aging method.

Percentage of Net Sales Method

The percentage of net sales method asks the question, How much of this year's net sales will not be collected? The answer determines the amount of uncollectible accounts expense for the year.

For example, the following balances represent the ending figures for Hassel Company for the year 19x9:

Sales			Sales Returns and Allowances		
	Dec. 31	645,000	Dec. 31	40,000	

Sales Discounts			Allowance for Uncollectible Accounts		
Dec. 31	5,000			Dec. 31	3,600

The actual losses from uncollectible accounts for the past three years have been as follows:

Year	Net Sales	Losses from Uncollectible Accounts	Percentage
19x6	$ 520,000	$10,200	1.96
19x7	595,000	13,900	2.34
19x8	585,000	9,900	1.69
Total	$1,700,000	$34,000	2.00

In many businesses, net sales is understood to approximate net credit sales. If there are substantial cash sales, then net credit sales should be used. Management believes that uncollectible accounts will continue to average about 2 percent of net sales. The uncollectible accounts expense for the year 19x9 is therefore estimated to be

$$.02 \times (\$645,000 - \$40,000 - \$5,000) = .02 \times \$600,000 = \$12,000$$

The entry to record this estimate is

Dec. 31	Uncollectible Accounts Expense	12,000	
	Allowance for Uncollectible Accounts		12,000
	To record uncollectible		
	accounts expense at 2 percent		
	of $600,000 net sales		

After the above entry is posted, Allowance for Uncollectible Accounts will have a balance of $15,600, as follows:

Allowance for Uncollectible Accounts

	Dec. 31	3,600
	Dec. 31 adjustment	12,000
	Dec. 31 balance	15,600

The balance consists of the $12,000 estimated uncollectible accounts receivable from 19x9 sales and the $3,600 estimated uncollectible accounts receivable from previous years. The $3,600 is the result of previous adjustments and writeoffs. The amount was not written off in previous years.

Accounts Receivable Aging Method   The accounts receivable aging method asks the question, How much of the year-end balance of accounts receivable will not be collected? Under this method, the year-end balance of Allowance for Uncollectible Accounts is determined directly by an analysis of accounts receivable. The difference between the amount determined to be uncollectible and the actual balance of Allowance for Uncollectible Accounts is the expense for the year. In theory, this method should produce the same result as the percentage of net sales method, but in practice it rarely does.

The aging of accounts receivable is the process of listing each accounts receivable customer according to the due date of the account. If the customer's account is past due, there is a possibility that the account will not be paid. And the further past due an account is, the greater that possibility. The aging of accounts receivable helps management to evaluate its credit and collection policies and alerts it to possible problems. The aging of accounts receivable for Myer Company is shown in Exhibit 7-2. Each account receivable is classified as being not yet due or as 1–30 days, 31–60 days, 61–90 days, or over 90 days past due. The estimated percentage uncollectible in each category is multiplied by the amount in each category to determine the estimated or target balance of Allowance for Uncollectible Accounts. In total, it is estimated that $2,459 of the $44,400 accounts receivable will not be collected.

Once the target balance for the Allowance for Uncollectible Accounts has been found, it is necessary to determine how much the adjustment needs to be. The amount of the adjustment depends on the current balance of the allowance account. Let us assume two cases for the December 31 balance of Allowance for Uncollectible Accounts for Myer Company: (1) a credit balance of $800 and (2) a debit balance of $800.

In the first case, an adjustment of $1,659 is needed to bring the balance of the allowance account to $2,459, calculated as follows:

Exhibit 7-2. Analysis of Accounts Receivable by Age

Myer Company
Analysis of Accounts Receivable by Age
December 31, 19xx

Customer	Total	Not Yet Due	1–30 Days Past Due	31–60 Days Past Due	61–90 Days Past Due	Over 90 Days Past Due
A. Arnold	$ 150		$ 150			
M. Benoit	400			$ 400		
J. Connolly	1,000	$ 900	100			
R. DiCarlo	250				$ 250	
Others	42,600	21,000	14,000	3,800	2,200	$1,600
Totals	$44,400	$21,900	$14,250	$4,200	$2,450	$1,600
Estimated Percentage Uncollectible		1.0	2.0	10.0	30.0	50.0
Allowance for Uncollectible Accounts	$ 2,459	$ 219	$ 285	$ 420	$ 735	$ 800

Targeted Balance for Uncollectible Accounts	$2,459
Less Credit Balance—Allowance for Uncollectible Accounts	800
Uncollectible Accounts Expense	$1,659

The uncollectible accounts expense is recorded as follows:

Dec. 31	Uncollectible Accounts Expense	1,659	
	Allowance for Uncollectible Accounts		1,659
	To record the allowance for		
	uncollectible accounts to the		
	level of estimated losses		

The resulting balance of Allowance for Uncollectible Accounts is $2,459:

Allowance for Uncollectible Accounts

		Dec. 31	800
		Dec. 31 adjustment	1,659
		Dec. 31 balance	2,459

In the second case, since the Allowance for Uncollectible Accounts has a debit balance of $800, the estimated uncollectible accounts expense for the year will have to be $3,259 to reach the targeted balance of $2,459, calculated as follows:

Targeted Balance for Uncollectible Accounts	$2,459
Plus Debit Balance—Allowance for Uncollectible Accounts	800
Uncollectible Accounts Expense	$3,259

The uncollectible accounts expense will be recorded as follows:

Dec. 31	Uncollectible Accounts Expense	3,259	
	Allowance for Uncollectible Accounts		3,259
	To record the allowance for		
	uncollectible accounts to the		
	level of estimated losses		

After this entry, Allowance for Uncollectible Accounts has a credit balance of $2,459, as follows:

Allowance for Uncollectible Accounts

Dec. 31	800	Dec. 31 adjustment	3,259
		Dec. 31 balance	2,459

Comparison of the Two Methods   Both the percentage of net sales method and the accounts receivable aging method estimate the uncollectible accounts expense in accordance with the matching rule, but they do so in different ways, as shown in Figure 7-6. The percentage of net sales method is an income statement approach. It assumes that a certain proportion of each dollar of sales will not be collected, and this proportion is the *amount of Uncollectible Accounts Expense* for the year. The accounts receivable aging method is a balance sheet approach. It assumes that a certain proportion of each dollar of accounts receivable outstanding will not be collected. This proportion is the *targeted balance of the Allowance for Uncollectible Accounts account.* The expense for the year is the difference between the targeted balance and the current balance of the allowance account.

Figure 7-6. Two Methods of Estimating Uncollectible Accounts

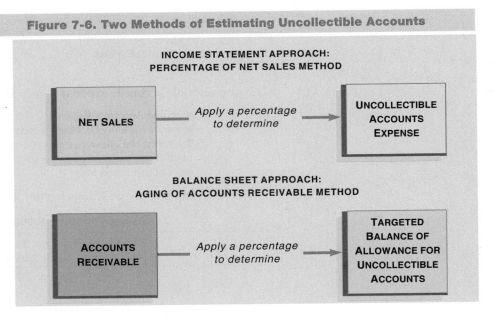

INCOME STATEMENT APPROACH:
PERCENTAGE OF NET SALES METHOD

NET SALES → *Apply a percentage to determine* → UNCOLLECTIBLE ACCOUNTS EXPENSE

BALANCE SHEET APPROACH:
AGING OF ACCOUNTS RECEIVABLE METHOD

ACCOUNTS RECEIVABLE → *Apply a percentage to determine* → TARGETED BALANCE OF ALLOWANCE FOR UNCOLLECTIBLE ACCOUNTS

Why Accounts Written Off Will Differ from Estimates   Regardless of the method used to estimate uncollectible accounts, the total of accounts receivable actually written off in any given year will rarely equal the estimated uncollectible accounts. The allowance account will show a credit balance when the accounts written off are less than the estimated uncollectible accounts. The allowance account will show a debit balance when the accounts written off are greater than the estimated uncollectible accounts.

BUSINESS BULLETIN: TECHNOLOGY IN PRACTICE

Accountants generally believe that the accounts receivable aging method is the best way to estimate uncollectible accounts because it takes into consideration current conditions, such as payment rates and economic conditions. However, since it is time-consuming to do an aging of accounts manually, in the past, the percentage of net sales method was generally used for preparing interim financial statements, such as monthly and quarterly reports. Now that most companies' accounts receivable are computerized, the aging of accounts receivable can be done much more easily and quickly. Indeed, many companies track the collection and aging of accounts receivables on a weekly or even a daily basis. As a result, the percentage of net sales method is used less often. ═══

WRITING OFF AN UNCOLLECTIBLE ACCOUNT

When it becomes clear that a specific account receivable will not be collected, the amount should be written off to Allowance for Uncollectible Accounts.

Remember that the uncollectible amount was already accounted for as an expense when the allowance was established. For example, assume that R. Deering, who owes Myer Company $250, is declared bankrupt on January 15 by a federal court. The entry to *write off* this account is as follows:

Jan. 15	Allowance for Uncollectible Accounts	250	
	Accounts Receivable		250
	To write off receivable from		
	R. Deering as uncollectible;		
	Deering declared bankrupt		
	on January 15		

Although the write-off removes the uncollectible amount from Accounts Receivable, it does not affect the estimated net realizable value of accounts receivable. The write-off simply reduces R. Deering's account to zero and reduces Allowance for Uncollectible Accounts by a similar amount, as the following table shows:

	Balances Before Write-off	Balances After Write-off
Accounts Receivable	$44,400	$44,150
Less Allowance for Uncollectible Accounts	2,459	2,209
Estimated Net Realizable Value of Accounts Receivable	$41,941	$41,941

Recovery of Accounts Receivable Written Off   Sometimes a customer whose account has been written off as uncollectible will later be able to pay the amount owed in full or in part. When this happens, two journal entries must be made: one to reverse the earlier write-off (which is now incorrect) and another to show the collection of the account.

For example, assume that on September 1, R. Deering, after his bankruptcy on January 15, notified the company that he would be able to pay $100 of his account and sent a check for $50. The entries to record this transaction are as follows:

Sept. 1	Accounts Receivable	100	
	Allowance for Uncollectible Accounts		100
	To reinstate the portion of		
	the account of R. Deering		
	now considered collectible;		
	originally written off		
	January 15		
1	Cash	50	
	Accounts Receivable		50
	Collection from R. Deering		

The collectible portion of R. Deering's account must be restored to his account and credited to Allowance for Uncollectible Accounts for two reasons. First, it turned out to be wrong to write off the full $250 on January 15 because only $150 was actually uncollectible. Second, the accounts receivable subsidiary account for R. Deering should reflect his ability to pay a portion of the money he owed in spite of his bankruptcy. Documentation of this action will give a clear picture of his credit record for future credit action.

NOTES RECEIVABLE

A promissory note is an unconditional promise to pay a definite sum of money on demand or at a future date. The entity who signs the note and thereby promises to pay is called the *maker* of the note. The entity to whom payment is to be made is called the *payee*. The promissory note in Figure 7-7 is dated May 20, 19x1, and is an unconditional promise by the maker, Samuel Mason, to pay a definite sum, or principal ($1,000), to the payee, Cook County Bank & Trust Company, at the future date of August 18, 19x1. The promissory note bears an interest rate of 8 percent. The payee regards all promissory notes it holds that are due in less than one year as notes receivable in the current assets section of the balance sheet. The makers regard them as notes payable in the current liability section of the balance sheet.

This portion of the chapter is concerned primarily with notes received from customers. The nature of a business generally determines how frequently promissory notes are received from customers. Firms selling durable goods of high value, such as farm machinery and automobiles, will often accept promissory notes. Among the advantages of promissory notes are that they produce interest income and represent a stronger legal claim against the creditor than do accounts receivable. In addition, selling promissory notes to banks is a common financing method. Almost all companies will occasionally receive a note, and many companies obtain notes receivable in settlement of past-due accounts.

COMPUTATIONS FOR PROMISSORY NOTES

In accounting for promissory notes, several terms are important to remember. These terms are (1) maturity date, (2) duration of note, (3) interest and interest rate, and (4) maturity value.

Figure 7-7. A Promissory Note

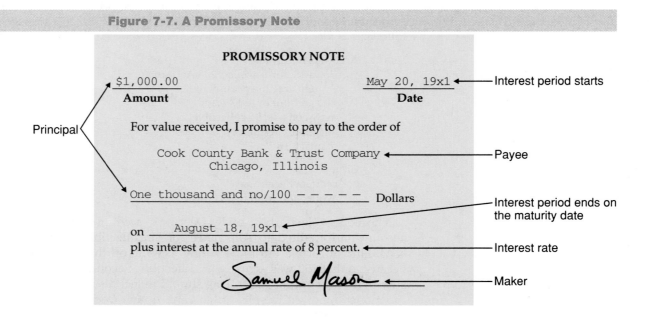

PROMISSORY NOTE

$1,000.00   May 20, 19x1 ← Interest period starts
Amount   **Date**

Principal

For value received, I promise to pay to the order of

Cook County Bank & Trust Company ← Payee
Chicago, Illinois

One thousand and no/100 – – – – – Dollars ← Interest period ends on the maturity date

on _____ August 18, 19x1 _____ ← Interest period ends on the maturity date

plus interest at the annual rate of 8 percent. ← Interest rate

Samuel Mason ← Maker

Maturity Date   The maturity date is the date on which the note must be paid. This date must either be stated on the promissory note or be determinable from the facts stated on the note. Among the most common statements of maturity date are the following:

1. A specific date, such as "November 14, 19xx"
2. A specific number of months after the date of the note, for example, "3 months after date"
3. A specific number of days after the date of the note, for example, "60 days after date"

There is no problem in determining the maturity date when it is stated. When the maturity date is a number of months from the date of the note, one simply uses the same day in the appropriate future month. For example, a note dated January 20 that is due in two months would be due on March 20.

When the maturity date is a specific number of days from the date of the note, it must be based on the exact number of days. In computing the maturity date, it is important to exclude the date of the note. For example, a note dated May 20 and due in 90 days would be due on August 18, computed as follows:

Days remaining in May (31 − 20)	11
Days in June	30
Days in July	31
Days in August	18
Total days	90

Duration of Note   Determining the duration of note, or its length of time in days, is the opposite problem from determining the maturity date. Knowing the duration of the note is important because interest is calculated for the exact number of days. There is no problem when the maturity date is stated as a specific number of days from the date of the note. However, if the maturity date is a specified date, the exact number of days must be determined. Assume that a note issued on May 10 matures on August 10. The duration of the note is 92 days, determined as follows:

Days remaining in May (31 − 10)	21
Days in June	30
Days in July	31
Days in August	10
Total days	92

Interest and Interest Rate   The interest is the cost of borrowing money or the return for lending money, depending on whether one is the borrower or the lender. The amount of interest is based on three factors: the principal (the amount of money borrowed or lent), the rate of interest, and the loan's length of time. The formula used in computing interest is as follows:

$$\text{Principal} \times \text{rate of interest} \times \text{time} = \text{interest}$$

Interest rates are usually stated on an annual basis. For example, the interest on a $1,000, one-year, 8 percent note would be $80 ($1,000 $\times$ 8/100 $\times$ 1 = $80). If the term, or time period, of the note were three months instead of a year, the interest charge would be $20 ($1,000 $\times$ 8/100 $\times$ 3/12 = $20).

When the term of a note is expressed in days, the exact number of days must be used in computing the interest. To keep the computation simple, let us compute interest on the basis of 360 days per year.[8] Therefore, if the term of the above note were 45 days, the interest would be $10, computed as follows: $1,000 $\times$ 8/100 $\times$ 45/360 = $10.

Maturity Value   The maturity value is the total proceeds of the note at the maturity date. Maturity value is the face value of the note plus interest. The maturity value of a 90-day, 8 percent, $1,000 note is computed as follows:

$$
\begin{aligned}
\text{Maturity value} &= \text{principal} + \text{interest} \\
&= \$1,000 + (\$1,000 \times 8/100 \times 90/360) \\
&= \$1,000 + \$20 \\
&= \$1,020
\end{aligned}
$$

There are also so-called non-interest-bearing notes. The maturity value is the face value, or principal amount. In this case, the principal includes an implied interest cost.

ILLUSTRATIVE ACCOUNTING ENTRIES

The accounting entries for promissory notes receivable fall into four groups: (1) receipt of a note, (2) collection on a note, (3) recording a dishonored note, and (4) recording adjusting entries.

Receipt of a Note   Assume that on June 1 a 12 percent, 30-day note is received from a customer, J. Halsted, in settlement of an existing account receivable of $4,000. The entry for this transaction is as follows:

June 1	Notes Receivable	4,000	
	Accounts Receivable		4,000
	Received 12 percent, 30-day note in payment of account of J. Halsted		

Collection on a Note   When the note plus interest is collected 30 days later, the entry is as follows:

July 1	Cash	4,040	
	Notes Receivable		4,000
	Interest Income		40
	Collected 12 percent, 30-day note from J. Halsted $4,000 \times 12/100 \times 30/360 = \$40$		

Recording a Dishonored Note   When the maker of a note does not pay the note at maturity, the note is said to be dishonored. The holder, or payee, of a dishonored note should make an entry to transfer the total amount due from Notes Receivable to an account receivable from the debtor. If J. Halsted dishonors his note on July 1, the following entry would be made:

July 1	Accounts Receivable	4,040	
	Notes Receivable		4,000
	Interest Income		40
	12 percent, 30-day note dishonored by J. Halsted		

8. Practice varies on the computation of interest. Most banks use a 365-day year for all loans, but some use a 360-day year for commercial loans. In Europe, use of a 360-day year is common. In this book, we use a 360-day year to keep the computations simple.

The interest earned is recorded because, although J. Halsted did not pay the note, he is still obligated to pay both the principal and the interest.

Two things are accomplished by transferring a dishonored note receivable into an Accounts Receivable account. First, it leaves the Notes Receivable account with only notes that have not matured and are presumably negotiable and collectible. Second, it establishes a record in the borrower's accounts receivable account that he or she has dishonored a note receivable. This information may be helpful in deciding whether to extend future credit to this customer.

Recording Adjusting Entries   A promissory note received in one period may not be due until a following accounting period. Because the interest on a note accrues by a small amount each day of the note's duration, it is necessary, according to the matching rule, to apportion the interest earned to the period in which it belongs. For example, assume that on August 31 a 60-day, 8 percent, $2,000 note was received and that the company prepares financial statements monthly. The following adjusting entry is necessary on September 30 to show how the interest earned for September has accrued:

Sept. 30	Interest Receivable	13.33	
	Interest Income		13.33
	To accrue 30 days' interest		
	earned on a note receivable		
	$2,000 \times 8/100 \times 30/360 = \$13.33$		

The account Interest Receivable is a current asset on the balance sheet. Upon receiving payment of the note plus interest on October 30, the following entry is made:[9]

Oct. 30	Cash	2,026.67	
	Notes Receivable		2,000.00
	Interest Receivable		13.33
	Interest Income		13.34
	Receipt of note receivable		
	plus interest		

As seen from these transactions, both September and October receive the benefit of one-half the interest earned.

Supplemental
OBJECTIVE

 Account for credit card transactions

CREDIT CARD SALES

Many retailers allow customers to charge their purchases to a third-party company that the customer will pay later. These transactions are normally handled with credit cards. Five of the most widely used credit cards are American Express, Diners Club, MasterCard, VISA, and Discover Card. The customer establishes credit with the lender (the credit card issuer) and receives a plastic card to use in making charge purchases. If the seller accepts the card, an invoice is prepared and signed by the customer at the time of the sale. The seller then sends the invoice to the lender and receives cash. Because the seller does not have to establish the customer's credit, collect from the customer, or tie money up in accounts receivable, the seller receives an economic benefit that is provided by the lender. For this reason, the lender

9. Some firms may follow the practice of reversing the September 30 adjusting entry. Here we assume that a reversing entry is not made.

does not pay 100 percent of the total amount of the invoices. The lender takes a discount of 2 to 6 percent on the credit card sales invoices.

One of two procedures is used in accounting for credit card sales, depending on whether the seller must wait for collection from the lender or may deposit the sales invoices in a checking account immediately. The following example illustrates the first procedure. Assume that, at the end of the day, a restaurant has American Express invoices totaling $1,000 and that the discount charged by American Express is 4 percent. These sales are recorded as follows:

Accounts Receivable	960	
Credit Card Discount Expense	40	
Sales		1,000
Sales made on American Express		
cards; discount fee is 4 percent		

The seller sends the invoices to American Express and later receives payment for them at 96 percent of their face value. When cash is received, the entry is as follows:

Cash	960	
Accounts Receivable		960
Receipt of payment from American		
Express for invoices at 96 percent of		
face value		

The second procedure is typical of sales made through bank credit cards such as VISA and MasterCard. Assume that the restaurant made sales of $1,000 on VISA credit cards and that VISA takes a 4 percent discount on the sales. Assume also that the sales invoices are deposited in a special VISA bank account in the name of the company, in much the same way that checks from cash sales are deposited. These sales are recorded as follows:

Cash	960	
Credit Card Discount Expense	40	
Sales		1,000
Sales on VISA cards		

CHAPTER REVIEW

REVIEW OF LEARNING OBJECTIVES

1. **Indentify and explain the management issues related to short-term liquid assets.** In managing short-term liquid assets, management must (1) consider the effects of seasonal cycles on the need for short-term investing and borrowing as the business's balance of cash fluctuates, (2) establish credit policies that balance the need for sales with the ability to collect, and (3) assess the need for additional cash flows through the financing of receivables.

2. **Explain cash and cash equivalents and prepare a bank reconciliation.** Cash consists of coins and currency on hand, checks and money orders received from customers, and deposits in bank accounts. Cash equivalents are investments that have a term of less than ninety days. A bank reconciliation accounts for the difference between the balance that appears on the bank statement and the balance in the company's Cash account. It involves adjusting both balances to arrive at the adjusted cash balance. The bank balance is adjusted for outstanding checks and

deposits in transit. The depositor's book balance is adjusted for service charges, NSF checks, interest earned, and miscellaneous debits and credits.

3. **Account for short-term investments.** Short-term investments may be classified as held-to-maturity securities, trading securities, and available-for-sale securities. Held-to-maturity securities are debt securities that management intends to hold to the maturity date; they are valued on the balance sheet at cost adjusted for the effects of interest. Trading securities are debt and equity securities that are bought and held principally for the purpose of being sold in the near term; they are valued at fair value or at market value. Unrealized gains or losses on trading securities appear on the income statement. Available-for-sale securities are debt and equity securities that do not meet the criteria for either held-to-maturity or trading securities. They are accounted for in the same way as trading securities, except that the unrealized gain or loss is reported as a special item in the stockholders' equity section of the balance sheet.

4. **Define *accounts receivable* and apply the allowance method of accounting for uncollectible accounts, using both the percentage of net sales method and the accounts receivable aging method.** Accounts receivable are amounts still to be collected from credit sales to customers. The amounts still owed by individual customers are found in the subsidiary ledger.

   Because credit is offered to increase sales, uncollectible accounts associated with the sales should be charged as expenses in the period in which the sales are made. However, because of the time lag between the sales and the time the accounts are judged to be uncollectible, the accountant must estimate the amount of bad debts in any given period.

   Uncollectible accounts expense is estimated by either the percentage of net sales method or the accounts receivable aging method. When the first method is used, bad debts are judged to be a certain percentage of sales during the period. When the second method is used, certain percentages are applied to groups of accounts receivable that have been arranged by due dates. A third method, the direct charge-off method, is used by some small companies, but because it does not follow the matching rule, it is not used by companies that follow generally accepted accounting principles.

   Allowance for Uncollectible Accounts is a contra-asset account to Accounts Receivable. The estimate of uncollectible accounts is debited to Uncollectible Accounts Expense and credited to the allowance account. When an individual account is determined to be uncollectible, it is removed from Accounts Receivable by debiting the allowance account and crediting Accounts Receivable. If the written-off account should later be collected, the earlier entry should be reversed and the collection recorded in the normal way.

5. **Define and describe a *promissory note*, and make calculations and journal entries involving promissory notes.** A promissory note is an unconditional promise to pay a definite sum of money on demand or at a future date. Companies selling durable goods of high value, such as farm machinery and automobiles, often accept promissory notes, which can be sold to banks as a financing method.

   In accounting for promissory notes, it is important to know how to calculate the maturity date, duration of note, interest and interest rate, and maturity value. The accounting entries for promissory notes receivable fall into four groups: receipt of a note, collection on a note, recording a dishonored note, and recording adjusting entries.

SUPPLEMENTAL OBJECTIVE

6. **Account for credit card transactions.** The use of third-party credit cards allows a company to sell on credit without incurring the cost of a credit department, keeping records of the account, and absorbing the losses from bad debts. In return, the company pays a fee, which is recorded as an expense at the time of the sale. Some credit card companies allow the merchant to deposit the credit card receipts in the bank immediately, while others require the merchant to wait for payment.

REVIEW OF CONCEPTS AND TERMINOLOGY

The following concepts and terms were introduced in this chapter:

L O 4   **Accounts receivable:** Short-term liquid assets that arise from sales on credit at the wholesale or retail level.

L O 4   **Accounts receivable aging method:** A method of estimating uncollectible accounts based on the assumption that a predictable portion of accounts receivable will not be collected.

L O 4   **Aging of accounts receivable:** The process of listing each accounts receivable customer according to the due date of the account.

L O 4   **Allowance for Uncollectible Accounts:** A contra-asset account that reduces accounts receivable to the amount that is expected to be collected in cash; also called *allowance for bad debts*.

L O 4   **Allowance method:** A method of accounting for uncollectible accounts whereby estimated uncollectible accounts are expensed in the period in which the related sales take place.

L O 3   **Available-for-sale securities:** Debt and equity securities that do not meet the criteria for either held-to-maturity or trading securities.

L O 1   **Average days' sales uncollected:** A ratio that shows on average how long it takes to collect accounts receivable; 365 days divided by receivable turnover.

L O 2   **Bank reconciliation:** The process of accounting for the difference between the balance appearing on a bank statement and the cash balance in the company records.

L O 2   **Bank statement:** A report sent by a bank to a customer that shows the status of the customer's account.

L O 2   **Cash:** Coins and currency on hand, checks and money orders from customers, and deposits in bank checking accounts.

L O 2   **Cash equivalents:** Short-term investments that will revert to cash in less than ninety days from when they are purchased.

L O 2   **Compensating balance:** A minimum amount that a bank requires be kept in an account as part of a credit-granting arrangement.

L O 1   **Contingent liability:** A potential liability that can develop into a real liability if a possible subsequent event occurs.

L O 4   **Controlling (or control) account:** An account in the general ledger for which there exists a subsidiary ledger.

L O 4   **Direct charge-off method:** A method of accounting for uncollectible accounts by directly debiting expenses when bad debts are discovered instead of using the allowance method; this method violates the matching rule but is required for federal income tax computations.

L O 1   **Discounting:** A method of selling notes receivable in which the bank deducts the interest from the maturity value of the note to determine the proceeds.

L O 5   **Dishonored note:** A promissory note that the maker cannot or will not pay at the maturity date.

L O 5   **Duration of note:** Length of time in days between a promissory note's issue date and its maturity date.

L O 2   **Electronic funds transfer (EFT):** The transfer of funds from one bank to another through electronic communication.

L O 1   **Factor:** An entity that buys accounts receivable.

L O 1   **Factoring:** The selling or transferring of accounts receivable.

L O 3   **Held-to-maturity securities:** Debt securities that management intends to hold to their maturity or payment date and whose cash value is not needed until that date.

L O 2   **Imprest system:** A system for controlling small cash disbursements by establishing a fund at a fixed amount and periodically reimbursing the fund by the amount necessary to restore its original cash balance.

L O 4   **Installment accounts receivable:** Accounts receivable that are payable in a series of time payments.

L O 5   **Interest:** The cost of borrowing money or the return for lending money, depending on whether one is the borrower or the lender.

L O 3   **Marketable securities:** Short-term investments intended to be held until needed to pay current obligations. Also called *short-term investments.*

L O 5   **Maturity date:** The due date of a promissory note.

L O 5   **Maturity value:** The total proceeds of a promissory note, including principal and interest, at the maturity date.

L O 5   **Notes payable:** Collective term for promissory notes owed by the entity (maker) who promises payment to other entities.

L O 5   **Notes receivable:** Collective term for promissory notes held by the entity to whom payment is promised (payee).

L O 4   **Percentage of net sales method:** A method of estimating uncollectible accounts based on the assumption that a predictable portion of sales will not be collected.

L O 2   **Petty cash fund:** A fund established by a business for making small payments of cash.

L O 5   **Promissory note:** An unconditional promise to pay a definite sum of money on demand or at a future date.

L O 1   **Quick ratio:** A ratio for measuring the adequacy of short-term liquid assets; quick assets divided by current liabilities.

L O 1   **Receivable turnover:** A ratio for measuring the average number of times receivables were turned into cash during an accounting period; net sales divided by average net accounts receivable.

L O 3   **Short-term investments:** Temporary investments of excess cash, intended to be held until needed to pay current obligations. Also called *marketable securities.*

L O 1   **Short-term liquid assets:** Financial assets that arise from cash transactions, the investment of cash, and the extension of credit.

L O 4   **Subsidiary ledger:** A separate ledger consisting of accounts whose total agrees with the balance of an account in the general ledger.

L O 4   **Trade credit:** Credit granted to customers by wholesalers or retailers.

L O 3   **Trading securities:** Debt and equity securities that are bought and held principally for the purpose of being sold in the near term.

L O 4   **Uncollectible accounts:** Accounts receivable owed by customers who cannot or will not pay. Also called *bad debts.*

REVIEW PROBLEM
ENTRIES FOR UNCOLLECTIBLE ACCOUNTS
EXPENSE AND NOTES RECEIVABLE TRANSACTIONS

L O 4, 5   The Farm Implement Company sells merchandise on credit and also accepts notes for payment. During the year ended June 30, the company had net sales of $1,200,000, and at the end of the year it had Accounts Receivable of $400,000 and a debit balance in Allowance for Uncollectible Accounts of $2,100. In the past, approximately 1.5 percent of net sales have proved uncollectible. Also, an aging analysis of accounts receivable reveals that $17,000 in accounts receivable appears to be uncollectible.

   The Farm Implement Company sold a tractor to R. C. Sims. Payment was received in the form of a $15,000, 9 percent, 90-day note dated March 16. On June 14, Sims dishonored the note. On June 29, the company received payment in full from Sims plus additional interest from the date of the dishonored note.

REQUIRED   1. Prepare journal entries to record uncollectible accounts expense using (a) the percentage of net sales method and (b) the accounts receivable aging method.
2. Prepare journal entries relating to the note received from R. C. Sims.

ANSWER TO REVIEW PROBLEM

1. Prepare journal entries to record uncollectible accounts expense.

   a. Percentage of net sales method:

June 30	Uncollectible Accounts Expense	18,000	
	Allowance for Uncollectible Accounts		18,000
	To record estimated uncollectible accounts expense at 1.5 percent of $1,200,000		

   b. Accounts receivable aging method:

June 30	Uncollectible Accounts Expense	19,100	
	Allowance for Uncollectible Accounts		19,100
	To record estimated uncollectible accounts expense. The debit balance in the allowance account must be added to the estimated uncollectible accounts: $2,100 + $17,000 = $19,100		

2. Prepare journal entries related to note.

Mar. 16	Notes Receivable	15,000.00	
	Sales		15,000.00
	Tractor sold to R. C. Sims; terms of note: 9 percent, 90 days		
June 14	Accounts Receivable	15,337.50	
	Notes Receivable		15,000.00
	Interest Income		337.50
	The note was dishonored by R. C. Sims Maturity value: $15,000 + ($15,000 × 9/100 × 90/360) = $15,337.50		
29	Cash	15,395.02	
	Accounts Receivable		15,337.50
	Interest Income		57.52
	Received payment in full from R. C. Sims $15,337.50 + ($15,337.50 × 9/100 × 15/360) $15,337.50 + $57.52 = $15,395.02		

CHAPTER ASSIGNMENTS

KNOWLEDGE AND UNDERSTANDING

Questions

1. Why does a business need short-term liquid assets? What three issues does management face in managing short-term liquid assets?
2. What is a factor, and what do the terms *factoring with recourse* and *factoring without recourse* mean?
3. What items are included in the Cash account? What is a compensating balance?

4. How do cash equivalents differ from cash? From short-term investments?

5. What are the three kinds of securities held as short-term investments and how are they valued at the balance sheet date?

6. What are unrealized gains and losses on trading securities? On what statement are they reported?

7. Which of the following lettered items should be in Accounts Receivable? For those that do not belong in Accounts Receivable, tell where on the balance sheet they do belong: (a) installment accounts receivable from regular customers, due monthly for three years; (b) debit balances in customers' accounts; (c) receivables from employees; (d) credit balances in customers' accounts; (e) receivables from officers of the company.

8. What is the function of the accounts receivable subsidiary ledger and how is it related to Accounts Receivable?

9. Why does a company sell on credit if it expects that some of the accounts will not be paid? What role does a credit department play in selling on credit?

10. What accounting rule is violated by the direct charge-off method of recognizing uncollectible accounts? Why?

11. According to generally accepted accounting principles, at what point in the cycle of selling and collecting does a bad debt loss occur?

12. Are the following terms different in any way: allowance for bad debts, allowance for doubtful accounts, allowance for uncollectible accounts?

13. What is the effect on net income of an optimistic versus a pessimistic view by management of estimated uncollectible accounts?

14. In what ways is Allowance for Uncollectible Accounts similar to Accumulated Depreciation? In what ways is it different?

15. What is the underlying reasoning behind the percentage of net sales method and the accounts receivable aging method of estimating uncollectible accounts?

16. What procedure for estimating uncollectible accounts also gives management a view of the status of collections and the overall quality of accounts receivable?

17. After adjusting and closing entries at the end of the year, suppose that Accounts Receivable is $176,000 and Allowance for Uncollectible Accounts is $14,500. (a) What is the collectible value of Accounts Receivable? (b) If the $450 account of a bankrupt customer is written off in the first month of the new year, what will be the resulting collectible value of Accounts Receivable?

18. Why should an account that has been written off as uncollectible be reinstated if the amount owed is subsequently collected?

19. What is a promissory note? Who is the maker? Who is the payee?

20. What are the maturity dates of the following notes: (a) a 3-month note dated August 16, (b) a 90-day note dated August 16, (c) a 60-day note dated March 25?

21. Why are merchants willing to pay a fee to credit card companies to be able to accept their cards from customers?

Short Exercises

SE 7-1.
L O 1   *Management Issues*

Indicate whether each of the actions below is related to (a) managing cash needs during seasonal cycles, (b) setting credit policies, or (c) financing receivables.

1. Selling accounts receivable to a factor.
2. Borrowing funds for short-term needs during slow periods.
3. Conducting thorough checks of new customers' ability to pay.
4. Investing cash that is not currently needed for operations.

SE 7-2.
L O 1   *Short-Term Liquidity Ratios*

Slater Company has cash of $20,000, short-term investments of $25,000, net accounts receivable of $45,000, inventory of $44,000, accounts payable of $60,000, and net sales of $360,000. Last year's net accounts receivable were $35,000. Compute the following ratios: quick ratio, receivable turnover, and average days' sales uncollected.

SE 7-3.
L O 2 *Bank Reconciliation*

Prepare a bank reconciliation from the following information:

a. Balance per bank statement as of June 30, $2,586.58
b. Balance per books as of June 30, $1,308.87
c. Deposits in transit, $348.00
d. Outstanding checks, $1,611.11
e. Interest on checking, $14.60

SE 7-4.
L O 3 *Held-to-Maturity Securities*

On May 31, Renata Company invests $49,000 in U.S. Treasury bills. The bills mature in 120 days at $50,000. Prepare entries to record the purchase on June 1; the adjustment to accrue interest on June 30, which is the end of the fiscal year; and the receipt of cash at the maturity date of September 28.

SE 7-5.
L O 3 *Trading Securities*

Monika Corporation began investing in trading securities this year. At the end of the year, the following trading portfolio existed:

Security	Cost	Market Value
Sara Lee (10,000 shares)	$220,000	$330,000
Skyline (5,000 shares)	100,000	75,000
Totals	$320,000	$405,000

Prepare the necessary year-end adjusting entry on December 31 and the entry for the sale of all the Skyline shares on the following March 23 for $95,000.

SE 7-6.
L O 4 *Percentage of Net Sales Method*

At the end of October, Mafa Company management estimates the uncollectible accounts expense to be 1.0 percent of net sales of $2,770,000. Give the entry to record the uncollectible accounts expense, assuming that the Allowance for Uncollectible Accounts has a debit balance of $14,000.

SE 7-7.
L O 4 *Accounts Receivable Aging Method*

An aging analysis on June 30 of the accounts receivable of Texbar Corporation indicates uncollectible accounts of $43,000. Give the entry to record uncollectible accounts expense under each of the following independent assumptions: (a) Allowance for Uncollectible Accounts has a credit balance of $9,000 before adjustment, and (b) Allowance for Uncollectible Accounts has a debit balance of $7,000 before adjustment.

SE 7-8.
L O 4 *Write-off of Accounts Receivable*

Key Company, which uses the allowance method, has an account receivable from Sandy Burgess of $4,400 that it deems to be uncollectible. Prepare the entries on May 31 to write off the account and on August 13 to record an unexpected receipt from Burgess of $1,000. The company is not expecting to collect more from Burgess.

SE 7-9.
L O 5 *Note Receivable Calculations*

On June 15, Rostin Company receives a 90-day, 6 percent note in the amount of $5,000. What are the maturity date and the maturity value of the note?

SE 7-10.
L O 5 *Notes Receivable Entries*

On August 25, Rostin Company receives a 90-day, 9 percent note in settlement of an account receivable in the amount of $10,000. Record the receipt of the note, the accrual of interest at fiscal year end on September 30, and collection of the note on the due date.

APPLICATION

Exercises

E 7-1.
L O 1 *Management Issues*

Indicate whether each of the actions below is primarily related to (a) managing cash needs during seasonal cycles, (b) setting credit policies, or (c) financing receivables.

1. Buying a U.S. Treasury bill with cash that is not needed for a few months.
2. Comparing receivable turnovers for two years.
3. Setting policy on which customers may buy on credit.
4. Selling notes receivable to a financing company.

5. Borrowing funds for short-term needs during the period of the year when sales are low.
6. Changing terms of sale in an effort to reduce the average days' sales uncollected.
7. Using a factor to provide operating funds.
8. Establishing a department whose responsibility is to approve customers' credit.

E 7-2.
L O 1 *Short-Term Liquidity Ratios*

Using the following information selected from the financial statements of Li Company, compute the quick ratio, the receivable turnover, and the average days' sales uncollected:

Current Assets	
Cash	$ 35,000
Short-Term Investments	85,000
Notes Receivable	120,000
Accounts Receivable, net	100,000
Inventory	250,000
Prepaid Assets	25,000
Total Current Assets	$615,000
Current Liabilities	
Notes Payable	$150,000
Accounts Payable	75,000
Accrued Liabilities	10,000
Total Current Liabilities	$235,000
Net Sales	$800,000
Last Period's Accounts Receivable, net	$ 90,000

E 7-3.
L O 2 *Bank Reconciliation*

Prepare a bank reconciliation from the following information:

a. Balance per bank statement as of May 31, $4,227.27
b. Balance per books as of May 31, $3,069.02
c. Deposits in transit, $567.21
d. Outstanding checks, $1,727.96
e. Bank service charge, $2.50

E 7-4.
L O 2 *Bank Reconciliation: Missing Data*

Compute the correct amount to replace each letter in the following table:

Balance per bank statement	$ a	$8,900	$315	$1,990
Deposits in transit	600	b	50	125
Outstanding checks	1,500	1,000	c	75
Balance per books	3,450	9,400	225	d

E 7-5.
L O 3 *Held-to-Maturity Securities*

Swick Company experiences heavy sales in the summer and early fall, after which time it has excess cash to invest until the next spring. On November 1, 19x1, the company invests $194,000 in U.S. Treasury bills. The bills mature in 180 days at $200,000. Prepare entries to record the purchase on November 1; the adjustment to accrue interest on December 31, which is the end of the fiscal year; and the receipt of cash at the maturity date of April 30.

E 7-6.
L O 3 *Trading Securities*

Saito Corporation began investing in trading securities and engaged in the following transactions:

Jan. 6 Purchased 7,000 shares of Chemical Bank shares, $30 per share.
Feb. 15 Purchased 9,000 shares of EG&G, $22 per share.

At June 30 year end, Chemical Bank was trading at $40 per share and EG&G was trading at $18 per share. Record the entries for the purchases. Then record the necessary year-end adjusting entry. (Include a schedule of the trading portfolio cost and market in the explanation.) Also record the entry for the sale of all the EG&G shares on August 20 for $16 per share. Is the last entry affected by the adjustment made on June 30?

E 7-7.
L O 4 *Percentage of Net Sales Method*

At the end of the year, Lockport Enterprises estimates the uncollectible accounts expense to be .7 percent of net sales of $30,300,000. The current credit balance of Allowance for Uncollectible Accounts is $51,600. Give the general journal entry to record the uncollectible accounts expense. What is the balance of the Allowance for Uncollectible Accounts after this adjustment?

E 7-8.
L O 4 *Accounts Receivable Aging Method*

Accounts Receivable of Kinsella Company shows a debit balance of $52,000 at the end of the year. An aging analysis of the individual accounts indicates estimated uncollectible accounts to be $3,350.

Give the general journal entry to record the uncollectible accounts expense under each of the following independent assumptions: (a) Allowance for Uncollectible Accounts has a credit balance of $400 before adjustment and (b) Allowance for Uncollectible Accounts has a debit balance of $400 before adjustment. What is the balance of Allowance for Uncollectible Accounts after each of these adjustments?

E 7-9.
L O 4 *Aging Method and Net Sales Method Contrasted*

At the beginning of 19xx, the balances for Accounts Receivable and Allowance for Uncollectible Accounts were $430,000 and $31,400, respectively. During the current year, credit sales were $3,200,000 and collections on account were $2,950,000. In addition, $35,000 in uncollectible accounts were written off. Using T accounts, determine the year-end balances of Accounts Receivable and Allowance for Uncollectible Accounts. Then, make the year-end adjusting entry to record the uncollectible accounts expense, and show the year-end balance sheet presentation of Accounts Receivable and Allowance for Uncollectible Accounts under each of the following conditions:

a. Management estimates the percentage of uncollectible credit sales to be 1.2 percent of total credit sales.
b. Based on an aging of accounts receivable, management estimates the end-of-year uncollectible accounts receivable to be $38,700.

Post the results of each entry to the T account for Allowance for Uncollectible Accounts.

E 7-10.
L O 4 *Aging Method and Net Sales Method Contrasted*

During 19x1 General Road Company had net sales of $2,850,000. Most of the sales were on credit. At the end of 19x1 the balance of accounts receivable was $350,000 and the Allowance for Uncollectible Accounts had a debit balance of $12,000. Management has two methods of estimating uncollectible accounts expense: (a) The percentage of uncollectible sales is 1.5 percent, and (b) based on an aging of accounts receivable, the end-of-year uncollectible accounts total $35,000. Make the end-of-year adjusting entry for uncollectible accounts expense under each method and tell what the balance of Allowance for Uncollectible Accounts will be after each adjustment. Why are the results different, and which method is likely to be more reliable?

E 7-11.
L O 4 *Entries for Uncollectible Accounts Expense*

The Cordero Office Supply Company sells merchandise on credit. During the fiscal year ended July 31, the company had net sales of $4,600,000. At the end of the year, it had Accounts Receivable of $1,200,000 and a debit balance in Allowance for Uncollectible Accounts of $6,800. In the past, approximately 1.4 percent of net sales have proved uncollectible. Also, an aging analysis of accounts receivable reveals that $60,000 of the receivables appear to be uncollectible. Prepare journal entries to record uncollectible accounts expense using (a) the percentage of net sales method and (b) the accounts receivable aging method.

What is the resulting balance of Allowance for Uncollectible Accounts under each method? How would your answers under each method change if Allowance for Uncollectible Accounts had a credit balance of $6,800 instead of a debit balance? Why do the methods result in different balances?

E 7-12.
L O 4 *Accounts Receivable Transactions*

Assuming that the allowance method is being used, prepare journal entries to record the following transactions:

July 12, 19x4 Sold merchandise to Vera Barnes for $1,800, terms n/10.
Oct. 18, 19x4 Received $600 from Vera Barnes on account.

May 8, 19x5   Wrote off as uncollectible the balance of the Vera Barnes account when she was declared bankrupt.

June 22, 19x5   Unexpectedly received a check for $200 from Vera Barnes. No additional amount is expected to be collected from Barnes.

E 7-13.
L O 5
Interest Computations

Determine the interest on the following notes:

a. $22,800 at 10 percent for 90 days
b. $16,000 at 12 percent for 60 days
c. $18,000 at 9 percent for 30 days
d. $30,000 at 15 percent for 120 days
e. $10,800 at 6 percent for 60 days

E 7-14.
L O 5
Notes Receivable Transactions

Prepare general journal entries to record the following transactions:

Jan. 16   Sold merchandise to Brighton Corporation on account for $36,000, terms n/30.

Feb. 15   Accepted a $36,000, 10 percent, 90-day note from Brighton Corporation in lieu of payment on account.

May 16   Brighton Corporation dishonored the note.

June 15   Received payment in full from Brighton Corporation, including interest at 10 percent from the date the note was dishonored.

E 7-15.
L O 5
Adjusting Entries: Interest Expense

Prepare journal entries (assuming reversing entries are not made) to record the following:

Dec. 1   Received a 90-day, 12 percent note for $10,000 from a customer for the sale of merchandise.

31   Made end-of-year adjustment for interest income.

Mar. 1   Received payment in full for note and interest.

E 7-16.
L O 5
Notes Receivable Transactions

Prepare general journal entries to record these transactions:

Jan. 5   Accepted a $4,800, 60-day, 10 percent note dated this day in granting a time extension on the past-due account of B. Martinez.

Mar. 6   B. Martinez paid the maturity value of his $4,800 note.

9   Accepted a $3,000, 60-day, 12 percent note dated this day in granting a time extension on the past-due account of L. Waters.

May 8   When asked for payment, L. Waters dishonored his note.

June 7   L. Waters paid in full the maturity value of the note plus interest at 12 percent for the period since May 8.

E 7-17.
S O 6
Credit Card Sales Transactions

Prepare journal entries to record the following transactions for Toni's Novelties Store:

Apr. 8   A tabulation of invoices at the end of the day showed $2,200 in American Express invoices and $1,200 in Diners Club invoices. American Express takes a discount of 4 percent, and Diners Club takes a 5 percent discount.

15   Received payment from American Express at 96 percent of face value and from Diners Club at 95 percent of face value.

19   A tabulation of invoices at the end of the day showed $800 in VISA invoices, which are deposited in a special bank account at full value less 5 percent discount.

Problem Set A

7A-1.
L O 2
Bank Reconciliation

The following information is available for Hernandez Company as of November 30, 19xx:

a. Cash on the books as of November 30 amounted to $113,675.28. Cash on the bank statement for the same date was $141,717.08.

b. A deposit of $14,249.84, representing cash receipts of November 30, did not appear on the bank statement.

c. Outstanding checks totaled $7,293.64.

d. A check for $2,420.00 returned with the statement was recorded in the cash payments journal as $2,024.00. The check was for advertising.

e. The bank service charge for November amounted to $26.00.

332

Chapter 7

f. The bank collected $36,400.00 for Hernandez Company on a note. The face value of the note was $36,000.00.

g. An NSF check for $1,140.00 from a customer, Emma Matthews, was returned with the statement.

h. The bank mistakenly deducted a check for $800.00 drawn by Mota Corporation.

i. The bank reported a credit of $960.00 for interest on the average balance.

REQUIRED

1. Prepare a bank reconciliation for Hernandez Company as of November 30, 19xx.
2. Prepare the journal entries necessary from the reconciliation.
3. State the amount of cash that should appear on the balance sheet as of November 30.

7A-2.
L O 2   *Bank Reconciliation*

The information presented below and on the top of the next page comes from the records of the Kowalski Company:

TURNBULL NATIONAL BANK

Statement of Kowalski Company
Jarvis and Oak Streets

Checks/Debits			Deposits/Credits		Daily Balances	
Posting Date	Check No.	Amount	Posting Date	Amount	Date	Amount
					4/01	3,785.00
4/03	500	100.00	4/03	914.00	4/03	4,099.00
4/03	505	500.00	4/09	1,012.00	4/05	3,625.00
4/05	530	460.00	4/16	3,240.00	4/07	3,209.00
4/05	531	14.00	4/23	2,646.00	4/09	4,194.00
4/07	533	416.00	4/27	408.00CM	4/13	4,174.00
4/09	534	27.00	4/30	42.00IN	4/15	3,267.00
4/13	536	5.00			4/16	6,507.00
4/13		15.00NSF			4/23	9,153.00
4/15	538	907.00			4/25	3,407.00
4/25	537	5,746.00			4/27	3,739.00
4/27	540	76.00			4/30	3,777.00
4/30		4.00SC				

Code: CM–Credit Memo   IN–Interest   NSF–Nonsufficient Funds
DM–Debit Memo   SC–Service Charge

From the Cash Receipts Journal	Page 9		From the Cash Payments Journal	Page 12
Date	Debit Cash	Date	Check Number	Credit Cash
Apr. 1	914	Apr. 1	531	14
8	1,012	3	532	283
15	3,240	4	533	416
22	2,646	5	534	27
30	1,942		535 (voided)	
	9,754	6	536	5
		11	537	5,746
		12	538	709
		21	539	1,246
		22	540	76
				8,522

From the General Ledger

Cash   Account No. 111

Date		Item	Post. Ref.	Debit	Credit	Balance	
						Debit	Credit
Mar.	31	Balance				2,465	
Apr.	30		CR9	9,754		12,219	
	30		CP12		8,522	3,697	

The NSF check was received from customer P. Kemp for merchandise. The credit memorandum represents a $400 note, plus interest, collected by the bank. Check number 535 was prepared improperly and has been voided. Check number 538 for a purchase of merchandise was recorded incorrectly in the cash payments journal as $709 instead of $907. On April 1, the following checks were outstanding: no. 500 for $100, no. 505 for $500, no. 529 for $260, and no. 530 for $460.

REQUIRED

1. Prepare a bank reconciliation as of April 30, 19xx.
2. Prepare the general journal entries necessary to adjust the accounts.
3. What amount should appear on the balance sheet for cash as of April 30?

7A-3.

L O 3 *Held-to-Maturity and Trading Securities*

During certain periods, Nicks Company invests its excess cash until it is needed. During 19x1 and 19x2, the company engaged in the following transactions:

19x1

Jan. 16 Invested $146,000 in 120-day U.S. Treasury bills that had a maturity value of $150,000.

Apr. 15 Purchased 10,000 shares of Goodrich Paper common stock at $40 per share and 5,000 shares of Keuron Power Company common stock at $30 per share as trading securities.

May 16 Received maturity value of U.S. Treasury bills in cash.

June 2 Received dividends of $2.00 per share from Goodrich Paper and $1.50 per share from Keuron Power.

June 30 Made year-end adjusting entry for trading securities. Market price of Goodrich Paper shares is $32 per share and of Keuron Power is $35 per share.

Nov. 14 Sold all the shares of Goodrich Paper for $42 per share.

19x2

Feb. 15 Purchased 9,000 shares of Beacon Communications for $50 per share.

Apr. 1 Invested $195,500 in 120-day U.S. Treasury bills that had a maturity value of $200,000.

June 1 Received dividends of $2.20 per share from Keuron Power.

June 30 Made year-end adjusting entry for held-to-maturity securities.

        30 Made year-end adjusting entry for trading securities. Market price of Keuron Power shares is $33 per share and of Beacon Communications is $60 per share.

REQUIRED

1. Prepare journal entries to record these transactions assuming that Nicks Company's fiscal year ends on June 30.
2. Show the balance sheet presentation of short-term investments on June 30, 19x2.

7A-4.

L O 4 *Percentage of Net Sales Method*

On December 31 of last year, the balance sheet of Marzano Company had Accounts Receivable of $298,000 and a credit balance in Allowance for Uncollectible Accounts of $20,300. During the current year, the company's records included the following selected activities: sales on account, $1,195,000; sales returns and allowances, $73,000; collections from customers, $1,150,000; accounts written off as worthless, $16,000; and written-off accounts unexpectedly collected, $2,000. In the past, the company had found that 1.6 percent of net sales would not be collected.

REQUIRED

1. Open ledger accounts for the Accounts Receivable controlling account (112) and Allowance for Uncollectible Accounts (113). Then enter the beginning balances in these accounts.
2. Prepare separate journal entries to record in summary form each of the five activities listed above.
3. Give the general journal entry on December 31 of the current year to record the estimated uncollectible accounts expense for the year.
4. Post the appropriate parts of the transactions in **2** and **3** to the accounts opened in **1**.

7A-5.
L O 4   *Accounts Receivable*
            Aging Method

Pokorny Company uses the accounts receivable aging method to estimate uncollectible accounts. The Accounts Receivable controlling account had a debit balance of $88,430 and Allowance for Uncollectible Accounts had a credit balance of $7,200 at the beginning of the year. During the year, the company had sales on account of $473,000, sales returns and allowances of $4,200, worthless accounts written off of $7,900, and collections from customers of $450,730. At the end of the year (December 31), a junior accountant for the company was preparing an aging analysis of accounts receivable. At the top of page 6 of the report, the following totals appeared:

Customer Account	Total	Not Yet Due	1–30 Days Past Due	31–60 Days Past Due	61–90 Days Past Due	Over 90 Days Past Due
Balance Forward	$89,640	$49,030	$24,110	$9,210	$3,990	$3,300

The following accounts remained to finish the analysis:

Account	Amount	Due Date
K. Foust	$ 930	Jan. 14 (next year)
K. Groth	620	Dec. 24
R. Mejias	1,955	Sept. 28
C. Polk	2,100	Aug. 16
M. Spears	375	Dec. 14
J. Yong	2,685	Jan. 23 (next year)
A. Zorr	295	Nov. 5
	$8,960	

The company has found from past experience that the following rates are realistic to estimate uncollectible accounts:

Time	Percentage Considered Uncollectible
Not yet due	2
1–30 days past due	4
31–60 days past due	20
61–90 days past due	30
Over 90 days past due	50

REQUIRED

1. Complete the aging analysis of accounts receivable.
2. Determine the end-of-year balances (before adjustments) of the Accounts Receivable controlling account and Allowance for Uncollectible Accounts.
3. Prepare an analysis computing the estimated uncollectible accounts.
4. Prepare a general journal entry to record the estimated uncollectible accounts expense for the year. (Round adjustment to the nearest dollar.)

7A-6.
L O 5   *Notes Receivable*
            Transactions

Calderon Manufacturing Company engaged in the following transactions involving promissory notes:

Jan. 14 Sold merchandise to Wynton Bell Company for $37,000, terms n/30.
Feb. 13 Received $8,400 in cash from Wynton Bell Company and a 90-day, 8 percent promissory note for the balance of the account.
May 14 Received payment in full from Wynton Bell Company.

May 15 Received a 60-day, 12 percent note from Ted Feller Company in payment of a past-due account, $12,000.
July 14 When asked to pay, Ted Feller Company dishonored the note.
20 Received a check from Ted Feller Company for payment of the maturity value of the note, and interest at 12 percent for the six days beyond maturity.
25 Sold merchandise to Marie Luciano Company for $36,000, with payment of $6,000 cash and the remainder on account.
31 Received a $30,000, 45-day, 10 percent promissory note from Marie Luciano Company for the outstanding account receivable.
Sept. 14 When asked to pay, Marie Luciano Company dishonored the note.
25 Wrote off the Marie Luciano Company account as uncollectible following news that the company had been declared bankrupt.

REQUIRED   Prepare general journal entries to record these transactions.

Problem Set B

7B-1.
L O 2 *Bank Reconciliation*

This information is available for Jorge Mendoza Company as of October 31, 19xx:

a. Cash on the books as of October 31 amounted to $21,327.08. Cash on the bank statement for the same date was $26,175.73.
b. A deposit of $2,610.47, representing cash receipts of October 31, did not appear on the bank statement.
c. Outstanding checks totaled $1,968.40.
d. A check for $960.00 returned with the statement was recorded incorrectly in the check register as $690.00. The check was made for a cash purchase of merchandise.
e. Bank service charges for October amounted to $12.50.
f. The bank collected for Jorge Mendoza Company $6,120.00 on a note. The face value of the note was $6,000.00.
g. An NSF check for $91.78 from a client, Beth Franco, came back with the statement.
h. The bank mistakenly charged to the company account a check for $425.00 drawn by another company.
i. The bank reported that it had credited the account for $170.00 in interest on the average balance for October.

REQUIRED
1. Prepare a bank reconciliation for Jorge Mendoza Company as of October 31, 19xx.
2. Prepare the journal entries necessary to adjust the accounts.
3. State the amount of cash that should appear on the balance sheet as of October 31.

7B-2.
L O 2 *Bank Reconciliation*

The information presented below and on the next page comes from the records of the Vandermeer Company:

From the Cash Receipts Journal	Page 22		From the Cash Payments Journal		Page 106
Date	Debit Cash		Date	Check Number	Credit Cash
Sept. 1	2,832		Sept. 1	1551	2,436
9	28,972		4	1552	44
16	26,428		7	1553	12
23	20,974		8	1554	38,800
30	15,604		9	1555	5,240
	94,810		13	1556	18,270
			17	1557	28
			18	1558	372
			19	1559	11,324
					76,526

From the General Ledger

Cash   Account No. 111

Date		Item	Post. Ref.	Debit	Credit	Balance Debit	Balance Credit
Aug.	31	Balance				21,140	
Sept.	30		CR22	94,810		115,950	
	30		CP106		76,526	39,424	

FIRST NATIONAL BANK   **Statement of Vandermeer Company**
Vandermeer, MO

Checks/Debits Posting Date	Check No.	Amount	Deposits/Credits Posting Date	Amount	Daily Balances Date	Amount
					9/01	24,832.00
9/03	1531	1,020.00	9/03	3,228.00	9/03	26,976.00
9/03	1550	64.00	9/10	28,972.00	9/04	24,532.00
9/04	1551	2,436.00	9/13	3,308.00CM	9/06	24,488.00
9/04	˙1547	8.00	9/17	26,428.00	9/10	53,460.00
9/06	1552	44.00	9/24	20,974.00	9/11	12,130.00
9/11	1554	38,800.00	9/30	202.00IN	9/12	6,890.00
9/11	1549	2,530.00			9/13	10,198.00
9/12	1555	5,240.00			9/17	36,626.00
9/18	1556	18,270.00			9/18	18,328.00
9/18	1557	28.00			9/19	18,248.00
9/19		80.00NSF			9/24	39,222.00
9/25	1559	11,324.00			9/25	27,898.00
9/30		34.00SC			9/30	28,066.00

Code: CM–Credit Memo   IN–Interest   NSF–Nonsufficient Funds
      DM–Debit Memo   SC–Service Charge

The NSF check was received from customer P. James for merchandise. The credit memorandum represents a $3,200 note, plus interest, collected by the bank. The September 1 deposit, recorded by Vandermeer as $2,832 in cash sales, was recorded correctly by the bank as $3,228. On September 1, there were the following outstanding checks: no. 1531 for $1,020, no. 1547 for $8, no. 1548 for $70, no. 1549 for $2,530, and no. 1550 for $64.

REQUIRED

1. Prepare a bank reconciliation as of September 30, 19xx.
2. Prepare journal entries to update the accounts.
3. What amount should appear on the balance sheet for cash as of September 30?

7B-3.
L O 3   *Held-to-Maturity and Trading Securities*

F&M Distributors, Inc. follows a policy of investing excess cash until it is needed. During 19x1 and 19x2, the company engaged in the following transactions:

19x1
Feb.   1   Invested $97,000 in 120-day U.S. Treasury bills that had a maturity value of $100,000.

Mar. 30 Purchased 20,000 shares of Dataflex Company common stock at $16 per share and 12,000 shares of Gates Aviation, Inc. common stock at $10 per share as trading securities.

June 1 Received maturity value of U. S. Treasury bills in cash.

June 10 Received dividends of $0.50 per share from Dataflex Company and $0.25 per share from Gates Aviation, Inc.

June 30 Made year-end adjusting entry for trading securities. Market price of Dataflex Company shares is $13 per share and of Gates Aviation, Inc. is $12 per share.

Dec. 3 Sold all the shares of Dataflex Company for $12 per share.

19x2

Mar. 17 Purchased 15,000 shares of Biotech, Inc. for $9 per share.

Mar. 31 Invested $116,000 in 120-day U.S. Treasury bills that had a maturity value of $120,000.

June 10 Received dividends of $0.30 per share from Gates Aviation, Inc.

June 30 Made year-end adjusting entry for held-to-maturity securities.

30 Made year-end adjusting entry for trading securities. Market price of Gates Aviation, Inc. shares is $6 per share and of Biotech, Inc. is $11 per share.

REQUIRED

1. Prepare journal entries to record these transactions, assuming that F&M Distributors, Inc.'s fiscal year ends on June 30.
2. Show the balance sheet presentation of short-term investments on June 30, 19x2.

7B-4.

LO 4 *Percentage of Net Sales Method*

Chappell Company had an Accounts Receivable balance of $320,000 and a credit balance in Allowance for Uncollectible Accounts of $16,700 at January 1, 19xx. During the year, the company recorded the following transactions:

a. Sales on account, $1,052,000.
b. Sales returns and allowances by credit customers, $53,400.
c. Collections from customers, $993,000.
d. Worthless accounts written off, $19,800.
e. Written-off accounts collected, $4,200.

In addition, the company's past history indicates that 2.5 percent of net credit sales will not be collected.

REQUIRED

1. Open ledger accounts for the Accounts Receivable controlling account (112) and Allowance for Uncollectible Accounts (113). Then enter the beginning balances in these accounts.
2. Record separate general journal entries for each of the five items listed above, summarizing the year's activity.
3. Record the general journal entry on December 31 for the estimated uncollectible accounts expense for the year.
4. Post the appropriate parts of the transactions in **2** and **3** to Accounts Receivable and Allowance for Uncollectible Accounts.

7B-5.

LO 4 *Accounts Receivable Aging Method*

The DiPalma Jewelry Store uses the accounts receivable aging method to estimate uncollectible accounts. The balance of the Accounts Receivable controlling account was a debit of $446,341 and the balance of Allowance for Uncollectible Accounts was a credit of $43,000 at February 1, 19x1. During the year, the store had sales on account of $3,724,000, sales returns and allowances of $63,000, worthless accounts written off of $44,300, and collections from customers of $3,214,000. As part of end-of-year (January 31, 19x2) procedures, an aging analysis of accounts receivable is prepared. The totals of the analysis, which is partially complete, follow.

Customer Account	Total	Not Yet Due	1–30 Days Past Due	31–60 Days Past Due	61–90 Days Past Due	Over 90 Days Past Due
Balance. Forward	$793,791	$438,933	$149,614	$106,400	$57,442	$41,402

The following accounts remain to be classified in order to finish the analysis:

Account	Amount	Due Date
H. Caldwell	$10,977	January 15
D. Carlson	9,314	February 15 (next fiscal year)
M. Guokas	8,664	December 20
F. Javier	780	October 1
B. Loo	14,810	January 4
S. Qadri	6,316	November 15
A. Rosenthal	4,389	March 1 (next fiscal year)
	$55,250	

From past experience, the company has found that the following rates are realistic to estimate uncollectible accounts:

Time	Percentage Considered Uncollectible
Not yet due	2
1–30 days past due	5
31–60 days past due	15
61–90 days past due	25
Over 90 days past due	50

REQUIRED

1. Complete the aging analysis of accounts receivable.
2. Determine the end-of-year balances (before adjustments) of the Accounts Receivable controlling account and Allowance for Uncollectible Accounts.
3. Prepare an analysis computing the estimated uncollectible accounts.
4. Prepare a general journal entry to record the estimated uncollectible accounts expense for the year (round the adjustment to the nearest whole dollar).

7B-6.
L O 5   *Notes Receivable Transactions*

Minarcik Manufacturing Company sells truck beds. The company engaged in the following transactions involving promissory notes:

Jan. 10   Sold beds to Glynn Company for $60,000, terms n/10.
   20   Accepted a 90-day, 12 percent promissory note in settlement of the account from Glynn.
Apr. 20   Received payment from Glynn Company for the note and interest.
May 5   Sold beds to Nanni Company for $40,000, terms n/10.
   15   Received $8,000 cash and a 60-day, 13 percent note for $32,000 in settlement of the Nanni Company account.
July 14   When asked to pay, Nanni dishonored the note.
Aug. 2   Wrote off the Nanni Company account as uncollectible after news that the company had declared bankruptcy.
   5   Received a 90-day, 11 percent note for $30,000 from Sayeed Company in settlement of an account receivable.
Nov. 3   When asked to pay, Sayeed Company dishonored the note.
   9   Received payment in full from Sayeed Company, including 15 percent interest for the 6 days since the note was dishonored.

REQUIRED   Prepare general journal entries to record these transactions.

CRITICAL THINKING AND COMMUNICATION

Conceptual Mini-Cases

CMC 7-1.
L O 1   *Management of Cash*

Academia Publishing Company publishes college textbooks in the sciences and humanities. More than 50 percent of the company's sales occur in July, August, and December. Its cash balances are largest in August, September, and January. During the rest of the year, its cash receipts are low. The corporate treasurer keeps the cash in a bank checking account that pays little or no interest and pays bills from this account as they come due. In order to survive, the company has borrowed money during some slow sales months. The loans were repaid in the months when cash receipts were largest. A management group has suggested that the company institute a new cash management plan under which cash would be invested in marketable securities as it is received and securities would be sold when the funds are needed. In this way, the cash will earn an income and perhaps the company will realize a gain through an increase in the value of the securities, reducing the need for borrowing. What are the accounting implications of this cash management plan? Are there any disadvantages to the plan?

CMC 7-2.
L O 1 *Role of Credit Sales*

Mitsubishi Electric Corp.,[10] a broadly diversified Japanese corporation, instituted a credit plan, called Three Diamond, for customers who buy its major electronic products, such as large-screen televisions and videotape recorders, from specified retail dealers. Under this plan, which was introduced in 1990, approved customers who make purchases in November do not have to make any payments until April and pay no interest for the intervening months. Mitsubishi pays the dealer the full amount less a small fee, sends the customer a Mitsubishi credit card, and collects from the customer at the specified time. What is Mitsubishi's motivation for establishing these generous credit terms? What costs are involved? What are the accounting implications?

CMC 7-3.
L O 1 *Asset Financing*

Siegel Appliances, Inc. is a small manufacturer of washing machines and dryers located in central Michigan. Siegel sells most of its appliances to large, established discount retail companies that market the appliances under their own names. Siegel sells the appliances on trade credit terms of n/60. If a customer wants a longer term, however, Siegel will accept a note with a term of up to nine months. At present, the company is having cash flow troubles and needs $5 million immediately. Its cash balance is $200,000, its accounts receivable balance is $2.3 million, and its notes receivable balance is $3.7 million. How might Siegel's management use its accounts receivable and notes receivable to raise the cash it needs? What are the company's prospects for raising the needed cash?

CMC 7-4.
L O 4 *Percentage of Net Sales and Aging Methods Contrasted*

All companies that sell on credit face the risk of bad debt losses. For example, in 1992, *L.A. Gear Inc.,* the well-known maker of athletic footwear, had an allowance for uncollectible accounts of $6.9 million on accounts receivable of $63.0 million. Its 1992 sales were $430.2 million. What two methods are available to L.A. Gear Inc. for estimating uncollectible accounts expense? Contrast the two methods, including their relationships to the financial statements. Which method would you expect L.A. Gear Inc. to use? Why?

Ethics Mini-Case

EMC 7-1.
L O 1, 4 *Ethics, Uncollectible Accounts, and Short-Term Objectives*

Fitzsimmons Designs, a successful retail furniture company, is located in an affluent suburb where a major insurance company has just announced a restructuring that will lay off 4,000 employees. Fitzsimmons sells quality furniture, usually on credit. Accounts Receivable represents one of the major assets of the company and, although the company's annual uncollectible accounts losses are not out of line, they represent a sizable amount. The company depends on bank loans for its financing. Sales and net income in the past year have declined, and some customers are falling behind in paying their accounts. George Fitzsimmons, owner of the business, has instructed the controller to underestimate the uncollectible accounts this year in order to show a small growth in earnings because he knows that the bank's loan officer likes to see a steady performance. Fitzsimmons believes the short-term action is justified because future successful years will average out the losses, and since the company has a history of success, the adjustments are meaningless accounting measures anyway. Are Fitzsimmons's actions ethical? Would any parties be harmed by his actions? How important is it to try to be accurate in estimating losses from uncollectible accounts?

10. Information based on promotional brochures received from Mitsubishi Electric Corp.

Decision-Making Case

The *Bates Christmas Tree Company*'s business—the growing and selling of Christmas trees—is seasonal. By January 1, after a successful season, the company has cash on hand that will not be needed for several months. The company has minimal expenses from January to October and heavy expenses during the harvest and shipping months of November and December. The company's management follows the practice of investing the idle cash in marketable securities, which can be sold as the funds are needed for operations. The company's fiscal year ends on June 30. On January 10 of the current year, the company has cash of $408,300 on hand. It keeps $20,000 on hand for operating expenses and invests the rest as follows:

$100,000 3-month Treasury bill	$ 97,800
1,000 shares of Ford Motor Co. ($50 per share)	50,000
2,500 shares of McDonald's ($50 per share)	125,000
2,100 shares of IBM ($55 per share)	115,500
Total short-term investments	$388,300

During the next few months, the company receives two quarterly cash dividends from each company (assume February 10 and May 10): $.40 per share from Ford, $.10 per share from McDonald's, and $1.04 per share from IBM. The Treasury bill is redeemed at face value on April 10. On June 1 management sells 500 shares of McDonald's at $55 per share. On June 30 the market values of the investments are as follows:

Ford Motor Co.	$61 per share
McDonald's	$46 per share
IBM	$50 per share

Another quarterly dividend is received from each company (assume August 10). All the remaining shares are sold on November 1 at the following prices:

Ford Motor Co.	$55 per share
McDonald's	$44 per share
IBM	$60 per share

1. Record the investment transactions that occurred on January 10, February 10, April 10, May 10, and June 1. Prepare the required adjusting entry on June 30, and record the investment transactions on August 10 and November 1.
2. Explain how the short-term investments would be shown on the balance sheet on June 30.
3. After November 1, what is the balance of the account that is called Allowance to Reduce Short-Term Investments to Market, and what will happen to this account next June?
4. What is your assessment of Bates Christmas Tree Company's strategy with regard to idle cash?

Basic Research Activity

Find a recent issue of the *Wall Street Journal* in your school library. Turn to the third, or C, section, entitled "Money & Investing." From the index at the top of the page, locate the listing of New York Stock Exchange (NYSE) stocks and turn to that page. From the listing of stocks, find five companies you have heard of. They may be companies like IBM, Deere, McDonald's, or Ford. Copy down the range of the stock price for the last year and the current closing price. Also, copy down the dividend, if any, per share. How much did the market values of the common stocks you picked vary in the last year? Do these data demonstrate the need to value short-term investments of this type at market? How does accounting for short-term investments in these common stocks differ from accounting for short-term investments in U.S. Treasury bills? How are dividends received on investments in these common stocks accounted for? Be prepared to hand in your notes and to discuss the results of your investigation in class.

FINANCIAL REPORTING AND ANALYSIS

Interpretation Cases from Business

ICB 7-1.

L O 3, 4 *Short-Term Liquid Assets in Classic Government Bailout*

The automobile industry, especially *Chrysler Corporation,* had difficult financial problems in the early 1980s. Chrysler incurred operating losses of over $1 billion in both 1979 and 1980. At that time it received U.S. government loan guarantees of $1 billion and more. Chrysler's short-term liquid assets for 1979 and 1980 were presented in its annual report as follows (in millions of dollars):[11]

	1980	1979
Cash	$101.1	$ 188.2
Time Deposits	2.6	120.8
Marketable Securities—at lower of cost or market	193.6	165.3
Accounts Receivable (less allowance for doubtful accounts: 1980—$40.3 million; 1979—$34.9 million)	476.2	610.3
Total Short-Term Liquid Assets	$773.5	$1,084.6

The company also reported current liabilities of $3,231.6 million in 1979 and $3,029.3 million in 1980. Sales totaled $12,001.9 million in 1979 and $9,225.3 million in 1980. In management's discussion and analysis of financial conditions and results of operations, it was noted that "Chrysler had to defer paying its major suppliers until it received the proceeds from the additional $400 million of federally guaranteed debt. Chrysler's liquidity and its long-term viability are predicated on a return to sustained profitable operations."

Epilogue: At the end of 1983, Lee A. Iacocca, chief executive officer of Chrysler, could state in the annual report, "We repaid the $1.2 billion in loans guaranteed by the Federal Government. This action was taken seven years early." At the end of 1983, Chrysler had total short-term liquid assets of $1,360.6 million, consisting of Cash and Time Deposits of $111.6 million; Marketable Securities of $957.8 million; and Accounts Receivable (less allowance for uncollectible accounts of $25.5 million) of $291.2. Current liabilities were $3,453.9 million, and sales for 1983 were $13,240.4 million. By 1990, short-term liquid assets were $3,597 million, consisting of Cash and Time Deposits of $1,491 million, Marketable Securities of $1,473 million, and Accounts Receivable of $633 million. Current liabilities were $7,096 million, and sales for 1990 were $26,965 million. For comparison purposes, 1990 figures are shown for Chrysler operations without the finance and rental subsidiaries included. A separate allowance for uncollectible accounts was not disclosed for Chrysler operations.

REQUIRED

1. Compute Chrysler's ratio of short-term liquid assets to current liabilities for 1979 and 1980. Did Chrysler's short-term liquidity position improve or deteriorate from 1979 to 1980? What apparent effect did the 1980 federally guaranteed loan of $400 million have on the balance sheet and on the liquidity position?
2. It is important to Chrysler's survival that its customers pay their debts, and pay them on time. Compute for 1979 and 1980 the ratio of the allowance for doubtful accounts to *gross* accounts receivable and the ratio of *net* accounts receivable to sales. What can you conclude from these computations about Chrysler's ability to collect from its customers?
3. Compute for 1983 the three ratios you computed in questions **1** and **2** for 1979 and 1980; for 1990, compute the first and third ratios. Comment on Chrysler's situation in 1983 and 1990 compared to 1979–1980.

ICB 7-2.

L O 4 *Accounting for Accounts Receivable*

Winton Sharrer Co. is a major consumer goods company that sells over 3,000 products in 135 countries. From the company's annual report to the Securities and Exchange Commission, data pertaining to net sales and accounts related to accounts receivable for 1991, 1992, and 1993 were as follows (in thousands):

11. Chrysler Corporation, *Annual Reports,* 1980, 1983, and 1990.

	1993	1992	1991
Net Sales	$4,910,000	$4,865,000	$4,888,000
Accounts Receivable	523,000	524,000	504,000
Allowance for Uncollectible Accounts	18,600	21,200	24,500
Uncollectible Accounts Expense	15,000	16,700	15,800
Uncollectible Accounts Written Off	19,300	20,100	17,700
Recoveries of Accounts Previously Written Off	1,700	100	1,000

REQUIRED

1. Compute the ratios of Uncollectible Accounts Expense to Net Sales and to Accounts Receivable and of the Allowance for Uncollectible Accounts to Accounts Receivable for 1991, 1992, and 1993.
2. Compute the receivable turnover and days' sales uncollected for each year, assuming 1990 net accounts receivable is $465,000.
3. Make the general journal entries for 1993 related to the Allowance for Uncollectible Accounts and to recoveries of accounts previously written off.
4. What is your interpretation of the ratios? What appears to be management's attitude with respect to the collectibility of accounts receivable over the three-year period?

ICB 7-3.
L O 4, 5 *Loan Receivables and Estimated Losses by a Bank*

AmeriBank is a large banking and financial institution with branches throughout the world. The following data about AmeriBank's loans and lease financing come from its 1992 and 1993 annual reports (in millions of dollars):

	December 31, 1993	December 31, 1992
Loans and Lease Financing, Net (Notes 2, 3, and 4)		
Consumer (Net of unearned discount of $3,674 in 1991 and $4,154 in 1990)	$ 78,959	$ 68,243
Commercial (Net of unearned discount of $598 in 1991 and $467 in 1990)	55,754	59,439
Lease Financing	3,372	3,222
Loans and Lease Financing, Net of Unearned Discount	$138,085	$130,904
Allowance for Possible Credit Losses	(4,618)	(1,698)
Total Loans and Lease Financing, Net	$133,467	$129,206

The following additional data come from Note 4 of the same report (in millions of dollars):

4. Changes in the Allowance for Possible Credit Losses

	1993	1992
Balance at Beginning of Year	$1,698	$1,235
Deductions		
Consumer loan and lease losses	$1,271	$1,172
Consumer loan and lease recoveries	(247)	(214)
Net consumer loan and lease losses	$1,024	$ 958
Commercial loan and lease losses	$ 617	$ 489
Commercial loan and lease recoveries	(144)	(76)
Net commercial loan and lease losses	$ 473	$ 413
Additions		
Provision for possible credit losses	$4,410	$1,825
Other (Principally from allowance balances of acquired companies and translation of overseas allowance balances)	7	9
Balance at End of Year	$4,618	$1,698

REQUIRED

1. Did AmeriBank experience a higher loss rate for commercial loans or for consumer loans? Did AmeriBank's loss experience improve from 1992 to 1993? **Hint:** Compute the ratio of net consumer loan and lease losses to consumer loans and the ratio of net commercial loan and lease losses to commercial loans for both years. Ignore the effects of lease financing as immaterial.
2. Did AmeriBank's expectation about overall future losses become more optimistic or more pessimistic from 1992 to 1993? **Hint:** Calculate the ratio of the allowance for possible credit losses to loans and lease financing, net of unearned discount, for both years.
3. Prepare the general journal entries for 1993 to record the losses and recoveries for commercial loans and leases and consumer loans and leases and the provision for possible credit losses.
4. Both the consumer and the commercial loans are listed as net of unearned discount. What do you think an unearned discount is?

International Company Case

ICC 7-1.
L O 1 *Interpretation of Ratios*

Philips Electronics, N.V. and **Heineken, N.V.** are two of the most famous Dutch companies. Philips is a large, diversified electronics, music, and media company, and Heineken makes a well-known beer. Philips is about six times bigger than Heineken, with 1992 revenues of 58.5 billion guilders versus 8.9 billion guilders. Ratios can help in comparing and understanding the companies. For example, the receivable turnovers for the companies for two recent years are as follows:

	1992	**1991**
Philips	3.7 times	3.9 times
Heineken	8.9 times	9.1 times

What do these ratios tell you about the credit policies of the two companies? How long does it take each on average to collect a receivable? What do these ratios tell about the companies' relative needs for capital to finance receivables? Can you tell which company has a better credit policy? Explain your answers.

Toys "R" Us Case

TC 7-1.
L O 1, 2, 4 *Analysis of Short-Term Liquid Assets*

Refer to the annual report in the appendix on Toys "R" Us to answer the following questions:

1. How much cash and cash equivalents did Toys "R" Us have in 1994? Do you suppose most of this amount is cash in the bank or cash equivalents?
2. Toys "R" Us does not disclose an allowance for uncollectible accounts. How do you explain the lack of disclosure?
3. Compute the quick ratios for 1993 and 1994 and comment on them.
4. Compute receivable turnover and average days' sales uncollected for 1993 and 1994 and comment on Toys "R" Us credit policies. Accounts Receivable in 1992 were $64,078,000.

Inventories

J. C. Penney Company, Inc.

The management of inventory for profit is one of management's most complex and challenging tasks. In terms of dollars, the inventory of goods held for sale is one of the largest assets of a merchandising business. As a major retailer, with department stores in all fifty states and Puerto Rico, J. C. Penney Company, Inc. devotes almost 24 percent, or $3.2 billion, of its $13.6 billion in assets to inventories.[1] What challenges does J. C. Penney's management face in managing its inventory?

Not only must J. C. Penney's management purchase fashions and other merchandise that customers will want to buy, but it must also have the merchandise available in the right locations at the times when customers want to buy it. In addition, it must try to minimize the cost of inventory while maintaining quality. To these ends, J. C. Penney maintains purchasing offices throughout the world, including Hong Kong, Taipei, Osaka, Seoul, Bangkok, Singapore, Bombay, and Florence. Quality assurance experts operate out of twenty-two domestic and fourteen international offices. Further, the amount of money tied up in inventory must be controlled because of the high cost of borrowing funds and storing inventory. Important accounting decisions include what assumptions to make about the flow of inventory costs, what prices to put on inventory, what inventory systems to use, and how to protect inventory against loss. Proper management of inventory helped J. C. Penney earn net income of $777 million in 1992, but small variations in any inventory decision can mean the difference between a net profit and a net loss. ⁙

MANAGEMENT ISSUES ASSOCIATED WITH ACCOUNTING FOR INVENTORIES

OBJECTIVE

1 *Identify and explain the management issues associated with accounting for inventories*

Inventory is considered a current asset because it will normally be sold within a year's time or within a company's operating cycle. For a merchandising business like J. C. Penney or Toys "R" Us, merchandise inventory consists of all goods that are owned and held for sale in the regular course of business. Inventories are also important for manufacturing companies. Since these companies are engaged in the actual making of products, they have

1. J. C. Penney Company, Inc., *Annual Report*, 1992.

three kinds of inventory: raw materials to be used in the production of goods, partially completed products (often called work in process), and finished goods ready for sale. For example, in its 1991 annual report, The Goodyear Tire & Rubber Company disclosed the following inventory (in millions):

	1991	1990
Raw materials and supplies	$ 232.0	$ 234.5
Work in process	58.1	67.5
Finished product	1,022.6	1,044.0
Total inventories	$1,312.7	$1,346.0

In manufacturing operations, the cost of work in process and the cost of finished goods inventories include not only the cost of the raw materials that go into the product, but also the cost of the labor used to convert the raw materials to finished goods and the overhead costs that support the production process. Included in this latter category are such costs as indirect materials (for example, paint, glue, and nails), indirect labor (such as the salaries of supervisors), factory rent, depreciation of plant assets, utility costs, and insurance costs. The methods for maintaining and pricing inventory explained in this chapter are applicable to manufactured goods, but since the details of accounting for manufacturing companies are usually covered in managerial accounting courses, this chapter focuses on accounting for merchandising firms.

In the chapter on the merchandising income statement and internal control, the importance of management's choice of either the periodic or the perpetual inventory system for the processing of accounting information was discussed. The management issues in this chapter relate to the measurement of income through the allocation of the cost of inventories in accordance with the matching rule; assessing the impact of inventory decisions on such factors as net income, income taxes, and cash flows; and evaluating the level of inventory.

APPLYING THE MATCHING RULE TO INVENTORIES

The American Institute of Certified Public Accountants states, "A major objective of accounting for inventories is the proper determination of income through the process of matching appropriate costs against revenues."[2] Note that the objective of accounting for inventories is the proper determination of income through the matching of costs and revenues, not the determination of the most realistic inventory value. As will be shown, these two objectives are sometimes incompatible, in which case the objective of income determination takes precedence.

The reason inventory accounting is so important to income measurement is linked to the way income is measured on the merchandising income statement. Recall that gross margin is computed as the difference between net sales and cost of goods sold and that cost of goods sold is measured by deducting ending inventory from the cost of goods available for sale. Because

2. American Institute of Certified Public Accountants, *Accounting Research Bulletin No. 43* (New York: AICPA, 1953), Ch. 4.

of these relationships, the higher the cost of ending inventory, the lower the cost of goods sold and the higher the resulting gross margin. Conversely, the lower the value assigned to ending inventory, the higher the cost of goods sold and the lower the gross margin. Since the amount of gross margin has a direct effect on the amount of net income, the amount assigned to ending inventory directly affects the amount of net income. *In effect, the value assigned to the ending inventory determines what portion of the cost of goods available for sale is assigned to cost of goods sold and what portion is assigned to the balance sheet as inventory to be carried over into the next accounting period.*

Figure 8-1 shows the management choices related to the application of the matching rule to accounting for inventory. In the context of either the periodic inventory system or the perpetual inventory system, the amount of cost of goods available for sale allocated to cost of goods sold and to ending inventory depends on what assumptions are made about the flow of costs into the company as goods are purchased and out of the company as goods are sold. The methods available to management for assigning costs to these flows are the specific identification method, the average-cost method, the first-in, first-out (FIFO) method, and the last-in, first-out (LIFO) method. Further, at the end of the accounting period, the market value of the inventory is calculated to determine whether the inventory must be adjusted through the application

Figure 8-1. Management Choices in Accounting for Inventories

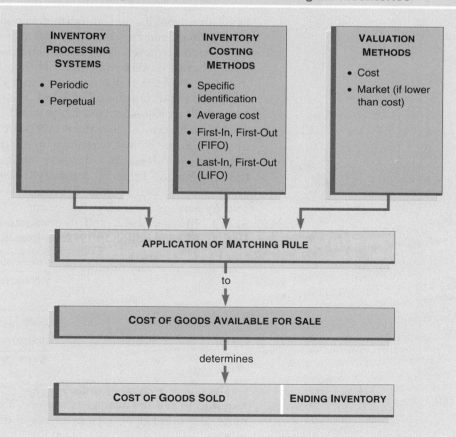

of the lower-of-cost-or-market rule. These choices are described and discussed in this chapter.

ASSESSING THE IMPACT OF INVENTORY DECISIONS

Figure 8-1 summarizes the management choices with regard to inventory systems and methods. The decisions usually result in different amounts of reported net income and, as a result, affect both the external evaluation of the company by investors and creditors and such internal evaluations as performance reviews, bonuses, and executive compensation. Further, because income is affected, the valuation of inventory may also have a considerable effect on the amount of income taxes paid. Federal income tax authorities have, therefore, been interested in the effects of various inventory valuation methods and have specific regulations about the acceptability of different methods. As a result, management is sometimes faced with the problem of balancing the goal of proper income determination with that of minimizing income taxes. Another consideration is that since the choice of inventory valuation method affects the amount of income taxes paid, it also affects a company's cash flows. The effects of management's decisions are discussed in more detail in this chapter after the inventory methods are presented.

EVALUATING THE LEVEL OF INVENTORY

Level of inventory has important economic consequences for a company. Ideally, management wants to have a great variety and quantity on hand so that customers have a large choice and do not have to wait. Such an inventory policy is not costless, however. The cost of handling and storage and the interest cost of the funds necessary to maintain high inventory levels are usually substantial. On the other hand, the maintenance of low inventory levels may result in lost sales and disgruntled customers. Common measures used in the evaluation of inventory levels are inventory turnover and its related measure, average days' inventory on hand.

Inventory turnover is a measure similar to receivable turnover. It indicates the number of times a company's average inventory is sold during an accounting period. Inventory turnover is computed by dividing cost of goods sold by average inventory. For example, J. C. Penney's cost of goods sold was $12.04 billion in 1992, and its merchandise inventory was $2.897 billion in 1991 and $3.258 billion in 1992. Its inventory turnover is computed as follows:

$$\text{Inventory turnover} = \frac{\text{cost of goods sold}}{\text{average inventory}}$$

$$= \frac{\$12,040,000,000}{(\$2,897,000,000 + \$3,258,000,000)/2}$$

$$= \frac{\$12,040,000,000}{\$3,077,500,000} = 3.9 \text{ times}$$

The average days' inventory on hand indicates the average number of days required to sell the average inventory. To find the average days' inventory on hand, the number of days in a year is divided by the inventory turnover, as follows:

Figure 8-2. Inventory Turnover for Selected Industries

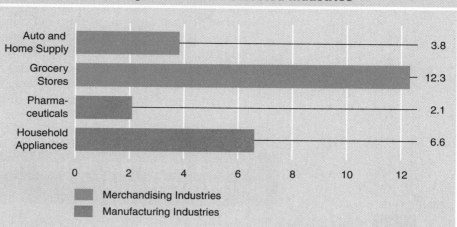

Source: Data from Dun and Bradstreet, *Industry Norms and Ratios*, 1992–93.

$$\text{Average days' inventory on hand} = \frac{\text{number of days in a year}}{\text{inventory turnover}}$$

$$= \frac{365 \text{ days}}{3.9 \text{ times}} = 93.6 \text{ days}$$

From this information, it may be seen that J. C. Penney turned its inventory over 3.9 times in 1992, or on average every 93.6 days. These figures are reasonable because J. C. Penney is in a business where fashions change every season, or about every ninety days. Management would want to sell all of each season's inventory within ninety days, even while making purchases for the next season. There are natural levels of inventory in every industry, as shown for selected merchandising and manufacturing industries in Figures 8-2 and 8-3. However, companies that are able to maintain their inventories at lower levels and still satisfy customer needs are the most successful.

Figure 8-3. Average Days' Inventory on Hand for Selected Industries

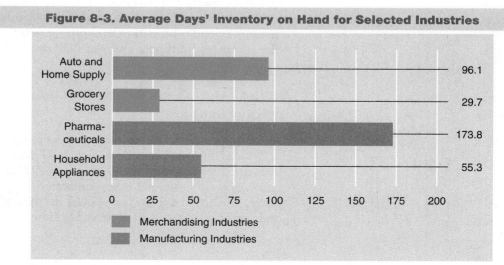

Source: Data from Dun and Bradstreet, *Industry Norms and Ratios*, 1992–93.

Many companies, both in merchandising and in manufacturing, are attempting to reduce their inventory assets by changing to a just-in-time operating environment. In this environment, rather than stockpiling inventories for later use, companies work closely with suppliers to coordinate and schedule shipments so that goods arrive just in time to be used or sold. Less money is thereby tied up in inventories, and the costs associated with carrying inventories are reduced. For example, Pacific Bell has been able to close six warehouses by implementing just-in-time inventory management.

PRICING INVENTORY UNDER THE PERIODIC INVENTORY SYSTEM

OBJECTIVE

2 *Define* **inventory cost** *and relate it to goods flow and cost flow*

According to the AICPA, "The primary basis of accounting for inventories is cost, which has been defined generally as the price paid or consideration given to acquire an asset."[3] This definition of inventory cost has generally been interpreted to include the following costs: (1) invoice price less purchases discounts; (2) freight or transportation in, including insurance in transit; and (3) applicable taxes and tariffs. Other costs—for ordering, receiving, and storing—should in principle also be included in inventory cost. In practice, however, it is so difficult to allocate these costs to specific inventory items that they are usually considered an expense of the accounting period instead of an inventory cost.

MERCHANDISE IN TRANSIT

Because merchandise inventory includes all items owned by a company and held for sale, the status of any merchandise in transit, either being sold or being purchased by the inventorying company, must be examined to determine if it should be included in the inventory count. As explained in the chapter on the merchandising income statement and internal control, the terms of the shipping agreement will indicate whether title has passed. Outgoing goods shipped FOB destination would be included in merchandise inventory, whereas those shipped FOB shipping point would not. Conversely, incoming goods shipped FOB shipping point would be included in merchandise inventory, but those shipped FOB destination would not.

MERCHANDISE ON HAND NOT INCLUDED IN INVENTORY

At the time a physical inventory is taken, there may be merchandise on hand to which the company does not hold title. One category of such goods includes merchandise that has been sold and is awaiting delivery to the buyer. Since the sale has been completed, title to the goods has passed to the buyer, and the merchandise should not be included in the inventory. A second category is goods held on consignment. A consignment is the placing of

---

3. Ibid.

goods by their owner (known as the *consignor*) on the premises of another company (the *consignee*). Title to consigned goods remains with the consignor until the consignee sells the goods. Thus, consigned goods should not be included in the physical inventory of the consignee because they still belong to the consignor.

METHODS OF PRICING INVENTORY AT COST

The prices of most kinds of merchandise vary during the year. Identical lots of merchandise may have been purchased at different prices. Also, when identical items are bought and sold, it is often impossible to tell which have been sold and which are still in inventory. For this reason, it is necessary to make an assumption about the order in which items have been sold. Because the assumed order of sale may or may not be the same as the actual order of sale, the assumption is really about the *flow of costs* rather than the *flow of physical inventory*.

Thus, the term goods flow refers to the actual physical movement of goods in the operations of a company, and the term cost flow refers to the association of costs with their *assumed* flow in the operations of a company. The assumed cost flow may or may not be the same as the actual goods flow. This statement may seem strange at first, but several assumed cost flows are available under generally accepted accounting principles. In fact, it is sometimes preferable to use an assumed cost flow that bears no relationship to goods flow because it gives a better estimate of income, which, as stated earlier, is the major goal of inventory valuation.

Accountants usually price inventory by using one of the following generally accepted methods, each based on a different assumption of cost flow: (1) specific identification method; (2) average-cost method; (3) first-in, first-out (FIFO) method; and (4) last-in, first-out (LIFO) method. The choice of method depends on the nature of the business, the financial effects of the methods, and the costs of implementing them.

To illustrate the four methods under the periodic inventory system, the following data for the month of June will be used:

Inventory Data, June 30

June	1	Inventory	50 units @ $1.00	$ 50
	6	Purchase	50 units @ $1.10	55
	13	Purchase	150 units @ $1.20	180
	20	Purchase	100 units @ $1.30	130
	25	Purchase	150 units @ $1.40	210
Goods Available for Sale			500 units	$625
Sales			280 units	
On hand June 30			220 units	

Notice that there is a total of 500 units available for sale at a total cost of $625. Stated simply, the problem of inventory pricing is to divide the $625 between the 280 units sold and the 220 units on hand. Recall that under the periodic inventory system, the inventory is not updated after each purchase and sale. Thus, it is not necessary to know when the individual sales take place.

OBJECTIVE

3a *Calculate the pricing of inventory, using the cost basis under the periodic inventory system according to the specific identification method*

Specific Identification Method

If the units in the ending inventory can be identified as coming from specific purchases, the specific identification method may be used to price the inventory. For instance, assume that the June 30 inventory consisted of 50 units from the June 1 inventory, 100 units from the purchase of June 13, and 70 units from the purchase of June 25. The cost assigned to the inventory under the specific identification method would be $268, determined as follows:

Periodic Inventory System—Specific Identification Method

50 units @ $1.00	$ 50	Cost of Goods Available	
100 units @ $1.20	120	for Sale	$625
70 units @ $1.40	98	→ Less June 30 Inventory	268
220 units at cost of	$268 ←	Cost of Goods Sold	$357

The specific identification method might be used in the purchase and sale of high-priced articles, such as automobiles, heavy equipment, and works of art. Although this method may appear logical, it is not used by many companies because it has two definite disadvantages. First, in many cases, it is difficult and impractical to keep track of the purchase and sale of individual items. Second, when a company deals in items of an identical nature, deciding which items are sold becomes arbitrary; thus, the company can raise or lower income by choosing to sell the high- or low-cost items.

OBJECTIVE

3b *Calculate the pricing of inventory, using the cost basis under the periodic inventory system according to the average-cost method*

Average-Cost Method

Under the average-cost method, inventory is priced at the average cost of the goods available for sale during the period. Average cost is computed by dividing the total cost of goods available for sale by the total units available for sale. This gives a weighted-average unit cost that is applied to the units in the ending inventory. In our illustration, the ending inventory would be $275, or $1.25 per unit, determined as follows:

Periodic Inventory System—Average-Cost Method

Cost of goods available for sale ÷ units available for sale = Average unit cost

$625 ÷ 500 units = $1.25

→ Ending inventory: 220 units @ $1.25 =	$275
Cost of Goods Available for Sale	$625
→ Less June 30 Inventory	275
Cost of Goods Sold	$350

The average-cost method tends to level out the effects of cost increases and decreases because the cost for the ending inventory calculated under this method is influenced by all the prices paid during the year and by the beginning inventory price. Some, however, criticize the average-cost method because they believe that recent costs are more relevant for income measurement and decision making.

First-In, First-Out (FIFO) Method

The first-in, first-out (FIFO) method is based on the assumption that the costs of the first items acquired should be

OBJECTIVE

3c *Calculate the pricing of inventory, using the cost basis under the periodic inventory system according to the first-in, first-out (FIFO) method*

assigned to the first items sold. The costs of the goods on hand at the end of a period are assumed to be from the most recent purchases, and the costs assigned to goods that have been sold are assumed to be from the earliest purchases. The FIFO method of determining inventory cost may be adopted by any business, regardless of the actual physical flow of goods, because the assumption is made regarding the flow of costs and not the flow of goods.

In our illustration, the June 30 inventory would be $301 when the FIFO method is used. It is computed as follows:

Periodic Inventory System—First-In, First-Out Method

150	units at $1.40 from purchase of June 25	$210
70	units at $1.30 from purchase of June 20	91
220	units at a cost of	$301
	Cost of Goods Available for Sale	$625
	Less June 30 Inventory	301
	Cost of Goods Sold	$324

The effect of the FIFO method is to value the ending inventory at the most recent costs and include earlier ones in cost of goods sold. During periods of consistently rising prices, the FIFO method yields the highest possible amount of net income, since cost of goods sold will show costs closer to the price level at the time the goods were purchased. Another reason for this result is that businesses tend to increase selling prices as costs rise, regardless of the fact that inventories may have been purchased before the price rise. The reverse effect occurs in periods of price decreases. For these reasons a major criticism of FIFO is that it magnifies the effects of the business cycle on income.

OBJECTIVE

3d *Calculate the pricing of inventory, using the cost basis under the periodic inventory system according to the last-in, first-out (LIFO) method*

Last-In, First-Out (LIFO) Method   The last-in, first-out (LIFO) method of costing inventories is based on the assumption that the costs of the last items purchased should be assigned to the first items used or sold and that the cost of the ending inventory reflects the cost of merchandise purchased earliest.

Under this method, the June 30 inventory would be $249, computed as follows:

Periodic Inventory System—Last-In, First-Out Method

50	units at $1.00 from June 1 inventory	$ 50
50	units at $1.10 from purchase of June 6	55
120	units at $1.20 from purchase of June 13	144
220	units at a cost of	$249
	Cost of Goods Available for Sale	$625
	Less June 30 Inventory	249
	Cost of Goods Sold	$376

The effect of LIFO is to value inventory at the earliest prices and to include in cost of goods sold the cost of the most recently purchased goods. This assumption, of course, does not agree with the actual physical movement of goods in most businesses.

However, there is a strong logical argument to support this method, based on the fact that a certain size inventory is necessary in a going concern. When inventory is sold, it must be replaced with more goods. The supporters of LIFO reason that the fairest determination of income occurs if the current costs of merchandise are matched against current sales prices, regardless of which physical units of merchandise are sold. When prices are moving either upward or downward, LIFO will mean that the cost of goods sold will show costs closer to the price level at the time the goods were sold. As a result, the LIFO method tends to show a smaller net income during inflationary times and a larger net income during deflationary times than other methods of inventory valuation. Thus, the peaks and valleys of the business cycle tend to be smoothed out. The important factor here is that in inventory valuation the flow of costs, and hence income determination, is more important than the physical movement of goods and balance sheet valuation.

An argument may also be made against the LIFO method. Because the inventory valuation on the balance sheet reflects earlier prices, it often gives an unrealistic picture of the current value of the inventory. Thus, such balance sheet measures as working capital and current ratio may be distorted and must be interpreted carefully.

BUSINESS BULLETIN: BUSINESS PRACTICE

A new type of retail business called the "category buster" seems to ignore the tenets of good inventory management. These retailers, such as The Home Depot, Inc. in home improvements, Barnes & Noble in book stores, Wal-Mart Stores, Inc. in groceries and dry goods, Toys "R" Us, Inc. in toys, and Blockbuster Entertainment, Inc. in videos, maintain huge inventories at such low prices that smaller competitors find it hard to compete. Although these companies do have a large amount of money tied up in inventories, they maintain very sophisticated just-in-time operating environments that require suppliers to meet demanding standards for delivery of products and reduction of inventory costs. Some suppliers are required to stock the shelves and keep track of inventory levels. By keeping handling and overhead costs down and buying at favorably low prices, the category busters achieve great success.

PRICING INVENTORY UNDER THE PERPETUAL INVENTORY SYSTEM

OBJECTIVE

4 *Apply the perpetual inventory system to the pricing of inventories at cost*

The pricing of inventories under the perpetual inventory system differs from pricing under the periodic inventory system. This difference occurs because under the perpetual inventory system, a continuous record of quantities and costs of merchandise is maintained as purchases and sales are made. Under the periodic inventory system, only the ending inventory is counted and priced. Cost of goods sold is determined by deducting the cost of the ending inventory from the cost of goods available for sale. Under the perpetual system, cost of goods sold is accumulated as sales are made and costs are transferred from the Inventory account to Cost of Goods Sold. The cost of the ending inventory is the balance of the Inventory account. In order to illustrate pricing methods under the perpetual inventory system, the same data will be used as before, but specific sales dates and amounts will be added, as follows:

Inventory Data—June 30

June 1	Inventory	50 units @ $1.00
6	Purchase	50 units @ $1.10
10	Sale	70 units
13	Purchase	150 units @ $1.20
20	Purchase	100 units @ $1.30
25	Purchase	150 units @ $1.40
30	Sale	210 units
30	Inventory	220 units

Pricing the inventory and cost of goods sold using the specific identification method is the same under the perpetual system as it was under the periodic system because cost of goods sold and ending inventory are based on the cost of the identified items sold and on hand. The perpetual system facilitates the use of the specific identification method because detailed records of purchases and sales are maintained.

Pricing the inventory and cost of goods sold using the average-cost method differs when the perpetual system is used. Under the periodic system, the average cost is computed for all goods available for sale during the month. Under the perpetual system, a moving average is computed after each purchase, as follows:

Perpetual Inventory System—Average-Cost Method

June 1	Inventory	50 units @ $1.00	$ 50.00
6	Purchase	50 units @ $1.10	55.00
6	Balance	100 units @ $1.05	$105.00
10	Sale	70 units @ $1.05	(73.50)
10	Balance	30 units @ $1.05	$ 31.50
13	Purchase	150 units @ $1.20	180.00
20	Purchase	100 units @ $1.30	130.00
25	Purchase	150 units @ $1.40	210.00
25	Balance	430 units @ $1.28*	$551.50
30	Sale	210 units @ $1.28*	(268.80)
30	Balance	220 units @ $1.28*	$282.70
Cost of Goods Sold		$73.50 + $268.80	$342.30

*Rounded.

The sum of the costs applied to sales becomes the cost of goods sold, $342.30. The ending inventory is the balance, or $282.70.

When pricing the inventory using the FIFO and LIFO methods, it is necessary to keep track of the components of inventory at each step of the way because as sales are made, the costs must be assigned in the proper order. To apply the FIFO method, the approach is as follows:

Perpetual Inventory System—FIFO Method

June 1	Inventory	50 units @ $1.00		$ 50.00
6	Purchase	50 units @ $1.10		55.00
10	Sale	50 units @ $1.00	($50.00)	
		20 units @ $1.10	(22.00)	(72.00)
10	Balance	30 units @ $1.10		$ 33.00
13	Purchase	150 units @ $1.20		180.00
20	Purchase	100 units @ $1.30		130.00
25	Purchase	150 units @ $1.40		210.00
30	Sale	30 units @ $1.10	($33.00)	
		150 units @ $1.20	(180.00)	
		30 units @ $1.30	(39.00)	(252.00)
30	Balance	70 units @ $1.30	$ 91.00	
		150 units @ $1.40	210.00	$301.00
Cost of Goods Sold		$72.00 + $252.00		$324.00

Note that the ending inventory of $301 and the cost of goods sold of $324 are the same as the figures computed earlier under the periodic inventory system. This will always occur because the ending inventory under both systems will always consist of the last items purchased—in this case, the entire purchase of June 25 and 70 units from the purchase of June 20.

To apply the LIFO method, the approach is as follows:

Perpetual Inventory System—LIFO Method

June 1	Inventory	50	units @ $1.00		$ 50.00
6	Purchase	50	units @ $1.10		55.00
10	Sale	50	units @ $1.10	($55.00)	
		20	units @ $1.00	(20.00)	(75.00)
10	Balance	30	units @ $1.00		$ 30.00
13	Purchase	150	units @ $1.20		180.00
20	Purchase	100	units @ $1.30		130.00
25	Purchase	150	units @ $1.40		210.00
30	Sale	150	units @ $1.40	($210.00)	
		60	units @ $1.30	(78.00)	(288.00)
30	Balance	30	units @ $1.00	$ 30.00	
		150	units @ $1.20	180.00	
		40	units @ $1.30	52.00	$262.00
Cost of Goods Sold		$75.00 + $288.00			$363.00

Note that the ending inventory of $262 includes 30 units from the beginning inventory, all units from the purchase of June 13, and 40 units from the purchase of June 20.

Using the LIFO method under the perpetual inventory system is a very tedious process, especially if done manually. However, the development of faster and less expensive computer systems over the past ten years has made it easier for many companies to switch to LIFO and still use the perpetual inventory system. The availability of better technology may partially account for the increasing use of LIFO in the United States and enable more companies to enjoy LIFO's economic benefits.

COMPARISON AND IMPACT OF INVENTORY DECISIONS AND MISSTATEMENTS

OBJECTIVE

5 *State the effects of inventory methods and misstatements of inventory on income determination and income taxes*

The specific identification, average-cost, FIFO, and LIFO methods of pricing inventory under both the periodic and the perpetual inventory systems have now been illustrated. The effects of the four methods on net income are shown in Exhibit 8-1, using the same data as before and assuming June sales of $500. Because the specific identification method is based on actual cost, it is the same under both systems.

Keeping in mind that June was a period of rising prices, we can see that LIFO, which charges the most recent and, in this case, the highest prices to cost of goods sold, resulted in the lowest gross margin under both systems.

Exhibit 8-1. Effects of Inventory Systems and Methods Computed

	Specific Identification Method	Periodic Inventory System			Perpetual Inventory System†		
		Average-Cost Method	First-In, First-Out Method	Last-In, First-Out Method	Average-Cost Method	First-In, First-Out Method	Last-In, First-Out Method
Sales	$500	$500	$500	$500	$500	$500	$500
Cost of Goods Sold							
Beginning Inventory	$ 50	$ 50	$ 50	$ 50			
Purchases	575	575	575	575			
Cost of Goods							
Available for Sale	$625	$625	$625	$625			
Less Ending Inventory	268	275	301	249	283*	301	262
Cost of Goods Sold	$357	$350	$324	$376	$342*	$324	$363
Gross Margin	$143	$150	$176	$124	$158	$176	$137

*Rounded.

†Ending inventory under the perpetual inventory system is provided for comparison only. It is not used in the computation of cost of goods sold.

Conversely, FIFO, which charges the earliest and, in this case, the lowest prices to cost of goods sold, produced the highest gross margin. The gross margin under the average-cost method is somewhere between those under LIFO and FIFO. Thus, it is clear that the average-cost method has a less pronounced effect. Note that the results under FIFO are the same under both systems.

During a period of declining prices, the reverse would occur. The LIFO method would produce a higher gross margin than the FIFO method. It is apparent that the method of inventory valuation has the greatest importance during prolonged periods of price changes in one direction, either up or down.

Because the specific identification method depends on the particular items sold, no generalization can be made about the effect of changing prices.

EFFECTS ON THE FINANCIAL STATEMENTS

Each of these four methods of inventory pricing is acceptable for use in published financial statements. The FIFO, LIFO, and average-cost methods are widely used, as can be seen in Figure 8-4, which shows the inventory cost methods used by six hundred large companies. Each has its advantages and disadvantages, and none can be considered best or perfect. The factors that should be considered in choosing an inventory method are the effects of each method on financial statements, income taxes, and management decisions.

A basic problem in determining the best inventory measure for a particular company stems from the fact that inventory affects both the balance sheet and the income statement. As we have seen, the LIFO method is best suited for the income statement because it matches revenues and cost of goods sold. But it is not the best measure of the current balance sheet value of inventory, particularly during a prolonged period of price increases or decreases. The FIFO method, on the other hand, is best suited to the balance sheet because the ending inventory is closest to current values and thus gives a more realistic

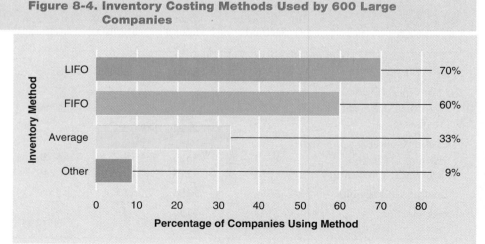

Figure 8-4. Inventory Costing Methods Used by 600 Large Companies

Total percentage exceeds 100 because some companies used different methods for different types of inventory.

Source: From *Accounting Trends & Techniques.* Copyright © 1992. Used by permission of the American Institute of Certified Public Accountants.

view of the current financial assets of a business. Readers of financial statements must be alert to inventory methods and be able to assess their effects.

EFFECTS ON INCOME TAXES

The Internal Revenue Service has developed several rules for valuing inventories for federal income tax purposes. A company has a wide choice of methods, including specific identification, average cost, FIFO, and LIFO, as well as lower of cost or market. But once a method has been chosen, it must be used consistently from one year to the next. The IRS must approve any change in the inventory valuation method for income tax purposes.[4] This requirement agrees with the rule of consistency in accounting, since changes in inventory method may cause income to fluctuate too much and would make income statements hard to interpret from year to year. A company may change its inventory method if there is a good reason for doing so. The nature and effect of the change must be shown on its financial statements.

Many accountants believe that the use of the FIFO and average-cost methods in periods of rising prices causes businesses to report more than their true profit, resulting in the payment of excess income taxes. The profit is overstated because cost of goods sold is understated, relative to current prices. The company must buy replacement inventory at higher prices, but additional funds are also needed to pay income taxes. During the rapid inflation of 1979 to 1982, billions of dollars reported as profits and paid in income taxes were believed to be the result of poor matching of current costs and revenues under the FIFO and average-cost methods. Consequently, many companies, encouraged by the belief that prices will continue to rise, have since switched to the LIFO inventory method.

If a company uses the LIFO method in reporting income for tax purposes, the IRS requires that the same method also be used in the accounting records. Also, the IRS will not allow the use of the lower-of-cost-or-market rule if LIFO is used to determine inventory cost. In this case, only the LIFO cost can be used. This rule, however, does not preclude a company from using lower of LIFO cost or market for financial reporting purposes. (The use of lower of cost or market is discussed later in this chapter.)

Over a period of rising prices, a business that uses the LIFO basis may find that for balance sheet purposes, its inventory is valued at a cost figure far below what it currently pays for the same items. Management must monitor this situation carefully, because if it should let the inventory quantity at year end fall below the beginning-of-the-year level, it will find itself paying income taxes on the difference between the current cost and the old LIFO cost in the records. When this occurs, it is called a LIFO liquidation because sales have reduced inventories below the levels established in prior years. A LIFO liquidation may be prevented by making enough purchases prior to year end to restore the desired inventory level. Sometimes a LIFO liquidation cannot be avoided because products are discontinued or supplies are interrupted, as in the case of a strike. In 1992, seventy-three of six hundred large companies reported a LIFO liquidation in which net income was increased because of the matching of older historical cost with present sales dollars.[5]

---

4. A single exception to this rule is that taxpayers must notify the IRS of a change to LIFO from another method, but do not need to have advance IRS approval.

5. American Institute of Certified Public Accountants, *Accounting Trends & Techniques* (New York: AICPA, 1992).

Amoco Corporation

As previously noted, a company's inventory methods affect not only its reported profitability, but also its reported liquidity. In the case of a large company like Amoco Corporation, the effects can be complex and material. Like many companies, Amoco uses three of the methods in this chapter to cost its various types of inventory, which in 1992 totaled almost $1 billion. In its statement of accounting policies, management explains its inventory methods: "Cost is determined under the last-in, first-out (LIFO) method for the majority of inventories of crude oil, petroleum products, and chemical products. The costs of remaining inventories are determined on the first-in, first-out (FIFO) or average cost methods." In a subsequent note, more detail is given:

> Inventories carried under the LIFO method represented approximately 48 percent of total year-end inventory carrying values in 1992 and 1991. It is estimated that inventories would have been approximately $1.3 billion higher than reported on December 31, 1992, and approximately $1.4 billion higher on December 31, 1991, if the quantities valued on the LIFO basis were instead valued on the FIFO basis.

The information in the note allows the reader to determine what Amoco's net income for 1992 would have been if FIFO had been used, excluding tax and currency effects and other variables. In this year of declining oil prices, Amoco's operating income after income taxes of $850 million would have decreased by $.1 billion ($1.4 billion − $1.3 billion) to $750 million, a decrease of 12 percent, if FIFO had been used. Finally, in management's discussion and analysis, the following clarifying remark is made:

> Amoco's short-term liquidity position is better than the reported figures indicate since the inventory component of working capital is valued in part under the LIFO method, whereas other elements of working capital are reported at amounts more indicative of their current values. If inventories were valued at current replacement costs, . . . the level of working capital would rise and an increase in the current ratio would result.[6]

EFFECTS OF MISSTATEMENTS IN INVENTORY MEASUREMENT

The basic problem of separating goods available for sale into two components—goods sold and goods not sold—is that of assigning a cost to the goods not sold, the ending inventory. That portion of the goods available for sale not assigned to the ending inventory is used to determine the cost of goods sold.

For this reason, a misstatement in the inventory figure at the end of the period will cause an equal misstatement in gross margin and net income in the income statement. The amount of assets and stockholders' equity on the balance sheet will also be misstated by the same amount. The consequences of overstatement and understatement of inventory are illustrated in the three simplified examples that follow. In each case, beginning inventory, net pur-

6. Amoco Corporation, *Annual Report*, 1992.

chases, and cost of goods available for sale have been stated correctly. In the first example, ending inventory has been stated correctly. In the second example, inventory is overstated by $6,000; in the third example, inventory is understated by $6,000.

Example 1. Ending Inventory Correctly Stated at $10,000

Cost of Goods Sold for the Year		Income Statement for the Year	
Beginning Inventory	$12,000	Net Sales	$100,000
Net Cost of Purchases	58,000	→Cost of Goods Sold	60,000
Cost of Goods Available for Sale	$70,000	Gross Margin	$ 40,000
Ending Inventory	10,000	Operating Expenses	32,000
Cost of Goods Sold	$60,000 ←	Net Income	$ 8,000

Example 2. Ending Inventory Overstated by $6,000

Cost of Goods Sold for the Year		Income Statement for the Year	
Beginning Inventory	$12,000	Net Sales	$100,000
Net Cost of Purchases	58,000	→Cost of Goods Sold	54,000
Cost of Goods Available for Sale	$70,000	Gross Margin	$ 46,000
Ending Inventory	16,000	Operating Expenses	32,000
Cost of Goods Sold	$54,000 ←	Net Income	$ 14,000

Example 3. Ending Inventory Understated by $6,000

Cost of Goods Sold for the Year		Income Statement for the Year	
Beginning Inventory	$12,000	Net Sales	$100,000
Net Cost of Purchases	58,000	→Cost of Goods Sold	66,000
Cost of Goods Available for Sale	$70,000	Gross Margin	$ 34,000
Ending Inventory	4,000	Operating Expenses	32,000
Cost of Goods Sold	$66,000 ←	Net Income	$ 2,000

In all three examples, the total cost of goods available for sale was $70,000. The difference in net income resulted from how this $70,000 was divided between ending inventory and cost of goods sold.

Because the ending inventory in one period becomes the beginning inventory in the following period, it is important to recognize that a misstatement in inventory valuation affects not only the current period, but also the following period. Note that over a two-year period the errors in net income will offset, or counterbalance, each other. In Example **2** above, for instance, the overstatement of ending inventory in 19x1 caused a $6,000 overstatement of beginning inventory in the following year, resulting in an understatement of income by $6,000 in the second year. This offsetting effect is illustrated in Table 8-1.

Because the total income for the two years is the same, there may be a tendency to think that one does not need to worry about inventory misstatements. However, the misstatements violate the matching rule. In addition, management, creditors, and investors make many decisions on an annual basis and depend on the accountant's determination of net income. The

Table 8-1. Ending Inventory Overstated by $6,000

	With Inventory Correctly Stated	With Inventory at Dec. 31, 19x1 Overstated	
		Reported Net Income Will Be	Reported Net Income Will Be Overstated (Understated)
Net Income for 19x1	$ 8,000	$14,000	$6,000
Net Income for 19x2	15,000	9,000	(6,000)
Total Net Income for Two Years	$23,000	$23,000	—

accountant has an obligation to make the net income figure for each year as useful as possible.

The effects of misstatements in inventory on net income are as follows:

Year 1	**Year 2**
Ending inventory overstated	**Beginning inventory overstated**
Cost of goods sold understated	Cost of goods sold overstated
Net income overstated	Net income understated
Ending inventory understated	**Beginning inventory understated**
Cost of goods sold overstated	Cost of goods sold understated
Net income understated	Net income overstated

If we assume no income tax effects, a misstatement in inventory results in a misstatement in net income of the same amount. Thus, the measurement of inventory is important.

BUSINESS BULLETIN: ETHICS IN PRACTICE

 Income may be easily manipulated through accounting for inventory. For example, it is easy to overstate or understate inventory by including end-of-the-year purchase and sale transactions in the wrong fiscal year or to misstate the amount of inventory. For example, the *Wall Street Journal* recently reported that Leslie Fay Company restated its earnings for the past three years to reverse $81 million of pretax earnings because of a "carefully concealed case of fraud" involving many members of the financial accounting staff. "Inventory was overstated, while the cost of making garments was understated in order to enhance profit figures." Such actions are obviously unethical and, in this case, led the company to bankruptcy and ruined the careers of most of its senior officers.[7]

7. Teri Agins, "Report Is Said to Show Pervasive Fraud at Leslie" and "Leslie Fay Co.'s. Profits Restated for Past 3 Years," *Wall Street Journal*, September 27 and 30, 1993.

VALUING THE INVENTORY AT THE LOWER OF COST OR MARKET (LCM)

OBJECTIVE

6 *Apply the lower-of-cost-or-market (LCM) rule to inventory valuation*

Although cost is usually the most appropriate basis for valuation of inventory, there are times when inventory may properly be shown in the financial statements at less than its cost. If by reason of physical deterioration, obsolescence, or decline in price level the market value of inventory falls below its cost, a loss has occurred. This loss may be recognized by writing the inventory down to market. The term market is used here to mean current replacement cost. For a merchandising company, market is the amount that the company would pay at the present time for the same goods, purchased from the usual suppliers and in the usual quantities. It may help in applying the lower-of-cost-or-market (LCM) rule to think of it as the "lower-of-cost-or-replacement-cost" rule.[8] Approximately 90 percent of six hundred large companies report applying the LCM rule to their inventories.[9]

There are three basic methods of valuing inventories at the lower of cost or market: (1) the item-by-item method, (2) the major category method, and (3) the total inventory method. For example, a stereo shop could determine lower of cost or market for each kind of speaker, receiver, and turntable (item by item); for all speakers, all receivers, and all turntables (major categories); or for all speakers, receivers, and turntables together (total inventory).

ITEM-BY-ITEM METHOD

When the item-by-item method is used, cost and market are compared for each item in inventory. The individual items are then valued at their lower price (see Table 8-2).

Table 8-2. Lower of Cost or Market with Item-by-Item Method

		Per Unit		Lower of
	Quantity	Cost	Market	Cost or Market
Category I				
Item a	200	**$1.50**	$1.70	$ 300
Item b	100	2.00	**1.80**	180
Item c	100	**2.50**	2.60	250
Category II				
Item d	300	5.00	**4.50**	1,350
Item e	200	**4.00**	4.10	800
Inventory at the lower of cost or market				**$2,880**

8. In some cases, *market value* is determined by the *realizable value* of the inventory—the amount for which the goods can be sold rather than the amount for which the goods can be replaced. The circumstances in which realizable value determines market value are encountered in practice only occasionally, and the valuation procedures are technical enough to be addressed in a more advanced accounting course.

9. American Institute of Certified Public Accountants, *Accounting Trends & Techniques* (New York: AICPA, 1992).

Table 8-3. Lower of Cost or Market with Major Category Method

		Per Unit		Total		Lower of Cost or Market
	Quantity	Cost	Market	Cost	Market	
Category I						
Item a	200	$1.50	$1.70	$ 300	$ 340	
Item b	100	2.00	1.80	200	180	
Item c	100	2.50	2.60	250	260	
Totals				$ 750	$ 780	$ 750
Category II						
Item d	300	5.00	4.50	$1,500	$1,350	
Item e	200	4.00	4.10	800	820	
Totals				$2,300	$2,170	2,170
Inventory at the lower of cost or market						$2,920

MAJOR CATEGORY METHOD

Under the major category method, the total cost and total market for each category of items are compared. Each category is then valued at its lower amount (See Table 8-3).

TOTAL INVENTORY METHOD

Under the total inventory method, the entire inventory is valued at both cost and market, and the lower amount is used to value inventory. Since this method is not acceptable for federal income tax purposes, it is not illustrated here.

VALUING INVENTORY BY ESTIMATION

It is sometimes necessary or desirable to estimate the value of ending inventory. The methods most commonly used for this purpose are the retail method and the gross profit method.

Supplemental OBJECTIVE

7a *Estimate the cost of ending inventory using the retail inventory method*

RETAIL METHOD OF INVENTORY ESTIMATION

The retail method, as its name implies, is used in retail merchandising businesses. There are two principal reasons for its use. First, management usually requires that financial statements be prepared at least once a month and, as taking a physical inventory is time-consuming and expensive, the retail method is used instead to estimate the value of inventory on hand. Second, because items in a retail store normally have a price tag or a universal product code, it is a common practice to take the physical inventory at retail from these price tags and codes and reduce the total value to cost through use of the retail method. The term *at retail* means the amount of the inventory at the marked selling prices of the inventory items.

When the retail method is used to estimate ending inventory, the records must show the beginning inventory at cost and at retail. The records must also show the amount of goods purchased during the period both at cost and at retail. The net sales at retail is, of course, the balance of the Sales account less returns and allowances. A simple example of the retail method is shown in Table 8-4.

Goods available for sale is determined both at cost and at retail by listing beginning inventory and net purchases for the period at cost and at the expected selling price of the goods, adding freight to the cost column, and totaling. The ratio of these two amounts (cost to retail price) provides an estimate of the cost of each dollar of retail sales value. The estimated ending inventory at retail is then determined by deducting sales for the period from the retail price of the goods that were available for sale during the period. The inventory at retail is then converted to cost on the basis of the ratio of cost to retail.

The cost of ending inventory may also be estimated by applying the ratio of cost to retail to the total retail value of the physical count of the ending inventory. Applying the retail method in practice is often more difficult than this simple example because of such complications as changes in retail price that take place during the year, different markups on different types of merchandise, and varying volumes of sales for different types of merchandise.

GROSS PROFIT METHOD OF INVENTORY ESTIMATION

Supplemental OBJECTIVE

7b *Estimate the cost of ending inventory using the gross profit method*

The gross profit method assumes that the ratio of gross margin for a business remains relatively stable from year to year. It is used in place of the retail method when records of the retail prices of beginning inventory and purchases are not kept. It is considered acceptable for estimating the cost of inventory for interim reports, but it is not acceptable for valuing inventory in the annual financial statements. It is also useful in estimating the amount of

---

Table 8-4. The Retail Method of Inventory Valuation

	Cost	Retail
Beginning Inventory	$ 40,000	$ 55,000
Net Purchases for the Period (excluding Freight In)	107,000	145,000
Freight In	3,000	
Goods Available for Sale	$150,000	$200,000
Ratio of Cost to Retail Price: $\dfrac{\$150,000}{\$200,000} = 75\%$		
Net Sales During the Period		160,000
Estimated Ending Inventory at Retail		$ 40,000
Ratio of Cost to Retail	75%	
Estimated Cost of Ending Inventory	$ 30,000	

Table 8-5. The Gross Profit Method of Inventory Valuation

1. Beginning Inventory at Cost		$ 50,000
Purchases at Cost (including Freight In)		290,000
Cost of Goods Available for Sale		$340,000
2. Less Estimated Cost of Goods Sold		
Sales at Selling Price	$400,000	
Less Estimated Gross Margin of 30%	120,000	
Estimated Cost of Goods Sold		280,000
3. Estimated Cost of Ending Inventory		$ 60,000

inventory lost or destroyed by theft, fire, or other hazards. Insurance companies often use this method to verify loss claims.

The gross profit method is simple to use. First, figure the cost of goods available for sale in the usual way (add purchases to beginning inventory). Second, estimate the cost of goods sold by deducting the estimated gross margin from sales. Finally, deduct the estimated cost of goods sold from the goods available for sale to arrive at the estimated cost of ending inventory. This method is shown in Table 8-5.

CHAPTER REVIEW

REVIEW OF LEARNING OBJECTIVES

1. **Identify and explain the management issues associated with accounting for inventories.** Included in inventory are goods owned, whether produced or purchased, that are held for sale in the normal course of business. Manufacturing companies also include raw materials and work in process. Among the issues management must face in accounting for inventories are allocating the cost of inventories in accordance with the matching rule, assessing the impact of inventory decisions, and evaluating the levels of inventory. The objective of accounting for inventories is the proper determination of income through the matching of costs and revenues, not the determination of the most realistic inventory value. Because the valuation of inventory has a direct effect on a company's net income, the choice of inventory systems and methods affects not only the amount of income taxes and cash flows, but also the external and internal evaluation of the company. The level of inventory as measured by the inventory turnover and its related measure, average days' inventory on hand, is important to managing the amount of investment needed by a company.

2. **Define *inventory cost* and relate it to goods flow and cost flow.** The cost of inventory includes (1) invoice price less purchases discounts, (2) freight or transportation in, including insurance in transit, and (3) applicable taxes and tariffs. Goods flow relates to the actual physical flow of merchandise, whereas cost flow refers to the assumed flow of costs in the operation of the business.

3. **Calculate the pricing of inventory, using the cost basis under the periodic inventory system according to the (a) specific identification method; (b) average-cost method; (c) first-in, first-out (FIFO) method; (d) last-in, first-out (LIFO) method.** The value assigned to ending inventory is the result of two measurements: quantity and price. Quantity is determined by taking a physical inventory. The

pricing of inventory is usually based on the assumed cost flow of the goods as they are bought and sold. One of four assumptions is usually made regarding cost flow. These assumptions are represented by four inventory methods. Inventory pricing could be determined by the specific identification method, which associates the actual cost with each item of inventory, but this method is rarely used. The average-cost method assumes that the cost of inventory is the average cost of goods available for sale during the period. The first-in, first-out (FIFO) method assumes that the costs of the first items acquired should be assigned to the first items sold. The last-in, first-out (LIFO) method assumes that the costs of the last items acquired should be assigned to the first items sold. The inventory method chosen may or may not be equivalent to the actual physical flow of goods.

4. **Apply the perpetual inventory system to the pricing of inventories at cost.** The pricing of inventories under the perpetual inventory system differs from pricing under the periodic system because under the perpetual system a continuous record of quantities and costs of merchandise is maintained as purchases and sales are made. Cost of goods sold is accumulated as sales are made and costs are transferred from the Inventory account to Cost of Goods Sold. The cost of the ending inventory is the balance of the Inventory account. Under the perpetual inventory system, the specific identification method and the FIFO method will produce the same results as under the periodic method. The results will differ for the average-cost method because a moving average is calculated prior to each sale rather than at the end of the accounting period and for the LIFO method because the cost components of inventory change constantly as goods are bought and sold.

5. **State the effects of inventory methods and misstatements of inventory on income determination and income taxes.** During periods of rising prices, the LIFO method will show the lowest net income; FIFO, the highest; and average cost, in between. The opposite effects occur in periods of falling prices. No generalization can be made regarding the specific identification method. The Internal Revenue Service requires that if LIFO is used for tax purposes, it must also be used for financial statement purposes, and that the lower-of-cost-or-market rule cannot be applied to the LIFO method. If the value of ending inventory is understated or overstated, a corresponding error—dollar for dollar—will be made in net income. Furthermore, because the ending inventory of one period is the beginning inventory of the next, the misstatement affects two accounting periods, although the effects are opposite.

6. **Apply the lower-of-cost-or-market (LCM) rule to inventory valuation.** The lower-of-cost-or-market rule can be applied to the above methods of determining inventory at cost. This rule states that if the replacement cost (market) of the inventory is lower than the inventory cost, the lower figure should be used.

SUPPLEMENTAL OBJECTIVE

7. **Estimate the cost of ending inventory using the (a) retail inventory method and (b) gross profit method.** Two methods of estimating the value of inventory are the retail inventory method and the gross profit method. Under the retail inventory method, inventory is determined at retail prices and is then reduced to estimated cost by applying a ratio of cost to retail price. Under the gross profit method, cost of goods sold is estimated by reducing sales by estimated gross margin. The estimated cost of goods sold is then deducted from cost of goods available for sale to estimate the inventory.

REVIEW OF CONCEPTS AND TERMINOLOGY

The following concepts and terms were introduced in this chapter:

L O 3 **Average-cost method:** An inventory cost method in which the price of inventory is determined by computing the average cost of all goods available for sale during the period.

L O 1 **Average days' inventory on hand:** The average number of days required to sell the inventory on hand; number of days in a year divided by inventory turnover.

L O 2 **Consignment:** The placing of goods by their owner (the consignor) on the premises of another company (the consignee).

L O 2 **Cost flow:** The association of costs with their assumed flow within the operations of a company.

L O 3 **First-in, first-out (FIFO) method:** An inventory cost method based on the assumption that the costs of the first items acquired should be assigned to the first items sold.

L O 2 **Goods flow:** The actual physical movement of goods in the operation of a company.

S O 7 **Gross profit method:** A method of inventory estimation based on the assumption that the ratio of gross margin for a business remains relatively stable from year to year.

L O 2 **Inventory cost:** The price paid or consideration given to acquire an asset; includes invoice price less purchases discounts, plus freight or transportation in and applicable taxes or tariffs.

L O 1 **Inventory turnover:** A ratio indicating the number of times a company's average inventory is sold during an accounting period; cost of goods sold divided by average inventory.

L O 6 **Item-by-item method:** A lower-of-cost-or-market method of valuing inventory in which cost and market are compared for each item in inventory, with each item then valued at its lower price.

L O 1 **Just-in-time operating environment:** An inventory management system in which companies seek to reduce their levels of inventory by working with suppliers to coordinate and schedule deliveries so that goods arrive just at the time they are needed.

L O 3 **Last-in, first-out (LIFO) method:** An inventory cost method based on the assumption that the costs of the last items purchased should be assigned to the first items sold.

L O 5 **LIFO liquidation:** The reduction of inventory below previous levels so that income is increased by the amount current prices exceed the historical cost of the inventory under LIFO.

L O 6 **Lower-of-cost-or-market (LCM) rule:** A method of valuing inventory at an amount below cost if the replacement (market) value is less than cost.

L O 6 **Major category method:** A lower-of-cost-or-market method for valuing inventory in which the total cost and total market for each category of items are compared, with each category then valued at its lower amount.

L O 6 **Market:** Current replacement cost of inventory.

L O 1 **Merchandise inventory:** All goods that are owned and held for sale in the regular course of business.

S O 7 **Retail method:** A method of inventory estimation used in retail businesses by which inventory at retail value is reduced by the ratio of cost to retail price.

L O 3 **Specific identification method:** An inventory cost method in which the price of inventory is computed by identifying the cost of each item in ending inventory as coming from a specific purchase.

L O 6 **Total inventory method:** A lower-of-cost-or-market method of valuing inventory in which the entire inventory is valued at both cost and market, and the lower price is used; not an acceptable method for federal income tax purposes.

REVIEW PROBLEM

PERIODIC AND PERPETUAL INVENTORY SYSTEMS

L O 3, 4 The following table summarizes the beginning inventory, purchases, and sales of Psi Company's single product during January.

	Beginning Inventory and Purchases			
Date	**Units**	**Cost**	**Total**	**Sales Units**
Jan. 1 Inventory	1,400	$19	$26,600	
4 Sale				300
8 Purchase	600	20	12,000	
10 Sale				1,300
12 Purchase	900	21	18,900	
15 Sale				150
18 Purchase	500	22	11,000	
24 Purchase	800	23	18,400	
31 Sale				1,350
Totals	4,200		$86,900	3,100

REQUIRED

1. Assuming that the company uses the periodic inventory system, compute the cost that should be assigned to ending inventory and to cost of goods sold using (a) the average-cost method, (b) the FIFO method, and (c) the LIFO method.
2. Assuming that the company uses the perpetual inventory system, compute the cost that should be assigned to ending inventory and to cost of goods sold using (a) the average-cost method, (b) the FIFO method, and (c) the LIFO method.

ANSWER TO REVIEW PROBLEM

	Units	**Dollars**
Beginning Inventory	1,400	$26,600
Purchases	2,800	60,300
Available for Sale	4,200	$86,900
Sales	3,100	
Ending Inventory	1,100	

1. Periodic inventory system

   a. Average-cost method

Cost of goods available for sale	$86,900
Ending inventory consists of 1,100 units at $20.69*	22,760[†]
Cost of goods sold	$64,140

   *$86,900 ÷ 4,200 = $20.69.
   [†]Rounded.

   b. FIFO method

Cost of goods available for sale		$86,900
Ending inventory consists of		
January 24 purchase (800 × $23)	$18,400	
January 18 purchase (300 × $22)	6,600	25,000
Cost of goods sold		$61,900

   c. LIFO method

Cost of goods available for sale	$86,900
Ending inventory consists of	
Beginning inventory (1,100 × $19)	20,900
Cost of goods sold	$66,000

2. Perpetual inventory system

a. Average-cost method

Date		Units	Cost*	Amount*
Jan. 1	Inventory	1,400	$19.00	$26,600
4	Sale	(300)	19.00	(5,700)
4	Balance	1,100	19.00	$20,900
8	Purchase	600	20.00	12,000
8	Balance	1,700	19.35	$32,900
10	Sale	(1,300)	19.35	(25,155)
10	Balance	400	19.35	$7,745
12	Purchase	900	21.00	18,900
12	Balance	1,300	20.50	$26,645
15	Sale	(150)	20.50	(3,075)
15	Balance	1,150	20.50	$23,570
18	Purchase	500	22.00	11,000
18	Balance	1,650	20.95	$34,570
24	Purchase	800	23.00	18,400
24	Balance	2,450	21.62	$52,970
31	Sale	(1,350)	21.62	(29,187)
31	Inventory	1,100	21.62	$23,783

Cost of Goods Sold: $5,700 + $25,155 + $3,075 + $29,187 = $63,117

*Rounded.

b. FIFO method

Date		Units	Cost	Amount
Jan. 1	Inventory	1,400	$19	$26,600
4	Sale	(300)	19	(5,700)
4	Balance	1,100	19	$20,900
8	Purchase	600	20	12,000
8	Balance	1,100	19	
		600	20	$32,900
10	Sale	(1,100)	19	
		(200)	20	(24,900)
10	Balance	400	20	$ 8,000
12	Purchase	900	21	18,900
12	Balance	400	20	
		900	21	$26,900
15	Sale	(150)	20	(3,000)
15	Balance	250	20	
		900	21	$23,900
18	Purchase	500	22	11,000
24	Purchase	800	23	18,400
24	Balance	250	20	
		900	21	
		500	22	
		800	23	$53,300
31	Sale	(250)	20	
		(900)	21	
		(200)	22	(28,300)
31	Inventory	300	22	
		800	23	$25,000

Cost of Goods Sold: $5,700 + $24,900 + $3,000 + $28,300 = $61,900

c. LIFO method

Date		Units	Cost	Amount
Jan. 1	Inventory	1,400	$19	$26,600
4	Sale	(300)	19	(5,700)
4	Balance	1,100	19	$20,900
8	Purchase	600	20	12,000
8	Balance	1,100	19	
		600	20	$32,900
10	Sale	(600)	20	
		(700)	19	(25,300)
10	Balance	400	19	$ 7,600
12	Purchase	900	21	18,900
12	Balance	400	19	
		900	21	$26,500
15	Sale	(150)	21	(3,150)
15	Balance	400	19	
		750	21	$23,350
18	Purchase	500	22	11,000
24	Purchase	800	23	18,400
24	Balance	400	19	
		750	21	
		500	22	
		800	23	$52,750
31	Sale	(800)	23	
		(500)	22	
		(50)	21	(30,450)
31	Inventory	400	19	
		700	21	$22,300

Cost of Goods Sold: $5,700 + $25,300 + $3,150 + $30,450 = $64,600

CHAPTER ASSIGNMENTS

KNOWLEDGE AND UNDERSTANDING

Questions

1. What is merchandise inventory, and what is the primary objective of inventory measurement?
2. How does inventory for a manufacturing company differ from that for a merchandising company?
3. Why is the level of inventory important, and what are two common measures of inventory level?
4. What items are included in the cost of inventory?
5. Fargo Sales Company is very busy at the end of its fiscal year on June 30. There is an order for 130 units of product in the warehouse. Although the shipping department tries, it cannot ship the product by June 30, and title has not yet passed. Should the 130 units be included in the year-end count of inventory? Why or why not?

6. What is the difference between goods flow and cost flow?

7. Do the FIFO and LIFO inventory methods result in different quantities of ending inventory?

8. Under which method of cost flow are (a) the earliest costs assigned to inventory, (b) the latest costs assigned to inventory, (c) the average costs assigned to inventory?

9. What are the relative advantages and disadvantages of FIFO and LIFO from management's point of view?

10. In periods of steadily rising prices, which inventory method—average-cost, FIFO, or LIFO—will give the (a) highest inventory cost, (b) lowest inventory cost, (c) highest net income, and (d) lowest net income?

11. May a company change its inventory cost method from year to year? Explain.

12. What are the relationships between income tax rules and inventory valuation methods?

13. If the merchandise inventory is mistakenly overstated at the end of 19x8, what is the effect on the (a) 19x8 net income, (b) 19x8 year-end balance sheet value, (c) 19x9 net income, and (d) 19x9 year-end balance sheet value?

14. Why do you think it is more expensive to maintain a perpetual inventory system?

15. In the phrase *lower of cost or market,* what is meant by the word *market?*

16. What methods can be used to determine lower of cost or market?

17. Does using the retail inventory method mean that inventories are measured at retail value on the balance sheet? Explain.

18. What are some of the reasons that may cause management to use the gross profit method of estimating inventory?

19. Which of the following inventory systems do not require taking a physical inventory: (a) perpetual, (b) periodic, (c) retail, (d) gross profit?

Short Exercises

SE 8-1.

L O 1 *Management Issues*

Indicate whether each item listed below is associated with (a) allocating the cost of inventories in accordance with the matching rule, (b) assessing the impact of inventory decisions, or (c) evaluating the level of inventory.

1. Calculating the average number of days' inventory on hand.
2. Ordering a supply of inventory to satisfy customer needs.
3. Calculating the income tax effect of an inventory method.
4. Deciding the price to place on ending inventory.

SE 8-2.

L O 1 *Inventory Turnover and Average Days' Inventory on Hand*

During 19x1, Certeen Clothiers had beginning inventory of $240,000, ending inventory of $280,000, and cost of goods sold of $1,100,000. Compute the inventory turnover and average days' inventory on hand.

SE 8-3.

L O 3 *Specific Identification Method*

Assume the following data with regard to inventory for Alexis Company:

Aug.	1	Inventory	80 units @ $10 per unit	$ 800
	8	Purchase	100 units @ $11 per unit	1,100
	22	Purchase	70 units @ $12 per unit	840
Goods Available for Sale			250 units	$2,740
Aug.	15	Sale	90 units	
	28	Sale	50 units	
Inventory, August 31			110 units	

Assuming that the inventory consists of 60 units from the August 8 purchase and 50 units from the purchase of August 22, calculate the cost of ending inventory and cost of goods sold.

SE 8-4.
L O 3
Average-Cost Method—Periodic Inventory System

Using the data in SE 8-3, calculate the cost of ending inventory and cost of goods sold using the average-cost method under the periodic inventory system.

SE 8-5.
L O 3
FIFO Method— Periodic Inventory System

Using the data in SE 8-3, calculate the cost of ending inventory and cost of goods sold using the FIFO method under the periodic inventory system.

SE 8-6.
L O 3
LIFO Method— Periodic Inventory System

Using the data in SE 8-3, calculate the cost of ending inventory and cost of goods sold using the LIFO method under the periodic inventory system.

SE 8-7.
L O 4
Average-Cost Method—Perpetual Inventory System

Using the data in SE 8-3, calculate the cost of ending inventory and cost of goods sold using the average-cost method under the perpetual inventory system.

SE 8-8.
L O 4
FIFO Method— Perpetual Inventory System

Using the data in SE 8-3, calculate the cost of ending inventory and cost of goods sold using the FIFO method under the perpetual inventory system.

SE 8-9.
L O 4
LIFO Method— Perpetual Inventory System

Using the data in SE 8-3, calculate the cost of ending inventory and cost of goods sold using the LIFO method under the perpetual inventory system.

SE 8-10.
L O 5
Effects of Methods and Changing Prices

Following the pattern of Exhibit 8-1, prepare a table with seven columns that shows the ending inventory and cost of goods sold for each of the results from your calculations in SE 8-3 through SE 8-9. Comment on the results, including the effects of different prices at which the merchandise was purchased. Which method(s) would result in the least amount of income taxes?

SE 8-11.
L O 6
Lower of Cost or Market

The following schedule is based on a physical inventory and replacement costs for one product line of men's shirts:

Item	Quantity	Cost per Unit	Market per Unit
Short sleeve	280	$24	$20
Long sleeve	190	28	29
Extra-long sleeve	80	34	35

Determine the value of this category of inventory at lower of cost or market using (1) the item-by-item method and (2) the major category method.

APPLICATION

Exercises

E 8-1.

L O 1 *Management Issues Related to Inventory*

Indicate whether each item listed below is associated with (a) allocating the cost of inventories in accordance with the matching rule, (b) assessing the impact of inventory decisions, or (c) evaluating the level of inventory.

1. Computing inventory turnover.
2. Application of the just-in-time operating environment.
3. Determining the effects of inventory decisions on cash flows.
4. Apportioning the cost of goods available for sale to ending inventory and cost of goods sold.
5. Determining the effects of inventory methods on income taxes.
6. Determining the assumption about the flow of costs into and out of the company.

E 8-2.

L O 1 *Inventory Ratios*

Costco Discount Stores is assessing its levels of inventory for 19x2 and 19x3 and has gathered the following data:

	19x3	19x2	19x1
Ending inventory	$ 64,000	$ 54,000	$46,000
Cost of goods sold	320,000	300,000	

Compute the inventory turnover and average days' inventory on hand for 19x2 and 19x3 and comment on the results.

E 8-3.

L O 3 *Inventory Costing Methods*

Helen's Farm Store had the following purchases and sales of fertilizer during the year:

Jan. 1	Beginning Inventory	250 cases @ $23	$ 5,750
Feb. 25	Purchase	100 cases @ $26	2,600
June 15	Purchase	400 cases @ $28	11,200
Aug. 15	Purchase	100 cases @ $26	2,600
Oct. 15	Purchase	300 cases @ $28	8,400
Dec. 15	Purchase	200 cases @ $30	6,000
	Total Goods Available for Sale	1,350	$36,550
	Total Sales	1,000 cases	
Dec. 31	Ending Inventory	350 cases	

Assume that the ending inventory included 50 cases from the beginning inventory, 100 cases from the February 25 purchase, 100 cases from the August 15 purchase, and 100 cases from the October 15 purchase.

Determine the costs that should be assigned to ending inventory and cost of goods sold under each of the following assumptions: (1) costs are assigned by the specific identification method; (2) costs are assigned by the average-cost method; (3) costs are assigned by the FIFO method; (4) costs are assigned by the LIFO method. What conclusions can be drawn about the effect of each method on the income statement and the balance sheet of Helen's Farm Store?

E 8-4.

L O 3 *Inventory Costing Methods*

During its first year of operation, Jefferson Company purchased 5,600 units of a product at $21 per unit. During the second year, it purchased 6,000 units of the same product at $24 per unit. During the third year, it purchased 5,000 units at $30 per unit. Jefferson Company managed to have an ending inventory each year of 1,000 units. The company sells goods at a 100 percent markup over cost.

Prepare cost of goods sold statements that compare the value of ending inventory and the cost of goods sold for each of the three years using (1) the FIFO method and (2) the LIFO method. What conclusions can you draw from the resulting data about the relationships between changes in unit price and changes in the value of ending inventory?

E 8-5.
L O 3 *Periodic Inventory System and Inventory Costing Methods*

In chronological order, the inventory, purchases, and sales of a single product for a recent month are as follows:

		Units	Amount per Unit
June 1	Beginning Inventory	300	$10
4	Purchase	800	11
8	Sale	400	20
12	Purchase	1,000	12
16	Sale	700	20
20	Sale	500	22
24	Purchase	1,200	13
28	Sale	600	22
29	Sale	400	22

Using the periodic inventory system, compute the cost of ending inventory, cost of goods sold, and gross margin. Use the average-cost, FIFO, and LIFO inventory costing methods. Explain the differences in gross margin produced by the three methods. Round unit costs to cents and totals to dollars.

E 8-6.
L O 4 *Perpetual Inventory System and Inventory Costing Methods*

Using the data provided in Exercise 8-5 and assuming the perpetual inventory system, compute the cost of ending inventory, cost of goods sold, and gross margin. Use the average-cost, FIFO, and LIFO inventory costing methods. Explain the difference in gross margin produced by the three methods. Round unit costs to cents and totals to dollars.

E 8-7.
L O 3, 4 *Inventory Costing Methods: Periodic and Perpetual Systems*

During July 19x2, Servex, Inc. sold 250 units of its product Dervex for $2,000. The following units were available:

	Units	Cost
Beginning Inventory	100	$1
Purchase 1	40	2
Purchase 2	60	3
Purchase 3	70	4
Purchase 4	80	5
Purchase 5	90	6

A sale of 100 units was made after purchase 1, and a sale of 150 units was made after purchase 4. Of the units sold, 100 came from beginning inventory and 150 from purchases 3 and 4.

Determine cost of goods available for sale and ending inventory in units. Then determine the costs that should be assigned to cost of goods sold and ending inventory under each of the following assumptions: (1) Costs are assigned under the periodic inventory system using (a) the specific identification method, (b) the average-cost method, (c) the FIFO method, and (d) the LIFO method. (2) Costs are assigned under the perpetual inventory system using (a) the average-cost method, (b) the FIFO method, and (c) the LIFO method. For each alternative, show the gross margin. Round unit costs to cents and totals to dollars.

E 8-8.
L O 5 *Effects of Inventory Methods on Cash Flows*

Ross Products, Inc. sold 120,000 cases of glue at $40 per case during 19x1. Its beginning inventory consisted of 20,000 cases at a cost of $24 per case. During 19x1 it purchased 60,000 cases at $28 per case and later 50,000 cases at $30 per case. Operating expenses were $1,100,000, and the applicable income tax rate was 30 percent.

Using the periodic inventory system, compute net income using the FIFO method and the LIFO method for costing inventory. Which alternative produces the larger cash flow? The company is considering a purchase of 10,000 cases at $30 per case just before the year end. What effect on net income and on cash flow will this proposed purchase have under each method? (**Hint:** What are the income tax consequences?)

E 8-9.

L O 3, 5 *Inventory Costing Method Characteristics*

The lettered items in the list below represent inventory costing methods. Write the letter of the method that each of the following statements *best* describes.

a. Specific identification
b. Average-cost
c. First-in, first-out (FIFO)
d. Last-in, first-out (LIFO)

1. Matches recent costs with recent revenues
2. Assumes that each item of inventory is identifiable
3. Results in most realistic balance sheet valuation
4. Results in lowest net income in periods of deflation
5. Results in lowest net income in periods of inflation
6. Matches oldest costs with recent revenues
7. Results in highest net income in periods of inflation
8. Results in highest net income in periods of deflation
9. Tends to level out the effects of inflation
10. Is unpredictable as to the effects of inflation

E 8-10.

L O 5 *Effects of Inventory Errors*

Condensed income statements for Hamlin Company for two years are shown below.

	19x4	19x3
Sales	$126,000	$105,000
Cost of Goods Sold	75,000	54,000
Gross Margin	$ 51,000	$ 51,000
Operating Expenses	30,000	30,000
Net Income	$ 21,000	$ 21,000

After the end of 19x4 it was discovered that an error had resulted in a $9,000 understatement of the 19x3 ending inventory.

Compute the corrected net income for 19x3 and 19x4. What effect will the error have on net income and stockholders' equity for 19x5?

E 8-11.

L O 6 *Lower-of-Cost-or-Market Rule*

Mercurio Company values its inventory, shown below, at the lower of cost or market. Compute Mercurio's inventory value using (1) the item-by-item method and (2) the major category method.

	Quantity	Per Unit Cost	Per Unit Market
Category I			
Item aa	200	$ 2.00	$ 1.80
Item bb	240	4.00	4.40
Item cc	400	8.00	7.50
Category II			
Item dd	300	12.00	13.00
Item ee	400	18.00	18.20

E 8-12.

S O 7 *Retail Method*

Roseanne's Dress Shop had net retail sales of $500,000 during the current year. The following additional information was obtained from the accounting records:

	At Cost	At Retail
Beginning Inventory	$ 80,000	$120,000
Net Purchases (excluding Freight In)	280,000	440,000
Freight In	20,800	

1. Estimate the company's ending inventory at cost using the retail method.
2. Assume that a physical inventory taken at year end revealed an inventory on hand of $36,000 at retail value. What is the estimated amount of inventory shrinkage (loss due to theft, damage, and so forth) at cost?

E 8-13.
S O 7   *Gross Profit Method*

Dale Nolan was at home watching television when he received a call from the fire department. His business was a total loss from fire. The insurance company asked him to prove his inventory loss. For the year, until the date of the fire, Dale's company had sales of $450,000 and purchases of $280,000. Freight in amounted to $13,700, and the beginning inventory was $45,000. It was Dale's custom to price goods to achieve a gross margin of 40 percent.

Compute Dale's estimated inventory loss.

Problem Set A

8A-1.
L O 3   *Inventory Costing Methods*

The Pascual Door Company sold 2,200 doors during 19x2 at $320 per door. Its beginning inventory on January 1 was 130 doors at $112. Purchases made during the year were as follows:

February	225 doors @ $124
April	350 doors @ $130
June	700 doors @ $140
August	300 doors @ $132
October	400 doors @ $136
November	250 doors @ $144

The company's selling and administrative expenses for the year were $202,000, and the company uses the periodic inventory system.

REQUIRED

1. Prepare a schedule to compute the cost of goods available for sale.
2. Prepare an income statement under each of the following assumptions: (a) costs are assigned to inventory using the average-cost method; (b) costs are assigned to inventory using the FIFO method; and (c) costs are assigned to inventory using the LIFO method.

8A-2.
L O 3   *Periodic Inventory System and Inventory Methods*

The inventory, purchases, and sales of Product LMR for May and June are presented below. The company closes its books at the end of each month and uses a periodic inventory system.

May	1	Inventory	60 units @ $147
	9	Sale	20 units
	12	Purchase	100 units @ $156
	25	Sale	70 units
	31	Inventory	70 units
June	5	Purchase	120 units @ $159
	9	Sale	110 units
	14	Purchase	50 units @ $162
	19	Sale	80 units
	24	Purchase	100 units @ $165
	28	Sale	100 units
	30	Inventory	50 units

REQUIRED

1. Compute the cost of the ending inventory on May 31 and June 30 using the average-cost method. In addition, determine cost of goods sold for May and June. Round unit costs to cents and totals to dollars.
2. Compute the cost of the ending inventory on May 31 and June 30 using the FIFO method. In addition, determine cost of goods sold for May and June.
3. Compute the cost of the ending inventory on May 31 and June 30 using the LIFO method. In addition, determine cost of goods sold for May and June.

8A-3.

L O 4 *Perpetual Inventory System and Inventory Methods*

Use the data provided in 8A-2, but assume that the company uses the perpetual inventory system. (**Hint:** In preparing the solutions below, it is helpful to determine the balance of inventory after each transaction, as shown in the Review Problem at the end of the chapter.)

REQUIRED

1. Determine the cost of ending inventory and cost of goods sold for May and June using the average-cost method. Round unit costs to cents and totals to dollars.
2. Determine the cost of ending inventory and cost of goods sold for May and June using the FIFO method.
3. Determine the cost of ending inventory and cost of goods sold for May and June using the LIFO method.

8A-4.

L O 6 *Lower-of-Cost-or-Market Rule*

The employees of Kuberski's Shoes completed their physical inventory as follows:

| | | Per Unit | |
	Pairs of Shoes	Cost	Market
Men			
Black	400	$44	$48
Brown	325	42	42
Blue	100	50	46
Tan	200	38	20
Women			
White	300	52	64
Red	150	46	40
Yellow	100	60	50
Blue	250	50	66
Brown	100	40	60
Black	150	40	50

REQUIRED

Determine the value of inventory at lower of cost or market using (1) the item-by-item method and (2) the major category method.

8A-5.

S O 7 *Retail Inventory Method*

Overland Company switched recently to the retail inventory method to estimate the cost of ending inventory. To test this method, the company took a physical inventory one month after its implementation. Cost, retail, and the physical inventory data are as follows:

	At Cost	At Retail
July 1 Beginning Inventory	$472,132	$ 622,800
Purchases	750,000	1,008,400
Purchases Returns and Allowances	(25,200)	(34,800)
Freight In	8,350	
Sales		1,060,000
Sales Returns and Allowances		(28,000)
July 31 Physical Inventory		508,200

REQUIRED

1. Prepare a schedule to estimate the dollar amount of Overland's July 31 inventory using the retail method.
2. Use Overland's cost ratio to reduce the retail value of the physical inventory to cost.
3. Calculate the estimated amount of inventory shortage at cost and at retail.

8A-6.

S O 7 *Gross Profit Method*

Brandon Oil Products stores its oil field products in a West Texas warehouse. The warehouse and most of its inventory were completely destroyed by a tornado on April 27. The company found some of its records, but it does not keep perpetual inventory records. The warehouse manager must estimate the amount of the loss. He found the following information in the records:

Beginning Inventory, January 1	$1,320,000
Purchases, January 2 to April 27	780,000
Purchases Returns, January 2 to April 27	(30,000)
Freight In since January 2	16,000
Sales, January 2 to April 27	1,840,000
Sales Returns, January 2 to April 27	(40,000)

Inventory costing $420,000 was recovered and could be sold. The manager remembers that the average gross margin on oil field products is 48 percent.

REQUIRED

Prepare a schedule to estimate the inventory destroyed by the tornado.

Problem Set B

8B-1.

L O 3 *Inventory Costing Methods*

Lattimer Company merchandises a single product called Rulex. The following data represent beginning inventory and purchases of Rulex during the past year: January 1 inventory, 68,000 units at $22.00; February purchases, 80,000 units at $24.00; March purchases, 160,000 units at $24.80; May purchases, 120,000 units at $25.20; July purchases, 200,000 units at $25.60; September purchases, 160,000 units at $25.20; and November purchases, 60,000 units at $26.00. Sales of Rulex totaled 786,000 units at $40 per unit. Selling and administrative expenses totaled $10,204,000 for the year, and Lattimer Company uses a periodic inventory system.

REQUIRED

1. Prepare a schedule to compute the cost of goods available for sale.
2. Prepare an income statement under each of the following assumptions: (a) costs are assigned to inventory using the average-cost method; (b) costs are assigned to inventory using the FIFO method; (c) costs are assigned to inventory using the LIFO method.

8B-2.

L O 3 *Periodic Inventory System and Inventory Methods*

The inventory of Product H and data on purchases and sales for a two-month period follow. The company closes its books at the end of each month. It uses a periodic inventory system.

Sept.	1	Inventory	50 units @ $204
	9	Sale	30 units
	15	Purchase	100 units @ $220
	20	Sale	60 units
	30	Inventory	60 units
Oct.	4	Purchase	100 units @ $216
	10	Sale	110 units
	16	Purchase	50 units @ $224
	20	Sale	40 units
	23	Purchase	60 units @ $234
	25	Sale	30 units
	30	Sale	20 units
	31	Inventory	70 units

REQUIRED

1. Compute the cost of ending inventory of Product H on September 30 and October 31 using the average-cost method. In addition, determine cost of goods sold for September and October. Round unit costs to cents and totals to dollars.
2. Compute the cost of the ending inventory of Product H on September 30 and October 31 using the FIFO method. In addition, determine cost of goods sold for September and October.
3. Compute the cost of the ending inventory of Product H on September 30 and October 31 using the LIFO method. In addition, determine cost of goods sold for September and October.

8B-3.

LO 4 *Perpetual Inventory System and Inventory Methods*

REQUIRED

Use the data provided in 8B-2, but assume that the company uses the perpetual inventory system. (**Hint:** In preparing the solutions below, it is helpful to determine the balance of inventory after each transaction, as shown in the Review Problem at the end of the chapter.)

1. Determine the cost of ending inventory and cost of goods sold for September and October using the average-cost method. Round unit costs to cents and totals to dollars.
2. Determine the cost of ending inventory and cost of goods sold for September and October using the FIFO method.
3. Determine the cost of ending inventory and cost of goods sold for September and October using the LIFO method.

8B-4.

LO 6 *Lower-of-Cost-or-Market Rule*

After taking the physical inventory, the accountant for Dorsey Company prepared the inventory schedule that follows:

	Quantity	Per Unit Cost	Per Unit Market
Product line 1			
Item 11	190	$ 27	$ 30
Item 12	270	12	15
Item 13	210	24	21
Product line 2			
Item 21	160	45	51
Item 22	400	63	60
Item 23	70	54	60
Product line 3			
Item 31	290	78	60
Item 32	310	90	84
Item 33	120	102	117

REQUIRED

Determine the value of the inventory at lower of cost or market using (1) the item-by-item method and (2) the major category method.

8B-5.

SO 7 *Retail Inventory Method*

Maywood Company operates a large discount store and uses the retail inventory method to estimate the cost of ending inventory. Management suspects that in recent weeks there have been unusually heavy losses from shoplifting or employee pilferage. To estimate the amount of the loss, the company has taken a physical inventory and will compare the results with the estimated cost of inventory. Data from the accounting records of Maywood Company are as follows:

	At Cost	At Retail
March 1 Beginning Inventory	$102,976	$148,600
Purchases	143,466	217,000
Purchases Returns and Allowances	(4,086)	(6,400)
Freight In	1,900	
Sales		218,366
Sales Returns and Allowances		(1,866)
March 31 Physical Inventory		124,900

REQUIRED

1. Prepare a schedule to estimate the dollar amount of the store's year-end inventory using the retail method.
2. Use the store's cost ratio to reduce the retail value of the physical inventory to cost.
3. Calculate the estimated amount of inventory shortage at cost and at retail.

8B-6.

S O 7 *Gross Profit Method*

Jauss and Sons is a large retail furniture company that operates in two adjacent warehouses. One warehouse is a showroom, and the other is used to store merchandise. On the night of May 9, a fire broke out in the storage warehouse and destroyed the merchandise stored there. Fortunately, the fire did not reach the showroom, so all the merchandise on display was saved.

Although the company maintained a perpetual inventory system, its records were rather haphazard, and the last reliable physical inventory was taken on December 31. In addition, there was no control of the flow of the goods between the showroom and the warehouse. Thus, it was impossible to tell what goods should be in either place. As a result, the insurance company required an independent estimate of the amount of loss. The insurance company examiners were satisfied when they were provided with the following information:

1. Merchandise Inventory on December 31	$1,454,800
2. Purchases, January 1 to May 9	2,412,200
3. Purchases Returns, January 1 to May 9	(10,706)
4. Freight In, January 1 to May 9	53,100
5. Sales, January 1 to May 9	3,959,050
6. Sales Returns, January 1 to May 9	(29,800)
7. Merchandise inventory in showroom on May 9	402,960
8. Average gross margin	44 percent

REQUIRED

Prepare a schedule that estimates the amount of the inventory lost in the fire.

CRITICAL THINKING AND COMMUNICATION

Conceptual Mini-Cases

CMC 8-1.

L O 1 *Evaluation of Inventory Levels*

The Gap, Inc. is one of the most important retailers of casual clothing for all members of the family. *Business Week* reports, "The Gap, Inc. is hell-bent on becoming to apparel what McDonald's is to food." With more than 1,100 stores already open, the company plans to open about 150 new stores per year for the next half decade. How does the company stay ahead of the competition? "One way is through frequent replenishment of mix-and-match inventory. That enables the company to clear out unpopular items fast—which prompts shoppers to check in on the new selections more often. . . . The Gap replaces inventory 7.5 times a year. That compares with 3.5 times at other specialty apparel stores."[10] One way in which The Gap controls inventory is by applying a just-in-time operating environment. How many days of inventory does The Gap have on hand on average compared to the competition? Discuss why these comparisons are important to The Gap. (Think of as many business and financial reasons as you can.) What is a just-in-time operating environment? Why is it important to achieving a favorable inventory turnover?

CMC 8-2.

L O 5 *LIFO Inventory Method*

In 1992, 95 percent of paper companies used the LIFO inventory method for the costing of inventories, whereas only 19 percent of electronic equipment companies used LIFO.[11] Describe the LIFO inventory method. What effects does it have on reported income and income taxes during periods of price changes? Discuss why the paper industry would use LIFO, but most of the electronics industry would not.

CMC 8-3.

L O 5 *Inventory Methods, Income Taxes, and Cash Flows*

The *Kyoto Trading Company* began business in 19x1 for the purpose of importing and marketing an electronics component used widely in digital appliances. It is now December 20, 19x1, and management is considering its options. Among its considerations is which inventory method to choose. It has decided to choose either the FIFO or the LIFO method. Under the periodic inventory system, the effects on net income of using the two methods are as follows:

10. "Everybody's Falling into The Gap," *Business Week,* September 23, 1991, p. 36.
11. American Institute of Certified Public Accountants, *Accounting Trends & Techniques* (New York: AICPA, 1993), p. 146.

	FIFO Method	LIFO Method
Sales: 500,000 units × $6	$3,000,000	$3,000,000
Cost of Goods Sold		
Purchases		
200,000 × $2	$ 400,000	$ 400,000
400,000 × $3	1,200,000	1,200,000
Total Purchases	$1,600,000	$1,600,000
Less Ending Inventory		
FIFO: 100,000 × $3	(300,000)	
LIFO: 100,000 × $2		(200,000)
Cost of Goods Sold	$1,300,000	$1,400,000
Gross Margin	$1,700,000	$1,600,000
Operating Expenses	1,200,000	1,200,000
Income Before Income Taxes	$ 500,000	$ 400,000
Income Taxes	150,000	120,000
Net Income	$ 350,000	$ 280,000

Also, management has an option to purchase an additional 100,000 units of inventory before year end at a price of $4 per unit, the price that is expected to prevail during 19x2. The income tax rate applicable to the company in 19x1 is 30 percent.

Business conditions are expected to be favorable in 19x2, as they were in 19x1. Management has asked you for advice. Analyze the effects of making the additional purchase. Then prepare a memorandum to management that compares cash outcomes under the four alternatives and advise management on which inventory method to choose and whether to order the additional inventory. Be prepared to discuss your recommendations.

Ethics Mini-Case

EMC 8-1.
L O 1 *Inventories, Income Determination, and Ethics*

Flare, Inc., which has a December 31 year end, designs and sells fashions for young professional women. Sandra Mason, president of the company, feared that the forecasted 1992 profitability goals would not be reached. She was pleased when Flare received a large order on December 30 from The Executive Woman, a retail chain of upscale stores for business women. Mason immediately directed the controller to record the sale, which represented 13 percent of Flare's annual sales, but directed the inventory control department not to separate the goods for shipment until after January 1. Separated goods are not included in inventory because they have been sold. On December 31 the company's auditors arrived to observe the year-end taking of the physical inventory under the periodic inventory system. What will be the effect of Mason's action on Flare's 1992 profitability? What will be the effect on 1993 profitability? Is Mason's action ethical?

Decision-Making Case

DMC 8-1.
L O 3, 5 *FIFO versus LIFO Analysis*

Bell Refrigerated Trucks Company (BRT Company) buys large refrigerated trucks from the manufacturer and sells them to companies and independent truckers who haul perishable goods for long distances. BRT has been successful in this specialized niche of the industry because it provides a unique product and service. Because of the high cost of the trucks and of financing inventory, BRT tries to maintain as small an inventory as possible. In fact, at the beginning of July the company had no inventory or liabilities, as shown by the balance sheet on page 381.

On July 9, BRT takes delivery of a truck at a price of $300,000. On July 19, an identical truck is delivered to the company at a price of $320,000. On July 28, the company sells one of the trucks for $390,000. During July expenses totaled $30,000. All transactions were paid in cash.

BRT Company
Balance Sheet
July 1, 19xx

Assets		Stockholders' Equity	
Cash	$800,000	Common Stock	$800,000
Total Assets	$800,000	Total Stockholders' Equity	$800,000

REQUIRED

1. Prepare income statements and balance sheets for BRT on July 31 using (a) the FIFO method of inventory valuation and (b) the LIFO method of inventory valuation. Assume an income tax rate of 40 percent. Explain the effects that each method has on the financial statements.
2. Assume that Larry Bell, the owner of BRT Company, follows the policy of declaring a cash dividend each period that is exactly equal to net income. What effects does this action have on each balance sheet prepared in **1**, and how do they compare with the balance sheet at the beginning of the month? Which inventory method, if either, do you feel is more realistic in representing BRT's income?
3. Assume that BRT receives notice of another price increase of $20,000 on refrigerated trucks, to take effect on August 1. How does this information relate to the owner's dividend policy, and how will it affect next month's operations?

Basic Research Activity

RA 8-1.
L O 2, 4 *Retail Business Inventories*

Make an appointment to visit a local retail business—a grocery, clothing, book, music, or appliance store, for example—and interview the manager for thirty minutes about the company's inventory accounting system. The store may be a branch of a larger company. Find out answers to the following questions, summarize your findings in a paper to be handed in, and be prepared to discuss your results in class.

What is the physical flow of merchandise into the store, and what documents are used in connection with this flow?

What documents are prepared when merchandise is sold?

Does the store keep perpetual inventory records? If so, does it keep the records in units only or does it keep track of cost as well? If not, what system does the store use?

How often does the company take a physical inventory?

How are financial statements generated for the store?

What method does the company use to price its inventory for financial statements?

FINANCIAL REPORTING AND ANALYSIS

Interpretation Cases from Business

ICB 8-1.
L O 2, 5 *LIFO, FIFO, and Income Taxes*

A portion of the income statements for 1992 and 1991 for **Hershey Foods Corp.,** famous for its chocolate and confectionery products, follows (in thousands).[12]

12. Hershey Foods Corp., *Annual Report*, 1992.

	1992	1991
Net Sales	$3,219,805	$2,899,165
Cost of Goods Sold	1,833,388	1,694,404
Gross Margin	$1,386,417	$1,204,761
Selling, General and Administrative Expense	958,189	814,459
Income from Operations	$ 428,228	$ 390,302
Interest Expense, Net	27,240	26,845
Income Before Income Taxes	$ 400,988	$ 363,457
Provision for Income Taxes	158,390	143,929
Net Income	$ 242,598	$ 219,528

In a note on supplemental balance sheet information, Hershey indicated that most of its inventories are maintained using the last-in, first-out (LIFO) method. The company also reported that inventories using the LIFO method were $436,917 in 1991 and $457,179 in 1992. In addition, it reported that if valued using the first-in, first-out (FIFO) method, inventories would have been $494,290 in 1991 and $505,521 in 1992.

REQUIRED

1. Prepare a schedule comparing net income for 1992 using the LIFO method with what it would have been under FIFO. Use a corporate income tax rate of 39 percent (Hershey's average tax rate in 1992).
2. Why do you suppose Hershey's management chooses to use the LIFO inventory method? On what economic conditions, if any, do these reasons depend? Given your calculations in **1** above, do you believe the economic conditions relevant to Hershey were advantageous for using LIFO in 1992? Explain your answer.

ICB 8-2.
L O 5 *Misstatement of Inventory*

The *Wall Street Journal* reported on November 20, 1987, that ***Crazy Eddie Inc.***, a discount consumer electronics chain, seemed to be missing $45 million in merchandise inventory. "It was a shock," Elias Zinn, the new president and chief executive officer, was quoted as saying.[13]

The article went on to say that Mr. Zinn headed a management team that took control of Crazy Eddie after a new board of directors was elected at a shareholders' meeting on November 6. A count on November 9 turned up only $75 million, compared with $126.7 million reported by the old management on August 30. Net sales could account for only $6.7 million of the difference. Mr. Zinn said he didn't know whether bookkeeping errors or an actual physical loss created the shortfall, although at least one store manager felt it was a bookkeeping error, because security is strong. "It would be hard for someone to steal anything," he says.

REQUIRED

1. What has been the effect of the misstatement of inventory on Crazy Eddie's reported earnings in prior accounting periods?
2. Is this a situation you would expect in a company that is experiencing financial difficulty? Explain.

ICB 8-3.
L O 5 *LIFO Liquidation*

In 1985 and 1986 ***General Motors Corp.*** experienced what is called a LIFO liquidation, as explained in its 1986 annual report: "Certain LIFO inventories carried at lower costs prevailing in prior years, as compared with the costs of current purchases, were liquidated in 1986 and 1985. These inventory adjustments favorably affected income before income taxes by approximately $38.2 million in 1986 and $20.9 million in 1985."[14] General Motors' average income tax rate for 1985 and 1986 was 22 percent.

REQUIRED

1. Explain why a reduction in the quantity of inventory resulted in favorable effects on income before income taxes. Would the same result have occurred if General Motors had used the FIFO method to value inventory? Explain your answer.
2. What is the income tax effect of the LIFO liquidation? Is it really a "favorable" outcome?

13. Based on Ann Hagedorn, "Crazy Eddie Says About $45 Million of Goods Missing," *Wall Street Journal*, November 20, 1987, p. 47.
14. General Motors, *Annual Report*, 1986.

International Company Case

ICC 8-1.
L O 1, 5 *Inventory Levels and Methods*

Two large Japanese diversified electronics companies are ***Pioneer Electronic Corporation*** and ***Yamaha Motor Co., Ltd.*** Both companies use the average-cost method and the lower-of-cost-or-market rule to account for inventories. The following data are for their 1992 fiscal years (in millions of yen):

	Pioneer	Yamaha
Beginning Inventory	¥ 76,324	¥123,768
Ending Inventory	93,148	113,766
Cost of Goods Sold	376,739	506,863

Compare the inventory efficiency of Pioneer and Yamaha by computing the inventory turnover and average days' inventory on hand for both companies in 1992. Comment on the results. Most companies in the United States use the LIFO inventory method. How would this affect your evaluation if you were to compare Pioneer and Yamaha to one of these companies? What could you do to make the results comparable?

Toys "R" Us Case

TC 8-1.
L O 3, 6
S O 7 *Retail Method and Inventory Ratios*

Refer to the note related to inventories in the appendix on Toys "R" Us to answer the following questions: What inventory method(s) does Toys "R" Us use? Why do you think that if LIFO inventories had been valued at FIFO, there would be no difference? Do you think many of the company's inventories are valued at market? Even though few companies use the retail inventory method, why do you think Toys "R" Us uses this method? Compute and compare the inventory turnover and average days' inventory on hand for Toys "R" Us for 1993 and 1994. According to management, in the "Operational Highlights" section of the annual report, what inventory policies contributed to the company's profitability?

Long-Term Assets

1. Identify the types of long-term assets and explain the management issues related to accounting for them.

2. Distinguish between capital and revenue expenditures, and account for the cost of property, plant, and equipment.

3. Define *depreciation,* state the factors that affect its computation, and show how to record it.

4. Compute periodic depreciation under the (a) straight-line method, (b) production method, and (c) declining-balance method.

5. Account for disposal of depreciable assets not involving exchanges.

6. Account for disposal of depreciable assets involving exchanges.

7. Identify natural resource accounting issues and compute depletion.

8. Apply the matching rule to intangible assets, including research and development costs and goodwill.

SUPPLEMENTAL OBJECTIVE

9. Apply depreciation methods to problems of partial years, revised rates, groups of similar items, special types of capital expenditures, and cost recovery.

DECISION POINT *H. J. Heinz Company*

The effects of management's decisions regarding long-term assets are most apparent in the areas of reported total assets and net income. How does one learn of the significance of these items to a company? An idea of the extent and importance of these assets can be gained from the financial statements. For example, the following list of assets is taken from the 1992 annual report of H. J. Heinz Company, one of the world's largest food companies (in thousands):

	1992	1991
Property, Plant, and Equipment:		
Land	$ 44,988	$ 39,918
Buildings and leasehold improvements	655,323	529,041
Equipment, furniture and other	2,279,471	2,195,511
	$2,979,782	$2,764,470
Less accumulated depreciation	1,067,673	1,041,729
Total property, plant and equipment, net	$1,912,109	$1,722,741
Other Noncurrent Assets:		
Investments, advances and other assets	$ 560,144	$ 343,526
Goodwill (net of amortization: 1992—$88,892 and 1991—$67,553)	822,100	498,029
Other intangibles (net of amortization: 1992—$63,197 and 1991—$44,285)	357,236	251,301
Total other noncurrent assets	$1,739,480	$1,092,856

Of the company's almost $6 billion in total assets, about one-third consists of property, plant, and equipment, and another 20 percent is goodwill and other intangibles. Further, on the income statement, depreciation and amortization expenses associated with these assets are $212 million, or about one-third of net income, and on the statement of cash flows, more than $331 million was spent on new long-term assets. This chapter deals with the long-term assets of property, plant, and equipment and intangible assets. Noncurrent, or long-term, investments are dealt with in the chapter on international accounting and intercompany investments.[1] • • • • •

1. H. J. Heinz Company, *Annual Report,* 1992.

MANAGEMENT ISSUES RELATED TO ACCOUNTING FOR LONG-TERM ASSETS

Long-term assets are assets that (1) have a useful life of more than one year, (2) are acquired for use in the operation of the business, and (3) are not intended for resale to customers. For many years, it was common to refer to long-term assets as *fixed assets,* but use of this term is declining because the word *fixed* implies that they last forever. The relative importance of long-term assets to various industries is shown in Figure 9-1. Long-term assets range from 16.7 percent of total assets in auto and home supply to 37.3 percent in interstate trucking.

Although there is no strict minimum useful life for an asset to be classified as long term, the most common criterion is that the asset must be capable of repeated use for a period of at least a year. Included in this category is equipment that is used only in peak or emergency periods, such as a generator.

Assets not used in the normal course of business should not be included in this category. Thus, land held for speculative reasons or buildings that are no longer used in ordinary business operations should not be included in the property, plant, and equipment category. Instead, they should be classified as long-term investments.

Finally, if an item is held for resale to customers, it should be classified as inventory—not plant and equipment—no matter how durable it is. For example, a printing press held for sale by a printing press manufacturer would be considered inventory, whereas the same printing press would be plant and equipment for a printing company that buys the press to use in its operations.

Long-term assets are customarily divided into the following categories:

Asset	Expense
Tangible Assets	
Land	None
Plant, buildings, and equipment (plant assets)	Depreciation
Natural resources	Depletion
Intangible Assets	Amortization

Tangible assets have physical substance. Land is a tangible asset, and because it has an unlimited life it is the only tangible asset not subject to depreciation or other expense. Plant, buildings, and equipment (referred to hereafter as plant assets) are subject to depreciation. **Depreciation** is the periodic allocation of the cost of a tangible long-lived asset (other than land and natural resources) over its estimated useful life. The term applies to manufactured assets only. Note that accounting for depreciation is an allocation process, not a valuation process. This point is discussed in more detail later.

Natural resources differ from land in that they are purchased for the substances that can be taken from the land and used up rather than for the value of their location. Among natural resources are ore from mines, oil and gas from oil and gas fields, and lumber from forests. Natural resources are subject to depletion rather than to depreciation. The term **depletion** refers to the exhaustion of a natural resource through mining, cutting, pumping, or other extraction and to the way in which the cost is allocated.

Intangible assets are long-term assets that do not have physical substance and in most cases relate to legal rights or advantages held. Intangible assets include patents, copyrights, trademarks, franchises, organization costs, lease-

Figure 9-1. Long-Term Assets as a Percentage of Total Assets for Selected Industries

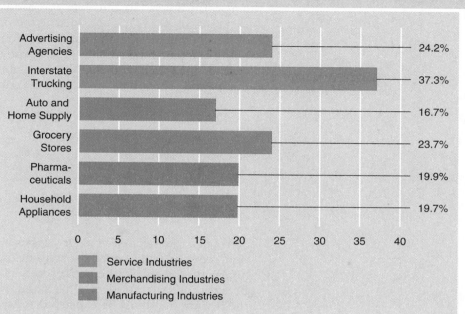

Source: Data from Dun and Bradstreet, *Industry Norms and Ratios*, 1992–93.

holds, leasehold improvements, and goodwill. The allocation of the cost of intangible assets to the periods they benefit is called amortization. Although the current assets accounts receivable and prepaid expenses do not have physical substance, they are not intangible assets because they are not long term.

The unexpired part of the cost of an asset is generally called its book value, or carrying value. The latter term is used in this book when referring to long-term assets. The carrying value of plant assets, for instance, is cost less accumulated depreciation.

Long-term assets differ from current assets in that they support the operating cycle instead of being a part of it. They are also expected to benefit the business for a longer period than do current assets. Current assets are expected to be realized within one year or during the operating cycle, whichever is longer. Long-term assets are expected to last beyond that period. For example, Wickes Furniture, Inc., a retail business, purchases furniture as inventory that it in turn sells to customers. Wickes' buildings that will last thirty years or more are used to store and showcase inventory. Wickes' delivery trucks that will last five years or more are used to deliver furniture to customers' homes. The management issues related to long-term assets revolve around the decision to acquire these assets, the means of financing the assets, and the methods of accounting for the assets.

DECIDING TO ACQUIRE LONG-TERM ASSETS

The decision to acquire a long-term asset involves a complex process. Methods of evaluating data to make rational decisions in this area are grouped under a topic called capital budgeting, which is usually covered in a managerial accounting course. However, an awareness of the general nature of the problem is helpful in understanding the accounting issues related to long-term assets. To illustrate the acquisition decision, let us assume that Irena Markova, M.D. is considering the purchase of a $5,000 computer for her office. By purchasing the computer, she estimates that she can reduce the hours of a part-time employee sufficiently to save net cash flows of $3,000 per year for four years and that the computer will be worth $1,000 at the end of that period. These data are summarized as follows:

	19x1	19x2	19x3	19x4
Acquisition Cost	($5,000)			
Net Annual Savings in Cash Flows	$3,000	$3,000	$3,000	$3,000
Disposal Price				1,000
Net Cash Flows	($2,000)	$3,000	$3,000	$4,000

To reach a rational decision, Dr. Markova must compare the negative cash out-flow required by the purchase with the positive cash flows to be received over a period of years. This comparison is not always as obvious as it may seem because the dollars that will be saved in future years are not as valuable as the dollars that must be expended today for the acquisition. (Techniques for considering such differences in the timing of cash flows are covered in the chapter on current liabilities and the time value of money.) Other important factors in the decision process are the costs of training and maintenance, and the possibility that, because of unforeseen circumstances, the savings may not be as great as expected. In Dr. Markova's case, the decision to purchase is likely to be a good one because the positive cash flows from the acquisition are substantially more than the purchase price.

Information about a company's acquisitions of long-term assets may be found under investing activities in the statement of cash flows. For example, in referring to this section of its annual report, the management of Bausch & Lomb, one of the largest makers of health care products, makes the following statement:

> Cash flows used in investing activities reflect payments for purchases of property, plant, and equipment, which increased $30.7 million or 35% to $119.3 million in 1992.[2]

FINANCING LONG-TERM ASSETS

In addition to deciding whether or not to acquire a long-term asset, management must decide how to finance the asset if it is acquired. Some companies are profitable enough to pay for long-term assets out of cash flows from operations, but when financing is needed, some form of long-term financing related to the life of the asset usually is most appropriate. For example, an automobile loan is generally four or five years, whereas a mortgage loan on a house may be thirty years. For a major long-term acquisition, a company may issue capital stock and long-term notes or bonds. A good place to study a company's long-term financing is in the financing activities section of the statement of cash flows. For instance, in discussing this section, Bausch & Lomb's management states that the company's increase in borrowings "was

2. Bausch & Lomb, Inc., *Annual Report*, 1992.

attributable to the higher level of capital spending."[3] Another option a company may have is to lease long-term assets instead of buying them. All these options related to long-term financing are discussed in the chapters on long-term liabilities and contributed capital.

APPLYING THE MATCHING RULE TO LONG-TERM ASSETS

As with inventories and prepaid expenses, accounting for long-term assets requires the proper application of the matching rule through the resolution of two important issues. The first is how much of the total cost should be allocated to expense in the current accounting period. The second is how much should remain on the balance sheet as an asset to benefit future periods. To resolve these issues, four important questions about the acquisition, use, and disposal of each long-term asset, as illustrated in Figure 9-2, must be answered:

1. How is the cost of the long-term asset determined?
2. How should the expired portion of the cost of the long-term asset be allocated against revenues over time?
3. How should subsequent expenditures, such as repairs and additions, be treated?
4. How should disposal of the long-term asset be recorded?

Because of the long life of long-term assets and the complexity of the transactions involving them, management is faced with a great many choices and

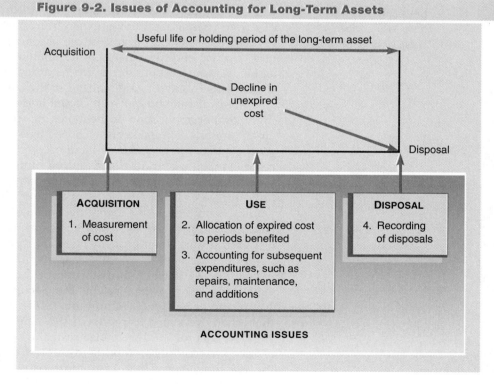

Figure 9-2. Issues of Accounting for Long-Term Assets

3. Ibid.

estimates. For example, acquisition cost may be complicated by group purchases, trade-ins, or construction costs. In addition, to allocate the cost of the asset to future periods effectively, management must estimate how long the asset will last and what it will be worth at the end of its use. In making these estimates, it is helpful to think of a long-term asset as a bundle of services to be used in the operation of the business over a period of years. A delivery truck may provide 100,000 miles of service over its life. A piece of equipment may have the potential to produce 500,000 parts. A building may provide shelter for fifty years. As each of these assets is purchased, the company is paying in advance for 100,000 miles, the capacity to produce 500,000 parts, or fifty years of service. In essence, each of these assets is a type of long-term prepaid expense. The accounting problem is to spread the cost of these services over the useful life of the asset. As the services benefit the company over the years, the cost becomes an expense rather than an asset.

The remainder of this chapter will address the issues raised in Figure 9-2 as they relate to property, plant, and equipment, natural resources, and intangible assets.

ACQUISITION COST OF PROPERTY, PLANT, AND EQUIPMENT

OBJECTIVE

2 *Distinguish between capital and revenue expenditures, and account for the cost of property, plant, and equipment*

The term expenditure refers to a payment or an obligation to make future payment for an asset, such as a truck, or a service received, such as a repair. Expenditures may be classified as capital expenditures or revenue expenditures. A capital expenditure is an expenditure for the purchase or expansion of a long-term asset. Capital expenditures are recorded in the asset accounts because they benefit several future accounting periods. A revenue expenditure is an expenditure related to the maintenance and operation of long-term assets. Revenue expenditures are recorded in the expense accounts because the benefits from them are realized in the current period.

Careful distinction between capital and revenue expenditures is important to the proper application of the matching rule. For example, if the purchase of an automobile is mistakenly recorded as a revenue expenditure, the expense for the current period is overstated on the income statement. As a result, current net income is understated, and in future periods net income will be overstated. If, on the other hand, a revenue expenditure such as the painting of a building were charged to an asset account, the expense of the current period would be understated. Current net income would be overstated by the same amount, and net income of future periods would be understated.

Determining when a payment is an expense and when it is an asset is a matter of judgment in which management takes a leading role. Such latitude, however, does not permit distortion of the financial results. For example, in 1991, after an investigation by the Securities and Exchange Commission, Amre, Inc., a maker of aluminum siding and kitchen cabinets, announced that it had overstated its profits in 1987 and 1988 and understated its losses in 1989. Results for 1990 were also restated, and the company's two top officers resigned. According to reports in the *Wall Street Journal*, a primary reason for the adjustments was that Amre improperly recorded its marketing costs, such as the cost of purchasing mailing lists, as assets instead of as expenses.

Because the costs were treated as assets, they appeared on Amre's balance sheet and the company was able to spread them over time, thereby improving its profits. For example, its 1988 net income should have been $2.9 million, not the reported $7.3 million.[4]

GENERAL APPROACH TO ACQUISITION COST

The acquisition cost of property, plant, and equipment includes all expenditures reasonable and necessary to get it in place and ready for use. For example, the cost of installing and testing a machine is a legitimate cost of the machine. However, if the machine is damaged while it is being installed, the cost of repairing the machine is an operating expense and not an acquisition cost.

Cost is easiest to determine when a transaction is made for cash. In this case, the cost of the asset is equal to the cash paid for the asset plus expenditures for freight, insurance while in transit, installation, and other necessary related costs. If a debt is incurred in the purchase of the asset, the interest charges are not a cost of the asset but a cost of borrowing the money to buy the asset. They are therefore an operating expense. An exception to this principle is that interest costs during the construction of an asset are properly included as a cost of the asset.[5]

Expenditures such as freight, insurance while in transit, and installation are included in the cost of the asset because they are necessary if the asset is to function. Following the matching rule, they are allocated to the useful life of the asset rather than charged as expenses in the current period.

For practical purposes many companies establish policies defining when an expenditure should be recorded as an expense or an asset. For example, small expenditures for items that normally would be treated as assets may be treated as expenses because the amounts involved are not material in relation to net income. Thus, a wastebasket, which might last for years, would be recorded as a supplies expense rather than as a depreciable asset.

Some of the problems of determining the cost of a long-lived asset are demonstrated in the illustrations for land, buildings, equipment, land improvements, and group purchases presented in the next few sections.

Land   There are often expenditures in addition to the purchase price of land that should be debited to the Land account. Some examples are commissions to real estate agents; lawyers' fees; accrued taxes paid by the purchaser; cost of preparing the land to build on, such as draining, tearing down old buildings, clearing, and grading; and assessments for local improvements, such as streets and sewage systems. The cost of landscaping is usually debited to the Land account because these improvements are relatively permanent. Land is not subject to depreciation because land does not have a limited useful life.

Let us assume that a company buys land for a new retail operation. It pays a net purchase price of $170,000, pays brokerage fees of $6,000 and legal fees

---

4. Karen Blumenthal, "Amre Overstated Financial Results for Three Fiscal Years," *Wall Street Journal*, August 7, 1991, p. B8.
5. "Capitalization of Interest Cost," *Statement of Financial Accounting Standards No. 34* (Stamford, Conn.: Financial Accounting Standards Board, 1979), par. 9–11.

of $2,000, pays $10,000 to have an old building on the site torn down, receives $4,000 salvage from the old building, and pays $1,000 to have the site graded. The cost of the land will be $185,000, determined as follows:

Net purchase price		$170,000
Brokerage fees		6,000
Legal fees		2,000
Tearing down old building	$10,000	
Less salvage	4,000	6,000
Grading		1,000
Total cost		$185,000

Land Improvements　　Improvements to real estate, such as driveways, parking lots, and fences, have a limited life and thus are subject to depreciation. They should be recorded in an account called Land Improvements rather than in the Land account.

Buildings　　When an existing building is purchased, its cost includes the purchase price plus all repairs and other expenses required to put it in usable condition. Buildings are subject to depreciation because they have a limited useful life. When a business constructs its own building, the cost includes all reasonable and necessary expenditures, such as those for materials, labor, part of the overhead and other indirect costs, the architects' fees, insurance during construction, interest on construction loans during the period of construction, lawyers' fees, and building permits. If outside contractors are used in the construction, the net contract price plus other expenditures necessary to put the building in usable condition are included.

Equipment　　The cost of equipment includes all expenditures connected with purchasing the equipment and preparing it for use. These expenditures include invoice price less cash discounts; freight or transportation, including insurance; excise taxes and tariffs; buying expenses; installation costs; and test runs to ready the equipment for operation. Equipment is subject to depreciation.

Group Purchases　　Sometimes land and other assets are purchased for a lump sum. Because land is a nondepreciable asset that has an unlimited life, it must have a separate ledger account, and the lump-sum purchase price must be apportioned between the land and the other assets. For example, assume that a building and the land on which it is situated are purchased for a lump-sum payment of $85,000. The apportionment can be made by determining the price of each if purchased separately and applying the appropriate percentages to the lump-sum price. Assume that appraisals yield estimates of $10,000 for the land and $90,000 for the building, if purchased separately. In that case, 10 percent of the lump-sum price, or $8,500, would be allocated to the land and 90 percent, or $76,500, would be allocated to the building, as shown below:

	Appraisal	**Percentage**	**Apportionment**
Land	$ 10,000	10 ($10,000/$100,000)	$ 8,500 ($85,000 × 10%)
Building	90,000	90 ($90,000/$100,000)	76,500 ($85,000 × 90%)
Totals	$100,000	100	$85,000

Determining the acquisition price of a long-term asset is not always as clear-cut as some might imagine, especially in the case of constructed assets. Management has considerable leeway, but choices that are questioned can sometimes be costly. The *Wall Street Journal* reported that Chambers Development Co., a waste-disposal company, wrote off nearly $50 million when it decided to stop deferring costs related to the development of landfills. Previously, Chambers had been including certain indirect costs, such as executives' salaries and travel, legal, and public relations fees, as capital expenditures to be written off over the life of the landfill. The *Wall Street Journal* states, "Accounting experts consider the practice unorthodox and aggressive, but not necessarily outside generally accepted accounting principles." Further write-offs may follow because of the large amount of interest the company is capitalizing as a cost of the landfill. On news of the accounting change, the company's stock price dropped 63 percent in one day.[6]

ACCOUNTING FOR DEPRECIATION

OBJECTIVE

3 *Define* depreciation, *state the factors that affect its computation, and show how to record it*

Depreciation accounting is described by the AICPA as follows:

> The cost of a productive facility is one of the costs of the services it renders during its useful economic life. Generally accepted accounting principles require that this cost be spread over the expected useful life of the facility in such a way as to allocate it as equitably as possible to the periods during which services are obtained from the use of the facility. This procedure is known as depreciation accounting, a system of accounting which aims to distribute the cost or other basic value of tangible capital assets, less salvage (if any), over the estimated useful life of the unit . . . in a systematic and rational manner. It is a process of allocation, not of valuation.[7]

This description contains several important points. First, all tangible assets except land have a limited useful life. Because of this limited useful life, the costs of these assets must be distributed as expenses over the years they benefit. Physical deterioration and obsolescence are the major causes of the limited useful life of a depreciable asset. The physical deterioration of tangible assets results from use and from exposure to the elements, such as wind and sun. Periodic repairs and a sound maintenance policy may keep buildings and equipment in good operating order and extract the maximum useful life from them, but every machine or building at some point must be discarded. The need for depreciation is not eliminated by repairs. Obsolescence is the process of becoming out of date. With fast-changing technology as well as

6. Gabriella Stern, "Chambers Development Co. May Face Further Write-offs Over Accounting," *Wall Street Journal,* April 10, 1992.

7. *Financial Accounting Standards: Original Pronouncements as of July 1, 1977* (Stamford, Conn.: Financial Accounting Standards Board, 1977), ARB No. 43, Ch. 9, Sec. C, par. 5.

fast-changing demands, machinery and even buildings often become obsolete before they wear out. Accountants do not distinguish between physical deterioration and obsolescence because they are interested in the length of the useful life of the asset regardless of what limits that useful life.

Second, the term *depreciation,* as used in accounting, does not refer to the physical deterioration of an asset or the decrease in market value of an asset over time. Depreciation means the allocation of the cost of a plant asset to the periods that benefit from the services of the asset. The term is used to describe the gradual conversion of the cost of the asset into an expense.

Third, depreciation is not a process of valuation. Accounting records are kept in accordance with the cost principle; they are not indicators of changing price levels. It is possible that, through an advantageous buy and specific market conditions, the market value of a building may rise. Nevertheless, depreciation must continue to be recorded because it is the result of an allocation, not a valuation, process. Eventually the building will wear out or become obsolete regardless of interim fluctuations in market value.

FACTORS THAT AFFECT THE COMPUTATION OF DEPRECIATION

Four factors affect the computation of depreciation. They are (1) cost, (2) residual value, (3) depreciable cost, and (4) estimated useful life.

Cost As explained earlier in the chapter, cost is the net purchase price plus all reasonable and necessary expenditures to get the asset in place and ready for use.

Residual Value The residual value of an asset is its estimated net scrap, salvage, or trade-in value as of the estimated date of disposal. Other terms often used to describe residual value are *salvage value* and *disposal value.*

Depreciable Cost The depreciable cost of an asset is its cost less its residual value. For example, a truck that costs $12,000 and has a residual value of $3,000 would have a depreciable cost of $9,000. Depreciable cost must be allocated over the useful life of the asset.

Estimated Useful Life The estimated useful life of an asset is the total number of service units expected from the asset. Service units may be measured in terms of years the asset is expected to be used, units expected to be produced, miles expected to be driven, or similar measures. In computing the estimated useful life of an asset, the accountant should consider all relevant information, including (1) past experience with similar assets, (2) the asset's present condition, (3) the company's repair and maintenance policy, (4) current technological and industry trends, and (5) local conditions such as weather.

As introduced in the chapter on measuring business income, depreciation is recorded at the end of the accounting period by an adjusting entry that takes the following form:

Depreciation Expense, Asset Name	xxx	
Accumulated Depreciation, Asset Name		xxx
To record depreciation for the period		

METHODS OF COMPUTING DEPRECIATION

Many methods are used to allocate the cost of plant assets to accounting periods through depreciation. Each of them is proper for certain circumstances. The most common methods are (1) the straight-line method, (2) the production method, and (3) an accelerated method known as the declining-balance method.

Straight-Line Method   When the straight-line method is used to allocate depreciation, the depreciable cost of the asset is spread evenly over the estimated useful life of the asset. The straight-line method is based on the assumption that depreciation depends only on the passage of time. The depreciation expense for each period is computed by dividing the depreciable cost (cost of the depreciating asset less its estimated residual value) by the number of accounting periods in the asset's estimated useful life. The rate of depreciation is the same in each year. Suppose, for example, that a delivery truck costs $10,000 and has an estimated residual value of $1,000 at the end of its estimated useful life of five years. The annual depreciation would be $1,800 under the straight-line method, calculated as follows:

$$\frac{\text{Cost} - \text{residual value}}{\text{Estimated useful life}} = \frac{\$10,000 - \$1,000}{5 \text{ years}} = \$1,800$$

The depreciation for the five years would be as follows:

Depreciation Schedule, Straight-Line Method

	Cost	Yearly Depreciation	Accumulated Depreciation	Carrying Value
Date of purchase	$10,000	—	—	$10,000
End of first year	10,000	$1,800	$1,800	8,200
End of second year	10,000	1,800	3,600	6,400
End of third year	10,000	1,800	5,400	4,600
End of fourth year	10,000	1,800	7,200	2,800
End of fifth year	10,000	1,800	9,000	1,000

There are three important points to note from the depreciation schedule for the straight-line depreciation method. First, the depreciation is the same each year. Second, the accumulated depreciation increases uniformly. Third, the carrying value decreases uniformly until it reaches the estimated residual value.

Production Method   The production method of depreciation is based on the assumption that depreciation is solely the result of use and that the passage of time plays no role in the depreciation process. If we assume that the delivery truck from the previous example has an estimated useful life of 90,000 miles, the depreciation cost per mile would be determined as follows:

$$\frac{\text{Cost} - \text{residual value}}{\text{Estimated units of useful life}} = \frac{\$10,000 - \$1,000}{90,000 \text{ miles}} = \$.10 \text{ per mile}$$

If we assume that the use of the truck was 20,000 miles for the first year, 30,000 miles for the second, 10,000 miles for the third, 20,000 miles for the fourth, and 10,000 miles for the fifth, the depreciation schedule for the delivery truck would appear as follows:

Depreciation Schedule, Production Method

	Cost	Miles	Yearly Depreciation	Accumulated Depreciation	Carrying Value
Date of purchase	$10,000	—	—	—	$10,000
End of first year	10,000	20,000	$2,000	$2,000	8,000
End of second year	10,000	30,000	3,000	5,000	5,000
End of third year	10,000	10,000	1,000	6,000	4,000
End of fourth year	10,000	20,000	2,000	8,000	2,000
End of fifth year	10,000	10,000	1,000	9,000	1,000

There is a direct relation between the amount of depreciation each year and the units of output or use. Also, the accumulated depreciation increases each year in direct relation to units of output or use. Finally, the carrying value decreases each year in direct relation to units of output or use until it reaches the estimated residual value.

Under the production method, the unit of output or use that is used to measure estimated useful life for each asset should be appropriate for that asset. For example, number of items produced may be an appropriate measure for one machine, but number of hours of use may be a better measure for another. The production method should be used only when the output of an asset over its useful life can be estimated with reasonable accuracy.

OBJECTIVE

4c *Compute periodic depreciation under the declining-balance method*

Declining-Balance Method

An accelerated method of depreciation results in relatively large amounts of depreciation in the early years of an asset's life and smaller amounts in later years. Such a method, which is based on the passage of time, assumes that many kinds of plant assets are most efficient when new, and so they provide more and better service in the early years of useful life. It is consistent with the matching rule to allocate more depreciation to the early years than to later years if the benefits or services received in the early years are greater.

An accelerated method also recognizes that changing technologies make some equipment lose service value rapidly. Thus, it is realistic to allocate more to depreciation in the early years than in later years. New inventions and products result in obsolescence of equipment bought earlier, making it necessary to replace equipment sooner than if technology changed more slowly.

Another argument in favor of an accelerated method is that repair expense is likely to be greater in later years than in early years. Thus, the total of repair and depreciation expense remains fairly constant over a period of years. This result naturally assumes that the services received from the asset are roughly equal from year to year.

The declining-balance method is the most common accelerated method of depreciation. Under this method, depreciation is computed by applying a fixed rate to the carrying value (the declining balance) of a long-lived asset, resulting in higher depreciation charges during the early years of the asset's life. Though any fixed rate might be used under the method, the most common rate is a percentage equal to twice the straight-line percentage. When twice the straight-line rate is used, the method is usually called the double-declining-balance method.

In our earlier example, the delivery truck had an estimated useful life of five years. Consequently, under the straight-line method, the depreciation rate for each year was 20 percent (100 percent ÷ 5 years).

Under the double-declining-balance method, the fixed rate is 40 percent (2 × 20 percent). This fixed rate of 40 percent is applied to the *remaining carrying value* at the end of each year. Estimated residual value is not taken into account in figuring depreciation except in the last year of an asset's useful life, when depreciation is limited to the amount necessary to bring the carrying value down to the estimated residual value. The depreciation schedule for this method is as follows:

Depreciation Schedule, Double-Declining-Balance Method

	Cost	Yearly Depreciation		Accumulated Depreciation	Carrying Value
Date of purchase	$10,000	—		—	$10,000
End of first year	10,000	(40% × $10,000)	$4,000	$4,000	6,000
End of second year	10,000	(40% × $6,000)	2,400	6,400	3,600
End of third year	10,000	(40% × $3,600)	1,440	7,840	2,160
End of fourth year	10,000	(40% × $2,160)	864	8,704	1,296
End of fifth year	10,000		296*	9,000	1,000

*Depreciation limited to amount necessary to reduce carrying value to residual value:
$296 = $1,296 (previous carrying value) − $1,000 (residual value).

Note that the fixed rate is always applied to the carrying value at the end of the previous year. The depreciation is greatest in the first year and declines each year after that. Finally, the depreciation in the last year is limited to the amount necessary to reduce carrying value to residual value.

Comparing the Three Methods   A visual comparison may provide a better understanding of the three depreciation methods described above. Figure 9-3 compares yearly depreciation and carrying value under the three methods. In the graph that shows yearly depreciation, straight-line depreciation is

Figure 9-3. Graphical Comparison of Three Methods of Determining Depreciation

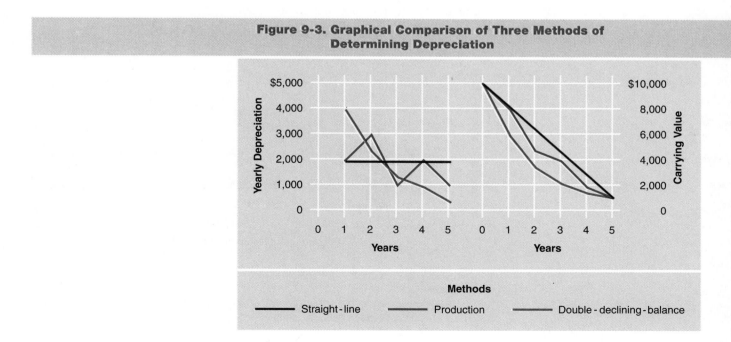

uniform at $1,800 per year over the five-year period. However, the declining-balance method begins at an amount greater than straight-line ($4,000) and decreases each year to amounts that are less than straight-line (ultimately, $296). The production method does not generate a regular pattern because of the random fluctuation of the depreciation from year to year. The three yearly depreciation patterns are reflected in the graph of carrying value. In that graph, each method starts in the same place (cost of $10,000) and ends at the same place (residual value of $1,000). It is the patterns during the useful life of the asset that differ for each method. For instance, the carrying value under the straight-line method is always greater than that under the double-declining-balance method, except at the beginning and the end of useful life.

BUSINESS BULLETIN: BUSINESS PRACTICE

Most companies choose the straight-line method of depreciation for financial reporting purposes, as shown in Figure 9-4. Only about 17 percent use some type of accelerated method and 8 percent use the production method. These figures tend to be misleading about the importance of accelerated depreciation methods, however, especially when it comes to income taxes. Federal income tax laws allow either the straight-line method or an accelerated method, and for tax purposes, according to *Accounting Trends and Techniques,* about 75 percent of the six hundred large companies studied preferred an accelerated method. Companies use different methods of depreciation for good reason. The straight-line method can be advantageous for financial reporting because it can produce the highest net income, and an accelerated method can be beneficial for tax purposes because it can result in lower income taxes.

Figure 9-4. Depreciation Methods Used by 600 Large Companies

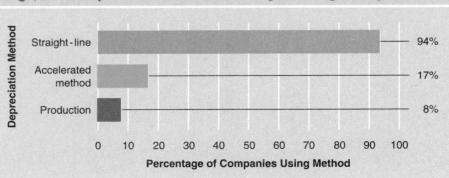

Total percentage exceeds 100 because some companies used different methods for different types of depreciable assets.

Source: From *Accounting Trends & Techniques.* Copyright © 1993. Used by permission of the American Institute of Certified Public Accountants.

DISPOSAL OF DEPRECIABLE ASSETS

When plant assets are no longer useful because they are worn out or obsolete, they may be discarded, sold, or traded in on the purchase of new plant and equipment. A comprehensive illustration will be used to show how these disposals are recorded in the accounting records.

ASSUMPTIONS FOR THE COMPREHENSIVE ILLUSTRATION

For accounting purposes, a plant asset may be disposed of in three ways: It may be (1) discarded, (2) sold for cash, or (3) exchanged for another asset. To illustrate how each of these cases is recorded, assume that MGC Corporation purchased a machine on January 1, 19x0 for $6,500 and depreciated it on a straight-line basis over an estimated useful life of ten years. The residual value at the end of ten years was estimated to be $500. On January 1, 19x7, the balances of the relevant accounts in the plant asset ledger appear as follows:

Machinery		Accumulated Depreciation, Machinery	
6,500			4,200

On September 30, 19x7, management disposes of the asset. The next few sections illustrate the accounting treatment to record depreciation for the partial year and the disposal under several assumptions.

DEPRECIATION FOR PARTIAL YEAR PRIOR TO DISPOSAL

When a plant asset is discarded or disposed of in some other way, it is first necessary to record depreciation expense for the partial year up to the date of disposal. This step is required because the asset was used until that date and, under the matching rule, the accounting period should receive the proper allocation of depreciation expense.

In this comprehensive illustration, MGC Corporation disposes of the machinery on September 30. The entry to record the depreciation for the first nine months of 19x7 (nine-twelfths of a year) is as follows:

Sept. 30	Depreciation Expense, Machinery	450	
	Accumulated Depreciation, Machinery		450
	To record depreciation up to date of disposal		

$$\frac{\$6,500 - \$500}{10} \times \frac{9}{12} = \$450$$

The relevant accounts in the plant asset ledger appear as follows after the entry is posted:

Machinery		Accumulated Depreciation, Machinery	
6,500			4,650

RECORDING DISCARDED PLANT ASSETS

A plant asset rarely lasts exactly as long as its estimated life. If it lasts longer than its estimated life, it is not depreciated past the point at which its carrying value equals its residual value. The purpose of depreciation is to spread the depreciable cost of the asset over the life of the asset. Thus, the total accumulated depreciation should never exceed the total depreciable cost. If the asset is still used in the business beyond the end of its estimated life, its cost and accumulated depreciation remain in the ledger accounts. Proper records will thus be available for maintaining control over plant assets. If the residual value is zero, the carrying value of a fully depreciated asset is zero until the asset is disposed of. If such an asset is discarded, no gain or loss results.

In the comprehensive illustration, however, the discarded equipment has a carrying value of $1,850 at the time of disposal. The carrying value from the ledger account above is computed as machinery of $6,500 less accumulated depreciation of $4,650. A loss equal to the carrying value should be recorded when the machine is discarded:

Sept. 30	Accumulated Depreciation, Machinery	4,650	
	Loss on Disposal of Machinery	1,850	
	Machinery		6,500
	Discarded machine no longer used in the business		

Gains and losses on disposals of long-term assets are classified as other revenues and expenses on the income statement.

RECORDING PLANT ASSETS SOLD FOR CASH

The entry to record an asset sold for cash is similar to the one illustrated above except that the receipt of cash should also be recorded. The following entries show how to record the sale of a machine under three assumptions about the selling price. In the first case, the $1,850 cash received is exactly equal to the carrying value of the machine ($1,850); therefore, no gain or loss results.

Sept. 30	Cash	1,850	
	Accumulated Depreciation, Machinery	4,650	
	Machinery		6,500
	Sale of machine for carrying value; no gain or loss		

In the second case, the $1,000 cash received is less than the carrying value of $1,850, so a loss of $850 is recorded.

Sept. 30	Cash	1,000	
	Accumulated Depreciation, Machinery	4,650	
	Loss on Sale of Machinery	850	
	Machinery		6,500
	Sale of machine at less than carrying value; loss of $850 ($1,850 − $1,000) recorded		

In the third case, the $2,000 cash received exceeds the carrying value of $1,850, so a gain of $150 is recorded.

Sept. 30	Cash	2,000	
	Accumulated Depreciation, Machinery	4,650	
	Gain on Sale of Machinery		150
	Machinery		6,500
	Sale of machine at more than the		
	carrying value; gain of $150		
	($2,000 − $1,850) recorded		

RECORDING EXCHANGES OF PLANT ASSETS

OBJECTIVE

6 *Account for disposal of depreciable assets involving exchanges*

Businesses also dispose of plant assets by trading them in on the purchase of other plant assets. Exchanges may involve similar assets, such as an old machine traded in on a newer model, or dissimilar assets, such as a machine traded in on a truck. In either case, the purchase price is reduced by the amount of the trade-in allowance.

The basic accounting for exchanges of plant assets is similar to accounting for sales of plant assets for cash. If the trade-in allowance received is greater than the carrying value of the asset surrendered, there has been a gain. If the allowance is less, there has been a loss. There are special rules for recognizing these gains and losses, depending on the nature of the assets exchanged.

Exchange	Losses Recognized	Gains Recognized
For financial accounting purposes		
Of dissimilar assets	Yes	Yes
Of similar assets	Yes	No
For income tax purposes		
Of dissimilar assets	Yes	Yes
Of similar assets	No	No

Both gains and losses are recognized when a company exchanges dissimilar assets. Assets are dissimilar when they perform different functions; assets are similar when they perform the same function. For financial accounting purposes, gains on exchanges of similar assets are not recognized because the earning lives of the assets surrendered are not considered to be completed. When a company trades in an older machine on a newer machine of the same type, the economic substance of the transaction is the same as that of a major renovation and upgrading of the older machine. You could think of the trade-in as an extension of the life and usefulness of the original machine. Instead of recognizing a gain at the time of the exchange, the company records the new machine at the sum of the book value of the older machine plus any cash paid.[8]

Accounting for exchanges of similar assets is complicated by the fact that neither gains nor losses are recognized for income tax purposes. This is important because many companies choose to follow this practice in their accounting records, usually for convenience. Thus, in practice, accountants

8. Accounting Principles Board, *Opinion No. 29,* "Accounting for Nonmonetary Transactions" (New York: American Institute of Certified Public Accountants, 1973); also see James B. Hobbs and D. R. Bainbridge, "Nonmonetary Exchange Transactions: Clarification of APB Opinion No. 29," *The Accounting Review* (January 1982).

face cases where both gains and losses are recognized (exchanges of dissimilar assets), where losses are recognized and gains are not (exchanges of similar assets), and where neither gains nor losses are recognized (exchanges of similar assets for income tax purposes). Since all these options are used in practice, they are all illustrated in the following paragraphs.

Loss Recognized on the Exchange   A loss is recognized for financial accounting purposes on all exchanges in which a material loss occurs. To illustrate the recognition of a loss, let us assume that the firm in our comprehensive example exchanges the machine for a newer, more modern machine on the following terms:

Price of new machine	$12,000
Trade-in allowance for old machine	(1,000)
Cash payment required	$11,000

In this case the trade-in allowance ($1,000) is less than the carrying value ($1,850) of the old machine. The loss on the exchange is $850 ($1,850 − $1,000). The following journal entry records this transaction under the assumption that the loss is to be recognized:

Sept. 30	Machinery (new)	12,000	
	Accumulated Depreciation, Machinery	4,650	
	Loss on Exchange of Machinery	850	
	Machinery (old)		6,500
	Cash		11,000
	Exchange of machines—cost of old machine and its accumulated depreciation removed from the records; new machine recorded at list price; loss recognized		

Loss Not Recognized on the Exchange   In the previous example, in which a loss was recognized, the new asset was recorded at the purchase price of $12,000 and a loss of $850 was recorded. If the transaction is for similar assets and is to be recorded for income tax purposes, the loss should not be recognized. In this case, the cost basis of the new asset will reflect the effect of the unrecorded loss. The cost basis is computed by adding the cash payment to the carrying value of the old asset:

Carrying value of old machine	$ 1,850
Cash paid	11,000
Cost basis of new machine	$12,850

Note that no loss is recognized in the entry to record this transaction:

Sept. 30	Machinery (new)	12,850	
	Accumulated Depreciation, Machinery	4,650	
	Machinery (old)		6,500
	Cash		11,000
	Exchange of machines—cost of old machine and its accumulated depreciation removed from the records; new machine recorded at amount equal to carrying value of old machine plus cash paid; no loss recognized		

Note that the new machinery is reported at the purchase price of $12,000 plus the unrecognized loss of $850. The nonrecognition of the loss on the exchange is, in effect, a postponement of the loss. Since depreciation of the new machine will be computed based on a cost of $12,850 instead of $12,000, the "unrecognized" loss results in more depreciation each year on a new machine than if the loss had been recognized.

Gain Recognized on the Exchange

Gains on exchanges are recognized for accounting purposes when dissimilar assets are exchanged. To illustrate the recognition of a gain, we continue with our example, assuming the following terms in which the machines being exchanged serve different functions:

Price of new machine	$12,000
Trade-in allowance for old machine	(3,000)
Cash payment required	$ 9,000

Here the trade-in allowance ($3,000) exceeds the carrying value ($1,850) of the old machine by $1,150. Thus, there is a gain on the exchange, assuming that the price of the new machine has not been inflated to allow for an excessive trade-in value. In other words, a gain exists if the trade-in allowance represents the fair market value of the old machine. Assuming that this condition is true, the entry to record the transaction is as follows:

Sept. 30	Machinery (new)	12,000	
	Accumulated Depreciation, Machinery	4,650	
	Gain on Exchange of Machinery		1,150
	Machinery (old)		6,500
	Cash		9,000
	Exchange of machines—cost of		
	old machine and its accumulated		
	depreciation removed from the		
	records; new machine recorded		
	at sales price; gain recognized		

Gain Not Recognized on the Exchange

A gain on an exchange should not be recognized in the accounting records if the machines perform similar functions. The cost basis of the new machine must indicate the effect of the unrecorded gain. This cost basis is computed by adding the cash payment to the carrying value of the old asset:

Carrying value of old machine	$ 1,850
Cash paid	9,000
Cost basis of new machine	$10,850

The entry to record the transaction is as follows:

Sept. 30	Machinery (new)	10,850	
	Accumulated Depreciation, Machinery	4,650	
	Machinery (old)		6,500
	Cash		9,000
	Exchange of machines—cost of		
	old machine and its accumulated		
	depreciation removed from the		
	records; new machine recorded at		
	amount equal to carrying value of		
	old machine plus cash paid; no		
	gain recognized		

As with the nonrecognition of losses, the nonrecognition of the gain on exchange is, in effect, a postponement of the gain. In the previous illustration, when the new machine is eventually discarded or sold, its cost basis will be $10,850 instead of its original price of $12,000. Since depreciation will be computed on the cost basis of $10,850, the "unrecognized" gain is reflected in less depreciation each year on new equipment than if the gain had been recognized.

ACCOUNTING FOR NATURAL RESOURCES

OBJECTIVE

7 *Identify natural resource accounting issues and compute depletion*

Natural resources are also known as *wasting assets.* Examples of natural resources are standing timber, oil and gas fields, and mineral deposits. The distinguishing characteristic of these wasting assets is that they are converted into inventory by cutting, pumping, or mining. For example, an oil field is a reservoir of unpumped oil, and a coal mine is a deposit of unmined coal.

Natural resources are shown on the balance sheet as long-term assets with such descriptive titles as Timber Lands, Oil and Gas Reserves, and Mineral Deposits. When the timber is cut, the oil is pumped, or the coal is mined, it becomes an inventory of the product to be sold. Natural resources are recorded at acquisition cost, which may also include some costs of development. As the resource is converted through the process of cutting, pumping, or mining, the asset account must be proportionally reduced. The carrying value of oil reserves on the balance sheet, for example, is reduced by a small amount for each barrel of oil pumped. As a result, the original cost of the oil reserves is gradually reduced, and depletion is recognized by the amount of the decrease.

DEPLETION

The term *depletion* is used to describe not only the exhaustion of a natural resource but also the proportional allocation of the cost of a natural resource to the units extracted. The costs are allocated in a way that is much like the production method used to calculate depreciation. When a natural resource is purchased or developed, there must be an estimate of the total units that will be available, such as barrels of oil, tons of coal, or board-feet of lumber. The depletion cost per unit is determined by dividing the cost (less residual value, if any) of the natural resource by the estimated number of units available. The amount of the depletion cost for each accounting period is then computed by multiplying the depletion cost per unit by the number of units pumped, mined, or cut. For example, for a mine having an estimated 1,500,000 tons of coal, a cost of $1,800,000, and an estimated residual value of $300,000, the depletion charge per ton of coal is $1. Thus, if 115,000 tons of coal are mined and sold during the first year, the depletion charge for the year is $115,000. This charge is recorded as follows:

Dec. 31	Depletion Expense, Coal Deposits	115,000	
	Accumulated Depletion, Coal Deposits		115,000
	To record depletion of coal mine:		
	$1 per ton for 115,000 tons mined		
	and sold		

On the balance sheet, the mine would be presented as follows:

Coal Deposits	$1,800,000	
Less Accumulated Depletion	115,000	$1,685,000

Sometimes a natural resource that is extracted in one year is not sold until a later year. It is important to note that it would then be recorded as a depletion *expense* in the year it is *sold*. The part not sold is considered inventory.

DEPRECIATION OF CLOSELY RELATED PLANT ASSETS

Natural resources often require special on-site buildings and equipment, such as conveyors, roads, tracks, and drilling and pumping devices that are necessary to extract the resource. If the useful life of these assets is longer than the estimated time it will take to deplete the resource, a special problem arises. Because these long-term assets are often abandoned and have no useful purpose once all the resources have been extracted, they should be depreciated on the same basis as the depletion is computed. For example, if machinery with a useful life of ten years is installed on an oil field that is expected to be depleted in eight years, the machinery should be depreciated over the eight-year period using the production method. In other words, each year's depreciation should be proportional to the year's depletion. If one-sixth of the oil field's total reserves is pumped in one year, then the depreciation should be one-sixth of the machinery's cost minus the scrap value. If the useful life of a long-term asset is less than the expected life of the depleting asset, the shorter life should be used to compute depreciation. In this case or when an asset is not to be abandoned when the reserves are fully depleted, other depreciation methods, such as the straight-line method or the declining-balance method, are appropriate.

DEVELOPMENT AND EXPLORATION COSTS IN THE OIL AND GAS INDUSTRY

The costs of exploration and development of oil and gas resources can be accounted for under either of two methods. Under successful efforts accounting, successful exploration—for example, the cost of a producing oil well—is a cost of the resource. This cost should be recorded as an asset and depleted over the estimated life of the resource. An unsuccessful exploration—such as the cost of a dry well—is written off immediately as a loss. Because of these immediate write-offs, successful efforts accounting is considered the more conservative method and is used by most large oil companies.

Exploration-minded independent oil companies, on the other hand, argue that the cost of the dry wells is part of the overall cost of the systematic development of the oil field and thus a part of the cost of producing wells. Under this full-costing method, all costs, including the cost of dry wells, are recorded as assets and depleted over the estimated life of the producing resources. This method tends to improve earnings performance in the early years for companies using it. Either method is permitted by the Financial Accounting Standards Board.[9]

9. *Statement of Financial Accounting Standards No. 25,* "Suspension of Certain Accounting Requirements for Oil and Gas Producing Companies" (Stamford, Conn.: Financial Accounting Standards Board, 1979).

U.S. Congress

DECISION POINT

Historically, intangible assets have not been considered very significant for either financial reporting or income taxes. Whether or not the amortization of intangibles was deductible in determining a company's income tax liability was not considered important. Write-offs of the costs of most intangibles have not been allowed for income tax purposes. However, in recent years, the U.S. Congress has been considering a change that would allow the write-off of most intangible assets over a period of fourteen years. Why is there a sudden interest in intangible assets?

Interest in the tax deductibility of the amortization of intangible assets has grown because companies are paying more for such assets. In the past the value of trademarks and other intangible assets tended to rise gradually as a company grew and prospered. Today, many intangible assets are purchased for high prices. This includes not only traditional intangible assets, such as trademarks and copyrights, but also newer assets, such as customer lists for mail order companies, takeoff and landing rights at busy airports, and cellular telephone licenses. During the 1980s, companies became more aggressive in writing off these expensive intangible assets, which led to numerous challenges by the Internal Revenue Service. The write-offs claimed by taxpayers for intangible assets grew from $45 billion in 1980 to $262 billion in 1987.[10] The growing financial significance of intangibles has increased their importance as an accounting issue, as shown in the following sections. ⦂⦂⦂⦂⦂

ACCOUNTING FOR INTANGIBLE ASSETS

OBJECTIVE

8 *Apply the matching rule to intangible assets, including research and development costs and goodwill*

The purchase of an intangible asset is a special kind of capital expenditure. An intangible asset is long term, but it has no physical substance. Its value comes from the long-term rights or advantages that it offers to the owner. Among the most common examples are patents, copyrights, leaseholds, leasehold improvements, trademarks and brand names, franchises, licenses, formulas, processes, and goodwill. Some current assets, such as accounts receivable and certain prepaid expenses, have no physical nature, but they are not classified as intangible assets because they are short term. Intangible assets are both long term and nonphysical.

Intangible assets are accounted for at acquisition cost, that is, the amount paid for them. Some intangible assets, such as goodwill and trademarks, may be acquired at little or no cost. Even though they may have great value and be needed for profitable operations, they should not appear on the balance sheet unless they have been purchased from another party at a price established in the marketplace.

10. Paul Merrion, "The Taxing Battle Over Intangibles," *Crain's Chicago Business,* October 14, 1991, p. 3.

The accounting issues connected with intangible assets are the same as those connected with other long-lived assets. The Accounting Principles Board, in its *Opinion No. 17*, lists them as follows:

1. Determining an initial carrying amount
2. Accounting for that amount after acquisition under normal business conditions—that is, through periodic write-off or amortization—in a manner similar to depreciation
3. Accounting for that amount if the value declines substantially and permanently[11]

Besides these three problems, an intangible asset has no physical qualities and so in some cases may be impossible to identify. For these reasons, its value and its useful life may be quite hard to estimate.

The Accounting Principles Board has decided that a company should record as assets the costs of intangible assets acquired from others. However, the company should record as expenses the costs of developing intangible assets. Also, intangible assets that have a determinable useful life, such as patents, copyrights, and leaseholds, should be written off through periodic amortization over that useful life in much the same way that plant assets are depreciated. Even though some intangible assets, such as goodwill and trademarks, have no measurable limit on their lives, they should also be amortized over a reasonable length of time (not to exceed forty years).

To illustrate these procedures, assume that Soda Bottling Company purchases a patent on a unique bottle cap for $18,000. The entry to record the patent would be as follows:

Patent	18,000	
Cash		18,000
Purchase of bottle cap patent		

Note that if Soda Bottling Company had developed the bottle cap internally instead of purchasing it from a third party, the costs of developing the cap, such as salaries of researchers, supplies used in testing, and costs of equipment, would have been expensed as incurred.

Assume now that Soda's management determines that, although the patent for the bottle cap will last for seventeen years, the product using the cap will be sold only for the next six years. The entry to record the annual amortization would be as follows:

Amortization Expense	3,000	
Patent		3,000
Annual amortization of patent		
$18,000 \div 6$ years $= \$3,000$		

Note that the Patent account is reduced directly by the amount of the amortization expense. This is in contrast to other long-term asset accounts in which depreciation or depletion is accumulated in a separate contra account.

If the patent becomes worthless before it is fully amortized, the remaining carrying value is written off as a loss. For instance, assume that after the first year Soda Bottling Company's chief competitor offers a bottle with a new type of cap that makes Soda's cap obsolete. The entry to record the loss is at the top of the next page.

11. Adapted from Accounting Principles Board, *Opinion No. 17*, "Intangible Assets" (New York: American Institute of Certified Public Accountants, 1970), par. 2.

Loss on Patent	15,000	
Patent		15,000
Loss resulting from patent's becoming worthless		

Accounting for several different types of intangible assets is outlined in Table 9-1.

Table 9-1. Accounting for Intangible Assets

Type	Description	Special Accounting Problems
Patent	An exclusive right granted by the federal government for a period of seventeen years to make a particular product or use a specific process.	The cost of successfully defending a patent in a patent infringement suit is added to the acquisition cost of the patent. Amortize over the useful life, which may be less than the legal life of seventeen years.
Copyright	An exclusive right granted by the federal government to the possessor to publish and sell literary, musical, and other artistic materials for a period of the author's life plus fifty years; includes computer programs.	Record at acquisition cost and amortize over the useful life, which is often much shorter than the legal life, but not to exceed forty years. For example, the cost of paperback rights to a popular novel would typically be amortized over a useful life of two to four years.
Leasehold	A right to occupy land or buildings under a long-term rental contract. For example, Company A, which owns but does not want to use a prime retail location, sells Company B the right to use it for ten years in return for one or more rental payments. Company B has purchased a leasehold.	Debit Leasehold for the amount of the rental payment, and amortize it over the remaining life of the lease. Payments to the lessor during the life of the lease should be debited to Lease Expense.
Leasehold improvements	Improvements to leased property that become the property of the lessor (the person who owns the property) at the end of the lease.	Debit Leasehold Improvements for the cost of improvements, and amortize the cost of the improvements over the remaining life of the lease.
Trademark, brand name	A registered symbol or name that can be used only by its owner to identify a product or service.	Debit the trademark or brand name for the acquisition cost, and amortize it over a reasonable life, not to exceed forty years.
Franchise, license	A right to an exclusive territory or to exclusive use of a formula, technique, process, or design.	Debit the franchise or license for the acquisition cost, and amortize it over a reasonable life, not to exceed forty years.
Goodwill	The excess of the cost of a group of assets (usually a business) over the fair market value of the net assets if purchased individually.	Debit Goodwill for the acquisition cost, and amortize it over a reasonable life, not to exceed forty years.

One of the most valuable intangible assets some companies have is a list of subscribers. For example, the Newark Morning Ledger Co., a newspaper chain, purchased a chain of Michigan newspapers whose list of 460,000 subscribers was valued at $68 million. In a 1993 decision, the Supreme Court upheld the company's right to amortize the value of the subscribers list because the company showed that the list had a limited useful life. The Internal Revenue Service had argued that the list had an indefinite life and therefore could not provide tax deductions through amortization. This ruling will benefit other types of businesses that purchase everything from bank deposits to pharmacy prescription files.[12] ═══

RESEARCH AND DEVELOPMENT COSTS

Most successful companies carry out activities, possibly within a separate department, involving research and development. Among these activities are development of new products, testing of existing and proposed products, and pure research. In the past, some companies would record as an asset those costs of research and development that could be directly traced to the development of specific patents, formulas, or other rights. Other costs, such as those for testing and pure research, were treated as expenses of the accounting period and deducted from income.

The Financial Accounting Standards Board has stated that all research and development costs should be treated as revenue expenditures and charged to expense in the period when incurred.[13] The board argues that it is too hard to trace specific costs to specific profitable developments. Also, the costs of research and development are continuous and necessary for the success of a business and so should be treated as current expenses. To support this conclusion, the board cites studies showing that 30 to 90 percent of all new products fail and that three-fourths of new-product expenses go to unsuccessful products. Thus, their costs do not represent future benefits.

COMPUTER SOFTWARE COSTS

Many companies develop computer programs or software to be sold or leased to individuals and companies. The costs incurred in creating a computer software product are considered research and development costs until the product has been proved to be technologically feasible. As a result, costs incurred to that point in the process should be charged to expense as incurred. A product is deemed to be technologically feasible when a detailed working program has been designed. After the working program has been developed, all software production costs are recorded as assets and amortized over the estimated economic life of the product using the straight-line method. If at

---

12. "What's In a Name?" *Time,* May 3, 1993.
13. *Statement of Financial Accounting Standards No. 2,* "Accounting for Research and Development Costs" (Stamford, Conn.: Financial Accounting Standards Board, 1974), par. 12.

any time the company cannot expect to realize from a software product the amount of its unamortized costs on the balance sheet, the asset should be written down to the amount expected to be realized.[14]

BUSINESS BULLETIN: BUSINESS PRACTICE

Research and development expenditures can be substantial for many companies. For example, General Motors and IBM spent $5.9 billion and $5.1 billion, respectively, on research and development in 1992. Those amounts are about 5 percent of the companies' revenues. Research and development can be even costlier in high-tech fields like biotechnology, where Genentech and Biogen spent 54.4 percent and 48.8 percent, respectively, of revenues.[15] The pharmaceutical industry also invests heavily in research and development. It is estimated that a new drug can cost from $125 million to $500 million before taxes to bring to market.[16] Which of these costs are capitalized and amortized and which must be expensed immediately are obviously important questions for both the management and the stockholders of these companies. ═══

GOODWILL

The term goodwill is widely used by business people, lawyers, and the public to mean different things. In most cases goodwill is taken to mean the good reputation of a company. From an accounting standpoint, goodwill exists when a purchaser pays more for a business than the fair market value of the net assets if purchased separately. Because the purchaser has paid more than the fair market value of the physical assets, there must be intangible assets. If the company being purchased does not have patents, copyrights, trademarks, or other identifiable intangible assets of value, the excess payment is assumed to be for goodwill. Goodwill exists because most businesses are worth more as going concerns than as collections of assets. Goodwill reflects all the factors that allow a company to earn a higher-than-market rate of return on its assets, including customer satisfaction, good management, manufacturing efficiency, the advantages of holding a monopoly, good locations, and good employee relations. The payment above and beyond the fair market value of the tangible assets and other specific intangible assets is properly recorded in the Goodwill account.

In *Opinion No. 17*, the Accounting Principles Board states that the benefits arising from purchased goodwill will in time disappear. It is hard for a company to keep having above-average earnings unless new factors of goodwill replace the old ones. For this reason, goodwill should be amortized or written

---

14. *Statement of Financial Accounting Standards No. 86,* "Accounting for the Costs of Computer Software to Be Sold, Leased, or Otherwise Marketed" (Stamford, Conn.: Financial Accounting Standards Board, 1985).
15. "R&D's Biggest Spenders," *Business Week,* June 28, 1993.
16. George Anders, "Vital Statistic: Disputed Cost of Creating a Drug," *Wall Street Journal,* November 9, 1993.

off by systematic charges to income over a reasonable number of future time periods. The total time period should in no case be more than forty years.[17]

Goodwill, as stated, should not be recorded unless it is paid for in connection with the purchase of a whole business. The amount to be recorded as goodwill can be determined by writing the identifiable net assets up to their fair market values at the time of purchase and subtracting the total from the purchase price. For example, assume that the owners of Company A agree to sell the company for $11,400,000. If the net assets (total assets − total liabilities) are fairly valued at $10,000,000, then the amount of the goodwill is $1,400,000 ($11,400,000 − $10,000,000). If the fair market value of the net assets is later determined to be more or less than $10,000,000, an entry is made in the accounting records to adjust the assets to the fair market value. The goodwill would then represent the difference between the adjusted net assets and the purchase price of $11,400,000.

Supplemental OBJECTIVE

9 *Apply depreciation methods to problems of partial years, revised rates, groups of similar items, special types of capital expenditures, and cost recovery*

SPECIAL PROBLEMS OF DEPRECIATING PLANT ASSETS

The illustrations used so far in this chapter have been simplified to explain the concepts and methods of depreciation. In real business practice, there is often a need to (1) calculate depreciation for partial years, (2) revise depreciation rates on the basis of new estimates of the useful life or residual value, (3) group together items that are alike in order to calculate depreciation, (4) account for special types of capital expenditures, and (5) use the accelerated cost recovery method for tax purposes. The next sections discuss these five cases.

DEPRECIATION FOR PARTIAL YEARS

So far, the illustrations of the depreciation methods have assumed that the plant assets were purchased at the beginning or end of the accounting period. However, businesses do not often buy assets exactly at the beginning or end of the accounting period. In most cases, they buy the assets when they are needed and sell or discard them when they are no longer useful or needed. The time of year is normally not a factor in the decision. Consequently, it is often necessary to calculate depreciation for partial years.

For example, assume that a piece of equipment is purchased for $3,500 and that it has an estimated useful life of six years, and an estimated residual value of $500. Assume also that it is purchased on September 5 and that the yearly accounting period ends on December 31. Depreciation must be recorded for four months, September through December, or four-twelfths of the year. This factor is applied to the calculated depreciation for the entire year. The four months' depreciation under the straight-line method is calculated as follows:

$$\frac{\$3,500 - \$500}{6 \text{ years}} \times \frac{4}{12} = \$167$$

For the other depreciation methods, most companies will compute the first year's depreciation and then multiply by the partial year factor. For example,

17. Accounting Principles Board, *Opinion No. 17*, par. 29.

if the company used the double-declining-balance method on the above equipment, the depreciation on the asset would be computed as follows:

$$\$3,500 \times .33 \times 4/12 = \$385$$

Typically, the depreciation calculation is rounded off to the nearest whole month because a partial month's depreciation is not usually material and the calculation is easier. In this case, depreciation was recorded from the beginning of September even though the purchase was made on September 5. If the equipment had been purchased on September 16 or thereafter, depreciation would be charged beginning October 1, as if the equipment were purchased on that date. Some companies round off all partial years to the nearest one-half year for ease of calculation (half-year convention).

For all methods, the remainder (eight-twelfths) of the first year's depreciation is recorded in the next annual accounting period together with four-twelfths of the second year's depreciation.

REVISION OF DEPRECIATION RATES

Because a depreciation rate is based on an estimate of an asset's useful life, the periodic depreciation charge is seldom precisely accurate. Sometimes it is very inadequate or excessive. This situation may result from an underestimate or overestimate of the asset's useful life or from a wrong estimate of the residual value. What action should be taken when it is found, after several years of use, that a piece of equipment will not last as long as—or will last longer than—originally thought? Sometimes it is necessary to revise the estimate of useful life, so that the periodic depreciation expense increases or decreases. Then, to correct the situation, the remaining depreciable cost of the asset is spread over the remaining years of useful life.

With this technique, the annual depreciation expense is increased or decreased to reduce the asset's carrying value to its residual value at the end of its remaining useful life. To illustrate, assume that a delivery truck was purchased for a price of $7,000, with a residual value of $1,000. At the time of the purchase, the truck was expected to last six years, and it was depreciated on the straight-line basis. However, after two years of intensive use, it is determined that the delivery truck will last only two more years, but that the estimated residual value at the end of the two years will still be $1,000. In other words, at the end of the second year, the estimated useful life is reduced from six years to four years. At that time, the asset account and its related accumulated depreciation account would appear as follows:

Delivery Truck		Accumulated Depreciation, Delivery Truck	
Cost 7,000		Depreciation, year 1	1,000
		Depreciation, year 2	1,000

The remaining depreciable cost is computed as follows:

cost	minus	depreciation already taken	minus	residual value	
$7,000	−	$2,000	−	$1,000	= $4,000

The new annual periodic depreciation charge is computed by dividing the remaining depreciable cost of $4,000 by the remaining useful life of two years. Therefore, the new periodic depreciation charge is $2,000. The annual adjusting entry for depreciation for the next two years would be as follows:

Dec. 31	Depreciation Expense, Delivery Truck	2,000
	Accumulated Depreciation, Delivery Truck	2,000
	To record depreciation expense for the year	

This method of revising depreciation is used widely in industry. It is also supported by the Accounting Principles Board of the AICPA in Accounting Principles Board *Opinion No. 9* and *Opinion No. 20.*

GROUP DEPRECIATION

To say that the estimated useful life of an asset, such as a piece of equipment, is six years means that the average piece of equipment of that type is expected to last six years. In reality, some equipment may last only two or three years, and other equipment may last eight or nine years, or longer. For this reason, and for reasons of convenience, large companies will group similar items, such as trucks, power lines, office equipment, or transformers, for purposes of calculating depreciation. This method is called group depreciation. Group depreciation is used widely in all fields of industry and business. A survey of large businesses indicated that 65 percent used group depreciation for all or part of their plant assets.[18]

SPECIAL TYPES OF CAPITAL EXPENDITURES

In addition to the acquisition of plant assets, natural resources, and intangible assets, capital expenditures also include additions and betterments. An addition is an enlargement to the physical layout of a plant asset. If a new wing is added to a building, the benefits from the expenditure will be received over several years, and the amount paid for it should be debited to the asset account. A betterment is an improvement that does not add to the physical layout of the asset. Installation of an air-conditioning system is an example of a betterment that will offer benefits over a period of years, so its cost should be charged to an asset account.

Among the more usual kinds of revenue expenditures for plant equipment are the repairs, maintenance, lubrication, cleaning, and inspection necessary to keep an asset in good working condition. Repairs fall into two categories: ordinary repairs and extraordinary repairs. Ordinary repairs are expenditures that are necessary to maintain an asset in good operating condition. Trucks must have tune-ups, their tires and batteries must be replaced regularly, and other routine repairs must be made. Offices and halls must be painted regularly, and broken tiles or woodwork must be replaced. Such repairs are a current expense.

Extraordinary repairs are repairs of a more significant nature—they affect the estimated residual value or estimated useful life of an asset. For example, a boiler for heating a building may be given a complete overhaul, at a cost of several thousand dollars, that will extend its useful life by five years.

---

18. Edward P. McTague, "Accounting for Trade-Ins of Operational Assets," *The National Public Accountant* (January 1986), p. 39.

Typically, extraordinary repairs are recorded by debiting the Accumulated Depreciation account, under the assumption that some of the depreciation previously recorded has now been eliminated. The effect of this reduction in the Accumulated Depreciation account is to increase the carrying value of the asset by the cost of the extraordinary repair. Consequently, the new carrying value of the asset should be depreciated over the new estimated useful life.

Let us assume that a machine costing $10,000 had no estimated residual value and an original estimated useful life of ten years. After eight years, the accumulated depreciation under the straight-line method was $8,000, and the carrying value was $2,000 ($10,000 − $8,000). At that point, the machine was given a major overhaul costing $1,500. This expenditure extended the useful life three years beyond the original ten years. The entry for the extraordinary repair would be as follows:

Jan. 4	Accumulated Depreciation, Machinery	1,500	
	Cash		1,500
	Extraordinary repair		
	to machinery		

The annual periodic depreciation for each of the five years remaining in the machine's useful life would be calculated as follows:

Carrying value before extraordinary repairs	$2,000
Extraordinary repairs	1,500
Total	$3,500

$$\text{Annual periodic depreciation} = \frac{\$3,500}{5 \text{ years}} = \$700$$

If the machine remains in use for the five years expected after the major overhaul, the total of the annual depreciation charges of $700 will exactly equal the new carrying value, including the cost of the extraordinary repair.

COST RECOVERY FOR FEDERAL INCOME TAX PURPOSES

In 1986, Congress passed the Tax Reform Act of 1986, arguably the most sweeping revision of federal tax laws since the original enactment of the Internal Revenue Code in 1913. The new Modified Accelerated Cost Recovery System (MACRS) discards the concepts of estimated useful life and residual value. Instead, it requires that a cost recovery allowance be computed (1) on the unadjusted cost of property being recovered, and (2) over a period of years prescribed by the law for all property of similar types. The accelerated method prescribed under MACRS for most property other than real estate is 200 percent declining balance with a half-year convention (only one half-year's depreciation is allowed in the year of purchase, and one half-year is taken in the last year). In addition, the period over which the cost may be recovered is specified. Recovery of the cost of property placed in service after December 31, 1986 is calculated as prescribed in the 1986 law.

Congress hoped that MACRS would encourage businesses to invest in new plant and equipment by allowing them to write the assets off rapidly. MACRS accelerates the write-off of these investments in two ways. First, the prescribed recovery periods are often shorter than the estimated useful lives used for calculating depreciation for the financial statements. Second, the accelerated method allowed under the new law enables businesses to recover most of the cost of their investments early in the depreciation process.

Tax methods of depreciation are not usually acceptable for financial reporting under generally accepted accounting principles because the recovery periods are shorter than the depreciable assets' estimated useful lives. Accounting for the differences between tax and book depreciation is discussed in the chapter on retained earnings and corporate income statements.

CHAPTER REVIEW

REVIEW OF LEARNING OBJECTIVES

1. **Identify the types of long-term assets and explain the management issues related to accounting for them.** Long-term assets are assets that are used in the operation of a business, are not intended for resale, and have a useful life of more than one year. Long-term assets are either tangible or intangible. In the former category are land, plant assets, and natural resources. In the latter are trademarks, patents, franchises, goodwill, and other rights. The issues associated with accounting for long-term assets relate to the decision to acquire the assets, the means of financing the assets, and the methods of accounting for the assets.

2. **Distinguish between capital and revenue expenditures, and account for the cost of property, plant, and equipment.** It is important to distinguish between capital expenditures, which are recorded as assets, and revenue expenditures, which are recorded as expenses. The error of classifying one as the other will have an important effect on net income. The acquisition cost of property, plant, and equipment includes all expenditures that are reasonable and necessary to get the asset in place and ready for use. These expenditures include such payments as purchase price, installation cost, freight charges, and insurance.

3. **Define *depreciation*, state the factors that affect its computation, and show how to record it.** Depreciation is the periodic allocation of the cost of a plant asset over its estimated useful life. It is recorded by debiting Depreciation Expense and crediting a related contra-asset account called Accumulated Depreciation. Factors that affect the computation of depreciation are cost, residual value, depreciable cost, and estimated useful life.

4. **Compute periodic depreciation under the (a) straight-line method, (b) production method, and (c) declining-balance method.** Depreciation is commonly computed by the straight-line method, the production method, or an accelerated method. The straight-line method is related directly to the passage of time, whereas the production method is related directly to use. An accelerated method, which results in relatively large amounts of depreciation in the early years and reduced amounts in later years, is based on the assumption that plant assets provide greater economic benefit in their early years than in later years. The most common accelerated method is the declining-balance method.

5. **Account for disposal of depreciable assets not involving exchanges.** Long-term assets may be disposed of by being discarded, sold, or exchanged. When long-term assets are disposed of, it is necessary to record the depreciation up to the date of disposal and to remove the carrying value from the accounts by removing the cost from the asset account and the depreciation to date from the accumulated depreciation account. If a long-term asset is sold at a price that differs from its carrying value, there is a gain or loss that should be recorded and reported on the income statement.

6. **Account for disposal of depreciable assets involving exchanges.** In recording exchanges of similar plant assets, a gain or loss may also arise. According to the Accounting Principles Board, losses, but not gains, should be recognized at the

time of the exchange. When a gain is not recognized, the new asset is recorded at the carrying value of the old asset plus any cash paid. For income tax purposes, neither gains nor losses are recognized in the exchange of similar assets. When dissimilar assets are exchanged, gains and losses are recognized under both accounting and income tax rules.

7. **Identify natural resource accounting issues and compute depletion.** Natural resources are wasting assets that are converted to inventory by cutting, pumping, mining, or other forms of extraction. Natural resources are recorded at cost as long-term assets. They are allocated as expenses through depletion charges as the resources are sold. The depletion charge is based on the ratio of the resource extracted to the total estimated resource. A major issue related to this subject is accounting for oil and gas reserves.

8. **Apply the matching rule to intangible assets, including research and development costs and goodwill.** The purchase of an intangible asset should be treated as a capital expenditure and recorded at acquisition cost, which in turn should be amortized over the useful life of the asset (limited by the type of intangible asset). The FASB requires that research and development costs be treated as revenue expenditures and charged as expenses in the periods of the expenditures. Software costs are treated as research and development costs and expensed until a feasible working program is developed, after which time the costs may be capitalized and amortized over a reasonable estimated life. Goodwill is the excess of the amount paid over the fair market value of the net assets in the purchase of a business and is usually related to the superior earning potential of the business. It should be recorded only if paid for in connection with the purchase of a business, and it should be amortized over a period not to exceed forty years.

SUPPLEMENTAL OBJECTIVE

9. **Apply depreciation methods to problems of partial years, revised rates, groups of similar items, special types of capital expenditures, and cost recovery.** In actual business practice, many factors affect depreciation calculations. It may be necessary to calculate depreciation for partial years because assets are bought and sold throughout the year, or to revise depreciation rates because of changed conditions. Because it is often difficult to estimate the useful life of a single item, and because it is more convenient, many large businesses group similar items for purposes of depreciation. Companies must also consider certain special capital expenditures when calculating depreciation. For example, expenditures for additions and betterments are capital expenditures. Extraordinary repairs, which increase the residual value or extend the life of an asset, are also treated as capital expenditures, but ordinary repairs are revenue expenditures. For income tax purposes, rapid write-offs of depreciable assets are allowed through the Modified Accelerated Cost Recovery System. Such rapid write-offs are not usually acceptable for financial accounting because the shortened recovery periods violate the matching rule.

REVIEW OF CONCEPTS AND TERMINOLOGY

The following concepts and terms were introduced in this chapter:

L O 4 **Accelerated method:** A method of depreciation that allocates relatively large amounts of the depreciable cost of an asset to earlier years and reduced amounts to later years.

S O 9 **Addition:** An enlargement to the physical layout of a plant asset.

L O 1 **Amortization:** The periodic allocation of the cost of an intangible asset over its useful life.

S O 9 **Betterment:** An improvement that does not add to the physical layout of a plant asset.

L O 8 **Brand name:** A registered name that can be used only by its owner to identify a product or service.

L O 2 **Capital expenditure:** An expenditure for the purchase or expansion of a long-term asset, recorded in the asset accounts.

L O 1   **Carrying value:** The unexpired part of the cost of an asset. Also called *book value.*

L O 8   **Copyright:** An exclusive right granted by the federal government to the possessor to publish and sell literary, musical, and other artistic materials for a period of the author's life plus fifty years; includes computer programs.

L O 4   **Declining-balance method:** An accelerated method of depreciation in which depreciation is computed by applying a fixed rate to the carrying value (the declining balance) of a tangible long-lived asset.

L O 1   **Depletion:** The exhaustion of a natural resource through mining, cutting, pumping, or other extraction, and the way in which the cost is allocated.

L O 3   **Depreciable cost:** The cost of an asset less its residual value.

L O 1   **Depreciation:** The periodic allocation of the cost of a tangible long-lived asset (other than land and natural resources) over its estimated useful life.

L O 4   **Double-declining-balance method:** An accelerated method of depreciation in which a fixed rate percentage equal to twice the straight-line percentage is applied to the carrying value of a tangible long-term asset.

L O 3   **Estimated useful life:** The total number of service units expected from a long-term asset.

L O 2   **Expenditure:** A payment or an obligation to make future payment for an asset or a service received.

S O 9   **Extraordinary repairs:** Repairs that affect the estimated residual value or estimated useful life of an asset.

L O 8   **Franchise:** The right to an exclusive territory or market.

L O 7   **Full-costing:** A method of accounting for the costs of exploration and development of oil and gas resources in which all costs are recorded as assets and depleted over the estimated life of the producing resources.

L O 8   **Goodwill:** The excess of the cost of a group of assets (usually a business) over the market value of the net assets if purchased individually.

S O 9   **Group depreciation:** The grouping of similar items for purposes of calculating depreciation.

L O 1   **Intangible assets:** Long-term assets that have no physical substance but have a value based on rights or advantages accruing to the owner.

L O 8   **Leasehold:** A right to occupy land or buildings under a long-term rental contract.

L O 8   **Leasehold improvements:** Improvements to leased property that become the property of the lessor at the end of the lease.

L O 8   **License:** Official or legal permission to do or own a specific thing.

L O 1   **Long-term assets:** Assets that (1) have a useful life of more than one year, (2) are acquired for use in the operation of a business, and (3) are not intended for resale to customers. Less commonly called *fixed assets.*

S O 9   **Modified Accelerated Cost Recovery System (MACRS):** A mandatory system enacted by Congress in 1986 that requires that a cost recovery allowance be computed (1) on the unadjusted cost of property being recovered, and (2) over a period of years prescribed by the law for all property of similar types.

L O 1   **Natural resources:** Long-term assets purchased for the physical substances that can be taken from the land and used up rather than for the value of their location. Also called *wasting assets.*

L O 3   **Obsolescence:** The process of becoming out of date; a contributor, together with physical deterioration, to the limited useful life of tangible assets.

S O 9   **Ordinary repairs:** Expenditures, usually of a recurring nature, that are necessary to maintain an asset in good operating condition.

L O 8   **Patent:** An exclusive right granted by the federal government for a period of seventeen years to make a particular product or use a specific process.

L O 3   **Physical deterioration:** Limitations on the useful life of a depreciable asset resulting from use and from exposure to the elements.

L O 4   **Production method:** A method of depreciation that bases the depreciation charge for a period of time solely on the amount of the asset's use during the period of time.

L O 3   **Residual value:** The estimated net scrap, salvage, or trade-in value of a tangible asset at the estimated date of disposal. Also called *salvage value* or *disposal value.*

L O 2   **Revenue expenditure:** An expenditure for repairs, maintenance, or other services needed to maintain or operate plant assets, recorded by a debit to an expense account.

L O 4   **Straight-line method:** A method of depreciation that assumes that depreciation depends only on the passage of time and that allocates an equal amount of depreciation to each period of time.

L O 7   **Successful efforts accounting:** A method of accounting for oil and gas resources in which successful exploration is recorded as an asset and depleted over the estimated life of the resource and all unsuccessful efforts are immediately written off as a loss.

L O 1   **Tangible assets:** Long-term assets that have physical substance.

L O 8   **Trademark:** A registered symbol that can be used only by its owner to identify a product or service.

REVIEW PROBLEM

COMPARISON OF DEPRECIATION METHODS

L O 3, 4   Norton Construction Company purchased a cement mixer on January 1, 19x1 for $14,500. The mixer is expected to have a useful life of five years and a residual value of $1,000. The company engineers estimate that the mixer will have a useful life of 7,500 hours. It was used 1,500 hours in 19x1, 2,625 hours in 19x2, 2,250 hours in 19x3, 750 hours in 19x4, and 375 hours in 19x5. The company's year end is December 31.

REQUIRED

1. Compute the depreciation expense and carrying value for 19x1 to 19x5, using the following three methods: (a) straight-line, (b) production, and (c) double-declining-balance.
2. Prepare the adjusting entry to record the depreciation for 19x1 calculated in **1 (a).**
3. Show the balance sheet presentation for the cement mixer after the entry in **2** on December 31, 19x1.
4. What conclusions can you draw from the patterns of yearly depreciation?

ANSWER TO REVIEW PROBLEM

1. Depreciation computed:

Depreciation Method	Year	Computation	Depreciation	Carrying Value
a. Straight-line	19x1	$13,500 × 1/5	$2,700	$11,800
	19x2	13,500 × 1/5	2,700	9,100
	19x3	13,500 × 1/5	2,700	6,400
	19x4	13,500 × 1/5	2,700	3,700
	19x5	13,500 × 1/5	2,700	1,000
b. Production	19x1	$13,500 × $\frac{1,500}{7,500}$	$2,700	$11,800
	19x2	13,500 × $\frac{2,625}{7,500}$	4,725	7,075
	19x3	13,500 × $\frac{2,250}{7,500}$	4,050	3,025
	19x4	13,500 × $\frac{750}{7,500}$	1,350	1,675
	19x5	13,500 × $\frac{375}{7,500}$	675	1,000

Depreciation Method	Year	Computation	Depreciation	Carrying Value
c. Double-declining-balance	19x1	$14,500 × .4	$5,800	$8,700
	19x2	8,700 × .4	3,480	5,220
	19x3	5,220 × .4	2,088	3,132
	19x4	3,132 × .4	1,253*	1,879
	19x5		879*†	1,000

*Rounded.

†Remaining depreciation to reduce carrying value to residual value ($1,879 − $1,000 = $879).

2. Adjusting entry prepared—straight-line method:

19x1

Dec. 31	Depreciation Expense, Cement Mixer	2,700	
	Accumulated Depreciation, Cement Mixer		2,700
	To record depreciation expense, straight-line method		

3. Balance sheet presentation for 19x1 shown:

Cement Mixer	$14,500
Less Accumulated Depreciation	2,700
	$11,800

4. Conclusions drawn from depreciation patterns: The pattern of depreciation for the straight-line method differs significantly from that for the double-declining-balance method. In the early years, the depreciation using the double-declining-balance method is significantly more than that using the straight-line method. In the later years, the opposite is true. The carrying value under the straight-line method is greater than that under the double-declining-balance method in all years except at the end of the fifth year. Depreciation under the production method differs from that under the other methods in that it follows no regular pattern. It varies with the amount of use. Consequently, depreciation is greatest in 19x2 and 19x3, which are the years of greatest use. Use declined significantly in the last two years.

CHAPTER ASSIGNMENTS

KNOWLEDGE AND UNDERSTANDING

Questions

1. What are the characteristics of long-term assets?
2. Which of the following items would be classified as plant assets on the balance sheet? (a) A truck held for sale by a truck dealer, (b) an office building that was once the company headquarters but is now to be sold, (c) a typewriter used by a secretary of the company, (d) a machine that is used in manufacturing operations but is now fully depreciated, (e) pollution-control equipment that does not reduce the cost or improve the efficiency of a factory, (f) a parking lot for company employees.
3. Why is land different from other long-term assets?
4. What do accountants mean by the term *depreciation,* and what is its relationship to depletion and amortization?
5. How do cash flows relate to the decisions on acquiring long-term assets and how does the useful life of the assets relate to the means of financing them?
6. Why is it useful to think of a plant asset as a bundle of services?

7. What is the distinction between revenue expenditures and capital expenditures, and what in general is included in the cost of a long-term asset?

8. Which of the following expenditures incurred in connection with the purchase of a computer system would be charged to the asset account? (a) The purchase price of the equipment, (b) interest on the debt incurred to purchase the equipment, (c) freight charges, (d) installation charges, (e) the cost of special communications outlets at the computer site, (f) the cost of repairing a door that was damaged during installation, (g) the cost of adjustments to the system during the first month of operation.

9. Hale's Grocery obtained bids on the construction of a dock for receiving goods at the back of its store. The lowest bid was $22,000. The company decided to build the dock itself, however, and was able to do it for $20,000, which it borrowed. The activity was recorded as a debit to Buildings for $22,000 and credits to Notes Payable for $20,000 and Gain on Construction for $2,000. Do you agree with the entry?

10. A firm buys a piece of technical equipment that is expected to last twelve years. Why might the equipment have to be depreciated over a shorter period of time?

11. A company purchased a building five years ago. The market value of the building is now greater than it was when the building was purchased. Explain why the company should continue depreciating the building.

12. Evaluate the following statement: "A parking lot should not be depreciated because adequate repairs will make it last forever."

13. Is the purpose of depreciation to determine the value of equipment? Explain your answer.

14. Contrast the assumptions underlying the straight-line depreciation method with the assumptions underlying the production depreciation method.

15. What is the principal argument supporting an accelerated depreciation method?

16. If a plant asset is sold during the year, why should depreciation be computed for the partial year prior to the date of the sale?

17. If a plant asset is discarded before the end of its useful life, how is the amount of loss measured?

18. When similar assets are exchanged, at what amount is the new asset recorded for federal income tax purposes?

19. When an exchange of similar assets occurs in which there is an unrecorded loss, is the taxpayer ever able to deduct or receive federal income tax credit for the loss?

20. Old Stake Mining Company computes the depletion rate of ore to be $2 per ton. During 19xx the company mined 400,000 tons of ore and sold 370,000 tons. What is the total depletion for the year?

21. Under what circumstances can a mining company depreciate its plant assets over a period of time that is less than their useful lives?

22. Because accounts receivable have no physical substance, can they be classified as intangible assets?

23. Under what circumstances can a company have intangible assets that do not appear on the balance sheet?

24. When the Accounting Principles Board indicates that accounting for intangible assets involves the same issues as accounting for tangible assets, what issues is it referring to?

25. How does the Financial Accounting Standards Board recommend that research and development costs be treated?

26. Archi Draw Company spent three years developing a new software program for designing office buildings and recently completed the detailed working program. How does accounting for the costs of software development differ before and after the completion of a successful working program?

27. How is accounting for software development costs similar to and different from accounting for research and development costs?

28. Under what conditions should goodwill be recorded? Should it remain in the records permanently once it is recorded?
29. What basic procedure should be followed in revising a depreciation rate?
30. On what basis can depreciation be taken on a group of assets rather than on individual items?
31. What will be the effect on future years' income of charging an addition to a building to repair expense?
32. In what ways do an addition, a betterment, and an extraordinary repair differ?
33. How does an extraordinary repair differ from an ordinary repair? What is the accounting treatment for each?
34. What is the difference between depreciation for accounting purposes and the Modified Accelerated Cost Recovery System for income tax purposes?

Short Exercises

SE 9-1.
L O 1 *Management Issues*

Indicate whether each of the following actions is primarily related to (a) acquisition of long-term assets, (b) financing of long-term assets, or (c) choosing methods and estimates related to long-term assets.

1. Deciding between common stock and long-term notes for the raising of funds.
2. Relating the acquisition cost of a long-term asset to cash flows generated by the asset.
3. Determining how long an asset will benefit the company.
4. Deciding to use cash flows from operations to purchase long-term assets.
5. Determining how much an asset will sell for when it is no longer useful to the company.

SE 9-2.
L O 2 *Determining Cost of Long-Term Assets*

Haines Auto, Inc. purchased a neighboring lot for a new building and parking lot. Indicate whether each of the following expenditures is properly charged to (a) Land, (b) Land Improvements, or (c) Buildings.

1. Paving costs
2. Architects' fee for building design
3. Cost of clearing the property
4. Cost of the property
5. Structure construction costs
6. Lights around the property
7. Building permit
8. Interest on the construction loan

SE 9-3.
L O 2 *Group Purchase*

Rezaki Company purchased property with a warehouse and parking lot for $750,000. An appraiser valued the property if purchased separately as follows:

Land	$200,000
Land improvements	100,000
Building	500,000
Total	$800,000

Determine the amount of cost to be assigned to each component.

SE 9-4.
L O 4 *Straight-Line Method*

Hubbard Woods Fitness Center, Inc. purchased a new step machine for $5,500. The apparatus is expected to last four years and have a residual value of $500. What will be the depreciation expense for each year using the straight-line method?

SE 9-5.
L O 4 *Production Method*

Assuming that the step machine in SE 9-4 has an estimated useful life of 8,000 hours and was used 2,400 hours in year 1, 2,000 hours in year 2, 2,200 hours in year 3, and 1,400 hours in year 4, how much would depreciation expense be in each year?

SE 9-6.
L O 4 *Double-Declining-Balance Method*

Assuming that the step machine in SE 9-4 is depreciated using the declining-balance method at double the straight-line rate, how much would depreciation expense be in each year?

SE 9-7.

L O 5 *Disposal of Plant Assets: No Trade-In*

Shanequa Printing, Inc. had a piece of equipment that cost $8,100 and on which $4,500 of accumulated depreciation had been recorded. The equipment was disposed of on January 4, the first day of business of the current year. Give the journal entries to record the disposal under each of the following assumptions:

1. It was discarded as having no value.
2. It was sold for $1,500 cash.
3. It was sold for $4,000 cash.

SE 9-8.

L O 6 *Disposal of Plant Assets: Trade-In*

Give the journal entries to record the disposal referred to in SE 9-7 under the following assumptions:

1. The equipment was traded in on dissimilar equipment having a list price of $12,000. A $3,800 trade-in was allowed, and the balance was paid in cash. Gains and losses are to be recognized.
2. The equipment was traded in on dissimilar equipment having a list price of $12,000. A $1,750 trade-in was allowed, and the balance was paid in cash. Gains and losses are to be recognized.
3. Same as **2**, except that the items are similar and gains and losses are not to be recognized.

SE 9-9.

L O 7 *Natural Resources*

Tulsa Corp. purchased land containing an estimated 4,000,000 tons of ore for $8,000,000. The land will be worth $1,200,000 without the ore after the eight-year period in which the mining is expected to be active. Although equipment needed for the mining will have a useful life of twenty years, it is not expected to be usable and will have no value after the mining on this site is complete. Compute the depletion charge per ton and the amount of depletion expense for the first year of operation, assuming that 600,000 tons of ore were mined and sold. Also, compute the first-year depreciation on the mining equipment using the straight-line method, assuming a cost of $9,600,000 with no residual value.

SE 9-10.

L O 8 *Intangible Assets: Computer Software*

Beta-Micro created a new software application for PCs. Its costs in the research and development stage were $500,000, and its costs after the working program was developed were $350,000. Although the copyright lasts longer, management believes that the product will be viable for only five years. How should the costs be accounted for? At what value will the software appear on the balance sheet after one year?

APPLICATION

Exercises

E 9-1.

L O 1 *Management Issues*

Indicate whether each of the following actions is primarily related to (a) acquisition of long-term assets, (b) financing of long-term assets, or (c) choosing methods and estimates related to long-term assets.

1. Deciding to use the production method of depreciation.
2. Allocating costs on a group purchase.
3. Determining the total units a machine will produce.
4. Deciding to borrow funds to purchase equipment.
5. Estimating the savings a new machine will produce and comparing the amount to cost.
6. Deciding whether to rent or buy a piece of equipment.

E 9-2.

L O 2 *Determining Cost of Long-Term Assets*

Decatur Manufacturing purchased land next to its factory to be used as a parking lot. Expenditures incurred by the company were as follows: purchase price, $150,000; broker's fees, $12,000; title search and other fees, $1,100; demolition of a shack on the property, $4,000; general grading of property, $2,100; paving parking lot, $20,000; lighting for parking lot, $16,000; and signs for parking lot, $3,200. Determine the amount that should be debited to the Land account and to the Land Improvements account.

E 9-3.
LO 2
Group Purchase

Linda Regalado went into business by purchasing a car wash for $480,000. The car wash assets included land, building, and equipment. If purchased separately, the land would have cost $120,000, the building $270,000, and the equipment $210,000. Determine the amount that should be recorded in the new business's records for land, building, and equipment.

E 9-4.
LO 2, 4
Cost of Long-Term Asset and Depreciation

Myron Walker purchased a used tractor for $35,000. Before the tractor could be used, it required new tires, which cost $2,200, and an overhaul, which cost $2,800. Its first tank of fuel cost $150. The tractor is expected to last six years and have a residual value of $4,000. Determine the cost and depreciable cost of the tractor and calculate the first year's depreciation under the straight-line method.

E 9-5.
LO 3, 4
Depreciation Methods

Findlay Oil Corporation purchased a drilling truck for $90,000. The company expected the truck to last five years or 200,000 miles, with an estimated residual value of $15,000 at the end of that time. During 19x5, the truck was driven 48,000 miles. The company's year end is December 31.

Compute the depreciation for 19x5 under each of the following methods, assuming that the truck was purchased on January 13, 19x4: (1) straight-line, (2) production, and (3) double-declining-balance. Using the amount computed in **3**, prepare the general journal entry to record depreciation expense for the second year and show how drilling trucks would appear on the balance sheet.

E 9-6.
LO 4
Declining-Balance Method

Schwab Burglar Alarm Systems Company purchased a word processor for $2,240. It has an estimated useful life of four years and an estimated residual value of $240. Compute the depreciation charge for each of the four years using the double-declining-balance method.

E 9-7.
LO 5, 6
Disposal of Plant Assets

A piece of equipment that cost $32,400 and on which $18,000 of accumulated depreciation had been recorded was disposed of on January 2, the first day of business of the current year. Give general journal entries to record the disposal under each of the following assumptions:

1. It was discarded as having no value.
2. It was sold for $6,000 cash.
3. It was sold for $16,000 cash.
4. It was traded in on dissimilar equipment having a list price of $48,000. A $15,600 trade-in was allowed, and the balance was paid in cash. Gains and losses are to be recognized.
5. It was traded in on dissimilar equipment having a list price of $48,000. A $7,500 trade-in was allowed, and the balance was paid in cash. Gains and losses are to be recognized.
6. Same as **5** except that the items are similar and gains and losses are not to be recognized.

E 9-8.
LO 6
Disposal of Plant Assets

A commercial vacuum cleaner costing $2,450, with accumulated depreciation of $1,800, was traded in on a new model that had a list price of $3,050. A trade-in allowance of $500 was given.

1. Compute the carrying value of the old vacuum cleaner.
2. Determine the amount of cash required to purchase the new vacuum cleaner.
3. Compute the amount of loss on the exchange.
4. Determine the cost basis of the new vacuum cleaner, assuming (a) the loss is recognized and (b) the loss is not recognized.
5. Compute the yearly depreciation on the new vacuum cleaner for both assumptions in **4,** assuming a useful life of five years, a residual value of $800, and straight-line depreciation.

E 9-9.
LO 5, 6
Disposal of Plant Assets

A microcomputer was purchased by Juniper Company on January 1, 19x1 at a cost of $5,000. It is expected to have a useful life of five years and a residual value of $500. Assuming that the computer is disposed of on July 1, 19x4, record the partial year's depreciation for 19x4 using the straight-line method, and record the disposal under each of the following assumptions:

1. The microcomputer is discarded.
2. The microcomputer is sold for $800.
3. The microcomputer is sold for $2,200.
4. The microcomputer is exchanged for a new microcomputer with a list price of $9,000. A $1,200 trade-in is allowed on the cash purchase. The accounting approach to gains and losses is followed.
5. Same as **4** except a $2,400 trade-in is allowed.
6. Same as **4** except the income tax approach is followed.
7. Same as **5** except the income tax approach is followed.
8. Same as **4** except the microcomputer is exchanged for dissimilar office equipment.
9. Same as **5** except the microcomputer is exchanged for dissimilar office equipment.

E 9-10.
L O 7 *Natural Resource Depletion and Depreciation of Related Plant Assets*

Church Mining Corporation purchased land containing an estimated 10 million tons of ore for a cost of $8,800,000. The land without the ore is estimated to be worth $1,600,000. The company expects that all the usable ore can be mined in ten years. Buildings costing $800,000 with an estimated useful life of thirty years were erected on the site. Equipment costing $960,000 with an estimated useful life of ten years was installed. Because of the remote location, neither the buildings nor the equipment has an estimated residual value. During its first year of operation, the company mined and sold 800,000 tons of ore.

1. Compute the depletion charge per ton.
2. Compute the depletion expense that Church Mining Corporation should record for the year.
3. Determine the annual depreciation expense for the buildings, making it proportional to the depletion.
4. Determine the annual depreciation expense for the equipment under two alternatives: (a) using the straight-line method and (b) making the expense proportional to the depletion.

E 9-11.
L O 8 *Amortization of Copyrights and Trademarks*

1. Fortunato Publishing Company purchased the copyright to a basic computer textbook for $20,000. The usual life of a textbook is about four years. However, the copyright will remain in effect for at least another fifty years. Calculate the annual amortization of the copyright.
2. Guzman Company purchased a trademark from a well-known supermarket for $160,000. The management of the company argued that because the trademark value would last forever and might even increase, no amortization should be charged. Calculate the minimum amount of annual amortization that should be charged, according to guidelines of the appropriate Accounting Principles Board opinion.

E 9-12.
S O 9 *Depreciation Methods: Partial Years*

Using the same data given for Findlay Oil Corporation in E 9-5, compute the depreciation for calendar year 19x5 under each of the following methods, assuming that the truck was purchased on July 1, 19x4: (1) straight-line, (2) production, and (3) double-declining-balance.

E 9-13.
S O 9 *Straight-Line Method: Partial Years*

Idriss Manufacturing Corporation purchased three machines during the year:

February 10	Machine 1	$ 3,600
July 26	Machine 2	24,000
October 11	Machine 3	43,200

Each machine is expected to last six years and have no estimated residual value. The company's fiscal year corresponds to the calendar year. Using the straight-line method, compute the depreciation charge for each machine for the year.

E 9-14.
S O 9 *Revision of Depreciation Rates*

Broadleigh Hospital purchased a special x-ray machine for its operating room. The machine, which cost $311,560, was expected to last ten years, with an estimated residual value of $31,560. After two years of operation (and depreciation charges using the straight-line rate), it became evident that the x-ray machine would last a total of only seven years. The estimated residual value, however, would remain the same. Given this information, determine the new depreciation charge for the third year on the basis of the revised estimated useful life.

E 9-15.
L O 2
S O 9
Special Types of Capital Expenditures

Tell whether each of the following transactions related to an office building is a revenue expenditure (RE) or a capital expenditure (CE). In addition, indicate whether each transaction is an ordinary repair (OR), an extraordinary repair (ER), and addition (A), a betterment (B), or none of these (N).

1. The hallways and ceilings in the building are repainted at a cost of $8,300.
2. The hallways, which have tile floors, are carpeted at a cost of $28,000.
3. A new wing is added to the building at a cost of $175,000.
4. Furniture is purchased for the entrance to the building at a cost of $16,500.
5. The air-conditioning system is overhauled at a cost of $28,500. The overhaul extends the useful life of the air-conditioning system by ten years.
6. A cleaning firm is paid $200 per week to clean the newly installed carpets.

E 9-16.
S O 9
Extraordinary Repairs

Regalado Manufacturing has an incinerator that originally cost $187,200 and now has accumulated depreciation of $132,800. The incinerator just completed its fifteenth year of service in an estimated useful life of twenty years. At the beginning of the sixteenth year, the company spent $42,800 repairing and modernizing the incinerator to comply with pollution-control standards. Therefore, the incinerator is now expected to last ten more years instead of five more years. It will not, however, have more capacity than it did in the past or a residual value at the end of its useful life.

1. Prepare the entry to record the cost of the repair.
2. Compute the book value of the incinerator after the entry.
3. Prepare the entry to record the straight-line depreciation for the current year.

Problem Set A

9A-1.
L O 2
Determining Cost of Assets

Muraskas Computers, Inc. constructed a new training center in 19x2. You have been hired to manage the training center. A review of the accounting records lists the following expenditures debited to the Training Center account:

Attorney's fee, land acquisition	$ 34,900
Cost of land	598,000
Architect's fee, building design	102,000
Contractor's cost, building	1,020,000
Contractor's cost, parking lot and sidewalk	135,600
Contractor's cost, electrical (for building)	164,000
Landscaping	55,000
Costs of surveying land	9,200
Training equipment, tables, and chairs	136,400
Contractor's cost, installing training equipment	68,000
Cost of grading the land	14,000
Cost of changes in building to soundproof rooms	59,200
Total account balance	$2,396,300

During the center's construction, someone from Muraskas Computers, Inc. worked full time on the project. She spent two months on the purchase and preparation of the site, six months on the construction, one month on land improvements, and one month on equipment installation and training room furniture purchase and set-up. Her salary of $64,000 during this ten-month period was charged to Administrative Expense. The training center was placed in operation on November 1.

REQUIRED

1. Prepare a schedule with the following four column (Account) headings: Land, Land Improvements, Building, and Equipment. Place each of the expenditures above in the appropriate column. Total the columns.
2. Prepare an entry on December 31 to correct the accounts associated with the training center, assuming that the company's accounts have not been closed at the end of the year.

9A-2.
L O 3, 4
Comparison of Depreciation Methods

Larson Manufacturing Company purchased a robot for its manufacturing operations at a cost of $1,440,000 at the beginning of year 1. The robot has an estimated useful life of four years and an estimated residual value of $120,000. The robot is expected to last 20,000 hours. The robot was operated 6,000 hours in year 1; 8,000 hours in year 2; 4,000 hours in year 3; and 2,000 hours in year 4.

REQUIRED

1. Compute the annual depreciation and carrying value for the robot for each year, assuming the following depreciation methods: (a) straight-line, (b) production, and (c) double-declining-balance.
2. Prepare the adjusting entry that would be made each year to record the depreciation calculated under the straight-line method.
3. Show the balance sheet presentation for the robot after the adjusting entry in year 2 using the straight-line method.
4. What conclusions can you draw from the patterns of yearly depreciation and carrying value in **1**?

9A-3.
L O 5, 6 *Recording Disposals*

Laughlin Designs, Inc. purchased a computer that will assist it in designing factory layouts. The cost of the computer was $23,500. Its expected useful life is six years. The company can probably sell the computer for $2,500 at the end of six years.

REQUIRED

Prepare journal entries to record the disposal of the computer at the end of the third year, after the depreciation is recorded, assuming that it was depreciated using the straight-line method and making the following assumptions:

a. The computer is sold for $19,000.
b. It is sold for $10,000.
c. It is traded in on a dissimilar item (equipment) costing $36,000, a trade-in allowance of $17,500 is given, the balance is paid in cash, and gains and losses are recognized.
d. Same as **c** except the trade-in allowance is $11,000.
e. Same as **c** except it is traded for a similar computer and APB accounting rules are followed with regard to the recognition of gains or losses.
f. Same as **d** except it is traded for a similar computer and APB accounting rules are followed with regard to the recognition of gains or losses.
g. Same as **c** except it is traded for a similar computer and gains and losses are not recognized (income tax method).
h. Same as **d** except it is traded for a similar computer and gains and losses are not recognized (income tax method).

9A-4.
L O 7 *Comprehensive Natural Resources Entries*

The Troy Coal Company purchased property that is estimated to contain 50,000,000 tons of coal. Troy paid $12,000,000 for the property on January 2, 19x3. The property should be worth $2,000,000 after all the coal is extracted. At the same time Troy purchased equipment costing $2,392,000 to extract the coal. The equipment has an eight-year useful life with a residual value of $192,000 and can be moved to a new site when this site is depleted. Also, an on-site office had to be constructed for $240,000. The office has an estimated useful life of ten years with no residual value. The office will be abandoned when the site is depleted. The coal extracted from this site will be sold to retail companies that will load and deliver the coal directly from Troy's property. Troy's management estimates that all the coal will be mined in four years and the mine will be closed. During 19x3, 13,000,000 tons of coal were mined and sold.

REQUIRED

1. Prepare general journal entries to record the purchase of the property and the equipment, and the construction of the office.
2. Prepare adjusting entries to record depletion and depreciation for 19x3. Assume that the depreciation rate is equal to the percentage of the total coal mined during the year unless the asset is movable, and that the straight-line method of depreciation is used for the movable assets.

9A-5.
L O 8 *Leasehold, Leasehold Improvements, and Amortization of Patent*

Part 1
At the beginning of the fiscal year, Chang Company purchased an eight-year sublease on a warehouse in Peoria for $48,000. Chang will also pay rent of $1,000 a month. The warehouse needs the following improvements to meet Chang's needs:

Lighting fixtures	$18,000
Replacement of a wall	25,000
Office carpet	14,400
Heating system	30,000
Break room	12,200
Loading dock	8,400

The expected life of the loading dock and carpet is eight years. The other items are expected to last ten years. None of the improvements will have a residual value.

REQUIRED

Prepare general journal entries to record the following: (a) payment for the sublease; (b) first-year lease payment; (c) payments for the improvements; (d) amortization of the leasehold for the year; (e) leasehold improvement amortization for the year.

Part 2

At the beginning of the fiscal year, Ricks Company purchased for $1,030,000 a patent that applies to the manufacture of a unique tamper-proof lid for medicine bottles. Ricks incurred legal costs of $450,000 in successfully defending the patent against use of the lid by a competitor. Ricks estimated that the patent would be valuable for at least ten years. During the first two years of operation, Ricks successfully marketed the lid. At the beginning of the third year, a study appeared in a consumers' magazine showing that the lid could, in fact, be removed by children. As a result, all orders for the lids were canceled, and the patent was rendered worthless.

REQUIRED

Prepare journal entries to record the following: (a) purchase of the patent; (b) successful defense of the patent; (c) amortization expense for the first year; and (d) write-off of the patent as worthless.

9A-6.

L O 4

S O 9

Depreciation Methods and Partial Years

Isabel Lim purchased a laundry company that caters to college students. In addition to the washing machines, Lim installed a tanning machine and a refreshment center. Because each type of asset performs a different function, she has decided to use different depreciation methods. Data on each type of asset are summarized in the table below.

The tanning machine was operated 2,100 hours in 19x5, 3,000 hours in 19x6, and 2,400 hours in 19x7.

Asset	Date Purchased	Cost	Installation Cost	Residual Value	Estimated Life	Depreciation Method
Washing machines	3/5/x5	$30,000	$4,000	$5,200	4 years	Straight-line
Tanning machine	4/1/x5	68,000	6,000	2,000	7,500 hours	Production
Refreshment center	10/1/x5	6,800	1,200	1,200	10 years	Double-declining-balance

REQUIRED

Assuming that the fiscal year ends December 31, compute the depreciation charges for each item and in total for 19x5, 19x6, and 19x7. Round your answers to the nearest dollar and present them by filling in a table with the headings shown below.

			Depreciation		
Asset	Year	Computations	19x5	19x6	19x7

Problem Set B

9B-1.

L O 2

Determining Cost of Assets

Flair Corporation began operation on January 1 of the current year. At the end of the year, the company's auditor discovered that all expenditures involving long-term assets had been debited to an account called Fixed Assets. An analysis of the account, which had a balance at the end of the year of $2,644,972, disclosed that it contained the items presented on the following page.

The timber that was cleared from the land was sold to a firewood dealer for $5,000. This amount was credited to Miscellaneous Income. During the construction period, two supervisors devoted their full time to the construction project. These people earn annual salaries of $48,000 and $42,000, respectively. They spent two months on the purchase and preparation of the land, six months on the construction of the building (approximately one-sixth of which was devoted to improvements on the grounds), and one month on installation of machinery. The plant began operation on October 1, and the supervisors returned to their regular duties. Their salaries were debited to Factory Salary Expense.

Cost of land	$ 316,600
Surveying costs	4,100
Transfer of title and other fees required by the county	920
Broker's fees	21,144
Attorney's fees associated with land acquisition	7,048
Cost of removing unusable timber from land	50,400
Cost of grading land	4,200
Cost of digging building foundation	34,600
Architect's fee for building and land improvements (80 percent building)	64,800
Cost of building	710,000
Cost of sidewalks	11,400
Cost of parking lots	54,400
Cost of lighting for grounds	80,300
Cost of landscaping	11,800
Cost of machinery	989,000
Shipping cost on machinery	55,300
Cost of installing machinery	176,200
Cost of testing machinery	22,100
Cost of changes in building due to safety regulations required because of machinery	12,540
Cost of repairing building that was damaged in the installation of machinery	8,900
Cost of medical bill for injury received by employee while installing machinery	2,400
Cost of water damage to building during heavy rains prior to opening the plant for operation	6,820
Account balance	$2,644,972

REQUIRED

1. Prepare a schedule with the following column headings: Land, Land Improvements, Buildings, Machinery, and Losses. List the items and place each in the proper account. Negative amounts should be shown in parentheses. Total the columns.
2. Prepare an entry to adjust the accounts based on all the information given, assuming that the company's accounts have not been closed at the end of the year.

9B-2.

L O 3, 4 *Comparison of Depreciation Methods*

Riggio Construction Company purchased a new crane for $360,500 at the beginning of year 1. The crane has an estimated residual value of $35,000 and an estimated useful life of six years. The crane is expected to last 10,000 hours. It was used 1,800 hours in year 1; 2,000 hours in year 2; 2,500 hours in year 3; 1,500 hours in year 4; 1,200 hours in year 5; and 1,000 hours in year 6.

REQUIRED

1. Compute the annual depreciation and carrying value for the new crane for each of the six years (round to nearest dollar where necessary) under each of the following methods: (a) straight-line, (b) production, and (c) double-declining-balance.
2. Prepare the adjusting entry that would be made each year to record the depreciation calculated under the straight-line method.
3. Show the balance sheet presentation for the crane after the adjusting entry in year 2 using the straight-line method.
4. What conclusions can you draw from the patterns of yearly depreciation and carrying value in **1**?

9B-3.

L O 5, 6 *Recording Disposals*

Pavlic Construction Company purchased a road grader for $58,000. The road grader is expected to have a useful life of five years and a residual value of $4,000 at the end of that time.

REQUIRED

Prepare journal entries to record the disposal of the road grader at the end of the second year, after the depreciation is recorded, assuming that the straight-line method is used and making the following additional assumptions:

a. The road grader is sold for $40,000 cash.
b. It is sold for $32,000 cash.

c. It is traded in on a dissimilar item (machinery) having a price of $66,000, a trade-in allowance of $40,000 is given, the balance is paid in cash, and gains or losses are recognized.

d. It is traded in on a dissimilar item (machinery) having a price of $66,000, a trade-in allowance of $32,000 is given, the balance is paid in cash, and gains or losses are recognized.

e. Same as **c** except it is traded for a similar road grader and Pavlic Construction Company follows APB accounting rules with regard to the recognition of gains or losses.

f. Same as **d** except it is traded for a similar road grader and Pavlic Construction Company follows APB accounting rules with regard to the recognition of gains or losses.

g. Same as **c** except it is traded for a similar road grader and gains or losses are not recognized (income tax purposes).

h. Same as **d** except it is traded for a similar road grader and gains or losses are not recognized (income tax purposes).

9B-4.

L O 7 *Comprehensive Natural Resources Entries*

Maria Morales is a limestone supplier from New Mexico. On January 3, 19x2, Morales purchased a piece of property with a limestone quarry for $13,020,000. She estimated that the quarry contained 2,350,000 cubic yards of limestone, which is used for making roads. After the limestone is gone, the land, which is in the desert, will be worth only about $800,000. The equipment required to extract the limestone cost $2,904,000. In addition, Morales decided to build a small frame building to house the quarry office and a small dining hall for the workers. The building cost $304,000 and would have no residual value after its estimated useful life of ten years. It cannot be moved from the quarry site. The equipment, which has an estimated useful life of six years, has no residual value and cannot be removed from the quarry site. Trucks for the project cost $616,000 (estimated life, six years; residual value, $40,000). The trucks, of course, can be used at a different site. Morales estimated that in five years all the limestone would be mined and the quarry would be shut down. During 19x2, 470,000 cubic yards of limestone were mined and sold.

REQUIRED

1. Prepare general journal entries to record the purchase of the property and all the buildings and equipment associated with the quarry.
2. Prepare adjusting entries to record depletion and depreciation for the first year of operation (19x2). Assume that the depreciation rate is equal to the percentage of the total limestone mined during the year, unless the asset is movable. For movable assets, use the straight-line method.

9B-5.

L O 8 *Amortization of Exclusive License, Leasehold, and Leasehold Improvements*

Part 1

On January 1, Miracle Games, Inc. purchased the exclusive license to make dolls based on the characters in a new hit television series called "Space Kids." The exclusive license cost $4,200,000, and there was no termination date on the rights. Immediately after signing the contract, the company sued a rival firm that claimed it had already received the exclusive license to the series characters. Miracle Games successfully defended its rights at a cost of $720,000. During the first year and the next, Miracle Games marketed toys based on the series. Because a successful television series lasts about five years, the company felt it could market the toys for three more years. However, before the third year of the series could get under way, a controversy arose between the two stars of the series and the producer. As a result, the stars refused to work the third year and the show was canceled, rendering exclusive rights worthless.

REQUIRED

Prepare journal entries to record the following: (a) purchase of the exclusive license; (b) successful defense of the license; (c) amortization expense, if any, for the first year; and (d) write-off of the license as worthless.

Part 2

Evelyn Miripol purchased a six-year sublease on a building from the estate of the former tenant, who had died suddenly. It was a good location for her business, and the annual rent of $7,200, which had been established ten years before, was low for such a good location. The cost of the sublease was $18,900. To use the building, Miripol had to make certain alterations. First she moved some panels at a cost of $3,400 and installed others for $12,200. Then she added carpet, lighting fixtures, and a sign at costs of $5,800, $6,200, and $2,400, respectively. All items except the carpet would last for at least twelve years. The expected life of the carpet was six years. None of the improvements would have a residual value at the end of those times.

REQUIRED

Prepare general journal entries to record the following: (a) the payment for the sublease; (b) the payments for the alterations, panels, carpet, lighting fixtures, and sign; (c) the lease payment for the first year; (d) the amortization expense, if any, associated with the sublease; and (e) the amortization expense, if any, associated with the alterations, panels, carpet, lighting fixtures, and sign.

9B-6.
L O 4 *Depreciation*
S O 9 *Methods and Partial Years*

Gottlieb Corporation operates three types of equipment. Because of the equipment's varied functions, company accounting policy requires the application of three different depreciation methods. Data on this equipment are summarized in the table below.

Assume that production for Equipment 3 was 2,000 hours in 19x5; 4,200 hours in 19x6; and 3,200 hours in 19x7.

Equipment	Date Purchased	Cost	Installation Cost	Estimated Residual Value	Estimated Life	Depreciation Method
1	1/12/x5	$171,000	$ 9,000	$18,000	10 years	Double-declining-balance
2	7/9/x5	191,100	15,900	21,000	10 years	Straight-line
3	10/2/x5	290,700	8,100	33,600	20,000 hours	Production

REQUIRED

Assuming that the fiscal year ends December 31, compute the depreciation charges on each type of equipment and in total for 19x5, 19x6, and 19x7 by filling in a table with the headings shown below.

Equipment No.	Year	Computations	Depreciation		
			19x5	19x6	19x7

CRITICAL THINKING AND COMMUNICATION

Conceptual Mini-Cases

CMC 9-1.
L O 1, 3 *Nature of Depreciation and Amortization and Estimated Useful Lives*

General Motors Corp., in its 1987 annual report, states, "In the third quarter of 1987, the Corporation revised the estimated service lives of its plants and equipment and special tools retroactive to January 1, 1987. These revisions, which were based on 1987 studies of actual useful lives and periods of use, recognized current estimates of service lives of the assets and had the effect of reducing 1987 depreciation and amortization charges by $1,236.6 million or $2.55 per share of $1-2/3 par value common stock." In 1987, General Motors' income before income taxes was $2,005.4 million. Discuss the purpose of depreciation and amortization. What is the estimated service life, and on what basis did General Motors change the estimates of the service lives of plants and equipment and special tools? What was the effect of this change on the corporation's income before income taxes? Is it likely that the company is in better condition economically as a result of the change? Does the company have more cash at the end of the year as a result? (Ignore income tax effects.)

CMC 9-2.
L O 3, 4 *Choice of Depreciation Methods*

Ford Motor Co., one of the nation's largest manufacturers of automobiles, does not use the straight-line depreciation method for financial reporting purposes even though, as shown in Figure 9-4, most companies do choose this depreciation method. As noted in Ford's 1990 annual report:

> Depreciation is computed using an accelerated method that results in accumulated depreciation of approximately two-thirds of asset cost during the first half of the asset's estimated useful life.

What reasons can you give for Ford's choosing this method of depreciation over the straight-line method? What is the role of the matching rule? Discuss which of these two methods is the more conservative.

CMC 9-3.

L O 8   *Trademarks*

The Quaker Oats Company's advertising campaign, "Gatorade is thirst aid for that deep down body thirst," infringed on a trademark held by Sands Taylor & Wood of Norwich, Vermont, according to a 1990 ruling by a federal judge.[19] Sands Taylor & Wood had acquired the trademark "thirst aid" in a 1973 acquisition but did not use the trademark at the time the 1990 ruling was handed down. The judge determined that Gatorade had produced $247.3 million in income over the previous six years and reasoned that the advertising campaign was responsible for 10 percent of the product's sales. As a result, he awarded Sands Taylor & Wood $24.7 million plus legal fees and interest from 1984. He also prohibited Quaker Oats from further use of the phrase "thirst aid" in any advertising campaign for Gatorade, its largest-selling product.

What is a trademark, and why is it considered an intangible asset? Why does a trademark have value? To whom does a trademark have value? Be prepared to discuss how your answers apply to the case of Quaker Oats Company's use of "thirst aid."

Ethics Mini-Case

EMC 9-1.

L O 2   *Ethics and Allocation of Acquisition Costs*

Signal Corporation has purchased land and a warehouse for $18,000,000. The warehouse is expected to last twenty years and to have an estimated salvage value equal to 10 percent of its cost. The chief financial officer (CFO) and controller are discussing the allocation of the purchase price. The CFO believes most of the cost should be assigned to the land because this action will improve reported net income in the future. Depreciation expense will be lower because land is not depreciated. He suggests allocating one-third, or $6,000,000, of the cost to the land. This results in depreciation expense each year of $540,000 [($12,000,000 − $1,200,000)/20 years]. The controller disagrees, arguing that the smallest amount possible, say one-fifth of the purchase price, should be allocated to the land, thereby saving income taxes, since the depreciation, which is tax deductible, will be greater. Under this plan, annual depreciation would be $648,000 [($14,400,000 − $1,440,000)/20 years]. The annual tax savings at a 30 percent tax rate is $32,400 [($648,000 − $540,000) × .30]. How will this decision affect the company's cash flows? How should the purchase cost ethically be allocated? Who will be affected by the decision?

Decision-Making Case

DMC 9-1.

L O 4, 7   *Natural Resource Accounting*

Billy Bob Daniels is in the gravel business in Oklahoma and has engaged you to assist in evaluating his company, *Daniels Gravel Company.* Your first step is to collect the facts about the company's operations. On January 3, 19x2, Billy Bob purchased a piece of property with gravel deposits for $6,310,000. He estimated that the gravel deposits contained 4,700,000 cubic yards of gravel. The gravel is used for making roads. After the gravel is gone, the land, which is in the desert, will be worth only about $200,000.

The equipment required to extract the gravel cost $1,452,000. In addition, Billy Bob had to build a small frame building to house the mine office and a small dining hall for the workers. The building cost $152,000 and will have no residual value after its estimated useful life of ten years. It cannot be moved from the mine site. The equipment has an estimated useful life of six years (with no residual value) and also cannot be moved from the mine site.

Trucks for the project cost $308,000 (estimated life, six years; residual value, $20,000). The trucks, of course, can be used at a different site.

Billy Bob estimated that in five years all the gravel would be mined and the mine would be shut down. During 19x2, 1,175,000 cubic yards of gravel were mined. The average selling price during the year was $2.66 per cubic yard, and at the end of the year 125,000 cubic yards remained unsold. Operating expenses were $852,000 for labor and $232,000 for other expenses.

REQUIRED

1. Prepare general journal entries to record the purchase of the property and the building and equipment associated with the mine. Assume purchases are made with cash on January 3.

19. James P. Miller, "Quaker Oats Loses Trademark Battle Over Gatorade Ad," *Wall Street Journal,* December 19, 1990.

2. Prepare adjusting entries to record depletion and depreciation for the first year of operation (19x2). Assume that the depreciation rate is equal to the percentage of the total gravel mined during the year, unless the asset is movable. For movable assets, use the straight-line method.
3. Prepare an income statement for 19x2 for Daniels Gravel Company.
4. What is your evaluation of the company's operations? What are the reasons for your evaluation? Ignore income tax effects.

Basic Research Activity

RA 9-1.
L O 5, 6   *SEC and Form 10-K*

Public corporations are required not only to communicate with their stockholders by means of an annual report, but also to submit an annual report to the Securities and Exchange Commission (SEC). The annual report to the SEC is called a 10-K and contains information in addition to that provided to stockholders. Most college and university libraries provide access to at least a selected number of 10-Ks. These 10-Ks may be on microfiche or on file with the companies' annual reports to stockholders. In your school's library, find the 10-K for a single company. In that 10-K, Schedule 5 will contain information about the dispositions and acquisitions of property, plant, and equipment at carrying value. Schedule 6 will show the increases and decreases in the accumulated depreciation accounts. In the statement of cash flows under investing activities, the cash proceeds from dispositions of property, plant, and equipment will be shown. Using the information from this statement and the two related schedules, determine whether or not the company had a gain or loss from dispositions of property, plant, and equipment during the year. Be prepared to discuss your results in class.

FINANCIAL REPORTING AND ANALYSIS

Interpretation Cases from Business

ICB 9-1.
L O 3, 4   *Effects of Change in*
S O 9   *Accounting Method*

Depreciation expense is a significant expense for companies in industries where plant assets are a high proportion of assets. The amount of depreciation expense in a given year is affected by estimates of useful life and choice of depreciation method. In 1993, *Century Steelworks Company,* a major integrated steel producer, changed the estimated useful lives for its major production assets. It also changed the method of depreciation for other steel-making assets from straight-line to the production method.

The company's 1993 annual report states, "A recent study conducted by management shows that actual years-in-service figures for our major production equipment and machinery are, in most cases, higher than the estimated useful lives assigned to these assets. We have recast the depreciable lives of such assets so that equipment previously assigned a useful life of 8 to 26 years now has an extended depreciable life of 10 to 32 years." The report goes on to explain that the new production method of depreciation "recognizes that depreciation of production equipment and machinery correlates directly to both physical wear and tear and the passage of time. The production method of depreciation, which we have now initiated, more closely allocates the cost of these assets to the periods in which products are manufactured."

The report summarized the effects of both actions on the year 1993 as follows:

Incremental Increase in Net Income	In Millions	Per Share
Lengthened lives	$11.0	$ .80
Production method		
Current year	7.3	.53
Prior years	2.8	.20
Total increase	$21.1	$1.53

During 1993, Century Steelworks reported a net loss of $83,156,500 ($6.03 per share). Depreciation expense for 1993 was $87,707,200.

In explaining the changes, the controller of Century Steelworks was quoted in an article in *Business Journal* as follows: "There is no reason why Century Steelworks should continue to depreciate our assets more conservatively than our competitors do." But the article quotes an industry analyst who argues that, by slowing its method of depreciation, Century Steelworks could be viewed as reporting lower-quality earnings.

REQUIRED

1. Explain the accounting treatment when there is a change in the estimated lives of depreciable assets. What circumstances must exist for the production method to produce the effect it did in relation to the straight-line method? What would have been Century Steelworks' net income or loss if the changes had not been made? What may have motivated management to make the changes?

2. What does the controller of Century Steelworks mean when he says that Century had been depreciating "more conservatively than our competitors"? Why might the changes at Century Steelworks indicate, as the analyst asserts, "lower-quality earnings"? What risks might Century face as a result of its decision to use the production method of depreciation?

ICB 9-2.
L O 6 *Exchange of Assets*

The *Wall Street Journal* reported on October 14, 1983 that "*Pan American World Airways* and *American Airlines* are in the final stages of negotiating the biggest swap in the industry's history. . . . According to industry sources, Pan Am would trade fifteen of its DC 10's to American Airlines. In return, Pan Am would get eight of American's much bigger Boeing 747 jumbo jets."

The article also stated that "New Boeing 747's currently sell for about $85 million, indicating that the eight involved in the swap could be valued at nearly $700 million. But the market for used wide-body jets is weak. One industry source estimated that a used 747 might fetch only about $20 million, indicating the eight could be valued as low as $160 million."

A note to Pan Am's 1983 annual report indicated that by the end of 1983 the title to fifteen DC 10's had been transferred to American Airlines, but that only one of the eight Boeing 747's had been received from American. It reported, "An Aircraft Exchange Receivable of approximately $111,652,000 has been recorded on the balance sheet at December 31, 1983, in connection with the exchange. No gain or loss has been recorded on the exchange."[20]

REQUIRED

1. Since no gain or loss was recognized on the exchange, how did Pan Am arrive at a value to be placed on the Boeing 747's? Assuming that each Boeing 747 was valued at the same amount, what was the total value of the exchange? How does this amount compare with the market value of the planes? Why was market value not used to value the transaction?

2. Prepare as completely as possible the journal entry Pan Am made to record the exchange. How would the account Aircraft Exchange Receivable be classified in the financial statements? Assume that Pan Am received delivery of two Boeing 747's on February 1, 1984. What entry would be made?

ICB 9-3.
S O 9 *Special Capital and Revenue Expenditures*

Selected accounting policies involving long-term assets of **Ocean Drilling and Exploration Company** (ODECO), one of the largest oil and gas contract drilling companies, appear below:[21]

1. Provisions are made for major repairs on the company's drilling barges by monthly charges to expense. The cost of major repairs incurred is charged against the related allowance created by the monthly provisions.

2. All other maintenance and repair costs are charged to expense.

3. Renewals (extraordinary repairs) are capitalized by reducing accumulated depreciation, and betterments are capitalized by increasing the asset account.

20. William M. Carley, "American Air, Pan Am Prepare to Swap Planes," *Wall Street Journal,* October 14, 1983, pp. 3, 18.
21. Ocean Drilling and Exploration Company, *Annual Report,* 1986.

The following data apply to the year 1986:

Major Barge Repairs

Provisions	$ 4,541,000
Charges	2,588,000
Repairs and maintenance	27,165,000
Renewals to drilling barges (estimated)	10,000,000
Betterments to drilling barges (estimated)	20,000,000

REQUIRED

1. Explain the reasoning behind each of the accounting policies listed above.
2. Prepare journal entries to record each of the amounts listed (assume that expenditures are made in cash).

International Company Case

ICC 9-1.

L O 8

Accounting for Trademarks: U.S. and British Rules

When the British company *Grand Metropolitan* (Grand Met) purchased *Pillsbury* in 1989, it adopted British accounting policies with regard to intangibles. Many analysts feel this gives British companies advantages over U.S. companies, especially in buyout situations.[22] There are two major differences in accounting for intangibles between U.S. accounting standards and British accounting standards. First, under the U.S. rules as discussed in this chapter, intangible assets such as trademarks are recorded at their acquisition cost, which is often nominal, and the cost is amortized over a reasonable life. Under British accounting standards, on the other hand, firms are able to record the value of trademarks for the purpose of increasing the total assets on their balance sheets. Further, they do not have to amortize the value if management can show that the value can be preserved through extensive brand support. Grand Met, therefore, elected to record such famous Pillsbury trademarks as the Pillsbury Doughboy, Green Giant vegetables, Haagen Dazs ice cream, and Van de Kamp fish at an estimated value and not to amortize them. Second, when one company purchases another company for more than the market value of the assets if purchased individually, under U.S. rules the excess is recorded as the asset goodwill, which must be amortized over a period not to exceed forty years. Although companies are required to show the expense, they cannot, under U.S. income tax laws, deduct the goodwill amortization for tax purposes. Under British accounting rules, any goodwill resulting from a purchase lowers stockholders' equity directly, rather than being recorded as an asset and lowering net income through amortization over a number of years. Analysts say that these two rules made Pillsbury more valuable to Grand Met than to Pillsbury stockholders and thus led to Pillsbury's being bought by the British firm. Write a one- or two-page paper that addresses the following questions: What is the rationale behind the argument that the British company has an advantage because of the differences between U.S. and British accounting principles? Do you agree with the U.S. or British accounting rules with regard to intangibles and goodwill? Give reasons for your answers.

Toys "R" Us Case

TC 9-1.

L O 2, 3, 4 *Long-Term Assets*

1. Refer to the consolidated balance sheets and to the note on property and equipment in the notes to consolidated financial statements in the appendix on Toys "R" Us to answer the following questions: What percentage of total assets in 1994 was Property and Equipment? What is the most significant type of property and equipment? Does Toys "R" Us have a significant investment in land? What kinds of things are included in the "Other, net" category? (Ignore leased property under capital leases for now. It will be covered in the chapter on long-term liabilities.)

22. Joanne Lipman, "British Value Brand Names—Literally," *Wall Street Journal*, February 9, 1989, p. B4; and "Brand Name Policy Boosts Assets," *Accountancy*, October 1988, pp. 38–39.

2. Refer to the summary of significant accounting policies and to the note on property and equipment in the appendix on Toys "R" Us. What method of depreciation does Toys "R" Us use? How is interest on construction of long-term assets accounted for? How long does management estimate its buildings to last as compared to furniture and equipment? What does this say about the need for remodeling?

3. Refer to the statement of cash flows in the appendix on Toys "R" Us. How much did Toys "R" Us spend on property and equipment (capital expenditures, net) during 1994? Is this an increase or a decrease from prior years?

LEARNING OBJECTIVES

1. Identify the management issues related to recognition, valuation, classification, and disclosure of current liabilities.

2. Identify, compute, and record definitely determinable and estimated current liabilities.

3. Define *contingent liability*.

4. Define interest and distinguish between simple and compound interest.

5. Use compound interest tables to compute the future value of a single invested sum at compound interest and of an ordinary annuity.

6. Use compound interest tables to compute the present value of a single sum due in the future and of an ordinary annuity.

7. Apply the concept of present value to simple accounting situations.

USAir, Inc.

Liabilities are one of the three major parts of the balance sheet. They are legal obligations for the future payment of assets or the future performance of services that result from past transactions. For example, the current and long-term liabilities of USAir, Inc., which has total assets of almost $6.6 billion, are as follows (in millions):[1]

	1992	1991
Current Liabilities		
Current maturities of long-term debt	$ 250,019	$ 104,508
Accounts payable	390,583	392,995
Traffic balances payable and unused tickets	622,428	513,356
Accrued expenses	1,169,632	927,970
Total current liabilities	2,432,662	1,938,829
Long-Term Debt, Net of Current Maturities	2,264,944	2,114,902

Current Maturities of Long-Term Debt, Accounts Payable, and Accrued Expenses for the most part will require an outlay of cash in the next year. Traffic Balances Payable will require payments to other airlines, but these may be partially offset by amounts owed from other airlines. Unused Tickets are tickets already paid for by passengers and represent services that must be performed. Long-Term Debt will require cash outlays in future years. Altogether these liabilities represent more than 70 percent of total assets. How does the decision of USAir, Inc.'s management to incur so much debt relate to the goals of the business?

Liabilities are important because they are closely related to the goals of profitability and liquidity. Liabilities are sources of cash for operating, investing, and financing activities when they are incurred, but they are also obligations that use cash when they are paid as required. Achieving the appropriate level of liabilities is critical to business success. A company that has too few liabilities may not be earning up to its potential. A company that has too many liabilities may be incurring excessive risks. This chapter focuses on the management and accounting issues involving current liabilities, contingent liabilities, and the time value of money. The following chapter will present the management and accounting issues involving long-term liabilities. ⁚ ⁚ ⁚ ⁚ ⁚

1. USAir, Inc., *Annual Report,* 1992.

MANAGEMENT ISSUES RELATED TO ACCOUNTING FOR CURRENT LIABILITIES

OBJECTIVE

1 *Identify the management issues related to recognition, valuation, classification, and disclosure of current liabilities*

The primary reason for incurring current liabilities is to meet needs for cash during the operating cycle. In a previous chapter, the operating cycle was presented as the process of converting cash to purchases, to sales, to accounts receivable, and back to cash. Most current liabilities arise in support of this cycle, as when accounts payable arise from purchases of inventory, accrued expenses arise from operating costs, and unearned revenues arise from customers' advance payments. Short-term debt is used to raise cash during periods of inventory build-up or while waiting for collection of receivables. Sometimes cash is siphoned off to pay current maturities of long-term debt, to make investments in long-term assets, or to pay cash dividends.

Failure to manage the cash flows related to current liabilities can have serious consequences for a business. For instance, if suppliers are not paid in a timely manner, they may withhold shipments that are vital to a company's operations. Continued failure to pay current liabilities can lead to bankruptcy. To evaluate a company's ability to pay its current liabilities, three measures of liquidity presented in previous chapters—working capital, the current ratio, and the quick ratio—are often used. Current liabilities is a key component of each of these measures. It typically equals from 25 to 40 percent of total assets, as may be seen in Figure 10-1. To properly identify and manage current liabilities requires an understanding of how they are recognized, valued, classified, and disclosed.

RECOGNITION OF LIABILITIES

Timing is important in the recognition of liabilities. Failure to record a liability in an accounting period very often goes along with failure to record an expense. This leads to an understatement of expense and an overstatement of income. A liability is recorded when an obligation occurs. This rule is harder to apply than it might appear. When a transaction obligates a company to make future payments, a liability arises and is recognized, as when goods are bought on credit. However, current liabilities are often not represented by direct transactions. One of the major reasons for adjusting entries at the end of an accounting period is to recognize unrecorded liabilities. Among these accrued liabilities are salaries payable and interest payable. Other liabilities that can only be estimated, such as taxes payable, must also be recognized through adjusting entries.

On the other hand, companies often enter into agreements for future transactions. For instance, a company may agree to pay an executive $50,000 a year for a period of three years, or a public utility may agree to buy an unspecified quantity of coal at a certain price over the next five years. These contracts, though they are definite commitments, are not considered liabilities because they are for future—not past—transactions. As there is no current obligation, no liability is recognized.

VALUATION OF LIABILITIES

A liability is generally valued on the balance sheet at the amount of money needed to pay the debt or at the fair market value of goods or services to be delivered. For most liabilities the amount is definitely known, but for some it

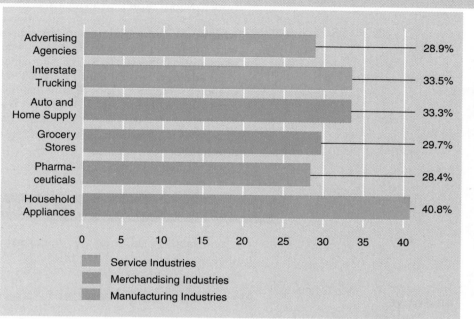

Figure 10-1. Current Liabilities as a Percentage of Total Assets for Selected Industries

Source: Data from Dun and Bradstreet, *Industry Norms and Ratios,* 1992–93.

must be estimated. For example, an automobile dealer who sells a car with a one-year warranty must provide parts and service during the year. The obligation is definite because the sale of the car has occurred, but the amount must be estimated. These estimates are usually based on past experience and anticipated changes in the business environment. Additional disclosures of the fair value of liabilities may be required in the notes to the financial statements, as explained below.

CLASSIFICATION OF LIABILITIES

The classification of liabilities directly matches the classification of assets. Current liabilities are debts and obligations that are expected to be satisfied within one year or within the normal operating cycle, whichever is longer. These liabilities are normally paid out of current assets or with cash generated from operations. Long-term liabilities, which are liabilities that are due beyond one year or beyond the normal operating cycle, have a different purpose. They are used to finance long-term assets, such as aircraft in the case of USAir, Inc. These distinctions are important because they affect the evaluation of a company's liquidity.

DISCLOSURE OF LIABILITIES

To explain some accounts, supplemental disclosure may be required in the notes to the financial statements. For example, if a company has a large amount of notes payable, an explanatory note may disclose the balances, maturities, interest rates, and other features of the debts. Any special credit arrangements, such as issues of commercial paper and lines of credit should also be disclosed. For example, Lowe's Companies, Inc., a large home center and consumer durables company, discloses its credit arrangements as follows:

> **Note 4, Short-Term Borrowings and Lines of Credit:**
>
> The Company had agreements with a group of banks at January 31, 1992, which provided for short-term unsecured borrowings of up to $60 million with interest at the lower of prime or bank transaction rate. These agreements were increased to $100 million effective February 1, 1992.
>
> In addition, several banks have extended lines of credit aggregating $75 million for the purpose of issuing documentary letters of credit and standby letters of credit. Another $240 million is available for purpose of short-term borrowings on a bid basis from various banks.[2]

This type of disclosure is helpful in assessing whether or not a company has additional borrowing power.

COMMON CATEGORIES OF CURRENT LIABILITIES

Current liabilities fall into two major groups: (1) definitely determinable liabilities and (2) estimated liabilities.

DEFINITELY DETERMINABLE LIABILITIES

OBJECTIVE

2 *Identify, compute, and record definitely determinable and estimated current liabilities*

Current liabilities that are set by contract or by statute and can be measured exactly are called definitely determinable liabilities. The related accounting problems are to determine the existence and amount of each such liability and to see that it is recorded properly. Definitely determinable liabilities include trade accounts payable, bank loans and commercial paper, notes payable, accrued liabilities, dividends payable, sales and excise taxes payable, current portions of long-term debt, payroll liabilities, and unearned or deferred revenues.

Accounts Payable   Accounts payable, sometimes called trade accounts payable, are short-term obligations to suppliers for goods and services. The amount in the Accounts Payable account is generally supported by an accounts payable subsidiary ledger, which contains an individual account for each person or company to whom money is owed.

Bank Loans and Commercial Paper   Management will often establish a line of credit from a bank; this arrangement allows the company to borrow funds when they are needed to finance current operations. For example, Nordstrom, Inc., a chain of quality department stores, reported in its 1993 annual report that the finance division had "a $150 [million] unsecured line of credit with a group of commerical banks which is available as liquidity support for short-term debt."[3] A promissory note for the full amount of the line of credit is signed when the credit is granted, but the company has great flexibility in using the available funds. The company can increase its borrowing up to the limit when it needs cash and reduce the amount borrowed when it generates enough cash of its own. Both the amount borrowed and the interest rate charged by the bank may change daily. The bank may require the company to meet certain financial goals (such as maintaining certain profit

2. Lowe's Companies, Inc., *Annual Report,* 1992.
3. Nordstrom, Inc., *Annual Report,* 1993.

margins, current ratios, or debt to equity ratios) to retain the line of credit. Companies with excellent credit ratings may borrow short-term funds by issuing commercial paper, unsecured loans that are sold to the public, usually through professionally managed investment firms. The portion of a line of credit that is currently borrowed and the amount of commercial paper issued are usually combined with notes payable in the current liabilities section of the balance sheet. Details are disclosed in a note to the financial statements.

Notes Payable   Short-term notes payable, which also arise out of the ordinary course of business, are obligations represented by promissory notes. These notes may be used to secure bank loans, to pay suppliers for goods and services, and to secure credit from other sources.

As with notes receivable, presented in the chapter on short-term liquid assets, the interest on notes may be stated separately on the face of the note (Case 1 in Figure 10-2), or it may be deducted in advance by discounting it from the face value of the note (Case 2). The entries to record the note in each case are as follows:

Case 1—Interest stated separately

Aug. 31	Cash	5,000	
	Notes Payable		5,000
	To record 60-day, 12% promissory note with interest stated separately		

Case 2—Interest in face amount

Aug. 31	Cash	4,900	
	Discount on Notes Payable	100	
	Notes Payable		5,000
	To record 60-day promissory note with $100 interest included in face amount		

Figure 10-2. Two Promissory Notes: One with Interest Stated Separately; One with Interest in Face Amount

CASE 1: INTEREST STATED SEPARATELY

Chicago, Illinois   August 31, 19xx

Sixty days after date I promise to pay First Federal Bank the sum of $5,000 with interest at the rate of 12% per annum.

Sandra Caron
Caron Corporation

CASE 2: INTEREST IN FACE AMOUNT

Chicago, Illinois   August 31, 19xx

Sixty days after date I promise to pay First Federal Bank the sum of $5,000.

Sandra Caron
Caron Corporation

Note that in Case 1 the money borrowed equaled the face value of the note, whereas in Case 2 the money borrowed ($4,900) was less than the face value ($5,000) of the note. The amount of the discount equals the amount of the interest for sixty days. Although the dollar amount of interest on each of these notes is the same, the effective interest rate is slightly more in Case 2 because the amount borrowed is slightly less ($4,900 in Case 2 versus $5,000 in Case 1). Discount on Notes Payable is a contra account to Notes Payable and is deducted from Notes Payable on the balance sheet.

On October 30, when the note is paid, each alternative is recorded as follows:

Case 1—Interest stated separately

Oct. 30	Notes Payable	5,000	
	Interest Expense	100	
	Cash		5,100
	Payment of note with interest stated separately		

Case 2—Interest in face amount

Oct. 30	Notes Payable	5,000	
	Cash		5,000
	Payment of note with interest included in face amount		
30	Interest Expense	100	
	Discount on Notes Payable		100
	Interest expense on matured note		

Accrued Liabilities

A key reason for adjusting entries at the end of an accounting period is to recognize and record liabilities that are not already in the accounting records. This practice applies to any type of liability. For example, in the chapter on measuring business income, adjustments relating to wages payable were made. As you will see, accrued liabilities can also include estimated liabilities.

Here the focus is on interest payable, a definitely determinable liability. Interest accrues daily on interest-bearing notes. At the end of the accounting period, an adjusting entry should be made in accordance with the matching rule to record the interest obligation up to that point in time. Let us again use the example of the two notes presented earlier in this chapter. If we assume that the accounting period ends on September 30, or thirty days after the issuance of the sixty-day notes, the adjusting entries for each case would be as follows:

Case 1—Interest stated separately

Sept. 30	Interest Expense	50	
	Interest Payable		50
	To record interest expense for 30 days on note with interest stated separately		

$$\$5,000 \times \frac{30}{360} \times .12 = \$50$$

Case 2—Interest in face amount

Sept. 30	Interest Expense	50	
	Discount on Notes Payable		50
	To record interest expense for 30 days on note with interest included in face amount		

$$\$100 \times \frac{30}{60} = \$50$$

In Case 2, Discount on Notes Payable will now have a debit balance of $50, which will become interest expense during the next thirty days.

Dividends Payable

Cash dividends are a distribution of earnings by a corporation. The payment of dividends is solely the decision of the coporation's board of directors. A liability does not exist until the board declares the dividends. There is usually a short time between the date of declaration and the date of payment of dividends. During that short time, the dividends declared are current liabilities of the corporation. Accounting for dividends is treated extensively in the chapter on retained earnings and corporate income statements.

Sales and Excise Taxes Payable

Most states and many cities levy a sales tax on retail transactions. There are federal excise taxes on some products, such as automobile tires. A merchant who sells goods subject to these taxes must collect the taxes and forward them periodically to the appropriate government agency. The amount of tax collected represents a current liability until it is remitted to the government. For example, assume that a merchant makes a $100 sale that is subject to a 5 percent sales tax and a 10 percent excise tax. Assuming that the sale takes place on June 1, the correct entry to record the sale is as follows:

June 1	Cash	115	
	Sales		100
	Sales Tax Payable		5
	Excise Tax Payable		10
	Sale of merchandise and collection		
	of sales and excise taxes		

The sale is properly recorded at $100, and tax collections are recorded as liabilities to be remitted at the proper time to the appropriate government agency.

Current Portions of Long-Term Debt

If a portion of long-term debt is due within the next year and is to be paid from current assets, then the current portion of long-term debt is properly classified as a current liability. For example, suppose that a $500,000 debt is to be paid in installments of $100,000 per year for the next five years. The $100,000 installment due in the current year should be classified as a current liability. The remaining $400,000 should be classified as a long-term liability. Note that no journal entry is necessary. The total debt of $500,000 is simply reclassified when the financial statements are prepared, as follows:

Current Liabilities	
Current Portion of Long-Term Debt	$100,000
Long-Term Liabilities	
Long-Term Debt	400,000

Payroll Liabilities

For most companies, the cost of labor and related payroll taxes is a major expense. In some industries, such as banking and airlines, payroll costs represent more than half of all operating costs. Payroll accounting is important because complex laws and significant liabilities are involved. The employer is liable to employees for wages and salaries and to various agencies for amounts withheld from wages and salaries and for related taxes. The term **wages** refers to payment for the services of employees at an hourly rate. The term **salaries** refers to the compensation of employees who are paid at a monthly or yearly rate.

Figure 10-3 provides an illustration of payroll liabilities and their relation to employee earnings and employer taxes and other costs. Two important observations may be made. First, the amount payable to employees is less than the amount of earnings. This occurs because employers are required by law or are requested by employees to withhold certain amounts from wages and send them directly to government agencies or other organizations. Second, the total employer liabilities exceed employee earnings because the employer must pay additional taxes and make other contributions, such as for pensions and medical care, that increase the cost. The most common withholdings, taxes, and other payroll costs are described below.

Federal Income Taxes   Federal income taxes are collected on a "pay as you go" basis. Employers are required to withhold appropriate taxes from employees' paychecks and pay them to the Internal Revenue Service.

State and Local Income Taxes   Most states and some local governments have income taxes. In most cases, the procedures for withholding are similar to those for federal income taxes.

Social Security (FICA) Taxes   The social security program offers retirement and disability benefits and survivor's benefits. About 90 percent of the people working in the United States fall under the provisions of this program. The 1994 social security tax rate of 6.20 percent is paid by *both* employee and employer on the first $60,600 earned by an employee during the calendar year. Both the rate and the base to which it applies are subject to change in future years.

Medicare Taxes   A major extension of the social security program is Medicare, which provides hospitalization and medical insurance for persons over 65. In 1994, the Medicare tax rate is 1.45 percent of gross income with no limit, paid by *both* employee and employer.

Medical Insurance   Many companies provide medical benefits to employees. Often, the employee contributes a portion of the cost through withholdings from income and the employer pays the rest, usually a greater amount, to the insurance company. The U.S. Congress is currently considering legislation that could change substantially the way medical insurance is funded and provided in this country.

Pension Contributions   Many companies also provide pension benefits to employees. In a manner similar to medical insurance, a portion of the pension contribution is withdrawn from the employee's income and the rest is paid by the company to the pension fund.

Federal Unemployment Insurance (FUTA) Tax   This tax, abbreviated FUTA after the Federal Unemployment Tax Act, is intended to pay for programs to help unemployed workers. It is paid *only* by employers and recently was 6.2 percent of the first $9,000 earned by each employee. The employer, however, is allowed a credit against this federal tax for unemployment taxes paid to the state. The maximum credit is 5.4 percent of the first $9,000 earned by each employee. Most states set their rate at this maximum. Thus, the FUTA tax most often paid is .8 percent (6.2 percent − 5.4 percent) of the taxable wages.

State Unemployment Insurance Tax   All state unemployment programs provide for unemployment compensation to be paid to eligible unemployed workers. This compensation is paid out of the fund provided by the 5.4 percent of the first $9,000 earned by each employee. In some states, employers with favorable employment records may be entitled to pay less than 5.4 percent.

To illustrate the recording of the payroll, assume that on February 15 gross employee wages are $32,500, with withholdings of $5,400 for federal income taxes, $1,200 for state income taxes, $2,015 for social security taxes, $471 for

Figure 10-3. Illustration of Payroll Liabilities

EMPLOYEE EARNINGS, TAXES, AND OTHER COSTS	EMPLOYER TAXES AND OTHER COSTS	EMPLOYER LIABILITIES PAYABLE TO
Take-Home Pay		Employee
Federal Income Taxes		Federal Government
State and Local Income Taxes		State and Local Government
FICA Taxes	Employer's Share of FICA Taxes	Federal Government
Medicare	Employer's Share of Medicare	
Medical Insurance	Employer's Share of Medical Insurance	Federal Government
Pension	Employer's Share of Pension	Insurance Company
	Federal Unemployment Taxes	Pension Fund
	State Unemployment Taxes	Federal Government
		State Government

Medicare taxes, $900 for medical insurance, and $1,300 for pension contributions. The entry to record this payroll is

Feb. 15	Wages Expense	32,500	
	Employees' Federal Income Taxes Payable		5,400
	Employees' State Income Taxes Payable		1,200
	Social Security Taxes Payable		2,015
	Medicare Taxes Payable		471
	Medical Insurance Payable		900
	Pension Contributions Payable		1,300
	Wages Payable		21,214
	To record payroll		

Note that the employees' take-home pay is only $21,214 out of $32,500 earned. Using the same data, the additional employer taxes and other costs would be recorded as follows, assuming that the payroll taxes correspond to the discussion above and that the employer pays 80 percent of the medical insurance premiums and half of the pension contributions:

Feb. 15	Payroll Expense	9,401	
	Social Security Taxes Payable		2,015
	Medicare Taxes Payable		471
	Medical Insurance Payable		3,600
	Pension Contributions Payable		1,300
	Federal Unemployment Taxes Payable		260
	State Unemployment Taxes Payable		1,755
	To record payroll taxes and other costs		

Note that the payroll taxes increase the total cost of the payroll to $41,901 ($9,401 + $32,500), which exceeds by almost 29 percent the amount earned by employees. This is a typical situation.

BUSINESS BULLETIN: TECHNOLOGY IN PRACTICE

The processing of payroll is an ideal application of computers because it is one of the most routine procedures in accounting and very complex, and it must be done with absolute accuracy: Employees want to be paid exactly what they are owed and failure to pay the taxes and other costs as required can result in severe penalties and high interest charges. As a result, many companies purchase carefully designed and tested computer software for use in preparing the payroll. Other companies do not process their own payroll but rely on outside businesses that specialize in providing such services. Many of these outside businesses, such as Automatic Data Processing, Inc., are successful and fast growing. ====

Unearned Revenues   Unearned revenues represent obligations for goods or services that the company must provide or deliver in a future accounting period in return for an advance payment from a customer. For example, a publisher of a monthly magazine who receives annual subscriptions totaling $240 would make the following entry:

Cash	240	
Unearned Subscriptions		240
Receipt of annual subscriptions		
in advance		

The publisher now has a liability of $240 that will be reduced gradually as monthly issues of the magazine are mailed, as follows:

Unearned Subscriptions	20	
Subscription Revenues		20
Delivery of monthly magazine issues		

Many businesses, such as repair companies, construction companies, and special-order firms, ask for a deposit or advance from a customer before they will begin work. These advances are also current liabilities until the goods or services are delivered.

ESTIMATED LIABILITIES

Estimated liabilities are debts or obligations of a company for which the exact amount cannot be known until a later date. Since there is no doubt about the existence of the legal obligation, the primary accounting problem is to estimate and record the amount of the liability. Examples of estimated liabilities are income taxes, property taxes, product warranties, and vacation pay.

Income Taxes Payable   The income of a corporation is taxed by the federal government, most state governments, and some cities and towns. The amount of income tax liability depends on the results of operations. Often that is not certain until after the end of the year. However, because income taxes are an expense in the year in which income is earned, an adjusting entry is necessary to record the estimated tax liability. An example of this entry follows:

Dec. 31	Federal Income Tax Expense	53,000	
	Federal Income Tax Payable		53,000
	To record estimated federal		
	income tax		

Remember that sole proprietorships and partnerships do *not* pay income taxes. Their owners must report their share of the firm's income on their individual tax returns.

Property Taxes Payable   Property taxes are taxes levied on real property, such as land and buildings, and on personal property, such as inventory and equipment. Property taxes are a main source of revenue for local governments. Usually they are assessed annually against the property involved. Because the fiscal years of local governments and their assessment dates rarely correspond to a firm's fiscal year, it is necessary to estimate the amount of property taxes that applies to each month of the year. Assume, for instance, that a local government has a fiscal year of July 1 to June 30, that its assessment date is November 1 for the current fiscal year that began on July 1, and that its payment date is December 15. Assume also that on July 1, Janis Corporation estimates that its property tax assessment for the coming year will be $24,000. The adjusting entry to be made on July 31, which would be repeated on August 31, September 30, and October 31, would be as follows:

July 31	Property Taxes Expense	2,000	
	Estimated Property Taxes Payable		2,000
	To record estimated property taxes		
	expense for the month		
	$24,000 ÷ 12 months = $2,000		

On November 1, the firm receives a property tax bill for $24,720. The estimate made in July was too low. The charge should have been $2,060 per month. Because the difference between the actual assessment and the estimate is small, the company decides to absorb in November the amount undercharged in the previous four months. Therefore, the property tax expense for November is $2,300 [$2,060 + 4($60)] and is recorded as follows:

Nov. 30	Property Taxes Expense	2,300	
	Estimated Property Taxes Payable		2,300
	To record estimated property taxes		

The Estimated Property Taxes Payable account now has a balance of $10,300. The entry to record payment on December 15 would be as follows:

Dec. 15	Estimated Property Taxes Payable	10,300	
	Prepaid Property Taxes	14,420	
	Cash		24,720
	Payment of property taxes		

Beginning December 31 and each month afterward until June 30, property tax expense is recorded by a debit to Property Taxes Expense and a credit to Prepaid Property Taxes in the amount of $2,060. The total of these seven entries will reduce the Prepaid Property Taxes account to zero on June 30.

Product Warranty Liability　　　　When a firm places a warranty or guarantee on its product at the time of sale, a liability exists for the length of the warranty. The cost of the warranty is properly debited to an expense account in the period of sale because it is a feature of the product or service sold and thus is included in the price paid by the customer for the product. On the basis of experience, it should be possible to estimate the amount the warranty will cost in the future. Some products or services will require little warranty service; others may require much. Thus, there will be an average cost per product or service.

For example, assume that a muffler company guarantees that it will replace any muffler free of charge if it fails during the time you own your car. The company charges a small service fee for replacing the muffler. This guarantee is an important selling feature for the firm's mufflers. In the past, 6 percent of the mufflers sold have been returned for replacement under the guarantee. The average cost of a muffler is $25. Assume that during July, 350 mufflers were sold. This accrued liability would be recorded as an adjustment at the end of July as follows:

July 31	Product Warranty Expense	525	
	Estimated Product Warranty Liability		525
	To record estimated product		
	warranty expense:		
	Number of units sold	350	
	Rate of replacement under warranty	× .06	
	Estimated units to be replaced	21	
	Estimated cost per unit	× $ 25	
	Estimated liability for product warranty	$525	

When a muffler is returned for replacement under the product warranty, the cost of the muffler is charged against the Estimated Product Warranty Liability account. For example, assume that a customer returns on December 5 with a defective muffler and pays a $10 service fee to have the muffler replaced. Assume that this particular muffler cost $20. The entry is as follows:

Dec. 5	Cash	10	
	Estimated Product Warranty Liability	20	
	Service Revenue		10
	Merchandise Inventory		20
	Replacement of muffler		
	under warranty		

BUSINESS BULLETIN: BUSINESS PRACTICE

Many companies promote their products by issuing coupons that offer "cents off" or other enticements for purchasers. Since four out of five shoppers use coupons, companies are forced by competition to use them. The total value of these coupons, each of which represents a potential liability for the issuing company, is truly staggering. NCH Promotional Services, a company owned by Dun & Bradstreet, estimates that more than 300 billion coupons were issued in 1993. Of course, the liability depends on how many of the coupons will actually be redeemed. NCH estimates that approximately 7 billion, or about 2.3 percent, will be redeemed. This is not a large percentage, but the value of the redeemed coupons is estimated to be more than $4 billion.[4]

Vacation Pay Liability　　　In most companies, employees earn the right to paid vacation days or weeks as they work during the year. For example, an employee may earn two weeks of paid vacation for each fifty weeks of work. Therefore, she or he is paid fifty-two weeks' salary for fifty weeks' work. Theoretically, the cost of the two weeks' vacation should be allocated as an expense over the whole year so that month-to-month costs will not be distorted. The vacation pay represents 4 percent (two weeks' vacation divided by fifty weeks) of a worker's pay. Every week worked earns the employee a small fraction (4 percent) of his or her vacation pay. Vacation pay liability can amount to a substantial amount of money. For example, Delta Airlines reported at its 1992 year end a vacation pay liability of $192,198,000.[5]

Suppose that a company with this vacation policy has a payroll of $21,000, of which $1,000 was paid to employees on vacation for the week ended April 20. Since not all employees in every company will collect vacation pay because of turnover and rules regarding term of employment, it is assumed that 75 percent of employees will ultimately collect vacation pay. The computation of vacation pay expense based on the payroll of employees not on vacation ($21,000 − $1,000) is as follows: $20,000 × 4 percent × 75 percent =

---

4. "Coupons Show Less Redeeming Value," *Chicago Tribune,* July 16, 1993.
5. Delta Airlines, *Annual Report,* 1992.

$600. The entry to record vacation pay expense for the week ended April 20 is as follows:

Apr. 20	Vacation Pay Expense	600	
	Estimated Liability for Vacation Pay		600
	Estimated vacation pay expense		

At the time employees receive their vacation pay, an entry is made debiting Estimated Liability for Vacation Pay and crediting Cash or Wages Payable. For example, the entry to record the $1,000 paid to employees on vacation is as follows:

Aug. 31	Estimated Liability for Vacation Pay	1,000	
	Cash (or Wages Payable)		1,000
	Wages of employees on vacation		

The treatment presented in this example for vacation pay may also be applied to other payroll costs, such as bonus plans and contributions to pension plans.

CONTINGENT LIABILITIES

OBJECTIVE

3 *Define* contingent liability

A contingent liability is not an existing liability. Rather, it is a potential liability because it depends on a future event arising out of a past transaction. For instance, a construction company that built a bridge may have been sued by the state for using poor materials. The past transaction is the building of the bridge under contract. The future event is the outcome of the lawsuit, which is not yet known.

Two conditions have been established by the FASB for determining when a contingency should be entered in the accounting records: (1) the liability must be probable and (2) it must be reasonably estimated.[6] Estimated liabilities such as the estimated income taxes liability, warranty liability, and vacation pay liability that were described earlier in this chapter meet these conditions. Therefore, they are accrued in the accounting records. Potential liabilities that do not meet both conditions (probable and reasonably estimated) are reported in the notes to the financial statements. Losses from such potential liabilities are recorded when the conditions set by the FASB are met. The following example comes from the notes in a recent annual report of Humana Inc., one of the largest health services organizations:

> Management continually evaluates contingencies based upon the best available evidence. In addition, allowances for loss are provided currently for disputed items that have continuing significance, such as certain third-party reimbursements and deductions that continue to be claimed in current cost reports and tax returns.
>
> Management believes that allowances for loss have been provided to the extent necessary and that its assessment of contingencies is reasonable. To the extent that resolution of contingencies results in amounts that vary from management's estimates, earnings will be charged or credited.
>
> Humana's principal contingencies are described below:
>
> *Revenues*—Certain third-party payments are subject to examination by agencies administering the programs. Management is contesting certain issues raised in audits of prior year cost reports.

---

6. *Statement of Financial Accounting Standards No. 5*, "Accounting for Contingencies" (Stamford, Conn.: Financial Accounting Standards Board, 1975).

Professional Liability Risks—Humana has provided for loss for professional liability risks based upon actuarially determined estimates. Actual settlements and expenses incident thereto may differ from the provisions for loss. See Note 5.

Interest Rate Agreements—Humana has entered into agreements which reduce the impact of changes in interest rates on its floating rate long-term debt. In the event of nonperformance by other parties to these agreements, Humana may incur a loss based on the difference between market rates and the contract rates.

Income Taxes—Management is contesting adjustments proposed by the Internal Revenue Service for years 1988 and 1989.

Litigation—Various suits and claims arising in the ordinary course of business are pending against Humana.[7]

Contingent liabilities may also arise from failure to follow government regulations, from discounted notes receivable, and from guarantees of the debt of other companies.

THE TIME VALUE OF MONEY

OBJECTIVE

4 *Define* interest *and distinguish between simple and compound interest*

Interest is the cost associated with the use of money for a specific period of time. It is an important cost to the debtor and an important revenue to the creditor. Because interest is a cost associated with time, and "time is money," it is also an important consideration in any business decision. For example, an individual who holds $100 for one year without putting that $100 in a savings account has forgone the interest that could have been earned. Thus, there is a cost associated with holding this money equal to the interest that could have been earned. Similarly, a businessperson who accepts a non-interest-bearing note instead of cash for the sale of merchandise is not forgoing the interest that could have been earned on that money but is including the interest implicitly in the price of the merchandise. These examples illustrate the point that the timing of the receipt and payment of cash must be considered in making business decisions.

BUSINESS BULLETIN: BUSINESS PRACTICE

Choosing the right interest rate to use in making decisions is difficult because interest rates can vary greatly depending on the length to maturity and the risk associated with the borrower's ability to pay. For example, Figure 10-4 shows the relationship of interest rates to length of maturity and risk for U.S. Treasury debt (lower line) and corporate debt (higher line). As the maturities become longer, the interest rates increase because the longer the time until a debt is paid, the greater the risk that it will not be paid. Creditors require a higher interest rate if they are going to wait longer for payment. The interest rates for corporate debt are higher at all maturities because corporations are considered to have more risk of nonpayment

7. Humana, Inc., *Annual Report*, 1992.

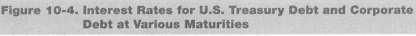

Figure 10-4. Interest Rates for U.S. Treasury Debt and Corporate Debt at Various Maturities

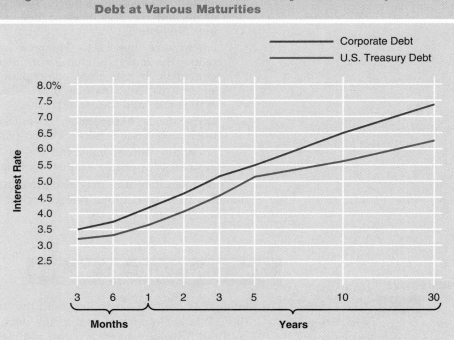

Source: Market quotations, December 1993.

than the U.S. Treasury. Also, interest rates and thus the lines on Figure 10-4 can move up or down by large amounts depending on the economy. Just a few years ago, interest rates were as much as three times higher than those shown on the graph because the rate of inflation was much higher. The rate of inflation affects interest rates because the interest must compensate the creditor for the money loaned but also for the loss in purchasing power from the inflation. When interest rates are low, corporate management tries to lock in the low rates through long-term borrowing, but such rates are still higher than short-term rates for the reason that more risk is associated with long-term loans. ════

SIMPLE INTEREST AND COMPOUND INTEREST

Simple interest is the interest cost for one or more periods if we assume that the amount on which the interest is computed stays the same from period to period. Compound interest is the interest cost for two or more periods if we assume that after each period the interest of that period is added to the amount on which interest is computed in future periods. In other words, compound interest is interest earned on a principal sum that is increased at the end of each period by the interest of that period.

Example: Simple Interest   Joe Sanchez accepts an 8 percent, $30,000 note due in ninety days. How much will he receive in total at that time? Remember the formula for calculating simple interest, which was presented in the chapter on short-term liquid assets as part of the discussion of notes receivable:

$$\begin{aligned}
\text{Interest} &= \text{principal} \times \text{rate} \times \text{time} \\
&= \$30,000 \times 8/100 \times 90/360 \\
&= \$600
\end{aligned}$$

The total that Sanchez will receive is computed as follows:

$$\begin{aligned}
\text{Total} &= \text{principal} + \text{interest} \\
&= \$30,000 + \$600 \\
&= \$30,600
\end{aligned}$$

Example: Compound Interest   Ann Clary deposits $5,000 in a savings account that pays 6 percent interest. She expects to leave the principal and accumulated interest in the account for three years. How much will her account total at the end of three years? Assume that the interest is paid at the end of the year, that it is added to the principal at that time, and that this total in turn earns interest. The amount at the end of three years may be computed as follows:

(1) Year	(2) Principal Amount at Beginning of Year	(3) Annual Amount of Interest (col. 2 × .06)	(4) Accumulated Amount at End of Year (col. 2 + col. 3)
1	$5,000.00	$300.00	$5,300.00
2	5,300.00	318.00	5,618.00
3	5,618.00	337.08	5,955.08

At the end of three years, Clary will have $5,955.08 in her savings account. Note that the annual amount of interest increases each year by the interest rate times the interest of the previous year. For example, between year 1 and year 2, the interest increased by $18 ($318 − $300), which exactly equals .06 times $300.

OBJECTIVE

5 *Use compound interest tables to compute the future value of a single invested sum at compound interest and of an ordinary annuity*

Future Value of a Single Invested Sum at Compound Interest   Another way to ask the question in the example of compound interest above is, What is the future value of a single sum ($5,000) at compound interest (6 percent) for three years? Future value is the amount that an investment will be worth at a future date if invested at compound interest. A business person often wants to know future value, but the method of computing the future value illustrated above is too time-consuming in practice. Imagine how tedious the calculation would be if the investment spanned ten years instead of three. Fortunately, there are tables that make problems involving compound interest much simpler and quicker to solve. Table 10-1, showing the future value of $1 after a range of time periods, is an example. It is actually part of a larger table, Table 1 in the appendix on future value and present value tables. Suppose that we want to solve the problem of Clary's savings account above. We simply look down the 6 percent column in Table 10-1 until we reach period 3 and find the factor 1.191. This factor, when multiplied by $1, gives the future value of that $1 at compound interest of 6 percent for three periods (years in this case). Thus, we solve the problem as shown on the next page:

Table 10-1. Future Value of $1 after a Given Number of Time Periods

Periods	1%	2%	3%	4%	5%	6%	7%	8%	9%	10%	12%	14%	15%
1	1.010	1.020	1.030	1.040	1.050	1.060	1.070	1.080	1.090	1.100	1.120	1.140	1.150
2	1.020	1.040	1.061	1.082	1.103	1.124	1.145	1.166	1.188	1.210	1.254	1.300	1.323
3	1.030	1.061	1.093	1.125	1.158	1.191	1.225	1.260	1.295	1.331	1.405	1.482	1.521
4	1.041	1.082	1.126	1.170	1.216	1.262	1.311	1.360	1.412	1.464	1.574	1.689	1.749
5	1.051	1.104	1.159	1.217	1.276	1.338	1.403	1.469	1.539	1.611	1.762	1.925	2.011
6	1.062	1.126	1.194	1.265	1.340	1.419	1.501	1.587	1.677	1.772	1.974	2.195	2.313
7	1.072	1.149	1.230	1.316	1.407	1.504	1.606	1.714	1.828	1.949	2.211	2.502	2.660
8	1.083	1.172	1.267	1.369	1.477	1.594	1.718	1.851	1.993	2.144	2.476	2.853	3.059
9	1.094	1.195	1.305	1.423	1.551	1.689	1.838	1.999	2.172	2.358	2.773	3.252	3.518
10	1.105	1.219	1.344	1.480	1.629	1.791	1.967	2.159	2.367	2.594	3.106	3.707	4.046

Source: Excerpt from Table 1 in the appendix on future value and present value tables.

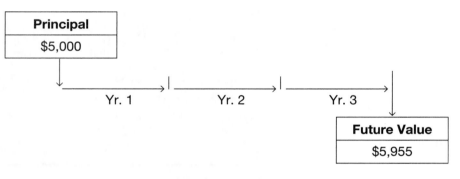

Principal × factor = future value
$5,000 × 1.191 = $5,955

Except for a rounding difference of $.08, the answer is exactly the same as that calculated on the previous page.

Future Value of an Ordinary Annuity   Another common problem involves an ordinary annuity, which is a series of equal payments made at the end of equal intervals of time, with compound interest on the payments.

The following example shows how to find the future value of an ordinary annuity. Assume that Ben Katz makes a $200 payment at the end of each of the next three years into a savings account that pays 5 percent interest. How much money will he have in his account at the end of the three years? One way of computing the amount is shown in the following table:

(1) Year	(2) Beginning Balance	(3) Interest Earned (5% × col. 2)	(4) Periodic Payment	(5) Accumulated at End of Period (col. 2 + col. 3 + col. 4)
1	$ —	$ —	$200	$200.00
2	200.00	10.00	200	410.00
3	410.00	20.50	200	630.50

Katz would have $630.50 in his account at the end of three years, consisting of $600.00 in periodic payments and $30.50 in interest.

This calculation can also be simplified by using Table 10-2. We look down the 5 percent column until we reach period 3 and find the factor 3.153. This factor, when multiplied by $1, gives the future value of a series of three $1 payments made at the end of these periods (years in this case) at compound interest of 5 percent. Thus, we solve the problem as shown below.

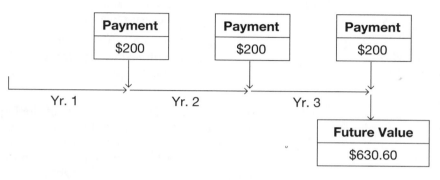

Periodic payment × factor = future value
$200.00   × 3.153 = $630.60

Except for a rounding difference of $0.10, this result is the same as the one calculated earlier.

PRESENT VALUE

OBJECTIVE

6 *Use compound interest tables to compute the present value of a single sum due in the future and of an ordinary annuity*

Suppose that you had the choice of receiving $100 today or one year from today. Intuitively, you would choose to receive the $100 today. Why? You know that if you have the $100 today, you can put it in a savings account to earn interest, so that you will have more than $100 a year from today. Therefore, we can say that an amount to be received in the future (future value) is not worth as much today as an amount to be received today (present value) because of the cost associated with the passage of time. In fact, present value and future value are closely related. Present value is the amount that

Table 10-2. Future Value of an Ordinary Annuity of $1 Paid in Each Period for a Given Number of Time Periods

Periods	1%	2%	3%	4%	5%	6%	7%	8%	9%	10%	12%	14%	15%
1	1.000	1.000	1.000	1.000	1.000	1.000	1.000	1.000	1.000	1.000	1.000	1.000	1.000
2	2.010	2.020	2.030	2.040	2.050	2.060	2.070	2.080	2.090	2.100	2.120	2.140	2.150
3	3.030	3.060	3.091	3.122	3.153	3.184	3.215	3.246	3.278	3.310	3.374	3.440	3.473
4	4.060	4.122	4.184	4.246	4.310	4.375	4.440	4.506	4.573	4.641	4.779	4.921	4.993
5	5.101	5.204	5.309	5.416	5.526	5.637	5.751	5.867	5.985	6.105	6.353	6.610	6.742
6	6.152	6.308	6.468	6.633	6.802	6.975	7.153	7.336	7.523	7.716	8.115	8.536	8.754
7	7.214	7.434	7.662	7.898	8.142	8.394	8.654	8.923	9.200	9.487	10.09	10.73	11.07
8	8.286	8.583	8.892	9.214	9.549	9.897	10.26	10.64	11.03	11.44	12.30	13.23	13.73
9	9.369	9.755	10.16	10.58	11.03	11.49	11.98	12.49	13.02	13.58	14.78	16.09	16.79
10	10.46	10.95	11.46	12.01	12.58	13.18	13.82	14.49	15.19	15.94	17.55	19.34	20.30

Source: Excerpt from Table 2 in the appendix on future value and present value tables.

must be invested now at a given rate of interest to produce a given future value.

For example, assume that Sue Dapper needs $1,000 one year from now. How much should she invest today to achieve that goal if the interest rate is 5 percent? From earlier examples, the following equation may be established:

Present value $\times$ (1.0 + interest rate) = future value
Present value $\times$ 1.05   = $1,000.00
Present value   = $1,000.00 ÷ 1.05
Present value   = $ 952.38

Thus, to achieve a future value of $1,000.00, a present value of $952.38 must be invested. Interest of 5 percent on $952.38 for one year equals $47.62, and these two amounts added together equal $1,000.00.

Present Value of a Single Sum Due in the Future   When more than one time period is involved, the calculation of present value is more complicated. Consider the following example. Don Riley wants to be sure of having $4,000 at the end of three years. How much must he invest today in a 5 percent savings account to achieve this goal? Adapting the above equation, we compute the present value of $4,000 at compound interest of 5 percent for three years in the future.

Year	Amount at End of Year	Divide by			Present Value at Beginning of Year
3	$4,000.00	÷	1.05	=	$3,809.52
2	3,809.52	÷	1.05	=	3,628.11
1	3,628.11	÷	1.05	=	3,455.34

Riley must invest a present value of $3,455.34 to achieve a future value of $4,000.00 in three years.

This calculation is again made much easier by using the appropriate table. In Table 10-3, we look down the 5 percent column until we reach period 3 and find the factor .864. This factor, when multiplied by $1, gives the present value of $1 to be received three years from now at 5 percent interest. Thus, we solve the problem:

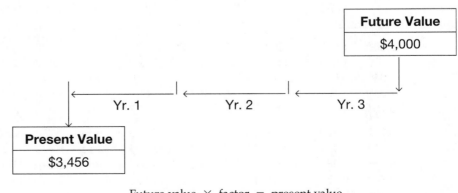

Future value $\times$ factor = present value
$4,000 $\times$ .864 = $3,456

Table 10-3. Present Value of $1 to Be Received at the End of a Given Number of Time Periods

Periods	1%	2%	3%	4%	5%	6%	7%	8%	9%	10%
1	0.990	0.980	0.971	0.962	0.952	0.943	0.935	0.926	0.917	0.909
2	0.980	0.961	0.943	0.925	0.907	0.890	0.873	0.857	0.842	0.826
3	0.971	0.942	0.915	0.889	0.864	0.840	0.816	0.794	0.772	0.751
4	0.961	0.924	0.888	0.855	0.823	0.792	0.763	0.735	0.708	0.683
5	0.951	0.906	0.883	0.822	0.784	0.747	0.713	0.681	0.650	0.621
6	0.942	0.888	0.837	0.790	0.746	0.705	0.666	0.630	0.596	0.564
7	0.933	0.871	0.813	0.760	0.711	0.665	0.623	0.583	0.547	0.513
8	0.923	0.853	0.789	0.731	0.677	0.627	0.582	0.540	0.502	0.467
9	0.914	0.837	0.766	0.703	0.645	0.592	0.544	0.500	0.460	0.424
10	0.905	0.820	0.744	0.676	0.614	0.558	0.508	0.463	0.422	0.386

Source: Excerpt from Table 3 in the appendix on future value and present value tables.

Except for a rounding difference of $.66, this result is the same as the one above.

Present Value of an Ordinary Annuity   It is often necessary to compute the present value of a series of receipts or payments. When we calculate the present value of equal amounts equally spaced over a period of time, we are computing the present value of an ordinary annuity.

For example, assume that Kathy Foster has sold a piece of property and is to receive $15,000 in three equal annual payments of $5,000, beginning one year from today. What is the present value of this sale, assuming a current interest rate of 5 percent? This present value may be computed by calculating a separate present value for each of the three payments (using Table 10-3) and summing the results, as follows:

Future Receipts (Annuity)				Present Value Factor at 5 Percent (from Table 10-3)		Present Value
Year 1	Year 2	Year 3				
$5,000			×	.952	=	$ 4,760
	$5,000		×	.907	=	4,535
		$5,000	×	.864	=	4,320
Total Present Value						$13,615

The present value of this sale is $13,615. Thus, there is an implied interest cost (given the 5 percent rate) of $1,385 associated with the payment plan that allows the purchaser to pay in three installments.

We can make this calculation more easily by using Table 10-4. We look down the 5 percent column until we reach period 3 and find the factor 2.723. This factor, when multiplied by $1, gives the present value of a series of three $1 payments (spaced one year apart) at compound interest of 5 percent. Thus, we solve the problem as shown on the next page.

Table 10-4. Present Value of an Ordinary Annuity of $1 Received Each Period for a Given Number of Time Periods

Periods	1%	2%	3%	4%	5%	6%	7%	8%	9%	10%
1	0.990	0.980	0.971	0.962	0.952	0.943	0.935	0.926	0.917	0.909
2	1.970	1.942	1.913	1.886	1.859	1.833	1.808	1.783	1.759	1.736
3	2.941	2.884	2.829	2.775	2.723	2.673	2.624	2.577	2.531	2.487
4	3.902	3.808	3.717	3.630	3.546	3.465	3.387	3.312	3.240	3.170
5	4.853	4.713	4.580	4.452	4.329	4.212	4.100	3.993	3.890	3.791
6	5.795	5.601	5.417	5.242	5.076	4.917	4.767	4.623	4.486	4.355
7	6.728	6.472	6.230	6.002	5.786	5.582	5.389	5.206	5.033	4.868
8	7.652	7.325	7.020	6.733	6.463	6.210	5.971	5.747	5.535	5.335
9	8.566	8.162	7.786	7.435	7.108	6.802	6.515	6.247	5.995	5.759
10	9.471	8.983	8.530	8.111	7.722	7.360	7.024	6.710	6.418	6.145

Source: Excerpt from Table 4 in the appendix on future value and present value tables.

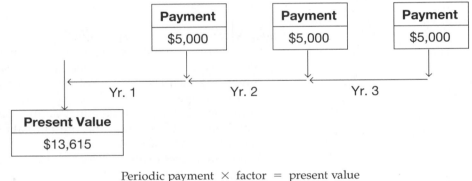

Periodic payment × factor = present value
$5,000 × 2.723 = $13,615

This result is the same as the one computed earlier.

TIME PERIODS

In all of the previous examples, and in most other cases, the compounding period is one year, and the interest rate is stated on an annual basis. However, in each of the four tables the left-hand column refers to periods, not to years. This is intended to accommodate compounding periods of less than one year. Savings accounts that record interest quarterly and bonds that pay interest semiannually are cases where the compounding period is less than one year. To use the tables in such cases, it is necessary to (1) divide the annual interest rate by the number of periods in the year, and (2) multiply the number of periods in one year by the number of years.

For example, assume that a $6,000 note is to be paid in two years and carries an annual interest rate of 8 percent. Compute the maturity (future) value of the note, assuming that the compounding period is semiannual. Before using the table, it is necessary to compute the interest rate that applies to each compounding period and the total number of compounding periods. First, the interest rate to use is 4 percent (8% annual rate ÷ 2 periods per year). Second, the total number of compounding periods is 4 (2 periods per year × 2 years). From Table 10-1, therefore, the maturity value of the note may be computed as follows:

$$\text{Principal} \times \text{factor} = \text{future value}$$
$$\$6,000 \times 1.170 = \$7,020$$

The note will be worth $7,020 in two years.

This procedure for determining the interest rate and the number of periods when the compounding period is less than one year may be used with all four tables.

Safety-Net Corporation

DECISION POINT

The fair market value of individual assets is sometimes difficult to determine. Valuing a business is even more difficult. The seller and buyer may have different views of a businesses's value. How can present value methods be used to resolve the differences between buyer and seller by illuminating the effects of each party's assumptions?

Robert Taft, president of Safety-Net Corporation, a manufacturer of a car safety restraint for children, wants to sell the business. He wants to receive $12,000,000 for the company, which has stockholders' equity (net assets) of $10,000,000. He argues that this price is a bargain because the company will generate annual cash flows of $2,000,000 for twenty years. Given an annual return of 15 percent, he says, the present value of the business should be $12,518,000, calculated from Table 4 in the appendix on future value and present value tables (20 years, 15 percent) as follows:

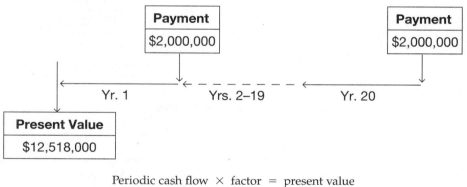

$$\text{Periodic cash flow} \times \text{factor} = \text{present value}$$
$$\$2,000,000 \times 6.259 = \$12,518,000$$

Susan Arnett, who represents a group of investors, is willing to pay no more than $10,000,000, the amount of stockholders' equity, because she believes Taft's assumptions are overly optimistic. First, she would reduce the twenty-year time period to twelve years because she is convinced that after that time, prospects for the business become uncertain. Using the same table as Taft did, she recalculates the present value of the business based on twelve years (12 years, 15 percent) as follows:

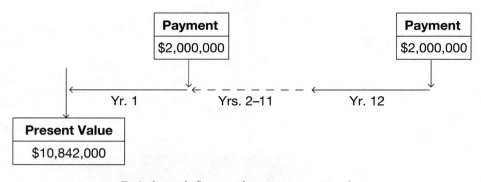

$$
\begin{array}{llll}
\text{Periodic cash flow} & \times & \text{factor} & = & \text{present value} \\
\$2,000,000 & \times & 5.421 & = & \$10,842,000
\end{array}
$$

Under Arnett's assumptions, the present value of the business decreases by \$1,676,000 (\$12,518,000 − \$10,842,000). Note that under the present value method, the effect of decreasing the time frame from twenty to twelve years is much less than the \$16,000,000 (\$2,000,000 × 8 years) realized through cash flows because the cash flows from distant years have low present values.

Second, Arnett questions whether the company can produce an annual cash flow of \$2,000,000. She believes that an annual cash flow of \$1,800,000 is more realistic. The present value of the business, using the same factor from the same table (12 years, 15 percent), would be calculated as follows:

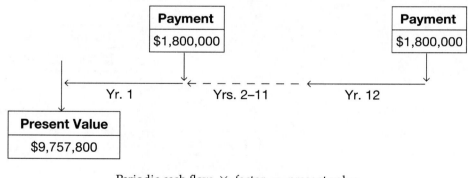

$$
\begin{array}{llll}
\text{Periodic cash flow} & \times & \text{factor} & = & \text{present value} \\
\$1,800,000 & \times & 5.421 & = & \$9,757,800
\end{array}
$$

Under this assumption of reduced annual cash flow, the present value of the business drops by another \$1,084,200 (\$10,842,000 − \$9,757,800) to \$9,757,800, an amount that is very much in line with Arnett's offer. Taft and Arnett now have a bargaining range within which they may be able to resolve their differences. Whether or not the two parties will be able to reach an agreement is open to question, but at least they know the source of their differences: the number of years over which the annual cash flows should be projected, and the amount of the annual cash flows. : : : :

APPLICATIONS OF PRESENT VALUE TO ACCOUNTING

The concept of present value is widely applicable in the discipline of accounting. Here, the purpose is to demonstrate its usefulness in some simple applications. In-depth study of present value is deferred to more advanced courses.

OBJECTIVE

Apply the concept of present value to simple accounting situations

Imputing Interest on Non-Interest-Bearing Notes   Clearly there is no such thing as an interest-free debt, regardless of whether the interest rate is explicitly stated. The Accounting Principles Board has declared that when a long-term note does not explicitly state an interest rate (or the interest rate is unreasonably low), a rate based on the normal interest cost of the company in question should be assigned, or imputed.[8]

The following example applies this principle. On January 1, 19x8, Gato, Inc. purchases merchandise from Haines Corp. by issuing an $8,000 non-interest-bearing note due in two years. Gato can borrow money from the bank at 9 percent interest. Gato pays the note in full after two years.

Note that the $8,000 note represents partly a payment for merchandise and partly a payment of interest for two years. In recording the purchase and sale, it is necessary to use Table 10-3 to determine the present value of the note. The calculation follows.

$$\text{Future payment} \times \text{present value factor (9\%, 2 years)} = \text{present value}$$
$$\$8,000 \qquad \times \qquad .842 \qquad = \qquad \$6,736$$

The imputed interest cost is $1,264 ($8,000 − $6,736). This is recorded as a discount on notes payable in Gato's records and as a discount on notes receivable in Haines's records. The entries necessary to record the purchase in the Gato records and the sale in the Haines records are as follows:

Gato, Inc. Journal			Haines Corp. Journal		
Purchases	6,736		Notes Receivable	8,000	
Discount on			Discount on		
Notes Payable	1,264		Notes Receivable		1,264
Notes Payable		8,000	Sales		6,736
Purchase of			Sale of		
Merchandise			Merchandise		

On December 31, 19x8, the adjustments to recognize the interest expense and interest income will be

Gato, Inc. Journal			Haines Corp. Journal		
Interest Expense	606.24		Discount on		
Discount on		606.24	Notes Receivable	606.24	
Notes Payable			Interest Income		606.24
Interest expense			Interest income		
for one year			for one year		

8. Accounting Principles Board, *Opinion No. 21*, "Interest on Receivables and Payables" (New York: American Institute of Certified Public Accountants, 1971), par. 13.

The interest is calculated by multiplying the original purchase by the interest for one year ($6,736.00 × .09 = $606.24). When payment is made on December 31, 19x9, the entries below will be made in the respective journals:

Gato, Inc. Journal				**Haines Corp. Journal**		
Interest Expense	657.76			Discount on		
Notes Payable	8,000.00			Notes Receivable	657.76	
Discount on				Cash	8,000.00	
Notes Payable		657.76		Interest Income		657.76
Cash		8,000.00		Notes Receivable		8,000.00
Payment of note				Payment of note		

The interest entries represent the remaining interest to be expensed or realized ($1,264 − $606.24 = $657.76). This amount approximates (because of rounding differences in the table) the interest for one year on the purchase plus last year's interest [($6,736 + $606.24) × .09 = $660.80].

Valuing an Asset   An asset is recorded because it will provide future benefits to the company that owns it. This future benefit is the basis for the definition of an asset. Usually, the purchase price of the asset represents the present value of these future benefits. It is possible to evaluate a proposed purchase price of an asset by comparing that price with the present value of the asset to the company.

For example, Sam Hurst is thinking of buying a new labor-saving machine that will reduce his annual labor cost by $700 per year. The machine will last eight years. The interest rate that Hurst assumes for making managerial decisions is 10 percent. What is the maximum amount (present value) that Hurst should pay for the machine?

The present value of the machine to Hurst is equal to the present value of an ordinary annuity of $700 per year for eight years at compound interest of 10 percent. From Table 10-4, we compute the value as follows:

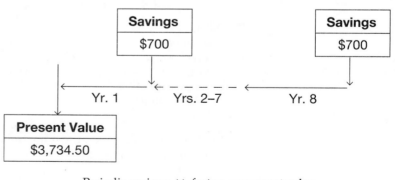

Periodic savings × factor = present value
$700.00   × 5.335 = $3,734.50

Hurst should not pay more than $3,734.50 for the new machine because this amount equals the present value of the benefits that will be received from owning the machine.

Deferred Payment   A seller will sometimes agree to defer payment for a sale to encourage the buyer to make the purchase. This practice is common, for example, in the farm implement industry, where a farmer needs equipment in the spring but cannot pay for it until the fall crop is in. Assume that Plains Implement Corporation sells a tractor to Dana Washington for $50,000 on February 1, agreeing to take payment ten months later on December 1. When this type of agreement is made, the future payment includes not only the sales price of the tractor but also an implied (imputed) interest cost. If the prevailing annual interest rate for such transactions is 12 percent compounded monthly, the actual sale (purchase) price of the tractor would be the present value of the future payment, computed according to Table 10-3 (10 periods, 1 percent), as follows:

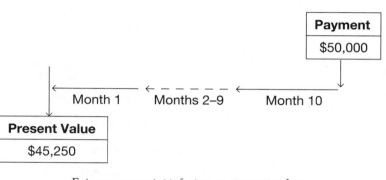

$$\text{Future payment} \times \text{factor} = \text{present value}$$
$$\$50,000 \qquad \times \quad .905 \quad = \qquad \$45,250$$

The purchase in Washington's records and the sale in Plains's records are recorded at the present value, $45,250. The balance consists of interest expense or interest income. The entries necessary to record the purchase in Washington's records and the sale in Plains's records are as follows:

	Washington's Journal			**Plains's Journal**		
Feb. 1	Tractor	45,250		Accounts Receivable	45,250	
	Accounts Payable		45,250	Sales		45,250
	Purchase of tractor			Sale of tractor		

When Washington pays for the tractor, the entries are as follows:

	Washington's Journal			**Plains's Journal**		
Dec. 1	Accounts Payable	45,250		Cash	50,000	
	Interest Expense	4,750		Accounts Receivable		45,250
	Cash		50,000	Interest Income		4,750
	Payment on account			Receipt on account from		
	including imputed			Washington including		
	interest expense			imputed interest earned		

Investment of Idle Cash   Childware Corporation, a toy manufacturer, has just completed a successful fall selling season and has $10,000,000 in cash to invest for six months. The company places the cash in a money market account that is expected to pay 12 percent annual interest. Interest is compounded monthly and credited to the company's account each month. How much cash will the company have at the end of six months, and what entries will be made to record the investment and the monthly interest? From Table

10-1, the future value factor is based on six monthly periods of 1 percent (12 percent divided by 12 months), and the future value is computed as follows:

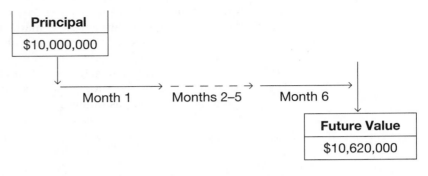

$$\text{Investment} \times \text{factor} = \text{future value}$$
$$\$10,000,000 \times 1.062 = \$10,620,000$$

When the investment is made, the journal entry is as follows:

Short-Term Investments	10,000,000	
Cash		10,000,000
Investment of cash		

After the first month, the interest is recorded by increasing the Short-Term Investments account, as follows:

Short-Term Investments	100,000	
Interest Income		100,000
One month's interest income		
$\$10,000,000 \times .01 = \$100,000$		

After the second month, the interest is earned on the new balance of the Short-Term Investments account, as follows:

Short-Term Investments	101,000	
Interest Income		101,000
One month's interest income		
$\$10,100,000 \times .01 = \$101,000$		

Entries would continue in a similar manner for four more months, at which time the balance of Short-Term Investments would be about $10,620,000. The actual amount accumulated may vary from this total because the interest rate paid on money market accounts can vary over time as a result of changes in market conditions.

Accumulation of a Fund   When a company owes a large fixed amount due in several years, management would be wise to accumulate a fund with which to pay off the debt at maturity. Sometimes creditors, when they agree to provide a loan, require that such a fund be established. In establishing the fund, management must determine how much cash to set aside each period to pay the debt. The amount will depend on the estimated rate of interest the investments will earn. Assume that Vason Corporation agrees with a creditor to set aside cash at the end of each year to accumulate enough to pay off a $100,000 note due in five years. Since the first contribution to the fund will be made in one year, five annual contributions will be made by the time the note is due. Assume also that the fund is projected to earn 8 percent, compounded annually. The amount of each annual payment is calculated from Table 10-2 (5 periods, 8 percent), as follows:

Payment	Payment	Payment	Payment	Payment
$17,044	$17,044	$17,044	$17,044	$17,044

Yr. 1   Yr. 2   Yr. 3   Yr. 4   Yr. 5

Future Value
$100,000

$$\text{Future value of fund} \div \text{factor} = \text{annual investment}$$
$$\$100,000 \div 5.867 = \$17,044 \text{ (rounded)}$$

Each year's contribution to the fund is $17,044. This contribution is recorded as follows:

Loan Repayment Fund	17,044	
Cash		17,044
Annual contribution to loan		
repayment fund		

Other Accounting Applications   There are many other applications of present value in accounting. The uses of present value in accounting for installment notes, valuing a bond, and recording lease obligations are shown in the chapter on long-term liabilities. Present value is also applied in such areas as pension obligations; premium and discount on debt; depreciation of property, plant, and equipment; capital expenditure decisions; and generally any situation where time is a factor.

CHAPTER REVIEW

REVIEW OF LEARNING OBJECTIVES

1.   **Identify the management issues related to recognition, valuation, classification, and disclosure of current liabilities.** Liabilities represent present legal obligations for future payment of assets or future performance of services. They result from past transactions and should be recognized when there is a transaction that obligates the company to make future payments. Liabilities are valued at the amount of money necessary to satisfy the obligation or the fair value of goods or services that must be delivered. Liabilities are classified as current or long term. Supplemental disclosure is required when the nature or details of the obligations would help in understanding the liability.

2.   **Identify, compute, and record definitely determinable and estimated current liabilities.** Two principal categories of current liabilities are definitely determinable liabilities and estimated liabilities. Although definitely determinable liabilities, such as accounts payable, notes payable, dividends payable, accrued liabilities, and the current portion of long-term debt, can be measured exactly, the accountant must still be careful not to overlook existing liabilities in these categories. Estimated liabilities, such as liabilities for income taxes, property taxes, and product warranties, definitely exist, but the amounts must be estimated and recorded properly.

3. **Define *contingent liability.*** A contingent liability is a potential liability arising from a past transaction and dependent on a future event. Examples are lawsuits, income tax disputes, discounted notes receivable, guarantees of debt, and the potential cost of changes in government regulations.

4. **Define *interest* and distinguish between simple and compound interest.** Interest is the cost of using money for a period of time. In computing simple interest, the amount on which the interest is computed stays the same from period to period. However, in computing compound interest, the interest for a period is added to the principal amount before the interest for the next period is computed.

5. **Use compound interest tables to compute the future value of a single invested sum at compound interest and of an ordinary annuity.** Future value is the amount that an investment will be worth at a future date if invested at compound interest. An ordinary annuity is a series of equal payments made at the end of equal intervals of time, with compound interest on the payments. Use Table 1 in the appendix on future value and present value tables to compute the future value of a single sum and Table 2 in the same appendix to compute the future value of an ordinary annuity.

6. **Use compound interest tables to compute the present value of a single sum due in the future and of an ordinary annuity.** Present value is the amount that must be invested now at a given rate of interest to produce a given future value. The present value of an ordinary annuity is the present value of a series of payments. Use Table 3 in the appendix on future value and present value tables to compute the present value of a single sum and Table 4 in the same appendix to compute the present value of an ordinary annuity.

7. **Apply the concept of present value to simple accounting situations.** Present value may be used to compute interest on non-interest-bearing notes, to value a bond or other asset, to compute the present value of deferred payments, to determine a bargaining range in negotiating the sale of a business, to determine the future value of an investment of idle cash or the accumulation of a fund, to record lease obligations, and in other accounting situations.

REVIEW OF CONCEPTS AND TERMINOLOGY

The following concepts and terms were introduced in this chapter:

L O 2 **Commercial paper:** A means of borrowing funds by unsecured loans that are sold directly to the public, usually through professionally managed investment firms.

L O 4 **Compound interest:** The interest cost for two or more periods if we assume that after each period the interest of that period is added to the amount on which interest is computed in future periods.

L O 3 **Contingent liability:** A potential liability that depends on a future event arising out of a past transaction.

L O 1 **Current liabilities:** Debts and obligations that are expected to be satisfied within one year or within the normal operating cycle, whichever is longer.

L O 2 **Definitely determinable liabilities:** Current liabilities that are set by contract or by statute and can be measured exactly.

L O 2 **Estimated liabilities:** Definite debts or obligations for which the exact amounts cannot be known until a later date.

L O 5 **Future value:** The amount that an investment will be worth at a future date if invested at compound interest.

L O 4 **Interest:** The cost associated with the use of money for a specific period of time.

L O 1 **Liabilities:** Legal obligations for the future payment of assets or the future performance of services that result from past transactions.

L O 2 **Line of credit:** A preapproved arrangement with a commercial bank that allows a company to borrow funds as needed.

L O 1 **Long-term liabilities:** Debts or obligations that are due beyond one year or beyond the normal operating cycle.

L O 5   **Ordinary annuity:** A series of equal payments made at the end of equal intervals of time, with compound interest on the payments.

L O 6   **Present value:** The amount that must be invested now at a given rate of interest to produce a given future value.

L O 2   **Salaries:** Compensation to employees who are paid at a monthly or yearly rate.

L O 4   **Simple interest:** The interest cost for one or more periods if we assume that the amount on which the interest is computed stays the same from period to period.

L O 2   **Unearned revenues:** Revenues received in advance for which the goods will not be delivered or the services not performed during the current accounting period.

L O 2   **Wages:** Payment for services of employees at an hourly rate or on a piecework basis.

REVIEW PROBLEM

TIME VALUE OF MONEY APPLICATIONS

L O 5, 6, 7   Effective January 1, 19x1, the board of directors of Jefferson Company approved the following actions, each of which is an application of the time value of money:

a. Approved purchase of a parcel of land for future plant expansion. Payments are to start January 1, 19x2, at $100,000 per year for 4 years.

b. Determined that a new building to be built on the property in **a** would cost $800,000 and authorized four annual payments to be paid starting January 1, 19x2, into a fund for its construction.

c. Issued a four-year non-interest-bearing note for $200,000 to an officer in connection with a termination agreement.

d. Established in a single payment of $200,000 a contingency fund for the possible settlement of a lawsuit. The suit is expected to be settled in three years.

e. Asked for another fund to be established by a single payment to accumulate to $500,000 in five years.

REQUIRED   Assuming an annual interest rate of 9 percent and using Tables 10-1, 10-2, 10-3, and 10-4, answer the following questions:

1. In action **a,** what is the purchase price (present value) of the land?
2. In action **b,** how much would the equal annual payments need to be to accumulate enough money to construct the building?
3. In action **c,** what is the actual price of the termination agreement (present value of the note)?
4. In action **d,** how much will the fund accumulate to in three years?
5. In action **e,** how much will need to be initially deposited to accumulate the desired amount?

ANSWER TO REVIEW PROBLEM

1. Present Value of an Ordinary Annuity (Table 10-4)

   Factor: 9%, 4 periods
   $100,000 × 3.240 = $324,000
   Purchase price = $324,000

2. Future Value of an Ordinary Annuity (Table 10-2)

   Factor: 9%, 4 periods
   $800,000 ÷ 4.573 = $174,939.86
   Annual payments = $174,939.86

3. Present Value of a Single Payment (Table 10-3)

   Factor: 9%, 4 periods
   $200,000 × .708 = $141,600
   Price = $141,600

4. Future Value of a Single Payment (Table 10-1)

Factor: 9%, 3 periods
$200,000 × 1.295 = $259,000
Fund balance = $259,000

5. Present Value of a Single Payment (Table 10-3)
Factor: 9%, 5 periods
$500,000 × .650 = $325,000
Initial deposit = $325,000

CHAPTER ASSIGNMENTS

KNOWLEDGE AND UNDERSTANDING

Questions

1. What are liabilities?
2. Why is the timing of liability recognition important in accounting?
3. At the end of the accounting period, Janson Company had a legal obligation to accept delivery and pay for a truckload of hospital supplies the following week. Is this legal obligation a liability?
4. Ned Johnson, a star college basketball player, received a contract from the Midwest Blazers to play professional basketball. The contract calls for a salary of $300,000 a year for four years, dependent on his making the team in each of those years. Should this contract be considered a liability and recorded on the books of the basketball team?
5. What is the rule for classifying a liability as current?
6. What are a line of credit and commercial paper? Where do they appear on the balance sheet?
7. Where should the Discount on Notes Payable account appear on the balance sheet?
8. When can a portion of long-term debt be classified as a current liability?
9. Why is payroll accounting important?
10. Who pays social security and Medicare taxes?
11. Why are unearned revenues classified as liabilities?
12. What is definite about an estimated liability?
13. Why are income taxes payable considered to be estimated liabilities?
14. When does a company incur a liability for a product warranty?
15. What is a contingent liability, and how does it differ from an estimated liability?
16. What are some examples of contingent liabilities? For what reason is each a contingent liability?
17. What is an ordinary annuity?
18. What is the key variable that distinguishes present value from future value?
19. How does the use of a compounding period of less than one year affect the computation of present value?
20. Why is present value important to accounting? (Illustrate your answer by giving concrete examples of applications in accounting.)

Short Exercises

SE 10-1.
L O 1 *Issues in Accounting for Liabilities*

Indicate whether each of the following actions relates to (a) recognition of liabilities, (b) valuation of liabilities, (c) classification of liabilities, or (d) disclosure of liabilities.

1. Determining that a liability will be paid in less than one year.
2. Estimating the amount of a liability.

3. Providing information on when liabilities are due and the interest rate that they carry.
4. Determining when a liability arises.

SE 10-2.
L O 2, 3 *Types of Liabilities*

Indicate whether each of the following is (a) a definitely determinable liability, (b) an estimated liability, or (c) a contingent liability.

1. Dividends Payable
2. Pending litigation
3. Income Taxes Payable
4. Current portion of long-term debt
5. Vacation Pay Liability
6. Guaranteed loans of another company

SE 10-3.
L O 2 *Interest Expense: Interest Not Included in Face Value of Note*

On the last day of August, Gross Company borrows $60,000 on a bank note for sixty days at 10 percent interest. Assume that interest is not included in the face amount. Prepare the following general journal entries: (1) August 31, recording of note; (2) October 30, payment of note plus interest.

SE 10-4.
L O 2 *Interest Expense: Interest Included in Face Value of Note*

Assume the same facts as in SE 10-3, except that interest of $1,000 is included in the face amount of the note and the note is discounted at the bank on August 31. Prepare the following general journal entries: (1) August 31, recording of note; (2) October 30, payment of note and recording of interest expense.

SE 10-5.
L O 2 *Product Warranty Liability*

Rainbow Corp. manufactures and sells travel clocks. Each clock costs $25 to produce and sells for $50. In addition, each clock carries a warranty that provides for free replacement if it fails for any reason during the two years following the sale. In the past, 5 percent of the clocks sold have had to be replaced under the warranty. During October, Rainbow sold 52,000 clocks, and 2,800 clocks were replaced under the warranty. Prepare general journal entries to record the estimated liability for product warranties during the month and the clocks replaced under warranty during the month.

SE 10-6.
L O 2 *Payroll Entries*

The following payroll totals for the month of April were taken from the payroll register of Coover Corporation: salaries, $223,000; social security taxes withheld, $13,826; Medicare taxes withheld, $3,233.50; federal income taxes withheld, $31,440; medical insurance deductions, $6,580; salaries subject to unemployment taxes, $156,600. Prepare general journal entries to record (1) accrual of the monthly payroll and (2) accrual of employer's payroll expense, assuming social security and Medicare taxes equal to the amounts for employees, a federal unemployment insurance tax of .8 percent, a state unemployment tax of 5.4 percent, and medical insurance cost, for which the employer's contribution is 80 percent.

SE 10-7.
L O 4 *Simple and Compound Interest*

Naber Motors, Inc. receives a one-year note that carries a 12 percent annual interest rate on $1,500 for the sale of a used car.

Compute the maturity value under each of the following assumptions: (1) Simple interest is charged. (2) The interest is compounded semiannually. (3) The interest is compounded quarterly. (4) The interest is compounded monthly.

SE 10-8.
L O 5 *Future Value Calculations*

Find the future value of (1) a single payment of $10,000 at 7 percent for ten years, (2) ten annual payments of $1,000 at 7 percent, (3) a single payment of $3,000 at 9 percent for seven years, and (4) seven annual payments of $3,000 at 9 percent.

SE 10-9.
L O 6 *Present Value Calculations*

Find the present value of (1) a single payment of $12,000 at 6 percent for twelve years, (2) twelve annual payments of $1,000 at 6 percent, (3) a single payment of $2,500 at 9 percent for five years, and (4) five annual payments of $2,500 at 9 percent.

SE 10-10.

L O 7 *Valuing an Asset for the Purpose of Making a Purchasing Decision*

Masa owns a machine shop and has the opportunity to purchase a new machine for $15,000. After carefully studying projected costs and revenues, Masa estimates that the new machine will produce a net cash flow of $3,600 annually and will last for eight years. Masa feels that an interest rate of 10 percent is adequate for his business.

Calculate the present value of the machine to Masa. Does the purchase appear to be a correct business decision?

APPLICATION

Exercises

E 10-1.

L O 1 *Issues in Accounting for Liabilities*

Indicate whether each of the following actions relates to (a) recognition of liabilities, (b) valuation of liabilities, (c) classification of liabilities, or (d) disclosure of liabilities.

1. Setting a liability at the fair market value of goods to be delivered.
2. Relating the payment date of a liability to the length of the operating cycle.
3. Recording a liability in accordance with the matching rule.
4. Providing information about financial instruments on the balance sheet.
5. Estimating the amount of "cents off" coupons that will be redeemed.
6. Placing a liability in long-term debt.

E 10-2.

L O 2 *Interest Expense: Interest Not Included in Face Value of Note*

On the last day of October, Ostrand Company borrows $30,000 on a bank note for sixty days at 12 percent interest. Assume that interest is not included in the face amount. Prepare the following general journal entries: (1) October 31, recording of note; (2) November 30, accrual of interest expense; (3) December 30, payment of note plus interest.

E 10-3.

L O 2 *Interest Expense: Interest Included in Face Value of Note*

Assume the same facts as in E 10-2, except that the $600 in interest is included in the face amount of the note and the note is discounted at the bank on October 31. Prepare the following general journal entries: (1) October 31, recording of note; (2) November 30, recognition of interest accrued on note; (3) December 30, payment of note and recording of interest expense.

E 10-4.

L O 2 *Sales and Excise Taxes*

Alert Dial Service billed its customers a total of $980,400 for the month of August, including 9 percent federal excise tax and 5 percent sales tax.

1. Determine the proper amount of revenue to report for the month.
2. Prepare a general journal entry to record the revenue and related liabilities for the month.

E 10-5.

L O 2 *Payroll Entries*

At the end of October, the payroll register for Escalera Corporation contained the following totals: salaries, $371,000; social security taxes withheld, $23,200; Medicare taxes withheld, $5,379.50; federal income taxes withheld, $94,884; state income taxes withheld, $15,636; medical insurance deductions, $12,870; life insurance deductions, $11,712; union dues deductions, $1,368; and salaries subject to unemployment taxes, $57,240.

Prepare general journal entries to record (1) accrual of the monthly payroll and (2) accrual of employer payroll expenses, assuming social security and Medicare taxes equal to the amount for employees, a federal unemployment insurance tax of .8 percent, a state unemployment tax of 5.4 percent, and medical insurance costs for which the employer pays 80 percent of the premium.

E 10-6.

L O 2 *Payroll Transactions*

Clarence Henry earns a salary of $70,000 per year. Social security taxes are 6.20 percent up to $60,600 and Medicare taxes are 1.45 percent. Federal unemployment insurance taxes are 6.2 percent of the first $9,000; however, a credit is allowed equal to the state unemployment insurance taxes of 5.4 percent on the $9,000. During the year, $15,000 was withheld for federal income taxes, $3,000 for state income taxes, and $1,500 for medical insurance.

1. Prepare a general journal entry summarizing the payment of $70,000 to Henry during the year.
2. Prepare a general journal entry summarizing the employer payroll taxes and other costs on Henry's salary for the year. Assume the company pays 80 percent of the total premiums for medical insurance.
3. Determine the total cost paid by Clarence Henry's employer to employ Henry for the year.

E 10-7.
L O 2 *Product Warranty Liability*

Keystone Company manufactures and sells electronic games. Each game costs $25 to produce and sells for $45. In addition, each game carries a warranty that provides for free replacement if it fails for any reason during the two years following the sale. In the past, 7 percent of the games sold had to be replaced under the warranty. During July, Keystone sold 26,000 games and 2,800 games were replaced under the warranty.

1. Prepare a general journal entry to record the estimated liability for product warranties during the month.
2. Prepare a general journal entry to record the games replaced under warranty during the month.

E 10-8.
L O 2 *Vacation Pay Liability*

Crosstown Corporation currently allows each employee three weeks' paid vacation after one year of employment. Based on studies of employee turnover and previous experience, management estimates that 65 percent of the employees will qualify for vacation pay this year.

1. Assume that Crosstown's July payroll is $600,000, of which $40,000 is paid to employees on vacation. Figure the estimated employee vacation benefit for the month.
2. Prepare a general journal entry to record the employee benefit for July.
3. Prepare a general journal entry to record the pay to employees on vacation.

E 10-9.
L O 2 *Estimated Liability*

Great Plains Airways has initiated a frequent flyer program in which enrolled passengers accumulate miles of travel that may be redeemed for rewards such as free trips or upgrades from coach to first class. Great Plains estimates that approximately 2 percent of its passengers are traveling for free as a result of this program. During 19x1, Great Plains Airways had total revenues of $16,000,000,000.

In January 19x2, passengers representing tickets of $300,000 flew free. Prepare the December 19x1 year-end adjusting entry to record the estimated liability for this program and the January 19x2 entry for the free tickets used. Can you suggest how these transactions would be recorded if the estimate of the free tickets were to be considered a deferred revenue (revenue received in advance) rather than an estimated liability? How is each treatment an application of the matching rule?

Note: Tables 1 to 4 in the appendix on future value and present value tables may be used where appropriate to solve the following exercises.

E 10-10.
L O 5 *Future Value Calculations*

Wieland signs a one-year note for $3,000 that carries a 12 percent annual interest rate for the purchase of a used car.

Compute the maturity value under each of the following assumptions: (1) Simple interest is charged. (2) The interest is compounded semiannually. (3) The interest is compounded quarterly. (4) The interest is compounded monthly.

E 10-11.
L O 5 *Future Value Calculations*

Find the future value of (1) a single payment of $20,000 at 7 percent for ten years, (2) ten annual payments of $2,000 at 7 percent, (3) a single payment of $6,000 at 9 percent for seven years, and (4) seven annual payments of $6,000 at 9 percent.

E 10-12.
L O 5 *Future Value Calculations*

Assume that $40,000 is invested today. Compute the amount that would accumulate at the end of seven years when the interest rate is (1) 8 percent compounded annually, (2) 8 percent compounded semiannually, and (3) 8 percent compounded quarterly.

E 10-13.
L O 5 *Future Value Calculations*

Calculate the accumulation of periodic payments of $1,000 made at the end of each of four years, assuming (1) 10 percent annual interest compounded annually, (2) 10 percent annual interest compounded semiannually, (3) 4 percent annual interest compounded annually, and (4) 16 percent annual interest compounded quarterly.

E 10-14.
L O 5 *Future Value Applications*

a. Two parents have $20,000 to invest for their child's college tuition, which they estimate will cost $40,000 when the child enters college twelve years from now.

Calculate the approximate rate of annual interest that the investment must earn to reach the $40,000 goal in twelve years. (**Hint:** Make a calculation; then use Table 1 in the appendix on future value and present value tables.)

b. Ted Pruitt is saving to purchase a summer home that will cost about $64,000. He has $40,000 now, on which he can earn 7 percent annual interest.

Calculate the approximate length of time he will have to wait to purchase the summer home. (**Hint:** Make a calculation; then use Table 1 in the appendix on future value and present value tables.)

E 10-15.
L O 5 *Working Backward from a Future Value*

Gloria Faraquez has a debt of $90,000 due in four years. She wants to save money to pay it off by making annual deposits in an investment account that earns 8 percent annual interest.

Calculate the amount she must deposit each year to reach her goal. (**Hint:** Use Table 2 in the appendix on future value and present value tables; then make a calculation.)

E 10-16.
L O 6 *Determining an Advance Payment*

Ellen Saber is contemplating paying five years' rent in advance. Her annual rent is $9,600. Calculate the single sum that would have to be paid now for the advance rent, if we assume compound interest of 8 percent.

E 10-17.
L O 6 *Present Value Calculations*

Find the present value of (1) a single payment of $24,000 at 6 percent for twelve years, (2) twelve annual payments of $2,000 at 6 percent, (3) a single payment of $5,000 at 9 percent for five years, and (4) five annual payments of $5,000 at 9 percent.

E 10-18.
L O 6 *Present Value of a Lump-Sum Contract*

A contract calls for a lump-sum payment of $60,000. Find the present value of the contract, assuming that (1) the payment is due in five years, and the current interest rate is 9 percent; (2) the payment is due in ten years, and the current interest rate is 9 percent; (3) the payment is due in five years, and the current interest rate is 5 percent; and (4) the payment is due in ten years, and the current interest rate is 5 percent.

E 10-19.
L O 6 *Present Value of an Annuity Contract*

A contract calls for annual payments of $1,200. Find the present value of the contract, assuming that (1) the number of payments is seven, and the current interest rate is 6 percent; (2) the number of payments is fourteen, and the current interest rate is 6 percent; (3) the number of payments is seven, and the current interest rate is 8 percent; and (4) the number of payments is fourteen, and the current interest rate is 8 percent.

E 10-20.
L O 7 *Non-Interest-Bearing Note*

On January 1, 19x8, Pendleton purchases a machine from Leyland by signing a two-year, non-interest-bearing $32,000 note. Pendleton currently pays 12 percent interest to borrow money at the bank.

Prepare entries in Pendleton's and Leyland's journals to (1) record the purchase and the note, (2) adjust the accounts after one year, and (3) record payment of the note after two years (on December 31, 19x9).

E 10-21.
L O 7 *Valuing an Asset for the Purpose of Making a Purchasing Decision*

Oscaro owns a service station and has the opportunity to purchase a car wash machine for $30,000. After carefully studying projected costs and revenues, Oscaro estimates that the car wash will produce a net cash flow of $5,200 annually and will last for eight years. Oscaro feels that an interest rate of 14 percent is adequate for his business.

Calculate the present value of the machine to Oscaro. Does the purchase appear to be a correct business decision?

E 10-22.
L O 7 *Deferred Payment*

Johnson Equipment Corporation sells a precision machine tool with computer controls to Borst Corporation for $800,000 on January 1, agreeing to take payment nine months later, on October 1. Assuming that the prevailing annual interest rate for such a transaction is 16 percent compounded quarterly, what is the actual price of the machine tool, and what journal entries will be made at the time of the purchase and at the time of the payment on the records of both Borst and Johnson?

E 10-23.

L O 7 *Investment of Idle Cash*

Scientific Publishing Company, a publisher of college books, has just completed a successful fall selling season and has $5,000,000 in cash to invest for nine months, beginning on January 1. The company places the cash in an investment account that is expected to pay 12 percent annual interest compounded monthly. Interest is credited to the company's account each month. How much cash will the company have at the end of nine months, and what entries are made to record the investment and the first two monthly (February 1 and March 1) interest amounts?

E 10-24.

L O 7 *Accumulation of a Fund*

Laferia Corporation borrows $3,000,000 from an insurance company on a four-year note. Management agrees to set aside enough cash at the end of each year to accumulate the amount needed to pay off the note at maturity. Since the first contribution to the fund will be made in one year, four annual contributions are needed. Assuming that the fund will earn 10 percent compounded annually, how much will the annual contribution to the fund be (round to nearest dollar), and what will be the journal entry for the first contribution?

E 10-25.

L O 7 *Negotiating the Sale of a Business*

Horace Raftson is attempting to sell his business to Ernando Ruiz. The company has assets of $900,000, liabilities of $800,000, and stockholders' equity of $100,000. Both parties agree that the proper rate of return to expect is 12 percent; however, they differ on other assumptions. Raftson believes that the business will generate at least $100,000 of cash flows per year for twenty years. Ruiz thinks that $80,000 in cash flows per year is more reasonable and that only ten years in the future should be considered. Using Table 4 in the appendix on future value and present value tables, determine the range for negotiation by computing the present value of Raftson's offer to sell and of Ruiz's offer to buy.

Problem Set A

10A-1.

L O 2 *Notes Payable Transactions and End-of-Period Entries*

Landover Corporation, whose fiscal year ends June 30, 19x1, completed the following transactions involving notes payable:

May   11   Signed a 90-day, $66,000 note payable to Village Bank for a working capital loan. The face value included interest of $1,980. Proceeds received were $64,020.

21   Obtained a sixty-day extension on an $18,000 trade account payable owed to a supplier by signing a 60-day, $18,000 note. Interest is in addition to the face value, at the rate of 14 percent.

June   30   Made end-of-year adjusting entry to accrue interest expense.

30   Made end-of-year adjusting entry to recognize interest expired on the note.

July   20   Paid off the note plus interest due the supplier.

Aug.   9   Paid the amount due to the bank on the 90-day note.

REQUIRED

Prepare general journal entries for the notes payable transactions.

10A-2.

L O 2 *Property Tax and Vacation Pay Liabilities*

Kubek Corporation prepares monthly financial statements and ends its fiscal year on June 30, the same as the local government. In July, 19x1, your first month as accountant for the company, you find that the company has not previously accrued estimated liabilities. In the past, the company, which has a large property tax bill, has charged property taxes to the month in which the bill is paid. The tax bill for the year ended June 30, 19x1 was $72,000, and it is estimated that the tax will increase by 8 percent for the year ending June 30, 19x2. The tax bill is usually received on September 1, to be paid November 1.

You also discover that employees who have worked for the company for one year are allowed to take two weeks' paid vacation each year. The cost of these vacations has been charged to expense in the month of payment. Approximately 80 percent of the employees qualify for this benefit. You suggest to management that proper accounting treatment of these expenses is to spread their cost over the entire year. Management agrees and asks you to make the necessary adjustments.

REQUIRED

1. Figure the proper monthly charge to property tax expense and prepare general journal entries for the following:

   July 31   Accrual of property tax expense
   Aug. 31   Accrual of property tax expense
   Sept. 30   Accrual of property tax expense (assume the actual bill is $81,720)
   Oct. 31   Accrual of property tax expense
   Nov. 1   Payment of property tax
         30   Adjustment for property tax expense

2. Assume that the total payroll for July is $1,136,000. This amount includes $42,600 paid to employees on paid vacations. (a) Compute the vacation pay expense for July. (b) Prepare a general journal entry on July 31 to record the accrual of vacation pay expense for July. (c) Prepare a general journal entry, dated July 31, to record the wages of employees on vacation in July (ignore payroll deductions and taxes).

10A-3.

L O 2

Product Warranty Liability

Marrero Company is engaged in the retail sale of washing machines. Each machine has a twenty-four-month warranty on parts. If a repair under warranty is required, a charge for the labor is made. Management has found that 20 percent of the machines sold require some work before the warranty expires. Furthermore, the average cost of replacement parts has been $120 per repair. At the beginning of June, the account for the estimated liability for product warranties had a credit balance of $28,600. During June, 112 machines were returned under the warranty. The cost of the parts used in repairing the machines was $17,530, and $18,884 was collected as service revenue for the labor involved. During the month, Marrero Company sold 450 new machines.

REQUIRED

1. Prepare general journal entries to record each of the following: (a) the warranty work completed during the month, including related revenue, and (b) the estimated liability for product warranties for machines sold during the month.
2. Compute the balance of the Estimated Product Warranty Liability account at the end of the month.

10A-4.

L O 2

Product Warranty Liability

Among other things, Broadway Car Outlet, Inc. sells tires and guarantees them for as long as the customer owns them. If a tire fails, the customer is charged a percentage of the retail price based on the percentage of the tire that is worn, plus a service charge for putting the tire on the car. In the past, management has found that only 2 percent of the tires sold require replacement under warranty, and of those replaced, an average of 20 percent of the cost is collected under the percentage pricing system. The average tire costs the company $55. At the beginning of July, the account for estimated liability for product warranties had a credit balance of $22,746. During July, 125 tires were returned under the warranty. The cost of the replacement tires was $4,625, of which $1,125 was recovered under the percentage-worn formula. Service revenue amounted to $531. During the month, the company sold 3,525 tires.

REQUIRED

1. Prepare general journal entries to record each of the following: (a) the warranty work completed during the month, including related revenues, and (b) the estimated liability for product warranties for tires sold during the month.
2. Compute the balance of the estimated product warranty liabilities at the end of the month.

10A-5.

L O 2, 6, 7

Non-Interest-Bearing Note and Valuing an Asset for the Purpose of Making a Purchasing Decision

Part A: Munro, Inc. provides heavy-duty industrial cleaning services to manufacturing companies. On July 1, 19x1, Munro, Inc. purchases a new truck from Lake Corporation by signing a two-year, non-interest-bearing $24,000 note. Lake currently pays 15 percent interest to borrow money at the bank.

REQUIRED

Prepare journal entries in Munro's and Lake's records to (1) record the purchase and the note, (2) adjust the accounts after one year (assuming June 30 year end), and (3) record payment of the note after two years (on June 30, 19x3). (Reversing entries are not made by either company.)

Part B: Becker Corporation is in the lawn-care business. Management is considering the purchase of a special type of spraying machine for $38,000. After carefully studying projected costs and revenues, management estimates that the machine will produce a net cash flow of $10,500 for the next seven years. Management also believes that an interest rate of 18 percent is appropriate for this analysis.

REQUIRED

Calculate the present value of the machine to Becker Corporation. Does the purchase appear to be a correct business decision?

10A-6.

L O 5, 6, 7 *Time Value of Money Applications*

Effective January 1, 19x1, the board of directors of Riordan, Inc. approved the following actions, each of which is an application of the time value of money:

a. Established in a single payment of $100,000 a contingency fund for the possible settlement of a lawsuit. The suit is expected to be settled in two years.
b. Asked for another fund to be established by a single payment to accumulate to $300,000 in four years.
c. Approved purchase of a parcel of land for future plant expansion. Payments are to start January 1, 19x2, at $50,000 per year for 5 years.
d. Determined that a new building to be built on the property in **c** would cost $800,000 and authorized five annual payments to be paid starting January 1, 19x2, into a fund for its construction.
e. Purchased Riordan common stock from a stockholder who wanted to be bought out by issuing a four-year non-interest-bearing note for $200,000.

REQUIRED

Assuming an annual interest rate of 8 percent and using Tables 10-1, 10-2, 10-3, and 10-4, answer the following questions:

1. In action **a,** how much will the fund accumulate to in two years?
2. In action **b,** how much will need to be deposited initially to accumulate the desired amount?
3. In action **c,** what is the purchase price (present value) of the land?
4. In action **d,** how much would the equal annual payments need to be to accumulate enough money to build the building?
5. In action **e,** assuming semiannual compounding of interest, what is the actual purchase price of the stock (present value of the note)?

Problem Set B

10B-1.

L O 2 *Notes Payable Transactions and End-of-Period Entries*

Prentiss Paper Company, whose fiscal year ends December 31, completed the following transactions involving notes payable:

19x1
Nov. 25   Purchased a new loading cart by issuing a 60-day, 10 percent note for $21,600.
Dec. 16   Borrowed $25,000 from the bank to finance inventory by signing a 90-day note. The face value of the note includes interest of $750. Proceeds received were $24,250.
      31   Made end-of-year adjusting entry to accrue interest expense.
      31   Made end-of-year adjusting entry to recognize interest expired on note.
19x2
Jan. 24   Paid off the loading cart note.
Mar. 16   Paid off the inventory note to the bank.

REQUIRED

Prepare general journal entries for these transactions.

10B-2.

L O 2 *Property Tax and Vacation Pay Liabilities*

Lawrence Corporation accrues estimated liabilities for property taxes and vacation pay. The company's and the government's fiscal years end June 30, 19x1. The property taxes for the year ended June 30, 19x1 were $72,000, and they are expected to increase 6 percent for the year ended June 30, 19x2. Two weeks' vacation pay is given to each employee after one year of service. Lawrence management estimates that 75 percent of its employees will qualify for this benefit in the current year.

In addition, the following information is available: The property tax bill of $79,104 for the June 30, 19x2 fiscal year was received in September and paid on November 1. Total payroll for July was $196,400, which includes $18,032 paid to employees on paid vacations.

REQUIRED

1. Prepare the monthly journal entries to record accrued property taxes for July through October, actual property taxes paid, and the adjustments for property tax expense at November 30.
2. a. Prepare a general journal entry to record the vacation accrual expense for July. (Round to nearest dollar.)
   b. Prepare a general journal entry to record the wages of employees on vacation in July. (Ignore payroll deductions and taxes.)

10B-3.
L O 2 *Product Warranty Liability*

The Citation Company manufactures and sells food processors. The company guarantees the processors for five years. If a processor fails, it is replaced free but the customer is charged a service fee for handling. In the past, management has found that only 3 percent of the processors sold required replacement under the warranty. The average food processor costs the company $120. At the beginning of September, the account for estimated liability for product warranties had a credit balance of $104,000. During September, 250 processors were returned under the warranty. The cost of replacement was $27,000. Service fees of $4,930 were collected for handling. During the month, the company sold 2,800 food processors.

REQUIRED

1. Prepare general journal entries to record the cost of food processors replaced under warranty and the estimated liability for product warranties for processors sold during the month.
2. Compute the balance of the estimated product warranty liabilities at the end of the month.

10B-4.
L O 2 *Product Warranty Liability*

Western Tire Company guarantees the tires it sells until they wear out. If a tire fails, the customer is charged a percentage of the retail price based on the percentage of the tire that is worn, plus a service charge for putting the tire on the car. In the past, management has found that only 2 percent of the tires sold require replacement under warranty, and of those replaced, an average of 20 percent of the cost is collected under the percentage pricing system. The average tire costs the company $70. At the beginning of July, the account for estimated liability for product warranties had a credit balance of $45,492. During July, 250 tires were returned under the warranty. The cost of the replacement tires was $9,250, of which $2,250 was recovered under the percentage-worn formula. Service revenue amounted to $1,062. During the month, the company sold 7,050 tires.

REQUIRED

1. Prepare general journal entries to record each of the following: (a) the warranty work completed during the month, including related revenue, and (b) the estimated liability for product warranties for tires sold during the month.
2. Compute the balance of the estimated product warranty liabilities at the end of the month.

10B-5.
L O 2, 6, 7 *Non-Interest-Bearing Note and Valuing an Asset for the Purpose of Making a Purchasing Decision*

Part A: Fender Corp., a candy manufacturer, needs a machine to heat chocolate. On January 1, 19x1, Fender purchases a machine to accomplish this task from Royce Company by signing a two-year, non-interest-bearing $24,000 note. Fender currently pays 12 percent interest to borrow money at the bank.

REQUIRED

Prepare journal entries in Fender's and Royce's records to (1) record the purchase and the note, (2) adjust the accounts after one year, and (3) record payment of the note after two years (on December 31, 19x2). (Assume that reversing entries are not made by either party.)

Part B: Sanchez owns a printing service and has the opportunity to purchase a high-speed copy machine for $20,000. After carefully studying projected costs and revenues, Sanchez estimates that the copy machine will produce a net cash flow of $3,000 annually and will last for eight years. Sanchez feels that an interest rate of 14 percent is adequate for his business.

REQUIRED

Calculate the present value of the machine to Sanchez. Does the purchase appear to be a correct business decision?

10B-6.
L O 5, 6, 7 *Time Value of Money Applications*

Neiman Corporation's management took several actions, each of which was to be effective on January 1, 19x1, and each of which involved an application of the time value of money:

a. Established a new retirement plan to take effect in three years and authorized three annual payments of $500,000 starting January 1, 19x2, to establish the retirement fund.

b. Approved plans for a new distribution center to be built for $1,000,000 and authorized five annual payments, starting January 1, 19x2, to accumulate the funds for the new center.

c. Bought out the contract of a member of top management for a payment of $50,000 per year for four years beginning January 1, 19x2.

d. Accepted a two-year non-interest-bearing note for $100,000 as payment for equipment that the company sold.

e. Set aside $300,000 for possible losses from lawsuits over a defective product. The lawsuits are not expected to be settled for three years.

REQUIRED

Assuming an annual interest rate of 10 percent and using Tables 10-1, 10-2, 10-3, and 10-4, answer the following questions:

1. In action **a,** how much will the retirement fund accumulate in three years?
2. In action **b,** how much must the annual payment be to reach the goal?
3. In action **c,** what is the cost (present value) of the buy-out?
4. In action **d,** assuming that interest is compounded semiannually, what is the selling price (present value) of the equipment?
5. In action **e,** how much will the fund accumulate to in three years?

CRITICAL THINKING AND COMMUNICATION

Conceptual Mini-Cases

CMC 10-1.
L O 2 *Identification of Current Liabilities*

Several businesses and organizations and a current liability from the balance sheet of each are listed below. Discuss the nature of each current liability (definitely determinable or estimated), how each arose, and how the obligation is likely to be fulfilled.

Institute of Management Accountants: Deferred Revenues—Membership Dues
The Foxboro Company: Advances on Sales Contracts
UNC Incorporated: Current Portion of Long-Term Debt
Hurco Companies, Inc.: Accrued Warranty Expense
Affiliated Publications, Inc.: Deferred Subscription Revenues
Geo. A Hormel & Company: Accrued Advertising

CMC 10-2.
L O 2 *Frequent Flyer Plan*

America South Airways instituted a frequent flyer program under which passengers accumulate points based on the number of miles they fly on the airline. One point is awarded for each mile flown, with a minimum of 750 miles given for any flight. Because of competition and a drop in passenger air travel in 1991, the company began a triple mileage bonus plan under which passengers received triple the normal mileage points. In the past, about 1.5 percent of passenger miles were flown by passengers who had converted points to free flights. Under the triple mileage program, it is expected that a 2.5 percent rate will be more appropriate for future years. During 1991 the company had passenger revenues of $966.3 million and passenger transportation operating expenses of $802.8 million before depreciation and amortization. Operating income was $86.1 million. The AICPA is considering requiring airline companies to recognize frequent flyer plans in their accounting records. What is the appropriate rate to use to estimate free miles? What would be the effect of the estimated liability for free travel by frequent flyers on 1991 net income? Describe several ways to estimate the amount of this liability. Be prepared to discuss the arguments for and against recognizing this liability.

CMC 10-3.
L O 7   *Baseball Contract*

The St. Louis Browns' fifth-year center fielder Carlos Hayes made the All-Star team and won the most valuable player award in 1991. St. Louis, a major league ball club, went to the World Series and lost to Oakland in six games. Hayes has three years left on a contract that is to pay him $800,000 per year. He wants to renegotiate his contract because other players who have equally outstanding records (although they do have more experience) are receiving as much as $3.5 million per year for five years. Management has a policy of never renegotiating a current contract but is willing to consider extending the contract to additional years. In fact, the Browns have offered Hayes an additional three years at $2.0 million, $3.0 million, and $4.0 million, respectively. In addition, they have added an option year at $5.0 million. Management points out that this package is worth $14.0 million, or $3.5 million per year on average. Hayes is considering this offer and is also considering asking for a bonus to be paid upon the signing of the contract. Comment on management's position. What is your evaluation of the offer, assuming a current prime (best bank rate) interest rate of 10 percent? (**Hint:** Use present values.) Hayes is considering asking for a signing bonus. Propose a range for the signing bonus. What other considerations may affect the value of the offer?

Ethics Mini-Case

EMC 10-1.
L O 2   *Ethical Dilemma*

Tower Restaurant is a large seafood restaurant in the suburbs of Chicago. Last summer, Joe Murray, an accounting student at the local college, secured a full-time accounting job at the restaurant. Joe felt fortunate to have a good job that accommodated his class schedule because the local economy was very bad. After a few weeks on the job, Joe realized that his boss, the owner of the business, was paying the kitchen workers in cash and was not withholding federal and state income taxes or social security and Medicare taxes. Joe understands that federal and state laws require that these taxes be withheld and paid in a timely manner to the appropriate agency. Joe also realizes that if he raises this issue, he may lose his job. What alternatives are available to Joe? What action would you take if you were in Joe's position? Why did you make this choice?

Decision-Making Case

DMC 10-1.
L O 6, 7   *Time Value of Money Application*

O'Hara Machine Works, Inc. has successfully obtained a subcontract to manufacture parts for a new military aircraft. The parts are to be delivered over the next five years, and O'Hara will be paid as the parts are delivered. To make the parts, new equipment will have to be purchased. Two types of equipment are available. Type A is conventional equipment that can be put into service immediately, and Type B requires one year to be put into service but is more efficient. Type A requires an immediate cash investment of $500,000 and will produce enough parts to provide net cash receipts of $170,000 each year for the five years. Type B may be purchased by signing a two-year non-interest-bearing note for $673,000. It is projected that Type B will produce net cash receipts of zero in year 1, $250,000 in year 2, $300,000 in year 3, $300,000 in year 4, and the remaining $100,000 in year 5. Neither type of equipment can be used on other contracts or will have any useful life remaining at the end of the contract. O'Hara currently pays an interest rate of 16 percent to borrow money.

REQUIRED

1. What is the present value of the investment required for each type of equipment? (Use Table 3 in the appendix on future value and present value tables.)
2. Compute the present value of the net cash receipts projected to be received from each type of equipment. (Use Tables 3 and 4 in the same appendix.)
3. Which option appears to be best for O'Hara, based on your analysis, and why?

Basic Research Activity

RA 10-1.
L O 2, 3   *Basic Research Skills*

Your school library has indexes for business periodicals in which you can look up articles on topics of interest. Three of the most important of these indexes are *Business Periodicals Index*, the *Wall Street Journal Index*, and the *Accountants' Index*. Using one or more of these indexes, locate and photocopy two articles related to bank financing, commercial paper, product warranties, airline frequent flyer plans, or contingent liabilities. Keep in mind that you may have to look under related topics to find an article. For example, to find articles about contingent liabilities, you might look under litigation, debt guarantees, environmental losses, or other topics. For each of the two articles, write a short summary of the situation and tell how it relates to accounting for the topic as described in the text. Be prepared to discuss your results in class.

FINANCIAL REPORTING AND ANALYSIS

Interpretation Cases from Business

ICB 10-1.

L O 1, 2 *Analysis of Current Liabilities for a Bankrupt Company*

Trans World Airlines, Inc. is a major airline that experienced financial difficulties in 1988 and 1989. In TWA's 1989 annual report, management refers to the company's deteriorating liquidity situation as follows:[9]

TWA's net working capital deficit was $55.5 million at December 31, 1989, representing a reduction of $82.6 million from net working capital of $27.1 million at December 31, 1988. Working capital deficits are not unusual in the airline industry because of the large advance ticket sales current liability account.

In 1991, the company declared bankruptcy. By 1993, the company had reorganized and was planning to come out of bankruptcy. The company's current liabilities and current assets at December 31 for 1989 and 1992 are as follows (in thousands):

	1992	1989
Current liabilities:		
Short-term notes payable	$ 75,000	—
Current maturities of long-term debt	252,023	$ 127,301
Current obligations under capital leases	228	93,194
Advance ticket sales	151,221	276,549
Accounts payable, principally trade	114,467	387,256
Accounts payable to affiliated companies	22,815	8,828
Securities sold, not yet purchased	—	82,302
Accrued expenses:		
Employee compensation and vacations earned	100,013	148,175
Contributions to retirement and pension trusts	4,583	14,711
Interest on debt and capital leases	6,543	86,761
Taxes	17,069	33,388
Other accrued expenses	148,714	122,295
Total	$892,676	$1,380,760

	1992	1989
Current assets:		
Cash and cash equivalents	$ 42,389	$ 454,415
Marketable securities	—	10,355
Receivables, less allowance for doubtful accounts, $13,432 in 1989 and $10,361 in 1992	311,915	435,061
Receivables from affiliated companies	2,925	15,506
Due from brokers	—	70,636
Spare parts, materials, and supplies, less allowance for obsolescence, $38,423 in 1989 and $47,872 in 1992	175,235	227,098
Prepaid expenses and other	44,047	112,232
Total	$576,511	$1,325,303

9. Trans World Airlines, Inc., *Annual Reports,* 1989 and 1992.

REQUIRED

1. Identify any current liabilities that do not require a current outlay of cash and identify any current estimated liabilities for 1989 and 1992. Why is management not worried about the cash flow consequences of advance ticket sales?
2. For 1989 and 1992, which current assets will not generate cash inflow, and which will most likely be available to pay for the remaining current liabilities? Compare the amount of these current assets to the amount of current liabilities other than those identified in **1** as not requiring a cash outlay.
3. In light of the calculations in **2**, comment on TWA's liquidity position for 1989 and 1992 and its ability to operate successfully after bankruptcy. Identify several alternative sources of additional cash.

ICB 10-2.

L O 3   *Contingent Liabilities*

Texaco, Inc., one of the largest integrated oil companies in the world, reported its loss of the largest damage judgment in history in its 1986 annual report as follows:[10]

> **Note 17.** Contingent Liabilities
> Pennzoil Litigation
>
> *State Court Action.* On December 10, 1985, the 151st District Court of Harris County, Texas, entered judgment for Pennzoil Company of $7.5 billion actual damages, $3 billion punitive damages, and approximately $600 million prejudgment interest in *Pennzoil Company v. Texaco, Inc.,* an action in which Pennzoil claims that Texaco, Inc., tortiously interfered with Pennzoil's alleged contract to acquire a ⅜ths interest in Getty. Interest began accruing on the judgment at the simple rate of 10% per annum from the date of judgment. Texaco, Inc., believes that there is no legal basis for the judgment, which it believes is contrary to the evidence and applicable law. Texaco, Inc., is pursuing all available remedies to set aside or to reverse the judgment.
>
> * * *
>
> The outcome of the appeal on the preliminary injunction and the ultimate outcome of the Pennzoil litigation are not presently determinable, but could have a material adverse effect on the consolidated financial position and the results of the consolidated operations of Texaco, Inc.

At December 31, 1986, Texaco's retained earnings were $12.882 billion, and its cash and marketable securities totaled $3.0 billion. The company's net income for 1986 was $.725 billion.

After a series of court reversals and filing for bankruptcy in 1987, Texaco announced in December 1987 an out-of-court settlement with Pennzoil for $3.0 billion. Although less than the original amount, it is still the largest damage payment in history.

REQUIRED

1. The FASB has established two conditions that a contingent liability must meet before it is recorded in the accounting records. What are the two conditions? Does the situation described in "Note 17. Contingent Liabilities" meet those conditions? Explain your answer.
2. Do the events of 1987 change your answer to **1**? Explain your response.
3. What will be the effect of the settlement on Texaco's retained earnings, cash and marketable securities, and net income?

ICB 10-3.

L O 6   *Time Value of Money Application*

When an asset is sold on credit, the purchaser usually pays interest on the amount owed, and the seller must include the interest received in income and pay income taxes on it. Some taxpayers have tried to understate interest in reported income by using an unrealistically low stated interest rate. For example, an asset was sold on January 1, 1993, for $28,000 under a contract that provides for four equal payments of principal and a stated interest rate of 9 percent as shown on page 483.

Every six months the *Internal Revenue Service (IRS)* determines a "federal" rate of interest based on the average yield of certain marketable securities of the U.S. government. Any sale such as the one above must have an effective interest rate at least equal to 110 percent of the "federal" rate. If it does not, the IRS will use a rate equal to 120 percent of the "federal" rate to compute the amount of unstated interest that must be reported as interest income in addition to the stated interest.

10. Texaco, Inc., *Annual Report,* 1986.

Date of Payment	Payment	Stated Interest (9%)	Total Paid	Balance Due
Jan. 1, 1993				$28,000
Jan. 1, 1994	$ 7,000	$2,520	$ 9,520	21,000
Jan. 1, 1995	7,000	1,890	8,890	14,000
Jan. 1, 1996	7,000	1,260	8,260	7,000
Jan. 1, 1997	7,000	630	7,630	—
	$28,000	$6,300	$34,300	

If the 110 percent test is not met, the amount of unstated interest that must be reported as income may be determined by subtracting the present value of the total payments using present value factors based on 120 percent of the "federal" rate from the original sale price.

REQUIRED

Assuming that the "federal" rate is 10 percent, does the agreement in this question meet the IRS test for stated interest? If not, use the third present value table in the appendix on future value and present value tables to determine the present value of the four payments. Then determine the total unstated interest that must be reported as taxable interest income in addition to the stated interest.

International Company Case

ICC 10-1.
LO 1, 2, 3   *Classification and Disclosure of Current Liabilities and Contingent Liabilities*

The German company *Volkswagen AG* is one of the largest automobile companies in the world. Accounting in Germany differs in some respects from that in the United States. A good example of this difference is the placement and classification of liabilities. On the balance sheet, Volkswagen places liabilities below a detailed stockholders' equity section. Volkswagen does not distinguish between current and long-term liabilities; however, a note to the financial statements does disclose the amount of the liabilities that are due within one year. These liabilities are primarily what we call *definitely determinable liabilities,* such as loans, accounts and notes payable, and unearned revenues. Estimated liabilities do not seem to appear in this category. In contrast, there is an asset category called *current assets,* which is similar to that found in the United States. In another note to the financial statements, the company lists what it calls *contingent liabilities,* which have not been recorded and do not appear on the balance sheet. These include liabilities for notes that have been discounted, 299 million DM; guarantees of loans of other companies, 140 million DM; and warranties on automobiles, 200 million DM.[11] What do you think of the idea of combining all liabilities, whether short term or long term, as a single item on the balance sheet? Do you think any of the contingent liabilities should be recorded and shown on the balance sheet?

Toys "R" Us Case

TC 10-1.
LO 1   *Short-Term Liabilities and Seasonality*

Refer to the balance sheet and the liquidity and capital resources section of Management's Discussion—Results of Operations and Financial Condition in the annual report in the appendix on Toys "R" Us to answer the following questions. What percentage of total assets are current liabilities for Toys "R" Us, and how does this percentage compare to that in other industries as represented by Figure 10-1? Toys "R" Us is a seasonal business. Would you expect short-term borrowings and accounts payable to be unusually high or unusually low at the balance sheet date of January 29, 1994? How does management make use of short-term financing to meet its needs for cash during the year?

11. Volkswagen AG, *Annual Report,* 1992.

Long-Term Liabilities

LEARNING OBJECTIVES

1. Explain the advantages and disadvantages of issuing long-term debt.
2. Identify and contrast the major characteristics of bonds.
3. Record the issuance of bonds at face value and at a discount or premium.
4. Determine the value of bonds using present values.
5. Amortize (a) bond discounts and (b) bond premiums using the straight-line and effective interest methods.
6. Account for bonds issued between interest dates and make year-end adjustments.
7. Account for the retirement of bonds and the conversion of bonds into stock.
8. Explain the basic features of mortgages payable, installment notes payable, long-term leases, and pensions and other postretirement benefits as long-term liabilities.

RJR Nabisco

During the 1980s, there was an explosion in the amount of long-term debt issued by companies either to refinance their own operations or to finance takeovers of other companies. Much of this financing was accomplished through so-called junk bonds, unsecured, high-risk, long-term bonds that carried high rates of interest. Carrying a large amount of debt is risky for a company, and interest charges on this kind of debt are especially high in relation to earnings and cash flows. If a company is unable to pay the interest on its bonds, it can be forced to declare bankruptcy. Even if a company can pay the interest, its ability to improve and expand operations can be limited severely.

A record was set in the takeover of RJR Nabisco by Kohlberg Kravis Roberts & Co. when $26 billion in junk bonds was issued. The heavy debt load proved to be a burden to RJR Nabisco. The biggest problem the company faced involved bonds whose interest rate had to be increased if the prices of the bonds on the open market declined, as they did in 1990. Some interest rates would have had to be reset at 20 percent or higher, more than double the interest rates on less risky bonds. Management now had to decide how to alleviate the situation or face the potential bankruptcy or breakup of the company.

As reported in the *Asian Wall Street Journal,* after six months of intense negotiations, RJR Nabisco's management resolved its immediate problems through a $6.9 billion refinancing plan.[1] This large refinancing package was designed to strengthen the balance sheet and ward off a potential financial crisis. Louis Gerstner, the company's chief financial officer, called the refinancing package "a comprehensive, creative program." Under the plan, RJR Nabisco would have billions of dollars at its disposal. Among the components of the plan were new long-term bonds, adjustments of interest rates on existing bonds, new issues of capital stock, new bank loans, and expansion of existing bank lines of credit. Although this financing plan is among the most complex in history, it can be understood using the concepts described in this chapter. : : : :

1. George Anders, "RJR Nabisco Moves to Retire Most Troublesome Junk Bonds," *Asian Wall Street Journal,* July 17, 1990.

OBJECTIVE

1 *Explain the advantages and disadvantages of issuing long-term debt*

A corporation has many sources of funds to finance operations and expansion. As you learned earlier, corporations can acquire cash and other assets from profitable operations and short-term credit. These sources, however, are seldom sufficient for a growing business that must invest in long-term assets, research and development, and other assets or activities that will produce income in future years. For these assets and activities, the company requires funds that will be available for a longer period of time. Two principal sources of long-term funds are the issuance of common stock and the issuance of long-term debt in the form of bonds, notes, mortgages, and leases. Although some companies carry an amount of long-term debt that exceeds 50 percent of their total assets, the average company carries less, as can be seen from Figure 11-1, which shows the average long-term debt to total assets for selected industries.

Since long-term debts represent financial commitments that must be paid at maturity and interest or other payments that must be paid periodically, common stock would seem to have two advantages over long-term debt: it does not have to be paid back, and dividends on common stock are usually paid only if the company earns sufficient income. There are, however, some advantages of long-term debt over common stock.

Stockholder control. Since bondholders or other creditors do not have voting rights, common stockholders do not relinquish any control of the company.

Tax effects. The interest on debt is tax deductible, whereas dividends on common stock are not. For example, if a corporation pays $100,000 in interest and the income tax rate is 30 percent, the net cost to the corporation is $70,000 because it will save $30,000 on its income taxes. To pay $100,000 in dividends, the company would have to earn $142,857 before taxes ($100,000 ÷ .70).

Financial leverage. If a corporation is able to earn more on its assets than it pays in interest on debt, all of the excess will increase its earnings for stockholders. This concept is called **financial leverage** or **trading on the equity.** For example, if a company is able to earn 12 percent or $120,000 on a $1,000,000 investment financed by long-term 10 percent notes, it will earn $20,000 before taxes ($120,000 − $100,000). Financial leverage makes heavily debt-financed investments in office buildings and shopping centers attractive to investors: They hope to earn a higher return than the interest cost. The debt to equity ratio is considered an overall measure of the financial leverage of a company.

In spite of these advantages, using debt financing is not always in a company's best interest. First, since cash is required to make periodic interest payments and to pay back the principal amount of the debt at the maturity date, a company whose plans for earnings do not pan out, whose operations are subject to ups and downs, or whose cash flow is weak can be in danger; if it fails to meet its obligations, it can be forced into bankruptcy by creditors. In other words, a company may become overcommitted. Consider, for example, the heavily debt-financed airline industry in recent years. Companies such as TWA, Inc. and Continental Airlines became bankrupt because they could not make payments on their long-term debt and other liabilities. Second, financial leverage can reverse direction and work against a company if the investments do not earn more than the interest payments. This happened during the savings and loan crisis of a few years ago, when long-term debt was used to finance the construction of office buildings that subsequently could not be leased for enough money to cover interest payments.

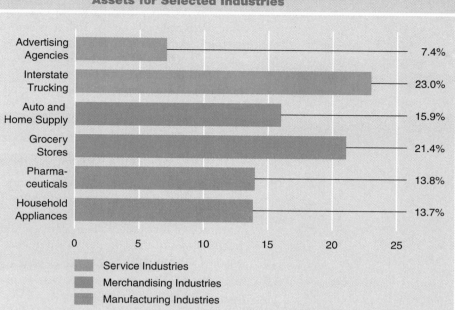

Figure 11-1. Average Long-Term Debt as a Percentage of Total Assets for Selected Industries

Source: Data from Dun and Bradstreet, *Industry Norms and Ratios*, 1992–93.

THE NATURE OF BONDS

OBJECTIVE

2 *Identify and contrast the major characteristics of bonds*

A bond is a security, usually long term, representing money borrowed by a corporation from the investing public. (Other kinds of bonds are issued by the U.S. government, state and local governments, and foreign companies and countries to raise money.) Bonds must be repaid at a certain time and require periodic payments of interest.[2] Interest usually is paid semiannually (twice a year). Bonds must not be confused with stocks. Because stocks are shares of ownership, stockholders are owners. Bondholders are creditors. Bonds are promises to repay the amount borrowed, called the *principal,* and interest at a certain rate on specified future dates.

The bondholder receives a bond certificate as evidence of the company's debt. In most cases, the face value (denomination) or principal of the bond is $1,000 or some multiple of $1,000. A bond issue is the total amount of bonds issued at one time. For example, a $1,000,000 bond issue could consist of a thousand $1,000 bonds. Because a bond issue can be bought and held by many investors, the corporation usually enters into a supplementary agreement, called a bond indenture. The bond indenture defines the rights, privileges, and limitations of the bondholders. It generally describes such things as the maturity date of the bonds, interest payment dates, interest rate, and characteristics of the bonds such as call features. Repayment plans and restrictions also may be covered.

2. At the time this chapter was written, the market interest rates on corporate bonds were volatile. Therefore, the examples and problems in this chapter use a variety of interest rates to demonstrate the concepts.

The prices of bonds are stated in terms of a percentage of face value. A bond issue quoted at 103½ means that a $1,000 bond costs $1,035 ($1,000 × 1.035). When a bond sells at exactly 100, it is said to sell at face or par value. When it sells above 100, it is said to sell at a premium; below 100, at a discount. For example, a $1,000 bond quoted at 87.62 would be selling at a discount and would cost the buyer $876.20.

A bond indenture can be written to fit the financing needs of an individual company. As a result, the bonds being issued by corporations in today's financial markets have many different features. Several of the more important ones are described here.

SECURED OR UNSECURED BONDS

Bonds can be either secured or unsecured. If issued on the general credit of the company, they are unsecured bonds (also called *debenture bonds*). Secured bonds give the bondholders a pledge of certain assets of the company as a guarantee of repayment. The security identified by a secured bond can be any specific asset of the company or a general category of asset, such as property, plant, or equipment.

TERM OR SERIAL BONDS

When all the bonds of an issue mature at the same time, they are called term bonds. For instance, a company may issue $1,000,000 worth of bonds, all due twenty years from the date of issue. If the bonds in an issue mature on several different dates, the bonds are serial bonds. An example of serial bonds would be a $1,000,000 issue that calls for retiring $200,000 of the principal every five years. This arrangement means that after the first $200,000 payment is made, $800,000 of the bonds would remain outstanding for the next five years. In other words, $1,000,000 is outstanding for the first five years, $800,000 for the second five years, and so on. A company may issue serial bonds to ease the task of retiring its debt.

REGISTERED OR COUPON BONDS

Most bonds that are issued today are registered bonds. The names and addresses of the owners of these bonds must be recorded with the issuing company. The company keeps a register of the owners and pays interest by check to the bondholders of record on the interest payment date. Coupon bonds generally are not registered with the corporation; instead, they bear interest coupons stating the amount of interest due and the payment date. The bondholder removes the coupons from the bonds on the interest payment dates and presents them at a bank for collection.

ACCOUNTING FOR BONDS PAYABLE

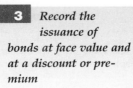

OBJECTIVE

3 *Record the issuance of bonds at face value and at a discount or premium*

When the board of directors decides to issue bonds, it generally presents the proposal to the stockholders. If the stockholders agree to the issue, the company prints the certificates and draws up an appropriate legal document. The bonds then are authorized for issuance. It is not necessary to make a journal entry for the authorization, but most companies prepare a memorandum in the Bonds Payable account describing the issue. This note lists the number and value of bonds authorized, the interest rate, the interest payment dates, and the life of the bonds.

Once the bonds are issued, the corporation must pay interest to the bond-holders over the life of the bonds (in most cases, semiannually) and the principal (face value) of the bonds at maturity.

BALANCE SHEET DISCLOSURE OF BONDS

Bonds payable and either unamortized discounts or premiums (which we explain later) generally are shown on a company's balance sheet as long-term liabilities. However, as explained in the chapter on current liabilities and the time value of money, if the maturity date of the bond issue is one year or less and the bonds will be retired using current assets, bonds payable should be listed as a current liability. If the issue is to be paid with segregated assets or replaced by another bond issue, the bonds still should be shown as a long-term liability.

Important provisions of the bond indenture are reported in the notes to the financial statements. Often reported with them is a list of all bond issues, the kinds of bonds, interest rates, any securities connected with the bonds, interest payment dates, maturity dates, and effective interest rates.

BONDS ISSUED AT FACE VALUE

Suppose that the Vason Corporation has authorized the issuance of $100,000 of 9 percent, five-year bonds on January 1, 19x0. According to the bond indenture, interest is to be paid on January 1 and July 1 of each year. Assume that the bonds are sold on January 1, 19x0 for their face value. The entry to record the issuance is as follows:

19x0			
Jan. 1	Cash	100,000	
	Bonds Payable		100,000
	Sold $100,000 of 9%, 5-year bonds at face value		

As stated above, interest is paid on January 1 and July 1 of each year. Therefore, the corporation would owe the bondholders $4,500 interest on July 1, 19x0:

$$\text{Interest} = \text{principal} \times \text{rate} \times \text{time}$$
$$= \$100,000 \times .09 \times {}^1/_2 \text{ year}$$
$$= \$4,500$$

The interest paid to the bondholders on each semiannual interest payment date (January 1 or July 1) would be recorded as follows:

Bond Interest Expense	4,500	
Cash		4,500
Paid semiannual interest to bondholders of 9%, 5-year bonds		

FACE INTEREST RATE AND MARKET INTEREST RATE

When issuing bonds, most companies try to set the face interest rate as close as possible to the market interest rate. The face interest rate is the rate of interest paid to bondholders based on the face value or principal of the bonds. The rate and amount are fixed over the life of the bond. The market interest rate is the rate of interest paid in the market on bonds of similar risk. It is also referred to as the *effective interest rate.* The market interest rate fluctuates daily. However, a company must decide in advance what the face interest rate will be to allow time to file with regulatory bodies, publicize the issue, and print the certificates. Because the company has no control over the market interest rate, there is often a difference between the market or effective interest rate and the face interest rate on the issue date. The result is that the issue price of the bonds does not always equal the principal or face value of the bonds. If the market rate of interest is greater than the face interest rate, the issue price will be less than the face value and the bonds are said to be issued at a discount. The discount equals the excess of the face value over the issue price. On the other hand, if the market rate of interest is less than the face interest rate, the issue price will be more than the face value and the bonds are said to be issued at a premium. The premium equals the excess of the issue price over the face value.

BONDS ISSUED AT A DISCOUNT

Suppose that the Vason Corporation issues its $100,000 of 9 percent, five-year bonds at 96.149 on January 1, 19x0, when the market rate of interest is 10 percent. In this case, the bonds are being issued at a discount because the market rate of interest exceeds the face interest rate. This entry records the issuance of the bonds at a discount:

19x0				
Jan. 1	Cash		96,149	
	Unamortized Bond Discount		3,851	
	Bonds Payable			100,000
	Sold $100,000 of 9%, 5-year			
	bonds at 96.149			
	Face amount of bonds	$100,000		
	Less purchase price of bonds			
	($100,000 × .96149)	96,149		
	Unamortized bond discount	$ 3,851		

As shown, Cash is debited for the amount received ($96,149), Bonds Payable is credited for the face amount ($100,000) of the bond liability, and the difference ($3,851) is debited to Unamortized Bond Discount. If a balance sheet is prepared right after the bonds are issued at a discount, the liability for bonds payable is as follows:

Long-Term Liabilities		
9% Bonds Payable, due 1/1/x5	$100,000	
Less Unamortized Bond Discount	3,851	$96,149

Unamortized Bond Discount is a contra-liability account: Its balance is deducted from the face amount of the bonds to arrive at the carrying value or present value of the bonds. The bond discount is described as unamortized because it will be amortized (written off) over the life of the bonds.

BONDS ISSUED AT A PREMIUM

When bonds have a face interest rate above the market rate for similar investments, they are issued at a price above the face value, or at a premium. For example, assume that the Vason Corporation issues $100,000 of 9 percent, five-year bonds for $104,100 on January 1, 19x0, when the market rate of interest is 8 percent. This means that investors will purchase the bonds at 104.1 percent of their face value. The issuance would be recorded as follows:

19x0			
Jan. 1	Cash	104,100	
	Unamortized Bond Premium		4,100
	Bonds Payable		100,000
	Sold $100,000 of 9%, 5-year		
	bonds at 104.1		
	($100,000 × 1.041)		

Right after this entry is made, bonds payable would be presented on the balance sheet as follows:

Long-Term Liabilities		
9% Bonds Payable, due 1/1/x5	$100,000	
Unamortized Bond Premium	4,100	$104,100

The carrying value of the bonds payable is $104,100, which equals the face value of the bonds plus the unamortized bond premium. The cash received from the bond issue is also $104,100. This means that the purchasers were willing to pay a premium of $4,100 to buy these bonds because the face interest on them was greater than the market rate.

BOND ISSUE COSTS

Most bonds are sold through underwriters, who receive a fee for taking care of the details of marketing the issue or for taking a chance on getting the selling price. These costs are connected with the issuance of bonds. Because bond issue costs benefit the whole life of a bond issue, it makes sense to spread the costs over that period. It is generally accepted practice to establish a separate account for bond issue costs and to amortize them over the life of the bonds. However, issue costs decrease the amount of money received by the company through the bond issue. They have the effect, then, of raising the discount or lowering the premium on the issue. As a result, bond issue costs can be spread over the life of the bonds through the amortization of a discount or premium. Because this method simplifies the recordkeeping, we assume in the text and problems of this book that all bond issue costs increase the discounts or decrease the premiums of bond issues.

USING PRESENT VALUE TO VALUE A BOND

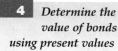

OBJECTIVE

4 *Determine the value of bonds using present values*

Present value[3] is relevant here because the value of a bond is based on the present value of two components of cash flow: (1) a series of fixed interest payments and (2) a single payment at maturity. The amount of interest that a bond pays is fixed over its life. During its life, however, the market rate of interest varies from day to day. Thus, the amount that investors are willing to pay for the bond changes as well.

Assume, for example, that a particular bond has a face value of $10,000 and pays a fixed amount of interest of $450 every six months (a 9 percent

---

3. A knowledge of present value concepts, as presented in the chapter on current liabilities and the time value of money is necessary to understand this section.

annual rate). The bond is due in five years. If the market rate of interest today is 14 percent, what is the present value of the bond?

To determine the present value of the bond, we use Table 4 in the appendix on future value and present value tables to calculate the present value of the periodic interest payments of $450, and we use Table 3 to calculate the present value of the single payment of $10,000 at maturity. Since interest payments are made every six months, the compounding period is half a year. Because of this, it is necessary to convert the annual rate to a semiannual rate of 7 percent (14 percent divided by two six-month periods per year) and to use ten periods (five years multiplied by two six-month periods per year). Using this information, we compute the present value of the bond:

Present value of 10 periodic payments at 7%
  (from Table 4 in the appendix on future value
  and present value tables): $450 × 7.024   = $3,160.80
Present value of a single payment at the end of
  10 periods at 7% (from Table 3 in the appendix
  on future value and present value tables):
  $10,000 × .508   =   5,080.00
Present value of $10,000 bond   = $8,240.80

The market rate of interest has increased so much since the bond was issued (from 9 percent to 14 percent) that the value of the bond is only $8,240.80 today. This amount is all that investors would be willing to pay at this time for income from this bond of $450 every six months and a return of the $10,000 principal in five years.

If the market rate of interest falls below the face interest rate, say to 8 percent (4 percent semiannually), the present value of the bond will be greater than the face value of $10,000:

Present value of 10 periodic payments at 4%
  (from Table 4 in the appendix on future value
  and present value tables): $450 × 8.111   = $ 3,649.95
Present value of a single payment at the end of
  10 periods at 4% (from Table 3 in the appendix
  on future value and present value tables):
  $10,000 × .676   =   6,760.00
Present value of $10,000 bond   = $10,409.95

BUSINESS BULLETIN: BUSINESS PRACTICE

In 1993, interest rates on long-term debt were at historically low levels, and this induced some companies to attempt to lock in these low costs for long periods. One of the most aggressive companies in this regard was The Walt Disney Company, which issued $150 million of 100-year bonds at a yield of only 7.5 percent. This was the first time since 1954 that 100-year bonds had been issued. Some analysts wondered if even Mickey Mouse could survive 100 years. Investors who purchase these bonds are taking a financial risk because if interest rates rise, which they are likely to do, the value of the bonds on the market will decrease.[4] ═══

AMORTIZING A BOND DISCOUNT

OBJECTIVE

5a *Amortize bond discounts using the straight-line and effective interest methods*

In the example on page 490, Vason Corporation issued $100,000 of five-year bonds at a discount because the market interest rate of 10 percent exceeded the face interest rate of 9 percent. The bonds were sold for $96,149, resulting in an unamortized bond discount of $3,851. Because this discount, as you will see, affects interest expense in each year of the bond issue, the bond discount should be amortized (reduced gradually) over the life of the issue. This means that the unamortized bond discount will decrease gradually over time, and that the carrying value of the bond issue (face value less unamortized discount) will increase gradually. By the maturity date of the bond, the carrying value of the issue will equal its face value, and the unamortized bond discount will be zero.

CALCULATION OF TOTAL INTEREST COST

When bonds are issued at a discount, the effective interest rate paid by the company is greater than the face interest rate on the bonds. The reason is that the interest cost to the company is the stated interest payments *plus* the amount of the bond discount. That is, although the company does not receive the full face value of the bonds on issue, it still must pay back the full face value at maturity. The difference between the issue price and the face value must be added to the total interest payments to arrive at the actual interest expense. The full cost to the corporation of issuing the bonds at a discount is as follows:

Cash to be paid to bondholders	
Face value at maturity	$100,000
Interest payments ($100,000 × .09 × 5 years)	45,000
Total cash paid to bondholders	$145,000
Less cash received from bondholders	96,149
Total interest cost	$ 48,851

Or, alternatively:

Interest payments ($100,000 × .09 × 5 years)	$ 45,000
Bond discount	3,851
Total interest cost	$ 48,851

The total interest cost of $48,851 is made up of $45,000 in interest payments and the $3,851 bond discount. So, the bond discount increases the interest paid on the bonds from the stated to the effective interest rate. The *effective interest rate* is the real interest cost of the bond over its life.

In order for each year's interest expense to reflect the effective interest rate, the discount must be allocated over the remaining life of the bonds as an

4. Thomas T. Vogel, Jr., "Disney Amazes Investors With Sale of 100-Year Bonds," *Wall Street Journal,* July 21, 1993.

increase in the interest expense each period. The process of allocating this expense is called *amortization of the bond discount*. Thus, interest expense for each period will exceed the actual payment of interest by the amount of the bond discount amortized over the period.

BUSINESS BULLETIN: BUSINESS PRACTICE

Some companies and governmental units have begun to issue bonds that do not require periodic interest payments. These bonds, called zero coupon bonds, are simply a promise to pay a fixed amount at the maturity date. They are issued at a large discount because the only interest earned by the buyer or paid by the issuer is the discount. For example, a five-year $100,000 bond issued at a time when the market rate is 14 percent, compounded semiannually, would sell for only $50,800. This amount is the present value of a single payment of $100,000 at the end of five years. The discount of $49,200 ($100,000 − $50,800) is the total interest cost; it is amortized over the life of the bond and payment is recorded in total at maturity.

METHODS OF AMORTIZING A BOND DISCOUNT

There are two ways of amortizing bond discounts or premiums: the straight-line method and the effective interest method.

Straight-Line Method   The straight-line method is the easier of the two, with equal amortization of the discount for each interest period. Suppose that the interest payment dates for the Vason Corporation bond issue are January 1 and July 1. The amount of the bond discount amortized and the interest cost for each semiannual period are figured in four steps:

1. Total interest payments = interest payments per year × life of bonds

$$= 2 \times 5$$
$$= 10$$

2. Amortization of bond discount per interest period $= \dfrac{\text{bond discount}}{\text{total interest payments}}$

$$= \frac{\$3,851}{10}$$
$$= \$385*$$

3. Regular cash interest payment = face value × face interest rate × time

$$= \$100,000 \times .09 \times {}^{6}/_{12}$$
$$= \$4,500$$

4. Total interest cost per interest period = interest payment + amortization of bond discount

$$= \$4,500 + \$385$$

*Rounded.   = $4,885

On July 1, 19x0, the first semiannual interest date, the entry would be:

19x0

July 1	Bond Interest Expense	4,885	
	Unamortized Bond Discount		385
	Cash		4,500
	Paid semiannual interest to bondholders and amortized the discount on 9%, 5-year bonds		

Notice that the bond interest expense is $4,885, but the amount paid to the bondholders is the $4,500 face interest payment. The difference of $385 is the credit to Unamortized Bond Discount. This lowers the debit balance of the Unamortized Bond Discount account and raises the carrying value of the bonds payable by $385 each interest period. Assuming that no changes occur in the bond issue, this entry will be made every six months for the life of the bonds. At the time when the bond issue matures, there will be no balance in the Unamortized Bond Discount account, and the carrying value of the bonds will be $100,000—exactly equal to the amount due the bondholders.

The straight-line method has long been used, but it has a certain weakness. Because the carrying value goes up each period and the bond interest expense stays the same, the rate of interest falls over time. Conversely, when the straight-line method is used to amortize a premium, the rate of interest rises over time. This is why the Accounting Principles Board has ruled that the straight-line method can be used only when it does not lead to a material difference from the effective interest method.[5] As we discuss next, the effective interest method presupposes a constant rate of interest over the life of the bonds. It is constant because the total interest expense changes a little each interest period in response to the changing carrying value of the bonds.

ALTERNATIVE METHOD

Effective Interest Method   To compute the interest and amortization of a bond discount for each interest period under the effective interest method, we have to apply a constant interest rate to the carrying value of the bonds at the beginning of each interest period. This constant rate equals the market rate or effective rate at the time the bonds are issued. The amount of Unamortized Bond Discount to be amortized each period is the difference between the interest computed by using the effective rate and the actual interest paid to bondholders.

As an example, we use the same facts presented earlier—a $100,000 bond issue at 9 percent, with a five-year maturity, interest to be paid twice a year. The market or effective rate of interest at the time the bonds were issued was 10 percent. The bonds were sold for $96,149, a discount of $3,851. The interest and amortization of the bond discount are shown in Table 11-1.

Here are explanations of how the amounts in the table are computed:

Column A: The carrying value of the bonds is the face value of the bonds less the unamortized bond discount at the beginning of the period ($100,000 − $3,851 = $96,149).

Column B: The interest expense to be recorded is the effective interest. It is found by multiplying the carrying value of the bonds by the effective interest rate for one-half year ($96,149 × .10 × $^{6}/_{12}$ = $4,807).

Column C: The interest paid in the period is a constant amount that is computed by multiplying the face value of the bonds by the face interest rate for the bonds by the interest time period ($100,000 × .09 × $^{6}/_{12}$ = $4,500).

5. Accounting Principles Board, *Opinion No. 21,* "Interest on Receivables and Payables" (New York: American Institute of Certified Public Accountants, 1971), par. 15.

Table 11-1. Interest and Amortization of Bond Discount: Effective Interest Method

	A	B	C	D	E	F
Semiannual Interest Period	Carrying Value at Beginning of Period	Semiannual Interest Expense at 10% to Be Recorded* (5% × A)	Semiannual Interest to Be Paid to Bondholders (4½% × $100,000)	Amortization of Discount (B − C)	Unamortized Bond Discount at End of Period	Carrying Value at End of Period (A + D)
0					$3,851	$ 96,149
1	$96,149	$4,807	$4,500	$307	3,544	96,456
2	96,456	4,823	4,500	323	3,221	96,779
3	96,779	4,839	4,500	339	2,882	97,118
4	97,118	4,856	4,500	356	2,526	97,474
5	97,474	4,874	4,500	374	2,152	97,848
6	97,848	4,892	4,500	392	1,760	98,240
7	98,240	4,912	4,500	412	1,348	98,652
8	98,652	4,933	4,500	433	915	99,085
9	99,085	4,954	4,500	454	461	99,539
10	99,539	4,961†	4,500	461	—	100,000

*Rounded to nearest dollar.   †Difference due to rounding.

Column D: The discount amortized is the difference between the effective interest expense to be recorded and the interest to be paid on the interest payment date ($4,807 − $4,500 = $307).

Column E: The unamortized bond discount is the balance of the bond discount at the beginning of the period less the current period amortization of the discount ($3,851 − $307 = $3,544). The unamortized discount decreases each interest payment period because it is amortized as a portion of interest expense.

Column F: The carrying value of the bonds at the end of the period is the carrying value at the beginning of the period plus the amortization during the period ($96,149 + $307 = $96,456). Notice that the sum of the carrying value and the unamortized discount (Column F + Column E) always equals the face value of the bonds ($96,456 + $3,544 = $100,000).

The entry to record the interest expense is exactly like the one used when the straight-line method is applied. However, the amounts debited and credited to the various accounts are different. Using the effective interest method, the entry for July 1, 19x0 would be as follows:

```
19x0
July 1   Bond Interest Expense                    4,807
             Unamortized Bond Discount                      307
             Cash                                          4,500
             Paid semiannual interest to
             bondholders and amortized
             the discount on 9%, 5-year
             bonds
```

Notice that it is not necessary to prepare an interest and amortization table to determine the amortization of a discount for any one interest payment period. It is necessary only to multiply the carrying value by the effective

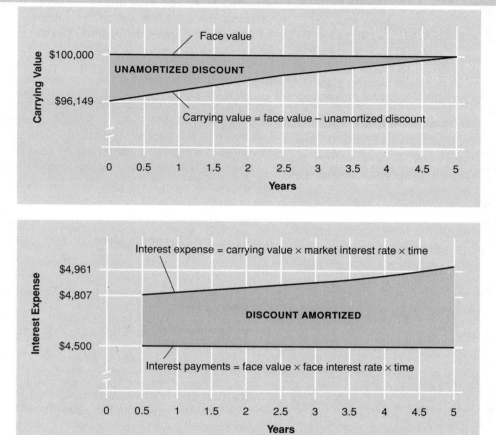

Figure 11-2. Carrying Value and Interest Expense—Bonds Issued at a Discount

interest rate and subtract the interest payment from the result. For example, the amount of discount to be amortized in the seventh interest payment period equals $412 [($98,240 × .05) − $4,500].

Visual Summary of the Effective Interest Method   The effect of the amortization of a bond discount using the effective interest method on carrying value and interest expense can be seen in Figure 11-2 (based on the data from Table 11-1). Notice that initially the carrying value (issue price) is less than the face value, but that it gradually increases toward the face value over the life of the bond issue. Notice also that interest expense exceeds interest payments by the amount of the discount amortized. Interest expense increases gradually over the life of the bond because it is based on the gradually increasing carrying value (multiplied by the market interest rate).

AMORTIZING A BOND PREMIUM

In our example on page 491, Vason Corporation issued $100,000 of five-year bonds at a premium because the market interest rate of 8 percent was less than the face interest rate of 9 percent. The bonds were sold for $104,100,

OBJECTIVE

5b *Amortize bond premiums using the straight-line and effective interest methods*

resulting in an unamortized bond premium of $4,100. Like a bond discount, a bond premium must be amortized over the life of the bonds so that it can be matched to its effect on interest expense during that period. In the following sections, the total interest cost is calculated and the bond premium is amortized using the straight-line and effective interest methods.

CALCULATION OF TOTAL INTEREST COST

Because the bondholders paid in excess of face value for the bonds, the premium of $4,100 ($104,100 − $100,000) represents an amount that the bondholders will not receive at maturity. The premium is in effect a reduction, in advance, of the total interest paid on the bonds over the life of the bond issue.

The total interest cost over the issue's life can be computed as follows:

Cash to be paid to bondholders	
Face value at maturity	$100,000
Interest payments ($100,000 × .09 × 5 years)	45,000
Total cash paid to bondholders	$145,000
Less cash received from bondholders	104,100
Total interest cost	$ 40,900

Or, alternatively:

Interest payments ($100,000 × .09 × 5 years)	$ 45,000
Less bond premium	4,100
Total interest cost	$ 40,900

Notice that the total interest payments of $45,000 exceed the total interest costs of $40,900 by $4,100, the amount of the bond premium.

METHODS OF AMORTIZING A BOND PREMIUM

The two methods of amortizing a bond premium are the straight-line method and the effective interest method.

Straight-Line Method   Under the straight-line method, the bond premiums are spread evenly over the life of the bond issue. As with bond discounts, the amount of the bond premium amortized and the interest cost for each semiannual period are computed in four steps:

1. Total interest payments = interest payments per year × life of bonds

$$= 2 \times 5$$

$$= 10$$

2. Amortization of bond premium per interest period $= \dfrac{\text{bond premium}}{\text{total interest payments}}$

$$= \dfrac{\$4,100}{10}$$

$$= \$410$$

3. Regular cash interest payment $=$ face value $\times$ face interest rate $\times$ time

$$= \$100,000 \times .09 \times {}^6/_{12}$$

$$= \$4,500$$

4. Total interest cost per interest period $=$ interest payment $-$ amortization of bond premium

$$= \$4,500 - \$410$$

$$= \$4,090$$

On July 1, 19x0, the first semiannual interest date, the entry would be:

19x0			
July 1	Bond Interest Expense	4,090	
	Unamortized Bond Premium	410	
	Cash		4,500
	Paid semiannual interest to bondholders		
	and amortized the premium on 9%,		
	5-year bonds		

Notice that the bond interest expense is $4,090, but the amount received by the bondholders is the $4,500 face interest payment. The difference of $410 is the debit to Unamortized Bond Premium. This lowers the credit balance of the Unamortized Bond Premium account and the carrying value of the bonds payable by $410 each interest period. Assuming that the bond issue remains unchanged, the same entry will be made every six months over the life of the bond issue. When the bond issue matures, there will be no balance in the Unamortized Bond Premium account, and the carrying value of the bonds payable will be $100,000, exactly equal to the amount due the bondholders.

As noted before, the straight-line method should be used only when it does not lead to a material difference from the effective interest method.

ALTERNATIVE METHOD

Effective Interest Method   Under the straight-line method, the real or effective interest rate is changing every interest period, even though the interest expense is fixed, because the effective interest rate is determined by comparing the fixed interest expense with a carrying value that is changing as a result of amortizing the discount or premium. To apply a fixed interest rate over the life of the bonds based on the actual market rate at the time of the bond issue requires the use of the effective interest method. Under this method, the interest expense decreases slightly each period (see Table 11-2, Column B) because the amount of the bond premium amortized increases slightly (Column D). This occurs because a fixed rate is applied each period to the gradually decreasing carrying value (Column A).

The first interest payment is recorded as follows:

19x0			
July 1	Bond Interest Expense	4,164	
	Unamortized Bond Premium	336	
	Cash		4,500
	Paid semiannual interest to bondholders		
	and amortized the premium on 9%,		
	5-year bonds		

Notice that the unamortized bond premium (Column E) decreases gradually to zero as the carrying value decreases to the face value (Column F). To find the amount of premium amortized in any one interest payment period,

Table 11-2. Interest and Amortization of Bond Premium: Effective Interest Method

	A	B	C	D	E	F
Semiannual Interest Period	Carrying Value at Beginning of Period	Semiannual Interest Expense at 8% to Be Recorded* (4% × A)	Semiannual Interest to Be Paid to Bondholders (4½% × $100,000)	Amortization of Premium (C − B)	Unamortized Bond Premium at End of Period	Carrying Value at End of Period (A − D)
0					$4,100	$104,100
1	$104,100	$4,164	$4,500	$336	3,764	103,764
2	103,764	4,151	4,500	349	3,415	103,415
3	103,415	4,137	4,500	363	3,052	103,052
4	103,052	4,122	4,500	378	2,674	102,674
5	102,674	4,107	4,500	393	2,281	102,281
6	102,281	4,091	4,500	409	1,872	101,872
7	101,872	4,075	4,500	425	1,447	101,447
8	101,447	4,058	4,500	442	1,005	101,005
9	101,005	4,040	4,500	460	545	100,545
10	100,545	3,955†	4,500	545	—	100,000

*Rounded to nearest dollar.   †Difference due to rounding.

we subtract the effective interest expense (the carrying value times the effective interest rate, Column B) from the interest payment (Column C). In semiannual interest period 5, for example, the amortization of premium equals $393 [$4,500 − ($102,674 × .04)].

Visual Summary of the Effective Interest Method   The effect of the amortization of a bond premium using the effective interest method on carrying value and interest expense can be seen in Figure 11-3 (based on data from Table 11-2). Notice that initially the carrying value (issue price) is greater than the face value, but that it gradually decreases toward the face value over the life of the bond issue. Notice also that interest payments exceed interest expense by the amount of the premium amortized, and that interest expense decreases gradually over the life of the bond because it is based on the gradually decreasing carrying value (multiplied by the market interest rate).

BUSINESS BULLETIN: TECHNOLOGY IN PRACTICE

Interest and amortization tables like those in Tables 11-1 and 11-2 provide ideal applications for computer spreadsheet software such as Lotus 1-2-3 and Microsoft Excel. Once the tables have been constructed with the proper formula in each cell, only five variables must be entered to produce the entire table. These variables are the face value of the bonds, the selling price, the life of the bonds, the face interest rate, and the effective interest rate.

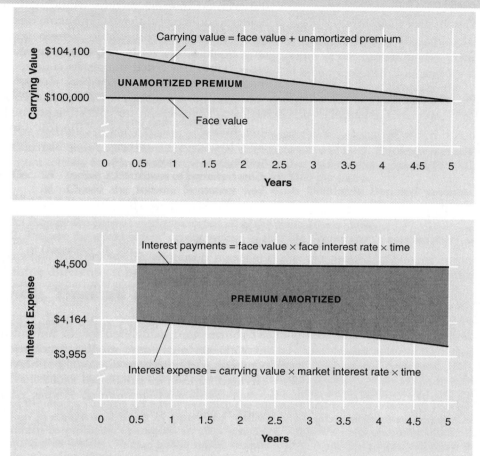

Figure 11-3. Carrying Value and Interest Expense—Bonds Issued at a Premium

OTHER BONDS PAYABLE ISSUES

Several other issues arise in accounting for bonds payable. Among them are the sale of bonds between interest payment dates, the year-end accrual of bond interest expense, the retirement of bonds, and the conversion of bonds into common stock.

SALE OF BONDS BETWEEN INTEREST DATES

Bonds can be issued on an interest payment date, as in the examples above, but often they are issued between interest payment dates. The generally accepted method of handling bonds issued in this manner is to collect from investors the interest that has accrued since the last interest payment date. Then, when the next interest period arrives, the corporation pays investors the interest for the entire period. Thus, the interest collected when bonds are sold is returned to investors on the next interest payment date.

There are two reasons for following this procedure. The first is a practical one. If a company issued bonds on several different days and did not collect the accrued interest, records would have to be maintained for each bond-holder and date of purchase. In such a case, the interest due each bondholder would have to be computed on the basis of different time periods. Clearly, large bookkeeping costs would be incurred under this kind of system. On the other hand, if accrued interest is collected when the bonds are sold, on the interest payment date the corporation can pay the interest due for the entire period, eliminating the extra computations and costs.

The second reason for collecting accrued interest in advance is that when this amount is netted against the full interest paid on the interest payment date, the resulting interest expense represents the amount for the time the money was borrowed.

For example, assume that the Vason Corporation sold $100,000 of 9 per-cent, five-year bonds for face value on May 1, 19x0, rather than on January 1, 19x0, the issue date. The entry to record the sale of the bonds follows:

19x0
May 1   Cash   103,000
           Bond Interest Expense   3,000
           Bonds Payable   100,000
             Sold 9%, 5-year bonds at face value
             plus 4 months' accrued interest
             $100,000 $\times$ .09 $\times$ $^4/_{12}$ = $3,000

As shown, Cash is debited for the amount received, $103,000 (the face value of $100,000 plus four months' accrued interest of $3,000). Bond Interest Expense is credited for the $3,000 of accrued interest, and Bonds Payable is credited for the face value of $100,000.

When the first semiannual interest payment date arrives, the following entry is made:

19x0
July 1   Bond Interest Expense   4,500
           Cash   4,500
             Paid semiannual interest
             $100,000 $\times$ .09 $\times$ $^6/_{12}$ = $4,500

Notice that here the entire half-year interest is both debited to Bond Interest Expense and credited to Cash because the corporation pays bond interest only once every six months, in full six-month amounts. This process is illus-trated in Figure 11-4. The actual interest expense for the two months that the bonds were outstanding is $1,500. This amount is the net balance of the $4,500 debit to Bond Interest Expense on July 1 less the $3,000 credit to Bond Interest Expense on May 1. You can see these steps clearly in the posted entries in the ledger account for Bond Interest Expense below:

Bond Interest Expense							Account No. 723
			Post.			Balance	
Date		Item	Ref.	Debit	Credit	Debit	Credit
19x0							
May	1				3,000		3,000
July	1			4,500		1,500	

Figure 11-4. Effect on Bond Interest Expense When Bonds Are Issued Between Interest Dates

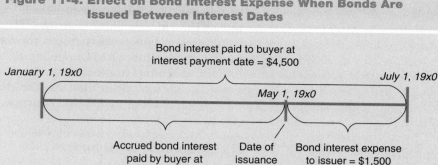

YEAR-END ACCRUAL FOR BOND INTEREST EXPENSE

It is not often that bond interest payment dates correspond with a company's fiscal year. Therefore, an adjustment must be made at the end of the accounting period to accrue the interest expense on the bonds from the last payment date to the end of the fiscal year. Further, if there is any discount or premium on the bonds, it also must be amortized for the fractional period.

Remember that in an earlier example, Vason Corporation issued $100,000 in bonds on January 1, 19x0 at 104.1 (see page 491). Suppose the company's fiscal year ends on September 30, 19x0. In the period since the interest payment and amortization of the premium on July 1, three months' worth of interest has accrued, and the following adjusting entry under the effective interest method must be made:

19x0			
Sept. 30	Bond Interest Expense	2,075.50	
	Unamortized Bond Premium	174.50	
	Interest Payable		2,250.00
	To record accrual of interest on 9% bonds payable for 3 months and amortization of one-half of the premium for the second interest payment period		

This entry covers one-half of the second interest period. Unamortized Bond Premium is debited for $174.50, which is one-half of $349, the amortization of the premium for the second period from Table 11-2. Interest Payable is credited for $2,250, three months' interest on the face value of the bonds ($100,000 $\times$ .09 $\times$ $^3/_{12}$). The net debit figure of $2,075.50 ($2,250 $-$ $174.50) is the bond interest expense for the three-month period.

When the January 1, 19x1 payment date arrives, the entry to pay the bondholders and amortize the premium is as follows:

19x1			
Jan. 1	Bond Interest Expense	2,075.50	
	Interest Payable	2,250.00	
	Unamortized Bond Premium	174.50	
	Cash		4,500.00
	Paid semiannual interest including interest previously accrued, and amortized the premium for the period since the end of the fiscal year		

As shown here, one-half ($2,250) of the amount paid ($4,500) was accrued on September 30. Unamortized Bond Premium is debited for $174.50, the remaining amount to be amortized for the period ($349.00 − $174.50). The resulting bond interest expense is the amount that applies to the three-month period from October 1 to December 31.

Bond discounts are recorded at year end in the same way as bond premiums. The difference is that the amortization of a bond discount increases interest expense instead of decreasing it, as a premium does.

OBJECTIVE

7 *Account for the retirement of bonds and the conversion of bonds into stock*

RETIREMENT OF BONDS

Most bond issues give the corporation a chance to buy back and retire the bonds at a specified call price, usually above face value, before maturity. Such bonds are known as callable bonds. They give the corporation flexibility in financing its operations. For example, if market interest rates drop, the company can call its bonds and reissue debt at a lower interest rate. Other reasons to call a company's bonds might be that the company has earned enough to pay off the debt, the reason for having the debt no longer exists, or the company wants to restructure its debt to equity ratio. The bond indenture states the time period and the prices at which the bonds can be redeemed. When a bond issue is retired before its maturity date, this is called early extinguishment of debt.

Let's assume that Vason Corporation can call or retire the $100,000 of bonds issued at a premium (page 491) at 105, and that it decides to do so on July 1, 19x3. (To simplify our example, we assume retirement on an interest payment date.) Because the bonds were issued on January 1, 19x0, the retirement takes place on the seventh interest payment date. Assume that the entry for the interest payment (which must be made) and for the amortization of the premium have been made. The entry to retire the bonds is as follows:

19x3			
July 1	Bonds Payable	100,000	
	Unamortized Bond Premium	1,447	
	Loss on Retirement of Bonds	3,553	
	Cash		105,000
	Retired 9% bonds at 105		

In this entry, the cash paid is the face value times the call price ($100,000 × 1.05 = $105,000). The unamortized bond premium can be found in Column E of Table 11-2. The loss on retirement of bonds occurs because the call price of the bonds is greater than the carrying value ($105,000 − $101,447 = $3,553). The loss, if material, is presented as an extraordinary item on the income statement, as explained in the chapter on retained earnings and corporate income statements.

Sometimes a rise in the market interest rate can cause the market value of bonds to fall considerably below the face value of the bonds. If it has the cash to do so, the company may find it advantageous to purchase the bonds on the open market and retire them, rather than wait and pay them off at face value. An extraordinary gain is recognized for the difference between the purchase price of the bonds and the face value of the retired bonds. For example, assume that because of a rise in interest rates, Vason Corporation is able to purchase the $100,000 bond issue on the open market at 85, making it unnecessary to call the bonds at the higher price of 105. Then, the entry would be as follows:

19x3
July 1 Bonds Payable   100,000
          Unamortized Bond Premium   1,447
            Cash   85,000
            Gain on Retirement of Bonds   16,447
              Purchased and retired
              9% bonds at 85

Inco Limited

DECISION POINT

On March 20, 1991, the *Wall Street Journal* reported that Inco Limited was issuing that day $172.5 million in 7¾ percent convertible debentures due in 2016. The debentures, which are callable, could be converted into common shares of the company at a conversion price of $38.25. In other words, a holder of a $1,000 bond could convert it into 26.14 ($1,000 ÷ $38.25) shares of common stock.[6] On the previous day, March 19, the company's common stock had sold on the New York Stock Exchange for $31.50. What advantages and disadvantages did Inco's management weigh in deciding to issue convertible bonds rather than another security, such as nonconvertible bonds or common stock?

Several factors are favorable to the issuance of convertible bonds. First, the interest rate of 7¾ percent is less than the company would have to offer if the bonds were not convertible. An investor is willing to give up some current interest for the prospect that the value of the underlying stock will increase, and therefore the value of the bonds will also increase. For example, if the common stock rises from $31.50 to above $38.25 per share, the value of the bond will begin to rise based on changes in the price of the common stock, not on changes in interest rates. If the common stock were to rise to $50, the market value of a $1,000 bond would rise to $1,307 (26.14 shares × $50). A second advantage is that Inco does not have to give up any current control of the company. Unlike stockholders, bondholders do not have voting rights. A third benefit is tax savings. Interest paid on bonds is fully deductible for income tax purposes, whereas cash dividends paid on common stock are not. Fourth, the company's income will be affected favorably if the company earns a return that exceeds the interest cost of the debentures. For example, if the company uses the funds for a purpose that earns 16 percent, this return will be more than twice the interest cost of 7¾ percent. Finally, the convertible feature offers financial flexibility. If the price of the stock rises above $38.25, management can avoid repaying the bonds by calling them for redemption, thereby forcing the bondholders to convert their bonds into common stock. The bondholders will agree to convert because the common stock they will

6. "$172,500,000 Inco Limited 7¾% Convertible Debentures Due 2016," *Wall Street Journal,* March 20, 1991.

receive will be worth more than the amount they would receive if the bonds were redeemed.

One major disadvantage of convertible debentures is that interest must be paid semiannually. Inability to make an interest payment could force the company into bankruptcy. Common stock dividends are declared and paid only when the board of directors decides to do so. Another disadvantage is that when the bonds are converted, they become new outstanding common stock and no longer have the features of bonds. Inco's management obviously felt that the advantages of its choice outweighed the disadvantages. :::::

CONVERSION OF BONDS INTO COMMON STOCK

Bonds that can be exchanged for other securities of the corporation (in most cases, common stock) are called convertible bonds. The conversion feature allows the investor to make more money because if the market price of the common stock rises, the value of the bonds rises. However, if the price of the common stock does not rise, the investor still holds the bonds and receives the periodic interest payment as well as the principal at the maturity date.

When a bondholder wishes to convert bonds into common stock, the rule is that the common stock is recorded at the carrying value of the bonds. The bond liability and the associated unamortized discount or premium are written off the books. For this reason, no gain or loss is recorded on the transaction. For example, suppose that Vason Corporation's bonds are not called on July 1, 19x3. Instead, the corporation's bondholders decide to convert all the bonds to $8 par value common stock under a convertible provision of 40 shares of common stock for each $1,000 bond. The entry would be as follows:

19x3			
July 1	Bonds Payable	100,000	
	Unamortized Bond Premium	1,447	
	Common Stock		32,000
	Paid-in Capital in Excess of Par		
	Value, Common		69,447
	Converted 9% bonds payable into		
	$8 par value common stock at a rate		
	of 40 shares for each $1,000 bond		

The unamortized bond premium is found in Column E of Table 11-2. At a rate of 40 shares for each $1,000 bond, 4,000 shares will be issued at a total par value of $32,000 (4,000 × $8). The Common Stock account is credited for the amount of the par value of the stock issued. The Paid-in Capital in Excess of Par Value, Common account is credited for the difference between the carrying value of the bonds and the par value of the stock issued ($101,447 − $32,000 = $69,447). No gain or loss is recorded.

OTHER LONG-TERM LIABILITIES

A company can have other long-term liabilities besides bonds. The most common are mortgages payable, installment notes payable, long-term leases, and pensions and other postretirement benefits.

OBJECTIVE

8 *Explain the basic features of mortgages payable, installment notes payable, long-term leases, and pensions and other postretirement benefits as long-term liabilities*

MORTGAGES PAYABLE

A mortgage is a long-term debt secured by real property. It usually is paid in equal monthly installments. Each monthly payment includes interest on the debt and a reduction in the principal. Table 11-3 shows the first three monthly payments on a $50,000, 12 percent mortgage. The mortgage was obtained on June 1, and the monthly payments are $800. According to the table, the entry to record the July 1 payment would be as follows:

July 1	Mortgage Payable	300	
	Mortgage Interest Expense	500	
	Cash		800
	Made monthly mortgage payment		

Notice from the entry and from Table 11-3 that the July 1 payment represents interest expense of $500 ($50,000 $\times$ .12 $\times$ $^1/_{12}$) and a reduction in the debt of $300 ($800 $-$ $500). Therefore, the unpaid balance is reduced by the July payment to $49,700. The interest expense for August is slightly less than July's because of the decrease in the debt.

INSTALLMENT NOTES PAYABLE

Long-term notes can be paid at the maturity date by making a lump-sum payment that includes the amount borrowed plus the interest. Often, however, the terms of the note will call for a series of periodic payments. When this situation occurs, the notes payable are called installment notes payable because each payment includes the interest from the previous payment to date plus a repayment of part of the amount which was borrowed. For example, let's assume that on December 31, 19x1, $100,000 is borrowed on a 15 percent installment note, to be paid annually over five years. The entry to record the note is as follows:

19x1			
Dec. 31	Cash	100,000	
	Notes Payable		100,000
	Borrowed $100,000 at 15%		
	on a 5-year installment note		

Table 11-3. Monthly Payment Schedule on $50,000, 12 Percent Mortgage

	A	B	C	D	E
Payment Date	Unpaid Balance at Beginning of Period	Monthly Payment	Interest for 1 Month at 1% on Unpaid Balance* (1% $\times$ A)	Reduction in Debt (B $-$ C)	Unpaid Balance at End of Period (A $-$ D)
June 1					$50,000
July 1	$50,000	$800	$500	$300	49,700
Aug. 1	49,700	800	497	303	49,397
Sept. 1	49,397	800	494	306	49,091

*Rounded to nearest dollar.

Payments of Accrued Interest Plus Equal Amounts of Principal

Installment notes most often call for payments consisting of accrued interest plus equal amounts of principal repayment. The amount of each installment decreases because the amount of principal on which the accrued interest is calculated decreases by the amount of the principal repaid. Banks use installment notes to finance equipment purchases by businesses; these notes are also common for other kinds of purchases when payment is spread over several years. They can be set up on a revolving basis whereby the borrower can borrow additional funds as the installments are paid. Moreover, the interest rate charged on installment notes can be adjusted periodically by the bank as market rates of interest change.

Under this method of payment, the principal declines by an equal amount each year for five years, or by $20,000 per year ($100,000 ÷ 5 years). The interest is calculated on the balance of the note that remains each year. Because the balance of the note declines each year, the amount of interest also declines. For example, the entries for the first two payments of the installment note are as follows:

```
19x2
Dec. 31  Notes Payable                        20,000
         Interest Expense                      15,000
             Cash                                          35,000
                 First installment payment
                 on note
                 $100,000 × .15 = $15,000
19x3
Dec. 31  Notes Payable                        20,000
         Interest Expense                      12,000
             Cash                                          32,000
                 Second installment payment
                 on note
                 $80,000 × .15 = $12,000
```

Notice that the amount of the payment decreases from $35,000 to $32,000 because the amount owed on the note has decreased from $100,000 to $80,000. The difference of $3,000 is the interest on the $20,000 that was repaid in 19x2. Each subsequent payment decreases by $3,000, as the note itself decreases by $20,000 each year until it is fully paid. This example assumes that the repayment of principal and the interest rate remain the same from year to year.

Payments of Accrued Interest Plus Increasing Amounts of Principal

Less commonly, the terms of an installment note, like those used for leasing equipment, may call for equal periodic (monthly or yearly) payments of accrued interest plus increasing amounts of principal. Under this method, the interest is deducted from the equal payments to determine the amount by which the principal will be reduced each year. This procedure, presented in Table 11-4, is very similar to that shown above for mortgages. Each equal payment of $29,833 is allocated between interest and reduction in debt (principal). Each year the interest is calculated on the remaining principal. As the principal decreases, the amount of interest also decreases, and because the payment remains the same, the amount by which the principal decreases becomes larger each year. The entries for the first two years, with data taken from Table 11-4, are as follows:

Table 11-4. Payment Schedule on $100,000, 15 Percent Installment Note

	A	B	C	D	E
Payment Date	Unpaid Principal at Beginning of Period	Equal Annual Payment	Interest for 1 Year at 15% on Unpaid Principal* (15% × A)	Reduction in Principal (B − C)	Unpaid Principal at End of Period (A − D)
					$100,000
19x2	$100,000	$29,833	$15,000	$14,833	85,167
19x3	85,167	29,833	12,775	17,058	68,109
19x4	68,109	29,833	10,216	19,617	48,492
19x5	48,492	29,833	7,274	22,559	25,933
19x6	25,933	29,833	3,900†	25,933	—

*Rounded to the nearest dollar.

†The last year's interest equals the installment payment minus the remaining unpaid principal ($29,833 − $25,933 = $3,900); it does not exactly equal $3,890 ($25,933 × .15) because of the cumulative effect of rounding

19x2			
Dec. 31	Notes Payable	14,833	
	Interest Expense	15,000	
	Cash		29,833
	First installment payment on note		

19x3			
Dec. 31	Notes Payable	17,058	
	Interest Expense	12,775	
	Cash		29,833
	Second installment payment on note		

Similar entries will be made for the next three years.

How is the equal annual payment calculated? Because the $100,000 borrowed is the present value of the five equal annual payments at 15 percent interest, present value tables can be used to calculate the annual payments. Using Table 4 from the appendix on future value and present value tables, the calculation is made as follows:

Periodic payment × factor (Table 4 in the present value appendix: 15%, 5 years) = present value

Periodic payment × 3.352 = $100,000

Periodic payment = $100,000 ÷ 3.352 = $29,833

Table 11-4 shows that five equal annual payments of $29,833 at 15 percent will reduce the principal balance to zero (except for the difference due to rounding).

LONG-TERM LEASES

There are several ways for a company to obtain new operating assets. One way is to borrow money and buy the asset. Another is to rent the equipment on a short-term lease. A third way is to obtain the equipment on a long-term lease. The first two methods do not create accounting problems. In the first case, the asset and liability are recorded at the amount paid, and the asset is subject to periodic depreciation. In the second case, the lease is short term or cancelable, and the risks of ownership lie with the lessor. This type of lease is called an operating lease. It is proper accounting to treat operating lease payments as an expense and to debit the amount of each monthly payment to Rent Expense.

The third case, a long-term lease, is one of the fastest-growing ways of financing operating equipment in the United States today. It has several advantages. For instance, a long-term lease requires no immediate cash payment, the rental payment may be fully deductible for tax purposes, and it costs less than a short-term lease. Acquiring the use of plant assets under long-term leases does cause several accounting problems, however. Often, these leases cannot be canceled. Also, their duration may be about the same as the useful life of the asset. Finally, they may provide for the lessee to buy the asset at a nominal price at the end of the lease. The lease is much like an installment purchase because the risks of ownership lie with the lessee. Both the lessee's available assets and its legal obligations (liabilities) increase because it must make a number of payments over the life of the asset.

Noting this problem, the Financial Accounting Standards Board has described this kind of long-term lease as a capital lease. The term reflects the provisions of the lease, which make the transaction more like a purchase or sale on installment. The FASB has ruled that in the case of a capital lease, the lessee must record an asset and a long-term liability equal to the present value of the total lease payments during the lease term. In doing so, the lessee must use the present value at the beginning of the lease.[7] In much the same way as mortgage payments are treated, each lease payment becomes partly interest expense and partly a repayment of debt. Further, depreciation expense is figured on the asset and entered on the records of the lessee.

Suppose, for example, that Isaacs Company enters into a long-term lease for a machine used in its manufacturing operations. The lease terms call for an annual payment of $4,000 for six years, which approximates the useful life of the machine (see Table 11-5.) At the end of the lease period, the title to the machine passes to Isaacs. This lease is clearly a capital lease and should be recorded according to FASB *Statement No. 13.*

A lease is a periodic payment for the right to use an asset or assets. Present value techniques, explained in the chapter on current liabilities and the time value of money, can be used to place a value on the asset and on the corresponding liability associated with a capital lease. If Isaacs's interest cost is 16 percent, the present value of the lease payments is computed as follows:

Periodic payment $\times$ factor (Table 4 in the present
value appendix: 16%, 6 years) = present value

$4,000 $\times$ 3.685 = $14,740

The entry to record the lease contract is as follows:

Equipment Under Capital Lease	14,740	
Obligations Under Capital Lease		14,740

Equipment under capital lease is classified as a long-term asset; obligations under capital lease are classified as a long-term liability. Each year, Isaacs must record depreciation on the leased asset. If we assume straight-line

7. *Statement of Financial Accounting Standards No. 13,* "Accounting for Leases" (Stamford, Conn.: Financial Accounting Standards Board, 1976), par. 10.

Table 11-5. Payment Schedule on 16 Percent Capital Lease*

	A	B	C	D
Year	Lease Payment	Interest (16%) on Unpaid Obligation (D × 16%)	Reduction of Lease Obligation (A − B)	Balance of Lease Obligation (D − C)
Beginning				$14,740
1	$ 4,000	$2,358	$ 1,642	13,098
2	4,000	2,096	1,904	11,194
3	4,000	1,791	2,209	8,985
4	4,000	1,438	2,562	6,423
5	4,000	1,028	2,972	3,451
6	4,000	549	3,451	—
	$24,000	$9,260	$14,740	

*Computations are rounded to the nearest dollar.

depreciation, a six-year life, and no salvage value, this entry would record the depreciation:

Depreciation Expense	2,457	
Accumulated Depreciation, Leased		
Equipment Under Capital Lease		2,457

The interest expense for each year is computed by multiplying the interest rate (16 percent) by the amount of the remaining lease obligation. Table 11-5 shows these calculations. Using the data in the table, the first lease payment would be recorded as follows:

Interest Expense (Column B)	2,358	
Obligations Under Capital Lease (Column C)	1,642	
Cash		4,000

PENSIONS

Most employees who work for medium-sized and large companies are covered by some sort of pension plan. A pension plan is a contract between the company and its employees, in which the company agrees to pay benefits to the employees after they retire. Most companies contribute the full cost of the pension, but sometimes the employees also pay part of their salary or wages toward their pension. The contributions from both parties generally are paid into a pension fund, from which benefits are paid out to retirees. In most cases, pension benefits consist of monthly payments to employees after retirement and other payments on disability or death.

There are two kinds of pension plans. Under *defined contribution plans,* the employer is required to contribute an annual amount determined in the current year on the basis of agreements between the company and its employees or a resolution of the board of directors. Retirement payments depend on the amount of pension payments the accumulated contributions can support. Under *defined benefit plans,* the employer's required annual contribution is the amount required to fund pension liabilities that arise as a result of employment in the current year but whose amount will not be determined finally until the retirement and death of the persons currently employed. Here, the amount of the contribution required in the current year depends on a fixed amount of future benefits but uncertain current contributions; under a defined contribution plan, the uncertain future amount of pension liabilities depends on the cumulative amounts of fixed current contributions.

Accounting for annual pension expense under defined contribution plans is simple. After the contribution required is determined, Pension Expense is debited and a liability (or Cash) is credited.

Accounting for annual expense under defined benefit plans is one of the most complex topics in accounting; thus, the intricacies are reserved for advanced courses. In concept, however, the procedure is simple. First, the amount of pension expense is determined. Then, if the amount of cash contributed to the fund is less than the pension expense, a liability results, which is reported on the balance sheet. If the amount of cash paid to the pension plan exceeds the pension expense, a prepaid expense arises and appears on the asset side of the balance sheet. For example, the December 31, 1991 annual report for Westinghouse Electric Corporation included among assets on the balance sheet a prepaid pension contribution of $864 million.

In accordance with the FASB's *Statement No. 87*, all companies should use the same actuarial method to compute pension expense.[8] However, because many factors, such as the average remaining service life of active employees, the expected long-run return on pension plan assets, and expected future salary increases, must be estimated, the computation of pension expense is not simple. In addition, actuarial terminology further complicates pension accounting. In nontechnical terms, the pension expense for the year includes not only the cost of the benefits earned by people working during the year but interest costs on the total pension obligation (which are calculated on the present value of future benefits to be paid) and other adjustments. These costs are reduced by the expected return on the pension fund assets.

Since 1989, all employers whose pension plans do not have sufficient assets to cover the present value of their pension benefit obligations (on a termination basis) must record the amount of the shortfall as a liability on their balance sheets. The investor no longer has to read the notes to the financial statements to learn whether the pension plan is fully funded. However, if a pension plan does have sufficient assets to cover its obligations, then no balance sheet reporting is required or permitted.

Lower interest rates—as have been experienced in recent years—normally are good news for businesses. This is not the case, however, when it comes to accounting for pension plans. The amount of the pension liabilities on the balance sheet depends on the assumed rate of return on the fund in the future. The lower the assumed rate, the higher the resulting liability will be. The *Wall Street Journal* reports that the Securities and Exchange Commission (SEC) is pressuring companies to revise

8. *Statement of Financial Accounting Standards No. 87*, "Employers' Accounting for Pensions" (Stamford, Conn.: Financial Accounting Standards Board, 1985).

their assumptions about future interest rates. The SEC is concerned that many companies have minimized their obligations to retirees by using high assumed interest rates to calculate today's pension liability. To better reflect 1993 rates, the SEC is urging companies to reduce the rate to about 7 percent, which approximates the current yield on long-term, high-grade corporate bonds. Companies such as General Electric, McDonnell Douglas, Rockwell International, Merck & Co., and Abbott Laboratories currently use rates of 9 percent. Lowering the interest rate by even 1 percent would increase the pension liabilities of these companies by 10 to 25 percent.[9]

OTHER POSTRETIREMENT BENEFITS

In addition to pension benefits, many companies provide health care and other benefits for employees after retirement. In the past, these other postretirement benefits were accounted for on a cash basis; that is, they were expensed when the benefits were paid, after an employee had retired. The FASB has concluded, however, that these benefits are earned by the employee, and that, in accordance with the matching rule, they should be estimated and accrued while the employee is working.[10] The estimates must take into account assumptions about retirement age, mortality, and, most significantly, future trends in health care benefits. As in accounting for pension benefits, these future benefits also should be discounted to the current period. In a field test conducted by the Financial Executives Research Foundation, it was determined that this move to accrual accounting increases postretirement benefits by two to seven times the amount recognized on a cash basis. Although the new requirement was not effective for businesses until 1993, some companies elected to implement it early. For example, IBM Corporation reported its first quarterly loss ever in the first quarter of 1991, when it recorded a one-time $2.26 billion charge associated with the adoption of *Statement No. 106.*[11] This charge covered costs of postretirement benefits earned by employees in the past up to that date. Future quarters would bear only the costs associated with earnings in those quarters.

BUSINESS BULLETIN: ETHICS IN PRACTICE

Accounting sometimes has a profound impact on our lives. When the FASB adopted SFAS No. 106, which requires companies to account for postretirement medical benefits on an accrual basis in accordance with the matching rule rather than on a cash basis in a distant year when the benefits are paid, companies had to face up to the cost of promising such benefits. Because the management of many companies, including Unisys Corporation, McDonnell Douglas Corporation, and Navistar

9. Laura Jereski, "SEC Is Challenging Funding for Plans," *Wall Street Journal,* November 17, 1993.
10. *Statement of Financial Accounting Standards No. 106,* "Employers' Accounting for Postretirement Benefits Other Than Pensions" (Stamford, Conn.: Financial Accounting Standards Board, 1990).
11. "Earnings Drop and One-Time Charge Produce $1.7 Billion Loss at IBM," *International Herald Tribune,* April 13–14, 1991.

International Corporation, had not realized the magnitude of the promises being made, they have been compelled to reduce health care benefits to retirees. As a result, many retirees are finding that they have lost benefits they had counted on receiving. According to one study, almost two-thirds of U.S. companies will have scaled back or eliminated benefits by 1994.[12] By pointing out to companies the real cost of health care, accounting has played a significant role in making health care reform a key political issue. Some people think the FASB should have left well enough alone and not required companies to report these costs. What do you think? ====

CHAPTER REVIEW

REVIEW OF LEARNING OBJECTIVES

1. **Explain the advantages and disadvantages of issuing long-term debt.** Long-term debt is used to finance long-term assets and business activities such as research and development that have long-run earnings potential for the business. Among the advantages of long-term debt financing are (1) common stockholders do not relinquish any control, (2) interest on debt is tax deductible, and (3) financial leverage may increase a company's earnings. Disadvantages of long-term financing are (1) interest and principal must be repaid on schedule, and (2) financial leverage can reverse direction and work against a company if a project is not successful.

2. **Identify and contrast the major characteristics of bonds.** A bond is a security that represents money borrowed from the investing public. When it issues bonds, the corporation enters into a contract, called a bond indenture, with the bondholders. The bond indenture identifies the major conditions of the bonds. A corporation can issue several types of bonds, each having different characteristics. For example, a bond issue may or may not require security (secured versus unsecured). It may be payable at a single time (term) or at several times (serial). And the holder may receive interest automatically (registered bond) or may have to return coupons to receive the interest (coupon bond). The bond may be callable in the future at a predetermined price or it may be converted into other securities in the future.

3. **Record the issuance of bonds at face value and at a discount or premium.** When bonds are issued, the bondholders pay an amount equal to, less than, or greater than the face value of the bond. Bondholders pay face value for bonds when the interest rate on the bonds approximates the market rate for similar investments. The issuing corporation records the bond issue as a long-term liability, in the Bonds Payable account, equal to the face value of the bonds.

   Bonds are issued at an amount less than face value when the bond interest rate is below the market rate for similar investments. The difference between the face value and the issue price is called a discount and is debited to Unamortized Bond Discount.

   When the interest rate on bonds is greater than the market rate on similar investments, investors are willing to pay more than face value for the bonds. The difference between the issue price and the face value is called a premium and is credited to Unamortized Bond Premium.

4. **Determine the value of bonds using present values.** The value of a bond is determined by summing the present values of (a) the series of fixed interest payments of a bond issue and (b) the single payment of the face value at maturity. The third and

12. Larry Light, Kelly Holland, and Kevin Kelly, "Honest Balance Sheets, Broken Promises," *Business Week*, November 23, 1992.

fourth tables in the appendix on future value and present value tables should be used in making these computations.

5. **Amortize (a) bond discounts and (b) bond premiums using the straight-line and effective interest methods.** When bonds are sold at a discount or a premium, the result is an adjustment of the interest rate on the bonds from the face rate to an effective rate that is close to the market rate when the bonds were issued. Therefore, bond discounts or premiums have the effect of increasing or decreasing the interest paid on the bonds over their life. Under these conditions, it is necessary to amortize the discount or premium over the life of the bonds by either the straight-line method or the effective interest method.

The straight-line method allocates a fixed portion of the bond discount or premium each interest period to adjust the interest payment to interest expense. The effective interest method, which is used when the effects of amortization are material, results in a constant rate of interest on the carrying value of the bonds. To find interest and the amortization of discounts or premiums, we apply the effective interest rate to the carrying value (face value minus the discount or plus the premium) of the bonds at the beginning of the interest period. The amount of the discount or premium to be amortized is the difference between the interest figured by using the effective rate and that obtained by using the stated or face rate. The effects of the effective interest method on bonds issued at par value, at a discount, and at a premium can be summarized as shown below.

	Bonds Issued at		
	Face Value	**Discount**	**Premium**
Trend in carrying value over bond term	Constant	Increasing	Decreasing
Trend in interest expense over bond term	Constant	Increasing	Decreasing
Interest expense versus interest payments	Interest expense = interest payments	Interest expense > interest payments	Interest expense < interest payments
Classification of bond discount or premium	Not applicable	Contra-liability (deducted from Bonds Payable)	Liability (added to Bonds Payable)

6. **Account for bonds issued between interest dates and make year-end adjustments.** When bonds are sold on dates between the interest payment dates, the issuing corporation collects from investors the interest that has accrued since the last interest payment date. When the next interest payment date arrives, the corporation pays the bondholders interest for the entire interest period.

When the end of a corporation's fiscal year does not fall on an interest payment date, the corporation must accrue bond interest expense from the last interest payment date to the end of the company's fiscal year. This accrual results in the inclusion of the interest expense in the year incurred.

7. **Account for the retirement of bonds and the conversion of bonds into stock.** Callable bonds can be retired before maturity at the option of the issuing corporation. The call price is usually an amount greater than the face value of the bonds,

so the corporation usually recognizes a loss on the retirement of bonds. An extraordinary gain can be recognized on the early extinguishment of debt, when a company purchases its bonds on the open market at a price below face value. This happens when a rise in the market interest rate causes the market value of the bonds to fall.

Convertible bonds allow the bondholder to convert bonds to stock in the issuing corporation. In this case, the common stock issued is recorded at the carrying value of the bonds being converted. No gain or loss is recognized.

8. **Explain the basic features of mortgages payable, installment notes payable, long-term leases, and pensions and other postretirement benefits as long-term liabilities.** A mortgage is a long-term debt secured by real property. It usually is paid in equal monthly installments. Each payment is partly interest expense and partly debt repayment. Installment notes payable are long-term notes that are paid in a series of payments. Part of each payment is interest, and part is repayment of principal. If a long-term lease is a capital lease, the risks of ownership lie with the lessee. Like a mortgage payment, each lease payment is partly interest and partly a reduction of debt. For a capital lease, both an asset and a long-term liability should be recorded. The liability should be equal to the present value at the beginning of the lease of the total lease payments over the lease term. The recorded asset is subject to depreciation. Pension expense must be recorded in the current period. Other postretirement benefits should be estimated and accrued while the employee still is working.

REVIEW OF CONCEPTS AND TERMINOLOGY

The following concepts and terms were introduced in this chapter:

L O 2 **Bond:** A security, usually long term, representing money borrowed by a corporation from the investing public.

L O 2 **Bond certificate:** Evidence of a company's debt to the bondholder.

L O 2 **Bond indenture:** A supplementary agreement to a bond issue that defines the rights, privileges, and limitations of bondholders.

L O 2 **Bond issue:** The total amount of bonds issued at one time.

L O 7 **Callable bonds:** Bonds that a corporation can buy back and retire at a call price before maturity.

L O 7 **Call price:** A specified price, usually above face value, at which a corporation may at its option buy back and retire bonds before maturity.

L O 8 **Capital lease:** A long-term lease in which the risk of ownership lies with the lessee and whose terms resemble a purchase or sale on installment.

L O 7 **Convertible bonds:** Bonds that can be exchanged for other securities of the corporation, usually its common stock.

L O 2 **Coupon bonds:** Bonds that generally are not registered with the issuing corporation but instead bear interest coupons stating the amount of interest due and the payment date.

L O 3 **Discount:** The amount by which the face value of a bond exceeds the issue price; for bonds issued when the market rate of interest is greater than the face interest rate.

L O 7 **Early extinguishment of debt:** The purchase by a company of its own bonds on the open market in order to retire the debt at less than face value.

L O 5 **Effective interest method:** A method of amortizing bond discounts or premiums that applies a constant interest rate, the market rate at the time the bonds were issued, to the carrying value of the bonds at the beginning of each interest period.

L O 3 **Face interest rate:** The rate of interest paid to bondholders based on the face value or principal of the bonds.

L O 1 **Financial leverage (trading on the equity):** The ability to increase earnings for stock-holders by earning more on an investment than is paid in interest on debt incurred to finance the investment.

L O 8 **Installment notes payable:** Long-term notes payable in a series of payments, of which part is interest and part is repayment of principal.

L O 1 **Junk bonds:** Unsecured, high-risk, long-term bonds that carry high rates of interest.

L O 3 **Market interest rate:** The rate of interest paid in the market on bonds of similar risk. Also called *effective interest rate.*

L O 8 **Mortgage:** A long-term debt secured by real property; usually paid in equal monthly installments.

L O 8 **Operating lease:** A short-term or cancelable lease in which the risks of ownership lie with the lessor, and whose payments are recorded as a rent expense.

L O 8 **Other postretirement benefits:** Health care and other nonpension benefits that are paid to a worker after retirement but that are earned while the employee is working.

L O 8 **Pension fund:** A fund established through contributions from an employer and some-times employees that pays pension benefits to employees after retirement or on their disability or death.

L O 8 **Pension plan:** A contract between a company and its employees under which the company agrees to pay benefits to the employees after they retire.

L O 3 **Premium:** The amount by which the issue price of a bond exceeds its face value; for bonds issued when the market rate of interest is less than the face interest rate.

L O 2 **Registered bonds:** Bonds for which the names and addresses of bondholders are recorded with the issuing company.

L O 2 **Secured bonds:** Bonds that give the bondholders a pledge of certain assets of the company as a guarantee of repayment.

L O 2 **Serial bonds:** A bond issue with several different maturity dates.

L O 5 **Straight-line method:** A method of amortizing bond discounts or premiums that allocates a discount or premium equally over each interest period of the life of the bond.

L O 2 **Term bonds:** Bonds of a bond issue that all mature at the same time.

L O 2 **Unsecured bonds:** Bonds issued on the general credit of a company. Also called *debenture bonds.*

L O 5 **Zero coupon bonds:** Bonds that do not pay periodic interest but that promise to pay a fixed amount on the maturity date.

REVIEW PROBLEM

INTEREST AND AMORTIZATION OF A BOND DISCOUNT, BOND RETIREMENT, AND BOND CONVERSION

L O 3, 5, 7 When the Merrill Manufacturing Company was expanding its metal window division, the company did not have enough capital to finance the expansion. So, management sought and received approval from the board of directors to issue bonds. The company planned to issue $5,000,000 of 8 percent, five-year bonds in 19x1. Interest would be paid on June 30 and December 31 of each year. The bonds would be callable at 104, and each $1,000 bond would be convertible into 30 shares of $10 par value common stock.

The bonds were sold at 96 on January 1, 19x1 because the market rate for similar investments was 9 percent. The company decided to amortize the bond discount by using the effective interest method. On July 1, 19x3 management called and retired half the bonds, and investors converted the other half into common stock.

REQUIRED

1. Prepare an interest and amortization schedule for the first five interest payment dates.
2. Prepare the journal entries to record the sale of the bonds, the first two interest payments, the bond retirement, and the bond conversion.

ANSWER TO REVIEW PROBLEM

1. Prepare a schedule for the first five interest periods.

Interest and Amortization of Bond Discount

Semiannual Interest Payment Date	Carrying Value at Beginning of Period	Semiannual Interest Expense* (9% × ¹/₂ × carrying value)	Semiannual Interest Paid per Period (8% × ¹/₂ × $5,000,000)	Amortization of Discount Discount	Unamortized Bond Discount at End of Period Period	Carrying Value at End of Period Period
Jan. 1, 19x1					$200,000	$4,800,000
June 30, 19x1	$4,800,000	$216,000	$200,000	$16,000	184,000	4,816,000
Dec. 31, 19x1	4,816,000	216,720	200,000	16,720	167,280	4,832,720
June 30, 19x2	4,832,720	217,472	200,000	17,472	149,808	4,850,192
Dec. 31, 19x2	4,850,192	218,259	200,000	18,259	131,549	4,868,451
June 30, 19x3	4,868,451	219,080	200,000	19,080	112,469	4,887,531

*Rounded to the nearest dollar.

2. Prepare the journal entries.

```
19x1
Jan.   1   Cash                                    4,800,000
               Unamortized Bond Discount             200,000
               Bonds Payable                                      5,000,000
                   Sold $5,000,000 of 8%,
                   5-year bonds at 96

       June 30  Bond Interest Expense                216,000
                   Unamortized Bond Discount                        16,000
                   Cash                                            200,000
                       Paid semiannual interest and
                       amortized the discount on 8%,
                       5-year bonds

       Dec. 31  Bond Interest Expense                216,720
                   Unamortized Bond Discount                        16,720
                   Cash                                            200,000
                       Paid semiannual interest and
                       amortized the discount on 8%,
                       5-year bonds

19x3
July   1   Bonds Payable                           2,500,000
           Loss on Retirement of Bonds               156,235
               Unamortized Bond Discount                           56,235
               Cash                                             2,600,000
                   Called $2,500,000 of 8% bonds
                   and retired them at 104
                   $112,469 × ¹/₂ = $56,235*

               *Rounded.
```

July 1	Bonds Payable	2,500,000	
	Unamortized Bond Discount		56,234
	Common Stock		750,000
	Paid-in Capital in Excess of Par		
	Value, Common		1,693,766

      Converted $2,500,000 of 8% bonds
into common stock:
2,500 × 30 shares = 75,000 shares
75,000 shares × $10 = $750,000
$112,469 − $56,235 = $56,234*
$2,500,000 − ($56,234 + $750,000)
= $1,693,766

*Rounded.

CHAPTER ASSIGNMENTS

KNOWLEDGE AND UNDERSTANDING

Questions

1. What are the advantages and disadvantages of issuing long-term debt?
2. What is the difference among a bond certificate, a bond issue, and a bond indenture? What are some examples of items found in a bond indenture?
3. What are the essential differences between (a) secured and debenture bonds, (b) term and serial bonds, and (c) registered and coupon bonds?
4. Napier Corporation sold $500,000 of 5 percent $1,000 bonds on the interest payment date. What would the proceeds from the sale be if the bonds were issued at 95, at 100, and at 102?
5. If you were buying bonds on which the face interest rate was less than the market interest rate, would you expect to pay more or less than par value for the bonds? Why?
6. Why does the amortization of a bond discount increase interest expense to an amount greater than interest paid? Why does the amortization of a premium have the opposite effect?
7. When the effective interest method of amortizing a bond discount or premium is used, why does the amount of interest expense change from period to period?
8. When bonds are issued between interest dates, why is it necessary for the issuer to collect an amount equal to accrued interest from the buyer?
9. Why would a company want to exercise the callable provision of a bond when it can wait to pay off the debt?
10. What are the advantages of convertible bonds to the company issuing them and to the investor?
11. What are the two components of a uniform monthly mortgage payment?
12. What are the two methods of repayment of installment notes?
13. Under what conditions is a long-term lease called a capital lease? Why should the accountant record both an asset and a liability in connection with this type of lease? What items should appear on the income statement as the result of a capital lease?
14. What is a pension plan? What assumptions must be made to account for the expenses of such a plan?
15. What is the difference between a defined contribution plan and a defined benefit plan?
16. What are other postretirement benefits, and how does the matching rule apply to them?

Short Exercises

SE 11-1.
L O 1
Bond versus Common Stock Financing

Indicate for each of the following statements whether it is an advantage or a disadvantage of using long-term bond financing rather than issuing common stock.

1. Interest paid on bonds is tax deductible.
2. Sometimes projects are not as successful as planned.
3. Financial leverage can have a negative effect when investments do not earn as much as the interest payments.
4. Bondholders do not have voting rights in a corporation.
5. Positive financial leverage may be achieved.

SE 11-2.
L O 3, 5
Interest Using the Straight-Line Method

Taylor Corporation issued $4,000,000 in 8$^1/_2$ percent, five-year bonds on April 1, 19x1, at 98. The semiannual interest payment dates are April 1 and October 1. Prepare journal entries for the issue of the bonds by Taylor on April 1, 19x1 and the first two interest payments on October 1, 19x1 and April 1, 19x2, using the straight-line method (ignore year-end accruals).

SE 11-3.
L O 3, 5, 6
Interest Using the Effective Interest Method

The River Front Freight Company sold $100,000 of its 9$^1/_2$ percent, twenty-year bonds on March 1, 19xx, at 106. The semiannual interest payment dates are March 1 and September 1. The effective interest rate is approximately 8.9 percent. The company's fiscal year ends August 31. Prepare journal entries to record the sale of the bonds on March 1, the accrual of interest and amortization of premium on August 31, and the first interest payment on September 1. Use the effective interest method to amortize the premium.

SE 11-4.
L O 4
Valuing Bonds Using Present Value

Mine-Mart, Inc. is considering two bond issues. (a) One is a $400,000 bond issue that pays semiannual interest of $32,000 and is due in twenty years. (b) The other is a $400,000 bond issue that pays semiannual interest of $30,000 and is due in fifteen years. Assume that the market rate of interest for each bond is 12 percent. Calculate the amount that Mine-Mart, Inc. will receive if both bond issues occur. (Calculate the present value of each bond issue and sum the two present values.)

SE 11-5.
L O 3, 6
Bond Issue Entries

Microfilm is authorized to issue $900,000 in bonds on June 1. The bonds carry a face interest rate of 8 percent, which is to be paid on June 1 and December 1. Prepare journal entries for the issue of the bonds by Microfilm under the following two independent assumptions that (a) the bonds are issued on September 1 at 100 and (b) the bonds are issued on June 1 at 103.

SE 11-6.
L O 3, 6
Sale of Bonds Between Interest Dates

Tripp Corporation sold $200,000 of 9 percent, ten-year bonds for face value on September 1, 19xx. The issue date of the bonds was May 1, 19xx. The company's fiscal year ends on December 31, and this is its only bond issue. Record the sale of the bonds on September 1 and the first semiannual interest payment on November 1, 19xx. What is the bond interest expense for the year ending December 31, 19xx?

SE 11-7.
L O 3, 5, 6
Year-End Accrual of Bond Interest

Alexus Corporation issued $500,000 of 9 percent bonds on October 1, 19x1, at 96. The bonds are dated October 1 and pay interest semiannually. The market rate of interest is 10 percent, and the company's year end is December 31. Prepare the entries to record the issuance of the bonds, the accrual of the interest on December 31, 19x1, and the payment of the first semiannual interest on April 1, 19x2. Assume that the company does not use reversing entries and uses the effective interest method to amortize bond discount.

SE 11-8.
L O 7
Bond Retirement Journal Entry

The Falstaf Corporation has outstanding $800,000 of 8 percent bonds callable at 104. On December 1, immediately after recording the payment of the semiannual interest and amortization of discount, the unamortized bond discount equaled $21,000. On that date, $480,000 of the bonds were called and retired. Prepare the entry to record the retirement of the bonds on December 1.

SE 11-9.
L O 7
Bond Conversion Journal Entry

The Degas Corporation has $1,000,000 of 6 percent bonds outstanding. There is $20,000 of unamortized discount remaining on these bonds after the March 1, 19x2 semiannual interest payment. The bonds are convertible at the rate of 20 shares of $10 par value common stock for each $1,000 bond. On March 1, 19x2, bondholders presented $600,000 of the bonds for conversion. Prepare the journal entry to record the conversion of the bonds.

SE 11-10.
L O 8   *Mortgage Payable*

Sternberg Corporation purchased a building by signing a $300,000 long-term mortgage with monthly payments of $2,400. The mortgage carries an interest rate of 8 percent. For the first three months, prepare a monthly payment schedule showing the monthly payment, the interest for the month, the reduction in debt, and the unpaid balance. (Round to the nearest dollar.)

APPLICATION

Exercises

E 11-1.
L O 3, 5   *Journal Entries for Interest Using the Straight-Line Method*

Berkshire Corporation issued $4,000,000 in $10^{1}/_2$ percent, ten-year bonds on February 1, 19x1, at 104. The semiannual interest payment dates are February 1 and August 1.

Prepare journal entries for the issue of bonds by Berkshire on February 1, 19x1 and the first two interest payments on August 1, 19x1 and February 1, 19x2, using the straight-line method. (Ignore year-end accruals).

E 11-2.
L O 3, 5   *Journal Entries for Interest Using the Straight-Line Method*

McAllister Corporation issued $8,000,000 in $8^{1}/_2$ percent, five-year bonds on March 1, 19x1, at 96. The semiannual interest payment dates are March 1 and September 1.

Prepare journal entries for the issue of the bonds by McAllister on March 1, 19x1 and the first two interest payments on September 1, 19x1 and March 1, 19x2, using the straight-line method. (Ignore year-end accruals).

E 11-3.
L O 3, 5, 6   *Journal Entries for Interest Using the Effective Interest Method*

The Mayfair Drapery Company sold $500,000 of its $9^{1}/_2$ percent, twenty-year bonds on April 1, 19xx, at 106. The semiannual interest payment dates are April 1 and October 1. The effective interest rate is approximately 8.9 percent. The company's fiscal year ends September 30.

Prepare journal entries to record the sale of the bonds on April 1, the accrual of interest and amortization of premium on September 30, and the first interest payment on October 1. Use the effective interest method to amortize the premium.

E 11-4.
L O 3, 5, 6   *Journal Entries for Interest Using the Effective Interest Method*

On March 1, 19x1, the Sperlazzo Corporation issued $1,200,000 of 10 percent, five-year bonds. The semiannual interest payment dates are March 1 and September 1. Because the market rate for similar investments was 11 percent, the bonds had to be issued at a discount. The discount on the issuance of the bonds was $48,670. The company's fiscal year ends February 28.

Prepare journal entries to record the bond issue on March 1, 19x1; the payment of interest and the amortization of the discount on September 1, 19x1; the accrual of interest and the amortization of the discount on February 28, 19x2; and the payment of interest on March 1, 19x2. Use the effective interest method. (Round answers to the nearest dollar.)

E 11-5.
L O 4   *Valuing Bonds Using Present Value*

Sessions, Inc. is considering two bond issues: (a) an $800,000 bond issue that pays semiannual interest of $64,000 and is due in twenty years; and (b) an $800,000 bond issue that pays semiannual interest of $60,000 and is due in fifteen years. Assume that the market rate of interest for each bond is 12 percent.

Calculate the amount that Sessions, Inc. will receive if both bond issues are made. (**Hint:** Calculate the present value of each bond issue and sum.)

E 11-6.
L O 4   *Valuing Bonds Using Present Value*

Using the present value tables in the appendix on future value and present value tables, calculate the issue price of a $1,200,000 bond issue in each of the following independent cases, assuming that interest is paid semiannually:

a. A ten-year, 8 percent bond issue; the market rate of interest is 10 percent.
b. A ten-year, 8 percent bond issue; the market rate of interest is 6 percent.
c. A ten-year, 10 percent bond issue; the market rate of interest is 8 percent.
d. A twenty-year, 10 percent bond issue; the market rate of interest is 12 percent.
e. A twenty-year, 10 percent bond issue; the market rate of interest is 6 percent.

E 11-7.
L O 4   *Zero Coupon Bonds*

The Commonwealth of Kentucky needs to raise $100,000,000 for highway repairs. Officials are considering issuing zero coupon bonds, which do not require periodic interest payments. The current market rate of interest for the bonds is 10 percent. What face value of bonds must be issued to raise the needed funds, assuming the bonds will be due in thirty years and compounded annually? How would your answer change if the bonds were due in fifty years? How would both answers change if the market rate of interest were 8 percent instead of 10 percent?

E 11-8.
L O 5   *Journal Entries for Interest Payments Using the Effective Interest Method*

The long-term debt section of the Fleming Corporation's balance sheet at the end of its fiscal year, December 31, 19x1, was as follows:

Long-Term Liabilities		
Bonds Payable—8%, interest payable		
1/1 and 7/1, due 12/31/20x3	$1,000,000	
Less Unamortized Bond Discount	80,000	$920,000

Prepare the journal entries relevant to the interest payments on July 1, 19x2, December 31, 19x2, and January 1, 19x3, using the effective interest method of amortization. Assume an effective interest rate of 10 percent.

E 11-9.
L O 3, 6   *Bond Issue Entries*

Graphic World, Inc. is authorized to issue $1,800,000 in bonds on June 1. The bonds carry a face interest rate of 9 percent, which is to be paid on June 1 and December 1.

Prepare journal entries for the issue of the bonds by Graphic World, Inc. under the assumptions that (a) the bonds are issued on September 1 at 100 and (b) the bonds are issued on June 1 at 105.

E 11-10.
L O 6   *Sale of Bonds Between Interest Dates*

Reese Corporation sold $400,000 of 12 percent, ten-year bonds at face value on September 1, 19xx. The issue date of the bonds was May 1, 19xx.

1. Record the sale of the bonds on September 1 and the first semiannual interest payment on November 1, 19xx.
2. The company's fiscal year ends on December 31 and this is its only bond issue. What is the bond interest expense for the year ending December 31, 19xx?

E 11-11.
L O 3, 5, 6   *Year-End Accrual of Bond Interest*

Swoboda Corporation issued $1,000,000 of 9 percent bonds on October 1, 19x1, at 96. The bonds are dated October 1 and pay interest semiannually. The market rate of interest is 10 percent, and the company's fiscal year ends on December 31.

Prepare the entries to record the issuance of the bonds, the accrual of the interest on December 31, 19x1, and the first semiannual interest payment on April 1, 19x2. Assume the company does not use reversing entries and uses the effective interest method to amortize the bond discount.

E 11-12.
L O 4, 7   *Time Value of Money and Early Extinguishment of Debt*

Feldman, Inc. has a $1,400,000, 8 percent bond issue that was issued a number of years ago at face value. There are now ten years left on the bond issue, and the market rate of interest is 16 percent. Interest is paid semiannually.

1. Using present value tables, figure the current market value of the bond issue.
2. Record the retirement of the bonds, assuming the company purchases the bonds on the open market at the calculated value.

E 11-13.
L O 7   *Bond Retirement*

The Okado Corporation has outstanding $1,600,000 of 8 percent bonds callable at 104. On September 1, immediately after recording the payment of the semiannual interest and the amortization of the discount, the unamortized bond discount equaled $42,000. On that date, $960,000 of the bonds were called and retired.

Prepare the entry to record the retirement of the bonds on September 1.

E 11-14.
L O 7   *Bond Conversion*

The Gallery Corporation has $400,000 of 6 percent bonds outstanding. There is $20,000 of unamortized discount remaining on these bonds after the July 1, 19x8 semiannual interest payment. The bonds are convertible at the rate of 40 shares of $5 par value common stock for each $1,000 bond. On July 1, 19x8, bondholders presented $300,000 of the bonds for conversion.

Prepare the journal entry to record the conversion of the bonds.

E 11-15.
L O 8 *Mortgage Payable*

Inland Corporation purchased a building by signing a $150,000 long-term mortgage with monthly payments of $2,000. The mortgage carries an interest rate of 12 percent.

1. For the first three months, prepare a monthly payment schedule showing the monthly payment, the interest for the month, the reduction in debt, and the unpaid balance. (Round to the nearest dollar.)
2. Prepare journal entries to record the purchase and the first two monthly payments.

E 11-16.
L O 8 *Recording Lease Obligations*

Ramos Corporation has leased a piece of equipment that has a useful life of twelve years. The terms of the lease are $43,000 per year for twelve years. Ramos currently is able to borrow money at a long-term interest rate of 15 percent. (Round answers to the nearest dollar.)

1. Calculate the present value of the lease.
2. Prepare the journal entry to record the lease agreement.
3. Prepare the entry to record depreciation of the equipment for the first year using the straight-line method.
4. Prepare the entries to record the lease payments for the first two years.

E 11-17.
L O 8 *Installment Notes Payable: Unequal Payments*

Assume that on December 31, 19x1, $40,000 is borrowed on a 12 percent installment note, to be paid annually over four years. Prepare the entry to record the note and the first two annual payments, assuming that the principal is paid in equal annual installments and the interest on the unpaid balance accrues annually. How would your answer change if the interest rate rose to 13 percent in the second year?

E 11-18.
L O 8 *Installment Notes Payable: Equal Payments*

Assume that on December 31, 19x1, $40,000 is borrowed on a 12 percent installment note, to be paid in equal annual payments over four years. Calculate to the nearest dollar the amount of each equal payment, using Table 4 from the appendix on future value and present value tables. Prepare a payment schedule table with four payments similar to Table 11-4, and record the first two annual payments.

Problem Set A

11A-1.
L O 3, 5, 6 *Bond Transactions— Straight-Line Method*

Weiskopf Corporation has $8,000,000 of 9½ percent, twenty-five-year bonds dated March 1, with interest payable on March 1 and September 1. The company's fiscal year ends on November 30. It uses the straight-line method to amortize bond premiums or discounts.

REQUIRED

1. Assume the bonds are issued at 103.5 on March 1. Prepare general journal entries for March 1, September 1, and November 30.
2. Assume the bonds are issued at 96.5 on March 1. Prepare general journal entries for March 1, September 1, and November 30.
3. Assume the bonds are issued on June 1 at face value plus accrued interest. Prepare general journal entries for June 1, September 1, and November 30.

11A-2.
L O 3, 5, 6 *Bond Transactions— Effective Interest Method*

Pandit Corporation has $20,000,000 of 10½ percent, twenty-year bonds dated June 1, with interest payment dates of May 30 and November 30. The company's fiscal year ends December 31. It uses the effective interest method to amortize bond premiums or discounts. (Round amounts to the nearest dollar.)

REQUIRED

1. Assume the bonds are issued at 103 on June 1, to yield an effective interest rate of 10.1 percent. Prepare general journal entries for June 1, November 30, and December 31.
2. Assume the bonds are issued at 97 on June 1, to yield an effective interest rate of 10.9 percent. Prepare general journal entries for June 1, November 30, and December 31.

3. Assume the bonds are issued at face value plus accrued interest on August 1. Prepare general journal entries for August 1, November 30, and December 31.

11A-3.

L O 3, 5, 6 *Bonds Issued at a Discount and a Premium*

Bannchi Corporation issued bonds twice during 19x1. The transactions were as follows:

19x1

Jan. 1   Issued $2,000,000 of $9^1/_5$ percent, ten-year bonds dated January 1, 19x1, with interest payable on June 30 and December 31. The bonds were sold at 98.1, resulting in an effective interest rate of 9.5 percent.

Apr. 1   Issued $4,000,000 of $9^4/_5$ percent, ten-year bonds dated April 1, 19x1, with interest payable on March 31 and September 30. The bonds were sold at 102, resulting in an effective interest rate of 9.5 percent.

June 30   Paid semiannual interest on the January 1 issue and amortized the discount, using the effective interest method.

Sept. 30   Paid semiannual interest on the April 1 issue and amortized the premium, using the effective interest method.

Dec. 31   Paid semiannual interest on the January 1 issue and amortized the discount, using the effective interest method.

      31   Made an end-of-year adjusting entry to accrue interest on the April 1 issue and to amortize half the premium applicable to the interest period.

19x2

Mar. 31   Paid semiannual interest on the April 1 issue and amortized the premium applicable to the second half of the interest period.

REQUIRED

Prepare general journal entries to record the bond transactions. (Round amounts to the nearest dollar.)

11A-4.

L O 3, 5, *Bond and Mortgage*
6, 8 *Transactions Contrasted*

Christakis Manufacturing Company, whose fiscal year ends on June 30, is expanding its operations by building and equipping a new plant. It is financing the building and land with a $20,000,000 mortgage, which carries an interest rate of 12 percent and requires monthly payments of $236,000. The company is financing the equipment and working capital for the new plant with a $20,000,000 twenty-year bond that carries a face interest rate of 11 percent, payable semiannually on March 31 and September 30. To date, selected transactions related to these two issues have been as follows:

Jan. 1   Signed mortgage in exchange for land and building. Land represents 10 percent of total price.

Feb. 1   Made first mortgage payment.

Mar. 1   Made second mortgage payment.

     31   Issued bonds for cash at 96, resulting in an effective interest rate of 11.5 percent.

Apr. 1   Made third mortgage payment.

May 1   Made fourth mortgage payment.

June 1   Made fifth mortgage payment.

     30   Made end-of-year adjusting entry to accrue interest on bonds and to amortize the discount, using the effective interest method.

July 1   Made sixth mortgage payment.

Aug. 1   Made seventh mortgage payment.

Sept. 1   Made eighth mortgage payment.

     30   Made first interest payment on bonds and amortized the discount for the time period since the end of the fiscal year.

19x2

Mar. 31   Made second interest payment on bonds and amortized the discount for the time period since the last interest payment.

REQUIRED

1. Prepare a monthly payment schedule for the mortgage for ten months using these headings (round amounts to the nearest dollar): Payment Date, Unpaid Balance at Beginning of Period, Monthly Payment, Interest for One Month at 1% on Unpaid Balance, Reduction in Debt, and Unpaid Balance at End of Period.
2. Prepare the journal entries for the selected transactions. (Ignore mortgage payments made after September 1, 19x1.)

11A-5.
L O 3, 5, 7
Bond Interest and Amortization Table and Bond Retirements

In 19x1, the Fender Corporation was authorized to issue $60,000,000 of six-year unsecured bonds. The bonds carried a face interest rate of 9 percent, payable semiannually on June 30 and December 31. The bonds were callable at 105 any time after June 30, 19x4. All of the bonds were issued on July 1, 19x1 at 95.568, a price yielding an effective interest rate of 10 percent. On July 1, 19x4, the company called and retired half the outstanding bonds.

REQUIRED

1. Prepare a table similar to Table 11-1, showing the interest and amortization of the bond discount for twelve interest payment periods. Use the effective interest method. (Round results to the nearest dollar.)
2. Prepare general journal entries for the bond issue, interest payments and amortization of the bond discount, and bond retirement on the following dates: July 1, 19x1; December 31, 19x1; June 30, 19x4; July 1, 19x4; and December 31, 19x4.

11A-6.
L O 3, 5,
6, 7
Comprehensive Bond Transactions

The Katz Corporation, a company whose fiscal year ends on June 30, engaged in the following long-term bond transactions over a three-year period:

19x5
Nov.   1   Issued $40,000,000 of 12 percent debenture bonds at face value plus accrued interest. Interest is payable on January 31 and July 31, and the bonds are callable at 104.

19x6
Jan.   31   Made the semiannual interest payment on the 12 percent bonds.
June   30   Made the year-end accrual of interest payment on the 12 percent bonds.
July   1   Issued $20,000,000 of 10 percent, fifteen-year convertible bonds at 105. Interest is payable on June 30 and December 31, and each $1,000 bond is convertible into 30 shares of $10 par value common stock. The market rate of interest is 9 percent.
       31   Made the semiannual interest payment on the 12 percent bonds.
Dec.   31   Made the semiannual interest payment on the 10 percent bonds and amortized the bond premium.

19x7
Jan.   31   Made the semiannual interest payment on the 12 percent bonds.
Feb.   28   Called and retired all of the 12 percent bonds, including accrued interest.
June   30   Made the semiannual interest payment on the 10 percent bonds and amortized the bond premium.
July   1   Accepted for conversion into common stock all of the 10 percent bonds.

REQUIRED

Prepare general journal entries to record the bond transactions, making all necessary accruals and using the effective interest method. (Round all calculations to the nearest dollar.)

Problem Set B

11B-1.
L O 3, 5, 6
Bond Transactions—Straight-Line Method

Marconi Corporation has $10,000,000 of 10 1/2 percent, twenty-year bonds dated June 1, with interest payment dates of May 30 and November 30. The company's fiscal year ends December 31, and it uses the straight-line method to amortize bond premiums or discounts.

REQUIRED

1. Assume the bonds are issued at 103 on June 1. Prepare general journal entries for June 1, November 30, and December 31.
2. Assume the bonds are issued at 97 on June 1. Prepare general journal entries for June 1, November 30, and December 31.
3. Assume the bonds are issued at face value plus accrued interest on August 1. Prepare general journal entries for August 1, November 30, and December 31.

11B-2.
L O 3, 5, 6
Bond Transactions—Effective Interest Method

Aparicio Corporation has $8,000,000 of 9 1/2 percent, twenty-five-year bonds dated March 1, with interest payable on March 1 and September 1. The company's fiscal year ends on November 30. It uses the effective interest method to amortize bond premiums or discounts. (Round amounts to the nearest dollar.)

1. Assume the bonds are issued at 102.5 on March 1, to yield an effective interest rate of 9.2 percent. Prepare general journal entries for March 1, September 1, and November 30.
2. Assume the bonds are issued at 97.5 on March 1, to yield an effective interest rate of 9.8 percent. Prepare general journal entries for March 1, September 1, and November 30.
3. Assume the bonds are issued on June 1 at face value plus accrued interest. Prepare general journal entries for June 1, September 1, and November 30.

11B-3.

L O 3, 5, 6   *Bonds Issued at a Discount and a Premium*

Maldonado Corporation sold bonds twice during 19x2. A summary of the transactions involving the bonds follows.

19x2

Jan.   1   Issued $6,000,000 of $9\,^9/_{10}$ percent, ten-year bonds dated January 1, 19x2, with interest payable on December 31 and June 30. The bonds were sold at 102.6, resulting in an effective interest rate of 9.4 percent.

Mar.   1   Issued $4,000,000 of $9\,^1/_5$ percent, ten-year bonds dated March 1, 19x2, with interest payable March 1 and September 1. The bonds were sold at 98.2, resulting in an effective interest rate of 9.5 percent.

June 30   Paid semiannual interest on the January 1 issue and amortized the premium, using the effective interest method.

Sept.   1   Paid semiannual interest on the March 1 issue and amortized the discount, using the effective interest method.

Dec. 31   Paid semiannual interest on the January 1 issue and amortized the premium, using the effective interest method.

      31   Made a year-end adjusting entry to accrue the interest on the March 1 issue and to amortize two-thirds of the discount applicable to the second interest period.

19x3

Mar.   1   Paid semiannual interest on the March 1 issue and amortized the remainder of the discount applicable to the second interest period.

Prepare general journal entries to record the bond transactions. (Round amounts to the nearest dollar.)

11B-4.

L O 3, 5,   *Bond and Mortgage*
6, 8   *Transactions Contrasted*

Idriss Grocery Stores, Inc. is expanding its operations by buying a chain of four outlets in another city. To finance the purchase of land and buildings, Idriss has obtained a $4,000,000 mortgage that carries an interest rate of 12 percent and requires monthly payments of $54,000. To finance the rest of the purchase, Idriss is issuing $4,000,000 of $12^1/_2$ percent unsecured bonds due in twenty years, with interest payable December 31 and June 30.

The company's fiscal year ends March 31. Selected transactions related to the two financing activities are as follows:

Jan.   1   Issued the bonds for cash at 104, to yield an effective rate of 12 percent.
Feb.   1   Issued the mortgage in exchange for land and buildings. The land represents 15 percent of the purchase price.
Mar.   1   Made first mortgage payment.
      31   Made the year-end adjusting entry to accrue interest on the bonds and amortize the premium, using the effective interest method.
Apr.   1   Made second mortgage payment.
May   1   Made third mortgage payment.
June   1   Made fourth mortgage payment.
      30   Made the first semiannual interest payment on the bonds and amortized the premium for the time period since the end of the fiscal year.
July   1   Made fifth mortgage payment.
Dec.   1   Made tenth mortgage payment.
      31   Made the second semiannual interest payment on the bonds and amortized the premium for the time period since the last payment.

REQUIRED

1. Prepare a payment schedule for the mortgage for ten months using these headings (round amounts to the nearest dollar): Payment Date, Unpaid Balance at Beginning of Period, Monthly Payment, Interest for One Month at 1% on Unpaid Balance, Reduction in Debt, and Unpaid Balance at End of Period.
2. Prepare the journal entries for the selected transactions. (Ignore the mortgage payments for August 1 through November 1.)

11B-5.

L O 3, 5, 7 *Bond Interest and Amortization Table and Bond Retirements*

In 19x1, Tully Corporation was authorized to issue $6,000,000 of unsecured bonds, due March 31, 19x6. The bonds carried a face interest rate of 11^3/$_5$ percent, payable semiannually on March 31 and September 30, and were callable at 104 any time after March 31, 19x4. All the bonds were issued on April 1, 19x1 at 102.261, a price that yielded an effective interest rate of 11 percent.

On April 1, 19x4, Tully Corporation called half of the outstanding bonds and retired them.

REQUIRED

1. Prepare a table similar to Table 11-2 to show the interest and amortization of the bond premium for ten interest payment periods, using the effective interest method. (Round results to the nearest dollar).
2. Prepare general journal entries for the bond issue, interest payments and amortization of the bond premium, and the bond retirement on the following dates: April 1, 19x1; September 30, 19x1; March 31, 19x4; April 1, 19x4; and September 30, 19x4.

11B-6.

L O 3, 5, *Comprehensive*
6, 7 *Bond Transactions*

Over a period of three years, DaSilva Corporation, a company whose fiscal year ends on December 31, engaged in the following transactions involving two bond issues:

19x1
July 1 Issued $20,000,000 of 12 percent convertible bonds at 96. The bonds are convertible into $20 par value common stock at the rate of 20 shares of stock for each $1,000 bond. Interest is payable on June 30 and December 31, and the market rate of interest is 13 percent.
Dec. 31 Made the semiannual interest payment and amortized the bond discount.

19x2
June 1 Issued $40,000,000 of 9 percent bonds at face value plus accrued interest. Interest is payable on February 28 and August 31. The bonds are callable at 105, and the market rate of interest is 9 percent.
30 Made the semiannual interest payment on the 12 percent bonds and amortized the bond discount.
Aug. 31 Made the semiannual interest payment on the 9 percent bonds.
Dec. 31 Made the semiannual interest payment and amortized the discount on the 12 percent bonds, and accrued interest on the 9 percent bonds.

19x3
Feb. 28 Made the semiannual interest payment on the 9 percent bonds.
June 30 Made the semiannual interest payment and amortized the bond discount on the 12 percent bonds.
July 1 Accepted for conversion into common stock all of the 12 percent bonds.
31 Called and retired all of the 9 percent bonds, including accrued interest.

REQUIRED

Prepare general journal entries to record the bond transactions, making all necessary accruals and using the effective interest method. (Round all calculations to the nearest dollar.)

CRITICAL THINKING AND COMMUNICATION

Conceptual Mini-Cases

CMC 11-1.

L O 3 *Bond Interest Rates and Market Prices*

RJR Nabisco's debt restructuring was the subject of the Decision Point that appeared at the beginning of this chapter. The following statement relates to the plan:

The refinancing plan's chief objective is to purge away most of the reset bonds of 2007 and 2009. These bonds have proved to be an immense headache for RJR.

. . . That's because the bonds' interest rate must be reset so that they trade at full face value. The bonds had sunk to a deep discount earlier this year, raising the prospect that RJR might have to accept a painfully high reset rate of 20% or more to meet its reset obligations.[13]

What is a "deep discount," and what causes bonds to sell at a deep discount? Who loses when they do? What does "the bonds' interest rate must be reset so that they trade at full face value" mean? Why would this provision in the covenant be "an immense headache" to RJR Nabisco?

CMC 11-2.

L O 5 *Nature of Zero Coupon Notes*

The *Wall Street Journal* reported, "Financially ailing Trans World Airlines has renegotiated its agreement to sell its 40 landing and takeoff slots and three gates at O'Hare International Airport to American Airlines." Instead of receiving a lump-sum cash payment in the amount of $162.5 million, TWA elected to receive a zero coupon note from American that would be paid off in monthly installments over a 20-year period. Since the 240 monthly payments total $500 million, TWA placed a value of $500 million on the note and indicated that the bankruptcy court would not have accepted the lower lump-sum cash payment. How does this zero coupon note differ from the zero coupon bonds described in this chapter? Explain the difference between the $162.5 million cash payment and the $500 million. Is TWA right in placing a $500 million price on the sale?[14]

CMC 11-3.

L O 8 *Lease Financing*

Federal Express Corporation, known for overnight delivery and distribution of high-priority goods and documents throughout the world, has an extensive fleet of aircraft and vehicles. Under lease commitments in its 1993 annual report, the company stated that it "utilizes certain aircraft, land, facilities, and equipment under capital and operating leases which expire at various dates through 2021. In addition, supplemental aircraft are leased under agreements which generally provide for cancellation upon 60 days' notice." The annual report further stated that the minimum commitments for capital leases and noncancelable operating leases for 1994 are $18,635,000 and $458,112,000, respectively.[15] What is the difference between a capital lease and an operating lease? How does the accounting treatment for the two types of leases differ? How do you interpret management's reasoning in placing some aircraft under capital leases and others under operating leases? Why do you think the management of Federal Express leases most of its aircraft instead of buying them?

CMC 11-4.

L O 1, 2, 8 *Issuance of Long-Term Bonds versus Leasing*

The *Coniglio Chemical Corporation* plans to build a new plant that will produce liquid fertilizer for the agricultural market. The plant is expected to cost $400,000,000 and will be located in the southwestern part of the United States. The company's chief financial officer, Terry Coniglio, has spent the last several weeks studying different means of financing the plant's construction. From his talks with bankers and other financiers, he has decided that there are two basic choices: The plant can be financed through the issuance of a long-term bond or a long-term lease. The two options follow:

a. Issuance of a $400,000,000, twenty-five-year, 16 percent bond secured by the new plant. Interest on the bonds would be payable semiannually.
b. Signing a twenty-five-year lease calling for lease payments of $32,700,000 on a semiannual basis.

Coniglio wants to know what the effect of each choice will be on the company's financial statements. He estimates that the useful life of the plant is twenty-five years, at which time it is expected to have an estimated residual value of $40,000,000.

Coniglio plans a meeting to discuss the alternatives. Prepare a short memorandum to him identifying the issues that should be considered in making this decision. (**Note:** You are not asked to discuss the factors or to recommend an action.)

13. George Anders, "RJR Nabisco Moves to Retire Most Troublesome Junk Bonds," *Asian Wall Street Journal,* July 17, 1990.
14. Stanley Ziemba, "TWA, American Revise O'Hare Gate Agreement," *Wall Street Journal,* May 13, 1992.
15. Federal Express Corporation, *Annual Report,* 1993.

Ethics Mini-Case

EMC 11-1.

L O 2 *Bond Indenture and Ethical Reporting*

Xetol Corporation, a biotech company, has a bond issue outstanding of $12,000,000 that has several restrictive provisions in its bond indenture. Among these are requirements that current assets exceed current liabilities by a ratio of 2 to 1 and that income before income taxes exceed the annual interest on the bonds by a ratio of 3 to 1. If these requirements are not met, the bondholders can force the company into bankruptcy. The company is still awaiting Food and Drug Administration (FDA) approval of its new product XTL-14, a cancer treatment drug. Management had been counting on sales of XTL-14 in 19x4 to meet the provisions of the bond indenture. As the end of the fiscal year approaches, the company does not have sufficient current assets or income before taxes to meet the requirements. Serge Sokolov, the chief financial officer, proposes, "Since we can assume that FDA approval will occur in early 19x5, I suggest we book sales and receivables from our major customers now in anticipation of the sales we know will take place next year. This action will increase our current assets and our income before taxes. It is absolutely essential that we do this in order to save the company. Look at all the people who will be hurt if we don't do it." Is Sokolov's proposal acceptable accounting? Is it ethical? Who could be harmed by this decision? What steps might management take?

Decision-Making Case

DMC 11-1.

L O 3, 4 *Contrasting Types of Bonds*

A bond or note with no periodic interest payments sounds like a car with no motor. But some large companies are issuing this kind of bond. For example, in 1981, **J.C. Penney Company, Inc.** advertised in the business press and sold $200,000,000 of zero coupon (no periodic interest) bonds due in 1989. The price, however, was not $200,000,000 but only 33.247 percent of $200,000,000. In other words, an investor paid about $332,470 initially for a bond that will pay the investor $1,000,000 in eight years. The advantage to J.C. Penney was that it did not have to pay a cent of interest for eight years. It did, of course, have to come up with the full face value of the notes at the maturity date. For the investor, a return would be guaranteed no matter what the market rate of interest was over the eight years, as long as J.C. Penney was able to pay off the notes at the maturity date. The J.C. Penney zero coupon bonds can be contrasted with the financing transactions taking place at about the same time at two other companies of similar quality: **Transamerica Corporation** and **Greyhound Corporation.** Transamerica sold $200,000,000 (face value) of thirty-year bonds with a $6^1/2$ percent coupon at a price of $480.67 per $1,000 bond. Greyhound issued $75,000,000 of ten-year notes carrying an interest rate of $14^1/4$ percent at 100.

REQUIRED

1. Using Tables 3 and 4 in the appendix on future value and present value tables, compute the effective interest rates for the three debt issues. Which issue would have been the most attractive to the investor?
2. Federal tax laws require the investor to pay income taxes on interest income that is amortized on low-coupon bonds and notes as well as on interest that is actually paid. In light of this, would your answer to **1** change? What factors other than the effective interest rate and income taxes would you consider important in deciding which of these bonds was the best investment?

Basic Research Activity

RA 11-1.

L O 3 *Reading the Bond Markets*

In your school or local library, obtain a copy of a recent issue of the *Wall Street Journal.* In the newspaper, find Section C, "Money & Investing," and turn to the page where the New York Exchange Bonds are listed. Notice, first, the Dow Jones Bond Averages of twenty bonds, ten utilities, and ten industrials. Are the averages above or below 100? Is this a premium or a discount? Is the market rate of interest above or below the face rate of the average bond? Now, identify three bonds from those listed. Choose one that sells at a discount, one that sells at a premium, and one that sells for approximately 100. For each bond, write the name of the company, the face interest rate, the year the bond is due, the current yield, and the current closing market price. (Some bonds have the letters *cv* in the Yield column. This means the bonds are convertible into common stock and the yield may not be meaningful.) For each bond, explain the relationship among the face interest rate, the current yield, and the closing price. What other factors affect the current yield of a bond? Be prepared to discuss your findings in class.

FINANCIAL REPORTING AND ANALYSIS

Interpretation Cases from Business

ICB 11-1.
L O 3, 5 *Long-Term Debt Transactions*

According to the long-term debt note in its annual report, the *Times Mirror Company,* publisher of the *Los Angeles Times, Newsday,* and other publications, engaged in the following long-term debt transactions in 1986:[16]

a. On April 1, 1986, the company issued $100,000,000 of ten-year, $8^{1}/_{4}$ percent notes with semiannual interest payments on April 1 and October 1 at face value.

b. On October 15, 1986, the company redeemed, prior to maturity dates, all of its outstanding 10 percent notes that had been issued in connection with the acquisition of Call-Chronicle Newspapers, Inc. The redemption price was $65,000,000 plus accrued interest. The carrying value of the notes on October 15 was $65,000,000 less an unamortized discount of $7,223,000. The semiannual interest dates were June 15 and December 15.

c. On December 8, 1986, the company issued $100,000,000 of 8 percent notes due December 15, 1996, with semiannual interest payments on June 15 and December 15. The notes were issued at face value plus accrued interest.

(**Note:** Long-term notes are accounted for in a manner similar to that for bonds.)

REQUIRED

1. Prepare journal entries to record the three transactions above.
2. Prepare the entries on the interest payment dates of October 1 and December 15, 1986, and the year-end adjustment on December 31, 1986.
3. What was the total interest expense during 1986 for the three long-term notes issued, assuming that the balance in Unamortized Discount was $7,493,000 at the beginning of the year? Assume the balance of Notes Outstanding was $65,000,000 at the beginning of the year.

ICB 11-2.
L O 3, 4, 5 *Bond Transactions*

A notice appeared in the *Wall Street Journal* stating that *Franklin Savings Association of Kansas* was issuing $2.9 billion in zero coupon bonds. "The Bonds do not pay interest periodically. The only scheduled payment to the holder of a Bond will be the amount at maturity,"[17] the ad read. The details of two components of the issue were as follows: $500,000,000 Bonds due December 12, 2014, at 3.254; $500,000,000 Bonds due December 12, 2024, at 1.380; plus accrued amortization, if any, of the original issue discount from December 12, 1984, to date of delivery.

REQUIRED

1. Assuming all the bonds were issued on December 12, 1984, make the general journal entry to record each component shown above.
2. Determine the approximate effective interest rate on each of the two components of the bond issue. Assume that interest is compounded annually. **Hint:** Use Table 3 in the appendix on future value and present value tables.
3. Prepare general journal entries to record bond interest expense for each of the first two years (December 12, 1985 and 1986) on the component of the bond due in 2014 (ignore effects of fiscal year ends). What advantages or disadvantages are there to Franklin in issuing zero coupon bonds?

ICB 11-3.
L O 8 *Lease Financing*

UAL Corporation, owner of United Airlines, states in its 1992 annual report that it leased 271 of its aircraft, 43 of which were capital leases.[18] United has leased many of these planes for terms of ten to twenty-two years. Some leases carry the right of first refusal to purchase the aircraft at fair market value at the end of the lease term and others at fair market value or a percentage of cost.

16. Times Mirror Company, *Annual Report,* 1986.
17. *Wall Street Journal,* November 16, 1984.
18. UAL Corporation, *Annual Report,* 1992.

On United's December 31, 1992 balance sheet, the following accounts appear (in thousands):

Owned—Flight Equipment	$7,790,100
Capital Leases—Flight Equipment	959,200
Current Obligations Under Capital Leases	53,700
Long-Term Obligations Under Capital Leases	812,400

Expected payments in 1993 for operating leases are $1,106,600 and for capital leases are $135,900.

REQUIRED

1. Why did UAL characterize some of the aircraft leases described in the first sentence as operating leases and others as capital leases? Explain your answer.
2. Explain in general the difference in accounting (a) for operating and capital leases and (b) for Owned—Flight Equipment and Capital Leases—Flight Equipment.

International Company Case

ICC 11-1.

L O 7 *Pros and Cons of Convertible Bonds*

Sumitomo Corporation, a Japanese company that is one of the world's leading merchandisers of commodities, industrial goods, and consumer goods, has a number of issues of long-term debt. Among them are almost ¥20,000 million ($15.9 million) of 1⅝% convertible bonds payable in Japanese yen in the year 2002.[19] (The interest rate illustrates the historically low rates in Japan.) The bonds are unsecured and are convertible into common stock at ¥1,193 per share. Since Japanese practice for issuing convertible debt is similar to that in the United States, what reasons can you suggest for the company's issuing bonds that are convertible into common stock rather than simply issuing nonconvertible bonds or issuing common stock directly? Are there any disadvantages to this approach?

Toys "R" Us Case

TC 11-1.

L O 1, 8 *Business Practice, Long-Term Debt, and Leases*

Refer to the Management's Discussion, Financial Statements, and Notes to Consolidated Financial Statements in the appendix on Toys "R" Us and answer the following questions:

1. Is it the practice of Toys "R" Us to own or lease most of its property and buildings?
2. What proportion of total assets is financed with long-term debt? What proportion of long-term debt is classified as current obligations due within the next year?
3. In what countries has Toys "R" Us incurred long-term debt? What maturity date is the farthest away from the present time?
4. Does Toys "R" Us lease property predominantly under capital leases or operating leases? Approximately how much will be paid out for each type of lease in 1995?

19. Sumitomo Corporation, *Annual Report*, 1992.

Contributed Capital

LEARNING OBJECTIVES

1. Define *corporation* and state the advantages and disadvantages of the corporate form of business.
2. Account for organization costs.
3. Identify the components of stockholders' equity.
4. Account for cash dividends.
5. Identify the characteristics of preferred stock, including the effect on division of dividends.
6. Account for the issuance of stock for cash and other assets.
7. Account for treasury stock.
8. Account for the exercise of stock options.

General Motors Corporation

In the chapter on long-term liabilities, bonds were presented as a popular way for corporations to raise new capital because of such factors as income tax advantages, flexibility, and leverage. Although much less prevalent than bonds, capital stock issues are still favored by many corporations. The *New York Times* recently reported that General Motors Corporation, a major automobile maker, successfully issued 55 million shares of common stock at $39 per share, raising more than $2.1 billion.[1] This is the fourth time in two years that the company has raised funds by issuing stock. In light of the advantages of bond financing, what are some possible reasons for General Motors Corporation to issue common stock?

As a means of financing, common stock has disadvantages. Unlike the interest expense on bonds, dividends paid on stock are not tax deductible. Also, by issuing more stock, the corporation dilutes its ownership. This means that the current shareholders must yield some control to the new stockholders. On the other hand, there are definite advantages to financing with common stock. First, financing with common stock issues is less risky than financing with bonds, because dividends on common stock are not paid unless management and the board of directors decide to pay them. In contrast, if the interest on bonds is not paid, a company can be forced into bankruptcy. Second, when a company does not pay a cash dividend, the cash generated by profitable operations can be invested in the company's operations. Third, and most important for a company such as General Motors, a company may need the proceeds of a common stock issue to improve the balance between liabilities and stockholders' equity. The company had lost more than $4.5 billion in the last year, drastically reducing its stockholders' equity. By issuing common stock, the company was able to improve its debt to equity ratio and its credit rating. It is important to understand the nature and characteristics of corporations as well as the process of accounting for a stock issue and other stock transactions. : : : : :

1. Susan Antilla, "Big G.M. Issue Lands and Price Holds Up," *New York Times*, May 21, 1992.

THE CORPORATION

OBJECTIVE

1 *Define* corporation *and state the advantages and disadvantages of the corporate form of business*

A corporation is defined as "a body of persons granted a charter legally recognizing them as a separate entity having its own rights, privileges, and liabilities distinct from those of its members."[2] In other words, the corporation is a legal entity separate and distinct from its owners. Although there are fewer corporations than sole proprietorships and partnerships in the United States, the corporate form of business dominates the economy in total dollars of assets and output of goods and services. Corporations are well suited to today's trends toward large organizations, international trade, and professional management. Figure 12-1 illustrates the corporation's ability to amass large amounts of capital by showing the amount and sources of new funds raised by corporations over the last five years for which data are available. There were dramatic increases in the amount of funds raised in 1991 and 1992. By 1992, the amount of new corporate capital reached $846.1 billion, of which $744.5 billion, or 88 percent, came from new bond issues; 72.4 billion, or 8.5 percent, came from new common stock issues; and 29.2 billion, or 3.5 percent, came from preferred stock issues. The choice of the corporate form of business is not automatic, however. The advantages and disadvantages of the corporate form must be considered.

THE ADVANTAGES OF A CORPORATION

The corporate form of business organization has several advantages over the sole proprietorship and the partnership. Among them are separate legal entity, limited liability, ease of capital generation, ease of transfer of ownership, lack of mutual agency, continuous existence, centralized authority and responsibility, and professional management.

Separate Legal Entity   A corporation is a separate legal entity that has most of the rights of a person except those of voting and marrying. As such, it can buy, sell, or own property; sue and be sued; enter into contracts; hire and fire employees; and be taxed.

Limited Liability   Because a corporation is a separate legal entity, it is responsible for its own actions and liabilities. This means that a corporation's creditors can satisfy their claims only against the assets of the corporation, not against the personal property of the owners of the company. Because the owners of a corporation are not responsible for the company's debts, their liability is limited to the amount of their investment. The personal property of sole proprietors and partners, however, generally is available to creditors.

Ease of Capital Generation   It is fairly easy for a corporation to raise capital because shares of ownership in the business are widely available to potential investors for a small amount of money. As a result, a single corporation can be owned by many people.

Ease of Transfer of Ownership   The ownership of a corporation is represented by a transferable unit, a share of stock. An owner of shares of stock, or a stockholder, normally can buy and sell shares of stock without affecting the activities of the corporation or needing the approval of other owners.

2. Copyright © 1992 Houghton Mifflin Company. Adapted and reprinted by permission from *The American Heritage Dictionary of the English Language,* Third Edition.

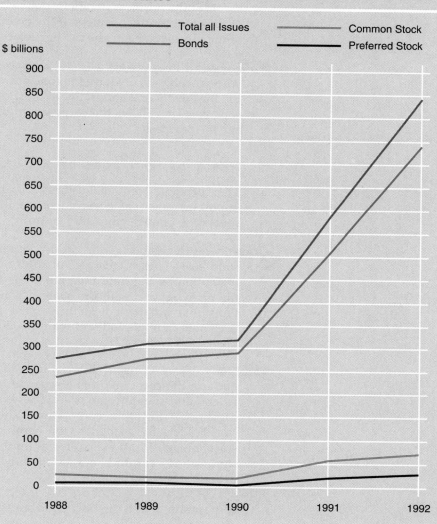

Figure 12-1. Sources of Capital Raised by Corporations in the United States

Source: Data from *Securities Industry Yearbook 1992–1993* (New York: Securities Industry Association, 1993), p. 947.

Lack of Mutual Agency   There is no mutual agency in the corporate form of business. If a stockholder, acting as an owner, tries to enter into a contract for the corporation, the corporation is not bound by the contract. But in a partnership, because of mutual agency, all the partners can be bound by one partner's actions.

Continuous Existence   Another advantage of the corporation's being a separate legal entity is that an owner's death, incapacity, or withdrawal does not affect the life of the corporation. The life of a corporation is set by its charter and regulated by state laws.

Centralized Authority and Responsibility   The board of directors represents the stockholders and delegates the responsibility and authority for the day-to-day operation of the corporation to a single person, usually the president of the organization. This power is not divided among the many owners of the business. The president may delegate authority for certain segments of the business to others, but he or she is held accountable to the board of directors for the business. If the board is dissatisfied with the performance of the president, he or she can be replaced.

Professional Management   Large corporations are owned by many people who probably do not have the time or training to make timely decisions about the business's operations. So, in most cases, management and ownership are separate. This allows the corporation to hire the best talent available to manage the business.

THE DISADVANTAGES OF A CORPORATION

The corporate form of business also has disadvantages. Among the more important ones are government regulation, taxation, limited liability, and separation of ownership and control.

Government Regulation   Corporations must meet the requirements of state laws. These "creatures of the state" are subject to greater control and regulation by the state than are other forms of business. Corporations must file many reports with the state in which they are chartered. Also, corporations that are traded publicly must file reports with the Securities and Exchange Commission and with the stock exchanges. Meeting these requirements is very costly.

Taxation   A major disadvantage of the corporation is double taxation. Because the corporation is a separate legal entity, its earnings are subject to federal and state income taxes. These taxes approach 35 percent of corporate earnings. If any of the corporation's after-tax earnings then are paid out to its stockholders as dividends, the earnings are taxed again as income to the stockholders. Taxation is different for the sole proprietorship and the partnership, whose earnings are taxed only as personal income to the owners.

Limited Liability   Above, we listed limited liability as an advantage of a corporation; it also can be a disadvantage. Limited liability restricts the ability of a small corporation to borrow money. Because creditors can lay claim only to the assets of the corporation, they limit their loans to the level secured by those assets or ask stockholders to guarantee the loans personally.

Separation of Ownership and Control   Just as limited liability can be a drawback, so can the separation of ownership and control. Sometimes management makes decisions that are not good for the corporation as a whole. Poor communication also can make it hard for stockholders to exercise control over the corporation or even to recognize that management's decisions are harmful.

ORGANIZATION COSTS

OBJECTIVE

2 *Account for organization costs*

The costs of forming a corporation are called organization costs. These costs, which are incurred before the corporation begins operation, include state incorporation fees and attorneys' fees for drawing up the articles of incorporation. They also include the cost of printing stock certificates, accountants' fees for services rendered in registering the firm's initial stock, and other expenditures necessary for forming the corporation.

Theoretically, organization costs benefit the entire life of the corporation. For this reason, a case can be made for recording organization costs as intangible assets and amortizing them over the years of the life of the corporation. However, the life of a corporation normally is not known, so accountants amortize these costs over the early years of a corporation's life. Because federal income tax regulations allow organization costs to be amortized over five years or more, most companies amortize these costs over a five-year (sixty-month) period.[3] Organization costs normally appear as other assets or as intangible assets on the balance sheet.

To show how organization costs are accounted for, we assume that a corporation pays a lawyer $5,000 for services rendered on July 1, 19x0 to prepare the application for a charter with the state. The entry to record this cost would be as follows:

19x0			
July 1	Organization Costs	5,000	
	Cash		5,000
	Lawyer's fee for services rendered in corporate organization		

If the corporation amortizes the organization costs over a five-year period, the entry to record the amortization at the end of the fiscal year, June 30, 19x1, would look like this:

19x1			
June 30	Amortization Expense, Organization Costs	1,000	
	Organization Costs		1,000
	To amortize organization costs for one year		
	$5,000 ÷ 5 years = $1,000		

THE COMPONENTS OF STOCKHOLDERS' EQUITY

OBJECTIVE

3 *Identify the components of stockholders' equity*

In a corporation's balance sheet, the owners' claims to the business are called stockholders' equity, as shown below.

Stockholders' Equity		
Contributed Capital		
Preferred Stock—$50 par value, 1,000 shares authorized, issued, and outstanding		$ 50,000
Common Stock—$5 par value, 30,000 shares authorized, 20,000 shares issued and outstanding	$100,000	
Paid-in Capital in Excess of Par Value, Common	50,000	150,000
Total Contributed Capital		$200,000
Retained Earnings		60,000
Total Stockholders' Equity		$260,000

3. The FASB allows organization costs to be amortized over a period of up to forty years.

Notice that the equity section of the corporate balance sheet is divided into two parts: (1) contributed capital and (2) retained earnings. Contributed capital represents the investments made by the stockholders in the corporation. Retained earnings are the earnings of the corporation since its inception less any losses, dividends, or transfers to contributed capital. Retained earnings are not a pool of funds to be distributed to the stockholders; they represent instead, earnings reinvested in the corporation.

The contributed-capital part of stockholders' equity on the balance sheet, in keeping with the convention of full disclosure, gives a great deal of information about the corporation's stock: the kinds of stock; their par value; and the number of shares authorized, issued, and outstanding. The information in the contributed-capital part of stockholders' equity is the subject of the rest of this chapter. We explain retained earnings fully in the chapter on retained earnings and corporate income statements.

CAPITAL STOCK

A share of stock is a unit of ownership in a corporation. A stock certificate is issued to the owner. It shows the number of shares of the corporation's stock owned by the stockholder. Stockholders can transfer their ownership at will. When they do, they must sign their stock certificate and send it to the corporation's secretary. In large corporations, those listed on the organized stock exchanges, it is hard to maintain stockholders' records. These companies can have millions of shares of stock, several thousand of which change ownership every day. Therefore, they often appoint independent registrars and transfer agents (usually banks and trust companies) to help perform the secretary's duties. They are responsible for transferring the corporation's stock, maintaining stockholders' records, preparing a list of stockholders for stockholders' meetings, and paying dividends. To help with the initial issue of capital stock, corporations often use an underwriter—an intermediary between the corporation and the investing public. For a fee—usually less than 1 percent of the selling price—the underwriter guarantees the sale of the stock. The corporation records the amount of the net proceeds of the offering—what the public paid less the underwriter's fee, legal and printing expenses, and any other direct costs of the offering—in its capital stock and additional paid-in capital accounts.

Authorized Stock   When a corporation applies for a charter, the articles of incorporation indicate the maximum number of shares of stock the corporation is allowed to issue. This number represents authorized stock. Most corporations are authorized to issue more shares of stock than are necessary at the time of organization, enabling them to issue stock in the future to raise additional capital. For example, if a corporation is planning to expand later, a possible source of capital would be the unissued shares of stock that were authorized in its charter. If all authorized stock is issued immediately, before it can issue more, the corporation must change its charter by applying to the state to increase its shares of authorized stock.

The charter also shows the par value of the stock that has been authorized. Par value is an arbitrary amount printed on each share of stock. It must be recorded in the Capital Stock accounts and constitutes the legal capital of a corporation. Legal capital equals the number of shares issued times the par value; it is the minimum amount that can be reported as contributed capital. Par value usually bears little if any relationship to the market value or book value of the shares. When the corporation is formed, a memorandum entry can be made in the general journal giving the number and description of authorized shares.

Issued and Outstanding Stock   The issued stock of a corporation is the shares sold or otherwise transferred to stockholders. For example, a corporation can be authorized to issue 500,000 shares of stock but may choose to issue only 300,000 shares when the company is organized. The holders of those 300,000 shares own 100 percent of the corporation. The remaining 200,000 shares of stock are unissued shares. No rights or privileges are associated with them until they are issued.

Outstanding stock is stock that has been issued and is still in circulation. A share of stock is not outstanding if it has been repurchased by the issuing corporation or given back to the company that issued it by a stockholder. So, a company can have more shares issued than are currently outstanding. Issued shares that are bought back and held by the corporation are called *treasury stock,* which we discuss in detail later in this chapter.

COMMON STOCK

A corporation can issue two basic types of stock: common stock and preferred stock. If only one kind of stock is issued by the corporation, it is called common stock. Common stock is the company's residual equity. This means that all other creditors' and preferred stockholders' claims to the company's assets rank ahead of those of the common stockholders in case of liquidation. Because common stock is generally the only stock that carries voting rights, it represents the means of controlling the corporation.

OBJECTIVE

 Account for cash dividends

DIVIDENDS

A dividend is the distribution of a corporation's assets to its stockholders. Each stockholder receives assets, usually cash, in proportion to the number of shares of stock held. The board of directors has sole authority to declare dividends.

Dividends can be paid quarterly, semiannually, annually, or at other times decided on by the board. Most states do not allow the board to declare a dividend that exceeds retained earnings. When this kind of dividend is declared, the corporation essentially is returning to the stockholders part of their contributed capital. This is called a liquidating dividend and normally is paid when a company is going out of business or is reducing its operations. Having sufficient retained earnings in itself does not justify the distribution of a dividend. If cash or other readily distributed assets are not available for distribution, the company might have to borrow money in order to pay a dividend—an action most boards of directors want to avoid.

There are three important dates associated with dividends. In order of occurrence, they are (1) the date of declaration, (2) the date of record, and (3) the date of payment. The *date of declaration* is the date the board of directors formally declares that a dividend is going to be paid. The *date of record* is the date on which ownership of the stock of a company, and therefore of the right to receive a dividend, is determined. Those individuals who own the stock on the date of record will receive the dividend. After that date, the stock is said to be ex-dividend: If one person sells the shares of stock to another, the right to the cash dividend remains with the first person; it does not transfer with the shares to the second person. The *date of payment* is the date on which the dividend is paid to the stockholders of record.

To illustrate the accounting for cash dividends, we assume that the board of directors has decided that sufficient cash is available to pay a $56,000 cash dividend to the common stockholders. The process has two steps. First, the board declares the dividend as of a certain date. Second, the dividend is paid. Assume that the dividend is declared on February 21, 19xx, for stockholders of record on March 1, 19xx, to be paid on March 11, 19xx. Here are the entries to record the declaration and payment of the cash dividend:

Date of Declaration

Feb. 21	Cash Dividends Declared	56,000	
	Cash Dividends Payable		56,000
	Declaration of a cash dividend		
	to common stockholders		

Date of Record

Mar. 1 No entry is required. This date is used simply to determine the owners of the stock who will receive the dividends. After this date (starting March 2), the shares are ex-dividend.

Date of Payment

Mar. 11	Cash Dividends Payable	56,000	
	Cash		56,000
	Payment of cash dividends		
	declared February 21		

Notice that the liability for the dividend is recorded on the date of declaration because the legal obligation to pay the dividend is established on that date. No entry is required on the date of record. The liability is liquidated, or settled, on the date of payment. The Cash Dividends Declared account is a temporary stockholders' equity account that is closed at the end of the accounting period by debiting Retained Earnings and crediting Cash Dividends Declared. Retained earnings are thereby reduced by the total dividends declared during the period.

Some companies do not pay dividends very often. A company may not have any earnings. Or, a corporation may need the assets generated by the earnings kept in the company for business purposes, perhaps expansion of the plant. Investors in growth companies expect a return on their investment in the form of an increase in the market value of their stock. Stock dividends, another kind of return, are discussed in the chapter on retained earnings and corporate income statements.

PREFERRED STOCK

OBJECTIVE

5 *Identify the characteristics of preferred stock, including the effect on division of dividends*

The second kind of stock a company can issue is called preferred stock. Both common stock and preferred stock are sold to raise money. But investors in preferred stock have different investment goals from investors in common stock. Preferred stock has preference over common stock in one or more areas. There can be several different classes of preferred stock, each with distinctive characteristics to attract different investors. Most preferred stock has one or more of the following characteristics: preference as to dividends, preference as to assets of the business in liquidation, convertibility, and a callable option.

J.C. Penney Company, Inc.

DECISION POINT

Preferred stock issues can be used strategically to accomplish management's objectives. For instance, an article in the *Wall Street Journal* reported that J.C. Penney Company, the large retailer, planned to sell an issue of preferred stock to its newly created Employee Stock Ownership Plan (ESOP) and use the $700 million in proceeds to buy back up to 11 percent of its outstanding common stock. The plan would result in the employees owning about 24 percent of the company. The new preferred stock would pay a dividend of 7.9 percent and would be convertible into common shares at $60 per share. The stock market reacted positively to the plan; the company's common stock rose almost $2 per share to $48 on the date of the announcement. What benefits to the company does management see from this elaborate plan?

As reported by the *Wall Street Journal*, "Analysts said the move should make the company less attractive as a takeover candidate by increasing its share price and per share earnings as well as by putting more shares in employees' hands."[4] Further, the company feels that its common stock is undervalued and that because there will be less common stock outstanding after the plan is put into effect, the market value of the company's stock will be enhanced. ⦂⦂⦂⦂⦂

Preference as to Dividends   Preferred stocks ordinarily have a *preference* over common stock in the receipt of dividends; that is, the holders of preferred shares must receive a certain amount of dividends before the holders of common shares can receive dividends. The amount that preferred stockholders must be paid before common stockholders can be paid usually is stated in dollars per share or as a percentage of the face value of the preferred shares. For example, a corporation can issue a preferred stock and pay a dividend of $4 per share, or it might issue a preferred stock at $50 par value and pay a yearly dividend of 8 percent of par value, $4 annually per share.

Preferred stockholders have no guarantee of ever receiving dividends: The company must have earnings and the board of directors must declare dividends on preferred shares before any liability to pay them arises. The consequences of not declaring a dividend to preferred stockholders in the current year vary according to the exact terms under which the shares were issued. In the case of noncumulative preferred stock, if the board of directors fails to declare a dividend to preferred stockholders in a given year, it is under no obligation to make up the missed dividend in future years. In the case of cumulative preferred stock, however, the fixed dividend amount per share

4. Karen Blumenthal, "J.C. Penney Plans to Buy Back Stock with ESOP Gains," *Wall Street Journal*, August 31, 1988.

accumulates from year to year, and the whole amount must be paid before any common dividends can be paid. Dividends that are not paid in the year they are due are called dividends in arrears.

Assume that a corporation has been authorized to issue 10,000 shares of $100 par value, 5 percent cumulative preferred stock, and that the shares have been issued and are outstanding. If no dividends were paid in 19x1, at the end of the year there would be preferred dividends of $50,000 (10,000 shares × $100 × .05 = $50,000) in arrears. If dividends are paid in 19x2, the preferred stockholders' dividends in arrears plus the 19x2 preferred dividends must be paid before any dividends on common stock can be paid.

Dividends in arrears are not recognized as liabilities of a corporation because there is no liability until the board declares a dividend. A corporation cannot be sure it is going to make a profit. So, of course, it cannot promise dividends to stockholders. However, if a company has dividends in arrears, they should be reported either in the body of the financial statements or in a footnote. The following footnote appeared in a steel company's annual report a few years ago:

> On January 1, 19xx, the company was in arrears by $37,851,000 ($1.25 per share) on dividends to its preferred stockholders. The company must pay all dividends in arrears to preferred stockholders before paying any dividends to common stockholders.

Suppose that on January 1, 19x1, a corporation issued 10,000 shares of $10 par, 6 percent cumulative preferred stock and 50,000 shares of common stock. The first year's operations resulted in income of only $4,000. The corporation's board of directors declared a $3,000 cash dividend to the preferred stockholders. The dividend picture at the end of 19x1 looked like this:

19x1 dividends due preferred stockholders ($100,000 × .06)	$6,000
Less 19x1 dividends declared to preferred stockholders	3,000
19x1 preferred stock dividends in arrears	$3,000

Now, suppose that in 19x2 the company earned income of $30,000 and wanted to pay dividends to both the preferred and the common stockholders. But the preferred stock is cumulative. So the corporation must pay the $3,000 in arrears on the preferred stock, plus the current year's dividends on its preferred stock, before it can distribute a dividend to the common stockholders. For example, assume that the corporation's board of directors declared a $12,000 dividend to be distributed to preferred and common stockholders. The dividend would be distributed as follows:

19x2 declaration of dividends	$12,000	
Less 19x1 preferred stock dividends in arrears	3,000	
Available for 19x2 dividends		$9,000
Less 19x2 dividends due preferred stockholders ($100,000 × .06)		6,000
Remainder available to common stockholders		$3,000

And this is the journal entry when the dividend is declared:

Dec. 31	Cash Dividends Declared	12,000	
	Cash Dividends Payable		12,000
	Declaration of a $9,000 cash dividend to preferred stockholders and a $3,000 cash dividend to common stockholders		

Preference as to Assets   Many preferred stocks have preference in terms of the assets of the corporation in the case of liquidation. So, when the business is ended, the preferred stockholders have a right to receive the par value of their stock or a larger stated liquidation value per share before the common stockholders receive any share of the company's assets. This preference also can include any dividends in arrears owed to the preferred stockholders.

Convertible Preferred Stock   A corporation can make its preferred stock more attractive to investors by adding a convertibility feature. People who hold convertible preferred stock can exchange their shares of preferred stock for shares of the company's common stock at a ratio stated in the preferred stock contract. Convertibility appeals to investors for two reasons. First, like all preferred stockholders, owners of convertible stock are more likely to receive regular dividends than are common stockholders. Second, if the market value of a company's common stock rises, the conversion feature allows the preferred stockholders to share in the increase. The rise in value would come either through equal increases in the value of the preferred stock or through conversion to common stock.

For example, suppose that a company issues 1,000 shares of 8 percent, $100 par value convertible preferred stock for $100 per share. Each share of stock can be converted into five shares of the company's common stock at any time. The market value of the common stock is now $15 per share. In the past, dividends on the common stock have been about $1 per share per year. The stockholder owning one share of preferred stock, on the other hand, now holds an investment that is approaching a worth of $100 on the market and is more likely to receive dividends than is the owner of common stock.

Assume that in the next several years, the corporation's earnings increase, and the dividends paid to common stockholders also increase, to $3 per share. In addition, the market value of a share of common stock goes up from $15 to $30. Preferred stockholders can convert each of their preferred shares into five common shares and increase their dividends from $8 on each preferred share to the equivalent of $15 ($3 on each of five common shares). Furthermore, the market value of each share of preferred stock will be close to the $150 value of the five shares of common stock because each share can be converted into five shares of common stock.

Callable Preferred Stock   Most preferred stocks are callable preferred stocks. That is, they can be redeemed or retired at the option of the issuing corporation at a price stated in the preferred stock contract. The stockholder must surrender a nonconvertible preferred stock to the corporation when asked to do so. If the preferred stock is convertible, the stockholder can either surrender the stock to the corporation or convert it into common stock when the corporation calls the stock. The *call price*, or redemption price, is usually higher than the par value of the stock. For example, a $100 par value preferred stock might be callable at $103 per share. When preferred stock is called and surrendered, the stockholder is entitled to (1) the par value of the stock, (2) the call premium, (3) any dividends in arrears, and (4) a prorated (by the proportion of the year to the call date) portion of the current period's dividend.

There are several reasons why a corporation would call its preferred stock. First, the company may want to force conversion of the preferred stock to common stock because the cash dividend being paid on the equivalent common stock is less than the dividend being paid on the preferred shares.

Second, it may be possible to replace the outstanding preferred stock on the current market with a preferred stock at a lower dividend rate or with long-term debt, which can have a lower after-tax cost. Third, the company may simply be profitable enough to retire the preferred stock.

BUSINESS BULLETIN: BUSINESS PRACTICE

To bolster their debt to equity ratios, which have deteriorated because of operating losses in recent years, General Motors Corporation and Ford Motor Company have issued $1.5 to $2.5 billion dollars of preferred stocks.[5] Preferred stocks are desirable because they are equity financing but they exhibit some of the favorable characteristics of debt, such as limiting the percentage of the dividend that will be paid and not carrying voting rights at stockholders' meetings. A popular new twist on preferred stock is a hybrid form called PERCs, or preferred equity redemption convertible stock. Citicorp issued $1 billion in PERCs to improve its equity capital ratio. These PERCs are popular with investors because they pay a higher dividend, 8.25 percent, than equivalent bonds and they have a mandatory retirement at the end of three years by conversion into common stock at a maximum 37.49 percent premium. PERCs are favored by companies like Citicorp because they provide flexibility through a redemption or call feature. If the financial condition of the company improves, it can substitute a cheaper form of financing by calling and retiring the PERCs.[6]

RETAINED EARNINGS

Retained earnings, the other component of stockholders' equity, represent stockholders' claims to the assets of the company resulting from profitable operations. The chapter on retained earnings and corporate income statements explains in detail the retained earnings section of the balance sheet.

ACCOUNTING FOR STOCK ISSUANCE

OBJECTIVE

6 *Account for the issuance of stock for cash and other assets*

A share of capital stock is either par or no-par stock. If the capital stock is par stock, the corporation charter states the par value, and this value must be printed on each share of stock. Par value can be $.10, $1, $5, $100, or any other amount worked out by the organizers of the corporation. The par values of common stocks tend to be lower than those of preferred stocks.

Par value is the amount per share that is entered into the corporation's Capital Stock accounts and that makes up the legal capital of the corporation.

5. Joseph B. White, "GM to Double Offer of Preference Stock to $1.5 Billion," *Wall Street Journal*, December 5, 1991.
6. Steven Lipin, "Citicorp Sells Over $1 Billion of Hybrid Stock," *Wall Street Journal*, October 15, 1992.

A corporation cannot declare a dividend that would cause stockholders' equity to fall below the legal capital of the firm. Therefore, the par value is a minimum cushion of capital that protects creditors. Any amount in excess of par value received from the issuance of stock is recorded in the Paid-in Capital in Excess of Par Value account and represents a portion of the company's contributed capital.

No-par stock is capital stock that does not have a par value. There are several reasons for issuing stock without a par value. One is that some investors confuse par value with the market value of stock instead of recognizing it as an arbitrary figure. Another reason is that most states do not allow an original stock issue below par value and thereby limit a corporation's flexibility in obtaining capital.

No-par stock can be issued with or without a stated value. The board of directors of the corporation issuing the no-par stock can be required by state law to place a stated value on each share of stock or may choose to do so as a matter of convenience. The stated value can be any value set by the board, although some states do indicate a minimum stated value per share. The stated value can be set before or after the shares are issued if the state law does not specify this point.

If a company issues no-par stock without a stated value, all proceeds of the issue are recorded in the Capital Stock account. This amount becomes the corporation's legal capital unless the amount is specified by state law. Because additional shares of the stock can be issued at different prices, the credit to the Capital Stock account per share will not be uniform. In this way, it differs from par value stock or no-par stock with a stated value.

When no-par stock with a stated value is issued, the shares are recorded in the Capital Stock account at the stated value. Any amount received in excess of the stated value is recorded in Paid-in Capital in Excess of Stated Value. The excess of the stated value is a part of the corporation's contributed capital. However, the stated value normally is considered to be the legal capital of the corporation.

PAR VALUE STOCK

When par value stock is issued, the appropriate capital stock account (usually Common Stock or Preferred Stock) is credited for the par value (legal capital) regardless of whether the proceeds are more or less than the par value. For example, assume that Bradley Corporation is authorized to issue 20,000 shares of $10 par value common stock and actually issues 10,000 shares at $10 per share on January 1, 19xx. The entry to record the stock issue at par value would be as follows:

Jan. 1	Cash	100,000	
	Common Stock		100,000
	Issued 10,000 shares of $10 par value common stock for $10 per share		

Cash is debited $100,000 (10,000 shares × $10), and Common Stock is credited an equal amount because the stock was sold for par value (legal capital).

If the stock had been issued for a price greater than par, the proceeds in excess of par would be credited to a capital account called Paid-in Capital in Excess of Par Value, Common. For example, assume that the 10,000 shares of Bradley common stock sold for $12 per share on January 1, 19xx. The entry to record the issuance of the stock at the price in excess of par value would be as follows:

Jan. 1	Cash	120,000	
	Common Stock		100,000
	Paid-in Capital in Excess of Par Value, Common		20,000
	Issued 10,000 shares of $10 par value common stock for $12 per share		

Cash is debited for the proceeds of $120,000 (10,000 shares × $12), and Common Stock is credited for the total par value of $100,000 (10,000 shares × $10). Paid-in Capital in Excess of Par Value, Common is credited for the difference of $20,000 (10,000 shares × $2). This amount is part of the corporation's contributed capital and will be included in the stockholders' equity section of the balance sheet. The stockholders' equity section for Bradley Corporation immediately following the stock issue would appear as follows:

Contributed Capital
Common Stock—$10 par value, 20,000 shares
authorized, 10,000 shares issued and outstanding $100,000
Paid-in Capital in Excess of Par Value, Common   20,000

Total Contributed Capital $120,000
Retained Earnings   —
Total Stockholders' Equity $120,000

If a corporation issues stock for less than par, an account called Discount on Capital Stock is debited for the difference. The issuance of stock at a discount rarely occurs because it is illegal in many states.

No-Par Stock

As mentioned earlier, stock can be issued without a par value. However, most states require that all or part of the proceeds from the issuance of no-par stock be designated as legal capital, which cannot be withdrawn except in liquidation. The purpose of this requirement is to protect the corporation's assets for creditors. Assume that the Bradley Corporation's capital stock is no-par common and that 10,000 shares are issued on January 1, 19xx at $15 per share. The $150,000 (10,000 shares × $15) in proceeds would be recorded as shown in the following entry:

Jan. 1	Cash	150,000	
	Common Stock		150,000
	Issued 10,000 shares of no-par common stock for $15 per share		

Because the stock does not have a stated or par value, all proceeds of the issue are credited to Common Stock and are part of the company's legal capital.

Most states allow the board of directors to put a stated value on no-par stock, and this value represents the corporation's legal capital. Assume that Bradley's board puts a $10 stated value on its no-par stock. The entry to record the issue of 10,000 shares of no-par common stock with a $10 stated value for $15 per share would appear as follows:

```
Jan. 1  Cash                               150,000
           Common Stock                              100,000
           Paid-in Capital in Excess of
             Stated Value, Common                     50,000
               Issued 10,000 shares of no-par
               common stock of $10 stated value
               for $15 per share
```

Notice that the legal capital credited to Common Stock is the stated value decided by the board of directors. Notice also that the account Paid-in Capital in Excess of Stated Value, Common is credited for $50,000. The $50,000 is the difference between the proceeds ($150,000) and the total stated value ($100,000). Paid-in Capital in Excess of Stated Value is presented on the balance sheet in the same way as Paid-in Capital in Excess of Par Value is presented.

ISSUANCE OF STOCK FOR NONCASH ASSETS

Stock can be issued for assets or services other than cash. The problem here is the dollar amount that should be recorded for the exchange. The generally preferred rule is to record the transaction at the fair market value of what the corporation is giving up—in this case, the stock. If the fair market value of the stock cannot be determined, the fair market value of the assets or services received can be used to record the transaction. Transactions of this kind usually involve the use of stock to pay for land or buildings or for the services of attorneys and others who helped organize the company.

Where there is an exchange of stock for noncash assets, the board of directors has the right to determine the fair market value of the property. Suppose that when the Bradley Corporation was formed on January 1, 19xx, its attorney agreed to accept 100 shares of its $10 par value common stock for services rendered. At the time the stock was issued, its market value could not be determined. However, for similar services the attorney would have billed the company $1,500. This is the entry to record the noncash transaction:

```
Jan. 1  Organization Costs                  1,500
           Common Stock                               1,000
           Paid-in Capital in Excess of
             Par Value, Common                          500
               Issued 100 shares of $10 par
               value common stock for attorney's
               services
```

Now suppose that two years later the Bradley Corporation exchanged 1,000 shares of its $10 par value common stock for a piece of land. At the time of the exchange, the stock was selling on the market for $16 per share. The entry to record this exchange would be as follows:

```
Jan. 1  Land                               16,000
           Common Stock                              10,000
           Paid-in Capital in Excess of
             Par Value, Common                        6,000
               Issued 1,000 shares of $10 par value
               common stock with a market value
               of $16 per share for a piece of land
```

The year 1993 proved to be a hot year for initial public offerings (IPOs); they reached an unprecedented $40 billion as small companies took advantage of all-time record highs in the stock market. IPOs are common stock issues of companies that are selling their stock to the public for the first time or "going public," and they are very popular with investors. For example, when Gateway 2000, a North Sioux City, South Dakota mail-order computer marketer, offered 10.9 million shares at $15 dollars per share, the price rose to above $20 per share on the first day of trading.[7] The stock of another company, Boston Chicken, a midwestern fast food company, more than doubled in price on the first day, climbing from $20 to over $48 per share. Some analysts note that the good fortune of Gateway and Boston Chicken will continue only as long as they maintain fast growth in sales. Disappointing sales could cause the stocks to plunge.[8] ══

TREASURY STOCK

OBJECTIVE

7 *Account for treasury stock*

Treasury stock is capital stock, either common or preferred, that has been issued and reacquired by the issuing company but has not been sold or retired. The company normally gets the stock back by purchasing the shares on the market.

It is common for companies to buy and hold their own stock. In 1991, 388, or 65 percent, of six hundred large companies held treasury stock.[9] There are several reasons why a company purchases its own stock:

1. It may want to have stock available to distribute to employees through stock option plans.
2. It may be trying to maintain a favorable market for the company's stock.
3. It may want to increase the company's earnings per share.
4. It may want to have additional shares of the company's stock available for such activities as purchasing other companies.
5. It may want to prevent a hostile takeover.

The effect of a treasury stock purchase is to reduce the assets and stockholders' equity of the company. It is not considered a purchase of assets, as the purchase of shares in another company would be. Treasury stock is capital stock that has been issued but is no longer outstanding. Treasury shares can be held for an indefinite period of time, reissued, or retired. Like unissued stock, treasury stock has no rights until it is reissued. Treasury stock does not have voting rights, rights to cash dividends or stock dividends, or rights to

7. Kyle Pope and Warren Getler, "Gateway 2000's New Shares Jump 28% Amid Keen Interest in Computer Issues," *Wall Street Journal*, December 9, 1993.
8. William Power, "Boston Chicken Soars by 143% on Its IPO Day," *Wall Street Journal*, November 10, 1993.
9. American Institute of Certified Public Accountants, *Accounting Trends & Techniques* (New York: AICPA, 1992), p. 240.

share in assets during liquidation of the company, and it is not considered to be outstanding in the calculation of book value. However, there is one major difference between unissued shares and treasury shares: A share of stock that originally was issued at par value or greater and fully paid for, and that then was reacquired as treasury stock, can be reissued at less than par value without negative consequences attaching to it.

The Purchase of Treasury Stock

When treasury stock is purchased, it normally is recorded at cost. The transaction reduces both the assets and the stockholders' equity of the firm. For example, assume that on September 15 the Caprock Corporation purchases 1,000 shares of its common stock on the market at a price of $50 per share. The purchase would be recorded as follows:

Sept. 15	Treasury Stock, Common	50,000	
	Cash		50,000
	Acquired 1,000 shares of the company's common stock for $50 per share		

Notice that the treasury shares are recorded at cost. The par value, stated value, or original issue price of the stock is ignored.

The stockholders' equity section of Caprock's balance sheet shows the cost of the treasury stock as a deduction from the total of contributed capital and retained earnings:

Contributed Capital	
Common Stock—$5 par value, 100,000 shares authorized, 30,000 shares issued, 29,000 shares outstanding	$ 150,000
Paid-in Capital in Excess of Par Value, Common	30,000
Total Contributed Capital	$ 180,000
Retained Earnings	900,000
Total Contributed Capital and Retained Earnings	$1,080,000
Less Treasury Stock, Common (1,000 shares at cost)	50,000
Total Stockholders' Equity	$1,030,000

Notice that the number of shares issued, and thus the legal capital, has not changed, although the number of outstanding shares has decreased as a result of the transaction.

The Sale of Treasury Stock

Treasury shares can be sold at cost, above cost, or below cost. For example, assume that on November 15 the 1,000 treasury shares of the Caprock Corporation are sold for $50 per share. This entry records the transaction:

Nov. 15	Cash	50,000	
	Treasury Stock, Common		50,000
	Reissued 1,000 shares of treasury stock for $50 per share		

When treasury shares are sold for an amount greater than their cost, the excess of the sales price over cost should be credited to Paid-in Capital, Treasury Stock. No gain should be recorded. For example, suppose that on

November 15 the 1,000 treasury shares of the Caprock Corporation are sold for $60 per share. The entry for the reissue would be as follows:

Nov. 15	Cash	60,000	
	Treasury Stock, Common		50,000
	Paid-in Capital, Treasury Stock		10,000
	Sale of 1,000 shares of treasury stock for $60 per share; cost was $50 per share		

If treasury shares are sold below their cost, the difference is deducted from Paid-in Capital, Treasury Stock. When this account does not exist or is insufficient to cover the excess of cost over the reissue price, Retained Earnings absorbs the excess. No loss is recorded. For example, suppose that on September 15, the Caprock Corporation bought 1,000 shares of its common stock on the market at a price of $50 per share. The company sold 400 shares of its stock on October 15 for $60 per share and the remaining 600 shares on December 15 for $42 per share. The entries to record these transactions are as follows:

Sept. 15	Treasury Stock, Common	50,000	
	Cash		50,000
	Purchase of 1,000 shares of treasury stock at $50 per share		
Oct. 15	Cash	24,000	
	Treasury Stock, Common		20,000
	Paid-in Capital, Treasury Stock		4,000
	Sale of 400 shares of treasury stock for $60 per share; cost was $50 per share		
Dec. 15	Cash	25,200	
	Paid-in Capital, Treasury Stock	4,000	
	Retained Earnings	800	
	Treasury Stock, Common		30,000
	Sale of 600 shares of treasury stock for $42 per share; cost was $50 per share		

In the entry for the December 15 transaction, Retained Earnings is debited $800 because the 600 shares were sold for $4,800 less than cost. That amount is $800 greater than the $4,000 of paid-in capital generated by the sale of the 400 shares on October 15.

The Retirement of Treasury Stock   If a company determines that it is not going to reissue stock it has purchased, with the approval of its stockholders it can retire the stock. When shares of stock are retired, all items related to those shares are removed from the related Capital accounts. When stock that cost less than the original contributed capital is retired, the difference is recognized in Paid-in Capital, Retirement of Stock. However, when stock that cost more than was received when the shares were first issued is retired, the difference is a reduction in stockholders' equity and is debited to Retained Earnings. For instance, suppose that instead of selling the 1,000 shares of treasury stock it purchased for $50,000, Caprock decides to retire the shares on November 15. Assuming that the $5 par value common stock originally was issued at $6 per share, this entry records the retirement:

Nov. 15	Common Stock	5,000	
	Paid-in Capital in Excess of		
	Par Value, Common	1,000	
	Retained Earnings	44,000	
	Treasury Stock, Common		50,000
	Retirement of 1,000 shares that		
	cost $50 per share and were		
	issued originally at $6 per share		

BUSINESS BULLETIN: INTERNATIONAL PRACTICE

 In the United States, it is accepted practice that a company does not report profits from trading in its own stock on the income statement, but this is not the case in other countries. Only if foreign companies raise money in the United States or are listed on a major U.S. stock exchange must they comply with U.S. accounting rules. Approximately 30 percent of all U.S. net purchases of foreign stocks are in emerging markets, and it is important that investors do not assume that U.S. accounting and disclosure rules apply. For example, in Mexico a company can record a gain from reselling its own treasury stock. *Forbes* reported that Cemex, a huge Mexican cement company, customarily reports nonoperating items with little explanation. Only by searching in the footnotes does one discover that one-third of its $495 million in 1991 pretax profits came from gains on treasury stock transactions.[10]

EXERCISING STOCK OPTIONS

OBJECTIVE

8 *Account for the exercise of stock options*

Many companies encourage the ownership of the company's common stock through a stock option plan, which is an agreement to issue stock to employees according to the terms of the plan. Under some plans, the option to purchase stock applies to all employees equally, and the purchase of stock is made at a price close to the market value at the time of purchase. In this situation, the stock issue is recorded in the same way any stock issue to an outsider is recorded. If, for example, we assume that on March 30 the employees of a company purchased 2,000 shares of $10 par value common stock at the current market value of $25 per share, the entry would be as follows:

Mar. 30	Cash	50,000	
	Common Stock		20,000
	Paid-in Capital in Excess of Par		
	Value, Common		30,000
	Issued 2,000 shares of $10 par		
	value common stock under		
	employee stock option plan		

10. Roula Khalaf, "Free-Style Accounting," *Forbes,* March 1, 1993.

In other cases, the stock option plan gives the employee the right to purchase stock in the future at a fixed price. This type of plan, which usually is offered only to management personnel, both compensates and motivates the employee because the market value of a company's stock is tied to its performance. As the market value of the stock goes up, the difference between the option price and the market price increases, increasing the employee's compensation. When an option eventually is exercised and the stock is issued, the entry is similar to the one above. For example, assume that on July 1, 19x1, a company grants its key management personnel the option to purchase 50,000 shares of $10 par value common stock at the market value (as of that date) of $15 per share. Suppose that one of the firm's vice presidents exercises the option to purchase 2,000 shares on March 30, 19x2, when the market price is $25 per share. This entry would record the issue:

19x2			
Mar. 30	Cash	30,000	
	Common Stock		20,000
	Paid-in Capital in Excess of Par		
	Value, Common		10,000
	Issued 2,000 shares of $10 par value common stock under the employee stock option plan		

Although the vice president has a gain of $20,000 (the $50,000 market value less the $30,000 option price), no compensation expense is recorded. Compensation expense would be recorded only if the option price is less than the $15 market price on July 1, 19x1, the date of grant. Methods of handling compensation in this situation are covered in more advanced courses.[11] Information pertaining to employee stock option plans should be discussed in the notes to the financial statements.

BUSINESS BULLETIN: BUSINESS PRACTICE

Stock options are also used to attract top managers to a company. When Eastman Kodak Company hired George Fisher away from Motorola, the company gave him options to purchase 750,000 shares of Kodak stock. Compensation consultants put a value on the package of between $13 million and $17 million and said that such compensation was appropriate for an executive hired to turn a company around, as Fisher was charged to do at Kodak. Fisher has options to purchase 742,000 shares at $57.97 per share and 7,910 shares at $63.19 per share. The average price per share at the time the options were granted was $63.19. Thus, if Fisher can increase the price of the shares by improving the company's profitability, he will stand to gain. In leaving Motorola, Fisher gave up unexercised options worth $6.4 million.[12] =====

---

11. Stock options are discussed here in the context of employee compensation. They also can be important features of complex corporate capitalization arrangements.
12. Wendy Bounds, "Kodak Gives Fisher Options to Purchase 750,000 of Its Shares," *Wall Street Journal,* December 20, 1993.

CHAPTER REVIEW

REVIEW OF LEARNING OBJECTIVES

1. **Define** *corporation* **and state the advantages and disadvantages of the corporate form of business.** A corporation is a separate legal entity that has its own rights, privileges, and liabilities distinct from its owners. Among the advantages of the corporate form of business are that (a) a corporation is a separate legal entity, (b) stockholders have limited liability, (c) it is easy to generate capital for a corporation, (d) stockholders can buy and sell shares of stock easily, (e) there is a lack of mutual agency, (f) the corporation has a continuous existence, (g) authority and responsibility are centralized, and (h) it is run by a professional management team. The disadvantages of corporations include (a) a large amount of government regulation, (b) double taxation, (c) difficulty of raising funds because of limited liability, and (d) separation of ownership and control.

2. **Account for organization costs.** The costs of organizing a corporation are recorded as an asset and are usually amortized over five years.

3. **Identify the components of stockholders' equity.** Stockholders' equity consists of contributed capital and retained earnings. Contributed capital includes two basic types of stock: common stock and preferred stock. When only one type of security is issued, it is common stock. Common stockholders have voting rights; they also share in the earnings of the corporation and in its assets in case of liquidation.

   Retained earnings, the other component of stockholders' equity, represents the claim of stockholders to the assets of the company resulting from profitable operations. These are earnings that have been reinvested in the corporation.

4. **Account for cash dividends.** The liability for payment of cash dividends arises on the date of declaration by the board of directors. The declaration is recorded with a debit to Cash Dividends Declared and a credit to Cash Dividends Payable. The date of record, on which no entry is required, establishes the stockholders who will receive the cash dividend on the date of payment. Payment is recorded with a debit to Cash Dividends Payable and a credit to Cash.

5. **Identify the characteristics of preferred stock, including the effect on division of dividends.** Preferred stock, like common stock, is sold to raise capital. But the investors have different objectives. To attract these investors, corporations usually give them a preference—in terms of receiving dividends and assets—over common stockholders. The dividend on preferred stock is generally figured first; then the remainder goes to common stock. If the preferred stock is cumulative and in arrears, the amount in arrears also has to be allocated to preferred stockholders before any allocation is made to common stockholders. In addition, certain preferred stock is convertible. Preferred stock is often callable at the option of the corporation.

6. **Account for the issuance of stock for cash and other assets.** A corporation's stock normally is issued for cash and other assets. The majority of states require that stock be issued at a minimum value called legal capital. Legal capital is represented by the par or stated value of the stock.

   When stock is issued for cash at par or stated value, Cash is debited and Common Stock or Preferred Stock is credited. When stock is sold at an amount greater than par or stated value, the excess is recorded in Paid-in Capital in Excess of Par or Stated Value.

   Sometimes stock is issued for noncash assets. Here, the accountant must decide how to value the stock. The general rule is to record the stock at its market value. If this value cannot be determined, then the fair market value of the asset received is used to record the transaction.

7. **Account for treasury stock.** The treasury stock of a company is stock that has been issued and reacquired but not resold or retired. A company acquires its own stock to create stock option plans, maintain a favorable market for the stock, increase earnings per share, or to purchase other companies. Treasury stock is similar to unissued stock in that it does not have rights until it is reissued. However, treasury

stock can be resold at less than par value without incurring a discount liability. The accounting treatment for treasury stock is as follows:

Treasury Stock Transaction	Accounting Treatment
Purchase of treasury stock	Debit Treasury Stock and credit Cash for the cost of the shares.
Sale of treasury stock at the same price as the cost of the shares	Debit Cash and credit Treasury Stock for the cost of the shares.
Sale of treasury stock at an amount greater than the cost of the shares	Debit Cash for the reissue price of the shares, and credit Treasury Stock for the cost of the shares and Paid-in Capital, Treasury Stock for the excess.
Sale of treasury stock at an amount less than the cost of the shares	Debit Cash for the reissue price; debit Paid-in Capital, Treasury Stock for the difference between the reissue price and the cost of the shares; and credit Treasury Stock for the cost of the shares. If Paid-in Capital, Treasury Stock does not exist or is not large enough to cover the difference, Retained Earnings should absorb the difference.

8. **Account for the exercise of stock options.** Companywide stock option plans are used to encourage employees to own a part of the company. Other plans are offered only to management personnel, both to compensate and to motivate them. Usually, the issue of stock to employees under stock option plans is recorded in a manner similar to the issue of stock to any outsider.

REVIEW OF CONCEPTS AND TERMINOLOGY

The following concepts and terms were introduced in this chapter:

L O 3   **Authorized stock:** The maximum number of shares a corporation can issue without changing its charter with the state.

L O 5   **Callable preferred stock:** Preferred stock that can be redeemed and retired at the option of the corporation.

L O 3   **Common stock:** Shares of stock that carry voting rights but that rank below preferred stock in terms of dividends and the distribution of assets in the event of liquidation.

L O 5   **Convertible preferred stock:** Preferred stock that can be exchanged for common stock at the option of the holder.

L O 1   **Corporation:** A separate legal entity having its own rights, privileges, and liabilities distinct from those of its owners.

L O 5   **Cumulative preferred stock:** Preferred stock on which unpaid dividends accumulate over time and must be satisfied in any given year before a dividend can be paid to common stockholders.

L O 4   **Dividend:** The distribution of a corporation's assets (usually cash) to its stockholders.

L O 5   **Dividends in arrears:** Dividends on cumulative preferred stock that are not paid in the year they are due.

L O 1   **Double taxation:** The act of taxing corporate earnings twice—once as the net income of the corporation and once when the dividends are distributed to stockholders.

L O 4   **Ex-dividend:** A description of capital stock between the date of record and the date of payment when the right to a dividend already declared on the stock remains with the person who sells the stock and does not transfer to the person who buys it.

L O 6   **Initial public offerings (IPOs):** Common stock issues of companies that are selling their stock to the public for the first time.

L O 3   **Issued stock:** The shares of stock sold or otherwise transferred to stockholders.

L O 3 **Legal capital:** The number of shares of stock issued times the par value; the minimum amount that can be reported as contributed capital.

L O 4 **Liquidating dividend:** A dividend that exceeds retained earnings; usually paid when a corporation goes out of business or reduces its operations.

L O 5 **Noncumulative preferred stock:** Preferred stock that does not carry an obligation to pay missed or undeclared dividends in future years.

L O 6 **No-par stock:** Capital stock that does not have a par value.

L O 2 **Organization costs:** The costs of forming a corporation.

L O 3 **Outstanding stock:** Stock that has been issued and is still in circulation.

L O 3 **Par value:** The arbitrary amount printed on each share of stock; used to determine the legal capital of a corporation.

L O 5 **Preferred stock:** Stock that has preference over common stock in terms of dividends and the distribution of assets in the event of liquidation.

L O 3 **Residual equity:** The common stock of a corporation.

L O 6 **Stated value:** A value assigned by the board of directors of a corporation to no-par stock.

L O 3 **Stock certificate:** A document issued to a stockholder indicating the number of shares of stock the stockholder owns.

L O 8 **Stock option plan:** An agreement to issue stock to employees according to the terms of a plan.

L O 7 **Treasury stock:** Capital stock, either common or preferred, that has been issued and reacquired by the issuing company but that has not been sold or retired.

L O 3 **Underwriter:** An intermediary between the corporation and the public who facilitates an issue of stock or other securities for a fee.

REVIEW PROBLEM
STOCK JOURNAL ENTRIES AND STOCKHOLDERS' EQUITY

L O 2, 3, 4, 5, 6, 7

The Beta Corporation was organized in 19xx in the state of Arizona. Its charter authorized the corporation to issue 1,000,000 shares of $1 par value common stock and an additional 25,000 shares of 4 percent, $20 par value cumulative convertible preferred stock. Here are the transactions that related to the company's stock during 19xx:

Feb. 12 Issued 100,000 shares of common stock for $125,000.
      20 Issued 3,000 shares of common stock for accounting and legal services. The services were billed to the company at $3,600.

Mar. 15 Issued 120,000 shares of common stock to Edward Jackson in exchange for a building and land that had an appraised value of $100,000 and $25,000, respectively.

Apr.   2 Purchased 20,000 shares of common stock for the treasury at $1.25 per share from an individual who changed his mind about being an investor in the company.

July   1 Issued 25,000 shares of preferred stock for $500,000.

Sept. 30 Sold 10,000 of the shares in the treasury for $1.50 per share.

Dec. 31 The company reported net income of $40,000 for 19xx, and the board declared dividends of $25,000, payable on January 15 to stockholders of record on January 8. Dividends included preferred stock cash dividends for one-half year.

REQUIRED

1. Prepare the journal entries necessary to record these transactions. Then close the Income Summary and Cash Dividends Declared accounts to Retained Earnings. Following the December 31 entry to record dividends, show dividends payable for each class of stock.

2. Prepare the stockholders' equity section of the Beta Corporation balance sheet as of December 31, 19xx.

ANSWER TO REVIEW PROBLEM

1. Prepare the journal entries.

19xx

Feb. 12	Cash	125,000	
	Common Stock		100,000
	Paid-in Capital in Excess of		
	Par Value, Common		25,000
	Sale of 100,000 shares of		
	$1 par value common		
	stock for $1.25 per share		
20	Organization Costs	3,600	
	Common Stock		3,000
	Paid-in Capital in Excess of		
	Par Value, Common		600
	Issue of 3,000 shares of		
	$1 par value common stock		
	for billed accounting and		
	legal services of $3,600		
Mar. 15	Building	100,000	
	Land	25,000	
	Common Stock		120,000
	Paid-in Capital in Excess of		
	Par Value, Common		5,000
	Issue of 120,000 shares of		
	$1 par value common stock		
	for a building and land		
	appraised at $100,000 and		
	$25,000, respectively		
Apr. 2	Treasury Stock, Common	25,000	
	Cash		25,000
	Purchase of 20,000 shares of		
	common stock for the treasury		
	at $1.25 per share		
July 1	Cash	500,000	
	Preferred Stock		500,000
	Sale of 25,000 shares of $20		
	par value preferred stock		
	for $20 per share		
Sept. 30	Cash	15,000	
	Treasury Stock, Common		12,500
	Paid-in Capital, Treasury Stock		2,500
	Sale of 10,000 shares of		
	treasury stock at $1.50 per		
	share; original cost was		
	$1.25 per share		
Dec. 31	Cash Dividends Declared	25,000	
	Cash Dividends Payable		25,000
	Declaration of a $25,000 cash		
	dividend to preferred and		
	common stockholders		

Total dividend	$25,000	
Less preferred stock cash		
dividend:		
$500,000 × .04 × 6/12	10,000	
Common stock cash dividend	$15,000	

Dec. 31	Income Summary	40,000	
	Retained Earnings		40,000
	To close the Income Summary account to Retained Earnings		
31	Retained Earnings	25,000	
	Cash Dividends Declared		25,000
	To close the Cash Dividends Declared account to Retained Earnings		

2. Prepare the stockholders' equity section of the balance sheet.

Beta Corporation
Stockholders' Equity
December 31, 19xx

Contributed Capital			
Preferred Stock—4% cumulative convertible,			
$20 par value, 25,000 shares authorized,			
issued, and outstanding			$500,000
Common Stock—$1 par value, 1,000,000			
shares authorized, 223,000 shares			
issued and 213,000 shares outstanding		$223,000	
Paid-in Capital in Excess of Par Value, Common		30,600	
Paid-in Capital, Treasury Stock		2,500	256,100
Total Contributed Capital			$756,100
Retained Earnings			15,000
Total Contributed Capital and Retained Earnings			$771,100
Less Treasury Stock, Common (10,000 shares, at cost)			12,500
Total Stockholders' Equity			$758,600

CHAPTER ASSIGNMENTS

KNOWLEDGE AND UNDERSTANDING

Questions

1. What is a corporation, and how is it formed?
2. Identify and explain several advantages of the corporate form of business.
3. Identify and explain several disadvantages of the corporate form of business.
4. What are the organization costs of a corporation?
5. What is the proper accounting treatment of organization costs?
6. What is the legal capital of a corporation, and what is its significance?
7. How is the value of stock determined when stock is issued for noncash assets?
8. Describe the significance of the following dates as they relate to dividends: (a) date of declaration, (b) date of record, and (c) date of payment.
9. Explain the accounting treatment of cash dividends.

10. Define the terms *cumulative, convertible,* and *callable* as they apply to preferred stock.

11. What are dividends in arrears, and how should they be disclosed in the financial statements?

12. What is the proper classification of the following accounts on the balance sheet? For stockholders' equity accounts, indicate whether they are contributed capital, retained earnings, or contra stockholders' equity. (a) Organization Costs; (b) Common Stock; (c) Treasury Stock; (d) Paid-in Capital, Treasury Stock; (e) Paid-in Capital in Excess of Par Value, Common; (f) Paid-in Capital in Excess of Stated Value, Common; and (g) Retained Earnings.

13. Define treasury stock and explain why a company would purchase its own stock.

14. What is a stock option plan and why does a company have one?

Short Exercises

SE 12-1.
L O 1 *Advantages and Disadvantages of the Corporation*

Identify whether each of the following characteristics is an advantage or disadvantage of the corporate form of business.

1. Ease of transfer of ownership
2. Taxation
3. Separate legal entity
4. Lack of mutual agency
5. Government regulation
6. Continuous existence

SE 12-2.
L O 2 *Journal Entries for Organization Costs*

At the beginning of 19x1, Scotch Company incurred the following costs in organizing the company: (1) Attorney's fees, market value of services, $5,000; paid with 3,000 shares of $1 par common stock. (2) Incorporation fees paid to the state, $3,000. Prepare the separate journal entries necessary to record these transactions and to amortize organization costs for the first year, assuming that the company elects to write off organization costs over five years.

SE 12-3.
L O 3, 7 *Stockholders' Equity*

Prepare a stockholders' equity section for Aguilar Corporation's balance sheet from the following accounts and balances on December 31, 19xx.

Account Name	Balance Debit	Balance Credit
Common Stock—$10 par value, 60,000 shares authorized, 40,000 shares issued, and 39,000 shares outstanding		$400,000
Paid-in Capital in Excess of Par Value, Common		200,000
Retained Earnings		30,000
Treasury Stock, Common (1,000 shares)	$15,000	

SE 12-4.
L O 4 *Cash Dividends*

Thai Corporation has authorized 100,000 shares of $1 par value common stock, of which 80,000 are issued and 70,000 are outstanding. On May 15, the board of directors declares a cash dividend of $.10 per share payable on June 15 to stockholders of record on June 1. Prepare the entries, as necessary, for each of the three dates.

SE 12-5.
L O 5 *Preferred Stock Dividends with Dividends in Arrears*

The Timonium Corporation has 1,000 shares of its $100, 8 percent cumulative preferred stock outstanding, and 20,000 shares of its $1 par value common stock outstanding. In its first three years of operation, the board of directors of Timonium Corporation paid cash dividends as follows: 19x1, none; 19x2, $20,000; and 19x3, $40,000.

Determine the total cash dividends and dividends per share paid to the preferred and common stockholders during each of the three years.

SE 12-6.
L O 6 *Issuance of Stock*

Carlotta Company is authorized to issue 100,000 shares of common stock. The company sold 5,000 shares at $12 per share. Prepare journal entries to record the sale of stock for cash under each of the following independent alternatives: (1) The stock has a par value of $5, and (2) the stock has no par value but a stated value of $1 per share.

SE 12-7.
L O 6 *Issuance of Stock for Noncash Assets*

Malaysia Corporation issued 8,000 shares of its $1 par value common stock for some land. The land had a fair market value of $50,000.

Prepare the journal entries necessary to record the issuance of the stock for the land under each of the following independent conditions: (1) The stock was selling for $7 per share on the day of the transaction, and (2) management attempted to place a value on the common stock but could not do so.

SE 12-8.
L O 7 *Treasury Stock Transactions*

Prepare the journal entries necessary to record the following stock transactions of the Curry Company during 19xx:

Oct. 5 Purchased 1,000 shares of its own $2 par value common stock for $20, the current market price.
17 Sold 250 shares of treasury stock purchased on Oct. 5 for $25 per share.
21 Sold 400 shares of treasury stock purchased on Oct. 5 for $18 per share.

SE 12-9.
L O 7 *Retirement of Treasury Stock*

Refer to SE 12-8. Assuming the remaining 350 shares in the treasury were retired on October 28, 19xx and that they were originally issued at $5 per share, prepare the entry to record the stock retirement.

SE 12-10.
L O 8 *Exercise of Stock Options*

On June 6, George Jensen exercised his option to purchase 10,000 shares of Marsalis Company $1 par value common stock at an option price of $4. The market price per share was $4 on the grant date and $18 on the exercise date. Record the transaction on Marsalis's books.

APPLICATION

Exercises

E 12-1.
L O 2, 6 *Journal Entries for Organization Costs*

The Wendt Corporation was organized during 19x7. At the beginning of the fiscal year, the company incurred the following organization costs: (1) Attorney's fees, market value of services, $6,000; paid with 2,000 shares of $2 par common stock. (2) Incorporation fees paid to the state, $5,000. (3) Accountant's services that normally would be billed at $3,000; paid with 1,100 shares of $2 par value common stock.

Prepare the separate journal entries necessary to record these transactions and to amortize organization costs for the first year, assuming that the company elects to write off organization costs over five years.

E 12-2.
L O 3, 7 *Stockholders' Equity*

The accounts and balances below were taken from the records of Jamil Corporation on December 31, 19xx.

	Balance	
Account	Debit	Credit
Preferred Stock—$100 par value, 9% cumulative, 20,000 shares authorized, 12,000 shares issued and outstanding		$1,200,000
Common Stock—$12 par value, 90,000 shares authorized, 60,000 shares issued, and 55,000 shares outstanding		720,000
Paid-in Capital in Excess of Par Value, Common		340,000
Retained Earnings		46,000
Treasury Stock, Common (5,000 shares)	$110,000	

Prepare a stockholders' equity section for Jamil Corporation's balance sheet.

E 12-3.

L O 3, 5   *Characteristics of Common and Preferred Stock*

For each of the characteristics listed below, indicate whether it is more closely associated with common stock (C) or with preferred stock (P).

1. Often receives dividends at a set rate
2. Is known as the residual equity of a company
3. Can be callable
4. Can be convertible
5. Amount of dividend more likely to vary from year to year
6. Can be entitled to receive dividends not paid in past years
7. Likely to have full voting rights
8. Receives assets first in liquidation
9. Generally receives dividends before other classes of stock

E 12-4.

L O 3, 6   *Journal Entries and Stockholders' Equity*

The Winkler Hospital Supply Corporation was organized in 19xx. The company was authorized to issue 100,000 shares of no-par common stock with a stated value of $5 per share, and 20,000 shares of $100 par value, 6 percent noncumulative preferred stock. On March 1 the company sold 60,000 shares of its common stock for $15 per share and 8,000 shares of its preferred stock for $100 per share.

1. Prepare the journal entries to record the sale of the stock.
2. Prepare the company's stockholders' equity section of the balance sheet immediately after the common and preferred stocks were issued.

E 12-5.

L O 4   *Cash Dividends*

Downey Corporation has secured authorization from the state for 200,000 shares of $10 par value common stock. There are 160,000 shares issued and 140,000 shares outstanding. On June 5, the board of directors declared a $.50 per share cash dividend to be paid on June 25 to stockholders of record on June 15. Prepare the journal entries necessary to record these events.

E 12-6.

L O 4   *Cash Dividends*

Gayle Corporation has 500,000 authorized shares of $1 par value common stock, of which 400,000 are issued and 360,000 are outstanding. On October 15, the board of directors declared a cash dividend of $.25 per share payable on November 15 to stockholders of record on November 1. Prepare the entries, as necessary, for each of the three dates.

E 12-7.

L O 4, 5   *Cash Dividends with Dividends in Arrears*

The Matsuta Corporation has 10,000 shares of its $100 par value, 7 percent cumulative preferred stock outstanding, and 50,000 shares of its $1 par value common stock outstanding. In its first four years of operation, the board of directors of Matsuta Corporation paid cash dividends as follows: 19x1, none; 19x2, $120,000; 19x3, $140,000; 19x4, $140,000.

Determine the dividends per share and total cash dividends paid to the preferred and common stockholders during each of the four years.

E 12-8.

L O 4, 5   *Preferred and Common Cash Dividends*

The Levinson Corporation pays dividends at the end of each year. The dividends paid for 19x1, 19x2, and 19x3 were $80,000, $60,000, and $180,000, respectively.

Calculate the total amount of dividends paid each year to the common and preferred stockholders if each of the following capital structures is assumed: (1) 20,000 shares of $100 par, 6 percent noncumulative preferred stock and 60,000 shares of $10 par common stock. (2) 10,000 shares of $100 par, 7 percent cumulative preferred stock and 60,000 shares of $10 par common stock. There were no dividends in arrears at the beginning of 19x1 and all shares were outstanding.

E 12-9.

L O 6   *Issuance of Stock*

Foth Company is authorized to issue 200,000 shares of common stock. On August 1, the company sold 10,000 shares at $25 per share. Prepare journal entries to record the sale of stock for cash under each of the following independent alternatives:

1. The stock has a par value of $25.
2. The stock has a par value of $10.
3. The stock has no par value or stated value.
4. The stock has a stated value of $1 per share.

E 12-10.
L O 6 *Journal Entries:*
Stated Value Stock

The Gladstone Corporation is authorized to issue 100,000 shares of no-par stock. The company recently sold 80,000 shares for $13 per share.

1. Prepare the journal entry to record the sale of the stock, assuming there is no stated value.
2. Prepare the journal entry if a $10 stated value is authorized by the company's board of directors.

E 12-11.
L O 6 *Issuance of Stock for*
Noncash Assets

On July 1, 19xx, Elk Grove, a new corporation, issued 20,000 shares of its common stock for a corporate headquarters building. The building has a fair market value of $600,000 and a book value of $400,000. Because the corporation is new, it is not possible to establish a market value for the common stock.

Record the issuance of stock for the building, assuming the following conditions: (1) The par value of the stock is $10 per share; (2) the stock has no par value; and (3) the stock has a stated value of $4 per share.

E 12-12.
L O 6 *Issuance of Stock for*
Noncash Assets

The Yang Corporation issued 2,000 shares of its $20 par value common stock for some land. The land had a fair market value of $60,000.

Prepare the journal entries necessary to record the stock issue for the land under each of the following conditions: (1) The stock was selling for $28 per share on the day of the transaction; and (2) management attempted to place a market value on the common stock but could not do so.

E 12-13.
L O 7 *Treasury Stock*
Transactions

Prepare the journal entries necessary to record the following stock transactions of the Henderson Company during 19xx:

May 5 Purchased 400 shares of its own $1 par value common stock for $10 per share, the current market price.
  17 Sold 150 shares of treasury stock purchased on May 5 for $11 per share.
  21 Sold 100 shares of treasury stock purchased on May 5 for $10 per share.
  28 Sold the remaining 150 shares of treasury stock purchased on May 5 for $9.50 per share.

E 12-14.
L O 7 *Treasury Stock*
Transactions
Including
Retirement

Prepare the journal entries necessary to record the following stock transactions of Nakate Corporation, which represent all treasury stock transactions entered into by the company.

June 1 Purchased 2,000 shares of its own $15 par value common stock for $35 per share, the current market price.
  10 Sold 500 shares of treasury stock purchased on June 1 for $40 per share.
  20 Sold 700 shares of treasury stock purchased on June 1 for $29 per share.
  30 Retired the remaining shares purchased on June 1. The original issue price was $21 per share.

E 12-15.
L O 8 *Exercise of Stock*
Options

Record the following equity transaction of the Evans Company in 19xx:

May 5 Walter Evans exercised his option to purchase 10,000 shares of $1 par value common stock at an option price of $12. The market price per share on the grant date was $12, and it was $25 on the exercise date.

Problem Set A

12A-1.
L O 2, 3, *Organization Costs,*
4, 6 *Stock and Dividend*
Journal Entries, and
Stockholders' Equity

Lasser Corporation began operations on September 1, 19xx. The corporation's charter authorized 300,000 shares of $8 par value common stock. Lasser Corporation engaged in the following transactions during its first quarter:

Sept. 1 Issued 50,000 shares of common stock, $500,000.
  1 Paid an attorney $32,000 to help organize the corporation and obtain the corporate charter from the state.
Oct. 2 Issued 80,000 shares of common stock, $960,000.
  24 Issued 24,000 shares of common stock for land and a warehouse. The land and warehouse had a fair market value of $50,000 and $200,000, respectively.
Nov. 30 The board of directors declared a cash dividend of $.40 per share to be paid on December 15 to stockholders of record on December 10.

Nov. 30   Closed the Income Summary and Cash Dividends Declared accounts for the first quarter. Revenues were $420,000 and expenses $340,000. (Assume revenues and expenses already have been closed to Income Summary.)

REQUIRED

1. Prepare general journal entries to record the first-quarter transactions and the closing entries.
2. Prepare the stockholders' equity section of Lasser Corporation's November 30, 19xx balance sheet.
3. Assuming that the payment to the attorney on September 1 was going to be amortized over five years, what adjusting entry was made on November 30?
4. How does the adjusting entry in **3** affect the balance sheet, including the resulting amount of organization costs?

12A-2.
L O 5   *Preferred and Common Stock Dividends*

The Rayner Corporation had both common stock and preferred stock outstanding from 19x4 through 19x6. Information about each stock for the three years is as follows:

Type	Par Value	Shares Outstanding	Other
Preferred	$100	40,000	7% cumulative
Common	20	600,000	

The company paid $140,000, $800,000, and $1,100,000 in dividends for 19x4 through 19x6, respectively.

REQUIRED

1. Determine the dividend per share paid to the common and preferred stockholders each year.
2. Repeat the computation performed in **1**, with the assumption that the preferred stock was noncumulative.

12A-3.
L O 7   *Treasury Stock Transactions*

The Spivy Corporation was involved in the following treasury stock transactions during 19x7:

a. Purchased 80,000 shares of its $1 par value common stock at $2.50 per share.
b. Purchased 16,000 shares of its common stock at $2.80 per share.
c. Sold 44,000 shares purchased in **a** for $131,000.
d. Sold the other 36,000 shares purchased in **a** for $72,000.
e. Sold 6,000 of the remaining shares of treasury stock for $1.60 per share.
f. Retired all the remaining shares of treasury stock. All shares originally were issued at $1.50 per share.

REQUIRED

Record the treasury stock transactions in general journal form.

12A-4.
L O 2, 3, 4, 5, 6, 7   *Comprehensive Stockholders' Equity Transactions*

The Loomis Plastics Corporation was chartered in the state of Wisconsin. The company was authorized to issue 20,000 shares of $100 par value, 6 percent preferred stock and 100,000 shares of no-par common stock. The common stock has a $2 stated value. The stock-related transactions for March and April 19xx were as follows:

Mar. 3   Issued 10,000 shares of common stock for $120,000 worth of services rendered in organizing and chartering the corporation.
     15   Issued 16,000 shares of common stock for land, which had an asking price of $200,000. The common stock had a market value of $12 per share.
     22   Issued 10,000 shares of preferred stock for $1,000,000.
     31   Closed the Income Summary account. Net income for March was $18,000.
Apr. 4   Issued 10,000 shares of common stock for $120,000.
     10   Purchased 5,000 shares of common stock for the treasury for $13,000.
     15   Declared a cash dividend for one month on the outstanding preferred stock and $.10 per share on common stock outstanding, payable on April 30 to stockholders of record on April 25.
     25   Date of record for cash dividends.
     30   Paid cash dividends.
     30   Closed the Income Summary and Cash Dividends Declared accounts. Net income for April was $28,000.

REQUIRED

1. Prepare general journal entries for March and April.
2. Prepare the stockholders' equity section of the company's balance sheet as of April 30, 19xx.

12A-5.

L O 2, 3, 4,
5, 6, 7, 8

Comprehensive
Stockholders' Equity
Transactions

The Omni Lighting Corporation was organized and authorized to issue 200,000 shares of 6 percent, $100 par value, noncumulative preferred stock and 3,000,000 shares of $10 par value common stock. The stock-related transactions for the first six months of 19xx operations were as follows:

Apr.   3   Issued 12,000 shares of common stock for legal and other organization fees valued at $120,000.

      29   Sold 300,000 shares of common stock for $12 per share.

May   5   Issued 40,000 shares of common stock for a building and land appraised at $300,000 and $160,000, respectively.

June 30   Closed the Income Summary account for the first quarter of operations. Net income for the first quarter was $400,000. (Assume that revenues and expenses already have been closed to Income Summary.)

July 10   Issued 2,000 shares of common stock to employees under a stock option plan. The plan allows employees to purchase the stock at the current market price, $12 per share.

      17   Purchased 20,000 shares of common stock for the treasury at $15 per share.

Aug.   8   Issued 200,000 shares of common stock for $16 per share.

Sept. 11   Declared a cash dividend of $.20 per common share to be paid on September 25 to stockholders of record on September 18.

      18   Cash dividend date of record.

      25   Paid the cash dividend to stockholders of record on September 18.

      26   Issued 10,000 shares of preferred stock at par value.

      29   Sold 8,000 shares held in the treasury for $20 per share.

      30   Closed the Income Summary and Cash Dividends Declared accounts for the second quarter of operations. Net income for the second quarter was $250,000.

REQUIRED

1. Prepare general journal entries to record the stock-related transactions of the Omni Lighting Corporation.
2. Prepare the stockholders' equity section of Omni Lighting Corporation's balance sheet as of September 30, 19xx.

Problem Set B

12B-1.

L O 2, 3,
4, 6

Organization Costs,
Stock and Dividend
Journal Entries, and
Stockholders' Equity

On March 1, 19xx, Blanco Corporation began operations with a charter from the state that authorized 100,000 shares of $4 par value common stock. Over the next quarter, the firm engaged in the following transactions:

Mar.   1   Issued 30,000 shares of common stock, $200,000.

      2   Paid fees associated with obtaining the charter and organizing the corporation, $24,000.

    10   Issued 30,000 shares of stock for land and a building with a fair market value of $38,000 and $128,000, respectively.

Apr. 10   Issued 13,000 shares of common stock, $130,000.

May 31   Closed the Income Summary account. Net income earned during the first quarter, $24,000.

      31   The board of directors declared a $.20 per share cash dividend to be paid on June 15 to shareholders of record on June 10.

      31   Closed Cash Dividends Declared to Retained Earnings.

REQUIRED

1. Prepare general journal entries to record the transactions and closing entries indicated above.
2. Prepare the stockholders' equity section of Blanco Corporation's balance sheet on May 31, 19xx.
3. Assuming that the payment for organization costs on March 2 was going to be amortized over five years, what adjusting entry was made on May 31 to record three months' amortization?

4. How does the adjusting entry in **3** affect the firm's balance sheet, including the resulting amount of organization costs?

12B-2.

L O 5 *Preferred and Common Stock Dividends*

The Fogel Corporation had the following stock outstanding from 19x1 through 19x4:

Preferred stock: $100 par value, 8 percent cumulative, 10,000 shares authorized, issued, and outstanding

Common stock: $10 par value, 200,000 shares authorized, issued, and outstanding

The company paid $60,000, $60,000, $188,000, and $260,000 in dividends during 19x1, 19x2, 19x3, and 19x4, respectively.

REQUIRED

1. Determine the dividend per share and the total dividends paid to common stockholders and preferred stockholders in 19x1, 19x2, 19x3, and 19x4.
2. Perform the same computations, with the assumption that the preferred stock was noncumulative.

12B-3.

L O 7 *Treasury Stock Transactions*

These treasury stock transactions occurred during 19xx for the Dwyer Company:

a. Purchased 52,000 shares of its $1 par value common stock on the market for $20 per share.
b. Sold 16,000 shares of the treasury stock for $21 per share.
c. Sold 12,000 shares of the treasury stock for $19 per share.
d. Sold 20,000 shares of the treasury stock remaining for $17 per share.
e. Purchased an additional 8,000 shares for $18 per share.
f. Retired all the remaining shares of treasury stock. All shares originally were issued at $8 per share.

REQUIRED

Record these transactions in general journal form.

12B-4.

L O 2, 3, 4, 5, 6, 7 *Comprehensive Stockholders' Equity Transactions*

Cabrini, Inc. was organized and authorized to issue 10,000 shares of $100 par value, 9 percent preferred stock and 100,000 shares of no-par, $5 stated value common stock on July 1, 19xx. Stock-related transactions for Cabrini were as follows:

July 1 Issued 20,000 shares of common stock at $11 per share.
   1 Issued 1,000 shares of common stock at $11 per share for services rendered in connection with the organization of the company.
   2 Issued 2,000 shares of preferred stock at par value for cash.
  10 Issued 5,000 shares of common stock for land on which the asking price was $70,000. Market value of the stock was $12. Management wishes to record the land at market value of the stock.
  31 Closed the Income Summary account. Net income earned during July was $13,000.
Aug. 2 Purchased 3,000 shares of common stock for the treasury at $13 per share.
  10 Declared a cash dividend for one month on the outstanding preferred stock and $.02 per share on common stock outstanding, payable on August 22 to stockholders of record on August 12.
  12 Date of record for cash dividends.
  22 Paid cash dividends.
  31 Closed the Income Summary and Cash Dividends Declared accounts. Net income during August was $12,000.

REQUIRED

1. Prepare general journal entries to record the above transactions.
2. Prepare the stockholders' equity section of the balance sheet as it would appear on August 31, 19xx.

12B-5.

L O 2, 3, 4, 5, 6, 7, 8 *Comprehensive Stockholders' Equity Transactions*

In January 19xx, the Rumilla Corporation was organized and authorized to issue 2,000,000 shares of no-par common stock and 50,000 shares of 5 percent, $100 par value, noncumulative preferred stock. The stock-related transactions for the first year's operations follow.

Jan. 19 Sold 30,000 shares of the common stock for $63,000. State law requires a minimum of $1 stated value per share.
  21 Issued 10,000 shares of common stock to attorneys and accountants for services valued at $22,000 and provided during the organization of the corporation.

Feb. 7 Issued 60,000 shares of common stock for a building that had an appraised value of $156,000. The current market value of the stock is unknown.

Mar. 22 Purchased 20,000 shares of common stock for the treasury at $3 per share.

June 30 Closed the Income Summary account. Reported $160,000 income for the first six months of operations, ended June 30.

July 15 Issued 10,000 shares of common stock to employees under a stock option plan that allows any employee to buy shares at the current market price, which today is $3 per share.

Aug. 1 Sold 5,000 shares of treasury stock for $4 per share.

Sept. 1 Declared a cash dividend of $.15 per common share to be paid on September 25 to stockholders of record on September 15.

15 Cash dividend date of record.

25 Paid cash dividend to stockholders of record on September 15.

Oct. 30 Issued 8,000 shares of common stock for a piece of land. The stock was selling for $3 per share, and the land had a fair market value of $25,000.

Dec. 15 Issued 2,200 shares of preferred stock for $100 per share.

31 Closed the Income Summary and Cash Dividends Declared accounts. Reported $40,000 income for the past six months of operations.

REQUIRED

1. Prepare the journal entries to record all of the transactions above.
2. Prepare the stockholders' equity section of Rumilla Corporation's balance sheet as of December 31, 19xx.

CRITICAL THINKING AND COMMUNICATION

Conceptual Mini-Cases

CMC 12-1.

L O 3 *Reasons for Issuing Common Stock*

For decades *Allstate Corporation,* one of the United States' largest automobile, home, and life insurance companies, was a division of *Sears, Roebuck & Co.* In June, 1993, the company had an initial public offering that raised $2.5 billion, as the public bought 19.9 percent of Allstate common shares for $27 per share. Sears retained 80.1 percent of the shares. Coming off a year in which the company had paid an estimated $2.5 billion in claims as a result of Hurricane Andrew in Florida, the company expects to return to profitable operations in 1993 and 1994. Allstate's chief executive officer is quoted as saying, "Going public really focused us."[13] What advantages are there to Sears and to Allstate in raising money by issuing common stock rather than bonds? Why would the chief executive officer say that going public "really focused us"?

CMC 12-2.

L O 5 *Effect of the Omission of Preferred Dividends*

Tucson Electric Company, the *Wall Street Journal* disclosed, discontinued all its preferred stock dividends indefinitely in an effort to improve liquidity. All of the company's cumulative preferred stock was affected. According to the article, "Some interpreted the drastic action as a requisite for the cash-strapped utility to secure a new credit agreement. . . . If the credit agreement falls through, the omission of preferred-stock dividends would suggest Tucson Electric is perilously close to filing for bankruptcy."[14] What are cumulative preferred shares? Why is the omission of dividends on these shares a "drastic action"? If new bank financing is not obtained, why would the company have to consider declaring bankruptcy?

CMC 12-3.

L O 5 *Reasons for Issuing Preferred Stock*

Preferred stock is a hybrid security that has some of the characteristics of stock and some of the characteristics of bonds. Historically, preferred stock has not been a popular means of financing. In the last few years, however, it has become more attractive to companies and individual investors alike, who are buying large amounts because of high yields. Large preferred stock issues have been made by banks such as *Chase Manhattan, Citicorp, Republic New York,* and *Wells Fargo,* as well as other companies.

13. Hillary Durgin, "A New Hand Dealt to 1990s Allstate," *Crain's Chicago Business,* December 20, 1993.

14. Rick Wartzman, "Tucson Electric Omits Dividends on Preferred Stock," *Wall Street Journal,* December 10, 1990.

The dividend yields on these stocks are over 9 percent, and interest rates on comparable bonds are less.[15] Especially popular are preferred equity redemption convertible stocks, or PERCs, which are automatically convertible into common stock after three years if the company does not redeem or call them first and retire them. What reasons can you give for the popularity of preferred stock, when the tax-deductible interest is less costly, and PERCs specifically, from the company's and investor's standpoints?

CMC 12-4.
L O 7 *Purposes of Treasury Stock*

This chapter discusses the recent popularity of issuing common or preferred stock. However, at the same time, other companies have bought back their common stock. For example, because its stock had declined under the uncertainty of the health care reforms, **Bristol-Myers Squibb** bought 25 million of its own shares. Other companies are awash in cash because of the decline in interest rates, the layoffs to cut costs, and the lack of a need to make new investments. **Quaker Oats** has purchased 4.8 million of its own shares for $323 million and plans to purchase 5 million more. The Quaker Oats treasurer is quoted as saying, "We spend on new products, we make acquisitions, we raise the dividend, and we still can't soak up the cash." **Sun Microsystems** has cut its outstanding shares by 9 percent with an aggressive buyback program, and **PepsiCo** has purchased 50 million shares at a cost of $1.8 billion. For what reasons would a company buy back its own shares?

Ethics Mini-Case

EMC 12-1.
L O 1 *The Corporate Form of Business and Ethical Considerations for the Accounting Profession*

Traditionally, accounting firms have organized as partnerships or as professional corporations, a form of corporation that in many ways resembles a partnership. In recent years, some accounting firms have suffered large judgments as a result of lawsuits by investors who lost money when they invested in companies that went bankrupt. In one case, a large international accounting firm went bankrupt mainly because of liabilities that were anticipated to arise from problems in the savings and loan industry. The partners dissolved the firm rather than put up the additional capital needed to keep it going. Because of the increased risk of large losses from malpractice suits, there is a movement to allow accounting firms to incorporate as long as they maintain a minimum level of partners' capital and carry malpractice insurance. Some accounting practitioners feel that incorporating would be a violation of their responsibility to the public. What features of the corporate form of business would be most advantageous to the partners of an accounting firm? Do you think it would be a violation of the public trust for an accounting firm to incorporate? (**Hint:** To refresh your memory on the characteristics of partnerships, refer to the appendix on accounting for unincorporated businesses.)

Decision-Making Case

DMC 12-1.
L O 3, 4, 5 *Analysis of Alternative Financing Methods*

Companies offering services to the computer technology industry are growing quickly. Participating in this growth, **Infinite Systems Corporation** has expanded rapidly in recent years. Because of its profitability, the company has been able to grow without obtaining external financing. This fact is reflected in its current balance sheet, which contains no long-term debt. The liability and stockholders' equity sections of the balance sheet are shown on the opposite page.

The company is now faced with the possibility of doubling its size by purchasing the operations of a rival company for $8,000,000. If the purchase goes through, Infinite Systems will become the top company in its specialized industry in the northeastern part of the country. The problem for management is how to finance the purchase. After much study and discussion with bankers and underwriters, management has prepared three financing alternatives to present to the board of directors, which must authorize the purchase and the financing.

15. Tom Herman, "Preferreds' Rich Yields Blind Some Investors to Risks," *Wall Street Journal,* March 24, 1992.

Alternative A: The company could issue $8,000,000 of long-term debt. Given the company's financial rating and the current market rates, management believes the company will have to pay an interest rate of 12 percent on the debt.

Alternative B: The company could issue 80,000 shares of 10 percent, $100 par value preferred stock.

Alternative C: The company could issue 100,000 additional shares of $20 par value common stock at $80 per share.

Management explains to the board that the interest on the long-term debt is tax deductible and that the applicable income tax rate is 40 percent. The board members know that a dividend of $1.60 per share of common stock was paid last year, up from $1.20 and $.80 per share in the two years before that. The board has had a policy of regular increases in dividends of $.40 per share. The board feels that each of the three financing alternatives is feasible and now wants to study the financial effects of each alternative.

Infinite Systems Corporation
Partial Balance Sheet

Liabilities

Current Liabilities		$ 1,000,000

Stockholders' Equity

Common Stock—$20 par value, 500,000 shares authorized, 100,000 shares issued and outstanding	$2,000,000	
Paid-in Capital in Excess of Par Value, Common	3,600,000	
Retained Earnings	3,400,000	
Total Stockholders' Equity		9,000,000
Total Liabilities and Stockholders' Equity		$10,000,000

REQUIRED

1. Prepare a schedule to show how the liabilities and stockholders' equity side of Infinite Systems' balance sheet would look under each alternative, and figure the debt to equity ratio (total liabilities ÷ total stockholders' equity) for each.
2. Compute and compare the cash needed to pay the interest or dividends for each kind of new financing net of income taxes in the first year.
3. How might the cash needed to pay for the financing change in future years?
4. Evaluate the alternatives, giving arguments for and against each one.

Basic Research Activity

RA 12-1.
L O 3, 4, 5, 6, 8   *Reading Corporate Annual Reports*

In your library, select the annual reports of three corporations. You can choose them from the same industry or at random, at the direction of your instructor. (**Note**: You will use these companies again in the Business Research Activities in later chapters.) Prepare a table with a column for each corporation. Then answer the following questions for each corporation: Does the corporation have preferred stock? If so, what are the par value and the indicated dividend, and is the preferred stock cumulative or convertible? Is the common stock par value or no-par? What is the par value or stated value? What cash dividends, if any, were paid in the past year? From the notes to the financial statements, determine whether the company has an employee stock option plan. What are some of its provisions? Be prepared to discuss the characteristics of the stocks and dividends for your selected companies in class.

FINANCIAL REPORTING AND ANALYSIS

Interpretation Cases from Business

ICB 12-1.
L O 3, 6 *Effect of Stock Issue*

UAL Corporation is a holding company whose primary subsidiary is United Airlines, which provides passenger and cargo air transportation to 141 airports worldwide. On March 21, 1991, UAL announced a common stock issue in a tombstone ad in the *Wall Street Journal:*

1,500,000 Shares
UAL Corporation
Common Stock
($5 par value)
Price $146 per share

In fact, UAL sold 1,733,100 shares of stock at $146 for net proceeds of $247.2 million.

Here is a portion of the stockholders' equity section of the balance sheet from UAL's 1990 annual report:

	1990	1989
	(in thousands)	
Common Stock, $5 par value; authorized 125,000,000 shares; issued 23,467,880 shares in 1990 and 23,419,953 shares in 1989	117,339	117,100
Additional Paid-in Capital	52,391	47,320
Retained Earnings	1,620,885	1,526,534

REQUIRED

1. Assuming that all the shares were issued at the price indicated and that UAL received the net proceeds, prepare the entry in UAL's accounting records to record the stock issue.
2. Prepare the portion of the stockholders' equity section of the balance sheet shown above after the issue of the common stock, based on the information given. Round all answers to the nearest thousand.
3. Based on your answer in **2**, did UAL have to increase its authorized shares to undertake this stock issue?
4. What amount per share did UAL receive and how much did UAL's underwriter receive to help in issuing the stock if investors paid $146 per share? What does the underwriter do to earn his or her fee?

ICB 12-2.
L O 4, 5 *Dividends and Preferred Stock*

Navistar International Corporation, a manufacturer of medium and heavy-duty diesel trucks, had several different types of preferred stock on October 31, 1986.[16] Two different series of preferred stock outstanding with different terms and amounts were as follows:

Series C: No-par, cumulative preferred, $5.76 dividend per share rate, 3,000,000 shares outstanding

Series E: No-par, noncumulative, convertible preferred, $120 dividend rate, commencing at the start of the first semiannual period in which a dividend is payable on common stock, in addition, a dividend not payable until all arrears are paid on Series C, conversion rate 100 shares of common stock per share of preferred stock, 160,960 shares outstanding.

There are 108,524,400 shares of no-par value common stock outstanding. As of October 31, 1986, there were $86.4 million ($28.80 per share) in cumulative dividends in arrears on Series C preferred stock.

Navistar, which suffered greatly from the farm recession in the 1980s, lost $12,240,000 in 1986 and has a deficit in Retained Earnings of $1,889,168,000.

REQUIRED

1. How likely is it that investors in Navistar common stock will receive cash dividends? Explain your answer.
2. Assume that in 1987 Navistar returned to profitable operations and eliminated the deficit in retained earnings. What amount of dividends in total must be declared

16. Navistar International Corporation, *Annual Report*, 1986.

before the common stockholders would be eligible to receive a dividend? Assuming that total dividends of $154,575,000 were declared by the board of directors in 1987, what would be the dividends per share paid to the common stockholders?

ICB 12-3.
L O 5, 6, 8   *Preferred Stock Characteristics and Stock Options*

At the beginning of fiscal 1986, ***Navistar International***, described in the preceding case, had 685,000 shares of Series A no-par, callable, convertible, cumulative preferred stock outstanding.[17] During fiscal 1986, 16,000 shares were called at $25.67 per share and retired. In addition, the remaining 669,000 shares were converted to 2,500,000 shares of no-par common stock. The total carrying value of the preferred stock after the redemption and before the conversion was $17,600,000.

In addition, employees exercised employee stock options on 56,000 shares of no-par common stock at $3.60 per share.

REQUIRED

1. There are four adjectives that describe Navistar's Series A preferred stock. Explain what each means.
2. Prepare journal entries to record the call and the conversion of preferred shares. Assume there is no gain or loss on the transaction.
3. Prepare the entry to record the exercise of stock options.
4. In 1986 Navistar had a net loss of $12,240,000 and a deficit in Retained Earnings of $1,889,168,000. The company has not paid a cash dividend since 1981. Why would the preferred stockholders and the employees want to own Navistar common stock?

ICB 12-4.
L O 7   *Purpose of Treasury Stock and Its Retirement*

Atlantic Richfield Company, in its 1989 annual report, indicated that the number of common shares held in the treasury decreased from 45,546,171 in 1988 to 3,397,381 in 1989. The following also was reported:

> By Board authorization, effective December 31, 1989 the Company cancelled 50 million shares of common stock held in treasury. As a result of the cancellation, common stock decreased by $125 million, capital in excess of par value of stock decreased by $228 million, and retained earnings decreased by $3,119 million.[18]

The shares canceled or retired represent almost 25 percent of the shares of common stock issued by Atlantic Richfield. Explain the accounting for the treasury shares by Atlantic Richfield. Did the company buy any treasury shares during the year? What journal entry was made to record the cancellation or retirement of the treasury shares? At what average price were the treasury shares purchased, and at what average price were they originally issued? What do you think was management's reason for purchasing the treasury shares?

ICB 12-5.
L O 7   *Analysis of Effects of Treasury Stock Transactions*

In November 1987, ***Ford Motor Company*** announced a plan to buy up to $2 billion of its common stock in the open market, constituting the company's second large-scale stock repurchase since 1984. At the then current market price of $71.75, Ford estimated that it could purchase more than 27 million shares, which would effectively reduce the number of outstanding shares by more than 11 percent.

The plan represented management's belief that Ford stock was undervalued and would be an exceptional investment for both the company and its shareholders. It was an action that demonstrated management's confidence in Ford's future in the highly competitive automobile market.

Another interpretation of the action might be that Ford had generated a tremendous amount of cash for which the company had limited investment opportunities other than its own stock. By the close of 1987, it was estimated that the company would have $8 billion in cash revenues.

On October 8, eleven days before the stock market crash of October 19, Ford proposed to shareholders a 2 for 1 stock split; the new shares were expected to be issued January 12. The calculations for the buyback move were based on presplit figures. October 8 was also the day of Ford's ninth dividend increase in the past seventeen quarters; the company's quarterly dividend rose from $.75 to $1.00 a share on a presplit basis.

17. Ibid.
18. Atlantic Richfield Company, *Annual Report*, 1989.

The condensed balance sheet for Ford Motor Company on December 31, 1986 is shown below.[19]

**Ford Motor Company
Condensed Balance Sheet
December 31, 1986
(in billions)**

Current Assets	$18.5	Current Liabilities	$15.6
Long-Term Assets	19.4	Long-Term Liabilities	7.5
	$37.9	Stockholders' Equity	
		Common Stock ($2 par value)	.5
		Paid-in Capital in Excess of	
		Par Value, Common	.6
		Retained Earnings	13.7
		Total Liabilities and	
		Stockholders' Equity	$37.9

REQUIRED

1. Assuming that the buyback was completed as planned (before December 31, 1987), prepare the journal entry to record the purchase of treasury stock (use the total dollar amount and date given above).
2. Prepare the condensed balance sheet after the buyback in **1** was recorded, assuming that the balance immediately before the buyback was the same as the balance sheet on December 31, 1986.
3. Tell whether the buyback would have increased or decreased the following ratios: current ratio, debt to equity, return on assets, return on equity, and earnings per share. Also indicate whether the increase or decrease was favorable or unfavorable.
4. Assuming that Ford decided to retire the repurchased stock, prepare the appropriate journal entry.
5. Assume that Ford did not retire the repurchased stock but went through with the proposed stock split. How do you think the balance sheet would differ from the one you prepared in **2**, and how much would the company have paid in total quarterly dividends?

International Company Case

**ICC 12-1.
LO 3, 4,
6, 8**

*Stockholders' Equity
Transactions*

Peugeot S.A. is France's largest automobile maker. Its brands are Peugeot and Citroen. The company's stockholders' equity section of the balance sheet appears as follows:

	1992	1991
Stockholders' Equity (in millions of French francs)		
Common stock (par value FF35 a share, 49,992,620 shares authorized and 49,964,000 shares issued and outstanding)	1,750	1,749
Capital in excess of par value of stock	5,214	5,203
Reserves	46,180	44,766
Total stockholders' equity	53,144	51,718

Reserves are similar to retained earnings in U.S. financial statements. During 1992, the company paid FF648 million in dividends. The changes in common stock and capital in excess of par value of stock represent stock issued to employees in connection with the exercise of employee stock options. Prepare the journal entries to record the

19. Ford Motor Company, *Annual Report*, 1986.

declaration and payment of dividends in 1992 and the issue of stock in connection with the employee stock options. Assuming that dividends and net income were the only factors that affected reserves during 1992, how much did Peugeot earn in 1992 in U.S. dollars (use an exchange rate of 5.8 French francs to the dollar)?

Toys "R" Us Case

TC 12-1.
L O 3, 4, 8   *Stockholders' Equity*

Refer to the Annual Report in the appendix on Toys "R" Us to answer the following questions:

1. What type of capital stock does Toys "R" Us have? What is the par value? How many shares are authorized, issued, and outstanding at the end of 1994?
2. What is the policy of Toys "R" Us with regard to dividends? Does the company rely mostly on stock or earnings for its stockholders' equity?
3. Does the company have a stock option plan? To whom do the stock options apply? Does senior management have significant stock options? Given the market price of the stock shown in the notes to the consolidated financial statements, do these options represent significant value to the executives?

Retained Earnings and Corporate Income Statements

1. Define *retained earnings* and prepare a statement of retained earnings.
2. Account for stock dividends and stock splits.
3. Describe the disclosure of restrictions on retained earnings.
4. Prepare a statement of stockholders' equity.
5. Calculate book value per share and distinguish it from market value.
6. Prepare a corporate income statement.
7. Show the relationships among income taxes expense, deferred income taxes, and net of taxes.
8. Describe the disclosure on the income statement of discontinued operations, extraordinary items, and accounting changes.
9. Compute earnings per share.

DECISION POINT *General Electric Company*

At a board meeting in December, 1993, the directors of General Electric Company raised the quarterly cash dividend on common stock by 14 percent and proposed a 2 for 1 stock split. The stock split was to be voted on by stockholders on April 27, 1994. In addition, the board recommended an increase from 1.1 billion authorized common shares to 2.2 billion. General Electric had about 926.5 million shares outstanding, and the current market price of the company's stock was $105 per share.[1] How does a stock split differ from a stock dividend and a cash dividend? Why would the board of directors take these actions? What are the implications for the stockholders?

These are important questions for internal management and external investors in the company. A 2 for 1 stock split gives stockholders one additional share of common stock for each share they own. Stock dividends also give stockholders additional shares based on the value of their holdings, but they have a different effect on the stockholders' equity section of the balance sheet, as will be explained in this chapter. A cash dividend is a distribution of cash based on the number of shares owned. In this case, the board of directors had to recommend increasing the number of authorized shares because there were not enough authorized shares available to give each stockholder another share. General Electric's prosperity is the probable reason for the proposal, as many companies view stock splits as symbols of success. By doubling the number of shares outstanding, the General Electric stock split will reduce the market value per share; this will make the stock more readily tradable and more easily available to the ordinary investor. The benefit to the stockholders is that although the market value per share will be about half of $105 per share, they will own twice as many shares. Transactions involving stock dividends and stock splits affect the financial structure of a company and are important strategic actions that both managers and investors should understand. This chapter examines these actions and their effects and shows how to read and interpret the statement of stockholders' equity and the corporate income statement. ⋮ ⋮ ⋮ ⋮ ⋮

1. "GE's Directors Raise Quarterly Dividend, Propose Stock Split," *Wall Street Journal*, December 20, 1993.

RETAINED EARNINGS TRANSACTIONS

OBJECTIVE

1 *Define* **retained earnings** *and prepare a statement of retained earnings*

Stockholders' equity, as presented earlier, has two parts: contributed capital and retained earnings. The retained earnings of a company are the part of stockholders' equity that represents claims to assets arising from the earnings of the business. Retained earnings equal a company's profits since the date of its inception, less any losses, dividends to stockholders, or transfers to contributed capital. Exhibit 13-1 shows a statement of retained earnings for Caprock Corporation for 19x2. The beginning balance of retained earnings of $854,000 is increased by net income of $76,000 and decreased by cash dividends of $30,000. The ending balance is $900,000. The statement of retained earnings also can disclose other transactions that are explained in this chapter.

It is important to remember that retained earnings are not the assets themselves. The existence of retained earnings means that assets generated by profitable operations have been kept in the company to help it grow or to meet other business needs. A credit balance in Retained Earnings does *not* mean that cash or any designated set of assets is associated directly with retained earnings. The fact that earnings have been retained means that assets as a whole have been increased.

Retained Earnings can carry a debit balance. Generally, this happens when a company's dividends and subsequent losses are greater than its accumulated profits from operations. In such a case, the firm is said to have a deficit (debit balance) in Retained Earnings. A deficit is shown in the stockholders' equity section of the balance sheet as a deduction from contributed capital.

Accountants use various terms to describe the retained earnings of a business. One is *surplus,* which implies that there are excess assets available for dividends. This usage is poor because the existence of retained earnings carries no connotation of "excess" or "surplus." Because of possible misinterpretation, the American Institute of Certified Public Accountants recommends more fitting terms, such as *retained income, retained earnings, accumulated earnings,* or *earnings retained for use in the business.*[2]

Prior period adjustments are events or transactions that relate to earlier accounting periods but that could not be determined in those earlier periods. When they occur, they are shown on the statement of retained earnings as an adjustment to the beginning balance. The Financial Accounting Standards Board identifies only two kinds of prior period adjustments. The first is to correct an error in the financial statements of a prior year. The second is needed if a company realizes an income tax gain from carrying forward a preacquisition operating loss of a purchased company.[3] Prior period adjustments are rare.

OBJECTIVE

2 *Account for stock dividends and stock splits*

STOCK DIVIDENDS

A stock dividend is a proportional distribution of shares of the corporation's stock to its shareholders. The distribution of stock does not change the assets or liabilities of the firm because there is no distribution of assets as there is when a cash dividend is distributed.

---

2. Committee on Accounting Terminology, *Accounting Terminology Bulletin No. 1,* "Review and Resume" (New York: American Institute of Certified Public Accountants, 1953), par. 69.
3. *Statement of Financial Accounting Standards No. 16,* "Prior Period Adjustments" (Stamford, Conn.: Financial Accounting Standards Board, 1977), par. 11.

Exhibit 13-1. A Statement of Retained Earnings

Caprock Corporation
Statement of Retained Earnings
For the Year Ended December 31, 19x2

Retained Earnings, December 31, 19x1	$854,000
Net Income, 19x2	76,000
Subtotal	$930,000
Less Cash Dividends, Common	30,000
Retained Earnings, December 31, 19x2	$900,000

The board of directors can declare a stock dividend for several reasons:

1. It may want to give stockholders some evidence of the success of the company without paying a cash dividend, which would affect the firm's working capital position.
2. It may seek to reduce the market price of the stock by increasing the number of shares outstanding, although this goal more often is met by stock splits.
3. It may want to make a nontaxable distribution to stockholders. Stock dividends that meet certain conditions are not considered income, so a tax is not levied on them.
4. It communicates that the permanent capital of the company has increased by transferring an amount from retained earnings to contributed capital.

The total stockholders' equity is not affected by a stock dividend. The effect of a stock dividend is to transfer a dollar amount from retained earnings to the contributed capital section on the date of declaration. The amount transferred is the fair market value (usually, the market price) of the additional shares to be issued. The laws of most states specify the minimum value of each share transferred under a stock dividend, which is normally the minimum legal capital (par or stated value). However, generally accepted accounting principles state that market value reflects the economic effect of small stock distributions (less than 20 to 25 percent of a company's outstanding common stock) better than par or stated value does. For this reason, market price should be used to account for small stock dividends.[4]

To illustrate the accounting for a stock dividend, we assume that Caprock Corporation has the following stockholders' equity structure:

Contributed Capital		
Common Stock—$5 par value, 100,000 shares		
authorized, 30,000 shares issued and outstanding		$ 150,000
Paid-in Capital in Excess of Par Value, Common		30,000
Total Contributed Capital		$ 180,000
Retained Earnings		900,000
Total Stockholders' Equity		$1,080,000

Suppose that the corporation's board of directors declares a 10 percent stock dividend on February 24, distributable on March 31 to stockholders of

4. *Accounting Research Bulletin No. 43* (New York: American Institute of Certified Public Accountants, 1953), chap. 7, sec. B, par 10.

record on March 15, and that the market price of the stock on February 24 is $20 per share. The entries to record the stock dividend declaration and distribution are as follows:

Date of Declaration

Feb. 24	Stock Dividends Declared		60,000	
	Common Stock Distributable			15,000
	Paid-in Capital in Excess of Par			
	Value, Common			45,000
	Declared a 10% stock dividend			
	on common stock, distributable on			
	March 31 to stockholders of record			
	on March 15:			
	30,000 shares $\times$ .10 = 3,000 shares			
	3,000 shares $\times$ \$20/share = \$60,000			
	3,000 shares $\times$ \$5/share = \$15,000			

The Stock Dividends Declared account is used to record stock dividends; the Cash Dividends Declared account is used for cash dividends, as shown in the chapter on contributed capital. Retained Earnings is reduced by the amount of the stock dividend by closing the Stock Dividends Declared account to Retained Earnings at the end of the accounting period in the same way that Cash Dividends Declared is closed.

Date of Record

Mar. 15   No entry required

Date of Distribution

Mar. 31	Common Stock Distributable	15,000	
	Common Stock		15,000
	Distributed a stock dividend of		
	3,000 shares		

The effect of this stock dividend is to permanently transfer the market value of the stock, $60,000, from retained earnings to contributed capital and to increase the number of shares outstanding by 3,000. Common Stock Distributable is credited for the par value of the stock to be distributed (3,000 $\times$ $5 = $15,000). In addition, when the market value is greater than the par value of the stock, Paid-in Capital in Excess of Par Value, Common must be credited for the amount by which the market value exceeds the par value. In this case, the total market value of the stock dividend ($60,000) exceeds the total par value ($15,000) by $45,000. No entry is required on the date of record. On the distribution date, the common stock is issued by debiting Common Stock Distributable and crediting Common Stock for the par value of the stock ($15,000).

Common Stock Distributable is not a liability because there is no obligation to distribute cash or other assets. The obligation is to distribute additional shares of capital stock. If financial statements are prepared between the date of declaration and the distribution of stock, Common Stock Distributable should be reported as part of contributed capital, as shown at the top of the next page.

Contributed Capital
   Common Stock—$5 par value, 100,000 shares

authorized, 30,000 shares issued and outstanding	$ 150,000
Common Stock Distributable, 3,000 shares	15,000
Paid-in Capital in Excess of Par Value, Common	75,000
Total Contributed Capital	$ 240,000
Retained Earnings	840,000
Total Stockholders' Equity	$1,080,000

    Three points can be made from this example. First, the total stockholders' equity is the same before and after the stock dividend. Second, the assets of the corporation are not reduced as in the case of a cash dividend. Third, the proportionate ownership in the corporation of any individual stockholder is the same before and after the stock dividend. To illustrate these points, assume that a stockholder owns 1,000 shares before the stock dividend. After the 10 percent stock dividend is distributed, this stockholder would own 1,100 shares.

Stockholders' Equity	**Before Dividend**	**After Dividend**
Common Stock	$ 150,000	$ 165,000
Paid-in Capital in Excess of Par Value, Common	30,000	75,000
Total Contributed Capital	$ 180,000	$ 240,000
Retained Earnings	900,000	840,000
Total Stockholders' Equity	$1,080,000	$1,080,000
Shares Outstanding	30,000	33,000
Stockholders' Equity per share	$ 36.00	$ 32.73

Stockholders' Investment

Shares owned	1,000	1,100
Shares outstanding	30,000	33,000
Percentage of ownership	3⅓%	3⅓%
Proportionate investment ($1,080,000 × .03⅓)	$ 36,000	$ 36,000

    Both before and after the stock dividend, the stockholders' equity totals $1,080,000 and the stockholder owns 3⅓ percent of the company. The proportionate investment (stockholders' equity times percentage ownership) stays at $36,000.

    All stock dividends have an effect on the market price of a company's stock. But some stock dividends are so large that they have a material effect on the price per share of the stock. For example, a 50 percent stock dividend would cause the market price of the stock to drop about 33 percent because there is a one-third increase in the number of shares outstanding. The AICPA arbitrarily has decided that large stock dividends, those greater than 20 to 25 percent, should be accounted for by transferring the par or stated value of the stock on the date of declaration from retained earnings to contributed capital.[5]

5. Ibid., par. 13.

STOCK SPLITS

A stock split occurs when a corporation increases the number of issued shares of stock and reduces the par or stated value proportionally. A company may plan a stock split when it wants to lower the market value per share of its stock and increase the liquidity of the stock. This action may be necessary if the market value per share has become so high that it hinders the trading of the company's stock. An example of this strategy is shown in the Decision Point on General Electric Company that introduced this chapter.

To illustrate a stock split, suppose that Caprock Corporation has 30,000 shares of $5.00 par value stock outstanding. The market value is $70.00 per share. The corporation plans a 2 for 1 split. This split will lower the par value to $2.50 and increase the number of shares outstanding to 60,000. A stockholder who previously owned 400 shares of the $5.00 par stock would own 800 shares of the $2.50 par stock after the split. When a stock split occurs, the market value tends to fall in proportion to the increase in outstanding shares of stock. For example, a 2 for 1 stock split would cause the price of the stock to drop by approximately 50 percent, to about $35.00. It would also halve earnings per share and cash dividends per share (if the board does not increase the dividend). The lower price plus the increase in shares tend to promote the buying and selling of shares.

A stock split does not increase the number of shares authorized. Nor does it change the balances in the stockholders' equity section of the balance sheet. It simply changes the par value and the number of shares issued, both those that are outstanding and those that are held as treasury shares. Therefore, an entry is not necessary. However, it is appropriate to document the change by making a memorandum entry in the general journal:

July 15   The 30,000 shares of $5 par value common stock that are issued and outstanding were split 2 for 1, resulting in 60,000 shares of $2.50 par value common stock issued and outstanding.

The change for the Caprock Corporation is as follows:

Before Stock Split (from page 575)

Contributed Capital	
Common Stock—$5 par value, 100,000 shares authorized, 30,000 shares issued and outstanding	$ 150,000
Paid-in Capital in Excess of Par Value, Common	30,000
Total Contributed Capital	$ 180,000
Retained Earnings	900,000
Total Stockholders' Equity	$1,080,000

After Stock Split

Contributed Capital	
Common Stock—$2.50 par value, 100,000 shares authorized, 60,000 shares issued and outstanding	$ 150,000
Paid-in Capital in Excess of Par Value, Common	30,000
Total Contributed Capital	$ 180,000
Retained Earnings	900,000
Total Stockholders' Equity	$1,080,000

Although the amount of stockholders' equity per share would be half as much, each stockholder's proportionate interest in the company would remain the same.

In cases where the number of split shares is going to exceed the number of authorized shares, the board of directors must secure state approval to increase the number of authorized shares prior to the issue of additional shares at the time of the split.

RESTRICTIONS ON RETAINED EARNINGS

OBJECTIVE

3 *Describe the disclosure of restrictions on retained earnings*

A corporation may be required or want to restrict all or a portion of retained earnings. A restriction on retained earnings means that dividends can be declared only to the extent of the *unrestricted* retained earnings. The following are several reasons a company might restrict retained earnings:

1. *A contractual agreement.* For example, bond indentures may place a limitation on the dividends the company can pay.
2. *State law.* Many states do not allow a corporation to distribute dividends or purchase treasury stock if doing so impairs the legal capital of the company.
3. *Voluntary action by the board of directors.* Many times a board decides to retain assets in the business for future needs. For example, the company may be planning to build a new plant and may want to show that dividends will be limited to save enough money for the building. A company also might restrict retained earnings to show a possible future loss of assets resulting from a lawsuit.

There are two ways of reporting restrictions on retained earnings to readers of financial statements: A restriction can be shown in the stockholders' equity section of the balance sheet, or it can be disclosed in a note to the financial statements.

A restriction on retained earnings does not change the total retained earnings or stockholders' equity of the company. It simply divides retained earnings into two parts, restricted and unrestricted. Assets in the restricted part cannot be used to pay dividends. The unrestricted amount represents earnings kept in the business that the company can use for dividends and other purposes.

Assuming that Caprock's board of directors has decided to restrict $300,000 in retained earnings because of plans for plant expansion, the disclosure in Caprock's stockholders' equity section would be as follows:

Contributed Capital
Common Stock—$5 par value, 100,000 shares
  authorized, 30,000 shares issued and

outstanding		$ 150,000
Paid-in Capital in Excess of Par Value, Common		30,000
Total Contributed Capital		$ 180,000
Retained Earnings		
Restricted for Plant Expansion	$300,000	
Unrestricted	600,000	
Total Retained Earnings		900,000
Total Stockholders' Equity		$1,080,000

The same facts about restricted retained earnings also could be presented by reference to a note to the financial statements. For example:

Retained Earnings (Note 15) $900,000

Note 15:
Because of plans to expand the capacity of the clothing division, the board of
directors has restricted retained earnings available for dividends by $300,000.

Notice that the restriction of retained earnings does not restrict cash or
other assets in any way. It simply explains to the readers of the financial
statements that a certain amount of assets generated by earnings will remain
in the business for the purpose stated. It is still management's job to make
sure that there is enough cash or assets on hand to fulfill the purpose. Also,
the removal of a restriction does not necessarily mean that the board of directors is now able to declare a dividend.

BUSINESS BULLETIN: INTERNATIONAL PRACTICE

Restrictions on retained earnings, called reserves,
are much more common in some foreign countries
than in the United States. In Sweden, for instance,
reserves are used to respond to fluctuations in the
economy. The tax code in Sweden allows companies to set up contingency reserves for the purpose
of maintaining financial stability. Appropriations to
these reserves reduce taxable income and income taxes. The reserves
become taxable when they are reversed, but they are available to absorb
losses should they occur. For example, although Skandia Group, a large
Swedish insurance company, incurred a net loss of SK2.4 billion in 1992, the
unrestricted retained earnings increased from SK1 billion to SK1.8 billion
because the company reduced its restricted reserves. Skandia Group paid
its customary cash dividend and still had SK4.2 billion in restricted
reserves.[6]

THE STATEMENT OF STOCKHOLDERS' EQUITY

OBJECTIVE

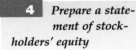

4 *Prepare a state-
ment of stock-
holders' equity*

The statement of stockholders' equity, also called the *statement of changes in
stockholders' equity,* summarizes the changes in the components of the stockholders' equity section of the balance sheet. Companies increasingly are
using this statement in place of the statement of retained earnings because it
reveals much more about the year's stockholders' equity transactions. In
Exhibit 13-2, for example, the Tri-State Corporation's statement of stockholders' equity, the first line contains the beginning balance (the last period's
ending balance) of each account in the stockholders' equity section. Each
additional line in the statement discloses the effects of transactions that affect
the accounts. It is possible to determine from this statement that during 19x2
Tri-State Corporation issued 5,000 shares of common stock for $250,000, had a

6. Skandia Group, *Annual Report,* 1992.

Exhibit 13-2. A Statement of Stockholders' Equity

Tri-State Corporation
Statement of Stockholders' Equity
For the Year Ended December 31, 19x2

	Preferred Stock $100 Par Value 8% Convertible	Common Stock $10 Par Value	Paid-in Capital in Excess of Par Value, Common	Retained Earnings	Treasury Stock	Total
Balance, December 31, 19x1	$400,000	$300,000	$300,000	$600,000	—	$1,600,000
Issuance of 5,000 Shares of Common Stock		50,000	200,000			250,000
Conversion of 1,000 Shares of Preferred Stock into 3,000 Shares of Common Stock	(100,000)	30,000	70,000			—
10 Percent Stock Dividend on Common Stock, 3,800 Shares		38,000	152,000	(190,000)		—
Purchase of 500 Shares of Treasury Stock					($24,000)	(24,000)
Net Income				270,000		270,000
Cash Dividends						
Preferred Stock				(24,000)		(24,000)
Common Stock				(47,600)		(47,600)
Balance, December 31, 19x2	$300,000	$418,000	$722,000	$608,400	($24,000)	$2,024,400

conversion of $100,000 of preferred stock into common stock, declared and issued a 10 percent stock dividend on common stock, had a net purchase of treasury shares of $24,000, earned net income of $270,000, and paid cash dividends on both preferred and common stock. The ending balances of the accounts are presented at the bottom of the statement. These accounts and balances make up the stockholders' equity section of Tri-State's balance sheet on December 31, 19x2, as shown in Exhibit 13-3. Notice that the Retained Earnings column has the same components as would the statement of retained earnings.

STOCK VALUES

The word *value* is associated with shares of stock in several ways. The terms *par value* and *stated value* already have been explained. They are each values per share that establish the legal capital of a company. Par value or stated value is set arbitrarily when the stock is authorized. Neither has any relationship to a stock's book value or market value.

Exhibit 13-3. Stockholders' Equity Section of a Balance Sheet

**Tri-State Corporation
Stockholders' Equity
December 31, 19x2**

Contributed Capital		
Preferred Stock—$100 par value, 8% convertible, 10,000 shares authorized, 3,000 shares issued and outstanding		$ 300,000
Common Stock—$10 par value, 100,000 shares authorized, 41,800 shares issued, 41,300 shares outstanding	$418,000	
Paid-in Capital in Excess of Par Value, Common	722,000	1,140,000
Total Contributed Capital		$1,440,000
Retained Earnings		608,400
Total Contributed Capital and Retained Earnings		$2,048,400
Less Treasury Stock, Common (500 shares, at cost)		24,000
Total Stockholders' Equity		$2,024,400

OBJECTIVE

5 *Calculate book value per share and distinguish it from market value*

BOOK VALUE

The book value of a company's stock represents the total assets of the company less its liabilities. It is simply the stockholders' equity of the company or, to look at it another way, the company's net assets. The book value per share, therefore, represents the equity of the owner of one share of stock in the net assets of the corporation. This value, of course, does not necessarily equal the amount the shareholder would receive if the company were sold or liquidated. It is probably different because most assets are recorded at historical cost, not at the current value at which they could be sold.

To determine the book value per share when the company has only common stock outstanding, divide the total stockholders' equity by the total common shares outstanding. In computing the shares outstanding, common stock distributable is included, but treasury stock (shares previously issued and now held by the company) is not included. For example, suppose that Caprock Corporation has total stockholders' equity of $1,030,000 and 29,000 shares outstanding after recording the purchase of treasury shares. The book value per share of Caprock's common stock is $35.52 ($1,030,000 ÷ 29,000 shares).

If a company has both preferred and common stock, the determination of book value per share is not so simple. The general rule is that the call value (or par value, if a call value is not specified) of the preferred stock plus any dividends in arrears is subtracted from total stockholders' equity to figure the equity pertaining to common stock. As an illustration, refer to the stockholders' equity section of Tri-State Corporation's balance sheet in Exhibit 13-3 above. Assuming that there are no dividends in arrears and the preferred stock is callable at $105, the equity pertaining to common stock is figured as shown at the top of the next page.

Total stockholders' equity	$2,024,400
Less equity allocated to preferred shareholders	
(3,000 shares × $105)	315,000
Equity pertaining to common shareholders	$1,709,400

There are 41,300 shares of common stock outstanding (41,800 shares issued less 500 shares of treasury stock). The book values per share are as follows:

Preferred Stock: $315,000 ÷ 3,000 shares = $105 per share
Common Stock: $1,709,400 ÷ 41,300 shares = $41.39 per share

If we assume the same facts except that the preferred stock is 8 percent cumulative and that one year of dividends is in arrears, the stockholders' equity would be allocated as follows:

Total stockholders' equity		$2,024,400
Less: Call value of outstanding preferred shares	$315,000	
Dividends in arrears ($300,000 × .08)	24,000	
Equity allocated to preferred shareholders		339,000
Equity pertaining to common shareholders		$1,685,400

The book values per share here are as follows:

Preferred Stock: $339,000 ÷ 3,000 shares = $113 per share
Common Stock: $1,685,400 ÷ 41,300 shares = $40.81 per share

Undeclared preferred dividends fall into arrears on the last day of the fiscal year (the date when the financial statements are prepared). Also, dividends in arrears do not apply to unissued preferred stock.

BUSINESS BULLETIN: BUSINESS PRACTICE

In a dramatic demonstration that investor expectations drive the market value of a company's stock, Eastman Kodak's stock price plunged nearly 12 percent in one day, from $63 to $55.50 per share, after the new chairman, George Fisher, warned financial analysts that their 1994 earnings estimates were too high. Fisher said that cost cutting alone would not overcome Kodak's poor showing in recent years and that the company would have to build a foundation for growth. Analysts had thought the new chairman would move faster to improve earnings. They are now revising their earnings estimates downward, which will negatively affect the stock price over the next year.[7]

MARKET VALUE

Market value is the price that investors are willing to pay for a share of stock on the open market. Whereas book value is based on historical cost, market

7. Joan E. Rigdon, "Kodak's Stock Plunges, Chairman Says Analysts' 1994 Forecasts Are High," *Wall Street Journal*, December 16, 1993.

value usually is determined by investors' expectations for the particular company and general economic conditions. That is, people's expectations about the company's future profitability and dividends per share, their perceptions of the risk attached to the company and of its current financial condition, and the state of the money market all play a part in determining the market value of a corporation's stock. Although book value per share often bears little relationship to market value per share, some investors use the relationship between the two measures as rough indicators of the relative value of the stock. For example, in early 1991, a large automobile company, Chrysler Corporation, had a market value per share of $14 and a book value per share of $31. By early 1994, the book value per share had dropped to $26 because of losses, but the market value of the stock had climbed to $54. Other factors being equal, investors were more optimistic about Chrysler's prospects in 1994 than they were in 1991.

THE CORPORATE INCOME STATEMENT

OBJECTIVE

6 *Prepare a corporate income statement*

This chapter and the chapter on contributed capital show how certain transactions are reflected in the stockholders' equity section of the corporate balance sheet and in the statement of retained earnings. A separate chapter deals with the statement of cash flows. The following sections briefly describe some of the features of the corporate income statement.

Accounting organizations have not specified the format of the income statement because flexibility has been considered more important than a standard format. Either the single-step or the multistep form can be used (see the chapter on financial reporting and analysis). However, the accounting profession has taken the position that income for a period should be all-inclusive, and, therefore, should represent comprehensive income.[8] This rule means that the income or loss for a period should include all revenues, expenses, gains, and losses over the period, except for prior period adjustments. This approach to the measurement of income has resulted in several items being added to the income statement, among them discontinued operations, extraordinary items, and accounting changes. In addition, earnings per share figures must be disclosed. Exhibit 13-4 illustrates a corporate income statement and the required disclosures. The following sections discuss the components of the corporate income statement, beginning with income taxes expense.

OBJECTIVE

7 *Show the relationships among income taxes expense, deferred income taxes, and net of taxes*

INCOME TAXES EXPENSE

Corporations determine their taxable income (the amount on which taxes are paid) by subtracting allowable business deductions from taxable gross income. The federal tax laws determine what business deductions are allowed and what must be included in taxable gross income.[9]

The tax rates that apply to a corporation's taxable income are shown in Table 13-1. A corporation with taxable income of $70,000 would have a federal

8. *Statement of Financial Accounting Concepts No. 6,* "Elements of Financial Statements" (Stamford, Conn.: Financial Accounting Standards Board, 1985), pars. 70–77.

9. Rules for calculating and reporting taxable income in specialized industries such as banking, insurance, mutual funds, and cooperatives are highly technical and may vary significantly from those discussed in this chapter.

Exhibit 13-4. A Corporate Income Statement

Junction Corporation
Income Statement
For the Year Ended December 31, 19xx

Revenues		$925,000
Less Costs and Expenses		500,000
Income from Continuing Operations Before Taxes		$425,000
Income Taxes Expense		119,000
Income from Continuing Operations		$306,000
Discontinued Operations		
Income from Operations of Discontinued Segment		
(net of taxes, $35,000)	$90,000	
Loss on Disposal of Segment (net of taxes, $42,000)	(73,000)	17,000
Income Before Extraordinary Items and		
Cumulative Effect of Accounting Change		$323,000
Extraordinary Gain (net of taxes, $17,000)		43,000
Subtotal		$366,000
Cumulative Effect of a Change in Accounting		
Principle (net of taxes, $5,000)		(6,000)
Net Income		$360,000
Earnings per Common Share:		
Income from Continuing Operations		$ 3.06
Discontinued Operations (net of taxes)		.17
Income Before Extraordinary Items and		
Cumulative Effect of Accounting Change		$ 3.23
Extraordinary Gain (net of taxes)		.43
Cumulative Effect of Accounting Change		
(net of taxes)		(.06)
Net Income		$ 3.60

Table 13-1. Tax Rate Schedule for Corporations, 1993*

Taxable Income		Tax Liability		
Over	But Not Over			Of the Amount Over
—	$ 50,000	0 + 15%		—
$ 50,000	75,000	$ 7,500 + 25%		$ 50,000
75,000	100,000	13,750 + 34%		75,000
100,000	335,000	22,250 + 39%		100,000
335,000	10,000,000	113,900 + 34%		335,000
10,000,000	15,000,000	3,496,650 + 35%		10,000,000
15,000,000	18,333,333	5,246,650 + 38%		15,000,000
18,333,333	—	6,513,317 + 35%		18,333,333

*Tax rates are subject to change by Congress.

income tax liability of $12,500: $7,500 (the tax on the first $50,000 of taxable income) plus $5,000 (25 percent of the $20,000 earned in excess of $50,000).

Income taxes expense is the expense recognized in the accounting records on an accrual basis to be applicable to income from continuing operations. This expense may or may not equal the amount of taxes actually paid by the corporation and recorded as income taxes payable in the current period. The amount payable is determined from taxable income, which is measured according to the rules and regulations of the income tax code. For convenience, most small businesses keep accounting records on the same basis as tax records so that the income taxes expense on the income statement equals the income taxes liability to be paid to the Internal Revenue Service (IRS). This practice is acceptable when there is no material difference between the income on an accounting basis and the income on an income tax basis. However, the purpose of accounting is to determine net income in accordance with generally accepted accounting principles, not to determine taxable income and tax liability.

Management has an incentive to use methods that minimize the firm's tax liability, but accountants, who are bound by accrual accounting and the materiality concept, cannot let tax procedures dictate their method of preparing financial statements if the result would be misleading. As a consequence, there can be a material difference between accounting and taxable incomes, especially in larger businesses. This difference between accounting and taxable incomes can result from differences in the timing of the recognition of revenues and expenses because of different methods used. Some possible alternatives are shown below.

Topic	Accounting Method	Tax Method
Expense recognition	Accrual or deferral	At time of expenditure
Accounts receivable	Allowance	Direct charge-off
Inventories	Average-cost	FIFO
Depreciation	Straight-line	Modified Accelerated Cost Recovery System (see the chapter on long-term assets)

BUSINESS BULLETIN: ETHICS IN PRACTICE

Generally accepted accounting principles allow companies considerable latitude in reporting certain gains and losses, but this latitude should not be used to mask the true situation. Although Rodman & Renshaw Capital Group Inc., a large Chicago brokerage firm, was rumored to have had a large loss in the fourth quarter ended June 25, 1993, the company reported that its earnings would be $854,000 for the period, including a gain on the sale of its London-based futures and options business. Even with the gain, earnings were expected to be "close to zero." The company was involved in negotiations to sell its business and needed to report good earnings. It turned out that the firm's auditors would not allow the company to record the gain because the sale had not been closed at the end of the quarter. In the final analysis, the company reported a net loss of $375,000 for the period.[10] ═════

DEFERRED INCOME TAXES

Accounting for the difference between income taxes expense based on accounting income and the actual income taxes payable based on taxable income is accomplished by a technique called income tax allocation. The amount by which income taxes expense differs from income taxes payable is reconciled in an account called Deferred Income Taxes. For example, suppose Junction Corporation shows income taxes expense of $119,000 on its income statement but has actual income taxes payable to the IRS of $92,000. The entry to record the estimated income taxes expense applicable to income from continuing operations using the income tax allocation procedure would be as follows:

Dec. 31	Income Taxes Expense	119,000	
	Income Taxes Payable		92,000
	Deferred Income Taxes		27,000
	To record estimated current and deferred income taxes		

In other years, it is possible for Income Taxes Payable to exceed Income Taxes Expense, in which case the same entry is made except that Deferred Income Taxes is debited.

The Financial Accounting Standards Board has issued new rules for recording, measuring, and classifying deferred income taxes.[11] When the Deferred Income Taxes account has a credit balance, which is its normal balance, it is classified as a liability on the balance sheet. Whether it is classified as a current or long-term (noncurrent) liability depends on when the timing difference is expected to reverse (to have the opposite effect). For instance, if an income tax deferral is caused by an expenditure that is deducted for income tax purposes in one year but is not an expense for accounting purposes until the next year, the deferral that is present in the first year will reverse in the second year. In this case, the income tax deferral in the first year is classified as a current liability. On the other hand, if the deferral is not expected to reverse for more than one year, the deferred income taxes are classified as a long-term liability. This situation can occur when the income tax deferral is caused by a difference in depreciation methods for items of plant and equipment that have useful lives of more than one year. In other words, an income tax liability is classified as short term or long term based on the nature of the transactions that gave rise to the deferral and the expected date of reversal.

The Deferred Income Taxes account can have a debit balance, in which case it should be classified as an asset. In this situation, the company has prepaid its income taxes because total income taxes paid exceed income taxes expensed. Classification of the debit balance as a current asset or as a long-term asset follows the same rules as for liabilities, but the amount of the asset is subject to certain limitations, which are covered in more advanced courses.

---

10. "Timing Is Everything," *Crain's Chicago Business,* October 16, 1993.
11. *Statement of Financial Accounting Standards No. 96,* "Accounting for Income Taxes" (Stamford, Conn.: Financial Accounting Standards Board, 1987).

Each year, the balance of the Deferred Income Taxes account is evaluated to determine whether it still accurately represents the expected asset or liability in light of legislated changes in income tax laws and regulations in the current year. If changes have occurred in the income tax laws, an adjusting entry is required to bring the account balance into line with the current laws. For example, a decrease in corporate income tax rates, like the one that occurred in 1987, means that a company with deferred income tax liabilities will pay less taxes in future years than indicated by the credit balance of its Deferred Income Taxes account. As a result, it would debit Deferred Income Taxes to reduce the liability and credit Gain from Reduction in Income Tax Rates. This credit increases the reported income on the income statement. If the tax rate increases in future years, a loss would be recorded and the deferred income tax liability increased.

In any given year, the amount a company pays in income taxes is determined by subtracting (or adding, as the case may be) the deferred income taxes for that year (as reported in the notes to the financial statements) from (or to) income taxes expense, which also is reported in the notes to the financial statements. In subsequent years, the amount of deferred income taxes can vary based on changes in tax laws and rates.

Some understanding of the importance of deferred income taxes to financial reporting can be gained from studying the financial statements of six hundred large companies surveyed in a recent year. About 82 percent reported deferred income taxes with a credit balance in the long-term liability section of the balance sheet.[12] About 8 percent reported deferred income taxes as a current liability.[13]

NET OF TAXES

The phrase net of taxes, as used in Exhibit 13-4 and in the discussion below, means that the effect of applicable taxes (usually income taxes) has been considered in determining the overall effect of the item on the financial statements. The phrase is used on the corporate income statement when a company has items (such as those explained below) that must be disclosed in a separate section of the income statement. Each of these items should be reported net of the income taxes applicable to that item to avoid distorting the net operating income figure.

For example, assume that a corporation with $120,000 operating income before taxes has a total tax liability of $66,000 based on taxable income, which is high because it includes a capital gain of $100,000 on which a tax of $30,000 is due. Assume also that the gain is an extraordinary item (see Extraordinary Items, pages 590–591) and must be disclosed as such. This is how the tax liability would be reported on the income statement:

Income from Continuing Operations Before Taxes	$120,000
Income Taxes Expense (actual taxes are $66,000, of which $30,000 is applicable to extraordinary gain)	36,000
Income Before Extraordinary Item	$ 84,000
Extraordinary Gain (net of taxes) ($100,000 − $30,000)	70,000
Net Income	$154,000

---

12. American Institute of Certified Public Accountants, *Accounting Trends & Techniques* (New York: AICPA, 1990), p. 178.
13. Ibid., p. 153.

If all the taxes payable were deducted from operating income before taxes, both the income before extraordinary items and the extraordinary gain would be distorted.

A company follows the same procedure in the case of an extraordinary loss. For example, assume the same facts as before except that total tax liability is only $6,000 because of a $100,000 extraordinary loss, which results in a $30,000 tax saving, as shown below.

Operating Income Before Taxes	$120,000
Income Taxes Expense (actual taxes of $6,000 as a result of an extraordinary loss)	36,000
Income Before Extraordinary Item	$ 84,000
Extraordinary Loss (net of taxes) ($100,000 − $30,000)	(70,000)
Net Income	$ 14,000

In Exhibit 13-4, the total of the income tax items is $124,000. This amount is allocated among five statement components, as follows:

Income taxes expense on income from continuing operations	$119,000
Income tax on income from a discontinued segment	35,000
Income tax saving on the loss on disposal of the segment	(42,000)
Income tax on the extraordinary gain	17,000
Income tax saving on the cumulative effect of a change in accounting principle	(5,000)
Total income taxes expense	$124,000

Pennzoil Company

DECISION POINT

Someone who does not understand the structure and use of corporate income statements may be confused by corporate earnings reports in the financial press. Pennzoil Company, a major oil and gas producer, reported net income of $21 million in 1991 and $128 million in 1992. Despite this seemingly tremendous increase in earnings, there was actually a decline from $40 million to $17 million in the company's income from operations.[14] How could Pennzoil Company have both a large rise in net income and a large decrease in operating earnings? What approach should the user take to analyze the corporate income statement?

As will be explained in the following sections, the corporate income statement has several components. On closer examination, Pennzoil had a negative $49 million cumulative effect of change in accounting principle in 1991 as a result of the change in accounting for postretirement benefits other than pensions under SFAS No. 106. It also experienced a positive $116 million cumulative effect from the change in accounting for income taxes under SFAS No. 109. In addition, in 1992 the company experienced

14. Pennzoil Company, *Annual Report*, 1992.

an extraordinary loss of almost $17 million and a gain on sale of certain operations of $1.5 billion.[15] Because of the complexity of the corporate income statement, analysts have learned not to look at just the bottom line but to study carefully the components of the corporate income statement to discover the long-term outlook for the company. ⋮⋮⋮⋮⋮

DISCONTINUED OPERATIONS

OBJECTIVE

8 *Describe the disclosure on the income statement of discontinued operations, extraordinary items, and accounting changes*

Large companies in the United States usually have many segments. A segment of a business can be a separate major line of business or serve a separate class of customer. For example, a company that makes heavy drilling equipment may also have another line of business, such as the manufacture of mobile homes. These large companies may discontinue or otherwise dispose of certain segments of their business that do not fit in with the company's future plans or are not profitable. Discontinued operations are segments of a business that are no longer part of its ongoing operations. Generally accepted accounting principles require that gains and losses from discontinued operations be reported separately in the income statement. The reason for this requirement is that the income statement is more useful for evaluating the ongoing activities of the business if results from continuing operations are reported separately from those of discontinued operations.

In Exhibit 13-4, the disclosure of discontinued operations has two parts. One part shows that the income during the year from operations of the segment of the business that has been disposed of (or will be disposed of) after the date of the decision to discontinue was $90,000 (net of $35,000 taxes). The other part shows that the loss from the disposal of the segment was $73,000 (net of $42,000 tax savings). Computation of the gains or losses is covered in more advanced accounting courses. The disclosure has been described, however, to give a complete view of the corporate income statement.

EXTRAORDINARY ITEMS

The Accounting Principles Board, in its *Opinion No. 30*, defines extraordinary items as those "events or transactions that are distinguished by their unusual nature *and* by the infrequency of their occurrence."[16] As stated in the definition, the major criteria for extraordinary items are that they must be unusual and must not happen very often. Unusual and infrequent occurrences are explained in the opinion as follows:

> Unusual Nature—the underlying event or transaction should possess a high degree of abnormality and be of a type clearly unrelated to, or only incidentally related to, the ordinary and typical activities of the entity, taking into account the environment in which the entity operates.

> Infrequency of Occurrence—the underlying event or transaction should be of a type that would not reasonably be expected to recur in the foreseeable future, taking into account the environment in which the entity operates.[17]

If an item is both unusual and infrequent (and material in amount), it should be reported separately from continuing operations on the income statement. This disclosure allows the reader of the statement to identify gains

---

15. Ibid.
16. Accounting Principles Board, *Opinion No. 30*, "Reporting the Results of Operations" (New York: American Institute of Certified Public Accountants, 1973), par. 20.
17. Ibid.

or losses shown in the computation of income that would not be expected to happen again soon. Items that usually are treated as extraordinary include (1) an uninsured loss from flood, earthquake, fire, or theft; (2) a gain or loss resulting from the passage of a new law; (3) the expropriation (taking) of property by a foreign government; and (4) a gain or loss from early retirement of debt. Gains or losses from extraordinary items should be reported on the income statement after discontinued operations. And they should be shown net of applicable taxes. In a recent year, fifty-eight (10 percent) of six hundred large companies reported extraordinary items on their income statements.[18] In Exhibit 13-4, the extraordinary gain was $43,000 after applicable taxes of $17,000.

ACCOUNTING CHANGES

Consistency, one of the basic conventions of accounting, means that for accounting purposes, companies must apply the same accounting principles from year to year. However, a company is allowed to make accounting changes if current procedures are incorrect or inappropriate. For example, a change from the FIFO to the LIFO inventory method can be made if there is adequate justification for the change. Adequate justification usually means that if the change occurs, the financial statements will better show the financial activities of the company. A company's wanting to lower the amount of income taxes it pays is not an adequate justification for an accounting change. If justification does exist and an accounting change is made during an accounting period, generally accepted accounting principles require the disclosure of the change in the financial statements.

The cumulative effect of an accounting change is the effect that the new accounting principle would have had on net income in prior periods if it, instead of the old principle, had been applied. This effect is shown on the income statement immediately after extraordinary items.[19] For example, assume that in the five years previous to 19xx, the Junction Corporation used the straight-line method to depreciate its machinery. This year, the company changes to the double-declining balance method of depreciation. The following depreciation charges (net of taxes) were arrived at by the controller:

Cumulative, 5-year double-declining balance depreciation	$16,000
Less cumulative, 5-year straight-line depreciation	10,000
Cumulative effect of accounting change	$ 6,000

Relevant information, such as the reasons for and the effects of the accounting change, is shown in the notes to the financial statements. The $6,000 difference (net of $5,000 income tax savings) is the cumulative effect of the change in depreciation methods. The change results in an additional $6,000 (net of taxes) depreciation expense for prior years being deducted in the current year in addition to the current year's depreciation costs included in the $500,000 costs and expenses section of the income statement. This expense must be shown in the current year's income statement as a reduction in income (see Exhibit 13-4). In a recent year, ninety (15 percent) of

18. American Institute of Certified Public Accountants, *Accounting Trends & Techniques* (New York: AICPA, 1992), p. 338.

19. Accounting Principles Board, *Opinion No. 20*, "Accounting Changes" (New York: American Institute of Certified Public Accountants, 1971), par. 20.

six hundred large companies reported changes in accounting procedures.[20] Further study of accounting changes is left to more advanced accounting courses.

OBJECTIVE

9 *Compute earnings per share*

EARNINGS PER SHARE

Readers of financial statements use earnings per share information to judge a company's performance and to compare that performance with the performance of other companies. The Accounting Principles Board recognized the importance of this information in its *Opinion No. 15*. There it concludes that earnings per share of common stock should be presented on the face of the income statement.[21] As shown in Exhibit 13-4, the information generally is disclosed just below the net income figure.

An earnings per share amount is always shown for (1) income from continuing operations, (2) income before extraordinary items and the cumulative effect of accounting changes, (3) the cumulative effect of accounting changes, and (4) net income. If the statement shows a gain or loss from discontinued operations or a gain or loss on extraordinary items, earnings per share amounts also can be presented for these items. The per share data from the income statement of Bally Manufacturing Corporation shows why it is a good idea to study the components of earnings per share.[22]

	Years ended December 31		
	1992	**1991**	**1990**
Per Common Share:			
Loss from continuing operations	($.05)	($1.79)	($10.22)
Discontinued operations—			
Income (loss) from operations		.16	(.35)
Gain on disposal of businesses		.53	
Extraordinary items—			
Credit for utilization of tax loss carryforwards	.26		
Gain on extinguishment of debt	.01	1.65	.42
Net income (loss)	$.22	$ .55	($10.15)

A basic earnings per share amount is found when a company has only common stock and has the same number of shares outstanding throughout the year. For example, Exhibit 13-4 tells us that Junction Corporation, with a net income of $360,000, had 100,000 shares of common stock outstanding for the entire year. The earnings per share of common stock were computed as follows:

$$\text{Earnings per share} = \frac{\text{net income}}{\text{shares outstanding}}$$

$$= \frac{\$360,000}{100,000 \text{ shares}}$$

$$= \$3.60 \text{ per share}$$

20. *Accounting Trends & Techniques* (New York: American Institute of Certified Public Accountants, 1992), p. 481.
21. Accounting Principles Board, *Opinion No. 15*, "Earnings per Share" (New York: American Institute of Certified Public Accountants, 1969), par. 12.
22. Bally Manufacturing Corporation, *Annual Report*, 1992.

If the number of shares outstanding changes during the year, it is necessary to figure a weighted-average number of shares outstanding for the year. Suppose that Junction Corporation had the following amounts of common shares outstanding during various periods of the year: January–March, 100,000 shares; April–September, 120,000 shares; and October–December, 130,000 shares. The weighted-average number of common shares outstanding and earnings per share would be found this way:

100,000 shares × ¼ year	25,000
120,000 shares × ½ year	60,000
130,000 shares × ¼ year	32,500
Weighted-average shares outstanding	117,500

$$\text{Earnings per share} = \frac{\$360,000}{117,500 \text{ shares}}$$

$$= \$3.06 \text{ per share}$$

If a company has nonconvertible preferred stock outstanding, the dividend for the stock must be subtracted from net income before earnings per share for common stock are computed. Suppose that Junction Corporation has preferred stock on which the annual dividend is $23,500. Earnings per share on common stock would be $2.86 [($360,000 − $23,500) ÷ 117,500 shares].

Companies with a capital structure in which there are no bonds, preferred stock, or stock options that could be converted into common stock are said to have a simple capital structure. The earnings per share for these companies are computed as shown on the previous page. Some companies, however, have a complex capital structure, which includes convertible stock and bonds. These convertible securities have the potential of diluting the earnings per share of common stock. *Potential dilution* means that a person's proportionate share of ownership in a company could be reduced through a conversion of stocks or bonds or the exercise of stock options, which would increase the total shares outstanding.

For example, suppose that a person owns 10,000 shares of a company, which equals 2 percent of the outstanding shares of 500,000. Now, suppose that holders of convertible bonds convert the bonds into 100,000 shares of stock. The person's 10,000 shares then would be only 1.67 percent (10,000 ÷ 600,000) of the outstanding shares. And the added shares outstanding would lower earnings per share and most likely would lower market price per share.

Because stock options and convertible preferred stocks or bonds have the potential to dilute earnings per share, they are referred to as potentially dilutive securities. A special subset of these convertible securities is called common stock equivalents because these securities are considered to be similar to common stock. A convertible preferred stock or bond is considered a common stock equivalent if the conversion feature is an important part of determining its original issue price. Special rules are applied by the accountant to determine if a convertible preferred stock or bond is a common stock equivalent. A stock option, on the other hand, is by definition a common stock equivalent. The significance of common stock equivalents is that when they exist, they are used in the earnings per share calculations explained in the next paragraph.

When a company has a complex capital structure, it must report two earnings per share figures: primary earnings per share and fully diluted earnings per share. Primary earnings per share are calculated by including in the denominator the total of weighted-average common shares outstanding and common stock equivalents. Fully diluted earnings per share are calculated by including in the denominator the additional potentially dilutive securities that are not common stock equivalents. The latter figure shows stockholders the maximum potential effect of dilution of their ownership in the company. Here is an example of this type of disclosure for the Tribune Company, a leading newspaper, broadcasting, and entertainment company:[23]

Net Income (Loss) Per Share	1992	1991
Primary:		
Before cumulative effects of changes in accounting principles	$1.82	$1.94
Cumulative effects of accounting changes, net	(.26)	—
Net income (loss)	$1.56	$1.94
Fully diluted:		
Before cumulative effects of changes in accounting principles	$1.70	$1.83
Cumulative effects of accounting changes, net	(.24)	—
Net income (loss)	$1.46	$1.83

The computation of these figures is a complex process reserved for more advanced courses.

BUSINESS BULLETIN:

Sometimes a change in accounting principle is mandated by the Financial Accounting Standards Board. For many companies, such a change has a dramatic effect on reported earnings. In 1992, Xerox Corporation, a major document processing company, reported a one-time mandated charge of $606 million for adopting SFAS No. 106 for post-retirement benefits other than pensions and a charge of $158 million for adopting SFAS No. 109 for accounting for income taxes. The total was reported on the income statement as a negative $764 million cumulative effect of a change in accounting principle, which, combined with the company's loss from operations of $256 million, gave a total net loss of $1.02 billion.

CHAPTER REVIEW

REVIEW OF LEARNING OBJECTIVES

1. **Define *retained earnings* and prepare a statement of retained earnings.** Retained earnings are the part of stockholders' equity that comes from retaining assets earned in business operations. They represent the claims of the stockholders against the assets of the company that arise from profitable operations. Retained earnings are different from contributed capital, which represents the claims against assets brought about by the initial and subsequent investments by the stockholders.

23. Tribune Company, *Annual Report*, 1992.

Both are claims against the general assets of the company, not against any specific assets that have been set aside. It is important not to confuse the assets themselves with the claims against the assets. The statement of retained earnings always shows the beginning and ending balance of retained earnings, net income or loss, and cash dividends. It also can show prior period adjustments, stock dividends, and other transactions that affect retained earnings.

2. **Account for stock dividends and stock splits.** A stock dividend is a proportional distribution of shares of the company's stock by a corporation to its stockholders. Here is a summary of the key dates and accounting treatment of stock dividends:

Key Date	**Stock Dividend**
Date of declaration	Debit Stock Dividends Declared for the market value of the stock to be distributed (if it is a small stock dividend), and credit Common Stock Distributable for the stock's par value and Paid-in Capital in Excess of Par Value, Common for the excess of the market value over the stock's par value.
Date of record	No entry.
Date of distribution	Debit Common Stock Distributable and credit Common Stock for the par value of the stock that has been distributed.

A stock split usually is undertaken to reduce the market value and improve the liquidity of a company's stock. Because there is normally a decrease in the par value of the stock in proportion to the number of additional shares issued, a stock split has no effect on the dollar amounts in the stockholders' equity accounts. The split should be recorded in the general journal by a memorandum entry only.

3. **Describe the disclosure of restrictions on retained earnings.** A restriction on retained earnings means that dividends can be declared only to the extent of unrestricted retained earnings. A corporation may be bound by contractual agreement or state law to restrict retained earnings, or it may do so voluntarily, to retain assets in the business for a plant expansion or a possible loss in a lawsuit. A restriction on retained earnings can be disclosed in two ways: in the stockholders' equity section of the balance sheet or, more commonly, as a note to the financial statements. Once a restriction is removed, its disclosure can be removed from the financial statements.

4. **Prepare a statement of stockholders' equity.** A statement of stockholders' equity shows changes over the period in each component (account) of the stockholders' equity section of the balance sheet. This statement reveals much more about the transactions that adjust stockholders' equity than does the statement of retained earnings.

5. **Calculate book value per share and distinguish it from market value.** Book value per share is the stockholders' equity per share. It is calculated by dividing stockholders' equity by the number of common shares outstanding plus shares distributable. When a company has both preferred and common stock, the call or par value of the preferred stock plus any dividends in arrears is deducted from total stockholders' equity before dividing by the common shares outstanding. Market value per share is the price investors are willing to pay based on their expectations about the future earning ability of the company and general economic conditions.

6. **Prepare a corporate income statement.** The corporate income statement shows comprehensive income—all revenues, expenses, gains, and losses for the accounting period, except for prior period adjustments. The top part of the corporate income statement includes all revenues, costs and expenses, and income taxes that pertain to continuing operations. The bottom part of the statement contains any or all of the following: discontinued operations, extraordinary items, and the cumulative effect of a change in accounting principle. Earnings per share data should be shown at the bottom of the statement, below net income.

7. **Show the relationships among income taxes expense, deferred income taxes, and net of taxes.** Income taxes expense is the taxes applicable to income from operations on an accrual basis. Income tax allocation is necessary when differences

between accrual-based accounting income and taxable income cause a material difference between income taxes expense as shown on the income statement and actual income tax liability. The difference between income taxes expense and income taxes payable is debited or credited to an account called Deferred Income Taxes. *Net of taxes* is a phrase used to indicate that the effect of taxes has been considered when showing an item on the income statement after income from continuing opreations.

8. **Describe the disclosure on the income statement of discontinued operations, extraordinary items, and accounting changes.** There are several accounting items that must be disclosed separately from continuing operations and net of income taxes on the income statement because of their unusual nature. These items include a gain or loss on discontinued operations and on extraordinary gains or losses, and the cumulative effect of accounting changes.

9. **Compute earnings per share.** Stockholders and other readers of financial statements use earnings per share data to evaluate a company's performance and to compare that performance with the performance of other companies. Therefore, earnings per share data are presented on the face of the income statement. The amounts are computed by dividing the income applicable to common stock by the common shares outstanding for the year. If the number of shares outstanding has varied during the year, then the weighted-average shares outstanding should be used in the computation. When the company has a complex capital structure, both primary and fully diluted earnings per share data must be disclosed on the face of the income statement.

REVIEW OF CONCEPTS AND TERMINOLOGY

The following concepts and terms were introduced in this chapter:

L O 5 **Book value:** The total assets of a company less its liabilities; stockholders' equity.

L O 9 **Common stock equivalents:** Convertible preferred stocks or bonds whose conversion feature is an important part of determining their original issue price.

L O 9 **Complex capital structure:** A capital structure that includes securities (convertible preferred stocks and bonds) that can be converted into common stock.

L O 6 **Comprehensive income:** The concept of income or loss for a period that includes all revenues, expenses, gains, and losses, except prior period adjustments.

L O 8 **Cumulative effect of an accounting change:** The effect that a new accounting principle would have had on the net income of prior periods if it had been used instead of the old principle.

L O 7 **Deferred Income Taxes:** The account used to record the difference between the Income Taxes Expense and the Income Taxes Payable accounts.

L O 1 **Deficit:** A debit balance in the Retained Earnings account.

L O 8 **Discontinued operations:** Segments of a business that are no longer part of the ongoing operations of the company.

L O 8 **Extraordinary items:** Events or transactions that are both unusual in nature and infrequent in occurrence.

L O 9 **Fully diluted earnings per share:** The net income applicable to common stock divided by the sum of the weighted average of common shares outstanding and common stock equivalents and other potentially dilutive securities.

L O 7 **Income tax allocation:** An accounting method used to accrue income taxes expense on the basis of accounting income whenever there are differences between accounting and taxable income.

L O 5 **Market value:** The price investors are willing to pay for a share of stock on the open market.

L O 7 **Net of taxes:** Taking into account the effect of applicable taxes (usually income taxes) on an item to determine the overall effect of the item on the financial statements.

L O 9 **Potentially dilutive securities:** Stock options and convertible preferred stocks or bonds, which have the potential to dilute earnings per share.

L O 9   **Primary earnings per share:** The net income applicable to common stock divided by the sum of the weighted average of common shares outstanding and common stock equivalents.

L O 1   **Prior period adjustments:** Events or transactions that relate to earlier accounting periods that could not be determined in the earlier periods.

L O 3   **Restriction on retained earnings:** The required or voluntary restriction of a portion of retained earnings that cannot be used to pay dividends.

L O 1   **Retained earnings:** Stockholders' claims to assets arising from the earnings of the business; the accumulated earnings of a corporation from its inception, minus any losses, dividends, or transfers to contributed capital.

L O 8   **Segments:** Distinct parts of business operations, such as lines of business or classes of customer.

L O 9   **Simple capital structure:** A capital structure with no other securities (stocks or bonds) or stock options that can be converted into common stock.

L O 4   **Statement of stockholders' equity:** A financial statement that summarizes changes in the components of the stockholders' equity section of the balance sheet; also called *statement of changes in stockholders' equity.*

L O 2   **Stock dividend:** A proportional distribution of shares of a corporation's stock to its stockholders.

L O 2   **Stock split:** An increase in the number of outstanding shares of stock accompanied by a proportionate reduction in the par or stated value.

REVIEW PROBLEM
COMPREHENSIVE STOCKHOLDERS' EQUITY TRANSACTIONS

L O 1, 2, 3, 4, 5

The stockholders' equity of the Szatkowski Company on June 30, 19x5 is shown below.

Contributed Capital	
Common Stock—no par value, $6 stated value, 1,000,000 shares authorized, 250,000 shares issued and outstanding	$1,500,000
Paid-in Capital in Excess of Stated Value, Common	820,000
Total Contributed Capital	$2,320,000
Retained Earnings	970,000
Total Stockholders' Equity	$3,290,000

Stockholders' equity transactions for the next fiscal year were as follows:

a. The board of directors declared a 2 for 1 split.

b. The board of directors obtained authorization to issue 50,000 shares of $100 par value, 6 percent noncumulative preferred stock, callable at $104.

c. Issued 12,000 shares of common stock for a building appraised at $96,000.

d. Purchased 8,000 shares of the company's common stock for $64,000.

e. Issued 20,000 shares of $100 par value preferred stock for $100 per share.

f. Sold 5,000 shares of the treasury stock for $35,000.

g. Declared cash dividends of $6 per share on the preferred stock and $.20 per share on the common stock.

h. Date of record.

i. Paid the preferred and common stock cash dividends.

j. Declared a 10 percent stock dividend on the common stock. The market value was $10 per share. The stock dividend is distributable after the end of the fiscal year.

k. Net income for the year was $340,000.

l. Closed the Cash Dividends Declared and Stock Dividends Declared accounts to Retained Earnings.

Because of a loan agreement, the company is not allowed to reduce retained earnings below $100,000. The board of directors determined that this restriction should be disclosed in the notes to the financial statements.

REQUIRED

1. Make the general journal entries to record the transactions above.
2. Prepare the company's statement of retained earnings for the year ended June 30, 19x6.
3. Prepare the stockholders' equity section of the company's balance sheet on June 30, 19x6, including appropriate disclosure of the restriction on retained earnings.
4. Compute the book values per share of common stock on June 30, 19x5 and 19x6, and of preferred stock on June 30, 19x6.

ANSWER TO REVIEW PROBLEM

1. Prepare the journal entries.

   a. Memorandum entry: 2 for 1 stock split, common, resulting in 500,000 shares issued and outstanding of no par value common stock with a stated value of $3

   b. No entry required

c. Building	96,000	
Common Stock		36,000
Paid-in Capital in Excess of Stated Value, Common		60,000
Issue of 12,000 shares of common stock for a building appraised at $96,000		
d. Treasury Stock, Common	64,000	
Cash		64,000
Purchase of 8,000 shares of common stock for the treasury for $8 per share		
e. Cash	2,000,000	
Preferred Stock		2,000,000
Sale of 20,000 shares of $100 par value preferred stock at $100 per share		
f. Cash	35,000	
Retained Earnings	5,000	
Treasury Stock, Common		40,000
Sale of 5,000 shares of treasury stock for $35,000, originally purchased for $8 per share		
g. Cash Dividends Declared	221,800	
Cash Dividends Payable		221,800
Declaration of cash dividends of $6 per share on 20,000 shares of preferred stock and $.20 per share on 509,000 shares of common stock:		

$$20,000 \times \$6 \quad = \$120,000$$
$$509,000 \times \$.20 = \underline{\quad 101,800 \quad}$$
$$\underline{\underline{\$221,800}}$$

h. No entry required		
i. Cash Dividends Payable	221,800	
Cash		221,800
Paid cash dividend to preferred and common stockholders		
j. Stock Dividends Declared	509,000	
Common Stock Distributable		152,700
Paid-in Capital in Excess of Stated Value, Common		356,300
Declaration of a 50,900-share stock dividend (509,000 × .10) on $3 stated value common stock at a market value of $509,000 (50,900 × $10)		

k. Income Summary   340,000

    Retained Earnings   340,000

      To close the Income Summary account

      to Retained Earnings

l. Retained Earnings   730,800

    Cash Dividends Declared   221,800

    Stock Dividends Declared   509,000

      To close the Cash Dividends Declared

      and Stock Dividends Declared accounts

      to Retained Earnings

2. Prepare a statement of retained earnings.

Szatkowski Company
Statement of Retained Earnings
For the Year Ended June 30, 19x6

Retained Earnings, June 30, 19x5		$ 970,000
Net Income, 19x6		340,000
Subtotal		$1,310,000
Less: Cash Dividends		
Preferred	$120,000	
Common	101,800	
Stock Dividends	509,000	
Treasury Stock Transaction	5,000	735,800
Retained Earnings, June 30, 19x6 (Note x)		$ 574,200

3. Prepare the stockholders' equity section of the balance sheet.

Szatkowski Company
Stockholders' Equity
June 30, 19x6

Contributed Capital		
Preferred Stock—$100 par value, 6%		
noncumulative, 50,000 shares authorized,		
20,000 shares issued and outstanding		$2,000,000
Common Stock—no par value, $3 stated value,		
1,000,000 shares authorized, 512,000 shares		
issued, 509,000 shares outstanding	$1,536,000	
Common Stock Distributable, 50,900 shares	152,700	
Paid-in Capital in Excess of Stated Value, Common	1,236,300	2,925,000
Total Contributed Capital		$4,925,000
Retained Earnings (Note x)		574,200
Total Contributed Capital and Retained Earnings		$5,499,200
Less Treasury Stock, Common (3,000 shares at cost)		24,000
Total Stockholders' Equity		$5,475,200

Note x: The board of directors has restricted retained earnings available for dividends by the amount of $100,000 as required under a loan agreement.

4. Compute the book values.

June 30, 19x5
   Common Stock: $3,290,000 ÷ 250,000 shares = $13.16 per share
June 30, 19x6
   Preferred Stock:
      Call price of $104 per share equals book value per share
   Common Stock:
      ($5,475,200 − $2,080,000) ÷ (509,000 shares + 50,900 shares) =
      $3,395,200 ÷ 559,900 shares = $6.06 per share

CHAPTER ASSIGNMENTS

KNOWLEDGE AND UNDERSTANDING

Questions

1. What are retained earnings, and how do they relate to the assets of a corporation?
2. When does a company have a deficit in retained earnings?
3. What items are identified by generally accepted accounting principles as prior period adjustments?
4. Explain how the accounting treatment of stock dividends differs from that of cash dividends.
5. What is the difference between a stock dividend and a stock split? What is the effect of each on the capital structure of a corporation?
6. What is the purpose of restricting retained earnings?
7. What is the difference between the statement of stockholders' equity and the stockholders' equity section of the balance sheet?
8. Would you expect a corporation's book value per share to equal its market value per share? Why or why not?
9. "Accounting income should be geared to the concept of taxable income because the public understands the concept of taxable income." Comment on this statement, and tell why income tax allocation is necessary.
10. Exxon Corporation had about $11.1 billion of deferred income taxes in 1992, equal to about 20 percent of total liabilities. This percentage has risen or remained steady for many years. Given management's desire to put off the payment of taxes as long as possible, the long-term growth of the economy and inflation, and the definition of a liability (probable future sacrifices of future benefits arising from present obligations), make an argument for not accounting for deferred income taxes.
11. Why should a gain or loss on discontinued operations be disclosed separately on the income statement?
12. Explain the two major criteria for extraordinary items. How should extraordinary items be disclosed in the financial statements?
13. How are earnings per share disclosed in financial statements?
14. When an accounting change occurs, what disclosures in the financial statements are necessary?
15. When does a company have a simple capital structure? A complex capital structure?
16. What is the difference between primary and fully diluted earnings per share?

Short Exercises

SE 13-1.
L O 1 *Statement of Retained Earnings*

The Snadhu Corporation had a balance in Retained Earnings on December 31, 19x1 of $260,000. During 19x2, the company reported a profit of $112,000 after taxes. During 19x2, the company declared cash dividends totaling $16,000. Prepare the company's statement of retained earnings for the year ended December 31, 19x2.

SE 13-2.
L O 2 *Stock Dividends*

On February 15, Oak Plaza Corporation's board of directors declared a 2 percent stock dividend applicable to the outstanding shares of its $10 par value common stock, of which 200,000 shares are authorized, 130,000 are issued, and 20,000 are held in the treasury. The stock dividend was distributable on March 15 to stockholders of record on March 1. On February 15, the market value of the common stock was $15 per share. On March 30, the board of directors declared a $.50 per share cash dividend. No other stock transactions have occurred. Record the necessary transactions on February 15, March 1, March 15, and March 30.

SE 13-3.
L O 2 *Stock Split*

On August 10, the board of directors of Nicolau International declared a 3 for 1 stock split of its $9 par value common stock, of which 800,000 shares were authorized and 250,000 were issued and outstanding. The market value on this date was $60 per share. On the same date, the balance of Paid-in Capital in Excess of Par Value, Common was $6,000,000, and the balance of Retained Earnings was $6,500,000. Prepare the stockholders' equity section of the company's balance sheet after the stock split. What journal entry, if any, is needed to record the stock split?

SE 13-4.
L O 3 *Restriction of Retained Earnings*

Thorne Company has a lawsuit filed against it. The board has taken action to restrict retained earnings of the company in the amount of $2,500,000 on May 31, 19x1, pending the outcome. On May 31, the company had retained earnings of $3,725,000. Show two ways in which the restriction on retained earnings can be disclosed.

SE 13-5.
L O 2, 3, 4 *Effects of Stockholders' Equity Actions*

Tell whether each of the following actions will increase, decrease, or have no effect on total assets, total liabilities, and total stockholders' equity.

1. Declaration of stock dividend
2. Declaration of cash dividend
3. Stock split
4. Restriction of retained earnings
5. Purchase of treasury stock

SE 13-6.
L O 4 *Statement of Stockholders' Equity*

Refer to the statement of stockholders' equity for Tri-State Corporation in Exhibit 13-2 and answer the following questions: (1) At what price per share were the 5,000 shares of common stock sold? (2) What was the conversion price per share of the preferred stock into common stock? (3) At what price was the common stock selling on the date of the stock dividend? (4) At what price per share was the treasury stock purchased?

SE 13-7.
L O 5 *Book Value for Preferred and Common Stock*

Given the stockholders' equity section of the Giszter Corporation's balance sheet shown below, what is the book value per share for both the preferred and the common stock?

Contributed Capital

Preferred Stock—$100 per share, 8 percent cumulative, 10,000 shares authorized, 500 shares issued and outstanding*		$ 50,000
Common Stock—$10 par value, 100,000 shares authorized, 40,000 shares issued and outstanding	$400,000	
Paid-in Capital in Excess of Par Value, Common	516,000	916,000
Total Contributed Capital		$ 966,000
Retained Earnings		275,000
Total Stockholders' Equity		$1,241,000

*The preferred stock is callable at $104 per share, and one year's dividends are in arrears.

SE 13-8.
L O 6 *Corporate Income Statement*

Assume that the Diah Company's chief financial officer gave you the following information: Net Sales, $720,000; Cost of Goods Sold, $350,000; Loss from Discontinued Operations (net of income tax benefit of $70,000), $200,000; Loss on Disposal of Discontinued Operations (net of income tax benefit of $16,000), $50,000; Operating Expenses, $130,000; Income Taxes Expense on Continuing Operations, $80,000. From this information, prepare the company's income statement for the year ended June 30, 19xx. (Ignore earnings per share information.)

SE 13-9.
L O 7 *Use of Corporate Income Tax Rate Schedule*

Using the corporate tax rate schedule in Table 13-1, compute the income tax liability for taxable income of (1) $400,000 and (2) $20,000,000.

SE 13-10.
L O 9 *Earnings per Share*

During 19x1, the Junifer Corporation reported a net income of $669,200. On January 1, Junifer had 360,000 shares of common stock outstanding. The company issued an additional 240,000 shares of common stock on August 1. In 19x1, the company had a simple capital structure. During 19x2, there were no transactions involving common stock, and the company reported net income of $870,000. Determine the weighted-average number of common shares outstanding for 19x1 and 19x2. Also, compute earnings per share for 19x1 and 19x2.

APPLICATION

Exercises

E 13-1.
L O 1 *Statement of Retained Earnings*

The Drennan Corporation had a balance in Retained Earnings on December 31, 19x1 of $520,000. During 19x2, the company reported a profit of $224,000 after taxes. In addition, the company located an $88,000 (net of taxes) error that resulted in an over-statement of prior years' income and meets the criteria for a prior period adjustment. During 19x2, the company declared cash dividends totaling $32,000.

Prepare the company's statement of retained earnings for the year ended December 31, 19x2.

E 13-2.
L O 2 *Journal Entries: Stock Dividends*

The Geyer Company has 30,000 shares of its $1 par value common stock outstanding. Record the following transactions as they relate to the company's common stock:

July 17 Declared a 10 percent stock dividend on common stock to be distributed on August 10 to stockholders of record on July 31. Market value of the stock was $5 per share on this date.
        31 Record date.
Aug. 10 Distributed the stock dividend declared on July 17.
Sept. 1 Declared a $.50 per share cash dividend on common stock to be paid on September 16 to stockholders of record on September 10.

E 13-3.
L O 2 *Journal Entries: Stock Dividends*

On August 26, Shipley Corporation's board of directors declared a 2 percent stock dividend applicable to the outstanding shares of its $5 par value common stock, of which 150,000 shares are authorized, 130,000 are issued, and 10,000 are held in the treasury. The stock dividend was distributable on September 25 to stockholders of record on September 10. On August 26, the market value of the common stock was $12 per share. On November 26, the board of directors declared a $.20 per share cash dividend. No other stock transactions have occurred. Record the transactions on August 26, September 10, September 25, and November 26. Make the December 31 entry to close Cash Dividends Declared and Stock Dividends Declared to Retained Earnings.

E 13-4.
L O 2 *Stock Split*

The Colson Company currently has 200,000 shares of $1 par value common stock outstanding. There are 500,000 shares authorized. The board of directors declared a 2 for 1 split on May 15, when the market value of the common stock was $2.50 per share. The Retained Earnings balance on May 15 was $700,000. Paid-in Capital in Excess of Par Value, Common on this date was $20,000.

Prepare the stockholders' equity section of the company's balance sheet before and after the stock split. What journal entry, if any, would be necessary to record the stock split?

E 13-5.
L O 2 *Stock Split*

On January 15, the board of directors of Fuquat International declared a 3 for 1 stock split of its $12 par value common stock, of which 800,000 shares were authorized and 200,000 were issued and outstanding. The market value on this date was $45 per share. On the same date, the balance of Paid-in Capital in Excess of Par Value, Common was $4,000,000, and the balance of Retained Earnings was $8,000,000.

Prepare the stockholders' equity section of the company's balance sheet before and after the stock split. What journal entry, if any, is needed to record the stock split?

E 13-6.
L O 3 *Restriction of Retained Earnings*

The board of directors of the Geroulis Company has approved plans to acquire another company during the coming year. The acquisition should cost approximately $1,100,000. The board took action to restrict retained earnings of the company in the amount of $1,100,000 on July 17, 19x1. On July 31, the company had retained earnings of $1,950,000.

1. Show two ways the restriction on retained earnings can be disclosed.
2. Assuming the purchase takes place as planned, what effect will it have on retained earnings and future disclosures?

E 13-7.
L O 4 *Statement of Stockholders' Equity*

The stockholders' equity section of Kolb Corporation's balance sheet on December 31, 19x2 appears as follows:

Contributed Capital	
Common Stock—$2 par value, 500,000 shares	
authorized, 400,000 issued and outstanding	$ 800,000
Paid-in Capital in Excess of Par Value, Common	1,200,000
Total Contributed Capital	$2,000,000
Retained Earnings	4,200,000
Total Stockholders' Equity	$6,200,000

Prepare a statement of stockholders' equity for the year ended December 31, 19x3, assuming the following transactions occurred in sequence during 19x3:

a. Issued 10,000 shares of $100 par value, 9 percent cumulative preferred stock at par after obtaining authorization from the state.
b. Issued 40,000 shares of common stock in connection with the conversion of bonds having a carrying value of $600,000.
c. Declared and issued a 2 percent common stock dividend. The market value on the date of declaration was $14 per share.
d. Purchased 10,000 shares of common stock for the treasury at a cost of $16 per share.
e. Earned net income of $460,000.
f. Declared and paid the full year's dividend on preferred stock and a dividend of $.40 per share on common stock outstanding at the end of the year.

E 13-8.
L O 5 *Book Value for Preferred and Common Stock*

The stockholders' equity section of the Colombus Corporation's balance sheet is shown below.

Contributed Capital		
Preferred Stock—$100 par value, 6 percent		
cumulative, 10,000 shares authorized,		
200 shares issued and outstanding*		$ 20,000
Common Stock—$5 par value, 100,000 shares		
authorized, 10,000 shares issued, 9,000 shares		
outstanding	$50,000	
Paid-in Capital in Excess of Par Value, Common	28,000	78,000
Total Contributed Capital		$ 98,000
Retained Earnings		95,000
Total Contributed Capital and Retained Earnings		$193,000
Less Treasury Stock, Common (1,000 shares, at cost)		15,000
Total Stockholders' Equity		$178,000

*The preferred stock is callable at $105 per share, and one year's dividends are in arrears.

Determine the book value per share for both the preferred and the common stock.

E 13-9.
L O 6 *Corporate Income Statement*

Assume that the Shortall Furniture Company's chief financial officer gave you the following information: Net Sales, $1,900,000; Cost of Goods Sold, $1,050,000; Extraordinary Gain (net of income taxes of $3,500), $12,500; Loss from Discontinued Operations (net of income tax benefit of $30,000), $50,000; Loss on Disposal of Discontinued Operations (net of income tax benefit of $13,000), $35,000; Selling Expenses, $50,000; Administrative Expenses, $40,000; Income Taxes Expense on Continuing Operations, $300,000.

From this information, prepare the company's income statement for the year ended June 30, 19xx. (Ignore earnings per share information.)

E 13-10.
L O 7 *Use of Corporate Income Tax Rate Schedule*

Using the corporate tax rate schedule in Table 13-1, compute the income tax liability for the following situations:

Situation	Taxable Income
A	$ 70,000
B	85,000
C	320,000

E 13-11.
L O 7 *Income Tax Allocation*

The Delcampo Corporation reported the following accounting income before income taxes, income taxes expense, and net income for 19x2 and 19x3:

	19x3	19x2
Accounting income before taxes	$280,000	$280,000
Income taxes expense	88,300	88,300
Net income	$191,700	$191,700

Also, on the balance sheet, deferred income taxes liability increased by $38,400 in 19x2 and decreased by $18,800 in 19x3.

1. How much did Delcampo Corporation actually pay in income taxes for 19x2 and 19x3?
2. Prepare journal entries to record income taxes expense for 19x2 and 19x3.

E 13-12.
L O 9 *Earnings per Share*

During 19x1, the Heath Corporation reported a net income of $1,529,500. On January 1, Heath had 700,000 shares of common stock outstanding. The company issued an additional 420,000 shares of common stock on October 1. In 19x1, the company had a simple capital structure. During 19x2, there were no transactions involving common stock, and the company reported net income of $2,016,000.

1. Determine the weighted-average number of common shares outstanding each year.
2. Compute earnings per share for each year.

E 13-13.
L O 6, 7, 8, 9 *Corporate Income Statement*

The following items are components in the income statement of Cohen Corporation for the year ended December 31, 19x1:

Sales	$500,000
Cost of Goods Sold	(275,000)
Operating Expenses	(112,500)
Total Income Taxes Expense for Period	(82,350)
Income from Operations of a Discontinued Segment	80,000
Gain on Disposal of Segment	70,000
Extraordinary Gain on Retirement of Bonds	36,000
Cumulative Effect of a Change in Accounting Principle	(24,000)
Net Income	$192,150
Earnings per share	$ .96

Recast the 19x1 income statement in proper multistep form, including allocating income taxes to appropriate items (assume a 30 percent income tax rate) and showing earnings per share figures (200,000 shares outstanding).

Problem Set A

13A-1.

L O 2 *Stock Dividend and Stock Split Transactions*

The stockholders' equity section of the balance sheet of Borkowski Corporation as of December 31, 19x6 was as follows:

Contributed Capital	
Common Stock—$4 par value, 500,000 shares authorized,	
200,000 shares issued and outstanding	$ 800,000
Paid-in Capital in Excess of Par Value, Common	1,000,000
Total Contributed Capital	$1,800,000
Retained Earnings	1,200,000
Total Stockholders' Equity	$3,000,000

The following transactions occurred in 19x7 for Borkowski Corporation:

Feb. 28   The board of directors declared a 10 percent stock dividend to stockholders of record on March 25 to be distributed on April 5. The market value on this date is $16.

Mar. 25   Date of record for stock dividend.

Apr. 5   Issued stock dividend.

Aug. 3   Declared a 2 for 1 stock split.

Dec. 31   Declared a 5 percent stock dividend to stockholders of record on January 25 to be distributed on February 5. The market value per share was $9.

Dec. 31   Closed Stock Dividends Declared to Retained Earnings.

REQUIRED

1. Record the transactions for Borkowski Corporation in general journal form.
2. Prepare the stockholders' equity section of the company's balance sheet as of December 31, 19x7. Assume net income for 19x7 is $108,000. (**Hint:** Use T accounts to keep track of transactions.)

13A-2.

L O 1, 2, 3 *Dividend and Stock Split Transactions, Retained Earnings, and Stockholders' Equity.*

The stockholders' equity section of the Kurland Blind and Awning Company's balance sheet as of December 31, 19x6 was as follows:

Contributed Capital	
Common Stock—$2 par value, 3,000,000 shares	
authorized, 500,000 shares issued and outstanding	$1,000,000
Paid-in Capital in Excess of Par Value, Common	400,000
Total Contributed Capital	$1,400,000
Retained Earnings	1,080,000
Total Stockholders' Equity	$2,480,000

The following stockholders' equity transactions occurred during 19x7:

Mar. 5   Declared a $.40 per share cash dividend to be paid on April 6 to stockholders of record on March 20.

20   Date of record.

Apr. 6   Paid the cash dividend.

June 17   Declared a 10 percent stock dividend to be distributed August 17 to stockholders of record on August 5. The market value of the stock was $14 per share.

Aug. 5   Date of record.

17   Distributed the stock dividend.

Oct. 2   Split its stock 3 for 1.

Dec. 27   Declared a cash dividend of $.10 payable January 27, 19x8, to stockholders of record on January 14, 19x8.

31   Closed Income Summary with a credit balance of $400,000 to Retained Earnings.

31   Closed Cash Dividends Declared and Stock Dividends Declared to Retained Earnings.

On December 9, the board of directors restricted retained earnings for a pending lawsuit in the amount of $200,000. The restriction should be shown on the firm's financial statements.

REQUIRED

1. Record the 19x7 transactions in general journal form.
2. Prepare a statement of retained earnings, with appropriate disclosure of the restriction.
3. Prepare the stockholders' equity section of the company's balance sheet as of December 31, 19x7, with an appropriate disclosure of the restriction on retained earnings. (**Hint:** Use T accounts to keep track of transactions.)

13A-3.

L O 6, 7, 8, 9

Corporate Income Statement

Income statement information for the Shah Corporation during 19x1 is as follows:

a. Administrative expenses, $220,000.
b. Cost of goods sold, $880,000.
c. Cumulative effect of a change in inventory methods that decreased income (net of taxes, $56,000), $120,000.
d. Extraordinary loss from a storm (net of taxes, $20,000), $40,000.
e. Income taxes expense, continuing operations, $84,000.
f. Net sales, $1,780,000.
g. Selling expenses, $380,000.

REQUIRED

Prepare Shah Corporation's income statement for the year ended December 31, 19x1, including earnings per share information assuming a weighted average of 200,000 shares of common stock outstanding for 19x1.

13A-4.

L O 6, 7, 8

Corporate Income Statement and Evaluation of Business Operations

During 19x3 Dasbol Corporation engaged in a number of complex transactions to restructure the business—selling off a division, retiring bonds, and changing accounting methods. The company has always issued a simple single-step income statement, and the accountant has accordingly prepared the following December 31 year-end income statements for 19x2 and 19x3:

Dasbol Corporation
Income Statements
For the Years Ended December 31, 19x3 and 19x2

	19x3	19x2
Sales	$1,000,000	$1,200,000
Cost of Goods Sold	(550,000)	(600,000)
Operating Expenses	(225,000)	(150,000)
Income Taxes Expense	(164,700)	(135,000)
Income from Operations of a Discontinued Segment	160,000	
Gain on Disposal of Segment	140,000	
Extraordinary Gain on Retirement of Bonds	72,000	
Cumulative Effect of a Change in Accounting Principle	(48,000)	
Net Income	$ 384,300	$ 315,000
Earnings per share	$ 1.92	$ 1.58

The president of the company, Joseph Dasbol, is pleased to see that both net income and earnings per share increased by 22 percent from 19x2 to 19x3 and intends to announce to the stockholders that the restructuring is a success.

REQUIRED

1. Recast the 19x3 income statement in proper multistep form, including allocating income taxes to appropriate items (assume a 30 percent income tax rate) and showing earnings per share figures (200,000 shares outstanding).
2. What is your assessment of the restructuring plan and business operations in 19x3?

13A-5.

LO 1, 2, *Comprehensive*
3, 5 *Stockholders' Equity*
Transactions

The stockholders' equity on June 30, 19x5 of the Gagliano Company is shown below:

Contributed Capital
  Common Stock—no par value, $4 stated value,
  500,000 shares authorized, 200,000 shares issued
  and outstanding .... $ 800,000
  Paid-in Capital in Excess of Stated Value, Common 1,280,000

  Total Contributed Capital $2,080,000
  Retained Earnings   840,000

  Total Stockholders' Equity $2,920,000

Stockholders' equity transactions for the next fiscal year are as follows:

a. The board of directors declared a 2 for 1 split.
b. The board of directors obtained authorization to issue 200,000 shares of $100 par value, $4 noncumulative preferred stock, callable at $105.
c. Issued 10,000 shares of common stock for a building appraised at $44,000.
d. Purchased 6,000 shares of the company's common stock for $30,000.
e. Issued 30,000 shares, $100 par value, of the preferred stock for $100 per share.
f. Sold 4,000 shares of the treasury stock for $18,000.
g. Declared cash dividends of $4 per share on the preferred stock and $.20 per share on the common stock.
h. Date of record.
i. Paid the preferred and common stock cash dividends.
j. Declared a 5 percent stock dividend on the common stock. The market value was $18 per share. The stock dividend was distributable after the end of the fiscal year.
k. Net income for the year was $420,000.
l. Closed the Cash Dividends Declared and Stock Dividends Declared accounts to Retained Earnings.

Because of a loan agreement, the company is not allowed to reduce retained earnings below $200,000. The board of directors determined that this restriction should be disclosed in the notes to the financial statements.

REQUIRED

1. Make the appropriate general journal entries to record the transactions.
2. Prepare the company's statement of retained earnings for the year ended June 30, 19x6, including disclosure of the restriction.
3. Prepare the stockholders' equity section of the company's balance sheet on June 30, 19x6, including an appropriate disclosure of the restriction on retained earnings. (**Hint:** Use T accounts to keep track of transactions.)
4. Compute the book values per share of preferred and common stock (including common stock distributable) on June 30, 19x5 and 19x6.

Problem Set B

13B-1.

LO 2 *Stock Dividend and*
Stock Split
Transactions

The stockholders' equity section of Klock Cotton Mills, Inc. as of December 31, 19x2 was as follows:

Contributed Capital
  Common Stock—$12 par value, 500,000 shares
  authorized, 80,000 shares issued and outstanding .... $ 960,000
  Paid-in Capital in Excess of Par Value, Common   300,000

  Total Contributed Capital $1,260,000
  Retained Earnings   960,000

  Total Stockholders' Equity $2,220,000

A review of the stockholders' equity records of Klock Cotton Mills, Inc. disclosed the following transactions during 19x3:

Mar. 25   The board of directors declared a 5 percent stock dividend to stockholders of record on April 20 to be distributed on May 1. The market value of the common stock was $22 per share.

Apr. 20 Date of record for the stock dividend.
May 1 Issued the stock dividend.
Sept. 10 Declared a 3 for 1 stock split.
Dec. 15 Declared a 10 percent stock dividend to stockholders of record on January 15 to be distributed on February 15. The market price on this date is $7 per share.
Dec. 31 Closed Stock Dividends Declared to Retained Earnings.

REQUIRED

1. Record the transactions for Klock Cotton Mills, Inc. in general journal form.
2. Prepare the stockholders' equity section of the company's balance sheet as of December 31, 19x3. Assume net income for 19x3 is $94,000. (Hint: Use T accounts to keep track of transactions.)

13B-2.
L O 1, 2, 3 *Dividend and Stock Split Transactions, Retained Earnings, and Stockholders' Equity*

The balance sheet of the Yao Clothing Company disclosed the following stockholders' equity as of September 30, 19x1:

Contributed Capital	
Common Stock—$4 par value, 1,000,000 shares authorized, 300,000 shares issued and outstanding	$1,200,000
Paid-in Capital in Excess of Par Value, Common	740,000
Total Contributed Capital	$1,940,000
Retained Earnings	700,000
Total Stockholders' Equity	$2,640,000

The following stockholders' equity transactions were completed during the next fiscal year in the order presented:

19x1
Dec. 17 Declared a 10 percent stock dividend to be distributed January 20 to stockholders of record on January 1. The market value per share on the date of declaration was $8.

19x2
Jan. 1 Date of record.
     20 Distributed the stock dividend.
Apr. 14 Declared a $.50 per share cash dividend. The cash dividend is payable May 15 to stockholders of record on May 1.
May 1 Date of record.
     15 Paid the cash dividend.
June 17 Split its stock 2 for 1.
Sept. 15 Declared a cash dividend of $.20 per share payable October 10 to stockholders of record October 1.
     30 Closed Income Summary with a credit balance of $300,000 to Retained Earnings.
     30 Closed Cash Dividends Declared and Stock Dividends Declared to Retained Earnings.

On September 14, the board of directors restricted retained earnings for plant expansion in the amount of $300,000. The restriction should be shown in the financial statements.

REQUIRED

1. Record the above transactions in general journal form.
2. Prepare a statement of retained earnings, including disclosure of the restriction.
3. Prepare the stockholders' equity section of the company's balance sheet as of September 30, 19x2, with an appropriate disclosure of the restriction of retained earnings. (**Hint:** Use T accounts to keep track of transactions.)

13B-3.
L O 6, 7, 8, 9 *Corporate Income Statement*

Information concerning operations of the Benedict Shoe Corporation during 19xx is as follows:

a. Administrative expenses, $180,000.
b. Cost of goods sold, $840,000.
c. Cumulative effect of an accounting change in depreciation methods that increased income (net of taxes, $40,000), $84,000.

d. Extraordinary loss from an earthquake (net of taxes, $72,000), $120,000.

e. Sales (net), $1,800,000.

f. Selling expenses, $160,000.

g. Income taxes expense applicable to continuing operations, $210,000.

REQUIRED

Prepare the corporation's income statement for the year ended December 31, 19xx, including earnings per share information. Assume a weighted average of 100,000 common shares outstanding during the year.

13B-4.

L O 6, 7, 8 *Corporate Income Statement and Evaluation of Business Operations*

During 19x4 Clever Corporation engaged in a number of complex transactions to restructure the business—selling off a division, retiring bonds, and changing accounting methods. The company has always issued a simple single-step income statement, and the accountant has accordingly prepared the following December 31 year-end income statements for 19x3 and 19x4:

Clever Corporation
Income Statements
For the Years Ended December 31, 19x4 and 19x3

	19x4	19x3
Sales	$1,750,000	$2,100,000
Cost of Goods Sold	(962,500)	(1,050,000)
Operating Expenses	(393,750)	(262,500)
Income Taxes Expense	(288,225)	(236,250)
Income from Operations of a Discontinued Segment	280,000	
Gain on Disposal of Segment	245,000	
Extraordinary Gain on Retirement of Bonds	126,000	
Cumulative Effect of a Change in Accounting Principle	(84,000)	
Net Income	$ 672,525	$ 551,250
Earnings per share	$ 3.36	$ 2.76

The president of the company, Thomas Clever, is pleased to see that both net income and earnings per share increased by 22 percent from 19x3 to 19x4 and intends to announce to the stockholders that the restructuring is a success.

REQUIRED

1. Recast the 19x4 income statement in proper multistep form, including allocating income taxes to appropriate items (assume a 30 percent income tax rate) and showing earnings per share figures (200,000 shares outstanding).

2. What is your assessment of the restructuring plan and business operations in 19x4?

13B-5.

L O 1, 2, *Comprehensive*
3, 5 *Stockholders' Equity Transactions*

On December 31, 19x1, the stockholders' equity section of the Pucinski Company's balance sheet appeared as follows:

Contributed Capital
Common Stock—$8 par value, 200,000 shares
authorized, 60,000 shares issued and outstanding $ 480,000
Paid-in Capital in Excess of Par Value, Common 1,280,000

Total Contributed Capital $1,760,000
Retained Earnings 824,000

Total Stockholders' Equity $2,584,000

Selected transactions involving stockholders' equity in 19x2 are as follows: On January 4, the board of directors obtained authorization for 20,000 shares of $40 par value non-cumulative preferred stock that carried an indicated dividend rate of $4 per share and was callable at $42 per share. On January 14, the company sold 12,000 shares of the preferred stock at $40 per share and issued another 2,000 in exchange for a building valued at $80,000. On March 8, the board of directors declared a 2 for 1 stock split on the common stock. On April 20, after the stock split, the company purchased 3,000 shares of common stock for the treasury at an average price of $12 per share; 1,000 of these shares subsequently were sold on May 4 at an average price of $16 per share. On July 15, the board of directors declared a cash dividend of $4 per share on the preferred stock and $.40 per share on the common stock. The date of record was July 25. The dividends were paid on August 15. The board of directors declared a 15 percent stock dividend on November 28, when the common stock was selling for $20. The record date for the stock dividend was December 15, and the dividend was to be distributed on January 5. Net loss for 19x2 was $218,000. On December 31, Income Summary, Cash Dividends Declared, and Stock Dividends Declared were closed. The board of directors noted that note disclosure must be made of a bank loan agreement that requires minimum retained earnings. No cash dividends can be declared or paid if retained earnings fall below $100,000.

REQUIRED

1. Prepare journal entries to record the transactions above.
2. Prepare the company's statement of retained earnings for the year ended December 31, 19x2, including disclosure of restriction.
3. Prepare the stockholders' equity section of the company's balance sheet as of December 31, 19x2, including an appropriate disclosure of the restrictions on retained earnings. (**Hint:** Use T accounts to keep track of transactions.)
4. Compute the book value per share for preferred and common stock on December 31, 19x1 and 19x2.

CRITICAL THINKING AND COMMUNICATION

Conceptual Mini-Cases

CMC 13-1.

L O 2

Motivation for Stock Dividends

Athey Products Corporation, a small maker of industrial products for the waste management industry, has followed the practice in recent years of issuing a 10 percent stock dividend annually. Although the company's net income has been almost $4 million in each of the last three years, retained earnings have declined from about $10 million to about $6 million.[24] What is the probable motivation for Athey's management's decision to issue an annual 10 percent stock dividend? What is the most likely explanation for the decrease in retained earnings? Given your explanation, would stockholders' equity also decrease by a like amount?

CMC 13-2.

L O 6, 8, 9

Interpretation of Corporate Income Statement

Westinghouse Electric Corporation is a major technology company whose main businesses are power systems, electronic systems, environmental services, transport temperature control, and broadcasting. In recent years, the company has faced difficult restructurings, including the sale of several of its businesses, and changes in accounting principles, indicated as follows in this excerpt from the report of the company's independent auditors, Price Waterhouse:[25]

> As discussed in Note 1 to these financial statements, the Corporation adopted Statement of Financial Accounting Standards (SFAS) No. 106, "Employers' Accounting for Postretirement Benefits Other Than Pensions," and SFAS No. 109, "Accounting for Income Taxes," in 1992. As discussed in Note 2 to these financial statements, the Corporation adopted a comprehensive plan in November 1992 that entails exiting the financial services business and certain other non-strategic businesses. These businesses have been accounted for as discontinued operations.

24. Athey Products Corporation, *Annual Report,* 1989.
25. Westinghouse Electric Company, *Annual Report,* 1992.

These changes are reflected in the company's 1991 and 1992 income statements, a portion of which appears below (amounts in millions of dollars except per share data):[26]

	1992	1991
Income from Continuing Operations	$ 348	$ 265
Discontinued Operations, net of income taxes (note 2):		
Loss from operations	(21)	(1,351)
Estimated loss on disposal of Discontinued Operations	(1,280)	—
Loss from Discontinued Operations	(1,301)	(1,351)
Income (loss) before cumulative effect of changes in accounting principles	(953)	(1,086)
Cumulative effect of changes in accounting principles:		
Postretirement benefits other than pensions (notes 1 and 4)	(742)	—
Income taxes (notes 1 and 5)	404	—
Net income (loss)	($1,291)	($1,086)
Earnings (loss) per common share (note 15):		
From Continuing Operations	$ .93	$ .84
From Discontinued Operations	(3.76)	(4.30)
From cumulative effect of changes in accounting principles	(.98)	—
Earnings (loss) per common share	($3.81)	($3.46)
Cash dividends per common share (note 15)	$ .72	$ 1.40

(1) Identify the amounts in the partial income statement for each item mentioned in the independent auditors' report. (2) Define discontinued operations and explain the difference between loss from operations and estimated loss on disposal of discontinued operations. Why are discontinued operations shown separately on the income statement? (3) Define the cumulative effect of changes in accounting principles. Were these changes instigated by management, or were they mandated by outside authorities? If mandated, by whom? (4) Why are several figures given for earnings per common share? Which earnings (loss) per common share figure would you say is most relevant to future operations? Why is this the most relevant?

CMC 13-3.

L O 6, 8 *Interpretation of Earnings Reports*

McDonnell Douglas Corporation, the large aerospace and defense company based in St. Louis, was the subject of an article in the *Wall Street Journal* reporting on its third-quarter 1990 results of operations. The following are excerpts from that article:

McDonnell Douglas Corp. posted a sharp rise in third-quarter net income after an accounting adjustment, but financial problems related to its C-17 military transport program raised questions about the strength of operating results.

Net [income] soared to $248 million, or $6.46 a share, from $38 million, or $.98 a share, in the year-earlier period on a 13% rise in revenue to $4.18 billion from $3.71 billion.

The accounting adjustment, which stems from the settlement of certain pension fund obligations announced in September, contributed $234 million, or $6.11 a share, leaving operating profit of only $14 million, or $.35 a share.

While McDonnell Douglas hailed its "improved performance," some Wall Street analysts weren't quite so upbeat. They took particular issue with the company's effort to paint a $58 million reversal of earnings on the C-17 program as a one-time, nonoperating adjustment, when in fact far more serious write-downs remain possible.

"I would consider the C-17 adjustment an operational issue because it stemmed from cost problems," said Lawrence Harris, an analyst.

. . . In making the C-17 adjustment, the company wiped out profit recorded on the program between 1985 and the first quarter of this year, indicating that it expects to bump against the $6.6 billion cost ceiling when the project is completed in the 1990s. Should it pierce that ceiling, things would get much worse.

26. Ibid.

At that point, the company could begin absorbing all expenses with the federal government no longer obliged to reimburse it.[27]

Is the increase shown by McDonnell Douglas's net income misleading? Why or why not? Defend your position by explaining the structure of McDonnell Douglas's income statement as suggested by the excerpt.

Ethics Mini-Case

EMC 13-1.
L O 2
Ethics and Stock Dividends

Bass Products Corporation, a public corporation, for twenty years has followed the practice of paying a cash dividend every quarter and has promoted itself to investors as a stable, reliable company. Recent competition from Asian companies in its industry has negatively affected its earnings and cash flows. As a result, Sandra Bass, president of the company, is proposing to the board of directors that the board declare a stock dividend of 5 percent this year instead of a cash dividend. She says, "This will maintain our consecutive dividend record and will not require any cash outflow." What is the difference between a cash dividend and a stock dividend? Why does a corporation usually issue them, and how does each affect the financial statements? Is the action proposed by Bass ethical?

Decision-Making Case

DMC 13-1.
L O 2, 5
Analyzing Effects of Stockholders' Equity Transactions

Borders Steel Corporation (BSC) is a small specialty steel manufacturer located in northern Alabama that has been owned by the Borders family for several generations. Myron Borders III is a major shareholder in BSC by virtue of having inherited 200,000 shares of common stock in the company. Myron has not shown much interest in the business because of his enthusiasm for archaeology, which takes him to far parts of the world. However, when he received minutes of the last board of directors meeting, he questioned a number of transactions involving the stockholders' equity of BSC. He asks you, as a person with a knowledge of accounting, to help him interpret the effect of these transactions on his interest in BSC.

You begin by examining the stockholders' equity section of BSC's January 1, 19xx balance sheet.

Borders Steel Corporation
Stockholders' Equity
January 1, 19xx

Contributed Capital	
Common Stock—$20 par value, 5,000,000 shares authorized, 1,000,000 shares issued and outstanding	$ 20,000,000
Paid-in Capital in Excess of Par Value, Common	50,000,000
Total Contributed Capital	$ 70,000,000
Retained Earnings	40,000,000
Total Stockholders' Equity	$110,000,000

Then you read the relevant parts of the minutes of the December 15, 19xx meeting of the firm's board of directors:

Item A: The president reported the following transactions involving the company's stock during the last quarter:

October 15. Sold 500,000 shares of authorized common stock through the investment banking firm of T. R. Kendall at a net price of $100 per share.

27. Rick Wartzman, "McDonnell's Net Rose in 3rd Period; Special Items Cited," *Wall Street Journal,* October 24, 1990. Reprinted by permission of *Wall Street Journal,* © 1994 Dow Jones & Company, Inc. All Rights Reserved.

November 1. Purchased 100,000 shares for the corporate treasury from Lucy Borders at a price of $110 per share.

Item B: The board declared a 2 for 1 stock split (accomplished by halving the par value, doubling each stockholder's shares, and increasing authorized shares to 10,000,000), followed by a 10 percent stock dividend. The board then declared a cash dividend of $4 per share on the resulting shares. All these transactions are applicable to stockholders of record on December 20 and are payable on January 10. The market value of Borders stock on the board meeting date after the stock split was estimated to be $60.

Item C: The chief financial officer stated that he expected the company to report net income for the year of $8,000,000.

REQUIRED

1. Prepare a stockholders' equity section of BSC's balance sheet as of December 31, 19xx that reflects the transactions above. (**Hint:** Use T accounts to analyze the transactions. Also, use a T account to keep track of the shares of common stock outstanding.)
2. Compute the book value per share and Myron's percentage of ownership of the company at the beginning and at the end of the year. Explain the differences. Would you say that Myron's position has improved during the year? Why or why not?

Basic Research Activity

RA 13-1.
L O 2, 4, 5,
6, 7, 8

Stockholders' Equity and Book Value Versus Market Price

In your library, select the annual reports of three corporations. You may choose them from the same industry or at random, at the direction of your instructor. (If you completed the related basic research activity in the chapter on contributed capital, use the same three companies.) Prepare a table with a column for each corporation. Then, for any year covered by the balance sheet, the statement of stockholders' equity, and the income statement, answer the following questions: Does the company own treasury stock? Was any treasury stock bought or retired? Did the company declare a stock dividend or a stock split? What other transactions appear in the statement of stockholders' equity? Has the company deferred any income taxes? Were there any discontinued operations, extraordinary items, or accounting changes? Compute the book value per common share for the company. In the *Wall Street Journal* or the financial section of another daily newspaper, find the current market price of each company's common stock and compare it to the book value you computed. Should there be any relationship between the two values? Be prepared to discuss your answers to these questions in class.

FINANCIAL REPORTING AND ANALYSIS

Interpretation Cases from Business

ICB 13-1.
L O 6, 8

Interpretation of Earnings Report in Financial Press

Presented below are several excerpts from an article that appeared in the February 2, 1982, *Wall Street Journal* entitled "Lockheed Had Loss in 4th Quarter, Year; $396 Million TriStar Write-Off is Cited."

As expected, ***Lockheed Corp.*** took a $396 million write-off to cover expenses of its production phase-out of L-1011 TriStar commercial jets, resulting in a net loss of . . . $289 million for the year.

Roy A. Anderson, Lockheed Chairman, said he believed the company had "recognized all costs, including those yet to be incurred, that are associated with the phase-out of the TriStar program." He said he thinks the company now is in a sound position to embark on a program of future growth and earnings improvement.

Included in the $396 million net write-off are remaining deferred production start-up costs, adjustments for redundant inventories, and provisions for losses and other costs expected to be incurred while TriStar production is completed. In addition to the write-off, discontinued operations include a $70 million after-tax loss associated with 1981 L-1011 operations. The comparable 1980 L-1011 loss was $108 million.

The $289 million net loss in 1981 consists of the TriStar losses, reduced by the previously reported [extraordinary after-tax] gain of $23 million from the exchange of debentures.

For the year, Lockheed had earnings from continuing operations of $154 million, a 14% gain from $135 million in 1980. In 1981 the company had a $466 million loss from discontinued operations, resulting in a net loss of $289 million. A year earlier, the concern had a $108 million loss from discontinued operations, resulting in a net profit of $28 million.[28]

REQUIRED

1. Interpret the financial information from the *Wall Street Journal* by preparing a partial income statement for Lockheed for 1981, beginning with "income from continuing operations." Be prepared to explain the nature of each item on the income statement.
2. How do you explain the fact that on the New York Stock Exchange, Lockheed common stock closed at $50 per share, up $.75 on the day after the quoted announcement of a net loss of $289 million and up from $41 per share two months earlier?

ICB 13-2.
L O 4 *Interpretation of Statement of Stockholders' Equity*

The consolidated statements of stockholders' equity for *Jackson Electronics, Inc.*, a manufacturer of a broad line of electrical components, appear as presented below.

Jackson Electronics, Inc.
Consolidated Statements of Stockholders' Equity
(in thousands)

	Preferred Stock	Common Stock	Paid-in Capital in Excess of Par Value	Retained Earnings	Common Stock in Treasury	Total
Balance at September 30, 1993	$2,756	$3,902	$14,149	$119,312	($ 942)	$139,177
Year Ended September 30, 1994:						
Net income	—	—	—	18,753	—	18,753
Redemption and retirement of Preferred Stock (27,560 shares)	(2,756)	—	—	—	—	(2,756)
Stock options exercised (89,000 shares)	—	89	847	—	—	936
Purchases of Common Stock for treasury (501,412 shares)	—	—	—	—	(12,552)	(12,552)
Issuance of Common Stock (148,000 shares) in exchange for convertible subordinated debentures	—	148	3,635	—	—	3,783
Issuance of Common Stock (715,000 shares) for cash	—	715	24,535	—	—	25,250
Issuance of 500,000 shares of Common Stock in exchange for investment interest in Electrix Company	—	500	17,263	—	—	17,763
Cash dividends—Common Stock ($.80 per share)	—	—	—	(3,086)	—	(3,086)
Balance at September 30, 1994	$ —	$5,354	$60,429	$134,979	($13,494)	$187,268

REQUIRED

Jackson Electronics, Inc.'s statement of stockholders' equity has eight summary transactions. Show that you understand this statement by preparing a general journal entry with an explanation for each. In each case, if applicable, determine the average price per common share. Sometimes you will also have to make assumptions about an offsetting part of the entry. For example, assume that there are no premiums or discounts on debentures (long-term bonds) and that employees pay cash for stock purchased under Jackson Electronics, Inc.'s employee incentive plans.

ICB 13-3.

L O 7 *Analysis of Income Taxes from Annual Report*

In its 1993 annual report, *Sara Lee Corporation,* an international food and packaged products company based in Chicago, provided the following data about its current and deferred income tax provisions (in millions):

	1993	
	Current	**Deferred**
Federal	$175	($ 7)
Foreign	159	17
State	33	1
	$367	$11

REQUIRED

1. How much in income taxes was paid in 1993? What was the income tax expense? Prepare a journal entry to record the overall income tax liability for 1993, using income tax allocation procedures.
2. In the long-term liability section of the balance sheet, Sara Lee shows deferred income taxes of $512 million in 1993 versus $488 million in 1992. This shows the amount of deferred income taxes to have grown. How do such deferred income taxes arise? Give an example of this process. Given the definition of a liability, do you see a potential problem with the company's classifying deferred income taxes as a liability while it is continuing to grow?

International Company Case

ICC 13-1.

L O 3 *Restriction of Retained Earnings*

In some countries, of which Japan is one, the availability of retained earnings for the payment of dividends is restricted. The following disclosure appears in the annual report of *Mazda Motor Corporation,* the Japanese automobile manufacturer:[29]

> Under the Commercial Code of Japan, the Company is required to appropriate to legal reserve an amount equal to at least 10% of cash dividends paid in each period through March 31, 1991, and at least 10% of the total amount of cash dividends paid and bonuses to directors and statutory auditors in the period ended March 31, 1992, until the reserve equals 25% of common stock.
>
> This reserve is not available for dividends but may be used to reduce a deficit by resolution of the shareholders or may be capitalized by resolution of the Board of Directors.

For Mazda, this legal reserve amounted to a substantial sum, Y14 billion or $105 million. How does this practice differ from that in the United States? Why do you think it is government policy in Japan? Do you think it is a good idea?

Toys "R" Us Case

TC 13-1.

L O 4, 5, *Corporate Income*
6, 8 *Statement, Statement of Stockholders' Equity, and Book Value per Share*

Refer to the Annual Report in the appendix on Toys "R" Us to answer the following questions:

1. Does Toys "R" Us have discontinued operations, extraordinary items, or cumulative changes in accounting principles? Would you say the income statement for Toys "R" Us is relatively simple or relatively complex?
2. What transactions most commonly affect the stockholders' equity section of the balance sheet of Toys "R" Us?
3. Compute the book value of Toys "R" Us stock in 1994 and 1993 and compare it to the market price. What interpretation do you place on these relationships?

29. Mazda Motor Corporation, *Annual Report,* 1992.

COMPREHENSIVE PROBLEM

SUNDIAL CORPORATION

Sundial Corporation filed articles of incorporation and obtained authorization for 500,000 shares of no-par common stock with a stated value of $1 per share and 10,000 shares of 9 percent cumulative preferred stock with a par value of $100 and a call price of $104. The company began business on January 1, 19xx as a high-tech startup in the business of making sophisticated time measuring devices. The company's first year of operation was an exciting and profitable one in which the company engaged in a number of transactions involving its stockholders' equity, which are listed below.

19xx

Jan. 1 Issued for cash 100,000 shares of common stock at $6.50 per share.

2 Issued 12,000 shares of common stock to attorneys and others who assisted with the organization of the corporation. The value of these services was put at $60,000.

3 Issued for cash 10,000 shares of preferred stock at par value.

Mar. 7 Issued 8,000 shares of common stock in exchange for a patent that had a value set at $50,000.

Apr. 2 Issued for cash 30,000 shares of common stock at a price of $6.

May 5 Purchased 30,000 common shares from a stockholder for $8 per share.

19 Sold 13,000 of the common shares purchased on May 5 for $9 per share.

June 30 Transferred by a closing entry the net income for the first half of the year to retained earnings, $250,000.

July 8 Sold 7,000 more of the common shares purchased on May 5 for $7.

Aug. 4 Declared a 10 percent common stock dividend distributable on Aug. 24 to stockholders of record Aug. 14. At this time the company's common stock is selling for $8 per share.

14 Date of record for stock dividend.

24 Date of distribution for stock dividend.

Sept. 9 Issued common stock for cash in connection with the exercise by management of employee stock options on 40,000 shares of common stock at $5 per share.

Oct. 10 Purchased 10,000 common shares from a stockholder for $9 per share.

20 Retired the shares purchased on October 10. The shares were originally issued at $6 per share.

Nov. 1 Declared cash dividends representing the annual dividend on preferred stock and $0.25 per share on common stock to stockholders of record November 11, payable on November 21.

11 Date of record for cash dividends.

21 Date of payment for cash dividends.

Dec. 16 Declared a 2 for 1 stock split. Assume that the stock split applies to treasury stock.

31 Transferred by closing entry the net income for the second half of the year of $230,000 to retained earnings.

31 Closed Cash Dividends Declared and Stock Dividends Declared to Retained Earnings.

31 Because of litigation and potential loss from a lawsuit over patent infringement, the board voted to restrict retained earnings to the extent of $100,000 and to disclose this information in a note to the financial statements.

REQUIRED

1. Record the above entries for Sundial Corporation in the general journal.
2. Prepare the statement of retained earnings for 19xx for Sundial Corporation.
3. Prepare the stockholders' equity section of Sundial's balance sheet on December 31, 19xx, including proper disclosure of the restriction on retained earnings.
4. Compute book value for preferred stock and common stock at year end.

This Comprehensive Problem covers all of the Learning Objectives in the chapter on contributed capital and Learning Objectives 1 through 5 in the chapter on retained earnings and corporate income statements.

Special Reports
and Analyses
of Accounting
Information

Because business organizations are so complex today, special reports are needed to present important information about their activities. To understand and evaluate financial statements, it is necessary to learn how to analyze them. **Part Three** deals with the statement of cash flows, the analysis of financial statements, international accounting, and intercompany investments.

CHAPTER 14
The Statement of
Cash Flows

presents the statement of cash flows, which explains the major operating, financing, and investing activities of a business. The chapter discusses this statement using both the direct approach and the indirect approach.

CHAPTER 15
Financial Statement
Analysis

explains the objectives and techniques of financial statement analysis from the standpoint of the financial analyst. As an extended illustration, the financial statements of Apple Computer, Inc. are analyzed.

CHAPTER 16
International Accounting
and Intercompany
Investments

addresses two areas of relevance to most corporations in today's complex and global environment. The first is international accounting, including the effects of changing rates of exchange for foreign currencies and of diversity of international accounting standards on the interpretations of financial statements. The second is accounting for investments by one company in the capital stock of another, including consolidated financial statements.

**LEARNING
OBJECTIVES**

1. Describe the statement of cash flows, and define *cash* and *cash equivalents*.

2. State the principal purposes and uses of the statement of cash flows.

3. Identify the principal components of the classifications of cash flows, and state the significance of noncash investing and financing transactions.

4. Determine cash flows from operating activities using the (a) direct and (b) indirect methods.

5. Determine cash flows from (a) investing activities and (b) financing activities.

6. Prepare a statement of cash flows using the (a) direct and (b) indirect methods.

7. Analyze the statement of cash flows.

SUPPLEMENTAL OBJECTIVE

8. Prepare a work sheet for the statement of cash flows.

Marriott International is a world leader in lodging and contract services. The company's annual report provides an excellent picture of management's philosophy and performance through its balance sheet, its income statement, and its statement of stockholders' equity. While these financial statements are essential to the evaluation of a company, some information that they do not cover is presented in a fourth statement, the statement of cash flows. It tells how much cash was generated by the company's operations during the year and how much was used or came from investing and financing activities. Marriott feels that maintaining adequate cash flow is important to the future of the company, as shown by the following statement in its annual report:

> Marriott places strong emphasis on maximizing cash flow, and its incentive compensation programs were revised in 1991 to reward managers based on cash flow rather than accounting earnings. In 1992, all nine of the company's major business units generated operating cash flow in excess of their capital expenditures, including outlays for expansion.[1]

Why would Marriott emphasize cash flow to such an extent?

A strong cash flow is essential to management's key goal of liquidity. If cash flow exceeds what is needed for operations and for expansion, the company will not have to borrow additional funds for expansion. The excess cash flow will be available to reduce the company's debt and improve its financial position by lowering its debt to equity ratio.

The statement of cash flows demonstrates management's commitments for the company in ways that are not readily apparent in the other financial statements. For example, the statement of cash flows can show whether management's focus is on the short term or the long term. This statement is required by the FASB[2] and satisfies the FASB's long-held position that a primary objective of financial statements is to provide investors and creditors with information on a company's cash flows.[3]

1. Marriott Corporation, *Annual Report*, 1992.
2. *Statement of Financial Accounting Standards No. 95*, "Statement of Cash Flows" (Stamford, Conn.: Financial Accounting Standards Board, 1987).
3. *Statement of Financial Accounting Concepts No. 1*, "Objectives of Financial Reporting for Business Enterprises" (Stamford, Conn.: Financial Accounting Standards Board, 1978), par. 37–39.

PURPOSES, USES, AND COMPONENTS OF THE STATEMENT OF CASH FLOWS

OBJECTIVE

> **1** *Describe the statement of cash flows, and define* **cash** *and* **cash equivalents**

The statement of cash flows shows the effect on cash of a company's operating, investing, and financing activities for an accounting period. It explains the net increase (or decrease) in cash during the accounting period. For purposes of preparing this statement, cash is defined to include both cash and cash equivalents. Cash equivalents are defined by the FASB as short-term, highly liquid investments, including money market accounts, commercial paper, and U.S. Treasury bills. A company maintains cash equivalents in order to earn interest on cash that otherwise would temporarily lie idle. Suppose, for example, that a company has $1,000,000 that it will not need for thirty days. To earn a return on this sum, the company may place the cash in an account that earns interest (for example, a money market account); it may loan the cash to another corporation by purchasing that corporation's short-term note (commercial paper); or it might purchase a short-term obligation of the U.S. government (a Treasury bill). In this context, short-term is defined as original maturities of ninety days or less. Since cash and cash equivalents are considered the same, transfers between the Cash account and cash equivalents are not treated as cash receipts or cash payments. In effect, cash equivalents are combined with the Cash account on the statement of cash flows.

Cash equivalents should not be confused with short-term investments or marketable securities, which are not combined with the Cash account on the statement of cash flows. Purchases of marketable securities are treated as cash outflows and sales of marketable securities as cash inflows on the statement of cash flows. In this chapter, cash will be assumed to include cash and cash equivalents.

PURPOSES OF THE STATEMENT OF CASH FLOWS

OBJECTIVE

> **2** *State the principal purposes and uses of the statement of cash flows*

The primary purpose of the statement of cash flows is to provide information about a company's cash receipts and cash payments during an accounting period. A secondary purpose of the statement is to provide information about a company's operating, investing, and financing activities during the accounting period. Some of the information on these activities may be inferred by examining other financial statements, but it is on the statement of cash flows that all the transactions affecting cash are summarized.

INTERNAL AND EXTERNAL USES OF THE STATEMENT OF CASH FLOWS

The statement of cash flows is useful internally to management and externally to investors and creditors. Management uses the statement to assess the liquidity of the business, to determine dividend policy, and to evaluate the effects of major policy decisions involving investments and financing. In other words, management may use the statement to determine if short-term financing is needed to pay current liabilities, to decide whether to raise or lower dividends, and to plan for investing and financing needs.

Investors and creditors will find the statement useful in assessing the company's ability to manage cash flows, to generate positive future cash flows, to pay its liabilities, to pay dividends and interest, and to anticipate its need for additional financing. Also, they may use the statement to explain the differences between net income on the income statement and the net cash flows generated from operations. In addition, the statement shows both the cash and noncash effects of investing and financing activities during the accounting period.

OBJECTIVE

3 *Identify the principal components of the classifications of cash flows, and state the significance of noncash investing and financing transactions*

CLASSIFICATION OF CASH FLOWS

The statement of cash flows classifies cash receipts and cash payments into the categories of operating, investing, and financing activities. The components of these activities are shown in Figure 14-1 and summarized as follows:

1. Operating activities include the cash effects of transactions and other events that enter into the determination of net income. Included in this category as cash inflows are cash receipts from customers for goods and services, interest and dividends received on loans and investments, and sales of trading securities. Included as cash outflows are cash payments for wages, goods and services, interest, taxes, and purchases of trading securities. In effect, the income statement is changed from an accrual to a cash basis.
2. Investing activities include the acquiring and selling of long-term assets, the acquiring and selling of marketable securities other than trading securities or cash equivalents, and the making and collecting of loans. Cash inflows include the cash received from selling long-term assets and marketable securities and from collecting loans. Cash outflows include the cash expended for purchases of long-term assets and marketable securities and the cash loaned to borrowers.
3. Financing activities include (1) obtaining or returning resources from or to owners and providing them with a return on their investment and (2) obtaining resources from creditors and repaying the amounts borrowed or otherwise settling the obligations. Cash inflows include the proceeds from issues of stocks and from short-term and long-term borrowing. Cash outflows include the repayments of loans and payments to owners, including cash dividends. Treasury stock transactions are also considered financing activities. Repayments of accounts payable or accrued liabilities are not considered repayments of loans under financing activities, but are classified as cash outflows under operating activities.

A company will occasionally engage in significant noncash investing and financing transactions involving only long-term assets, long-term liabilities, or stockholders' equity, such as the exchange of a long-term asset for a long-term liability or the settlement of a debt by issuing capital stock. For instance, a company might take out a long-term mortgage for the purchase of land and a building. Or it might convert long-term bonds into common stock. These transactions represent significant investing and financing activities, but they would not be reflected on the statement of cash flows because they do not involve either cash inflows or cash outflows. However, since one purpose of the statement of cash flows is to show investing and financing activities, and since transactions like these will affect future cash flows, the FASB has determined that they should be disclosed in a separate schedule as part of the statement of cash flows. In this way, the reader of the statement will see the company's investing and financing activities clearly.

FORMAT OF THE STATEMENT OF CASH FLOWS

The statement of cash flows, shown in Exhibit 14-1, is divided into three sections corresponding to the three categories of activities just discussed. The

Figure 14-1. Classification of Cash Inflows and Cash Outflows

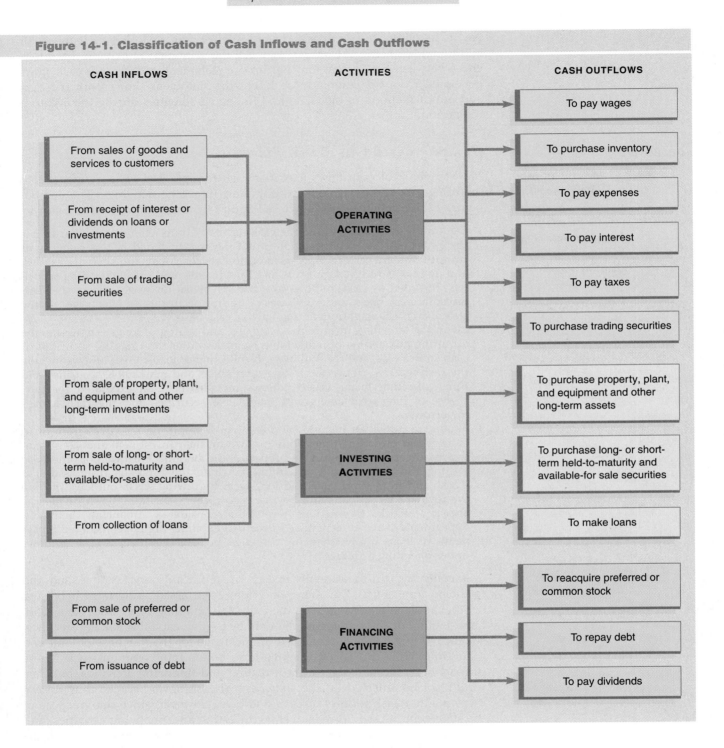

cash flows from operating activities are followed by cash flows from investing activities and cash flows from financing activities. The individual inflows and outflows from investing and financing activities are usually shown separately in their respective categories. For instance, cash inflows from the sale of property, plant, and equipment are shown separately from cash outflows for the purchase of property, plant, and equipment. Similarly, cash inflows from bor-

Exhibit 14-1. Format for the Statement of Cash Flows

Company Name
Statement of Cash Flows
Period Covered

Cash Flows from Operating Activities		
(List of individual inflows and outflows)	xxx	
Net Cash Flows from Operating Activities		xxx
Cash Flows from Investing Activities		
(List of individual inflows and outflows)	xxx	
Net Cash Flows from Investing Activities		xxx
Cash Flows from Financing Activities		
(List of individual inflows and outflows)	xxx	
Net Cash Flows from Financing Activities		xxx
Net Increase (Decrease) in Cash		xx
Cash at Beginning of Year		xx
Cash at End of Year		xx

Schedule of Noncash Investing and Financing Transactions

(List of individual transactions)	xxx

rowing are shown separately from cash outflows to retire loans. A reconciliation of the beginning and ending balances of cash is shown at the end of the statement. A list of noncash transactions appears in the schedule at the bottom of the statement.

PREPARING THE STATEMENT OF CASH FLOWS

To demonstrate the preparation of the statement of cash flows, we will work through an example step by step. The data for this example are presented in Exhibits 14-2 and 14-3. These two exhibits present Ryan Corporation's balance sheets for December 31, 19x1 and 19x2, and its 19x2 income statement, with additional data about transactions affecting noncurrent accounts during 19x2. Since the changes in the balance sheet accounts will be used for analysis, those changes are shown in Exhibit 14-2. Whether the change in each account is an increase or a decrease is also shown. In addition, Exhibit 14-3 contains data about transactions that affected noncurrent accounts. These transactions would be identified by the company's accountants from the records.

There are four steps in preparing the statement of cash flows:

1. Determine cash flows from operating activities.
2. Determine cash flows from investing activities.
3. Determine cash flows from financing activities.
4. Present the information obtained in the first three steps in the form of the statement of cash flows.

Exhibit 14-2. Comparative Balance Sheets with Changes in Accounts Indicated for Ryan Corporation

Ryan Corporation
Comparative Balance Sheets
December 31, 19x2 and 19x1

	19x2	19x1	Change	Increase or Decrease
Assets				
Current Assets				
Cash	$ 46,000	$ 15,000	$ 31,000	Increase
Accounts Receivable (net)	47,000	55,000	(8,000)	Decrease
Inventory	144,000	110,000	34,000	Increase
Prepaid Expenses	1,000	5,000	(4,000)	Decrease
Total Current Assets	$238,000	$185,000	$ 53,000	
Investments	$115,000	$127,000	($12,000)	Decrease
Plant Assets				
Plant Assets	$715,000	$505,000	$210,000	Increase
Accumulated Depreciation	(103,000)	(68,000)	(35,000)	Increase
Total Plant Assets	$612,000	$437,000	$175,000	
Total Assets	$965,000	$749,000	$216,000	
Liabilities				
Current Liabilities				
Accounts Payable	$ 50,000	$ 43,000	$ 7,000	Increase
Accrued Liabilities	12,000	9,000	3,000	Increase
Income Taxes Payable	3,000	5,000	(2,000)	Decrease
Total Current Liabilities	$ 65,000	$ 57,000	$ 8,000	
Long-Term Liabilities				
Bonds Payable	$295,000	$245,000	$ 50,000	Increase
Total Liabilities	$360,000	$302,000	$ 58,000	
Stockholders' Equity				
Common Stock, $5 par value	$276,000	$200,000	$ 76,000	Increase
Paid-in Capital in Excess of Par Value	189,000	115,000	74,000	Increase
Retained Earnings	140,000	132,000	8,000	Increase
Total Stockholders' Equity	$605,000	$447,000	$158,000	
Total Liabilities and Stockholders' Equity	$965,000	$749,000	$216,000	

DETERMINING CASH FLOWS FROM OPERATING ACTIVITIES

The first step in preparing the statement of cash flows is to determine cash flows from operating activities. The income statement indicates a business's

Ryan Corporation
Income Statement
For the Year Ended December 31, 19x2

Sales		$698,000
Cost of Goods Sold		520,000
Gross Margin		$178,000
Operating Expenses (including Depreciation Expense of $37,000)		147,000
Operating Income		$ 31,000
Other Income (Expenses)		
Interest Expense	($23,000)	
Interest Income	6,000	
Gain on Sale of Investments	12,000	
Loss on Sale of Plant Assets	(3,000)	(8,000)
Income Before Taxes		$ 23,000
Income Taxes		7,000
Net Income		$ 16,000

Other transactions affecting noncurrent accounts during 19x2:

1. Purchased investments in the amount of $78,000.
2. Sold investments classified as long-term and available-for-sale for $102,000. These investments cost $90,000.
3. Purchased plant assets in the amount of $120,000.
4. Sold plant assets that cost $10,000 with accumulated depreciation of $2,000 for $5,000.
5. Issued $100,000 of bonds at face value in a noncash exchange for plant assets.
6. Repaid $50,000 of bonds at face value at maturity.
7. Issued 15,200 shares of $5 par value common stock for $150,000.
8. Paid cash dividends in the amount of $8,000.

success or failure in earning an income from its operating activities, but it does not reflect the inflow and outflow of cash from those activities. The reason for this is that the income statement is prepared on an accrual basis. Revenues are recorded even though the cash for them may not have been received, and expenses are recorded even though the cash for them may not have been expended. As a result, to arrive at cash flows from operations, the figures on the income statement must be converted from an accrual basis to a cash basis by adjusting earned revenues to cash received from sales and incurred costs and expenses to cash expended, as shown in Figure 14-2.

There are two methods of converting the income statement from an accrual basis to a cash basis: the direct method and the indirect method. Under the direct method, each item in the income statement is adjusted from the accrual basis to the cash basis. The result is a statement that begins with cash receipts from sales and deducts cash payments for purchases, operating expenses,

OBJECTIVE

4a *Determine cash flows from operating activities using the direct method*

Figure 14-2. Relationship of Accrual and Cash Bases of Accounting

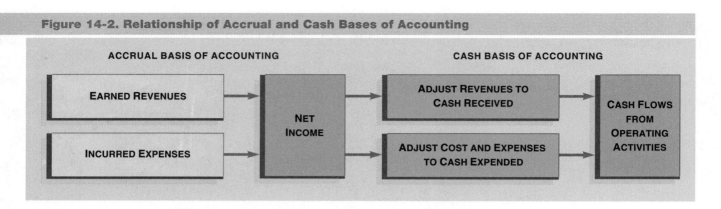

interest payments, and income taxes to arrive at net cash flows from operating activities:

Cash Flows from Operating Activities
Cash Receipts from
Sales	xxx	
Interest and Dividends Received	xxx	xxx

Cash Payments for
Purchases	xxx	
Operating Expenses	xxx	
Interest Payments	xxx	
Income Taxes	xxx	xxx
Net Cash Flows from Operating Activities		xxx

OBJECTIVE

4b *Determine cash flows from operating activities using the indirect method*

The indirect method, on the other hand, does not require the individual adjustment of each item in the income statement, but lists only those adjustments necessary to convert net income to cash flows from operations, as follows:

Cash Flows from Operating Activities
Net Income		xxx
Adjustments to Reconcile Net Income to Net Cash Flows from Operating Activities (List of individual items)	xxx	xxx
Net Cash Flows from Operating Activities		xxx

Both methods, however, analyze certain income statement items and changes in certain current assets and current liabilities. In the sections that follow, the direct method will be used to illustrate the conversion of the income statement to a cash basis, and the indirect method will be used to summarize the process.

Cash Receipts from Sales   Sales result in a positive cash flow for a company. Cash sales are direct cash inflows. Credit sales are not, because they are recorded originally as accounts receivable. When they are collected, they become cash inflows. You cannot, however, assume that credit sales are automatically inflows of cash, because the collections of accounts receivable in any one accounting period are not likely to equal credit sales. Receivables may be uncollectible, sales from a prior period may be collected in the current period, or sales from the current period may be collected next period. For example, if accounts receivable increases from one accounting period to the next, cash receipts from sales will not be as great as sales. On the other hand, if accounts receivable decreases from one accounting period to the next, cash receipts from sales will exceed sales.

The relationships among sales, changes in accounts receivable, and cash receipts from sales are reflected in the following formula:

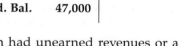

$$\begin{array}{c} \text{Cash Receipts} \\ \text{from Sales} \end{array} = \text{Sales} \left\{ \begin{array}{c} + \text{ Decrease in Accounts Receivable} \\ \text{or} \\ - \text{ Increase in Accounts Receivable} \end{array} \right.$$

Refer to the balance sheets and income statement for Ryan Corporation in Exhibits 14-2 and 14-3. Note that sales were $698,000 in 19x2, and accounts receivable decreased by $8,000. Thus, cash received from sales is $706,000:

$$\$706,000 = \$698,000 + \$8,000$$

Ryan Corporation collected $8,000 more from sales than it sold during the year. This relationship may be illustrated as follows:

Accounts Receivable

Sales to Customers	Beg. Bal.	55,000	706,000 →	Cash Receipts from Customers
	→	698,000		
	End. Bal.	**47,000**		

If Ryan Corporation had unearned revenues or advances from customers, an adjustment would be made for changes in those items as well.

DECISION POINT

Survey of Large Companies

The direct method and the indirect method of determining cash flows from operating activities produce the same results. Although it will accept either method, the FASB recommends that the direct method be used. If the direct method of reporting net cash flows from operating activities is used, reconciliation of net income to net cash flows from operating activities is to be provided in a separate schedule (the indirect method). Despite the FASB's recommendations, a survey of large companies in 1992 showed that an overwhelming majority, 97 percent, chose to use the indirect method. Of six hundred companies, only fifteen chose the direct approach.[4] Why did so many choose the indirect approach?

The reasons for this choice may vary, but chief financial officers tend to prefer the indirect method because it is easier and less expensive to prepare. Moreover, because the FASB requires the reconciliation of net income (accrual) to cash flow (operations) as a supplemental schedule, the indirect method has to be implemented anyway.

4. American Institute of Certified Public Accountants, *Accounting Trends & Techniques* (New York: AICPA, 1993), p. 452.

A knowledge of the direct method helps the manager and the reader of financial statements perceive the underlying causes for the difference between reported net income and cash flows from operations. The indirect method is a practical way of presenting the differences. Both methods have merit. ⦂ ⦂ ⦂ ⦂ ⦂

Cash Receipts from Interest and Dividends Received   Although interest and dividends received are most closely associated with investment activity and are often called investment income, the FASB has decided to classify the cash received from these items as operating activities. To simplify the examples in this text, it is assumed that interest income equals interest received and that dividend income equals dividends received. Thus, from Exhibit 14-3, interest received by Ryan Corporation is assumed to equal $6,000, which is the amount of interest income.

Cash Payments for Purchases   Cost of goods sold (from the income statement) must be adjusted for changes in two balance sheet accounts to arrive at cash payments for purchases. First, cost of goods sold must be adjusted for changes in inventory to arrive at net purchases. Then, net purchases must be adjusted for the change in accounts payable to arrive at cash payments for purchases. If inventory has increased from one accounting period to another, net purchases will be greater than cost of goods sold because net purchases during the period have exceeded the dollar amount of the items sold during the period. If inventory has decreased, net purchases will be less than cost of goods sold. Conversely, if accounts payable has increased, cash payments for purchases will be less than net purchases; if accounts payable has decreased, cash payments for purchases will be greater than net purchases.

These relationships may be stated in equation form as follows:

$$\text{Cash Payments for Purchases} = \text{Cost of Goods Sold} \begin{cases} + \text{ Increase in Inventory} \\ \text{or} \\ - \text{ Decrease in Inventory} \end{cases} \begin{cases} + \text{ Decrease in Accounts Payable} \\ \text{or} \\ - \text{ Increase in Accounts Payable} \end{cases}$$

From Exhibits 14-2 and 14-3, cost of goods sold is $520,000, inventory increased by $34,000, and accounts payable increased by $7,000. Thus, cash payments for purchases is $547,000, as the following calculation shows:

$$\$547,000 = \$520,000 + \$34,000 - \$7,000$$

In this example, Ryan Corporation purchased $34,000 more inventory than it sold and paid out $7,000 less in cash than it purchased. The net result is that cash payments for purchases exceeded cost of goods sold by $27,000 ($547,000 − $520,000). These relationships can be visualized as follows:

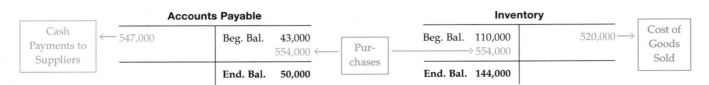

Cash Payments for Operating Expenses   Just as cost of goods sold does not represent the amount of cash paid for purchases during an accounting period, operating expenses do not match the amount of cash paid to employees, suppliers, and others for goods and services. Three adjustments must be made to operating expenses to arrive at the cash outflows. The first adjustment is for changes in prepaid expenses, such as prepaid insurance or prepaid rent. If prepaid assets increase during the accounting period, more cash will have been paid out than appears on the income statement as expenses. If prepaid assets decrease, the expenses shown on the income statement will exceed the cash spent.

The second adjustment is for changes in liabilities resulting from accrued expenses, such as wages payable and payroll taxes payable. If accrued liabilities increase during the accounting period, operating expenses on the income statement will exceed the cash spent. And if accrued liabilities decrease, operating expenses will fall short of cash spent.

The third adjustment is made because certain expenses do not require a current outlay of cash; these expenses must be subtracted from operating expenses to arrive at cash payments for operating expenses. The most common expenses in this category are depreciation expense, amortization expense, and depletion expense. Expenditures for plant assets, intangibles, and natural resources occur when these assets are purchased and are classified as an investing activity at that time. Depreciation expense, amortization expense, and depletion expense are simply allocations of the costs of those original purchases to the current accounting period; they do not affect cash flows in the current period. For example, Ryan Corporation recorded 19x2 depreciation expense as follows:

Depreciation Expense	37,000	
Accumulated Depreciation		37,000
To record depreciation on plant assets		

No cash payment was made in this transaction. Therefore, to the extent that operating expenses include depreciation and similar items, an adjustment is needed in order to reduce operating expenses to the amount of cash expended.

The three adjustments to operating expenses are summarized in the following equation.

$$\begin{matrix} \text{Cash Payments} \\ \text{for Operating} \\ \text{Expenses} \end{matrix} = \begin{matrix} \text{Operating} \\ \text{Expenses} \end{matrix} \left\{ \begin{matrix} + \text{ Increase in} \\ \text{Prepaid} \\ \text{Expenses} \\ \text{or} \\ - \text{ Decrease in} \\ \text{Prepaid} \\ \text{Expenses} \end{matrix} \right. \left\{ \begin{matrix} + \text{ Decrease in} \\ \text{Accrued} \\ \text{Liabilities} \\ \text{or} \\ - \text{ Increase in} \\ \text{Accrued} \\ \text{Liabilities} \end{matrix} \right. \left\{ \begin{matrix} - \text{ Depreciation} \\ \text{and Other} \\ \text{Noncash} \\ \text{Expenses} \end{matrix} \right.$$

From Exhibits 14-2 and 14-3, Ryan's operating expenses (including depreciation of $37,000) were $147,000; prepaid expenses decreased by $4,000; and accrued liabilities increased by $3,000. As a result, Ryan Corporation's cash payments for operating expenses are $103,000, computed as follows:

$$\$103,000 = \$147,000 - \$4,000 - \$3,000 - \$37,000$$

If prepaid expenses and accrued liabilities that are *not* related to specific operating expenses exist, they are not included in these computations. One example is income taxes payable, which is the accrued liability related to income taxes expense. The cash payment for income taxes is discussed in a later section of this chapter.

Cash Payments for Interest   The FASB classifies cash payments for interest as operating activities, although some authorities argue that they should be considered financing activities because of their association with loans incurred to finance the business. The FASB feels that interest expense is a cost of operating a business. We follow the FASB position in this text. Also, for the sake of simplicity, all examples in this text assume that interest payments are equal to interest expense on the income statement. Thus, from Exhibit 14-3, Ryan Corporation's interest payments are assumed to be $23,000 in 19x2.

Cash Payments for Income Taxes   The amount of income taxes expense that appears on the income statement rarely equals the amount of income taxes actually paid during the year. One reason for this difference is that the final payments for the income taxes of one year are not due until some time in the following year. A second reason is that there may be differences between what is deducted from or included in income for accounting purposes and what is deducted from or included in income for tax purposes. The latter reason often results in a deferred income tax liability. Its effects were discussed in the chapter on retained earnings and corporate income statements. Here, we deal only with the changes that result from increases or decreases in income taxes payable.

To determine cash payments for income taxes, income taxes expense (from the income statement) is adjusted by the change in income taxes payable. If income taxes payable increased during the accounting period, cash payments for taxes will be less than the expense shown on the income statement. If income taxes payable decreased, cash payments for taxes will exceed income taxes on the income statement. In other words, the following equation is applicable:

$$\begin{array}{ccc} \text{Cash Payments for} \\ \text{Income Taxes} \end{array} = \begin{array}{c} \text{Income} \\ \text{Taxes} \end{array} \left\{ \begin{array}{c} + \text{ Decrease in Income Taxes Payable} \\ \text{or} \\ - \text{ Increase in Income Taxes Payable} \end{array} \right.$$

In 19x2, Ryan Corporation showed income taxes of $7,000 on its income statement and a decrease of $2,000 in income taxes payable on its balance sheets (see Exhibits 14-2 and 14-3). As a result, cash payments for income taxes during 19x2 were $9,000, calculated as follows:

$$\$9,000 = \$7,000 + \$2,000$$

Other Income and Expenses   In computing cash flows from operations, some items classified on the income statement as other income and expenses are not considered operating items because they are more closely related to financing and investing activities. Items must be analyzed individually to determine their proper classification on the statement of cash flows. For instance, we have already dealt with interest income and interest expense as operating activities. Unlike interest, however, the effects of gains and losses are considered with the item that gave rise to the gain or loss. The effects of gains or losses on the sale of assets are considered with investing activities, and the effects of gains or losses related to liabilities are considered with financing activities. Consequently, the effects of the gain on sale of investments and of the loss on sale of plant assets reported on Ryan Corporation's income statement (Exhibit 14-3) are considered under cash flows from investing activities.

Schedule of Cash Flows from Operating Activities—Direct Method It is now possible to prepare a schedule of cash flows from operations using the direct method and the calculations made in the preceding paragraphs. In Exhibit 14-4, Ryan Corporation had cash receipts from sales and interest received of $712,000 and cash payments for purchases, operating expenses, interest payments, and income taxes of $682,000, resulting in net cash flows from operating activities of $30,000 in 19x2.

Schedule of Cash Flows from Operating Activities—Indirect Method It is also possible to calculate net cash flows from operations using the indirect method, as shown in Exhibit 14-5. Note that the amount for net cash flows from operating activities is the same as it was under the direct method (Exhibit 14-4).

First, the indirect method is based on the fact that cash flows from operations will not equal net income (or net loss). Under this method, net income is adjusted for expenses such as depreciation expense, amortization expense, depletion expense, and other income and expenses, such as gains and losses. These are items included on the income statement that do not affect cash flows. As a result, they are added or deducted as follows:

Adjustments to Convert Net Income to
Net Cash Flows from Operating Activities

	Add to (Deduct from) Net Income
Depreciation Expense	Add
Amortization Expense	Add
Depletion Expense	Add
Losses	Add
Gains	Deduct

Note that these adjustments to net income are made for several reasons. For example, depreciation expense is added because it is a noncash expense that was deducted in the income statement to arrive at net income. Adjustments are made for gains and losses for reasons that will become clear when investing activities and financing activities are discussed in the next two sections.

Second, the same adjustments for the changes in current assets and current liabilities are made as under the direct method, except that they are made as additions to or subtractions from net income instead of as adjustments to the individual income statement items. For instance, under the direct method, the decrease in accounts receivable was added to sales to adjust sales from an accrual basis to a cash basis. Since sales is included in the computation of net income, the same effect is achieved by adding the decrease in accounts receivable to net income. The same logic applies to adjustments to cost of goods sold, operating expenses, and income taxes, except that the signs will be opposite for these adjustments for the reason that the adjustments are to net income, not to the individual expense items. In general, in arriving at cash flows, the effects on net income of increases and decreases in current liabilities will be in the same direction and the effects of increases and decreases in current assets will be in the opposite direction, as summarized in the following table:

**Adjustments to Convert Net Income to
Net Cash Flows from Operating Activities**

	Add to Net Income	Deduct from Net Income
Current Assets		
Accounts Receivable (net)	Decrease	Increase
Inventory	Decrease	Increase
Prepaid Expenses	Decrease	Increase
Current Liabilities		
Accounts Payable	Increase	Decrease
Accrued Liabilities	Increase	Decrease
Income Taxes Payable	Increase	Decrease

DETERMINING CASH FLOWS FROM INVESTING ACTIVITIES

OBJECTIVE

5a *Determine cash flows from investing activities*

The second step in preparing the statement of cash flows is to determine cash flows from investing activities. Each account that involves cash receipts and cash payments from investing activities is examined individually. The objective is to explain the change in each account balance from one year to the next.

Investing activities center on the long-term assets shown on the balance sheet, but they also include transactions affecting short-term investments from the current asset section of the balance sheet and investment income from the income statement. From the balance sheet in Exhibit 14-2, we can see that Ryan Corporation has long-term assets of investments and plant assets, but no short-term investments. From the income statement in Exhibit 14-3, we see that Ryan has investment income in the form of interest income, a gain on sale of investments, and a loss on sale of plant assets. Also, from the schedule at the bottom of Exhibit 14-3, we find the following five items pertaining to investing activities in 19x2:

1. Purchased investments in the amount of $78,000.
2. Sold investments classified as long-term and available-for-sale for $102,000. These investments cost $90,000.
3. Purchased plant assets in the amount of $120,000.
4. Sold plant assets that cost $10,000 with accumulated depreciation of $2,000 for $5,000, resulting in a loss of $3,000.
5. Issued $100,000 of bonds at face value in a noncash exchange for plant assets.

The following paragraphs analyze the accounts related to investing activities to determine their effects on Ryan Corporation's cash flows.

Investments   The objective here is to explain the corporation's $12,000 decrease in investments, all of which are classified as available-for-sale securities, by analyzing the increases and decreases in the Investments account to determine the effects on the Cash account. Purchases increase investments

**Exhibit 14-4. Schedule of Cash Flows from Operating Activities—
Direct Method**

Ryan Corporation
Schedule of Cash Flows from Operating Activities
For the Year Ended December 31, 19x2

Cash Flows from Operating Activities		
Cash Receipts from		
Sales	$706,000	
Interest Received	6,000	$712,000
Cash Payments for		
Purchases	$547,000	
Operating Expenses	103,000	
Interest	23,000	
Income Taxes	9,000	682,000
Net Cash Flows from Operating Activities		$ 30,000

**Exhibit 14-5. Schedule of Cash Flows from Operating Activities—
Indirect Method**

Ryan Corporation
Schedule of Cash Flows from Operating Activities
For the Year Ended December 31, 19x2

Cash Flows from Operating Activities		
Net Income		$16,000
Adjustments to Reconcile Net Income to Net		
Cash Flows from Operating Activities		
Depreciation	$37,000	
Gain on Sale of Investments	(12,000)	
Loss on Sale of Plant Assets	3,000	
Changes in Current Assets and Current Liabilities		
Decrease in Accounts Receivable	8,000	
Increase in Inventory	(34,000)	
Decrease in Prepaid Expenses	4,000	
Increase in Accounts Payable	7,000	
Increase in Accrued Liabilities	3,000	
Decrease in Income Taxes Payable	(2,000)	14,000
Net Cash Flows from Operating Activities		$30,000

and sales decrease investments. Item **1** in the list of Ryan's investing activities shows purchases of $78,000 during 19x2. The transaction is recorded as follows:

Investments	78,000	
Cash		78,000
Purchase of investments		

As we can see from the entry, the effect of this transaction is a $78,000 decrease in cash flows.

Item **2** in the list shows a sale of investments at a gain. This transaction is recorded as follows:

Cash	102,000	
Investments		90,000
Gain on Sale of Investments		12,000
Sale of investments for a gain		

The effect of this transaction is a $102,000 increase in cash flows. Note that the gain on sale of investments is included in the $102,000. This is the reason it was excluded earlier in computing cash flows from operations. If it had been included in that section, it would have been counted twice.

The $12,000 decrease in the Investments account during 19x2 has now been explained, as may be seen in the following T account:

Investments

Beg. Bal.	127,000	Sales	90,000
Purchases	78,000		
End. Bal.	**115,000**		

The cash flow effects from these transactions are shown under the Cash Flows from Investing Activities section on the statement of cash flows as follows:

Purchase of Investments	($ 78,000)
Sale of Investments	102,000

Notice that purchases and sales are disclosed separately as cash outflows and cash inflows. They are not netted against each other into a single figure. This disclosure gives the reader of the statement a more complete view of investing activity.

If Ryan Corporation had short-term investments or marketable securities, the analysis of cash flows would be the same.

Plant Assets In the case of plant assets, it is necessary to explain the changes in both the asset account and the related accumulated depreciation account. According to Exhibit 14-2, plant assets increased by $210,000 and accumulated depreciation increased by $35,000. Purchases increase plant assets and sales decrease plant assets. Accumulated depreciation is increased by the amount of depreciation expense and decreased by the removal of the accumulated depreciation associated with plant assets that are sold. Three items listed in Exhibit 14-3 affect plant assets. Item **3** in the list on page 632 indicates that Ryan Corporation purchased plant assets totaling $120,000 during 19x2, as shown by this entry:

Plant Assets	120,000	
Cash		120,000
Purchase of plant assets		

This transaction results in a cash outflow of $120,000.

Item **4** states that Ryan Corporation sold plant assets for $5,000 that had cost $10,000 and had accumulated depreciation of $2,000. The entry to record this transaction is shown at the top of the next page:

Cash	5,000	
Accumulated Depreciation	2,000	
Loss on Sale of Plant Assets	3,000	
Plant Assets		10,000
Sale of plant assets at a loss		

Note that in this transaction the positive cash flow is equal to the amount of cash received, or $5,000. The loss on sale of plant assets is considered here rather than in the operating activities section. The amount of a loss or gain on the sale of an asset is determined by the amount of cash received and does not represent a cash outflow or inflow.

The disclosure of these two transactions in the investing activities section of the statement of cash flows is as follows:

Purchase of Plant Assets	($120,000)
Sale of Plant Assets	5,000

As with investments, cash outflows and cash inflows are not netted, but are presented separately to give full information to the statement reader.

Item **5** on the list of Ryan's investing activities is a noncash exchange that affects two long-term accounts, Plant Assets and Bonds Payable. It is recorded as follows:

Plant Assets	100,000	
Bonds Payable		100,000
Issued bonds at face value		
for plant assets		

Although this transaction is not an inflow or outflow of cash, it is a significant transaction involving both an investing activity (the purchase of plant assets) and a financing activity (the issue of bonds payable). Because one purpose of the statement of cash flows is to show important investing and financing activities, it is listed in a separate schedule, either at the bottom of the statement of cash flows or accompanying the statement, as follows:

Schedule of Noncash Investing and Financing Transactions

Issue of Bonds Payable for Plant Assets	$100,000

Through our analysis of these transactions and the depreciation expense for plant assets of $37,000, all the changes in the plant assets accounts have now been accounted for, as shown in these T accounts:

Plant Assets

Beg. Bal.	505,000	Sale	10,000
Purchase	120,000		
Noncash Purchase	100,000		
End. Bal.	**715,000**		

Accumulated Depreciation

Sale	2,000	Beg. Bal.	68,000
		Dep. Exp.	37,000
		End. Bal.	**103,000**

If the balance sheet had included specific plant asset accounts, such as Buildings and Equipment and their related accumulated depreciation accounts, or other long-term asset accounts, such as intangibles or natural resources, the analysis would be the same.

DETERMINING CASH FLOWS FROM FINANCING ACTIVITIES

OBJECTIVE

5b *Determine cash flows from financing activities*

The third step in preparing the statement of cash flows is to determine cash flows from financing activities. The procedure followed in this step is the same as that applied to the analysis of investing activities, including treatment of related gains or losses. The only difference between the two is that the accounts to be analyzed are the short-term borrowings, long-term liabilities, and stockholders' equity accounts. Cash dividends from the statement of stockholders' equity must also be considered. Since Ryan Corporation does not have short-term borrowings, only long-term liabilities and stockholders' equity accounts are considered here. The following items from Exhibit 14-3 pertain to Ryan Corporation's financing activities in 19x2:

5. Issued $100,000 of bonds at face value in a noncash exchange for plant assets.
6. Repaid $50,000 of bonds at face value at maturity.
7. Issued 15,200 shares of $5 par value common stock for $150,000.
8. Paid cash dividends in the amount of $8,000.

Bonds Payable Exhibit 14-2 shows that bonds payable increased by $50,000 in 19x2. This account is affected by items **5** and **6.** Item **5** was analyzed in connection with plant assets. It is reported on the schedule of noncash investing and financing transactions (see Exhibit 14-6 on page 639), but it must be remembered here in preparing the T account for bonds payable. Item **6** results in a cash outflow, a point that can be seen in the following transaction:

Bonds Payable	50,000	
Cash		50,000

Repayment of bonds at face value at maturity

This cash outflow is shown in the financing activities section of the statement of cash flows as follows:

Repayment of Bonds $(50,000)

From these transactions, the change in the Bonds Payable account can be explained as follows:

Bonds Payable

Repayment	50,000	Beg. Bal.	245,000
		Noncash Issue	100,000
		End. Bal.	**295,000**

If Ryan Corporation had notes payable, either short-term or long-term, the analysis would be the same.

Common Stock   As with plant assets, related stockholders' equity accounts should be analyzed together. For example, Paid-in Capital in Excess of Par Value should be examined together with Common Stock. In 19x2 Ryan Corporation's Common Stock account increased by $76,000 and Paid-in Capital in Excess of Par Value increased by $74,000. These increases are explained by item **7**, which states that Ryan Corporation issued 15,200 shares of stock for $150,000. The entry to record this cash inflow is as follows:

Cash	150,000	
Common Stock		76,000
Paid-in Capital in Excess of Par Value		74,000
Issue of 15,200 shares of $5 par		
value common stock		

This cash inflow is shown in the financing activities section of the statement of cash flows as follows:

Issue of Common Stock $150,000

The analysis of this transaction is all that is needed to explain the changes in the two accounts during 19x2, as follows:

Common Stock				Paid-in Capital in Excess of Par Value		
	Beg. Bal.	200,000			Beg. Bal.	115,000
	Issue	76,000			Issue	74,000
	End. Bal.	**276,000**			**End. Bal.**	**189,000**

Retained Earnings   At this point in the analysis, several items that affect Retained Earnings have already been dealt with. For instance, in the case of Ryan Corporation, net income was used as part of the analysis of cash flows from operating activities. The only other item affecting the Retained Earnings of Ryan Corporation is the payment of $8,000 in cash dividends (item **8** on the list on page 636), as reflected by the following transaction:

Retained Earnings	8,000	
Cash		8,000
Cash dividends for 19x2		

Ryan Corporation would have declared the dividend before paying it and debited the Dividends Declared account instead of Retained Earnings, but after paying the dividend and closing the Dividends Declared account to Retained Earnings, the effect is as shown. Cash dividends are displayed in the financing activities section of the statement of cash flows as follows:

Dividends Paid $(8,000)

The change in the Retained Earnings account is explained in the T account that follows:

Retained Earnings			
Dividends	8,000	Beg. Bal.	132,000
		Net Income	16,000
		End. Bal.	**140,000**

OBJECTIVE

> **6** *Prepare a state-
> ment of cash
> flows using the (a)
> direct and (b) indirect
> methods*

PRESENTING THE INFORMATION IN THE FORM OF THE STATEMENT OF CASH FLOWS

At this point in the analysis, all income statement items have been analyzed, all balance sheet changes have been explained, and all additional information has been taken into account. The resulting information may now be assembled into a statement of cash flows for Ryan Corporation. The statement in Exhibit 14-6 was prepared using the direct method and contains the operating activities section from Exhibit 14-4. The statement is just as easily prepared using the indirect approach and the data in Exhibit 14-5, as presented in Exhibit 14-7 (located on page 640). The Schedule of Noncash Investing and Financing Transactions is presented at the bottom of each statement. When the direct method is used, a schedule explaining the difference between reported net income and cash flows from operating activities must be provided, as shown in Exhibit 14-6. This reconciliation is the same as the cash flows from operating activities section of the indirect method form of the statement (Exhibit 14-7).

BUSINESS BULLETIN: INTERNATIONAL PRACTICE

The FASB in the United States is not the only body that makes changes in accounting standards that significantly affect financial reporting. A change in accounting standards in England caused consternation on the part of Saatchi & Saatchi, a British company that is one of the largest advertising agencies in the world. The chief executive announced that in 1992 the company had had the highest pretax loss—£595.1 million—in its history. According to the chief executive, the 1992 figures were caused by a £600 million writedown of assets, reflecting the fall in value of a large group of companies purchased by Saatchi & Saatchi during the 1980s. He explained that it was entirely a paper item that did not affect cash flows and described the new accounting standard as "a typical accounting trick which I do not understand."[5]

In fact, the new rule is understandable as good accounting practice. The writedowns are not a cash outflow in the *current* year because the companies were purchased in *prior* years; however, they are appropriately deducted in determining net income because if the values of the purchased companies have declined, as all agree they have, *future* cash flows will be negatively affected. A purpose of net income is to provide information about future cash flows. The net loss reported by Saatchi & Saatchi reflects reduced future cash flows. ▬▬▬

---

5. Martin Waller, "Writedown Condemns Saatchi to £595m Loss," *The London Times*, March 10, 1993.

Exhibit 14-6. Statement of Cash Flows—Direct Method

Ryan Corporation
Statement of Cash Flows
For the Year Ended December 31, 19x2

Cash Flows from Operating Activities

Cash Receipts from		
Sales	$706,000	
Interest Received	6,000	$712,000
Cash Payments for		
Purchases	$547,000	
Operating Expenses	103,000	
Interest	23,000	
Income Taxes	9,000	682,000
Net Cash Flows from Operating Activities		$ 30,000

Cash Flows from Investing Activities

Purchase of Investments	($ 78,000)	
Sale of Investments	102,000	
Purchase of Plant Assets	(120,000)	
Sale of Plant Assets	5,000	
Net Cash Flows from Investing Activities		(91,000)

Cash Flows from Financing Activities

Repayment of Bonds	($ 50,000)	
Issue of Common Stock	150,000	
Dividends Paid	(8,000)	
Net Cash Flows from Financing Activities		92,000
Net Increase (Decrease) in Cash		$ 31,000
Cash at Beginning of Year		15,000
Cash at End of Year		$ 46,000

Schedule of Noncash Investing and Financing Transactions

Issue of Bonds Payable for Plant Assets	$100,000

Reconciliation of Net Income to Net Cash Flows from Operating Activities

Net Income		$ 16,000
Adjustments to Reconcile Net Income to Net		
Cash Flows from Operating Activities		
Depreciation	$ 37,000	
Gain on Sale of Investments	(12,000)	
Loss on Sale of Plant Assets	3,000	
Changes in Current Assets and Current Liabilities		
Decrease in Accounts Receivable	8,000	
Increase in Inventory	(34,000)	
Decrease in Prepaid Expenses	4,000	
Increase in Accounts Payable	7,000	
Increase in Accrued Liabilities	3,000	
Decrease in Income Taxes Payable	(2,000)	14,000
Net Cash Flows from Operating Activities		$ 30,000

Exhibit 14-7. Statement of Cash Flows—Indirect Method

Ryan Corporation
Statement of Cash Flows
For the Year Ended December 31, 19x2

Cash Flows from Operating Activities		
Net Income		$ 16,000
Adjustments to Reconcile Net Income to Net		
Cash Flows from Operating Activities		
Depreciation	$ 37,000	
Gain on Sale of Investments	(12,000)	
Loss on Sale of Plant Assets	3,000	
Changes in Current Assets and Current Liabilities		
Decrease in Accounts Receivable	8,000	
Increase in Inventory	(34,000)	
Decrease in Prepaid Expenses	4,000	
Increase in Accounts Payable	7,000	
Increase in Accrued Liabilities	3,000	
Decrease in Income Taxes Payable	(2,000)	14,000
Net Cash Flows from Operating Activities		$ 30,000
Cash Flows from Investing Activities		
Purchase of Investments	($ 78,000)	
Sale of Investments	102,000	
Purchase of Plant Assets	(120,000)	
Sale of Plant Assets	5,000	
Net Cash Flows from Investing Activities		(91,000)
Cash Flows from Financing Activities		
Repayment of Bonds	($ 50,000)	
Issue of Common Stock	150,000	
Dividends Paid	(8,000)	
Net Cash Flows from Financing Activities		92,000
Net Increase (Decrease) in Cash		$ 31,000
Cash at Beginning of Year		15,000
Cash at End of Year		$ 46,000
Schedule of Noncash Investing and Financing Transactions		
Issue of Bonds Payable for Plant Assets		$100,000

ANALYSIS OF THE STATEMENT OF CASH FLOWS

OBJECTIVE

7 *Analyze the statement of cash flows*

Now that the statement is prepared, it is important to know how to interpret it. What can you learn about Ryan Corporation and its management by reading its statement of cash flows? As with the other financial statements, analysis can be used to show significant relationships. Two areas analysts look at in analyzing a company are its cash-generating efficiency and its free cash flow.

CASH-GENERATING EFFICIENCY

Analysts tend to focus first on the cash flows from operating activities in assessing the cash-generating efficiency of a company. Cash-generating efficiency is the ability of a company to generate cash from its current or continuing operations. Three ratios that are helpful in measuring cash-generating efficiency are the cash flow yield, cash flows to sales, and cash flows to assets. These ratios are computed and discussed below for Ryan Corporation. Data for the computations are obtained from Exhibits 14-2, 14-3, and 14-6.

Cash flow yield is the ratio of net cash flows from operating activities to net income, as follows:

$$\text{Cash flow yield} = \frac{\text{net cash flows from operating activities}}{\text{net income}}$$

$$= \frac{\$30,000}{\$16,000}$$

$$= 1.9 \text{ times}$$

Ryan Corporation provides a good cash flow yield of 1.9 times. This means that operating activities are generating almost twice as much cash flow as net income. If the company has material special items on the income statement, such as discontinued operations, income from continuing operations should be used as the denominator.

Cash flows to sales is the ratio of net cash flows from operating activities to sales, as follows:

$$\text{Cash flows to sales} = \frac{\text{net cash flows from operating activities}}{\text{net sales}}$$

$$= \frac{\$30,000}{\$698,000}$$

$$= 4.3\,\%$$

Ryan Corporation generates cash flows to sales of only 4.3 percent. This means that the company is not generating a high level of cash from sales.

Cash flows to assets is the ratio of net cash flows from operating activities to average total assets, as follows:

$$\text{Cash flows to assets} = \frac{\text{net cash flows from operating activities}}{\text{average total assets}}$$

$$= \frac{\$30,000}{(\$749,000 + \$965,000)/2}$$

$$= 3.5\%$$

The cash flows to assets is even lower than cash flows to sales because Ryan Corporation has a poor asset turnover ratio (sales ÷ average total assets) of less than 1.0 times. Cash flows to sales and cash flows to assets are closely related to the profitability measures profit margin and return on assets. They equal those measures times the amount of the cash flow yield ratio because cash flow yield is the ratio of net cash flows from operating activities to net income.

Although Ryan Corporation's cash flow yield is relatively strong, the latter two ratios show its efficiency at generating cash flows from operating activities to be low.

FREE CASH FLOW

It would be logical to move along in the analysis to investing and financing activities. Since there is a net cash outflow of $91,000 in the investing activities section, it is apparent that the company is expanding. However, this figure mixes net capital expenditures for plant assets, which reflect management's expansion of operations, with purchases and sales of investments. Also, cash flows from financing activities were a positive $92,000, but this figure combines financing activities associated with bonds and stocks with dividends paid to stockholders. While something can be learned by looking at these broad categories, many analysts find it more fruitful to go beyond them and focus on a new computation called free cash flow.

Free cash flow is the cash generated or cash deficiency after providing for commitments that must be made if a company is to continue operating at its planned level. These commitments are for current or continuing operations, interest, income taxes, dividends, and net capital expenditures. Cash requirements for current or continuing operations, interest, and income taxes must be paid or the company's creditors and the government can bring action against the company. Although the payment of dividends is not strictly required, dividends normally represent a commitment to stockholders. If they are reduced or eliminated, stockholders will be unhappy and the price of the company's stock will suffer. Net capital expenditures represent management's plans for the future.

If free cash flow is positive, it means that the company has met all of its planned cash commitments and has cash available to reduce debt or expand further. On the other hand, if free cash flow is negative, it means that the company will have to sell investments, borrow money, or issue stock in the short term to continue at its planned levels. If a negative situation continues for several years, a company may run out of sources of cash from selling investments or issuing stock or bonds.

Since cash commitments for current or continuing operations, interest, and income taxes are incorporated in cash flows from current operations, free cash flow for Ryan Corporation is computed as follows:

Free cash flow $=$ net cash flows from operating activities $-$ dividends $-$ purchases of plant assets $+$ sales of plant assets

$= \$30,000 - \$8,000 - \$120,000 + \$5,000$

$= (\$93,000)$

Purchases and sales of plant assets appear in the investing activities section of the statement of cash flows. Many companies provide this number as a "net" amount, using terms such as "net capital expenditures." Dividends are found in the financing activities section. Ryan Corporation has negative free cash flow of $93,000 and thus must make up the difference from sales of investments and from financing activities. Net sales of investments provided $24,000 ($102,000 − $78,000). Looking at the financing activities section, it may be seen that the company repaid debt of $50,000, while issuing common stock in the amount of $150,000, providing more than enough cash to overcome the negative free cash flow. Also, reducing debt while increasing equity is a wise action on management's part in light of the negative free cash flow. Unless the company improves its free cash flow, it may have difficulty meeting future debt repayments.

Because cash flows can vary from year to year, it is best to look at trends over several years when analyzing a company's cash flows.

Because the statement of cash flows has been around for less than a decade, no generally accepted analyses have yet been developed. For example, the term *free cash flow* is used commonly in the business press, but there is no agreement on its definition. A recent article in *Forbes* defines free cash flow as "cash available after paying out capital expenditures and dividends, *but before taxes and interest*"[6] [emphasis added]. In the *Wall Street Journal*, free cash flow was defined as "operating income less maintenance-level capital expenditures."[7] The definition we feel is best is the one used in *Business Week*, which is net cash flows from operating activities less net capital expenditures and dividends. This "measures truly discretionary funds—company money that an owner could pocket without harming the business."[8]

Supplemental OBJECTIVE

8 *Prepare a work sheet for the statement of cash flows*

PREPARING THE WORK SHEET

Previous sections illustrated the preparation of the statement of cash flows for Ryan Corporation, a relatively simple company. To assist in preparing the statement of cash flows in more complex companies, accountants developed a work sheet approach. The work sheet approach employs a special format that allows for the systematic analysis of all the changes in the balance sheet accounts to arrive at the statement of cash flows. In this section, the work sheet approach is demonstrated using the statement of cash flows for Ryan Corporation. The work sheet approach uses the indirect method of determining cash flows from operating activities because of its basis in changes in the balance sheet accounts.

PROCEDURES IN PREPARING THE WORK SHEET

The work sheet for Ryan Corporation is presented in Exhibit 14-8 on the next page. The work sheet has four columns, labeled as follows:

Column A: Description
Column B: Account balances for the end of the prior year (19x1)
Column C: Analysis of transactions for the current year
Column D: Account balances for the end of the current year (19x2)

Five steps are followed in the preparation of the work sheet. As you read each one, refer to Exhibit 14-8.

---

6. Gary Slutsker, "Look at the Birdie and Say: 'Cash Flow,' " *Forbes*, October 25, 1993.
7. Jonathan Clements, "Yacktman Fund is Bloodied but Unbowed," *Wall Street Journal*, November 8, 1993.
8. Jeffrey Laderman, "Earnings, Schmearnings—Look at the Cash," *Business Week*, July 24, 1989.

Exhibit 14-8. Work Sheet for the Statement of Cash Flows

Ryan Corporation
Work Sheet for Statement of Cash Flows
For the Year Ended December 31, 19x2

Description	Account Balances 12/31/x1	Analysis of Transactions Debit		Analysis of Transactions Credit		Account Balances 12/31/x2
Debits						
Cash	15,000	(x)	31,000			46,000
Accounts Receivable (net)	55,000			(b)	8,000	47,000
Inventory	110,000	(c)	34,000			144,000
Prepaid Expenses	5,000			(d)	4,000	1,000
Investments	127,000	(h)	78,000	(i)	90,000	115,000
Plant Assets	505,000	(j)	120,000	(k)	10,000	715,000
		(l)	100,000			
Total Debits	817,000					1,068,000
Credits						
Accumulated Depreciation	68,000	(k)	2,000	(m)	37,000	103,000
Accounts Payable	43,000			(e)	7,000	50,000
Accrued Liabilities	9,000			(f)	3,000	12,000
Income Taxes Payable	5,000	(g)	2,000			3,000
Bonds Payable	245,000	(n)	50,000	(l)	100,000	295,000
Common Stock	200,000			(o)	76,000	276,000
Paid-in Capital	115,000			(o)	74,000	189,000
Retained Earnings	132,000	(p)	8,000	(a)	16,000	140,000
Total Credits	817,000		425,000		425,000	1,068,000
Cash Flows from Operating Activities						
Net Income		(a)	16,000			
Decrease in Accounts Receivable		(b)	8,000			
Increase in Inventory				(c)	34,000	
Decrease in Prepaid Expenses		(d)	4,000			
Increase in Accounts Payable		(e)	7,000			
Increase in Accrued Liabilities		(f)	3,000			
Decrease in Income Taxes Payable				(g)	2,000	
Gain on Sale of Investments				(i)	12,000	
Loss on Sale of Plant Assets		(k)	3,000			
Depreciation Expense		(m)	37,000			
Cash Flows from Investing Activities						
Purchase of Investments				(h)	78,000	
Sale of Investments		(i)	102,000			
Purchase of Plant Assets				(j)	120,000	
Sale of Plant Assets		(k)	5,000			
Cash Flows from Financing Activities						
Repayment of Bonds				(n)	50,000	
Issue of Common Stock		(o)	150,000			
Dividends Paid				(p)	8,000	
			335,000		304,000	
Net Increase in Cash				(x)	31,000	
			335,000		335,000	

1. Enter the account names from the balance sheet (Exhibit 14-2) in column A. Note that all accounts with debit balances are listed first, followed by all accounts with credit balances.
2. Enter the account balances for 19x1 in column B and the account balances for 19x2 in column D. In each column, total the debits and the credits. The total debits should equal the total credits in each column. (This is a check of whether all accounts were transferred from the balance sheet correctly.)
3. Below the data entered in step **2**, insert the captions Cash Flows from Operating Activities, Cash Flows from Investing Activities, and Cash Flows from Financing Activities, leaving several lines of space between each one. As you do the analysis in step **4**, write the results in the appropriate categories.
4. Analyze the changes in each balance sheet account using information from both the income statement (see Exhibit 14-3) and other transactions affecting noncurrent accounts during 19x2. (The procedures for this analysis are presented in the next section.) Enter the results in the debit and credit columns. Identify each item with a letter. On the first line, identify the change in cash with an (x). In a complex situation, these letters will reference a list of explanations on another working paper.
5. When all the changes in the balance sheet accounts have been explained, add the debit and credit columns in both the top and bottom portions of column C. The debit and credit columns in the top portion should equal each other. They should *not* be equal in the bottom portion. If no errors have been made, the difference between columns in the bottom portion should equal the increase or decrease in the Cash account, identified with an (x) on the first line of the work sheet. Add this difference to the lesser of the two columns, and identify it as either an increase or a decrease in cash. Label the change with an (x) and compare it with the change in cash on the first line of the work sheet, also labeled (x). The amounts should be equal, as they are in Exhibit 14-8, where the net increase in cash is $31,000.

When the work sheet is complete, the statement of cash flows may be prepared using the information in the lower half of the work sheet.

ANALYZING THE CHANGES IN BALANCE SHEET ACCOUNTS

The most important step in the preparation of the work sheet is the analysis of the changes in the balance sheet accounts (step **4**). Although there are a number of transactions and reclassifications to analyze and record, the overall procedure is systematic and not overly complicated. It is as follows:

1. Record net income.
2. Account for changes in current assets and current liabilities.
3. Account for changes in noncurrent accounts using the information about other transactions.
4. Reclassify any other income and expense items not already dealt with. In the following explanations, the identification letters refer to the corresponding transactions and reclassifications in the work sheet.

a. Net Income   Net income results in an increase in Retained Earnings. It is also the starting point under the indirect method for determining cash flows from operating activities. Under this method, additions and deductions are made to net income to arrive at cash flows from operating activities. Work sheet entry **a** is as follows:

(a) Cash Flows from Operations: Net Income   16,000
       Retained Earnings   16,000

b–g. Changes in Current Assets and Current Liabilities   Entries **b** to **g** record the effects of the changes in current assets and current liabilities on cash flows. In each case, there is a debit or credit to the current asset or current liability to account for the change in the year and a corresponding debit or credit in the operating activities section of the work sheet. Recall that in the prior analysis, each item on the accrual-based income statement was adjusted for the change in the related current assets or current liabilities to arrive at the cash-based figure. The same reasoning applies in recording these changes in accounts as debits or credits in the operating activities section. For example, work sheet entry **b** records the decrease in Accounts Receivable as a credit (decrease) to Accounts Receivable and as a debit in the operating activities section because the decrease has a positive effect on cash flows, as follows:

(b) Cash Flows from Operating Activities:		
Decrease in Accounts Receivable	8,000	
Accounts Receivable		8,000

Work sheet entries **c–g** reflect the effects of the changes in the other current assets and current liabilities on cash flows from operating activities. As you study these entries, note how the effects of each entry on cash flows are automatically determined by debits or credits reflecting changes in the balance sheet accounts.

(c) Inventory	34,000	
Cash Flows from Operating Activities:		
Increase in Inventory		34,000
(d) Cash Flows from Operating Activities:		
Decrease in Prepaid Expenses	4,000	
Prepaid Expenses		4,000
(e) Cash Flows from Operating Activities:		
Increase in Accounts Payable	7,000	
Accounts Payable		7,000
(f) Cash Flows from Operating Activities:		
Increase in Accrued Liabilities	3,000	
Accrued Liabilities		3,000
(g) Income Taxes Payable	2,000	
Cash Flows from Operating Activities:		
Decrease in Income Taxes Payable		2,000

h–i. Investments   Among the other transactions affecting noncurrent accounts during 19x2 (see Exhibit 14-3), two items pertain to investments. One is the purchase for $78,000 and the other is the sale at $102,000. The purchase is recorded on the work sheet as a cash flow in the investing activities section, as follows:

(h) Investments	78,000	
Cash Flows from Investing Activities:		
Purchase of Investments		78,000

Note that instead of crediting Cash, a credit entry with the appropriate designation is made in the appropriate section in the lower half of the work sheet. The sale transaction is more complicated because it involves a gain that appears on the income statement and is included in net income. The work sheet entry accounts for this gain as follows:

(i) Cash Flows from Investing Activities:
    Sale of Investments   102,000
      Investments   90,000
      Cash Flows from Operating Activities:
        Gain on Sale of Investments   12,000

This entry records the cash inflow in the investing activities section, accounts for the remaining difference in the Investments account, and removes the gain on sale of investments from net income.

j–m. *Plant Assets and Accumulated Depreciation*   Four transactions affect plant assets and the related accumulated depreciation. These are the purchase of plant assets, the sale of plant assets at a loss, the noncash exchange of bonds for plant assets, and the depreciation expense for the year. Because these transactions may appear complicated, it is important to work through them systematically when preparing the work sheet. First, the purchase of plant assets for $120,000 is entered (entry **j**) in the same way the purchase of investments was entered in entry **h:**

(j) Plant Assets   120,000
    Cash Flows from Investing Activities:
      Purchase of Plant Assets   120,000

Second, the sale of plant assets is similar to the sale of investments, except that a loss is involved, as follows:

(k) Cash Flows from Investing Activities:
    Sale of Plant Assets   5,000
    Cash Flows from Operating Activities:
      Loss on Sale of Plant Assets   3,000
      Accumulated Depreciation   2,000
        Plant Assets   10,000

The cash inflow from this transaction is $5,000. The rest of the entry is necessary to add the loss back into net income in the operating activities section of the statement of cash flows (since it was deducted to arrive at net income and no cash outflow resulted) and to record the effects on plant assets and accumulated depreciation.

The third transaction (entry **l**) is the noncash issue of bonds for the purchase of plant assets, as follows:

(l) Plant Assets   100,000
    Bonds Payable   100,000

Note that this transaction does not affect cash. Still, it needs to be recorded because the objective is to account for all the changes in the balance sheet accounts. It is listed at the end of the statement of cash flows (Exhibit 14-7) in the schedule of noncash investing and financing transactions.

At this point the increase of $210,000 ($715,000 − $505,000) in plant assets has been explained by the two purchases less the sale ($120,000 + $100,000 − $10,000 = $210,000), but the change in Accumulated Depreciation has not been completely explained. The depreciation expense for the year needs to be entered, as follows:

(m) Cash Flows from Operating Activities:
    Depreciation Expense   37,000
      Accumulated Depreciation   37,000

The debit is to the operating activities section of the work sheet because, as explained earlier in the chapter, no current cash outflow is required for depreciation expense. The effect of this debit is to add the amount for depreciation expense back into net income. The $35,000 increase in Accumulated Depreciation has now been explained by the sale transaction and the depreciation expense (−$2,000 + $37,000 = $35,000).

n. Bonds Payable　　　Part of the change in Bonds Payable was explained in entry l when a noncash transaction, a $100,000 issue of bonds in exchange for plant assets, was entered. All that remains is to enter the repayment, as follows:

(n) Bonds Payable	50,000	
Cash Flows from Financing Activities:		
Repayment of Bonds		50,000

o. Common Stock and Paid-in Capital in Excess of Par Value　　　One transaction affects both these accounts. It is an issue of 15,200 shares of $5 par value common stock for a total of $150,000. The work sheet entry is

(o) Cash Flows from Financing Activities:		
Issue of Common Stock	150,000	
Common Stock		76,000
Paid-in Capital in Excess of Par Value		74,000

p. Retained Earnings　　　Part of the change in Retained Earnings was recognized when net income was entered (entry **a**). The only remaining effect to be recognized is the $8,000 in cash dividends paid during the year, as follows:

(p) Retained Earnings	8,000	
Cash Flows from Financing Activities:		
Dividends Paid		8,000

x. Cash　　　The final step is to total the debit and credit columns in the top and bottom portions of the work sheet and then to enter the net change in cash at the bottom of the work sheet. The columns in the upper half equal $425,000. In the lower half, the debit column totals $335,000 and the credit column totals $304,000. The credit difference of $31,000 (entry **x**) equals the debit change in cash on the first line of the work sheet.

CHAPTER REVIEW

REVIEW OF LEARNING OBJECTIVES

1. **Describe the statement of cash flows, and define *cash* and *cash equivalents.*** The statement of cash flows explains the changes in cash and cash equivalents from one accounting period to the next by showing cash inflows and cash outflows from the operating, investing, and financing activities of a company for an accounting period. For purposes of preparing the statement of cash flows, *cash* is defined to include cash and cash equivalents. *Cash equivalents* are short-term (ninety days or less), highly liquid investments, including money market accounts, commercial paper, and U.S. Treasury bills.

2. **State the principal purposes and uses of the statement of cash flows.** The primary purpose of the statement of cash flows is to provide information about a company's cash receipts and cash payments during an accounting period. Its secondary purpose is to provide information about a company's operating, investing, and financing activities. It is useful to management as well as to investors and creditors in assessing the liquidity of a business, including the ability of the business to generate future cash flows and to pay its debts and dividends.

3. **Identify the principal components of the classifications of cash flows, and state the significance of noncash investing and financing transactions.** Cash flows may be classified as (1) operating activities, which include the cash effects of transactions and other events that enter into the determination of net income; (2) investing activities, which include the acquiring and selling of long- and short-term marketable securities, property, plant, and equipment, and the making and collecting of loans, excluding interest; or (3) financing activities, which include the obtaining and returning or repaying of resources, excluding interest to owners and creditors. Noncash investing and financing transactions are particularly important because they are exchanges of assets and/or liabilities that are of interest to investors and creditors when evaluating the financing and investing activities of a business.

4. **Determine cash flows from operating activities using the (a) direct and (b) indirect methods.** The direct method of determining cash flows from operating activities is accomplished by adjusting each item in the income statement from an accrual basis to a cash basis, in the following form:

Cash Flows from Operating Activities		
Cash Receipts from		
Sales	xxx	
Interest and Dividends Received	xxx	xxx
Cash Payments for		
Purchases	xxx	
Operating Expenses	xxx	
Interest	xxx	
Income Taxes	xxx	xxx
Net Cash Flows from Operating Activities		xxx

    In the indirect method, net income is adjusted for all noncash effects to arrive at a cash flow basis, as follows:

Cash Flows from Operating Activities		
Net Income		xxx
Adjustments to Reconcile Net Income to		
Net Cash Flows from Operating Activities		
(List of individual items)	xxx	xxx
Net Cash Flows from Operating Activities		xxx

5. **Determine cash flows from (a) investing activities and (b) financing activities.** Cash flows from investing activities are determined by identifying the cash flow effects of the transactions that affect each account relevant to investing activities. These accounts include all long-term assets and short-term marketable securities. The same procedure is followed for financing activities, except that the accounts involved are short-term notes payable, long-term liabilities, and stockholders' equity accounts. The effects on related accounts of gains and losses reported on the income statement must also be considered. When the change in a balance sheet account from one accounting period to the next has been explained, all the cash flow effects should have been identified.

6. **Prepare a statement of cash flows using the (a) direct and (b) indirect methods.** The statement of cash flows lists cash flows from operating activities, investing activities, and financing activities, in that order. The section on operating activities may be prepared using either the direct or the indirect method of determining cash

flows from operating activities. The sections on investing and financing activities are prepared by examining individual accounts involving cash receipts and cash payments in order to explain year-to-year changes in the account balances. Significant noncash transactions are included in a schedule of noncash investing and financing transactions that accompanies the statement of cash flows. Whenever the direct method is used, a reconciliation of net income to net cash flows from operating activities is required.

7. **Analyze the statement of cash flows.** In analyzing a company's statement of cash flows, analysts tend to focus on the company's cash-generating efficiency and free cash flow. Cash-generating efficiency is a company's ability to generate cash from its current or continuing operations. Three ratios used in measuring cash-generating efficiency are cash flow yield, cash flows to sales, and cash flows to assets. Free cash flow is the cash generated or cash deficiency after providing for commitments that must be made if a company is to continue operating at its planned level. These commitments are for current or continuing operations, interest, income taxes, dividends, and net capital expenditures.

SUPPLEMENTAL OBJECTIVE

8. **Prepare a work sheet for the statement of cash flows.** A work sheet is useful in preparing the statement of cash flows for complex companies. The basic procedures in the work sheet approach are to analyze the changes in the balance sheet accounts for their effects on cash flows (in the top portion of the work sheet) and to classify those effects according to the format of the statement of cash flows (in the lower portion of the work sheet). When all the changes in the balance sheet accounts have been explained and entered on the work sheet, the change in the cash account will also be explained, and the information will be available to prepare the statement of cash flows. The work sheet approach lends itself to the indirect method of preparing the statement of cash flows.

REVIEW OF CONCEPTS AND TERMINOLOGY

The following concepts and terms were introduced in this chapter:

L O 1 **Cash:** For purposes of the statement of cash flows, both cash and cash equivalents.

L O 1 **Cash equivalents:** Short-term (ninety days or less), highly liquid investments, including money market accounts, commercial paper, and U.S. Treasury bills.

L O 7 **Cash flows to assets:** The ratio of net cash flows from operating activities to average total assets.

L O 7 **Cash flows to sales:** The ratio of net cash flows from operating activities to sales.

L O 7 **Cash flow yield:** The ratio of net cash flows from operating activities to net income.

L O 7 **Cash-generating efficiency:** The ability of a company to generate cash from its current or continuing operations.

L O 4 **Direct method:** The procedure for converting the income statement from an accrual basis to a cash basis by adjusting each item in the income statement separately.

L O 3 **Financing activities:** Business activities that involve obtaining or returning resources from or to owners and providing them with a return on their investment, and obtaining resources from creditors and repaying the amounts borrowed or otherwise settling the obligations.

L O 7 **Free cash flow:** The cash generated or cash deficiency after providing for commitments that must be made if a company is to continue operating at its planned level; net cash flows from operating activities minus dividends minus net capital expenditures.

L O 4 **Indirect method:** The procedure for converting the income statement from an accrual basis to a cash basis by adjusting net income for items that do not affect cash flows, including depreciation, amortization, depletion, gains, losses, and changes in current assets and current liabilities.

L O 3 **Investing activities:** Business activities that include the acquiring and selling of long-term assets, the acquiring and selling of marketable securities other than cash equivalents, and the making and collecting of loans.

L O 3 **Noncash investing and financing transactions:** Significant investing and financing transactions that do not involve an actual cash inflow or outflow but involve only long-term assets, long-term liabilities, or stockholders' equity, such as the exchange of a long-term asset for a long-term liability or the settlement of a debt by the issue of capital stock.

L O 3 **Operating activities:** Business activities that include the cash effects of transactions and other events that enter into the determination of net income.

L O 1 **Statement of cash flows:** A primary financial statement that shows the effect on cash of a company's operating, investing, and financing activities for an accounting period.

REVIEW PROBLEM
THE STATEMENT OF CASH FLOWS

L O 4, 5, 6 The comparative balance sheets for Northwest Corporation for the years 19x7 and 19x6 are presented below; the 19x7 income statement is shown on the following page.

Northwest Corporation
Comparative Balance Sheets
December 31, 19x7 and 19x6

	19x7	19x6	Change	Increase or Decrease
Assets				
Cash	$ 115,850	$ 121,850	($ 6,000)	Decrease
Accounts Receivable (net)	296,000	314,500	(18,500)	Decrease
Inventory	322,000	301,000	21,000	Increase
Prepaid Expenses	7,800	5,800	2,000	Increase
Long-Term Investments	36,000	86,000	(50,000)	Decrease
Land	150,000	125,000	25,000	Increase
Building	462,000	462,000	—	—
Accumulated Depreciation, Building	(91,000)	(79,000)	(12,000)	Increase
Equipment	159,730	167,230	(7,500)	Decrease
Accumulated Depreciation, Equipment	(43,400)	(45,600)	2,200	Decrease
Intangible Assets	19,200	24,000	(4,800)	Decrease
Total Assets	$1,434,180	$1,482,780	($ 48,600)	
Liabilities and Stockholders' Equity				
Accounts Payable	$ 133,750	$ 233,750	($100,000)	Decrease
Notes Payable (current)	75,700	145,700	(70,000)	Decrease
Accrued Liabilities	5,000	—	5,000	Increase
Income Taxes Payable	20,000	—	20,000	Increase
Bonds Payable	210,000	310,000	(100,000)	Decrease
Mortgage Payable	330,000	350,000	(20,000)	Decrease
Common Stock—$10 par value	360,000	300,000	60,000	Increase
Paid-in Capital in Excess of Par Value	90,000	50,000	40,000	Increase
Retained Earnings	209,730	93,330	116,400	Increase
Total Liabilities and Stockholders' Equity	$1,434,180	$1,482,780	($ 48,600)	

Northwest Corporation
Income Statement
For the Year Ended December 31, 19x7

Sales		$1,650,000
Cost of Goods Sold		920,000
Gross Margin from Sales		$ 730,000
Operating Expenses (including Depreciation Expense of $12,000 on Buildings and $23,100 on Equipment and Amortization Expense of $4,800)		470,000
Operating Income		$ 260,000
Other Income (Expense)		
Interest Expense	($55,000)	
Dividend Income	3,400	
Gain on Sale of Investments	12,500	
Loss on Disposal of Equipment	(2,300)	(41,400)
Income Before Taxes		$ 218,600
Income Taxes		52,200
Net Income		$ 166,400

The following additional information was taken from the company's records:

a. Long-term investments (available-for-sale securities) that cost $70,000 were sold at a gain of $12,500; additional long-term investments were made in the amount of $20,000.

b. Five acres of land were purchased for $25,000 for a parking lot.

c. Equipment that cost $37,500 with accumulated depreciation of $25,300 was sold at a loss of $2,300; new equipment costing $30,000 was purchased.

d. Notes payable in the amount of $100,000 were repaid; an additional $30,000 was borrowed by signing notes payable.

e. Bonds payable in the amount of $100,000 were converted into 6,000 shares of common stock.

f. The Mortgage Payable account was reduced by $20,000 during the year.

g. Cash dividends declared and paid were $50,000.

REQUIRED

1. Prepare a schedule of cash flows from operating activities using the (a) direct method and (b) indirect method.
2. Prepare a statement of cash flows using the indirect method.

ANSWER TO REVIEW PROBLEM

1. (a) Prepare a schedule of cash flows from operating activities—direct method.

Northwest Corporation
Schedule of Cash Flows from Operating Activities
For the Year Ended December 31, 19x7

Cash Flows from Operating Activities		
Cash Receipts from		
Sales	$1,668,500[1]	
Dividends Received	3,400	$1,671,900
Cash Payments for		
Purchases	$1,041,000[2]	
Operating Expenses	427,100[3]	
Interest	55,000	
Income Taxes	32,200[4]	1,555,300
Net Cash Flows from Operating Activities		$ 116,600

1. $1,650,000 + $18,500 = $1,668,500
2. $920,000 + $100,000 + $21,000 = $1,041,000
3. $470,000 + $2,000 − $5,000 − ($12,000 + $23,100 + $4,800) = $427,100
4. $52,200 − $20,000 = $32,200

1. (b) Prepare a schedule of cash flows from operating activities—indirect method.

Northwest Corporation
Schedule of Cash Flows from Operating Activities
For the Year Ended December 31, 19x7

Cash Flows from Operating Activities		
Net Income		$166,400
Adjustments to Reconcile Net Income to		
Net Cash Flows from Operating Activities		
Depreciation Expense, Buildings	$ 12,000	
Depreciation Expense, Equipment	23,100	
Amortization Expense, Intangible Assets	4,800	
Gain on Sale of Investments	(12,500)	
Loss on Disposal of Equipment	2,300	
Changes in Current Assets		
and Current Liabilities		
Decrease in Accounts Receivable	18,500	
Increase in Inventory	(21,000)	
Increase in Prepaid Expenses	(2,000)	
Decrease in Accounts Payable	(100,000)	
Increase in Accrued Liabilities	5,000	
Increase in Income Taxes Payable	20,000	(49,800)
Net Cash Flows from Operating Activities		$116,600

2. Prepare a statement of cash flows—indirect method.

Northwest Corporation
Statement of Cash Flows
For the Year Ended December 31, 19x7

Cash Flows from Operating Activities		
Net Income		$166,400
Adjustments to Reconcile Net Income to		
Net Cash Flows from Operating Activities		
Depreciation Expense, Buildings	$ 12,000	
Depreciation Expense, Equipment	23,100	
Amortization Expense, Intangible Assets	4,800	
Gain on Sale of Investments	(12,500)	
Loss on Disposal of Equipment	2,300	
Changes in Current Assets and		
Current Liabilities		
Decrease in Accounts Receivable	18,500	
Increase in Inventory	(21,000)	
Increase in Prepaid Expenses	(2,000)	
Decrease in Accounts Payable	(100,000)	
Increase in Accrued Liabilities	5,000	
Increase in Income Taxes Payable	20,000	(49,800)
Net Cash Flows from Operating Activities		$116,600
Cash Flows from Investing Activities		
Sale of Long-Term Investments	$ 82,500[1]	
Purchase of Long-Term Investments	(20,000)	
Purchase of Land	(25,000)	
Sale of Equipment	9,900[2]	
Purchase of Equipment	(30,000)	
Net Cash Flows from Investing Activities		17,400
Cash Flows from Financing Activities		
Repayment of Notes Payable	($ 100,000)	
Issuance of Notes Payable	30,000	
Reduction in Mortgage	(20,000)	
Dividends Paid	(50,000)	
Net Cash Flows from Financing Activities		(140,000)
Net Increase (Decrease) in Cash		($ 6,000)
Cash at Beginning of Year		121,850
Cash at End of Year		$115,850

Schedule of Noncash Investing and Financing Transactions

Conversion of Bonds Payable into Common Stock	$100,000

1. $70,000 + $12,500 (gain) = $82,500
2. $37,500 − $25,300 = $12,200 (book value) − $2,300 (loss) = $9,900

CHAPTER ASSIGNMENTS

KNOWLEDGE AND UNDERSTANDING

Questions

1. What is the term *cash* in the statement of cash flows understood to include?

2. In order to earn a return on cash on hand during 19x3, Sallas Corporation transferred $45,000 from its checking account to a money market account, purchased a $25,000 Treasury bill, and bought $35,000 in common stocks. How will each of these transactions affect the statement of cash flows?

3. What are the purposes of the statement of cash flows?

4. Why is the statement of cash flows needed when most of the information in it is available from a company's comparative balance sheets and the income statement?

5. What are the three classifications of cash flows? Give some examples of each.

6. Why is it important to disclose certain noncash transactions? How should they be disclosed?

7. What are the essential differences between the direct method and the indirect method of determining cash flows from operations?

8. Are the following items shown as increases or decreases in cash flows from operations (assuming the direct method is used): (a) an increase in accounts receivable, (b) a decrease in inventory, (c) an increase in accounts payable, (d) a decrease in wages payable, (e) depreciation expense, and (f) amortization of patents?

9. Glen Corporation has the following other income and expense items: interest expense, $12,000; interest income, $3,000; dividend income, $5,000; and loss on retirement of bonds, $6,000. How does each of these items appear on or affect the statement of cash flows (assuming the direct method is used)?

10. Cell-Borne Corporation has a net loss of $12,000 in 19x1 but has positive cash flows from operations of $9,000. What conditions may have caused this situation?

11. What is the proper treatment on the statement of cash flows of a transaction in which a building that cost $50,000 with accumulated depreciation of $32,000 is sold for a loss of $5,000?

12. What is the proper treatment on the statement of cash flows of (a) a transaction in which buildings and land are purchased by the issuance of a mortgage for $234,000 and (b) a conversion of $50,000 in bonds payable into 2,500 shares of $6 par value common stock?

13. Define *cash-generating efficiency* and identify three ratios that measure cash-generating efficiency.

14. Define free cash flow and identify its components. What does it mean to have a positive or a negative free cash flow?

15. Why is the work sheet approach considered to be more compatible with the indirect method than with the direct method of determining cash flows from operations?

16. Assuming in each of the following independent cases that only one transaction occurred, what transactions would be likely to cause (a) a decrease in investments and (b) an increase in common stock? How would each case be treated on the work sheet for the statement of cash flows?

Short Exercises

SE 14-1.

L O 3 *Classification of Cash Flow Transactions*

Turandot Corporation engaged in the following transactions. Identify each as (a) an operating activity, (b) an investing activity, (c) a financing activity, (d) a noncash transaction, or (e) none of the above.

1. Sold land for a gain.
2. Declared and paid a cash dividend.
3. Paid interest.

4. Issued common stock for plant assets.
5. Issued preferred stock for cash.
6. Borrowed cash on a bank loan.

SE 14-2.
L O 4
Cash Receipts from Sales

During 19x2, Maine Grain Company, a marketer of whole-grain products, had sales of $426,500. The ending balance of Accounts Receivable was $127,400 in 19x1 and $96,200 in 19x2. Calculate cash receipts from sales in 19x2.

SE 14-3.
L O 4
Cash Payments for Purchases

During 19x2, Maine Grain Company had cost of goods sold of $294,200. The ending balance of Inventory was $36,400 in 19x1 and $44,800 in 19x2. The ending balance of Accounts Payable was $28,100 in 19x1 and $25,900 in 19x2. Calculate cash payments for purchases in 19x2.

SE 14-4.
L O 4
Cash Payments for Operating Expenses and Income Taxes

During 19x2, Maine Grain Company had operating expenses of $79,000 and income taxes expense of $12,500. Depreciation expense of $20,000 for 19x2 was included in operating expenses. The ending balance of Prepaid Expenses was $3,600 in 19x1 and $2,300 in 19x2. The ending balance of Accrued Liabilities (excluding Income Taxes Payable) was $3,000 in 19x1 and $2,000 in 19x2. The ending balance of Income Taxes Payable was $4,100 in 19x1 and $3,500 in 19x2. Calculate cash payments for operating expenses and income taxes in 19x2.

SE 14-5.
L O 4
Preparing a Schedule of Cash Flows from Operating Activities—Direct Method

The income statement for the Ridge Corporation follows.

Ridge Corporation
Income Statement
For the Year Ended June 30, 19xx

Sales		$60,000
Cost of Goods Sold		30,000
Gross Margin		$30,000
Operating Expenses		
Salaries Expense	$16,000	
Rent Expense	8,400	
Depreciation Expense	1,000	25,400
Income Before Income Taxes		$ 4,600
Income Taxes		1,200
Net Income		$ 3,400

Additional information: (a) All sales were on credit, and accounts receivable increased by $2,000 during the year. (b) All merchandise purchased was on credit. Inventories increased by $3,000, and accounts payable increased by $7,000 during the year. (c) Prepaid rent decreased by $700, and salaries payable increased by $500. (d) Income taxes payable decreased by $200 during the year. Prepare a schedule of cash flows from operating activities using the direct method.

SE 14-6.
L O 4
Computing Cash Flows from Operating Activities—Indirect Method

During 19x1, Akabah Corporation had a net income of $72,000. Included on the income statement was depreciation expense of $8,000 and amortization expense of $900. During the year, accounts receivable decreased by $4,100, inventories increased by $2,700, prepaid expenses decreased by $500, accounts payable decreased by $7,000, and accrued liabilities decreased by $850. Determine cash flows from operating activities using the indirect method.

SE 14-7.

L O 5 *Cash Flows from Investing Activities and Noncash Transactions*

During 19x1, Maryland Company purchased land for $750,000. The company paid $250,000 in cash and signed a $500,000 mortgage for the rest. The company also sold a building that had originally cost $180,000, on which it had $140,000 of accumulated depreciation, for $190,000 cash and a gain of $150,000. Prepare the cash flows from investing activities and schedule of noncash investing and financing transactions sections of the statement of cash flows.

SE 14-8.

L O 5 *Cash Flows from Financing Activities*

During 19x1, Maryland Company issued $1,000,000 in long-term bonds at 96, repaid $150,000 of bonds at face value, paid interest of $80,000, and paid dividends of $50,000. Prepare the cash flows from financing activities section of the statement of cash flows.

SE 14-9.

L O 4, 6 *Direct Method Versus Indirect Method*

Indicate whether each of the following items would appear in the operating activities section of the statement of cash flows under (a) the direct method, (b) the indirect method, or (c) neither.

1. Depreciation Expense
2. Cash Receipts from Sales
3. Increase in Accounts Receivable
4. Cash Payments for Purchases
5. Dividends Paid
6. Gain on Sale of Investments

SE 14-10.

L O 7 *Cash-Generating Efficiency Ratios and Free Cash Flow*

In 19x2, Wong Corporation had total assets of $550,000, net sales of $790,000, net income of $90,000, net cash from operations of $180,000, dividends of $40,000, purchases of plant assets of $120,000, and sales of plant assets of $20,000. In 19x1, total assets were $500,000. Calculate the cash-generating efficiency ratios of cash flow yield, cash flows to sales, and cash flows to assets. Also calculate free cash flow.

APPLICATION

Exercises

E 14-1.

L O 3 *Classification of Cash Flow Transactions*

Horizon Corporation engaged in the following transactions. Identify each as (a) an operating activity, (b) an investing activity, (c) a financing activity, (d) a noncash transaction, or (e) none of the above.

1. Declared and paid a cash dividend.
2. Purchased a long-term investment.
3. Received cash from customers.
4. Paid interest.
5. Sold equipment at a loss.
6. Issued long-term bonds for plant assets.
7. Received dividends on securities held.
8. Issued common stock.
9. Declared and issued a stock dividend.
10. Repaid notes payable.
11. Paid employees their wages.
12. Purchased a 60-day Treasury bill.
13. Purchased land.

E 14-2.

L O 4 *Cash Receipts from Sales*

During 19x2, Union Chemical Company, a distributor of farm fertilizers and herbicides, had sales of $6,500,000. The ending balance of Accounts Receivable was $850,000 in 19x1 and $1,200,000 in 19x2. Calculate cash receipts from sales in 19x2.

E 14-3.

L O 4 *Cash Payments for Purchases*

During 19x2, Union Chemical Company had cost of goods sold of $3,800,000. The ending balance of Inventory was $510,000 in 19x1 and $420,000 in 19x2. The ending balance of Accounts Payable was $360,000 in 19x1 and $480,000 in 19x2. Calculate cash payments for purchases in 19x2.

E 14-4.

L O 4 *Cash Payments for Operating Expenses and Income Taxes*

During 19x2, Union Chemical Company had operating expenses of $1,900,000 and income taxes expense of $200,000. Depreciation expense of $410,000 for 19x2 was included in operating expenses. The ending balance of Prepaid Expenses was $90,000 in 19x1 and $130,000 in 19x2. The ending balance of Accrued Liabilities (excluding Income Taxes Payable) was $50,000 in 19x1 and $30,000 in 19x2. The ending balance of Income Taxes Payable was $60,000 in 19x1 and $70,000 in 19x2. Calculate cash payments for operating expenses and income taxes in 19x2.

E 14-5.
L O 4 *Cash Flows from Operating Activities—Direct Method*

Using the computations you made in E14-2, 14-3, and 14-4, prepare in good form a schedule of cash flows from operating activities for 19x2, using the direct method. The company has a December 31 year end.

E 14-6.
L O 4 *Cash Flows from Operating Activities—Indirect Method*

The condensed single-step income statement of Union Chemical Company, a distributor of farm fertilizers and herbicides, appears as follows:

Sales		$6,500,000
Less: Cost of Goods Sold	$3,800,000	
Operating Expenses (including depreciation of $410,000)	1,900,000	
Income Taxes	200,000	5,900,000
Net Income		$ 600,000

Selected accounts from the company's balance sheets for 19x1 and 19x2 appear as shown below:

	19x2	19x1
Accounts Receivable	$1,200,000	$850,000
Inventory	420,000	510,000
Prepaid Expenses	130,000	90,000
Accounts Payable	480,000	360,000
Accrued Liabilities	30,000	50,000
Income Taxes Payable	70,000	60,000

Present in good form a schedule of cash flows from operating activities using the indirect method.

E 14-7.
L O 4 *Computing Cash Flows from Operating Activities—Direct Method*

Europa Corporation engaged in the following transactions in 19x2. Using the direct method, compute the various cash flows from operating activities as required.

a. During 19x2, Europa Corporation had cash sales of $41,300 and sales on credit of $123,000. During the same year, accounts receivable decreased by $18,000. Determine the cash received from sales during 19x2.
b. During 19x2, Europa Corporation's cost of goods sold was $119,000. During the same year, merchandise inventory increased by $12,500 and accounts payable decreased by $4,300. Determine the cash payments for purchases during 19x2.
c. During 19x2, Europa Corporation had operating expenses of $45,000, including depreciation of $15,600. Also during 19x2, related prepaid expenses decreased by $3,100 and relevant accrued liabilities increased by $1,200. Determine the cash payments for operating expenses to suppliers of goods and services during 19x2.
d. Europa Corporation's income taxes expense for 19x2 was $4,300. Income taxes payable decreased by $230 that year. Determine the cash payment for income taxes during 19x2.

E 14-8.
L O 4 *Computing Cash Flows from Operating Activities—Indirect Method*

During 19x1, Mayfair Corporation had a net income of $41,000. Included on the income statement was depreciation expense of $2,300 and amortization expense of $300. During the year, accounts receivable increased by $3,400, inventories decreased by $1,900, prepaid expenses decreased by $200, accounts payable increased by $5,000, and accrued liabilities decreased by $450. Determine cash flows from operating activities using the indirect method.

E 14-9.
L O 4 *Preparing a Schedule of Cash Flows from Operating Activities—Direct Method*

The income statement for the Karsko Corporation appears at the top of the next page. The following is additional information: (a) All sales were on credit, and accounts receivable increased by $4,400 during the year; (b) all merchandise purchased was on credit; inventories increased by $7,000, and accounts payable increased by $14,000 during the year; (c) prepaid rent decreased by $1,400, while salaries payable increased by $1,000; and (d) income taxes payable decreased by $600 during the year. Prepare a schedule of cash flows from operating activities using the direct method.

Karsko Corporation
Income Statement
For the Year Ended June 30, 19xx

Sales		$122,000
Cost of Goods Sold		60,000
Gross Margin		$ 62,000
Operating Expenses		
Salaries Expense	$32,000	
Rent Expense	16,800	
Depreciation Expense	2,000	50,800
Income Before Income Taxes		$ 11,200
Income Taxes		2,400
Net Income		$ 8,800

E 14-10.
L O 4 *Preparing a Schedule of Cash Flows from Operating Activities—Indirect Method*

Using the data provided in E 14-9, prepare a schedule of cash flows from operating activities using the indirect method.

E 14-11.
L O 5 *Computing Cash Flows from Investing Activities— Investments*

Krieger Company's T account for long-term available-for-sale investments at the end of 19x3 is shown below.

Investments

Beg. Bal.	38,500	Sales	39,000
Purchases	58,000		
End. Bal.	**57,500**		

In addition, Krieger's income statement shows a loss on the sale of investments of $6,500. Compute the amounts to be shown as cash flows from investing activities and show how they are to appear on the statement of cash flows.

E 14-12.
L O 5 *Computing Cash Flows from Investing Activities—Plant Assets*

The T accounts for the Plant Assets and Accumulated Depreciation accounts for Krieger Company at the end of 19x3 are as follows:

Plant Assets

Beg. Bal.	65,000	Disposals	23,000
Purchases	33,600		
End. Bal.	**75,600**		

Accumulated Depreciation

Disposals	14,700	Beg. Bal.	34,500
		19x3 Depreciation	10,200
		End. Bal.	**30,000**

In addition, Krieger Company's income statement shows a gain on sale of plant assets of $4,400. Compute the amounts to be shown as cash flows from investing activities and show how they are to appear on the statement of cash flows.

E 14-13.

L O 5   *Determining Cash Flows from Investing and Financing Activities*

All transactions involving Notes Payable and related accounts engaged in by Krieger Company during 19x3 are as follows:

Cash	18,000	
Notes Payable		18,000
Bank loan		

Patent	30,000	
Notes Payable		30,000
Purchase of patent by issuing note payable		

Notes Payable	5,000	
Interest Expense	500	
Cash		5,500
Repayment of note payable at maturity		

Determine the amounts and how these transactions are to be shown in the statement of cash flows for 19x3.

E 14-14.

L O 6   *Preparing the Statement of Cash Flows*

Bradbury Corporation's 19x2 income statement and its comparative balance sheets for June 30, 19x2 and 19x1 follow.

Bradbury Corporation
Income Statement
For the Year Ended June 30, 19x2

Sales	$468,000
Cost of Goods Sold	312,000
Gross Margin	$156,000
Operating Expenses	90,000
Operating Income	$ 66,000
Interest Expense	5,600
Income Before Income Taxes	$ 60,400
Income Taxes	24,600
Net Income	$ 35,800

Bradbury Corporation
Comparative Balance Sheets
June 30, 19x2 and 19x1

	19x2	19x1
Assets		
Cash	$139,800	$ 25,000
Accounts Receivable (net)	42,000	52,000
Inventory	86,800	96,800
Prepaid Expenses	6,400	5,200
Furniture	110,000	120,000
Accumulated Depreciation, Furniture	(18,000)	(10,000)
Total Assets	$367,000	$289,000
Liabilities and Stockholders' Equity		
Accounts Payable	$ 26,000	$ 28,000
Income Taxes Payable	2,400	3,600
Notes Payable (long-term)	74,000	70,000
Common Stock—$10 par value	230,000	180,000
Retained Earnings	34,600	7,400
Total Liabilities and Stockholders' Equity	$367,000	$289,000

Additional information: (a) Issued a $44,000 note payable for the purchase of furniture; (b) sold furniture that cost $54,000 with accumulated depreciation of $30,600 at carrying value; (c) recorded depreciation on the furniture during the year, $38,600; (d) repaid a note in the amount of $40,000 and issued $50,000 of common stock at par value; and (e) declared and paid dividends of $8,600. Without using a work sheet, prepare a statement of cash flows for 19x2 using the direct method.

E 14-15.
L O 7 *Cash-Generating Efficiency Ratios and Free Cash Flow*

In 19x2, Kenetics Corporation had total assets of $2,400,000, net sales of $3,300,000, net income of $280,000, net cash from operations of $390,000, dividends of $120,000, and net capital expenditures of $410,000. In 19x1, total assets were $2,100,000. Calculate the cash-generating efficiency ratios of cash flow yield, cash flows to sales, and cash flows to assets. Also calculate free cash flow.

E 14-16.
L O 6 *Preparing a Work*
S O 8 *Sheet for the Statement of Cash Flows*

Using the information in E 14-14, prepare a work sheet for the statement of cash flows for Bradbury Corporation for 19x2. From the work sheet, prepare a statement of cash flows using the indirect method.

Problem Set A

14A-1.
L O 3 *Classification of Transactions*

Analyze each transaction in the following schedule and place an X in the appropriate columns to indicate its classification and its effect on cash flows using the direct method.

Transaction	Cash Flow Classification				Effect on Cash		
	Operating Activity	Investing Activity	Financing Activity	Noncash Transaction	Increase	Decrease	No Effect
1. Earned a net income.							
2. Declared and paid cash dividend.							
3. Issued stock for cash.							
4. Retired long-term debt by issuing stock.							
5. Paid accounts payable.							
6. Purchased inventory for cash.							
7. Purchased a one-year insurance policy for cash.							
8. Purchased a long-term investment with cash.							
9. Sold trading securities at a gain.							
10. Sold a machine at a loss.							
11. Retired fully depreciated equipment.							
12. Paid interest on debt.							
13. Purchased available-for-sale securities (long-term).							
14. Received dividend income.							
15. Received cash on account.							
16. Converted bonds to common stock.							
17. Purchased ninety-day Treasury bill.							

14A-2.

L O 4   *Cash Flows from Operating Activities*

The income statement for Broadwell Clothing Store is presented below.

Broadwell Clothing Store
Income Statement
For the Year Ended June 30, 19xx

Sales		$4,900,000
Cost of Goods Sold		
Beginning Inventory	$1,240,000	
Net Cost of Purchases	3,040,000	
Goods Available for Sale	$4,280,000	
Ending Inventory	1,400,000	
Cost of Goods Sold		2,880,000
Gross Margin		$2,020,000
Operating Expenses		
Sales and Administrative Salaries Expense	$1,112,000	
Other Sales and Administrative Expenses	624,000	
Total Operating Expenses		1,736,000
Income Before Income Taxes		$ 284,000
Income Taxes		78,000
Net Income		$ 206,000

Additional information: (a) Other sales and administrative expenses include depreciation expense of $104,000 and amortization expense of $36,000; (b) accrued liabilities for salaries were $24,000 less than the previous year and prepaid expenses were $40,000 more than the previous year; and (c) during the year accounts receivable (net) increased by $288,000, accounts payable increased by $228,000, and income taxes payable decreased by $14,400.

REQUIRED

1. Prepare a schedule of cash flows from operating activities using the direct method.
2. Prepare a schedule of cash flows from operating activities using the indirect method.

14A-3.

L O 4   *Cash Flows from Operating Activities*

The income statement for Springer Greeting Card Company is as follows:

Springer Greeting Card Company
Income Statement
For the Year Ended December 31, 19x2

Sales		$944,000
Cost of Goods Sold		573,400
Gross Margin		$370,600
Operating Expenses (including Depreciation Expense of $42,860)		174,800
Operating Income		$195,800
Other Income (Expenses)		
Interest Expense	($ 16,800)	
Interest Income	8,600	
Loss on Sale of Investments	(11,600)	(19,800)
Income Before Income Taxes		$176,000
Income Taxes		37,000
Net Income		$139,000

Relevant accounts from the comparative balance sheets for December 31, 19x2 and 19x1 are as follows:

	19x2	19x1
Accounts Receivable (net)	$37,060	$47,340
Inventory	79,280	69,980
Prepaid Expenses	4,800	17,800
Accounts Payable	69,880	45,400
Accrued Liabilities	9,380	17,660
Income Taxes Payable	9,500	35,200

REQUIRED

1. Prepare a schedule of cash flows from operating activities using the direct method.
2. Prepare a schedule of cash flows from operating activities using the indirect method.

14A-4.

L O 6, 7 *The Statement of Cash Flows—Direct Method*

Gutierrez Corporation's 19x7 income statement and its comparative balance sheets as of June 30, 19x7 and 19x6 appear as follows:

Gutierrez Corporation
Income Statement
For the Year Ended June 30, 19x7

Sales		$2,081,800
Cost of Goods Sold		1,312,600
Gross Margin		$ 769,200
Operating Expenses (including Depreciation Expense of $120,000)		378,400
Income from Operations		$ 390,800
Other Income (Expenses)		
Loss on Sale of Equipment	($ 8,000)	
Interest Expense	(75,200)	(83,200)
Income Before Income Taxes		$ 307,600
Income Taxes		68,400
Net Income		$ 239,200

Gutierrez Corporation
Comparative Balance Sheets
June 30, 19x7 and 19x6

	19x7	19x6
Assets		
Cash	$ 334,000	$ 40,000
Accounts Receivable (net)	200,000	240,000
Finished Goods Inventory	360,000	440,000
Prepaid Expenses	1,200	2,000
Property, Plant, and Equipment	1,256,000	1,104,000
Accumulated Depreciation, Property, Plant, and Equipment	(366,000)	(280,000)
Total Assets	$1,785,200	$1,546,000
Liabilities and Stockholders' Equity		
Accounts Payable	$ 128,000	$ 84,000
Notes Payable (due in 90 days)	60,000	160,000
Income Taxes Payable	52,000	36,000
Mortgage Payable	720,000	560,000
Common Stock—$5 par value	400,000	400,000
Retained Earnings	425,200	306,000
Total Liabilities and Stockholders' Equity	$1,785,200	$1,546,000

Additional information about 19x7: (a) Equipment that cost $48,000 with accumulated depreciation of $34,000 was sold at a loss of $8,000; (b) land and building were purchased in the amount of $200,000 through an increase of $200,000 in the mortgage payable; (c) a $40,000 payment was made on the mortgage; (d) the notes were repaid, but the company borrowed an additional $60,000 through the issuance of new notes payable; and (e) a $120,000 cash dividend was declared and paid.

REQUIRED

1. Prepare a statement of cash flows using the direct method. Include a supporting schedule of noncash investing and financing transactions.
2. What are the primary reasons for Gutierrez Corporation's large increase in cash from 19x6 to 19x7?
3. Compute and assess cash flow yield and free cash flow for 19x7.

14A-5.
L O 6, 7 *The Statement of Cash Flows— Indirect Method*

Use the information for Gutierrez Corporation given in 14A-4 to answer the requirements below.

REQUIRED

1. Prepare a statement of cash flows using the indirect method. Include a supporting schedule of noncash investing and financing transactions.
2. Answer requirements 2 and 3 in 14A-4 if that problem was not assigned.

14A-6.
L O 6, 7 *The Work Sheet and*
S O 8 *the Statement of Cash Flows— Indirect Method*

The comparative balance sheets for Bausch Ceramics, Inc. for December 31, 19x3 and 19x2 appear below.

Bausch Ceramics, Inc.
Comparative Balance Sheets
December 31, 19x3 and 19x2

	19x3	19x2
Assets		
Cash	$ 277,600	$ 305,600
Accounts Receivable (net)	738,800	758,800
Inventory	960,000	800,000
Prepaid Expenses	14,800	26,800
Long-Term Investments (available-for-sale)	440,000	440,000
Land	361,200	321,200
Building	1,200,000	920,000
Accumulated Depreciation, Building	(240,000)	(160,000)
Equipment	480,000	480,000
Accumulated Depreciation, Equipment	(116,000)	(56,000)
Intangible Assets	20,000	40,000
Total Assets	$4,136,400	$3,876,400
Liabilities and Stockholders' Equity		
Accounts Payable	$ 470,800	$ 660,800
Notes Payable (current)	40,000	160,000
Accrued Liabilities	10,800	20,800
Mortgage Payable	1,080,000	800,000
Bonds Payable	1,000,000	760,000
Common Stock	1,200,000	1,200,000
Paid-in Capital in Excess of Par Value	80,000	80,000
Retained Earnings	254,800	194,800
Total Liabilities and Stockholders' Equity	$4,136,400	$3,876,400

Additional information about Bausch Ceramics' operations during 19x3: (a) Net income was $96,000; (b) building and equipment depreciation expense amounts were $80,000 and $60,000, respectively; (c) intangible assets were amortized in the amount of $20,000; (d) investments in the amount of $116,000 were purchased; (e) investments were sold for $150,000, on which a gain of $34,000 was made; (f) the company issued $240,000 in long-term bonds at face value; (g) a small warehouse building with the accompanying land was purchased through the issue of a $320,000 mortgage; (h) the company paid $40,000 to reduce mortgage payable during 19x3; (i) the company borrowed funds in the amount of $60,000 by issuing notes payable and repaid notes payable in the amount of $180,000; and (j) cash dividends in the amount of $36,000 were declared and paid.

REQUIRED

1. Prepare a work sheet for the statement of cash flows for Bausch Ceramics.
2. Prepare a statement of cash flows from the information in the work sheet using the indirect method. Include a supporting schedule of noncash investing and financing transactions.
3. Why did Bausch Ceramics experience a decrease in cash in a year in which it had a net income of $96,000? Discuss and interpret.
4. Compute and assess cash flow yield and free cash flow for 19x3.

Problem Set B

14B-1.

L O 3 *Classification of Transactions*

Analyze each transaction in the following schedule and place an X in the appropriate columns to indicate its classification and its effect on cash flows using the direct method.

	Cash Flow Classification				Effect on Cash		
Transaction	Operating Activity	Investing Activity	Financing Activity	Noncash Transaction	Increase	Decrease	No Effect
1. Incurred a net loss.							
2. Declared and issued a stock dividend.							
3. Paid a cash dividend.							
4. Collected accounts receivable.							
5. Purchased inventory with cash.							
6. Retired long-term debt with cash.							
7. Sold available-for-sale securities for a loss.							
8. Issued stock for equipment.							
9. Purchased a one-year insurance policy for cash.							
10. Purchased treasury stock with cash.							
11. Retired a fully depreciated truck (no gain or loss).							
12. Paid interest on note.							
13. Received cash dividend on investment.							
14. Sold treasury stock.							
15. Paid income taxes.							
16. Transferred cash to money market account.							
17. Purchased land and building with a mortgage.							

14B-2.

L O 4 *Cash Flows from Operating Activities*

The income statement for Lui Food Corporation is as follows:

Lui Food Corporation
Income Statement
For the Year Ended December 31, 19xx

Sales		$980,000
Cost of Goods Sold		
Beginning Inventory	$ 440,000	
Net Cost of Purchases	800,000	
Goods Available for Sale	$1,240,000	
Ending Inventory	500,000	
Cost of Goods Sold		740,000
Gross Margin		$240,000
Selling and Administrative Expenses		
Selling and Administrative Salaries Expense	$ 100,000	
Other Selling and Administrative Expenses	23,000	
Depreciation Expense	36,000	
Amortization Expense (Intangible Assets)	3,000	162,000
Income Before Income Taxes		$ 78,000
Income Taxes		25,000
Net Income		$ 53,000

Additional information: (a) Accounts receivable (net) increased by $36,000 and accounts payable decreased by $52,000 during the year; (b) salaries payable at the end of the year were $14,000 more than last year; (c) the expired amount of prepaid insurance for the year is $1,000 and equals the decrease in the Prepaid Insurance account; and (d) income taxes payable decreased by $10,800 from last year.

REQUIRED

1. Prepare a schedule of cash flows from operating activities using the direct method.
2. Prepare a schedule of cash flows from operating activities using the indirect method.

14B-3.

L O 4 *Cash Flows from Operating Activities*

The income statement of Rosen Electronics, Inc. appears at the top of the next page. Relevant accounts from the comparative balance sheets for February 28, 19x3 and 19x2 are as follows:

	19x3	19x2
Accounts Receivable (net)	$130,980	$ 97,840
Inventory	197,520	205,120
Prepaid Expenses	20,900	10,980
Accounts Payable	84,760	111,380
Accrued Liabilities	7,120	17,580
Income Taxes Payable	49,260	27,600

REQUIRED

1. Prepare a schedule of cash flows from operating activities using the direct method.
2. Prepare a schedule of cash flows from operating activities using the indirect method.

Rosen Electronics, Inc.
Income Statement
For the Year Ended February 28, 19x3

Sales		$1,838,000
Cost of Goods Sold		1,287,000
Gross Margin		$ 551,000
Operating Expenses (including Depreciation Expense of $42,860)		353,800
Operating Income		$ 197,200
Other Income (Expenses)		
Interest Expense	($ 55,600)	
Dividend Income	28,400	
Loss on Sale of Investments	(24,200)	(51,400)
Income Before Income Taxes		$ 145,800
Income Taxes		43,000
Net Income		$ 102,800

14B-4.

L O 6, 7 *The Statement of Cash Flows—Direct Method*

Meridian Corporation's comparative balance sheets as of December 31, 19x2 and 19x1 appear below. Meridian's 19x2 income statement appears at the top of page 668.

Meridian Corporation
Comparative Balance Sheets
December 31, 19x2 and 19x1

	19x2	19x1
Assets		
Cash	$ 82,400	$ 25,000
Accounts Receivable (net)	82,600	100,000
Merchandise Inventory	175,000	225,000
Prepaid Rent	1,000	1,500
Furniture and Fixtures	74,000	72,000
Accumulated Depreciation, Furniture and Fixtures	(21,000)	(12,000)
Total Assets	$394,000	$411,500
Liabilities and Stockholders' Equity		
Accounts Payable	$ 71,700	$100,200
Notes Payable (long-term)	20,000	10,000
Bonds Payable	50,000	100,000
Income Taxes Payable	700	2,200
Common Stock—$10 par value	120,000	100,000
Paid-in Capital in Excess of Par Value	90,720	60,720
Retained Earnings	40,880	38,380
Total Liabilities and Stockholders' Equity	$394,000	$411,500

Meridian Corporation
Income Statement
For the Year Ended December 31, 19x2

Sales		$804,500
Cost of Goods Sold		563,900
Gross Margin		$240,600
Operating Expenses (including Depreciation Expense of $23,400)		224,700
Income from Operations		$ 15,900
Other Income (Expenses)		
Gain on Sale of Furniture and Fixtures	$ 3,500	
Interest Expense	(11,600)	(8,100)
Income Before Income Taxes		$ 7,800
Income Taxes		2,300
Net Income		$ 5,500

Additional information about 19x2: (a) Furniture and fixtures that cost $17,800 with accumulated depreciation of $14,400 were sold at a gain of $3,500; (b) furniture and fixtures were purchased in the amount of $19,800; (c) a $10,000 note payable was paid and $20,000 was borrowed on new notes; (d) bonds payable in the amount of $50,000 were converted into 2,000 shares of common stock; and (e) $3,000 in cash dividends were declared and paid.

REQUIRED

1. Prepare a statement of cash flows using the direct method. Include a supporting schedule of noncash investing and financing transactions. (Do not use a work sheet.)
2. What are the primary reasons for Meridian Corporation's large increase in cash from 19x1 to 19x2, despite its low net income?
3. Compute and assess cash flow yield and free cash flow for 19x2.

14B-5.
L O 6, 7 *The Statement of Cash Flows— Indirect Method*

Use the information for Meridian Corporation given in 14B-4 to answer the following requirements.

REQUIRED

1. Prepare a statement of cash flows using the indirect approach. Include a supporting schedule of noncash investing and financing transactions.
2. Answer requirements **2** and **3** in 14B-4 if that problem was not assigned.

14B-6.
L O 6, 7
S O 8 *The Work Sheet and the Statement of Cash Flows— Indirect Method*

The comparative balance sheets for Mateo Fabrics, Inc. for December 31, 19x3 and 19x2 appear at the top of the next page. The following is additional information about Mateo Fabrics' operations during 19x3: (a) net loss, $56,000; (b) building and equipment depreciation expense amounts, $30,000 and $6,000, respectively; (c) equipment that cost $27,000 with accumulated depreciation of $25,000 sold for a gain of $10,600; (d) equipment purchases, $25,000; (e) patent amortization, $6,000; purchase of patent, $2,000; (f) borrowed funds by issuing notes payable, $50,000; notes payable repaid, $30,000; (g) land and building purchased for $324,000 by signing a mortgage for the total cost; (h) 3,000 shares of $20 par value common stock issued for a total of $100,000; and (i) cash dividend, $18,000.

Mateo Fabrics, Inc.
Comparative Balance Sheets
December 31, 19x3 and 19x2

	19x3	19x2
Assets		
Cash	$ 77,120	$ 54,720
Accounts Receivable (net)	204,860	150,860
Inventory	225,780	275,780
Prepaid Expenses	—	40,000
Land	50,000	—
Building	274,000	—
Accumulated Depreciation, Building	(30,000)	—
Equipment	66,000	68,000
Accumulated Depreciation, Equipment	(29,000)	(48,000)
Patents	8,000	12,000
Total Assets	$846,760	$553,360
Liabilities and Stockholders' Equity		
Accounts Payable	$ 21,500	$ 73,500
Notes Payable (current)	20,000	—
Accrued Liabilities	—	24,600
Mortgage Payable	324,000	—
Common Stock—$20 par value	360,000	300,000
Paid-in Capital in Excess of Par Value	114,400	74,400
Retained Earnings	6,860	80,860
Total Liabilities and Stockholders' Equity	$846,760	$553,360

REQUIRED

1. Prepare a work sheet for the statement of cash flows for Mateo Fabrics, Inc.
2. Prepare a statement of cash flows from the information in the work sheet using the indirect method.
3. Why did Mateo Fabrics have an increase in cash in a year in which it recorded a net loss of $56,000? Discuss and interpret.
4. Compute and assess cash flow yield and free cash flow for 19x3.

CRITICAL THINKING AND COMMUNICATION

Conceptual Mini-Cases

CMC 14-1.
L O 4 *Direct Versus Indirect Method*

Compaq Computer Corporation, a leading manufacturer of personal computers, uses the direct method of presenting the cash flows from operating activities in its statement of cash flows.[9] As noted in the text, 97 percent of large companies use the indirect method. State clearly the difference between the direct and indirect methods of presenting cash flows from operating activities. Then take either the direct or the indirect method and develop an argument for it as the best way of presenting cash flows from operations. Be prepared to present your opinion in class.

CMC 14-2.
L O 7 *Cash-Generating Efficiency and Free Cash Flow*

The statement of cash flows for *Tandy Corporation,* the owner of Radio Shack and other retail store chains, appears on page 671. For the two years shown, compute the cash-generating efficiency ratios of cash flow yield, cash flows to sales, and cash flows to assets. Also compute free cash flow for the two years. Assess Tandy's cash-generating efficiency and evaluate its available free cash flow in light of its financing activities. Were there any special operating circumstances that should be taken into consideration? Is the concept of free cash flow a useful one in light of your evaluation? Be prepared to discuss your analysis in class. The following data come from the supplemental information in Tandy's annual report (in thousands):

	1992	1991	1990
Net Sales	$4,680,156	$4,561,782	$4,499,604
Total Assets	$3,165,164	$3,078,145	$3,239,980

Ethics Mini-Case

EMC 14-1.
L O 3 *Ethics and Cash Flow Classifications*

Chemical Waste Treatment, Inc. is a fast-growing company that disposes of chemical wastes. The company has a $800,000 line of credit at its bank. One convenant in the loan agreement stipulates that the ratio of cash flows from operations to interest expense must exceed 3.0. If this ratio falls below 3.0, the company must pay down its line of credit to one-half if the funds borrowed against it currently exceed that amount. After the end of the fiscal year, the controller informs the president: "We will not meet our ratio requirements on our line of credit in 19x2 because interest expense was $1.2 million and cash flows from operations were $3.2 million. Also, we have borrowed 100 percent of our line of credit. We do not have the cash to reduce the credit line by $400,000." The president says, "This is a serious situation. To be able to pay our ongoing bills, we need our bank to increase our line of credit, not decrease it. What can we do?" "Do you recall the $500,000 two-year note payable for equipment?" replied the controller. "It is now classified as 'Proceeds from Notes Payable' in cash flows provided from financing activities in the statement of cash flows. If we move it up to cash flows from operations and call it 'Increase in Payables,' it would put us over the limit at $3.7 million." "Well, do it," ordered the president. "It surely doesn't make any difference where it is on the statement. It is an increase in both places. It would be much worse for our company in the long term if we failed to meet this ratio requirement." What is your opinion of the president's reasoning? Is the president's order ethical? Who benefits and who is harmed if the controller follows the president's order? What are management's alternatives? What would you do?

9. American Institute of Certified Public Accountants, *Accounting Trends & Techniques* (New York: AICPA, 1993), p. 452.

Tandy Corporation
Statements of Cash Flows
Years Ended June 30,
(in thousands)

	1992	1991
Cash flows from operating activities		
Net income	$183,847	$195,444
Adjustments to reconcile net income to net cash provided by operating activities:		
Cumulative effect on prior years of change in accounting principle, net of taxes	—	10,619
Depreciation and amortization	103,281	99,698
Deferred income taxes and other items	9,302	(29,633)
Provision for credit losses and bad debts	67,388	60,643
Gain on sale of subsidiary, assets of which were primarily real estate	(18,987)	—
Changes in operating assets and liabilities, excluding the effect of businesses acquired:		
Securitization of customer receivables	—	350,000
Receivables	(121,719)	(256,445)
Inventories	(89,441)	151,339
Other current assets	(2,955)	(2,028)
Accounts payable, accrued expenses and income taxes	16,066	37,716
Net cash provided by operating activities	146,782	617,353
Investing activities		
Additions to property, plant and equipment, net of retirements	(123,430)	(139,453)
Proceeds from sale of subsidiary, assets of which were primarily real estate	20,293	—
Acquisition of Victor Technologies	—	—
Payment received on InterTAN note	—	—
Other investing activities	947	(1,046)
Net cash used by investing activities	(102,190)	(140,499)
Financing activities		
Purchases of treasury stock	(527,773)	(83,086)
Sales of treasury stock to employee stock purchase program	49,590	50,383
Issuance of Series C PERCS	429,982	—
Issuance of preferred stock to TESOP	—	100,000
Dividends paid, net of taxes	(56,132)	(51,478)
Changes in short-term borrowings—net	57,533	(598,763)
Additions to long-term borrowings	21,071	210,167
Repayments of long-term borrowings	(98,702)	(52,981)
Net cash provided (used) by financing activities	(124,431)	(425,758)
Increase (decrease) in cash and short-term investments	(79,839)	51,096
Cash and short-term investments at the beginning of the year	186,293	135,197
Cash and short-term investments at the end of the year	$106,454	$186,293

Decision-Making Case

May Hashimi, president of *Hashimi Print Gallery, Inc.,* is examining the following income statement, which has just been handed to her by her accountant, Lou Klein, CPA. After looking at the statement, Ms. Hashimi said to Mr. Klein, "Lou, the statement seems to be well done, but what I need to know is why I don't have enough cash to pay my bills this month. You show that I have earned $120,000 in 19x2, but I have only $24,000 in the bank. I know I bought a building on a mortgage and paid a cash dividend of $48,000, but what else is going on?" Mr. Klein replied, "To answer your question, we have to look at comparative balance sheets and prepare another type of statement. Take a look at these balance sheets." The statements handed to Ms. Hashimi follow.

Hashimi Print Gallery, Inc.
Income Statement
For the Year Ended December 31, 19x2

Sales	$884,000
Cost of Goods Sold	508,000
Gross Margin	$376,000
Operating Expenses (including Depreciation Expense of $20,000)	204,000
Operating Income	$172,000
Interest Expense	24,000
Income Before Taxes	$148,000
Income Taxes	28,000
Net Income	$120,000

Hashimi Print Gallery, Inc.
Comparative Balance Sheets
December 31, 19x2 and 19x1

	19x2	19x1
Assets		
Cash	$ 24,000	$ 40,000
Accounts Receivable (net)	178,000	146,000
Inventory	240,000	180,000
Prepaid Expenses	10,000	14,000
Building	400,000	—
Accumulated Depreciation	(20,000)	—
Total Assets	$832,000	$380,000
Liabilities and Stockholders' Equity		
Accounts Payable	$ 74,000	$ 96,000
Income Taxes Payable	6,000	4,000
Mortgage Payable	400,000	—
Common Stock	200,000	200,000
Retained Earnings	152,000	80,000
Total Liabilities and Stockholders' Equity	$832,000	$380,000

<table>
<tr><td>**REQUIRED**</td><td>

1. To what statement is Mr. Klein referring? From the information given, prepare the additional statement using the direct method.
2. Hashimi Print Gallery, Inc. has a cash problem despite profitable operations. Why?

</td></tr>
</table>

Basic Research Activity

RA 14-1.

L O 7 *Basic Research Skills*

In your library, select the annual reports of three corporations. You may choose them from the same industry or at random, at the direction of your instructor. (If you did a related exercise in a previous chapter, use the same three companies.) Prepare a table with a column for each corporation. Then, for any year covered by the statement of cash flows, answer the following questions: Does the company use the direct or the indirect approach? Is net income more or less than net cash flows from operating activities? What are the major causes of differences between net income and net cash flows from operating activities? Compute cash flow efficiency ratios and free cash flow. Does the dividend appear secure? Did the company make significant capital expenditures during the year? How were the expenditures financed? Do you notice anything unusual about the investing and financing activities of your companies? Do the investing and financing activities provide any insights into management's plan for each company? If so, what are they? Be prepared to discuss the answers to these questions in class.

FINANCIAL REPORTING AND ANALYSIS

Interpretation Cases from Business

ICB 14-1.

L O 6, 7 *Presentation and Interpretation of Statement of Cash Flows*

The statements of cash flows from the annual report of *National Communications, Inc.,* a major television network broadcaster and publisher, appear on page 674. Note that they do not follow the format recommended by the FASB.

REQUIRED

1. Recast the statements of cash flows using the indirect method as shown in this chapter (ignore noncash investing and financing transactions).
2. National Communications, Inc. places an emphasis on "available cash flow from operations." Evaluate this approach as compared to "net cash flows from operating activities" in the statement of cash flows.
3. Although net cash flow from operating activities increased from 1993 to 1994, cash and cash equivalents decreased significantly (from $687,413,000 to $134,324,000). What are the primary causes of this decline in cash and cash equivalents?

National Communications, Inc.
Statements of Cash Flows
For the Years Ended January 31, 1994 and 1993
(in thousands)

	1994	1993
Cash provided		
Operations		
Net income	$ 267,693	$242,222
Depreciation	95,202	37,992
Amortization of intangible assets	63,403	19,712
Other noncash items, net	28,930	23,370
Total cash from operations	$ 455,228	$323,296
Capital expenditures for operations	(153,087)	(75,383)
Program licenses and rights, net	(2,732)	(1,734)
Available cash flow from operations	$ 299,409	$246,179
Issuance of common stock	517,500	—
Issuance of common stock warrants	97,197	—
Issuance of long-term debt	1,350,503	493,322
Long-term debt assumed on acquisitions	123,678	—
Disposition of operating properties, net of current taxes	625,677	7,229
Disposition of real estate	162,166	—
Other dispositions, net	29,495	3,114
	$3,205,625	$749,844
Cash applied		
Acquisition of television stations	$3,270,972	$ —
Common stock warrants purchased and redeemed	16,688	—
Acquisition of other operating properties	12,599	103,109
Reduction of long-term debt	367,521	7,874
Changes in other working capital items	86,645	2,322
Purchase of common stock for treasury	1,079	485
Dividends	3,210	2,594
	$3,758,714	$116,384
(Decrease) increase in cash and cash investments	($ 553,089)	$633,460
Cash and cash equivalents		
Beginning of period	687,413	53,953
End of period	$ 134,324	$687,413

ICB 14-2.
L O 7   *Analysis of the Statement of Cash Flows*

Airborne Freight Corporation, which is known as Airborne Express, is an air express transportation company, providing next-day, morning delivery of small packages and documents throughout the United States. Airborne Express is one of three major participants, along with Federal Express and United Parcel Service, in the air express industry. The following statement appears in "Management's discussion and analysis of results of operations and financial condition" from the company's 1992 annual report: "Capital expenditures and financing associated with those expenditures have been the primary factors affecting the financial condition of the company over the last three years."[10] The company's consolidated statements of cash flows for 1992, 1991, and 1990 follow. The following data (in thousands) are also available.

	1992	1991	1990	1989
Net Sales	$1,484,316	$1,367,047	$1,181,890	$949,896
Total Assets	964,739	823,647	613,534	470,605

10. Airborne Freight Corporation, *Annual Report*, 1992.

Airborne Freight Corporation and Subsidiaries
Consolidated Statements of Cash Flows
Year Ended December 31
(in thousands)

	1992	1991	1990
Operating Activities			
Net earnings	$ 5,157	$ 29,999	$ 33,577
Adjustments to reconcile net earnings to net cash provided by operating activities:			
Depreciation and amortization	110,206	90,586	69,055
Provision for aircraft engine overhauls	10,426	8,445	6,224
Deferred income taxes	(9,930)	(3,256)	536
Other	5,949	8,125	1,921
Cash Provided by Operations	121,808	133,899	111,313
Change in:			
Receivables	(16,158)	(11,880)	(19,722)
Inventories and prepaid expenses	(5,635)	(7,594)	(6,496)
Accounts payable	16	(3,177)	14,514
Accrued expenses, salaries and taxes payable	5,167	19,229	10,715
Net Cash Provided by Operating Activities	105,198	130,477	110,324
Investing Activities			
Additions to property and equipment	(252,733)	(248,165)	(217,926)
Disposition of property and equipment	1,068	1,674	2,286
Expenditures for engine overhauls	(1,933)	(4,970)	(7,483)
Other	206	1,094	(1,868)
Net Cash Used in Investing Activities	(253,392)	(250,367)	(224,991)
Financing Activities			
Proceeds from bank note borrowings, net	30,700	17,900	(6,800)
Proceeds from debt issuances	132,786	126,479	—
Principal payments on debt	(6,273)	(19,190)	(8,642)
Proceeds from sale-leaseback of aircraft	—	—	28,464
Proceeds from redeemable preferred stock issuance	—	—	40,000
Proceeds from common stock issuance	1,641	2,370	69,461
Dividends paid	(8,503)	(8,442)	(7,609)
Net Cash Provided by Financing Activities	150,351	119,117	114,874
Net Increase (Decrease) in Cash	2,157	(773)	207
Cash at Beginning of Year	8,022	8,795	8,588
Cash at End of Year	$ 10,179	$ 8,022	$ 8,795

REQUIRED

1. Have operations provided significant cash flows over the past three years? What is the role of net earnings in this provision? Other than net earnings, what is the most significant factor in providing the cash flows? Have changes in working capital accounts been a significant factor?
2. Calculate and assess Airborne Express's cash-generating ability for the three years.
3. Calculate free cash flow for the three years. Is management's statement about capital expenditures and associated financing substantiated by the figures? If your answer is yes, what were Airborne Express's primary means of financing the expansion in 1992?

International Company Case

ICC 14-1.

L O 3, 7   *Format and
Interpretation of
Statement of Cash
Flows*

The format of the statement of cash flows can differ from country to country. One of the more interesting presentations is that of *Guinness PLC,* a large British liquor company that distributes Johnny Walker Scotch, among many other products.[11] Refer to the group cash flow statement below to answer the following questions. (The word *group* means the same as *consolidated* in the United States.) What differences can you identify between this British statement of cash flows and the one used in the United States? In what ways do you find the Guinness format more useful than the format used in the United States? Assume that net cash flow from operating activities is computed similarly in both countries, except for the items shown.

Guinness PLC
Group Cash Flow Statement
For the Years Ended 31 December 1992 and 1991

	1992 £m	1991 £m
NET CASH INFLOW FROM OPERATING ACTIVITIES*	**891**	**833**
Interest received	106	43
Interest paid	(284)	(197)
Dividends received from associated undertakings	58	32
Dividends paid	(221)	(193)
NET CASH OUTFLOW FROM RETURNS ON INVESTMENTS AND SERVICING OF FINANCE	(341)	(315)
United Kingdom corporation tax paid	(72)	(129)
Overseas tax paid	(73)	(56)
TOTAL TAX PAID	(145)	(185)
NET CASH INFLOW BEFORE INVESTING ACTIVITIES	**405**	**333**
Purchase of tangible fixed assets	(218)	(224)
Sale of tangible fixed assets	18	14
Purchase of subsidiary undertakings	(16)	(679)
Other investments	(126)	(46)
Disposals	6	50
NET CASH OUTFLOW FROM INVESTING ACTIVITIES	(336)	(885)
NET CASH INFLOW/(OUTFLOW) BEFORE FINANCING ACTIVITIES	69	(552)
Proceeds of new borrowings	736	1,635
Borrowings repaid	(1,252)	(1,272)
Issue of shares (employee share schemes)	15	20
NET CASH (OUTFLOW)/INFLOW FROM FINANCING ACTIVITIES	(501)	383
(DECREASE) IN CASH AND CASH EQUIVALENTS	(432)	(169)
ANALYSIS OF FREE CASH FLOW		
Net cash inflow before investing activities	405	333
Purchase of tangible fixed assets	(218)	(224)
Sale of tangible fixed assets	18	14
FREE CASH FLOW (AFTER DIVIDENDS)	**205**	**123**
FREE CASH FLOW (BEFORE DIVIDENDS)	**426**	**316**

*The company provides the detail for this item in a note to the financial statements.

11. Guinness PLC, *Annual Report,* 1992.

Toys "R" Us Case

TC 14-1.
L O 7 *Analysis of the
Statement of Cash
Flows*

Refer to the statement of cash flows in the appendix on Toys "R" Us to answer the following questions:

1. Does Toys "R" Us use the direct or the indirect method of reporting cash flows from operating activities? Other than net earnings, what are the three most important factors affecting cash flows from operating activities? Explain the trend of each.
2. Based on the cash flows from investing activities, would you say that Toys "R" Us is a contracting or an expanding company?
3. Calculate the cash flow yield, cash flows to sales, cash flows to assets, and free cash flow for the last three years for Toys "R" Us. How would you evaluate the company's cash-generating efficiency? Does Toys "R" Us need external financing? If so, where has it come from?

LEARNING
OBJECTIVES

1. Describe and discuss the objectives of financial statement analysis.

2. Describe and discuss the standards for financial statement analysis.

3. State the sources of information for financial statement analysis.

4. Identify the issues related to evaluating the quality of a company's earnings.

5. Apply horizontal analysis, trend analysis, and vertical analysis to financial statements.

6. Apply ratio analysis to financial statements in a comprehensive analysis of a company's financial situation.

DECISION POINT
Moody's Investors Service, Inc.

Moody's Investors Service, Inc. rates the bonds and other indebtedness of companies on the basis of safety, that is, the likelihood of repayment. Investors rely on this service when making investments in bonds and other long-term company debt. The *Wall Street Journal* reported on September 19, 1990 that Moody's was reviewing $40 million of Ford Motor Co.'s debt for possible downgrade.[1] Moody's cited the softness in the U.S. auto market. Ford replied that the action was not warranted and questioned Moody's decision to review this debt, given that the market problem might be short term. One month later, on October 25, 1990, Moody's did in fact lower the rating on Ford's long-term debt. The new rating was still in the high-grade area, but the downgrade meant that Ford would pay higher interest rates because, according to Moody's, its debt was not quite as secure as it had been. On what basis would Moody's decide to upgrade or lower the bond rating of a company?

According to the *Wall Street Journal*, "Moody's said it took the actions because Ford's returns and cash flow are vulnerable to a weaker U.S. economy, softer European sales, and volatile fuel prices. At the same time, Moody's said, Ford has committed to huge capital spending plans."[2] Ford Motor Co. officials, according to the same article, said they were disappointed with the decision, as the reasons given were cyclical and transitional. This case demonstrates several features of the evaluation of a company's financial prospects. First, the analysis is rooted in the financial statements (for example, returns and cash flow). Second, it is directed toward the future (for example, capital spending plans). Third, the operating environment must be taken into consideration (for example, a weaker U.S. economy, softer European sales, and volatile fuel prices). Fourth, judgment is involved (for example, the disagreement between Moody's and Ford about the seriousness of the situation).

1. "Ford Motor's Debt Reviewed by Moody's; Downgrade Is Possible," *Wall Street Journal*, September 19, 1990.
2. Bradley A. Stertz, "Ratings on Ford and Units' Debt Cut by Moody's," *Wall Street Journal*, October 25, 1990.

OBJECTIVES OF FINANCIAL STATEMENT ANALYSIS

1 *Describe and discuss the objectives of financial statement analysis*

Financial statement analysis comprises all the techniques employed by users of financial statements to show important relationships in the financial statements. Users of financial statements fall into two broad categories: internal and external. Management is the main internal user. However, because those who run a company have inside information on operations, other techniques are available to them. Since these techniques are covered in managerial accounting courses, the main focus here is on the external use of financial analysis.

Creditors make loans in the form of trade accounts, notes, or bonds, on which they receive interest. They expect a loan to be repaid according to its terms. Investors buy capital stock, from which they hope to receive dividends and an increase in value. Both groups face risks. The creditor faces the risk that the debtor will fail to pay back the loan. The investor faces the risk that dividends will be reduced or not paid or that the market price of the stock will drop. For both groups, the goal is to achieve a return that makes up for the risk. In general, the greater the risk taken, the greater the return required as compensation.

Any one loan or any one investment can turn out badly. As a result, most creditors and investors put their funds into a portfolio, or group of loans or investments. The portfolio allows them to average both the returns and the risks. Nevertheless, the portfolio is made up of a number of loans or stocks on which individual decisions must be made. It is in making these individual decisions that financial statement analysis is most useful. Creditors and investors use financial statement analysis in two general ways: (1) to judge past performance and current position and (2) to judge future potential and the risk connected with the potential.

ASSESSMENT OF PAST PERFORMANCE AND CURRENT POSITION

Past performance is often a good indicator of future performance. Therefore, an investor or creditor looks at the trend of past sales, expenses, net income, cash flow, and return on investment not only as a means for judging management's past performance but also as a possible indicator of future performance. In addition, an analysis of current position will tell, for example, what assets the business owns and what liabilities must be paid. It will also tell what the cash position is, how much debt the company has in relation to equity, and how reasonable the inventories and receivables are. Knowing a company's past performance and current position is often important in achieving the second general objective of financial analysis.

ASSESSMENT OF FUTURE POTENTIAL AND RELATED RISK

Information about the past and present is useful only to the extent that it bears on decisions about the future. An investor judges the potential earning ability of a company because that ability will affect the market price of the company's stock and the amount of dividends the company will pay. A creditor judges the potential debt-paying ability of the company.

The potentials of some companies are easier to predict than those of others, and so there is less risk associated with them. The riskiness of an investment or loan depends on how easy it is to predict future profitability or liquidity. If an investor can predict with confidence that a company's earnings per share will be between $2.50 and $2.60 next year, the investment is less risky than if the earnings per share are expected to fall between $2.00 and $3.00. For example, the potential associated with an investment in an established and stable electric utility, or a loan to it, is relatively easy to predict on the basis of the company's past performance and current position. The potential associated with a small microcomputer manufacturer, on the other hand, may be much harder to predict. For this reason, the investment or loan to the electric utility carries less risk than the investment or loan to the small microcomputer company.

Often, in return for taking a greater risk, an investor in the microcomputer company will demand a higher expected return (increase in market price plus dividends) than will an investor in the utility company. Also, a creditor of the microcomputer company will demand a higher interest rate and possibly more assurance of repayment (a secured loan, for instance) than a creditor of the utility company. The higher interest rate reimburses the creditor for assuming a higher risk.

STANDARDS FOR FINANCIAL STATEMENT ANALYSIS

OBJECTIVE

2 *Describe and discuss the standards for financial statement analysis*

In using financial statement analysis, decision makers must judge whether the relationships they have found are favorable or unfavorable. Three standards of comparison often used are (1) rule-of-thumb measures, (2) past performance of the company, and (3) industry norms.

RULE-OF-THUMB MEASURES

Many financial analysts, investors, and lenders employ ideal or rule-of-thumb measures for key financial ratios. For example, it has long been thought that a current ratio (current assets divided by current liabilities) of 2:1 is acceptable. The credit rating firm of Dun & Bradstreet, in its *Key Business Ratios*, offers these guidelines:

Current debt to tangible net worth. Ordinarily, a business begins to pile up trouble when this relationship exceeds 80%.

Inventory to net working capital. Ordinarily, this relationship should not exceed 80%.

Although such measures may suggest areas that need further investigation, there is no proof that these levels are the best for any company. A company with a current ratio higher than 2:1 may have a poor credit policy (resulting in accounts receivable being too large), too much or out-of-date inventory, or poor cash management. Another company may have a ratio lower than 2:1 as a result of excellent management in these three areas. Thus, rule-of-thumb measures must be used with great care.

PAST PERFORMANCE OF THE COMPANY

An improvement over rule-of-thumb measures is the comparison of financial measures or ratios of the same company over a period of time. This standard will at least give the analyst some basis for judging whether the measure or ratio is getting better or worse. It may also be helpful in showing possible future trends. However, since trends do reverse at times, such projections must be made with care. Another problem with trend analysis is that the past may not be a useful measure of adequacy. In other words, past performance may not be enough to meet present needs. For example, even if return on total investment improved from 3 percent last year to 4 percent this year, the 4 percent return may in fact not be adequate.

INDUSTRY NORMS

One way of making up for the limitations of using past performance as a standard is to use industry norms. This standard will tell how the company being analyzed compares with other companies in the same industry. For example, suppose that other companies in an industry have an average rate of return on total investment of 8 percent. In such a case, 3 and 4 percent returns are probably not adequate. Industry norms can also be used to judge trends. Suppose that, because of a downward turn in the economy, a company's profit margin dropped from 12 to 10 percent. A finding that other companies in the same industry had experienced an average drop in profit margin from 12 to 4 percent would indicate that the company being analyzed did relatively well.

There are three limitations to using industry norms as standards. First, two companies that seem to be in the same industry may not be strictly comparable. Consider two companies said to be in the oil industry. The main business of one may be marketing oil products it buys from other producers through service stations. The other, an international company, may discover, produce, refine, and market its own oil products. The operations of these two companies cannot be compared because they are different.

Second, most large companies today operate in more than one industry. Some of these diversified companies, or *conglomerates,* operate in many unrelated industries. The individual segments of a diversified company generally have different rates of profitability and different degrees of risk. In analyzing the consolidated financial statements of these companies, it is often impossible to use industry norms as standards. There are simply no other companies that are similar enough. A requirement by the Financial Accounting Standards Board in *Statement No. 14* provides a partial solution to this problem. This requirement states that diversified companies must report revenues, income from operations, and identifiable assets for each of their operating segments. Depending on specific criteria, segment information may be reported for operations in different industries, in foreign markets, or to major customers.[3]

The third limitation of industry norms is that companies in the same industry with similar operations may use different acceptable accounting procedures. That is, inventories may be valued using different methods, or different depreciation methods may be used for similar assets. Even so, if little information about a company's prior performance is available, industry norms probably offer the best available standards for judging current performance. They should be used with care.

3. *Statement of Financial Accounting Standards No. 14,* "Financial Reporting for Segments of a Business Enterprise" (Stamford, Conn.: Financial Accounting Standards Board, 1976).

PepsiCo, Inc.

Most people think of PepsiCo, Inc. as a maker of soft drinks, but in fact, the company is also involved in diversified food products (Frito-Lay) and restaurants (Pizza Hut, Taco Bell, and KFC). Since these businesses are different, the overall success of PepsiCo as reflected in its financial statements will be affected by the relative amount of investment and earnings in each of its businesses. How should a financial analyst assess the impact of each of these three segments on the company's overall financial performance?

In accordance with FASB *Statement No. 14,* PepsiCo reports the information about its three segments in a note to the financial statements in its annual report (see Exhibit 15-1 on page 684). The analyst can learn a lot about the company from this information. For example, domestic and international net sales and operating profits for each segment are shown for the past three years. Note that in all three segments, international net sales and operating profits are growing much more rapidly than those in the United States. Identifiable assets, capital spending, and depreciation and amortization expense are also shown. This information allows the analyst to see the profitability of each segment and to identify where management is investing most for the future. For example, snack foods is the most profitable segment, earning a return on identifiable assets of 21.3 percent ($984.7 million ÷ $4,628.0 million) in 1992. The largest amount of capital spending is going into the restaurant segment. ⦂⦂⦂⦂⦂

SOURCES OF INFORMATION

OBJECTIVE

3 *State the sources of information for financial statement analysis*

The external analyst is often limited to publicly available information about a company. The major sources of information about publicly held corporations are reports published by the company, SEC reports, business periodicals, and credit and investment advisory services.

REPORTS PUBLISHED BY THE COMPANY

The annual report of a publicly held corporation is an important source of financial information. The major parts of this annual report are (1) management's analysis of the past year's operations, (2) the financial statements, (3) the notes to the statements, including the principal accounting procedures used by the company, (4) the auditors' report, and (5) a summary of operations for a five- or ten-year period. Most publicly held companies also publish interim financial statements each quarter. These reports present limited information in the form of condensed financial statements, which may be subject to a limited review or a full audit by the independent auditor. The interim

Exhibit 15-1. Segment Information for PepsiCo, Inc.

Industry Segments:		Net Sales			Operating Profits			Identifiable Assets[a]		
		1992	1991	1990	1992	1991	1990	1992	1991	1990
Beverages:	Domestic	$ 5,485.2	$ 5,171.5	$ 5,034.5	$ 686.3	$ 746.2	$ 673.8			
	International	2,120.4	1,743.7	1,488.5	112.3	117.1	93.8			
		7,605.6	6,915.2	6,523.0	798.6	863.3	767.6	$ 7,857.5	$ 6,832.6	$ 6,465.2
Snack Foods:	Domestic	3,950.4	3,737.9	3,471.5	775.5	616.6	732.3			
	International	2,181.7	1,512.2	1,295.3	209.2	140.1	160.3			
		6,132.1	5,250.1	4,766.8	984.7	756.7	892.6	4,628.0	4,114.3	3,892.4
Restaurants:	Domestic	7,115.4	6,258.4	5,540.9	597.8	479.4	447.2			
	International	1,116.9	868.5	684.8	120.7	96.2	75.2			
		8,232.3	7,126.9	6,225.7	718.5	575.6	522.4	5,097.1	4,254.2	3,448.9
Total:	Domestic	16,551.0	15,167.8	14,046.9	2,059.6	1,842.2	1,853.3			
	International	5,419.0	4,124.4	3,468.6	442.2	353.4	329.3			
		$21,970.0	$19,292.2	$17,515.5	$2,501.8	$2,195.6	$2,182.6	$17,582.6	$15,201.1	$13,806.5
Geographic Areas[b]:										
United States		$16,551.0	$15,167.8	$14,046.9	$2,059.6	$1,842.2	$1,853.3	$11,957.0	$10,777.8	$ 9,980.7
Canada and Mexico		2,214.2	1,434.7	1,089.2	251.0	198.7	164.2	2,395.2	917.3	689.5
Europe		1,349.0	1,170.3	1,057.5	52.6	30.9	66.7	1,948.4	2,367.3	2,255.2
Other		1,855.8	1,519.4	1,321.9	138.6	123.8	98.4	1,282.0	1,138.7	881.1
								17,582.6	15,201.1	13,806.5
Corporate Assets								3,368.6	3,574.0	3,336.9
Total		$21,970.0	$19,292.2	$17,515.5	2,501.8	2,195.6	2,182.6	$20,951.2	$18,775.1	$17,143.4
Interest and Other Corporate Expenses, net					(603.0)	(535.9)	(528.8)			
Income from Continuing Operations Before Income Taxes and Cumulative Effect of Accounting Changes					$1,898.8	$1,659.7	$1,653.8			

Net Sales
($ In Millions)

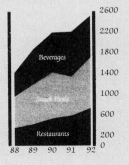

	Capital Spending[a]			Depreciation and Amortization Expense[a]		
	1992	1991	1990	1992	1991	1990
Beverages	$ 343.7	$ 425.8	$ 334.1	$ 456.9	$393.2	$338.1
Snack Foods	446.2	406.0	381.6	291.7	253.5	232.5
Restaurants	757.2	648.4	460.6	456.2	379.6	306.5
Corporate	18.0	4.1	21.9	10.1	8.2	6.9
	$1,565.1	$1,484.3	$1,198.2	$1,214.9	$1,034.5	$884.0

Results by Restaurant Chain:	Net Sales			Operating Profits		
Pizza Hut	$3,603.5	$3,258.3	$2,949.9	$335.4	$314.5	$245.9
Taco Bell	2,460.0	2,038.1	1,745.5	214.3	180.6	149.6
KFC	2,168.8	1,830.5	1,530.3	168.8	80.5	126.9
	$8,232.3	$7,126.9	$6,225.7	$718.5	$575.6	$522.4

(a) Due to immateriality, identifiable assets, capital spending and depreciation and amortization expense were not restated for certain previously consolidated international snack food businesses contributed to the new SVE joint venture. (See Note 1.)

(b) The results of centralized concentrate manufacturing operations in Puerto Rico and Ireland have been allocated based upon sales to the respective areas.

Segment Operating Profits
($ In Millions)

Source: Courtesy, PepsiCo, Inc © 1992.

statements are watched closely by the financial community for early signs of important changes in a company's earnings trend.[4]

SEC REPORTS

Publicly held corporations must file annual reports, quarterly reports, and current reports with the Securities and Exchange Commission (SEC). All such reports are available to the public at a small charge. The SEC calls for a standard form for the annual report (Form 10-K) that has more information than the published annual report. Form 10-K is, for this reason, a valuable source of information. It is available free of charge to stockholders of the company. The quarterly report (Form 10-Q) presents important facts about interim financial performance. The current report (Form 8-K) must be filed within a few days of the date of certain major events. It is often the first indicator of important changes that may affect the company's financial performance in the future.

BUSINESS PERIODICALS AND CREDIT AND INVESTMENT ADVISORY SERVICES

Financial analysts must keep up with current events in the financial world. Probably the best source of financial news is the *Wall Street Journal*, which is published every business day and is the most complete financial newspaper in the United States. Some helpful magazines, published every week or every two weeks, are *Forbes, Barron's, Fortune*, and the *Commercial and Financial Chronicle*.

For further details about the financial history of companies, the publications of such services as Moody's Investors Service, Inc. and Standard & Poor's are useful. Data on industry norms, average ratios and relationships, and credit ratings are available from such agencies as The Dun & Bradstreet Corp. Dun & Bradstreet offers an annual analysis using 14 ratios of 125 industry groups classified as retailing, wholesaling, manufacturing, and construction in its *Key Business Ratios. Annual Statement Studies*, published by Robert Morris Associates, presents many facts and ratios for 223 different industries. Also, a number of private services are available to the analyst for a yearly fee.

An example of specialized financial reporting readily available to the public is Moody's *Handbook of Dividend Achievers*, which profiles companies that have increased their dividends consistently over the past ten years. A sample listing from this publication—for PepsiCo, Inc.—is shown in Exhibit 15-2. Within one page, a wealth of information about the company is summarized: the market action of the stock; summaries of the business operations, recent developments, and prospects; earnings and dividend data; annual financial data for the past six or seven years; and other information. From the data it is possible to do many of the trend analyses and ratios that are explained in this chapter.

---

4. Accounting Principles Board, *Opinion No. 28*, "Interim Financial Reporting" (New York: American Institute of Certified Public Accountants, 1973); and *Statement of Financial Accounting Standards No. 3*, "Reporting Accounting Change in Interim Financial Statements" (Stamford, Conn.: Financial Accounting Standards Board, 1974).

Exhibit 15-2. Sample Listing from Moody's *Handbook of Dividend Achievers*

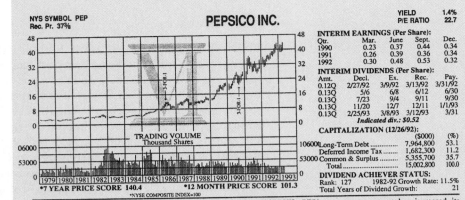

NYS SYMBOL PEP
Rec. Pr. 37⅜

PEPSICO INC.

YIELD 1.4%
P/E RATIO 22.7

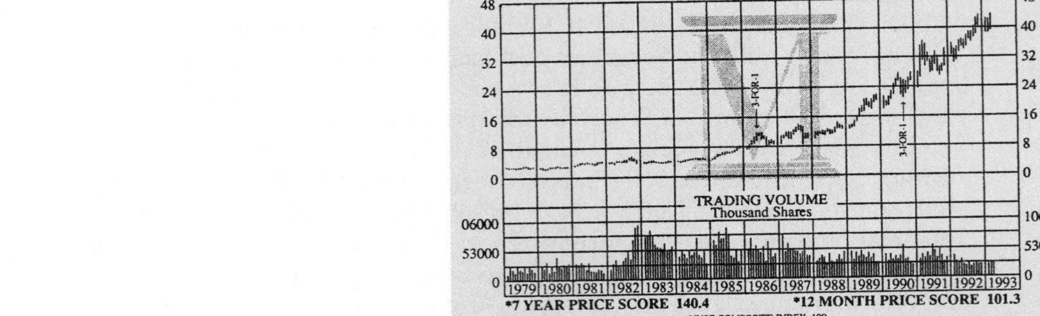
48
40
32
24
16
8
0
3-FOR-1
3-FOR-1
TRADING VOLUME
Thousand Shares
106000
53000
0
1979 1980 1981 1982 1983 1984 1985 1986 1987 1988 1989 1990 1991 1992 1993

*7 YEAR PRICE SCORE 140.4 *12 MONTH PRICE SCORE 101.3

*NYSE COMPOSITE INDEX=100

INTERIM EARNINGS (Per Share):

Qtr.	Mar.	June	Sept.	Dec.
1990	0.23	0.37	0.44	0.34
1991	0.26	0.39	0.36	0.34
1992	0.30	0.48	0.53	0.32

INTERIM DIVIDENDS (Per Share):

Amt.	Decl.	Ex.	Rec.	Pay.
0.12Q	2/27/92	3/9/92	3/13/92	3/31/92
0.13Q	5/6	6/8	6/12	6/30
0.13Q	7/23	9/4	9/11	9/30
0.13Q	11/20	12/7	12/11	1/1/93
0.13Q	2/25/93	3/8/93	3/12/93	3/31

Indicated div.: $0.52

CAPITALIZATION (12/26/92):

	($000)	(%)
Long-Term Debt	7,964,800	53.1
Deferred Income Tax	1,682,300	11.2
Common & Surplus	5,355,700	35.7
Total	15,002,800	100.0

DIVIDEND ACHIEVER STATUS:
Rank: 127 1982-92 Growth Rate: 11.5%
Total Years of Dividend Growth: 21

RECENT DEVELOPMENTS: Income before an accounting charge for the year ended 12/26/92 increased 14% to $1.30 billion from $1.08 billion in 1991. Sales rose to $22.0 billion. Worldwide beverage profits grew 12% on sales that increased 10% to $7.6 billion. U.S. bottler case sales grew more than 1%, reflecting growth in the Mountain Dew and Diet Pepsi brands. International bottler case sales increased 7%. Worldwide snacks had higher profits on sales of $6.1 billion, up 17%. Domestic profits were up 13% as gains were posted by Lay's and Ruffles. Restaurant profits advanced 19% and sales grew 16%.

PROSPECTS: PEP's restaurant segment has increased its market share and stands to benefit from unit additions in the near term. However, moderate growth is expected as chain expansion nears saturation. PEP will expand its operations in the former Soviet Union. PEP's Frito-Lay unit is already rebounding. A new line of Taco Bell products for the supermarket will be rolled out soon.

BUSINESS

PEPSICO, INC. operates on a worldwide basis within three distinct business segments; soft drinks, snackfoods and restaurants. The soft drinks segment, manufactures concentrates, and markets Pepsi-Cola, Diet Pepsi, Mountain Dew, Slice and allied brands worldwide, and 7-up internationally. This segment also conducts soft drink bottling businesses principally in the United States. Snack Foods manufactures and markets snack chips through Frito-Lay Inc. Well known brands include: Doritos, Ruffles and Lays. Restaurants consists of Pizza Hut, Taco Bell and Kentucky Fried Chicken.

BUSINESS LINE ANALYSIS

(12/26/92)	Rev(%)	Inc(%)
Beverages	34.6	31.9
Snack Foods	27.9	39.4
Restaurants	37.5	28.7
Total	100.0	100.0

ANNUAL EARNINGS AND DIVIDENDS PER SHARE

	12/26/92	12/28/91	12/29/90	12/30/89	12/31/88	12/28/87	12/27/86
Earnings Per Share	1.61	1.35	1.37	1.13	0.97	[1] 0.77	0.58
Dividends Per Share	0.50	0.44	0.367	0.31	0.25	0.22	[2] 0.205
Dividend Payout %	31.1	32.6	26.8	27.1	26.2	28.7	35.3

[1] Before disc. oper. [2] 3-for-1 stk split, 5/86

ANNUAL FINANCIAL DATA

	12/26/92	12/28/91	12/29/90	12/30/89	12/31/88	12/28/87	12/27/86
RECORD OF EARNINGS (IN MILLIONS):							
Total Revenues	21,970.0	19,607.9	17,802.7	15,242.4	13,007.0	11,485.2	9,290.8
Costs and Expenses	19,332.9	17,276.3	15,558.0	13,309.1	11,017.7	9,778.9	[1] 8,470.2
Depreciation & Amort	1,214.9	1,034.5	884.0	772.0	629.3	563.0	...
Operating Income	2,371.2	2,122.9	2,055.6	1,782.9	1,360.0	1,143.3	820.6
Income Bef Income Taxes	1,898.8	1,670.3	1,667.4	1,350.5	1,137.6	960.4	680.3
Provision for Inc Taxes	597.1	590.1	576.8	449.1	375.4	355.3	222.5
Net Income	374.3	1,080.2	[2] 1,090.6	901.4	762.2	[3] 605.1	457.8
Aver. Shs. Outstg. (000)	806,700	802,500	798,700	795,900	790,500	789,300	393,300

[1] Incl. Dep. [2] Before disc. op. dr$13,700,000. [3] Before disc. op. dr$10,300,000.

	12/26/92	12/28/91	12/29/90	12/30/89	12/31/88	12/28/87	12/27/86
BALANCE SHEET (IN MILLIONS):							
Tot Cash & Sh-tm Invests	2,058.4	2,036.0	1,815.7	1,533.9	1,617.8	1,352.6	920.5
Receivables, Net	1,588.5	1,481.7	1,414.7	1,239.7	979.3	885.6	820.2
Inventories	768.8	661.5	585.8	546.1	442.4	433.0	431.5
Gross Property	12,095.2	10,501.7	8,977.7	7,818.4	6,658.4	6,000.6	5,389.1
Accumulated Depreciation	4,653.2	3,907.0	3,266.8	2,688.2	2,195.9	1,883.2	1,549.0
Long-Term Debt	7,964.8	7,806.2	5,600.1	5,777.1	2,356.6	2,150.6	2,492.9
Capital Lease Obligations	...	...	...	...	...	129.3	139.7
Net Stockholders' Equity	5,355.7	5,545.4	4,904.2	3,891.1	3,161.0	2,508.6	2,059.1
Total Assets	20,951.2	18,775.1	17,143.4	15,126.7	11,135.3	9,022.7	8,028.6
Total Current Assets	4,842.3	4,566.1	4,081.4	3,550.8	3,264.7	2,939.6	2,503.8
Total Current Liabilities	4,324.4	3,722.1	4,770.5	3,691.8	3,873.6	2,722.8	2,223.1
Net Working Capital	517.9	844.0	d689.1	d141.0	d608.9	216.8	280.7
Year End Shs Outstg (000)	798,800	789,101	788,389	791,057	863,100	781,239	780,957
STATISTICAL RECORD:							
Operating Profit Margin %	10.8	10.8	11.5	11.7	10.5	10.0	8.8
Book Value Per Share	...	...	...	...	0.67	1.44	0.99
Return on Equity %	24.3	19.5	22.2	23.2	24.1	24.1	22.2
Return on Assets %	6.2	5.8	6.4	6.0	6.8	6.7	5.7
Average Yield %	1.4	1.5	1.6	1.8	2.0	1.9	2.1
P/E Ratio	26.9-18.9	27.0-17.4	20.3-13.1	19.5-11.2	14.9-10.3	18.3-11.0	20.5-12.7
Price Range	43⅜-30½	36½-23½	27⅞-18	22-12⅝	14½-10	14⅛-8½	11⅞-7⅜

Statistics are as originally reported.

OFFICERS:
D.W. Calloway, Chmn. & C.E.O.
R.G. Dettmer, Exec. V.P. & C.F.O.
E.V. Lahey, Jr., Sr. V.P., Gen. Coun. & Sec.
L. Schutzman, Sr. V.P. & Treas.
INCORPORATED: NC, Dec., 1986
PRINCIPAL OFFICE: Purchase, NY 10577

TELEPHONE NUMBER: (914) 253-2000
NO. OF EMPLOYEES: 338,000
ANNUAL MEETING: In May
SHAREHOLDERS: 135,000
INSTITUTIONAL HOLDINGS:
No. of Institutions: 1,106
Shares Held: 468,147,988

REGISTRAR(S): Chemical Bank, New York, NY

TRANSFER AGENT(S): Chemical Bank, New York, NY

Source: From Moody's *Handbook of Dividend Achievers*. Copyright © 1993. Used by permission of Moody's Investor Services.

EVALUATING A COMPANY'S QUALITY OF EARNINGS

OBJECTIVE

4 *Identify the issues related to evaluating the quality of a company's earnings*

It is clear from the preceding sections that current and expected earnings play an important role in the analysis of a company's prospects. In fact, a survey of two thousand members of the Association for Investment Management and Research indicated that the two most important economic indicators in evaluating common stocks were expected changes in earnings per share and expected return on equity.[5] Net income is a key component of both measures. Because of the importance of net income, or the "bottom line," in measures of a company's prospects, there is significant interest in evaluating the quality of the net income figure, or the *quality of earnings*. The quality of a company's earnings may be affected by (1) the accounting methods and estimates the company's management chooses and/or (2) the nature of nonoperating items in the income statement.

CHOICE OF ACCOUNTING METHODS AND ESTIMATES

Two aspects of the choice of accounting methods affect the quality of earnings. First, some accounting methods are by nature more conservative than others because they tend to produce a lower net income in the current period. Second, there is considerable latitude in the choice of the estimated useful life over which assets are written off and in the amount of estimated residual value. In general, an accounting method or estimated useful life and/or residual value that results in lower current earnings is considered to produce better-quality earnings.

In earlier chapters, various acceptable methods were used in applying the matching rule. These methods are based on allocation procedures, which in turn are based on certain assumptions. Here are some of these procedures:

---

5. Cited in *The Week in Review* (Deloitte Haskins & Sells), February 28, 1985.

1. For estimating uncollectible accounts expense: percentage of net sales method and accounts receivable aging method
2. For pricing the ending inventory: average-cost method; first-in, first-out (FIFO) method; and last-in, first-out (LIFO) method
3. For estimating depreciation expense: straight-line method, production method, and declining-balance method
4. For estimating depletion expense: production (extraction) method
5. For estimating amortization of intangibles: straight-line method

All these procedures are designed to allocate the costs of assets to the periods in which those costs contribute to the production of revenue. They are based on a determination of the benefits to the current period (expenses) versus the benefits to future periods (assets). They are estimates, and the period or periods benefited cannot be demonstrated conclusively. They are also subjective, because in practice it is hard to justify one method of estimation over another.

For this reason, it is important for both the accountant and the financial statement user to understand the possible effects of different accounting procedures on net income and financial position. For example, suppose that two companies have similar operations, but that one uses FIFO for inventory pricing and the straight-line (SL) method for computing depreciation and the other uses LIFO for inventory pricing and the double-declining-balance (DDB) method for computing depreciation. The income statements of the two companies might appear as follows:

	FIFO and SL	LIFO and DDB
Sales	$500,000	$500,000
Goods Available for Sale	$300,000	$300,000
Less Ending Inventory	60,000	50,000
Cost of Goods Sold	$240,000	$250,000
Gross Margin from Sales	$260,000	$250,000
Less: Depreciation Expense	$ 40,000	$ 80,000
Other Expenses	170,000	170,000
Total Operating Expenses	$210,000	$250,000
Net Income Before Income Taxes	$ 50,000	$ 0

This $50,000 difference in income before income taxes stems only from the differences in accounting methods. Differences in the estimated lives and residual values of the plant assets could lead to an even greater variation. In practice, of course, differences in net income occur for many reasons, but the user must be aware of the discrepancies that can occur as a result of the methods chosen by management.

The existence of these alternatives could cause problems in the interpretation of financial statements were it not for the conventions of full disclosure and consistency described in the chapter on financial reporting and analysis. Full disclosure requires that management explain the significant accounting policies used in preparing the financial statements in a note to the statements. Consistency requires that the same accounting procedure be followed from year to year. If a change in procedure is made, the nature of the change and its monetary effect must be explained in a note.

NATURE OF NONOPERATING ITEMS

As seen in the chapter on retained earnings and corporate income statements, the corporate income statement consists of several components. The top of the statement presents earnings from current ongoing operations, called income from operations. The lower part of the statement can contain such nonoperating items as discontinued operations, extraordinary gains and losses, and effects of accounting changes. These items may drastically affect the bottom line, or net income, of the company.

For practical reasons, the calculations of trends and ratios are based on the assumption that net income and other components are comparable from year to year and from company to company. However, in making interpretations the astute analyst will always look beyond the ratios to the quality of the components. For example, recall that in the chapter on long-term liabilities, many companies were cited as reporting large write-offs because of the cumulative effects of the change in accounting principles to recognize liabilities for postretirement medical benefits. In a recent year, AT&T wrote off $7 billion for retiree health benefits and another $1.3 billion to cover future disability and severance payments. Despite these huge losses, the company's stock price has been higher because income from operations before these charges was up for the year.[6] Although such write-offs reduce a company's net worth, they do not affect current operations or cash flows and are usually ignored by analysts assessing current performance.

In some cases, a company may boost income by selling assets on which it can report a gain. For example, the *Wall Street Journal* recently reported that Lotus Development Corporation, the well-known software company, reported a 40 percent increase in net income when earnings from operations actually decreased by 66 percent. Weak sales and earnings were camouflaged by a one-time $33.3 million gain after taxes from the sale of shares that Lotus owns in another company.[7] The quality of Lotus's earnings is lower than might appear on the surface. Unless analysts go beyond the "bottom line" in analyzing and interpreting financial reports, they can come to the wrong conclusions.

BUSINESS BULLETIN: ETHICS IN PRACTICE

External users of financial statements depend on management's honesty and openness in disclosing factual information about a company. In the vast majority of cases, management's reports are reliable, but on occasion, employees (called whistle-blowers) may publicly disclose wrongdoing on the part of their company. For instance, employees have accused various divisions of Teledyne, Inc., a large defense contractor, of financial misdeeds. The charges include keeping two sets of records, overbilling the government, and making illegal payments to Egyptian officials.

6. "Accounting Rule Change Will Erase AT&T Earnings," *Chicago Tribune,* January 15, 1994.
7. John R. Wilke, "Lotus Net Rises 40% on One-Time Gain While Operating Earnings Plunge 66%," *Wall Street Journal,* October 16, 1992.

Although whistle-blowers are protected by law, their actions often harm their careers. A former Teledyne employee, for example, who complained about poor equipment, improper training, and shipments of untested components claims to have been banished to a dingy corner of the plant. The company is now subject to a possible $1.1 billion in damages and a congressional hearing.[8] Whether or not these allegations are true, they will have a negative effect on the market's view of Teledyne and must be considered when analyzing the company. ▬▬▬

TOOLS AND TECHNIQUES OF FINANCIAL ANALYSIS

Few numbers by themselves mean very much. It is their relationship to other numbers or their change from one period to another that is important. The tools of financial analysis are intended to show relationships and changes. Among the more widely used of these financial analysis techniques are horizontal analysis, trend analysis, vertical analysis, and ratio analysis.

HORIZONTAL ANALYSIS

OBJECTIVE

5 *Apply horizontal analysis, trend analysis, and vertical analysis to financial statements*

Generally accepted accounting principles call for the presentation of comparative financial statements that give the current year's and past year's financial information. A common starting point for studying such statements is **horizontal analysis**, which begins with the computation of dollar amount changes and percentage changes from the previous to the current year. The percentage change must be computed to show how the size of the change relates to the size of the amounts involved. A change of $1 million in sales is not so drastic as a change of $1 million in net income, because sales is a larger amount than net income.

Exhibits 15-3 and 15-4 present the comparative balance sheets and income statements, respectively, for Apple Computer, Inc., with the dollar and percentage changes shown. The percentage change is computed as follows:

$$\text{Percentage change} = 100\left(\frac{\text{amount of change}}{\text{previous year amount}}\right)$$

The **base year** in any set of data is always the first year being studied. For example, from 1992 to 1993, Apple's total assets increased by $948 million, from $4,224 million to $5,171 million, or by 22.4 percent, computed as follows:

$$\text{Percentage increase} = 100\left(\frac{\$948 \text{ million}}{\$4,224 \text{ million}}\right) = 22.4\%$$

An examination of the comparative balance sheets shows much change from 1992 to 1993. Total assets increased by 22.4 percent. There was an especially large increase in inventories of 159.7 percent and a decrease in short-term investments of 77.0 percent. The percentage increase in current liabilities of 76.4 percent was more than three times the percentage increase in current assets of 21.9 percent. Notes payable showed a large increase of 346.3 percent. Total stockholders' equity decreased by 7.4 percent. Overall, Apple became less liquid and more heavily financed by short-term debt.

---

8. "At Teledyne, A Chorus of Whistle-blowers," *Business Week*, December 14, 1992.

Exhibit 15-3. Comparative Balance Sheets with Horizontal Analysis

Apple Computer, Inc.
Consolidated Balance Sheets
September 24, 1993, and September 25, 1992

	(Dollars in thousands)		Increase (Decrease)	
	1993	1992	Amount	Percentage
Assets:				
Current assets:				
Cash and cash equivalents	$ 676,413	$ 498,557	$ 177,856	35.7
Short-term investments	215,890	936,943	(721,053)	(77.0)
Accounts receivable, net of allowance for				
doubtful accounts of $83,776 ($83,048 in 1992)	1,381,946	1,087,185	294,761	27.1
Inventories	1,506,638	580,097	926,541	159.7
Prepaid income taxes	268,085	199,139	68,946	34.6
Other current assets	289,383	256,473	32,910	12.8
Total current assets	$4,338,355	$3,558,394	$ 779,961	21.9
Property, plant, and equipment:				
Land and buildings	$ 404,688	$ 255,808	$ 148,880	58.2
Machinery and equipment	578,272	516,335	61,937	12.0
Office furniture and equipment	167,905	155,317	12,588	8.1
Leasehold improvements	261,792	208,180	53,612	25.8
Total property, plant, and equipment	$1,412,657	$1,135,640	$ 277,017	24.4
Accumulated depreciation and amortization	(753,111)	(673,419)	(79,692)	11.8
Net property, plant, and equipment	$ 659,546	$ 462,221	$ 197,325	42.7
Other assets	$ 173,511	$ 203,078	($29,567)	(14.6)
Total assets	$5,171,412	$4,223,693	$ 947,719	22.4
Liabilities and Shareholders' Equity:				
Current liabilities:				
Notes payable	$ 823,182	$ 184,461	$ 638,721	346.3
Accounts payable	742,622	426,936	315,686	73.9
Accrued compensation and employee benefits	144,779	142,382	2,397	1.7
Income taxes payable	23,658	78,382	(54,724)	(69.8)
Accrued marketing and distribution	174,547	187,767	(13,220)	(7.0)
Accrued restructuring costs	307,932	105,038	202,894	193.2
Other current liabilities	298,482	300,554	(2,072)	(.7)
Total current liabilities	$2,515,202	$1,425,520	$1,089,682	76.4
Deferred income taxes	$ 629,832	$ 610,803	$ 19,029	3.1
Commitments and contingencies	—	—	—	—
Shareholders' equity:				
Common stock, no par value; 320,000,000 shares				
authorized; 116,147,035 shares issued and				
outstanding in 1993 (118,478,825 shares in 1992)	$ 203,613	$ 282,310	($78,697)	(27.9)
Retained earnings	1,842,600	1,904,519	(61,919)	(3.3)
Accumulated translation adjustment	(19,835)	541	(20,376)	(3,766.4)
Total shareholders' equity	$2,026,378	$2,187,370	($160,992)	(7.4)
Total liabilities and stockholders' equity	$5,171,412	$4,223,693	$ 947,719	22.4

Exhibit 15-4. Comparative Income Statements with Horizontal Analysis

Apple Computer, Inc.
Consolidated Statements of Income
For the Years Ended September 24, 1993 and September 25, 1992

| | (In thousands, except per share amounts) | | Increase (Decrease) | |
	1993	1992	Amount	Percentage
Net sales	$7,976,954	$7,086,542	$ 890,412	12.6
Costs and expenses:				
Cost of sales	$5,248,834	$3,991,337	$1,257,497	31.5
Research and development	664,564	602,135	62,429	10.4
Selling, general and administrative	1,632,362	1,687,262	(54,900)	(3.3)
Restructuring costs and other	320,856	—	320,856	NA
Total costs and expenses	$7,866,616	$6,280,734	$1,585,882	25.2
Operating income	$ 110,338	$ 805,808	($695,470)	(86.3)
Interest and other income, net	29,321	49,634	(20,313)	(40.9)
Income before income taxes	$ 139,659	$ 855,442	($715,783)	(83.7)
Provision for income taxes	53,070	325,069	(271,999)	(83.7)
Net income	$ 86,589	$ 530,373	($443,784)	(83.7)
Earnings per common and common equivalent share	$ 0.73	$ 4.33	($3.60)	(83.1)
Common and common equivalent shares used in the calculations of earnings per share	119,125	122,490	(3,365)	(2.7)

From the income statements in Exhibit 15-4, the most obvious conclusion is that the increases in cost of sales of 31.5 percent and in total costs and expenses of 25.2 percent exceeded the increase in sales of 12.6 percent, resulting in a decline in operating income of 86.3 percent. In 1993, Apple had restructuring costs associated with the downsizing of certain operations. Also note that in both years interest and other income, net is a positive amount, meaning that other income exceeded interest expense in each year.

Care must be taken in the analysis of percentage changes. For example, in Exhibit 15-3, one might view the 34.6 percent increase in prepaid income taxes as more important than the 27.1 percent increase in accounts receivable, net. However, this is not the proper conclusion because in dollars the increase of $295 million in accounts receivable, net is more than four times the increase of $69 million in prepaid income taxes.

TREND ANALYSIS

A variation of horizontal analysis is trend analysis, in which percentage changes are calculated for several successive years instead of two years. Trend analysis is important because, with its long-run view, it may point to basic changes in the nature of a business. In addition to comparative financial statements, most companies present a summary of operations and data on other key indicators for five or more years. Domestic and international net sales from Apple's summary of operations together with a trend analysis are presented in Exhibit 15-5.

Exhibit 15-5. Trend Analysis

Apple Computer, Inc.
Domestic and International Net Sales
Trend Analysis

	1993	1992	1991	1990	1989
Net Sales (in thousands)					
Domestic Net Sales	$4,387,674	$3,885,042	$3,484,533	$3,241,061	$3,401,462
International Net Sales	3,589,280	3,201,500	2,824,316	2,317,374	1,882,551
Trend Analysis (in percentages)					
Domestic Net Sales	129.0	114.2	102.4	95.3	100.0
International Net Sales	190.7	170.1	150.0	123.1	100.0

Trend analysis uses an index number to show changes in related items over a period of time. For index numbers, one year, the base year, is equal to 100 percent. Other years are measured in relation to that amount. For example, the 1993 index for domestic net sales was figured as follows:

$$\text{Index} = 100 \left(\frac{\text{index year amount}}{\text{base year amount}} \right) = 100 \left(\frac{\$4,387,674}{\$3,401,462} \right) = 129.0$$

An index number of 129.0 means that the 1993 sales are 129.0 percent of, or 1.290 times, the 1989 sales.

A study of the trend analysis in Exhibit 15-5 clearly shows that Apple's international sales have been rising more rapidly than domestic sales over the past five years. Domestic sales were flat from 1989 to 1991 before beginning to grow to a five-year index of 129.0. International sales have risen substantially in every year to a five-year index of 190.7. These contrasting trends are presented graphically in Figure 15-1.

Figure 15-1. Trend Analysis Presented Graphically for Apple Computer, Inc.

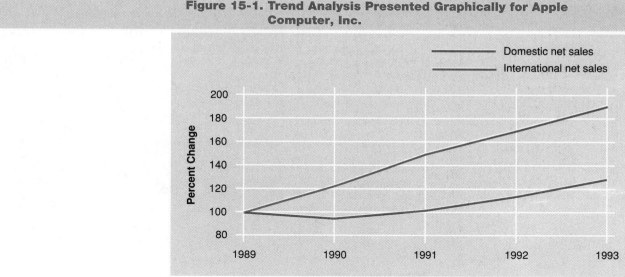

VERTICAL ANALYSIS

In vertical analysis, percentages are used to show the relationship of the different parts to the total in a single statement. The accountant sets a total figure in the statement equal to 100 percent and computes each component's percentage of that total. (The figure would be total assets or total liabilities and stockholders' equity on the balance sheet, and revenues or sales on the income statement.) The resulting statement of percentages is called a common-size statement. Common-size balance sheets and income statements for Apple are shown in pie-chart form in Figures 15-2 and 15-3, and in financial-statement form in Exhibits 15-6 and 15-7.

Vertical analysis is useful for comparing the importance of certain components in the operation of a business. It is also useful for pointing out important changes in the components from one year to the next in comparative common-size statements. For Apple, the composition of assets in Exhibit 15-6 did not change significantly from 1992 to 1993. A slightly larger proportion of assets was in properties (12.7 percent versus 10.9 percent), with a corresponding decrease in current assets (83.9 percent versus 84.3 percent) between 1993 and 1992. The composition of liabilities shows more change. Current liabilities increased from 33.8 percent to 48.6 percent. Correspondingly, stockholders' equity decreased from 51.7 percent to 39.2 percent.

The common-size income statements (Exhibit 15-7) show the importance of the increase in costs and expenses from 88.6 to 98.6 percent of sales. Two factors caused this increase. One was the one-time increase in restructuring costs, but the other was an unfavorable increase in cost of sales from 56.3 percent to 65.8 percent. These factors were major causes of the decrease in operating income from 11.4 to 1.4 percent. Consequently, net earnings as a percent of sales decreased from 7.5 percent in 1992 to only 1.1 percent in 1993.

Figure 15-2. Common-Size Balance Sheets Presented Graphically

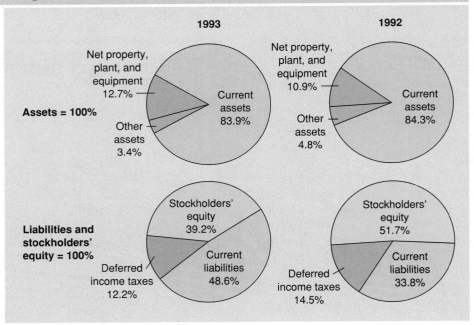

Rounding causes some additions not to total precisely.

Exhibit 15-6. Common-Size Balance Sheets

Apple Computer, Inc.
Common-Size Balance Sheets
September 24, 1993 and September 25, 1992

	1993*	1992*
Assets		
Current assets	83.9%	84.3%
Net property, plant, and equipment	12.7	10.9
Other assets	3.4	4.8
Total assets	100.0%	100.0%
Liabilities		
Current liabilities	48.6%	33.8%
Deferred income taxes	12.2	14.5
Total liabilities and deferred taxes	60.8%	48.3%
Total stockholders' equity	39.2%	51.7%
Total liabilities and stockholders' equity	100.0%	100.0%

*Results are rounded in some cases to equal 100%.

Common-size statements are often used to make comparisons between companies. They allow an analyst to compare the operating and financing characteristics of two companies of different size in the same industry. For example, the analyst may want to compare Apple to other companies in terms of the percentage of total assets financed by debt or the percentage of selling, general and administrative expenses to sales. Common-size statements would show these and other relationships.

Figure 15-3. Common-Size Income Statements Presented Graphically

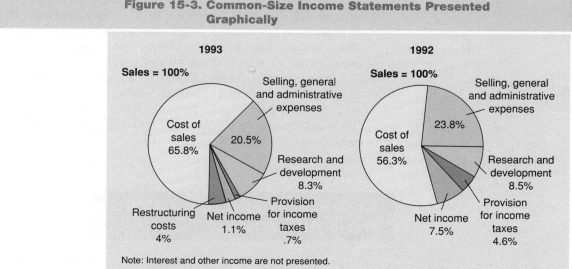

Note: Interest and other income are not presented.

Rounding causes some additions not to total precisely.

Exhibit 15-7. Common-Size Income Statements

Apple Computer, Inc.
Common-Size Income Statements
For Years Ended September 24, 1993 and September 25, 1992

	1993*	1992*
Sales	100.0%	100.0%
Costs and expenses		
Cost of sales	65.8%	56.3%
Research and development	8.3	8.5
Selling, general and administrative	20.5	23.8
Restructuring costs and other	4.0	—
Total costs and expenses	98.6%	88.6%
Operating income	1.4%	11.4%
Interest and other income, net	.4	.7
Income before income taxes	1.8%	12.1%
Provision for income taxes	.7	4.6
Net income	1.1%	7.5%

*Rounding causes some additions and subtractions not to total precisely.

OBJECTIVE

6 *Apply ratio analysis to financial statements in a comprehensive analysis of a company's financial situation*

RATIO ANALYSIS

Ratio analysis is an important way to state meaningful relationships between two components of a financial statement. To be most useful, the interpretation of ratios must include a study of the underlying data. Ratios are guides or shortcuts that are useful in evaluating a company's financial position and operations and making comparisons with results in previous years or with other companies. The primary purpose of ratios is to point out areas needing further investigation. They should be used in connection with a general understanding of the company and its environment. Ratios for financial analysis were introduced in the chapter on financial reporting and analysis. The following section briefly reviews the ratios covered in that chapter and expands the analysis to cover new ratios.

Ratios may be expressed in several ways. For example, a ratio of net income of $100,000 to sales of $1,000,000 may be stated as (1) net income is 1/10, or 10 percent of sales; (2) the ratio of sales to net income is 10 to 1 (10:1), or 10 times net income; or (3) for every dollar of sales, the company has an average net income of 10 cents.

COMPREHENSIVE ILLUSTRATION OF RATIO ANALYSIS

In prior chapters, financial ratios have been introduced at appropriate points. The purpose of this section is to show a comprehensive ratio analysis of a real company, Apple Computer, Inc., using the ratios that have been introduced and a few new ones. These ratios are used to compare Apple's performance for the years 1992 and 1993 in achieving the following objectives: (1) liquidity, (2) profitability, (3) long-term solvency, (4) cash flow adequacy, and (5) market strength. Most data for the analyses come from the financial statements of Apple presented in Exhibits 15-3 and 15-4. Other data are presented as needed.

EVALUATING LIQUIDITY

Liquidity is the ability to pay bills when they are due and to meet unexpected needs for cash. The ratios that relate to this goal all have to do with working capital or some part of it, because it is out of working capital that debts are paid. The objective of liquidity is also closely related to the cash flow ratios discussed in a following section.

The liquidity ratios for Apple Computer in 1992 and 1993 are presented in Exhibit 15-8. The current ratio and the quick ratio are measures of short-term debt-paying ability. The major difference between the two ratios is that the current ratio includes inventories in the numerator. Inventories take longer to convert to cash than the other current assets included in the numerator of the quick ratio. Both ratios declined from 1992 to 1993. The primary reasons for the declines were the large increase in current liabilities and the decrease in marketable securities. The current ratio decreased less (2.5 to 1.7 times) than the quick ratio (1.8 to .9 times) because inventories increased from 1992 to 1993. Overall, Apple's short-term debt-paying ability declined, but the company is still not in danger.

Analysis of two major components of current assets, receivables and inventories, also shows declines in liquidity from 1992 to 1993. The relative size of accounts receivable and the effectiveness of credit policies are measured by the receivable turnover, which decreased from 7.1 to 6.5 times. The relative size of inventories is measured by inventory turnover, which dropped from 6.4 to 5.0 times. The related ratios of average days' sales uncollected and average days' inventory on hand increased from 51.4 to 56.2 days and from 57.0 to 73.0 days, respectively. These results mean that Apple's operating cycle, or the time it takes to sell and collect for products sold, increased from 108.4 days (51.4 days + 57.0 days) in 1992 to 129.2 days (56.2 days + 73.0 days) in 1993. This significant increase has a negative effect on Apple's liquidity because the company has to wait 20.8 additional days (129.2 days − 108.4 days) to receive cash from sales. Apple's management explains the situation as follows:

> These higher levels of inventory, in turn, reduced the company's liquidity position and resulted in increased levels of short-term borrowings under the company's commercial paper program and from certain banks. The company has commenced a number of measures that it expects will result in improved inventory over the course of the next year.[9]

EVALUATING PROFITABILITY

The objective of profitability relates to a company's ability to earn a satisfactory income so that investors and stockholders will continue to provide capital to it. A company's profitability is also closely linked to its liquidity because earnings ultimately produce cash flow. For this reason, evaluating

9. "Management's Discussion and Analysis of Financial Condition and Results of Operations," *Annual Report,* Apple Computer, Inc., 1993.

Exhibit 15-8. Liquidity Ratios of Apple Computer, Inc.

	1993	1992

Current ratio: Measure of short-term debt-paying ability

$$\frac{\text{Current assets}}{\text{Current liabilities}} \qquad \frac{\$4,338,355}{\$2,515,202} = 1.7 \text{ times} \qquad \frac{\$3,558,394}{\$1,425,520} = 2.5 \text{ times}$$

Quick ratio: Measure of short-term debt-paying ability

$$\frac{\text{Cash + marketable securities + receivables}}{\text{Current liabilities}} \qquad \frac{\$676,413 + \$215,890 + \$1,381,946}{\$2,515,202} \qquad \frac{\$498,557 + \$936,943 + \$1,087,185}{\$1,425,520}$$

$$= \frac{\$2,274,249}{\$2,515,202} = .9 \text{ times} \qquad = \frac{\$2,522,685}{\$1,425,520} = 1.8 \text{ times}$$

Receivable turnover: Measure of relative size of accounts receivable balance and effectiveness of credit policies

$$\frac{\text{Net sales}}{\text{Average accounts receivable*}} \qquad \frac{\$7,976,954}{(\$1,381,946 + \$1,087,185)/2} \qquad \frac{\$7,086,542}{(\$1,087,185 + \$907,159)/2}$$

$$= \frac{\$7,976,954}{\$1,234,566} = 6.5 \text{ times} \qquad = \frac{\$7,086,542}{\$997,172} = 7.1 \text{ times}$$

Average days' sales uncollected: Measure of average time taken to collect receivables

$$\frac{\text{Days in year}}{\text{Receivable turnover}} \qquad \frac{365 \text{ days}}{6.5 \text{ times}} = 56.2 \text{ days} \qquad \frac{365 \text{ days}}{7.1 \text{ times}} = 51.4 \text{ days}$$

Inventory turnover: Measure of relative size of inventory

$$\frac{\text{Cost of goods sold}}{\text{Average inventory*}} \qquad \frac{\$5,248,834}{(\$1,506,638 + \$580,097)/2} \qquad \frac{\$3,991,337}{(\$580,097 + \$671,655)/2}$$

$$= \frac{\$5,248,834}{\$1,043,368} = 5.0 \text{ times} \qquad = \frac{\$3,991,337}{\$625,876} = 6.4 \text{ times}$$

Average days' inventory on hand: Measure of average days taken to sell inventory

$$\frac{\text{Days in year}}{\text{Inventory turnover}} \qquad \frac{365 \text{ days}}{5.0 \text{ times}} = 73.0 \text{ days} \qquad \frac{365 \text{ days}}{6.4 \text{ times}} = 57.0 \text{ days}$$

*1991 figures are from the eleven-year financial history in Apple Computer's annual report.

profitability is important to both investors and creditors. The profitability ratios and analysis of Apple Computer, Inc. are shown in Exhibit 15-9.

Apple's profitability declined by all measures from 1992 to 1993 primarily because of the large decrease in net income. The reasons for this decrease were discussed previously in the sections on horizontal and vertical analysis. Profit margin, which measures the net income produced by each dollar of sales, declined from 7.5 to 1.1 percent, and asset turnover, which measures the efficiency of assets in producing sales, declined from 1.8 to 1.7 times. The result is a decline in the overall earning power of the company, or return on assets, from 13.7 to 1.8 percent. These relationships may be illustrated as follows:

Exhibit 15-9. Profitability Ratios of Apple Computer, Inc.

	1993	1992

Profit margin: Measure of net income produced by each dollar of sales

$$\frac{\text{Net income*}}{\text{Net sales}} \qquad \frac{\$86,589}{\$7,976,954} = 1.1\% \qquad \frac{\$530,373}{\$7,086,542} = 7.5\%$$

Asset turnover: Measure of how efficiently assets are used to produce sales

$$\frac{\text{Net sales}}{\text{Average total assets}} \qquad \frac{\$7,976,954}{(\$5,171,412 + \$4,223,693)/2} \qquad \frac{\$7,086,542}{(\$4,223,693 + \$3,493,597)/2}$$

$$= \frac{\$7,976,954}{\$4,697,553} \qquad\qquad = \frac{\$7,086,542}{\$3,858,645}$$

$$= 1.7 \text{ times} \qquad\qquad = 1.8 \text{ times}$$

Return on assets: Measure of overall earning power or profitability

$$\frac{\text{Net income}}{\text{Average total assets}} \qquad \frac{\$86,589}{\$4,697,553} = 1.8\% \qquad \frac{\$530,373}{\$3,858,645} = 13.7\%$$

Return on equity: Measure of the profitability of stockholders' investments

$$\frac{\text{Net income}}{\text{Average stockholders' equity}} \qquad \frac{\$86,589}{(\$2,026,378 + \$2,187,370)/2} \qquad \frac{\$530,373}{(\$2,187,370 + \$1,766,676)/2}$$

$$= \frac{\$86,589}{\$2,106,874} \qquad\qquad = \frac{\$530,373}{\$1,977,023}$$

$$= 4.1\% \qquad\qquad = 26.8\%$$

*In comparing companies in an industry, some analysts use net income before income taxes as the numerator to eliminate the effect of differing tax rates among firms.

	Profit Margin		**Asset Turnover**		**Return on Assets**
	$\dfrac{\text{Net income}}{\text{Net sales}}$	$\times$	$\dfrac{\text{net sales}}{\text{average total assets}}$	$=$	$\dfrac{\text{net income}}{\text{average total assets}}$
1993	1.1%	$\times$	1.7	$=$	1.9%
1992	7.5%	$\times$	1.8	$=$	13.5%

The slight differences in the two sets of return on assets figures result from the rounding of the ratios in the second set of computations.

Finally, the profitability of stockholders' investments, or **return on equity**, declined from a generous 26.8 percent to an inadequate 4.1 percent. Management anticipates that pressures on profit margins will continue:

> The Company anticipates that gross margins for its personal computers will remain under pressure and below historic levels due to a variety of factors, including continued pricing pressures, increased competition, and advances in technology. In response to these factors, the Company has implemented various pricing and promotional actions, and as a result, expects continued lower gross margins as a percentage of net sales in 1994 compared with 1993.[10]

10. Ibid.

BUSINESS BULLETIN: INTERNATIONAL PRACTICE

Just because a company lists substantial cash and cash equivalents on its balance sheet does not necessarily mean that this cash is available to pay short-term debt in the United States. For example, although Apple shows almost $.7 billion dollars in cash and cash equivalents at the end of 1993, management warns that continued short-term borrowing will be necessary "because a substantial portion of the company's cash, cash equivalents, and short-term investments is held by foreign subsidiaries. . . . Amounts held by foreign subsidiaries would be subject to U.S. income taxation upon repatriation to the United States."[11]

EVALUATING LONG-TERM SOLVENCY

Long-term solvency has to do with a company's ability to survive for many years. The aim of long-term solvency analysis is to point out early that a company is on the road to bankruptcy. Studies have shown that accounting ratios can show as much as five years in advance that a company may fail.[12] Declining profitability and liquidity ratios are key signs of possible business failure. Two other ratios that analysts often consider when assessing long-term solvency are debt to equity and interest coverage. These ratios are shown in Exhibit 15-10.

Increasing amounts of debt in a company's capital structure mean that the company is becoming more heavily leveraged. This condition negatively affects long-term solvency because it represents increasing legal obligations to pay interest periodically and the principal at maturity. Failure to make these payments can result in bankruptcy. The debt to equity ratio measures capital structure and leverage by showing the amount of a company's assets provided by creditors in relation to the amount provided by stockholders. Apple's capital structure became much more leveraged from 1992 to 1993, during which time the debt to equity ratio increased significantly, from .9 times to 1.6 times. At the latter level, Apple has about one and a half times as much debt as equity. It is especially noteworthy to recall from Exhibit 15-3 that the increase in debt came from short-term financing rather than long-term financing. Short-term financing places demands on cash flows sooner than long-term debt does. Apple's management commented on this increase in short-term debt as follows: "The company expects that during 1994, its liquidity position will improve from recent levels, as the measures the company has identified to reduce inventory levels are implemented and take effect."[13]

If debt is bad, why have any? The answer is that the level of debt is a matter of balance. In spite of its riskiness, debt is a flexible means of financing certain business operations. Apple is using debt to finance what management plans to be a temporary increase in inventory. The interest paid on this debt

11. Ibid.
12. William H. Beaver, "Alternative Accounting Measures as Indicators of Failure," *Accounting Review,* January 1968; and Edward Altman, "Financial Ratios, Discriminant Analysis and the Prediction of Corporate Bankruptcy," *Journal of Finance,* September 1968.
13. "Management's Discussion and Analysis of Financial Condition and Results of Operations," *Annual Report,* Apple Computer, Inc., 1993.

Exhibit 15-10. Long-Term Solvency Ratios of Apple Computer, Inc.

	1993	1992

Debt to equity ratio: Measure of capital structure and leverage

$$\frac{\text{Total liabilities}}{\text{Stockholders' equity}} \qquad \frac{\$3,145,034}{\$2,026,378} = 1.6 \text{ times} \qquad \frac{\$2,036,323}{\$2,187,370} = .9 \text{ times}$$

Interest coverage ratio: Measure of creditors' protection from default on interest payments

$$\frac{\text{Net income before taxes + interest expense*}}{\text{Interest expense*}} \qquad \frac{\$139,659 + \$28,811}{\$28,811} \qquad \frac{\$855,442 + \$6,456}{\$6,456}$$

$$= 5.8 \text{ times} \qquad = 133.5 \text{ times}$$

*Interest expense was estimated based on information in the notes to the financial statements.

is deductible for income tax purposes, whereas dividends on stock are not. Also, because debt usually carries a fixed interest charge, the cost of financing can be limited and leverage can be used to advantage. If the company is able to earn a return on assets greater than the cost of the interest, it makes an overall profit.[14] However, the company runs the risk of not earning a return on assets equal to the cost of financing those assets, thereby incurring a loss.

The interest coverage ratio measures the degree of protection creditors have from a default on interest payments. This ratio declined sharply, from 133.5 times in 1992 to 5.8 times in 1993, because of the decrease in net income and the increase in short-term debt. An interest coverage ratio of 5.8 times is normally considered adequate, so unless it declines further in 1994, it is not a problem for Apple.

EVALUATING CASH FLOW ADEQUACY

Because cash flows are needed to pay debts when they are due, cash flow measures are closely related to the objectives of liquidity and long-term solvency. Apple's cash flow adequacy ratios are presented in Exhibit 15-11. By all measures, Apple's ability to generate positive operating cash flows declined from 1992 to 1993. Key to these declines is the decline in cash flow yield, or the relationship of cash flows from operating activities to net income, from a positive 1.7 times to a negative 7.6 times. This occurred because net cash flows from operating activities, as presented in the statement of cash flows, showed an extraordinary decline from a positive $920,582,000 in 1992 to a negative $661,837,000 in 1993. The principal reasons for the decline in operating cash flows were the decrease in net income and the large increases in receivables and inventories, which we have already discussed. As a result of the decline in cash flow yield, the other cash flow ratios also declined significantly. Cash flows to sales, or the ability of sales to generate operating cash flows, declined from a positive 13.0 percent to a negative 8.3 percent. Cash flows to assets, or the ability of assets to generate operating cash flows, declined from a positive 23.9 percent to a negative 14.1 percent. Overall, Apple's free cash flow, or cash generated or deficiency after providing for

14. In addition, there are advantages to being a debtor in periods of inflation because the debt, which is fixed in dollar amount, may be repaid with cheaper dollars.

Exhibit 15-11. Cash Flow Adequacy Ratios of Apple Computer, Inc.

	1993	1992

Cash flow yield: Measure of a company's ability to generate operating cash flows in relation to net income

$$\frac{\text{Net cash flows from operating activities}}{\text{Net income}} \qquad \frac{(\$661,837)}{\$86,589} = -7.6 \text{ times} \qquad \frac{\$920,582}{\$530,373} = 1.7 \text{ times}$$

Cash flows to sales: Measure of the ability of sales to generate operating cash flows

$$\frac{\text{Net cash flows from operating activities}}{\text{Net sales}} \qquad \frac{(\$661,837)}{\$7,976,954} = -8.3\% \qquad \frac{\$920,582}{\$7,086,542} = 13.0\%$$

Cash flows to assets: Measure of the ability of assets to generate operating cash flows

$$\frac{\text{Net cash flows from operating activities}}{\text{Average total assets}} \qquad \frac{(\$661,837)}{(\$5,171,412 + \$4,223,693)/2} \qquad \frac{\$920,582}{(\$4,223,693 + \$3,493,597)/2}$$

$$= \frac{(\$661,837)}{\$4,697,553} = -14.1\% \qquad = \frac{\$920,582}{\$3,858,645} = 23.9\%$$

Free cash flow: Measure of cash generated or cash deficiency after providing for commitments

Net cash flows from operating activities − dividends − net capital expenditures

$$-\$661,837 - \$55,593 - \$213,118 = -\$930,548 \qquad \$920,582 - \$57,196 - \$194,853 = \$668,533$$

commitments, went from an acceptable positive $668,533,000 to a dangerously negative $930,548,000. These computations include dividends of $57,196,000 in 1992 and $213,118,000 in 1993 and net capital expenditures of $194,853,000 in 1992 and $213,118,000 in 1993, as presented in the statement of cash flows.

EVALUATING MARKET RATIOS

The market price of a company's stock is of interest to the analyst because it represents what investors as a whole think of the company at a point in time. Market price is the price at which people are willing to buy or sell the stock. It provides information about how investors view the potential return and risk connected with owning the company's stock. Market price by itself is not very informative for this purpose, however. Companies differ in number of out-standing shares and amount of underlying earnings and dividends. Thus, market price must be related to earnings by considering the price/earnings ratio and the dividends yield. These ratios for Apple appear in Exhibit 15-12 and have been computed using the average market price for Apple's stock during 1992 and 1993.

The price/earnings (P/E) ratio, which measures investor confidence in a company, is the ratio of the market price per share to earnings per share. The P/E ratio is useful in comparing the relative values placed on the earnings of different companies and in comparing the value placed on a company's shares in relation to the overall market. Apple's price/earnings ratio increased from 11.5 times in 1992 to 53.4 times in 1993 because although its

Exhibit 15-12. Market Strength Ratios of Apple Computer, Inc.

	1993	1992

Price/earnings ratio: Measure of investor confidence in a company

$$\frac{\text{Market price per share*}}{\text{Earnings per share}} \qquad = \frac{\$39}{\$.73} = 53.4 \text{ times} \qquad = \frac{\$50}{\$4.33} = 11.5 \text{ times}$$

Dividends yield: Measure of the current return to an investor in a stock

$$\frac{\text{Dividends per share*}}{\text{Market price per share}} \qquad = \frac{\$.48}{\$39} = 1.2\% \qquad = \frac{\$.48}{\$50} = 1.0\%$$

*Market price and dividends are from Apple's annual report.

net income dropped significantly, the market price of its stock did not decline as much. This would indicate that investors are confident that Apple will rebound in profitability in 1994 and beyond. The dividends yield measures a stock's current return to an investor in the form of dividends. Apple's dividends yield inched up from 1.0 percent in 1992 to 1.2 percent in 1993 because the market price of the stock declined, but the dividends per share were the same. Because these are very low dividends yields, it may be concluded that investors expect to earn a greater return from increases in the market value of Apple's stock than from dividends.

SUMMARY OF FINANCIAL ANALYSIS OF APPLE COMPUTER, INC.

This ratio analysis clearly shows that Apple's liquidity, profitability, long-term solvency, and cash flow position declined from 1992 to 1993. The primary reasons were the drop in earnings and the greater need for short-term financing as a result of the increases in current assets, especially inventories, and the decrease in operating cash flows. As pointed out above, management has concrete plans to address the challenges of declining liquidity and profitability. It will be interesting to see whether an improvement occurs in 1994. Based on the market ratios, investors seem willing to give Apple the benefit of the doubt.

CHAPTER REVIEW

REVIEW OF LEARNING OBJECTIVES

1. **Describe and discuss the objectives of financial statement analysis.** Creditors and investors, as well as managers, use financial statement analysis to judge the past performance and current position of a company. In this way they also judge its future potential and the risk associated with it. Creditors use the information gained from their analysis to make reliable loans that will be repaid with interest. Investors use the information to make investments that will provide a return that is worth the risk.

2. **Describe and discuss the standards for financial statement analysis.** Three commonly used standards for financial statement analysis are rule-of-thumb measures,

past performance of the company, and industry norms. Rule-of-thumb measures are weak because of the lack of evidence that they can be applied widely. The past performance of a company can offer a guideline for measuring improvement but is not helpful in judging performance relative to other companies. Although the use of industry norms overcomes this last problem, its disadvantage is that firms are not always comparable, even in the same industry.

3. **State the sources of information for financial statement analysis.** The major sources of information about publicly held corporations are company-published reports such as annual reports and interim financial statements, SEC reports, business periodicals, and credit and investment advisory services.

4. **Identify the issues related to evaluating the quality of a company's earnings.** Current and prospective net income is an important component in many ratios used to evaluate a company. The user should recognize that the quality of reported net income can be influenced by certain choices made by management. First, management exercises judgment in choosing the accounting methods and estimates used in computing net income. Second, discontinued operations, extraordinary gains or losses, and changes in accounting methods may affect net income positively or negatively.

5. **Apply horizontal analysis, trend analysis, and vertical analysis to financial statements.** Horizontal analysis involves the computation of dollar amount changes and percentage changes from year to year. Trend analysis is an extension of horizontal analysis in that percentage changes are calculated for several years. The changes are usually computed by setting a base year equal to 100 and calculating the results for subsequent years as a percentage of that base year. Vertical analysis uses percentages to show the relationship of the component parts to the total in a single statement. The resulting financial statements, which are expressed entirely in percentages, are called common-size statements.

6. **Apply ratio analysis to financial statements in a comprehensive analysis of a company's financial situation.** A comprehensive ratio analysis includes the evaluation of a company's liquidity, profitability, long-term solvency, cash flow adequacy, and market ratios. The ratios for measuring these characteristics are found in Exhibits 15-8 to 15-12.

REVIEW OF CONCEPTS AND TERMINOLOGY

The following concepts and terms were introduced in this chapter:

L O 6 **Asset turnover:** Net sales divided by average total assets. Used to measure how efficiently assets are used to produce sales.

L O 6 **Average days' inventory on hand:** Days in year divided by inventory turnover. Shows the average number of days taken to sell inventory.

L O 6 **Average days' sales uncollected:** Days in year divided by receivable turnover. Shows the speed at which receivables are turned over—literally, the number of days, on average, that a company must wait to receive payment for credit sales.

L O 5 **Base year:** In financial analysis, the first year to be considered in any set of data.

L O 6 **Cash flows to assets:** Net cash flows from operating activities divided by average total assets. Used to measure the ability of assets to generate operating cash flows.

L O 6 **Cash flows to sales:** Net cash flows from operating activities divided by net sales. Used to measure the ability of sales to generate operating cash flows.

L O 6 **Cash flow yield:** Net cash flows from operating activities divided by net income. Used to measure the ability of a company to generate operating cash flows in relation to net income.

L O 5 **Common-size statement:** A financial statement in which the components of a total figure are stated in terms of percentages of the total.

L O 6 **Current ratio:** Current assets divided by current liabilities. Used as an indicator of a company's liquidity and short-term debt-paying ability.

L O 6   **Debt to equity ratio:** Total liabilities divided by stockholders' equity. Used to measure the relationship of debt financing to equity financing, or the extent to which a company is leveraged.

L O 2   **Diversified companies:** Companies that operate in more than one industry. Also called *conglomerates*.

L O 6   **Dividends yield:** Dividends per share divided by market price per share. Used as a measure of the current return to an investor in a stock.

L O 1   **Financial statement analysis:** All techniques used to show important relationships among figures in financial statements.

L O 6   **Free cash flow** Net cash flows from operating activities minus dividends minus net capital expenditures. Used to measure cash generated or cash deficiency after providing for commitments.

L O 5   **Horizontal analysis:** A technique for analyzing financial statements that involves the computation of dollar amount changes and percentage changes from the previous to the current year.

L O 5   **Index number:** In trend analysis, a number against which changes in related items over a period of time are measured. Calculated by setting the base year equal to 100 percent.

L O 6   **Interest coverage ratio:** Net income before taxes plus interest expense divided by interest expense. Used as a measure of the degree of protection creditors have from a default on interest payments.

L O 3   **Interim financial statements:** Financial statements issued for a period of less than one year, usually quarterly or monthly.

L O 6   **Inventory turnover:** The cost of goods sold divided by average inventory. Used to measure the relative size of inventory.

L O 6   **Operating cycle:** Time it takes to sell and collect for products sold; average days' inventory on hand plus average days' sales uncollected.

L O 1   **Portfolio:** A group of loans or investments designed to average the returns and risks of a creditor or investor.

L O 6   **Price/earnings (P/E) ratio:** Market price per share divided by earnings per share. Used as a measure of investor confidence in a company and as a means of comparison among stocks.

L O 6   **Profit margin:** Net income divided by net sales. Used to measure the percentage of each revenue dollar that contributes to net income.

L O 6   **Quick ratio:** The more liquid current assets—cash, marketable securities or short-term investments, and receivables—divided by current liabilities. Used as a measure of short-term liquidity.

L O 6   **Ratio analysis:** A technique of financial analysis in which meaningful relationships are shown between components of financial statements.

L O 6   **Receivable turnover:** Net sales divided by average accounts receivable. Used as a measure of the relative size of a company's accounts receivable and the success of its credit and collection policies; shows how many times, on average, receivables were turned into cash during the period.

L O 6   **Return on assets:** Net income divided by average total assets. Used to measure the amount earned on each dollar of assets invested. An overall measure of earning power or profitability.

L O 6   **Return on equity:** Net income divided by average stockholders' equity. Used to measure how much income was earned on each dollar invested by stockholders.

L O 5   **Trend analysis:** A type of horizontal analysis in which percentage changes are calculated for several successive years instead of two years.

L O 5   **Vertical analysis:** A technique for analyzing financial statements that uses percentages to show the relationships of the different parts to the total in a single statement.

L O 4   **Whistle-blowers:** Employees who publicly disclose wrongdoing on the part of the company they work for.

REVIEW PROBLEM

COMPARATIVE ANALYSIS OF TWO COMPANIES

L O 6 Maggie Washington is considering an investment in one of two fast-food restaurant chains because she believes the trend toward eating out more often will continue. Her choices have been narrowed to Quik Burger and Big Steak, whose balance sheets and income statements follow.

Balance Sheets
(in thousands)

	Quik Burger	Big Steak
Assets		
Cash	$ 2,000	$ 4,500
Accounts Receivable (net)	2,000	6,500
Inventory	2,000	5,000
Property, Plant, and Equipment (net)	20,000	35,000
Other Assets	4,000	5,000
Total Assets	$30,000	$56,000
Liabilities and Stockholders' Equity		
Accounts Payable	$ 2,500	$ 3,000
Notes Payable	1,500	4,000
Bonds Payable	10,000	30,000
Common Stock ($1 par value)	1,000	3,000
Paid-in Capital in Excess of Par Value, Common	9,000	9,000
Retained Earnings	6,000	7,000
Total Liabilities and Stockholders' Equity	$30,000	$56,000

Income Statements
(in thousands, except per share amounts)

	Quik Burger	Big Steak
Net Sales	$53,000	$86,000
Cost of Goods Sold (including restaurant operating expenses)	37,000	61,000
Gross Margin	$16,000	$25,000
General Operating Expenses		
Selling Expenses	$ 7,000	$10,000
Administrative Expenses	4,000	5,000
Interest Expense	1,400	3,200
Income Taxes Expense	1,800	3,400
Total Operating Expenses	$14,200	$21,600
Net Income	$ 1,800	$ 3,400
Earnings per share	$ 1.80	$ 1.13

From the statement of cash flows, net cash flows from operations were $2,200,000 for Quik Burger and $3,000,000 for Big Steak. Net capital expenditures were $2,100,000 for Quik Burger and $1,800,000 for Big Steak. Dividends of $500,000 were paid for Quik Burger and $600,000 for Big Steak. The market prices of the stocks for Quik Burger and Big Steak were $30 and $20, respectively. Financial information pertaining to prior years is not readily available to Maggie Washington. Assume that all notes payable are current liabilities and that all bonds payable are long-term liabilities.

REQUIRED

Conduct a comprehensive ratio analysis of Quik Burger and Big Steak and compare the results. The analysis should be performed using the following steps (round all ratios and percentages to one decimal place):

1. Prepare an analysis of liquidity.
2. Prepare an analysis of profitability.
3. Prepare an analysis of long-term solvency.
4. Prepare an analysis of cash flow adequacy.
5. Prepare an analysis of market strength.
6. Compare the two companies by inserting the ratio calculations from the preceding five steps in a table with the following column headings: Ratio Name, Quik Burger, Big Steak, and Company with More Favorable Ratio. Indicate in the last column the company that apparently had the more favorable ratio in each case. (Consider changes of .1 or less to be neutral.)
7. In what ways would having access to prior years' information aid this analysis?

ANSWER TO REVIEW PROBLEM

Ratio Name	Quik Burger	Big Steak
1. Liquidity analysis		

1. Liquidity analysis

a. Current ratio

$$\frac{\$2,000 + \$2,000 + \$2,000}{\$2,500 + \$1,500}$$

$$= \frac{\$6,000}{\$4,000} = 1.5 \text{ times}$$

$$\frac{\$4,500 + \$6,500 + \$5,000}{\$3,000 + \$4,000}$$

$$= \frac{\$16,000}{\$7,000} = 2.3 \text{ times}$$

b. Quick ratio

$$\frac{\$2,000 + \$2,000}{\$2,500 + \$1,500}$$

$$= \frac{\$4,000}{\$4,000} = 1.0 \text{ times}$$

$$\frac{\$4,500 + \$6,500}{\$3,000 + \$4,000}$$

$$= \frac{\$11,000}{\$7,000} = 1.6 \text{ times}$$

c. Receivable turnover

$$\frac{\$53,000}{\$2,000} = 26.5 \text{ times}$$

$$\frac{\$86,000}{\$6,500} = 13.2 \text{ times}$$

d. Average days' sales uncollected

$$\frac{365}{26.5} = 13.8 \text{ days}$$

$$\frac{365}{13.2} = 27.7 \text{ days}$$

e. Inventory turnover

$$\frac{\$37,000}{\$2,000} = 18.5 \text{ times}$$

$$\frac{\$61,000}{\$5,000} = 12.2 \text{ times}$$

f. Average days' inventory on hand

$$\frac{365}{18.5} = 19.7 \text{ days}$$

$$\frac{365}{12.2} = 29.9 \text{ days}$$

2. Profitability analysis

a. Profit margin

$$\frac{\$1,800}{\$53,000} = 3.4\%$$

$$\frac{\$3,400}{\$86,000} = 4.0\%$$

b. Asset turnover

$$\frac{\$53,000}{\$30,000} = 1.8 \text{ times}$$

$$\frac{\$86,000}{\$56,000} = 1.5 \text{ times}$$

Ratio Name	Quik Burger	Big Steak

c. Return on assets

$$\frac{\$1,800}{\$30,000} = 6.0\% \qquad\qquad \frac{\$3,400}{\$56,000} = 6.1\%$$

d. Return on equity

$$\frac{\$1,800}{\$1,000 + \$9,000 + \$6,000} \qquad \frac{\$3,400}{\$3,000 + \$9,000 + \$7,000}$$

$$= \frac{\$1,800}{\$16,000} = 11.3\% \qquad = \frac{\$3,400}{\$19,000} = 17.9\%$$

3. Long-term solvency analysis

a. Debt to equity ratio

$$\frac{\$2,500 + \$1,500 + \$10,000}{\$1,000 + \$9,000 + \$6,000} \qquad \frac{\$3,000 + \$4,000 + \$30,000}{\$3,000 + \$9,000 + \$7,000}$$

$$= \frac{\$14,000}{\$16,000} = .9 \text{ times} \qquad = \frac{\$37,000}{\$19,000} = 1.9 \text{ times}$$

b. Interest coverage ratio

$$\frac{\$1,800 + \$1,800 + \$1,400}{\$1,400} \qquad \frac{\$3,400 + \$3,400 + \$3,200}{\$3,200}$$

$$= \frac{\$5,000}{\$1,400} = 3.6 \text{ times} \qquad = \frac{\$10,000}{\$3,200} = 3.1 \text{ times}$$

4. Cash flow adequacy analysis

a. Cash flow yield

$$\frac{\$2,200}{\$1,800} = 1.2 \text{ times} \qquad\qquad \frac{\$3,000}{\$3,400} = .9 \text{ times}$$

b. Cash flows to sales

$$\frac{\$2,200}{\$53,000} = 4.2\% \qquad\qquad \frac{\$3,000}{\$86,000} = 3.5\%$$

c. Cash flows to assets

$$\frac{\$2,200}{\$30,000} = 7.3\% \qquad\qquad \frac{\$3,000}{\$56,000} = 5.4\%$$

d. Free cash flow (in thousands)

$$\$2,200 - \$500 - \$2,100 \qquad \$3,000 - \$600 - \$1,800$$
$$= -\$400 \qquad\qquad = \$600$$

5. Market strength analysis

a. Price/earnings ratio

$$\frac{\$30}{\$1.80} = 16.7 \text{ times} \qquad\qquad \frac{\$20}{\$1.13} = 17.7 \text{ times}$$

b. Dividends yield

$$\frac{\$500,000 \div 1,000,000}{\$30} = 1.7\% \qquad \frac{\$600,000 \div 3,000,000}{\$20} = 1.0\%$$

6. Comparative analysis

Ratio Name	Quik Burger	Big Steak	Company with More Favorable Ratio*
1. Liquidity analysis			
a. Current ratio	1.5 times	2.3 times	Big Steak
b. Quick ratio	1.0 times	1.6 times	Big Steak
c. Receivable turnover	26.5 times	13.2 times	Quik Burger
d. Average days' sales uncollected	13.8 days	27.7 days	Quik Burger
e. Inventory turnover	18.5 times	12.2 times	Quik Burger
f. Average days' inventory on hand	19.7 days	29.9 days	Quik Burger
2. Profitability analysis			
a. Profit margin	3.4%	4.0%	Big Steak
b. Asset turnover	1.8 times	1.5 times	Quik Burger
c. Return on assets	6.0%	6.1%	Neutral
d. Return on equity	11.3%	17.9%	Big Steak
3. Long-term solvency analysis			
a. Debt to equity ratio	0.9	1.9 times	Quik Burger
b. Interest coverage ratio	3.6 times	3.1 times	Quik Burger
4. Cash flow adequacy analysis			
a. Cash flow yield	1.2 times	.9 times	Quik Burger
b. Cash flows to sales	4.2%	3.5%	Quik Burger
c. Cash flows to assets	7.3%	5.4%	Quik Burger
d. Free cash flow	−$400,000	$600,000	Big Steak
5. Market strength analysis			
a. Price/earnings ratio	16.7 times	17.7 times	Big Steak
b. Dividends yield	1.7%	1.0%	Quik Burger

*This analysis indicates the company with the apparently more favorable ratio. Class discussion may focus on conditions under which different conclusions may be drawn.

7. Usefulness of prior years' information

Prior years' information would be helpful in two ways. First, turnover, return and cash flows to assets ratios could be based on average amounts. Second, a trend analysis could be performed for each company.

CHAPTER ASSIGNMENTS

KNOWLEDGE AND UNDERSTANDING

Questions

1. What are the differences and similarities in the objectives of investors and creditors in using financial statement analysis?
2. What role does risk play in making loans and investments?
3. What standards are commonly used to evaluate financial statements, and what are their relative merits?
4. Why would a financial analyst compare the ratios of Steelco, a steel company, with the ratios of other companies in the steel industry? What factors might invalidate such a comparison?

5. Where may an investor look to find information about a publicly held company in which he or she is thinking of investing?

6. What is the basis of the statement "Accounting income is a useless measurement because it is based on so many arbitrary decisions"? Is the statement true?

7. Why would an investor want to see both horizontal and trend analyses of a company's financial statements?

8. What does the following sentence mean: "Based on 1980 equaling 100, net income increased from 240 in 1992 to 260 in 1993"?

9. What is the difference between horizontal and vertical analysis?

10. What is the purpose of ratio analysis?

11. Under what circumstances would a current ratio of 3:1 be good? Under what circumstances would it be bad?

12. In a period of high interest rates, why are receivable and inventory turnover especially important?

13. The following statements were made on page 35 of the November 6, 1978 issue of *Fortune* magazine: "Supermarket executives are beginning to look back with some nostalgia on the days when the standard profit margin was 1 percent of sales. Last year the industry overall margin came to a thin 0.72 percent." How could a supermarket earn a satisfactory return on assets with such a small profit margin?

14. Company A and Company B both have net incomes of $1,000,000. Is it possible to say that these companies are equally successful? Why or why not?

15. Circo Company has a return on assets of 12 percent and a debt to equity ratio of .5. Would you expect return on equity to be more or less than 12 percent?

16. What amount is common to all cash flow adequacy ratios? To what other groups of ratios are the cash flow adequacy ratios most closely related?

17. The market price of Company J's stock is the same as that of Company Q's. How might you determine whether investors are equally confident about the future of these companies?

Short Exercises

SE 15-1.
L O 1, 2 *Objectives and Standards of Financial Statement Analysis*

Indicate whether each of the following items is (a) an objective or (b) a standard of comparison of financial statement analysis.

1. Industry norms
2. Assessment of the company's past performance
3. The company's past performance
4. Assessment of future potential and related risk
5. Rule-of-thumb measures

SE 15-2.
L O 3 *Sources of Information*

For each piece of information listed below, indicate whether the *best* source would be (a) reports published by the company, (b) SEC reports, (c) business periodicals, or (d) credit and investment advisory services.

1. Current market value of a company's stock
2. Management's analysis of the past year's operations
3. Objective assessment of a company's financial performance
4. Most complete body of financial disclosures
5. Current events affecting the company

SE 15-3.
L O 5 *Trend Analysis*

Prepare a trend analysis for the following data using 19x1 as the base year, and tell whether the results suggest a favorable or unfavorable trend. (Round your answers to one decimal place.)

	19x3	19x2	19x1
Net Sales	$158,000	$136,000	$112,000
Accounts Receivable (net)	$43,000	$32,000	$21,000

SE 15-4.

L O 5 *Horizontal Analysis*

Compute the amount and percentage changes for the following income statements, and comment on the changes from 19x1 to 19x2. (Round the percentage changes to one decimal place.)

Nu-Way, Inc.
Comparative Income Statements
For the Years Ended December 31, 19x2 and 19x1

	19x2	19x1
Net Sales	$180,000	$145,000
Cost of Goods Sold	112,000	88,000
Gross Margin	$ 68,000	$ 57,000
Operating Expenses	40,000	30,000
Operating Income	$ 28,000	$ 27,000
Interest Expense	7,000	5,000
Income Before Taxes	$ 21,000	$ 22,000
Income Taxes	7,000	8,000
Net Income	$ 14,000	$ 14,000

SE 15-5.

L O 5 *Vertical Analysis*

Express the comparative balance sheets that follow as common-size statements, and comment on the changes from 19x1 to 19x2. (Round computations to one decimal place.)

Nu-Way, Inc.
Comparative Balance Sheets
December 31, 19x2 and 19x1

	19x2	19x1
Assets		
Current Assets	$ 24,000	$ 20,000
Property, Plant, and Equipment (net)	130,000	100,000
Total Assets	$154,000	$120,000
Liabilities and Stockholders' Equity		
Current Liabilities	$ 18,000	$ 22,000
Long-Term Liabilities	90,000	60,000
Stockholders' Equity	46,000	38,000
Total Liabilities and Stockholders' Equity	$154,000	$120,000

SE 15-6.

L O 6 *Liquidity Analysis*

Using the information for Nu-Way, Inc. in SE 15-4 and SE 15-5, compute the current ratio, quick ratio, receivable turnover, average days' sales uncollected, inventory turnover, and average days' inventory on hand for 19x1 and 19x2. Inventories were $4,000 in 19x0, $5,000 in 19x1, and $7,000 in 19x2. Accounts Receivable were $6,000 in 19x0, $8,000 in 19x1, and $10,000 in 19x2. There were no marketable securities or prepaid assets. Comment on the results. (Round computations to one decimal place.)

SE 15-7.
L O 6 *Profitability Analysis*

Using the information for Nu-Way, Inc. in SE 15-4 and SE 15-5, compute the profit margin, asset turnover, return on assets, and return on equity for 19x1 and 19x2. In 19x0, total assets were $100,000 and total stockholders' equity was $30,000. Comment on the results. (Round computations to one decimal place.)

SE 15-8.
L O 6 *Long-Term Solvency Analysis*

Using the information for Nu-Way, Inc. in SE 15-4 and SE 15-5, compute the debt to equity and interest coverage ratios for 19x1 and 19x2. Comment on the results. (Round computations to one decimal place.)

SE 15-9.
L O 6 *Cash Flow Adequacy Analysis*

Using the information for Nu-Way, Inc. in SE 15-4, SE 15-5, and SE 15-7, compute the cash flow yield, cash flows to sales, cash flows to assets, and free cash flow for 19x1 and 19x2. Net cash flows from operating activities were $21,000 in 19x1 and $16,000 in 19x2. Net capital expenditures were $30,000 in 19x1 and $40,000 in 19x2. Cash dividends were $6,000 in both years. Comment on the results. (Round computations to one decimal place.)

SE 15-10.
L O 6 *Market Strength Analysis*

Using the information for Nu-Way, Inc. in SE 15-4, SE 15-5, and SE 15-9, compute the price/earnings and dividends yield ratios for 19x1 and 19x2. The company had 10,000 shares of common stock outstanding in both years. The price of Nu-Way's common stock was $30 in 19x1 and $20 in 19x2. Comment on the results. (Round computations to one decimal place.)

APPLICATION

Exercises

E 15-1.
L O 4 *Effect of Alternative Accounting Methods*

At the end of its first year of operations, a company could calculate its ending merchandise inventory according to three different accounting methods, as follows: FIFO, $95,000; average-cost, $90,000; LIFO, $86,000. If the company uses the average-cost method, net income for the year would be $34,000.

1. Determine net income if the FIFO method is used.
2. Determine net income if the LIFO method is used.
3. Which method is more conservative?
4. Will the consistency convention be violated if the company chooses to use the LIFO method?
5. Does the full-disclosure convention require disclosure of the inventory method selected by management in the financial statements?

E 15-2.
L O 4, 6 *Effect of Alternative Accounting Methods*

Jeans F' All and Jeans 'R' Us are very similar companies in size and operation. Jeans F' All uses FIFO and straight-line depreciation methods, and Jeans 'R' Us uses LIFO and accelerated depreciation. Prices have been rising during the past several years. Each company has paid its taxes in full for the current year, and each uses the same method for figuring income taxes as for financial reporting. Identify which company will report the greater amount for each of the following ratios:

1. Current ratio
2. Inventory turnover
3. Profit margin
4. Return on assets

If you cannot tell which company will report the greater amount, explain why.

E 15-3.
L O 5 *Horizontal Analysis*

Compute the amount and percentage changes for the following balance sheets, and comment on the changes from 19x1 to 19x2. (Round the percentage changes to one decimal place.)

Lindquist Company
Comparative Balance Sheets
December 31, 19x2 and 19x1

	19x2	19x1
Assets		
Current Assets	$ 37,200	$ 25,600
Property, Plant, and Equipment (net)	218,928	194,400
Total Assets	$256,128	$220,000
Liabilities and Stockholders' Equity		
Current Liabilities	$ 22,400	$ 6,400
Long-Term Liabilities	70,000	80,000
Stockholders' Equity	163,728	133,600
Total Liabilities and Stockholders' Equity	$256,128	$220,000

E 15-4.

L O 5 *Trend Analysis*

Prepare a trend analysis of the following data using 19x1 as the base year, and tell whether the situation shown by the trends is favorable or unfavorable. (Round your answers to one decimal place.)

	19x5	19x4	19x3	19x2	19x1
Net Sales	$25,520	$23,980	$24,200	$22,880	$22,000
Cost of Goods Sold	17,220	15,400	15,540	14,700	14,000
General and Administrative Expenses	5,280	5,184	5,088	4,896	4,800
Operating Income	3,020	3,396	3,572	3,284	3,200

E 15-5.

L O 5 *Vertical Analysis*

Express the comparative income statements that follow as common-size statements, and comment on the changes from 19x1 to 19x2. (Round computations to one decimal place.)

Lindquist Company
Comparative Income Statements
For the Years Ended December 31, 19x2 and 19x1

	19x2	19x1
Net Sales	$424,000	$368,000
Cost of Goods Sold	254,400	239,200
Gross Margin	$169,600	$128,800
Selling Expenses	$106,000	$ 73,600
General Expenses	50,880	36,800
Total Operating Expenses	$156,880	$110,400
Net Operating Income	$ 12,720	$ 18,400

E 15-6.
L O 6 *Liquidity Analysis*

Partial comparative balance sheet and income statement information for Lum Company follows.

	19x2	19x1
Cash	$ 6,800	$ 5,200
Marketable Securities	3,600	8,600
Accounts Receivable (net)	22,400	17,800
Inventory	27,200	24,800
Total Current Assets	$ 60,000	$ 56,400
Current Liabilities	$ 20,000	$ 14,100
Net Sales	$161,280	$110,360
Cost of Goods Sold	108,800	101,680
Gross Margin	$ 52,480	$ 8,680

The year-end balances for Accounts Receivable and Inventory in 19x0 were $16,200 and $25,600, respectively. Compute the current ratio, quick ratio, receivable turnover, average days' sales uncollected, inventory turnover, and average days' inventory on hand for each year. (Round computations to one decimal place.) Comment on the change in the company's liquidity position from 19x1 to 19x2.

E 15-7.
L O 6 *Turnover Analysis*

Alberto's Men's Shop has been in business for four years. Because the company has recently had a cash flow problem, management wonders whether there is a problem with receivables or inventories. Here are selected figures from the company's financial statements (in thousands):

	19x4	19x3	19x2	19x1
Net Sales	$288	$224	$192	$160
Cost of Goods Sold	180	144	120	96
Accounts Receivable (net)	48	40	32	24
Merchandise Inventory	56	44	32	20

Compute receivable turnover and inventory turnover for each of the four years, and comment on the results relative to the cash flow problem that Alberto's Men's Shop has been experiencing. Round computations to one decimal place.

E 15-8.
L O 6 *Profitability Analysis*

At year end, Canzoneri Company had total assets of $640,000 in 19x0, $680,000 in 19x1, and $760,000 in 19x2. Its debt to equity ratio was .67 in all three years. In 19x1, the company earned a net income of $77,112 on revenues of $1,224,000. In 19x2, the company earned a net income of $98,952 on revenues of $1,596,000. Compute the profit margin, asset turnover, return on assets, and return on equity for 19x1 and 19x2. Comment on the apparent cause of the increase or decrease in profitability. (Round the percentages and other ratios to one decimal place.)

E 15-9.
L O 6 *Long-Term Solvency and Market Strength Ratios*

An investor is considering investing in the long-term bonds and common stock of Companies X and Y. Both companies operate in the same industry. In addition, both companies pay a dividend per share of $4 and a yield of 10 percent on their long-term bonds. Other data for the two companies follow:

	Company X	Company Y
Total Assets	$2,400,000	$1,080,000
Total Liabilities	1,080,000	594,000
Net Income Before Taxes	288,000	129,600
Interest Expense	97,200	53,460
Earnings per Share	3.20	5.00
Market Price of Common Stock	40	47.50

Compute the debt to equity, interest coverage, and price/earnings (P/E) ratios, and the dividends yield, and then comment on the results. (Round computations to one decimal place.)

E 15-10.

L O 6 *Cash Flow Adequacy Analysis*

Using the data below, taken from the financial statements of Furri, Inc., compute the cash flow yield, cash flows to sales, cash flows to assets, and free cash flow.

Net Sales	$3,200,000
Net Income	352,000
Net Cash Flows from Operating Activities	456,000
Total Assets, Beginning of Year	2,890,000
Total Assets, End of Year	3,120,000
Cash Dividends	120,000
Net Capital Expenditures	298,000

E 15-11.

L O 6 *Preparation of Statements from Ratios and Incomplete Data*

Following are the income statement and balance sheet of Pandit Corporation, with most of the amounts missing.

Pandit Corporation
Income Statement
For the Year Ended December 31, 19x1
(in thousands of dollars)

Net Sales		$18,000
Cost of Goods Sold		?
Gross Margin		$?
Operating Expenses		
Selling Expenses	$?	
Administrative Expenses	234	
Interest Expense	162	
Income Taxes Expense	620	
Total Operating Expenses		?
Net Income		$?

Pandit Corporation
Balance Sheet
December 31, 19x1
(in thousands of dollars)

Assets

Cash	$?	
Accounts Receivable (net)	?	
Inventories	?	
Total Current Assets		$?
Property, Plant, and Equipment (net)		5,400
Total Assets		$?

Liabilities and Stockholders' Equity

Current Liabilities	$?	
Bonds Payable, 9% interest	?	
Total Liabilities		$?
Common Stock—$20 par value	$3,000	
Paid-in Capital in Excess of Par Value, Common	2,600	
Retained Earnings	4,000	
Total Stockholders' Equity		9,600
Total Liabilities and Stockholders' Equity		$?

Pandit's only interest expense is on long-term debt. Its debt to equity ratio is .5, its current ratio 3:1, its quick ratio 2:1, the receivable turnover 4.5, and its inventory turnover 4.0. The return on assets is 10 percent. All ratios are based on the current year's information. Complete the financial statements using the information presented. Show supporting computations.

Problem Set A

15A-1.

L O 4, 6   *Effect of Alternative Accounting Methods*

Albers Company began operations this year. At the beginning of the year the company purchased plant assets of $900,000, with an estimated useful life of ten years and a salvage value of $130,000. During the year, the company had sales of $1,300,000, salary expense of $200,000, and other expenses of $80,000, excluding depreciation. In addition, Albers Company purchased inventory as follows:

January 15	400 units at $400	$160,000
March 20	200 units at $408	81,600
June 15	800 units at $416	332,800
September 18	600 units at $412	247,200
December 9	300 units at $420	126,000
Total	2,300 units	$947,600

At the end of the year on December 31, a physical inventory disclosed 500 units still on hand. The managers of Albers Company know that they have a choice of accounting methods, but are unsure how these methods will affect net income. They have heard of the FIFO and LIFO inventory methods and the straight-line and double-declining-balance depreciation methods.

REQUIRED

1. Prepare two income statements for Albers Company, one using the FIFO and straight-line methods, the other using the LIFO and double-declining-balance methods.
2. Prepare a schedule accounting for the difference in the two net income figures obtained in **1.**
3. What effect does the choice of accounting methods have on Albers's inventory turnover? What conclusions can you draw?
4. How does the choice of accounting methods affect Albers's return on assets?

Use year-end balances to compute the ratios. Assume that the only asset other than plant assets and inventory is $80,000 cash. Is your evaluation of Albers's profitability affected by the choice of accounting methods?

15A-2.

L O 5   *Horizontal and Vertical Analysis*

The condensed comparative income statements and balance sheets of Mariano Corporation follow. All figures are given in thousands of dollars.

Mariano Corporation
Comparative Income Statements
For the Years Ended December 31, 19x2 and 19x1

	19x2	19x1
Net Sales	$3,276,800	$3,146,400
Cost of Goods Sold	2,088,800	2,008,400
Gross Margin	$1,188,000	$1,138,000
Operating Expenses		
Selling Expenses	$ 476,800	$ 518,000
Administrative Expenses	447,200	423,200
Interest Expense	65,600	39,200
Income Taxes Expense	62,400	56,800
Total Operating Expenses	$1,052,000	$1,037,200
Net Income	$ 136,000	$ 100,800

Mariano Corporation
Comparative Balance Sheets
December 31, 19x2 and 19x1

	19x2	19x1
Assets		
Cash	$ 81,200	$ 40,800
Accounts Receivable (net)	235,600	229,200
Inventory	574,800	594,800
Property, Plant, and Equipment (net)	750,000	720,000
Total Assets	$1,641,600	$1,584,800
Liabilities and Stockholders' Equity		
Accounts Payable	$ 267,600	$ 477,200
Notes Payable	200,000	400,000
Bonds Payable	400,000	—
Common Stock—$10 par value	400,000	400,000
Retained Earnings	374,000	307,600
Total Liabilities and Stockholders' Equity	$1,641,600	$1,584,800

REQUIRED

Perform the following analyses. Round percentages to one decimal place.

1. Prepare schedules showing the amount and percentage changes from 19x1 to 19x2 for Mariano's comparative income statements and balance sheets.
2. Prepare common-size income statements and balance sheets for 19x1 and 19x2.
3. Comment on the results in **1** and **2** by identifying favorable and unfavorable changes in the components and composition of the statements.

15A-3.

L O 6 *Analyzing the Effects of Transactions on Ratios*

Straight Corporation engaged in the transactions listed in the first column of the following table. Opposite each transaction is a ratio and space to indicate the effect of each transaction on the ratio.

		Effect		
Transaction	**Ratio**	**Increase**	**Decrease**	**None**
a. Sold merchandise on account.	Current ratio			
b. Sold merchandise on account.	Inventory turnover			
c. Collected on accounts receivable.	Quick ratio			
d. Wrote off an uncollectible account.	Receivable turnover			
e. Paid on accounts payable.	Current ratio			
f. Declared cash dividend.	Return on equity			
g. Incurred advertising expense.	Profit margin			
h. Issued stock dividend.	Debt to equity ratio			
i. Issued bond payable.	Asset turnover			
j. Accrued interest expense.	Current ratio			
k. Paid previously declared cash dividend.	Dividends yield			
l. Purchased treasury stock.	Return on assets			
m. Recorded depreciation expense.	Cash flow yield			

REQUIRED

Place an X in the appropriate column to show whether the transaction increased, decreased, or had no effect on the indicated ratio.

15A-4.

L O 6   *Ratio Analysis*

Additional data for Mariano Corporation in 19x2 and 19x1 follow. This information should be used with the data in **15A-2** to answer the requirements below.

	19x2	**19x1**
Net Cash Flows from Operating Activities	$213,000,000	$172,500,000
Net Capital Expenditures	$ 45,000,000	$ 32,000,000
Dividends Paid	$ 44,000,000	$ 34,400,000
Number of Common Shares	40,000,000	40,000,000
Market Price per Share	$18	$30
Earnings per Share	$3.40	$2.52

Balances of selected accounts (in thousands) at the end of 19x0 were Accounts Receivable (net), $206,800; Inventory, $547,200; Total Assets, $1,465,600; and Stockholders' Equity, $641,200. All of Mariano's notes payable were current liabilities; all of the bonds payable were long-term liabilities.

REQUIRED

Perform the following analyses. Round percentages and ratios to one decimal place, and consider changes of .1 or less to be neutral. After making the calculations, indicate whether each ratio had a favorable (F) or unfavorable (U) change from 19x1 to 19x2.

1. Conduct a liquidity analysis by calculating for each year the (a) current ratio, (b) quick ratio, (c) receivable turnover, (d) average days' sales uncollected, (e) inventory turnover, and (f) average days' inventory on hand.
2. Conduct a profitability analysis by calculating for each year the (a) profit margin, (b) asset turnover, (c) return on assets, and (d) return on equity.
3. Conduct a long-term solvency analysis by calculating for each year the (a) debt to equity ratio and (b) interest coverage ratio.
4. Conduct a cash flow adequacy analysis by calculating for each year the (a) cash flow yield, (b) cash flows to sales, (c) cash flows to assets, and (d) free cash flow.
5. Conduct a market strength analysis by calculating for each year the (a) price/earnings ratio and (b) dividends yield.

15A-5.

L O 6   *Comprehensive Ratio Analysis of Two Companies*

Willis Rowe is considering an investment in the common stock of a chain of retail department stores. He has narrowed his choice to two retail companies, Allison Corporation and Marker Corporation, whose income statements and balance sheets follow.

	Allison Corporation	**Marker Corporation**
Net Sales	$25,120,000	$50,420,000
Cost of Goods Sold	12,284,000	29,668,000
Gross Margin	$12,836,000	$20,752,000
Operating Expenses		
Sales Expense	$ 9,645,200	$14,216,400
Administrative Expense	1,972,000	4,868,000
Interest Expense	388,000	456,000
Income Taxes Expense	400,000	600,000
Total Operating Expenses	$12,405,200	$20,140,400
Net Income	$ 430,800	$ 611,600
Earnings per share	$ 4.31	$ 10.19

	Allison Corporation	Marker Corporation
Assets		
Cash	$ 160,000	$ 384,800
Marketable Securities (at cost)	406,800	169,200
Accounts Receivable (net)	1,105,600	1,970,800
Inventory	1,259,600	2,506,800
Prepaid Expenses	108,800	228,000
Property, Plant, and Equipment (net)	5,827,200	13,104,000
Intangibles and Other Assets	1,106,400	289,600
Total Assets	$9,974,400	$18,653,200
Liabilities and Stockholders' Equity		
Accounts Payable	$ 688,000	$ 1,145,200
Notes Payable	300,000	800,000
Accrued Liabilities	100,400	146,800
Bonds Payable	4,000,000	4,000,000
Common Stock—$20 par value	2,000,000	1,200,000
Paid-in Capital in Excess of Par Value, Common	1,219,600	7,137,200
Retained Earnings	1,666,400	4,224,000
Total Liabilities and Stockholders' Equity	$9,974,400	$18,653,200

During the year, Allison Corporation paid a total of $100,000 in dividends. The market price per share of its stock is currently $60. In comparison, Marker Corporation paid a total of $228,000 in dividends, and the current market price of its stock is $76 per share. Allison Corporation had net cash flows from operations of $543,000 and net capital expenditures of $1,250,000. Marker Corporation had net cash flows from operations of $985,000 and net capital expenditures of $2,100,000. Information for prior years is not readily available. Assume that all notes payable are current liabilities and all bonds payable are long-term liabilities.

REQUIRED

Conduct a comprehensive ratio analysis for each company using the available information and compare the results. Round percentages and ratios to one decimal place, and consider differences of .1 or less to be indeterminate. This analysis should be done in the following steps:

1. Prepare an analysis of liquidity by calculating for each company the (a) current ratio, (b) quick ratio, (c) receivable turnover, (d) average days' sales uncollected, (e) inventory turnover, and (f) average days' inventory on hand.
2. Prepare an analysis of profitability by calculating for each company the (a) profit margin, (b) asset turnover, (c) return on assets, and (d) return on equity.
3. Prepare an analysis of long-term solvency by calculating for each company the (a) debt to equity ratio and (b) interest coverage ratio.
4. Prepare an analysis of cash flow adequacy by calculating for each company the (a) cash flow yield, (b) cash flows to sales, (c) cash flows to assets, and (d) free cash flow.
5. Prepare an analysis of market strength by calculating for each company the (a) price/earnings ratio and (b) dividends yield.
6. Compare the two companies by inserting the ratio calculations from 1 through 5 in a table with the following column heads: Ratio Name, Allison Corporation, Marker Corporation, and Company with More Favorable Ratio. Indicate in the right-hand column which company had the more favorable ratio in each case.
7. How could the analysis be improved if prior years' information were available?

Problem Set B

15B-1.

L O 4, 6 *Effect of Alternative Accounting Methods*

Le Beau Company began operations by purchasing $660,000 in equipment that had an estimated useful life of ten years and an estimated residual value of $60,000.

During the year, Le Beau Company purchased inventory as presented in the following chart:

January	2,000 units at $50	$ 100,000
March	4,000 units at $48	192,000
May	1,000 units at $54	54,000
July	5,000 units at $54	270,000
September	6,000 units at $56	336,000
November	2,000 units at $58	116,000
December	3,000 units at $56	168,000
Total	23,000 units	$1,236,000

During the year the company sold 19,000 units for a total of $1,820,000 and incurred salary expenses of $340,000 and expenses other than depreciation of $240,000. The company's year ends on December 31.

Le Beau's management is anxious to present its income statement fairly in its first year of operation. It realizes that alternative accounting methods are available for accounting for inventory and equipment. Management wants to determine the effect of various alternatives on this year's income. Two sets of alternatives are required.

REQUIRED

1. Prepare two income statements for Le Beau Company: one using the FIFO and straight-line methods, the other using the LIFO and the double-declining-balance methods.
2. Prepare a schedule accounting for the difference in the two net income figures obtained in **1.**
3. What effect does the choice of accounting methods have on Le Beau Company's inventory turnover? What conclusions can you draw?
4. What effect does the choice of accounting methods have on Le Beau Company's return on assets?

Use year-end balances to compute the ratios. Round all ratios and percentages to one decimal place. Assume that the only asset other than plant assets and inventory is $60,000 cash. Is your evaluation of Le Beau's profitability affected by the choice of accounting methods?

15B-2.

L O 5 *Horizontal and Vertical Analysis*

The condensed comparative income statements and balance sheets for Kelso Corporation follow.

Kelso Corporation
Comparative Income Statements
For the Years Ended December 31, 19x2 and 19x1

	19x2	19x1
Net Sales	$800,400	$742,600
Cost of Goods Sold	454,100	396,200
Gross Margin	$346,300	$346,400
Operating Expenses		
Selling Expenses	$130,100	$104,600
Administrative Expenses	140,300	115,500
Interest Expense	25,000	20,000
Income Taxes Expense	14,000	35,000
Total Operating Expenses	$309,400	$275,100
Net Income	$ 36,900	$ 71,300

Kelso Corporation
Comparative Balance Sheets
December 31, 19x2 and 19x1

	19x2	19x1
Assets		
Cash	$ 31,100	$ 27,200
Accounts Receivable (net)	72,500	42,700
Inventory	122,600	107,800
Property, Plant, and Equipment (net)	577,700	507,500
Total Assets	$803,900	$685,200
Liabilities and Stockholders' Equity		
Accounts Payable	$104,700	$ 72,300
Notes Payable	50,000	50,000
Bonds Payable	200,000	110,000
Common Stock—$10 par value	300,000	300,000
Retained Earnings	149,200	152,900
Total Liabilities and Stockholders' Equity	$803,900	$685,200

REQUIRED

Perform the following analyses. Round all ratios and percentages to one decimal place.

1. Prepare a schedule showing the amount and percentage changes from 19x1 to 19x2 for the comparative income statements and the balance sheets.
2. Prepare common-size income statements and balance sheets for 19x1 and 19x2.
3. Comment on the results in **1** and **2** by identifying favorable and unfavorable changes in the components and composition of the statements.

15B-3.
L O 6 *Analyzing the Effects of Transactions on Ratios*

Estevez Corporation engaged in the transactions listed in the first column of the following table. Opposite each transaction is a ratio and space to mark the effect of each transaction on the ratio.

			Effect	
Transaction	Ratio	Increase	Decrease	None
a. Issued common stock for cash.	Asset turnover			
b. Declared cash dividend.	Current ratio			
c. Sold treasury stock.	Return on equity			
d. Borrowed cash by issuing note payable.	Debt to equity ratio			
e. Paid salary expense.	Inventory turnover			
f. Purchased merchandise for cash.	Current ratio			
g. Sold equipment for cash.	Receivable turnover			
h. Sold merchandise on account.	Quick ratio			
i. Paid current portion of long-term debt.	Return on assets			
j. Gave sales discount.	Profit margin			
k. Purchased marketable securities for cash.	Quick ratio			
l. Declared 5% stock dividend.	Current ratio			
m. Purchased a building.	Free cash flow			

REQUIRED

Place an X in the appropriate column to show whether the transaction increased, decreased, or had no effect on the indicated ratio.

15B-4.

L O 6 *Ratio Analysis*

Additional data for Kelso Corporation in 19x2 and 19x1 follow. These data should be used in conjunction with the data in 15B-2.

	19x2	19x1
Net Cash Flows from Operating Activities	$ 64,000	$99,000
Net Capital Expenditures	$119,000	$38,000
Dividends Paid	$ 31,400	$35,000
Number of Common Shares	30,000	30,000
Market Price per Share	$40	$60
Earnings per Share	$1.23	$2.38

Balances of selected accounts at the end of 19x0 were Accounts Receivable (net), $52,700; Inventory, $99,400; Total Assets, $647,800; and Stockholders' Equity, $376,600. All of Kelso's notes payable were current liabilities; all of the bonds payable were long-term liabilities.

REQUIRED

Perform the following analyses. Round all answers to one decimal place, and consider changes of .1 or less to be neutral. After making the calculations, indicate whether each ratio improved or deteriorated from 19x1 to 19x2 by writing F for favorable or U for unfavorable.

1. Prepare a liquidity analysis by calculating for each year the (a) current ratio, (b) quick ratio, (c) receivable turnover, (d) average days' sales uncollected, (e) inventory turnover, and (f) average days' inventory on hand.
2. Prepare a profitability analysis by calculating for each year the (a) profit margin, (b) asset turnover, (c) return on assets, and (d) return on equity.
3. Prepare a long-term solvency analysis by calculating for each year the (a) debt to equity ratio and (b) interest coverage ratio.
4. Conduct a cash flow adequacy analysis by calculating for each year the (a) cash flow yield, (b) cash flows to sales, (c) cash flows to assets, and (d) free cash flow.
5. Conduct a market strength analysis by calculating for each year the (a) price/earnings ratio and (b) dividends yield.

15B-5.

L O 6 *Comprehensive Ratio Analysis of Two Companies*

June Kim has decided to invest some of her savings in common stock. She feels that the chemical industry has good growth prospects, and she has narrowed her choice to two companies in that industry. As a final step in making the choice, she has decided to make a comprehensive ratio analysis of the two companies, Evander and Lord. Income statement and balance sheet data for the two companies follow.

	Evander	Lord
Net Sales	$18,972,400	$54,574,600
Cost of Goods Sold	11,624,400	36,744,800
Gross Margin	$ 7,348,000	$17,829,800
Operating Expenses		
Selling Expenses	$ 2,388,000	$ 3,911,400
Administrative Expenses	2,434,800	8,252,000
Interest Expense	540,000	2,720,000
Income Taxes Expense	900,000	1,200,000
Total Operating Expenses	$ 6,262,800	$16,083,400
Net Income	$ 1,085,200	$ 1,746,400
Earnings per share	$ 3.10	$ 1.75

	Evander	Lord
Assets		
Cash	$ 252,200	$ 1,028,600
Marketable Securities (at cost)	235,000	2,400,000
Accounts Receivable (net)	913,400	5,200,000
Inventories	3,760,000	9,912,000
Prepaid Expenses	145,200	313,200
Property, Plant, and Equipment (net)	10,684,400	38,712,000
Intangibles and Other Assets	434,000	1,160,000
Total Assets	$16,424,200	$58,725,800
Liabilities and Stockholders' Equity		
Accounts Payable	$ 1,034,800	$ 4,684,000
Notes Payable	2,000,000	4,000,000
Income Taxes Payable	170,400	235,800
Bonds Payable	4,000,000	30,000,000
Common Stock—$2 par value	700,000	2,000,000
Paid-in Capital in Excess of Par Value, Common	3,494,600	10,866,600
Retained Earnings	5,024,400	6,939,400
Total Liabilities and Stockholders' Equity	$16,424,200	$58,725,800

During the year, Evander paid a total of $280,000 in dividends, and its current market price per share is $40. Lord paid a total of $1,200,000 in dividends during the year, and its current market price per share is $18. Evander has net cash flows from operations of $1,543,000 and net capital expenditures of $900,000. Lord has net cash flows from operations of $1,686,000 and net capital expenditures of $3,100,000. Information pertaining to prior years is not readily available. Assume that all notes payable are current liabilities and that all bonds payable are long-term liabilities.

REQUIRED

Conduct a comprehensive ratio analysis of Evander and of Lord using the current end-of-year data. Compare the results. Round all ratios and percentages to one decimal place. This analysis should be done in the following steps:

1. Prepare an analysis of liquidity by calculating for each company the (a) current ratio, (b) quick ratio, (c) receivable turnover, (d) average days' sales uncollected, (e) inventory turnover, and (f) average days' inventory on hand.
2. Prepare an analysis of profitability by calculating for each company the (a) profit margin, (b) asset turnover, (c) return on assets, and (d) return on equity.
3. Prepare an analysis of long-term solvency by calculating for each company the (a) debt to equity ratio and (b) interest coverage ratio.
4. Prepare an analysis of cash flow adequacy by calculating for each company the (a) cash flow yield, (b) cash flows to sales, (c) cash flows to assets, and (d) free cash flow.
5. Prepare an analysis of market strength by calculating for each company the (a) price/earnings ratio and (b) dividends yield.
6. Compare the two companies by inserting the ratio calculations from **1** through **5** in a table with the following column heads: Ratio Name, Evander, Lord, and Company with More Favorable Ratio. Indicate in the right-hand column of the table which company had the more favorable ratio in each case.
7. How could the analysis be improved if from prior years information were made available?

CRITICAL THINKING AND COMMUNICATION

Conceptual Mini-Cases

CMC 15-1.
L O 2 *Standards for Financial Analysis*

Helene Curtis is a well-known, publicly owned corporation. "By almost any standard, Chicago-based Helene Curtis rates as one of America's worst-managed personal care companies. In recent years its return on equity has hovered between 10% and 13%, well below the industry average of 18% to 19%. Net profit margins of 2% to 3% are half that of competitors. . . . As a result, while leading names like Revlon and Avon are trading at three and four times book value, Curtis's trades at less than two-thirds book value."[15] Considering that many companies in other industries are happy with a return on equity of 10 percent to 13 percent, why is this analysis so critical of Curtis's performance? Assuming that Curtis could double its profit margin, what other information would be necessary to project the resulting return on stockholders' investment? Why are Revlon's and Avon's stocks trading for more than Curtis's? Be prepared to discuss your answers to these questions in class.

CMC 15-2.
L O 4 *Quality of Earnings*

On Tuesday, January 19, 1988, *International Business Machines Corp.* (IBM), the world's largest computer manufacturer, reported greatly increased earnings for the fourth quarter of 1987. Despite this reported gain in earnings, the price of IBM's stock on the New York Stock Exchange declined by $6 per share to $111.75. In sympathy with this move, most other technology stocks also declined.[16]

IBM's fourth-quarter net earnings rose from $1.39 billion, or $2.28 a share, to $2.08 billion, or $3.47 a share, an increase of 49.6 percent and 52.2 percent over the year-earlier period. Management declared that these results demonstrated the effectiveness of IBM's efforts to become more competitive, and that, despite the economic uncertainties of 1988, the company was planning for growth.

The apparent cause of the stock price decline was that the huge increase in income could be traced to nonrecurring gains. Investment analysts pointed out that IBM's high earnings stemmed primarily from factors such as a lower tax rate. Despite most analysts' expectations of a tax rate between 40 and 42 percent, IBM's rate was a low 36.4 percent, down from the previous year's 45.3 percent.

In addition, analysts were disappointed in IBM's revenue growth. Revenues within the United States were down, and much of the growth in revenues came through favorable currency translations, increases that might not be repeated. In fact, some estimates of the fourth-quarter earnings attributed $.50 per share to currency translations and another $.25 to tax-rate changes.

Other factors contributing to the rise in earnings were one-time transactions, such as the sale of Intel Corporation stock and bond redemptions, along with a corporate stock buyback program that reduced the amount of stock outstanding in the fourth quarter by 7.4 million shares.

The analysts were concerned about the quality of IBM's earnings. Identify four quality of earnings issues reported in the case and the analysts' concern about each. In percentage terms, what is the impact of the currency changes on fourth-quarter earnings? Comment on management's assessment of IBM's performance. Do you agree with management? (Optional question: What was IBM's subsequent performance through 1993?) Be prepared to discuss your answers to the questions in class.

CMC 15-3.
L O 3 *Use of Investors' Service*

Refer to Exhibit 15-2, which contains the listing of *PepsiCo, Inc.* from Moody's *Handbook of Dividend Achievers.* Write a short report that describes PepsiCo's business segments and their relative importance (In what three business segments does PepsiCo, Inc. operate and what is the relative size of each in terms of sales and operating profit? Which business segment appears to be the most profitable?), PepsiCo's

---

15. *Forbes*, November 13, 1978, p. 154.
16. "Technology Firms Post Strong Earnings But Stock Prices Decline Sharply," *Wall Street Journal*, January 21, 1988; Donald R. Seace, "Industrials Plunge 57.2 Points—Technology Stocks' Woes Cited," *Wall Street Journal*, January 21, 1988.

earnings history (What generally has been the relationship between PepsiCo's return on assets and its return on equity over the years 1986 to 1992? What does this tell you about the way the company is financed? What figures back up your conclusion?), the trend of PepsiCo's stock price and price/earnings ratio for the seven years shown, and PepsiCo's prospects, including developments that are likely to affect the future of the company.

Ethics Mini-Case

EMC 15-1.
L O 4 *Management of Earnings*

Recently, the *Wall Street Journal* reported that **H. J. Heinz Co.**, the famous maker of catsup and many other food products, earned a quarterly income of $.75 per share, including a gain on sale of assets of $.24 per share. Income from continuing operations was only $.51 per share, or 16 percent below last year's figure. The paper was critical of Heinz's use of a one-time gain to increase earnings: "In recent years, H. J. Heinz Co. has been spicing up its earnings with special items. The latest quarter is no exception." An analyst is quoted as saying that Heinz has not admitted the slump in its business but has "started including nonrecurring items in the results they were showing. That created an artificially high base of earnings that they can no longer match."[17] Do you think it is unethical for a company's management to increase earnings periodically through the use of one-time transactions, such as sales of assets, on which it has a profit? What potential long-term negative effects might this practice have for Heinz?

Decision-Making Case

DMC 15-1.
L O 4 *Effect of Alternative Accounting Methods on Executive Compensation*

At the beginning of 19x1, Victor Uribe retired as president and principal stockholder in **Uribe Corporation,** a successful producer of personal computer equipment. As an incentive to the new management, Uribe supported the board of directors' new executive compensation plan, which provides cash bonuses to key executives for years in which the company's earnings per share equal or exceed the current dividends per share of $4.00, plus a $.40 per share increase in dividends for each future year. Thus, for management to receive the bonuses, the company must earn per-share income of $4.00 the first year, $4.40 the second, $4.80 the third, and so forth. Since Uribe owns 500,000 of the one million common shares outstanding, the dividend income will provide for his retirement years. He is also protected against inflation by the regular increase in dividends. Earnings and dividends per share for the first three years of operation under the new management were as follows:

	19x3	19x2	19x1
Earnings per share	$5.00	$5.00	$5.00
Dividends per share	4.80	4.40	4.00

During this time, management earned bonuses totaling more than $2 million under the compensation plan. Uribe, who had taken no active part on the board of directors, began to worry about the unchanging level of earnings and decided to study the company's annual report more carefully. The notes to the annual report revealed the following information:

a. Management changed from the LIFO inventory method to the FIFO method in 19x1. The effect of the change was to decrease cost of goods sold by $400,000 in 19x1, $600,000 in 19x2, and $800,000 in 19x3.
b. Management changed from the double-declining-balance accelerated depreciation method to the straight-line method in 19x2. The effect of this change was to decrease depreciation by $800,000 in 19x2 and by $1,000,000 in 19x3.

---

17. "Heinz's 25% Jump in 2nd-Period Profit Masks Weakness," *Wall Street Journal*, December 8, 1993.

c. In 19x3, management increased the estimated useful life of intangible assets from five to ten years. The effect of this change was to decrease amortization expense by $200,000 in 19x3.

REQUIRED

1. Compute earnings per share for each year according to the accounting methods in use at the beginning of 19x1. (Use common shares outstanding.)
2. Have the executives earned their bonuses? What serious effect has the compensation package apparently had on the net assets of Uribe Corporation? How could Uribe have protected himself from what has happened?

Basic Research Activity

RA 15-1.
L O 3
Use of Investment Services

In your school library, find either *Moody's Investors Service, Standard & Poor's Industry Guide,* or *The Value Line Investment Survey.* Locate the reports on three corporations. You may choose the corporations at random or choose them from the same industry, if directed to do so by your instructor. (If you did a related exercise in a previous chapter, use the same three companies.) Write a summary of what you learn about each company from the reference works and be prepared to discuss your findings in class.

FINANCIAL REPORTING AND ANALYSIS

Interpretation Cases from Business

ICB 15-1.
L O 4
Quality of Earnings

The Walt Disney Company is, of course, a famous entertainment company that produces films and operates theme parks, among other things. The company is also well known as a profitable and well-managed business. On November 15, 1984, the *Wall Street Journal* ran the following article by Michael Cieply, under the title "Disney Reports Fiscal 4th-Period Loss After Taking $166 Million Write-Down."

Walt Disney Productions reported a $64 million net loss for its fiscal fourth quarter ended Sept. 30, after writing down a record $166 million in movies and other properties.

In the year-earlier quarter, Disney had net income of $24.5 million, or 70 cents a share. Fourth-quarter revenue this year rose 28% to $463.2 million from $363 million.

In the fiscal year, the entertainment company's earnings rose 5% to $97.8 million, or $2.73 a share, from $93.2 million, or $2.70 a share, a year earlier. Revenue rose 27% to $1.66 billion from $1.31 billion.

The company said it wrote down $112 million in motion picture and television properties. The write-down involves productions that already have been released as well as ones still under development, but Disney declined to identify the productions or projects involved.

"This just reflects the judgment of new management about the ultimate value of projects we had under way," said Michael Bagnall, Disney's executive vice president for finance. . . .

The company also said it charged off $40 million to reflect the "abandonment" of a number of planned projects at its various theme parks. An additional $14 million was charged off as a reserve to cover possible legal obligations resulting from the company's fight to ward off a pair of successive takeover attempts last summer, Mr. Bagnall said.

Disney said its full-year net included a $76 million gain from a change in its method of accounting for investment tax credits. The change was made retroactive to the fiscal first quarter ended Dec. 31, and will boost that quarter's reported net to $85 million, from $9 million.

Mr. Bagnall said the $76 million credit stemmed largely from construction of Disney's Epcot Center theme park in Florida. By switching to flow-through from deferral accounting, the company was able to take the entire credit immediately instead of amortizing it over 18 years, as originally planned, Mr. Bagnall said. Flow-through accounting is usual in the entertainment industry.[18]

REQUIRED

1. What two categories of issues does the user of financial statements want to consider when evaluating the quality of a company's reported earnings? Did Disney have one or both types of items in fiscal 1984?
2. Compare the fourth-period earnings or losses for 1983 and 1984 and full fiscal 1983 and 1984 earnings or losses before and after adjusting for the item or items described in **1.** Which comparisons do you believe give the best picture of Disney's performance?

ICB 15-2.

L O 6   *Analysis for Bond Ratings*

Standard & Poor's Corporation (S & P) offers a wide range of financial information services to investors. One of its services is rating the quality of the bond issues of U.S. corporations. Its top bond rating is AAA, followed by AA, A, BBB, BB, B, and so forth. The lowest rating, C, is reserved for companies that are in or near bankruptcy. *Business Week* reported on February 2, 1981, that S & P had downgraded the bond rating for **Ford Motor Co.**, a leading U.S. automobile maker, from AAA to AA. The cause of the downgrading was a deterioration in Ford's financial strength as indicated by certain ratios considered important by S & P. The ratios, S & P's guidelines, and Ford's performance are summarized in the following table.[19]

Ratio	S & P Guidelines for AAA Rating	Ford's Performance		
		1980	1979	1978
Interest Coverage	15 times	Loss	6.5 times	15.3 times
Pretax Return on Assets	15% to 20%	Loss	6.6%	13.4%
Debt to Equity	50%	63.4%	37.8%	34%
Cash Flow as a Percentage of Total Debt*	100%	91%	118.5%	152.6%
Short-Term Debt as a Percentage of Total Debt	25%	52.5%	48.3%	43.1%

*Cash flow includes net income plus noncash charges to earnings.

REQUIRED

1. Identify the objective (profitability, liquidity, long-term solvency) measured by each of the S & P ratios. Why is each ratio important to the rating of Ford's long-term bonds?
2. The *Business Week* article suggested several actions that Ford might take to regain its previous rating. Tell which of the ratios each of the following actions would improve: (a) cutting operating costs; (b) scrapping at least part of its massive spending plans over the next several years; (c) eliminating cash dividends to stockholders; and (d) selling profitable non-automobile-related operations, such as its steelmaker, aerospace company, and electronic concerns.

18. "Disney Reports Fiscal 4th-Period Loss After Taking $166 Million Write-Down," *Wall Street Journal,* November 15, 1984. Reprinted by permission of *Wall Street Journal,* © 1984 Dow Jones & Company, Inc. All Rights Reserved.
19. Ford Motor Co., *Annual Reports,* 1978, 1979, and 1980.

ICB 15-3.

L O 6   *Analysis for Bond Ratings*

Part A

By 1983, *S & P* had dropped the rating on *Ford's* bond issues to BBB. Selected data for the years ended December 31, 1982 and 1983, from Ford Motor Co.'s 1983 annual report, follow (in millions):[20]

	1983	1982
Balance Sheet Data		
Short-Term Debt	$10,315.9	$10,424.0
Long-Term Debt	2,712.9	2,353.3
Stockholders' Equity	7,545.3	6,077.5
Total Assets	23,868.9	21,961.7
Income Statement Data		
Income (Loss) Before Income Taxes	2,166.3	(407.9)
Interest Expense	567.2	745.5
Statement of Changes in Financial Position		
Funds (Cash Basis) Provided by Operations	5,001.5	2,632.0

REQUIRED

1. Compute for 1982 and 1983 the same ratios that were used by S & P in ICB 15-2.
2. If you were S & P, would you raise the rating on Ford's long-term bonds in 1984? Why or why not?

Part B

By the end of 1986, Ford's financial situation had improved enough to warrant an A rating from Standard & Poor's. Then in 1990, as discussed in the Decision Point at the beginning of this chapter, Ford's rating was lowered by Moody's, another bond rating company. Selected data for the years ended December 31, 1986 and 1989, from Ford Motor Co.'s 1986 and 1989 annual reports, follow (in millions):[21]

	1989	1986
Balance Sheet Data		
Short-Term Debt	$20,180.6	$15,625.6
Long-Term Debt	1,137.0	2,137.1
Stockholders' Equity	22,727.8	14,859.5
Total Assets	45,819.2	37,993.0
Income Statement Data		
Income Before Income Taxes	6,029.6	5,552.2
Interest Expense	321.1	482.9
Statement of Cash Flows		
Net Cash Flows from Operating Activities	5,623.6	7,624.4

Total assets were $31,603.6 million in 1985 and $43,127.7 million in 1988.

REQUIRED

1. Compute for 1986 and 1989 the same ratios that were used by Standard & Poor's in ICB 15-2.
2. Do you agree that Ford's performance had improved enough by 1986 (see Part A) to warrant an increase to an A rating?
3. Do the 1989 figures warrant a reduction in the bond rating? If not, how do you explain the downgrade described in the Decision Point at the beginning of the chapter?

20. Ford Motor Co., *Annual Report,* 1983.
21. Ford Motor Co., *Annual Reports,* 1986 and 1989.

International Company Case

ICC 15-1.
L O 6
Analyzing Non-U.S.
Financial Statements

When dealing with non-U.S. companies, the analyst is often faced with financial statements that do not follow the same format as the statements of U.S. companies. The 1990 group balance sheet shown below and the group profit and loss account (income statement) shown on page 730 for *Maxwell Communication Corporation plc,* a British publishing firm, present such a situation.

Maxwell Communication Corporation plc
Group Balance Sheet
At 31st March

	1990 £ million
Fixed Assets	
Intangible assets	2,162.7
Tangible assets	337.3
Investments in convertible loan notes	—
Partnerships and associated companies	582.5
Investments	188.1
	3,270.6
Current Assets	
Stocks	108.4
Debtors	757.6
Investments	1.3
Cash at bank and in hand	65.3
	932.6
Creditors—amounts falling due within one year	(1,024.5)
Net Current Assets/(Liabilities)	(91.9)
Total Assets Less Current Liabilities	3,178.7
Creditors—amounts falling due after more than one year	(1,679.7)
Provisions for liabilities and charges	(55.1)
Accruals and deferred income	(140.4)
	1,303.5
Capital and Reserves	
Called up ordinary share capital	161.5
Share premium account	60.3
Special reserve	566.7
Capital reserve	59.2
Revaluation reserve	2.7
Profit and loss account	155.9
	1,006.3
Minority shareholders' interests	297.2
	1,303.5

These are the financial statements for the year immediately preceding the chairman of this company's being lost at sea off the company yacht and the subsequent bankruptcy and sale of the company. In these statements, the word *group* is used in the same way that the word *consolidated* is used in U.S. financial statements. It means that the company's financial statements present the combined results of a number of subsidiary companies.[22]

Maxwell Communication Corporation plc
Group Profit and Loss Account
For the Year Ended 31st March 1990

	Year 1990 £ million
Sales	1,242.1
Operating costs	(1,006.1)
Share of profits of partnership and associated companies	25.2
Operating Profit Before Exceptional Item	261.2
Exceptional item	19.2
Total Operating Profit	280.4
Net interest and investment income	(108.1)
Profit Before Taxation	172.3
Taxation on profit on ordinary activities	(34.5)
Profit on Ordinary Activities After Taxation	137.8
Minority shareholders' interests	(11.0)
Extraordinary items less taxation	(25.7)
Profit Attributable to Shareholders	101.1
Dividends paid and proposed	(95.8)
Retained Profit for the Period	5.3
Retained Profits at Beginning of Period	173.3
Transfer of depreciation from revaluation reserve	—
Exchange translation differences	(22.7)
Retained Profits at End of Period	155.9
Earnings per Share	20.0p

Show that you can read these British financial statements by computing as many of the following ratios as you can: (a) current ratio, (b) receivable turnover, (c) inventory turnover, (d) profit margin, (e) asset turnover, (f) return on assets, (g) return on equity, and (h) debt to equity. Use year-end figures to compute ratios that normally require averages. Indicate what data are missing for any ratio you are not able to compute. What terms or accounts did you have trouble interpreting? How do you evaluate the usefulness of the formats of the British financial statements relative to those of U.S. financial statements?

Toys "R" Us Case

TC 15-1.
L O 6 *Comprehensive Ratio Analysis*

Refer to the Annual Report in the appendix on Toys "R" Us, and conduct a comprehensive ratio analysis that compares data from 1994 and 1993. If you have been computing ratios for Toys "R" Us in previous chapters, you may prepare a table that summarizes the ratios for 1994 and 1993 and show calculations only for the ratios not

22. Maxwell Communication Corporation plc, *Annual Report*, 1990.

previously calculated. If this is the first time you are doing a ratio analysis for Toys "R" Us, show all your computations. In either case, comment on Toys "R" Us's performance after each group of ratios. Round your calculations to one decimal place. Prepare and comment on the following categories of ratios:

Liquidity analysis: Current ratio, quick ratio, receivable turnover, average days' sales uncollected, inventory turnover, and average days' inventory on hand.

Profitability analysis: Profit margin, asset turnover, return on assets, and return on equity.

Long-term solvency analysis: Debt to equity and interest coverage.

Cash flow adequacy: Cash flow yield, cash flows to sales, cash flows to assets, and free cash flow.

Market strength analysis: Price/earnings ratio and dividends yield. (For market price, use the average of the fourth-quarter prices.)

International Accounting and Intercompany Investments

1. Define *exchange rate* and record transactions that are affected by changes in foreign exchange rates.
2. Describe the restatement of a foreign subsidiary's financial statements in U.S. dollars.
3. Describe progress toward international accounting standards.
4. Apply the cost adjusted to market method and the equity method to the appropriate situations in accounting for long-term investments.
5. Explain when to prepare consolidated financial statements, and describe their uses.
6. Prepare consolidated balance sheets at acquisition date for purchase at (a) book value and (b) other than book value.
7. Prepare consolidated income statements for intercompany transactions.

DECISION POINT · *Schneider S.A. and Square D Company (Part 1)*

Schneider S.A., a French company, is a $10 billion business whose sales are divided equally between electrical products and construction. On March 4, 1991, Schneider made a hostile takeover offer for Square D Company, a U.S. electrical products company. Schneider offered $78 per share, 55 percent above market price, or a total of $2 billion. Didier Pineau-Valencienne, chairman of Schneider and a tough negotiator, launched the attack after discussions of joint efforts between the two companies were unsuccessful. *Business Week* reported that "The French executive faces an equally tough rival, however, in Square D's dug-in chairman, Jerre L. Stead. Stead blames an artificially cheap dollar for the 'unfair' French raid. Schneider's boss shrugs. 'When the dollar was strong, Americans came over and bought up French paintings,' says Pineau-Valencienne, an art collector. 'Now,' he says, 'it's our turn to buy.'" What role does a "cheap dollar" play in this takeover battle?[1]

In transactions between U.S. firms or between French firms, the relative values of the currencies of the two countries do not play a part in the negotiations because both parties are dealing in the same currency. However, when companies that operate in different countries engage in transactions, the relative values of the two currencies play an important role in the negotiations. If the U.S. dollar is "cheap" relative to the French franc, French francs will "purchase" more dollars. Although the dollar purchase price of assets in the United States, such as the Square D Company, may be the same as it was before, their purchase costs Schneider less in terms of French francs. Stead considers this situation "unfair" because Schneider is taking advantage of the relatively low value of the dollar to attempt a bargain purchase in the United States. The low value of the U.S. dollar relative to other currencies has been behind many of the purchases of U.S. assets and companies by Japanese, British, German, and French companies over the past few years. :::::

1. Based on information in Stewart Toy, "Schneider: 'Dr. Attila' Has Big Plans," *Business Week*, March 18, 1991, quotation on p. 36; Charles Storch, "Square D Co. Accepts $2.2 Billion for Merger with French Firm," *Chicago Tribune*, May 13, 1991; James P. Miller, "Square D Accepts Sweetened Bid of $2.23 Billion from Schneider," *Wall Street Journal*, May 13, 1991.

OBJECTIVE

1 *Define* exchange rate *and record transactions that are affected by changes in foreign exchange rates*

As businesses grow, they naturally look for new sources of supply and new markets in other countries. Today, it is common for businesses, called multinational or transnational corporations, to operate in more than one country, and many of them operate throughout the world. Table 16-1 shows the extent of foreign business of a few multinational corporations. IBM, for example, has operations in eighty countries and receives almost two-thirds of its sales and income from outside the United States. Unilever, the giant British/Dutch company, operates around the world and receives 75 percent of its revenues from outside its home countries. Together, the economies of such industrial countries as the United States, Japan, Great Britain, Germany, and France have given rise to numerous worldwide corporations. More than five hundred companies are listed on at least one stock exchange outside their home country.

In addition, sophisticated investors no longer restrict their investment activities to domestic securities markets. Many Americans invest in foreign securities markets, and non-Americans invest heavily in the stock market in the United States. Figure 16-1 shows that from 1980 to 1991, the total value of securities traded on the world's stock markets has increased almost eightfold, while the U.S. share of the pie has declined from 55 to 40 percent.

Foreign business transactions have two major effects on accounting. First, most sales or purchases of goods and services in other countries involve different currencies. Thus, one currency needs to be translated into another, using exchange rates.[2] An exchange rate is the value of one currency in terms of another. For example, an English person purchasing goods from a U.S. company and paying in U.S. dollars must exchange British pounds for U.S. dollars before making payment. In effect, currencies are goods that can be bought and sold. Table 16-2 lists the exchange rates of several currencies in terms of dollars. It shows the exchange rate for the British pound as $1.49 per pound on a particular date. Like the price of any good or service, these prices change daily according to supply and demand for the currencies. Accounting for these price changes in recording foreign transactions and preparing financial statements for foreign subsidiaries is the subject of the next two sections.

The second major effect of international business on accounting is that financial standards differ from country to country, which hampers comparisons among companies from different countries. Some of the obstacles to achieving comparability and some of the progress in solving the problem are discussed later in this chapter.

ACCOUNTING FOR TRANSACTIONS IN FOREIGN CURRENCIES

Among the first activities of an expanding company in the international market are the buying and selling of goods and services. For example, a U.S. maker of precision tools may expand by selling its product to foreign customers. Or it might lower its product cost by buying a less expensive part from a source in another country. In previous chapters, all transactions were

---

2. At the time this chapter was written, exchange rates were fluctuating rapidly. Thus, the examples, exercises, and problems in this book use exchange rates in the general range for the countries involved.

Table 16-1. Extent of Foreign Business for Selected Companies

Company	Home Country	1989 Total Sales (Billions)	Sales Outside Home Country	Assets Outside Home Country	Shares Held Outside Home Country
Michelin	France	$ 9.4	78.0%	NA	0.0
Hoechst	Germany	27.3	77.0	NA	42.0%
Unilever	Britain/Neth.	35.3	75.0*	70.0%*	27.0
Air Liquide	France	5.0	70.0	66.0	6.0
Canon	Japan	9.4	69.0	32.0	14.0
Northern Telecom	Canada	6.1	67.1	70.5	16.0
Sony	Japan	16.3	66.0	NA	13.6
Bayer	Germany	25.8	65.4	NA	48.0
BASF	Germany	13.3	65.0	NA	NA
Gillette	U.S.	3.8	65.0	63.0	10.0*
Colgate	U.S.	5.0	64.0	47.0	10.0*
Honda	Japan	26.4	63.0	35.7	6.9
Daimler Benz	Germany	45.5	61.0	NA	25.0*
IBM	U.S.	62.7	59.0	NA	NA

Business Week estimates.

Source: "The Stateless Corporation: Forget Multinationals—Today's Giants Are Really Leaping Boundaries." Reprinted from May 14, 1990 issue of *Business Week* by special permission, copyright © 1990 by McGraw-Hill, Inc.

recorded in dollars, and it was assumed that the dollar is a uniform measure in the same way that inches and centimeters are. But in the international marketplace, a transaction may take place in Japanese yen, British pounds, or some other currency. The values of these currencies rise and fall daily in relation to the dollar.

Figure 16-1. Value of Securitites Traded on the World's Stock Markets

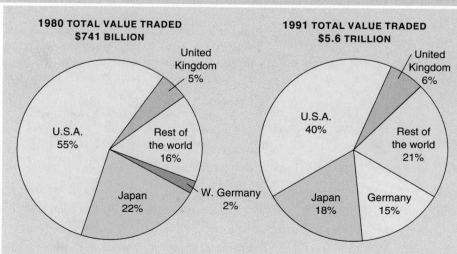

Source: From *Emerging Stock Markets Factbook* . Copyright © 1993. Used by permission of International Finance Corporation.

Table 16-2. Partial Listing of Foreign Exchange Rates

Country	Prices in $ U.S.	Country	Prices in $ U.S.
Britain (pound)	1.49	Italy (lira)	.0006
Canada (dollar)	.74	Japan (yen)	.0025
France (franc)	.17	Mexico (peso)	.31
Germany (mark)	.59	Philippines (peso)	.037
Hong Kong (dollar)	.13	Taiwan (dollar)	.037

Source: From "World Markets/Foreign Exchange," *Wall Street Journal,* February 28, 1994. Reprinted by permission of *The Wall Street Journal,* © 1994 Dow Jones & Company, Inc. All Rights Reserved Worldwide.

Foreign Sales When a domestic company sells merchandise abroad, it may bill either in its own country's currency or in the foreign currency. If the billing and the subsequent payment are both in the domestic currency, no accounting problem arises. For example, assume that the precision toolmaker sells $160,000 worth of tools to a British company and bills the British company in dollars. The entry to record the sale and payment is familiar:

Date of sale

Accounts Receivable, British company	160,000	
Sales		160,000

Date of payment

Cash	160,000	
Accounts Receivable, British company		160,000

However, if the U.S. company bills the British company in British pounds and accepts payment in pounds, the U.S. company may incur an exchange gain or loss. A gain or loss will occur if the exchange rate of dollars to pounds changes between the date of sale and the date of payment. Since gains and losses tend to offset one another, a single account is used during the year to accumulate the activity. The net exchange gain or loss is reported on the income statement. For example, assume that the sale of $160,000 above was billed as £100,000, reflecting an exchange rate of 1.60 (that is, $1.60 per pound) on the sale date. Now assume that by the date of payment, the exchange rate has fallen to 1.50. The entries to record the transactions follow:

Date of sale

Accounts Receivable, British company	160,000	
Sales		160,000
£100,000 × $1.60 = $160,000		

Date of payment

Cash	150,000	
Exchange Gain or Loss	10,000	
Accounts Receivable, British company		160,000
£100,000 × $1.50 = $150,000		

The U.S. company has incurred an exchange loss of $10,000 because it agreed to accept a fixed number of British pounds in payment, and the value of each pound dropped before the payment was made. Had the value of the pound in relation to the dollar increased, the U.S. company would have made an exchange gain.

Foreign Purchases Purchases are the opposite of sales. The same logic applies to them, except that the relationship of exchange gains and losses to changes in exchange rates is reversed. For example, assume that the maker of precision tools purchases $15,000 of a certain part from a Japanese supplier. If the purchase and subsequent payment are made in U.S. dollars, no accounting problem arises.

Date of purchase

Purchases	15,000	
Accounts Payable, Japanese company		15,000

Date of payment

Accounts Payable, Japanese company	15,000	
Cash		15,000

However, the Japanese company may bill the U.S. company in yen and be paid in yen. If so, the U.S. company will incur an exchange gain or loss if the exchange rate changes between the date of purchase and the date of payment. For example, assume that the transaction is for 2,500,000 yen and the exchange rates on the dates of purchase and payment are $.0060 and $.0055 per yen, respectively. The entries follow.

Date of purchase

Purchases	15,000	
Accounts Payable, Japanese company		15,000
¥2,500,000 × $.0060 = $15,000		

Date of payment

Accounts Payable, Japanese company	15,000	
Exchange Gain or Loss		1,250
Cash		13,750
¥2,500,000 × $.0055 = $13,750		

In this case the U.S. company received an exchange gain of $1,250 because it agreed to pay a fixed ¥2,500,000, and between the dates of purchase and payment the exchange value of the yen decreased in relation to the dollar.

Realized Versus Unrealized Exchange Gain or Loss The preceding illustration dealt with completed transactions (in the sense that payment was completed). In each case the exchange gain or loss was recognized on the date of payment. If financial statements are prepared between the sale or purchase and the subsequent receipt or payment, and exchange rates have changed, there will be unrealized gains or losses. The Financial Accounting Standards Board, in its *Statement No. 52*, requires that exchange gains and losses "shall be included in determining net income for the period in which the exchange rate changes."[3] The requirement includes interim (quarterly) statements and applies whether or not a transaction is complete.

This ruling has caused much debate. Critics charge that it gives too much weight to fleeting changes in exchange rates, causing random changes in earnings that hide long-run trends. Others believe that the use of current exchange rates to value receivables and payables as of the balance sheet date is a major step toward economic reality (current values).

3. *Statement of Financial Accounting Standards No. 52,* "Foreign Currency Translation" (Stamford, Conn.: Financial Accounting Standards Board, 1981), par. 15.

To illustrate, we will use the preceding case, in which a U.S. company buys parts from a Japanese supplier. We will assume that the transaction has not been completed by the balance sheet date, when the exchange rate is $.0051 per yen:

Date		Exchange Rate ($ per Yen)
Date of purchase	Dec. 1	.0060
Balance sheet date	Dec. 31	.0051
Date of payment	Feb. 1	.0055

The accounting effects of the unrealized gain are as follows:

	Dec. 1	Dec. 31	Feb. 1
Purchase recorded in U.S. dollars (billed as ¥2,500,000)	$15,000	$15,000	$15,000
Dollars to be paid to equal ¥2,500,000 (¥2,500,000 × exchange rate)	15,000	12,750	13,750
Unrealized gain (or loss)	—	$ 2,250	
Realized gain (or loss)			$ 1,250

Dec. 1	Purchases	15,000	
	Accounts Payable, Japanese company		15,000
Dec. 31	Accounts Payable, Japanese company	2,250	
	Exchange Gain or Loss		2,250
Feb. 1	Accounts Payable, Japanese company	12,750	
	Exchange Gain or Loss	1,000	
	Cash		13,750

In this case, the original sale was billed in yen by the Japanese company. Following the rules of *Statement No. 52*, an exchange gain of $2,250 is recorded on December 31, and an exchange loss of $1,000 is recorded on February 1. Even though these large fluctuations do not affect the net exchange gain of $1,250 for the whole transaction, the effect on each year's income statements may be important.

RESTATEMENT OF FOREIGN SUBSIDIARY FINANCIAL STATEMENTS

OBJECTIVE

2 *Describe the restatement of a foreign subsidiary's financial statements in U.S. dollars*

Growing companies often expand by setting up or buying foreign subsidiaries. If a foreign subsidiary is more than 50 percent owned and the parent company exercises control, then the foreign subsidiary should be included in the consolidated financial statements (see the discussion of parent and subsidiary companies later in this chapter). The consolidation procedure is the same as that for domestic subsidiaries, except that the statements of the foreign subsidiary must be restated in the reporting currency before consolidation takes place. The reporting currency is the currency in which the consolidated financial statements are presented. Clearly, it makes no sense to combine the assets of a Mexican subsidiary stated in pesos with the assets of the U.S. parent company stated in dollars. Most U.S. companies present their financial statements in U.S. dollars, so the following discussion assumes that the U.S. dollar is the reporting currency used.[4]

Restatement is the stating of one currency in terms of another. The method of restatement depends on the foreign subsidiary's functional currency. The functional currency is the currency of the place where the subsidiary carries on most of its business. Generally, it is the currency in which a company earns and spends its cash. The functional currency to be used depends on the kind of foreign operation in which the subsidiary takes part. There are two broad types of foreign operation. Type I includes those that are fairly self-contained and integrated within a certain country or economy. Type II includes those that are mainly a direct and integral part or extension of the parent company's operations. As a general rule, Type I subsidiaries use the currency of the country in which they are located, and Type II subsidiaries use the currency of the parent company. If the parent company is a U.S. company, the functional currency of a Type I subsidiary will be the currency of the country where the subsidiary carries on its business, and the functional currency of a Type II subsidiary will be the U.S. dollar. *Statement No. 52* makes an exception when a Type I subsidiary operates in a country where there is hyperinflation (as a rule of thumb, more than 100 percent cumulative inflation over three years), such as Brazil or Argentina. In such a case, the subsidiary is treated as a Type II subsidiary, with the functional currency being the U.S. dollar.

BUSINESS BULLETIN: ETHICS IN PRACTICE

In the United States, insider trading, or making use of insider information for personal gain, is unethical and usually illegal. The officers and employees of a public company are not allowed to buy or sell shares of stock in their own company in advance of the release of significant information; only after the information is released to the stockholders and the general public can insiders make such trades. The Securities and Exchange Commission (SEC) vigorously prosecutes any individual, whether employed by the company in question or not, who buys or sells shares of a publicly held company based on information that is not yet available to the public. This is not true in some other countries. For example, when the shares of a German retailing company, ASKO Deutsche Kauthaus A.G., dropped from $547 per share to $510 per share prior to the announcement that poor operating results would force the company to cut its dividend, it was suspected that insider trading forced the price down. But, because insider trading is not illegal in Germany, there is no agency comparable to the SEC for investigating what in the United States would constitute suspicious trading.[5]

---

4. This section is based on the requirements of *Statement of Financial Accounting Standards No. 52,* "Foreign Currency Translation" (Stamford, Conn.: Financial Accounting Standards Board, 1981).
5. Richard C. Morais, "Insider, auf Deutsch," *Forbes,* November 9, 1992.

THE SEARCH FOR COMPARABILITY OF INTERNATIONAL ACCOUNTING STANDARDS

International investors need to compare the financial position and results of operations of companies from different countries. At present, however, few standards of accounting are recognized worldwide. For example, the LIFO method of valuing inventory is the most popular in the United States, but it is not acceptable in most European countries. As another example, historical cost is strictly followed in Germany, replacement cost is used by some companies in the Netherlands, and a mixed system, allowing lower of cost or market in some cases, is used in the United States and England. Even the formats of financial statements differ from country to country. In England and France, for example, the order in which the balance sheets are presented is almost the reverse of that in the United States. In those countries, property, plant, and equipment is the first listing in the assets section.

A number of major problems stand in the way of setting international standards. One is that accountants and users of accounting information have not been able to agree on the goals of financial statements. Some other problems are differences in the way the accounting profession has developed in various countries, differences in the laws regulating companies, and differences in government and other requirements. Further difficulties are the failure to deal with differences among countries in the basic economic factors affecting financial reporting, inconsistencies in practices recommended by the accounting profession in different countries, and the influence of tax laws on financial reporting.[6] In the last area, for example, a survey for a major accounting firm found widely differing requirements. In nine countries, strict adherence to tax accounting was required. In eleven countries, adherence to tax accounting was required in some areas. In four countries (including the United States), adherence to tax practice was mostly forbidden.[7]

Some efforts have been made to achieve greater international understanding and uniformity of accounting practice. The Accountants International Study Group, formed in 1966 and consisting of the AICPA and similar bodies in Canada, England and Wales, Ireland, and Scotland, has issued reports that survey and compare accounting practices in the member countries. Probably the best hopes for finding areas of agreement among all the different countries are the International Accounting Standards Committee (IASC) and the International Federation of Accountants (IFAC). The IASC was formed in 1973 as a result of an agreement by accountancy bodies in Australia, Canada, France, Germany, Japan, Mexico, the Netherlands, the United Kingdom and Ireland, and the United States. More than one hundred professional accountancy bodies from over seventy countries now support the IASC.

The role of the IASC is to contribute to the development and adoption of accounting principles that are relevant, balanced, and comparable throughout the world by formulating and publicizing accounting standards and encouraging their observance in the presentation of financial statements.[8] The standards issued by the IASC are generally followed by large multinational

---

6. *Accounting Standards for Business Enterprises Throughout the World* (Chicago: Arthur Andersen, 1974), pp. 2–3.
7. *Accounting Principles and Reporting Practices: A Survey in 38 Countries* (New York: Price Waterhouse International, 1973), sec. 233.
8. "International Accounting Standards Committee Objectives and Procedures," *Professional Standards* (New York: American Institute of Certified Public Accountants, 1988), Volume B, Section 9000, par. 24–27.

companies that are clients of international accounting firms. The IASC has been especially helpful to companies in developing economies that do not have the financial history or resources to develop accounting standards. The IASC is currently engaged in a major project to enhance the comparability of financial statements worldwide by reducing the number of acceptable accounting methods in twelve areas, including inventory and depreciation accounting and accounting for investments and business combinations.

The IFAC, which was formed in 1977 and also consists of most of the world's accountancy organizations, fully supports the work of the IASC and recognizes the IASC as the sole body having responsibility and authority to issue pronouncements on international accounting standards. The IFAC's objective is to develop international guidelines for auditing, ethics, education, and management accounting. Every five years an International Congress is held to judge the progress toward achieving these objectives. In Europe, attempts are also being made to harmonize accounting standards. The European Community has issued a directive (4th) requiring certain minimum and uniform reporting and disclosure standards for financial statements. Other directives deal with uniform rules for preparing consolidated financial statements (7th) and qualifications of auditors (8th). In recent years, the European Community has paid considerable attention to the comparability of financial reporting as the organization moves toward the goal of a single European market.[9]

The road to international harmony is a difficult one. However, there is reason for optimism because an increasing number of countries are recognizing the appropriateness of international accounting standards in international trade and commerce.

DECISION POINT

Schneider S.A. and Square D Company (Part 2)

Corporations often find it desirable to invest in the securities of other corporations with the intent of holding them for an indefinite period. There are many reasons for making such long-term investments. One reason, of course, is simple: the prospect of earning a return on the investment. Another might be to establish a more formal business relationship with a company with which the acquiring company has ties. As noted in the first Decision Point in this chapter, on March 4, 1991, Schneider, a French electrical and construction company, made a hostile takeover offer for Square D Company, a U.S. electrical products company, after negotiations for a friendly arrangement broke down. What reasons may Schneider's chairman, Didier Pineau-Valencienne, have had for persisting in this takeover attempt when the chief executive of Square D Company, Jerre L. Stead, clearly did not want to cooperate?

Takeovers are often attempted when one company wants another company's assets or other advantages, such as established customers, markets,

9. "Comparability of Financial Statements," *Exposure Draft No. 32* (New York: International Accounting Standards Committee, 1989).

products, expertise, or operations. According to *Business Week*, Pineau-Valencienne "covets the U.S. company for two reasons: to broaden the payoff from Schneider's $400 million research budget and to sell each other's products in the other's home market. Pineau-Valencienne assails Square D's business strategy as far too inward-looking. 'Their idea is small is beautiful,' says he, noting that only 10.4% of Square D's sales are in Europe."[10] Schneider finds it easier and less expensive to buy Square D, even when Square D does not want to be taken over, than to start a whole operation independently. Furthermore, legally and for tax purposes, it is easier to buy or invest in a company than to start a new business.[11] There are significant accounting implications of takeovers like this and of other long-term investments of one corporation in another. The following sections explore these implications. ⦂ ⦂ ⦂ ⦂ ⦂

LONG-TERM INTERCOMPANY INVESTMENTS

OBJECTIVE

4 *Apply the cost adjusted to market method and the equity method to the appropriate situations in accounting for long-term investments*

One corporation may invest in another corporation by purchasing bonds or stocks. These investments may be either short term or long term. In this section, we are concerned with long-term investments in stocks. Long-term investments in bonds are covered in an appendix.

All long-term investments in stocks are recorded at cost, in accordance with generally accepted accounting principles. The treatment of the investment in the accounting records after the initial purchase depends on the extent to which the investing company can exercise significant influence or control over the operating and financial policies of the other company.

The Accounting Principles Board defined the important terms *significant influence* and *control* in its *Opinion No. 18*. Significant influence is the ability to affect the operating and financial policies of the company whose shares are owned, even though the investor holds less than 50 percent of the voting stock. Ability to influence a company may be shown by representation on the board of directors, participation in policy making, material transactions between the companies, exchange of managerial personnel, and technological dependency. For the sake of uniformity, the APB decided that unless there is proof to the contrary, an investment of 20 percent or more of the voting stock should be presumed to confer significant influence. An investment of less than 20 percent of the voting stock would not confer significant influence.[12]

---

10. Stewart Toy, "Schneider: 'Dr. Attila' Has Big Plans," *Business Week,* March 18, 1991, p. 36.
11. Schneider was successful in its attempt to take over Square D Company. Square D's board accepted an offer of $88 per share, or a total of $2.23 billion, on May 12, 1991. (*Wall Street Journal,* May 13, 1991.)
12. The Financial Accounting Standards Board points out in its *Interpretation No. 35* (May 1981) that though the presumption of significant influence applies when 20 percent or more of the voting stock is held, the rule is not a rigid one. All relevant facts and circumstances should be examined in each case to find out whether or not significant influence exists. For example, the FASB notes five circumstances that may remove the element of significant influence: (1) The company files a lawsuit against the investor or complains to a government agency; (2) the investor tries and fails to become a director; (3) the investor agrees not to increase its holdings; (4) the company is operated by a small group that ignores the investor's wishes; (5) the investor tries and fails to obtain additional information from the company that is not available to other stockholders.

Control is defined as the ability of the investing company to decide the operating and financial policies of the other company. Control is said to exist when the investing company owns more than 50 percent of the voting stock of the company in which it has invested.

Thus, in the absence of information to the contrary, a noninfluential and noncontrolling investment would be less than 20 percent ownership. An influential but noncontrolling investment would be 20 to 50 percent ownership. And a controlling investment would be more than 50 percent ownership. The accounting treatment differs for each kind of investment.

BUSINESS BULLETIN: TECHNOLOGY IN PRACTICE

The global transmission of financial and other information is a rapidly growing business. Global revenues from network services, which include data network management and data interchanges among suppliers and banks, were approximately $4.6 billion in 1992 and are growing at about 15 percent per year. Because of the substantial investments needed to tap this market, large companies are forming alliances by making long-term investments in other companies. For example, Ameritech Corporation, a Chicago-based telephone company, is investing $472 million for a 30 percent share in General Electric Information Services Company, a company that creates and markets data-transmission products and services to businesses. In this way, Ameritech is able to get a toehold in the market without having to develop it from scratch.[13]

NONINFLUENTIAL AND NONCONTROLLING INVESTMENT

As defined in the chapter on short-term liquid assets, available-for-sale securities are debt or equity securities that are not classified as trading or held-to-maturity securities. When equity securities are involved, the further criterion is that they be noninfluential and noncontrolling investments of less than 20 percent of the voting stock. The Financial Accounting Standards Board requires a cost adjusted to market method for accounting for available-for-sale securities. Under this method, available-for-sale securities must be recorded initially at cost and thereafter adjusted periodically through the use of an allowance account to reflect changes in the market value of the securities.[14] They are classified as long term if management intends to hold them for more than one year. The only difference between accounting for long-term available-for-sale securities and accounting for trading securities is that the unrealized gain or loss resulting from the adjustment is not reported on the income statement, but is reported as a special item in the stockholders' equity section of the balance sheet.

---

13. John J. Keller, "Ameritech, GE Plan $472 Million Data Venture," *Wall Street Journal*, December 21, 1993.
14. *Statement of Financial Accounting Standards No. 115*, "Accounting for Certain Investments in Debt and Equity Securities" (Stamford, Conn.: Financial Accounting Standards Board, 1993).

At the end of each accounting period, the total cost and the total market value of these long-term stock investments must be determined. If the total market value is less than the total cost, the difference must be credited to a contra-asset account called Allowance to Adjust Long-Term Investments to Market. Because of the long-term nature of the investment, the debit part of the entry, which represents a decrease in value below cost, is treated as a temporary decrease and does not appear as a loss on the income statement. It is shown in a contra-stockholders' equity account called Unrealized Loss on Long-Term Investments. Thus, both of these accounts are balance sheet accounts. If the market value exceeds the cost, the allowance account is added to Long-Term Investments and the unrealized gain appears as an addition to stockholders' equity.[15]

When long-term investments in stock are sold, the difference between the sale price and what the stock cost is recorded and reported as a realized gain or loss on the income statement. Dividend income from such investments is recorded by a debit to Cash and a credit to Dividend Income.

For example, assume the following facts about the long-term stock investments of Coleman Corporation:

June 1, 19x0	Paid cash for the following long-term investments: 10,000 shares of Durbin Corporation common stock (representing 2 percent of outstanding stock) at $25 per share; 5,000 shares of Kotes Corporation common stock (representing 3 percent of outstanding stock) at $15 per share.
Dec. 31, 19x0	Quoted market prices at year end: Durbin common stock, $21; Kotes common stock, $17.
Apr. 1, 19x1	Change in policy required sale of 2,000 shares of Durbin Corporation common stock at $23.
July 1, 19x1	Received cash dividend from Kotes Corporation equal to $.20 per share.
Dec. 31, 19x1	Quoted market prices at year end: Durbin common stock, $24; Kotes common stock, $13.

Entries to record these transactions follow:

Investment

19x0				
June	1	Long-Term Investments	325,000	
		Cash		325,000
		Investments in Durbin common stock (10,000 shares × $25 = $250,000) and Kotes common stock (5,000 shares × $15 = $75,000)		

Year-End Adjustment

19x0			
Dec. 31	Unrealized Loss on Long-Term Investments	30,000	
	Allowance to Adjust Long-Term Investments to Market		30,000
	To record reduction of long-term investment to market		

---

15. If the decrease in value is deemed permanent, a different procedure is followed to record the decline in market value of the long-term investment. A loss account that appears on the income statement is debited instead of the Unrealized Loss account.

Company	Shares	Market Price	Total Market	Total Cost
Durbin	10,000	$21	$210,000	$250,000
Kotes	5,000	17	85,000	75,000
			$295,000	$325,000

Cost − market value = $325,000 − $295,000 = $30,000

Sale

19x1
Apr. 1 Cash 46,000
   Loss on Sale of Investment 4,000
    Long-Term Investments 50,000
     Sale of 2,000 shares of Durbin
     common stock
     2,000 × $23 = $46,000
     2,000 × $25 = 50,000

     Loss $ 4,000

Dividend Received

19x1
July 1 Cash 1,000
   Dividend Income 1,000
    Receipt of cash dividends from
    Kotes stock
    5,000 × $.20 = $1,000*

Year-End Adjustment

19x1
Dec. 31 Allowance to Adjust Long-Term
    Investments to Market 12,000
     Unrealized Loss on Long-Term
     Investments 12,000
      To record the adjustment in long-
      term investment so it is reported
      at market

The adjustment equals the previous balance ($30,000 from the December 31, 19x0 entry) minus the new balance ($18,000), or $12,000. The new balance of $18,000 is the difference at the present time between the total market value and the total cost of all investments. It is figured as follows:

Company	Shares	Market Price	Total Market	Total Cost
Durbin	8,000	$24	$192,000	$200,000
Kotes	5,000	13	65,000	75,000
			$257,000	$275,000

Cost − market value = $275,000 − $257,000 = $18,000

The Allowance to Adjust Long-Term Investments to Market and the Unrealized Loss on Long-Term Investments are reciprocal contra accounts, each with the same dollar balance, as can be shown by the effects of these transactions on the T accounts:

Contra-Asset Account				**Contra-Stockholders' Equity Account**			
Allowance to Adjust				**Unrealized Loss on**			
Long-Term Investments to Market				**Long-Term Investments**			
19x1	12,000	19x0	30,000	19x0	30,000	19x1	12,000
		Bal. 19x1	18,000	Bal. 19x1	18,000		

The Allowance account reduces long-term investments by the amount by which cost exceeds market of the investments; the Unrealized Loss account reduces stockholders' equity by a similar amount. The opposite effects will exist if market value exceeds cost, resulting in an unrealized gain.

INFLUENTIAL BUT NONCONTROLLING INVESTMENT

As we have seen, ownership of 20 percent or more of a company's voting stock is considered sufficient to influence the operations of another corporation. When this is the case, the investment in the stock of the influenced company should be accounted for using the equity method. The equity method presumes that an investment of 20 percent or more is more than a passive investment, and that therefore the investing company should share proportionately in the success or failure of the investee company. The three main features of this method are as follows:

1. The investor records the original purchase of the stock at cost.
2. The investor records its share of the investee's periodic net income as an increase in the Investment account, with a corresponding credit to an income account. In like manner, the investor records its share of the investee's periodic loss as a decrease in the Investment account, with a corresponding debit to a loss account.
3. When the investor receives a cash dividend, the asset account Cash is increased and the Investment account decreased.

To illustrate the equity method of accounting, we will assume the following facts about an investment by the Vassor Corporation. On January 1 of the current year, Vassor Corporation acquired 40 percent of the voting common stock of the Block Corporation for $180,000. With this share of ownership, the Vassor Corporation can exert significant influence over the operations of the Block Corporation. During the year, the Block Corporation reported net income of $80,000 and paid cash dividends of $20,000. The entries to record these transactions by the Vassor Corporation are

Investment

Investment in Block Corporation	180,000	
Cash		180,000
Investment in Block Corporation common stock		

Recognition of Income

Investment in Block Corporation	32,000	
Income, Block Corporation Investment		32,000
Recognition of 40% of income reported by Block Corporation		
40% × $80,000 = $32,000		

Receipt of Cash Dividend

Cash	8,000	
Investment in Block Corporation		8,000
Cash dividend from Block Corporation		
40% × $20,000 = $8,000		

The balance of the Investment in Block Corporation account after these transactions is $204,000, as shown here:

Investment in Block Corporation

Investment	180,000	Dividends received	8,000
Share of income	32,000		
Balance	204,000		

CONTROLLING INVESTMENT

In some cases, an investor who owns less than 50 percent of the voting stock of a company may exercise such powerful influence that for all practical purposes the investor controls the policies of the other company. Nevertheless, ownership of more than 50 percent of the voting stock is required for accounting recognition of control. When a controlling interest is owned, a parent-subsidiary relationship is said to exist. The investing company is known as the parent company, the other company as the subsidiary. Because both corporations are separate legal entities, each prepares separate financial statements. However, owing to their special relationship, they are viewed for public financial reporting purposes as a single economic entity. For this reason, they must combine their financial statements into a single set of statements called consolidated financial statements.

Accounting for consolidated financial statements is very complex. It is usually the subject of an advanced accounting course. However, most large public corporations have subsidiaries and must prepare consolidated financial statements. It is therefore important to have some understanding of accounting for consolidations.

The proper accounting treatments for long-term investments in stock are summarized in Table 16-3.

BUSINESS BULLETIN: BUSINESS PRACTICE

Companies sometimes engage in bidding wars in attempts to take over and consolidate with other companies. A well-publicized confrontation recently occurred between QVC Network, Inc., the owner of Home Shopping Network, and Viacom, Inc., the owner of the MTV channel. They sought to take over Paramount Communications, Inc., a major publisher and entertainment (movies and television) company. The action started when Paramount announced a friendly takeover by Viacom at a total price of about $8 billion. QVC Network immediately made a higher counter-offer. To bring more money to the table, Viacom merged with Blockbuster Entertainment Company, owner of Blockbuster Video, and upped its bid. The

Table 16-3. Accounting Treatments of Long-Term Investments in Stock

Level of Ownership	Percentage of Ownership	Accounting Treatment
Noninfluential and noncontrolling	Less than 20%	Cost initially; investment adjusted subsequent to purchase for changes in market value.
Influential but noncontrolling	Between 20% and 50%	Equity method; investment valued subsequently at cost plus investor's share of income (or minus investor's share of loss) minus dividends received.
Controlling	More than 50%	Financial statements consolidated.

fierce back-and-forth bidding over a five-month period in late 1993 and early 1994 finally pushed the price past $10 billion as Viacom made the winning bid with a complex combination of cash and exchanges of stocks. The values of the bids were especially difficult to determine because they depended on the market prices of the respective stocks, which fluctuated daily. Accounting for this complex transaction, which created one of the largest entertainment and communications companies in the world, will be a vast challenge.[16] ═══

CONSOLIDATED FINANCIAL STATEMENTS

OBJECTIVE

5 *Explain when to prepare consolidated financial statements, and describe their uses*

Most major corporations find it convenient for economic, legal, tax, or other reasons to operate in parent-subsidiary relationships. When we speak of a large company such as Ford, IBM, or Texas Instruments, we generally think of the parent company, not of its many subsidiaries. When considering investment in one of these firms, however, the investor wants a clear financial picture of the total economic entity. The main purpose of consolidated financial statements is to give such a view of the parent and subsidiary firms by treating them as if they were one company. On a consolidated balance sheet, the Inventory account includes the inventory held by the parent and all its subsidiaries. Similarly, on the consolidated income statement, the Sales account is the total revenue from sales by the parent and all its subsidiaries. This overview helps management and stockholders of the parent company judge the company's progress in meeting its goals. Long-term creditors of the par-

16. Laura Landro and Johnnie L. Roberts, "Viacom Is Set to Grow Into Media Colossus—or Burdened Giant," *Wall Street Journal*, February 16, 1994.

ent also find consolidated statements useful because of their interest in the long-range financial health of the company.

In the past, it was acceptable not to consolidate the statements of certain subsidiaries, even though the parent owned a controlling interest, when the business of the subsidiary was not homogeneous with that of the parent. For instance, a retail company or an automobile manufacturer might have had a wholly-owned finance subsidiary that was not consolidated. However, such practices were criticized because they tended to remove certain assets (accounts and notes receivable) and certain liabilities (borrowing by the finance subsidiary) from the consolidated financial statements. For example, in 1986, General Motors's financing subsidiary, GMAC, with assets of $90 billion and liabilities of $84 billion, was carried as a long-term investment of $6 billion on GM's balance sheet. It was also argued by those who favored consolidation that financing arrangements such as these are an integral part of the overall business. The Financial Accounting Standards Board ruled, effective in 1988, that all subsidiaries in which the parent owns a controlling interest (more than 50 percent) must be consolidated with the parent for financial reporting purposes.[17] As a result, with few exceptions, the financial statements of all majority-owned subsidiaries must now be consolidated with the parent company's financial statements for external reporting purposes.

METHODS OF ACCOUNTING FOR BUSINESS COMBINATIONS

Interests in subsidiary companies may be acquired by paying cash; issuing long-term bonds, other debt, or common or preferred stock; or working out some combination of these forms of payment, such as exchanging shares of the parent's own unissued capital stock for the outstanding shares of the subsidiary's capital stock. For parent-subsidiary relationships that arise when cash is paid or debt or preferred stock is issued, it is mandatory to use the purchase method, which is explained below. For simplicity, our illustrations assume payment in cash. In the special case of establishing a parent-subsidiary relationship through an exchange of common stock, the pooling of interests method may be appropriate. This latter method is the subject of more advanced courses.

CONSOLIDATED BALANCE SHEET

In preparing consolidated financial statements under the purchase method, similar accounts from the separate statements of the parent and the subsidiaries are combined. Some accounts result from transactions between the parent and the subsidiary. Examples are debt owed by one of the entities to the other and sales and purchases between the two entities. When considering the group of companies as a single business, it is not appropriate to include these accounts in the group financial statements; the purchases and sales are only transfers between different parts of the business, and the payables and receivables do not represent amounts due to or receivable from outside parties. For this reason, it is important that certain eliminations be made. These eliminations avoid the duplication of accounts and reflect the financial position and operations from the standpoint of a single entity.

17. *Statement of Financial Accounting Standards No. 94*, "Consolidation of All Majority-Owned Subsidiaries" (Stamford, Conn.: Financial Accounting Standards Board, 1987).

Eliminations appear only on the work sheets used in preparing consolidated financial statements. They are never shown in the accounting records of either the parent or the subsidiary. There are no consolidated journals or ledgers.

Another good example of accounts that result from transactions between the two entities is the Investment in Subsidiary account in the parent's balance sheet and the stockholders' equity section of the subsidiary. When the balance sheets of the two companies are combined, these accounts must be eliminated to avoid duplicating these items in the consolidated financial statements.

To illustrate the preparation of a consolidated balance sheet under the purchase method, we will use the following balance sheets for Parent and Subsidiary companies:

Accounts	Parent Company	Subsidiary Company
Cash	$100,000	$25,000
Other Assets	760,000	60,000
Total Assets	$860,000	$85,000
Liabilities	$ 60,000	$10,000
Common Stock—$10 par value	600,000	55,000
Retained Earnings	200,000	20,000
Total Liabilities and Stockholders' Equity	$860,000	$85,000

OBJECTIVE

6a *Prepare consolidated balance sheets at acquisition date for purchase at book value*

100 Percent Purchase at Book Value   Suppose that Parent Company purchases 100 percent of the stock of Subsidiary Company for an amount exactly equal to Subsidiary's book value. The book value of Subsidiary Company is $75,000 ($85,000 − $10,000). Parent Company would record the purchase as shown below:

Investment in Subsidiary Company	75,000	
Cash		75,000
Purchase of 100 percent of Subsidiary		
Company at book value		

It is helpful to use a work sheet like the one shown in Exhibit 16-1 in preparing consolidated financial statements. Note that the balance of Parent Company's Cash account is now $25,000 and that Investment in Subsidiary Company is shown as an asset in Parent Company's balance sheet, reflecting the purchase of the subsidiary. To prepare a consolidated balance sheet, it is necessary to eliminate the investment in the subsidiary. This procedure is shown by elimination entry **1** in Exhibit 16-1. This elimination entry does two things. First, it eliminates the double counting that would take place when the net assets of the two companies are combined. Second, it eliminates the stockholders' equity section of Subsidiary Company.

The theory underlying consolidated financial statements is that parent and subsidiary are a single entity. The stockholders' equity section of the consolidated balance sheet is the same as that of Parent Company. So after eliminating the Investment in Subsidiary Company and the stockholders' equity of

Exhibit 16-1. Work Sheet for Preparation of Consolidated Balance Sheet

Parent and Subsidiary Companies
Work Sheet for Consolidated Balance Sheet
As of Acquisition Date

Accounts	Balance Sheet Parent Company	Balance Sheet Subsidiary Company	Eliminations		Consolidated Balance Sheet
			Debit	Credit	
Cash	25,000	25,000			50,000
Investment in Subsidiary Company	75,000			(1) 75,000	
Other Assets	760,000	60,000			820,000
Total Assets	860,000	85,000			870,000
Liabilities	60,000	10,000			70,000
Common Stock— $10 par value	600,000	55,000	(1) 55,000		600,000
Retained Earnings	200,000	20,000	(1) 20,000		200,000
Total Liabilities and Stockholders' Equity	860,000	85,000	75,000	75,000	870,000

(1) Elimination of intercompany investment.

the subsidiary, we can take the information from the right-hand column in Exhibit 16-1 and present it in the following form:

Parent and Subsidiary Companies
Consolidated Balance Sheet
As of Acquisition Date

Cash	$ 50,000	Liabilities	$ 70,000
Other Assets	820,000	Common Stock	600,000
		Retained Earnings	200,000
		Total Liabilities and	
Total Assets	$870,000	Stockholders' Equity	$870,000

Less than 100 Percent Purchase at Book Value   A parent company does not have to purchase 100 percent of a subsidiary to control it. If it purchases more than 50 percent of the voting stock of the subsidiary company, it will have legal control. In the consolidated financial statements, therefore, the total assets and liabilities of the subsidiary are combined with the assets and liabilities of the parent. However, it is still necessary to account for the interests of those stockholders of the subsidiary company who own less than 50 percent of the voting stock. These are the minority stockholders, and their minority interest must appear on the consolidated balance sheet as an amount equal to their percentage of ownership times the net assets of the subsidiary.

Suppose that the same Parent Company buys, for $67,500, only 90 percent of Subsidiary Company's voting stock. In this case, the portion of the company purchased has a book value of $67,500 (90% × $75,000). The work sheet used for preparing the consolidated balance sheet appears in Exhibit 16-2. The elimination is made in the same way as in the case above, except that the minority interest must be accounted for. All of the Investment in Subsidiary Company ($67,500) is eliminated against all of Subsidiary Company's stockholders' equity ($75,000). The difference ($7,500, or 10% × $75,000) is set as minority interest.

There are two ways to classify minority interest on the consolidated balance sheet. One is to place it between long-term liabilities and stockholders' equity. The other is to consider the stockholders' equity section as consisting of (1) minority interest and (2) Parent Company's stockholders' equity, as shown here:

Minority Interest	$ 7,500
Common Stock	600,000
Retained Earnings	200,000
Total Stockholders' Equity	$807,500

OBJECTIVE

6b *Prepare consolidated balance sheets at acquisition date for purchase at other than book value*

Purchase at More or Less than Book Value

The purchase price of a business depends on many factors, such as the current market price, the relative strength of the buyer's and seller's bargaining positions, and the prospects for future earnings. Thus, it is only by chance that the purchase price of a subsidiary will equal the book value of the subsidiary's equity. Usually, it will not. For example, a parent company may pay more than the book value of a subsidiary to purchase a controlling interest if the assets of the subsidiary are understated. In that case, the recorded historical cost less depreciation of the subsidiary's assets may not reflect current market values. The parent may also pay more than book value if the subsidiary has something that the parent wants, such as an important technical process, a new and different product, or a new market. On the other hand, the parent may pay less than book value for its share of the subsidiary's stock if the subsidiary's assets are not worth their depreciated cost. Or the subsidiary may have suffered heavy losses, causing its stock to sell at rather low prices.

The Accounting Principles Board has provided the following guidelines for consolidating a purchased subsidiary and its parent:

> First, all identifiable assets acquired . . . and liabilities assumed in a business combination . . . should be assigned a portion of the cost of the acquired company, normally equal to their fair values at date of acquisition.
>
> Second, the excess of the cost of the acquired company over the sum of the amounts assigned to identifiable assets acquired less liabilities assumed should be recorded as goodwill.[18]

To illustrate the application of these principles, we will assume that Parent Company purchases 100 percent of Subsidiary Company's voting stock for $92,500, or $17,500 more than book value. Parent Company considers $10,000 of the $17,500 to be due to the increased value of Subsidiary's other assets and $7,500 of the $17,500 to be due to the overall strength that Subsidiary Company would add to Parent Company's organization. The work

---

18. Accounting Principles Board, *Opinion No. 16*, "Business Combinations" (New York: Accounting Principles Board, 1970), par. 87.

Exhibit 16-2. Work Sheet Showing Elimination of Less than 100 Percent Ownership

Parent and Subsidiary Companies
Work Sheet for Consolidated Balance Sheet
As of Acquisition Date

Accounts	Balance Sheet Parent Company	Balance Sheet Subsidiary Company	Eliminations		Consolidated Balance Sheet
			Debit	Credit	
Cash	32,500	25,000			57,500
Investment in Subsidiary Company	67,500			(1) 67,500	—
Other Assets	760,000	60,000			820,000
Total Assets	860,000	85,000			877,500
Liabilities	60,000	10,000			70,000
Common Stock— $10 par value	600,000	55,000	(1) 55,000		600,000
Retained Earnings	200,000	20,000	(1) 20,000		200,000
Minority Interest				(1) 7,500	7,500
Total Liabilities and Stockholders' Equity	860,000	85,000	75,000	75,000	877,500

(1) Elimination of intercompany investment. Minority interest equals 10 percent of subsidiary's stockholders' equity.

sheet used for preparing the consolidated balance sheet appears in Exhibit 16-3. All of the Investment in Subsidiary Company ($92,500) has been eliminated against all of the Subsidiary Company's stockholders' equity ($75,000). The excess of cost over book value ($17,500) has been debited in the amounts of $10,000 to Other Long-Term Assets and $7,500 to a new account called Goodwill, or Goodwill from Consolidation.

The amount of goodwill is determined as follows:

Cost of investment in subsidiary	$92,500
Book value of subsidiary	75,000
Excess of cost over book value	$17,500
Portion of excess attributable to undervalued long-term assets of subsidiary	10,000
Portion of excess attributable to goodwill	$ 7,500

Goodwill appears as an asset on the consolidated balance sheet representing the excess of the cost of the investment over book value that cannot be allocated to any specific asset. Other Assets appears on the consolidated balance sheet at the combined total of $830,000 ($760,000 + $60,000 + $10,000).

When the parent pays less than book value for its investment in the subsidiary, Accounting Principles Board *Opinion No. 16,* paragraph 87, requires that the excess of book value over cost of the investment be used to lower the carrying value of the subsidiary's long-term assets. The reasoning behind this

Exhibit 16-3. Work Sheet Showing Elimination When Purchase Cost IS Greater than Book Value

Parent and Subsidiary Companies
Work Sheet for Consolidated Balance Sheet
As of Acquisition Date

Accounts	Balance Sheet Parent Company	Balance Sheet Subsidiary Company	Eliminations		Consolidated Balance Sheet
			Debit	Credit	
Cash	7,500	25,000			32,500
Investment in Subsidiary Company	92,500			(1) 92,500	
Other Assets	760,000	60,000	(1) 10,000		830,000
Goodwill			(1) 7,500		7,500
Total Assets	860,000	85,000			870,000
Liabilities	60,000	10,000			70,000
Common Stock— $10 par value	600,000	55,000	(1) 55,000		600,000
Retained Earnings	200,000	20,000	(1) 20,000		200,000
Total Liabilities and Stockholders' Equity	860,000	85,000	92,500	92,500	870,000

(1) Elimination of intercompany investment. Excess of cost over book value ($92,500 − $75,000 = $17,500) allocated $10,000 to Other Assets and $7,500 to Goodwill.

is that market values of long-lived assets (other than marketable securities) are among the least reliable of estimates, since a ready market does not usually exist for such assets. In other words, the APB advises against using negative goodwill, except in very special cases.

Intercompany Receivables and Payables   If either the parent or the subsidiary company owes money to the other, there will be a receivable on the creditor company's individual balance sheet and a payable on the debtor company's individual balance sheet. When a consolidated balance sheet is prepared, both the receivable and the payable should be eliminated because, from the viewpoint of the consolidated entity, neither the asset nor the liability exists. In other words, it does not make sense for a company to owe money to itself. The eliminating entry would be made on the work sheet by debiting the payable and crediting the receivable for the amount of the intercompany loan.

CONSOLIDATED INCOME STATEMENT

OBJECTIVE

7 *Prepare consolidated income statements for intercompany transactions*

The consolidated income statement for a consolidated entity is prepared by combining the revenues and expenses of the parent and subsidiary companies. The procedure is the same as that for preparing a consolidated balance sheet. That is, intercompany transactions are eliminated to prevent double counting of revenues and expenses. Several intercompany transactions affect the consolidated income statement. They are: (1) sales and purchases of goods and services between parent and subsidiary (purchases for the buying company and sales for the selling company); (2) income and expenses on loans, receivables, or bond indebtedness between parent and subsidiary; and (3) other income and expenses from intercompany transactions.

To illustrate the eliminating entries, we will assume the following transactions between a parent and its wholly-owned subsidiary. Parent Company made sales of $120,000 in goods to Subsidiary Company, which in turn sold all the goods to others. Subsidiary Company paid Parent Company $2,000 interest on a loan from the parent.

The work sheet in Exhibit 16-4 shows how to prepare a consolidated income statement. The purpose of the eliminating entries is to treat the two companies as a single entity. Thus, it is important to include in Sales only those sales made to outsiders and to include in Cost of Goods Sold only those purchases made from outsiders. This goal is met with the first eliminating entry, which eliminates the $120,000 of intercompany sales and purchases by a debit of that amount to Sales and a credit of that amount to Cost of Goods Sold. As a result, only sales to outsiders ($510,000) and purchases from outsiders ($240,000) are included in the Consolidated Income Statement column. The intercompany interest income and expense are eliminated by a debit to Other Revenues and a credit to Other Expenses.

OTHER CONSOLIDATED FINANCIAL STATEMENTS

Public corporations also prepare consolidated statements of retained earnings and consolidated statements of cash flows. For examples of these statements, see the appendix containing the financial statements of Toys "R" Us, Inc.

Exhibit 16-4. Work Sheet Showing Eliminations for Preparing a Consolidated Income Statement

Parent and Subsidiary Companies
Work Sheet for Consolidated Income Statement
For the Year Ended December 31, 19xx

Accounts	Income Statement Parent Company	Income Statement Subsidiary Company	Eliminations Debit	Eliminations Credit	Consolidated Income Statement
Sales	430,000	200,000	(1) 120,000		510,000
Other Revenues	60,000	10,000	(2) 2,000		68,000
Total Revenues	490,000	210,000			578,000
Cost of Goods Sold	210,000	150,000		(1) 120,000	240,000
Other Expenses	140,000	50,000		(2) 2,000	188,000
Total Cost and Expenses	350,000	200,000			428,000
Net Income	140,000	10,000	122,000	122,000	150,000

(1) Elimination of intercompany sales and purchases.
(2) Elimination of intercompany interest income and interest expense.

CHAPTER REVIEW

REVIEW OF LEARNING OBJECTIVES

1. **Define** *exchange rate* **and record transactions that are affected by changes in foreign exchange rates.** An *exchange rate* is the value of one currency stated in terms of another. A domestic company may make sales or purchases abroad in either its own country's currency or the foreign currency. If a transaction (sale or purchase) and its resolution (receipt or payment) are made in the domestic currency, no accounting problem arises. However, if the transaction and its resolution are made in a foreign currency and the exchange rate changes between the time of the transaction and its resolution, an exchange gain or loss will occur and should be recorded.

2. **Describe the restatement of a foreign subsidiary's financial statements in U.S. dollars.** Foreign financial statements are converted to U.S. dollars by multiplying the appropriate exchange rates by the amounts in the foreign financial statements. In general, the rates that apply depend on whether the subsidiary is separate and self-contained (Type I) or an integral part of the parent company (Type II).

3. **Describe progress toward international accounting standards.** There has been some progress toward establishing international accounting standards, especially through the efforts of the International Accounting Standards Committee and the International Federation of Accountants. However, there still are serious inconsistencies in financial reporting among countries. These inconsistencies make the comparison of financial statements from different countries difficult.

4. **Apply the cost adjusted to market method and the equity method to the appropriate situations in accounting for long-term investments.** Long-term stock investments fall into three categories. First are noninfluential and noncontrolling investments, representing less than 20 percent ownership. To account for these investments, use the cost adjusted to market method, adjusting the investment to market for financial statement purposes. Second are influential but noncontrolling investments, representing 20 percent to 50 percent ownership. Use the equity method to account for these investments. Third are controlling interest investments, representing more than 50 percent ownership. Account for them using consolidated financial statements.

5. **Explain when to prepare consolidated financial statements, and describe their uses.** The FASB requires that consolidated financial statements be prepared when an investing company has legal and effective control over another company. Control exists when the parent company owns more than 50 percent of the voting stock of the subsidiary company. Consolidated financial statements are useful to investors and others because they treat the parent company and its subsidiaries realistically, as an integrated economic unit.

6. **Prepare consolidated balance sheets at acquisition date for purchase at (a) book value and (b) other than book value.** At the date of acquisition, a work sheet entry is made to eliminate the investment from the parent company's financial statements and the stockholders' equity section of the subsidiary's financial statements. The assets and liabilities of the two companies are combined. If the parent owns less than 100 percent of the subsidiary, minority interest will appear on the consolidated balance sheet equal to the percentage of the subsidiary owned by minority stockholders multiplied by the stockholders' equity in the subsidiary. If the cost of the parent's investment in the subsidiary is greater than the subsidiary's book value, an amount equal to the excess of cost over book value will be allocated on the consolidated balance sheet to undervalued subsidiary assets and to goodwill. If the cost of the parent's investment in the subsidiary is less than book value, the excess of book value over cost should be used to reduce the book value of the long-term assets (other than long-term marketable securities) of the subsidiary.

7. **Prepare consolidated income statements for intercompany transactions.** When consolidated income statements are prepared, intercompany sales, purchases, interest income, interest expense, and other income and expenses from intercompany transactions must be eliminated to avoid double counting of these items.

REVIEW OF CONCEPTS AND TERMINOLOGY

The following concepts and terms were introduced in this chapter:

L O 4 **Consolidated financial statements:** Financial statements that reflect the combined operations of parent company and subsidiaries.

L O 4 **Control:** The ability of the investing company to decide the operating and financial policies of another company through ownership of more than 50 percent of its voting stock.

L O 4 **Cost adjusted to market method:** A method of accounting for available-for-sale securities at cost adjusted for changes in market value of the securities.

L O 5 **Eliminations:** Entries made on consolidated work sheets to eliminate transactions between parent and subsidiary companies.

L O 4 **Equity method:** The method of accounting for long-term investments in which the investor records its share of the investee's periodic net income or loss as an increase or decrease in the Investment account. Used when the investing company exercises significant influence over the other company.

L O 1 **Exchange gains or losses:** Changes due to exchange rate fluctuations that are reported on the income statement.

L O 1 **Exchange rate:** The value of one currency in terms of another.

L O 2 **Functional currency:** The currency of the place where a subsidiary carries on most of its business.

L O 6 **Goodwill (Goodwill from Consolidation):** The amount paid for a subsidiary that exceeds the fair value of the subsidiary's assets less its liabilities.

L O 3 **Insider trading:** The practice of buying or selling shares of a publicly held company based on information that has not yet been made available to the public.

L O 6 **Minority interest:** The amount recorded on a consolidated balance sheet that represents the holdings of stockholders who own less than 50 percent of the voting stock of a subsidiary.

L O 1 **Multinational (transnational) corporation:** A company that operates in more than one country.

L O 4 **Parent company:** An investing company that owns a controlling interest in another company.

L O 5 **Purchase method:** A method of accounting for parent/subsidiary relationships in which similar accounts from separate statements are combined. Used when the investing company owns more than 50 percent of a subsidiary.

L O 2 **Reporting currency:** The currency in which consolidated financial statements are presented.

L O 2 **Restatement:** The stating of one currency in terms of another.

L O 4 **Significant influence:** The ability of an investing company to affect the operating and financial policies of another company, even though the investor holds 50 percent or less of the voting stock.

L O 4 **Subsidiary:** An investee company in which a controlling interest is owned by another company.

REVIEW PROBLEM
CONSOLIDATED BALANCE SHEET: LESS THAN 100 PERCENT OWNERSHIP

L O 6 In a cash transaction, Taylor Company purchased 90 percent of the outstanding stock of Schumacher Company for $763,200 on June 30, 19xx. Directly after the acquisition, separate balance sheets of the companies appeared as follows:

	Taylor Company	Schumacher Company
Assets		
Cash	$ 400,000	$ 48,000
Accounts Receivable	650,000	240,000
Inventory	1,000,000	520,000
Investment in Schumacher Company	763,200	—
Plant and Equipment (net)	1,500,000	880,000
Other Assets	50,000	160,000
Total Assets	$4,363,200	$1,848,000
Liabilities and Stockholders' Equity		
Accounts Payable	$ 800,000	$ 400,000
Long-Term Debt	1,000,000	600,000
Common Stock—$5 par value	2,000,000	800,000
Retained Earnings	563,200	48,000
Total Liabilities and Stockholders' Equity	$4,363,200	$1,848,000

Additional information: (a) Schumacher Company's other assets represent a long-term investment in Taylor Company's long-term debt. The debt was purchased for an amount equal to Taylor's carrying value of the debt. (b) Taylor Company owes Schumacher Company $100,000 for services rendered.

REQUIRED Prepare a work sheet as of the acquisition date for preparing a consolidated balance sheet.

ANSWER TO REVIEW PROBLEM

Taylor and Schumacher Companies
Work Sheet for Consolidated Balance Sheet
June 30, 19xx

Accounts	Balance Sheet Taylor Company	Balance Sheet Schumacher Company	Eliminations		Consolidated Balance Sheet
			Debit	Credit	
Cash	400,000	48,000			448,000
Accounts Receivable	650,000	240,000		(3) 100,000	790,000
Inventory	1,000,000	520,000			1,520,000
Investment in					
Schumacher Company	763,200	—		(1) 763,200	—
Plant and Equipment (net)	1,500,000	880,000			2,380,000
Other Assets	50,000	160,000		(2) 160,000	50,000
Total Assets	4,363,200	1,848,000			5,188,000
Accounts Payable	800,000	400,000	(3) 100,000		1,100,000
Long-Term Debt	1,000,000	600,000	(2) 160,000		1,440,000
Common Stock—					
$5 par value	2,000,000	800,000	(1) 800,000		2,000,000
Retained Earnings	563,200	48,000	(1) 48,000		563,200
Minority Interest				(1) 84,800	84,800
Total Liabilities and					
Stockholders' Equity	4,363,200	1,848,000	1,108,000	1,108,000	5,188,000

(1) Elimination of intercompany investment. Minority interest equals 10 percent of Schumacher Company stockholders' equity
   (10% × [$800,000 + $48,000] = $84,800).
(2) Elimination of intercompany long-term debt.
(3) Elimination of intercompany receivables and payables.

CHAPTER ASSIGNMENTS

KNOWLEDGE AND UNDERSTANDING

Questions

1. What does it mean to say that the exchange rate for a French franc in terms of the U.S. dollar is .15? If a bottle of French perfume costs 200 francs, how much will it cost in dollars?

2. If an American firm does business with a German firm and all their transactions take place in German marks, which firm may incur exchange gains or losses, and why?

3. What is the difference between a reporting currency and a functional currency?

4. If you as an investor were trying to evaluate the relative performance of General Motors, Volkswagen, and Toyota Motors from their published financial statements, what problems might you encounter (other than a language problem)?

5. What are some of the obstacles to uniform international accounting standards, and what efforts are being made to overcome them?

6. Why are the concepts of significant influence and control important in accounting for long-term investments?

7. For each of the following categories of long-term investments, briefly describe the applicable percentage of ownership and accounting treatment: (a) noninfluential and noncontrolling investment, (b) influential but noncontrolling investment, and (c) controlling investment.

8. What is meant by a parent-subsidiary relationship?

9. Would the stockholders of American Home Products Corporation be more interested in the consolidated financial statements of the overall company than in the statements of its many subsidiaries? Explain.

10. The 1987 annual report for Merchant Corporation included the following statement in its Summary of Principal Accounting Policies: "*Principles applied in consolidation.*—Majority-owned subsidiaries are consolidated, except for leasing and finance companies and those subsidiaries not considered to be material." How did this practice change in 1988, and why?

11. Also in Merchant's annual report, in the Summary of Principal Accounting Policies, was the following statement: "*Investments.*—Investments in companies, in which Merchant has significant influence in management and control, are on the equity basis." What is the equity basis of accounting for investments, and why did Merchant use it in this case?

12. Why should intercompany receivables, payables, sales, and purchases be eliminated in the preparation of consolidated financial statements?

13. The following item appears on Merchant's consolidated balance sheet: "Minority Interest—$50,000." Explain how this item arose and where you would expect to find it on the consolidated balance sheet.

14. Why may the price paid to acquire a controlling interest in a subsidiary company exceed the subsidiary's book value?

15. The following item also appears on Merchant's consolidated balance sheet: "Goodwill from Consolidation—$70,000." Explain how this item arose and where you would expect to find it on the consolidated balance sheet.

16. Subsidiary Corporation has a book value of $100,000, of which Parent Corporation purchases 100 percent for $115,000. None of the excess of cost over book value is attributed to tangible assets. What is the amount of goodwill from consolidation?

17. Subsidiary Corporation, a wholly-owned subsidiary, has total sales of $500,000, $100,000 of which were made to Parent Corporation. Parent Corporation has total sales of $1,000,000, including sales of all items purchased from Subsidiary Corporation. What is the amount of sales on the consolidated income statement?

Short Exercises

SE 16-1.
L O 1
Recording Sales: Fluctuating Exchange Rate

Prepare an entry to record a sale by a U.S. company on account on September 12 in the amount of DM420,000 to a German company and its subsequent collection in full in marks on October 12. On September 12, the exchange rate was $.70 per mark, and on October 12 it was $.60 per mark.

SE 16-2.
L O 1
Recording Purchases: Fluctuating Exchange Rate

Prepare an entry to record a purchase by a U.S. company on account on September 12 in the amount of DM420,000 from a German company and its subsequent payment in full in marks on October 12. On September 12, the exchange rate was $.70 per mark, and on October 12 it was $.60 per mark.

SE 16-3.
L O 4
Cost Adjusted to Market Method

At December 31, 19x1 the market value of Terrace Company's portfolio of long-term available-for-sale securities was $320,000. The cost of these securities was $285,000. Prepare the entry to adjust the portfolio to market at year end, assuming that the company did not have any long-term investments prior to 19x1.

SE 16-4.

L O 4 *Cost Adjusted to Market Method*

Refer to your answer to SE 16-3 and assume that at December 31, 19x2 the cost of Terrace Company's portfolio of long-term available-for-sale securities was $640,000 and its market value was $600,000. Prepare the entry to record the 19x2 year-end adjustment.

SE 16-5.

L O 4 *Equity Method*

Matson Company owns 30 percent of Zorex Company. In 19x1, Zorex Company earned $120,000 and paid $80,000 in dividends. Prepare journal entries for Matson Company's records on December 31 to reflect this information. Assume that the dividends are received on December 31.

SE 16-6.

L O 4, 5 *Methods of Accounting for Long-Term Investments*

For each of the investments listed below, tell which of the following methods should be used for external financial reporting: (a) cost adjusted to market method, (b) equity method, (c) consolidation of parent and subsidiary financial statements.

1. 49 percent investment in Motir Corporation.
2. 51 percent investment in Saris Corporation.
3. 5 percent investment in Ransor Corporation.

SE 16-7.

L O 6 *Purchase of 100 Percent at Book Value*

Sugar Corporation buys 100 percent ownership of Spice Corporation for $50,000. At the time of the purchase, Spice's stockholders' equity consists of $10,000 in common stock and $40,000 in retained earnings, and Sugar's stockholders' equity consists of $100,000 in common stock and $200,000 in retained earnings. After the purchase, what would be the amount, if any, of the following accounts on the consolidated balance sheet: Goodwill, Minority Interest, Common Stock, and Retained Earnings?

SE 16-8.

L O 6 *Purchase of Less than 100 Percent at Book Value*

Assume the same facts as in SE 16-7 except that the purchase was 80 percent of Spice Corporation for $40,000. After the purchase, what would be the amount, if any, of the following accounts on the consolidated balance sheet: Goodwill, Minority Interest, Common Stock, and Retained Earnings?

SE 16-9.

L O 6 *Purchase of 100 Percent at More than Book Value*

Assume the same facts as in SE 16-7 except that the purchase of 100 percent of Spice Corporation was for $60,000. After the purchase, what would be the amount, if any, of the following accounts on the consolidated balance sheet: Goodwill, Minority Interest, Common Stock, and Retained Earnings?

SE 16-10.

L O 6, 7 *Intercompany Transactions*

P Company owns 100 percent of S Company. Some of the separate accounts from the balance sheets and income statements for P Company and S Company appear below:

	P Company	**S Company**
Accounts Receivable	$230,000	$150,000
Accounts Payable	180,000	90,000
Sales	1,200,000	890,000
Cost of Goods Sold	710,000	540,000

What would be the combined amount of each of the above accounts on the consolidated financial statements assuming the following additional information: (a) S Company sold to P Company merchandise at cost in the amount of $270,000; (b) all of the merchandise sold by S Company to P Company had been resold by P Company to customers, but it still owes S Company $60,000 for the merchandise.

APPLICATION

Exercises

E 16-1.

L O 1 *Recording International Transactions: Fluctuating Exchange Rate*

States Corporation purchased a special-purpose machine from Hamburg Corporation on credit for DM 50,000. At the date of purchase, the exchange rate was $.55 per mark. On the date of the payment, which was made in marks, the value of the mark had increased to $.60.

Prepare journal entries to record the purchase and payment in States Corporation's accounting records.

E 16-2.
L O 1 *Recording International Transactions*

U.S. Corporation made a sale on account to U.K. Company on November 15 in the amount of £300,000. Payment was to be made in British pounds on February 15. U.S. Corporation's fiscal year is the same as the calendar year. The British pound was worth $1.70 on November 15, $1.58 on December 31, and $1.78 on February 15.

Prepare journal entries to record the sale, year-end adjustment, and collection on U.S. Corporation's books.

E 16-3.
L O 4 *Long-Term Investments*

Heard Corporation has the following portfolio of long-term available-for-sale securities at year end:

Company	Percentage of Voting Stock Held	Cost	Year-End Market Value
N Corporation	4	$160,000	$190,000
O Corporation	12	750,000	550,000
P Corporation	5	60,000	110,000
Total		$970,000	$850,000

The Unrealized Loss on Long-Term Investments account and the Allowance to Adjust Long-Term Investments to Market account both currently have a balance of $80,000 from the last accounting period. Prepare the year-end adjustment to reflect the above information.

E 16-4.
L O 4 *Long-Term Investments: Cost Adjusted to Market and Equity Methods*

On January 1, Mueller Corporation purchased, as long-term investments, 8 percent of the voting stock of Schott Corporation for $500,000 and 45 percent of the voting stock of Choy Corporation for $2 million. During the year, Schott Corporation had earnings of $200,000 and paid dividends of $80,000. Choy Corporation had earnings of $600,000 and paid dividends of $400,000. The market value of neither investment declined during the year. Which of these investments should be accounted for using the cost adjusted to market method? Which with the equity method? At what amount should each investment be carried on the balance sheet at year end? Give a reason for each choice.

E 16-5.
L O 4 *Long-Term Investments: Equity Method*

On January 1, 19xx, Romano Corporation acquired 40 percent of the voting stock of Burke Corporation for $2,400,000 in cash, an amount sufficient to exercise significant influence over Burke Corporation's activities. On December 31, Romano determined that Burke paid dividends of $400,000 but incurred a net loss of $200,000 for 19xx. Prepare journal entries in Romano Corporation's records to reflect this information.

E 16-6.
L O 4, 5 *Methods of Accounting for Long-Term Investments*

Diversified Corporation has the following long-term investments:

1. 60 percent of the common stock of Calcor Corporation
2. 13 percent of the common stock of Virginia, Inc.
3. 50 percent of the nonvoting preferred stock of Camrad Corporation
4. 100 percent of the common stock of its financing subsidiary, DCF, Inc.
5. 35 percent of the common stock of the French company Maison de Boutaine
6. 70 percent of the common stock of the Canadian company Alberta Mining Company

For each of these investments, tell which of the following methods should be used for external financial reporting.

a. Cost adjusted to market method
b. Equity method
c. Consolidation of parent and subsidiary financial statements

E 16-7.
L O 6 *Elimination Entry for a Purchase at Book Value*

The Lardner Manufacturing Company purchased 100 percent of the common stock of the Gwynn Manufacturing Company for $300,000. Gwynn's stockholders' equity included common stock of $200,000 and retained earnings of $100,000. Prepare the eliminating entry in general journal form that would appear on the work sheet for consolidating the balance sheets of these two entities as of the acquisition date.

E 16-8.
L O 6 *Elimination Entry and Minority Interest*

The stockholders' equity section of the Brandt Corporation's balance sheet appeared as follows on December 31:

Common Stock—$10 par value, 40,000 shares authorized and issued	$400,000
Retained Earnings	48,000
Total Stockholders' Equity	$448,000

Assume that Wegner Manufacturing Company owns 80 percent of the voting stock of Brandt Corporation and paid $11.20 for each share. In general journal form, prepare the entry (including minority interest) to eliminate Wegner's investment and Brandt's stockholders' equity that would appear on the work sheet used in preparing the consolidated balance sheet for the two firms.

E 16-9.
L O 6 *Consolidated Balance Sheet with Goodwill*

On September 1, Y Company purchased 100 percent of the voting stock of Z Company for $960,000 in cash. The separate condensed balance sheets immediately after the purchase follow:

	Y Company	Z Company
Other Assets	$2,206,000	$1,089,000
Investment in Z Company	960,000	—
	$3,166,000	$1,089,000
Liabilities	$ 871,000	$ 189,000
Common Stock—$1 par value	1,000,000	300,000
Retained Earnings	1,295,000	600,000
	$3,166,000	$1,089,000

Prepare a work sheet for preparing the consolidated balance sheet immediately after Y Company acquired control of Z Company. Assume that any excess cost of the investment in the subsidiary over book value is attributable to goodwill from consolidation.

E 16-10.
L O 6 *Analyzing the Effects of Elimination Entries*

Some of the separate accounts from the balance sheets for A Company and B Company, just after A Company purchased 85 percent of B Company's voting stock for $1,530,000 in cash, follow:

	A Company	B Company
Accounts Receivable	$2,600,000	$ 800,000
Interest Receivable, Bonds of B Company	14,400	—
Investment in B Company	1,530,000	—
Investment in B Company Bonds	360,000	—
Accounts Payable	1,060,000	380,000
Interest Payable, Bonds	64,000	40,000
Bonds Payable	1,600,000	1,000,000
Common Stock	2,000,000	1,200,000
Retained Earnings	1,120,000	600,000

Accounts Receivable and Accounts Payable included the following: B Company owed A Company $100,000 for services rendered, and A Company owed B Company $132,000 for purchases of merchandise. A bought B Company's bonds for an amount equal to B's carrying value of the bonds. Determine the amount, including minority interest, that would appear on the consolidated balance sheet for each of the accounts listed.

E 16-11.
L O 7 *Preparation of Consolidated Income Statement*

Polonia Company has owned 100 percent of Cardwell Company since 19x0. The income statements of these two companies for the year ended December 31, 19x1 appear on page 764. Also assume the following information: (a) Cardwell Company purchased $560,000 of inventory from Polonia Company, which had been sold to Cardwell Company customers by the end of the year. (b) Cardwell Company leased its building from Polonia Company for $120,000 per year. Prepare a consolidated income statement work sheet for the two companies for the year ended December 31, 19x1. Ignore income taxes.

	Polonia Company	Cardwell Company
Net Sales	$3,000,000	$1,200,000
Cost of Goods Sold	1,500,000	800,000
Gross Margin	$1,500,000	$ 400,000
Less: Selling Expenses	$ 500,000	$ 100,000
General and Administrative Expenses	600,000	200,000
Total Operating Expenses	$1,100,000	$ 300,000
Income from Operations	$ 400,000	$ 100,000
Other Income	120,000	—
Net Income	$ 520,000	$ 100,000

Problem Set A

Since foreign exchange rates can fluctuate widely, a variety of rates have been used in Problem Sets A and B.

16A-1.

L O 1 *International Transactions*

Mountain States Company, whose year end is June 30, engaged in the following international transactions (exchange rates in parentheses):

May 15 Purchased goods from a Japanese firm for $110,000; terms n/10 in U.S. dollars (yen = $.0080).

17 Sold goods to a German company for $165,000; terms n/30 in marks (mark = $.55).

21 Purchased goods from a Mexican company for $120,000; terms n/30 in pesos (peso = $.30).

25 Paid for the goods purchased on May 15 (yen = $.0085).

31 Sold goods to an Italian firm for $200,000; terms n/60 in lire (lira = $.0005).

June 5 Sold goods to a British firm for $56,000; terms n/10 in U.S. dollars (pound = $1.30).

7 Purchased goods from a Japanese firm for $221,000; terms n/30 in yen (yen = $.0085).

15 Received payment for the sale made on June 5 (pound = $1.80).

16 Received payment for the sale made on May 17 (mark = $.60).

17 Purchased goods from a French firm for $66,000; terms n/30 in U.S. dollars (franc = $.16).

20 Paid for the goods purchased on May 21 (peso = $.25).

22 Sold goods to a British firm for $108,000; terms n/30 in pounds (pound = $1.80).

30 Made year-end adjusting entries for incomplete foreign exchange transactions (franc = $.17; peso = $.30; mark = $.60; lira = $.0003; pound = $1.70; yen = $.0090).

July 7 Paid for the goods purchased on June 7 (yen = $.0085).

17 Paid for the goods purchased on June 17 (franc = $.15).

22 Received payment for the goods sold on June 22 (pound = $1.60).

30 Received payment for the goods sold on May 31 (lira = $.0004).

REQUIRED Prepare general journal entries for these transactions.

16A-2.

L O 4 *Long-Term Investments*

Mazurek Corporation made the following transactions in its Long-Term Investments account over a two-year period:

19x0

Apr. 1 Purchased with cash 20,000 shares of Cheevers Company stock for $152 per share.

June 1 Purchased with cash 15,000 shares of Abbado Corporation stock for $72 per share.

Sept. 1 Received a $1 per share dividend from Cheevers Company.

Nov. 1 Purchased with cash 25,000 shares of Frankel Corporation stock for $110 per share.

Dec. 31 Market values per share of shares held in the Long-Term Investments account were as follows: Cheevers Company, $140; Abbado Corporation, $32; and Frankel Corporation, $122.

19x1

Feb. 1 Because of unfavorable prospects for Abbado Corporation, sold Abbado stock for cash at $40 per share.

May 1 Purchased with cash 10,000 shares of Schulian Corporation for $224 per share.

Sept. 1 Received $2 per share dividend from Cheevers Company.

Dec. 31 At year end, market values per share of shares held in the Long-Term Investments account were as follows: Cheevers Company, $160; Frankel Corporation, $140; and Schulian Corporation, $200.

REQUIRED

Prepare entries to record these transactions in the Mazurek Corporation records. Assume that all investments represent less than 20 percent of the voting stock of the company whose stock was acquired.

16A-3.

L O 4 *Long-Term Investments: Equity Method*

The Samir Company owns 40 percent of the voting stock of the Gorman Company. The Investment account for this company on the Samir Company's balance sheet had a balance of $600,000 on January 1, 19xx. During 19xx, the Gorman Company reported the following quarterly earnings and dividends paid:

Quarter	Earnings	Dividends Paid
1	$ 80,000	$ 40,000
2	60,000	40,000
3	160,000	40,000
4	(40,000)	40,000
	$260,000	$160,000

The Samir Company exercises a significant influence over the operations of the Gorman Company and therefore uses the equity method to account for its investment.

REQUIRED

1. Prepare the journal entries that the Samir Company must make each quarter in accounting for its investment in the Gorman Company.
2. Prepare a ledger account for the investment in common stock of the Gorman Company. Enter the beginning balance and post relevant portions of the entries made in **1.**

16A-4.

L O 6 *Consolidated Balance Sheet: Less than 100 Percent Ownership*

In a cash transaction, Kamper Company purchased 70 percent of the outstanding stock of Woolf Company for $593,600 cash on June 30, 19xx. Immediately after the acquisition, the separate balance sheets of the companies appeared as shown on the next page. Also assume the following additional information: (a) Woolf Company's other assets represent a long-term investment in Kamper Company's long-term debt. The debt was purchased for an amount equal to Kamper's carrying value of the debt. (b) Kamper Company owes Woolf Company $80,000 for services rendered.

REQUIRED

Prepare a work sheet for preparing a consolidated balance sheet as of the acquisition date.

	Kamper Company	Woolf Company
Assets		
Cash	$ 320,000	$ 48,000
Accounts Receivable	520,000	240,000
Inventory	800,000	520,000
Investment in Woolf Company	593,600	—
Plant and Equipment (net)	1,200,000	880,000
Other Assets	40,000	160,000
Total Assets	$3,473,600	$1,848,000
Liabilities and Stockholders' Equity		
Accounts Payable	$ 640,000	$ 400,000
Long-Term Debt	800,000	600,000
Common Stock—$10 par value	1,600,000	800,000
Retained Earnings	433,600	48,000
Total Liabilities and Stockholders' Equity	$3,473,600	$1,848,000

16A-5.

L O 6 *Consolidated Balance Sheet: Cost Exceeding Book Value*

The balance sheets of Magreb and Nicario Companies as of December 31, 19xx are shown below.

	Magreb Company	Nicario Company
Assets		
Cash	$ 120,000	$ 80,000
Accounts Receivable	200,000	60,000
Investment in Nicario Company	700,000	—
Other Assets	200,000	360,000
Total Assets	$1,220,000	$500,000
Liabilities and Stockholders' Equity		
Liabilities	$ 220,000	$ 60,000
Common Stock—$20 par value	800,000	400,000
Retained Earnings	200,000	40,000
Total Liabilities and Stockholders' Equity	$1,220,000	$500,000

REQUIRED

Prepare a consolidated balance sheet work sheet for the Magreb and Nicario Companies. Assume that the Magreb Company purchased 100 percent of Nicario's common stock for $700,000 immediately before the balance sheet date. Also assume that $160,000 of the excess of cost over book value is attributable to the increased value of Nicario Company's other assets. The rest of the excess is considered by the Magreb Company to be goodwill.

Problem Set B

16B-1.

L O 1 *International Transactions*

Tsin Import/Export Company, whose year end is December 31, engaged in the following transactions (exchange rates in parentheses):

Oct. 14 Sold goods to a Mexican firm for $20,000; terms n/30 in U.S. dollars (peso = $.31).

26 Purchased goods from a Japanese firm for $40,000; terms n/20 in yen (yen = $.0040).

Nov. 4 Sold goods to a British firm for $39,000; terms n/30 in pounds (pound = $1.30).

13 Received payment in full for October 14 sale (peso = $.28).

15 Paid for the goods purchased on October 26 (yen = $.0044).

23 Purchased goods from an Italian firm for $28,000; terms n/10 in U.S. dollars (lira = $.0008).

30 Purchased goods from a Japanese firm for $35,200; terms n/60 in yen (yen = $.0044).

Dec. 2 Paid for the goods purchased on November 23 (lira = $.0007).

3 Received payment in full for the goods sold on November 4 (pound = $1.20).

8 Sold goods to a French firm for $66,000; terms n/30 in francs (franc = $.11).

17 Purchased goods from a Mexican firm for $37,000; terms n/30 in U.S. dollars (peso = $.35).

18 Sold goods to a German firm for $90,000; terms n/30 in marks (mark = $.30).

31 Made year-end adjusting entries for incomplete foreign exchange transactions (franc = $.09; peso = $.30; pound = $1.10; mark = $.35; lira = $.0008; yen = $.0050).

Jan. 7 Received payment for the goods sold on December 8 (franc = $.10).

16 Paid for the goods purchased on December 17 (peso = $.32).

17 Received payment for the goods sold on December 18 (mark = $.40).

28 Paid for the goods purchased on November 30 (yen = $.0045).

REQUIRED

Prepare general journal entries for these transactions.

16B-2.

L O 4 *Long-Term Investments*

On January 2, 19x0, the Healey Company made several long-term investments in the voting stock of various companies. It purchased 10,000 shares of Zweig at $4.00 a share, 15,000 shares of Kamb at $6.00 a share, and 6,000 shares of Rodriguez at $9.00 a share. Each investment represents less than 20 percent of the voting stock of the company. The remaining transactions of Healey in securities during 19x0 were as follows:

May 15 Purchased with cash 6,000 shares of Drennan stock for $6.00 per share. This investment comprises less than 20 percent of the Drennan voting stock.

July 16 Sold the 10,000 shares of Zweig stock for $3.60 per share.

Sept. 30 Purchased with cash 5,000 additional shares of Kamb for $6.40 per share.

Dec. 31 The market values per share of the stock in the Long-Term Investments account at year end were as follows: Kamb, $6.50; Rodriguez, $8.00; and Drennan, $4.00.

Healey's transactions in securities during 19x1 were as follows:

Feb. 1 Received a cash dividend from Kamb of $.20 per share.

July 15 Sold the 6,000 Rodriguez shares for $8.00 per share.

Aug. 1 Received a cash dividend from Kamb of $.20 per share.

Sept. 10 Purchased 3,000 shares of Parmet for $14.00 per share.

Dec. 31 The market values per share of the stock in the Long-Term Investments account were as follows: Kamb, $7.50; Drennan, $5.00; and Parmet, $13.00.

REQUIRED

Prepare the journal entries to record all of Healey Company's transactions in long-term investments during 19x0 and 19x1.

16B-3.

L O 4 *Long-Term Investments: Equity Method*

Keith Corporation owns 35 percent of the voting stock of Kang Corporation. Keith Corporation's Investment account as of January 1, 19xx was $720,000. During 19xx, Kang Corporation reported the following quarterly earnings and dividends:

Quarter	Earnings	Dividends Paid
1	$160,000	$100,000
2	240,000	100,000
3	120,000	100,000
4	(80,000)	100,000
	$440,000	$400,000

Because of the percentage of voting shares Keith owns, it can exercise significant influence over the operations of Kang Corporation. Under these conditions, Keith Corporation must account for the investment using the equity method.

REQUIRED

1. Prepare the journal entries that Keith Corporation must make each quarter to record its share of earnings and dividends.
2. Prepare a ledger account for Keith Corporation's investment in Kang, enter the beginning balance, and post the relevant entries from **1**.

16B-4.

L O 6 *Consolidated Balance Sheet: Less than 100 Percent Ownership*

The Lobos Corporation purchased 80 percent of the outstanding voting stock of the Yost Corporation for $820,800 in cash. The balance sheets of the two companies immediately after acquisition were as shown below.

	Lobos Corporation	Yost Corporation
Assets		
Cash	$ 150,000	$ 60,000
Accounts Receivable	360,000	200,000
Inventory	1,600,000	700,000
Investment in Yost	820,800	—
Property, Plant, and Equipment (net)	2,500,000	1,000,000
Other Assets	100,000	40,000
Total Assets	$5,530,800	$2,000,000
Liabilities and Stockholders' Equity		
Accounts Payable	$ 400,000	$ 150,000
Salaries Payable	50,000	20,000
Taxes Payable	20,000	4,000
Bonds Payable	1,300,000	800,000
Common Stock	2,500,000	900,000
Retained Earnings	1,260,800	126,000
Total Liabilities and Stockholders' Equity	$5,530,800	$2,000,000

Additional information: (a) The Other Assets account on the Yost balance sheet represents an investment in Lobos's Bonds Payable. The investment in Lobos was made at an amount equal to Lobos's carrying value of the bonds. (b) $50,000 of the Accounts Receivable of Lobos Corporation represents receivables due from Yost.

REQUIRED

Prepare a work sheet as of the acquisition date for the preparation of a consolidated balance sheet.

16B-5.

L O 6 *Consolidated Balance Sheet: Cost Exceeding Book Value*

The balance sheets of Cheever and Ham Corporations as of December 31, 19xx are shown as follows.

	Cheever Corporation	Ham Corporation
Assets		
Cash	$ 600,000	$ 120,000
Accounts Receivable	700,000	600,000
Inventory	250,000	600,000
Investment in Ham Corporation	800,000	—
Property, Plant, and Equipment (net)	1,350,000	850,000
Other Assets	20,000	50,000
Total Assets	$3,720,000	$2,220,000
Liabilities and Stockholders' Equity		
Accounts Payable	$ 750,000	$ 500,000
Salaries Payable	300,000	270,000
Bonds Payable	350,000	800,000
Common Stock	1,500,000	500,000
Retained Earnings	820,000	150,000
Total Liabilities and Stockholders' Equity	$3,720,000	$2,220,000

REQUIRED

Prepare a consolidated balance sheet work sheet for the two companies, assuming that Cheever purchased 100 percent of the common stock of Ham for $800,000 immediately prior to December 31, 19xx and that $70,000 of the excess of cost over book value is attributable to the increased value of Ham Corporation's inventory. The rest of the excess is considered goodwill.

CRITICAL THINKING AND COMMUNICATION

Conceptual Mini-Cases

CMC 16-1.

L O 1 *Effect of Change in Exchange Rate*

Compagnie Générale des Etablissements Michelin, the famous French maker of Michelin tires, became the world's largest tiremaker when it purchased the U.S. tire-maker Uniroyal Goodrich Tire Company in 1990. The *Wall Street Journal* reported that excluding Uniroyal Goodrich sales, sales revenue in fiscal 1990 decreased 4.4 percent to 52.74 billion francs. The decrease was due mainly to the weak dollar in 1990. Michelin executives said, the article reported, that about 25 percent of Michelin's sales, not counting those of Uniroyal Goodrich, were exports to the United States. Without the dollar's drop, revenue expressed in francs would have increased instead of decreased.[19] Explain why a weak dollar would lead to a decrease in Michelin's sales. Why are sales of Uniroyal Goodrich excluded from this discussion?

CMC 16-2.

L O 1 *Effects of Changes in Exchange Rates*

Japan Air Lines, one of the world's top-ranking airlines, has an extensive global network of passenger and cargo services. The company engages in sales and purchase transactions throughout the world. At the end of the year, it will have receivables and payables in many currencies that must be translated into yen for preparation of its consolidated financial statements. The company's 1990 annual report notes that these receivables and payables are translated at the applicable year-end rates. What will be

19. E. S. Browning, "Michelin Sees Heavy Net Loss for the Year," *Wall Street Journal,* October 19, 1990.

the financial effects (exchange gain or loss) under each of the following independent assumptions about changes in the exchange rates since the transactions that gave rise to the receivables or payables occurred? (1) Receivables exceed payables, and on average the yen has risen relative to other currencies. (2) Receivables exceed payables, and on average the yen has fallen relative to other currencies. (3) Payables exceed receivables, and on average the yen has risen relative to other currencies. (4) Payables exceed receivables, and on average the yen has fallen relative to other currencies. Suggest some ways in which Japan Air Lines can minimize the effects of the fluctuations in exchange rates as they relate to receivables and payables.

Ethics Mini-Case

EMC 16-1.
L O 3   *Insider Trading*

Refer to the Business Bulletin: Ethics in Practice on page 739 in the chapter to answer the following questions:

1. What is meant by the phrase "insider trading"?
2. Why do you think insider trading is unethical and illegal in the United States?
3. Why do you think insider trading is an allowable practice in countries such as Germany?
4. Do you think the prohibition of insider trading in the United States is the correct approach? Why or why not?

Decision-Making Case

DMC 16-1.
L O 4   *Accounting for Investments*

San Antonio Corporation is a successful oil and gas exploration business in the southwestern part of the United States. At the beginning of 19xx, the company made investments in three companies that perform services in the oil and gas industry. The details of each of these investments are presented in the next three paragraphs.

San Antonio purchased 100,000 shares in Bellows Service Corporation at a cost of $8 per share. Bellows has 1.5 million shares outstanding, and during 19xx paid dividends of $.40 per share on earnings of $.80 per share. At the end of the year, Bellows's shares were selling for $12 per share.

San Antonio also purchased 2 million shares of Sunrise Drilling Company at $4 per share. Sunrise has 10 million shares outstanding. In 19xx, Sunrise paid a dividend of $.20 per share on earnings of $.40 per share. During the current year the president of San Antonio was appointed to the board of directors of Sunrise. At the end of the year, Sunrise's stock was selling for $6 per share.

In another action, San Antonio purchased 1 million of Blue Sky Oil Field Supplies Company's 5 million outstanding shares at $6 per share. The president of San Antonio sought membership on the board of directors of Blue Sky but was rebuffed by Blue Sky's board when shareholders representing a majority of Blue Sky's outstanding stock stated that they did not want to be associated with San Antonio. Blue Sky paid a dividend of $.40 per share and reported a net income of only $.20 per share for the year. By the end of the year, the price of its stock had dropped to $2 per share.

REQUIRED

1. What principal factors must you consider in order to determine how to account for San Antonio's investments? Should they be shown on the balance sheet as short-term or long-term investments? What factors affect this decision?
2. For each of the three investments, make general journal entries for each of the following: (a) initial investment, (b) receipt of cash dividend, and (c) recognition of income (if appropriate).
3. What adjusting entry (if any) is required at the end of the year?
4. Assuming that San Antonio's investment in Blue Sky is sold after the first of the year for $3 per share, what general journal entry would be made? Assuming that the market value of the remaining investments held by San Antonio exceeds cost by $1,200,000 at the end of the second year, what adjusting entry (if any) would be required?

Basic Research Activity

RA 16-1.

L O 1 *Reading and Analyzing Foreign Currency Markets*

Go to the section of the library where recent issues of the *Wall Street Journal* are located. From the index on the front page of Section C, "Money & Investing," find the page number of world markets. In the "Currency Trading" portion of that page, find a table entitled "Exchange Rates." This table shows the exchange rates of the currencies of about fifty countries with the U.S. dollar. Choose the currency of any country in which you are interested. Write down the value of that currency in U.S. dollar equivalents for one day in the first week of each month for the past six months, as reported in the *Wall Street Journal*. Prepare a chart that shows the variation in exchange rate for this currency over this time period. Assuming that you run a company that exports goods to the country you chose, would you find the change in exchange rate over the past six months favorable or unfavorable? Assuming that you run a company that imports goods from the country you chose, would you find the change in exchange rate over the past six months favorable or unfavorable? Explain your answers and tell what business practices you would follow to offset any adverse effects of exchange rate fluctuations. Be prepared to discuss your results in class.

FINANCIAL REPORTING AND ANALYSIS

Interpretation Cases from Business

ICB 16-1.

L O 5, 6 *Effects of Consolidating Finance Subsidiaries*

Metropolitan Stores Corporation is one of the largest owners of discount appliance stores in the United States. It owns Highway Superstores, among several other discount chains. The company has a wholly-owned finance subsidiary to finance its accounts receivable. Condensed 1991 financial statements for Metropolitan Stores and its finance subsidiary (in millions) are shown below. The fiscal year ends January 31.

	Metropolitan Stores Corporation	Finance Subsidiary
Assets		
Current Assets (except Accounts Receivable)	$ 866	$ 1
Accounts Receivable (net)	293	869
Property, Equipment, and Other Assets	933	—
Investment in Finance Subsidiary	143	—
Total Assets	$2,235	$870
Liabilities and Stockholders' Equity		
Current Liabilities	$ 717	$ 10
Long-Term Liabilities	859	717
Stockholders' Equity	659	143
Total Liabilities and Stockholders' Equity	$2,235	$870

Total sales to customers were $4 billion. The Financial Accounting Standards Board's *Statement No. 94* requires all majority-owned subsidiaries to be consolidated in the parent company's financial statements. Metropolitan's management believes that it is misleading to consolidate the finance subsidiary because it distorts the real operations of the company. You are asked to assess the effects of the statement on Metropolitan Stores' financial position.

REQUIRED

1. Prepare a consolidated balance sheet for Metropolitan Stores and its finance subsidiary.
2. Demonstrate the effects of FASB *Statement No. 94* by computing the following ratios for Metropolitan Stores before and after the consolidation in **1**: receivable turnover, average days' sales uncollected, and debt to equity (use year-end balances).

3. What other ratios will be affected by the implementation of FASB *Statement No. 94*? Does consolidation assist investors and creditors in assessing the risk of investing in Metropolitan Stores securities or loaning the company money? Relate your answer to your calculations in **2**. What do you think of management's position?

ICB 16-2.
L O 6 *Consolidation of Two Large Companies*

One of the major corporate buyouts in 1986 was *General Electric Company*'s purchase of *RCA Corporation.* This transaction is described in a note to GE's financial statements in its 1986 annual report as follows:

> On June 9, 1986, GE acquired RCA Corporation and its subsidiaries (RCA) in a transaction for which the total consideration to former RCA shareholders was $6.406 billion in cash. RCA businesses include the manufacture and sale of a wide range of electronic products and related research and services for consumer, commercial, military and space applications; the National Broadcasting Company's (NBC) radio and television stations and network broadcasting services; and domestic and international message and data communications services.

> The acquisition was accounted for as a purchase, and the operating results of RCA have been consolidated with those of GE since June 1, 1986. In preparing 1986 financial information, the purchase price ($6.426 billion, including an estimated $20 million of related costs) has been allocated to the assets and liabilities of RCA based on estimates of fair market values. The excess of purchase price over the estimate of fair values of net assets acquired (goodwill) was $2.7 billion, which is being amortized on a straight-line basis over 40 years.[20]

REQUIRED

1. Show the entry in GE's records to record the purchase of RCA.
2. Did GE pay more or less than book value for RCA?
3. Show the year-end adjusting entry on GE's records related to the amortization of goodwill. (GE's year end is December 31.)

ICB 16-3.
L O 6 *Analysis of an Acquisition*

In 1981 *USX Corporation* fought *Mobil Oil Corporation* for control of *Marathon Oil Company.* USX won this battle of the giants by reaching an agreement to purchase all of Marathon's stock. The *Chicago Tribune* reported on March 12, 1982 that the $6 billion merger, as approved by the stockholders of Marathon, was the second largest in history and created the twelfth largest industrial corporation in the United States.

In a note to USX's 1981 annual report, the details of the purchase were revealed. USX "purchased 30 million common shares of Marathon Oil Company for $125 per share . . . as the first step in its planned acquisition of the entire equity of Marathon." Additional Marathon shares would be purchased by issuing $100 principal amount of 12½ percent notes due in 1994 for each share of stock. These notes were estimated by the financial press to have a fair market value of $80 per note. The total number of Marathon shares prior to these two transactions was 59.0 million. On December 31, 1981, just before the merger, the condensed balance sheets of USX and Marathon Oil appeared as shown at the top of the next page (in millions).

Further information in USX's annual report indicated that when consolidated financial statements were prepared using the purchase method, management would adjust Marathon's assets and liabilities in the following manner. It would (a) increase inventory by $1,244 million; (b) increase current liabilities by $392 million; and (c) decrease deferred income taxes by $588 million. After these adjustments, any remaining excess of the purchase price over book value of Marathon's shares would be attributed to property, plant, and equipment.[21]

REQUIRED

1. Prepare the entry in USX's journals to record the purchase of Marathon Oil.
2. Prepare the eliminating entry, including the adjustments indicated, that would be made to consolidate USX and Marathon.
3. Prepare a consolidated balance sheet for the merged companies.
4. Did USX pay more or less than book value for Marathon? Why would USX take this action? Did the purchase raise or lower USX's book value per share?

20. General Electric, *Annual Report*, 1986.
21. USX Corporation, *Annual Report*, 1981.

	USX	Marathon Oil
Assets		
Current Assets, Excluding Inventories	$ 4,214	$ 907
Inventories	1,198	576
Property, Plant, and Equipment (net)	6,676	4,233
Other Assets	1,228	278
Total Assets	$13,316	$5,994
Liabilities and Stockholders' Equity		
Current Liabilities	$ 2,823	$1,475
Long-Term Debt	2,340	1,368
Deferred Income Taxes	732	588
Other Liabilities	1,161	501
Total Liabilities	$ 7,056	$3,932
Stockholders' Equity	6,260	2,062
Total Liabilities and Stockholders' Equity	$13,316	$5,994

International Company Case

ICC 16-1.

L O 3 *Differences Between U.S. and U.K. Accounting Principles*

Cadbury Schweppes is a major global beverage and confectionery company, with such well-known brands as Schweppes, Sunkist, Canada Dry, and Cadbury. This United Kingdom company publishes its financial statements in accordance with generally accepted accounting principles (GAAP) in the United Kingdom but includes in its annual report a very interesting summary of the differences that would result if selected financial data were presented in accordance with GAAP in the United States, as follows:[22]

	Per U.K. GAAP		Per U.S. GAAP	
Effect of Differences	1991 £m	**1992 £m**	1991 £m	**1992 £m**
Operating income	360.2	**370.7**	359.4	**348.5**
Income before tax	314.7	**332.7**	289.2	**290.2**
Net income (as below)	192.7	**195.6**	165.8	**136.0**
Stockholders' equity	874.9	**1,084.1**	1,456.4	**1,755.6**

	1991 £m	**1992 £m**
Net income for Ordinary shareholders per U.K. GAAP	192.7	**195.6**
U.S. GAAP adjustments (net of tax):		
Goodwill/intangibles	(25.2)	**(28.0)**
Capitalization of interest	2.1	**1.3**
Elimination of revaluation surplus	2.5	**0.7**
One-time credits/(charges)	(7.7)	**(18.6)**
Deferred taxation	(1.3)	**(1.7)**
Pension costs	2.9	**(12.7)**
Other items	(0.2)	**(0.6)**
Net income per U.S. GAAP	165.8	**136.0**

22. Cadbury Schweppes, *Annual Report*, 1992.

Calculate return on equity for 1991 and 1992 under U.K. GAAP and U.S. GAAP. The GAAP from which country shows the best results? What role does goodwill and intangibles play in this difference? (**Hint:** Recall from the chapter on long-term assets that purchased goodwill is shown as an asset and is amortized on the income statement in the United States; it is deducted from stockholders' equity and is not amortized in the United Kingdom.) What are two other important differences in accounting principles between U.K. GAAP and U.S. GAAP? Do accounting principles appear to be more conservative under U.K. GAAP or U.S. GAAP?

Toys "R" Us Case

TC 16-1.

L O 1, 2   *Effects of Foreign Exchange*

Refer to the Annual Report in the appendix on Toys "R" Us to answer the following questions. In Management's Discussion, management states that "International sales and operating earnings were unfavorably impacted by the translation of local currency results into U.S. dollars at lower average exchange rates in 1993 than in 1992. However, the strong dollar had a favorable impact on the cost of international capital in 1993." In another paragraph, management indicates that the company has borrowed money in Japanese yen. Why does a strong dollar have an unfavorable impact on results and a favorable effect on the cost of international capital?

Toys "R" Us
Annual Report

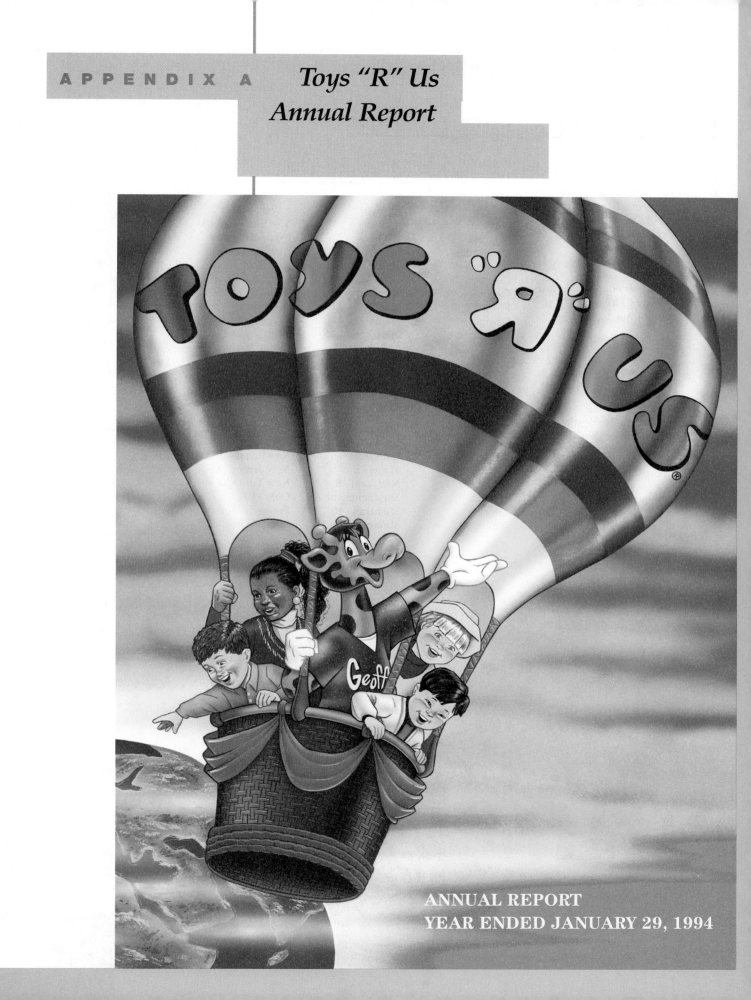

**ANNUAL REPORT
YEAR ENDED JANUARY 29, 1994**

TABLE OF CONTENTS

Toys "R" Us is the world's largest and fastest growing children's specialty retail chain in terms of both sales and earnings. At January 29, 1994, the Company operated 581 toy stores in the United States, 234 international toy stores and 217 Kids "R" Us children's clothing stores.

STORE LOCATIONS

TOYS "R" US UNITED STATES - 581 LOCATIONS

Alabama - 7	Indiana - 12	Nebraska - 3	Tennessee - 11
Alaska - 1	Iowa - 6	Nevada - 3	Texas - 43
Arizona - 10	Kansas - 4	New Hampshire - 5	Utah - 5
Arkansas - 2	Kentucky - 7	New Jersey - 21	Virginia - 17
California - 74	Louisiana - 8	New Mexico - 3	Washington - 10
Colorado - 9	Maine - 2	New York - 36	West Virginia - 3
Connecticut - 8	Maryland - 16	North Carolina - 15	Wisconsin - 11
Delaware - 2	Massachusetts - 16	Ohio - 27	
Florida - 36	Michigan - 23	Oklahoma - 4	Puerto Rico - 4
Georgia - 14	Minnesota - 11	Oregon - 5	
Hawaii - 1	Mississippi - 3	Pennsylvania - 27	
Idaho - 1	Missouri - 12	Rhode Island - 1	
Illinois - 33	Montana - 1	South Carolina - 8	

KIDS "R" US - 217 LOCATIONS

Alabama - 1	Indiana - 7	Missouri - 4	Tennessee - 1
Arizona - 4	Iowa - 1	Nebraska - 1	Texas - 5
California - 31	Kansas - 1	New Hampshire - 2	Utah - 3
Connecticut - 6	Maine - 2	New Jersey - 17	Virginia - 7
Delaware - 1	Maryland - 8	New York - 20	Wisconsin - 3
Florida - 7	Massachusetts - 4	Ohio - 19	
Georgia - 4	Michigan - 13	Pennsylvania - 14	Puerto Rico - 3
Illinois - 21	Minnesota - 6	Rhode Island - 1	

TOYS "R" US INTERNATIONAL - 234 LOCATIONS

Australia - 7	Hong Kong - 4	Spain - 17
Austria - 5	Japan - 16	Switzerland - 4
Belgium - 2	Malaysia - 2	Taiwan - 3
Canada - 50	Netherlands - 5	United Kingdom - 45
France - 25	Portugal - 2	
Germany - 44	Singapore - 3	

Printed on
recycled paper

TOYS"R"US, INC. AND SUBSIDIARIES

FINANCIAL HIGHLIGHTS

(Dollars in millions except per share information)   *Fiscal Year Ended*

	Jan 29, 1994	Jan. 30, 1993	Feb. 1, 1992	Feb. 2, 1991	Jan. 28, 1990	Jan. 29, 1989	Jan. 31, 1988	Feb. 1, 1987	Feb. 2, 1986	Feb. 3, 1985
OPERATIONS:										
Net Sales	$ 7,946	$ 7,169	$ 6,124	$ 5,510	$ 4,788	$ 4,000	$ 3,137	$ 2,445	$ 1,976	$ 1,702
Net Earnings	483	438	340	326	321	268	204	152	120	111
Earnings Per Share	1.63	1.47	1.15	1.11	1.09	.91	.69	.52	.41	.39
FINANCIAL POSITION AT YEAR END:										
Working Capital	633	797	328	177	238	255	225	155	181	222
Real Estate-Net	2,040	1,877	1,751	1,433	1,142	952	762	601	423	279
Total Assets	6,150	5,323	4,583	3,582	3,075	2,555	2,027	1,523	1,226	1,099
Long-Term Obligations	724	671	391	195	173	174	177	85	88	88
Stockholders' Equity	3,148	2,889	2,426	2,046	1,705	1,424	1,135	901	717	579
NUMBER OF STORES AT YEAR END:										
Toys"R"Us - United States	581	540	497	451	404	358	313	271	233	198
Toys"R"Us - International	234	167	126	97	74	52	37	24	13	5
Kids"R"Us	217	211	189	164	137	112	74	43	23	10

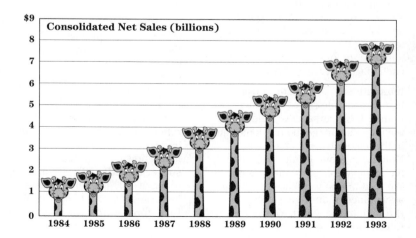

Consolidated Net Sales (billions)

1

TO OUR STOCKHOLDERS

FINANCIAL HIGHLIGHTS

We are pleased to report another excellent year for Toys "R" Us. In 1993, we once again achieved record sales and earnings as well as significant market share gains. Since Toys "R" Us became a public company, we have reported 15 consecutive years of sales and earnings increases, with an annual compounded growth rate over that period of 25%.

Our sales reached $7.9 billion, an 11% increase over the $7.2 billion reported in the previous year. Pre-tax earnings increased 12% while net earnings rose to $483 million, a 10% increase over the $438 million in 1992. Earnings per share were $1.63 compared to $1.47 a year ago. Our stockholders' equity increased to $3.1 billion by the end of 1993.

We achieved these outstanding results by having the best selection of merchandise, being stocked in depth, and by being competitive with our everyday low prices. Our strong performance also reflects several new marketing and merchandising initiatives implemented this year; including the wider distribution of our Holiday Toy Catalog, the expansion of Books "R" Us shops within our U.S.A. toy stores and increased customer service initiatives.

Our existing and new strategies contributed to comparable store sales increases in our U.S.A. toy stores of 6.5% in the fourth quarter and 3.3% for the year. These results are particularly impressive as they come on top of strong increases in each of the last two years.

Internationally, Germany and Japan had comparable store sales decreases in their local currencies, reflecting the recessionary economic conditions in those countries. Canada, the United Kingdom, France and Spain had comparable store sales increases. We continue to be pleased with the acceptance of our new stores throughout the world. Our International division once again, demonstrated its ability to improve inventory management and increase

Robert C. Nakasone, President and Chief Operating Officer and Michael Goldstein, Vice Chairman and Chief Executive Officer.

labor and distribution productivity in spite of the difficult economic environment in Europe and Japan.

We have created a franchising division that will enable us to bring additional countries into the Toys "R" Us family on an accelerated basis, and provide for the opening of stores in additional parts of the world. We have already signed two franchise agreements which allow for the opening of Toys "R" Us stores in the Middle East commencing in 1994. We will receive royalty and other related franchise service fees providing meaningful cash flow and earnings for our International division.

Our Kids "R" Us children's clothing stores' sales improved throughout the second half of the year, and despite a difficult apparel sales environment, ended the year with a slight increase. Operating profits increased approximately 25% following a 50% increase in 1992 reflecting the improved expense and inventory control as well as new marketing and merchandising strategies. Kids "R" Us continues to make strategic improvements to increase its profitability. In 1993, four stores were closed and we anticipate closing another 15 to 20 stores which are not meeting expectations.

Lastly, we announced a plan to buy back $1 billion of our common stock over the next several years. Even with our aggressive expansion, Toys "R" Us expects to generate excess cash flow. We believe that in addition to investing in our ongoing business, the repurchase of Toys "R" Us common stock will increase shareholder value.

OPERATIONAL HIGHLIGHTS

We are proud of our ability to provide our customers with the best selection of merchandise, stocked in depth with everyday low prices, while maintaining one of the lowest expense structures in the industry. The following highlights some 1993 accomplishments along with our plans for 1994.

In 1993, we significantly expanded the distribution of our Holiday Toy Catalog providing our customers with even more coupons than in prior years. The catalog was very successful and allowed us to highlight the broad selection of merchandise that can be found at Toys "R" Us. Customers used the catalog as a shopping aid throughout the Holiday season.

We have continued testing various "specialty shops" within our stores: the most notable being "Books "R" Us".

2

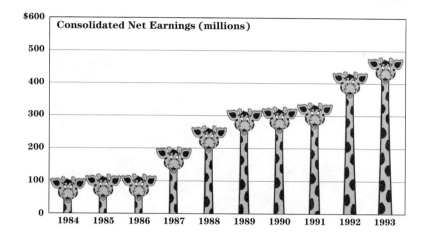

Consolidated Net Earnings (millions)

The Books "R" Us shops offer a broad selection of children's books and encourage children to read. In 1993, we added about 160 "Books "R" Us" shops and plan to have over 300 shops by the end of 1994. We have also been experimenting with other shops such as construction toys, large outdoor playsets and stuffed animals. We believe that these shops help distinguish Toys "R" Us from our competitors.

Enhancing customer service continues to be a primary focus for Toys "R" Us. In 1993, we expanded our successful "Geoffrey Helper" program in both the U.S.A. and International toy stores. In 1994, we will install customer friendly in-aisle price scanners and other service oriented technology to assist our customers who are our number one priority.

In 1990, we began remodeling about fifteen of our older U.S.A. toy stores each year. The remodeled stores enhance the customers' shopping experience while increasing in-store productivity. In 1993, we accelerated this program to about 25 stores and expect to remodel another 25 to 30 stores in 1994.

The use of technology to control expenses is a priority at Toys "R" Us. We again increased productivity and improved our ability to replenish stores by building an automated state-of-the-art distribution facility in southern Germany and retrofitting an existing facility in California with our new automated systems. In 1994, we plan to replace four U.S.A. toy distribution centers with two automated facilities in Missouri and Florida. Distribution facilities in France, Germany and Spain will also be retrofitted with new automated systems.

All U.S.A. toy stores were provided with laser radio terminal (LRT) technology in 1993, which takes advantage of wireless radio frequency communications within our stores. This equipment enhances shelf replenishment and improves employee productivity.

We installed satellite technology in North America. This technology instantaneously links our stores with our headquarters' computer databases as well as our customer transaction authorization networks in a more cost effective manner. We have also been able to utilize business television in our North American stores.

STORE GROWTH

In 1993, we opened 41 toy stores in the United States. Internationally, 67 stores opened in 11 countries, including our first stores in Australia, Portugal, Belgium, Switzerland and the Netherlands. For the first time, our International division opened more toy stores than the United States division. We also opened 10 Kids "R" Us stores. At the end of 1993, we had 815 toy stores operating in 46 states and Puerto Rico, Canada; Europe - the United Kingdom, Germany, France, Spain, Austria, Switzerland, the Netherlands, Belgium and Portugal; Asia - Japan, Hong Kong, Singapore, Malaysia and Taiwan; and Australia. We also had 217 Kids "R" Us stores operating in 29 states.

In 1994, we plan to open 40 to 45 toy stores in the U.S.A. and 65 to 70 stores internationally, including our first stores in Scandinavia. The new Scandinavian stores will be serviced from the United Kingdom. Once again, our anticipated opening of international stores will exceed the openings in the U.S.A. The international stores will capitalize on the existing infrastructure thereby enhancing the profitability of new

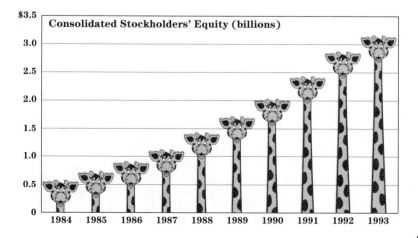

Consolidated Stockholders' Equity (billions)

and existing stores. We plan to open about 10 new Kids "R" Us stores.

With our financial strength, we intend to capitalize on our strong competitive position throughout the world, by continued expansion to achieve greater sales, earnings and market share gains.

CORPORATE CITIZENSHIP

Toys "R" Us maintains a corporate-wide giving program focusing on improving the health care needs of children by supporting many national and regional children's health care organizations. In 1993, we contributed funds to more than 10 new children's health care organizations. We expanded our Hospital Playroom Program in 1993 by opening 4 additional playrooms bringing the total to 18. This program fixtures and equips quality children's play centers in hospitals. We expect to expand our program into eight additional hospitals in 1994.

Once again we were very involved in assisting those in need in the aftermath of the floods in the Midwest and the Southern California earthquake by providing free diapers and other basic consumables.

Toys "R" Us is a signatory to a Fair Share Agreement with the NAACP and has taken steps to support women and other minorities in the workplace. We are the leading purchaser of products from several minority-owned toy companies.

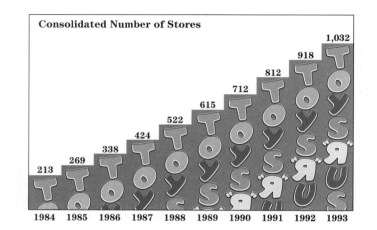

Consolidated Number of Stores

1984	1985	1986	1987	1988	1989	1990	1991	1992	1993
213	269	338	424	522	615	712	812	918	1,032

Toys "R" Us continues to have a strong toy safety program which includes the inspection of directly imported toys. Furthermore, we continue to take numerous pro-active initiatives, including a leadership position in eliminating the sale of look-a-like toy guns.

Through our new Books "R" Us shops, we are promoting literacy by demonstrating to children that reading is fun. We introduced a reading initiative called Geoffrey's Reading Railroad which offers a free reading kit with prize incentives for reading up to nine books. In conjunction with the opening of Books "R" Us shops, Toys "R" Us reached out to the community and selected Reading Is Fundamental (RIF) as the recipient of a grant. Part of this grant went towards RIF's Project Open Book, a program that provides books to children in homeless shelters.

HUMAN RESOURCES

The excellence of our management team and associates enables Toys "R" Us to expand aggressively and profitably.

We have made the following important promotions and additions to our executive ranks:

Corporate and Administrative:

Michael J. Corrigan, Vice President - Compensation and Benefits

Toys "R" Us, United States:

Lee Richardson, Vice President - Advertising

Karl S. Taylor, Vice President - Merchandise Planning and Allocation

Toys "R" Us, International:

Ken Bonning, Vice President - Logistics

Keith C. Spurgeon, Vice President - Toys "R" Us, Asia/Australia

Kids "R" Us:

Virginia Harris, Senior Vice President- General Merchandise Manager

Lorna E. Nagler, Vice President - Divisional Merchandise Manager

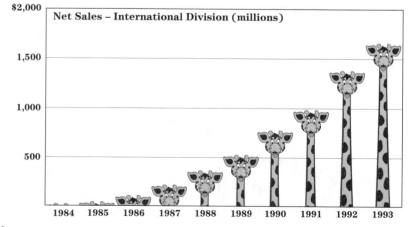

Net Sales – International Division (millions)

	1984	1985	1986	1987	1988	1989	1990	1991	1992	1993

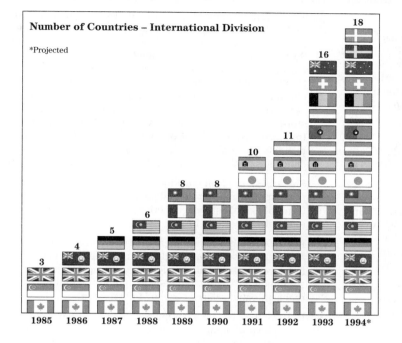

Number of Countries – International Division

*Projected

3 — 1985
4 — 1986
5 — 1987
6 — 1988
8 — 1989
8 — 1990
10 — 1991
11 — 1992
16 — 1993
18 — 1994*

Charles Lazarus, Chairman of the Board

SUMMARY

The exciting world of Toys "R" Us continues to expand. We look forward to a strong year in 1994, with profit improvement in all three divisions. We will work hard to continue being the most trusted store in town.

We value our excellent relationships with our innovative suppliers and commend them for their products, which create excitement in our stores. Our assessment of the February New York Toy Fair indicates an exciting year in basic categories such as crafts, construction, action figures, preschool and dolls with reasonably priced quality product.

We recognize the dedication and quality work of our associates around the world who have made this another record year. Our appreciation is also extended to you, our stockholders, for your commitment and loyalty to Toys "R" Us.

Finally, we would like to thank Charles Lazarus, our founder and the Chairman of the Board for his confidence in us and the rest of the Toys "R" Us team. He has created an impressive organization and a great legacy. We intend to fully meet his expectations and live up to the standards he set.

Sincerely,

Michael Goldstein

Michael Goldstein
Vice Chairman and
Chief Executive Officer

Robert C. Nakasone

Robert C. Nakasone
President and
Chief Operating Officer

March 30, 1994

LETTER FROM THE CHAIRMAN

Over the past 46 years since I opened my first toy store in Washington, D.C., I have seen Toys "R" Us grow to become a sophisticated, multinational company with stores throughout the world. Many people have contributed to the success of our company, none more than Mike Goldstein, our new Vice Chairman and Chief Executive Officer, and Bob Nakasone, our new President and Chief Operating Officer. These appointments are an integral part of our succession planning process and give added responsibilities to our two most senior executives.

In my new role, I will continue to be significantly involved with Toys "R" Us in a variety of ways. First and foremost, I will ensure that the vision of Toys "R" Us remains intact by visiting our U.S.A. and International operations. I will also be providing guidance in the development of new merchandising and marketing concepts. Lastly, I will be working with governmental officials throughout the world to ensure that Toys "R" Us is able to continue its global expansion.

I look forward to my new role and remain as excited about the future prospects of Toys "R" Us today, as I first did more than four decades ago.

Charles Lazarus

Charles Lazarus
Chairman of the Board

MANAGEMENT'S DISCUSSION-RESULTS OF OPERATIONS AND FINANCIAL CONDITION

RESULTS OF OPERATIONS*

The Company has experienced sales growth in each of its last three years; sales were up 10.8% in 1993, 17.1% in 1992 and 11.1% in 1991. Part of the growth is attributable to the opening of 130 new U.S.A. toy stores, 137 international toy stores and 57 children's clothing stores during the three year period, and a portion of the increase is due to comparable U.S.A. toy store sales increases of 3.3%, 6.9% and 2.4% in 1993, 1992 and 1991, respectively.

Cost of sales as a percentage of sales decreased to 69.2% in 1993 from 69.3% in 1992 and from 70.0% in 1991 due to a more favorable merchandise mix.

Selling, advertising, general and administrative expenses as a percentage of sales increased to 18.8% in 1993 from 18.7% in 1992 primarily as a result of start-up costs for the opening of our new market in Australia. These expenses decreased in 1992 from 18.8% in 1991 as a result of labor productivity gains and other cost cutting measures.

Interest expense increased in 1993 and 1992 compared to 1991 due to increased average borrowings, the mix between short-term and long-term borrowings and the mix between countries, partially offset by lower short-term interest rates. Short-term interest income increased during these periods due to an increase in cash available for investment.

The effective tax rate increased to 37.5% in 1993 from 36.5% in 1992, due to a 1% increase in the U.S. Federal corporate income tax rate and an adjustment for the retroactive impact of this tax change. The effective tax rate decreased to 36.5% in 1992 from 37.0% in 1991, due to a change in the mix of foreign earnings and certain foreign tax benefits. The Company believes its deferred tax assets, as reported, are fully realizable.

The Company believes that its risks attendant to foreign operations are minimal as it operates in sixteen different countries which are politically stable. International sales and operating earnings were unfavorably impacted by the translation of local currency results into U.S. dollars at lower average exchange rates in 1993 than in 1992. However, the strong dollar had a favorable impact on the cost of international capital investment in 1993.

Inflation has had little effect on the Company's operations in the last three years.

LIQUIDITY AND CAPITAL RESOURCES

The Company continues to maintain a strong financial position as evidenced by its working capital of $633 million at January 29, 1994 and $797 million at January 30, 1993. The long-term debt to equity percentage is 23.0% at January 29, 1994 as compared to 23.2% at January 30, 1993.

The Company plans to open 105 to 115 toy stores in 1994 in the United States, Australia, Austria, Belgium, Canada, France, Germany, Japan, the Netherlands, Portugal, Spain, Switzerland and the United Kingdom, as well as the new markets of Denmark and Sweden. Additionally, the Company plans to open about 10 Kids "R" Us children's clothing stores and close approximately 15 to 20 stores (4 stores closed in 1993). The Company believes that the store closings will not have a significant impact on its financial position. The Company opened 108 toy stores in 1993, 84 in 1992 and 75 in 1991 and 10 Kids "R" Us children's clothing stores in 1993, 23 in 1992 and 25 in 1991.

Since 1981, the Company has purchased a significant portion of its real estate and plans to continue this policy. Generally, real estate acquisitions are financed through internally generated funds.

For 1994, capital requirements for real estate, store and warehouse fixtures and equipment, leasehold improvements and other additions to property and equipment are estimated at $650 million (including real estate and related costs of $400 million).

In 1993, the Company completed its five million share repurchase program and announced a new one billion dollar share repurchase program which will occur over the next several years. During the three years ended January 29, 1994, the Company repurchased 5,648,000 shares of its common stock for $210,477,000 pursuant to these programs. The repurchase of shares during 1994 is anticipated to be financed by internally generated funds.

The seasonal nature of the business (approximately 49% of sales take place in the fourth quarter) typically causes cash to decline from the beginning of the year through October as inventory increases for the Christmas season and funds are used for land purchases and construction of new stores, which usually open in the first ten months of the year. Therefore, the Company has commitments and backup lines from numerous financial institutions to adequately support its short-term financing needs. Management expects that seasonal cash requirements will continue to be met primarily through operations, issuance of short-term commercial paper and bank borrowings for its foreign subsidiaries.

Where appropriate, the Company may convert short-term borrowings to long-term debt to achieve a balance between fixed and variable interest rates. In this regard, during 1993 the Company's Japanese subsidiary borrowed 4 billion yen (approximately $36 million) at various interest rates with a third party in Japan.

---

* References to 1993, 1992 and 1991 are for the 52 weeks ended January 29, 1994, January 30, 1993 and February 1, 1992, respectively.

TOYS"R"US, INC. AND SUBSIDIARIES

CONSOLIDATED STATEMENTS OF EARNINGS

(In thousands except per share information)   *Year Ended*

	January 29, 1994	January 30, 1993	February 1, 1992
Net sales	$ 7,946,067	$ 7,169,290	$ 6,124,209
Costs and expenses:			
Cost of sales	5,494,766	4,968,555	4,286,639
Selling, advertising, general and administrative	1,497,011	1,342,262	1,153,576
Depreciation and amortization	133,370	119,034	100,701
Interest expense	72,283	69,134	57,885
Interest and other income	(24,116)	(18,719)	(13,521)
	7,173,314	6,480,266	5,585,280
Earnings before taxes on income	772,753	689,024	538,929
Taxes on income	289,800	251,500	199,400
Net earnings	$ 482,953	$ 437,524	$ 339,529
Earnings per share	$ 1.63	$ 1.47	$ 1.15

See notes to consolidated financial statements.

7

TOYS"R"US, INC. AND SUBSIDIARIES

CONSOLIDATED BALANCE SHEETS

(In thousands)

	January 29, 1994	January 30, 1993
ASSETS		
Current Assets:		
Cash and cash equivalents	$ 791,893	$ 763,721
Accounts and other receivables	98,534	69,385
Merchandise inventories	1,777,569	1,498,671
Prepaid expenses and other	40,400	52,731
Total Current Assets	2,708,396	2,384,508
Property and Equipment:		
Real estate, net	2,035,673	1,876,835
Other, net	1,148,794	926,715
Total Property and Equipment	3,184,467	2,803,550
Other Assets	256,746	134,794
	$ 6,149,609	$ 5,322,852
LIABILITIES AND STOCKHOLDERS' EQUITY		
Current Liabilities:		
Short-term borrowings	$ 239,862	$ 120,772
Accounts payable	1,156,411	941,375
Accrued expenses and other current liabilities	471,782	361,661
Income taxes payable	206,996	163,841
Total Current Liabilities	2,075,051	1,587,649
Deferred Income Taxes	202,663	175,430
Long-Term Debt	710,365	660,488
Obligations Under Capital Leases	13,248	10,264
Stockholders' Equity:		
Common stock	29,794	29,794
Additional paid-in capital	454,061	465,494
Retained earnings	3,012,806	2,529,853
Foreign currency translation adjustments	(56,021)	14,317
Treasury shares, at cost	(292,358)	(150,437)
	3,148,282	2,889,021
	$ 6,149,609	$ 5,322,852

See notes to consolidated financial statements.

TOYS"R"US, INC. AND SUBSIDIARIES
CONSOLIDATED STATEMENTS OF CASH FLOWS

(In thousands)

	January 29, 1994	January 30, 1993	February 1, 1992
CASH FLOWS FROM OPERATING ACTIVITIES			
Net earnings	$ 482,953	$ 437,524	$ 339,529
Adjustments to reconcile net earnings to net cash provided by operating activities:			
Depreciation and amortization	133,370	119,034	100,701
Deferred income taxes	36,534	13,998	15,817
Changes in operating assets and liabilities:			
Accounts and other receivables	(29,149)	(5,307)	9,092
Merchandise inventories	(278,898)	(108,066)	(115,436)
Prepaid expenses and other operating assets	(39,448)	(36,249)	(16,176)
Accounts payable, accrued expenses and other liabilities	325,165	112,232	462,152
Income taxes payable	26,588	40,091	7,071
Total adjustments	174,162	135,733	463,221
Net cash provided by operating activities	657,115	573,257	802,750
CASH FLOWS FROM INVESTING ACTIVITIES			
Capital expenditures, net	(555,258)	(421,564)	(548,538)
Other assets	(58,383)	(22,175)	(17,110)
Net cash used in investing activities	(613,641)	(443,739)	(565,648)
CASH FLOWS FROM FINANCING ACTIVITIES			
Short-term borrowings, net	119,090	(170,887)	(94,811)
Long-term borrowings	40,576	318,035	197,802
Long-term debt repayments	(1,335)	(7,926)	(1,590)
Exercise of stock options	29,879	86,323	32,707
Share repurchase program	(183,233)	(27,244)	--
Net cash provided by financing activities	4,977	198,301	134,108
Effect of exchange rate changes on cash and cash equivalents	(20,279)	(8,691)	38,378
CASH AND CASH EQUIVALENTS			
Increase during year	28,172	319,128	409,588
Beginning of year	763,721	444,593	35,005
End of year	$ 791,893	$ 763,721	$ 444,593

SUPPLEMENTAL DISCLOSURES OF CASH FLOW INFORMATION

The Company considers its highly liquid investments purchased as part of its daily cash management activities to be cash equivalents. During the years ended January 29, 1994, January 30, 1993 and February 1, 1992, the Company made income tax payments of $220,229, $151,722 and $155,469 and interest payments (net of amounts capitalized) of $104,281, $83,584 and $46,763, respectively.

See notes to consolidated financial statements.

TOYS"R"US, INC. AND SUBSIDIARIES

CONSOLIDATED STATEMENTS OF STOCKHOLDERS' EQUITY

(In thousands)	Shares	Issued Amount	Common Stock In Treasury Amount	Additional paid-in capital	Retained earnings
Balance, February 2, 1991	297,938	$ 29,794	$ (129,340)	$ 353,924	$ 1,752,800
Net earnings for the year	–	–	–	–	339,529
Exercise of stock options (1,640 Treasury shares)	–	–	1,623	15,259	
Tax benefit from exercise of stock options	–	–	–	15,620	-
Balance, February 1, 1992	297,938	29,794	(127,717)	384,803	2,092,329
Net earnings for the year	–	–	–	–	437,524
Share repurchase program (708 Treasury shares)	–	–	(27,244)	–	–
Exercise of stock options (4,479 Treasury shares)	–	–	4,524	35,301	–
Tax benefit from exercise of stock options	–	–	–	45,390	–
Balance, January 30, 1993	297,938	29,794	(150,437)	465,494	2,529,853
Net earnings for the year	–	–	–	–	482,953
Share repurchase program (4,940 Treasury shares)	–	–	(183,233)	–	–
Exercise of stock options (1,394 Treasury shares)	–	–	41,312	(21,464)	–
Tax benefit from exercise of stock options	–	–	–	10,031	–
Balance, January 29, 1994	297,938	$ 29,794	$ (292,358)	$ 454,061	$ 3,012,806

See notes to consolidated financial statements.

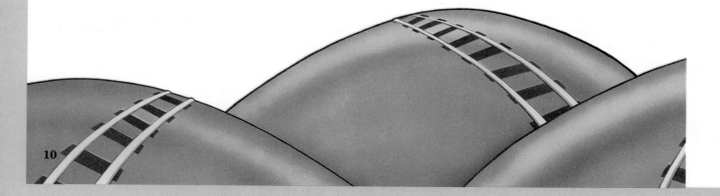

TOYS"R"US, INC. AND SUBSIDIARIES

NOTES TO CONSOLIDATED FINANCIAL STATEMENTS

SUMMARY OF SIGNIFICANT ACCOUNTING POLICIES

Fiscal Year

The Company's fiscal year ends on the Saturday nearest to January 31. References to 1993, 1992 and 1991 are for the 52 weeks ended January 29, 1994, January 30, 1993 and February 1, 1992, respectively.

Principles of Consolidation

The consolidated financial statements include the accounts of the Company and its subsidiaries. All material intercompany balances and transactions have been eliminated. Assets and liabilities of foreign operations are translated at current rates of exchange at the balance sheet date while results of operations are translated at average rates in effect for the period. Translation gains or losses are shown as a separate component of stockholders' equity. The increase (decrease) in the foreign currency translation adjustment was ($70,338,000), ($33,650,000), and $7,539,000 for 1993, 1992 and 1991, respectively.

Merchandise Inventories

Merchandise inventories for the U.S.A. toy store operations, which represent over 66% of total inventories, are stated at the lower of LIFO (last-in, first-out) cost or market as determined by the retail inventory method. If inventories had been valued at the lower of FIFO (first-in, first-out) cost or market, inventories would show no change at January 29, 1994 or January 30, 1993. All other merchandise inventories are stated at the lower of FIFO cost or market as determined by the retail inventory method.

Property and Equipment

Property and equipment are recorded at cost. Depreciation and amortization are provided using the straight-line method over the estimated useful lives of the assets or, where applicable, the terms of the respective leases, whichever is shorter.

Preopening Costs

Preopening costs, which consist primarily of advertising, occupancy and payroll expenses, are amortized over expected sales to the end of the fiscal year in which the store opens.

Capitalized Interest

Interest on borrowed funds is capitalized during construction of property and is amortized by charges to earnings over the depreciable lives of the related assets. Interest of $7,300,000, $8,403,000 and $12,237,000 was capitalized during 1993, 1992 and 1991, respectively.

Financial Instruments

The carrying amounts reported in the balance sheets for cash and cash equivalents and short-term borrowings approximate their fair market values.

Forward Foreign Exchange Contracts

The Company enters into forward foreign exchange contracts to eliminate currency movement relating to certain transactions denominated in foreign currency. Gains and losses which offset the movement in the underlying transactions are recognized as part of such transactions. As of January 29, 1994, the Company had $290,000,000 of outstanding forward contracts maturing in 1994. There were no open contracts at January 30, 1993. The Company does not expect to incur any losses as a result of counterparty defaults.

PROPERTY AND EQUIPMENT

(In thousands)	Useful Life (in years)	January 29, 1994	January 30, 1993
Land		$ 693,737	$ 642,368
Buildings	45-50	1,446,277	1,280,850
Furniture and equipment	5-20	953,360	809,772
Leaseholds and leasehold improvements	12 1/2-50	658,191	510,780
Construction in progress		41,855	72,895
Leased property under capital leases		24,360	20,193
		3,817,780	3,336,858
Less accumulated depreciation and amortization		633,313	533,308
		$ 3,184,467	$ 2,803,550

11

LONG - TERM DEBT

(In thousands)	January 29, 1994	January 30, 1993
Industrial revenue bonds, net of expenses (a)	$ 74,208	$ 74,174
Mortgage notes payable at annual interest rates from 7 1/8% to 11% (b)	13,318	13,708
Japanese yen loans payable at annual interest rates from 3.85% to 6.46%, due in varying amounts through 2012	142,688	93,904
British pound sterling 11% Stepped Coupon Guaranteed Bonds, due 2017	194,415	193,180
8 1/4% sinking fund debentures, due 2017, net of discounts	88,117	88,013
8 3/4% debentures, due 2021, net of expenses	197,978	197,906
	710,724	660,885
Less current portion	359	397
	$ 710,365	$ 660,488

(a) Bank letters of credit of $57,135,000, expiring in 1995, support certain industrial revenue bonds. The Company expects the bank letters of credit expiring in 1995 will be renewed. The bonds have fixed or variable interest rates with an average of 2.5% at January 29, 1994.

(b) Mortgage notes payable are collateralized by property and equipment with an aggregate carrying value of $18,628,000 at January 29, 1994.

The fair market value of the Company's long-term debt at January 29, 1994 is approximately $846,000,000. The fair market value was estimated using quoted market rates for publicly traded debt and estimated current interest rates for non-public debt.

The annual maturities of long-term debt at January 29, 1994 are as follows:

Year ending in	(In thousands)
1995	$ 359
1996	1,655
1997	3,045
1998	4,360
1999	5,310
2000 and subsequent	695,995
	$ 710,724

LEASES

The Company leases a portion of the real estate used in its operations. Most leases require the Company to pay real estate taxes and other expenses; some require additional amounts based on percentages of sales.

Obligations under capital leases require minimum payments as follows:

Year ending in	(In thousands)
1995	$ 2,582
1996	2,630
1997	2,475
1998	2,255
1999	1,996
2000 and subsequent	12,451
Total minimum lease payments	24,389
Less amount representing interest	9,957
Obligations under capital leases	14,432
Less current portion	1,184
	$ 13,248

Minimum rental commitments under noncancellable operating leases having a term of more than one year as of January 29, 1994 were as follows:

(In thousands) Year ending in	Gross minimum rentals	Sublease income	Net minimum rentals
1995	$ 207,664	$ 7,139	$ 200,525
1996	207,462	6,593	200,869
1997	204,867	5,754	199,113
1998	204,730	5,587	199,143
1999	203,461	4,688	198,773
2000 and subsequent	2,770,005	31,359	2,738,646
	$ 3,798,189	$ 61,120	$ 3,737,069

Total rental expense was as follows:

(In thousands)	January 29, 1994	January 30, 1993	February 1, 1992
Minimum rentals	$ 180,118	$ 149,027	$ 118,583
Additional amounts computed as percentages of sales	5,604	5,447	5,140
	185,722	154,474	123,723
Less sublease income	7,935	5,788	2,629
	$ 177,787	$ 148,686	$ 121,094

STOCKHOLDERS' EQUITY

The common shares of the Company, par value $.10 per share, were as follows:

(In thousands)	January 29, 1994	January 30, 1993
Authorized shares..............................	550,000	550,000
Issued shares.....................................	297,938	297,938
Treasury shares................................	8,416	4,870

Earnings per share is computed by dividing net earnings by the weighted average number of common shares outstanding after reduction for treasury shares and assuming exercise of dilutive stock options computed by the treasury stock method using the average market price during the year.

Weighted average numbers of shares used in computing earnings per share were as follows:

		Year ended	
(In thousands)	January 29, 1994	January 30, 1993	February 1, 1992
Common and common equivalent shares....................	296,463	297,718	296,139

TAXES ON INCOME

The provisions for income taxes consist of the following:

		Year ended	
(In thousands)	January 29, 1994	January 30, 1993	February 1, 1992
Current:			
Federal	$ 200,303	$ 186,013	$ 138,779
Foreign	17,259	15,605	15,378
State	35,704	35,884	29,426
	253,266	237,502	183,583
Deferred:			
Federal	49,961	17,187	19,545
Foreign	(16,186)	(6,705)	(7,678)
State	2,759	3,516	3,950
	36,534	13,998	15,817
Total	$ 289,800	$ 251,500	$ 199,400

Deferred tax liabilities and deferred tax assets reflect the net tax effects of temporary differences between the carrying amounts of assets and liabilities for financial reporting purposes and the amounts used for income tax purposes. The Company has gross deferred tax liabilities of $251.7 million at January 29, 1994 and $190.4 million at January 30, 1993 which consist primarily of temporary differences related to fixed assets of $194.0 million and $171.9 million, respectively. The Company had gross deferred tax assets of $92.8 million at January 29, 1994 and $63.8 million at January 30, 1993, which consist primarily of net operating losses of foreign start-up operations of $60.4 million and $38.5 million, and operating costs not currently deductible for tax purposes of $23.2 million and $18.6 million, respectively. Valuation allowances are not significant.

A reconciliation of the federal statutory tax rate with the effective tax rate follows:

		Year ended	
(In thousands)	January 29, 1994	January 30, 1993	February 1, 1992
Statutory tax rate.....................	35.0%	34.0%	34.0%
State income taxes, net of federal income tax benefit...	3.2	4.0	4.1
Foreign......................................	(0.5)	(1.2)	(0.5)
Other, net.................................	(0.2)	(0.3)	(0.6)
	37.5%	36.5%	37.0%

Deferred income taxes were not provided on unremitted earnings of foreign subsidiaries that are intended to be indefinitely invested. Unremitted earnings were approximately $101 million at January 29, 1994, exclusive of amounts that if remitted would result in little or no tax under current U.S. tax laws. Net income taxes of approximately $35 million would be due if these earnings were to be remitted.

PROFIT SHARING PLAN

The Company has a profit sharing plan with a 401(k) salary deferral feature for eligible domestic employees. The terms of the plan call for annual contributions by the Company as determined by the Board of Directors, subject to certain limitations. The profit sharing plan may be terminated at the Company's discretion. Provisions of $29,961,000, $29,824,000 and $15,513,000 have been charged to operations in 1993, 1992 and 1991, respectively.

STOCK OPTIONS

The Company has Stock Option Plans (the "Plans"), including a new plan subject to shareholder approval, which provide for the granting of options to purchase the Company's common stock to substantially all employees and non-employee directors of the Company. The Plans provide for the issuance of non-qualified options, incentive stock options, performance share options, performance units, stock appreciation rights, restricted shares and unrestricted shares. The majority of the options become exercisable four years and nine months from the date of grant. Certain non-qualified options become exercisable nine years from the date of grant, however the exercise date of all or a portion of such options may be accelerated if the price of the Company's common stock reaches certain target amounts. The options granted to non-employee directors are exercisable 20% each year on a cumulative basis commencing one year from the date of grant.

In addition to the aforementioned Plans, stock options aggregating 6,659,375 shares were granted to certain senior executives during the period from 1984 to 1993 pursuant to individual plans. These options are exercisable 20% each year on a cumulative basis commencing one year from the date of grant.

The exercise price per share of all options granted has been the market price of the Company's common stock on the date of grant. Outstanding options must be exercised within ten years from the date of grant.

At January 29, 1994, 13,327,781 shares were available for future grants under the Plans and 4,807,607 options were exercisable. All outstanding options expire at dates varying from May 1994 to December 2003.

At January 29, 1994, an aggregate of 30,574,872 shares of authorized common stock was reserved for all of the Plans noted above.

Stock option transactions are summarized as follows:

| | | Shares Under Option | |
(In thousands except price range)	Incentive	Non-Qualified	Price Range
Outstanding January 30, 1993	752	13,201	$ 7.03 - 39.63
Granted	--	5,645	36.44 - 40.94
Exercised	(224)	(1,170)	7.03 - 36.94
Cancelled	(1)	(956)	9.74 - 39.88
Outstanding January 29, 1994	527	16,720	$ 7.68 - 40.94

The exercise of non-qualified stock options results in state and federal income tax benefits to the Company related to the difference between the market price at the date of exercise and the option price. During 1993, 1992 and 1991, $10,031,000, $45,390,000 and $15,620,000, respectively, was credited to additional paid-in capital.

FOREIGN OPERATIONS

Certain information relating to the Company's foreign operations is set forth below. Corporate assets include all cash and cash equivalents and other related assets.

| | | | Year ended |
(In thousands)	January 29, 1994	January 30, 1993	February 1, 1992
Sales			
Domestic	$ 6,278,591	$ 5,795,119	$ 5,154,215
Foreign	1,667,476	1,374,171	969,994
Total	$ 7,946,067	$ 7,169,290	$ 6,124,209
Operating Profit			
Domestic	$ 724,818	$ 647,640	$ 527,695
Foreign	102,923	101,132	62,846
General corporate expenses	(6,821)	(9,333)	(7,248)
Interest expense, net	(48,167)	(50,415)	(44,364)
Earnings before taxes on income	$ 772,753	$ 689,024	$ 538,929
Identifiable Assets			
Domestic	$ 3,630,921	$ 3,277,527	$ 3,095,178
Foreign	1,694,565	1,248,827	1,009,455
Corporate	824,123	796,498	477,975
Total	$ 6,149,609	$ 5,322,852	$ 4,582,608

QUARTERLY FINANCIAL DATA

The following table sets forth certain unaudited quarterly financial information.

(In thousands except per share information)	First Quarter	Second Quarter	Third Quarter	Fourth Quarter
YEAR ENDED JANUARY 29, 1994				
Net Sales	$1,286,479	$ 1,317,012	$ 1,449,118	$ 3,893,458
Cost of Sales	882,876	902,414	982,151	2,727,325
Net Earnings	35,436	35,505	37,457	374,555
Earnings per Share	$ .12	$ .12	$ .13	$1.27
YEAR ENDED JANUARY 30, 1993				
Net Sales	$1,172,476	$ 1,249,144	$ 1,345,835	$ 3,401,835
Cost of Sales	809,929	864,511	922,619	2,371,496
Net Earnings	28,304	32,709	36,796	339,715
Earnings per Share	$ .10	$ .11	$ .12	$1.14

REPORT OF MANAGEMENT

Responsibility for the integrity and objectivity of the financial information presented in this Annual Report rests with Toys "R" Us management. The accompanying financial statements have been prepared from accounting records which management believes fairly and accurately reflect the operations and financial position of the Company. Management has established a system of internal controls to provide reasonable assurance that assets are maintained and accounted for in accordance with its policies and that transactions are recorded accurately on the Company's books and records.

The Company's comprehensive internal audit program provides for constant evaluation of the adequacy of the adherence to management's established policies and procedures. The Company has distributed to key employees its policies for conducting business affairs in a lawful and ethical manner.

The 1993 and 1992 financial statements of the Company have been audited by Ernst & Young, independent auditors, in accordance with generally accepted auditing standards, including a review of financial reporting matters and internal controls to the extent necessary to express an opinion on the consolidated financial statements.

Michael Goldstein
Vice Chairman and
Chief Executive Officer

Louis Lipschitz
Senior Vice President-Finance
and Chief Financial Officer

MARKET INFORMATION

The Company's common stock is listed on the New York Stock Exchange. The following table reflects the high and low prices (rounded to the nearest one-eighth) based on New York Stock Exchange trading since February 1, 1992.

The Company has not paid any cash dividends and a change in this policy is not under consideration by the Board of Directors.

The number of stockholders of record of common stock on March 9, 1994 was approximately 25,500.

	High	Low
1992		
1st Quarter	38 5/8	30 3/8
2nd Quarter	37 1/8	31
3rd Quarter	41	34 3/4
4th Quarter	41 1/4	35 5/8
1993		
1st Quarter	42 3/8	36 5/8
2nd Quarter	39 3/4	32 3/8
3rd Quarter	40 3/8	33 3/4
4th Quarter	42 7/8	36

REPORT OF INDEPENDENT AUDITORS

The Board of Directors and Stockholders
Toys "R" Us, Inc.

We have audited the accompanying consolidated balance sheets of Toys "R" Us, Inc. and subsidiaries, as of January 29, 1994 and January 30, 1993, and the related consolidated statements of earnings, stockholders' equity and cash flows for the years then ended. These financial statements are the responsibility of the Company's management. Our responsibility is to express an opinion on these financial statements based on our audit. The consolidated statements of earnings, stockholders' equity and cash flows of Toys "R" Us, Inc. and subsidiaries for the year ended February 1, 1992 were audited by other auditors whose report dated March 11, 1992, expressed an unqualified opinion on those statements.

We conducted our audits in accordance with generally accepted auditing standards. Those standards require that we plan and perform the audit to obtain reasonable assurance about whether the financial statements are free of material misstatement. An audit includes examining, on a test basis, evidence supporting the amounts and disclosures in the financial statements. An audit also includes assessing the accounting principles used and significant estimates made by management, as well as evaluating the overall financial statement presentation. We believe that our audits provide a reasonable basis for our opinion.

In our opinion, the 1993 and 1992 financial statements referred to above present fairly, in all material respects, the consolidated financial position of Toys "R" Us, Inc. and subsidiaries at January 29, 1994 and January 30, 1993 and the consolidated results of their operations and their cash flows for the years then ended in conformity with generally accepted accounting principles.

Ernst & Young

New York, New York
March 9, 1994

DIRECTORS AND OFFICERS

DIRECTORS

Charles Lazarus
Chairman of the Board
of the Company

Robert A. Bernhard
Real Estate Developer

Michael Goldstein
Vice Chairman and Chief Executive
Officer of the Company

Milton S. Gould
Attorney-at-law;
Partner - Shea & Gould

Shirley Strum Kenny
President, Queens College of The City
University of New York

Reuben Mark
Chairman and CEO
Colgate-Palmolive Company

Howard W. Moore
Former Executive
Vice President-General
Merchandise Manager of
the Company; Consultant

Robert C. Nakasone
President and Chief Operating
Officer of the Company

Norman M. Schneider
Former Chairman, Leisure Products
Division of Beatrice Foods
Company; Consultant

Harold M. Wit
Managing Director,
Allen & Company Incorporated;
Investment Bankers

OFFICERS - CORPORATE AND ADMINISTRATIVE

Michael Goldstein
Vice Chairman and
Chief Executive Officer

Robert C. Nakasone
President and
Chief Operating Officer

Dennis Healey
Senior Vice President -
Management Information Systems

Louis Lipschitz
Senior Vice President - Finance and
Chief Financial Officer

Michael P. Miller
Senior Vice President - Real Estate

Jeffrey S. Wells
Senior Vice President -
Human Resources

Gayle C. Aertker
Vice President - Real Estate

Michael J. Corrigan
Vice President - Compensation
and Benefits

Jonathan M. Friedman
Vice President - Controller

Eileen C. Gabriel
Vice President -
Information Systems

Jon W. Kimmins
Vice President - Treasurer

Matthew J. Lombardi
Vice President -
Information Technology

Eric A. Swartwood
Vice President -
Architecture and Construction

Michael L. Tumolo
Vice President -
Real Estate Counsel

Peter W. Weiss
Vice President - Taxes

Andre Weiss
Secretary - Attorney-at-law;
Partner-Schulte Roth & Zabel

TOYS "R" US UNITED STATES - OFFICERS AND GENERAL MANAGERS

Roger V. Goddu
Executive Vice President -
General Merchandise Manager

Van H. Butler
Senior Vice President - Marketing and
Divisional Merchandise Manager

Bruce C. Hall
Senior Vice President - Store
Operations and Support Services

Michael J. Madden
Senior Vice President - Distribution

Thomas J. Reinebach
Senior Vice President -
Chief Financial Officer

Ernest V. Speranza
Senior Vice President -
Advertising/Marketing

Robert J. Weinberg
Senior Vice President -
Divisional Merchandise Manager

Kristopher M. Brown
Vice President - Distribution Operations

Richard N. Cudrin
Vice President - Employee and
Labor Relations

Harvey J. Finkel
Vice President - Operations

Martin Fogelman
Vice President -
Divisional Merchandise Manager

Lee Richardson
Vice President - Advertising

John P. Sullivan
Vice President - Divisional
Merchandise Manager

Karl S. Taylor
Vice President - Merchandise
Planning and Allocation

GENERAL MANAGERS

Robert F. Price
Vice President
New York/Northern New Jersey

Larry D. Gardner
Pacific Northwest/Alaska

Michael A. Gerety
Georgia/South Carolina/
Tennessee/Alabama

Gary H. Gilliard
Colorado/Utah/New Mexico/Montana

Mark H. Haag
Southern California/
Arizona/Nevada/Hawaii

Daniel D. Hlavaty
Central Ohio/Indiana/Kentucky

Debra M. Kachurak
New England

Richard A. Moyer
S. Texas/Louisiana/Mississippi

Gerald S. Parker
Northern California

John J. Prawlocki
Florida/Puerto Rico

J. Michael Roberts
Pennsylvania/Delaware/
Southern New Jersey

Edward F. Siegler
Kansas/Missouri/Iowa/Nebraska

Carl P. Spaulding
N.E. Ohio/W. Pennsylvania/N. New York

William A. Stephenson
Illinois/Wisconsin/Minnesota

John P. Suozzo
Maryland/Virginia/North Carolina

Brian L. Voorhees
N. Texas/Oklahoma/Arkansas

Dennis J. Williams
Michigan/N.W. Ohio

KIDS "R" US - OFFICERS

Richard L. Markee
President

Virginia Harris
Senior Vice President - General
Merchandise Manager

James L. Easton
Vice President -
Divisional Merchandise Manager

Jerel G. Hollens
Vice President -
Merchandise Planning and
Management Information Systems

Debra G. Hyman
Vice President -
Divisional Merchandise Manager

Elizabeth S. Jordan
Vice President -
Human Resources

Lorna E. Nagler
Vice President - Divisional
Merchandise Manager

James G. Parros
Vice President - Stores and
Physical Distribution

TOYS "R" US INTERNATIONAL - OFFICERS AND COUNTRY MANAGEMENT

Larry D. Bouts
President

Gregory R. Staley
Senior Vice President -
General Merchandise Manager

Lawrence H. Meyer
Vice President -
Chief Financial Officer

Philip Bloom
Vice President -
General Merchandise Manager

Ken Bonning
Vice President-Logistics

Joseph Giamelli
Vice President -
Information Systems

Adam Szopinski
Vice President - Operations

Keith Van Beek
Vice President - Development

COUNTRY MANAGEMENT

David Rurka
President - Toys "R" Us Europe
Managing Director -
Toys "R" Us Holdings PLC
(United Kingdom)

Arnt Klöser
President - Toys "R" Us
Central Europe
Managing Director - TRU A.G.
(Switzerland)

Jacques Le Foll
President - Toys "R" Us
S.A.R.L. (France)

Carl Olsen
Managing Director - Toys "R" Us
(Australia) Pty. Ltd.

Guillermo Porrati
Managing Director - Toys "R" Us
Iberia, S.A. (Spain)

Manabu Tazaki
President - Toys "R" Us Japan, Ltd.

Elliott Wahle
President - Toys "R" Us (Canada) Ltd.

Keith C. Spurgeon
Vice President -Asia/Australia

Scott Chen
General Manager - Toys "R" Us
Lifung Taiwan Limited

Michael Yeo
General Manager - Toys "R" Us
Metro Pte. Ltd. (Singapore)

CORPORATE DATA

ANNUAL MEETING

The Annual Meeting of the
Stockholders of Toys "R" Us will be
held at the offices of the Company,
461 From Road, Paramus, New Jersey
on Wednesday, June 8, 1994 at 10:00 a.m.

STOCKHOLDER INFORMATION

The Company will supply to any
owner of Common Stock, upon
written request to Mr. Louis Lipschitz
of the Company at the address set
forth below, and without charge, a
copy of the Annual Report on Form
10-K for the year ended January 29,
1994, which has been filed with the
Securities and Exchange Commission.

COMMON STOCK LISTED

New York Stock Exchange, Symbol: TOY

THE OFFICE OF THE COMPANY
IS LOCATED AT

461 From Road
Paramus, New Jersey 07652
Telephone: 201-262-7800

GENERAL COUNSEL

Schulte Roth & Zabel
900 Third Avenue
New York, New York 10022

INDEPENDENT AUDITORS

Ernst & Young
787 Seventh Avenue
New York, New York 10019

REGISTRAR AND TRANSFER AGENT

American Stock Transfer
and Trust Company
40 Wall Street
New York, New York 10005
Telephone: 718-921-8200

Printed on
recycled paper

The Merchandising Work Sheet and Closing Entries

LEARNING OBJECTIVES

1. Prepare a work sheet and closing entries for a merchandising concern using the periodic inventory system.

2. Prepare a work sheet and closing entries for a merchandising concern using the perpetual inventory system.

In the chapter on completion of the accounting cycle, the work sheet is presented as a useful tool in preparing financial statements and adjusting and closing entries. This appendix shows how the work sheet and closing entries are prepared for merchandising companies. The work sheet for a merchandising company is basically the same as that for a service business, except that it includes the additional accounts that are needed to handle merchandising transactions. The treatment of these new accounts differs depending on whether a company uses the periodic or the perpetual inventory system.

THE PERIODIC INVENTORY SYSTEM

OBJECTIVE

1 *Prepare a work sheet and closing entries for a merchandising concern using the periodic inventory system*

The new accounts for a merchandising company using the periodic inventory system generally include Sales, Sales Returns and Allowances, Sales Discounts, Purchases, Purchases Returns and Allowances, Purchases Discounts, Freight In, and Merchandise Inventory. Except for Merchandise Inventory, these accounts are treated in much the same way as revenue and expense accounts for a service company. They are transferred to the Income Summary account in the closing process. On the work sheet, they are extended to the Income Statement columns.

Merchandise Inventory requires special treatment under the periodic inventory system because purchases of merchandise are accumulated in the Purchases account. No entries are made to the Merchandise Inventory account during the accounting period. Its balance at the end of the period, before adjusting and closing entries, is the same as it was at the beginning of the period. Thus, its balance at this point represents beginning merchandise inventory. Remember also that the cost of goods sold is determined by adding beginning merchandise inventory to net cost of purchases and then subtracting ending merchandise inventory. The objectives of handling merchandise inventory in the closing entries at the end of the period are to (1) remove the beginning balance from the Merchandise Inventory account, (2) enter the ending balance into the Merchandise Inventory account, and (3) enter the beginning inventory as a debit and the ending inventory as a credit to the Income Summary account to calculate net income. Using the figures for the Fenwick Fashions Corporation example in the chapter on accounting for merchandising operations, the T accounts below show how these objectives can be met:

Merchandise Inventory

Jan. 1	Beginning Balance	52,800	Dec. 31	52,800
Dec. 31	Ending Balance	48,300		

Effect A   Effect B

Income Summary

Dec. 31		52,800	Dec. 31	48,300

In this example, merchandise inventory was $52,800 at the beginning of the year and $48,300 at the end of the year. Effect A removes the $52,800 from Merchandise Inventory, leaving a zero balance, and transfers it to Income Summary. In Income Summary, the $52,800 is in effect added to net purchases because, like expenses, the balance of the Purchases account is debited to Income Summary in a closing entry. Effect B establishes the ending balance of Merchandise Inventory, $48,300, and enters it as a credit in the Income Summary account. The credit entry in Income Summary has the effect of deducting the ending inventory from goods available for sale because both purchases and beginning inventory are entered on the debit side. In other words, beginning merchandise inventory and purchases are debits to Income Summary, and ending merchandise inventory is a credit to Income Summary.

Keep these effects in mind while studying the work sheet for Fenwick Fashions Corporation shown in Exhibit 1. Each pair of columns in the work sheet and the closing entries are discussed below.

TRIAL BALANCE COLUMNS

The first step in the preparation of the work sheet is to enter the balances from the ledger accounts into the Trial Balance columns. You are already familiar with this procedure.

ADJUSTMENTS COLUMNS

The adjusting entries for Fenwick Fashions Corporation are entered in the Adjustments columns in the same way that they were for service companies. They involve insurance expired during the period (adjustment **a**), store and office supplies used during the period (adjustments **b** and **c**), the depreciation of building and office equipment (adjustments **d** and **e**), and accrued income taxes (adjustment **f**). No adjusting entry is made for merchandise inventory.

Exhibit 1. Work Sheet for Fenwick Fashions Corporation: Periodic Inventory System

Fenwick Fashions Corporation
Work Sheet
For the Year Ended December 31, 19xx

Account Name	Trial Balance Debit	Trial Balance Credit	Adjustments Debit	Adjustments Credit	Income Statement Debit	Income Statement Credit	Balance Sheet Debit	Balance Sheet Credit
Cash	29,410						29,410	
Accounts Receivable	42,400						42,400	
Merchandise Inventory	52,800				52,800	48,300	48,300	
Prepaid Insurance	17,400			(a) 5,800			11,600	
Store Supplies	2,600			(b) 1,540			1,060	
Office Supplies	1,840			(c) 1,204			636	
Land	4,500						4,500	
Building	20,260						20,260	
Accumulated Depreciation, Building		5,650		(d) 2,600				8,250
Office Equipment	8,600						8,600	
Accumulated Depreciation, Office Equipment		2,800		(e) 2,200				5,000
Accounts Payable		25,683						25,683
Common Stock		50,000						50,000
Retained Earnings		68,352						68,352
Dividends	20,000						20,000	
Sales		246,350				246,350		
Sales Returns and Allowances	2,750				2,750			
Sales Discounts	4,275				4,275			
Purchases	126,400				126,400			
Purchases Returns and Allowances		5,640				5,640		
Purchases Discounts		2,136				2,136		
Freight In	8,236				8,236			
Sales Salaries Expense	22,500				22,500			
Freight Out Expense	5,740				5,740			
Advertising Expense	10,000				10,000			
Office Salaries Expense	26,900				26,900			
	406,611	406,611						
Insurance Expense, Selling			(a) 1,600		1,600			
Insurance Expense, General			(a) 4,200		4,200			
Store Supplies Expense			(b) 1,540		1,540			
Office Supplies Expense			(c) 1,204		1,204			
Depreciation Expense, Building			(d) 2,600		2,600			
Depreciation Expense, Office Equipment			(e) 2,200		2,200			
Income Taxes Expense			(f) 5,000		5,000			
Income Taxes Payable				(f) 5,000				5,000
			18,344	18,344	277,945	302,426	186,766	162,285
Net Income					24,481			24,481
					302,426	302,426	186,766	186,766

After the adjusting entries are entered on the work sheet, the columns are totaled to prove that total debits equal total credits.

OMISSION OF ADJUSTED TRIAL BALANCE COLUMNS

These two columns, which appeared in the work sheet for a service company, can be omitted. They are optional and are used when there are many adjusting entries to record. When only a few adjusting entries are required, as is the case for Fenwick Fashions Corporation, these columns are not necessary and may be omitted to save time.

INCOME STATEMENT AND BALANCE SHEET COLUMNS

After the Trial Balance columns have been totaled, the adjustments entered, and the equality of the columns proved, the balances are extended to the Income Statement and Balance Sheet columns. Again, begin with the Cash account at the top of the work sheet and move sequentially down the work sheet, one account at a time, entering each account balance in the correct Income Statement or Balance Sheet column.

The "problem" extension here is in the Merchandise Inventory row. The beginning inventory balance of $52,800 (which is already in the trial balance) is extended to the debit column of the Income Statement columns, as shown in Exhibit 1. This procedure has the effect of adding beginning inventory to net purchases because the Purchases account is also in the debit column of the Income Statement columns. The ending inventory balance of $48,300 (which is determined by the physical inventory and is not in the trial balance) is then inserted in the credit column of the Income Statement columns. This procedure has the effect of subtracting the ending inventory from goods available for sale in order to calculate the cost of goods sold. Finally, the ending merchandise inventory ($48,300) is inserted in the debit side of the Balance Sheet columns because it will appear on the balance sheet.

After all the items have been extended into the correct columns, the four columns are totaled. The net income or net loss is the difference between the debit and credit Income Statement columns. In this case, Fenwick Fashions Corporation has earned a net income of $24,481, which is extended to the credit side of the Balance Sheet columns. The four columns are then added to prove that total debits equal total credits.

ADJUSTING ENTRIES

The adjusting entries from the work sheet are now entered into the general journal and posted to the ledger, as they would be in a service company. Under the closing entry method, there is no difference in this procedure between a service company and a merchandising company.

CLOSING ENTRIES

The closing entries for Fenwick Fashions Corporation appear in Exhibit 2. Notice that Merchandise Inventory is credited for the amount of beginning inventory ($52,800) in the first entry and debited for the amount of the

Exhibit 2. Closing Entries for a Merchandising Concern: Periodic Inventory System

			General Journal			**Page 10**
Date			**Description**	**Post. Ref.**	**Debit**	**Credit**
19xx			*Closing entries:*			
Dec.	31		Income Summary		277,945	
			Merchandise Inventory			52,800
			Sales Returns and Allowances			2,750
			Sales Discounts			4,275
			Purchases			126,400
			Freight In			8,236
			Sales Salaries Expense			22,500
			Freight Out Expense			5,740
			Advertising Expense			10,000
			Office Salaries Expense			26,900
			Insurance Expense, Selling			1,600
			Insurance Expense, General			4,200
			Store Supplies Expense			1,540
			Office Supplies Expense			1,204
			Depreciation Expense, Building			2,600
			Depreciation Expense, Office Equipment			2,200
			Income Taxes Expense			5,000
			To close temporary expense and revenue accounts with debit balances and to remove the beginning inventory			
	31		Merchandise Inventory		48,300	
			Sales		246,350	
			Purchases Returns and Allowances		5,640	
			Purchases Discounts		2,136	
			Income Summary			302,426
			To close temporary expense and revenue accounts with credit balances and to establish the ending inventory			
	31		Income Summary		24,481	
			Retained Earnings			24,481
			To close the Income Summary account			
	31		Retained Earnings		20,000	
			Dividends			20,000
			To close the Dividends account			

ending inventory ($48,300) in the second entry, as shown on page 798. Otherwise, these closing entries are very similar to those for a service company except that the merchandising accounts also must be closed to Income Summary. All income statement accounts with debit balances, including the merchandising accounts of Sales Returns and Allowances, Sales Discounts, Purchases, and Freight In, are credited in the first entry. The total of these accounts ($277,945) equals the total of the debit column in the Income Statement columns of the work sheet. All income statement accounts with credit balances—Sales, Purchases Returns and Allowances, and Purchases Discounts—and ending Merchandise Inventory are debited in the second entry. The total of these accounts ($302,426) equals the total of the Income Statement credit column in the work sheet. The third and fourth entries are used to close the Income Summary account and transfer net income to Retained Earnings, and to close the Dividends account to Retained Earnings.

THE PERPETUAL INVENTORY SYSTEM

OBJECTIVE

2 *Prepare a work sheet and closing entries for a merchandising concern using the perpetual inventory system*

Under the perpetual inventory system, the Merchandise Inventory account is up to date at the end of the accounting period and therefore is not involved in the closing process. The reason for this is that purchases of merchandise are recorded directly in the Merchandise Inventory account and costs are transferred from the Merchandise Inventory account to the Cost of Goods Sold account as merchandise is sold. The work sheet for Fenwick Fashions Corporation, assuming the company uses the perpetual inventory system, is shown in Exhibit 3 on page 800. Note that the ending merchandise inventory is $48,300 in both the Trial Balance and the Balance Sheet columns.

The closing entries for Fenwick Fashions Corporation, assuming that the perpetual inventory system is used, are shown in Exhibit 4 on page 801. The Cost of Goods Sold account is closed to Income Summary along with the expense accounts because it has a debit balance. There are no entries to the Merchandise Inventory account.

Questions

1. Why is the handling of merchandise inventory at the end of the accounting period of special importance in the determination of net income under the periodic inventory system? What must be achieved in the account?

2. What are the principal differences between the work sheet for a merchandising company and that for a service company?

3. What are the principal differences in closing entries between a merchandising company using the periodic inventory system and one using the perpetual inventory system?

Exhibit 3. Work Sheet for Fenwick Fashions Corporation: Perpetual Inventory System

Fenwick Fashions Corporation
Work Sheet
For the Year Ended December 31, 19xx

Account Name	Trial Balance Debit	Trial Balance Credit	Adjustments Debit	Adjustments Credit	Income Statement Debit	Income Statement Credit	Balance Sheet Debit	Balance Sheet Credit
Cash	29,410						29,410	
Accounts Receivable	42,400						42,400	
Merchandise Inventory	48,300						48,300	
Prepaid Insurance	17,400			(a) 5,800			11,600	
Store Supplies	2,600			(b) 1,540			1,060	
Office Supplies	1,840			(c) 1,204			636	
Land	4,500						4,500	
Building	20,260						20,260	
Accumulated Depreciation, Building		5,650		(d) 2,600				8,250
Office Equipment	8,600						8,600	
Accumulated Depreciation, Office Equipment		2,800		(e) 2,200				5,000
Accounts Payable		25,683						25,683
Common Stock		50,000						50,000
Retained Earnings		68,352						68,352
Dividends	20,000						20,000	
Sales		246,350				246,350		
Sales Returns and Allowances	2,750				2,750			
Sales Discounts	4,275				4,275			
Cost of Goods Sold	123,124				123,124			
Freight In	8,236				8,236			
Sales Salaries Expense	22,500				22,500			
Freight Out Expense	5,740				5,740			
Advertising Expense	10,000				10,000			
Office Salaries Expense	26,900				26,900			
	398,835	398,835						
Insurance Expense, Selling			(a) 1,600		1,600			
Insurance Expense, General			(a) 4,200		4,200			
Store Supplies Expense			(b) 1,540		1,540			
Office Supplies Expense			(c) 1,204		1,204			
Depreciation Expense, Building			(d) 2,600		2,600			
Depreciation Expense, Office Equipment			(e) 2,200		2,200			
Income Taxes Expense			(f) 5,000		5,000			
Income Taxes Payable				(f) 5,000				5,000
			18,344	18,344	221,869	246,350	186,766	162,285
Net Income					24,481			24,481
					246,350	246,350	186,766	186,766

Exhibit 4. Closing Entries for a Merchandising Concern: Perpetual Inventory System

		General Journal			Page 10
Date		Description	Post. Ref.	Debit	Credit
19xx Dec.	31	*Closing entries:* Income Summary		221,869	
		Sales Returns and Allowances			2,750
		Sales Discounts			4,275
		Cost of Goods Sold			123,124
		Freight In			8,236
		Sales Salaries Expense			22,500
		Freight Out Expense			5,740
		Advertising Expense			10,000
		Office Salaries Expense			26,900
		Insurance Expense, Selling			1,600
		Insurance Expense, General			4,200
		Store Supplies Expense			1,540
		Office Supplies Expense			1,204
		Depreciation Expense, Building			2,600
		Depreciation Expense, Office Equipment			2,200
		Income Taxes Expense			5,000
		To close temporary expense and revenue accounts with debit balances			
	31	Sales		246,350	
		Income Summary			246,350
		To close temporary revenue account with credit balance			
	31	Income Summary		24,481	
		Retained Earnings			24,481
		To close the Income Summary account			
	31	Retained Earnings		20,000	
		Dividends			20,000
		To close the Dividends			

Exercises

EB-1.

L O 1 *Preparation of Closing Entries: Periodic Inventory System*

Selected December 31, 19xx account balances of the Mill Pond General Store for the year ended December 31, 19xx appear below:

Account Name	Debit	Credit
Sales		297,000
Sales Returns and Allowances	11,000	
Sales Discounts	4,200	
Purchases	114,800	
Purchases Returns and Allowances		1,800
Purchases Discounts		2,200
Freight In	5,600	
Selling Expenses	48,500	
General and Administrative Expenses	37,200	
Income Taxes Expense	15,000	

Beginning merchandise inventory was $26,000, and ending merchandise inventory is $22,000. Prepare closing entries, assuming that Mill Pond General Store declared and paid dividends of $34,000 during the year.

EB-2.

L O 2 *Preparation of Closing Entries: Perpetual Inventory System*

Selected December 31, 19xx account balances of Certin Company for the year ended December 31, 19xx appear below:

Account Name	Debit	Credit
Sales		297,000
Sales Returns and Allowances	15,200	
Cost of Goods Sold	113,000	
Freight In	5,600	
Selling Expenses	48,500	
General and Administrative Expenses	37,200	
Income Taxes Expense	15,000	

Prepare closing entries, assuming that Certin Company declared and paid dividends of $40,000 during the year.

Problems

B-1.

L O 1 *Work Sheet, Financial Statements, and Closing Entries for a Merchandising Company: Periodic Inventory System*

The trial balance shown at the top of page 803 was taken from the ledger of Metzler Music Store, Inc. at the end of its annual accounting period.

REQUIRED

1. Enter the trial balance on a work sheet, and complete the work sheet using the following information: ending merchandise inventory, $99,681; ending store supplies inventory, $912; unexpired prepaid insurance, $600; estimated depreciation on store equipment, $12,900; sales salaries payable, $240; accrued utility expense, $450; and estimated income taxes expense, $15,000.
2. Prepare an income statement, a statement of retained earnings, and a balance sheet. Sales Salaries Expense; Other Selling Expenses; Store Supplies Expense; and Depreciation Expense, Store Equipment are all selling expenses.
3. From the work sheet, prepare the closing entries.

Metzler Music Store, Inc.
Trial Balance
November 30, 19x4

Cash	$ 18,075	
Accounts Receivable	27,840	
Merchandise Inventory	88,350	
Store Supplies	5,733	
Prepaid Insurance	4,800	
Store Equipment	111,600	
Accumulated Depreciation, Store Equipment		$ 46,800
Accounts Payable		36,900
Common Stock		30,000
Retained Earnings		95,982
Dividends	36,000	
Sales		306,750
Sales Returns and Allowances	2,961	
Purchases	189,600	
Purchases Returns and Allowances		58,965
Purchases Discounts		4,068
Freight In	6,783	
Sales Salaries Expense	64,050	
Rent Expense	10,800	
Other Selling Expenses	7,842	
Utility Expense	5,031	
	$579,465	$579,465

B-2.

L O 2 *Work Sheet, Financial Statements, and Closing Entries for a Merchandising Company: Perpetual Inventory System*

The year-end trial balance shown below was taken from the ledger of Kirby Party Costumes Corporation at the end of its annual accounting period on June 30, 19x2.

Kirby Party Costumes Corporation
Trial Balance
June 30, 19x2

Cash	$ 7,050	
Accounts Receivable	24,830	
Merchandise Inventory	88,900	
Store Supplies	3,800	
Prepaid Insurance	4,800	
Store Equipment	151,300	
Accumulated Depreciation, Store Equipment		$ 25,500
Accounts Payable		38,950
Common Stock		50,000
Retained Earnings		111,350
Dividends	24,000	
Sales		475,250
Sales Returns and Allowances	4,690	
Cost of Goods Sold	231,840	
Freight In	10,400	
Sales Salaries Expense	64,600	
Rent Expense	48,000	
Other Selling Expenses	32,910	
Utility Expense	3,930	
	$701,050	$701,050

1. Enter the trial balance on a work sheet, and complete the work sheet using the following information: (a) ending store supplies inventory, $550; (b) expired insurance, $2,400; (c) estimated depreciation on store equipment, $5,000; (d) sales salaries payable, $650; (e) accrued utility expense, $100; and (f) estimated income taxes expense, $20,000.
2. Prepare an income statement, a statement of retained earnings, and a balance sheet. Sales Salaries Expense; Other Selling Expenses; Store Supplies Expense; and Depreciation Expense, Store Equipment are to be considered selling expenses.
3. From the work sheet, prepare closing entries.

Special-Purpose Journals

1. Explain the objectives and uses of special-purpose journals.
2. Construct and use the following types of special-purpose journals: sales journal, purchases journal, cash receipts journal, cash payments journal, and others as needed.
3. Explain the purposes and relationships of controlling accounts and subsidiary ledgers.

Companies that are faced with large numbers of transactions, perhaps hundreds or thousands every week or every day, must have a more efficient and economical way of recording transactions in the journal and posting entries to the ledger. The easiest approach is to group the company's typical transactions into common categories and use an input device called a special-purpose journal for each category. The objectives of special-purpose journals are efficiency, economy, and control. In addition, although manual special-purpose journals are used by companies that have not yet computerized their systems, the concepts underlying special-purpose journals also underlie the programs that drive computerized accounting systems.

TYPES OF SPECIAL-PURPOSE JOURNALS

OBJECTIVE

1 *Explain the objectives and uses of special-purpose journals*

Most business transactions—90 to 95 percent—fall into one of four categories. Each kind of transaction can be recorded in a special-purpose journal:

Transaction	Special-Purpose Journal	Posting Abbreviation
Sale of merchandise on credit	Sales journal	S
Purchase on credit	Purchases journal	P
Receipt of cash	Cash receipts journal	CR
Disbursement of cash	Cash payments journal	CP

The general journal is used to record transactions that do not fall into any of the special categories. For example, purchases returns and sales returns not involving cash and adjusting and closing entries are recorded in the general journal. (When transactions are posted from the general journal to the ledger accounts, the posting abbreviation used is **J**.)

Using special-purpose journals greatly reduces the work involved in entering and posting transactions. For example, instead of posting every debit and credit for each transaction, in most cases only column totals—the sum of many transactions—are posted. In addition, labor can be divided, with each journal assigned to a different employee. This division of labor is important in establishing good internal control, as we discussed in the chapter on the merchandising income statement and internal control.

SALES JOURNAL

OBJECTIVE

2 *Construct and use the following types of special-purpose journals: sales journal, purchases journal, cash receipts journal, cash payments journal, and others as needed*

Special-purpose journals are designed to record particular kinds of transactions. Thus, all transactions in a special-purpose journal result in debits and credits to the same accounts. The sales journal, for example, is designed to handle all credit sales. Cash sales are recorded in the cash receipts journal.

Exhibit 1 illustrates a page from a typical sales journal. Six sales transactions involving five customers are recorded in this sales journal. As each sale takes place, several copies of the sales invoice are made. The seller's accounting department uses one copy to make the entry in the sales journal. The date, the customer's name, the invoice number, the amount of the sale, and sometimes the credit terms are copied from the invoice. These data correspond to the columns of the sales journal.

Notice how the sales journal saves time:

1. Only one line is needed to record each transaction. Each entry consists of a debit to each customer in Accounts Receivable. The corresponding credit to Sales is understood.
2. The account names do not have to be written out because each entry automatically is debited to Accounts Receivable and credited to Sales.
3. No explanations are necessary because the function of the special-purpose journal is to record just one type of transaction. Only credit sales are recorded in the sales journal. Sales for cash are recorded in the cash receipts journal.
4. Only one amount—the total credit sales for the month—has to be posted. It is posted twice: once as a debit to Accounts Receivable and once as a credit to Sales. You can see the time this saves in Exhibit 1, with just six transactions. Imagine the time saved when there are hundreds of sales transactions.

Controlling Accounts and Subsidiary Ledgers   Every entry in the sales journal represents a debit to a customer's account in Accounts Receivable. In previous chapters, we've posted all of these transactions to Accounts Receivable. However, a single entry in Accounts Receivable does not tell us how much each customer has bought and paid for or how much each customer still owes. In practice, almost all companies that sell to customers on credit keep an individual accounts receivable record for each customer. If the company has 6,000 credit customers, there are 6,000 accounts receivable. To include all these accounts in the ledger with the other asset, liability, and stockholders' equity accounts would make it very bulky. Consequently, most companies take the individual customers' accounts out of the general ledger and place them in a separate ledger, called a subsidiary ledger. In the accounts receivable subsidiary ledger, customers' accounts are filed either alphabetically or numerically (if account numbers are used).

When a company puts its individual customers' accounts in an accounts receivable subsidiary ledger, it still must maintain an Accounts Receivable

OBJECTIVE

3 *Explain the purposes and relationships of controlling accounts and subsidiary ledgers*

Exhibit 1. Sales Journal and Related Ledger Accounts

				Sales Journal						Page 1

Date		Account Debited	Invoice Number	Post. Ref.	Amount (Debit/Credit Accounts Receivable/ Sales)
July	1	Peter Clark	721	✓	750
	5	Georgetta Jones	722	✓	500
	8	Eugene Cumberland	723	✓	335
	12	Maxwell Gertz	724	✓	1,165
	18	Peter Clark	725	✓	1,225
	25	Michael Powers	726	✓	975
					4,950
					(114/411)

Post total at end of month.

Accounts Receivable 114

Date	Post. Ref.	Debit	Credit	Balance Debit	Balance Credit
July 31	S1	4,950		4,950	

Sales 411

Date	Post. Ref.	Debit	Credit	Balance Debit	Balance Credit
July 31	S1		4,950		4,950

account in the general ledger. The Accounts Receivable account "controls" the subsidiary ledger and is called a controlling account, or *control account*. It controls in the sense that the total of the individual account balances in the subsidiary ledger must equal the balance in the controlling account. The balance of this account on the balance sheet date appears as Accounts Receivable on the balance sheet. In transactions that involve accounts receivable, such as credit sales, entries must be posted to the individual customers' accounts every day. Postings to the controlling account in the general ledger are made at least once a month. If a wrong amount has been posted, the sum of all the customers' account balances in the subsidiary accounts receivable ledger will not equal the balance of the Accounts Receivable controlling account in the general ledger. When these amounts do not match, the accountant knows there is an error to find and correct.

Exhibit 2 shows how controlling accounts work. The single controlling account in the general ledger summarizes all the individual accounts in the subsidiary ledger. Because the individual accounts are recorded daily and the controlling account is posted monthly, the total of the individual accounts in the accounts receivable ledger equals the controlling account only after the monthly posting. The monthly trial balance is prepared using only the general ledger accounts.

Most companies use an accounts payable subsidiary ledger as well. It is also possible to use a subsidiary ledger for almost any account in the general ledger for which management wants a specific account for individual items,

Exhibit 2. Relationship of Sales Journal, General Ledger, and Accounts Receivable Subsidiary Ledger and the Posting Procedure

Sales Journal   Page 1

Date		Account Debited	Invoice Number	Post. Ref.	Amount (Debit/Credit Accounts Receivable/ Sales)
July	1	Peter Clark	721	✓	750
	5	Georgetta Jones	722	✓	500
	8	Eugene Cumberland	723	✓	335
	12	Maxwell Gertz	724	✓	1,165
	18	Peter Clark	725	✓	1,225
	25	Michael Powers	726	✓	975
					4,950
					(114/411)

Post individual amounts **daily** to subsidiary ledger accounts.

Post total at **end of month** to general ledger accounts.

Accounts Receivable Subs. Ledger

Peter Clark

Date		Post. Ref.	Debit	Credit	Balance
July	1	S1	750		750
	18	S1	1,225		1,975

Eugene Cumberland

Date		Post. Ref.	Debit	Credit	Balance
July	8	S1	335		335

Continue posting to Maxwell Gertz, Georgetta Jones, and Michael Powers.

General Ledger

Accounts Receivable   114

Date		Post. Ref.	Debit	Credit	Balance Debit	Balance Credit
July	31	S1	4,950		4,950	

Sales   411

Date		Post. Ref.	Debit	Credit	Balance Debit	Balance Credit
July	31	S1		4,950		4,950

such as Merchandise Inventory, Notes Receivable, Temporary Investments, and Equipment.

Summary of the Sales Journal Procedure   Exhibit 2 illustrates the procedure for using a sales journal:

1. Enter each sales invoice in the sales journal on a single line. Record the date, the customer's name, the invoice number, and the amount. No column is needed for the terms if the terms on all sales are the same.

2. At the end of each day, post each individual sale to the customer's account in the accounts receivable subsidiary ledger. As each sale is posted, place a check-mark (or customer account number, if used) in the Post. Ref. (posting reference) column of the sales journal to indicate that it has been posted. In the Post. Ref. column of each customer's account, place an **S** and the sales journal page number (**S1** means Sales Journal—Page 1) to indicate the source of the entry.

3. At the end of the month, sum the Amount column in the sales journal to determine the total credit sales, and post the total to the general ledger accounts (debit Accounts Receivable and credit Sales). Place the numbers of the accounts debited and credited beneath the total in the sales journal to indicate that this step has been completed. In the general ledger, indicate the source of the entry in the Post. Ref. column of each account.

4. Verify the accuracy of the posting by adding the account balances of the accounts receivable subsidiary ledger and by matching the total with the Accounts Receivable controlling account balance in the general ledger. You can do this by listing the accounts in a schedule of accounts receivable, like the one shown in Exhibit 3, in the order in which the accounts are maintained. This step is performed after collections on account in the cash receipts journal have been posted.

Sales Taxes   Other columns, such as a column for credit terms, can be added to the sales journal. The nature of the company's business determines whether they are needed.

Many cities and states require retailers to collect a sales tax from their customers and periodically remit the total collected to the city or state. In this case, an additional column is needed in the sales journal to record the credit to Sales Taxes Payable on credit sales. The form of the entry is shown in Exhibit 4. The procedure for posting to the ledger is exactly the same as described above except that the total of the Sales Taxes Payable column must be posted as a credit to the Sales Taxes Payable account at the end of the month.

Most companies also make cash sales. Cash sales usually are recorded in a column of the cash receipts journal, as discussed later in this appendix.

PURCHASES JOURNAL

The purchases journal is used to record purchases on credit. It can take the form of either a single-column journal or a multicolumn journal. In the

Exhibit 3. Schedule of Accounts Receivable

Mitchell's Used Car Sales Schedule of Accounts Receivable July 31, 19xx	
Peter Clark	$1,975
Eugene Cumberland	335
Maxwell Gertz	1,165
Georgetta Jones	500
Michael Powers	975
Total Accounts Receivable	$4,950

Exhibit 4. Section of a Sales Journal with a Column for Sales Taxes

Sales Journal						Page 2
				Debit	**Credits**	
Date	**Account Debited**	**Invoice Number**	**Post. Ref.**	**Accounts Receivable**	**Sales Taxes Payable**	**Sales**
Aug. 1	Ralph P. Hake	727	✓	206	6	200

single-column journal, shown in Exhibit 5, only credit purchases of merchandise for resale to customers are recorded. This kind of transaction is recorded with a debit to Purchases and a credit to Accounts Payable. When the single-column purchases journal is used, credit purchases of things other than merchandise are recorded in the general journal. Cash purchases are never recorded in the purchases journal; they are recorded in the cash payments journal, which we explain later.

Like the Accounts Receivable account, the Accounts Payable account in the general ledger is used by most companies as a controlling account. So that the company knows how much it owes each supplier, it keeps a separate account for each supplier in an accounts payable subsidiary ledger. The process described above for using the accounts receivable subsidiary ledger and general ledger controlling account also applies to the accounts payable subsidiary ledger and general ledger controlling account. Thus, the total of the separate accounts in the accounts payable subsidiary ledger should equal the balance of the Accounts Payable controlling account in the general ledger. Here, too, the monthly total of the credit purchases posted to the individual accounts each day must equal the total credit purchases posted to the controlling account each month.

The procedure for using the purchases journal is much like that for using the sales journal:

1. Enter each purchase invoice in the purchases journal on a single line. Record the date, the supplier's name, the invoice date, the terms (if given), and the amount. It is not necessary to record the shipping terms in the terms column because they do not affect the payment date.
2. At the end of each day, post each individual purchase to the supplier's account in the accounts payable subsidiary ledger. As each purchase is posted, place a checkmark in the Post. Ref. column of the purchases journal to show that it has been posted. Also place a **P** and the page number in the purchases journal (**P1** stands for Purchases Journal—Page 1) in the Post. Ref. column of each supplier's account to show the source of the entry.
3. At the end of the month, sum the Amount column, and post the total to the general ledger accounts (a debit to Purchases and a credit to Accounts Payable). Place the numbers of the accounts debited and credited beneath the totals in the purchases journal to show that this step has been carried out.
4. Check the accuracy of the posting by adding the balances of the accounts payable subsidiary ledger accounts and matching the total with the balance of the Accounts Payable controlling account in the general ledger. This step can be done by preparing a schedule of accounts payable subsidiary ledger.

The single-column purchases journal can be expanded to record credit purchases of items other than merchandise by adding separate debit

Exhibit 5. Relationship of Single-Column Purchases Journal to the General Ledger and the Accounts Payable Subsidiary Ledger

Purchases Journal — Page 1

Date		Account Credited	Date of Invoice	Terms	Post. Ref.	Amount (Debit/Credit Purchases/ Accounts Payable)
July	1	Jones Chevrolet	7/1	2/10, n/30	✓	2,500
	2	Marshall Ford	7/2	2/15, n/30	✓	300
	3	Dealer Sales	7/3	n/30	✓	700
	12	Thomas Auto	7/11	n/30	✓	1,400
	17	Dealer Sales	7/17	2/10, n/30	✓	3,200
	19	Thomas Auto	7/17	n/30	✓	1,100
						9,200
						(511/212)

Post individual amounts **daily.**   Post total at **end of month.**

Accounts Payable Subs. Ledger

Dealer Sales

Date		Post. Ref.	Debit	Credit	Balance
July	3	P1		700	700
	17	P1		3,200	3,900

Jones Chevrolet

Date		Post. Ref.	Debit	Credit	Balance
July	1	P1		2,500	2,500

Continue posting to Marshall Ford and Thomas Auto.

General Ledger

Accounts Payable — 212

Date		Post. Ref.	Debit	Credit	Balance Debit	Balance Credit
July	31	P1		9,200		9,200

Purchases — 511

Date		Post. Ref.	Debit	Credit	Balance Debit	Balance Credit
July	31	P1	9,200		9,200	

columns for other accounts that are used often. For example, the multicolumn purchases journal in Exhibit 6 has columns for Freight In, Store Supplies, Office Supplies, and Other Accounts. Here, the total credits to Accounts Payable ($9,637) equal the total debits to Purchases, Freight In, Store Supplies, Office Supplies, and Parts ($9,200 + $50 + $145 + $42 + $200). Again, the individual transactions in the Accounts Payable column are posted regularly to the accounts payable subsidiary ledger, and the totals of each column in the journal are posted monthly to the correct general ledger accounts.

Exhibit 6. A Multicolumn Purchases Journal

						Credit	Debits				Other Accounts		
Date	Account Credited	Date of Invoice	Terms	Post. Ref.		Accounts Payable	Purchases	Freight In	Store Supplies	Office Supplies	Account	Post. Ref.	Amount
July 1	Jones Chevrolet	7/1	2/10, n/30	✓		2,500	2,500						
2	Marshall Ford	7/2	2/15, n/30	✓		300	300						
2	Shelby Car Delivery	7/2	n/30	✓		50		50					
3	Dealer Sales	7/3	n/30	✓		700	700						
12	Thomas Auto	7/11	n/30	✓		1,400	1,400						
17	Dealer Sales	7/17	2/10, n/30	✓		3,200	3,200						
19	Thomas Auto	7/17	n/30	✓		1,100	1,100						
25	Osborne Supply	7/21	n/10	✓		187			145	42			
28	Auto Supply	7/28	n/10	✓		200					Parts	120	200
						9,637	9,200	50	145	42			200
						(212)	(511)	(514)	(132)	(133)			(✓)

Purchases Journal — Page 1

CASH RECEIPTS JOURNAL

All transactions involving receipts of cash are recorded in the cash receipts journal. Examples of these transactions are cash from cash sales, cash from credit customers in payment of their accounts, and cash from other sources. The cash receipts journal must have several columns because, although all cash receipts are alike in that they require a debit to Cash, they are different in that they require a variety of credit entries. The Other Accounts column is used to record credits to accounts not specifically represented by a column. The account numbers are entered in the Post. Ref. column and the amounts are posted daily to the appropriate account in the general ledger.

The cash receipts journal illustrated in Exhibit 7 is based on the following selected transactions for July:

July 1   Henry Mitchell invested $20,000 in exchange for common stock.
    5   Sold a used car for $1,200 cash.
    8   Collected $500 less a 2 percent sales discount from Georgetta Jones.
   13   Sold a used car for $1,400 cash.
   16   Collected $750 from Peter Clark.
   19   Sold a used car for $1,000 cash.
   20   Sold some equipment not used in the business for $500 cash. The carrying value of the equipment was $500.
   24   Signed a note at the bank for a loan of $5,000.
   26   Sold a used car for $1,600 cash.
   28   Collected partial payment of $600 less a 2 percent sales discount from Peter Clark.

The cash receipts journal shown in Exhibit 7 has three debit columns and three credit columns. The three debit columns are as follows:

1. *Cash* Each entry must have an amount in this column because each transaction must be a receipt of cash.

Exhibit 7. Relationship of the Cash Receipts Journal to the General Ledger and the Accounts Receivable Subsidiary Ledger

Cash Receipts Journal

Page 1

Date		Account Debited/Credited	Post. Ref.	Debits — Cash	Debits — Sales Discounts	Debits — Other Accounts	Credits — Accounts Receivable	Credits — Sales	Credits — Other Accounts
July	1	Common Stock	311	20,000					20,000
	5	Sales		1,200				1,200	
	8	Georgetta Jones	✓	490	10		500		
	13	Sales		1,400				1,400	
	16	Peter Clark	✓	750			750		
	19	Sales		1,000				1,000	
	20	Equipment	151	500					500
	24	Notes Payable	213	5,000					5,000
	26	Sales		1,600				1,600	
	28	Peter Clark	✓	588	12		600		
				32,528	22		1,850	5,200	25,500
				(111)	(412)		(114)	(411)	(✓)

Post individual amounts in Accounts Receivable Subsidiary Ledger columns **daily**.

Post totals at end of month.

Total not posted.

Post individual amounts in Other Accounts column **daily**.

General Ledger

Cash 111

Date	Post. Ref.	Debit	Credit	Balance Debit	Balance Credit
July 31	CR1	32,528		32,528	

Accounts Receivable 114

Date	Post. Ref.	Debit	Credit	Balance Debit	Balance Credit
July 31	S1	4,950		4,950	
31	CR1		1,850	3,100	

Equipment 151

Date	Post. Ref.	Debit	Credit	Balance Debit	Balance Credit
Bal.				500	
July 20	CR1		500	—	

Accounts Receivable Subsidiary Ledger

Peter Clark

Date	Post. Ref.	Debit	Credit	Balance
July 1	S1	750		750
16	CR1		750	—
18	S1	1,225		1,225
28	CR1		600	625

Georgetta Jones

Date	Post. Ref.	Debit	Credit	Balance
July 5	S1	500		500
8	CR1		500	—

Continue posting to Notes Payable and Common Stock.

Continue posting to Sales and Sales Discounts.

2. *Sales Discounts* This company allows a 2 percent discount for prompt payment. Therefore, it is useful to have a column for sales discounts. Notice that in the transactions of July 8 and 28, the debits to Cash and Sales Discounts equal the credits to Accounts Receivable.
3. *Other Accounts* The Other Accounts column (sometimes called *Sundry Accounts*) is used for transactions that involve both a debit to Cash and a debit to some account other than Sales Discounts.

These are the credit columns:

1. *Accounts Receivable* This column is used to record collections on account from customers. The customer's name is written in the Account Debited/Credited column so that the payment can be entered in the corresponding account in the accounts receivable subsidiary ledger. Posting to the individual accounts receivable accounts is usually done daily so that each customer's account balance is up to date.
2. *Sales* This column is used to record all cash sales during the month. Retail firms that use cash registers would make an entry at the end of each day for the total sales from each cash register for that day. The debit, of course, is in the Cash debit column.
3. *Other Accounts* This column is used for the credit portion of any entry that is neither a cash collection from accounts receivable nor a cash sale. The name of the account to be credited is indicated in the Account Debited/Credited column. For example, the transactions of July 1, 20, and 24 involve credits to accounts other than Accounts Receivable or Sales. These individual postings should be done daily (or weekly if there are just a few of them). If a company finds that it consistently is crediting a certain account in the Other Accounts column, it can add another credit column to the cash receipts journal for that particular account.

The procedure for posting the cash receipts journal, shown in Exhibit 7, is as follows:

1. Post the Accounts Receivable column daily to each individual account in the accounts receivable subsidiary ledger. The amount credited to the customer's account is the same as that credited to Accounts Receivable. A checkmark in the Post. Ref. column of the cash receipts journal indicates that the amount has been posted, and a **CR1** (Cash Receipts Journal—Page 1) in the Post. Ref. column of each subsidiary ledger account indicates the source of the entry.
2. Post the debits/credits in the Other Accounts columns daily, or at convenient short intervals during the month, to the general ledger accounts. Write the account number in the Post. Ref. column of the cash receipts journal as the individual items are posted to indicate that the posting has been done, and write **CR1** in the Post. Ref. column of each subsidiary ledger account to indicate the source of the entry.
3. At the end of the month, total the columns in the cash receipts journal. The sum of the Debits column totals must equal the sum of the Credits column totals:

Debits Column Totals		Credits Column Totals	
Cash	$32,528	Accounts Receivable	$ 1,850
Sales Discounts	22	Sales	5,200
Other Accounts	0	Other Accounts	25,500
Total Debits	$32,550	Total Credits	$32,550

This step is called *crossfooting*—a procedure we encountered earlier.

4. Post the Debits column totals as follows:
    a. *Cash* Posted as a debit to the Cash account.
    b. *Sales Discounts* Posted as a debit to the Sales Discounts account.
5. Post the Credits column totals as follows:
    a. *Accounts Receivable* Posted as a credit to the Accounts Receivable controlling account.
    b. *Sales* Posted as a credit to the Sales account.
6. Write the account numbers below each column in the cash receipts journal as they are posted to indicate that this step has been completed. A **CR1** is written in the Post. Ref. column of each account in the general ledger to indicate the source of the entry.
7. Notice that the Other Accounts column totals are not posted because each entry was posted separately when the transaction occurred. The individual accounts were posted in step **2.** Place a checkmark at the bottom of each column to show that postings in that column have been made and that the total is not posted.

CASH PAYMENTS JOURNAL

All transactions involving payments of cash are recorded in the cash payments journal (also called the *cash disbursements journal*). Examples of these transactions are cash purchases and payments of obligations resulting from earlier purchases on credit. The form of the cash payments journal is much like that of the cash receipts journal.

The cash payments journal illustrated in Exhibit 8 is based on the following selected transactions of Mitchell's Used Car Sales in July:

July 2 Issued check no. 101 for merchandise (a used car) from Sondra Tidmore, $400.

6 Issued check no. 102 for newspaper advertising in the *Daily Journal*, $200.

8 Issued check no. 103 for one month's land and building rent to Siviglia Agency, $250.

11 Issued check no. 104 to Jones Chevrolet for July 1 invoice (recorded in the purchases journal in Exhibit 5), $2,500 less 2 percent purchases discount.

16 Issued check no. 105 to Charles Kuntz, a salesperson, for his salary, $600.

17 Issued check no. 106 to Marshall Ford for July 2 invoice (recorded in the purchases journal in Exhibit 5), $300 less 2 percent purchases discount.

24 Issued check no. 107 to Grabow & Company for two-year insurance policy, $480.

27 Issued check no. 108 to Dealer Sales for July 17 invoice (recorded in the purchases journal in Exhibit 5), $3,200 less 2 percent purchases discount.

30 Purchased office equipment for $400 and service equipment for $500 from A&B Equipment Company. Issued check no. 109 for the total amount.

31 Purchased land for $15,000 from Burns Real Estate. Issued check no. 110 for $5,000 and note payable for $10,000.

The cash payments journal shown in Exhibit 8 has three credit columns and two debit columns. The credit columns for the cash payments journal are as follows:

1. *Cash* Each entry must have an amount in this column because each transaction must involve a payment of cash.
2. *Purchases Discounts* When purchases discounts are taken, they are recorded in this column.
3. *Other Accounts* This column is used to record credits to accounts other than Cash or Purchases Discounts. Notice that the July 31 transaction shows a purchase of Land for $15,000, with a check for $5,000 and a note payable for $10,000.

Exhibit 8. Relationship of the Cash Payments Journal to the General Ledger and the Accounts Payable Subsidiary Ledger

Cash Payments Journal Page 1

| | | | | | | Credits | | | Debits | |
Date	Ck. No.	Payee	Account Credited/Debited	Post. Ref.	Cash	Purchases Discounts	Other Accounts	Accounts Payable	Other Accounts
July 2	101	Sondra Tidmore	Purchases	511	400				400
6	102	Daily Journal	Advertising Expense	612	200				200
8	103	Siviglia Agency	Rent Expense	631	250				250
11	104	Jones Chevrolet		✓	2,450	50		2,500	
16	105	Charles Kuntz	Salaries Expense	611	600				600
17	106	Marshall Ford		✓	294	6		300	
24	107	Grabow & Company	Prepaid Insurance	119	480				480
27	108	Dealer Sales		✓	3,136	64		3,200	
30	109	A&B Equipment Company	Office Equipment Service Equipment	144 146	900				400 500
31	110	Burns Real Estate	Notes Payable Land	213 141	5,000		10,000		15,000
					13,710	120	10,000	6,000	17,830
					(111)	(512)	(✓)	(212)	(✓)

Post individual amounts in Other Accounts column **daily**.

Post individual amounts in Accounts Payable Subsidiary Ledger column **daily**.

Post totals at end of month.

Totals not posted.

General Ledger

Cash 111

Date	Post. Ref.	Debit	Credit	Balance Debit	Balance Credit
July 31	CR1	32,528		32,528	
31	CP1		13,710	18,818	

Prepaid Insurance 119

Date	Post. Ref.	Debit	Credit	Balance Debit	Balance Credit
July 24	CP1	480		480	

Continue posting to Land, Office Equipment, Service Equipment, Notes Payable, Purchases, Salaries Expense, Advertising Expense, and Rent Expense

Continue posting to Purchases Discounts and Accounts Payable.

Accounts Payable Subsidiary Ledger

Jones Chevrolet

Date	Post. Ref.	Debit	Credit	Balance
July 1	P1		2,500	2,500
11	CP1	2,500		—

Marshall Ford

Date	Post. Ref.	Debit	Credit	Balance
July 2	P1		300	300
17	CP1	300		—

Dealer Sales

Date	Post. Ref.	Debit	Credit	Balance
July 3	P1		700	700
17	P1		3,200	3,900
27	CP1	3,200		700

The debit columns are as follows:

1. *Accounts Payable* This column total is used to record payments to suppliers that have extended credit to the company. Each supplier's name is written in the Payee column so that the payment can be entered in his or her account in the accounts payable subsidiary ledger.
2. *Other Accounts* Cash can be expended for many reasons. Thus, an Other Accounts or Sundry Accounts column is needed in the cash payments journal. The title of the account to be debited is written in the Account Credited/Debited column, and the amount is entered in the Other Accounts debit column. If a company finds that a particular account appears often in the Other Accounts column, it can add another debit column to the cash payments journal.

The procedure for posting the cash payments journal, shown in Exhibit 8, is as follows:

1. Post the Accounts Payable column daily to each individual account in the accounts payable subsidiary ledger. Place a checkmark in the Post. Ref. column of the cash payments journal to indicate that the posting has been made.
2. Post the debits/credits in the Other Accounts debit/credit columns to the general ledger daily or at convenient short intervals during the month. Write the account number in the Post. Ref. column of the cash payments journal as the individual items are posted to indicate that the posting has been completed and **CP1** (Cash Payments Journal—Page 1) in the Post. Ref. column of each ledger account.
3. At the end of the month, the columns are footed and crossfooted. That is, the sum of the Credits column totals must equal the sum of the Debits column totals, as follows:

Credits Column Totals		**Debits Column Totals**	
Cash	$13,710	Accounts Payable	$ 6,000
Purchases Discounts	120	Other Accounts	17,830
Other Accounts	10,000	Total Debits	$23,830
Total Credits	$23,830		

4. Post the column totals for Cash, Purchases Discounts, and Accounts Payable at the end of the month to their respective accounts in the general ledger. Write the account number below each column in the cash payments journal as it is posted to indicate that this step has been completed and CP1 in the Post. Ref. column of each ledger account. Place a checkmark under the total of each Other Accounts column in the cash payments journal to indicate that the postings in the column have been made and that the total is not posted.

GENERAL JOURNAL

Transactions that do not involve sales, purchases, cash receipts, or cash payments should be recorded in the general journal. Usually, there are only a few of these transactions. The two examples that follow require entries that do not fit in a special-purpose journal: a return of merchandise bought on account and an allowance from a supplier for credit. Adjusting and closing entries also are recorded in the general journal.

July 25   Returned one of the two used cars purchased on credit from Thomas Auto on July 12, $700 credit.

26   Agreed to give Maxwell Gertz a $35 allowance on his account because a tire blew out on the car he purchased.

Exhibit 9. Transactions Recorded in the General Journal

		General Journal			Page 1
Date		Description	Post. Ref.	Debit	Credit
July	25	Accounts Payable, Thomas Auto Purchases Returns and Allowances Returned used car for credit; invoice date: 7/11	212/✓ 513	700	700
	26	Sales Returns and Allowances Accounts Receivable, Maxwell Gertz Allowance for faulty tire	413 114/✓	35	35

These entries are shown in Exhibit 9. Notice that the entries include a debit or a credit to a controlling account (Accounts Payable or Accounts Receivable). The name of the customer or supplier also is given here. When this kind of debit or credit is made to a controlling account in the general journal, the entry must be posted twice: once in the controlling account and once in the individual account in the subsidiary ledger. This procedure keeps the subsidiary ledger equal to the controlling account. Notice that the July 26 transaction is posted by a debit to Sales Returns and Allowances in the general ledger (shown by the account number 413), a credit to the Accounts Receivable controlling account in the general ledger (account number 114), and a credit to the Maxwell Gertz account in the accounts receivable subsidiary ledger (checkmark).

THE FLEXIBILITY OF SPECIAL-PURPOSE JOURNALS

Special-purpose journals reduce and simplify the work in accounting and allow for the division of labor. These journals should be designed to fit the business in which they are used. As noted earlier, if certain accounts show up often in the Other Accounts column of a journal, it is a good idea to add a column for those accounts when a new page of a special-purpose journal is prepared. Also, if certain transactions appear repeatedly in the general journal, it is a good idea to set up a new special-purpose journal. For example, if Mitchell's Used Car Sales finds that it often gives allowances to customers, it may want to set up a sales returns and allowances journal specifically for these transactions. Sometimes a purchases returns and allowances journal is in order. In short, special-purpose journals should be designed to take care of the kinds of transactions a company commonly encounters.

Questions

1. How do special-purpose journals save time in entering and posting transactions?
2. Long Transit had 1,700 sales on credit during the current month.
   a. If the firm uses a two-column general journal to record sales, how many times will the word *Sales* be written?

b. How many postings to the Sales account will have to be made?

c. If the firm uses a sales journal, how many times will the word *Sales* be written?

d. How many postings to the Sales account will have to be made?

3. What is the purpose of the Accounts Receivable controlling account? What is its relationship to the accounts receivable subsidiary ledger?

4. Why are the cash receipts journal and cash payments journal crossfooted? When is this step performed?

5. A company has the following numbers of accounts with balances: 18 asset accounts, including the Accounts Receivable account but not the individual customers' accounts; 200 customer accounts; 8 liability accounts, including the Accounts Payable account but not the individual creditors' accounts; 100 creditor accounts; and 35 stockholders' equity accounts, including income statement accounts—a total of 361 accounts. How many accounts in total would appear in the general ledger?

Exercises

EC-1.

L O 1 *Matching Transactions to Special-Purpose Journals*

A company uses a single-column sales journal, a single-column purchases journal, a cash receipts journal, a cash payments journal, and a general journal. In which journal would each of the following transactions be recorded?

1. Sold merchandise on credit
2. Sold merchandise for cash
3. Gave a customer credit for merchandise purchased on credit and returned
4. Paid a creditor
5. Paid office salaries
6. Customer paid for merchandise previously purchased on credit
7. Recorded adjusting and closing entries
8. Purchased merchandise on credit
9. Purchased sales department supplies on credit
10. Purchased office equipment for cash
11. Returned merchandise purchased on credit
12. Paid taxes

EC-2.

L O 1, 3 *Characteristics of Special-Purpose Journals*

Kua Corporation uses a single-column sales journal, a single-column purchases journal, a cash receipts journal, a cash payments journal, and a general journal.

1. In which of the journals listed above would you expect to find the fewest transactions recorded?
2. At the end of the accounting period, to which account or accounts should the total of the sales journal be posted as a debit and/or credit?
3. At the end of the accounting period, to which account or accounts should the total of the purchases journal be posted as a debit and/or credit?
4. What two subsidiary ledgers probably would be associated with the journals listed above? From which journals would postings normally be made to each of the two subsidiary ledgers?
5. In which of the journals are adjusting and closing entries made?

Problems

C-1.

L O 2 *Cash Receipts and Cash Payments Journals*

The items below detail all cash transactions by Baylor Company for the month of July. The company uses multicolumn cash receipts and cash payments journals similar to those illustrated in this appendix.

July 1 The owner, Eugene Baylor, invested $50,000 cash and $24,000 in equipment in the business in exchange for common stock.

2 Paid rent to Leonard Agency, $600, with check no. 75.

3 Cash sales, $2,200.

6 Purchased store equipment for $5,000 from Gilmore Company, with check no. 76.

7 Purchased merchandise for cash, $6,500, from Pascual Company, with check no. 77.

July 8 Paid Audretti Company invoice, $1,800, less 2 percent discount, with check no. 78 (assume that a payable has already been recorded).

9 Paid advertising bill, $350, to WOSU, with check no. 79.

10 Cash sales, $3,910.

12 Received $800 on account from B. Erring.

13 Purchased used truck for cash, $3,520, from Pettit Company, with check no. 80.

19 Received $4,180 from Monroe Company, in settlement of a $4,000 note plus interest.

20 Received $1,078 ($1,100 less $22 cash discount) from Young Lee.

21 Declared and paid Baylor a dividend, $2,000, by issuing check no. 81.

23 Paid Dautley Company invoice, $2,500, less 2 percent discount, with check no. 82.

26 Paid Haywood Company for freight on merchandise received, $60, with check no. 83.

27 Cash sales, $4,800.

28 Paid C. Murphy for monthly salary, $1,400, with check no. 84.

31 Purchased land from N. Archibald for $20,000, paying $5,000 with check no. 85 and signing a note payable for $15,000.

REQUIRED

1. Enter the preceding transactions in the cash receipts and cash payments journals.
2. Foot and crossfoot the journals.

C-2.
L O 2, 3 *Purchases and General Journals*

The following items represent the credit transactions for McGarry Company during the month of August. The company uses a multicolumn purchases journal and a general journal similar to those illustrated in this appendix.

Aug. 2 Purchased merchandise from Alvarez Company, $1,400.

5 Purchased truck to be used in the business from Meriweather Company, $8,000.

8 Purchased office supplies from Daudridge Company, $400.

12 Purchased filing cabinets from Daudridge Company, $550.

14 Purchased merchandise, $1,400, and store supplies, $200, from Petrie Company.

17 Purchased store supplies from Alvarez Company, $100, and office supplies from Hollins Company, $50.

20 Purchased merchandise from Petrie Company, $1,472.

24 Purchased merchandise from Alvarez Company, $2,452; the $2,452 invoice total included shipping charges, $232.

26 Purchased office supplies from Daudridge Company, $150.

29 Purchased merchandise from Petrie Company, $290.

30 Returned defective merchandise purchased from Petrie Company on August 20 for full credit, $432.

REQUIRED

1. Enter the preceding transactions in the purchases journal and the general journal. Assume that all terms are n/30 and that invoice dates are the same as the transaction dates. Use Page 1 for all references.
2. Foot and crossfoot the purchases journal.
3. Open the following general ledger accounts: Store Supplies (116), Office Supplies (117), Trucks (142), Office Equipment (144), Accounts Payable (211), Purchases (611), Purchases Returns and Allowances (612), and Freight In (613). Open accounts payable subsidiary ledger accounts as needed. Post from the journals to the ledger accounts.

C-3.
L O 2, 3 *Comprehensive Use of Special-Purpose Journals*

During October, Sanchez Refrigeration Company completed the following transactions:

Oct. 1 Received merchandise from Keagy Company, $5,000, invoice dated September 29, terms 2/10, n/30, FOB shipping point.

3 Issued check no. 230 to Starbuck Realtors for October rent, $4,000.

4 Received merchandise from Passarelli Manufacturing, $10,800, invoice dated October 1, terms 2/10, n/30, FOB shipping point.

6 Issued check no. 231 to Hare Company for repairs, $1,120.

Oct. 7 Received $800 credit memorandum pertaining to October 4 shipment from Passarelli Manufacturing for return of unsatisfactory merchandise.

8 Issued check no. 232 to Gem Company for freight charges on October 1 and October 4 shipments, $368.

9 Sold merchandise to B. Kahn, $2,000, terms 1/10, n/30, invoice no. 725.

10 Issued check no. 233 to Keagy Company for full payment less discount.

11 Sold merchandise to L. Nomura for $2,500, terms 1/10, n/30, invoice no. 726.

12 Issued check no. 234 to Passarelli Manufacturing for balance of account less discount.

13 Purchased advertising on credit from WMBT, invoice dated October 13, $900, terms n/20.

15 Issued credit memorandum to L. Nomura for $100 for merchandise returned.

16 Cash sales for the first half of the month, $19,340. (To shorten this problem, cash sales are recorded only twice a month instead of daily, as they would be in actual practice.)

17 Sold merchandise to C. Jambois, $1,400, terms 1/10, n/30, invoice no. 727.

18 Received check from B. Kahn for October 9 sale less discount.

19 Received check from L. Nomura for balance of account less discount.

20 Received merchandise from Keagy Company, $5,600, invoice dated October 19, terms 2/10, n/30, FOB shipping point.

21 Received freight bill from Chacon Company for merchandise purchased on October 20, invoice dated October 19, $1,140, terms n/5.

22 Issued check no. 235 for advertising purchase of October 13.

24 Received merchandise from Passarelli Manufacturing, $7,200, invoice dated October 23, terms 2/10, n/30, FOB shipping point.

25 Issued check no. 236 for freight charge of October 21.

26 Sold merchandise to B. Kahn, $1,600, terms 1/10, n/30, invoice no. 728.

28 Received credit memorandum from Passarelli Manufacturing for defective merchandise received October 24, $600.

29 Issued check no. 237 to Makita Company for purchase of office equipment, $700.

30 Issued check no. 238 to Keagy Company for half of October 20 purchase less discount.

30 Received check in full from C. Jambois, no discount allowed.

31 Cash sales for the last half of the month, $23,120.

31 Issued check no. 239, payable to Payroll Account, for monthly sales salaries, $8,600.

REQUIRED

1. Prepare a sales journal, a multicolumn purchases journal, a cash receipts journal, a cash payments journal, and a general journal for Sanchez Refrigeration Company similar to the ones illustrated in this appendix. Use Page 1 for all journal references.

2. Open the following general ledger accounts: Cash (111), Accounts Receivable (112), Office Equipment (141), Accounts Payable (211), Sales (411), Sales Discounts (412), Sales Returns and Allowances (413), Purchases (511), Purchases Discounts (512), Purchases Returns and Allowances (513), Freight In (514), Sales Salaries Expense (521), Advertising Expense (522), Rent Expense (531), and Repairs Expense (532).

3. Open the following accounts receivable subsidiary ledger accounts: C. Jambois, B. Kahn, and L. Nomura.

4. Open the following accounts payable subsidiary ledger accounts: Chacon Company, Keagy Company, Passarelli Manufacturing, and WMBT.

5. Enter the transactions in the journals and post as appropriate.

6. Foot and crossfoot the journals, and make the end-of-month postings.

7. Prepare a trial balance of the general ledger and prove the control balances of Accounts Receivable and Accounts Payable by preparing schedules of accounts receivable and accounts payable.

Accounting for Unincorporated Businesses

LEARNING OBJECTIVES

1. Record the basic transactions affecting the owner's equity of a sole proprietorship.
2. Identify the major characteristics of a partnership.
3. Record investments of cash and of other assets by the partners in forming a partnership.
4. Compute and record the income or losses that partners share, based on stated ratios, capital balance ratios, and partners' salaries and interest.
5. Record the admission of a new partner.
6. Describe the implications of the withdrawal or death of a partner and of the liquidation of a partnership.

Accountants need to understand the three major forms of business organization: sole proprietorships, partnerships, and corporations. Accountants recognize each form as an economic unit separate from its owners, though legally only the corporation is considered separate from its owners. The main focus of this book has been on corporations. In this appendix, however, the focus is on sole proprietorships and partnerships.

ACCOUNTING FOR SOLE PROPRIETORSHIPS

OBJECTIVE

1 *Record the basic transactions affecting the owner's equity of a sole proprietorship*

A sole proprietorship is a business owned by one person. This business form gives the individual a means of controlling the business apart from his or her personal interests. Legally, however, the proprietorship is the same economic unit as the individual. The individual business owner receives all the profits or losses and is liable for all the obligations of the proprietorship. Proprietorships represent the largest number of businesses in the United States, but typically they are the smallest in size. The life of a proprietorship ends when the owner wishes it to or at the owner's death or incapacity.

When someone invests in his or her own company, the amount of the investment is recorded in a capital account. For example, the entry to record the initial investment of $10,000 by Clara Hooper in her new mail-order business would be:

Cash	10,000	
Clara Hooper, Capital		10,000
To record initial investment		
in sole proprietorship		

During the period, Clara will probably withdraw assets from the business for personal living expenses. Since legally there is no separation between the owner and the sole proprietorship, it is not necessary to make a formal declaration of a withdrawal, as would be required in the case of corporate dividends. The withdrawal of $500 by Clara is recorded as follows:

Clara Hooper, Withdrawals	500	
Cash		500
To record withdrawal of $500		
for personal use		

Revenue and expense accounts are closed out to Income Summary in the same way for sole proprietorships as they are for corporations. Income Summary, however, is closed to the Capital account instead of to Retained Earnings. For example, the closing entry, assuming a net income of $1,000, is as follows:

Income Summary	1,000	
Clara Hooper, Capital		1,000
To close Income Summary in		
a sole proprietorship		

Further, the Withdrawals account is closed to the Capital account as follows:

Clara Hooper, Capital	500	
Clara Hooper, Withdrawals		500
To close Withdrawals		

ACCOUNTING FOR PARTNERSHIPS

The Uniform Partnership Act, which has been adopted by a majority of the states, defines a partnership as "an association of two or more persons to carry on as co-owners of a business for profit." Normally, partnerships are formed when owners of small businesses wish to combine capital or managerial talents for some common business purpose.

PARTNERSHIP CHARACTERISTICS

OBJECTIVE

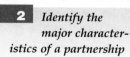

2 *Identify the major characteristics of a partnership*

Partnerships are treated as separate entities in accounting. They differ in many ways from the other forms of business. The next few paragraphs describe some of the important characteristics of a partnership.

VOLUNTARY ASSOCIATION

A partnership is a voluntary association of individuals rather than a legal entity in itself. Therefore, a partner is responsible under the law for his or her partners' business actions within the scope of the partnership. A partner also has unlimited liability for the debts of the partnership. Because of these potential liabilities, an individual must be allowed to choose the people who join the partnership.

PARTNERSHIP AGREEMENT

A partnership is easy to form. Two or more competent people simply agree to be partners in some common business purpose. This agreement is known as a partnership agreement. The partnership agreement does not have to be in writing; however, it is good business practice to have a written document that clearly states the details of the partnership. The contract should describe the name, location, and purpose of the business; the partners and their respective duties; the investments of each partner; the methods for distributing income and losses; and procedures for the admission and withdrawal of partners, the withdrawal of assets allowed each partner, and the liquidation (termination) of the business.

LIMITED LIFE

Because a partnership is formed by a contract between partners, it has a limited life: Anything that ends the contract dissolves the partnership. A partnership is dissolved when (1) a new partner is admitted, (2) a partner withdraws, (3) a partner goes bankrupt, (4) a partner is incapacitated (to the point at which he or she cannot perform as obligated), (5) a partner retires, (6) a partner dies, or (7) the terms set out in the partnership agreement come to pass (for example, when a major project is completed). The partnership agreement can be written to cover each of these situations, allowing the partnership to continue legally.

MUTUAL AGENCY

Each partner is an agent of the partnership within the scope of the business. Because of this mutual agency, any partner can bind the partnership to a business agreement as long as he or she acts within the scope of the company's normal operations. For example, a partner in a used-car business can bind the partnership through the purchase or sale of used cars. But this partner cannot bind the partnership to a contract for buying men's clothing or any other goods that are not related to the used-car business.

UNLIMITED LIABILITY

Each partner has personal unlimited liability for all the debts of the partnership. If a partnership is in poor financial condition and cannot pay its debts, the creditors first must satisfy their claims from the assets of the partnership. If the assets of the business are not enough to pay all debts, the creditors can seek payment from the personal assets of each partner. If a partner's personal assets are used up before the debts are paid, the creditors can claim additional assets from the remaining partners who are able to pay. Each partner, then, could be required by law to pay all the debts of the partnership.

CO-OWNERSHIP OF PARTNERSHIP PROPERTY

When individuals invest property in a partnership, they give up the right to their separate use of the property. The property becomes an asset of the partnership and is owned jointly by all the partners.

PARTICIPATION IN PARTNERSHIP INCOME

Each partner has the right to share in the company's income and the responsibility to share in its losses. The partnership agreement should state the method of distributing income and losses to each partner. If the agreement describes how income should be shared but does not mention losses, losses are distributed in the same way as income. If the partners fail to describe the method of income and loss distribution in the partnership agreement, the law states that income and losses must be shared equally.

ACCOUNTING FOR PARTNERS' EQUITY

OBJECTIVE

3 *Record investments of cash and of other assets by the partners in forming a partnership*

The owners' equity of a partnership is called partners' equity. In accounting for partners' equity, it is necessary to maintain separate Capital and Withdrawals accounts for each partner and to divide the income and losses of the company among the partners. The differences in the Capital accounts of a sole proprietorship and a partnership are shown below.

Sole Proprietorship

Blake, Capital	
	50,000

Blake, Withdrawals	
12,000	

Partnership

Desmond, Capital		Frank, Capital	
	30,000		40,000

Desmond, Withdrawals		Frank, Withdrawals	
5,000		6,000	

In the partners' equity section of the balance sheet, the balance of each partner's Capital account is listed separately:

Liabilities and Partners' Equity

Total Liabilities		$28,000
Partners' Equity		
Desmond, Capital	$25,000	
Frank, Capital	34,000	
Total Partners' Equity		59,000
Total Liabilities and Partners' Equity		$87,000

Each partner invests cash, other assets, or a combination in the partnership according to the partnership agreement. Noncash assets should be valued at their fair market value on the date they are transferred to the partnership. The assets invested by a partner are debited to the proper account, and the total amount is credited to the partner's Capital account.

To show how partners' investments are recorded, let's assume that Jerry Adcock and Rose Villa have agreed to combine their capital and equipment in a partnership to operate a jewelry store. According to their partnership agreement, Adcock will invest $28,000 cash and $37,000 of furniture and displays, and Villa will invest $40,000 cash and $20,000 of equipment. The general journal entries to record the partners' initial investments are as follows:

```
19x1
July 1    Cash                              28,000
          Furniture and Displays            37,000
              Jerry Adcock, Capital                     65,000
                  Initial investment of Jerry
                  Adcock in Adcock and Villa

      1   Cash                              40,000
          Equipment                         20,000
              Rose Villa, Capital                       60,000
                  Initial Investment of Rose
                  Villa in Adcock and Villa
```

The values assigned to the assets in our example would have had to be included in the partnership agreement. These values can differ from those carried on the partners' personal books. For example, the equipment that Rose Villa contributed may have had a value of only $12,000 on her books. But suppose that after she purchased the equipment, its market value increased considerably. The book value of Villa's equipment is not important. The fair market value of the equipment at the time of transfer *is* important, however, because that value represents the amount invested by Villa in the partnership. Later investments are recorded the same way.

The partnership also can assume liabilities that are related to investments. For example, suppose that after seven months, Villa invests additional equipment with a fair market value of $45,000 in the partnership. Related to the equipment is a note payable for $37,000, which the partnership assumes. This entry records the transaction:

```
19x2
Feb. 1    Equipment                         45,000
              Notes Payable                             37,000
              Rose Villa, Capital                        8,000
                  Additional investment by Rose
                  Villa in Adcock and Villa
```

DISTRIBUTION OF PARTNERSHIP INCOME AND LOSSES

OBJECTIVE

4 *Compute and record the income or losses that partners share, based on stated ratios, capital balance ratios, and partners' salaries and interest*

A partnership's income and losses can be distributed according to whatever method the partners specify in the partnership agreement. The agreement should be specific and clear, to avoid later disputes. If a partnership agreement does not mention the distribution of income and losses, the law requires that they be shared equally by all partners. Also, if a partnership agreement mentions only the distribution of income, the law requires that losses be distributed in the same ratio as income.

The income of a partnership normally has three components: (1) return to the partners for the use of their capital (called *interest on partners' capital*), (2) compensation for direct services the partners have rendered (partners' salaries), and (3) other income for any special characteristics individual partners may bring to the partnership or risks they may take. The breakdown of total income into its three components helps clarify how much each partner has contributed to the firm.

If all partners are contributing equal capital, have similar talents, and are spending the same amount of time in the business, then an equal distribution of income and losses would be fair. However, if one partner works full time in the firm and another devotes only a fourth of his or her time, then the distribution of income or losses should reflect this difference. (This concept would apply to any situation in which the partners contribute unequally to the business.)

Several ways for partners to share income are (1) by stated ratios, (2) by capital balance ratios, and (3) by salaries to the partners and interest on partners' capital, with the remaining income shared according to stated ratios. *Salaries* and *interest* here are not *salaries expense* or *interest expense* in the ordinary sense of the terms. They do not affect the amount of reported net income. Instead, they refer to ways of determining each partner's share of net income or loss on the basis of time spent and money invested in the partnership.

STATED RATIOS

One method of distributing income and losses is to give each partner a stated ratio of the total income or loss. If each partner is making an equal contribution to the firm, each can assume the same share of income and losses. It is important to understand that an equal contribution to the firm does not necessarily mean an equal capital investment in the firm. One partner may be devoting more time and talent to the firm, whereas the second partner may make a larger capital investment. And, if the partners contribute unequally to the firm, unequal stated ratios—60 percent and 40 percent, perhaps—can be appropriate.

Let's assume that Adcock and Villa had a net income last year of $140,000. The partnership agreement states that the percentages of income and losses distributed to Jerry Adcock and Rose Villa should be 60 percent and 40 percent, respectively. The computation of each partner's share of the income and the journal entry to show the distribution are as follows:

Adcock ($140,000 × .60)	$84,000
Villa ($140,000 × .40)	56,000
Net Income	$140,000

19x2			
June 30	Income Summary	140,000	
	Jerry Adcock, Capital		84,000
	Rose Villa, Capital		56,000
	Distribution of income for the year		
	to the partners' Capital accounts		

CAPITAL BALANCE RATIOS

If invested capital produces the most income for the partnership, then income and losses may be distributed according to capital balance. One way of distributing income and losses here is to use a ratio based on each partner's capital balance at the beginning of the year. Another way is to use the average capital balance of each partner during the year. The partnership agreement must describe the method that is going to be used.

Ratios Based on Beginning Capital Balances

To show how the first method works, let's look at the beginning capital balance of the partners in Adcock and Villa. At the start of the fiscal year, July 1, 19x1, Jerry Adcock, Capital showed a $65,000 balance, and Rose Villa, Capital showed a $60,000 balance. (Actually, these balances reflect the partners' initial investment; the partnership was formed on July 1, 19x1.) The total partners' equity in the firm, then, was $125,000 ($65,000 + $60,000). Each partner's capital balance at the beginning of the year divided by the total partners' equity at the beginning of the year is that partner's beginning capital balance ratio:

	Beginning Capital Balance	Beginning Capital Balance Ratio
Jerry Adcock	$ 65,000	65 ÷ 125 = .52 = 52%
Rose Villa	60,000	60 ÷ 125 = .48 = 48%
	$125,000	

The income that each partner should receive when distribution is based on beginning capital balance ratios is figured by multiplying the total income by each partner's capital ratio. If we assume that income for the year was $140,000, Jerry Adcock's share of that income was $72,800, and Rose Villa's share was $67,200:

Jerry Adcock	$140,000 × .52 =	$ 72,800
Rose Villa	$140,000 × .48 =	67,200
		$140,000

This journal entry shows the distribution of income to Jerry Adcock and Rose Villa:

```
19x2
June 30   Income Summary                          140,000
              Jerry Adcock, Capital                          72,800
              Rose Villa, Capital                            67,200
                  Distribution of income for the year
                  to the partners' Capital accounts
```

Ratios Based on Average Capital Balances

If Adcock and Villa use beginning capital balance ratios to determine the distribution of income, they do not consider any investments or withdrawals made during the year. But these investments and withdrawals usually change the partners' capital ratio. If the partners believe that their capital balances are going to change dramatically during the year, they can choose average capital balance ratios as a fairer means of distributing income and losses.

These T accounts show the activity over the year in Adcock and Villa's partners' Capital and Withdrawals accounts:

Jerry Adcock, Capital			Jerry Adcock, Withdrawals		
	7/1/x1	65,000	1/1/x2	10,000	

Rose Villa, Capital			Rose Villa, Withdrawals		
	7/1/x1	60,000	11/1/x1	10,000	
	2/1/x2	8,000			

Jerry Adcock withdrew $10,000 on January 1, 19x2. Rose Villa withdrew $10,000 on November 1, 19x1 and invested an additional $8,000 of equipment on February 1, 19x2. Again, the income for the year's operation (7/1/x1–6/30/x2) was $140,000. The calculations for the average capital balances and the distribution of income are as follows:

Average Capital Balances

Partner	Date	Capital Balance ×	Months Unchanged =	Total	Average Capital Balance
Adcock	July–Dec.	$65,000 ×	6 =	$390,000	
	Jan.–June	55,000 ×	6 =	330,000	
			12	$720,000 ÷ 12 =	$ 60,000
Villa	July–Oct.	$60,000 ×	4 =	$240,000	
	Nov.–Jan.	50,000 ×	3 =	150,000	
	Feb.–June	58,000 ×	5 =	290,000	
			12	$680,000 ÷ 12 =	56,667
				Total average capital	$116,667

Average Capital Balance Ratios

$$\text{Adcock} = \frac{\text{Adcock's average capital balance}}{\text{Total average capital}} = \frac{\$60,000}{\$116,667} = .514 = 51.4\%$$

$$\text{Villa} = \frac{\text{Villa's average capital balance}}{\text{Total average capital}} = \frac{\$56,667}{\$116,667} = .486 = 48.6\%$$

Distribution of Income

Partner	Income	×	Ratio	=	Share of Income
Adcock	$140,000	×	.514	=	$ 71,960
Villa	$140,000	×	.486	=	68,040
			Total income		$140,000

Notice that in order to determine the distribution of income (or loss), you have to determine (1) the average capital balances, (2) the average capital balance ratios, and (3) each partner's share of income or loss. To compute a partner's average capital balance, you have to examine the changes that have taken place during the year in that partner's capital balance, changes that are the product of further investments and withdrawals. The partner's beginning capital is multiplied by the number of months the balance remains unchanged. After the balance changes, the new balance is multiplied by the number of months it remains unchanged. The process continues until the end of the year. The totals of these computations are added together and then divided by 12 to determine the average capital balance. Once all the partners' average capital balances have been determined, the method of figuring capital balance ratios for sharing income and losses is the same as that used for beginning capital balances.

The journal entry showing how the earnings for the year are distributed to the partners' Capital accounts appears on the top of the next page.

Appendix D

19x2

June 30	Income Summary	140,000	
	Jerry Adcock, Capital		71,960
	Rose Villa, Capital		68,040
	Distribution of income for the year to the partners' Capital accounts		

SALARIES, INTEREST, AND STATED RATIOS

Partners generally do not contribute equally to a firm. To make up for unequal contributions, a partnership agreement can allow for partners' salaries, interest on partners' capital balances, or a combination of both in the distribution of income. Again, salaries and interest of this kind are not deducted as expenses before the partnership income is determined. They represent a method of arriving at an equitable distribution of income or loss.

To illustrate an allowance for partners' salaries, we assume that Adcock and Villa have agreed that they will receive salaries—$8,000 for Adcock and $7,000 for Villa—and that any remaining income will be divided equally between them. Each salary is charged to the appropriate partner's Withdrawals account when paid. If we assume the same $140,000 income for the first year, the calculations for Adcock and Villa are as follows:

| | Income of Partner | | Income Distributed |
	Adcock	Villa	
Total Income for Distribution			$140,000
Distribution of Salaries			
Adcock	$ 8,000		
Villa		$ 7,000	(15,000)
Remaining Income After Salaries			$125,000
Equal Distribution of Remaining Income			
Adcock ($125,000 × .50)	62,500		
Villa ($125,000 × .50)		62,500	(125,000)
Remaining Income			—
Income of Partners	$70,500	$69,500	$140,000

The journal entry is as follows:

19x2

June 30	Income Summary	140,000	
	Jerry Adcock, Capital		70,500
	Rose Villa, Capital		69,500
	Distribution of income for the year to the partners' Capital accounts		

Salaries allow for differences in the services that partners provide the business. However, they do not take into account differences in invested capital. To allow for capital differences, in addition to salary, each partner can receive a stated interest on his or her invested capital. Suppose that Jerry Adcock and Rose Villa agree to receive annual salaries of $8,000 for Adcock and $7,000 for Villa, as well as 10 percent interest on their beginning capital balances, and to share any remaining income equally. These are the calculations for Adcock and Villa, if we assume income of $140,000:

| | Income of Partner | | Income Distributed |
	Adcock	Villa	
Total Income for Distribution			$140,000
Distribution of Salaries			
Adcock	$ 8,000		
Villa		$ 7,000	(15,000)
Remaining Income After Salaries			$125,000
Distribution of Interest			
Adcock ($65,000 × .10)	6,500		
Villa ($60,000 × .10)		6,000	(12,500)
Remaining Income After Salaries and Interest			$112,500
Equal Distribution of Remaining Income			
Adcock ($112,500 × .50)	56,250		
Villa ($112,500 × .50)		56,250	(112,500)
Remaining Income			—
Income of Partners	$70,750	$69,250	$140,000

The journal entry is as follows:

19x2			
June 30	Income Summary	140,000	
	Jerry Adcock, Capital		70,750
	Rose Villa, Capital		69,250
	Distribution of income for the year		
	to the partners' Capital accounts		

If the partnership agreement allows for the distribution of salaries or interest or both, the amounts must be allocated to the partners even if profits are not enough to cover the salaries and interest. In fact, even if the company has a loss, these allocations still must be made. The negative balance or loss after the allocation of salaries and interest must be distributed according to the stated ratio in the partnership agreement, or equally if the agreement does not mention a ratio.

For example, let's assume that Adcock and Villa agreed to the following conditions for the distribution of income and losses:

	Salaries	Interest	Beginning Capital Balance
Adcock	$70,000	10 percent of beginning	$65,000
Villa	60,000	capital balances	60,000

The income for the first year of operation was $140,000. This is the computation for the distribution of the income and loss:

	Income of Partner		Income Distributed
	Adcock	Villa	
Total Income for Distribution			$140,000
Distribution of Salaries			
Adcock	$70,000		
Villa		$60,000	(130,000)
Remaining Income After Salaries			$ 10,000
Distribution of Interest			
Adcock ($65,000 × .10)	6,500		
Villa ($60,000 × .10)		6,000	(12,500)
Negative Balance After Salaries and Interest			$ (2,500)
Equal Distribution of Negative Balance*			
Adcock ($2,500 × .50)	(1,250)		
Villa ($2,500 × .50)		(1,250)	2,500
Remaining Income			—
Income of Partners	$75,250	$64,750	$140,000

*Notice that the negative balance is distributed equally because the agreement does not indicate how income and losses should be distributed after salaries and interest are paid.

The journal entry is as follows:

```
19x2
June 30    Income Summary                          140,000
                Jerry Adcock, Capital                          75,250
                Rose Villa, Capital                            64,750
                    Distribution of income for the year
                    to the partners' Capital accounts
```

DISSOLUTION OF A PARTNERSHIP

Dissolution of a partnership occurs whenever there is a change in the original association of partners. When a partnership is dissolved, the partners lose their authority to continue the business as a going concern. This does not mean that the business operation necessarily is ended or interrupted, but it does mean—from a legal and accounting standpoint—that the separate entity ceases to exist. The remaining partners can act for the partnership in finishing the affairs of the business or in forming a new partnership that will be a new accounting entity. The dissolution of a partnership takes place through the admission of a new partner, the withdrawal of a partner, or the death of a partner.

OBJECTIVE

 Record the admission of a new partner

ADMISSION OF A NEW PARTNER

The admission of a new partner dissolves the old partnership because a new association has been formed. Dissolving the old partnership and creating a new one require the consent of all the old partners and the ratification of a new partnership agreement. When a new partner is admitted, a new partnership agreement should be in place.

An individual can be admitted into a firm in one of two ways: (1) by purchasing an interest in the partnership from one or more of the original partners or (2) by investing assets in the partnership.

Purchasing an Interest from a Partner

When an individual is admitted to a firm by purchasing an interest from an old partner, each partner must agree to the change. The transaction is a personal one between the old and new partners, but the interest purchased must be transferred from the Capital account of the selling partner to the Capital account of the new partner.

Suppose that Jerry Adcock decides to sell his interest, assumed to be $70,000, in Adcock and Villa to Richard Davis for $100,000 on August 31, 19x3, and that Rose Villa agrees to the sale. The entry to record the sale on the partnership books looks like this:

19x3			
Aug. 31	Jerry Adcock, Capital	70,000	
	Richard Davis, Capital		70,000
	Transfer of Jerry Adcock's equity		
	to Richard Davis		

Notice that the entry records the book value of the equity, not the amount Davis pays. The amount Davis pays is a personal matter between him and Adcock. Because the amount paid does not affect the assets or liabilities of the firm, it is not entered in the records.

Here's another example of a purchase: Assume that Richard Davis purchases half of Jerry Adcock's $70,000 and half of Rose Villa's interest, assumed to be $80,000, in the partnership by paying a total of $100,000 to the two partners on August 31, 19x3. The entry to record this transaction on the partnership books would be as follows:

19x3			
Aug. 31	Jerry Adcock, Capital	35,000	
	Rose Villa, Capital	40,000	
	Richard Davis, Capital		75,000
	Transfer of half of Jerry Adcock's		
	and Rose Villa's equity to		
	Richard Davis		

Investing Assets in a Partnership

When a new partner is admitted through an investment in the partnership, both the assets and the partners' equity in the firm increase. Why is this so? Because the assets the new partner invests become partnership assets, and as partnership assets increase, partners' equity increases as well.

For example, assume that Richard Davis wants to invest $75,000 for a one-third interest in the partnership of Adcock and Villa. The Capital accounts of Jerry Adcock and Rose Villa are assumed to be $70,000 and $80,000, respectively. The assets of the firm are valued correctly. So, the partners agree to sell Davis a one-third interest in the firm for $75,000. Davis's $75,000 investment equals a one-third interest in the firm after the investment is added to the previously existing capital of the partnership:

Jerry Adcock, Capital	$ 70,000
Rose Villa, Capital	80,000
Davis's investment	75,000
Total capital after Davis's investment	$225,000

One-third interest = $225,000 ÷ 3 =	$ 75,000

The journal entry to record Davis's investment is as follows:

19x3			
Aug. 31	Cash	75,000	
	Richard Davis, Capital		75,000
	Admission of Richard Davis for a one-third interest in the company		

Bonus to the Old Partners   Sometimes a partnership may be so profitable or otherwise advantageous that a new investor is willing to pay more than the actual dollar interest that he or she receives in the partnership. Suppose an individual pays $100,000 for an $80,000 interest in a partnership. The $20,000 excess of the payment over the interest purchased is a **bonus** to the original partners. The bonus must be distributed to the original partners according to the partnership agreement. When the agreement does not cover the distribution of bonuses, it should be distributed to the original partners in accordance with the method of distributing income and losses.

Assume that the Adcock and Villa Company has operated for several years and that the partners' capital balances and the stated ratios for distribution of income and loss are as follows:

Partners	Capital Balances	Stated Ratios
Adcock	$160,000	55%
Villa	140,000	45%
	$300,000	100%

Richard Davis wants to join the firm. He offers to invest $100,000 on December 1 for a one-fifth interest in the business and income. The original partners agree to the offer. This is the computation of the bonus to the original partners:

Partners' equity in the original partnership		$300,000
Cash investment by Richard Davis		100,000
Partners' equity in the new partnership		$400,000
Partners' equity assigned to Richard Davis ($400,000 × ⅕)		$ 80,000
Bonus to the original partners		
Investment by Richard Davis	$100,000	
Less equity assigned to Richard Davis	80,000	$ 20,000
Distribution of bonus to original partners		
Jerry Adcock ($20,000 × .55)	$ 11,000	
Rose Villa ($20,000 × .45)	9,000	$ 20,000

And this is the journal entry that records Davis's admission to the partnership:

```
19x3
Dec. 1  Cash                                    100,000
             Jerry Adcock, Capital                        11,000
             Rose Villa, Capital                           9,000
             Richard Davis, Capital                       80,000
                  Investment by Richard Davis for
                  a one-fifth interest in the firm,
                  and the bonus distributed to the
                  original partners
```

Bonus to the New Partner   There are several reasons why a partnership might want a new partner. A firm in financial trouble might need additional cash. Or the original partners, wanting to expand the firm's markets, might need more capital than they themselves can provide. Also, the partners might know a person who would bring a unique talent to the firm. Under these conditions, a new partner could be admitted to the partnership with the understanding that part of the original partners' capital will be transferred (credited) to the new partner's Capital account as a bonus.

OBJECTIVE

6 *Describe the implications of the withdrawal or death of a partner and of the liquidation of a partnership*

WITHDRAWAL OF A PARTNER

Generally, a partner has the right to withdraw from a partnership in accord with legal requirements. However, to avoid disputes when a partner does decide to withdraw or retire from the firm, the partnership agreement should describe the procedures to be followed. The agreement should specify (1) whether or not an audit will be performed, (2) how the assets will be reappraised, (3) how a bonus will be determined, and (4) by what method the withdrawing partner will be paid.

There are several ways in which an individual can withdraw from a partnership. A partner can (1) sell his or her interest to another partner with the consent of the remaining partners, (2) sell his or her interest to an outsider with the consent of the remaining partners, (3) withdraw assets equal to his or her capital balance, (4) withdraw assets that are less than his or her capital balance (in this case, the remaining partners receive a bonus), or (5) withdraw assets that are greater than his or her capital balance (in this case, the withdrawing partner receives a bonus). Bonuses are allocated in a manner similar to those that arise when a new partner is admitted. These alternatives are illustrated in Figure 1.

DEATH OF A PARTNER

When a partner dies, the partnership is dissolved because the original association has changed. The partnership agreement should state the actions to be taken. Normally, the books are closed and financial statements prepared. These actions are necessary to determine the capital balance of each partner on the date of the death. The agreement also may indicate whether an audit should be conducted, assets appraised, and a bonus recorded, as well as the procedures for settling with the deceased partner's heirs. The remaining partners may purchase the deceased's equity, sell it to outsiders, or deliver certain business assets to the estate. If the firm intends to continue, a new partnership must be formed.

Figure 1. Alternative Ways for a Partner to Withdraw

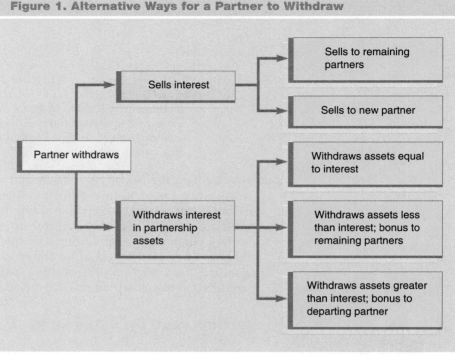

LIQUIDATION OF A PARTNERSHIP

Liquidation of a partnership is the process of ending the business, of selling enough assets to pay the partnership's liabilities and distributing any remaining assets among the partners. Liquidation is a special form of dissolution. When a partnership is liquidated, the business will not continue.

The partnership agreement should indicate the procedures to be followed in case of liquidation. Usually, the books are adjusted and closed, with the income or loss distributed to the partners. As the assets of the business are sold, any gain or loss should be distributed to the partners according to the stated ratios. As cash becomes available, it must be applied first to outside creditors, then to partners' loans, and finally to the partners' capital balances. Any deficits in partners' capital accounts must be made up from personal assets.

Questions

1. In what ways is accounting for withdrawals by sole proprietorships similar to and different from accounting for dividends by corporations?
2. Briefly define *partnership* and list several major characteristics of the partnership form of business.
3. What is the meaning of unlimited liability when applied to a partnership?
4. Abe and Bill are partners in a drilling operation. Abe purchased a drilling rig to be used in the partnership's operations. Is this purchase binding on Bill even though he was not involved in it? Explain your answer.
5. The partnership agreement for Karla and Jean's partnership does not disclose how they will share income and losses. How would the income and losses be shared in this partnership?

6. What characteristics of a partnership could be interpreted as disadvantages?

7. What characteristics of a partnership differ from those of a sole proprietorship and a corporation?

8. In the liquidation of a partnership, Robert's Capital account showed a $5,000 deficit balance after all the creditors were paid. What obligation does Robert have to the partnership?

9. Describe how a dissolution of a partnership may differ from a liquidation of a partnership.

10. Tom Howard and Sharon Thomas are forming a partnership. What are some of the factors they should consider in deciding how income might be divided?

Exercises

ED-1.

L O 1 *Proprietorship Transactions*

Perceiving a need for a message service to serve downtown businesses, Clare Alvarez established Alvarez Message Delivery on July 1. Prepare general journal entries to record the following transactions that affect the company's proprietorship accounts.

July 1 Alvarez invested $5,000 in cash and an automobile valued at $6,000 in the business.

15 Withdrew $750 in cash from the business for living expenses.

31 Closed the following revenue and expense accounts:

Service Revenue	$1,000
Rent Expense	300
Telephone Expense	50
Utility Expense	200
Depreciation Expense, Automobile	100

31 Closed Income Summary account

31 Closed Withdrawals account

ED-2.

L O 4 *Distribution of Income*

Walker Parks and Lonnie Tucker agreed to form a partnership. Parks contributed $200,000 in cash, and Tucker contributed assets with a fair market value of $400,000. The partnership, in its initial year, reported net income of $120,000.

Prepare the journal entry to distribute the first year's income to the partners under each of the following conditions:

1. Parks and Tucker failed to include stated ratios in the partnership agreement.
2. Parks and Tucker agreed to share income and losses in a 3:2 ratio.
3. Parks and Tucker agreed to share income and losses in the ratio of their original investments.
4. Parks and Tucker agreed to share income and losses by allowing 10 percent interest on original investments and sharing any remainder equally.

ED-3.

L O 5 *Admission of a New Partner: Recording a Bonus*

Jorge, Ramon, and Hubert have equity in a partnership of $40,000, $40,000, and $60,000, respectively, and they share income and losses in a ratio of 1:1:3. The partners have agreed to admit Jesse to the partnership.

Prepare journal entries to record the admission of Jesse to the partnership under the following conditions:

1. Jesse invests $60,000 for a 20 percent interest in the partnership, and a bonus is recorded for the original partners.
2. Jesse invests $60,000 for a 40 percent interest in the partnership, and a bonus is recorded for Jesse.

Problems

D-1.

L O 3, 4 *Partnership Formation and Distribution of Income*

In January 19x1, Tom Himes and Jeff Palmer agreed to produce and sell chocolate candies. Himes contributed $240,000 in cash to the business. Palmer contributed the building and equipment, valued at $220,000 and $140,000, respectively. The partnership had an income of $84,000 during 19x1 but was less successful during 19x2, when income was only $40,000.

REQUIRED

1. Prepare the journal entry to record the investment of both partners in the partnership.
2. Determine the share of income for each partner in 19x1 and 19x2 under each of the following conditions: (a) The partners agreed to share income equally. (b) The partners failed to agree on an income-sharing arrangement. (c) The partners agreed to share income according to the ratio of their original investments. (d) The partners agreed to share income by allowing interest of 10 percent on their original investments and dividing the remainder equally. (e) The partners agreed to share income by allowing salaries of $40,000 for Himes and $28,000 for Palmer, and dividing the remainder equally. (f) The partners agreed to share income by paying salaries of $40,000 to Himes and $28,000 to Palmer, allowing interest of 9 percent on their original investments, and dividing the remainder equally.

D-2.

L O 5, 6 *Admission and Withdrawal of a Partner*

Pat, Connie, and Janice are partners in Manitow Woodwork Company. Their capital balances as of July 31, 19x4, are as follows:

Pat, Capital	Connie, Capital	Janice, Capital
45,000	15,000	30,000

Each partner has agreed to admit Felicia to the partnership.

REQUIRED

Prepare the journal entries to record Felicia's admission to or Pat's withdrawal from the partnership under each of the following independent conditions: (a) Felicia pays Pat $12,500 for 20 percent of Pat's interest in the partnership. (b) Felicia invests $20,000 cash in the partnership and receives an interest equal to her investment. (c) Felicia invests $30,000 cash in the partnership for a 20 percent interest in the business. A bonus is to be recorded for the original partners on the basis of their capital balances. (d) Felicia invests $30,000 cash in the partnership for a 40 percent interest in the business. The original partners give Felicia a bonus according to the ratio of their capital balances on July 31, 19x4. (e) Pat withdraws from the partnership, taking $52,500. The excess of assets over the partnership interest is distributed according to the balances of the Capital accounts. (f) Pat withdraws by selling her interest directly to Felicia for $60,000.

APPENDIX E   *Overview of Governmental and Not-for-Profit Accounting*

LEARNING OBJECTIVES

1. Explain and differentiate some basic concepts related to governmental and not-for-profit accounting.
2. Describe the types of funds used in governmental accounting.
3. Explain the modified accrual basis of accounting used by state and local governments.
4. Describe the financial reporting system used in governmental accounting.
5. Provide a brief introduction to other types of not-for-profit accounting.

State and local governments and not-for-profit organizations account for a significant share of all spending in the American economy. This appendix provides a brief introduction to financial accounting for several categories of governmental and not-for-profit groups. They include state and local governments, colleges and universities, hospitals, and voluntary health and welfare organizations.

GOVERNMENTAL, NOT-FOR-PROFIT, AND BUSINESS ACCOUNTING

Businesses in the United States are organized to produce profits for their owners or shareholders. This fact requires that the accounting system provide shareholders, creditors, and other interested parties with information that will help them evaluate the firm's success in making a profit. The rules and practices of business accounting are referred to as generally accepted accounting principles (GAAP), which are established by the Financial Accounting Standards Board (FASB). Historically, governmental GAAP have been the responsibility of the National Council on Governmental Accounting (NCGA). In 1984 the Financial Accounting Foundation founded the Governmental Accounting Standards Board (GASB). The GASB has the power to establish accounting rules and practices for governmental units. Its responsibilities parallel those of the FASB in that it defines generally accepted accounting principles for governmental units. Standards set by the GASB do not apply to nongovernmental not-for-profit organizations like private universities and hospitals. Accounting practices for these nongovernmental not-for-profit organizations fall under the pronouncements of the FASB.

FINANCIAL REPORTING OBJECTIVES OF GOVERNMENTAL UNITS

OBJECTIVE

1 *Explain and differentiate some basic concepts related to governmental and not-for-profit accounting*

State and local governments have different objectives from those of businesses, and thus they have traditionally had different GAAP. Governmental units chiefly provide services to citizens, with expenditures for these services limited to the amounts legally available. Governmental units need not be profitable in the business sense; however, they do need to limit their spending to the funds made available for specific purposes. For these reasons, the GASB has established the following financial reporting objectives for governmental units:

1. Financial reporting should assist in fulfilling government's duty to be publicly accountable and should enable users to assess that accountability.
2. Financial reporting should assist users in evaluating the operating results of the governmental entity for the year.
3. Financial reporting should assist users in assessing the level of services that can be provided by the entity and its ability to meet its obligations when due.[1]

The primary objective of governmental GAAP is, therefore, not profit measurement but the assessment and accountability of the funds available for governmental activities. To help satisfy this objective, governmental GAAP have several unique accounting features, the most important of which are the use of funds to account for various activities and the use of modified accrual accounting. A fund is defined as a fiscal and accounting entity. Modified accrual accounting attempts to provide an accurate measure of increases and decreases in resources available (especially cash) to fulfill governmental obligations.

The operations of state and local governments are recorded in a variety of funds, each of which is designated for a specific purpose. This means that each fund simultaneously shows (1) the financial position and results of operations during the period and (2) compliance with legal requirements of the state or local government. State and local governments rely on the following types of funds:

OBJECTIVE

2 *Describe the types of funds used in governmental accounting*

General fund   To account for all financial resources not accounted for in any other fund. This fund accounts for most of the current operating activities of the governmental unit (administration, police, fire, health, and sanitation, for example).

Special revenue funds   To account for revenues legally restricted to specific purposes.

Capital projects funds   To account for the acquisition and construction of major capital projects.

Debt service fund   To account for resources accumulated to pay the interest and principal of general obligation long-term debt.

Enterprise funds   To account for activities that are financed and operated in a manner similar to private business activities. These funds are most appropriate for activities that charge the public for goods or services, such as municipal golf courses or utilities.

Internal service funds   To account for the financing of goods or services provided by one department or agency of a governmental unit to other departments or agencies of governmental units.

---

1. *Concept Statement No. 1*, "Objectives of Financial Reporting" (Stamford, Conn.: Governmental Accounting Standards Board, 1987).

Trust and agency funds   To account for assets held by a governmental unit acting as a trustee or agent for individuals, private organizations, or other funds.

The first four funds are called governmental funds. The enterprise and internal service funds are proprietary funds. Trust and agency funds are fiduciary funds. A political unit may properly have only one general fund. There is no limit, however, on the number of other funds used. There is also no requirement that a state or local government have all of these funds; individual needs govern the type and number of funds used.

In addition to the above funds, state and local governments use two unique entities called account groups to record certain fixed assets and long-term liabilities.

General fixed assets account group   To account for all long-term assets of a governmental unit except long-term assets related to specific proprietary or trust funds. This account group does not record depreciation.

General long-term debt group   To account for all long-term liabilities of a governmental unit except for long-term liabilities related to specific proprietary or trust funds. This account group records the principal amounts of long-term debt as well as the amounts available in the debt service fund and the amounts to be provided in the future for the retirement of the debt.

Long-term assets and long-term liabilities related to proprietary and trust funds are accounted for in essentially the same manner as in business accounting.

MODIFIED ACCRUAL ACCOUNTING

OBJECTIVE

3   *Explain the modified accrual basis of accounting used by state and local governments*

Governmental funds, as well as certain types of trust funds, use the modified accrual method of accounting. Proprietary funds, as well as certain types of trust funds, use the familiar full accrual accounting common to business organizations. This section will concentrate on the less familiar modified accrual basis of accounting.

Modified accrual accounting has several features that distinguish it from accrual accounting used in business. The measurement and recognition of revenues and expenditures, the incorporation of the budget into the formal accounting system, and the use of encumbrances to account for purchase commitments will each be described briefly.

In governmental accounting, revenues are defined as increases in fund resources from sources other than interfund transactions or proceeds of long-term debt. They are recognized in the accounts when "measurable and available." In most cases these conditions are met when cash is received. Expenditures are defined as decreases in fund resources that are caused by transactions other than interfund transfers. These concepts of revenues and expenditures result in some unusual situations, as the following examples illustrate.

1. Assume that a city sells a used police car for $2,500 cash. This transaction would be recorded in the general fund as follows:

Cash	2,500	
Revenues		2,500
Sale of used police car		

2. When a city purchases a new police car for $12,000 cash, the transaction would be recorded in the general fund as shown at the top of the next page.

| Expenditures | 12,000 | |
| Cash | | 12,000 |

Purchase of new police car

The transactions are recorded in this way because they satisfy the definitions of revenues and expenditures.

To further illustrate the contrast between governmental and business-type accrual accounting, we can examine the way in which a business would record the above transactions:

1. Assume that a firm sells a used car for $2,500 cash and that the car has a carrying value of $2,000 (cost of $7,500 less accumulated depreciation of $5,500):

Cash	2,500	
Accumulated Depreciation, Car	5,500	
Car		7,500
Gain on Disposal		500

Sale of used car

Unlike governmental accounting, accrual accounting recognizes revenues only to the extent that cash received exceeds carrying value.

2. If a firm purchases a new car for $12,000 cash, the transaction would be recorded as follows:

| Car | 12,000 | |
| Cash | | 12,000 |

Purchase of new car

The car would be shown as an asset on the firm's balance sheet. No expense would be recorded until depreciation is recognized in subsequent years. As discussed throughout this book, business accounting focuses on the matching of revenues and expenses to compute net income or loss for the period. Governmental accounting, in contrast, concentrates on inflows and outflows of fund resources.

Another unique feature of governmental accounting is the formal incorporation of the budget into the accounts of the particular fund. This approach is required for the general fund and the special revenue fund and is optional for the other governmental funds. The general fund, for example, would record its budget as follows:

Estimated Revenues	1,000,000	
Appropriations		950,000
Fund Balance		50,000

To record budget for fiscal year

This example assumes that the governmental unit expects revenues to exceed legally mandated expenditures (or appropriations). The use of budgetary accounts enables the governmental unit to have a continuous check or control on whether actual revenues and expenditures correspond to original estimates. In addition, the various funds' financial statements will show both the budgeted and actual amounts of major revenue and expenditure categories. At the end of the accounting period, the budget entry would be reversed, since its control function is no longer needed. A new budget would then be recorded in the subsequent period to control revenues and expenditures in that period. Businesses also use budgets, but they do not integrate those budgets formally into the regular accounting system.

A third unique feature of governmental accounting is the use of encumbrance accounting. Since governments cannot legally spend more than the amounts appropriated for specific purposes, it is necessary to keep track of anticipated, as well as actual, expenditures. Whenever a significant lapse of time is expected between a commitment to spend and the actual expenditure, governmental GAAP require the use of encumbrance accounting.

For example, a city orders $10,000 of supplies on July 1, but does not expect to receive the supplies until September 1. The bill received on September 1 amounts to $10,200. The general fund would record this transaction as follows:

July 1	Encumbrances	10,000	
	Reserve for Encumbrances		10,000
	Order of supplies		
Sept. 1	Reserve for Encumbrances	10,000	
	Encumbrances		10,000
	Reverse encumbrance upon receipt		
	of bill for supplies		
1	Expenditures	10,200	
	Cash (or Vouchers Payable)		10,200
	Payment for supplies		

The purpose of an encumbrance system is to ensure that the governmental unit does not exceed its spending authority. This is accomplished by recording not only actual expenditures but also anticipated expenditures under the current period's appropriations. In addition to normal expenditures, the Reserve for Encumbrances account represents that portion of the fund balance already committed to future expenditures. Regardless of the original estimated encumbrance amounts, on September 1, the encumbrance is eliminated by reversing the original entry of July 1, and Expenditures is debited for the actual amount spent.

FINANCIAL REPORTING SYSTEM

OBJECTIVE

4 *Describe the financial reporting system used in governmental accounting*

The accounting system we have described is designed to produce periodic financial statements. The financial statements recommended by the NCGA in its Government Accounting Standard No. 1 include the following:

Combined balance sheet This statement is prepared for all fund types and account groups. Each fund type and account group lists major categories of assets, liabilities, and either fund balances or owners' equity accounts.

Combined statement of revenues, expenditures, and changes in fund balances—all governmental funds This statement is prepared for all governmental fund types. Since only governmental funds are reported in this statement, all revenues and expenditures would be measured according to the principles of modified accrual accounting.

Combined statement of revenues, expenditures, and changes in fund balances—budget and actual—general and special revenue funds This statement presents budget and actual amounts for general and special revenue fund types. The statement includes the budgetary data described earlier and directly compares actual revenues and expenditures to budgeted revenues and expenditures. It indicates, for each type of revenue and expenditure, the amount by which actual amounts differ from budgeted amounts.

Combined statement of revenues, expenses, and changes in retained earnings (or equity) This statement is prepared for all proprietary fund types. It is prepared on the full accrual basis and resembles the financial statements prepared by businesses.

Combined statement of changes in financial position This statement is prepared for all proprietary fund types.

NOT-FOR-PROFIT ORGANIZATIONS

OBJECTIVE

5 *Provide a brief introduction to other types of not-for-profit accounting*

Colleges and universities, hospitals, and voluntary health and welfare organizations, among others, share characteristics of both governmental and business entities. Like governments, they are not intended to make a profit; however, they lack the taxing ability of a government. Because the lack of taxing ability requires that the revenues of not-for-profit organizations at least equal expenses over the long run, these organizations rely on accrual accounting for most of their activities. These organizations also use funds to account for different types of resources and activities. The use of funds is necessary because of the legal restrictions imposed on many of the resources available to these groups.

COLLEGES AND UNIVERSITIES

Colleges and universities, with a few exceptions, use full accrual accounting. Until recently, one notable exception was that depreciation on plant and equipment did not have to be recorded. However, the FASB issued Statement No. 93 to eliminate this exception. For example, even Harvard University began to report a deficit when it began to recognize depreciation of $76 million per year.[2] Another exception is that revenues from restricted sources can be recognized only when expenditures are made for the purposes specified by the revenue source.

Financial statements used by colleges and universities include the following: (a) statement of current funds, revenues, expenditures, and other changes; (b) combined balance sheet; and (c) statement of changes in fund balances.

HOSPITALS

Accounting for not-for-profit hospitals closely resembles the accrual accounting methods used by businesses. An important aspect of hospital accounting, however, is the classification of revenues and expenses. Revenues must be separated by *source,* including patient service and other operating and nonoperating revenues. Expenses must be classified by *function,* including nursing services, other professional services, administrative services, and so forth. Hospitals recognize depreciation on plant assets.

VOLUNTARY HEALTH AND WELFARE ORGANIZATIONS

Voluntary health and welfare organizations encompass a broad variety of groups, such as the Sierra Club, the American Cancer Society, and the National Rifle Association. Even though accounting practices vary considerably, these organizations usually follow the full accrual basis of accounting. Their fund structure is as follows: current unrestricted fund; current restricted fund; land, building, and equipment fund; endowment funds; custodial (similar to agency) funds; and loan and annuity funds.

2. Gary Putka, "Harvard University Reports Deficits Totaling $79.1 Million for the Past 2 Years," *Wall Street Journal,* February 14, 1992.

ACCOUNTING FOR CONTRIBUTIONS

The FASB requires that all not-for-profit organizations, including charitable organizations, and private colleges and universities, recognize as revenues and list as assets all gifts promised to them whenever such a promise to give is unconditional or any conditions have been met.[3]

The FASB also requires that not-for-profit organizations report amounts for their total assets, liabilities, and net assets in a statement of financial position; the changes in their net assets in a statement of activities; and the changes in their cash and cash equivalents in a statement of cash flows. Net assets and revenues, expenses, gains, and losses must be classified based on the existence or absence of donor-imposed restrictions. Assets must be shown in the statement of financial position for three classes of assets: permanently restricted, temporarily restricted, and unrestricted. The amounts of change in each class must be shown on the statement of activities.[4]

Questions

1. How do the objectives of governmental accounting differ from the objectives of business accounting?
2. What is the purpose of a *fund,* as that term is used in governmental accounting?
3. What is a proprietary fund in governmental accounting? Why do such funds use accrual accounting?
4. Contrast the measurement of revenues and expenditures in governmental accounting with the measurement of revenues and expenses in business accounting.
5. What is the purpose of budgetary accounts in governmental accounting?
6. What are the major characteristics of modified accrual accounting as used in governmental accounting?
7. What are the purposes of recording encumbrances?
8. In what ways does accounting for colleges and universities resemble business accounting? How does it differ from business accounting?
9. Describe how revenues and expenses are classified in hospital accounting.

Exercise

EE-1.

L O 2, 3, 5 *Basic Concepts and Funds*

Select the most appropriate answer for the following questions.

1. The fund that accounts for the day-to-day operating activities of a local government is the

   a. enterprise fund.
   b. general fund.
   c. operating fund.
   d. special revenue fund.

2. Accrual accounting is recommended for which of the following funds?

   a. Debt service fund
   b. General fund
   c. Internal service fund
   d. Capital projects fund

3. *Statement of Financial Accounting Standards No. 116,* "Accounting for Contributions Received and Contributions Made" (Stamford, Conn.: Financial Accounting Standards Board, 1993).
4. *Statement of Financial Accounting Standards No. 117,* "Financial Statements of Not-for-Profit Organizations" (Stamford, Conn.: Financial Accounting Standards Board, 1993).

3. A debt service fund of a municipality is an example of what type of fund?

    a. Account fund
    b. Governmental fund
    c. Proprietary fund
    d. Fiduciary fund

4. What basis of accounting would a not-for-profit hospital use?

    a. Cash basis for all funds
    b. Modified accrual basis for all funds
    c. Accrual basis for all funds
    d. Accrual basis for some funds and modified accrual basis for other funds

5. After the implementation of FASB No. 93, which of the following types of organization does not record depreciation expense on property, plant, and equipment?

    a. State and local governments
    b. Private colleges and universities
    c. Hospitals
    d. Businesses

Problem

E-1.

L O 3 *Journal Entries for the General Fund*

The following transactions occurred in the city of Worthington during 19x1.

19x1

Jan. 1   The budget was adopted. Estimated revenues are $8,000,000; appropriations are $8,200,000.

Feb. 11   Supplies with an estimated cost of $44,000 were ordered.

Mar. 1   Property taxes totaling $7,000,000 were levied. Worthington expects 2 percent of this amount to be uncollectible.

Apr. 10   The supplies ordered on February 11 were received. The actual bill for these supplies amounted to $43,500.

June 1   Property tax collections totaled $6,900,000. The rest were classified as delinquent.

Aug. 10   Equipment costing $22,600 was purchased for cash.

Dec. 31   Actual revenues for 19x1 totaled $8,100,000. Actual expenditures totaled $7,950,000.

REQUIRED

Record the journal entries for these transactions in Worthington's general fund.

Accounting for Bond Investments

LEARNING OBJECTIVES

1. Account for the purchase of bonds between interest dates.

2. Amortize the premium or discount of a bond.

3. Account for the sale of bonds.

In the chapter on long-term liabilities, bond transactions and disclosures were discussed from the issuing corporation's viewpoint. Bonds may also be held for investment. If bonds are held as trading securities or available-for-sale securities, they are accounted for at fair value in a manner similar to that of accounting for equity investments described in the chapter on short-term liquid assets and the chapter on international accounting and intercompany investments. This appendix presents the accounting for bond investments when they are classified as held-to-maturity securities. In this case, bonds are accounted for at amortized value, taking into account any premium or discount at which the bond was purchased.

PURCHASE OF BONDS BETWEEN INTEREST DATES

OBJECTIVE

1 *Account for the purchase of bonds between interest dates*

The purchase price of bonds includes the price of the bonds plus the broker's commission. When the bonds are purchased between interest dates, the purchaser must also pay an amount equal to the interest that has accrued on the bonds since the last interest payment date. On the next interest payment date, the purchaser will receive an interest payment for the whole period. The payment for accrued interest should be recorded as a debit to Interest Income, to be offset later by a credit to Interest Income when the semiannual interest is received.

Suppose that on May 1 Vason Corporation purchases twenty $1,000 MGR Corporation bonds that carry a face interest rate of 9 percent at 88 plus accrued interest and a broker's commission of $400. The interest payment dates are January 1 and July 1. Management intends to hold the bonds to maturity. The entry on the next page records this purchase transaction.

May 1	Investment in Bonds	18,000	
	Interest Income	600	
	Cash		18,600
	Purchase of MGR Corporation bonds at 88 plus $400 commission and accrued interest $20,000 × 9% × ⁴⁄₁₂ = $600		

Note that the purchase is recorded at cost, as are all purchases of assets. The debit to Investment in Bonds of $18,000 equals the purchase price of $17,600 ($20,000 × .88) plus the commission of $400. This case is contrasted with that of the issuing corporation, which will record the bonds payable at face value and establish a discount on bonds payable.

The debit to Interest Income of $600 represents four months' interest (from January 1 to May 1) that was paid to the seller of the bonds.

AMORTIZATION OF PREMIUM OR DISCOUNT

OBJECTIVE

2 *Amortize the premium or discount of a bond*

Because the investing company does not use separate accounts for the face value and any related discount or premium, the entry to amortize the premium or discount is made directly to the investment account. The amortization of a premium calls for a credit to the investment account to reduce the carrying value gradually to face value. The amortization of a discount calls for a debit to the investment account to increase the carrying value gradually to face value.

Returning to the case of Vason Corporation's purchase of bonds at a discount, we assume that the effective interest rate is 10½ percent. Remember that the amount of amortization of a premium or discount is the difference between (1) the face interest rate times the face value and (2) the effective interest rate times the carrying value. On July 1, the first interest date after the purchase, two months will have passed. The amount of discount to be amortized is as follows:

Two months' effective interest:
  $18,000 × 10½% × ²⁄₁₂ = $315
Two months' face interest:
  $20,000 × 9% × ²⁄₁₂ = 300
Discount to be amortized $ 15

The entry to record the receipt of an interest check on July 1 would be as follows:

July 1	Cash	900	
	Investment in Bonds	15	
	Interest Income		915
	Receipt of semiannual interest, some of which was previously accrued, and amortization of discount		

In this entry, Cash is debited for the semiannual interest payment ($20,000 × 9% × ½ = $900), Investment in Bonds is debited for the amortization of discount, or $15, and Interest Income is credited for the sum of the two debits, or $915. Note that the net interest earned is $315, which is the net amount of the $600 debit on May 1 and the $915 credit on July 1 to Interest Income. This amount is equal to the two months' effective interest just computed.

To continue the example, assume that Vason Corporation's fiscal year corresponds to the calendar year. Although the interest payment will not be received until January, it is necessary to accrue the interest and amortize the discount for the six months since July 1 in accordance with the matching concept. The entry to record the accrual of interest on December 31 is as follows:

Dec. 31	Interest Receivable	900.00	
	Investment in Bonds	45.79	
	Interest Income		945.79
	Accrual of interest income and		
	amortization of discount on bond		
	investment		

The period covered by this entry is six months. Therefore, the amounts to be debited and credited are as follows:

Six months' effective interest:
$$\$18,015 \times 10\tfrac{1}{2}\% \times \tfrac{1}{2} = \$945.79$$
Six months' face interest:
$$\$20,000 \times 9\% \times \tfrac{1}{2} = 900.00$$
Discount to be amortized $ 45.79

Note that the effective interest rate is applied to the new carrying value of $18,015.00. The next time the effective interest is calculated, the effective rate will be applied to $18,060.79 ($18,015.00 + $45.79). The entry to record receipt of the interest payment check on January 1 is as follows:[1]

Jan. 1	Cash	900.00	
	Interest Receivable		900.00
	Receipt of interest on bonds		

Similar calculations are made when a company purchases bonds at a premium. The only difference is that Investment in Bonds is credited rather than debited to reduce the carrying value, and the interest earned is less than the face interest.

SALE OF BONDS

OBJECTIVE

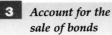

Account for the sale of bonds

Sometimes it is necessary to sell held-to-maturity securities even though that was not the original intent. When this happens, the sale is recorded by debiting Cash for the amount received and crediting Investment in Bonds for the carrying value of the investment. Any difference in the proceeds from the sale and the carrying value of the bonds is debited or credited to Loss or Gain on Sale of Investments. If the sale is made between interest payment dates, the company is entitled to the accrued interest from the last interest date, just as it had to pay the accrued interest when the bonds were purchased.

If we assume that Vason Corporation sells the bonds in our continuing example at 94 plus accrued interest less commission of $400 on March 1, two entries are required. The first entry, which appears at the top of the next page, is necessary to amortize the discount for two months.

---

1. This entry assumes that reversing entries are not made. Some companies may prefer to use reversing entries.

Mar. 1	Investment in Bonds	16.06	
	Interest Income		16.06
	Amortization of 2 months' bond discount		

Effective interest:

$18,060.79 × 10½% × 2/12 = $316.06

Face interest:

$20,000 × 9% × 2/12 = 300.00

Discount to be amortized $ 16.06

The second entry is to record the sale:

Mar. 1	Cash	18,700.00	
	Gain on Sale of Investments		323.15
	Investment in Bonds		18,076.85
	Interest Income		300.00
	Sale of bonds at 94 less $400 commission plus accrued interest		

The cash received is the selling price of $18,800 ($20,000 × .94) less the commission of $400 plus the accrued interest for two months of $300 ($20,000 × 9% × ⅙). The gain on the sale of investments is the difference between the selling price less commission ($18,400) and the carrying value of $18,076.85. The carrying value represents the assigned purchase price plus all amortization of discount:

May 1 purchase	$18,000.00
July 1 amortization	15.00
Dec. 31 amortization	45.79
Mar. 1 amortization	16.06
Carrying value of bond investment	$18,076.85

Questions

1. Why does the buying company record a bond investment at cost when the issuing company will record the same issue at face value and adjust a separate account for any discount or premium?
2. What special accounting problem arises when bonds are purchased between interest dates, even if the purchase is made at face value?

Exercise

EF-1.

L O 1, 2, 3 *Bond Investment Transactions*

On November 1, DiCenza Corporation purchased one thousand $2,000 bonds for $2,100,000 plus accrued interest and intends to hold them to maturity. The bonds carried a face interest rate of 10½ percent paid semiannually on July 1 and January 1. Because of a change in investment plans, management decided to sell the bonds on January 1 for $2,140,000. Prepare journal entries to record the purchase on November 1, the receipt of interest and amortization of premium on January 1, assuming an effective interest rate of 9½ percent, and the sale of the bonds on January 1. Assume that the company's fiscal year does not fall between November 1 and January 1.

Problems

F-1.

L O 1, 2, 3 *Bond Investment Transactions*

Transactions involving bond investments intended to be held to maturity made by Lang Corporation appear as shown on page 851. Lang has a June 30 year end.

19x1

July 1 Purchased $1,000,000 of Mead Corporation's 12½ percent bonds at 104, a price that yields an effective interest rate of 11½ percent. These bonds have semiannual interest payment dates of June 30 and December 31.

Nov. 1 Purchased $600,000 of Crown Company's 9 percent bonds, dated August 1, at face value plus accrued interest. These bonds have semiannual interest payment dates of February 1 and August 1.

Dec. 31 Received a check from Mead for semiannual interest and amortized the premium using the effective interest method.

19x2

Feb. 1 Received a check from Crown for the semiannual interest.

June 30 Received a check from Mead for the semiannual interest and amortized the premium using the effective interest method.

30 Made a year-end adjusting entry to accrue the interest on the Crown bonds.

Aug. 1 Received a check from Crown for the semiannual interest (reversing entries were not used).

Nov. 1 Sold the Crown bonds at 98 plus accrued interest.

Dec. 31 Received a check from Mead for the semiannual interest and amortized the premium using the effective interest method.

19x3

Jan. 1 Sold one-half of the Mead bonds at 101.

REQUIRED

Prepare general journal entries to record these transactions.

F-2.
L O 1, 2, 3   *Bond Investment Transactions*

Jennings Corporation purchases bonds as long-term investments with the intent to hold them to maturity. Jennings' long-term bond investment transactions for 19x1 and 19x2 follow. Jennings' year end is December 31.

19x1

Jan. 1 Purchased on the semiannual interest payment date $800,000 of Garr Company 10 percent bonds at 91, a price yielding an effective interest rate of 12 percent.

Apr. 1 Purchased $400,000 of Raines Corporation 12 percent, twenty-year bonds dated March 1 at face value plus accrued interest. These bonds have semiannual interest payment dates of March 4 and September 1.

July 1 Received a check from Garr Company for semiannual interest and amortized the discount using the effective interest method.

Sept. 1 Received a check from Raines for semiannual interest.

Dec. 31 Made year-end adjusting entries to accrue interest on the Garr and Raines bonds and to amortize the discount on the Garr bonds using the effective interest method.

19x2

Jan. 1 Received a check from Garr for semiannual interest (reversing entries were not made).

Mar. 1 Received a check from Raines Corporation for semiannual interest.

July 1 Received a check from Garr for semiannual interest and amortized the discount using the effective interest method.

1 Sold one-half of the Garr bonds at 96.

Sept. 1 Received a check from Raines for semiannual interest.

Nov. 1 Sold the Raines bonds at 99 plus accrued interest.

Dec. 31 Made year-end adjusting entry to accrue interest on the remaining Garr bonds and to amortize the discount using the effective interest method.

REQUIRED

Prepare general journal entries to record these transactions.

APPENDIX G

Future Value and Present Value Tables

Table 1 provides the multipliers necessary to compute the future value of a *single* cash deposit made at the *beginning* of year 1. Three factors must be known before the future value can be computed: (1) the time period in years, (2) the stated annual rate of interest to be earned, and (3) the dollar amount invested or deposited.

Example

Determine the future value of $5,000 deposited now that will earn 9 percent interest compounded annually for five years. From Table 1, the necessary multiplier for five years at 9 percent is 1.539, and the answer is

$$\$5,000 \times 1.539 = \$7,695$$

Where r is the interest rate and n is the number of periods, the factor values for Table 1 are

$$FV = PV(1 + r)^n$$

Situations requiring the use of Table 2 are similar to those requiring Table 1 except that Table 2 is used to compute the future value of a *series* of *equal* annual deposits at the end of each period.

Example

What will be the future value at the end of thirty years if $1,000 is deposited each year on January 1, beginning in one year, assuming 12 percent interest compounded annually? The required multiplier from Table 2 is 241.3, and the answer is

$$\$1,000 \times 241.3 = \$241,300$$

The factor values for Table 2 are

$$FVa = \left[\frac{(1 + r)^n - 1}{r} \right]$$

Table 3 is used to compute the value today of a *single* amount of cash to be received sometime in the future. To use Table 3, you must first know: (1) the time period in years until funds will be received, (2) the stated annual rate of interest, and (3) the dollar amount to be received at the end of the time period.

Example

What is the present value of $30,000 to be received twenty-five years from now, assuming a 14 percent interest rate? From Table 3, the required multiplier is .038, and the answer is

$$\$30,000 \times .038 = \$1,140$$

The factor values for Table 3 are

$$PV = FV \times (1 + r)^{-n}$$

Appendix G

Table 3 is the reciprocal of Table 1.

Table 4 is used to compute the present value of a *series* of *equal* annual cash flows.

Example

Arthur Howard won a contest on January 1, 1993, in which the prize was $30,000, payable in fifteen annual installments of $2,000 every December 31, beginning in 1993. Assuming a 9 percent interest rate, what is the present value of Mr. Howard's prize on January 1, 1993? From Table 4, the required multiplier is 8.061, and the answer is:

$$\$2,000 \times 8.061 = \$16,122$$

Table 1. Future Value of $1 After a Given Number of Time Periods

Periods	1%	2%	3%	4%	5%	6%	7%	8%	9%	10%	12%	14%	15%
1	1.010	1.020	1.030	1.040	1.050	1.060	1.070	1.080	1.090	1.100	1.120	1.140	1.150
2	1.020	1.040	1.061	1.082	1.103	1.124	1.145	1.166	1.188	1.210	1.254	1.300	1.323
3	1.030	1.061	1.093	1.125	1.158	1.191	1.225	1.260	1.295	1.331	1.405	1.482	1.521
4	1.041	1.082	1.126	1.170	1.216	1.262	1.311	1.360	1.412	1.464	1.574	1.689	1.749
5	1.051	1.104	1.159	1.217	1.276	1.338	1.403	1.469	1.539	1.611	1.762	1.925	2.011
6	1.062	1.126	1.194	1.265	1.340	1.419	1.501	1.587	1.677	1.772	1.974	2.195	2.313
7	1.072	1.149	1.230	1.316	1.407	1.504	1.606	1.714	1.828	1.949	2.211	2.502	2.660
8	1.083	1.172	1.267	1.369	1.477	1.594	1.718	1.851	1.993	2.144	2.476	2.853	3.059
9	1.094	1.195	1.305	1.423	1.551	1.689	1.838	1.999	2.172	2.358	2.773	3.252	3.518
10	1.105	1.219	1.344	1.480	1.629	1.791	1.967	2.159	2.367	2.594	3.106	3.707	4.046
11	1.116	1.243	1.384	1.539	1.710	1.898	2.105	2.332	2.580	2.853	3.479	4.226	4.652
12	1.127	1.268	1.426	1.601	1.796	2.012	2.252	2.518	2.813	3.138	3.896	4.818	5.350
13	1.138	1.294	1.469	1.665	1.886	2.133	2.410	2.720	3.066	3.452	4.363	5.492	6.153
14	1.149	1.319	1.513	1.732	1.980	2.261	2.579	2.937	3.342	3.798	4.887	6.261	7.076
15	1.161	1.346	1.558	1.801	2.079	2.397	2.759	3.172	3.642	4.177	5.474	7.138	8.137
16	1.173	1.373	1.605	1.873	2.183	2.540	2.952	3.426	3.970	4.595	6.130	8.137	9.358
17	1.184	1.400	1.653	1.948	2.292	2.693	3.159	3.700	4.328	5.054	6.866	9.276	10.76
18	1.196	1.428	1.702	2.026	2.407	2.854	3.380	3.996	4.717	5.560	7.690	10.58	12.38
19	1.208	1.457	1.754	2.107	2.527	3.026	3.617	4.316	5.142	6.116	8.613	12.06	14.23
20	1.220	1.486	1.806	2.191	2.653	3.207	3.870	4.661	5.604	6.728	9.646	13.74	16.37
21	1.232	1.516	1.860	2.279	2.786	3.400	4.141	5.034	6.109	7.400	10.80	15.67	18.82
22	1.245	1.546	1.916	2.370	2.925	3.604	4.430	5.437	6.659	8.140	12.10	17.86	21.64
23	1.257	1.577	1.974	2.465	3.072	3.820	4.741	5.871	7.258	8.954	13.55	20.36	24.89
24	1.270	1.608	2.033	2.563	3.225	4.049	5.072	6.341	7.911	9.850	15.18	23.21	28.63
25	1.282	1.641	2.094	2.666	3.386	4.292	5.427	6.848	8.623	10.83	17.00	26.46	32.92
26	1.295	1.673	2.157	2.772	3.556	4.549	5.807	7.396	9.399	11.92	19.04	30.17	37.86
27	1.308	1.707	2.221	2.883	3.733	4.822	6.214	7.988	10.25	13.11	21.32	34.39	43.54
28	1.321	1.741	2.288	2.999	3.920	5.112	6.649	8.627	11.17	14.42	23.88	39.20	50.07
29	1.335	1.776	2.357	3.119	4.116	5.418	7.114	9.317	12.17	15.86	26.75	44.69	57.58
30	1.348	1.811	2.427	3.243	4.322	5.743	7.612	10.06	13.27	17.45	29.96	50.95	66.21
40	1.489	2.208	3.262	4.801	7.040	10.29	14.97	21.72	31.41	45.26	93.05	188.9	267.9
50	1.645	2.692	4.384	7.107	11.47	18.42	29.46	46.90	74.36	117.4	289.0	700.2	1,084

The factor values for Table 4 are

$$PVa = \left[\frac{1 - (1 + r)^{-n}}{r} \right]$$

Table 4 is the columnar sum of Table 3.

Table 4 applies to *ordinary annuities,* in which the first cash flow occurs one time period beyond the date for which the present value is to be computed.

An *annuity due* is a series of equal cash flows for N time periods, but the first payment occurs immediately. The present value of the first payment equals the face value of the cash flow; Table 4 then is used to measure the present value of $N - 1$ remaining cash flows.

Table 2. Future Value of $1 Paid in Each Period for a Given Number of Time Periods

Periods	1%	2%	3%	4%	5%	6%	7%	8%	9%	10%	12%	14%	15%
1	1.000	1.000	1.000	1.000	1.000	1.000	1.000	1.000	1.000	1.000	1.000	1.000	1.000
2	2.010	2.020	2.030	2.040	2.050	2.060	2.070	2.080	2.090	2.100	2.120	2.140	2.150
3	3.030	3.060	3.091	3.122	3.153	3.184	3.215	3.246	3.278	3.310	3.374	3.440	3.473
4	4.060	4.122	4.184	4.246	4.310	4.375	4.440	4.506	4.573	4.641	4.779	4.921	4.993
5	5.101	5.204	5.309	5.416	5.526	5.637	5.751	5.867	5.985	6.105	6.353	6.610	6.742
6	6.152	6.308	6.468	6.633	6.802	6.975	7.153	7.336	7.523	7.716	8.115	8.536	8.754
7	7.214	7.434	7.662	7.898	8.142	8.394	8.654	8.923	9.200	9.487	10.09	10.73	11.07
8	8.286	8.583	8.892	9.214	9.549	9.897	10.26	10.64	11.03	11.44	12.30	13.23	13.73
9	9.369	9.755	10.16	10.58	11.03	11.49	11.98	12.49	13.02	13.58	14.78	16.09	16.79
10	10.46	10.95	11.46	12.01	12.58	13.18	13.82	14.49	15.19	15.94	17.55	19.34	20.30
11	11.57	12.17	12.81	13.49	14.21	14.97	15.78	16.65	17.56	18.53	20.65	23.04	24.35
12	12.68	13.41	14.19	15.03	15.92	16.87	17.89	18.98	20.14	21.38	24.13	27.27	29.00
13	13.81	14.68	15.62	16.63	17.71	18.88	20.14	21.50	22.95	24.52	28.03	32.09	34.35
14	14.95	15.97	17.09	18.29	19.60	21.02	22.55	24.21	26.02	27.98	32.39	37.58	40.50
15	16.10	17.29	18.60	20.02	21.58	23.28	25.13	27.15	29.36	31.77	37.28	43.84	47.58
16	17.26	18.64	20.16	21.82	23.66	25.67	27.89	30.32	33.00	35.95	42.75	50.98	55.72
17	18.43	20.01	21.76	23.70	25.84	28.21	30.84	33.75	36.97	40.54	48.88	59.12	65.08
18	19.61	21.41	23.41	25.65	28.13	30.91	34.00	37.45	41.30	45.60	55.75	68.39	75.84
19	20.81	22.84	25.12	27.67	30.54	33.76	37.38	41.45	46.02	51.16	63.44	78.97	88.21
20	22.02	24.30	26.87	29.78	33.07	36.79	41.00	45.76	51.16	57.28	72.05	91.02	102.4
21	23.24	25.78	28.68	31.97	35.72	39.99	44.87	50.42	56.76	64.00	81.70	104.8	118.8
22	24.47	27.30	30.54	34.25	38.51	43.39	49.01	55.46	62.87	71.40	92.50	120.4	137.6
23	25.72	28.85	32.45	36.62	41.43	47.00	53.44	60.89	69.53	79.54	104.6	138.3	159.3
24	26.97	30.42	34.43	39.08	44.50	50.82	58.18	66.76	76.79	88.50	118.2	158.7	184.2
25	28.24	32.03	36.46	41.65	47.73	54.86	63.25	73.11	84.70	98.35	133.3	181.9	212.8
26	29.53	33.67	38.55	44.31	51.11	59.16	68.68	79.95	93.32	109.2	150.3	208.3	245.7
27	30.82	35.34	40.71	47.08	54.67	63.71	74.48	87.35	102.7	121.1	169.4	238.5	283.6
28	32.13	37.05	42.93	49.97	58.40	68.53	80.70	95.34	113.0	134.2	190.7	272.9	327.1
29	33.45	38.79	45.22	52.97	62.32	73.64	87.35	104.0	124.1	148.6	214.6	312.1	377.2
30	34.78	40.57	47.58	56.08	66.44	79.06	94.46	113.3	136.3	164.5	241.3	356.8	434.7
40	48.89	60.40	75.40	95.03	120.8	154.8	199.6	259.1	337.9	442.6	767.1	1,342	1,779
50	64.46	84.58	112.8	152.7	209.3	290.3	406.5	573.8	815.1	1,164	2,400	4.995	7,218

Table 3. Present Value of $1 to be Received at the End of a Given Number of Time Periods

Periods	1%	2%	3%	4%	5%	6%	7%	8%	9%	10%	12%
1	0.990	0.980	0.971	0.962	0.952	0.943	0.935	0.926	0.917	0.909	0.893
2	0.980	0.961	0.943	0.925	0.907	0.890	0.873	0.857	0.842	0.826	0.797
3	0.971	0.942	0.915	0.889	0.864	0.840	0.816	0.794	0.772	0.751	0.712
4	0.961	0.924	0.888	0.855	0.823	0.792	0.763	0.735	0.708	0.683	0.636
5	0.951	0.906	0.883	0.822	0.784	0.747	0.713	0.681	0.650	0.621	0.567
6	0.942	0.888	0.837	0.790	0.746	0.705	0.666	0.630	0.596	0.564	0.507
7	0.933	0.871	0.813	0.760	0.711	0.665	0.623	0.583	0.547	0.513	0.452
8	0.923	0.853	0.789	0.731	0.677	0.627	0.582	0.540	0.502	0.467	0.404
9	0.914	0.837	0.766	0.703	0.645	0.592	0.544	0.500	0.460	0.424	0.361
10	0.905	0.820	0.744	0.676	0.614	0.558	0.508	0.463	0.422	0.386	0.322
11	0.896	0.804	0.722	0.650	0.585	0.527	0.475	0.429	0.388	0.350	0.287
12	0.887	0.788	0.701	0.625	0.557	0.497	0.444	0.397	0.356	0.319	0.257
13	0.879	0.773	0.681	0.601	0.530	0.469	0.415	0.368	0.326	0.290	0.229
14	0.870	0.758	0.661	0.577	0.505	0.442	0.388	0.340	0.299	0.263	0.205
15	0.861	0.743	0.642	0.555	0.481	0.417	0.362	0.315	0.275	0.239	0.183
16	0.853	0.728	0.623	0.534	0.458	0.394	0.339	0.292	0.252	0.218	0.163
17	0.844	0.714	0.605	0.513	0.436	0.371	0.317	0.270	0.231	0.198	0.146
18	0.836	0.700	0.587	0.494	0.416	0.350	0.296	0.250	0.212	0.180	0.130
19	0.828	0.686	0.570	0.475	0.396	0.331	0.277	0.232	0.194	0.164	0.116
20	0.820	0.673	0.554	0.456	0.377	0.312	0.258	0.215	0.178	0.149	0.104
21	0.811	0.660	0.538	0.439	0.359	0.294	0.242	0.199	0.164	0.135	0.093
22	0.803	0.647	0.522	0.422	0.342	0.278	0.226	0.184	0.150	0.123	0.083
23	0.795	0.634	0.507	0.406	0.326	0.262	0.211	0.170	0.138	0.112	0.074
24	0.788	0.622	0.492	0.390	0.310	0.247	0.197	0.158	0.126	0.102	0.066
25	0.780	0.610	0.478	0.375	0.295	0.233	0.184	0.146	0.116	0.092	0.059
26	0.772	0.598	0.464	0.361	0.281	0.220	0.172	0.135	0.106	0.084	0.053
27	0.764	0.586	0.450	0.347	0.268	0.207	0.161	0.125	0.098	0.076	0.047
28	0.757	0.574	0.437	0.333	0.255	0.196	0.150	0.116	0.090	0.069	0.042
29	0.749	0.563	0.424	0.321	0.243	0.185	0.141	0.107	0.082	0.063	0.037
30	0.742	0.552	0.412	0.308	0.231	0.174	0.131	0.099	0.075	0.057	0.033
40	0.672	0.453	0.307	0.208	0.142	0.097	0.067	0.046	0.032	0.022	0.011
50	0.608	0.372	0.228	0.141	0.087	0.054	0.034	0.021	0.013	0.009	0.003

Example

Determine the present value on January 1, 1993, of twenty lease payments; each payment of $10,000 is due on January 1, beginning in 1993. Assume an interest rate of 8 percent.

Present value = immediate payment + $\left\{\begin{array}{l}\text{present value of 19 subsequent}\\ \text{payments at 8\%}\end{array}\right.$

= $10,000 + ($10,000 × 9.604) = $106,040

Future Value and Present Value Tables

Table 3. (continued)

14%	15%	16%	18%	20%	25%	30%	35%	40%	45%	50%	Periods
0.877	0.870	0.862	0.847	0.833	0.800	0.769	0.741	0.714	0.690	0.667	1
0.769	0.756	0.743	0.718	0.694	0.640	0.592	0.549	0.510	0.476	0.444	2
0.675	0.658	0.641	0.609	0.579	0.512	0.455	0.406	0.364	0.328	0.296	3
0.592	0.572	0.552	0.516	0.482	0.410	0.350	0.301	0.260	0.226	0.198	4
0.519	0.497	0.476	0.437	0.402	0.328	0.269	0.223	0.186	0.156	0.132	5
0.456	0.432	0.410	0.370	0.335	0.262	0.207	0.165	0.133	0.108	0.088	6
0.400	0.376	0.354	0.314	0.279	0.210	0.159	0.122	0.095	0.074	0.059	7
0.351	0.327	0.305	0.266	0.233	0.168	0.123	0.091	0.068	0.051	0.039	8
0.308	0.284	0.263	0.225	0.194	0.134	0.094	0.067	0.048	0.035	0.026	9
0.270	0.247	0.227	0.191	0.162	0.107	0.073	0.050	0.035	0.024	0.017	10
0.237	0.215	0.195	0.162	0.135	0.086	0.056	0.037	0.025	0.017	0.012	11
0.208	0.187	0.168	0.137	0.112	0.069	0.043	0.027	0.018	0.012	0.008	12
0.182	0.163	0.145	0.116	0.093	0.055	0.033	0.020	0.013	0.008	0.005	13
0.160	0.141	0.125	0.099	0.078	0.044	0.025	0.015	0.009	0.006	0.003	14
0.140	0.123	0.108	0.084	0.065	0.035	0.020	0.011	0.006	0.004	0.002	15
0.123	0.107	0.093	0.071	0.054	0.028	0.015	0.008	0.005	0.003	0.002	16
0.108	0.093	0.080	0.060	0.045	0.023	0.012	0.006	0.003	0.002	0.001	17
0.095	0.081	0.069	0.051	0.038	0.018	0.009	0.005	0.002	0.001	0.001	18
0.083	0.070	0.060	0.043	0.031	0.014	0.007	0.003	0.002	0.001		19
0.073	0.061	0.051	0.037	0.026	0.012	0.005	0.002	0.001	0.001		20
0.064	0.053	0.044	0.031	0.022	0.009	0.004	0.002	0.001			21
0.056	0.046	0.038	0.026	0.018	0.007	0.003	0.001	0.001			22
0.049	0.040	0.033	0.022	0.015	0.006	0.002	0.001				23
0.043	0.035	0.028	0.019	0.013	0.005	0.002	0.001				24
0.038	0.030	0.024	0.016	0.010	0.004	0.001	0.001				25
0.033	0.026	0.021	0.014	0.009	0.003	0.001					26
0.029	0.023	0.018	0.011	0.007	0.002	0.001					27
0.026	0.020	0.016	0.010	0.006	0.002	0.001					28
0.022	0.017	0.014	0.008	0.005	0.002						29
0.020	0.015	0.012	0.007	0.004	0.001						30
0.005	0.004	0.003	0.001	0.001							40
0.001	0.001	0.001									50

Table 4. Present Value of $1 Received Each Period for a Given Number of Time Periods

Periods	1%	2%	3%	4%	5%	6%	7%	8%	9%	10%	12%
1	0.990	0.980	0.971	0.962	0.952	0.943	0.935	0.926	0.917	0.909	0.893
2	1.970	1.942	1.913	1.886	1.859	1.833	1.808	1.783	1.759	1.736	1.690
3	2.941	2.884	2.829	2.775	2.723	2.673	2.624	2.577	2.531	2.487	2.402
4	3.902	3.808	3.717	3.630	3.546	3.465	3.387	3.312	3.240	3.170	3.037
5	4.853	4.713	4.580	4.452	4.329	4.212	4.100	3.993	3.890	3.791	3.605
6	5.795	5.601	5.417	5.242	5.076	4.917	4.767	4.623	4.486	4.355	4.111
7	6.728	6.472	6.230	6.002	5.786	5.582	5.389	5.206	5.033	4.868	4.564
8	7.652	7.325	7.020	6.733	6.463	6.210	5.971	5.747	5.535	5.335	4.968
9	8.566	8.162	7.786	7.435	7.108	6.802	6.515	6.247	5.995	5.759	5.328
10	9.471	8.983	8.530	8.111	7.722	7.360	7.024	6.710	6.418	6.145	5.650
11	10.368	9.787	9.253	8.760	8.306	7.887	7.499	7.139	6.805	6.495	5.938
12	11.255	10.575	9.954	9.385	8.863	8.384	7.943	7.536	7.161	6.814	6.194
13	12.134	11.348	10.635	9.986	9.394	8.853	8.358	7.904	7.487	7.103	6.424
14	13.004	12.106	11.296	10.563	9.899	9.295	8.745	8.244	7.786	7.367	6.628
15	13.865	12.849	11.938	11.118	10.380	9.712	9.108	8.559	8.061	7.606	6.811
16	14.718	13.578	12.561	11.652	10.838	10.106	9.447	8.851	8.313	7.824	6.974
17	15.562	14.292	13.166	12.166	11.274	10.477	9.763	9.122	8.544	8.022	7.120
18	16.398	14.992	13.754	12.659	11.690	10.828	10.059	9.372	8.756	8.201	7.250
19	17.226	15.678	14.324	13.134	12.085	11.158	10.336	9.604	8.950	8.365	7.366
20	18.046	16.351	14.878	13.590	12.462	11.470	10.594	9.818	9.129	8.514	7.469
21	18.857	17.011	15.415	14.029	12.821	11.764	10.836	10.017	9.292	8.649	7.562
22	19.660	17.658	15.937	14.451	13.163	12.042	11.061	10.201	9.442	8.772	7.645
23	20.456	18.292	16.444	14.857	13.489	12.303	11.272	10.371	9.580	8.883	7.718
24	21.243	18.914	16.936	15.247	13.799	12.550	11.469	10.529	9.707	8.985	7.784
25	22.023	19.523	17.413	15.622	14.094	12.783	11.654	10.675	9.823	9.077	7.843
26	22.795	20.121	17.877	15.983	14.375	13.003	11.826	10.810	9.929	9.161	7.896
27	23.560	20.707	18.327	16.330	14.643	13.211	11.987	10.935	10.027	9.237	7.943
28	24.316	21.281	18.764	16.663	14.898	13.406	12.137	11.051	10.116	9.307	7.984
29	25.066	21.844	19.189	16.984	15.141	13.591	12.278	11.158	10.198	9.370	8.022
30	25.808	22.396	19.600	17.292	15.373	13.765	12.409	11.258	10.274	9.427	8.055
40	32.835	27.355	23.115	19.793	17.159	15.046	13.332	11.925	10.757	9.779	8.244
50	39.196	31.424	25.730	21.482	18.256	15.762	13.801	12.234	10.962	9.915	8.305

Table 4. (*continued*)

14%	15%	16%	18%	20%	25%	30%	35%	40%	45%	50%	Periods
0.877	0.870	0.862	0.847	0.833	0.800	0.769	0.741	0.714	0.690	0.667	1
1.647	1.626	1.605	1.566	1.528	1.440	1.361	1.289	1.224	1.165	1.111	2
2.322	2.283	2.246	2.174	2.106	1.952	1.816	1.696	1.589	1.493	1.407	3
2.914	2.855	2.798	2.690	2.589	2.362	2.166	1.997	1.849	1.720	1.605	4
3.433	3.352	3.274	3.127	2.991	2.689	2.436	2.220	2.035	1.876	1.737	5
3.889	3.784	3.685	3.498	3.326	2.951	2.643	2.385	2.168	1.983	1.824	6
4.288	4.160	4.039	3.812	3.605	3.161	2.802	2.508	2.263	2.057	1.883	7
4.639	4.487	4.344	4.078	3.837	3.329	2.925	2.598	2.331	2.109	1.922	8
4.946	4.772	4.607	4.303	4.031	3.463	3.019	2.665	2.379	2.144	1.948	9
5.216	5.019	4.833	4.494	4.192	3.571	3.092	2.715	2.414	2.168	1.965	10
5.453	5.234	5.029	4.656	4.327	3.656	3.147	2.752	2.438	2.185	1.977	11
5.660	5.421	5.197	4.793	4.439	3.725	3.190	2.779	2.456	2.197	1.985	12
5.842	5.583	5.342	4.910	4.533	3.780	3.223	2.799	2.469	2.204	1.990	13
6.002	5.724	5.468	5.008	4.611	3.824	3.249	2.814	2.478	2.210	1.993	14
6.142	5.847	5.575	5.092	4.675	3.859	3.268	2.825	2.484	2.214	1.995	15
6.265	5.954	5.669	5.162	4.730	3.887	3.283	2.834	2.489	2.216	1.997	16
6.373	6.047	5.749	5.222	4.775	3.910	3.295	2.840	2.492	2.218	1.998	17
6.467	6.128	5.818	5.273	4.812	3.928	3.304	2.844	2.494	2.219	1.999	18
6.550	6.198	5.877	5.316	4.844	3.942	3.311	2.848	2.496	2.220	1.999	19
6.623	6.259	5.929	5.353	4.870	3.954	3.316	2.850	2.497	2.221	1.999	20
6.687	6.312	5.973	5.384	4.891	3.963	3.320	2.852	2.498	2.221	2.000	21
6.743	6.359	6.011	5.410	4.909	3.970	3.323	2.853	2.498	2.222	2.000	22
6.792	6.399	6.044	5.432	4.925	3.976	3.325	2.854	2.499	2.222	2.000	23
6.835	6.434	6.073	5.451	4.937	3.981	3.327	2.855	2.499	2.222	2.000	24
6.873	6.464	6.097	5.467	4.948	3.985	3.329	2.856	2.499	2.222	2.000	25
6.906	6.491	6.118	5.480	4.956	3.988	3.330	2.856	2.500	2.222	2.000	26
6.935	6.514	6.136	5.492	4.964	3.990	3.331	2.856	2.500	2.222	2.000	27
6.961	6.534	6.152	5.502	4.970	3.992	3.331	2.857	2.500	2.222	2.000	28
6.983	6.551	6.166	5.510	4.975	3.994	3.332	2.857	2.500	2.222	2.000	29
7.003	6.566	6.177	5.517	4.979	3.995	3.332	2.857	2.500	2.222	2.000	30
7.105	6.642	6.234	5.548	4.997	3.999	3.333	2.857	2.500	2.222	2.000	40
7.133	6.661	6.246	5.554	4.999	4.000	3.333	2.857	2.500	2.222	2.000	50

COMPANY NAME INDEX

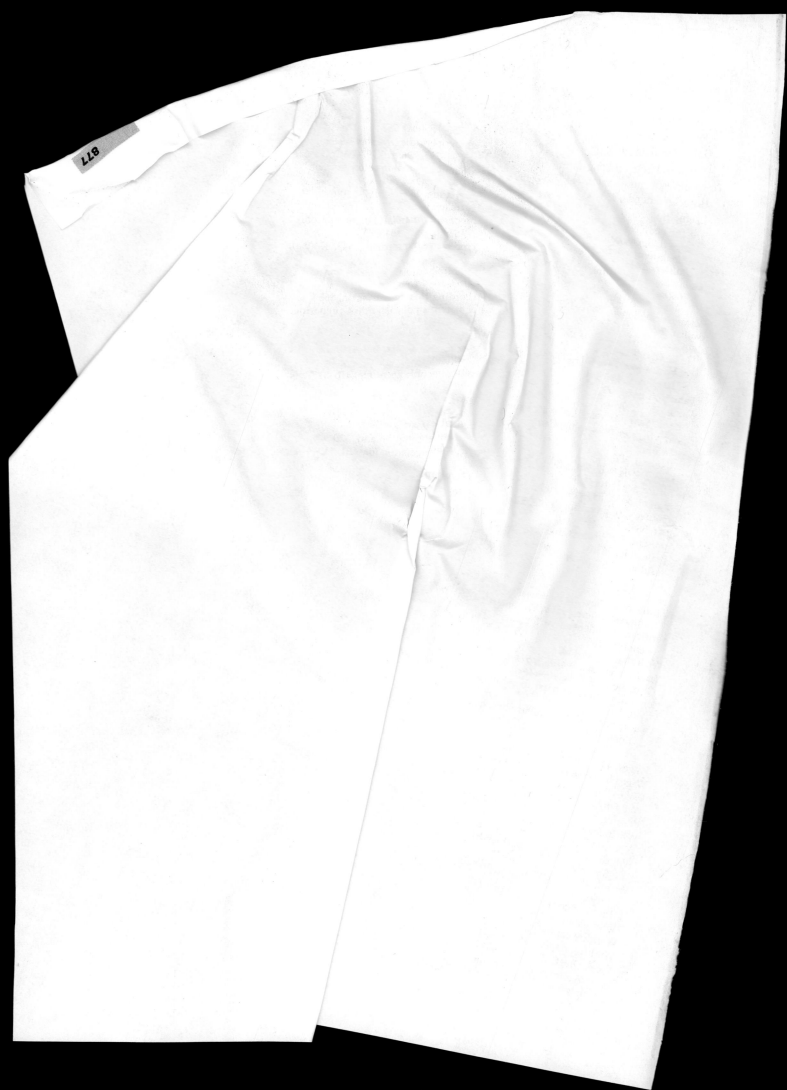

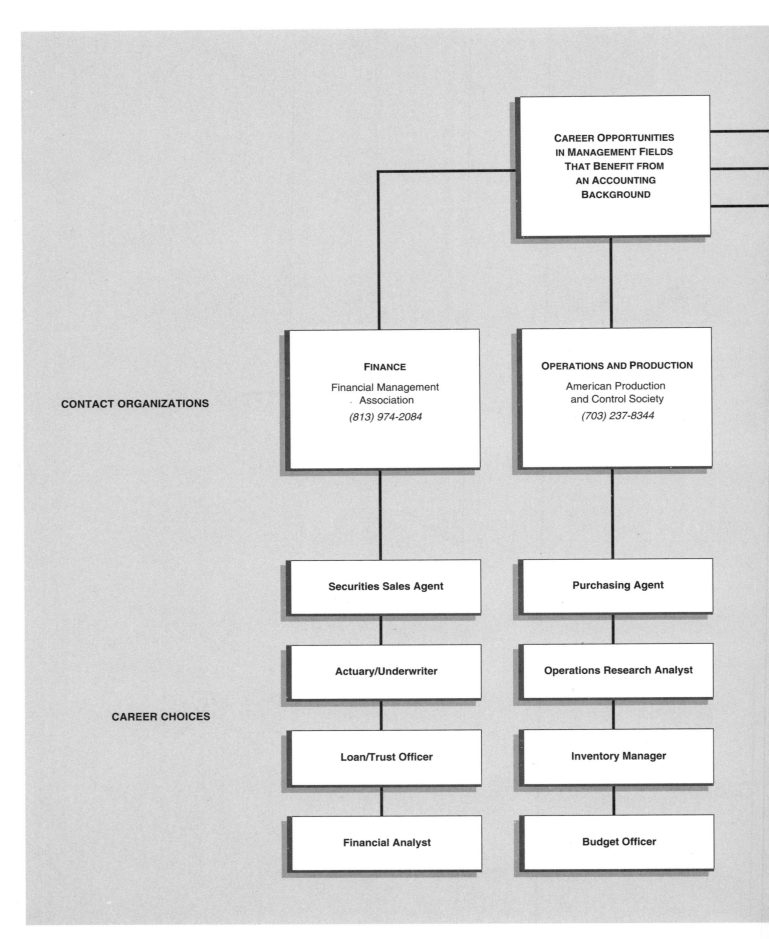

CAREER OPPORTUNITIES IN MANAGEMENT FIELDS THAT BENEFIT FROM AN ACCOUNTING BACKGROUND

CONTACT ORGANIZATIONS

FINANCE

Financial Management Association

(813) 974-2084

OPERATIONS AND PRODUCTION

American Production and Control Society

(703) 237-8344

CAREER CHOICES

Securities Sales Agent

Purchasing Agent

Actuary/Underwriter

Operations Research Analyst

Loan/Trust Officer

Inventory Manager

Financial Analyst

Budget Officer